MYTH

KENNETH MCLEISH

MYTH

MYTHS AND LEGENDS OF THE WORLD EXPLORED

BLOOMSBURY

First published in 1996 by
Bloomsbury Publishing plc
2 Soho Square
London, W1V 6HB

Copyright © 1996 by Kenneth McLeish

The moral right of the author has been asserted

A copy of the CIP entry for this book is available from the British Library

ISBN 0 7475 2502 1

10 9 8 7 6 5 4 3 2 1

Jacket design by Sarah Maxey
Designed by AB3
Typeset by Andrew McLeish and Hewer Text Composition Services, Edinburgh
Printed by Clays Ltd, St Ives Plc

INTRODUCTION

The word 'myth' (*mythos*) originated in ancient Athens, as the antithesis of *logos*. *Logos* was an objective account of an event or phenomenon, following the rules of reason and logic. Myth was an account of the same subject-matter organized to give specific information or to make a particular effect. *Mythos* was associated with the spoken word (which Greek poets imagined as a bird fluttering from one person's lips to another's ears). *Logos* was connected with the worlds of law and accounting, and referred especially to evidence presented in court or to the balance-sheet state officials were compelled to submit for moral and ethical (as well as financial) audit at the end of each year in office.

As early as the fourth century BCE, the same distinction was being applied to accounts of grander matters: the origins of the universe, the hierarchy of creation, the nature and demands of supernatural powers, the causes of things, the reasons for certain social customs and popular beliefs and the self-image of this or that community. Philosophers discussed such matters in terms of *logos*, trying to reach the truth by a purely intellectual process of reduction and elimination of the inessential. Poets and historians used *mythos*, aiming to discover truth in flashes of insight triggered by a mass of evocation and anecdote. Neither method was considered more fallible than the other – though if anyone had asked, the Greeks might have claimed that the conclusions of philosophy were less 'true' than myth, since they were the results of an activity practised and understood by a select few only, whereas myths were universally accepted and governed the lives and attitudes of all who used them. They offered a focus for thought; they put people in touch not only with one another's minds but with those of their forebears and ancestors; they validated each present moment in terms of a wider picture, both in time and space; they were a net of ideas and attitudes which guaranteed identity.

In recent years, it is this last function of myth which has chiefly interested those who study them professionally. Bronislaw Malinowski and others used myth-stories as windows, so to speak, into the mind and soul of the communities which created them. Unlike law, politics and the other systems which 'validate' a society, myths are not substantially altered by influences from outside the community; they are primary evidence. Other researchers, led by Claude Lévi-Strauss, deconstructed the myths to discover the cultural, psychological, religious and other impulses which underlay the stories; they hoped that the process would reveal basic structures of human thought, universal ways of dealing with the world as we perceive it. Still other scholars treat a society's myths not as a 'primitive' stage in its historical evolution, but as the persistent and undeviating context itself, the continuum of identity which allows the community to make sense of everything it experiences or thinks.

The myths in this book come from every part of the world, and represent a score of such continuums. They reveal a wealth of individual, local feelings and attitudes: the mindset of (say) Melanesian myth is easily distinguishable from that of North American, Celtic or Japanese, and recognizing such differences is part of the pleasure the stories give outsiders. But immersion in the whole pool of myth also shows a far wider consistency, in which the stories reveal a single, overarching human attitude to our universe and its inhabitants. Jung talked of 'archetypes' (Hero, Magician, Orphan, Wanderer and so on) arising not as the inventions of individual communities or creators, but from the 'collective unconscious' of the whole human race. This is more than just phrase-making. Human beings everywhere, at all periods of world history (at least until the scientific present) have had much the same attitudes to sex, birth, the supernatural, morality and mortality, and have also used remarkably similar images and fancies to embody those attitudes in stories. To put it grandly, myths give us for the whole of humanity what Malinowski claimed for individual communities: a window into mind and soul, into the condition of the species.

Such assertions directly challenge another attitude of the recent past: that myths have no validity outside the society which devises them, that once a culture or a religion is dead, its myths are no more than fairy-tales – interesting, colourful or both, but invested with only a fraction of their original importance. We live in an age, the argument goes, in which *logos* has made *mythos* obsolete. Stories are for children; grownups concern themselves with scientific exploration, religious or political 'truth' (that is, orthodoxy) and the serious concerns of everyday living. We deal with facts; we have no need of the poetic, the inspired, the evocative.

All this may be arguable, but it is also deplorable. In a world where 'truth' is regularly confused with 'fact', in which knowledge is measured in terms not of quality but of quantity – facts learned, examinations passed – our humanness itself can be easily dismissed, our reality reduced to figures in a computer or a checklist of attitudes on some pollster's or advertiser's clipboard. The mass of us become malleable clay in other people's hands, invited to use imagination less often than amazement, to 'look at this' rather than to 'think about this', to relate to the wider world not as participants but as spectators, tourists. The connection is not proven between this diminution of individual involvement and the collapse of moral and ethical values which many people, at least in 'advanced' society, currently and increasingly perceive – but it is undeniable that the two phenomena characterize our age more than any other in history.

Myth offers a completely different view of the human condition. It is concerned not with tidiness but with the gaps, chinks, hinges, holes, awkwardnesses, uncertainties and epiphanies of life. It deals, by definition, with what is unpredictable, unquantifiable, uncontrollable, terrifying, inspiring. This gives the stories their simple narrative appeal – one of the main reasons for their survival outside the times and societies which created them. But it also lets them seduce us into walking the border between what exists and what we think *might* exist, reminds us that 'truth' is not an objective but a subjective phenomenon, that in terms of our humanity, what we imagine is just as important as what we know.

*

Robert Yeatman commissioned my first myth-retellings of Greek, Roman and British myth: a few extracts have survived into the present book. Hilary Rubinstein first encouraged me to tackle the entire subject in a single volume, and Kathy Rooney and Kate Bouverie guided the project from outline proposal to publication. Valerie McLeish did much research and compiled the index and cross-references; Cesare Marino read and commented on the American myths here included. David Grant and Andrew McLeish prepared the book for press. To them all, warm thanks.

Kenneth McLeish, 1996

Note: The myths are told in alphabetical sequence. Embedded in this are general articles each of which mentions or lists all the stories retold in this book on its particular subject. They are: African Myth, American Myth, animal-gods, archers, Australian Myth, beauty, bulls and cows, Celtic Myth, childbirth and infant care, Chinese Myth, civilization, crafts, creation, death, demons, disease and healing, dragons, earthquakes, Egyptian Myth, farming, fate, fertility, Finnish Myth, fire, floods, food and drink of immortality, Germanic Myth, ghosts, giants, good luck, Great Goddess, Greek Myth, guardians, Heaven, heroes, household and family, human ancestors, hunting, immortality, Indian Myth, Japanese Myth, justice and universal order, light and dark, lightning, love, Mesopotamian Myth, messengers, monsters, Moon, Mother Earth, mountains, music and dance, mysteries, Nordic Myth, Oceanian Myth, prophecy, prosperity, rain, Rainbow Snake, Roman Myth, sea, sex, shape-changers, Sky, Slavic Myth, smiths, snakes, storms, Sun, supreme deity, thunder, time, tricksters, twins, Underworld, war, water, wind, wisdom and writing.

Throughout the book, BCE after a date means 'before Christian (or Common) Era'; CE means 'Christian (or Common) Era'.

All the myths retold and discussed in this book, grouped by traditions:

AFRICAN MYTH

Abassi and Atai
Adroa
Aigamuxa
Ajok
Akongo
Amma
Anansi
Andriambahomanana and
Andriamahilala
Ataokoloinona
Bumba
Chuku
Da
Ditaolane
Deng
Dubiaku
Dxui
Eshu
Gauna
Gu
Haiuri
Heitsi-Eibib
Holawaka
Huveane
Imana
Imilozi
Itherther
Juok
Kaang
Kabundungulu
Kalumba

Katonda
Khonvum
Kintu and Nambi
Legba
Leza and Honeybird
Libanza
Mawu-Lisa
Modimo
Muluku
Mulungu
Mwambu and Sela
Mwuetsi and Morongo
Ngewo
Njinji
Nyambe
Nyambi
Oduduwa
Ogo
Ogun
Onyankopon
Ruhanga
Ruwa
Shango
Sudika-Mbambi
Unkulunkulu
Wak
Wele
Woyengi
Zamba
Zanahary

AMERICAN MYTH

Adekagagwaa
Agwe
Ah Puch
Ahsonnutli
Aiomum Kondi
Amana
Amotken
Annency
Ariconte and Tamendonare
Asgaya Gigagei
Ataentsic
Atsehastin and Atseestan
Auchimalgen
Aulanerk
Aunyainá
Awonawilona
Bachue
Baxbakualanuchsiwae
Black God
Bochica
Bossu
Catequil
Chac
Chalchihuitlicue
Chantico
Chiminigagué
Chinigchinich
Chonchonyi
Cihuacóatl
Coatlicue
Coniraya
Copper Woman
Corn Woman
Coyolxauhqui
Coyote
Cupay
Dajoji
Damballah
Dayunsi
Disemboweller

Doquebuth
Dzoavits
Eeyeekalduk
Ehecatl
Ekkekko
El Dorado
Ellall
Enumclaw and Kapoonis
Erzulie
Esaugetuh Emissee
Estsanatlehi
First Made Man
Five Sisters
Flying Head
Ga-oh
Gendenwitha
Ghede
Gluskap
Gudratrigakwitl
Guecufu
Guinechen
Gukumatz
Gunnodayak
Hahgwehdiyu and Hahgwehdaetgah
Hinun
Huitzilopochtli
Humanmaker
Hunab
Hurukan
Ictinike
Igaluk
Ilamatecuhtli
Ilyap'a
Inti
Ioskeha
Itzamná
Itzpapalotl
Ixchel
Ixtab
Ixtlilton

Kadlu
Kananeski Amaiyehi
Kanassa
Kasogonaga
Kilya
Kitshi Manitu
Kloskurbeh
Kodoyanpe
Kokyangwuti
Komokwa
Kononatoo
Kuat
Kukulkan
Kumokum
Kumush
Kururumany
Kwatee
Legba
Macuilxóchitl
Maheo
Mait' Carrefour
Malsum
Mama Brigitte
Mama Quilla
Manco Capac
Mani
Mayauel
Michabo
Mictlan
Mictlantecuhtli
Mixcóatl
Na'pi
Nagaitcho
Nanabush
Nanook
Nayenezgani and Tobadzistsini
Nipinoukhe and Pipinoukhe
Nocoma
Nokomis
Ogoun
Ometecuhtli
Onatah
Oshadagea

Owiot
Pachacamac
Page Abe
Pah
Paraparawa
Payatamu
Pillan
Pinga
Poshaiyankayo
Qamaits
Quaayayp
Quetzalcóatl
Raven
Sedna
Sinaa
Snoqalm and Beaver
Star Country
Szeukha
Tamusi and Tamulu
Tawiskaron
Temazcalteci
Ten Corn Maidens
Tezcatlipoca
Thunderbirds
Tirawa
Tlaloc
Tlazoltéotl
Tochopa and Hokomata
Tonatiuh
Tonenili
Torngarsak
Tsohanoai
Tupan
Uaica
Umai-hulhlya-wit
Uncegila
Underwater Panthers
Unelanuki
Utset
Vaimatse
Valedjád
Viracocha
Wahari and Buoka Wakan Tanka

Wakonda
Wheememeowah
White She-Buffalo
Wishpoosh
Wonomi
Xipetotec

Xiutecuhtli
Xochipili
Xochiquetzal
Xólotl
Yacatecuhtli
Yanauluha

AUSTRALIAN MYTH

Bagadjimbiri
Bildjiwuaroju
Bobbi-Bobbi
Darana
Great Rainbow Snake
Julunggul
Jurawadbad
Jurumu
Kunapipi
Kurukadi and Mumba
Mangarkungerkunja
Marindi and Adnoartina
Mimi

Minawara and Multultu
Miralaldu and Djanggawul
Mudungkala
Namorodo
Ngurunderi
Purukapali
Tjinimin and Pilirin
Uluru
Waramurungundju and Wuraka
Widjingara
Wondjina
Yalungur

CELTIC MYTH

Albion
Annwn
Arawn
Arthur
Avalon
Aywell
Balor
Belenus
Beowulf
Bran
Bres
Brigid
Brit
Camelot
Cernunnos
Cormac MacAirt
Cuculain
Danaan
Deirdre
Dian Cecht
Excalibur
Finn MacCool
Fintan
Galahad
Gawain
Gogmagog
Grail

Guinevere
Lady of the Lake
Lleu Law Gyffes
Mabinogion
Manannan MacLir
Medb
Merlin
Mm
Modred
Morgan le Fay
Morrigan
Nimue
Oberon
Ogmios
Oisin
Pelles
Perceval
Pwyll
Rosmerta
Sucellus
Taliesin
Taranis
Teutatis
Tristram and Yseult
Uther Pendragon
Volund
Wyrd sisters

CHINESE MYTH

Ba Ja
Begdu San
Di
Di Jun
Di Kanh Wang
Eight Gods
Eight Immortals
Erh Jang
Erh Long
Fan Guei
Fei Lian
Five Buddhas
Five Elements
Five Emperors
Four Diamond Kings
Four Dragon Kings
Four Kings of Hell
Fu Xi
Gong Gong
Guan Di
Guan Yin
Hang Ha
Heng O
Huai Nan Zu
Huang Di
Huang Gun
Hun Dun
Jang Xien
Jou Wang
Jun Di
Kuafu
Kui
Lei Gong
Lei Jen Zu
Li No Zha

Li Papai
Long Wang
Lu Ban
Mi Hung Tang
Mi Lo
Nü Gua
Pan Gu
Penglai Shan
Qi Yu
Qian Nu and Zhi Nu
Shang Di
Shen Nong
Shi Zong Di
Shou Lao
Shun
Song Jiang
Sun Bin
Ten Yama Kings
Three Door Gods
Three Gods of Happiness
Three Lavatory Ladies
Three Sovereigns
Tian
Tsai Shen
Tsao Jun
Wen Jang
Xi He
Yao
Yen Lo
Yi
Yu
Yu Huang
Yu Zu
Zhuan Hu

EGYPTIAN MYTH

Aapep
Amaunet
Ammut
Amun
Anubis
Aset
Aten
Bastet
Benu Bird
Bes
Duat
Ennead
Geb
Hap
Hapi
Hapy
Hathor
Heqet
Horus
Imhotep
Khepri
Khnum
Maat

Mahaf
Meskhent
Min
Mut
Naunet
Nebthet
Nefertem
Nehebkau
Neit
Nun
Nut
Ogdoad
Osiris
Ptah
Ra
Sekhmet
Serapis
Serqet
Seshat
Set
Taweret
Thoth

ғINNISH MYTH

Ahto
Akka
Antero Vipunen
Ilma
Ilmarinen
Joukahainen
Jumala
Kalevala
Kalma
Kipu-Tyttö
Kuu
Kylliki
Lemminkäinen
Louhi
Loviatar

Kullervo
Luonnotar
Otava
Ovda
Päivä
Pohjola
Sampo
Surma
Tapio
Tuonela
Tuonetar
Tuoni
Ukko
Väinämöinen

GENERAL

animal-gods
archers
beauty
bulls and cows
childbirth and infant care
civilization
crafts
creation
death
demons
disease and healing
dragons
earthquakes
farming
fate
fertility
fire
floods
food and drink of immortality
ghosts
giants
good luck
guardians
Heaven
heroes
household and family
human ancestors
hunting
immortality
justice and universal order
light and dark

lightning
love
messengers
monsters
Moon
Mother Earth
mountains
music and dance
mysteries
prophecy
prosperity
rain
Rainbow Snake
sea
sex
shape-changers
Sky
smiths
snakes
storms
Sun
supreme deity
thunder
time
tricksters
twins
Underworld
war
water
wind
wisdom and writing

GERMANIC MYTH

Andvari
Atli
Donar
Faust
Flying Dutchman
Mephistopheles
Nibelungs

Norns
Sigmund
Signy
Sinfiotl
Tiwaz
Woden

GREEK MYTH

Achates
Achelous
Acheron
Achilles
Adonis
Aegeus
Aegisthus
Aeneas
Aeolus
Aesculapius
Agamemnon
Agave
Ajax
Alcinous
Alcmaeon
Alcmena
Amazons
ambrosia
Amphion
Amphitrite
Amphitryon
Andromache
Antigone
Antiope
Aphrodite
Apollo
Arachne
Ares
Arethusa
Argonauts
Argus
Ariadne
Aristaeus
Arne
Artemis
Astyanax
Atalanta
Ate
Athamas
Athene
Atlas

Atreus
Atropus
Attis
Augeas
Aurora
Autolycus
Bellerophon
Boreas
Briareus
Cadmus
Caeneus
Calchas
Calypso
Campe
Cassandra
centaurs
Cerberus
Chaos
Charon
Chimaera
Chiron
Chrysothemis
Circe
Clashing Rocks
Clytemnestra
Cocytus
Creon
Cretan Bull
Cronus
Cyclopes
Dactyls
Daedalus
Danaë
Deiphobus
Demeter
Deucalion and Pyrrha
Diomedes
Dionysus
Dioscuri
Earthborn Giants
Electra

Elpenor
Elysium
Empusa
Endymion
Eos
Eriphyle
Eris
Eros
Erymanthian Boar
Erysichthon
Eteocles
Europa
Eurynome
Eurystheus
Fates
Five Ages of Mortals
Furies
Gaia
Ganymede
Geryon
Golden Fleece
Gorgons
Graces
Graeae
Hades
Harpies
Hebe
Hecate
Hecuba
Helen
Helenus
Helius
Helle
Hephaestus
Hera
Heracles
Hermes
Hermione
Hesperides
Hippolyta
Hippolytus
Hundred-handed Giants
Hyacinthus

Hydra
Hylas
Hymen
Hyperion
Hypnus
Hypsipyle
Icarus
Idomeneus
Ilythia
Io
Ion
Iphigenia
Iris
Ismene
Ixion
Jason
Jocasta
Keryneian Hind
Laertes
Laius
Lamia
Laomedon
Leda
Leo
Lethe
Lotus-eaters
Lycaon
Lycurgus
Medea
Medusa
Melampus
Menelaus
Metis
Midas
Minotaur
Mount
Muses
Narcissus
Nauplius
Nausicaä
nectar
Nemean Lion
Nemesis

Neoptolemus
Nephele
Nereus
Nike
Niobe
Nisus and Euryalus
Odysseus
Oenomaus
Olympian Gods
Olympus
Omphale
Orestes
Orpheus
Ouranos
Palamedes
Palladium
Pallas
Pan
Pandora
Paris
Pasiphaë
Patroclus
Pegasus
Peleus
Pelias
Pelops
Penelope
Pentheus
Persephone
Perseus
Phaedra
Phaethon
Philoctetes
Phineus
Phion
Phlegethon
Phrixus
Pirithous
Polydorus
Polynices
Polyphemus
Polyxena
Poseidon

Priam
Priapus
Procrustes
Prometheus
Proteus
Psyche
Pygmalion
Pylades
Pyrrha
Pyrrhus
Rhadamanthus
Rhea
Rhesus
Salmoneus
Satyrs
Scamander
Scylla and Charybdis
Selene
Semele
Seven Against Thebes
Sibyls
Silenus
Sirens
Sisyphus
Sown Men
Sphinx
Stymphalian Birds
Styx
Tantalus
Telchines
Telemachus
Tereus
Thanatos
Thebes
Tiresias
Titans
Trojan War
Trophonius
Tyndareus
Typhon
Wooden Horse
Zephyrus
Zeus

INDIAN MYTH

Aditi
Agastya
Ages of Brahma
Agni
Airavata
Ambalika
Ambika
Amitabha
amrita
Ananda
Anjana
apsaras
Ardhanarishvara
Arjuna
Ashvathaman
Ashvins
Asuras
Atri
Avalokiteshvara
Balarama
Bali
Balin
Bhagiratha
Bharata
Bhima
Bhisma
Bhutas
boddhisattvas
Brahma
Brighu
Brighus
Brihaspati
Buddha
Candramus
Chandra
Chyavana
Daityas
Daksha
Dasaratha
Deva

Devadatta
Devaki
devas and *devis*
Devi
Dhanvantari
Dharma
Dhatar
Dhritarashtra
Diti
Draupadi
Drona
Drumalika
Durga
Dyaus
Dyavaprivithi
Gandharvas
Ganesh
Ganga
Garuda
Gommateshvara
Hanuman
Harihara
Hayagriva
Hiranyakishipu
Hiranyaksha
Ida
Indra
Jaganath
Jalandhara
Jambavan
Janaka
Jara
Jarasandha
Jatayu
Kadru
Kaikeyi
Kalanemi
Kali
Kaliya
Kalki

Kama
Kamadhenu
Kansa
Karttikeya
Kasyapa
Kauravas
Kausalya
Krishna
Kubera
Kumbhaka
Kunti
Kurma
Lakshma
Lakshmi
Madri
Mahabharata
Mahavira
Maitreya
Manasa
Manu
Mara
Maruts
Matsya
Maya
Meru
Mithra
Mount
Muchalinda
nagas and *naginis*
Nakula
Nanda
Nandi
Narasimha
Pandavas
Pandu
Parashurama
Parjanya
Parshva
Parsu
Parvati
Pavanareka
Pisakas
Prahlada

Prajapati
Prisni
Privithi
Purusha
Pushan
Putana
Radha
Rahu
Rakshasas
Rama
Rashnu
Rati
Ratri
Ravana
Ribhus
Rig Veda
Rishabha
Rishis
Rohini
Rudra
Rudrani
Rukmini
Sagara
Sahadeva
Saktasura
Sandhya
Saranyu
Sarasvati
Sati
Savitri
Seven Seers
Shashti
Shatrughna
Shesha
Shitala
Shiva
Siddhartha Gautama
Sisupala
Sita
Skanda
soma
Sugriva
Surya

Tara
Taraka
tirkanthara
Trinavarta
Tripitaka
Tvashtri
Ugrasena
Ugrasura
Uma
Urvashi
Ushas
Vamana
Varaha
Varuna
Varuni
Vashishtra

Vasudeva
Vasuki
Vasus
Vibishana
Vinata
Viraj
Vishnu
Vishvakarman
Vivasvat
Vritra
Vyasa
Yama
Yashodhara
Yasoda
Yudhishthira

JAPANESE MYTH

Ajisukitakahikone
Amaterasu
Bimbogami
Chimatano
Daikoku
Fujiyama
Futen
Gaki
Hachiman
In and Yo
Inari
Izanami and Izanagi
Jizo
Kagutsuchi
Kappa
Kojin

Kotoamatsukami
Moshirikkwechep
Musubi
Ninigi
Okuninushi
Oni
Raiden and Raiju
Seven Gods of Good Luck
Susano
Tide Jewels
Tsukuyomi
Ukemochi
Umashiashikabihikoji
Yamasachi
Yomi
Yuriwaka

MESOPOTAMIAN MYTH

Adam and Eve
Adad
Adapa
Ahriman
Ahura Mazda
An
Anat
Ashur
Astarte
Atrahis
Baal
Beelzebub
Borak
Cain
Dagon
Ea
El
Enki
Enlil
Ereshkigal
Gabriel
Gilgamesh
houris
Illuyankas
Imdugud
Kusor

Leviathan
Lilith
Mammitu
Marduk
Mary
Nabu
Nabu
Nanna
Nergal
Ninhursaga
Ninurta
Noah
Og
Samson
Satan
Shamash
Sheol
Sin
Telepinu
Tengri
Teshub
Tiamat
Utnapishtim
Utu
Yahweh

NORDIC MYTH

Aegir	Hrungnir
Aesir	Hrym
Agnar	Hymir
Alvis	Idun
Andvari	Jormungand
Asegeir	Kvasir
Asgard	Lif
Ask and Embla	Loki
Audumla	Midgard
Baldur	Mimir
Bergelmir	Muspell
Berserkers	Nerthus
Bestla	Nidhogg
Bifröst	Niflheim
Bor	Nine Wave-maidens
Bragi	Nine
Brisingamen	orlds
Brynhild	Njörd
Buri	Norns
Donar	Od
Elli	Odin
Fafnir	Odin
Forseti	Otr
Frey	Ragnarök
Freyja	Ran
Freyja	Regin
Frigg	Sif
Gefion	Sigmund
Geirröd (giant)	Sigurd
Geirröd (mortal)	Skadi
Gilling	Skrymsli
Ginungagap	Sleipnir
Grid	Surt
Gunnlod	Suttung
Heimdall	Thiazi
Hel	Thor
Hlin	Thor
Höd	Tiwaz
Honir	Tyr
Hraesvelg	Ull

Utgard
Valhalla
Valkyries
Vanir
Ve
Vidar

Vili
Wyrd
Yambe-Akka
Yggdrasil
Ymir

OCEANIAN MYTH

Areop-Enap
Atea
Dudugera
Ha'iaka
Hina
Honoyeta
Jari and Kamarong
Jugumishanta and Morufonu
Kamapua'a
Kava
Loa
Maui
Na Kaa
Nareau
Nu'u
Olifat

Papa
Pele
Rangi
Rangi's and Papa's Immortal Children
Ruaumoko
Haumea
Sido
Soido
Sosom
Ta'aroa
Tagaro
Tane
Tangaloa
Tangaroa
To Kabinana and To Karvuvu
Totoima

ROMAN MYTH

Achates
Aeneid
Anchises
Angerona
Baucis and Philemon
Bellona
Cacus
Dido
Epona
Faunus
Flora
Fortuna
Hersilia
Horatius Cocles
Janus
Jupiter
Lar
Latinus
Lavinia

Lucretia
manes
Mania
Mars
Metamorphoses
Mors
Nisus and Euryalus
Penates
Picus and Canens
Pomona and Vertumnus
Psyche
Pylades
Pyrrhus
Romulus and Remus
Saturnus
Tiber
Troilus and Cressida
Turnus

SLAVIC MYTH

Baba Yaga
bogatiri
Byelobog
Dazhbog
Domovoi
Dugnai
Ilya Muromets
Leshy
Mati-Syra-Zemlya
Meness
Miktula
Polevik
Potok-Mikhailo Ivanovich
Priparchis
Pyerun

Rod
Rugievit
Russalki
Sadko
Saule
Simorg
Stribog
Svarozich
Svyatogor
Varpulis
Vodyanoi
Yarilo
Zoryas
Zosim

ΑΑΡΕΡ
Africa (North)

Aapep ('**moon**-snake', also known as Apep and, in Greek, Apophis, 'Aa-snake'), in Egyptian myth, was Nothingness, the gulf that swallows Light. He took the form of a huge snake, not coiling but forming a concertina of S-bends, and instead of hissing he uttered a silent roar – the opening of the abyss – which filled the entire world and terrified all who heard it. This roar was also his own nourishment, and he needed no other food. His main task was to snatch the souls of the Dead in their precarious journey between one life and the next; those he swallowed entered non-existence, and stayed there until one of the gods rescued them. Aapep lay in wait for **Ra** the **Sun** each day, opening his mouth to engulf him as he sailed towards evening on the Sun-ship. It took the concerted efforts of gods and mortals to kill Aapep and help Ra to escape each day: in one typical story, everyone else was eaten and it was only when **Set** speared Aapep in the gullet that he disgorged his prey again. Each time Aapep was destroyed, all the souls he had eaten were regurgitated and could travel on to judgement in the **Underworld**. But Aapep himself regenerated, ready to lie in wait on the Western Mountains at the edge of the universe for the next day's Sun.

ABASSI AND ATAI
Africa

Abassi ('god') and Atai ('fate'), in the myths of the Efik people of Nigeria, had two children. When the children were grown, they wanted to leave **Heaven** and settle on Earth. Abassi hesitated,

1

Stele with Amitābha Buddha. Northern Wei Dynasty. A.D. 535.

Apsaras (*Chinese rubbing, c14th century*)

in case they bred a warrior-people and attacked him. But Atai persuaded him to let the children live on Earth providing that they never mated or worked and that they came to Heaven to eat whenever he rang the dinner-bell. For a time this arrangement worked, but then the children began experimenting with ploughing, sowing, harvesting and **sex** – and soon Earth was swarming with their descendants. Atai solved this by giving them two gifts of her own: argument and death. The primordial parents died immediately, and their offspring have been brawling and death-haunted ever since. As for Abassi and Atai, they were so disenchanted with their descendants that they lived utterly aloof in Heaven, taking no heed whatever of the human race.

ACHATES
Europe (South)

Achates ('agate'), in Greek and Roman myth, was a Trojan warrior. In some accounts he was the man who killed Protesilaus, the first Greek to leap ashore when the expedition reached Troy to fetch **Helen** back. Achates became **Aeneas'** close friend (and some say, squire), accompanying him on all his subsequent adventures except the journey to the **Underworld**.

Achates would be a shadowy figure if it were not for his featured role in Virgil's **Aeneid***. Even there he does little but act as Aeneas' squire and confidant, so much so that the phrase* fidus Achates *('faithful Achates') became proverbial for someone whose devotion is unthinking, unquestioning, doglike. The phrase is, in fact, the* origin of the name 'Fido' sometimes given to dogs in English-speaking nations.

ACHELOUS
Europe (South)

Achelous (Acheloös, 'who drives out grief'), in Greek and Roman myth, the son of Ocean and **Gaia** (**Mother Earth**) – or, some say, of the **Sun** and Tethys – was a river-god, a **giant** with a serpent's tail, a man's body and a bull's head from whose beard and mane streams of river-water unceasingly flowed. He wanted to take Deianira for wife, and wrestled **Heracles** for her. Achelous wriggled like a serpent, wrestled like a man, and finally lowered his head like a bull and charged. This was the end of the fight: for Heracles remembered how he had tamed the fire-breathing **Cretan bull**, took hold of one of Achelous' horns and vaulted on to his back. The horn snapped off in his hand, and Achelous, disfigured and ashamed, withdrew from the contest and left Deianira to Heracles. Heracles gave the broken horn to the **nymphs** of fields and woods, who filled it with an unceasing supply of fruits, nuts and berries of all kinds and presented it to Plutus god of wealth: the Horn of Plenty.
≫→ **water**

ACHERON
Europe (South)

Acheron ('distress'), in Greek and Roman myth, was the son of **Demeter**, goddess of harvest, who conceived him without a father. In some accounts, he supported the gods against

3

the **Titans**, and was so terrified of retribution that he hid in the **Underworld**. In others, he helped the Titans, taking them **water** during their fight with the gods, and **Zeus** punished him by hurling him into the Underworld. Once there, he turned into a river of bitter water, became a tributary of the river **Styx**, and took charge of mortal bodies as soon as their souls left them, beginning the process of decay.

ACHILLES
Europe (South)

Achilles (Achilleus, 'child of sorrow'), in Greek myth, was the son of a mortal, **Peleus**, and the sea-**nymph Thetis**. He was thus a **hero**: immortal and mortal striving to coexist in the same mind and body. His mother tried to make him fully immortal, either by charring his bones clean of flesh or by dipping him in the river **Styx**. The treatment failed, but made Achilles invulnerable to weapons – except for one heel, by which Peleus grabbed him to save him from the fire, or Thetis held him while dipping him in the Styx.

Achilles before the Trojan War. Like all Greek heroes, Achilles was fated to fight at Troy. Thetis, knowing that he was also doomed to die there, tried to prevent him hearing the call to arms by dressing him as a woman and hiding him in the harem of King Lycomedes of Scyros. But when the recruiting-party blew an alarm-call, Achilles ran out in dress and veil, brandishing a sword. His arrival among the Greeks was opportune. To appease **Artemis** (who was holding back the winds and keeping the fleet from sailing), the Greek leader

Agamemnon had been ordered to sacrifice his daughter **Iphigenia**. He sent word to **Clytemnestra**, his wife, that Achilles had demanded Iphigenia's hand in marriage, and Clytemnestra sent the child to Aulis, the harbour from which the Greeks sailed.

Achilles at Troy. For much of the ten years of the **Trojan War**, Achilles' unpredictable blend of bravery and bravado terrified all who faced him. In the end the gods used it to engineer the end of the fighting. The underlying reason was rivalry between Achilles and Agamemnon, and the immediate causes were Briseis and Chryseis, beautiful Trojan prisoners-of-war allocated to each of them respectively. Chryseis' father, the priest Chryses, demanded his daughter back, and when Agamemnon refused, he cursed the Greeks with plague. Hastily, Agamemnon returned Chryseis, and compensated himself by taking Briseis from Achilles. At once Achilles withdrew himself and his Myrmidons from the fighting and refused to play any further part in the war.

The Trojans massed for a final attack. Agamemnon proposed that the war be settled by single combat between the two rivals for **Helen**, Greek **Menelaus** and Trojan **Paris**. But before this could happen, the gods acted. They sent Chryseis back from Troy to Agamemnon, and the Trojans claimed treachery and rallied to destroy the Greeks. Agamemnon sent a deputation to Achilles, led by the silver-tongued **Odysseus**, offering him Briseis again and begging him to change his mind. Achilles sulkily refused.

Hector and Patroclus. Next morning, Prince **Hector** of Troy and his soldiers sliced through the Greek lines and attacked the Greek ships. Achilles still refused to fight in person. But he told his friend and lover **Patroclus** to put on his (Achilles') armour and ride out to protect the ships. Thinking that Patroclus was Achilles, the Greeks rallied and the Trojans fled. Patroclus climbed a siege-ladder to lead his men into the city, but **Apollo** heard Hector's prayer for aid and knocked Patroclus to the ground. His helmet flew off, the Greeks saw that he was not Achilles and fell back, and the Trojans swarmed out of the city. Hector stabbed Patroclus dead and carried Achilles' armour back in triumph.

Achilles and Hector. Achilles swore not to rest until Patroclus was avenged. His mother Thetis gave him magnificent new armour, crafted by **Hephaestus** himself, and he challenged Hector to single combat. Trying to tire Achilles, Hector ran away round the city, taunting him: he hoped that the divine armour would slow him down. But Achilles caught him, killed him, and dragged his body behind a chariot three times round the city walls.

Achilles' death. Hector's father **Priam** offered Achilles Hector's weight in gold in return for the body – and when the amount fell short, Priam's daughter **Polyxena** offered her earrings to make up the total. Overwhelmed by her beauty, Achilles rejected the gold and asked for her instead. The Greeks accused him of taking her as a bribe to desert them, and once more he went back to his tent and sulked.

This time the gods sent the Egyptian warlord Memnon to stir Achilles' fury. Memnon killed Antiochus, who had replaced Patroclus as Achilles' catamite, and Achilles ran out in rage, chasing Memnon and his followers right into Troy. The gods now took final action. Apollo guided Paris' hand and he killed Achilles by shooting him in the (vulnerable) ankle with a poisoned arrow. There was a fierce battle over his body, ended only by a thunderstorm from Zeus. The Greeks cremated the body and buried Achilles' ashes with those of Patroclus, in a golden urn made by Hephaestus. He travelled to the **Underworld**, where he married **Medea** and spent his afterlife in the Fields of the Blessed.

Another version of Achilles' death says that Polyxena cajoled from him the secret of his invulnerability and passed it to Paris, who lay in hiding at Achilles' and Polyxena's marriage, then leapt out and stabbed his heel. After the war, Polyxena was given to Achilles' son **Neoptolemus**, who sacrificed her on his father's grave.

Achilles is a central character in Homer's Iliad, *from the tenth or ninth century BCE. This took a powerful hold on later Greek imagination: it was, for example, read aloud at a huge annual festival in Athens, and vase-painters made exquisite drawings of practically every scene described above. The events of the* Iliad *were revisited and reinvented by the great fifth-century Greek dramatists, notably Aeschylus and Euripides, and figured in rhetoric and poetry. In the fourth century BCE, the* Iliad *dominated the thinking of no less a person than Alexander the Great. He is reputed to have regarded himself as Achilles reborn, to have carried an* Iliad *everywhere, and to have consciously set out to repeat Achilles' more spectacular exploits.*

In later times, however, the Iliad lost favour, yielding its place to the Odyssey and to Virgil's Aeneid. Curiously, it hardly influenced later European epics, such as those telling of King Arthur's knights or Charlemagne's paladins. In modern times it has inspired a few creative artists (for example the British writers John Cowper Powys and Christopher Logue), but it has never recaptured the pre-eminence it had in ancient Greece. This, in turn, has led to Achilles becoming sidelined as a 'favourite' Graeco-Roman hero. Agamemnon, Heracles, Odysseus or Aeneas easily outrank him in modern eyes.

ACHIMI: *see* Itherther and Achimi

ADAD
Asia (West)

Adad ('crasher'; also spelled Addad, Addu and Haddad), in Sumerian myth, was the **thunder**-god, storm-bringer and giver of **rain**. He was one of the seventy children of the **sea**-goddess Asherat, but moved inland to control fresh water, supervising in particular the annual **floods** of the rivers Tigris and Euphrates. In some accounts he was reborn each year, manifesting himself to mortals in the vegetation which grew in the fields when the floods subsided and died when it was harvested: to eat the crop was to take in the god. In art he was shown as a warrior, brandishing a thunderbolt and striding into battle, or riding a cloud-chariot or a white bull whose horns he wore on his helmet, not erect but flat like folded wings. Bulls were

sacrificed to him each winter, to ensure the flood and successful planting. His sacred fruit, the pomegranate, was thought to contain the **Sun**'s blood: life.

Adad, Prince Sea and Mot. In some Syrian and Canaanite accounts, Adad created the world from chaos. In the beginning, Prince Sea, the primordial ocean, ruled, but then his son Adad dethroned him by the power of **lightning**. Adad sliced Prince Sea into pieces, and put ramparts of land between them to prevent them ever reassembling again. Prince Sea still flails and roars against the land, and Adad is the only god able to stop him, channelling his energy into rivers and irrigation-channels.

In some accounts, Adad was so proud of defeating Prince Sea that he called himself Baal-Hadad ('Thunderprince'), built himself a palace on the slopes of Mount Saphon, and announced that he had power even over Mot, god of **death**. Mot challenged him to prove it by visiting the **Underworld**, eating the food of the Dead (mud) and surviving. Adad did so, and as soon as the mud passed his lips he died. His wife **Anat** dragged his body to the Upper World and tried to revive him. But he lay inert on the mountainside, and Anat hauled Mot out of the Underworld, chopped him to pieces and soaked the mountain with his blood. This sacrifice brought Adad back to life, and he grew to full strength as a seed becomes a tree. This event, the myth ends, has been endlessly repeated in the cycle of the seasons, and unless Adad dies and is reborn through sacrifice each year, the world's **fertility** will end.

The story of Adad and Mot is sometimes told of another Syrian god, Rimmon. But most scholars think that the two names, Rimmon ('roarer') and Adad ('crasher') are simply alternative honorific names for the same god, whose main identity is lost.
⟫→ creation, supreme deity

ADAM AND EVE
Asia (West)

Adam ('clay-red'), in Hebrew myth, was the first human being, moulded by **Yahweh** and given the breath of life on the sixth day of **creation**. Eve (Hawwah, 'life') was made soon afterwards (in some accounts, from one of Adam's ribs). Adam invented language, naming everything in creation – and in some accounts, this gave him and his descendants authority over all other creatures.

Adam and Eve lived in Eden, the earthly paradise where grew the Tree of All-knowledge and the Tree of **Immortality**. Yahweh allowed them to eat the fruits of every plant on Earth, except for these trees, the divine prerogative. But Eve (in some accounts tempted by **Satan** in the form of a **snake**) picked the fruit of the Tree of All-knowledge and shared it with Adam. At once they acquired the knowledge of **sex**, the ability to create life – and Yahweh, fearing that they might go on to eat the fruit of the Tree of Immortality and become gods, sent **Gabriel** to banish them from Eden and punished them further, forcing Adam to till the ground and grow food instead of picking it at random, and giving Eve and her female descendants the pains of **childbirth**.

The Bible account of this myth adds the element of shame. As soon as Adam and Eve ate the fruit of Knowledge, they realized that they were naked, and made clothes to cover themselves, first from fig-leaves and then from animal-skins.
⟫→ farming

ADAPA
Asia (West)

Adapa, creation of the **water**-god **Ea** in Mesopotamian myth, was the first human being. The mud from which he was moulded made him half mortal, but the god's creating hand made him half divine; he had immortal strength and Ea taught him everything he knew, one third of all the knowledge in the universe. Adapa lived with the rest of humanity (made later from the same mould which had formed him), and taught them language. He spent his days glorifying his maker and the other gods. But one day, when he was sailing in the estuary of the river Euphrates, Shutu the South Wind bore down on the ship and all but sank it – and Adapa lost his temper, snatched Shutu's bird-like wings and tore them off. The god's wings were immortal and grew back, but in the time that took, the sky-lord **An** noticed the calm which had fallen on the world and summoned Adapa to **Heaven** to explain it. Adapa asked his father Ea what to do, and Ea told him to dress in mourning, speak humbly and refuse any food and drink he was offered. The first two pieces of advice got Adapa safely through his trial before the Heavenly court. But the third was a trap, for An offered Adapa the gods' food and drink of **immortality**, and when Adapa refused he condemned the entire human race, Ea's creation, to be bound by **death**.

Adapa was the first of the seven Apkallu, sages created by Ea to be intermediaries between gods and mortals, to teach human beings as much as they could understand of the knowledge of the gods. (Ea himself was the Apkallu of the gods.) All human wisdom was later attributed to these Seven Sages: among other things, one of them was said to have composed the Epic of **Gilgamesh**.

ADEKAGAGWAA
Americas (North)

Adekagagwaa, in the myths of the Iroquois people of the Northeastern US woodlands, was the spirit of Summer. For half the year he ruled the Northern forests and fields, blessing them with **fertility**, but then he went South for six months' holiday, leaving his 'sleep spirit' to watch over the people. The sleep spirit was watchful but powerless, unable to stand up to **Ga-oh** the wind-lord, Gohone the frost-spirit or **Hinu** the thunder-god, who did as they pleased until Adekagagwaa returned and brought back Spring.

ADITI
India

Aditi ('boundless') came to India from ancient Iran with the Aryan invasions of the seventeenth century BCE. She was the vault of **Heaven** and the mother of the gods. In Aryan myth, her children, each of whom was called Aditya ('Aditi's child' or 'heavenly light') after her, included **Dhatar**, **Indra**, **Mithra**, **Savitri**, **Surya**, **Varuna** and **Vivasvat**. In some later myths the number was increased to twelve, and each took charge of the **Sun** and the revolution of night and day for one month of the year; by the fifth century BCE Aditi was often honoured as the mother of all the gods. But there is no consistency: in some accounts, for example, **Vishnu** was her only son, in others just one of them.
➤ sky

ADNOARTINA: *see* Marindi and Adnoartina

ADONIS
Europe (South)

Adonis ('prince'), in Greek myth, was one of the few mortals favoured with the amorous attentions of **Aphrodite**, goddess of love. His birth was unusual. King Cinyras of Assyria boasted that his daughter, Smyrna, was more beautiful than Aphrodite herself. As punishment, Aphrodite filled him with lust for Smyrna, and he raped her and made her pregnant. Realizing this, he tried to kill her, but Aphrodite rescued her and turned her into a myrrh tree. This particular tree splits its trunk in the spring to allow new growth – and Adonis was discovered inside.

As soon as Aphrodite saw Adonis, she fell in love with him and planned to make him her lover when he was old enough. She hid him in a box and gave it to **Persephone** to guard. However, Persephone too fell in love with Adonis and refused to give him up. The goddess asked Calliope, **Muse** of eloquence, to settle the dispute, and she ordered Adonis to spend four months with

Aphrodite, four with Persephone and the rest of the year with whichever he chose.

At the end of Aphrodite's four months, she charmed Adonis with her girdle of desire and he swore to stay with her always. Persephone went to the war-god **Ares** (who was himself in love with Aphrodite), and told him he had a mortal rival. The next time Adonis went hunting, Ares disguised himself as a boar and killed him. Wherever drops of Adonis' blood fell, wood anemones sprang up.

Now **Zeus** took a hand, decreeing that half of Adonis' year should be spent with Aphrodite, and the other half with Persephone (the six months she spent as queen of the **Underworld**). Adonis and Aphrodite had three children. Two of these, Golgus and Beroe, were mortal and beautiful; the third, **Priapus**, was immortal, ugly, and so shamelessly lustful that the other gods refused to have him in Olympus.

>>+ **beauty, Endymion, Ganymede, Hylas, Narcissus**

ADROA
Africa

Adroa ('up there'), in the myths of the Lugbara people of Zaïre and Uganda, created the universe and everything in it, including himself. He was thought alone, shapeless, all-good, remote. But to make his second creation, Adro (Earth), he had to divide himself in two and give the new half form. Adro the Earth-spirit was like half of a human body divided from crown of head to toes: one eye, half a mouth, one arm, one leg and no generative organs.

Deprived of union with its heavenly half, it swam eternally in the rivers of the world, and was the spirit of evil. It and its children, the water-snakes known as Adroanzi (produced from a slit in their parent's single side), were permanently on watch for humans to drown and eat.

>>+ **creation, Haiuri**

AEGEUS
Europe (South)

Aegeus (Aigeus, 'goaty'), son of King Pandion of Athens in Greek myth, inherited his father's throne. But he had no children, and was afraid that after his death his kingdom would be snatched by one or another of his quarrelsome brothers Lycus, Nisus and Pallas, or by one of Pallas' fifty warrior-sons. He asked advice from the Delphic oracle, and the priests told him 'not to unfasten the wineskin's foot' until he reached the Acropolis, or he would cause his own death. Finding this advice incomprehensible, Aegeus went to ask his old friend Pittheus, prophet-king of Troezen, if he could explain it. On the way he visited **Medea** in Corinth. Tormented with rage because **Jason** had just taken a new wife, she told Aegeus that if he promised her shelter in Athens she would end his childlessness.

In Troezen, King Pittheus gave a banquet in Aegeus' honour, and Aegeus enjoyed himself so much that he forgot the oracle's advice. Wineskin after wineskin was unfastened and drained, and he staggered drunk to bed without telling Pittheus why he'd come. Not only that, but the bed he staggered to belonged to Pittheus' daughter Aethra. He made love with her – and then in the sober dawn, rather than face her father, slipped out of Troezen and hurried back to Athens. Before he went, he buried a golden sword and a pair of sandals under a rock, and told Aethra, if she proved to be pregnant and bore a son, to wait until the boy grew up and then tell him about the sword. If the gods gave him strength to lift the rock and find the sword he should go to Athens, where he would be welcomed as Aegeus' heir.

Back in Athens, Aegeus found that Medea had reached the city before him, having killed her children by Jason and fled from Corinth. She used her magic powers to protect the city against Aegeus' quarrelsome family, and she also fed Aegeus herbs to increase his potency, so that he and she had a son, Medus. Aegeus lived happily with her for twenty years. Then a young stranger arrived from Troezen: **Theseus**. Medea at once realized that he was a threat to her power. She tried to poison him – and Aegeus, just in time, recognized the golden sword he'd left under the rock, dashed the poison-cup from Theseus' hand and welcomed him as the son he never knew he'd fathered. (Medea stormed off to the **Underworld**, and Medus fled to Asia Minor, where he became the ancestor of the Median people.)

As soon as Medea was gone, Aegeus' brothers and nephews ran to attack Athens. But Theseus killed all of them, and Aegeus made him heir-apparent. He would have abdicated in Theseus' favour, but Theseus left almost immediately for Crete to put an end to the **Minotaur**, and Aegeus agreed to rule in Athens until he

returned. He told Theseus that he would watch for a signal each day from the heights of the Acropolis (or some say, from Cape Sunium overlooking the sea). If Theseus succeeded, he should hang purple-red (or some say white) sails on the ship that brought him back to Athens; if he failed, his crew should hang a black sail. Each day, as agreed, Aegeus climbed to the top of Acropolis hill (or rode to Sunium) and gazed out to sea. At last he saw a ship – and it had black sails. In fact, Theseus *had* killed the Minotaur and was coming back alive, but **Dionysus** had blurred his memory, making him forget the arrangement about the sail. As soon as Aegeus saw the black sail he hurled himself to his death, either dashing his brains out on the rocks below the Acropolis, or throwing himself from Sunium into the sea which was later called the Aegean after him.

Aegeus' best-known appearance in literature is as the doddering old fool charmed by Medea in Euripides' play. Euripides started his characterization from one myth-account that Aegeus had ruled in Athens for four mortal generations, and the reason he was childless was that he was over a hundred years old. To the Athenian spectators, who regarded Aegeus as one of the founders of their city, this characterization must have come as a surprise, but it has affected Aegeus' depiction in all subsequent literature and art.

AEGIR
Europe (North)

Aegir, personification of the primordial ocean in Nordic myth, held himself aloof from such newer families of gods as the **Vanir** and **Aesir**, living with his wife **Ran** in a golden underwater palace. He contented himself with rule over the **sea** and all its creatures, and sent his rage to the surface in storms and tidal waves to frighten off any gods, **giants** or mortals rash enough to stray into his domain. Occasionally he held underwater parties, feasting the gods on seafood and ale brewed in an enormous pot which **Thor** and **Tyr** stole for him from Tyr's father, the giant **Hymir**.

Aegir's aloofness led him to ignore the presence in his realm of **Jormungand**, the world-snake which bound the waters together. Unknown to him, Jormungand is continually growing, and when **Ragnarök** comes and the sea-serpent surges to the surface to overwhelm **creation**, Aegir will be so feeble in comparison that he will be unable to stop it.

AEGISTHUS
Europe (South)

Aegisthus (Aegisthos, 'strength of goats'), in Greek myth, was born of the incest between his father **Thyestes** and Thyestes' daughter Pelopia. As soon as he was born he was sent to be brought up by goatherds, but was later rescued and taken to the court of King **Atreus** of Mycenae, who brought him up as a ·royal prince together with Atreus' own sons **Agamemnon** and **Menelaus**.

What no one knew was that Aegisthus' birth had been ordered by the gods. He was to take revenge for an atrocity committed years before by Atreus, who had butchered Thyestes'

other children and served them in a stew to their father. Atreus had no idea that Aegisthus was related to Thyestes. Thinking him a foundling, he gave him the name Aegisthus because of the goatherds. But when Aegisthus grew up his true birth was revealed, and he avenged his dead brothers and sisters by murdering Atreus, exactly as the gods had planned.

For a few weeks after the murder, Aegisthus ruled Mycenae. But Atreus' son Agamemnon raised an army in Sparta, deposed him and took the throne, ruling with his queen **Clytemnestra**. Agamemnon thought that there was nothing to fear from Aegisthus. He had no idea that Aegisthus was conducting a long-standing affair with Clytemnestra, and planning revenge on him. When Agamemnon was chosen as commander of the Greeks who went to fight the **Trojan War**, he rashly left Mycenae in Clytemnestra's and Aegisthus' joint charge – and by the time he came home, after ten years away, they had become tyrants, and murdered him. They continued their reign of terror until Agamemnon's son **Orestes** (who had been exiled soon after Agamemnon sailed for Troy) returned in secret and killed them both.

AENEAS
Europe (South)

Aeneas' youth. Aeneas (Aineias, 'praiseworthy'), in Greek and Roman myth, was the son of Prince **Anchises** of Troy and the goddess **Aphrodite**. Even as a child he was admired for his attention to duty, his respect for gods and family and his qualities of leadership. As a youth he fought in the **Trojan War**, and though he was too young to play a large part in either fighting or counsels – both of which were dominated by **Priam**'s fifty sons, the senior branch of the royal family – he made his mark for diligence and bravery. **Poseidon** prophesied that when Troy fell Aeneas would lead his people to a new kingdom and new greatness, and the gods protected him during the fighting, rescuing him from such powerful adversaries as **Achilles** and **Diomedes**.

Aeneas after the fall of Troy. As soon as the Greeks breached the walls of Troy and began pillaging and burning the city, the gods told Aeneas to gather several shiploads of survivors, including his aged father Anchises, and sail with them to a new destiny far to the South. Aeneas took with him the ancestral gods of Troy, intending to make them the hub of whatever new city the gods found for him. He sailed past the **Clashing Rocks** into the Aegean, South along the coastline, and then through dangerous open water to landfall in Sicily, where his crew narrowly avoided being eaten by the **Cyclopes**, whose leader **Polyphemus** had already tried to kill **Odysseus** and his men.

Aeneas and Rome. From Sicily Aeneas went to Africa, where he visited Queen **Dido** of Carthage. He would have stayed there with her forever, allowing his people to intermarry with the Carthaginians and building Carthage into the second Troy promised by the gods. But **Zeus** intervened, sending **Hermes** to tell Aeneas that his destiny lay in Italy, not Africa. The Trojans sailed, leaving Dido heartbroken, and landed in Cumae, whose **Sibyl** took Aeneas into the **Underworld** where Anchises' ghost showed him the whole future of his people: the city of Rome and the generations of **heroes** still unborn. Fortified by this vision, he sailed up the coast to Latium, at the mouth of the river Tiber, where he made an alliance with King **Latinus** and agreed to marry Latinus' daughter **Lavinia**. At this **Turnus**, king of the Rutulians (the most powerful of the local peoples), to whom Lavinia had previously been promised, declared war against the Trojans and Latins, and it was not until after months of fierce fighting that the gods helped Aeneas to kill Turnus in single combat, to unite the warring peoples and declare himself king of the whole area.

The end of Aeneas' life. Not long after killing Turnus, Aeneas vanished. In some accounts he was either killed in a skirmish or dived for safety into the river Numicus, and the current swept his body away so that it was never found. His people claimed that he had been taken into **Heaven**, and worshipped him as a god. In other accounts, he handed his throne to his son **Ascanius** (Iulus), and went alone on a second journey, either back to Carthage (whose people murdered him for betraying Dido years before) or North to the ruins of Troy, where his mother Aphrodite took him into Heaven.

In Greek myth, Aeneas is a minor figure, a lordling who fights bravely for Troy but disappears from the action as soon as the city falls. In Roman myth, however, he is central: he is the link between the gods (his mother Venus/Aphrodite) and the Roman people (descended from his son Iulus/Ascanius), and an important intercessor between mortals and immortals. The story of his wanderings was sketched by a number of writers, from Hyginus to Ovid, but was given definitive form in Virgil's **Aeneid** in the early first century CE. Virgil modelled the Aeneid on the grandest epics he knew, Homer's Iliad and Odyssey – and he built into it sustained, if dignified, propaganda about Rome's divine destiny and the nobility and honour of the Roman character. These last qualities are embodied by Aeneas himself, and some scholars think that Virgil invented several episodes of the Aeneid to highlight them, not least the story of Aeneas' love-affair with Dido.

In the Middle Ages, the Aeneid was known throughout Europe, and its vision of heroic obedience to the will of Heaven, of self-denying heroism and unfaltering nobility – Aeneas' character, in short – became a model for the knights of Charlemagne's court, and from there the foundation of the chivalric code of social morality and Christian ethics.

AENEID

The *Aeneid* ('story of Aeneas') is a Latin epic poem by Virgil, brought out after his death in 19BCE. Its twelve sections tell of the fall of Troy, the wanderings of **Aeneas** and his companions in search of a new homeland, and their battles to win the area of Italy which became the site of the future Rome. Virgil modelled his style and form on Homer's *Iliad* and *Odyssey*, and reworked several episodes from those books, for example the funeral games held for Aeneas' father **Anchises**, Aeneas' hand-to-hand duels with various Italian leaders, and – most

memorably of all – Aeneas' descent into the **Underworld**, to hear from his father's ghost the future destiny of Rome. The *Aeneid*'s purposes were patriotic, even propagandist: to trace the descent of the ruling Julian dynasty from Aeneas' son Ascanius (Iulus), and therefore from his ancestors the gods, and to hymn the virtues of obedience, moral uprightness and discipline which were highly regarded in aristocratic Roman circles of the time. The *Aeneid* was popular not only in ancient Rome, but throughout medieval Europe, where it was the second most copied book after the Bible.

Because of its popularity, the *Aeneid* is one of the most frequently illustrated books of Western literature. Artists, from medieval monks decorating manuscripts to nineteenth-century painters of vast panoramic scenes, concentrated on such sequences as Virgil's account of the Fall of Troy, the funeral games for Anchises, the suffering souls in the Underworld, Aeneas' battle with **Turnus** and – on a more domestic if hardly less stiff-upper-lip scale – the parting of **Dido** and Aeneas and Dido's subsequent madness and suicide.

AEOLUS
Europe (South)

Aeolus (Aiolos, 'Destroyer'), in Greek myth, was the son of **Poseidon** and the mortal Arne, wife of King Desmontes. His twin brother was Boeotus. Desmontes realized that he was not the children's father, and was so furious that he blinded Arne, imprisoned her in an underground pit and left the children on a mountainside to die.

Here, however, a shepherd found them and took them to his employer, Queen Theaeno. She brought them up as princes in the palace until they were adolescents, when she began to fear that they would steal the throne from her own two sons. She and her sons tried to kill them in a hunting accident, but Aeolus and Boeotus, equipped with supernatural strength by their father Poseidon, easily killed the two mortal princes, and Theaeno stabbed herself dead from grief.

The gods now told Aeolus and Boeotus the true story of their parentage, and they hurried home, killed Desmontes and rescued their mother Arne from her pit. Boeotus settled to farm the part of Greece later called Boeotia after him. The gods gave Aeolus a kingdom on the floating island of Lipara. **Zeus** and Poseidon honeycombed it with caves and tunnels, and Zeus forced the winds into them, sealing the entrances. Whenever the gods wanted help from a wind, Aeolus used his trident (a replica of the **earthquake**-causing trident of Poseidon, his father) to prise open a vent-hole, allowed the chosen wind to escape, and then resealed the hole.

Aeolus and Odysseus. **Odysseus** visited Lipara on his journey home from the **Trojan War**. Aeolus gave him a bagful of winds, and showed him how to untie the magic knot which fastened it if he ever needed to fill his sails. Odysseus' crew, however, jealous that he was the only one to be given a present, waited until he dozed – it was just after he'd caught the first glimpse of Ithaca on the horizon – and slashed open the bag with knives. The winds rushed out and blew them all the way back to Lipara. This time Aeolus refused to help them, and they were left to limp to Ithaca under their own oar-power.

Some later writers claimed that Aeolus was not a supernatural figure at all but a real person, Aeolus King of Aeolia. Whether myth or legend came first is a moot point – and by Homer's time (c10th century BCE) the two were inextricably intertwined.

≫→ **twins**

AESCULAPIUS
Europe (South)

Aesculapius (or Asclepius, Greek Asklepeios, 'always gentle'), in Greek myth, was the son of **Apollo** and the mortal princess Koronis. While Koronis was pregnant, she had an affair with a mortal, Ischys, and for this Apollo and **Artemis** shot her dead. However, even as the flames burned Koronis' body on the funeral pyre, Apollo remembered his child and cut Aesculapius free.

Aesculapius was educated by the centaur **Chiron**, who taught him medicine. **Athene** gave him two bottles of **Gorgon**'s blood: one held poison and the other a potion which could raise mortals from death. At Artemis' request, he used the latter to save **Hippolytus**, and for this **Zeus** struck him dead with a thunderbolt. At once, Apollo began killing the **Cyclopes** who made Zeus' thunderbolts, and Zeus, afraid that he would lose the weapons which guaranteed his power, released Aesculapius from the **Underworld** and gave him all the rights and honours of an immortal.

Aesculapius was worshipped as a healing god and the founder of medicine for 2000 years, and people throughout the Greek and Roman world visited his shrines to be cured of illness. (One such shrine was at Epidaurus, where the theatre was part of a huge complex used for sacred rituals and for entertaining visitors.) The sick spent a night in the temple, and Aesculapius and his daughters Iaso ('healer') and Panacea ('cure-all') were supposed to move amongst them, telling them how they might be healed or even curing them on the spot. After this ceremony, Aesculapius' priests prescribed herbal medicines, or performed operations (though not surgery, which was anathema) to guarantee the cure.
≫→ disease and healing

AESIR
Europe (North)

The Aesir, in Nordic myth, were a vast family of war-gods and creator-gods. The first three, **Odin**, **Vili** and **Ve**, created the universe and everything in it from the corpse of the giant **Ymir**. Other gods joined them – later offspring of their parents **Bor** and **Bestla**, the first beings – and the family mated incestuously to produce still more gods. The chief Aesir were **Baldur**, **Bragi**, **Frigg**, **Heimdall**, **Höd**, **Honir**, **Idun**, **Loki**, **Mimir**, **Sif**, **Thor**, **Tyr** and Vali. They built a citadel, **Asgard**, and defended it against all-comers, particularly the **giants**, who were determined to steal the apples of **immortality** which Idun guarded and which gave the gods supremacy in the universe.

For the war between the Aesir and another group of gods, the Vanir, see **Vanir**.

No one knows the meaning or origin of the word 'Aesir'. In the thirteenth century CE, Snorri Sturluson drew a fanciful derivation from 'Asia', and this led him and others to make genealogical trees relating the Aesir to the gods of ancient Greece – or even to such figures as King **Priam** of Troy: they were the 'lost' Trojans who sailed North after the **Trojan War**, as **Aeneas** sailed South. A more plausible connection is with the root-word for 'ancient', and suggests that Aesir simply means 'Old Ones'.
≫→ creation

AFRICAN MYTH

If, as is currently believed, the earliest human beings came from East Africa, then one might logically expect African myth to include some of the primal ideas borrowed and elaborated by many other systems throughout the world. This may have been the case – a typical example is the idea, widespread in African myth, that the world was made by a single, beneficent deity – but evidence is scanty. In a way which at first seems incredible for a continent with so many thousands of peoples, languages and traditions, African myth is sparse and stark. Taken as a whole, and with a few areas of exception (such as ancient Egypt), the continent is richer in folk-tale than in true myth, more fertile in ritual practice than in the stories and ideas on which it is based.

The reasons are geographical and historical. The size of the continent, and the difficulties of travel in ancient times, tended to isolate communities. Except in huge empires like those along the Congo or Zambezi rivers, or the later Zulu kingdoms in the South, people lived in small groups. A few dozen might speak an entirely different language from their immediate neighbours, and have no contact with them whatever. Myths served single villages or small clusters of communities, and were not codified or systematized, remaining a kind of joint property like gossip or family history. When conquerors came – and the history of Africa for the last 2000 years has been one of continuous imperialism, both internal (as when the Bantu peoples swept into Southern Africa) and external (for example from Rome, Muslim Arabia, Viking and then Christian Europe, China and India) – they either assimilated local peoples into their empires or marginalized them: examples are the Pygmy peoples on the fringes of the equatorial forests or Bush people in the Kalahari desert.

Each of these procedures was damaging to myth. Marginalized communities tended to turn inwards, fighting for survival – as many still do today – and making their rituals and sustaining myths matters of pride-in-identity and above all secret, with the result that when the people disappeared, their myths vanished with them. The imperialists, almost without exception, treated the peoples they assimilated as second-class citizens, and dismissed their myths and practices as primitive. It was no part of the agenda to admit that myths might have serious ethical, philosophical and social point, particularly if the ideas they contained were different from those of the dominant culture. This attitude, which was eagerly shared by many of those assimilated, pushed ancient myths to the side

of the plate (so that former gods turned into the **demons** of the new religions) or off the table altogether (in which case the gods now survive only dimly, in folktale, or are entirely lost).

Surviving African myth – as opposed to a myriad folktales explaining local customs – is concerned largely with two questions: 'Who is God?' and 'Why do mortals die?' In almost all areas, God the creator is a single figure, a father, mother or grandfather (or in one case, **Itherther**, a buffalo). The deity – **Adroa, Amma, Akongo, Juok, Libanza, Mawu-Lisa, Modimo, Ngewo, Njinji, Ruwa, Unkulunkulu, Wak, Woyengi, Zanahary** – is a mysterious, amorphous being, creativity itself given energetic purpose. He, she or it makes the world sometimes as an expression of selfness, sometimes out of loneliness. The methods of **creation** are sometimes left unexplained, sometimes given in remarkable detail – **Bumba** vomits everything into existence, **Dxui** becomes each new thing in turn, **Nyambe** gathers created objects like fruit from the Tree of Life, **Ruhanga** dances the universe into being. God sometimes rejoices in the world, but more often comes to regret the way it turns out: **Deng** and **Onyankopon** are pounded, to the point of irritation, by the pole of a woman grinding corn, **Huveane** scrambles away from the world's noise up a series of sky-pegs, **Nyambi** is plagued by a neighbour who copies everything he does.

When it comes to human beings, the stories show a similar kind of unity-through-diversity. We are usually made from mud, and often descended from an original pair of parents such as

Andriambahomanana and **Andriama-hilala**, **Kintu** and **Nambi**, **Mwambu** and **Sela** or **Mwuetsi** and **Morongo**. Our first gift from God is **sex**, and our second is mortality. Sometimes **death** comes as a result of a war in **Heaven** – we are the prey of such demons as **Gauna**, **Ogo** and **Oduduwa** – but more usually it is because God sends fallible **messengers**, and the one which promises us **immortality** arrives later than the one guaranteeing death. **Leza** sends three sealed calabashes, with instructions to the Messenger (Honeybird) not to open the last one – and the results are predictable. In fact, messengers are invariably untrustworthy. **Anansi** and **Legba** are **tricksters** who delight in the confusion they cause by lying; the **Imilozi** give messages by whistling in a language no mortal can understand; **Mulungu** sends his instructions by a messenger-chain so long that they are completely garbled by the time they reach us, as are our prayers to him.

These core-myths are surrounded by others, more mundane. Some explain **thunder** and **lightning** as gods (for example **Sudika-Mbambi** and **Kabundungulu**). Others – **Aigamuxa**, **Haiuri** – tell of spectacular **monsters**, or of **heroes** such as **Ditaolane** and **Dubiaku** who deal with them. What may be one of the oldest of all African myths, the story of **Ataokoloinona**, tells why the human race spends most of its time searching for water. Above all, African myths have a slyness, a wit in the telling which is rivalled in few other systems. **Gu** the blacksmith-god is a lump of stone with a blade for a face. **Heitsi-Eibib**, god of difference, keeps falling over his own feet. Juok quickly tires of making human beings from mud, so he gives them sexual organs and leaves them to get on with it. **Muluku** offers civilized ways first to humans, and then to monkeys because their manners are better. **Imana** builds a universe like a tottering house of cards, and has to spend eternity shoring it up and repairing it to avoid catastrophe. The world of African myth is immense, unpredictable, dangerous – and, in all senses of the word, absurd.

≫→ **Abassi and Atai, Ajok, Chuku, Da, Eshu, Holawaka, Kaang, Kalumba, Katonda, Khonvum, Ogun, Olorun, Shango, Wele, Zamba**

AGAMEMNON
Europe (South)

Agamemnon ('very warlike'), in Greek myth, was the son of King **Atreus** of Argos and his queen Aerope, and the brother of **Menelaus**. When their uncle **Thyestes** killed Atreus and took his throne, Agamemnon and Menelaus fled, first to Aetolia and then to Sparta. In Sparta, they married twin princesses: Menelaus married **Helen** (and in due course succeeded to her father's throne in Sparta), Agamemnon married **Clytemnestra**. The Spartans gave Agamemnon an army, and he went back to Argos, killed Thyestes and took his rightful place on his father's throne, ruling from an impregnable citadel built at Mycenae, on a hill from which all Argos could be easily surveyed.

Agamemnon and Iphigenia. Agamemnon and Clytemnestra had four children: **Iphigenia**, **Electra**, **Chrysothemis** and **Orestes**. In a dozen years, they built Argos, and Mycenae its citadel, into two of the most powerful places in Greece. It was natural, therefore, that when **Paris** of Troy stole Helen from Menelaus, the Greeks should ask Agamemnon to lead the huge expedition which was to sack Troy and bring Helen home to Greece. While their fleet assembled at Aulis and prepared to sail, Agamemnon passed his time **hunting**. One day, he shot and killed a magnificent stag, not realizing that it was sacred to the goddess **Artemis**. She retaliated by holding back the winds, becalming the fleet — and when Agamemnon asked the gods what to do (using the prophet **Calchas** as go-between), she said that he could buy back the winds only by sacrificing his daughter Iphigenia. Agamemnon cut the child's throat over Artemis' altar, the winds returned and the Greeks sailed for Troy.

Agamemnon at Troy. During most of the **Trojan War**, Agamemnon showed true qualities of leadership, fighting bravely and guiding his unruly army of **heroes** with a firm hand. But as the siege dragged into its tenth year, his sureness of touch deserted him. He and **Achilles**, the greatest and touchiest of the Greek heroes, were allotted twin sisters as prisoners-of-war, Briseis and Chryseis, and when their father, the priest Chryses, demanded her back, Agamemnon commandeered Briseis from Achilles. In the flurry of sulking and recrimination which followed, he lost so much face that he surrendered control to his fellow-warlords (notably Menelaus and **Odysseus**). After the sack of Troy, his share of the spoils included **Cassandra**, the prophetess daughter of King **Priam** — and he shipped her home to Mycenae despite warnings that both she and he would die there.

Agamemnon's death. In Mycenae, Clytemnestra had spent the ten years of the war planning revenge for Agamemnon's murder of Iphigenia. She had taken as lover Agamemnon's cousin **Aegisthus**, and when Agamemnon's ships arrived she went to meet him at the Lion Gate of Mycenae, unrolling a red carpet in pretended welcome. She took him to the bath-house, tangled him in the blood-red cloth, and beckoned Aegisthus from the shadows to butcher him with a double-headed axe.

In the myth-cycle of Argos, Agamemnon is actually one of the least important or active figures: a figurehead king whose rank and position are more significant than anything he does. Importance attaches more to his father Atreus, to his uncle Thyestes, to his wife Clytemnestra, and to his children Electra and Orestes. But successive generations of Greek writers, from Homer to Aeschylus, Sophocles and Euripides, made him a focal point of both the Trojan War and the tangled account of what happened after he went home to Argos. In the Iliad, the Oresteia and Euripides' Trojan-War-set plays – not to mention such later accounts as Shakespeare's Troilus and Cressida – he is memorable chiefly for pomp and circumstance, shading into pomposity, and in Sophocles' Electra and Euripides' Argos-set plays he is a kind of totem of kingliness, used by Electra and Orestes as the model of all fine fathers unjustly slain, and as the trigger for nobility in others. Only Euripides' Iphigenia in Aulis, which deals with the events leading up to the sacrifice of Iphigenia, gives him anything like a truly tragic dilemma or depth of personality. Similarly, in art, he is often the gaudiest and grandest person in a painting, but seldom the most significant.

AGASTYA
India

Agastya (or Agasti), in the Vedic myths of the Aryan people who invaded India in the seventeenth century BCE, was the son of not one but two fathers, **Varuna** and **Mithra** (or some say **Surya**). One day they were so enraptured by the dancing of beautiful **Urvashi** that they had orgasms on the spot. Their semen was gathered and stored in a jar, and Agastya grew from it. He was not a god but a sage, and he became a kind of heavenly historian, writing the gods' stories down and passing them to mortals in the form of the **Rig Veda**.

Agastya was the implacable enemy of **demons**. Once, realizing that demons were hiding from him in the primordial ocean, he drank it, and they crept out of their muddy holes, cowering and blinking in the sunlight. He penned a horde of demons in Southern India, erecting a **mountain**-chain round them as a mortal might make a mud-fence to keep in cattle. He sheltered **Rama**, **Sita** and **Lakshmana** when they were exiled in the Dandaka Forest, and he lent Rama the fearsome weapon, the 'arrow of Brahma', which killed the demon-king **Ravana**.

AGAVE
Europe (South)

Agave (Agaue, 'princess'), in Greek myth, was the daughter of **Cadmus** and Harmony. She helped to bring up the infant **Dionysus** (son of **Zeus** and her sister **Semele**), and later married Echion (one of the **Sown Men**) and became queen of Thebes. After Echion's death their son **Pentheus** inherited the Theban throne, and Agave ruled with him as queen mother. Some years later, Dionysus returned to the city, bringing his ecstatic religion, and Agave became one of his first followers, leading the women of Thebes in dancing and ritual worship on Mount Cithaeron. Pentheus resisted the god, who took him to the mountain and told the women that he was a wild animal and a spy. Agave led the women in tearing Pentheus to pieces; she spiked his head on a pole and danced with it all the way back to Thebes – and it was only when she entered the city gates that the trance left her and she realized what she'd done. She fled to Illyria, where she married King Lycotherses. Many years later, when the aged Cadmus and Harmony left Thebes and wandered the world looking for a place to end their lives on earth, she took them in, and it was here that they, and she, shed their mortality and ascended to **Olympus**.

AGES OF BRAHMA
India

Numerologists of the Brahmanic religion, working in the 600s BCE, held that eternity is measured in years of **Brahma**'s life, which is eternal but is itself part of the cycle. Each turn of the wheel of eternity takes 100 years of Brahma's life (157,680 million mortal years). Each turn is followed by another

100 Brahmanic years of chaos (absence of *brahman*, the 'power which is in everything'), after which Brahma is reborn and the cycle begins again.

So far as the universe is concerned, each cycle of its existence, from **creation** to dissolution, is equal to a single day of Brahma's life, the time between him waking and sleeping: 4,320 million mortal years. This period is divided into four ages, each of them only three-quarters as long as the one before. The first age (1,728 million mortal years) is a time of virtue and contentment, during which **Dharma** god of justice walks on all four legs, created beings live in harmony and God is the colour of snow. The second age (1,296 million mortal years) is one quarter less virtuous and contented. Dharma walks on three legs, created beings are occasionally quarrelsome and God is the colour of fire. The third age (972,000 mortal years) is one quarter less contented. Dharma hobbles on two legs, created beings are discontented, God is the yellow of snake's venom and only the spiritual exercises of the devout maintain the world in harmony. The fourth age (432,000 mortal years), the one in which we currently live, is one of violence, quarrels and injustice. Dharma hops on a single leg, created beings have lost all integrity and God is the colour of tar. At the end of the fourth age, the world will be destroyed, all creation will be absorbed into *brahman* and there will be 4,320 million years of nothing (during which Brahma sleeps) before creation recurs and the cycle begins again.

AGNAR
Europe (North)

Agnar, in Nordic myth, was deprived of his father's throne by his younger brother **Geirröd**, who thought he had killed him by pushing him out to sea in a storm. But Agnar survived, returned to Geirröd's court disguised as a servant, and helped Grimnir (the god **Odin** in disguise) when Geirröd tortured him. For this Odin rewarded him by bringing about Geirröd's death and giving Agnar his rightful throne.

AGNI
India

Agni ('Fire') came to India in the Vedic period (seventeenth century BCE), perhaps from ancient Iran. His power equalled that of **Indra** and **Varuna**, and he had a thousand names, including Abhimani ('proud'), Grihaspati ('master of the house'), Pramati ('forethought'), Tanunapat ('ever-young') and Vaicnavara ('belongs to all'). He was the god of all **fire**, from **lightning** to the heat of inspiration, from the hearth-fire to the blaze of anger and the warmth which creates good digestion.

Agni's nature and powers. Above all else, Agni was the guardian of sacrifice and a mediator between gods and mortals. He sent columns of smoke to guide the gods to the place of sacrifice (and was the mouth which ate the offerings for them); he gathered the souls of mortals from funeral pyres, and carried them to **Heaven**. Because he himself was reborn each time he was kindled, he was the god of **immortality**. He created the **Sun** and stars, and hung them in the sky; he made smoke-pillars to support the firmament. He cleansed impurities, eradicated sin – and, on a more practical level, made implacable war on **demons**, creatures of dark and water: as soon as his piercing eyes saw them, he chased them, licked them up and swallowed them alive. He was hot-tempered: if you poked a **fire**, you disturbed him, making him grumble or flare into sudden rage.

Agni's birth. Agni was thrice-born: first from **water**, as the Sun is born from the **sea**; second in Air, as **lightning**; third on Earth, as humans kindled him everywhere. Some accounts are more specific: **Brahma** created him by rubbing a lotus-blossom, or Indra made him by striking a stone against the Thunderstone to make a spark, or he was made when two dry sticks were rubbed together (and was thus life created out of death). The commonest account says that he was made from the mating of **Privithi (Mother Earth)** and **Dyaus** (Father Sky), and was Indra's brother. Like Indra, he was born full-grown, and he was insatiably hungry. He ate his parents, and then, unsatisfied, grew seven tongues and began lapping purified butter from the sacrificial altar – a practice he continued ever afterwards, wherever sacrifice was made. In one story, he ate so much – or drank so much **soma** – that he exhausted himself, and was able to recover only by eating the huge Khandava Forest and everything in it – a feat which he still regularly equals, in forest-fires throughout the world.

Agni and Brighu. In one story, Agni was not born insatiable but was cursed with all-hunger by the sage Brighu. Brighu stole Puloma, a beautiful woman betrothed to a demon – and Agni, who sees and knows everything, told the demon where she was hidden. Brighu cursed Agni, saying that he would eat everything in the universe, pure or impure, and would never be satisfied. Agni objected that all he'd done was answer the demon's questions, and asked Brighu if he'd rather the mouth of the gods told lies. Brighu relented and changed the curse. Agni was still condemned insatiably to bite, and consume, everything put before him; but since the mouth of the god was all-pure, everything he ate would be purified as soon as it touched his jaws. Agni and impurity could never coexist. At the end of the world, the myth ends, Agni will surge from the **Underworld** and lick up all **creation**. There will be no more darkness, no more secrets; truth will prevail.

*Agni is a favourite subject for poets, and some of the more fanciful descriptions above come from the **Rig Veda**, and from flights of metaphor in the **Mahabharata** and **Ramayana**. In art he is shown as a red-fleshed, smoke-robed prince who rides a sacred ram or a wind-wheeled chariot drawn by flame-red horses. His back and face glisten gold with butter; his hair is flames; his two faces each have seven tongues, knife-jaws, gold teeth and flames arrowing from his mouths. Sometimes he has three arms, sometimes four; he carries a bundle of fruit, an axe, fan, torch and ladle. He has seven legs, and his body sends out seven rays of light. One myth tells how he* *changed his appearance to fight the flesh-eating demons the Kravyads. For this exploit he became a Kravyad himself, a bull with a boar's head armed with iron tusks – and some art-works show him in this uncompromising aspect.*

≫→ **light and dark**

AGWE
Americas (Caribbean)

Agwe ('water'), in Voodoo myth, is the god of salt and fresh **water**. He and his mermaid-consort La Sirene live in a palace on the underwater island of Z'ile Minfort. They are propitiated by an annual ceremony of feasting, dancing, and the sacrifice of a blue-dyed ram and a banquet, laid on a bed-shaped altar and slid into the water for Agwe and La Sirene to sleep on and guarantee prosperity for the coming year.

AH PUCH
Americas (South)

Ah Puch, in Mayan myth, was the god of **death**, a **demon** who ruled the deepest and darkest of the nine Underworlds. In the **Underworld** he had no shape, but every night, when darkness made it possible for him to visit the Upper World, he took the form of a putrefying, walking corpse and padded round the houses of mortals, knife at the ready, looking for victims. For this reason, relatives of sick and dying people used to leave food outside the sickroom door to distract Ah Puch's attention, and shrieked and howled to make him think that other demons had fallen on his prey before him.

AHRIMAN
Asia (West)

Ahriman (a contraction of Angra Mainya, 'destructive force'), in Iranian myth, was the power of darkness, leader of **demons**, **twin** and implacable opponent of **Ahura Mazda**, lord of light. He had no good qualities whatever. When he was still in the womb of the primeval being **Zurvan Akarana**, sharing it with Ahura Mazda, he overheard Zurvan Akarana saying 'the firstborn will be greatest' – and at once ripped the womb apart and jostled into the world ahead of Ahura Mazda. He created and ruled all the destructive forces in the universe, and used storms, disease and **death** to try to force Ahura Mazda's human worshippers to abandon light and worship him instead.

For all this, Zoroaster taught, Ahriman was essential for the continued existence and harmony of the universe. For if darkness did not exist, how we would understand the true nature of light, or how to value it?

≫→ **light and dark, twins**

AHSONNUTLI
Americas (North)

Ahsonnutli, in the myths of the Navajo people of the US Southwestern desert, created Earth and **Sky**, and kept them apart by propping Sky on four **giants**, one at each main compass point. (The giants' panting as they bore Sky's weight caused winds and storms.) Ahsonnutli was originally mortal, but mated with the shape-changing Turquoise Woman (a being who could throw off mortality like a dress, as often as she wanted, and assume a new life and identity). **Sex with her gave him a share of her immortality**, and to enjoy it in peace he withdrew to a remote palace far above Sky, where he still lives in solitude, keeping apart from all other gods and humans.

➵ **creation**

AHTO
Europe (North)

Ahto ('**water**') or Ahti, in Finnish myth, was the god of seas, lakes and rivers. His palace was the hollow heart of a black cliff curtained by clouds and protected by waves. Forever jealous of the gods of the **sky**, he spent his time brooding, and because human beings prayed to the sky-gods and not to him, he sent his servants, whirlpools, genies and water-sprites, to harry them.

➵ **sea**

AHURA MAZDA
Asia (West)

Ahura Mazda ('creative light'), in Iranian myth, was the ruler of the universe. He was the **twin** of **Ahriman**, and was his opposite in every way: light instead of dark, calmness instead of fury, giving instead of taking, forgiveness instead of implacability. He created human beings, whereas Ahriman sought to destroy them. When Ahriman sent his three-headed dragon **Azhi Dahaka** to eat the universe, Ahura Mazda created his own son, **Atar, fire**, and sent him to fight for the powers of light.

In the Zoroastrian religion, Ahura Mazda's name is contracted to Ormahzd.

➵ **creation, light and dark, twins**

AIGAMUXA
Africa

Aigamuxa, in the myths of the Khoisan (Hottentot) peoples of the Southern African deserts, were man-eating **monsters**. They were hampered in chasing their victims because their eyes were not in their heads but in their insteps, so that they had to run blind, and when they wanted to see where they were going they had to lie on the sand and lift up their feet, during which time their prey could easily escape.

AIOMUM KONDI
Americas (South)

Aiomum Kondi, in the myths of the Arawak people of the Guianas, was king of the gods and ruler of the **sky**. He created mortals in the image of the gods, but was so disgusted by their debauchery that he destroyed them in a fire from **Heaven**. He remade them, and once again they disappointed him and he sent a flood to wash them from Earth. However, this time there was one good man, Marerewana, and he and his wife were allowed to survive the flood and regenerate the human race. This is why good and evil are permanent characteristics of human beings, alone of all earthly creatures – and the presence of evil in the world is why Aiomum Kondi, and the rest of the gods, nowadays take so little interest in it.

➵ **supreme deity**

AIRAVATA
India

Airavata (or Airavana), in the Vedic myths of the Aryan people who invaded India in the seventeenth century BCE, was a four-tusked, white elephant as big as snow-capped Mount Kailasa (site of **Shiva**'s palace on Earth). Two different accounts are given of its birth and functions. In one, it was created from the churning of the Sea of Milk (see **amrita**), and was immediately appropriated by **Indra** as his war-steed. It was a cloud-creature, and when Indra rode it, it sucked trunksful of water from the **Underworld** and sprayed them on Earth as rain. In the other account, Airavata was created by **Brahma**. He broke an egg, holding half the shell in each hand. From the right-hand half he made eight male elephants, led by Airavata: they had four tusks each, and their hides were as milky as egg-white. From the left-hand half he made eight female elephants, their mates. Brahma set the sixteen elephants to support the Earth: one pair at each of the eight main compass-points.

AJAX, 'GREAT'
Europe (South)

'Great' or 'Telamonian' Ajax (Aias, 'earthman') – so-called, in Greek myth, to distinguish him from 'Little' Ajax – was the son of King Telamon of Salamis. **Heracles**, a friend of his father, visited Salamis for Ajax's naming feast, and gave him the gift of heroic strength, by wrapping him in his cloak made from the skin of the **Nemean Lion**. Wherever the cloak touched Ajax's skin, he could not be hurt by mortal weapons; only one armpit (where Heracles' quiver got in the way) was vulnerable.

Ajax in the Trojan War. Ajax grew up to be one of the strongest and ablest warrior-princes in Greece. At Troy, his feats of arms were surpassed only by **Achilles**, and the Greeks nicknamed him 'Wall'. On one occasion, he fought **Hector** single-handed. The duel lasted all day, and the pair were so evenly matched that neither disturbed even a hair on the other's body. At last, as dusk fell, they agreed to part, and gave each other presents: Hector gave Ajax a sword, and Ajax gave Hector a baldrick of purple leather. The **Fates** were watching, and later involved each gift in its new owner's death. When Achilles killed Hector and dragged him after his chariot round the walls of Troy, he used Ajax's baldrick to fasten his corpse to the chariot. When Ajax killed himself (see below) it was with Hector's sword.

Ajax's death. After the distribution of spoils which followed the fall of Troy, the goddess **Thetis** (Achilles' mother) added another treasure: the armour **Hephaestus** had made in **Heaven** for her son. Because Achilles' son **Neoptolemus** was too young to wear it, she offered it to the bravest Greek hero still left alive. Everyone agreed that the choice was between Ajax (who had carried Achilles' body back from the walls of Troy) and **Odysseus** (who had protected him while he did so). **Agamemnon** asked each hero to make his case before the assembled leaders, and Ajax (who was as slow with words as he was quick with weapons) was no match for the plausible Odysseus.

Odysseus was awarded the armour, and the humiliation of being rejected sent Ajax mad. He buckled on his own armour, snatched up the sword Hector had given him, and went to butcher all the Greek leaders in their beds. But all he attacked, in his madness, was a flock of sheep, and when his wits came back and he found himself surrounded by their carcasses, he stuck Hector's sword point-upwards in the ground and fell on it, trying to commit suicide. At first the point would not pierce his invulnerable skin. But his repeated efforts bent the sword into a bow-shape, and its point slipped upwards into his one vulnerable part (his armpit) and pierced his heart. Years later, when Odysseus visited the **Underworld** and met all his dead companions from the **Trojan War**, Ajax's ghost was still blazing with rage because of Achilles' armour, and refused to speak to him.

AJAX, 'LITTLE'
Europe (South)

'Little' Ajax (Aias, 'earthman') – so-called, in Greek myth, to distinguish him from 'Great' Ajax – was the son of King Oileus of Locris. He was one of the unsuccessful suitors of **Helen** of Sparta, and later took forty ships and an army of soldiers to Troy to help win her back from **Paris**. During the sack of Troy, he found **Cassandra** in **Athene**'s temple, clinging for safety to the holy statue. He dragged her out to rape her, and in the struggle pulled the statue from its pedestal. Athene, furious, borrowed one of **Zeus**' thunderbolts and blasted him dead. His soldiers took his ashes home and buried them on the island of Mykonos.

Not surprisingly, many accounts confuse the two Ajaxes, saying that it was 'Great' Ajax who raped Cassandra and that it was to punish him for this that Athene drove him mad after he failed to win Achilles' armour. Some scholars think that the story of 'Little' Ajax was invented in Locris, to explain a curious custom there. Even though Athene killed Ajax with a thunderbolt, she was still not satisfied. She sent plague on Locris, and lifted it only when the people agreed to send two girls to her temple in Troy – the new Troy, built from the ruins of the city sacked by the Greeks – each year for a thousand years. The girls had to climb secretly into Troy, make offerings in Athene's temple and then become temple slaves. If they were caught before they reached the temple, they were stoned to death.

AJISUKITAKAHIKONE
Asia (East)

Ajisukitakahikone, in Japanese myth, was the chief of many **thunder**-spirits, and the father of Takitsuhiko, Lord of Pouring **Rain**. When he was a baby he was so noisy that his nurses carried him up and down a flight of steps to soothe him, and then put him in a boat to sail endlessly round and round Japan – which is why thunder seems to approach and recede.
»→ Raiden and Raiju

AJOK
Africa

Ajok (or Adyok or Naijok), creator-god in the myths of the Sudanese Lotuko people, made human beings in his own image. When the child of the first human pair died, the woman begged him to bring it back to life. Ajok did so, and was preparing to grant it and all its descendants **immortality** when the child's father burst in. Furious that he had not been consulted, he killed his wife and baby – and Ajok was so annoyed that he left **death** to prey forever on human beings and never visited Earth again.

≫→ creation

AJYSYT
Arctic

Ajysyt ('birthgiver'), in the myths of the Yakuts people of Siberia, owned the Golden Book of **Fate**, containing the names and destinies of every human being ever born. At the instant of each new birth, she gave the baby a soul and entered its name in the book – and the child was from then on a fully-fledged member of the human race, equipped with all our potential, both for good and ill.

AKKA
Europe (North)

Akka ('old woman'), in Finnish myth, was queen of the gods, consort of **Ukko**. Like Ukko, she did nothing active in the world, and stayed aloof from it. But her existence was essential to its continuation, guaranteeing the stability of marriage, family and society among human beings. Her sacred tree was the mountain-ash (after which she was also called Rauni, 'rowan'), and people planted single trees beside their houses to honour her and ask her blessing.

≫→ justice and universal order

AKONGO
Africa

Akongo, supreme Sky-spirit in the myths of the Ngombe people of the river Congo, created human beings and regretted it. In some accounts, he lived with them on Earth until he could no longer stand their quarrelling, then moved away, either deep into the forest or up into the sky. In others, there were just two human beings and he shared his hut in **Heaven** with them; when they started arguing he lowered them on a rope to the as yet uninhabited Earth, giving them maize and sugarcane to plant and pulling up the rope as soon as they were safely down. In this version the two humans mated and had a daughter, who ran into the forest and had sex with the first wild animal that came along – the origin of every witch and demon on Earth, and yet another reason for Akongo to disdain his offspring.

≫→ creation, supreme deity

ALBERICH: *see* Andvari

ALBION
Europe (North)

Albion ('white'), in Celtic myth, was a **giant** who took part in the epic battle against the **Olympian** gods, escaped being killed by **Heracles** and fled to the remote islands later known as Britain. He took with him one of the golden apples of **immortality**, and planted an apple-tree in his new kingdom. But he quickly tired of life in a backwater, went on a recruiting-drive South to gather a second giant-army to attack the gods, met Heracles and was killed by him.

This story survives principally in Geoffrey of Monmouth's twelfth-century History of the Kings of Britain, and is a characteristic medieval attempt to marry the shreds of surviving indigenous myth (in this case Celtic) with lore distantly and imperfectly remembered from monkish classical education (in this case the story of the Greek giants' revolt against the gods). Albion was the original name for the islands; the name 'Britain' came later, and the myth of **Brit** *– a similar farrago of half-digested pagan lore – was invented to explain it.*

ALCINOUS
Europe (South)

Alcinous (Alkinoös, 'strong-mind'), in Greek myth, was the King of Phaeacia and father of **Nausicaä**. When **Odysseus** was washed up on the shores of his kingdom, he welcomed him, listened to the story of his wanderings, and then gave a ship and a crew to carry him home to Ithaca.

ALCMAEON
Europe (South)

Alcmaeon and Eriphyle. Alcmaeon (Alkmaion, 'mighty endeavour'), in Greek myth, was the son of Princess **Eriphyle** of Argos and the prophet Amphiaraus who was one of the **Seven Against Thebes**. When **Polynices'** son Thesander was collecting a second group of heroes, the Epigoni, the gods told him that the expedition would fail unless Alcmaeon led it. Alcmaeon was reluctant to fight, just as his father had been before him – and, just as his father had done, agreed to leave the decision to Eriphyle. Thesander bribed her with the golden wedding-dress made by the gods for Harmony when she married

Cadmus years before, and Eriphyle sent Alcmaeon to war.

Alcmaeon knew nothing of the bribery until Thesander boasted about it after the fall of Thebes. He asked the Delphic oracle what the punishment was for a woman who took gold to send her husband and son to war, and the oracle answered '**Death**'. Alcmaeon murdered his mother, and the **Furies** drove him mad for it. He wandered all over Greece in search of purification. King Phegeus of Psophis helped him, and in gratitude he married Phegeus' daughter Arsinoe and gave her Harmony's golden dress and necklace. But then the Furies returned, and Alcmaeon forgot Arsinoe and began his wanderings again. Before she died Eriphyle had cursed him, saying that he would never find purification on any land then existing. The gods guided him to a patch of new land, sand washed down since Eriphyle's death by the river **Achelous**; there Alcmaeon was purified at last from madness, and married the river-god's daughter Callirrhoe.

Alcmaeon and Callirrhoe. Alcmaeon and Callirrhoe had two sons. But then, like Eriphyle before her, Callirrhoe began to fear that she would grow ugly as she grew older. She refused to sleep with Alcmaeon unless he gave her Harmony's dress and necklace, which guaranteed eternal youth. Alcmaeon had to go to Psophis and steal them from Arsinoe, the wife he had long ago abandoned – and on the way home he was ambushed by Phegeus' sons and killed. Arsinoe, now truly a widow, cursed her father Phegeus and her brothers, and prayed to the gods to kill them before the next moon waned. Phegeus punished her for this by locking her in a box and selling her into slavery.

Meanwhile, word reached Callirrhoe of Alcmaeon's death, and she prayed to **Zeus** that her baby sons might grow to manhood in a single day and avenge him. Zeus granted her prayer. The babies jumped out of their cradle, turned into grown men before they touched the ground, went to Psophis and killed Phegeus and his sons. Harmony's golden dress and necklace were given for safety to the priests of **Apollo**, and lay for centuries in one of the treasuries at Delphi.

ALCMENA
Europe (South)

Alcmena (Alkmene, 'mighty in anger'), in Greek myth, was the daughter of King Electryon of Argos, and the wife of his heir **Amphitryon**. Electryon's cattle had all been stolen, and his eight sons murdered, by King Pterelaus of the Teleboans, and Amphitryon set out to take revenge. While he was away, **Zeus** took advantage and seduced Alcmena.

There was more to this seduction than the lust which normally inspired Zeus' affairs on Earth. After the gods defeated the **Titans** and became lords of the universe, they had successfully defended themselves against **giants**, **monsters** and supernatural creatures of every kind. But Zeus knew that however powerful the Olympians were, **Mother Earth**'s relatives Ocean, Night and **Chaos** still lurked in the recesses of the universe, and that one day gods and mortals could be swept away just as Zeus and his brothers had displaced

the Titans. He had decided therefore to create a son, a **hero** who would combine the finest qualities of gods and mortals, who would act as the gods' champion, defy the world of darkness and keep its creatures cowed.

It was to be the mother of such a champion that Zeus chose Alcmena, the noblest of all mortal women. And since he knew that she would never betray Amphitryon to make love with anyone else, he waited until Amphitryon was far from Argos, fighting the Teleboans, then disguised himself as Amphitryon, pretended he had come successfully home from the expedition, and made love to Alcmena in Amphitryon's place. The love-making lasted for three mortal nights: Zeus made the **Sun** stable his horses and stay at home, while the **Moon** lingered and Sleep sealed mortal eyes. Human beings leapt up refreshed after their three-day sleep – and in the meantime the real Amphitryon finished his business with the Teleboans, hurried home and replaced Zeus in Alcmena's bed without anyone knowing that the ruler of the universe had ever usurped him there.

No one would have been any the wiser until the birth of the child, except that on the morning the baby was due Zeus boasted that everyone in Argos would be subordinate to the next prince born there. At once **Hera** realized what had happened. She sent **Ilythia**, goddess of **childbirth**, to hold back the birth, and Ilythia sat outside Alcmena's door and clasped her hands tightly round her knees. This spell prevented Alcmena from giving birth, and in the meantime Hera helped another Argive princess, Nicippe, to give

birth to a seven-months' child. (His name was **Eurystheus**, and as soon as he was born, Zeus' prophecy came true for him.)

There was still the matter of Alcmena's unending pregnancy. Hera meant to leave Ilythia sitting on guard until Alcmena and her unborn child died of starvation. But Alcmena's maidservant Galanthis ran in shouting 'A boy! A boy!' She was reporting Eurystheus' birth, but Ilythia mistook her meaning, jumped up and broke the binding-spell. Angrily she changed Galanthis into a weasel; but she was too late to stop Alcmena giving birth at last, to **twins**: **Iphicles**, the mortal son of Amphitryon, and **Heracles**, the son of Zeus.

*This was a favourite story in ancient times – but only in comedy. Comic dramatists and poets found irresistible the idea of two Amphitryons, one false one real, rushing round the palace and trying to get into Alcmena's bed, and several writers – notably Plautus, who wrote the most influential version of the story – treated it from the point of view of the confidential slave of the real Amphitryon, totally confused by having two masters he couldn't tell apart. In other versions **Hermes** muddied the waters still further by disguising himself as the slave in question, so that confusion was doubly confused: the origin of a thousand such mistaken-identity farces in later European drama.*

ALKLHA
Arctic

Alklha, in the myths of ancient Siberia, was the darkness of the **sky**. It was a universe-filling **monster** whose wings and body were impenetrable blackness and which fed itself by gnawing and swallowing the **Moon** each month – and the **Sun** whenever it got the chance. Since both heavenly bodies were hot, they seared Alklha's gullet and guts, and the monster regurgitated them. We can see the gashes of Alklha's fangs on the Moon, and they would also be visible on the Sun if we could bear to look at it. ⟫⁺ **light and dark, monsters and dragons**

ALVIS
Europe (North)

Alvis, in Nordic myth, was a dwarf who rashly asked to marry **Thor**'s daughter Thrud. Normally Thor challenged all Thrud's suitors to trials of strength, and easily defeated them. But in Alvis' case, Thor challenged him to a riddle-contest. He spent the whole night asking him questions until day dawned, the rising Sun turned Alvis to stone and Thrud remained unmarried.

AMANA
Americas (South)

Amana, in the myths of the Caliña people, was the first being in the universe. Her **sea**-kingdom was the Milky Way, and its fish, whales, seals, otters and other **water**-creatures danced with her through the waters, while she rode on Turtle's back with her mermaid-tail streaming behind her like weed in the vastness.

The floor of Amana's kingdom was not sand but darkness, the gulf of space. From time to time volcanoes erupted from it, and the streams of spat-out rock floated in space as planets. Amana covered them with plants and creatures. All would have been serene and calm if it had not been for her very first creation, **Sun**. Eternal enemy of water, he fought to destroy both Amana and her creatures wherever she made them. He scorched life from most of the planets – we can still see the ashes of the cosmic fire which engulfed the **Moon** – and was prevented from destroying the most beautiful of all, Earth, only because Amana waited until he attacked in a huge fireball, then trapped the fireball in ocean. The fireball has seethed under the surface ever since, occasionally erupting in geysers and volcanoes sending their serpents of fire to scorch the land. To keep Sun's power at bay, and to allow herself to sail her sky-ocean without taking heed of Earth, Amana made two warriors, **Tamusi** (Light) and **Tamulu** (Darkness), and sent them to look after it.

≫→ **creation, light and dark**

AMATERASU
Asia (East)

Amaterasu's birth. Amaterasu, goddess of the **Sun** in Japanese myth, was Izanagi's daughter (see **Izanami and Izanagi**). When Izanagi came back to the world of light from **Yomi**, the **Underworld** (where he had gone, in vain, to bring his sister Izanami back from death), he stripped off his clothes and washed to remove the dust of the grave. When he took off his clothes twelve deities were created, when he scrubbed his body ten more appeared, and when he washed his face three great gods

were born (in some accounts from the water-drops which fell back into the basin, in others as points of light from the mirror he used to see what he was doing): **Susano** the storm-god from his nose, **Tsukuyomi** the **Moon** from his right eye and Amaterasu from his left eye. Izanagi gave Susano the sea to rule, and made Tsukuyomi and Amaterasu rulers, respectively, of night and day. Amaterasu's symbol of office was a necklace of light, the Milky Way, and her clothes (which she wove herself: the first garments ever made) were sewn with jewels, her radiance made into precious stones.

Amaterasu and Susano. Susano, furious at being supplanted by his sister, raged about the Earth so violently that seas dried up and mountains withered. Izanagi banished him to the Underworld, granting him just one favour before he left the world of light: to say goodbye to Amaterasu in **Heaven**. Susano now tricked Amaterasu. He pretended to be attacking Heaven, and when she reluctantly armed herself to fight him, said innocently that she was the aggressor, that he'd come in peace and that they should both perform wonders to prove their good faith. If her magic proved stronger than his, he'd go to the Underworld. If his proved stronger than hers, he'd stay with her in Heaven forever. He handed over his sword, and she gave him a hairband of five strung stars. Amaterasu broke the sword in three, chewed the pieces in her mouth and spat them out; they turned into three goddesses who (because they were made from Susano's sword) were sent to spend eternity on Earth. Susano washed the five stars in the Heaven-well of Eternal Life, crunched them in his mouth and spat out five gods; since these were made from Amaterasu's stars, they became rulers in Heaven.

Amaterasu and the Seasons. Amaterasu was by nature gentle and retiring. Her main activities were farming silkworms and spinning and weaving the resulting thread – skills she introduced to human beings. She was happy to let Susano racket round Heaven, so long as he left her and her maids in peace. But Susano wanted more attention. He hammered on the doors and howled through the windows of the weaving-house. When Amaterasu went to celebrate the feast of first fruits, Susano hurried to the temple ahead of her, and fouled the entire floor with dung. Finally, seeing Amaterasu alone in the weaving-house with her servant – or, in some accounts, with her sister the dawn-goddess Wakahirume – he killed one of the Horses of Heaven, flayed it and threw the carcass in the air so that it crashed through the roof and flopped to the floor. Amaterasu's servant jumped back in terror, and the shuttle of her loom stabbed her in the vagina and killed her. Driven out of patience at last, Amaterasu barricaded herself in a cave and refused to come out.

Amaterasu's exile deprived the universe of light – and with it, of growth and life. The eight hundred myriad gods tried unsuccessfully to persuade her to come out. They held a council on the banks of the Heaven-river, and Omoigane, god of wisdom, suggested a trick. He told the Heavenly Jewelmaster to make a star-necklace two metres long, the Heavenly Coppersmith to make a polished mirror and the others to plant *sakati* trees outside the cave-mouth and hang on the branches not only the necklace and mirror but strips of coloured cloth, prayer-scrolls and precious stones. Finally, he told **Uzume** the dancer to perform, and the other gods to make as much noise as they could. The gods sang and stamped their feet, Uzume's dancing grew more and more lascivious, the gods laughed louder and louder, and eventually Amaterasu moved aside one of the boulders blocking the cave-entrance – the light which emerged was the origin of the first dawn-light each day – and asked how they could be so happy when light was denied the world. Omoigane answered that it was simple: they'd found a god more radiant than she was, and were celebrating. Amaterasu pulled away a few more stones, saw her own reflection in the mirror hung on the tree, and came a little way out of the cave to see more. At once the Strong God dragged her fully out, the other gods strung a rope across the entrance to stop her going back, and two of the Elder Gods took her hands and begged her never to leave again.

Amaterasu's return brought light and **fertility** back to the world, and she marked it by showing human beings how to grow and cook rice. As for Susano, the Court of Heaven fined him, cut off his beard, fingernails and toenails and banished him to Earth.

Amaterasu and the Imperial Family. Susano's departure restored peace to Heaven. Although the time which then passed was the blink of an eye to gods, on Earth it took many human generations, during which Susano's half-human, half-**monster** offspring ruled. Then Amaterasu decided that Heavenly calm should be given to Earth as well, and asked her son Amenoosimasa to go there and rule. He refused, saying that he'd just had a son of his own and had responsibilities in Heaven. Amaterasu sent another god, Amenohohi, and when no news came back of him she asked his son Amenowakahiko to find out what had happened. But Amenowakahiko married one of Susano's descendants, and paid no more attention to Heaven. Amaterasu sent a pheasant-**messenger** to ask for news, and he shot it dead. Finally Amaterasu sent **Ninigi**, and gave him the mirror and necklace the gods had made to entice her from the cave, and the Heaven-sword Kusanagi. Carrying these emblems, Ninigi was escorted to Earth in majesty, and was accepted as ruler. He founded the Imperial dynasty – and with their coming, the story ends, the period of myth ended and the cycle of history began.

The Amaterasu story lies at the heart of the symbiosis of Shinto worship and the politics and social order of Imperial Japan. Scholars from outside Japan see it as an amalgamation of ancient myths – among the very few in the world in which the Sun is not male but female – legend and straightforward annalistic history. But in Japan, the interpenetration of religion and history was for centuries so powerful that heads of the Imperial family continued to be regarded by many people as gods, direct lineal descendants of Amaterasu, until Emperor Hirohito renounced this sta-tus after the Second World War. The centrality of Amaterasu makes her story one of the most often illustrated in all Japanese art, with a wealth of iconography – peacocks, pigs, gambolling monkeys, symbolic patterns of pebbles on the ground and branches on the trees – not present in myth-illustrations of other kinds.
»+ Great Goddess

AMAZONS
Europe (South)

The Amazons, in Greek myth, were warrior women, descended from **Ares** god of war. Their name either means 'without a breast', and refers to their (alleged) custom of cutting off one breast so that they could more easily sling their quivers (they were expert archers); or it means 'without cereal food', and refers to their (alleged) cannibalism. The Amazons lived on the shores of Ocean, the river which girds the Earth, and waited for unwary sailors. When the ships landed, they welcomed the sailors, had **sex** with them, killed them and ate them. Very few heroes in myth, apart from **Heracles** and **Theseus**, visited them and lived to tell the tale.

The Amazons seldom visited the rest of the world, and when they did they were usually defeated. Princess Penthesilea, for example, fought on **Priam**'s side in the **Trojan war** until she was killed by **Achilles**, and Princess **Antiope** (whom Theseus had taken to Athens as his mistress) called an Amazon army to attack Athens and kill Theseus after he abandoned her for **Phaedra**, but the Athenians defeated them.

AMBALIKA
India

Ambalika, in Hindu myth, was a queen whose husband Vichitravirya died before he could give her children. (She was senior to her fellow-queen **Ambika**.) As custom was, she agreed to let his brother father her child instead. She expected to entertain her handsome brother-in-law **Bhisma**, but instead found **Vyasa**, a filthy hermit, in her bed. She turned pale with horror – and consequently conceived an albino son, **Pandu** ('pale').

AMBIKA
India

Ambika, in Hindu myth, was a queen whose husband Vichitravirya died before he could give her children. (She was junior to her fellow-queen **Ambalika**.) As custom was, she agreed to let his brother father her child instead. She expected her handsome brother-in-law **Bhisma**, but instead found **Vyasa**, a filthy hermit, in her bed. At the moment of penetration she shut her eyes – and consequently the son she conceived, **Dhritarashtra**, was blind.

AMBROSIA
Europe (South)

Ambrosia ('**immortality**'), in Greek and Roman myth, was the food of the gods, as **nectar** was their drink. It gave and guaranteed **immortality**. The sweetness of its smell and its taste surpassed all earthly foods, and although mortals often tried to make it for themselves (for example by mixing honey, wine and herbs), they never succeeded.

The gods not only ate it, but distilled it into perfume and used it as ointment, rubbing themselves down with it after exercise and dropping it into wounds to heal them instantly.

AMERICAN MYTH

At some time between 35,000 and 10,000 years ago, during the last Ice Age, humans from Asia crossed the frozen Bering Strait into the American continent, and spread over its entire area. Over the succeeding millennia some 2000 individual peoples arose, some of them small communities (for example the fishers of Patagonia), others large empires or language-groups. (In its heyday, the Andean Inca empire was twice the size of the contemporary Frankish empire in Europe; at the same period the Iroquois-speaking confederacy dominated a vast area of what is now the Eastern United States.)

Despite such diversity, the strands of myth remained remarkably consistent throughout the continent. The idea, for example, that the Earth was created from mud drawn from the bottom of the primordial ocean, sometimes after an all-engulfing **flood**, was common to peoples from Canada and Argentina, the Great Lakes and the Amazon basin, Central America and – perhaps most tellingly of all, since there was unlikely to be any way in which they can ever have seen the **sea** – the Great Plains and Desert of the Central and Southwestern United States.

In the majority of these cultures, the Earth, home of human beings, was one of three worlds, the others being homes respectively of gods and spirits and of demons and the Dead. Usually the god-world was above the Earth and the demon-world below it. The gods were led by a bodiless entity, creativity made manifest, usually given a name such as Great Spirit, Maker, Nothing Lacking or Ancient One. Sometimes this Spirit remained concerned in and active for its own creation, but often it withdrew from activity, remaining in the universe but not of it, the object of speculation rather than of worship. The other gods were more manifest: offspring (usually in giant human form) of the Great Spirit, embodiments of such natural phenomena as Famine, **Lightning**, **Mother Earth**, **Rain** or **Sun**; rulers of the Dead. Animals were important. Many myth-systems – particularly those of the forests of the North and the Amazon basin – said that the Earth was originally the home of giant animals, which had the abilities to move freely between the three worlds, to take off their animal identity and hang it up like a skin on a peg, and to work magic (for example, many helped in the details of **creation**). This idea gave rise, first, to the adoption by many peoples of animals as guardian and guiding spirits (*totems*) and, second, to thousands of myths and folktales in which animals – Beaver in Canada, Coyote in the Southwest and California, Hare in the Great Lakes, Panther in Amazonia, Raven in the Pacific Northwest – were both archetypal **tricksters** and creation-gods. Other animals, particularly the Water-**snakes** (which ruled all rivers on Earth and were hostile to the Sun) and Thunderbirds (which controlled the weather), were common to cultures throughout the continent.

In Central America and the Peruvian Andes – and nowhere else, suggesting perhaps a common ancestry for this area – cosmologies of a different kind arose. These were present not only in the myths of such enormous empires as those of the Aztecs, Inca and Maya, but in smaller systems and individual stories from elsewhere. In all of them, the Sun and Moon predominated as original gods and creators. There was eternal conflict between **Light** and **Dark** (often embodied in a pair of warring god-**twins**), and human survival depended on keeping Dark (standing for evil and death) at bay and encouraging Light (standing for good and life). The lesser gods, those of harvest, rain, sickness, war and so forth, all tended towards one sphere of influence (usually that of their parent, good or bad), and had to be seduced to help mortals by unceasing prayer and sacrifice. The gods often mated with mortals to produce new warrior-gods or **fertility**-spirits, and many gods also chose to spend time as mortals, manifesting themselves in human society as empire-builders or glorious rulers.

Societies whose myths centred on the regular reappearance of the Sun and **Moon**, or on the cycle of the seasons, often immersed themselves in ritual to the point where observance itself began to seem to be what kept life going, not the gods in whose names the observances were made. Mayan myths, and the religious practices arising from them, depended on meticulous calculations of time, based on subdivisions of the year. Inca myths were obsessive in a similar way about spatial geometry, the location of each place or journey being exhaustively described. Aztec society drew from its myths (which hardly now seem to bear such a weight of interpretation) a system of rigorous ritual, sacrifice and self-denial which consumed its people's lives – and, if Spanish conquerors are to be believed, also their bodies, since holocausts of human victims, and cannibalism, were claimed to be standard practice at the shrines of even the most genial-seeming Aztec gods.

The question of biased description is one facet of a major problem for anyone investigating the myths of the Americas: transmission. However sophisticated the societies which gave rise to the myths, they were all non-literate, and what survives today is therefore largely a matter of what other people chose (and choose) to codify from an enormous, amorphous mass of ritual and oral storytelling. In the cases of the Incas, and particularly the Aztecs, the Spanish conquerors who were the first to write down their myths had a vested interest in making them seem as barbarous and bloodthirsty as possible. (The Maya survived this process by retreating into the jungle or the mountains, with the result that their myths, very recently rediscovered, are among the most dispersed and fragmentary of all major systems.) Similar disruption by Europeans of the culture of other societies (in North America in the sixteenth-nineteenth centuries CE, in Amazonia at this precise moment) have led to myth becoming, for many native peoples, a crucial factor in the survival of tribal identity – and consequently to its politicization. In one area, the Caribbean, native myth has all but disappeared, replaced by the Christianity of eighteenth-century plantation-owners from Europe, the myths of the African people they shipped in as slaves, and systems (such as the Voodoo religion in Haiti) which draw on both.

≫→ **Myths of the Arctic:** Aulanerk, Disemboweller, Eeyeekalduk, Igaluk, Kadlu, Nanook, Pinga, Sedna, Torngarsak

≫→ **Myths of the Northwest coast:** Amotken, Copper Woman, Enumclaw and Kapoonis, Five Sisters, Komokwa, Kwatee, Nagaitcho, Nocoma, Qamaits, Raven, Sisiutl, Snoqalm and Beaver, Wishpoosh

≫→ **Myths of the Northeastern woodlands:** Adekagagwaa, Ataentsic, Dajoji, Flying Head, Ga-oh, Gendenwitha, Gluskap, Gunnodayak, Hahgwehdiyu and Hahgwehdaetgah, Hinu, Ioskeha, Kitshi Manito, Nanabush, Nokomis, Onatah, Oshadagea, Tawiskaron, Underwater panthers

≫→ **Myths of the Northern forests:** Amotken, Baxbakualanuchsiwae, Gluskap, Malsum, Michabo, Nipinoukhe and Pipinoukhe, Underwater panthers

≫→ **Myths of the US/Canadian plains:** Ictinike, Maheo, Na'pi, Pah, Poia, Tirawa, Uncegila, Wakan Tanka, Wakonda, Wheememeowah, White She-Buffalo

≫→ **Myths of the Southeastern US:** Asgaya Gigagei, Corn Woman, Dayunsi, Esaugetuh Emissee, Kananeski Amaiyehi, Unelanuki, Utset

≫→ **Myths of the Southwestern US (desert):** Ahsonnutli, Atsehastin and Atseestan, Black God, Dzoavits, Estsanatlehi, Humanmaker, Nayenezgani and Tobadzistsini, Szeukha, Tonenili, Tsohanoai

≫→ Myths of the Southwestern US (Pueblos): Awonawilona, Doquebuth, First Made Man, Kloskurbeh, Kokyangwuti, Payatamu, Poshaiyankayo, Star Country, Ten Corn Maidens, Umai-hulhlya-wit, Wonomi, Yanauluha

≫→ Myths of the California coast: Chinigchinich, Gudratrigakwitl, Kodoyanpe, Kumokum, Kumush, Owiot, Quaayayp, Wonomi

≫→ Myths of Central America (including Aztec and Mayan): Chac, Chalchihuitlicue, Cihuacóatl, Coatlicue, Coyolxauhqui, Ehecatl, Gucumatz, Hunab, Hurukan, Ilamatecuhtli, Itzamná, Itzpapalotl, Ixchel, Ixtab, Ixtlilton, Kanassa, Kasogonaga, Kukulkan, Macuilxóchitl, Mayauel, Mictlan, Mixcóatl, Ometecuhtli, Quetzalcóatl, Temazcalteci, Tezcatlipoca, Tlaloc, Tlazoltéotl, Tochopa and Hokomata, Tonatiuh, Xipetotec, Xiutecuhtli, Xochipili, Xochiquetzal, Xólotl, Yacatecuhtli

≫→ Myths of the Caribbean (including Voodoo): Agwe, Annency, Azacca, Bossu, Damballah, Erzulie, Ghede, Legba, Mait' Carrefour, Mama Brigitte, Ogoun

≫→ Myths of South America (including Inca): Ah Puch, Aiomum Kondi, Amana, Ariconte and Tamendonare, Auchimalgen, Aunyainá, Bachue, Bochica, Catequil, Ceucy, Chantico, Chiminigagué, Chonchonyi, Coniraya, Cupay, Ekkekko, El Dorado, Ellal, Guecufu, Guinechen, Huitzilopochtli, Ilyap'a, Inti, Kilya, Kononatoo, Kuat, Kururumany, Mama Quilla, Manco Capac, Mani, Pachacamac, Page Abe, Para-

parawa, Pillan, Sinaa, Tamusi and Tamulu, Tupan, Uaica, Vaimatse, Valedjád, Viracocha, Wahari and Buoka

≫→ general: Coyote, Thunderbirds

AMFORTAS: *see* Pelles

AMITABHA
Asia (East); India

Amitabha, in some Buddhist myth and belief, is **Buddha**'s manifestation as God. He sits in his Western Paradise, enthroned on a lotus-flower, and welcomes all who truly believe in him and repent their sins. His Chinese name is Emituofo, and he is attended by **Avalokiteshvara**, who appears in Chinese in female form as **Guan Yin**, goddess of mercy.

≫→ supreme deity

AMMA
Africa

Amma, in the myths of the Dogon people of Mali, existed before the world. In some accounts, he was the disembodied principle of **creation**, and made the universe by conceiving an infinitesimally small particle, the nucleus of the atom of a seed, which grew and swelled to make the primordial egg. The egg was double-yolked, and its hatchlings, **Ogo** and Yasigi from one yolk, and the Nummo from the other, created all that exists.

In other accounts, Amma was the spirit not only of creation but of maleness. Desperate with sexual longing, he tried to make a female by moulding clay in two earthenware bowls. Having shaped **Mother Earth**, he threw the spare lumps of clay and the bowls into the sky – where the lumps became stars and the bowls the **Moon** and **Sun**. He tried to mate with Mother Earth, but her clitoris (a termite-hill) got in the way, so before he could penetrate her he had to circumcise her. From this union three children were born: Ogo and the Nummo twins (Yasigi does not feature in this account). Ogo was all-wicked, and to produce good creatures to counteract his evil Amma sacrificed the Nummo and scattered their blood on Mother Earth (to make her grow plants and animals), then reconstituted them and gave them new life: the first humans. (It was because they had died and come to life again that human beings are mortal.) The Nummo's children, Amma's grandchildren, were four males and four females. Each couple stood for one of the four elements (air, earth, fire, water), for one of the four cardinal compass points and for one of the four 'great skills': farming, magic, marketing and medicine.

»+ civilization

AMMUT
Africa (North)

Ammut ('corpse-eater'), in Egyptian myth, stood by the scales which weighed the sins of the Dead in the **Underworld**. She had a hippopotamus' back legs, a lion's body and a crocodile's head, and her job was to eat the hearts of the wicked.

»+ animal-gods, monsters and dragons

AMOTKEN
Americas (North)

Amotken, in the myths of the Salish-speaking peoples of the Pacific Northwest coast and interior US and Canada, created the world and everything in it. He made himself daughters, from five hairs from his head, and offered each of them any gift she asked. The first asked to become Mother of Evil, the second Mother of Good, the third Mother of Earth, the fourth Mother of **Fire** and the fifth Mother of **Water**. Amotken gave them their gifts. He decreed that Mother of Evil should rule the others for a day and a night, then Mother of Good, then Mother of Earth and so on. In the eyes of the gods, each of these periods of rule was short – but human time is different, and we are still labouring under the first reign of Mother of Evil, waiting for the second age to dawn. Benign and indifferent, Amotken sits in the sky like a doddering elder. His **messenger Coyote** carries his wishes to us on Earth, but the flow of information is one way only, and Amotken has no idea how we suffer under his daughter's tyranny.

»+ creation, five sisters

AMPHION AND ZETHUS
Europe (South)

Amphion ('of two lands') and Zethus (Zetos, 'seeker'), in Greek myth, were **twin** sons of **Zeus** and Princess **Antiope** of Boeotia. They built the city of **Thebes**, Zethus laying out the streets with mathematical skills taught him by **Athene**, Amphion (a pupil of **Hermes**) by playing his lyre so skilfully that stones leapt into place of their own accord to form the walls. They called the city after Zethus' wife Thebe, and ruled it together.

Amphion and Zethus both died as a result of sorrow caused by their own children. The children of Amphion and his wife **Niobe** were so beautiful that Thebe was jealous. She crept into the palace nursery one night to murder them, and in the darkness made a mistake and cut the throat of her own son Itylus. The gods turned her into a nightingale, forever singing mourning songs – and next morning, when Thebe's husband Zethus found out what had happened, he killed himself from grief. For her part, Niobe began boasting that her children outdid in beauty even **Apollo** himself and his sister **Artemis** – and Apollo responded by shooting them dead. Amphion, driven mad by grief, gathered an army and marched on Delphi to sack the holy shrine – and although Amphion was Zeus' own son, Zeus punished him for challenging the gods by taking away his **immortality** and banishing him to the **Underworld**.

AMPHITRITE
Europe (South)

Amphitrite ('embracer', that is, the **sea**), daughter of **Proteus** the Old Man of the Sea, in Greek myth, swore eternal virginity. But **Poseidon** chose her sister **Thetis** as consort – and when he was told that she was fated to bear a son who would be greater than his father, he abandoned her to a mortal, **Peleus**, and courted Amphitrite instead. Amphitrite would have nothing to do with him, and withdrew in an enormous tidal wave to the Atlas Mountains in Africa. (In some accounts, the wave drowned the continent of Atlantis.) Instead of raging after her, Poseidon sent an ambassador to woo her: Delphinus, king of the dolphins.

Charmed by Delphinus' antics – instead of speaking, he turned cartwheels, somersaulted and leapt in the air to convey his message – Amphitrite returned to the sea-kingdom to share Poseidon's bed. To her regret, she found that sending Delphinus was the one gentle thing Poseidon ever did for her. As soon as she married him, he returned to his former arrogance and lasciviousness, so that she spent much of her time in a fury, lashing herself into rages with storms and waves. Only Poseidon and her father could ever calm her, the one by threatening her with his trident, the other by lulling her asleep with warm West winds and soothing words.

AMPHITRYON
Europe (South)

Amphitryon ('harassing on each side'), son of Alcaeus and Hipponome in Greek myth, was a prince of **Thebes**. His elder sister had married King Electryon of Argos, and when Amphitryon grew up he married their daughter **Alcmena**. Electryon and his eight sons were cattle-lords, owning herds as far as the eye could see, and the cattle caught the eye of King Pterelaus of the Teleboans, who decided to steal them. He had one immortal hair, and unless it was discovered and plucked out of his head, he could not be harmed. Armed with this protection, Pterelaus raided

Argos, killed Electryon's sons and stole Electryon's cattle. Electryon planned to raise an army and go to punish the Teleboans, leaving Mycenae in Alcmena's care. But Amphitryon argued with him, saying that it was pointless to attack a man who could not be killed. He dashed his stick on the ground to emphasize what he was saying; the stick hit a stone, bounced up and killed Electryon.

Since this was an accident, Alcmena said that Amphitryon should not be banished for murder. But she refused to have anything more to do with him until he defeated the Teleboans and avenged the deaths of her eight brothers. Amphitryon went to Thebes to ask for help, and the Thebans offered him an army on condition that he rid their countryside of a monstrous fox: it was fated never to be caught or killed, and each month it ate or carried off a Theban child. Amphitryon hunted the fox with the famous dog Laelaps. This was a present given long ago by **Zeus** to **Europa**, and was fated always to catch and kill the animals it chased. So the hound which always caught its prey hunted the fox which could never be caught. In the end, to avoid breaking the laws of **Fate**, Zeus turned the pair of them to stone.

As soon as the fox was dealt with, the Thebans gave Amphitryon his army, and he went to fight the Teleboans. He was not at all sure how he was going to beat Pterelaus, who was still protected by his immortal hair. Fortunately, the gods made Pterelaus' daughter Comaetho fall in love with Amphitryon, and she plucked out the hair while her father slept and gave it to Amphitryon as a love-gift. Next day Amphitryon challenged Pterelaus to single combat, killed him, executed Comaetho for treachery and marched back to Argos driving his father-in-law's stolen cattle.

While all this was going on, Zeus, back in Argos, disguised himself as Amphitryon and made love to Alcmena – love-making which led to the birth of **Heracles**. As soon as Amphitryon arrived home he, too, made love to Alcmena, and their son Iphicles was born immediately after Heracles, as the hero's mortal twin.

AMRITA
India

Amrita ('immortal') was the food of the gods. In early Vedic accounts, by the Aryan people who invaded India in the seventeenth century BCE, it was the same thing as *soma*. But in later, Hindu myth it was created by the gods themselves. As the result of a curse laid on them by the wizard Durvasas, the gods' powers, and their ability to resist **demons**, began to decline. **Vishnu** said that they should make a truce with the demons, and join with them in creating a food which would guarantee strength and **immortality**. They should fill the primordial **sea**, the Sea of Milk, with seeds and plants of all kinds, and with the sperm of every animal; then, using a mountain as pole and the serpent **Vasuki** as cord, they should churn the mixture. To anchor the mountain in the void of non-being, Vishnu turned himself into a huge turtle, **Kurma**.

As the gods and demons churned, Vasuki writhed, groaned and spat out streams of poison, which **Shiva** swallowed before they could destroy **creation**. Gradually the mixture began to take on a rice-pudding-like texture, and beings were born from it: Surabji the sacred cow who grants all wishes, the wine-goddess **Varuni**, **Soma** the Moon-god, **Lakshmi** goddess of luck, **Parijata** the paradise-tree and **Dhanvantari**, doctor of the gods, holding a precious cup of *amrita*.

The battle for amrita. As soon as *amrita* appeared, gods and demons began squabbling for it. The demon **Rahu** snatched the cup and sipped – and if Vishnu had not sliced off the demon's head before *amrita* could flow through his whole body, he would have become ruler of the universe. As it was, the head remained immortal, a snarling, gaping thing which rolled round the heavens ever afterwards and tried to eat the stars. The quarrel continued, until the beautiful moon-goddess **Rohini** appeared and offered to settle it. She sat the gods and demons in long lines, facing one another, then took the cup of *amrita* and walked between them, letting each god taste it. The demons thought that when she reached the end of the row, she would turn round and start feeding them – but instead she revealed herself as Vishnu in disguise and disappeared, taking the *amrita*.

Battle flared once more, but now the gods had drunk *amrita* and outmatched the demons. They defeated them easily, and banished them underwater or into the crevices of dark where they have lurked ever since. The gods now owned *amrita* exclusively, and it guaranteed immortality to them and to anyone they allowed to taste it. But if the supply was to be renewed, it was essential that mortals make regular sacrifice to the gods. Each sacrifice had to be made according to exact ritual – and the demons lay waiting in the shadows each time, knowing that if the slightest ritual slip were made, the sacrifice would be void and a tiny drop of *amrita* would be subtracted from the heavenly store and descend to them.

AMUN
Africa (North)

Amun ('secret god'), or Amon or (Greek) Ammon, in Egyptian myth, was originally a god of the air, born with other deities from the voice of **Thoth**. He was protector of the area round Thebes (modern Luxor), and although he had no shape – he was all-pervasive and all-encompassing – he was worshipped as a curly-horned ram married to the goose which symbolized the River Nile. In the twentieth century BCE, when Thebes became Egypt's capital and a new royal dynasty was established, Amun was promoted to become god of gods, ruler of the universe, and the pharaohs added his name to their own as a symbol of authority: the founder of the Theban dynasty, for example, ruling from 1991-1961BCE, was Amunemhat ('Amun leads').

Amun's supremacy led him to take in the powers, myths and even names, of other gods. In particular, priests of his huge temples at Thebes and Karnak constructed an elaborate cult in his honour, taking over the **creation**-myth originally centred on **Atum**, and claiming that the Sun-god, **Ra**, was Amun's engendering power made manifest. (In this version, the Sun was renamed Amun-Ra.) These changes to the mythology gave Amun authority not only as creator and sustainer of the universe but as father and ruler of all gods – and his cult became so all-engulfing, in the next two millennia, that it was able to contain two mutually incompatible versions of his nature and power, and of the nature of the divine. In one, there were many gods, and Amun was the leader of a ruling trinity which also included **Ptah** and Ra. In the other, there was only one god, Amun, who was able to take any shape he chose – so that all other gods were merely his emanations, aspects of the One.

During the first 1400 years of Amun's hegemony, a ram was kept in the temple of Thebes. It was the god incarnate, and every year, in a glittering festival, it was carried across the Nile to visit Amun's relatives on the far bank (in what became the Valley of the Kings). Its companion in the divine barge (a model of the Sun-ship in which Ra sailed the sky each day) was the pharaoh, Amun-Ra's son and ruler of mortals as he ruled the gods. Thebes was sacked in the seventh century BCE, and physical power moved elsewhere (notably to Yunu or Heliopolis, now part of Cairo). But Amun-worship, as a focus of Egyptian nationalism, lasted a further six centuries, until the temples at Thebes and Karnak were damaged by earthquakes, and other gods, notably **Aset** and **Osiris**, became predominant.

≫→ supreme deity

AN
Asia (West)

An or Anu ('**sky**'), in Mesopotamian myth, was the child either of Apsu ('fresh **water**') and **Tiamat** ('salt water'), or of Anshar ('light') and Kishar ('horizon'). He threw dice with his sons **Ea** and **Enlil** for kingdoms; Ea won the **sea**, Enlil dry land and An the sky. An then divided the universe among them, creating the regions each had won. At first, after this, he was benevolent and interested in his own creation. But **Marduk** the **Sun**-god attacked him, flayed him, cut out his heart and beheaded him – after which An withdrew from the universe and became an invisible entity: space, all-embracing but uninvolved. (In some accounts, this aloofness made him an ideal judge, before whom quarrelling gods and mortals could plead their cases; but although he appeared to listen to such oratory, there was only one occasion, in the case of **Adapa**, when he stirred himself actually to issue judgement.)

*Despite – or perhaps because of – An's aloofness, he was thought to personify infallibility and omniscience. His shrines were oracular centres, the seven judges of the **Underworld** were called Annunaki ('An's children'), and kings often legitimized and dignified their reigns by incorporating his name into their own.*
≫→ justice and universal order, prophecy

ANANDA
India

Ananda, in Buddhist myth and legend, was born at the same moment as

Buddha, was his inseparable childhood companion and became his first disciple and follower after Buddha attained enlightenment. Some accounts make Ananda the same person as Buddha's half-brother **Nanda**.

ANANSI
Africa

Anansi ('spider'), in the myths of many West African peoples, was a **trickster**. He began his career as a creator-god, spinning the entire world at the request of the Great Sky-spirit, and was a **shape-changer**. Then he became one of the **messengers** between the Sky-spirit and human beings, teaching such things as how to pound corn in a mortar, how to use **fire** and how to tell stories.

The Sky-spirit had several messengers, all shape-changers, and there was constant bickering between them. Anansi and one of his rivals organized a contest, saying that whichever of them appeared in greatest splendour before the Sky-spirit would be his principal messenger thereafter. Anansi appeared first, turning himself into the yellow of a tiger's eye – and his rival matched him exactly. Anansi made himself the blue of sky reflected in a water-hole, the grey of the membrane on a lizard's eye, the pink of the blood-vessel in an antelope's ear – and was matched each time. Finally, exerting all his skill, he became the iridescence of sunlight in a dew-drop caught in a spider's web, and his rival turned into an entire rainbow and filled the sky. Anansi, defeated, wove a rope, let himself down from the Sky-spirit's hut and

settled on Earth forever, leaving the carrying of messages to his successful rival: Chameleon.

Mythographers suggest that this story is a folk-tale memory of the displacement of ancient deities by newer gods. It is also one of the very few tales in which Anansi is outwitted. Thousands of Anansi-tales survive, and all have the same pattern. Having decided, usually just for the fun of it, to trick someone, Anansi sets up a situation by boasting – for example that he will buy the songs of the Sky-spirit by fetching him a panther, a hornet, a ghost and his own self, or that he will bundle up the Sun, Moon and Darkness and bring them to Earth in a bag – and then fulfils each of the conditions by a trick. In some tales, he benefits other creatures – for example, he escapes from a bushfire by hiding in Antelope's ear and whispering to her the best way of escape, then rewards her by weaving a web to hide her fawn from marauding lions. But usually his tricks are done for their own sake, and the stories are invented simply for the pleasure of telling them, for the ingenious ways Anansi carries out each boast.

This insouciance marks a major difference between Anansi and the tricksters of such other areas as Australia and North America. In those parts, the tricksters (Gluskap; Manabozho; Spider Woman) are full-blown gods, with a serious and solemn role in the creation and continuance of life, and their folk-tale existence is distinctly secondary. Anansi's presence in the world, by contrast, not to mention his exploits, are almost all frivolous and told solely for entertainment.

In the Caribbean islands to which many West Africans were taken as slaves in the eighteenth century CE, *Anansi is known as* **Annency**.

ANANTA: *see* Shesha

ANAT
Asia (West)

Anat ('mountain-lady'), in Canaanite myth, was the sister and consort of **Baal** the storm-god. In some accounts she was not his sister but his mother, but this may be no more than a poetic way of referring to the story of how she rescued him from the **Underworld** after he rashly said that he could defeat anyone, even Mot god of the Dead. She herself was defeated only by one being, the mortal Aqhat. He owned a miraculous bow (the arch of the **sky**) made for him by the blacksmith-god Kothar. Anat coveted it, and when Aqhat refused to give it to her at any price, not even for **immortality**, she killed him. Aqhat's corpse fell into the Underworld, and his bow sank into the **sea** – and at once the darkness of chaos engulfed the Earth and plants and animals died. Anat was forced to beg help from **El**, king of **Heaven**, and he allowed her to rescue Aqhat from the Underworld, to give him back his bow (so propping the sky above the Earth once more) and to restart **creation**.

Anat is the Canaanite name for the goddess known in other West Asian myth-traditions as **Astarte**, **Cybele**, **Inanna** and **Ishtar**. She travelled to Egypt as consort of **Seth** and protector of the pharaohs when they rode into battle, and into European myth as the Greek **Artemis** and then the Roman **Diana**.
➤ **fertility**

ANCHISES
Europe (South)

Anchises ('associate of Isis'), in Greek and Roman myth, a distant cousin of King **Priam** of Troy, was the most handsome human being ever born, and **Aphrodite** herself was filled with lust for him. She disguised herself as a mortal princess, and seduced him, revealing her true identity only after he made her pregnant. She swore Anchises to secrecy, on pain of punishment from **Zeus** himself. But when Anchises' son **Aeneas** was born, he had inherited his mother's beauty as well as his father's, and Anchises found it almost unendurable to have to pretend that the child's mother was a mortal. Finally, he got drunk at a banquet and blurted out Aeneas' true identity – and Zeus hurled a thunderbolt which lamed him and turned him in an instant from handsome youth to wizened old man.

In Virgil's **Aeneid**, *one of whose main themes is Aeneas' sense of duty to* **Heaven** *and his family, Anchises is given somewhat more dignity than in this original myth. Aeneas carries him on his shoulders from the ruins of Troy, showing him no less respect than the statues of the ancestral gods, and when Anchises dies on the journey south (in Sicily) celebrates a huge funeral games in his honour. Later, he visits Anchises in the* **Underworld**, *where the old man, now a dignified sage and prophet, shows him the destiny of Rome and the generations of* **heroes** *and princes still unborn.*

ANDRIAMAHILALA: *see*
Andriambahomanana and
Andriamahilala

ANDRIAMBAHOMANANA AND ANDRIAMAHILALA
Africa

Andriambahomanana and Andriamahila-la, in Madagascan myth, were the first human beings. After they had lived for many centuries, and peopled the world, the **Sky**-spirit said that it was time to end their mortal existence, and asked where they would like to live in future. Andriam-bahomanana chose to spend some time underground and some on the surface, and the Sky-spirit made him a banana plant, being born, flourishing and dying each year. Andriamahilala chose to live on the **Moon**, and the Sky-spirit sent her there, where she is born, grows to maturity and dies every month.

ANDROMACHE
Europe (South)

Andromache ('battle of men'), in Greek myth, was the wife of Prince **Hector** of Troy, and the mother of his son and heir **Astyanax**. As senior princess of Troy, second in rank only to Queen **Hecuba**, she led the women throughout the **Trojan War**, and when the city fell never wavered in her dignity and re-straint despite being raped, enslaved and losing Astyanax (who was torn from her arms and thrown from the battlements). Together with her broth-er-in-law, the prophet **Helenus**, she was allocated as war-spoils to **Neoptolemus** and taken to Epirus. **Menelaus**, whose daughter **Hermione** had been promised in marriage to Neoptolemus, tried to kill her, but the gods (or some say **Peleus**) prevented it. After **Orestes** killed Neop-tolemus and married Hermione, Andro-mache married Helenus and they spent the rest of their lives as king and queen of Epirus.

*The bare bones of the Andromache myth were fleshed out by many writers, who made her one of the most long-suffering and dignified characters in European litera-ture. In Homer's Iliad she is the picture both of a princess and a noble wife and mother: in antiquity, her farewell to Hector as he goes to fight **Achilles** (Iliad Book 24) was considered one of the finest passages in all Greek poetry. Euripides made her a lead-ing character in Women of Troy – where she stoically endures the seizure and death of Astyanax – and the main character of Andromache, which dramatizes the strug-gle between her and Hermione. In more modern times, Racine's Andromache made her an emblem of royal duty and maternal devotion, maintained through great suffer-ing – a picture followed by most subsequent writers. Ancient vase-painters and sculp-tors, with their penchant for showing beau-tiful women in mourning, regularly depicted the moment when she surrendered Astya-nax to the Greeks who were to throw him from the battlements; a few more adventur-ous artists depicted her bravely facing Hermione and Menelaus as they tried to kill her in Epirus.*

ANDVARI
Europe (North)

Andvari ('fire-worker'), in Nordic myth, was a dwarf who crafted a magic ring, building into it the power endlessly to create more gold. He became master of all the gold in the universe, until **Loki** demanded that he hand it over to **Regin** and **Fafnir** to pay for Loki's murder of their brother **Otr**. Andvari offered all the gold except the magic ring, intending to use it to restock the dwarf-hoard. But Loki insisted on taking the ring as well, and Andvari cursed it, filling it with power to bring about the death of all who owned it.

In Wagner's Ring of the Nibelungs, *Andvari becomes Alberich. The gold-hoard is the treasure at the bottom of the river Rhine, and he renounces love in order to possess enough of it to make the magic ring. This variant from the original relates to the common myth-idea that dwarfs are immortal but unable to reproduce: they can craft anything they like, with wondrous skill, except their own offspring.*
≫→ **crafts, smiths**

ANGERONA
Europe (South)

Angerona ('raiser') was one of the most revered but least trumpeted goddesses in Rome. She guarded the city's secret name, an identity which the gods alone knew and which would cause the city's downfall if it were ever revealed to enemies. For this reason her statues showed her gagged and with her hand clutching her mouth to stop the name escaping by mistake. She had another secret skill, as her name suggests: she knew the raising-spell which made the **Sun** rise from its torpor at the end of the winter Solstice, and used it once a year at her festival on 21 December.

ANIMAL-GODS

In several cultures, particularly those of the Christian, Islamic and ancient Nordic worlds, animals were thought to exist on a lower rung than humans on the ladder of creation. But in many others they held an equal or higher place. They had skills and abilities which humans both lacked and coveted. In many myth-traditions, the gods and spirits who created the world were **shape-changers**, and assumed the forms not only of men or women but of such animals as coyotes, dogs, eagles, kangaroos, lizards, ravens, snakes and spiders. The power of the sky was often embodied as a **bull**, the nourishing power of **Mother Earth** as a **cow**, the primordial ocean as a **snake**. These animal-spirits, and thence all subsequent generations of animals, were thought to own part of universal wisdom, to know secrets denied to humans. Perhaps because of this, many cultures also told myths of animal-human hybrids – some beneficent (skilled, for example, in healing and **prophecy**), others **demons** and **monsters**, nightmares fleshed. Animal deities were especially common in mystery-cults, and sacrificing and consuming the cult-animal was thought to share its knowledge and power among all worshippers. But a proviso applied to all animal-myths: animals and animal-gods never entirely revealed their whole natures. Many were **tricksters**, and all kept some of their secrets, so that animal-gods and spirits could be dangerous as well as fascinating.
≫→ (Africa): Itherther and Achimi, Ogo; (Australia): Bagadjimbiri, Kurukadi and Mumba, Marindi and Adnoartina, Minawara and Multultu, Tjinimin and Pilirin; (Americas):

Coyote, Dayunsi, Gluskap, Michabo, Nanabush, Raven, Sinaa, Thunderbirds, Underwater Panthers, Wishpoosh, Xólotl; (Egypt): Ammut, Anubis, Bastet, Hap, Heqet, Khepri, Serqet, Tefnut; (Greece): Pan; (India): Balin, Ganesh, Garuda, Hanuman, Jambavan, Jatayu, Kurma, Matsya, Narasimha, Varaha; (Oceania): Areop-Enap and Rigi, Nareau, Totoima; (Rome): Faunus; (Tibet): Dorje Pahmo, sPyan-ras-gzigs

ANJANA
Indian

Anjana, in Hindu myth, was an **apsara** cursed with monkey shape. She lived alone in the forest, pining for a son. In some accounts a kite dropped a cake in her lap, and **Shiva** appeared before her and told her to eat it. When she did so, she became pregnant with **Hanuman**, the future monkey-king. In other accounts, **Vayu** the wind-god either raped her or blew the cake into her lap, to make her pregnant.

≫→ beauty

ANNENCY
Americas (Caribbean)

Annency, in the myths and folk-tales of Jamaica, Trinidad and Haiti (where he is also known as 'Ti Malice) is a **trickster** and **shape-changer**. He is able to take on any shape he pleases, but usually appears as human or spider. He is the African trickster-god **Anansi**, taken to the Caribbean by West Africans enslaved for plantation work.

ANNWN
Europe (North)

Annwn, or Anwfn ('not-world'), in Celtic myth, was the **Underworld**. Its other names included Affan ('invisible'), Affwys ('gulf') and Anghar ('loveless'). It was a mirror-image of the mortal world, replacing substance with emptiness, being with nonentity, time with infinity. Its ruler was **Arawn**, and its inhabitants were fairies, **demons** and goblins. In Annwn, they were serene and vacuous, shapes without identity; it was only when they spilled into the mortal world that they took on recognizable characteristics, usually mischievous or malign to humans who encountered them. Human beings who strayed into Annwn (for example by joining its inhabitants as they danced in the mortal world in a fairy ring) had the identity sucked out of them, and became wraiths, of neither one world nor the other. The only creatures able to pass easily in and out of Annwn were pigs: **shape-changers** who could assume, shed or mask their identity at will.

*Although in Christian times Annwn became sidelined, featuring chiefly in children's stories and fairy tales, its earlier importance in myth survives in two accounts above all others. In The **Mabinogion**, the story of **Pwyll** prince of Dyfed tells how Arawn persuaded Pwyll to change identities with him and win the throne of Annwn from its previous ruler Havgan. In the poem The Spoiling of Annwn, by **Taliesin**, King **Arthur** led a raiding party into Annwn to steal the Cauldron of Plenty, the never-failing source of* *the Underworld's prosperity and its inhabitants' inspiration and immortality.*

ANTERO VIPUNEN
Europe (North)

Antero Vipunen ('old Vipunen'), in Finnish myth, was a **giant** who spent his existence sleeping just under the surface of the land, using the topsoil as a blanket. He slept for so long that whole forests seeded themselves, grew, reseeded themselves and died above him. He knew every song and magic spell ever made, and when **Väinämöinen** failed to find in the **Underworld** the binding-spell he needed to finish his magic boat, a shepherd directed him to Antero Vipunen. Väinämöinen tried to wake the giant, unceremoniously poking his stick down Antero Vipunen's gullet. But Antero Vipunen yawned, swallowed him and went back to sleep. It was not until Väinämöinen made a smithy in the giant's belly and started working iron that Antero Vipunen woke up, vomiting, and spewed out both the hero and the binding-spells Väinämöinen had come to find.

ANTIGONE
Europe (South)

Antigone ('in place of a mother' or 'against her birth'), in Greek myth, was the eldest child of **Oedipus** and **Jocasta**. When Oedipus blinded himself and was sent into exile, she accompanied him, and eventually took him to Colonus near Athens where the gods received him into the **Underworld**. Antigone then went back to **Thebes**, just before her brothers **Eteocles** and **Polynices** quarrelled over the kingship, and Polynices gathered the army led by the **Seven Against Thebes** to win himself sole power.

When the Seven were defeated and the war was won by Thebes, Antigone's uncle **Creon**, regent of the city, proclaimed that all the dead Thebans, including Eteocles, were to be buried with honour, but that all the dead attackers, including Polynices, were to be left on the plain to rot. Antigone refused to accept the decree. Claiming to obey the laws of the gods, which said that all kin were to be treated with equal honour, whatever their crimes, she buried her brother Polynices, and faced arrest and punishment with a combination of innocence and determination which outraged Creon. He had her walled up in a cave to starve to death.

The bare bones of this myth give no hint of its enormous fecundity in classical and later times. Beginning with Sophocles' Antigone, which sets Antigone (embodiment of honour, duty and radiant trust in God) against Creon (embodiment of unyielding and self-destructive political arrogance, authoritarianism turned into a tragic flaw), the story has travelled throughout the world, engendering more than 20,000 known versions, derivatives and variants. Of all surviving literary works from ancient Greece and Rome, only Homer's Odyssey and Virgil's Aeneid have come close to it in influence. Some scholars believe that the reason for this is entirely Sophocles' genius, the power of his arguments and the characterization of Antigone and Creon in his play; a few go further, and say that he invented the story himself to articulate his themes, embroidering a

*myth-original even scantier than the outline
given here.*

ANTIOPE
Europe (South)

Antiope ('set face'), daughter of **Ares** in
Greek myth, was princess of the Amazon city of Themiscyra. When **Heracles**
came to the country of the **Amazons** to
steal the golden belt of **Hippolyta**, one
of his companions was **Theseus**. They
besieged Themiscyra, and Antiope saw
Theseus from the walls, fell in love with
him, and gave him the keys of the city as
a love-gift. He took her back to Athens
and they had one child, **Hippolytus**. But
then Theseus made a dynastic marriage
with Princess **Phaedra** of Crete, and
Antiope gathered a band of Amazon
warriors and broke into the wedding-
feast, trying to kidnap or kill the bride.
Theseus fought her off and killed her – a
crime for which the gods punished him
by making his innocent Cretan bride,
Phaedra, fall in love with his son Hippolytus.

In some versions, Antiope is confused with Hippolyta (possibly her
sister).

ANUBIS
Africa (North)

Anubis, son of the **Underworld** gods
Osiris and **Nebthet** in Egyptian myth,
was originally the god of putrefaction,
and took his shape – a crouching dog or
jackal – from the animals which sca-
venged in burial-grounds in the time
before deep grave-shafts and pyramids
were built. In later myth his role changed round completely. He became the
jackal which protected the dead against
robbers and marauders (and was often
depicted as a dog on guard); in the
Underworld, he supervised the weighing of dead people's hearts before
Osiris' judgement-seat. When bodies
were embalmed, the priest who supervised the workers wore a jackal-mask to
signify Anubis' presence.
⇒ **animal-gods**

APHRODITE
Europe (South)

Aphrodite ('foam-born'; Latin Venus),
in Greek and Roman myth, was created
from the foam arising when **Cronus**
threw the severed penis of **Ouranos**
(Father **Sky**) into the **sea**. She was
beauty incarnate, and the West Winds
gathered her up and carried her to
Cyprus, where she first appeared on
Earth. She was the goddess of desire,
and won gods and mortals by seduction. In **Heaven**, she had love-affairs
with **Ares** (their offspring was **Eros**),
Dionysus and **Hermes**; on Earth, she
slept with **Adonis** and **Anchises**. But
she was capricious, and hurt people
more often than she helped them. She
bribed **Paris** of Troy to judge her the
most beautiful goddess in **Olympus**,
and started the **Trojan War**. When
the women of Lemnos forgot to worship her, she made them first reject and
then slaughter their husbands. When
Eros fell in love with **Psyche**, she made
all-but impossible conditions before
Psyche could enter **Heaven** and find
happiness.

*In Greece, Aphrodite was depicted quite
differently by fine artists and writers. Artists*

48

showed her as the archetype of serene female beauty, while writers depicted her as usually charming but sometimes spiteful and sulky. In Rome, because she was the mother of **Aeneas**, founder of the Roman state, she was worshipped as 'Genetrix' ('mother [of the state]'), and was honoured less as a flighty young girl than as a mature and dignified woman, as benignly aloof from her people as a Roman aristocratic mother was from her children.

⫸→ beauty, Idun, sex

APOLLO
Europe (South)

Apollo (Apollon, 'destroyer'), in Greek myth, was the son of **Zeus** and **Leto**, and the **twin** brother of **Artemis**. They were born on the island of Delos, and the Sun flooded the island with its radiance, covering it with gold (hence the name Delos, 'shining'). Jealous of their birth, **Hera** summoned a gigantic serpent to hunt Leto to her death across the world. But four-day-old Apollo begged a bow and arrows from **Hephaestus**, cornered the serpent in the sacred cave at Delphi and shot him dead. (Later, the Pythian Games were held every four years in Delphi to celebrate this event. In some accounts, killing the serpent was what gave Apollo skill at **prophecy**: until then **Gaia**, **Mother Earth**, had been the only being able to foretell the future, and the serpent was one of her servants.) Next Hera sent a giant, Tityus, to hunt Leto. Once again Apollo, helped this time by Artemis, protected her with arrows, and at last Zeus hurled Tityus down into the **Underworld**, pegged him there on the rock floor and sent a pair of vultures to feast daily on his liver.

Apollo was the light of the **Sun** made manifest, and had the power either to sear to **death** or to give sudden illumination. He was thus both a bringer of disease and a healer, both a hunter and a rescuer, and a prophet whose oracles were ambiguous but always true. Throughout his youth he was fierce, quickly angered and unforgiving. For example, when people claimed that the singing and flute-playing of the satyr Marsyas was finer than anything Apollo could manage, Apollo challenged him to a contest: playing and singing at the same time. This was easy for Apollo, playing the lyre, but impossible for Marsyas – and Apollo punished him by skinning him alive and nailing his hide to a pine tree.

Apollo was equally merciless to women who refused to have **sex** with him. One was **Cassandra**, princess of Troy. He cursed her by giving her true knowledge of the future, and then arranging that no one would believe a word she said. Another was the **Sibyl** of Cumae in Italy. He offered her **immortality** if she slept with him; she refused and asked instead to be allowed to live as many years as she held grains of sand in her hand. Cruelly, he granted her wish – but she had forgotten to ask to remain young and beautiful, and shrivelled until she spent the rest of her life as a withered husk hung up in a bottle.

In the end Apollo's wildness angered even Zeus. Apollo's son **Aesculapius**, a skilful healer, brought back to life Artemis' mortal servant **Hippolytus**, something forbidden even to a god – and when Zeus punished Aesculapius by dashing him down to the **Underworld**, Apollo set arrows to bow and began killing the **Cyclopes** who made Zeus' thunderbolts.

Only the pleading of Apollo's mother Leto saved him from being sent to the Underworld himself. He remained resentful of Zeus, and joined **Hera** and **Poseidon** in a revolt against his power – for which he was punished by being forced to serve for a year as slave to a mortal, King **Laomedon** of Troy.

Apollo served his punishment and learned his lesson. He became one of the calmest and most dignified of all the gods, the senior male **Olympian** as **Athene** was the senior female. His favourite proverbs were 'Know yourself' and 'Moderation in all things', and his oracle at Delphi gave this advice to many enquirers. He spent his time healing gods and humans, and making music (a skill taught him by **Hermes**). He led the **Muses** in playing and singing, and danced on Mount Parnassus with **Dionysus** and his followers. When he played his lyre, the whole of creation stopped to listen, awestruck, and the syllables he sang – 'Ee-eh Pa-ee-an' – were the only examples ever heard on Earth of the language of the gods, sounds to haunt every listening ear. He kept aloof from mortals (though he sometimes desired individual men and women as much as they longed for him, and had brief affairs with them). But his main contact was by oracles, when he revealed, through the mouth of his priestesses the Sybils, the secrets of past, present and most especially future.

Apollo was one of the gods most often represented in ancient Greek sculpture and painting. He was shown as a handsome, serenely smiling young man ('kouros' in Greek), the ideal of male beauty as **Aphrodite** *was the ideal of female beauty. In literature he appears as a somewhat forbidding guide and guardian or (in pastoral poetry) as the leader of the Muses and sweetest singer ever heard. Euripides, alone of surviving writers, concentrates on his deviousness, asking how human beings can cope with a god who never lies but who often blurs or only partially reveals the truth. In more modern times, critics of the arts liked to make a distinction between the 'Apollonian' impulse, based on rationality and classical control, and the 'Dionysian', derived from emotion and romantic self-indulgence.*

≫→ archers, disease and healing

APSARAS
India

The *Apsaras* (or *Apsarasas*, 'essences of water') were the dancers of the gods. They were created from the mist which rose at the churning of the **Sea** of Milk (see **amrita**) or from fragments of **Prajapati**'s body, and there were (in some accounts) 'seven times six thousand' of them, or (in others) 35 million. They took many forms – doves, gazelles, butterflies, rainbows – but their favourite shapes were clouds or beautiful women. As clouds, they hovered in trees, waiting to seduce the unwary and draw them into fairy time. As women, they danced for the gods, and made love eagerly with the **Gandharvas**, the celestial musicians. As goddesses of **fertility**, they were always welcome at weddings, and they also had the power to bring good luck for their favoured mortals, in dice and other games of chance.

≫→ beauty, Graces, nymphs, shape-changers

ARACHNE
Europe (South)

Arachne ('spider'), in Greek myth, was the finest weaver in Athens. She was also a fool, and challenged **Athene** (goddess of weaving) to a contest of skill. Athene warned her by weaving a tapestry showing scenes of mortals who were punished for challenging the gods. But Arachne took no notice, and wove a tapestry full of scandalous scenes of the gods' love-affairs. Athene tore it to pieces and thrashed Arachne with her own shuttle. Arachne hanged herself in mortification, and Athene changed her into a spider, condemned to weave for the rest of time, and to use threads from her own body to do it.
≫→ **crafts**

ARAWN
Europe (North)

Arawn, in Celtic myth, was a prince of **Annwn** the **Underworld**. He was ambitious to rule it, but was not powerful enough to kill Havgan its overlord. He persuaded the **shape-changer Pwyll** to take his identity for a year and kill Havgan, then took his place as ruler of the Underworld. He spent his time roistering and racketing, and every so often, on stormy nights, led his **demon** followers in a riotous chase through the mortal world, riding black horses with hunting-dogs yapping at their heels.

ARCHERS

Archers are a small but select band in world myth, and their stories are among the most imaginatively detailed. Arrows were often identified with the sunshaft, which could kill, send flashes of prophetic insight, cause or cure disease. They were also linked with sexual ejaculation, so that (male) gods of lust were often archers, and human or heroic archers were notably lustful. Both associations linked archers and archer-gods with hunting (if male) and procreation and **childbirth** (if female); in such cases, a female god, by practising archery (with its male sexual associations), desexed herself, combining her role as patron of **fertility**, birth and the newborn with uncompromising chastity.

≫→ **(China): Jang Xien, Yi; (Greece): Apollo, Artemis, Eros, Heracles, Philoctetes; (India): Arjuna; (Japan): Raiden and Raiju, Yamasachi, Yuriwaka; (Nordic): Ull**

ARDHANARISHVARA
India

Ardhanarishvara, in Hindu myth, was a form of **Shiva** in which the left half was female (creative, impulsive, violent) and the right half was male (industrious, reflective, calm). The balance between them was a generative and constructive force – and that is what Ardhanarishvara represented.

AREOP-ENAP AND RIGI
Oceania

Areop-Enap ('old spider'), in the myths of the islanders of Nauru, searched for food in the darkness at the beginning of **creation**. She found an enormous clam, but before she could stun it, it swallowed her and snapped shut again.

Exploring the clam's insides, Areop-Enap found a tiny snail (or, in some accounts, a Triton's Horn shellfish). Instead of killing it, she asked it to climb to the hinge of the shell and prise the clam open. As the snail moved across the clam's flesh, it left a phosphorescent trail, in the light of which Areop-Enap saw a white worm (or some say a caterpillar), Rigi. Ignoring the snail, Areop-Enap put a strength-spell on Rigi, and persuaded him to try to snap the clam open.

Time and again Rigi set his head against the upper shell and his tail against the lower, and heaved. The clam resisted, and sweat poured from Rigi, making a pool in the lower shell, then a lake and finally a sea. The saltiness finally forced the clam open, and it lay there dead. Areop-Enap made its lower shell Earth and its upper shell Sky. She set the snail high in the sky-shell, where it became the **Moon**. She made islands from clam-flesh, and clothed them in vegetation made from her own web-thread. Finally she turned to Rigi, and found him drowned in his own sweat, killed by his own exertions. Areop-Enap wrapped him in a cocoon of silk and hung him in the sky: the Milky Way.

⫸➤ animal-gods, Nareau

ARES
Europe (South)

Ares ('fighter'), in Greek myth, was the son either of **Zeus** and **Hera**, or in some accounts of Hera alone without a male partner: her rage made into a god. He was the god of war, brawn without brains, anger beyond restraint, force without control, and spent his time swaggering round **Heaven** and Earth with his followers Deimos ('dread'), Enyo ('fierceness'), **Eris** ('quarrel') and Phobos ('terror'). His war-cry laid mortals dead in heaps, and gave the gods such headaches that they kept trying to find ways of throwing him out of **Olympus** – in vain, for none dared directly to challenge him, or his mother Hera. Sexually insatiable, he raped **nymphs**, goddesses, **Titans**, even rocks and trees, and fathered a gang of brutish **heroes** who lorded it on Earth as brainlessly as he did in Heaven. His only weakness was his love for **Aphrodite**, on whom he fathered **Eros** (and, some say, **Priapus**).

Although Ares was later identified with the Roman **Mars**, their characters were completely different.

ARETHUSA
Europe (South)

Arethusa ('waterer'), in Roman myth, was a **hunting-nymph**, a virgin follower of Diana (see **Artemis**). One day she went swimming in the river Alpheus, and the river-god tried to seize her and rape her. She picked up her clothes and ran – and the god assumed human form and ran after her. He was just about to snatch her when Diana hid her in a cloud. Alpheus tried to part the cloud-wisps with his hands, but when he had dispersed it all he found nothing: Arethusa had changed to water inside it, and slipped away into a crack in the ground, far out of his reach.

Alpheus, a river, was easily able to follow Arethusa underground. But as soon as she slipped below the surface the spirits of the **Underworld** led her by secret channels to Sicily, where she bubbled up in a stream of pure water near the town of Syracuse. Alpheus wandered in despair along the river-channels and streams of the Underworld for a thousand years, until the gods at last took pity, guided him to Syracuse and filled Arethusa's heart with love for him. She and he mingled their streams, and have been together ever since.

This folk-tale, typical of hundreds, was said to have been devised to explain a curious phenomenon: when offerings were thrown into the river Alpheus in Greece, they vanished underwater, only to reappear days later in Arethusa's Spring in Sicily.

»»→ water

ARGONAUTS
Europe (South)

The Argonauts, in Greek and Roman myth, were fifty **heroes** chosen by **Jason** to help him steal the **Golden Fleece**. Their name comes from their ship, *Argo*, built for them by Argus. There are many different lists of their names: each Greek state liked to claim that one of its ancestors had taken part in the expedition. Apart from Jason and Argus, the Argonauts most commonly listed include sixteen sons of gods (among them **Aesculapius**, Calais and Zetes, the **Dioscuri**, Echion, **Heracles**, **Nauplius** and Periclymenus), the musician **Orpheus**, two dozen heroes including Admetus, Euryalus, Idas and his twin Lynceus, **Laertes** and **Peleus**, one woman, **Atalanta**, and one boy, Heracles'

page **Hylas**. Most were chosen for their bravery, but some had special skills as well: Echion was a herald, Lynceus the sharpest-eyed man who ever lived, Nauplius a navigator and Periclymenus a **shape-changer**.

The adventures of the Argonauts, and the way each contributed to the expedition in his own specialized way, were comprehensively described in Apollonius of Rhodes' Homer-inspired epic Argonautica (The Voyage of Argo). It is from this that all later accounts, from tragic dramas to children's fairy-tales, are derived.

ARGUS (HUNTING DOG)
Europe (South)

Argus (Argos, 'eager'), in Greek myth, was **Odysseus**' old hunting-dog. For twenty years, while his master was away fighting in Troy or travelling home, Argus had been neglected, and now he lay on the dung-heap, aged and full of fleas. But when he saw Odysseus, who had returned to Ithaca disguised as a beggar, he lifted his head, flattened his ears and wagged his tail. He was the first living creature to recognize Odysseus returned, and (as Homer puts it in the *Odyssey*) 'he no sooner recognized his master than he gave himself up to death's dark hand.'

ARGUS (WATCHMAN)
Europe (South)

Argus (Argos, 'eager'), in Greek myth, was a **giant** with a hundred eyes (or in some accounts, a thousand). When **Hera** wanted to hide **Io** from **Zeus** (who was eager to seduce her), she changed her into a cow, hid her in the divine herd and set Argus on guard. He was the ideal choice, because even when most of his eyes closed in sleep, some always remained alert. Zeus asked **Hermes**, god of **tricksters**, to steal Io, and Hermes played Argus a tune on his lyre so sweet that all Argus' eyes closed at the same moment – whereupon Hermes snatched Io and cut Argus' head off to prevent him telling. When Hera found the head, she gathered Argus' eyes and set them to decorate the peacock's tail.

ARIADNE
Europe (South)

Ariadne ('purity'), in Greek myth, was the daughter of King **Minos** of Crete and sister of **Phaedra**. She fell in love with **Theseus**, and showed him how to find his way out of the **Minotaur**'s lair in the Cretan Labyrinth (by rewinding a spindle of wool which he had unwound on the way in). After he had killed the Minotaur, she sailed with him for Athens, hoping to become his queen. But on the way they landed on the island of Naxos, and Theseus deserted her. In some accounts, this was because he already had a wife in Athens (the **Amazon** princess **Antiope**); in others it was because **Dionysus** fell in love with Ariadne and put a spell on Theseus to make him forget her.

What happened next is also disputed. Some versions say that Ariadne was so broken-hearted at losing Theseus that she hanged herself, others that married King Onarus of Naxos and lived many happy years as his queen. The most common story says that Dionysus took

her into **Heaven** and made her his consort in his revels and dances across the universe, that he or **Aphrodite** gave her a crown of seven stars, and when she died – for he was unable to give her **immortality**, that possession of gods alone – the star-crown was placed in the sky forever as her memorial: the Corona Borealis or Northern Crown.

ARICONTE AND TAMENDONARE
Americas (South)

Ariconte and Tamendonare, in the myths of the Tupinamba people of Brazil, were **twins** but with different fathers – their mother (a mortal) was raped by a god at the exact moment when she was having **sex** with her mortal husband. Some time later she was eaten by cannibals, and the twins set out to avenge her murder and then to find their father. They cornered the cannibals on an island, and shifted the river-flow to swamp it; at the last moment the cannibals turned into panthers and escaped into the jungle.

In a lonely village the twins found an old, wise man, and asked him who their father was. He said that they could prove their identity by undertaking supernatural tests. They shot at targets, but their arrows vanished in thin air. They leapt between the two halves of a huge boulder, Itha-Irapi, which crashed together like snapping jaws. One twin was crushed, but the other reconstituted him and breathed new life into him. For the third test, they were told to steal bait from the demon Agnen, who fished food to feed the dead in the **Underworld**. The twins succeeded – but not before one of them was torn to pieces by Agnen and had to be remade and revived by his brother.

So each twin died and was reborn with his brother's help. They went back to the village wizard, who told them that he himself was their immortal father, Maira Ata. Their mortal father, Sarigoys, had died or disappeared long ago. Maira Ata had no idea which twin was mortal and which immortal, and Ariconte and Tamendonare spent their rest of their time on Earth sharing adventures, testing and watching each other, neither daring to kill the other or let him die in case he was the god.

Modern mythographers have given this story a neat (not to say wished-for) psychological explanation: Ariconte and Tamendonare are the two halves of each human being's nature, perpetually in rivalry but neither able to exist without the other. The Italian writer Italo Calvino reworked the story in his short novel The Cloven Viscount. *In this, a medieval crusader is sliced in two, and the two halves roam the world, each a separate identity, yearning for the moment when they can meet and unite again, letting the man who is compounded of both of them end his days in peace.*
≫→ animal-gods, creation

ARISTAEUS
Europe (South)

Aristaeus (Aristaios, 'best'), son of **Apollo** and the mountain-**nymph Cyrene** in Greek myth, was the god of beekeeping. A hunter like his father, he was following his hounds one day when he saw **Orpheus'** wife **Eurydice** bathing.

Filled with lust, he leapt into the water to rape her, and when she fled she trod on a **snake** and was killed. Her **nymph**-sisters punished Aristaeus by killing all his bees, and he wandered the world trying to find new swarms. His mother advised him to ask **Proteus**, the Old Man of the **Sea**, and Proteus told him to sacrifice four bulls and four cows in Eurydice's memory, but to leave the carcasses to rot instead of burning them. Aristaeus did so, and swarms of bees rose from the carcasses to fill his hives.

Apart from this one lapse, Aristaeus was gentle and kindly. **Zeus** gave him charge of the infant **Dionysus**, to whom he taught love of the countryside. He married Princess Autonoe of **Thebes** (sister of Dionysus' mother **Semele**), and settled with her on Mount Haemus. Their son, Actaeon, grew up to be a hunter like his father and grandfather before him – only to anger **Artemis**, Apollo's sister, and die for it.
≫→ farming, Zosim

ARJUNA
India

Arjuna, in Hindu myth, was the son of **Indra** and Queen **Kunti** of Bharata. He was the third-born of the five **Pandava** brothers, each of whom had a different god for father. He was a master **archer**, and his skills were crucial in the huge war between the Pandavas and their cousins the **Kauravas**. But he was a thoughtful and peaceable man, and tried to find reasons why he should kill not merely his own cousins (who had been friends and companions throughout their boyhood), but also countless hundreds of soldiers he'd never even met. His charioteer, the god **Krishna**, resolved his doubts, explaining that only the gods understand the pattern of each individual human destiny. Our duty is not to question but to have faith in God, obedience and willingness – and only this surrender will bring us true fulfilment.

*Arjuna's adventures are told in the **Ma-habharata**, the sixth part of which, the Bhagavad Gita ('Song of the Lord') contains his dialogue with Krishna, a main text in both Hindu philosophy and Sanskrit poetry.*

≫→ archers, heroes

ARTEMIS
Europe (South)

Artemis ('pure water-spring'; Latin Diana), in Greek and Roman myth, was the daughter of **Zeus** and **Leto**, and the twin sister of **Apollo**. When Zeus slept with Leto, to prevent **Hera** finding out he changed both himself and her into quails. Leto therefore bore her children with as few birth-pains as a mother quail suffers when it lays an egg. Ever afterwards women in **childbirth** used to pray to Artemis to ease their labour-pains. She brought to the childbed a pine-torch blazing with the light of life; its warmth and radiance were symbols of security for the newborn child. She shielded infants and baby animals from harm until they grew out of helplessness and could fend for themselves. She was the goddess of women's monthly cycle, protected innocence and virginity, and was herself untouched by god or mortal; in her honour her followers swore lifelong virginity.

As Apollo symbolized the sunshaft, so Artemis symbolized the moonbeam. She was a hunter, using a silver bow and arrows made for her by **Hephaestus** and a pack of immortal dogs bred for her by **Pan**. Sometimes her prey was human: when sudden death came to a mortal its cause was an arrow from Artemis, punishment for some crime of which the guilty person might not even be aware. She also punished mortals in other ways: for example, when **Agamemnon** mistakenly shot one of her sacred deer, she ordered him to pay for it by sacrificing his daughter **Iphigenia**. But her usual prey was deer and other wild animals. She hunted them either in a silver **moon**-chariot pulled by two horned hinds, or on foot with her company of **nymphs** and her pack of dogs.

Although Artemis and her nymphs would have nothing to do with males, they were among the most beautiful and graceful of all the immortals, and many gods and men pursued them and tried to have sex with them. This made Artemis shy of being seen by males at all, and merciless to any who came on her unawares. When Actaeon caught sight of her bathing naked in a river, she set his own dogs on him. On another occasion, on the island of Chios, when Orion surprised her in a forest clearing, she conjured from the ground a giant scorpion which stung him dead.

In Greek myth, although Artemis was terrifying, she was a comparatively minor goddess. Roman Diana, by contrast, was one of the main protectors of the stability of the state, and was worshipped both at huge public festivals and in secret **mysteries**, available to women alone.

*Artemis/Diana was shown as a young, beautiful woman, either in hunting dress or robed as a princess. Her companions were dogs, lions and panthers, and she was sometimes shown with wings arching above her head to symbolize the path of stars in the night sky. Her temple at Ephesus (which held a many-breasted statue, symbolizing **fertility** – said by some to be the **Palladium** of Troy) was one of the most important pilgrimage sites of the ancient Roman world – as Saint Paul acknowledged when he chose to preach a sermon there saying that the old gods were dead and Christianity had replaced them.*

»→ **archers, Great Goddess**

ARTHUR

Europe (North)

Arthur's birth and accession. The 'once and future king', in Celtic myth, was originally one of the most ancient gods of Northern Europe, Artos the Bear, brother of the war-goddess **Morrigan** (or **Morgan le Fay**). When Christianity came to Britain, the Celtic gods abandoned the world of mortals for the sky, and Artos became the constellation Arcturus. But from time to time he felt a longing to return to Earth, and slipped into a mortal woman's womb at the moment of conception. He did this when **Uther Pendragon** made adulterous love with Queen Ygern of Tintagel, and was brought up in secret as Uther's son. He succeeded to the throne by magic, pulling the sword **Excalibur** from a stone (or, some say, being given it by the **Lady of the Lake**).

The Round Table and the Holy Grail. The early years of Arthur's reign were happy and successful; with the help of wizards and **shape-changers** (such as **Merlin**) he made war on the Romans and united all Britain under his rule. He married Princess **Guinevere** and established a magic court at **Camelot**, a Round Table where **giants**, wizards and mortal warriors lived peaceably together. The Round Table was a force for good in the world, and existed in fairy time, untroubled by aging or mortality. But when the **(Holy) Grail** began to disappear from the mortal world, King **Pelles** of Carbonek sent his grandson **Galahad** to Camelot, and one by one Arthur's courtiers agreed to join Galahad in a quest to find the Grail. This Christian ambition upset the placid life of Camelot, dragging its warriors into the mortal world. Some returned, but most were killed, and the harmony of Camelot was destroyed forever.

The end of Arthur's reign. Soon after the Grail-quest, several of Arthur's courtiers, including his son **Modred**, conspired to snatch his throne. They told him that he was being cuckolded by **Lancelot**, his oldest friend and noblest warrior. Arthur banished Lancelot, and Modred and the others seized their chance and declared war. One by one Arthur's surviving courtiers were killed in the fighting, and finally the old king faced his son in single combat. Arthur killed Modred, but was so severely wounded that he had to withdraw once more from the mortal world. He went to the land of **Avalon**, the island of the blessed where the golden apples of **immortality** grew, and neither he nor Camelot were ever seen again. Still, today, the myth ends, Arthur and his warriors lie sleeping under a mountain, and when the need is great and the horn blows to waken them, they will gallop to restore the Golden Age.

*The Arthur story is a confection, made in early Christian times from several elements of Celtic myth. In medieval fable, it was further elaborated, incorporating stories from France (Lancelot and the Lady of the Lake) and Germany (Percival or **Parsifal**). In the fifteenth century Malory, in his Morte d'Arthur, gave it prescriptive literary form, the romance of Christian chivalry and betrayed love and friendship in which it is still bestknown today. These versions concentrate on the events of Arthur's youth, before and after he won his throne, on the tragic effects of the love of Lancelot and Guinevere, and on Arthur's battle with Modred and his death. In between these events, they often depict Arthur as the typical medieval roi fainéant, the figureheadking who sits in royal state, inactive and characterless, while his lords have all the adventures. This does nothing for Arthur, but greatly assists the problem of assimilating many different legends and folk-stories into a single narrative.*

The story of Arthur – and the ideas of chivalry and knight-errantry grafted on to it – have gripped the European imagination for fifteen hundred years. Scholars have conducted quests for the 'real' Arthur, identifying him as a Celtic prince who fought the Romans and excavating many of the sites of his supposed activities

(including several different versions of Camelot). Literary works range from the anonymous medieval poem Gawain and the Green Knight, through complex allegorical epics by such Christian apologists as Chrétien de Troyes and Malory (who gave the story, perhaps, its most definitive form) to such twentieth-century works as Steinbeck's translation/adaptation of Malory, The Acts of King Arthur and His Noble Knights and T.H. White's novel-trilogy The Once and Future King. In fine art, Pre-Raphaelite painters in Britain took Arthurian legend as a main source for their vision of a pure, simple and elegant medieval world, and their work in turn influenced other art-works of all kinds, ranging from a clutch of Hollywood swashbucklers (not to mention such Disney extravaganzas as The Once and Future King, an animated version of T.H. White's novel, and the comedy A Spaceman at the Court of King Arthur, drawing on Mark Twain's novel A Connecticut Yankee in King Arthur's Court) to Bresson's brooding film Lancelot du Lac and the stage musical Camelot.

⁂→ **heroes**

ARUNA
India

Aruna ('rose-coloured'), in Hindu myth, was god of the morning **sky**. He was hatched from the same clutch of eggs as **Garuda**, and would have been the most handsome god in **Heaven** except that his mother, eager to see him, broke the shell before he was fully formed, so that he had no feet. He was able to soar in the sky, but not to walk, and was barred forever from the gods' feasts and sacrifices.

ASCANIUS
Europe (South)

Ascanius (Askaneios, 'tentless'), in Greek myth, was the son of **Aeneas** and Creusa. When the Greeks captured Troy, Ascanius followed his father into exile, sailing with him to Sicily, Carthage and finally Italy. During the battles which followed the Trojans' landing near the mouth of the Tiber, Ascanius fought bravely, and when the war was won Aeneas declared him his heir. Shortly after this Aeneas died or disappeared, and Ascanius became king. He ruled for 30 years from Lavinium, his father's former city, then founded a new community, Alba Longa, on the site of the future Rome.

In the time of the Emperor Augustus, who was a member of the Julian (or Iulian) dynasty, enormous propaganda was organized to link the imperial family with the heroic founders of Rome and with the gods who were parents or ancestors of those founders. As part of this work, Livy and Virgil changed Ascanius' name to Iulus, borrowing the name of a later, less distinguished king of Alba Longa. This muddied the historical record, made the imperial descent seem even more distinguished, and caused the near disappearance of the name Ascanius from Julian circles, if not from myth, from that time on.

ASEGEIR
Europe (North)

The Asegeir, in Nordic myth, were twelve seers and scholars who set sail in a boat to try to convert all Scandinavia to wisdom instead of **war**. They were beset by a storm, but the god **Forseti** rescued them and steered their boat safely to the island of Heligoland, where they lived happily ever afterwards.

ASET
Africa (North)

Aset (or Eset, 'throne'; Greek Isis), in Egyptian myth, was the daughter of **Nut** and **Geb** and sister of **Osiris**, **Set** and **Nebthet**. She and Osiris had a dual function as **fertility** gods: she oversaw **love** and union, he was the god of growth. They ruled Egypt as wife and husband; he taught his subjects the rule of law and respect for the gods; she taught them marriage, household management and medicine.

After Osiris was drowned and dismembered by their jealous brother Set, Aset used her medical skills first to impregnate herself with the last drop of semen in her consort's penis, and then to reassemble the corpse and bring it back to life. The first magic worked, and she became pregnant with **Horus**. But the gods refused to let Osiris return to the world of mortals, and he went to rule in the **Underworld**, leaving Aset vowing revenge on Set. Instead of fighting him herself, she encouraged Horus to take every chance to try to kill him, and when this proved impossible she arranged for Horus to humiliate and disempower Set. In some accounts this happened when Horus castrated Set in a duel, fit punishment for Set's crime of cutting off Osiris' penis and throwing it into the Nile.

In other accounts, Set was defeated by a trick. Horus went to Aset, complaining that in one of their wrestling-bouts Set had raped him, and producing drops of the god's semen to prove it. Aset asked Horus to masturbate over a lettuce-bed, and when the lettuces were grown took the choicest to Set, who ate them greedily. Then she handcuffed him and took him before the court of the gods, claiming that he'd stolen what belonged to Horus. Set protested that he'd not stolen the lettuces but had been given them – at which point Horus' semen began flying out of his mouth like a flock of finches, returning to its creator.

*In a society most of whose gods concerned themselves with the sky or the Underworld, Aset was one of the few great powers identified exclusively with life on Earth. She was worshipped throughout Egypt as a queen in royal robes (paralleling the depiction of her brother Osiris as a king in the Underworld). She wore either a throne-shaped crown (symbolizing royal power) or cow's horns enfolding the Sundisc, and carried a talisman, the tyet, a knotted girdle symbolizing the interconnectedness of life and sometimes made from red jasper to symbolize menstrual blood. In other representations she was shown as a pregnant sow or as a cow of plenty (either the goddess **Hathor** or – in Thebes – the cow which **Ptah** fertilized and which gave birth to **Hap**, the sacred bull).*

*Under the Greek name of Isis, Aset was worshipped particularly in the Greek-Egyptian towns of the Nile Delta, where she was regarded not as one of a pantheon of goddesses but as the **Great Goddess** herself. In the Delta myth-cycle, Isis tricked Ra into giving her his powers and his obligation to keep the universe in balance. She did this by a trick. Ra's power depended on*

*his true, secret name, known to no other being in creation. But although he was immortal, he was subject to aging, and one day Aset/Isis gathered some of the spittle he'd drooled into the sand and moulded a water-snake which bit him in the ankle. Racked with pain, he begged her to use her medical skill to cure him – and she agreed only if he told her his secret name. He told her a whole litany of false names, but each one made the snake-venom torment him even more, until at last he spoke the true secret name and was cured. Devotees of the **Mysteries** of Isis, a popular cult in Greek Egypt and Rome from the first century BCE to the time of the Christian Empire (fourth century CE), believed that knowledge of the name made Isis the most powerful deity in the universe – and furthermore, that when they themselves were told the name on their initiation into the cult, it gave them a (limited) share of the goddess' magic: power to defeat illness, aging and even death.*

⇒ justice and universal order

ASGARD
Europe (North)

Asgard ('home of the **Aesir**'), in Nordic myth, was the realm of the gods, in the highest of the three levels of existence, above **Midgard** (home of human beings) and **Niflheim** (home of the Dead). It was not so much a citadel as an entire fortified country. The gods owned palaces, farms, meadows, forests and lakes. They spent their days as prosperous human landowners did in Midgard, tending their crops and animals, ruling their followers and meeting each other to enjoy hunting, feasting in their banqueting-hall Gladsheim ('joy-home') and listening to the songs of bards. Every morning they gathered in council at the Well of Urd, where the three **Norns** guarded one of the roots of **Yggdrasil**, tree of the universe.

Asgard was connected to Midgard by **Bifröst**, the rainbow bridge. But the gods, although they looked down into Midgard and supervised mortal lives, seldom visited it, and no mortal ever passed from Midgard to Asgard except the souls of dead **heroes**, carried by the **Valkyries** to **Valhalla**. The **giants**, by contrast, were always trying to invade Asgard, hoping to steal the golden apples of **immortality**. Against their attacks the Aesir surrounded Asgard with an enormous wall. It was built by immortals and could be destroyed only by immortals. During the war between Aesir and **Vanir**, the entire wall was smashed, and a giant mastermason offered to rebuild it. He demanded as price the **Sun**, the **Moon** and **Freyja**, guardian of immortality, and the gods tried to cheat him by setting a time-limit too short for the work to be done. But the giant was helped by his magic horse Svadilfari, and it was only when **Loki** disguised himself as a mare and seduced Svadilfari away from the work, three days before the deadline, that the gods both got their wall and kept their immortality.

Ever after this, the myth ends, since both Asgard's defences and the gods' continuing immortality depend on a trick, they have been imperfect and are therefore doomed. At **Ragnarök**, the end of the universe, the forces of evil will rise to do battle with the powers of light, and Asgard will be overwhelmed. Its walls, rebuilt not by gods but by a mortal giant, will fall and it and its inhabitants will pass from existence as if they had never been.
≫→ **Heaven**

ASGAYA GIGAGEI
Americas (North)

Asgaya Gigagei ('red person' or 'red man of lightning'), in the myths of the Cherokee people of the Southeastern US, was a healing spirit which indicated sympathy by assuming the same sex as the person who asked for its help.
≫→ **disease and healing**

ASHUR
Asia (West)

Ashur (or Ashshur or Assur), in Mesopotamian myth, was the chief god of the Assyrian people of what is now Kurdistan. In **Heaven** he was the principle of **justice and universal order**, and his defeat of chaos kept the universe in being. On Earth he was the guarantor of **fertility** (symbolized by his appearance in art as a goatherd), or a warrior, protector of the city named after him, and depicted either as a king standing on a bull or, even more symbolically, as a bow or thunderbolt enclosed in a winged **Sun**-disc.
≫→ **supreme deity**

ASHVATHAMAN
India

Ashvathaman, in Hindu myth, was the son of **Drona**, one of the **Kaurava** generals in their war with the **Pandavas**. The gods had told Drona that he would never die so long as Ashvathaman lived – and the Pandavas cheated him by telling him that Ashvathaman was dead, adding only in a whisper that it was not his son but Ashvathaman the elephant. Drona, heartbroken, allowed himself to be killed by the Pandava leader Dhrishtadyumna.

Ashvathaman swore to avenge his father's death. In the night he and two companions set out for the Pandava camp. Their way was barred by a **giant**, and Ashvathaman fought him until he suddenly recognized him as **Shiva** himself. He ran to the nearest watch-fire and threw himself on it, declaring that he was sacrificing himself to Shiva to atone for making war on God. Shiva punished him, filling him with unthinking rage as soon as his mortal flesh was burned away and sending him rampaging through the camp, where he killed not only Dhrishtadyumna (his father's murderer) but every soldier he could find. Ashvathaman took a bundle of heads back to the Kaurava camp, swinging them by the hair like onions in a bag – a sight that sickened mortals and gods alike.

»+ heroes

ASHVINS
India

The Ashvins ('horse-lords') were twin sons of **Vivasvat**, god of the rising **Sun**, and his wife **Saranyu**. (Other accounts say that they were born from 'Agni's tears', that is, sparks, or were children of the heavenly **sea**: foam-beings, white horses.) They galloped across the sky before the appearance of dawn each day, riding in a golden chariot pulled by winged horses. They were healers, and guarded the gates of **death**. In some accounts, they were the same people as the **Ribhus**.

»+ disease and healing

ASK AND EMBLA
Europe (North)

Ask ('ash'), in Nordic myth, was the first man and Embla ('elm') was the first woman in the world. After **Odin**, **Vili** and **Ve** had finished creating the universe from the flesh, bones and brains of the **giant Ymir**, they walked throughout their creation to inspect it. They found two trees, uprooted by storms on a seashore. They lifted them and made them free-standing, free-willed individuals: Ask and Embla. Odin gave them life, Vili gave them intelligence and emotion, Ve gave them sight and hearing. The gods built **Midgard** for them to live in, making them responsible for all its plants and creatures. Ask and Embla were the ancestors of the human race.

ASTARTE
Asia (West)

Astarte ('sky-lady'), or Ashtart, Athirat or Athtart, in Canaanite myth, was the **Great Goddess**, consort of **El** and both mother and consort of **Baal**. She was the guarantor of **fertility**, sometimes shown as a cow or a cow-headed woman, sometimes as a many-breasted woman or (in a complex image) a many-breasted vagina. Fertility streamed from her breasts like milk; on Earth it was the sap in plants and the semen which engendered animals; when it spattered across the sky it made the Milky Way.

*One of the customs practised at Astarte's shrines was ritual prostitution. Women went there, once in their lives, and offered **sex** to the first man who asked, returning immediately to the enclosed existences of their homes and marriages. Non-worshippers of Astarte, from the Greeks to the Hebrew prophets, thought this practice as degenerate as it was bizarre, and claimed that the temples were brothels, full of prostitutes and illegitimate babies. (There is no evidence whatever for this assertion.) Later scholars of religion say that the multifarious accounts in West Asian myth of people being born to a mortal mother and an immortal father may derive from the custom of ritual prostitution, and that the idea of virgin birth, common in many mystery-myths from the area, may have been invented to suggest that the person so born was not contaminated by promiscuous intercourse. (There is no evidence for these assertions either.)*

≫→ Anat, Cybele, Inanna, Ishtar

ASTYANAX
Europe (South)

Astyanax ('prince of the city'), in Greek myth, was a baby, the son of **Hector** and **Andromache**. After the capture of Troy, prophets told the Greeks that if he grew up he would rebuild the city and avenge his father, so they took him to a high tower and threw him to his death.

ASURAS
India

Asura comes from the ancient Iranian word Ahura ('lord'), but in Indian myth

the *asuras* are always **demons**, opposing the *devas* (gods). One myth explains. Originally both *asuras* and *devas* were equal, offspring of **Prajapati** and chief powers in the universe. But when they were given choice, the *asuras* chose darkness to live in and lies to speak, whereas the gods chose light and truth. The two groups have been at war ever since – and their enmity has been compounded since the gods acquired **soma** and with it **immortality**. The *asuras* could only guarantee continued existence by breeding, and spawned countless offspring in the crevices of Earth. But they watch ceaselessly, especially at sacrifices, for a chance to snatch a little *soma* for themselves, and so usurp the gods' privileges and prerogatives. Like gods, they have a vast hierarchical society, from princes to slaves, and their lords are perpetually busy in the universe, challenging the gods and making trouble for humans.

≫→ light and darkness

ATAENTSIC
Americas (North)

Ataentsic, in the myths of the Huron and Iroquois peoples of the Northeastern US woodlands, was a **sky** goddess. She married a sky-chief and became pregnant with his child. But the Northern Lights whispered in his ear that the child was someone else's, and he dug a hole in the floor of **Heaven** and threw Ataentsic into it. She would have drifted in space forever if birds had not caught her and floated her gently down to where Otter and Muskrat had built an island, piling earth on Turtle's back in the primordial ocean, for her to live on.

Ataentsic bore her child, Wind Breath, on the island, and the animals fed them both. Wind Breath grew up, and the Wind fell in love with her and mated with her. Twin sons were born – in some accounts called **Ioskeha** and Tawiskara, in others **Hahgwehdiyu** and **Hahgwehdaetgah**. They were rivals from the moment of conception, and fought so fiercely in Wind Breath's womb that she died of it, at the very moment of giving birth. In some accounts the twins used fragments of her body to make the Earth and all its plants and creatures. In others, Ataentsic created the world and the planets from her daughter's body and ordered the **twins** to create animals and human beings. Ioskeha's creations were successful, but Tawiskara's were poor imitations – which is why both good and bad still exist in us.

ATAI: *see* Abassi and Atai

ATALANTA
Europe (South)

Atalanta (Atalante, 'tireless'), in Greek myth, was the daughter of King Iasus of Calydon. But he wanted a son, and when Atalanta was born he left her on a hillside to die. **Artemis** sent a she-bear to suckle her, and later gave her to her servants the **Amazons** to bring up as a hunter and athlete. It was only after the hunting of the Calydonian Boar that Iasus accepted Atalanta as his daughter – and she was immediately besieged by suitors, all the young **heroes** who had tried to kill the boar. But the Delphic oracle had prophesied that Atalanta's marriage would end her life, and she was determined never to

take a husband. She challenged each of her suitors to race her, saying that she would marry anyone who beat her.

There are several accounts of what happened next. In some, Hippomenes won the race by dropping three golden apples in front of Atalanta, and passing her each time as she bent to pick them up. The trick (inspired by Hippomenes' patron **Aphrodite**) melted Atalanta's heart, and forgetting the oracle's warning she ran into the woods with Hippomenes to enjoy **sex**. Unfortunately they chose to do it in a grove sacred to **Rhea**, and she changed them into lions and yoked them forever to her chariot, so proving the oracle true.

In other accounts, the man who beat Atalanta was not Hippomenes but Melanion, and the place where they had sex was sacred to **Zeus**, not Rhea. In still others, Atalanta was not turned into a lion, but disclosed after the race that she was pregnant by **Ares** the war-god. When the baby was born, the gods took Atalanta into **Olympus**, and her father Iasus exposed the child to die on the same hillside as his daughter years before. Artemis rescued the baby and gave him to her Amazons to bring him up; his name was Parthenopaeus, and he was later one of the seven champions who laid siege to **Thebes**.

ATAOKOLOINONA
Africa

Ataokoloinona ('how strange'), in Madagascan myth, was the son of 'Ndriananahary the creator. 'Ndriananahary made the world from mud, and left it in the sun to bake dry. After a while he sent Ataokoloinona to see if it was cool enough to live on. As soon as Ataoko-loinona touched the surface he vanished, wriggling underground through the scorching sand. Ever since then, 'Ndriananahary has sent showers of rain to cool the surface and entice Ataokoloinona back – so far without success. He has also created human beings to scour the surface and find the child. We fail, and when we send messengers – the Dead – to **Heaven** to ask for new instructions, they prefer **Sky**'s coolness and never come back.

ATAR
Asia (West)

Atar ('fire'), in Iranian myth, was the son of **Ahura Mazda** god of light. Ahura Mazda's twin **Ahriman**, lord of darkness, created a dragon, **Azhi Dahaka**, to eat the universe with its three heads of pain, anguish and **death**. The only way it could be stopped was if Ahura Mazda had a son, Atar, and sent him to fight the dragon. Atar fought Azhi Dahaka for millions of mortal years, and finally trapped the dragon and chained it to a mountainside. But the battle is not yet over: when the moment comes for the end of time, Azhi Dahaka will break free, and the duel will begin again, the dragon destroying one third of all **creation** before Atar finally kills it and scatters its ashes in the gulf of oblivion.

ATE
Europe (South)

Ate ('negativeness'), daughter of **Zeus** in Greek myth, was a goddess of mischief. Originally she delighted the gods with her pranks and practical jokes. In particular, she loved intoxicating her victim, making him or her behave in **Heaven** as mortals do on Earth when full of wine. (The gods drank **nectar**, not wine, and so did not get drunk.) On one occasion, however, she went too far. For nine months Zeus had successfully kept secret from his jealous wife **Hera** his love-making with the Argive princess **Alcmena**. But on the day their child was due to be born, Ate fuddled Zeus' wits, and he boasted that the next boy to be born in Argos would grow up to be prince of all around him. Hera at once realized what was happening, and delayed the birth of Alcmena's child (**Heracles**) until another Argive princess had had a son.

Zeus was so angry that he banished Ate from **Olympus** forever. He snatched her by the hair and threw her to Earth. Her high spirits were replaced by furious brooding, and she began preying on mortals, not playing innocent practical jokes but twisting their minds with arrogance, trying to fill them so full of self-confidence that they would challenge and unseat the gods and win Ate back her place in Heaven. (The attempts always failed. Mortal character was too weak to sustain the full self-knowledge of an immortal god, and the people Ate worked on became puffed up with arrogance, set themselves against the gods or **Fate**, and suffered for it.)

ATEA
Oceania

Atea ('space'), in the myths of the people of Tuamotu, was the original deity, moulding himself out of emptiness and making himself a consort, Fa'ahotu. Their first children died because Fa'ahotu had no breasts to suckle them with, but then Atea himself took on this role, nursing and weaning his own sons Tahu, **Tane** and Ro'o (some say by letting them suck from his penis). When Tane grew up, he fought Atea for control of the universe, and wounded him so severely with a thunderbolt that Atea withdrew from the universe and took no further part in its affairs.

*In some accounts, Atea is amalgamated with **Rangi** (and Fa'ahotu with **Papa**), and the two sets of myths are run together. In parts of Tuamotu, people claimed that there had been some seventy mortal generations between Atea's time and the modern era, and that their own families could trace their ancestry all the way back to him.*
≫→ creation

ATEN
Africa (North)

Aten ('disc'), in Egyptian myth, was originally the body of **Ra** the **Sun**, imagined as a flat disc like the blaze of sunlight reflected in the polished bronze circle of a mirror (used for divination). Until the fourteenth century BCE Aten was only one aspect of Ra, a minor member of the vast Egyptian pantheon. But in the reign of Pharaoh Amenhotep IV (1372-54BCE) he was promoted to become the only god in existence – not the most senior of the gods, but their entire replacement. Amenhotep changed his own name to Akhenaten ('he who pleases Aten'), established rites and rituals

(centring on a huge new temple built at a place he called Aketaten ('Aten's horizon', modern el-Amarna).

The Aten cult, one of the first monotheistic and philosophical systems in all world religion, failed to survive Akhenaten's death. Political pressure from the priests of **Amun** forced the new Pharaoh, Tutankhamun, to restore the former religion and the temples and hierarchies dependent on it. Aten's shrines were desecrated, his followers were persecuted, and he himself dwindled once more to become one facet of Amun-Ra, the Sun in splendour.

In the first few years of Aten-worship, the god was shown as a hawk-headed warrior or as a king in human shape brandishing the Sun-disk above his head. But as the cult became more philosophical, representations became more abstract, showing Aten as a golden disk with rays coming from its sides like embracing arms or dangling like ropes from a basket. Aten-worship yielded one of the finest surviving pieces of ancient Egyptian literature, the Hymn to Aten which some authorities say was written by Akhenaten himself, and which was later set to music by the Greek Egyptian Mesomedes and survives in written form – the only piece of ancient music for which notation still exists.
≫→ supreme deity

ATHAMAS
Europe (South)

Athamas ('reaper on high'), in Greek myth, was the son of the wind-lord **Aeolus**, and the brother of **Salmoneus** and **Sisyphus**. Unlike his brothers, who were rogues and **tricksters**, he was a simpleton. He was the king of Boeotia, a servant of **Hera** – and even she took advantage of his simplicity. She gave him as wife the goddess **Nephele**, the image **Zeus** had made of Hera to confuse **Ixion** when he repaid the gods' hospitality by trying to rape Hera at her own dinner-table in **Olympus**.

Athamas and Phrixus. Although Athamas and Nephele had two children (a son, **Phrixus**, and a daughter, **Helle**), their marriage was unhappy. Athamas took a mistress, **Ino**, and they had two children, Learchus and Melicertes. Athamas built the three of them a palace at the foot of Mount Laphystium – a place so secret that when Zeus had to find somewhere to hide his infant son **Dionysus** (son of Ino's sister **Semele**) from Hera's jealousy, he thought it ideal. Ino dressed Dionysus as a girl and brought him up among the palace women.

Unfortunately, even with Zeus' approval Athamas was too stupid to manage two families at once, or even to keep them apart for long. Soon he had to face an angry cloud-goddess and an angry mortal woman, each determined to punish him. Nephele blighted the crops so that Athamas' people would rise up and kill him, and Ino bribed the Delphic oracle to say that Nephele's and Athamas' son Phrixus had caused the blight (by raping his aunt Biddice), and that the only way to end it was for his father to take him to Mount Laphystium and sacrifice him.

Weeping, Athamas, Phrixus and Helle climbed the mountain. On the peak, Athamas and Phrixus built an altar of stones, and Athamas laid Phrixus on it and drew his knife. Just in time, Zeus saw what was happening. He sent **Heracles** to the mountain-top, riding a winged ram with a golden fleece. Heracles caught Athamas' arm just as he was about to stab his son, explained about the false oracle and said that neither Phrixus nor Helle would be safe from Ino if they stayed in Boeotia. They should fly to safety on the back of the golden ram.

The ram soared into the sky and carried Phrixus and Helle away. Athamas, by now utterly confused, went home to face Nephele – and found even worse trouble waiting there. Hera had discovered the infant Dionysus, hidden among Ino's palace women. She sent Ino mad and drove her out to wander in the hills; then, saying that Athamas was too stupid to deserve even a cloud for wife, she took Nephele back to Olympus.

Athamas and Themisto. So, at one stroke, Athamas lost his wife, his mistress and two of his children. He still had Ino's sons Learchus and Melicertes, but they were babies. He lived alone and unhappy for a year or two, hoping that Ino would come back to him; then, convinced that she was dead, he married another woman, Themisto, and made her his queen.

Athamas and Themisto lived happily for several years, and had two children. Then Hera restored Ino's wandering wits, and sent her back to the palace. Once again Athamas was trapped between a pair of warring wives. For a while he tried to live with both, but in the end he gave way to Ino's insistence that she was his true wife, and sent Themisto away. Themisto plotted to kill Ino's two children so that her own sons could be brought up as princes in their place. She bribed one of the palace maids to dress her sons in black and Ino's in white; then, in the night, she crept into the palace and stabbed the white-robed children dead. Unfortunately for her, the maid had told Ino of the plot and Ino had changed round the children's clothes, so that the children Themisto murdered were her own.

They were also Athamas' sons, and their deaths sent him mad with grief. He was out **hunting** with Ino's son Learchus when the news was brought. In his insanity he took the boy for a lion and killed him; then he ran home, snatched up Melicertes and threw him into a cauldron of boiling water to try to make him immortal. Ino rescued Melicertes and fled. But in their haste they fell over a cliff into the sea and drowned.

Broken with grief, Athamas went to the Delphic oracle and begged it to tell him a place where he could live the rest of his life in peace, unharassed by the gods. The oracle replied that the end of his wandering would come when wild animals shared their meal with him: there he would set up a kingdom and live in peace. Athamas set out on his wanderings (in the same northerly direction as Phrixus and Helle had flown on the golden ram). One day he came on wolves attacking a flock of sheep. Ravenously hungry, he braved the wolves' jaws and snatched fragments of sheep-meat to fill his belly. So the oracle came true. Athamas named the place Athamania, sent for Themisto to be his queen, and settled in peace at last.

ATHENE
Europe (South)

Athene's birth and powers. Athene ('**Heaven**-queen'; Latin Minerva), in Greek and Roman myth, was born from the forehead of her father **Zeus** (who had swallowed her mother Metis): she was the physical manifestation of her father's power and her mother's intelligence. She was the most honoured of Zeus' children, ranked equal with **Apollo**, and was the only god Zeus trusted to wield his thunderbolts. She was a warrior, brandishing a spear (the origin, some say, of her honorific name Pallas, 'brandisher'; others say it came from the name of the giant **Pallas** whom she killed) and carrying the *aegis* (a shield covered with skin from the goats which suckled the infant Zeus in Crete, fringed with snakes and carrying the **Gorgon**'s head which turned all who saw it to stone). At her side, or sometimes carried in her hand, went the goddess **Nike** (Victory). She was the mistress of all arts and **crafts**, especially spinning and weaving, and taught them to mortals.

Athene and Hephaestus. Athene was sexless. She was, at least technically speaking, born without a mother, and remained celibate. In thanks for splitting his forehead and releasing her, Zeus gave **Hephaestus** permission to marry her – so long as she agreed. But she refused, and when Hephaestus (who had been told by **Poseidon** that this was out of shyness not disdain and that she really loved him) tried to rape her she brushed him off so vigorously that a drop of his semen spilled all the way from **Heaven** to Earth, where it fertilized the ground to create Erichthonius (who later became king of Athens).

Athene and Athens. Athene and Poseidon both wanted to rule Attica, and the city which controlled it. Zeus decreed a contest of gifts: whichever god gave mortals the greatest gift should rule. Poseidon gave a water-spring, bubbling from the summit of the Acropolis (or some say a horse). Athene gave the first olive tree ever seen on Earth. After long discussion, the gods agreed, by a single vote, that this was the greater gift, and would enrich all Attica. Athene became patron of the area, and her people called their city Athens after her.

*Athene features in classical literature and art more than any other god except Zeus. She played a major part in the **Trojan War**, advised **Odysseus** on his journey home afterwards, and was the subject of hundreds of legends and folk-tales, for example the story of **Arachne**. The grandest piece of art ever made of her was the thirteen-metre statue created by Phidias in the fifth century BCE for her temple on the Acropolis, showing her in full military majesty, and with viewing platforms to let visitors see the carved ivory of her face and the gold of her headdress. Small replicas were common throughout the Greek world, and Athene also figured on vases and in tapestries and embroideries – and not least on Athenian coins, where her likeness appeared on one side and her favoured bird, the owl, on the other.*

*Roman Minerva was a much less active deity. She was one of the trinity which ruled the universe (acting in concert with **Jupiter** and **Juno**), but her role was far more ceremonial than in ancient Greece, and she*

was majestic and aloof rather than busy in human life. She was the patron goddess of craft-guilds and flute-players (she was held to have invented the flute), and – not unexpectedly, given her role as a war-goddess – was particularly interested in military bands.

ATLANTIS: *see* Amphitrite, Atlas

ATLAS
Europe (South)

Atlas and Atlantis. Atlas ('daring'; 'sufferer'), in Greek myth, was the son of the **Titan** Iapetus and the ocean-**nymph** Clymene. His half-brothers were Epimetheus, Menoetus and **Prometheus**, and his kingdom was Atlantis, a huge island in the Far West of the world. It was as large as Asia and Africa combined, and its surrounding ocean was so vast that it made the Mediterranean, by comparison, seem like a landlocked harbour. Atlas' subjects were as numerous as ants. At first they were industrious and god-fearing, but as the generations passed they became ever more degenerate and vicious, until the gods sent a **flood** which destroyed them and swallowed their continent; where it used to be there is now a stormy ocean covering half the world.

Atlas and the gods. Atlas took revenge for the loss of his kingdom by agreeing to act as the Titans' war-leader in their battle with the gods. When the gods won, thanks to the help of Atlas' half-brother Prometheus, they punished Atlas by condemning him to support the sky on his shoulders forever. For a thousand mortal generations he stood there, his back bent under the weight of **Heaven**. Then **Perseus** passed by on his winged horse **Pegasus**, and Atlas glimpsed the **Gorgon**'s head and was turned at once to stone. He became the mountain-range now known as the Atlas Mountains in North Africa (not, as some accounts have it, the Atlas Mountain in Arcadia in Greece).

Atlas' children were the **Hesperides** who tended the golden apples of **immortality**, the Hyades and the Pleiades.

Atlas supporting the heavens is an enduring image in Western art – and thanks to its appearance on the cover of Rumer Mercator's 1595 publication of his father's maps, the name 'atlas' has now become standard for any map-book. Atlantis, the lost continent, is another abiding idea from this myth, though it figures more as a symbol in utopian philosophy and literature than as an entity in its own right: it is the dream-continent of the Golden Age, before human beings were corrupted from innocence, elegance and goodness.
≫→ Heracles

ATLI
Europe (North)

Atli, king of the Huns (and some say, brother of Brünnhilde), in Germanic myth, married Gudrun after the death of her first husband **Sigurd**. Gudrun disliked him intensely, and their two children Erp and Eitel were born as a result of marital rape.

Atli and Gunnar. Atli was greedy to own the dwarf-gold for which so many people had already died. To find out where it was, he captured and tortured Sigurd's blood-brother Gunnar. Gunnar said that only two people, he himself and his brother Högli, knew where the treasure was hidden – and that he would tell Atli everything only when Atli brought him Högli's heart. Atli tried to fob him off with someone else's heart, but the heart trembled and shook before Gunnar and Gunnar rejected it. Then Atli brought the true heart, and demanded to know where the treasure was. Gunnar said that he was now the only person in the world who knew, and was not telling – and Atli executed him by throwing him into a pit of vipers, realizing too late that the secret had died with him.

Atli's death. All this time, Gudrun's dislike of Atli had been festering into madness. When Atli came back to the feast-hall after executing Gunnar, she served him a banquet of pretended welcome. But the food was their own sons Erp and Eitel – stewed flesh, roast hearts and livers – and the drink was mead thickened with their blood and served in their skulls for goblets. Knowing nothing of this, Atli ate and drank heartily, and as soon as he had finished Gudrun told him what she had done, set fire to the palace and destroyed them both.

ATRAHIS
Asia (West)

Atrahis, in Mesopotamian myth, was one name for the mortal allowed to escape the **flood** sent by **Enlil** and the other gods to destroy the human race. Advised by **Enki**, he had already helped humanity survive two divine attempts to destroy them, by plague and drought. Before the flood, therefore, Enlil made all the gods swear not to tell any living thing what was about to happen – and Enki the **trickster** was able to warn Atrahis only by whispering the secret not to the king himself but to the walls of his palace. Atrahis loaded a boat with creatures of all kinds, sailed on the waters until the flood subsided, and then sacrificed to the gods – at which point, Enlil gave up his vendetta against mortals, gave Atrahis **immortality** and allowed him to father a reborn human race.

≫→ Deucalion and Pyrrha, Doque-buth, Manu, Noah, Nu'u, Utnapishtim

ATREUS
Europe (South)

Atreus and Artemis. Atreus ('fearless'), in Greek myth, was one of the sixteen sons of **Pelops** and Hippodamia. Jointly with his brother **Thyestes**, he ruled the small town of Midea near Mycenae. The brothers were shepherds, and Atreus promised one day to give the finest animal in all his herds to **Artemis**. To test him, the goddess hid among the sheep a ram with a golden fleece. Greed drove promises from Atreus' mind. He sacrificed the ram and gave Artemis the meat and bones, but kept the fleece for himself.

The throne of Mycenae. When **Eurystheus**, king of Mycenae, died, the Delphic oracle told his people to put a son of Pelops on the throne. The Mycenaeans asked Atreus and Thyestes to choose which one of them it should be, and Thyestes suggested that it should be whichever brother owned Artemis' golden fleece. When Atreus enthusiastically agreed, Thyestes, quick as a conjurer, produced the fleece. (It was no conjuring trick. Unknown to anyone, he had been having an affair with Atreus' wife Aerope, and she had given him the fleece as a love-token.) The Mycenaeans prepared to make Thyestes king. But now the **Sun**, seeing that a wrong choice was to be made, wheeled his chariot round and rode across the **sky** from West to East; the stars reversed their courses; the earth roared. Thyestes, terrified, confessed that Atreus was the rightful mortal owner of the fleece. The Mycenaeans made Atreus king, and Thyestes was banished.

Atreus and Thyestes. So Atreus punished the man who stole the fleece from him. But he had himself stolen it, and now its true owner Artemis sent him insane and made him commit a hideous crime. Atreus sent messengers to tell Thyestes that he was forgiven and could come home from exile. He welcomed him, gave him the seat of honour at a banqueting-table, and with his own hands served him a stew – of his own sons' flesh. Thyestes called on the gods to destroy Atreus and all his children. Then he fled into exile once more, this time to Sicyon where his daughter Pelopia was a priestess of **Athene**.

Atreus' death. The gods had still not finished with the brothers. Thyestes asked the oracle how he could avenge his dead children, and the oracle told him to father a child on his own daughter Pelopia. This Thyestes did, raping her in a sanctuary of Athene – and the resulting child, **Aegisthus**, was brought up by his uncle Atreus in Mycenae, without anyone knowing whose son he really was. The gods bided their time until Aegisthus, and Atreus' sons **Agamemnon** and **Menelaus**, grew to manhood. Then they sent plague on the city, and the Delphic oracle said that nothing but 'the death of a son of Pelops' would end it. Agamemnon and Menelaus arrested Thyestes, thinking that he was the man Apollo meant. But in Mycenae, Thyestes recognized his son Aegisthus, told him how Atreus had butchered his brothers and sisters long ago, and begged him to avenge them. Aegisthus stole into Atreus' bedroom and stabbed him dead.

Atreus' tomb. After this murder, Aegisthus set Thyestes on the throne and banished Agamemnon and Menelaus. They went to Sparta, where Agamemnon raised an army and besieged Mycenae. He took the town, exiled Thyestes and Aegisthus and established himself as king. He built a fortress inside a ring of walls crowned by the Lion Gate, constructed a huge beehive-shaped tomb just outside the citadel, and there buried Atreus' remains with a wealth of chariots, weapons and treasure of every kind, including the fleece of the golden ram whose theft had begun the decline in Atreus' life.

ATRI
India

Atri, in Hindu myth, was one of the **Seven Seers**. Throughout eternity, his task was to keep the **Sun** in the sky, preventing it falling into the darkness of the **Underworld**. He did this by mental powers alone: concentration and meditation. In some accounts, the strain of this occasionally made his eyes water –

and this was the origin of **soma**.

ATROPUS: *see* Fates

ATSEESTAN: *see* Atsehastin and Atseestan

ATSEHASTIN AND ATSEESTAN
Americas (North)

Atsehastin ('first man') and Atseestan ('first woman'), in the myths of the Navajo people of the Southwestern US, made our world. Their ancestors were the bats, birds and insects of Red World, lowest of the five superimposed layers which formed the universe. All these creatures were sexually promiscuous, and the gods flooded Red World to wipe them out. They escaped by flying through a smoke-hole in the roof of Red World, and came into Blue World. Here they were accepted until their licentiousness annoyed the chief – they tried to rape his wife – and they were forced to escape into Yellow World, where exactly the same thing happened. They arrived at last in the fourth, many-coloured world (the one below our own), and settled there.

The many-coloured world was already inhabited, by creatures exactly like human beings except that they had no intelligence. They browsed in the forests and on the plains, but made nothing and worshipped no gods. It was to put an end to this that the gods took two corn-seeds (one white, one yellow) and made Atsehastin and Atseestan, giving them human shape but also breathing into them the air of intelligence. Atsehastin and Atseestan, helped by **Coyote** the **trickster**, taught the browsing humans to believe in and worship gods, to form communities, hunt, farm, and live civilized lives. This exaltation of humans to rival the gods angered the water-monster Tieholtsodi, who flooded the world to drown them. Hawk flew up and clawed a hole in the sky, Badger widened it with his claws, and Atsehastin and Atseestan led the surviving humans and animals through it.

When the climbers passed through the clouds, they found themselves in a fifth world, our own. Nothing as yet existed there except water and one small island, and Atsehastin and Atseestan created **Sky**, **Sea**, **Mother Earth**, **Sun**, **Moon**, the stars and everything else which is. They appointed a Sun-bearer, **Tsohanoai**, and a Moon-bearer, Klehanoai, to carry the heavenly bodies across the sky. So our world began – and when it was finished and a fit home for the human race Atsehastin and Atseestan vanished, their work complete.

≫→ **Estsanatlehi, civilization, creation**

ATTIS
Europe (South)

Attis was originally a god from the Black Sea area, either the male half of the hermaphroditic Agditis or son of the river goddess Nana, conceived after she gathered blossom from a tree fertilized with blood from Agditis' severed penis. **Cybele**, the female half of Agditis, lusted after him, and tried to abduct him – and when he refused she drove him mad, so that he castrated himself and bled to death.

*The Attis cult became notorious in ancient Rome because of the extraordinary zeal of its adherents, who worked themselves up into religious ecstasy by taking drugs and dancing, and then castrated themselves in the god's honour. One of Catullus' best-known poems relates the emotions of such a devotee, mutilating himself for love of the divine on the sacred island of Cybele and Attis (even, Catullus implied, as he himself was so carried away by ecstatic love for Lesbia, his mistress, that he would willingly destroy his manhood). At a slightly (but not much) more decorous level, the Emperor himself used to preside, as high priest of Cybele, at an annual re-enactment of the story of Attis and Cybele, part **fertility** ritual part orgy.*

≫→ **mysteries**

ATUM
Africa (North)

Atum ('totality'), in Egyptian myth, was both primordial Chaos and the creator-god who emerged from it. In one version of the **creation**-myth, he gathered his own formlessness and gave it man-shape (himself), then masturbated (or some say spat) into the void to make **Shu** and **Tefnut**, ancestors of the gods.

In other accounts, Atum/Chaos was personified as a gigantic **snake**. At the end of this cycle of the universe, when all existence ended, he and **Horus** (also in the form of a snake) would slough their present existence as snakes shed their skins, and be reborn to begin the world anew.

Reluctant to accept the idea of a god masturbating, Atum's priests modified the *myth to say that the god was both male and female: his male part (penis) mated with his female part (hand) to begin creation. The 'Hand of Atum' was worshipped as a separate god. Atum was especially honoured in Heliopolis, where his cult pre-dated that of **Ra**. When the Ra cult took over, Atum was claimed to be one aspect of the Sun-god: Atum-Ra, the Evening Sun which returns to the womb of **Mother Earth** each evening to be reborn next morning as Ra-Harakhti, the Sun at dawn.*

In art, Atum was occasionally shown as a snake or snake-headed god, but more often as a king enthroned, wearing the royal crown and head-dress and holding the staff of office. His sacred animals, bull, ichneumon, lion and lizard, were sometimes shown attending him. In Heliopolis, as the Evening Sun preparing for reincarnation, he was occasionally depicted as an old man.

AUCHIMALGEN
Americas (South)

Auchimalgen, in the myths of the Araucanian people of Chile, was one of the two primordial beings. She was the goddess of the **Moon** and consort of her brother the **Sun**. The Sun played no part in the affairs of the world, and Auchimalgen was herself remote. But she took sufficient interest in human lives to turn red every time some catastrophe, such as a royal death, was imminent.

AUDUMLA
Europe (North)

Audumla ('nourisher'), in Nordic myth, was a cow, formed at the beginning of **creation** from the melting ice of **Niflheim**. She was the second being ever to exist, and the first being, **Ymir**, sucked nourishment from her udders. She herself licked the ice for salt, and uncovered the sleeping form of **Buri**, the third being, ancestor of the gods.

➤ **bulls and cows**

AUGEAS
Europe (South)

Augeas (or Augias, Greek Augeias, 'dazzling ray'), King of Elis in Greek myth, was the son of **Helius** the **Sun**-god, and like his father kept huge herds of cattle. These were immortal, and enormously fertile. None ever died, and every day thousands more calves were born. Because Augeas never cleaned out his cattle-pens, the dung overflowed and choked the fields on every side. As his fifth labour, **Heracles** was ordered to clean out the stables, and he bet Augeas one tenth of all his cattle that he could do it in a single day. Instead of laboriously forking and carting the dung away, he battered down the wall surrounding the cattle-pens, and diverted the river Alpheus through the yard. The water carried the dung out to sea, and Heracles returned the river to its course and rebuilt the wall.

Augeas now broke his bargain. He refused Heracles his share of the cattle, on the grounds that he had done the work by trickery – and when his own son Pyleus took Heracles' side, he lost his temper (as the Sun's children easily did) and banished him. Heracles bided his time for years – he had other labours to perform, not to mention travelling with the **Argonauts** and serving queen **Omphale** – but then went back to Elis, killed Augeas and put Pyleus on the throne.

*Eurystheus (who devised Heracles' labours) refused to accept the cleansing of Augeas' stables, on the grounds that Alpheus, not Heracles, had done all the work. He set Heracles an alternative, far more dangerous task: to steal **Cerberus**, guard-dog of the **Underworld**.*
>>→ Laomedon

AULANERK
Arctic

Aulanerk, in Eskimo myth, frolicked in his **sea**-kingdom, basking in its waters – and his movements warmed the water, kept back the ice and gave fishermen safe sailing home.

AUNYAINÁ
Americas (South)

Aunyainá, in the myths of the Tupari people of Brazil, was a **demon** from the early days of **creation**. It had human shape and boars' tusks, and fed on human children. One day it was hunting in the forest when its prey climbed up a high tree. Aunyainá followed them, scrambling up a liana – until Parrot gnawed through the liana and sent it crashing to the forest floor. Lizards seethed like maggots in Aunyainá's broken flesh, and crawled out to colonize land and river. As for the children who'd climbed into the trees to escape being eaten, they became monkeys.

AURORA: *see* Eos

AUSTRALIAN MYTH
Archaeologists suggest that Australia may have been continuously inhabited since the last Ice Age, some 50,000 years ago. The people were hunter-gatherers, living in small groups (between five and fifty families) wherever the terrain supported life. When European settlers arrived in the late eighteenth century, it is estimated that there were some 300-500 of these groups, each with its own language; 200 years later the Aboriginal population had declined to just over 150,000 people, and some fifty languages survived.

All such estimates of numbers and time would have been meaningless to the people who created the myths and lived by them. They existed simultaneously on two planes: everyday reality, dominated by hunting, food preparation and child-rearing, and the Dreaming or Dream Time. The Dream Time had temporal location: it was the period at the beginning of **creation** when enormous spirit-beings travelled across the continent, giving the land shape and identity and stocking it with plants and creatures, including the spirits of everyone ever to be born in the future. It also had a mystic dimension: if you followed ritual exactly, in the places sacred to the spirits of your group, you entered into communion with them, became part of a continuum of existence which transcended the everyday.

This second dimension of the Dream Time, and therefore of existence, was what myth supported and validated. The journeys of the spirits covered the entire continent in a skein of mystic pathways, and their rest-points – water-holes, hills, clumps of undergrowth – were areas of particular sacredness. Myths offered a kind of map of these journeys, and by reciting or re-enacting the stories you entered into the spirit-journeys and so into the Dream Time. Each human group was custodian of a small part of the total web, related to its own geographical area; but the myths themselves were blurred, coalescing, never-ending, the threads which bound all existence together.

Understanding nothing of this, baffled by the profusion of native languages, and convinced that 'primitive' religion was merely an early stage in the progress that would lead to Christianity, early European incomers ignored or trampled on Aboriginal culture. The net was torn, and the myths which had sustained it survived only fragmentarily, embedded in the songs and rituals which persisted despite the settlers. By the present century, some two thirds of all Aboriginal languages had disappeared, taking with them the myths and social framework they had upheld. Determined efforts were and still are being made to reconstruct the whole vast pattern – but in a system which depended entirely on memory, the loss of so many people, continent-wide over several generations, makes success, if not entirely doomed, unlikely. (Memories are chiefly stirred by surviving ceremonies and by a rich legacy of paintings, on rocks, bark or skin, and other artefacts. In this culture, all 'art' is narrative: every artefact has a story, and depends on it for meaningful existence, so that stories are enshrined in an iconography of styles and patterns which in some cases dates back 10,000 years.)

In the present book, whose organization is not by skeins but alphabetical, it is possible to give only glimpses of the full fabric of native Australian myth, as if one attempted to show the ocean by focusing, one at a time, on a few dozen individual water-drops. The continuum, not its interruption, makes the pattern. We have included stories of creator-spirits from different regions: the **Bagadjimbiri**, **Bildjiwuaroju**, **Miralaldu** and **Djanggawul**, **Kurukadi** and **Mumba**, **Mangarkungerkunja**, **Minawara** and **Multultu**, **Mudungkala**, **Ngurunderi**, **Waramurungundju** and **Wuraka**. The **Great Rainbow Snake** appears in several forms: as **Julunggul**, **Jurawadbad**, **Kunapipi** and the **Wondjina** rain spirits. Other stories tell of more specific matters: the separation of females from males (**Yalungur**); why humans die (**Bobbi-Bobbi**; **Purukapali**; **Widjingara**); how fire was discovered (**Jurumu**); the nature of spirits who preyed on unwary humans (the **Mimi**; the **Namorodo**); the rivalry between **Marindi** and **Adnoartina** in the Dream Time, as a result of which **Uluru** (Ayers Rock) is the colour of blood. There is also one trickster-tale (**Tjinimin** and **Pilirin**) and one (characteristically specific) tale explaining the presence in one community of particular sacred objects, in this case (**Darana**) the Stones of Destiny of the Dieri people of Lake Hope.

AUTOLYCUS
Europe (South)

Autolycus (Autolykos, 'lone wolf'), in Greek myth, was the son of **Hermes**, god of **tricksters**. He was a bandit-leader and cattle-rustler, using his semi-divine magic to change the brand-marks on the cattle he stole. The only person ever to outwit him was another trickster, **Sisyphus**, who hid additional marks on the bottom of his cows' hooves. Autolycus and Sisyphus became close friends, so much so that Autolycus allowed Sisyphus to have **sex** with his daughter Anticlea on the morning of her wedding to King **Laertes** of Ithaca – a union whose offspring, some accounts say, was **Odysseus**.

AVALOKITESHVARA

Asia (Central; East); India

Avalokiteshvara ('he who looks down'; 'the compassionate'), in Buddhist myth and belief, is **Buddha**'s manifestation as lord of forgiveness. In Tibet he is worshipped as **sPyan-ras-gzigs**, and in China he takes female form as **Guan Yin**, goddess of mercy.

In Indian art, Avalokiteshvara is usually shown as a standing prince wearing rich clothes and jewels and surrounded by attendants. In one hand he carries a lotus; the other is held straight down with the palm flat towards us – a gesture of reassurance. Particularly important are the calmness and compassion shown in his face.

AVALON

Europe (North)

Avalon ('apple-isle'), in Celtic myth, was an island existing outside mortal space and time, where the apples of **immortality** grew. In some versions of the story of King **Arthur**, he was taken there at the end of his life to be cured of his wounds, and lived on as one of the Blessed Immortals.

*Those modern scholars who hold that Arthur was a real person identify Avalon as Glastonbury in Southern England – a place medieval scholars had previously dignified by saying that its holiness and serenity led Joseph of Arimathea to take the **Holy Grail** to safety there when he fled from the Holy Land after Jesus' death.*

≫→ **Heaven**

AWONAWILONA

Americas (North)

Awonawilona ('all-container'), in the myths of the Zuñi people, Pueblos of the Southwestern US, existed before existence. It was thought alone, and in the course of time streams of thought issued from it in the form of mists and heat. The heat turned the mists to **water**, the primordial **sea**, and warmed the surface until green algae grew and covered it. Awonawilona, by willpower alone, turned some of the algae into Awitelin Tsta, **Mother Earth**, and the rest into Apoyan Tachi, Father **Sky**.

There were four enormous caves in the body of Mother Earth, and into each of them Awonawilona placed seeds of life and fertilized them with the heat of willpower. The seeds burst and grew, and the caves teemed with life. Eventually, one of the creatures, Poshaiyankayo, tunnelled his way to the surface and persuaded Awonawilona to open the caves and let all the creatures spill out on the surface of the Earth.

≫→ **creation**

AYWELL
Europe (North)

Aywell was the protector of the independent peoples of the North of England. He was inseparably linked with his consort **Mm**, and to this day they are always invoked together.

AZACCA
Americas (Caribbean)

Azacca ('cornman'), in Haitian myth, was the god of **farming**, a spirit of light just as his brother **Ghede** was a spirit of darkness. He was his brother's mirror-image in other ways: he was brainless and brutish, with voracious appetites for food, beer and **sex**. But he was also hardworking and honest, and – providing you could keep his appetites satisfied – would never desert you or your farm.

AZHI DAHAKA
Asia (West)

Azhi Dahaka, in Iranian myth, was a dragon created by **Ahriman** to eat the universe. Its three heads were pain, anguish and **death**, and its wings of darkness were so vast that they hid the stars. **Ahura Mazda** sent his son, **Atar**, to fight the dragon, and their battle covered all creation for millions of mortal years, until finally Atar chained Azhi Dahaka to a mountain, allowing mortals the chance of happiness. However, **Zurvan Akarana**, eternity, knows that Azhi Dahaka is not dead, and will break free at the end of human time, beginning a final battle between good and evil which will destroy one third of all creation and will end only when Atar finally kills Azhi Dahaka and scatters his ashes into the gulf of oblivion.

≫→ monsters and dragons

BAAL
Asia (West)

Baal ('keeper' or 'lord') was the title given to many gods of Palestine, Syria and the Phoenician region, as well as of the Phoenician settlements in North Africa. Their true names were too sacred to be spoken except by high priests in secret ceremonies, and 'Baal' was the public equivalent. There were hundreds of Baals, since any god could be given the name: examples are Baal Berith ('lord of contracts'), Baal Gad ('master of goats') and Baal Zebulon ('keeper of the house').

Most Baals were taken bodily into the religions and myths of the peoples who conquered each area, or were strenuously (and somewhat mindlessly) opposed by adherents of monotheistic religions. The North African sky-god Baal Hammon, for example, became the Egyptian **Amun**. Baal Tyre, the Tyrian sun-god, was made over as **Heracles** by the Greeks and was railed at by Old Testament prophets as Moloch. Baal Samin ('lord of the skies') and Baal Zebul (see **Beelzebub**) were reinvented in the Bible as **Yahweh**'s rival **Satan**.

»+ Adad

BABA-YAGA
Europe (East)

Baba-Yaga, goddess of **death** in Slavic myth, ate human flesh and lived in a house built of her victims' bones and surrounded by a bone fence topped with skulls whose eyes lit up in the dark. The whole thing was not stationary but ran about on enormous hen's legs. Baba-Yaga rode not in a chariot but in an enormous mortar, using the pestle to pole it along like a boat. Her teeth

Cotama Budha, Worshipped in Ceylon, Siam, China and other parts of the East.
Cotama Budha, a Addolir yn Ceylon, Siam, China, a Pharthau ereill o'r Dwyrain.

Buddha (*17th-century Welsh engraving*)

were knives and her eyes turned her victims to stone, in which state she took them back to home to unpetrify and eat.

*The Gothic details of this myth date from the Christian era. Before then, Baba-Yaga was also an aspect of the **Great Goddess**, helping all who worshipped her. In folktales, however, she was downgraded to become a mere **demon**. She often lay in wait for victims, opening her jaws like a cave-mouth to swallow anyone who passed inside – possibly a folk-memory of the gaping devil's jaws which, in medieval Christian drama, symbolized the gates of Hell.*

BABEL, THE TOWER OF
Asia (West)

The Tower of Babel, in Hebrew myth, was an ambitious project planned by **Noah**'s descendants after the **Flood**: that is, by all human beings left alive. They migrated to the plain of Shinar, and their king Nimrod decided to build a huge tower which would reach to **Heaven** and challenge **Yahweh**. Yahweh foiled them by confusing their speech, so that no one could understand what anyone else was saying. Without a single language to co-ordinate the work, the people began squabbling, the building was abandoned, and soon they separated and migrated to every corner of the world, taking their myriad languages with them.

*Scholars say that this myth was invented to explain the huge ziggurat at the heart of the city of Babylon, a temple in honour of **Marduk**. The 'Nimrod' who planned it, in the myth, was the same person as*

Gilgamesh. 'Babel' ('God's Gate') was Babylon's ancient name, and the idea of 'confusion of languages' came from a simple pun: 'Babel' is irresistibly close to the Hebrew word balal, 'to confuse'. The myth ends, egregiously, by saying that Hebrew, the original sole language of the universe, was reserved ever afterwards for Yahweh's own chosen people – and indeed was one of the proofs that he had chosen them.

BACCHUS: *see* Dionysus

BACHUE
Americas (South)

Bachue ('big-breasts'), in the myths of the Chibcha people of Colombia, was the mother of the whole human race. She rose from the primordial lake as a **snake**, changed into a woman and bore a son. Six years later, when he had grown to maturity, she mated with him; their offspring were the first human beings. As soon as the humans were born, Bachue and her son changed back into snakes and plunged to the bottom of the lake.

BADIMO: *see* Modimo and Badimo

BAGADJIMBIRI, THE
Australia

The Bagadjimbiri, in the myths of the Karadjeri people of the Kimberleys in Northwestern Australia, were brothers born spontaneously from **Mother Earth** in the Dream Time, in the form of wild dogs. At that time the world was desert, and they wandered everywhere making waterholes, trees, shrubs, insects and

animals. Finally they mated a toadstool (the first penis) with a fungus (the first vagina) and made the ancestors of the human race. When **creation** was complete their souls soared into the sky, and their bodies lived on as water-**snakes**.
»→ animal-gods, Kurukadi and Mumba, Minawara and Multultu

BA JA
Asia (Central; East)

Ba Ja, in the myths of the Mongolian nomads and in Chinese myth, was a general whose service on Earth was so outstanding that he was promoted, in extreme old age, to the Heavenly bureaucracy. His job was to fight locusts, and he was given an eagle's beak and talons to do it with – attributes which, together with the blue skin worn by every immortal, went somewhat incongruously with his general's cloak, snowy hair and sagging, old man's breasts. Farmers often put his image on poles in their fields and orchards, and if locust-swarms then devastated them they claimed, disarmingly, that the poor old man had dozed off, as was only to be expected.
»→ farming, guardians

BALARAMA
India

Balarama's birth. Balarama ('Powerful Rama'), in Hindu myth, was either the seventh son conceived by **Devaki** and **Vasudeva**, or a child placed in Devaki's womb by **Vishnu**, in the form of a white hair from the world-serpent **Shesha**. He would have been **Krishna**'s elder brother, since Krishna was placed in Devaki's womb at the same time, in the form of one of Vishnu's own black hairs. But when the gods prophesied that Devaki's son would kill the demon-king **Kansa**, and Kansa began murdering Devaki's children, Balarama was smuggled out of her womb into that of her sister **Rohini**, and grew up as Rohini's son; Krishna was left to be born as Devaki's seventh son. Balarama and Krishna were inseparable companions, both throughout their childhood (when they competed in killing **demons**) and when they grew up, in the war between the **Pandavas** and **Kauravas**, and in the battle they waged against Kansa and his followers.

Balarama's nature. Unlike Krishna, a god briefly assuming mortal form, Balarama was a human being with godly powers. He found it hard to control his supernatural self, and it surfaced with particular violence whenever he lost his temper, making him perform feats of strength out of all proportion to the situation. He was especially savage with demons, playing with them as a cat plays with mice and hurling their bodies about so that they lodged in inaccessible cliffsides or in the tops of trees. His favourite weapon was a ploughshare, and with it he battered down city walls or smashed the skulls of his enemies. On one occasion, when he was drunk, he shouted to the river Yamuna to come to him, as he wanted to bathe but was too lazy to walk to her – and when she refused he hooked her with his ploughshare and dragged her behind him across half India, flooding the countryside.

Balarama's death. One day, feeling drunk, Balarama lay under a banyan tree to sleep it off. In fact, he was full not of wine but of **water**: his father, the world-serpent Shesha, had flowed into him, and now gushed out, taking Balarama's spirit with him. Shesha splashed and gurgled to the **sea**, which rose with flowers to welcome him, and when Balarama's followers came looking for their master, all they found was his skin, as flaccid and featureless as a wineskin.

Balarama features in most of the literature about Krishna, sometimes as a hero with powers equal to the gods, but often as a bantering, irreverent companion halfway between elder brother and squire. In art he appears either as a mortal warrior armed with club and ploughshare, or as a figure with human head and shoulders and a body which is snake or rapidly-flowing river.

⟫→ **heroes**

BALDUR
Europe (North)

Baldur ('lord' or 'beautiful one'), or Balder, in Nordic myth, was the son of **Odin** and **Frigg**. He was the most desirable person in all **creation** – and unlike the rest of the warlike **Aesir**, he was sweet-natured and gentle. He lived in a golden palace with his wife Nanna (one of the goddesses-in-waiting of the love-goddess **Freyja**), and his radiance filled **Asgard** with wisdom, companionship and cheerfulness.

As time passed, Baldur began to suffer from nightmares: that he would die, killed by one of the other Aesir, and that his death would begin the destruction of the universe. Trying to cheat this fate, Baldur's mother Frigg asked everything in existence, gods, humans, animals, **water**, rocks, plants, to swear that they would never harm him. All swore except mistletoe, which Frigg thought too young and insignificant to ask. Baldur's invulnerability led the Aesir to bouts of horseplay. At banquets they delighted in hurling sticks, rocks, spears and firebrands at him and watching them bounce harmlessly away. But one day **Loki** put into the hands of the blind god **Höd** a mistletoe-twig sharpened like a dart – and guided his aim so that the mistletoe stabbed Baldur's heart and killed him.

Baldur's death took all joy from Asgard. Because he had been killed at a banquet, not on the battlefield, he was barred from **Valhalla** and forced to live with the Dead in the **Underworld**. Frigg sent Hermod, Baldur's brother, to **Hel** goddess of the Underworld to ask what must be done for Baldur to be given back to life. Hel said that just as every created thing had vowed not to harm Baldur, so, if all **creation** shed one tear for him, he could return. The gods sent messages throughout the universe, and creation promised to weep for Baldur all except one bent old giantess, festering in a cave deep underground. Her name was Thökk, and she refused to weep for Baldur, saying that he had never done anything for her.

So Baldur, joy of creation, was condemned to stay in the Underworld until **Ragnarök**, the end of the universe. And that event is now not long away. The gods discovered that Thökk was actually Loki in disguise. He tried to escape by changing into a salmon, but they caught him and bound him with chains made from his own son's guts. He lies imprisoned until the time comes for him to break free and send the forces of darkness charging into Asgard to destroy the gods.

Throughout Ragnarök, the tempestuous battle which will destroy **creation** as we know it, Baldur will remain imprisoned in the Underworld. But when all the forces of evil have been destroyed, he will be free, and will rule the children of the gods and the new race of mortals, for another age of the universe.

For an alternative, and strikingly different, account of Baldur's nature and his death, see Höd.

»+ beauty, light and dark

BALI
India

Bali ('rose-coloured'), in Hindu myth, was a **demon** king who conquered Earth and Middle Air and then attacked **Heaven** itself. **Vishnu** took the form of a dwarf, **Vamana**, begged Bali to give him as much land as he could cross in three steps – and then, when Bali agreed, soared to god-height and traversed the entire universe. In some accounts he then mercifully allowed Bali to rule the world below, and Bali became king of the **Underworld**. In others, he chained Bali in the fathomless depths below the Underworld. Bali lay there for an age of the world, then started stirring and roaring once again. This time, before he could surge from the Underworld and challenge the gods, **Indra** broke him to pieces with a thunderbolt. Instead of blood and flesh, Bali shattered into precious stones: the wealth of the universe, buried in the earth.

Bali is not the same person as **Balin**.

BALIN
India

Balin and Ravana. Balin, in Hindu myth, was the son of **Indra** the storm-god and a monkey-queen. He boasted that he could easily beat the **demon**-king **Ravana**, and challenged him to single combat anywhere, any time. Ravana crept up behind him one day as he was drinking at a lakeside, and grabbed his tail. Immediately, Balin flicked it round, and it grew so long that it pinioned Ravana's hands, his ten arms, his ten heads and finally his whole body. Balin capered round the world for twelve years with Ravana bundled in his tail, before setting the furious demon free.

Balin and Sugriva. Balin coveted the monkey-kingdom of his half-brother **Sugriva** (who had stayed at home, ruling, while Balin pranced round the world with Ravana). His grandfather **Brahma** had granted him an unusual gift: each time he looked hard at someone, he stole half their power. Armed with this, he challenged Sugriva to single combat. Sugriva asked **Rama** to help, and Rama hid behind a tree as the brothers circled one another. Each time Sugriva ran to attack, Balin stared hard at him, sapping half his strength, until the monkey-king was as weak and helpless as an ant. But each time Sugriva's strength was halved, Rama magically redoubled his own strength behind the tree, until finally, filled with the full power of **Vishnu** whose avatar he was, he set arrow to bow and shot Balin dead. It was in thanks for this help that Sugriva organized the army of monkeys and bears which helped Rama win back his wife **Sita** when she was kidnapped by Ravana.

Balin is not the same person as **Bali**.
≫→ animal-gods

BALOR
Europe (North)

Balor, in Celtic myth, was the god of **death**. He ruled the Fomori, **demons** who lived in the impenetrable darkness of the **sea**'s depths and in lakes and dark pools in the upper world. He had one eye. At first it was lidless, but Balor once spied on a group of wizards making a magic potion, and they threw the boiling liquid into his eye to poison him. The poison failed to kill Balor, but weakened his eye. He grew a drooping, baggy lid to cover it – and whenever his attendants lifted the lid (it took four of them to do it) and he looked directly at someone, that person was immediately claimed by the Fomori and died.

Warned by a prophecy that his own grandson would kill him, Balor shut his daughter Ethlin in a glass tower to prevent any male ever touching her. But the smith-god Cian disguised himself as a woman, visited Ethlin and made her pregnant, and in due course their son **Lug** killed Balor, avoiding his evil eye by fighting from a distance and shooting him dead with a sling-shot. After Balor's death his demons retreated to their dark depths. They live there still, without a leader but dangerous, no longer fed by Balor's victims but surging out to snatch prey for themselves, taking the forms of sea-monsters, lake-spirits and the boggarts who lurk in fens.

BANNIK, THE
Europe (East)

The *bannik* (from *banya*, 'bath'), in Slavic myth, was the spirit of the bath-house. He was unpredictable and had to be treated carefully: every fourth bath was his alone, and if you interrupted it, he might react by strangling you. The way to find out about your future was to back naked into the bath-house – if the *bannik* stroked your back you could expect good luck, if he scratched you were in for a hard time.
≫→ water

BASTET
Africa (North)

Bastet, in Egyptian myth, was the cat-headed goddess of **fertility**. She was **Ra**'s daughter, and may originally have been the same person as **Sekhmet** the destroyer, lion-rage made manifest. But as time passed, Sekhmet took all the anger, and Bastet became gentle and approachable. Her responsibilities were **sex** and **childbirth**, and her cat-servants also symbolized the luck of people's houses: in particular, when **fire** broke out, they were thought to run deliberately into the flames, to draw the power of the fire into themselves and so save the household at the expense of their own lives.

Bastet was particularly worshipped at the town of Bubastis ('Bastet's place') in the Nile Delta, where an annual festival was held in her honour. Dead cats were embalmed and sent to join her in the spirit world, and tens of thousands of their mummies have been found in the Bubastis region. In art she was shown as a cat-headed woman shaking a rattle, and often with kittens playing at her feet.

≫→ animal-gods

BATARA GURU
Indonesia

Batara Guru, in Indonesian myth, created the world. Originally nothing existed but **Heaven**, ruled by Batara Guru, and the primordial ocean, ruled by the serpent-king **Naga Pahoda**. One day Batara Guru's daughter fell out of Heaven into the ocean, and to prevent her drowning Batara Guru threw down handfuls of dust to make an enormous island – and this became the world.

≫→ creation

BAUCIS AND PHILEMON
Europe (South)

Baucis ('modest') and her husband Philemon ('hospitable'), in Roman myth, were an old couple who lived on a hillside beside a marsh. They had nothing but each other, and had lived content together for sixty years. When **Jupiter** decided to wipe out the human race, he and Mercury (**Hermes**) first went out into the world, disguised as tramps, to see if there were any mortals worth rescuing. They knocked on a thousand doors, asking for shelter, and a thousand householders set the dogs on them.

Finally the gods came to Baucis' and Philemon's cottage – and were welcomed with open arms. Baucis bustled about stirring the fire and putting water on to boil, while Philemon gathered vegetables for soup and cut a slice of salt pork to flavour it. They covered a rickety table with their best counterpane, and set it with cheese, pickles, cherries, a honeycomb. It was enough food to keep them for a week, but they served it gladly to their visitors. The gods sat down to eat – and Baucis and Philemon noticed that the wine-jug filled of its own accord each time it was emptied, and realized who their guests really were.

Overcome with embarrassment at the humble fare they had offered, Baucis and Philemon tried to catch their pet goose, to roast it for the visitors. But Jupiter stopped them, and promised to reward their kindness and simplicity of heart. Neptune (**Poseidon**) had already opened the floodgates of the **sea**, and the waters were rising. The gods led Baucis and Philemon up the hill – and as they looked back they saw the **flood** rise until there was nothing in any direction but glassy sea, and their old cottage transformed into a temple, with pillars of painted marble and a roof of gold instead of thatch.

Baucis and Philemon lived on as keepers of the temple until the time came to end their mortal lives. Then the gods turned them into trees. Baucis became a linden and Philemon an oak, and they just had time to lean towards each other, embrace and whisper a last goodbye before the transformation was complete.

BAXBAKUALANUCHSIWAE
Americas (North)

Baxbakualanuchsiwae ('cannibal-at-North-end-of-world'), in the myths of the Kwakiutl peoples of the Northwest coast of the US and Canada, was the guardian spirit of the universe. He lived in the Arctic, and humans never saw him. But they could see the smoke rising from his cooking fire. It was sometimes red (the Aurora Borealis), sometimes multicoloured (the rainbow), but more usually white (the Milky Way) – and it guaranteed that Baxbakualanuchsiwae was there, looking after his **creation**.

BEAUTY

All myth-traditions treated physical beauty as one of the absolutes of existence, a possession as character-defining as skill in **crafts** or **prophecy**, a force as irresistible as lust or rage. It had the power to enhance other qualities in the possessor, so that (for example) a gentle beauty was overwhelmingly desirable, an arrogant beauty was introverted to the point of self-destruction, an angry beauty was destruction incarnate. The quality attached itself (sometimes literally, as a bird or insect which flew from the gods) to males and females equally, and though it could be removed by an angry creator-god (in which case the beautiful creature became a **demon**), the possessor could neither transfer it to someone else nor wish it away. Also, since beauty required an admirer as well as a possessor, it involved relationships and was often the catalyst for enormous events of **creation** or destruction in the existence of mortals and gods alike.

➤➤ **(Americas):** Chalchihuitlicue, Coyolxauhqui, Ten Corn Maidens, Xochiquetzal; (Celtic): Deirdre, Guinevere, Morgan le Fay, Tristram and Yseult; (Egypt): Hathor; (Finnish): Kylliki; (Greece): Adonis, Aphrodite, Circe, Endymion, Eos, Ganymede, Graces, Helen, Hylas, Narcissus, nymphs; (India): Anjana, *apsaras*, Draupadi, Krishna, Parvati, Radha, Rati, Sandhya, Savitri, Sita, Surya, Urvashi; (Nordic): Baldur, Brynhild, Idun, Nine Wave-maidens; (West Asia): *houris*

BEAVER: *see* Snoqalm and Beaver

BEELZEBUB
Asia (West)

Beelzebub ('lord of flies'), in the Bible, is a name given to **Satan**, the Devil. Its origins are complex. There was an ancient Palestinian god Baal Zebul ('keeper of the house'), and when his function was taken over by the Jewish **Yahweh** he was downgraded and punningly reviled, with only one letter changed in his name, as Beelzebul ('keeper of filth'). There was also an ancient Canaanite god 'Fly' – and scholars suggest that the 'Beelzebul' pun was adapted to imply the lord of all devils, **demons** and others who feed on filth: Beelzebub.

BEGDU SAN
Asia (East)

Begdu San, the **mountain** range in Northeastern China, together with the lake Yong Dam ('dragon pool') and the rivers Tumun and Yalu, was formed by a **giant** banished from Korea because his enormous size blocked out the **Sun**. He survived for a while by eating trees and drinking rivers, but soon the whole countryside was desert, and he was forced to eat earth and drink **sea**. He fell ill with sickness and diarrhoea – and Begdu San and the waterways were the results.

BEL
Europe (Northern)

Bel ('bright'), or Belinus or Belenus, in Celtic myth, was a **fire**-god. He came to Earth in willow-trees, and was the chief god worshipped by the Druids. When the Romans began advancing through Europe, the Druids tried to save their religion by pointing out that Belenus' associations with light, healing and **music** identified him with **Apollo**. But this failed to convince the conquerors, who thought that the Druids inspired fanatical armed resistance to the legions, and the Bel-cult was so ruthlessly persecuted and scattered that no coherent myths remain.

Bel is variously associated with the Sumerian god **Baal**, and with the legendary British king Beli who sacked Rome. Legend says that he is buried in Billingsgate in London, though no accounts of his death survive.

BELENUS
Europe (South)

Belenus, in the Celtic myths of the Alpine region, was the god of sunlight. He was a healer, melting disease from human bodies in the same way as he dispersed mist and fog each morning. When the Romans conquered the area, they amalgamated him, not unnaturally, with **Apollo**.
➽ disease and healing

BELLEROPHON
Europe (South)

Bellerophon (Bellerophontes, 'killer of Bellerus'), in Greek myth, was the son of Glaucus and grandson of **Sisyphus**. He was originally called Hipponous, but took the name Bellerophon after he lost his temper with his brother Bellerus one day and murdered him. He fled from Corinth to Tiryns, and vowed never to give way to emotion again. In Tiryns, however, Queen Antea lusted after him and asked him to sleep with her – and when Bellerophon took this as a test of his vow to avoid emotion and rejected her, she told her husband King Proetus that he had raped her. Proetus, reluctant himself to harm Bellerophon, sent him with a sealed message to King Iobates of Lycia. Bellerophon took it gladly, not realizing that Iobates was Antea's father and that the message asked him to kill the messenger.

Without explanation, Iobates set Bellerophon a trial of strength: to kill **Chimaera**, a fire-breathing **monster** which lived on a nearby **mountain**. Bellerophon prayed to the gods for help. They gave him a bow, a quiver of arrows, a spear tipped with a large block of lead instead of a point, and helped him tame the winged horse **Pegasus**. He flew above Chimaera's lair, weakening her with arrows, and finally hurled the spear into her open jaws. Her fiery breath melted the lead and she choked to death. Bellerophon tossed her body into a volcano and went back to tell Iobates that he was innocent.

Iobates now set him further tasks: to kill Chimaeros (Chimaera's pirate father), and to deal with **giants** and a group of marauding **Amazons**. Bellerophon fulfilled these tasks by soaring above his enemies on Pegasus and pelting them with stones. Iobates next sent an army against him – and the gods gave him superhuman strength, so that he killed them all. Up until now, he had kept his promise to himself and avoided all emotion. But now Iobates showed him the secret message he had brought from King Proetus, and Bellerophon learned for the first time that Antea had falsely accused him of rape. The violent temper inherited from his grandfather Sisyphus boiled up in him. He bridled Pegasus, flew to Tiryns, snatched Antea into the air and dropped her to her **death**. Then, full of the excitement of flying, he decided to soar still higher and visit the gods themselves.

But no mortals can enter **Olympus** unless the gods invite them. **Zeus** sent a fly to sting Pegasus; Pegasus reared; Bellerophon plunged to Earth like a shooting star. He landed in a thornbush in a desert. Both legs were broken, and the thorns put out his eyes. He spent the rest of his life wandering, a blind beggar in the desert – punishment at last for murdering his brother.

≫→ heroes

BELLONA
Europe (South)

Bellona (or Duellona), in Roman myth, was the goddess of **war**, often thought of as daughter, sister or wife to **Mars**, and sometimes confused with Minerva (**Athene**). She prepared Mars' chariot in times of war.

Although Bellona had almost no mythology and no festivals, she was worshipped enthusiastically by the Romans: one of her temples, at Comana, housed 3000 priests. Her temple on the Campus Martius outside the boundary of the city of Rome was used, in Republican times, to give audience to foreign ambassadors and returning generals thought too dangerous to allow back into the city. It was also the site for official declarations of war: a spear was ceremonially hurled against a 'war column' which symbolized the borders of the enemies' territory.

BENU BIRD, THE
Africa (North)

The Benu Bird (*benu* means 'shiner' or 'self-creator'), in some Egyptian accounts of the **creation** of the world, was the first-ever living being. It flew out of light and landed in darkness; its flight brought warmth and creative energy, and its cry was the first sound ever heard.

*The Benu Bird was worshipped particularly in Heliopolis, where it was regarded as one facet of the Sun-god **Ra**. In native Egyptian art it was shown as a yellow wagtail or a Nile heron (with two feathers rising from its head like spears); the Greek writer Herodotus, however, following information given him by Egyptian Greeks, identified it as the phoenix, and reworked the myth to say that when the first cycle of the universe ended in fire and destruction, the Benu Bird flew out of the fire, the only being to survive, and settled on the primeval Earth-mound to restart creation. Benu were often carved on gemstones and buried with bodies, to help grant them a second life.*

≫→ light and dark

BEOWULf
Europe (North)

Beowulf in Denmark. Beowulf ('bee-wolf'), in Celtic myth, was king of the Geats of Southern Sweden. On a visit to Heorot, palace of the Danish king Hrothgar, he killed the **monster** Grendel which was preying on Hrothgar's people, snatching them with its one arm and eating them alive. Beowulf tore off Grendel's arm and hung it as a trophy from the ceiling of Heorot. That night Grendel's mother, a **water**-witch, surged from her underwater lair and took back the arm. Beowulf dived into the lake after her, killed her and had four of his men carry her head back to Heorot in triumph.

Beowulf's death. Back in Sweden, Beowulf ruled his people in peace and honour for fifty years. Then one of his servants stumbled by accident into the nest of a treasure-guarding **dragon**, and stole one drinking-cup to prove to his friends that the hoard existed. The dragon flew out to savage Beowulf's people. Although Beowulf was over seventy years old, he went to fight accompanied by only one attendant, Wiglaf. He and Wiglaf killed the dragon, but in the fight Beowulf was bitten in the shoulder, and died from his wounds. He was buried with honour on a headland, the dragon-hoard all round him, and the flames from his funeral-pyre could be seen far out to sea.

The story of Beowulf, a cross between a saga-narrative and one of the hundreds of medieval tales of saints and other champions battling monsters, is raised to unique status by its telling in an anonymous West Saxon poem of the eighth century, one of the earliest surviving examples of the English language, and a sonorous, rhetorical piece of bardic verse.

»→ heroes

BERGELMIR
Europe (North)

Bergelmir, in Nordic myth, was an ice-**giant**, descendant of **Ymir** the first living being. When **Odin**, **Vili** and **Ve** killed Ymir to make the world, and Ymir's blood streamed out in a **flood** which engulfed the giants, Bergelmir and his wife escaped by building a boat and riding out the flood. They then became parents of a new race of ice-giants, perpetually at war with the descendants of Odin, Vili and Ve: the gods.

BERSERKERS
Europe (North)

Berserkers ('bare-skins') were real Germanic warriors supposedly inspired by **Odin**'s mortal followers in Nordic myth. Before battle, they worked themselves into a frenzy on mead and magic mushrooms, then ran to fight stark naked, screaming with fury and biting the rims of their shields. In stories, this tactic never failed. In real life, it worked so long as the berserkers' enemies tried to ward them off with prayers and spells, but failed as soon as people began countering them with gunpowder.

BES
Africa (North)

Bes, also known as Aha ('fighter'), in Egyptian myth, protected houses and families. He was a bandy-legged, paunchy dwarf with big ears, a beard, a lolling tongue and twinkling eyes. He wore a lion-skin so threadbare that nothing remained but the tail and hind legs (wrapped round his waist like a belt). He was armed with a knife, the magic noose *sa* (which bound evil spirits before they could attack) and – in case all else failed – rattles, tambourines and other musical instruments to play his enemies into submission. Bes-statues were put at the doors of houses, and his image was carved into chairs, bedsteads, table-legs, fence-posts, and anywhere else where evil spirits might lie in wait to catch the unwary.

BESTLA
Europe (North)

Bestla, in Nordic myth, was an ice-giantess, a descendant of **Ymir**, the first living being. She married **Bor** son of **Buri**, and their children were **Odin**, **Vili** and **Ve**, creators of the world.
»→ giants

BHAGIRATHA
India

Bhagiratha, in Hindu myth, was a sage known chiefly for two things: he had 60,000 sons, and he advised the gods that the way to stop the Earth being choked and destroyed by drought was to divert the Ganges from **Heaven** – something which would have proved disastrous if **Shiva** had not taken the river's full weight on his head and divided it into the seven streams still known today.

BHARATA (KING)
India

Bharata ('brigand'), in Hindu myth, was the son of King **Dasaratha** and Queen **Kaikeyi**. His mother persuaded his father to put him on the throne in place of his elder brother **Rama**, but Bharata refused to agree, and instead acted as Rama's regent. Bharata is also the name, in myth, for Upper India, and perhaps King (or rather Regent) Bharata is its eponymous founder. The Hindu epic **Mahabharata** concerns a struggle for the kingdom; it has nothing to do with King Bharata himself.

BHARATA (PLACE)
India

Bharata ('booty'), in Hindu myth, was the land between the rivers Sarasvati and Yamuna, or between the Himalayan and Vindhyan mountains. It was named after King **Bharata**, and was fought over by his distant descendants the **Pandavas** and **Kauravas** – the war which is the subject of the *Mahabharata*.

BHIMA
India

Bhima ('fearsome'), in Hindu myth, was the son of **Vayu** the wind-god and Queen **Kunti** of **Bharata**. He was second-born of the five **Pandava** brothers, each of whom had a different god for father. From childhood he was the sworn enemy of his cousin **Duryodhana**, eldest and most devious of the **Kaurava** brothers. One day Duryodhana poisoned Bhima and threw his body into the Ganges. The water-**snakes** whose kingdom is under the river swarmed round him and sank their fangs into him — only to find that the earthly poison in his blood neutralized their venom, and vice versa. They welcomed him to their palace, and fed him on **amrita**, which gave him the strength of a hundred thousand elephants.

Bhima's strength was crucial in the Pandavas' epic war with the Kauravas for the throne of Bharata. He was especially skilled as a wrestler and boxer — he used to practise with an iron opponent, forged to look like Duryodhana — and he also whirled a wind-club which none could face. But his temper was ungovernable, and although he finally won the war for the Pandavas, the way he did it turned their victory to ashes. All the Kauravas had been killed except for their leader, Duryodhana, and he and the Pandavas agreed that he should fight the brothers one at a time, single-handed, winner take all. Bhima was the first to fight — and instead of following the rules of chivalry (which said that combatants should aim blows alternately, and none below the waist) he ran at Duryodhana, howling and whirling his wind-club, and smashed his thigh, leaving him crippled. It was the end of the war, but the gods were unsatisfied. The Pandavas, including Bhima, went on a pilgrimage of expiation to Mount **Meru**, and all except **Yudhishthira** their leader died on the way.
≫→ heroes

BHISMA
India

Bhisma and his parents. Bhisma ('fearsome'), in Hindu myth, was the son of King Santanu of **Bharata** and the river Ganges. The river bore Santanu eight children, but then she grew tired of mortal shape, changed back into **water** and left Santanu forever. She drowned her first seven children, leaving Bhisma as her mortal husband's heir-apparent. Santanu planned to marry a second wife, and Bhisma agreed to surrender all claims to the throne in her children's favour, and never to have sons of his own, who might grow up to challenge the succession.

Kauravas and Pandavas. Santanu and his new queen had two sons, both of whom married but died without fathering children. As custom was, their wives **Ambika** and **Ambalika** agreed to have sex with their dead husbands' nearest male relatives, so producing legal offspring. They expected Bhisma, their uncle, to come to them, but because Bhisma had sworn never to have children, the queens in fact found themselves in bed with their half-brother-in-law **Vyasa**. Ambika's son born of this relationship, **Dhritarashtra**, went on to have 100 children of his own, called the **Kauravas** after an ancestor. Ambalika's son **Pandu** was prevented from having children, so his queens **Kunti** and **Madri** had five sons (the **Pandavas**) by different gods.

Bhisma acted as tutor to the Kauravas and Pandavas, teaching them all military and athletic skills. But when the boys grew up and squabbled over whether Kauravas or Pandavas were the legitimate rulers of Bharata, and when the argument led to a huge dynastic war, he sided with the Kauravas. As son of a goddess, he owned a small inheritance of **immortality**: he could not be killed by god or mortal unless he consented to his own death, and was then taken unawares – and he would survive for 58 days wounds which in any other mortal would be immediately fatal. He was appointed the Kaurava general, and under him the Kaurava army was invincible.

Bhisma's death. Although Bhisma sided with the wicked Kauravas, he was not a wicked man, and the Pandavas went to him and pointed out that he was leading an army which included **demons**, wizards and every other force for evil in the world. They begged him to set the universal balance straight by allowing one of the Pandavas to kill him. Bhisma said that he would agree to die only at the hands of **Arjuna**. Arjuna was aghast – how could he kill the friend and tutor he'd revered all his life? In the end, Arjuna's charioteer **Krishna** explained that human feelings were not a consideration: every mortal has a destiny and a duty, and should live in obedience to it without seeking to understand it. Reluctantly, Arjuna shot a flight of arrows into the air, and they fell and fatally wounded Bhisma (who was momentarily off guard, laughing at a slave who had dared to challenge him). The Pandavas carried him back to their camp, where he survived for 58 days before his spirit left his body. **Indra** took his spirit into **Heaven**, and Bhisma's mother the Ganges carried his body away to the ocean which girds the world.
≫→ heroes

BHUTAS
India

Bhutas, in Hindu myth, were the offspring of **demons** and **ghosts**. They cast no shadows, and hovered over sleeping people and animals, dropping disease into their ears like poison. There were two ways to avoid them. If you knew they were there, you could lie flat on the ground, since *Bhutas* hovered in mid-air and never settled. If you were unsure they were there, you could burn turmeric – the one smell in all **creation** they could not abide.
≫→ monsters and dragons

BIFRÖST
Europe (North)

Bifröst, in Nordic myth, was the bridge between **Midgard** and **Asgard**, the mortal and immortal worlds. It consisted of three plaited strands of fire, and looked to mortals like a rainbow. It was guarded by the god **Heimdall**, who allowed the gods to pass into Midgard but no Midgard beings to ascend into Asgard except the souls of dead **heroes** on their way to **Valhalla**. At **Ragnarök**, the end of time (still in the future), the myth says that the frost-**giants** of **Jotunheim** will swarm up Bifröst in such numbers that it will collapse under their weight.

Some scholars say that Bifröst is a mythologized version of the Milky Way, others that it is the bridge between the natural and supernatural worlds which no living human can cross except in imagination. Irish folktellers expand this idea by saying that the gods, about to begin the laborious climb up the rainbow from our world to theirs, often put down their burdens, crocks of gold – and then forgot them later in the splendour of their supernatural kingdom. Find the rainbow's end, therefore, and you find the gold.

BILDJIWUAROJU, MIRALALDU AND DJANGGAWUL
Australia

In the myths of the Wulumba people of Arnhem Land in Northern Australia, the **Sun** had three children, Bildjiwuaroju, Miralaldu and Djanggawul. Bildjiwuaroju and Miralaldu had enormous genitals, simultaneously male and female; Djanggawul had merely a penis. They sailed from **Heaven** in a bark canoe, down the morning rays of their mother the Sun (or in some accounts crossed the primordial ocean from Bralgu, island of the Dead), and beached on the shore of the new Earth, as yet uninhabited. They began to walk inland, and as they went they copulated ceaselessly. Each mating produced a new plant or creature, and the Sun-children used them to stock the Earth. When night fell the Sun-children made camp, and while Djanggawul went hunting (in some accounts, with his mortal squire Bralbral), Bildjiwuaroju and Miralaldu fell asleep by the fire. In the darkness Djanggawul crept back and hacked off Bildjiwuaroju's and Miralaldu's genitals, leaving vagina-shaped wounds. Next morning the journey, the copulating and the stocking of Earth continued, but this time Djanggawul, as the male, led the way and the others followed. So it has been with men and women ever since.

⟫⟶ creation, sex

BIMBOGAMI
Asia (East)

Bimbogami, god of poverty in Japanese myth, was emaciated, ragged and dirty. He moped in the houses of those he visited, an unwelcome guest who required lengthy and expensive exorcism. Fortunately, if you held the right ceremonies before he arrived, you could send him somewhere else – and you always had warning that he was in the neighbourhood, because his servants the death-watch beetles (*bimbomushi*, 'poverty-beetles') began clicking with excitement that he was on his way.

BLACK GOD
Americas (North)

Black God, in the myths of the Navajo people of the Southwestern US, was darkness, the gulf of space. In a pouch at his belt he carried star-rocks, glowing like crystals filled with sunlight, and one by one he took them out and hung them in the gulf that was his body and the surrounding emptiness. The rocks that were to become the Pleiades fell and burned his foot, and he angrily ordered them to hop to his knee, his shoulder and finally to his temple, where they became the most important stars in the sky. The sound of his voice alerted **Coyote**, who ran up to see what was happening. Coyote asked if he could help, and when Black God crossly refused he snatched the pouch out of his hands, took the last star-rock from it in his jaws and spat it into the face of Black God, where it became the Dog-star Sirius. Black God snatched back the pouch, found it empty and turned it inside-out to shake out the last glowing fragments of star-dust: the Milky Way.

⟫⟶ light and dark

BOBBI-BOBBI
Australia

Bobbi-Bobbi, in the myths of the Binbinga people of Northern Australia, was one of the supernatural beings which shared the world with humans in the Dream Time. He was an enormous **snake**, and was originally benevolent towards humans. Looking down from **Heaven** and seeing that they were hungry, he created flying foxes for them to eat, and when the foxes flew too high for them to catch, he took out one of his own ribs and gave it to humans, who used it as the first-ever boomerang.

Unfortunately, some human beings were not satisfied using Bobbi-Bobbi's rib in humble gratitude. Anxious to see what **Heaven** looked like, two men pretended that they wanted to open a hole in the sky and thank him in person. They hurled the boomerang-rib and tore a huge rent in the clouds. Bobbi-Bobbi was so startled that he failed to catch the rib, and it fell back to Earth and killed the foolish men. So Death came to the human race, and from then until now Bobbi-Bobbi has stayed aloof in Heaven, making no more attempts to help us.

BOCHICA
Americas (South)

Bochica, in the myths of the Chibcha and Muyscaya peoples of Colombia, was a benefactor and protector of human beings. Possibly the god of the **Sun**, he appeared from the East and taught them house-building, **farming** and the ways of society. His jealous wife, Chia the **Moon**-goddess, sent a **flood** to drown humanity, and Bochica took a few chosen followers into the hills, sent his rays to dry up the floodwaters, and banished Chia to the **sky** forever. He spent the next two thousand years helping his people to rebuild human **civilization**, and then left the world, riding into the Western sky along a sun-shaft and leaving nothing but a footprint in the rock.

In some accounts, Bochica was not the Sun-god but a **giant**, and when he left the world he took on the task of supporting the sky on his shoulders. In others, the being who supported the sky was Chibchacum. He was originally the god of hard work, but helped Chia to flood the world – and Bochica punished him by making him hold the sky. In each account, whenever the sky-supporter shifts its weight from shoulder to shoulder, the Earth quakes.

BODDHISATTVAS
Asia (East); India

Boddhisattvas ('those whose essence is enlightenment'), in Buddhist myth and belief, are human beings so virtuous that they have achieved enlightenment and could, if they wished, merge with God – in a phrase, potential Buddhas. Instead of becoming part of the divine, however, they choose to stay in our world, sharing our mortality and helping others to find and follow the path towards enlightenment. There have been countless thousands of such beings, and in some accounts they are treated as reincarnations of each other, each an avatar of the one true God.
≫→ Avalokiteshvara

BOGATIRI, THE
Europe (East)

The *bogatiri* ('champions', singular *bogatyr*) were demi-gods and **heroes** in early Christian Russia. Their adventures are told in two cycles of epic poetry, mixing myth-elements with Christian belief, and thought by scholars to be a priestly way of accommodating ancient gods into the new religious system. The *bogatiri* fought God's enemies, dealing in particular with imps and **demons** sent by the Devil. One poem, *Why There Are No More Bogatiri In Holy Russia*, an attempt to eliminate their worship altogether, explains that they became too sure of themselves and attacked a supernatural army. Each time a warrior fell, two more sprang up in his place, until at last the *bogatiri* admitted defeat and fled to the mountains, where they were turned to stone. Many *bogatiri* had local associations: **Ilya Muromets**, for example, built Kiev Cathedral, and **Sadko** was connected both with Novgorod and the river Volga. Others included **Mikula**, **Potok-Mikhailo Ivanovich**, **Svyatogor** and **Volkh**.

BOR
Europe (North)

Bor, son of **Buri** in Nordic myth, married the ice-giantess **Bestla**, and their children were **Odin**, **Vili** and **Ve**, creators of the world.

BORAK
Asia (West)

Borak ('**lightning**'), in Islamic myth, was the half-animal, half-human steed on which Mohammed ascended into **Heaven**.

BOREAS
Europe (South)

Boreas (Boreias, 'devourer'), in Greek and Roman myth, was the son of Astraeus (or some say, the river Strymon) and the Dawn-goddess **Eos** (Aurora). He was the North Wind, with owl-brown wings, a dragon's tail, streaming white hair and a billowing raincloud cloak. He led a pirate-gang of winds that roared and bucketed across the world. Boreas once lusted after the beautiful nymph Orythia, and when she refused him **sex** he snatched her away to his stronghold in Thrace and imprisoned her there, raping her and fathering four children: Calais and Zetes, dragon-winged sons, and Chione and Cleopatra (not the Egyptian queen), daughters in human form. On another occasion he outraged **Poseidon** by disguising himself as a stallion and running riot through Poseidon's herd of three thousand mares. Twelve foals were later born, white horses that raced among the waves without so much as dampening their hooves.

It was largely because of such adventures that **Zeus** confined the winds on the hollow island of Lipara, installing **Aeolus** as their guardian and controller.

BOSSU
Americas (Caribbean)

Bossu ('horned'), in the Voodoo myths of Haiti, is a huge horned man, leader of

the demon bodyguard of **Ghede** (Baron Samedi).

≫→ **demons**

BRAGI
Europe (North)

Bragi ('poetry' or, some say, 'leader'), in Nordic myth, was the son of **Odin** and the giantess **Gunnlod**. When Odin learned the mysteries of **writing** (by hanging himself for nine days on **Yggdrasil**, tree of the universe) he gave the secret to Bragi, cutting runes on his tongue. He told him to let them out, like butterflies, at banquets of the gods and in **Valhalla**, in the form of poetry. In the course of time, Bragi also became the god of eloquence, speaker and ambassador of the gods. He married **Idun**, guardian of the golden apples of **immortality**, and was respected by all the other gods except **Loki**, who called him 'Braggy' and 'Windymouth'.

BRAHMA
India

Brahma, in Hindu myth is the god-form of the abstract force *brahman* ('the power which is self-creating and in everything'). With **Vishnu** (personification of preservation) and **Shiva** (personification of destruction) he forms the triad which rules the universe, three gods (or three principles) in one; or else he stands apart from Vishnu and Shiva, and mediates between them.

Brahma's birth and the wheel of time. In the beginning the Lord of the Universe brooded on the surface of the Universal Ocean. Neither had shape or form. A seed appeared in the navel of the Lord of the Universe, and from it, in a dazzle of light, grew a lotus from which Brahma was born: the power which is in all things, given form. Brahma encompasses all things and all time. One of his days lasts 4,320 million mortal years, and his life is a never-ending wheel in which each revolution is 100 of his years and 157,680 million of ours (see **Ages of Brahma**).

Brahma and Creation. Brahma began **creation** with little plan or purpose. He concentrated the force in himself, and waited to see what it would make. In one account, the first thing he made was **Sarasvati**, who began as a river gushing from his hip and became a beautiful goddess with whom he mated and made everything in the universe. Another account says that the first thing he created was a personification of his own ignorance about what the universe would be like. He threw it away, but it turned into Night and began spawning offspring of its own. Alarmed at these beings (the **rakshasas** and **yakshas**), Brahma hastily made gods and other light-beings, and then went on to create the stars, the Earth and everything in it. A third account says that he began by creating sages to make the universe by contemplation and mystic practice, as he had made them. But they preferred their exercises to creation, and he was so angry that fury burst from his forehead in a blast of storm and lightning, took form (**Rudra**) and completed Brahma's creative work.

Brahma's Heaven. Brahma lives in the highest of all Heavens, at the tip of the cone-shaped universe. His **Heaven**

lies on the peak of Mount **Meru**, 84,000 leagues above the mortal world. The Heavens of other gods surround it, on peaks and plateaus at lower levels. Brahma has no need to leave his Heaven and travel about the world, as other gods do. He is everything and everywhere. He sees and knows all that happens; he is all that happens. He spends his time in meditation and spiritual exercises, and they are what sustain the universe. He needs no distraction (such as the singing of **Gandharvas** and dancing of **Apsaras** which delight the other gods). He accepts no sacrifice, but can be approached – if he can be approached at all – through austerity and contemplation. His is a Heaven not of body or emotion but of purest intellect.

The problems of depicting pure intellect or indwelling principle led artists to show Brahma in a kind of idealized but earthly paradise. He reclines on his lotus or rides a sacred goose, peacock or swan. He is a handsome, somewhat fleshy prince with four faces (of which we often see just one, or two). He has four arms, and his hands hold the Vedas (sacred books), the sun-disk, a dish for alms and a spoon for sacrifice. Often, Sarasvati is at his side, and they look adoringly at one another.

≫→ justice and universal order, supreme deity

BRAN
Europe (North)

Bran ('raven'), in Celtic myth, was a **giant**, son of the **sea**-king **Lir** and a mortal woman. His sister Branwen married the king of Ireland, and Bran and his giant brothers were invited to the wedding feast. But Branwen's mortal half-brother Evnissyen, who had not been invited, crept into the stables of the king of Ireland and mutilated all his horses, and the king took revenge by setting Branwen to work as a skivvy in the royal kitchens. The giants, led by Bran, waded across the sea from Wales to Ireland, deposed the king and enthroned Bran's son Gwern. But Evnissyen intervened again, throwing Gwern into the fire, and in the ensuing battle Bran was fatally wounded by a poisoned arrow. He told his followers to cut off his head and bury it in the White Tower in London, facing France: it would keep watch against invasion forever. Removing the head to the Tower took many years – it was kept for a time in Wales, where it brought prosperity and sang prophecies – but eventually it was planted as Bran had requested, and England has been safe from invasion ever since.

One version of this story claimed that Bran owned the cauldron of rebirth, and gave it to the Irish king as one of Branwen's wedding-presents. When the fighting began, Bran's enemies threw their dead soldiers into the cauldron and revived them, until he himself jumped into it and broke it to pieces.

*In an alternative to the White Tower story, the head remained at the Tower until the time of King **Arthur**. He said that England needed no supernatural defenders while he was alive, dug it up and sent it back to Wales. None the less, the Bran-in-the-Tower story originated a superstition that the ravens of the Tower of London enshrine its good luck, and Britain's, and*

that if they ever leave the Tower, disaster will follow. The job of 'Raven-keeper' at the Tower is one of the oldest, and most bizarre, sinecures in British government service, and has been so since medieval times.
≫→ prophecy

BRES
Europe (North)

Bres, in Celtic myth, was the son of a goddess and a **demon**, and husband of the poetry-goddess **Brigid**. He was chosen king of all Ireland, leader of the forces of good against the **demons**, but ruled like a tyrant, humiliating his courtiers and oppressing the common people. In the end his wife inspired the bard Cairbe to satirize him so forcefully that his entire body became covered in boils and sores, and he abdicated from embarrassment and went to help the demons. In the huge battle which ensued he was captured, begged for his life, and was spared in exchange for revealing the best times of year to begin each of the four seasons.

BRIAREUS
Europe (South)

Briareus ('strong'), in Greek myth, was the most intelligent of the **Hundred-handed Giants** – but since none of them was brighter than a tree, this was not much of a distinction. With his brothers, he was hidden away in the **Underworld** as soon as he was born, and lay forgotten there until **Zeus** brought them to the surface to help the gods in their battle against the **Titans**. As soon as the war was won, the Hundred-handed Giants were sent

back to the Underworld, this time to guard the defeated Titans – a job they took for promotion. But when **Apollo**, **Hera** and **Poseidon** rebelled against Zeus, tying him to his own bed with a hundred unbreakable knots, Briareus was once more summoned. He swarmed up to **Olympus**, untied the knots, and then stood beside Zeus while the king of the gods forced his opponents to swear eternal allegiance. After this Briareus hoped that he'd be kept on in Olympus as some kind of celestial bouncer, but Zeus persuaded him that it was far more distinguished to go back to the Underworld, take command of his two ungainly brothers, and supervise the guarding of the Titans.
≫→ giants

BRIGHU
India

Brighu ('flame-born'), in the Vedic myths of the Aryans who invaded India in the seventeenth century BCE, was a descendant of **Manu**; he was one of the earliest humans on Earth and one of the ten patriarchs, or ten sages. He lived at a time when mortals, thanks to the power of sacrifice, were able to communicate easily with gods and **demons**, and to move at will between the worlds of **Heaven**, Earth and Middle Air. On one occasion, this power nearly cost Brighu his life. He stole Puloma, betrothed of a demon – and when **Agni** the **fire**-god told the demon where to find her, he rashly cursed Agni, only to retract hastily when Agni threatened him with a lightning-bolt. A second adventure was more successful. Brighu set out to discover which of the three great gods, **Brahma**, **Shiva** and **Vishnu**, most deserved human worship. First he visited Brahma, intentionally omitting one of the signs of respect which gods demand from humans – and Brahma scolded him but forgave him. Next he treated Shiva in the same way – and escaped being scorched to cinders only by making grovelling apologies. Finally he visited Vishnu, kicking him awake – and Vishnu, instead of raging, asked gently if he'd hurt himself, and massaged his foot. From this moment, on Brighu's advice, mortals respected Vishnu above all other gods.

In some accounts, Brighu's offspring were the storm-god **Brighus**. But this relationship seems to have more to do with etymology (the 'brightness' of intelligence; the 'brightness' of the **lightning**-flash) than with heredity.

BRIGHUS
India

The Brighus ('shining ones' or 'roasters'), in the Vedic myths of the Aryans who invaded India in the seventeenth century BCE, were storm-gods, descended either from **Agni** god of **lightning** or from the sage **Brighu**. In particular, they were lords of the lightning-bolt itself, the fire which fell from **Heaven** to Earth – and this gave them a special function, as **messengers** between gods and mortals.

BRIGID
Europe (North)

Brigid ('high one'), in Celtic myth, was the name given to all three daughters of the **sky**-god **Dagda** and his queen

Dana. The eldest Brigid was the goddess of the intellect (as shown especially in poetry and **crafts**), her younger sister Brigid oversaw healing, and the youngest Brigid was the goddess of metal-working.

*Some scholars suggest that since 'Brigid' is an honorific title like 'Highness', the goddess' names were actually too sacred to be spoken, or were the subject of **mysteries**, known only to initiates. In Christian times there was confusion between the eldest Brigid and Saint Brigid, guardian of the holy fire.*

➤ **disease and healing**

BRIHASPATI
India

Brihaspati ('lord of prayer'), in Hindu myth, was the chaplain and teacher of the gods. He was a kind of celestial majordomo and master of protocol, expert in the organization of festivals, feasts and sacrifices. He also acted as constable, shooting **fire**-arrows to char any **demons** impudent enough to try to enter **Heaven**. His honorific names included Dhishana ('Wise One'), Ganapati ('Leader of the Herd' – a title he shared with **Ganesh**), Jyeshtharaja ('Senior Elder') and Sadasapati ('Master of Gatherings'). He collected and stored the energy from human sacrifices on Earth, the source of all the gods' power in the universe. When **Soma** abducted his beautiful wife **Tara** and made her pregnant, it was only Brihaspati's willingness to accept and bring up her child that prevented civil war in Heaven.

BRISINGAMEN
Europe (North)

Brisingamen ('fire-band'), in Nordic myth, was a miraculous golden necklace (or, in some accounts, a belt) crafted by four dwarfs, Alfrigg, Berling, Dvalin and Grerr. **Freyja** coveted it, and won it from them by having **sex** with each of them in turn. Brisingamen then became one of the greatest treasures of the gods.

The golden circle, or fire-circle, was (and still is) a common sexual symbol, and as Freyja's necklace (or girdle) of desire, it guaranteed the fecundity of the entire universe. Needless to say, Brisingamen was a favourite inspiration of mortal goldsmiths, and many examples have been found in treasure-hoards throughout Northern Europe: necklaces and belts made of gold worked to look like interlocking flames. In later times, a 'Brisingamen' was a finger-ring, a gold band similarly mimicking a band of fire.

BRIT
Europe (North)

Brit, or Brut, in Celtic myth, was a Trojan who escaped North when the Greeks sacked his city in the **Trojan War**. He went to the British Isles – as they were later named after him – and set about exterminating the race of **giants** who lived there and replacing them with human inhabitants.
≫→ heroes

BRYNHILD
Europe (North)

Brynhild ('brown-hair'), in Nordic myth, was the most beautiful of the **Valkyries**. She refused to have **sex** with **Odin**, and he punished her by putting her to sleep in a ring of **fire** on a **mountain**-top. She would be woken only by a mortal brave enough to dare the fire, and her love for him would destroy them both. In due course **Sigurd**, king of the Volsungs, found her, fell in love with her – and gave her as betrothal-token the gold ring made by **Andvari** and filled by him with the power to destroy all who owned it. This curse was fulfilled. Sigurd (after being given a potion of forgetfulness) promised to marry Gudrun queen of the Nibelungs, sent his brother-in-law Gunnar to marry Brynhild – and when Gunnar was driven back by the circle of fire disguised himself as Gunnar and took the magic ring. Brynhild's revenge was to tell her own brother-in-law Guttorm of the one vulnerable spot on Sigurd's shoulder (where a leaf had stuck as he bathed in the blood of the dragon **Fafnir**). She persuaded Guttorm to kill Sigurd, and threw herself into Sigurd's funeral-pyre to die.

This version of the story is told in the Volsung Saga (thirteenth century). The German Nibelung Poem of the same period makes Brynhild an Icelandic princess and renames her Brünnhilde. Wagner in his Ring of the Nibelungs made her once more a Valkyrie, and stirred into the psychological mixture the idea that the ring, a token of true love, also had the power to destroy that love. In his version, Brünnhilde's suicide triggered Götterdämmerung (Ragnarök), the end of the universe.
≫→ beauty, Deirdre, Dido, Guinevere

BUDDHA
India

Buddha in Hindu myth. Buddha ('enlightened one') is **Vishnu**'s ninth avatar. He came into the world at the birth of the present age, and is still active in it. Unlike Vishnu's other avatars, who used physical strength and magic to overcome the gods' enemies, Buddha uses intellect. He preaches false ideas, seducing the gods' enemies with visions of vice, vainglory and excess. His object is to make those who reject the gods destroy themselves by whoring after wickedness; true believers, by contrast, will stay firm in their devotion to the gods, and will be rewarded. We have our chance, and for those who fail to take it the end will be the arrival of **Kalki**, Vishnu's tenth avatar, and the obliteration of this cycle of the universe.

Buddha in Buddhist myth and legend. Before coming into the world as **Siddhartha**, the future Buddha had appeared countless times before, as **Boddhisattvas** ('those preparing for enlightenment'). Each Boddhisattva appeared in a different age of the world, and they took many forms. When **Indra**, disguised as a wandering beggar, visited a holy hare, the hare offered to feed the god on its own flesh. (Indra honoured it by placing its image forever on the **Moon**.) A priest, challenged by a wicked rival to prove his holiness by a miracle, created a garden, a lake and a bejewelled palace in a single night. A monkey-king saved his subjects from hunters by stretching himself as a living bridge across the Ganges. A king offered his own flesh to a hawk (Indra in disguise again) to prevent it eating a captured dove. A prince let a starving tigress lap

strength from his own blood. Each Boddhisattva learned, and showed, that salvation is achieved through denial of self for others, and each Boddhisattva drew strength and power from previous existences and self-denial. The last Boddhisattva before Buddha visited the gods in **Heaven** and preached to them.

Buddha's birth. One night Queen **Maya** dreamed that a white elephant entered her womb, holding a lotus in its trunk – and all **creation** rejoiced, woods and hillsides bursting into blossom, rivers stopping in their tracks for wonder, musical instruments playing without being touched. Next morning in the quietness of her garden, Siddhartha was born miraculously from her side. At once he began walking: he took seven steps North, seven South, seven West and seven East, traversing the entire world – and a lotus blossomed in each footprint. On the fifth day his parents held a naming ceremony, with 100 godmothers, 108 officiating priests and 80,000 relatives.

Buddha's life and death. The events of Buddha's life – his royal childhood, during which his father tried in vain to keep all ugliness out of his sight; his decision to go into the world to seek enlightenment; his meditation under the *bho* tree; his forty-five years of preaching and his miracles – are matters for religious biography rather than myth. Myth-elements occasionally appear – as for example when **Muchalinda** the serpent spread his hood like an umbrella over the meditating Buddha during a thunderstorm, or the many occasions when **Devadatta** tried to kill Buddha or his followers – but by and large the stories are concerned more with Buddha's teaching and example than with myth. However, when he left the world (by his own choice, for he could have lived until the end of that cycle of the universe), the gods sent more signs and portents. As his soul passed into Nirvana, the Earth shuddered, rivers boiled and the sky was darkened. His funeral pyre took fire of its own accord, and his body was burned not to ash but to a pile of gleaming pearls.

Boddhisattva myths are told in the Jataka ('birth stories'), part of the Theravada Buddhist scriptures. The basic details of Buddha's life are the same in every Buddhist country, but each tradition has vigorous local additions and variations. In the same way, while the underlying themes of Buddhist religious art are the same throughout the world – the smiling, meditating figure is a standard icon – popular art often draws on local stories and traditions, so that Buddha is, so to speak, remade in the image of his followers in whatever part of the world they may be.
»+ Amitabha, Avalokiteshvara, Siddhartha Gautama, Hanuman, Maitreya

BUGA
Arctic

Buga ('god'), creator-god in the myths of the Tungus peoples of Siberia, made the first human beings by mixing earth (flesh and bones), **fire** (warmth), **water** (blood) and iron (heart).
»+ creation

BULLS AND COWS

Bulls and cows are at the heart of **creation**. Bulls were universal energy made flesh; cows embodied **Mother Earth**'s nourishing and sustaining power. In some accounts, once creation was complete, the **sky**-bull or earth-cow retired to some extra-celestial pasture and was never seen again. In a few myths, however, it remained in the universe, and gods summoned it, or assumed its identity, usually with destructive results which took generations of human endeavour to counteract.
»+ (Egypt): Hap, Hathor; (Greece): Cretan Bull, Io, Minotaur; (India): Kamadhenu, Nandi, Prisni, Rohini; (Nordic): Audumla; (Rome): Mithras; (Iran): Geush Urvan

BUMBA
Africa

Bumba, in the myths of the Bushongo people of the Congo, was the only being in existence. To provide himself with company, he began vomiting creatures of every kind. Because they had nowhere to live, he vomited Earth and **Sky** for them. At first, Earth and Sky lived together like husband and wife. But then Sky, tired of the racket made by Earth's myriad creatures, took his own offspring – stars, planets, clouds and birds – and left her. He still pines for her, however, and semen spills from him in the form of rain, encouraging still further her never-ending fecundity.
»+ creation, sex

BURI
Europe (North)

Buri, in Nordic myth, was the third

living being in **creation**, after **Ymir** and **Audumla**. He was formed from ice, when Audumla licked it to find salt and gave it shape. He created a son spontaneously: **Bor**, who grew up to father **Odin**, **Vili** and **Ve**, the creator-gods.

BUYAN
Europe (East)

Buyan, or Bouyan or Byelun, in Slavic myth, was paradise. In some accounts it was the island home of **Zorya** in the river of healing, and the **Sun** lived there tended by her servants the winds. In others, Buyan was a silent underwater city, where the Dead lived in endless peace.

➠ Byelobog and Chernobog, Heaven

BYELOBOG AND CHERNOBOG
Europe (East)

Byelobog ('white god'), beneficent god of light in Slavic myth, was dressed always in white, and was locked in permanent conflict with Chernobog ('black god'), lord of darkness and evil, cloaked always in black. In ancient Russian myth, Byelobog was also called Byelun – the name for paradise (see **Buyan**).

*Byelobog and Chernobog, two of the oldest of all Slavic gods, were possibly carried to the area by nomadic peoples from Western Asia or the Himalayas. They are related to **Ahura Mazda** and **Ahriman** in ancient Persian myth, and to the yin-and-yang duality of Buddhist belief: the opposites which unite to make a whole.*

➠ light and dark, Svarog

CACUS
Europe (South)

Cacus (Greek *kakos*, 'wicked'), in Roman myth, was the son of the blacksmith-god Vulcan (**Hephaestus**) and **Medusa**. He had a vast spider's body, legs and arms like saplings, and three fire-breathing heads on a single neck. He hated the **Sun**, and lurked all day in a cave beside the Tiber. He hunted at night, and preyed on anything warmblooded which crossed his path: owls on the wing, cattle from the fields, wolves and lions from the hills and human beings from their beds. The floor of his cave was greasy with blood, and he spiked his victims' heads on poles outside his lair.

Heracles, as one of his twelve **labours**, had stolen **Geryon's cattle** from their island in the river which girdles the world, and was driving them through Italy when he stopped to water them by the Tiber, not far from Cacus' den. While Heracles dozed, Cacus crept out to steal the cattle. He took four bulls and four heifers, turned them round and dragged them backwards to his cave, so that when dawn came there were no tracks leading from the herd to show where the animals had gone. But when Heracles woke up and began rounding up the cattle, the herd began lowing and one of the cows in Cacus' cave heard and answered. Heracles strode to the mouth of the cave – and Cacus blocked it with a boulder.

Three times Heracles tried to club his way through the rock, but it was too much even for him. Then he seized a jutting spur of rock, a perch for vultures waiting to feast on Cacus' victims, and wrenched it sideways, tearing the cliff apart. Cacus peered out of the hole, and began breathing fire to scorch Heracles

Charon (*Gustave Doré, 19th century*)

dead. But Heracles jumped into the cave, tied his neck in a knot and left him to choke to death. Then he battered a hole in the cave-wall from inside and dragged the carcass out. The heat of the Sun withered Cacus' flesh from his bones, leaving his skeleton like tree-branches after a lightning-strike. Heracles gathered his cattle and went on his way.

This story, perhaps devised to explain a specific land-formation near the Tiber, was told by such Roman writers as Ovid, Propertius and Virgil. Cacus' name in Latin became standard slang for a brigand. Despite the Greekness of the name, however, and the presence of Heracles in the story, this myth is unknown in Greece.

≫→ monsters and dragons

CADMUS
Europe (South)

Cadmus (Kadmos, 'easterner'), in Greek myth, was the youngest son of King Agenor of Phoenicia. When **Zeus** disguised himself as a bull and stole Agenor's daughter **Europa**, her brothers set out across the world to look for her. Instead of wandering aimlessly, Cadmus went to ask the Delphic oracle where she was, and the oracle told him to forget her. Instead, he was to buy a cow, drive it until it collapsed with exhaustion, and build a city where it lay.

Cadmus and his servants came down from the hills into meadowland filled with the grazing cattle of King Pelagon. They bought the prize cow from Pelagon's herd, and set out across the plain, driving the animal before them. They walked for a day and a night without rest, and at first the cow showed no sign of weariness. But at last, on the evening of the second day, it collapsed exhausted on its right side, exactly as the oracle had foretold.

Cadmus piled stones for an altar, ready to sacrifice the cow, and sent his servants to fetch water. But the spring was guarded by an enormous, fanged **snake**, a child of **Mother Earth** herself. It tore Cadmus' servants to pieces. While it ripped and gnawed their flesh, Cadmus crept up behind it and killed it, letting Mother Earth drink her own child's blood. As the snake writhed and died, **Athene** appeared, told Cadmus to sow its teeth like seed-corn, and gave him her golden helmet to hold them. As soon as Cadmus sowed the teeth, an army of men grew from them, Cadmus tossed a pebble among them, and they leapt for each other's throats and fought until all but five were dead. They knelt at Cadmus' feet and promised him loyalty. They were the **Sown Men**, ancestors of **Thebes**.

As punishment for killing Mother Earth's sacred snake, Cadmus had to spend eight years as a slave in **Olympus**. But when his time was done Zeus gave him a sign of particular favour. Although he was mortal, he was allowed to marry the goddess Harmony, daughter of **Ares** and **Aphrodite**. The wedding, attended by all the gods, was a dazzling event, held in the meadows through which the cow had wandered. Cadmus called the place Boeotia ('cow-land') after her. When the celebrations were over and the gods had gone back to Olympus, Cadmus and the Sown Men set to work to build a citadel. They called it Cadmeia, and it quickly became the heart of a thriving town.

All this entirely fitted the gods' hopes for the area. It was the most beautiful spot in the world, and they planned to make it their earthly paradise. But two things thwarted their plans. First was Cadmus' killing of the sacred snake. Its blood had polluted its own mother, Earth, and she now demanded the blood of every generation of the royal house of Thebes (as Cadmeia was later called). Second, Zeus slept with Cadmus' daughter **Semele** (fathering on her the god **Dionysus**), and his jealous consort **Hera** cursed Cadmus and all his descendants. All four daughters of Cadmus and Harmony, **Agave**, Autonoe, Ino and Semele, died in misery, and in extreme old age Cadmus and Harmony left Thebes forever. They settled as king and queen of Illyria, and when the time came for them to leave the Earth, the gods changed them into snakes and carried them away to live in the Islands of the Blessed.

CAENEUS
Europe (South)

Caeneus (Kaineus, 'new'), in Greek myth, was born a woman, Caenis. **Poseidon** raped her, and promised her any gift she asked. She asked to become a man, and he turned her into Caeneus, king of the Lapiths. Flushed with self-satisfaction, Caeneus now declared that the Lapiths had a god of their own, Might-in-War, far superior to **Zeus** – and Zeus ordered his servants the **Centaurs** to avenge this

blasphemy. The centaurs slaughtered the Lapiths, but their weapons had no effect on Caeneus, whom Poseidon had made invulnerable. At last Zeus told the Centaurs to put Caeneus in a hole and bury him with logs. A greybrown bird – some say a cuckoo – flew out, and the prophet Mopsus said that this was Caeneus' soul and that **Mother Earth** herself had killed him. But when the Centaurs pulled away the logs, they found the body of a woman: when Caeneus lost his invulnerability he turned back into Caenis.

CAENIS: *see* Caeneus

CAIN
Asia (West)

Cain ('smith'), in Hebrew myth, was the eldest son of **Adam** and **Eve**, and the third human being in the world. Jealous of his younger brother Abel, he murdered him, and when **Yahweh** asked where Abel was, Cain lied to him. Yahweh punished Cain by sending him into eternal exile, and put a portwine stain on the skin of his face to mark him forever.

Scholars say that this myth arose to explain the animosity between two early peoples, one of them nomadic farmers ('Abel's people') and the others settled craftworkers ('Cain's people'). In the Book of Genesis, the portwine stain was put on Cain's face to protect him – it 'marked him for the lord' and he was therefore not for human beings to kill. It was only later that the 'mark of Cain' came to be taken as a sign of criminal guilt whose wearers had to be hunted down.

CALCHAS
Europe (South)

Calchas (Kalchas, 'bronze-man'), in Greek myth, was a favourite of **Apollo**, who gave him such accuracy in interpreting the gods' messages that he was appointed official prophet to the Greeks who fought in the **Trojan War**. Before the expedition, he foretold that the Greeks would never capture Troy unless they recruited **Achilles** – and told them where Achilles' mother, **Thetis**, had hidden him, knowing that if he went to Troy he was doomed.

Calchas at Aulis. After the Greek fleet was becalmed at Aulis, Calchas explained that the reason was **Artemis'** fury at **Agamemnon**, and said that the gods would release the winds only if Agamemnon sacrificed his own daughter **Iphigenia**. He also predicted the exact length of the Trojan War. While Agamemnon was sacrificing, a snake climbed a tree to a sparrow's nest in the top branches, where it ate the mother and eight chicks before the gods turned it to stone and felled it to the ground. Calchas said that Troy would resist for nine years, and fall like a stone in the tenth, and Zeus sent lightning in a clear sky to prove him right.

Calchas' death. During the siege of Troy, Calchas guided the Greeks with good advice – predicting, for example, that the city would fall only if they brought **Philoctetes** and his infallible bow from exile in Lemnos. After the war he took his share of the spoils and settled in Colophon in Asia Minor. Here, forgetting the gods' warning that he would die on the day he met a prophet greater than himself, he foolishly challenged Mopsus, grandson of **Tiresias**, to a contest in soothsaying. He pointed to a fig-tree, asked Mopsus how many figs it would produce, and jeered when Mopsus answered 'Ten thousand and one' – an answer proved exactly right when the figs were gathered and counted. Calchas pointed to a pregnant sow, asked Mopsus how many piglets would be born – and when Mopsus correctly answered, 'One black male and nine black-and-white females', Calchas was so mortified that he dropped down dead.

⫸→ **prophecy**

CALYPSO
Europe (South)

Calypso (Kalypson, 'hider'), in Greek myth, was one of the daughters of **Ocean** (or, some say, of **Atlas**), and was the goddess of silence. She lived alone on a beautiful floating island, Ogygia, which travelled at the winds' whim all over her father's kingdom. When **Poseidon** drowned **Odysseus'** crewmen for eating the cattle of the **Sun**, Odysseus alone escaped. He was washed up on the shore of Ogygia, and Calypso fell in love with him. She planned to marry him, giving him **immortality** and a seat in the councils of the gods. But he wanted none of it. He spent seven years on the island, enduring Calypso's kindness and slipping away each day to gaze out to **sea** and weep for Ithaca and the mortal wife and son he thought he would never see again. At last the gods took pity, and **Zeus** ordered Calypso to set him free. Broken-hearted, she helped him build

and provision a boat, tearfully watched him sail away, then went back to her old life, even more reclusive than before.
➤ Circe, Deirdre

CAMELOT
Europe (North)

Camelot, in Celtic and medieval myth, was the site of King **Arthur**'s court, home of the Knights of the Round Table.

Those scholars determined to prove that Arthur was real have identified Camelot with a number of places, chief among them Winchester in Southern England (where a fake Round Table survives from the late Middle Ages). Others, more sceptical, say that the name was corrupted from Camelodunum (the Roman name for what became Colchester), and was engrafted in the Arthur story by mythographers whose grasp was stronger on fantasy than on history or geography.

CAMPE
Europe (South)

Campe (Kampe, 'twisted', 'arthritis'), in Greek myth, was the daughter of Tartarus, a being formed entirely from darkness. She guarded the entrance to her father's **Underworld** kingdom: an unseen presence, looming and terrible. At first Tartarus was empty, but then **Ouranos** stuffed into it the monstrous offspring of his consort **Gaia** – the **Cyclopes**, the **Hundred-handed Giants** – and Campe was ordered to keep them there. She remained on guard for unmeasurable time, until **Zeus**, on Gaia's advice, came down to Tartarus to recruit the Cyclopes and Hundred-handed Giants in the war against the **Titans**. He expected trouble from Campe, and carried a thunderbolt to blast her into submission. But when he reached Tartarus he found that she had long evaporated into her father's darkness, leaving nothing but a memory of terror and a musty smell.

CANDRAMUS
India

Candramus, in the earliest Vedic myths of the Aryans who invaded India in the seventeenth century BCE, was the **Moon**. He was one of the five primordial beings engendered by **Prajapati**; his sister was **Ushas** (Dawn) and his brothers were **Aditya** (**Sun**), **Agni** (**Fire**) and **Vayu** (Wind). Early in the cycle of myth, he was converted from a being into a piece of celestial real estate (the inert Moon-disc itself), and his active powers and functions were taken over by **Soma**.

CANENS: *see* Picus and Canens

CASSANDRA
Europe (South)

Cassandra (Kassandra, 'entangler of men'), in Greek myth, was the most beautiful daughter of King **Priam** of Troy and Queen **Hecuba** of Troy, and a prophetess. Some say that when she and her brother **Helenus** were babies, they were left overnight in **Apollo**'s temple, and the priests found them next morning entwined with **snakes**, which were licking their ears and eyes and giving them second hearing and second sight. Others say that Apollo lusted after Cassandra and, kissing her, offered her any gift she chose if she would make love with him. She asked for the gift of infallible **prophecy**, and he touched her tongue with his to grant it. But as soon as the gift was given she refused to have anything more to do with him – and, unable to take back her infallibility (for the gods' gifts are irrevocable), he spat in her mouth, thus making certain that her prophecies, infallible or not, would never be believed.

During the **Trojan War** Cassandra foretold the deaths of many heroes, and each time the people treated her like a madwoman, and no one believed her. When the Greeks breached the walls with the **Wooden Horse** and began sacking the city, Cassandra hid in the temple of **Artemis**, clutching the holy statue. 'Little' **Ajax** found her there and snatched her for his own, intending to take her home with him as spoils of war – and she clung so tightly to the statue that it, too, had to be counted as his booty. But later, at the division of the spoils, **Agamemnon** lusted after Cassandra, and **Odysseus** obligingly put about the story that Little Ajax had raped her and should be punished by being deprived of her. Cassandra was reallocated to Agamemnon; despite her prophecy that **Clytemnestra** would murder them both as soon as they set foot in Mycenae, he took her home – and the prophecy came true.

Cassandra is a favourite 'turn' in ancient literature: a tragic madwoman, a flawed beauty simultaneously blessed and cursed by the gods. In Aeschylus' Agamemnon and Euripides' Women of Troy she has two of Greek drama's most bravura scenes, and she makes spectacular appearances in Homer, Virgil, Ovid and many others. These scenes set a pattern for the melodramatic and pathetic depiction of madness which became standard in later Western literature: the range is from Virgil's **Dido** *to Shakespeare's Ophelia and the multifarious mad heroines of Donizetti, Bellini and other writers of Romantic opera.*

CASTOR: *see* Dioscuri

CATEQUIL
Americas (South)

Catequil, in Inca myth, was the god of **thunder** and **lightning**. He made thunder by battering the winds with his club, and lightning by hurling thunderbolts from his sling. Occasionally he turned himself into a lightning-bolt and entered a woman's womb as she made love with her husband, at the moment of conception. Whenever this happened, **twins** were born.

CELTIC MYTH
The Celts were a warrior people – their name means 'fighters' – who appeared in Eastern Europe in the second millennium BCE and swept West and South, even sacking Rome in 386 BCE. For some 1500 years theirs was the dominant culture in Northern Europe, rivalled only by those of Greece or Rome in the South. They were one of the few peoples who refused to accept Roman rule, and the Romans accordingly set out to annihilate them. This was a difficult task, as the Celts were not a unified people ruled from a single

centre (as were the Romans), but were a conglomeration of hundreds of small communities, hill- and forest-dwellers adept at guerrilla warfare. Caesar's war-commentaries and Tacitus' accounts of the anti-Celtic wars of the first century CE give some idea of the Celts' ferocity and tenacity, and of the Romans' utter incomprehension of their ways of life or thought.

By the fourth century CE, Roman persecution had driven the Celts to the fringes of the Roman Empire. In Spain, Northern France and Britain they survived in communities too small or too isolated to cause problems for the huge Roman political machine. They settled in Scandinavia, the Balearic Islands and such remote parts of the British Isles as the Orkneys, the Isle of Man and Ireland (one area untouched by Roman rule). Their religion and culture went with them, and since it was entirely oral it was modified to suit the needs of each community. Thus, the same gods, **heroes** and myths turn up in areas as far apart as Connaught and the Caucasus – and even in the British Isles, where the distances are smaller, there are such marked differences between Welsh and Irish versions of the same stories (separated by less than 100km) that they seem at times to be entirely different: **Lancelot**, **Lleu** and **Lug**, for example, are all aspects of the same original **Sun**-god who was the chief deity of all Celts everywhere.

Further change came in the Christian era. The Christians abominated Celtic religion, equating it with Devil-worship, and as the Celts were converted they responded by downgrading their gods to the status of fairies, trolls or other forms of 'the little people', and turning their myths into a vast treasury of folk-tales and small local legends and super-stitions. (In Ireland, for example, the entire family of gods was supposed to have become weakened because they lost the apples of **immortality**, and to have literally 'gone underground', becoming craftworkers and gold-hoarders under the rule of Lug Chromain, the original 'leprechaun'.) Often, Celtic gods became Christian saints – Saint Brigid, for example, is **Brigid** goddess of knowledge in a different guise – and such attributes of Celtic deities as dragon-slaying and soothsaying were re-attributed to Christian saints. (Saint Columba had an encounter with the Loch Ness Monster; Saint David possessed second hearing and second sight.) Others had less dignified fates: **Medb** the war-goddess became the sulky, sexually voracious Mab queen of the fairies; the **Wyrd sisters**, goddesses of fate, became cackling witches.

A final stage in the transmogrification of Celtic myth came in the Middle Ages, from the time of Charlemagne (eighth century CE) through to the Reformation. Christian writers in all parts of Europe, working to create a body of didactic and chivalric literature, reworked many of the myths in Christian terms. Sometimes the stitching was crude – the story of **Bran**'s head going to the Tower of London, or the tale of **Gawain**'s encounter with the Green Giant, are hardly convincing Christian narratives – but at their best, for example in the **Grail** sagas or the tales of King **Arthur**, the constructs of Christian fabulists match anything in their originals.

The result of all this is that Celtic myth is remarkably diffuse and obscure. Its purest form is the hero-stories of Ireland (**Cuculain**; **Finn MacCool**) or Wales (**Lleu Law Gyffes**; **Pwyll**); its most elusive form is stories of such deities as the **Dagda**, including fragments and hints from almost every part of Europe. The tellings vary wildly, from the saga-like robustness of the **Beowulf** narrative to the flowery fantasy of the stories in the **Mabinogion**, from the folktale simplicity of the stories of **Albion** or **Deirdre** to the preachiness of Chrétien de Troyes' **Perceval** or the literary sophistication of Malory's *Morte d'Arthur*. For mythographers, this diffusion and these descants on Celtic myth can be particularly tantalizing. Interesting though the variants and derivatives are, they are merely the wracks and ruins of a myth-culture which seems, once, to have been as vast and as compelling, both in detail and in social effect, as Hindu, Nordic or any of the other great surviving world mythologies.

≫+ Annwn, Arawn, Avalon, Aywell, Balor, Belenus, Bres, Brit, Camelot, Cernunnos, Cormac MacAirt, Danann, Dian Cecht, Excalibur, Fintan, Galahad, Gogmagog, Guinevere, Lady of the Lake, Manannan MacLir, Merlin, Mm, Modred, Morgan le Fay, Morrigan, Nimue, Oberon, Ogmios, Oisin, Pelles, Roland, Rosmerta, Sucellus, Taliesin, Taranis, Teutatis, Tristram and Yseult, Uther Pendragon, Volund

CENTAURS
Europe (South)

Centaurs, in Greek myth, were human from the waist up, horse from the waist down. They were the result of the mating of the **hero** Centaurus with a fieldful of mares, and combined their father's wildness with their mothers' gentleness. Sometimes, for no reason, they fell into wild fits and galloped crazily across the countryside; at others, they were placid and peaceful, fond of music and skilled at **prophecy** and healing. The gods admired them, and sent such favoured mortal heroes as **Theseus** and **Jason** to learn with them, to acquire a kind of supernatural higher education. (The Centaur king **Chiron** was especially renowned as a teacher of adolescent heroes.)

Centaurs and Lapiths. The Lapiths, descended from Centaurus' brother Lapithus, were horse-tamers, and there was, not surprisingly, no love lost between them and the Centaurs. Squabbles flared into war when the Lapiths held a feast to celebrate the wedding of their prince **Pirithous** to Hippodamia. Many gods were guests of honour, and the Centaurs were invited. But **Ares** had been left out, and revenged himself by giving the Centaurs wine, something they had never tasted. They got drunk, tried to rape all the women present, and the ensuing battle ended only when Theseus, another of the guests, picked up a sword and fought on the Lapiths' side.

The battle between Centaurs and Lapiths was a favourite subject for Greek sculpture, giving magnificent opportunities for showing humans and horses in a variety of heroic or tormented poses. A particularly famous example, on the Parthenon frieze, inspired the (otherwise unexplained) screaming horses of Picasso's Guernica.

CERBERUS
Europe (South)

Cerberus (Kerberos, 'pit devil'), in Greek and Roman myth, was born to the monsters **Typhon** and Echidna: a huge, three-headed (or, some say, fifty-headed) dog with a hundred serpent-tails, who prowled the entrance to the **Underworld**, on guard against intruders from the upper world. Dead souls were able to slip past him, flitting like the shadows they were. But the only way for living beings to escape his fangs was to feed him drugged food (as **Aeneas** did), lull him asleep (as **Orpheus** did) or terrify him (as **Heracles** did).

Cerberus and Heracles. As the last of Heracles' **Labours**, King **Eurystheus** of Mycenae ordered him to go to the Underworld, capture Cerberus and bring him back alive. Instead of bribing or cheating his way into the Underworld, Heracles used brute force, shouldering his way through the ghosts on the shore of the **Styx**, browbeating **Charon** into ferrying him across, and threatening Cerberus with his unerring bow until the huge hound ran whining to his master **Hades**.

Hades gave Heracles permission to take the dog, providing he first caught him and held him, unarmed, wearing only his lion-skin cloak. Heracles caught Cerberus by the neck and squeezed until the branching heads began to droop and loll; the serpent-tails' venom dribbled harmlessly against his lion-cloak. Then he fastened him with an iron chain and led him, docile as a puppy, back to Charon's boat, across the Styx and up the rock-passages to the upper world.

As soon as Cerberus sensed sunlight his jaws slavered, his eyes glittered like sparks from a blacksmith's anvil and his snake-tails hissed and writhed. But Heracles dragged him across the fields to Mycenae, where Eurystheus was in the middle of a sacrifice. Eurystheus saw Cerberus, dropped the knife and ran for safety – and Heracles unchained Cerberus and let him scamper back to the Underworld. The myth ends by saying that wherever drops of his saliva, or venom from his tails, touched the ground they scorched it like forest-fire, so that to this day they are barren.

CERES: *see* Demeter

CERNUNNOS
Europe (North)

Cernunnos ('horned one'), in Celtic myth, was a **fertility** god, ruler of wild beasts. He lived in the forests, where he either sat cross-legged in state, surrounded by his creatures, or led them in wild gallops through his kingdom, filling all who saw him with ecstatic madness. In form he was human, with stag's antlers; but he could also change shape (see **shape-changers**), and took the forms of snake, ram and wolf.

Cernunnos survived in Britain into Shakespeare's time, as Hern the Hunter, a mysterious being who lived in Windsor Great Park and was worshipped annually with morris-dancing and bucolic revelry. Falstaff, in The Merry Wives of Windsor, *has what he thinks is a close encounter (in fact a prank organized by the town children).*

CEUCY
Americas (South)

Ceucy, in the myths of the Tupi people of Amazonia, lived in the days when the entire world was ruled by women. The **Sun** preferred the supremacy of the male, and chose Ceucy as his means to bring this about on Earth. Ceucy one day was cutting branches from a cucura tree, when its sap spurted like semen and splashed her breasts. She became pregnant, and gave birth to a boy, Jurupari. From his birth Jurupari was a swaggerer, a hero with the strength of the Sun and the slyness of panthers. As soon as he was old enough, he began holding mystery feasts and ceremonies to which only men were invited, and persuaded his followers to take over rule and kill any woman who opposed them. The first woman to suffer in this way was Ceucy herself – and the world has been male-ruled ever since.

This myth comes equipped with an even more male-chauvinist ending. One day, Jurupari will find a woman equal to him, a perfect female as he is a perfect male. They will mate, and the world will be ruled by both sexes equally.

CHAC
Americas (South)

Chac ('red' or 'big' – called either after his droopy nose or his flaccid penis), in Mayan myth, was the god of **rain**. He was four deities in one: his white form guarded the North, his red form the East, his yellow form the South and his black form the West. Each was a warrior weeping streams of tears. But Chac was a benefactor as well as a destroyer. His rain, irrigating Mayan lands from all four compass-points, brought **fertility** to the land, and he often took human form and visited women at the moment of intercourse with their husbands, guaranteeing them conception.

CHALCHIHUITLICUE
Americas (Central)

Chalchihuitlicue ('jade skirt'), in Aztec myth, was the sister of **Tláloc** the **rain**-god, and was the goddess of **beauty**, personification of light playing on **water**. Her clothes were green and white, like silken water-streams, and her worshippers offered her flowers and leaves instead of the human sacrifice preferred by other gods. She was married for a time to her brother, but the presence of both of them in **Heaven** caused such storms and floods on Earth that **Quetzalcóatl** the wind took her back to Earth and turned her into a river. In its midst was a prickly-pear tree, covered with fruit – her heart, and (in its fruit) a symbol of all human hearts.

CHANDRA
India

Chandra ('radiant'), in Hindu myth, was the god of the **Moon**. He was born from the churning of the Sea of Milk (see **amrita**), and is reborn from it each evening. In most accounts he is the same god as **Soma**, and *chandra* is one of Soma's honorific titles.

CHANTICO
Americas (South)

Chantico, in Inca myth, was the goddess of the home, worshipped in the hearth-fire. She was made of pure gold, and controlled all the ore and precious stones hidden in the Earth. But she was capricious, and people who sought her treasures found death (from her **snake**-guardian, a tongue of living **fire**, or the spikes of poisoned cactus which formed her crown) as often as they discovered wealth.

CHAOS
Europe (South)

Chaos ('yawn'), in Greek myth, was what existed before existence. There were no shapes, no forms. All the elements and atoms that would one day make matter swirled and seethed in endless, meaningless movement. This movement, and the emptiness in which it took place, was Chaos.
➽➜ **Eros**

CHARON
Europe (South)

Charon ('fierce brightness'), in Greek and Roman myth, was the son of Darkness and Night. An aged ferryman, he poled a leaky boat across the river **Styx**, carrying dead souls to the **Underworld**. The fare was a copper coin, laid under the dead person's tongue, or a pair of coins placed on the eyes, and the journey was always one way, since once the Dead had crossed the Styx Charon could never be persuaded to ferry them back again. He also refused to carry living people (except for a handful of **heroes**, including **Aeneas**, **Heracles** and **Theseus**, who bribed, tricked or terrified him into accepting them) on the grounds that his boat was too fragile to take the weight of living flesh and bone. (He always suffered when he broke this rule. When he ferried Heracles, for example, **Hades** imprisoned him in a rock-cleft for an entire year, during which no souls at all were able to cross to the Underworld.)

CHARYBDIS: *see* Scylla and Charybdis

CHERNOBOG: *see* Byelobog and Chernobog

CHILDBIRTH AND INFANT CARE
In many cultures, the cycles of female **fertility**, birth and the protection of the newborn, in humans as in animals, were all under the care of the **Great Goddess**, who was either **Mother Earth**, the **Moon**, or both. She manifested herself in different forms, some of which became separated from her main identity and were worshipped independently. (In some, male-oriented myth-cultures, such separate gods were the heart of **mysteries**, frequented only by women.) A number of domestic, local gods also acted as midwives and child-minders – and their worship was, and is, among the most persistent in the world, surviving long after the disappearance of the religions which gave rise to them.
➽➜ **(Americas): Mayauel; (Australia): Yalungur; (China): Jang Xien,**

Three Lavatory Ladies; (Egypt): Hathor, Heqet, Meskhent, Neit, Taweret; (Greece): Artemis, Ilythia; (India): Shashti; (Japan): Kojin; (Mesopotamia): Ninhursaga; (Oceania): Haumea; (Slavic): Mokosh

CHIMAERA
Europe (South)

Chimaera (Chimaira, 'she-goat'), in Greek myth, was the daughter of the whirlwind **Typhon** and the **sea-monster** Echidna. Her brothers were **Cerberus**, guard-dog of the **Underworld**, and the **Nemean Lion**; her sisters were **Hydra**, the swamp monster killed by Heracles, and the **Sphinx** which tormented **Thebes**. For middle parts she had the legs and head of a gigantic goat, for lower parts the body of a **snake** and for foreparts the mane and head of a fire-breathing lion. For a time, the King of Caria kept her as a monstrous, three-headed pet, but she escaped and made her home on a volcanic mountain in Lycia, where she was eventually killed by **Bellerophon**.

After Chimaera's death, her name became proverbial for any monster so hideous and so improbable that people thought it must be imaginary.

CHIMATANO
Asia (East)

Chimatano, in Japanese myth, guarded crossroads, and hence decisions and journeys. He was made from Izanagi's stick when the creator-spirit laid it on the ground after visiting the World of Darkness (see **Izanami and Izanagi**). Chimatano was represented as a man

with an enormous, erect phallus, or sometimes as an upright phallus-post without an owner. As travellers used the crossroads, they stroked the phallus to bring good luck.

≫+ Hermes, Priapus

CHIMINIGAGUÉ
Americas (South)

Chiminigagué, in the myths of the Chibcha people of Colombia, was the original being: space incarnate. He gathered his darkness and formed it into a flock of huge-winged, black birds. Then he loaded the birds' backs with light and sent them flapping throughout the universe to scatter it as stars and constellations.

CHINESE MYTH

Chinese culture, and the language which sustains it, have existed in a turbulent but unbroken sequence for some 3000 years, longer than any others in world history. One effect of this is to blur the passage of time, so that distinctions between past and present become less marked, less pungent, than in shorter-winded societies. In myth, the same blurring takes place between reality and fantasy. Historical characters become part of the mythic pantheon, and myth figures are treated as if they were our real-life relatives or neighbours, in a way quite unlike the legendizing process which takes place in other cultures. **Fu Xi**, for example, first of the **Three Sovereigns** of primordial times, is as 'real' or 'unreal' a figure as **Guan Di** the war-god, a general of the third century BCE promoted to myth-hood, or as Kao Guojiu, a Daoist ascetic of some 1400 years later who became one of the mythical **Eight Immortals**. **Shang Di**, the original generative principle of the universe, worshipped from prehistoric times, was merged in the eleventh century CE with **Yu Huang** the Jade Emperor, assuming a new identity but remaining Supreme Being. In such a system, even figures as remote as the 'Yellow Emperor' **Huang Di** can be allocated historical dates (in his case the 2600sBCE), and can mingle with gods, dragons, **giants** and personified planets without the remotest sense of incongruity.

One reason for this is the over-riding Chinese view of life and **immortality**. In Chinese (and especially Daoist) culture, life was considered the most precious possession human beings owned, and its prolongation into immortality was therefore a blessing beyond all others. The great and the good tended to be promoted to immortality as soon as their mortal lives were over – or, in some cases, even while they were still alive, since mortal Emperors had the power to grant immortality, and used it to reward outstanding service or ability. (The qualifying act might be large, for example the abandonment of worldly ambition which earned many a Daoist sage immortality, or more trivial: the inventors of gunpowder, printing and shoes were all made gods.) More fallible beings went, at the end of their mortal lives, to the **Underworld**, where they endured a series of trials, judgements and spectacular punishments before passing to the Wheel of Transmigration to be returned to a new body, and another life, in the world above.

Collision between what might be called the poetic and the prosaic views of human existence made China particularly fertile soil for three substantial systems of philosophy: Confucianism and Daoism in the sixth-third centuries BCE, and Buddhism a thousand years later. Each of these systems, while prescriptive about behaviour, was remarkably tolerant about belief, accepting and modifying existing ideas rather than proscribing them. Religious belief, and the myths and folk-tales which grew up with it, became like a collection of treasures in a cupboard, to be taken out and returned as needed, without loss or diminution. Lack of astonishment, of awe, was an important part of this process. If **Nü Gua** the creator was a **snake** with a woman's head, or **Fei Lian** the wind-lord kept his subjects in a billowing bag, or **Yen Lo**, lord of the Underworld, was dethroned by his subordinates for being too forgiving, that was simply, matter-of-factly, how things were. The transcendental, in Chinese belief and myth, was a matter not of miraculous stories but of intellectual thought and ascetic practice.

Absence of awe led to, or was accompanied by, a strikingly cavalier attitude to the practical details of the mythical universe. The Chinese amiably assumed that the supernatural world was exactly like the natural world, except that its inhabitants lived forever. It had **mountains**, rivers, fields and farms just like our world; it was governed by a labyrinthine bureaucracy, just like ours, and promotion and demotion were regular, dependent on passing exams, doing favours, receiving patronage or staging *coups*. These ideas made it unnecessary to go into too much detail. There could be four paradises, or forty, or 108, depending on who told the story. The world might be a flat square or a fore-shortened pyramid. The sky was a bowl, or perhaps an umbrella, supported on eight rock-pillars or five mountains or the legs of a giant tortoise. Gods lived in space, or in mountain-top palaces, or walked the Earth in human form. In a system where everything was possible, logic was irrelevant. The truth of people's lives lay inside themselves, in their hearts and minds, and so long as that truth was respected, the external world could do, and be, anything it pleased.

In such a shifting, teeming myth-universe, there might seem little chance for stability or continuity. But just as in 'real' history some events and individuals make more mark than others, so in the supernatural world an inner core of gods and other beings outdid all others, and their powers and privileges remained constant through all the comings and goings of lesser beings. The group begins with some of the oldest myth-creations of all, **Hun Dun** (primal chaos), **Di (Mother Earth)**, **Tian** (Father Sky), **Kuafu** the giant, **Pan Gu** and Nü Gua who created the human race, **Yi** the Sun-archer and **Heng O** the Moon, **Erh Long** the hunter of **demons**, and the Three Sovereigns (Fu Xi, **Shen Nong**, Yen Di) and **Five Emperors** (Huang Di, **Zhuan Hu**, Ku, **Yao** and **Shun**) who regulated the world, brought **civilization** and ruled during the Golden Age. All these figures mixed cheerfully with weather-gods such as Fei Lian (wind), **Lei Gong** the thunder-lord, **Long Wang** and the other Dragon Kings (who, together with

their subordinates **Qi Yu, Yu Zu** and Yun Tun, brought rain), and with sky-gods such as **Di Jun** (father of the Suns and Moons), Heng O, **Jun Di** (dawn) and **Xi He** mother of the Suns and Heng Xi mother of the Moons.

Among **Heaven**'s more transient in-habitants was a huge *corps* of gods, many of whom had begun life as hu-mans and who spent their time visiting Earth to help specific groups or trades. Grandest of all were benefactors such as the **Three Gods of Happiness**, the **Three Lavatory Ladies** who supervised **childbirth**, **Tsao Jun** the kitchen god who looked after the household and protectors such as the **Hang Ha Erh Jang** who guarded temple gates and the **Three Door Gods**. But there were in-numerable lesser functionaries, whose jobs ranged from swelling rice-grains on the stalk (**Guan Yin**) to bringing success in exams (**Kui**), from ensuring **fertility** (**Jang Xien**) to overseeing car-penters (**Lu Ban**), cobblers (**Sun Bin**), incense burners (**Huang Gun**), sodo-mites (**Jou Wang**), thieves (**Song Jiang**) and writers (**Wen Jang**). For conveni-ence, gods were often remembered or worshipped in groups, such as the **Eight Gods** honoured by the (hu-man) Emperor in an annual cere-mony, the **Five Plague Demons** or the **Four Dragon Kings**. The family of humans and superhumans – every being who ever existed, and including animals, which were reborn souls that had lived particularly wicked previous lives as humans – was capacious, all-embracing, an entirety.

»+ Ba Ja, Begdu San, Di Kang Wang, Eight Immortals, Fan Guei, Five Buddhas, Five Elements, Four

Diamond Kings, Four Dragon Kings, Four Kings of Hell, Gong Gong, Huai Nan Zu, Lei Jen Zu, Li No Zha, Li Papai, Mi Hung Tang, Mi Lo, Penglai Shan, Qian Nu and Zhi Niu, Shi Zong Di, Shou Lao, Ten Yama Kings, Tsai Shen, Yu

CHINIGCHINICH
Americas (North)

Chinigchinich, in the myths of the Acagchemem (San Juan Capistrano people/Luiseño) of the Southern coast of California, was the offspring of **Owiot**, son of Father **Sky** and **Mother Earth**. Owiot was supposed to engender the human race, but died before he could find a mate. The spirits burned his body on a pyre, but before it was fully consumed **Coyote** stole a piece of his flesh and carried it away. A scrap of Owiot's skin fell on to Mother Earth and grew into Chinigchinich. Chinigchinich went to the spirits (who were still holding their vigil round Owiot's pyre), and told them that he would create a race of beings to serve them and honour them. He moulded mud-dolls and breathed life into them: the first human beings.

≫→ creation, Enki, Esaugetuh Emissee, Humanmaker, Hurukan, Na'pi, Prometheus, Tagaro, Woyengi

CHIRON
Europe (South)

Chiron (Cheiron, 'hand'), in Greek myth, was the child of a **Titan** (**Cronus**) and a mortal (Philyra). In order to mate with Philyra without attracting the attention of his wife **Rhea**, Cronus had taken the shape of a horse, and so

Chiron was half horse half human. He was brought up in **Olympus**, where **Apollo** and **Artemis** taught him **hunting**, medicine, **music** and **prophecy**; when he grew up **Zeus** made him king of the **Centaurs**. His wisdom and patience made him an ideal teacher, and many princes went to him to finish their education – his pupils included **Achilles**, **Aeneas**, **Heracles**, **Jason** and Apollo's son **Aesculapius**, to whom he taught medicine.

Chiron's death. Because Chiron's father was a Titan, he himself was immortal. Zeus hoped that he would rule the Centaurs throughout eternity. But when Heracles passed through Chiron's kingdom on his hunt for the **Erymanthian Boar**, the Centaur Pholus opened a jar of wine to entertain him, and the smell attracted a gang of wild Centaurs who galloped up and demanded a share. There was a pitched battle – and when Chiron tried to intervene he slipped in the mud and fell into the path of one of Heracles' arrows, poisoned by the blood of the **Hydra**. Chiron's **immortality** meant that the arrow could not kill him, but the festering wound gave him such torment that at last he asked Zeus to end his life. Zeus gave his immortality to **Prometheus** (so ending Prometheus' punishment for stealing **fire**), and set Chiron in the sky as the constellation Centaurus.

CHONCHONYI
Americas (South)

Chonchonyi, in the myths of the Araucanian people of Chile, was a vampire **demon**. It was a human head whose wings were its enormous ears and whose teeth were tigers' fangs. If sick people were left unattended even for an instant it flapped down and sucked their blood.

⋙→ Flying Head

CHRYSOTHEMIS
Europe (South)

Chrysothemis ('golden stability'), in Greek myth, was **Agamemnon**'s and **Clytemnestra**'s daughter, the younger sister of **Iphigenia, Electra** and **Orestes**. She sided with Clytemnestra and **Aegisthus** when they murdered Agamemnon, and refused to help Orestes when he returned from exile and plotted to murder Clytemnestra. In some accounts Orestes and Electra killed her for this; in others she escaped to Delos, where she married King Staphylus and established a royal dynasty.

CHUKU
Africa

Chuku ('great spirit'), also known as Chineke ('maker'), in the myths of the Ibo people of Nigeria, created the universe, and made Ale (**Mother Earth**) as a paradise for his favoured offspring, human beings. He wanted human beings to be immortal, and sent Sheep to tell them that if anyone died, they should lay the corpse on Mother Earth and cover it with ashes to bring it back to life. Unfortunately, Sheep garbled the message, saying that corpses should be burned to ash and then buried – which is why human beings die, and why the Earth is populated with **ghosts**, **demons** and other spirits.

CHYAVANA
India

Chyavana, in Hindu myth, was a hermit who married a beautiful young wife and took her to live in his forest retreat. By chance the **Ashvins** passed that way, and asked her to leave the decrepit old man and run away with them. She answered that she preferred to stay with Chyavana, the husband chosen for her by her father. Flirtatiously, the Ashvins asked what was wrong with them, and like a dutiful wife she asked her husband what to answer. 'Ask them how I can recover my youth,' said Chyavana, 'Then say you'll explain.' The Ashvins advised him to bathe in a magic pool, and as soon as he was out of the way invited his wife to run off with them. But she said that what was wrong with them was that they were incomplete, and they were incomplete because they had not been invited to a sacrifice which the gods were holding at that very moment in **Heaven**. Furious, the Ashvins hurried away – and Chyavana came back from the magic pool, restored to the youth and vigour his wife had known from the start were his.

CIHUACÓATL
Americas (Central)

Cihuacóatl ('snake woman'), in Aztec myth, was the **Great Goddess**. In some accounts she was herself alone, one and indivisible: goddess of the **Moon**, of women's **fertility** and of **war**. In others, she divided herself into several goddesses, each with a different responsibility: **Coatlicue** (**Mother Earth**: see also **Ilamatecuhtli**), **Itzpapalotl** ('flint butterfly', demon of desire), **Temazcal-teci** (goddess of purification), Tetoin-nan (mother of the gods) and Tonantzin ('our mother') nourisher of all **creation**.

»→ fertility

CIRCE
Europe (North)

Circe (Kirke, 'falcon'), in Greek myth, was the daughter of the **Sun** and **Hecate**, goddess of black magic, who took the form of an ocean-**nymph** to seduce the Sun. Her half-brother was Aeëtes, guardian of the **Golden Fleece**, and her half-sister was **Pasiphaë**, mother of the **Minotaur**.

Like many gods and goddesses, Circe was insatiably attracted to human lovers. But her own double nature always caused trouble. From her father she had inherited dazzling beauty, but her mother had given her slyness and black magic instead of charm. She wooed the Italian prince **Picus**, and when he refused her she changed him into a woodpecker. She tried to seduce Glaucus the sea god, but disgusted him by changing her rival **Scylla** into a monster. She married a prince of Colchis, but could not bear giving up her divine power to live in his harem, and killed him to inherit his throne. Her husband's subjects would have stoned her for this, if her father had not carried her away in his Sun-chariot and given her a land of her own to rule, the floating island of Aeaea.

Circe and Odysseus. On Aeaea, Circe spent her time waiting for mortal sailors to land, and seducing them when they did so. She sat at her loom in the palace, singing a song so beautiful that none could resist. She feasted her mortal guests and enjoyed **sex** with them – then changed them into pigs and left them grubbing in her pens, weeping for their lost mortality. She would have trapped **Odysseus** in the same way, except that **Hermes** warned him and gave him a herb, moly (wild garlic), to ward off her magic.

By the time Odysseus reached Circe's palace, she had turned all his men into pigs. She welcomed him, served him a banquet, had sex with him, then tapped him with her wand and ordered him to go and wallow with the other pigs. But the moly cancelled her magic, and Odysseus drew his sword and threatened to kill her unless she set free all the bewitched pig-men. Circe, being immortal, knew that no mortal sword could harm her; but she realized that Odysseus was there with the gods' protection, and that she must give way to him. She set the pig-men free, and entertained Odysseus and his men to a real banquet, without spells – except that what took one night for a goddess lasted several mortal months, and when the men woke next morning they found their nails and hair grown and their faces covered with flowing beards.

There are various versions of what happened next. In some, Circe kept Odysseus and his crew on Aeaea for seven years, and she and Odysseus had three sons, Agrius, Latinus and Telegonus. Then the gods summoned Odysseus home, and Circe lost him forever. She sent her sons to look for him, and Telegonus landed by chance on Ithaca, was taken for a pirate by his father (who had never seen him before) and killed him. Telegonus married Odysseus' former wife **Penelope**, and Odysseus' son **Telemachus** sailed to Aeaea, married Circe and was granted the **immortality** she had always longed to give her mortal husbands. In other accounts, Circe told Odysseus that he must visit the **Underworld**, see the **heroes** who had fought at Troy and learn his future. Horrified by this prophecy, he sailed from Aeaea in such a rush that he forgot his cabin-boy **Elpenor**, who rushed to the palace roof to shout after him, fell and was killed, so that his was the most unexpected ghost Odysseus saw in the Underworld.

≫+ beauty, Calypso, Deirdre

CIVILIZATION

Civilization was, with **immortality** and all-knowledge, one of the possessions of the gods which humans most coveted – and it was the one the gods were most willing to share. It was part of universal order, and its mortal forms guaranteed the same kind of stability and longevity in human institutions as the laws of the gods ensured in **creation** at large. Civilization, in these terms, consisted of practicalities such as **crafts** or **farming**, the use of law, practice of worship and the gamut of arts and other creative skills. In all its forms, mortals were able to cope only with a small part of what the gods themselves knew and did: if they had had it all, it would have destroyed them. No other creatures but mortals were, however, gifted by the gods with civilization – though some, for example **snakes** in many traditions, tried to learn it by parodying

the institutions they saw in human life, producing their own perverted, monstrous and often enormously powerful versions.

Often, creators themselves gave their humans the vestiges of civilization, or enough wisdom to work out forms of them suitable for earthbound beings. In some traditions, specific gods took over this function – and they were often **tricksters**, using their wiles for good instead of mischief. In a very few cases, the creator opposed human beings being taught civilized behaviour, and punished the god who did so – usually with justice, since once humans shared any of the gods' prerogatives, even in diluted form, the established balance of the universe tilted and the road lay open to apocalypse. (The idea that humans perverted divine knowledge underlay many myths of the Ages of the world, and of the cataclysmic **Flood** designed to wipe us out and start again.)

≫+ (Americas): Tochopa and Hokomata, Yanauluha; (Australia): Mangarkungerkunja, Wondjina; (China): Fu Xi, Huang Di, Three Sovereigns, Yao; (Egypt): Osiris; (Greece): Prometheus; (Mesopotamia): Ea, Kusor, Ninurta; (Rome): Saturnus; (general): crafts, farming, guardians, smiths

CLASHING ROCKS
Europe (South)

The Clashing Rocks (Symplegades, 'crashers together'), in Greek myth, were living beings, **Gaia**'s (**Mother Earth**'s) rock-children. They guarded the entrance to the Black Sea, the boundary between the mortal world to the South and the supernatural world to the North where the **Sun**, **Winds** and other weather-beings lived. Whenever they sensed a ship trying to pass between them, they slammed together with enormous force, crushing it and its crew – and the gods threatened them with **death** if any unauthorized mortals slipped past them. No humans ever succeeded until the **Argonauts**, on their way to steal the **Golden Fleece**, tricked the Rocks by sending a dove winging through ahead of *Argo*. When the ship itself escaped the gods' warning came true and the Rocks were stripped of their life and turned into islands. They lie at the mouth of the Dardanelles (the gully between Europe and Asia) to this day.

CLOTHO: *see* Fates

CLYTEMNESTRA
Europe (South)

Clytemnestra (Klytaimestre, 'famous wooing'), in Greek myth, was the daughter of **Zeus** and **Leda**, wife of King **Tyndareus** of Sparta. She was the twin of **Helen**, hatched from the same egg, and they were the sisters of Castor and Pollux (see **Dioscuri**), **twins** born from another egg fertilized at the same time. Helen and Clytemnestra married two brothers, **Menelaus** and **Agamemnon** – in some accounts Agamemnon murdered Clytemnestra's former husband, King Tantalus of Pisa, and married her by force – and they ruled in Sparta and Mycenae respectively. Clytemnestra and Agamemnon had four children: **Iphigenia**, **Electra**, **Chrysothemis** and **Orestes**.

When Prince **Paris** of Troy stole Helen from Menelaus, and Agamemnon led the Greek force which assembled to sack Troy and bring her back, Agamemnon won fair winds for the fleet by sacrificing his eldest child Iphigenia. In some accounts, this was what caused Clytemnestra's fury towards him and her determination on revenge. In others, she suffered from the split personality characteristic of all children of gods and mortals, and it gave her a man's spirit in a woman's body, making her despise all males. Whatever the reason, she took advantage of Agamemnon's ten-year absence in Troy to find a lover (her less-than-assertive cousin **Aegisthus**), plant him on the throne as regent of Mycenae, and rule in his name.

When Agamemnon came home from the war, Clytemnestra pretended to welcome him. She took him to the bath-house, and tangled him in a net (or, some say, in the rich red fabric over which she had invited him to enter Mycenae in triumph). Aegisthus stepped from the shadows and murdered him, splitting his skull with an axe. The pair then butchered all who supported Agamemnon, tyrannized their own daughters Electra and Chrysothemis, and ruled Mycenae in unchallenged arrogance for another dozen years. Clytemnestra's son Orestes, however, who had been smuggled out of the palace immediately after Agamemnon's murder, grew up in exile, and as soon as he was old enough came back to Mycenae, disguised, and killed Clytemnestra and Aegisthus.

Clytemnestra's death was not the end of her story. Because she was Zeus' daughter, only the gods could settle the true rights and wrongs of her murdering Agamemnon. Her ghost allied with the **Furies**, driving Orestes mad and pursuing him all over Greece, until at last he sought refuge at **Apollo**'s shrine in Delphi. Apollo took his side against the Furies, and **Athene** spoke for the still-raging Clytemnestra. In the end Zeus – or in some accounts, a jury of humans – decided that Orestes' crime was just and that Clytemnestra was guilty and had been punished as she deserved. Her ghost fled weeping to the **Underworld**, where it has remained ever since, cursing mortals and gods alike.

»+ **Nauplius, twins**

COATLICUE
Americas (Central)

Coatlicue ('snake-skirt'), in Aztec myth, was **Mother Earth**; in some accounts, the South American continent itself was formed from her body and upper jaw, after the lower jaw was torn off during a battle in which she took the form of a crocodile (*cipactli*) to fight **Quetzalcóatl**. Her other names included **Ilamatecuhtli** ('old goddess'), **Itzpapalotl** ('flint butterfly'), Tlatecuhtli ('earth-toad-knife') and Tonantzin ('our mother'). As some of these names suggest, she was a **shape-changer**, and her favourite form was that of a woman with talons for fingers, a skirt of snakes and a necklace of the skulls, hands and hearts of her sacrificial victims. Originally she was full-breasted, and her breasts spurted the milk of life; but she had 400 sons and innumerable daughters, and they drained the energy

from her, leaving her breasts pendulous and wrinkled.

Coatlicue and Huitzilopochtli. Coatlicue's husband, father of all her children, was the cloud-snake **Mixcóatl**, god of hunting. But one day when she was sweeping, a ball of feathers caught in her clothes, and when she tried to brush it off it slipped into her womb and impregnated her. Hearing that she was pregnant, her sons and daughters ran to kill her. One of them, **Coyolxauhqui**, hurried ahead to warn her, and the child in her womb, **Huitzilopochtli** god of war, thrust himself into life, grew to full size in an instant, and began slaughtering his own half-brothers and sisters until the survivors knelt and swore homage.

*The Coatlicue myths – at least as recounted by the Spanish conquerors of Mexico, who glossed them as the worst imaginable kinds of criminal paganism – end with a gruesome form of the common world belief that blood-sacrifice is necessary to ensure the fertility of the soil. Each year, Coatlicue mated with her own son, the corn-god **Xipetotec**, who planted corn-seeds deep in her womb. But to bring them to fruition, she had to have mortal encouragement – and her priests provided it by tearing the hearts from living victims, watering her soil with their blood and planting the heads, hands and hearts for her to add to her putrescent necklace.*

COCYTUS
Europe (South)

Cocytus (Kokytos, 'lament'), in Greek myth, was one of the tributaries of the river **Styx** which flowed through the

Underworld. Its **water** was as bitter as tears, and the only being able to live in it was Allecto, leader of the **Furies**, whose pastime was swimming in its icy rapids.

CONIRAYA
Americas (South)

Coniraya, in Inca myth, was one of the oldest gods in the universe. He was a creator not by intention but by accident: he was **fertility** incarnate, and whatever he touched swarmed and foamed with life. Despite, or perhaps because of, this uncontrollable fecundity, he could never find a mate. He tramped the universe as a beggar, and fruit-trees sprouted from his footsteps. The goddess Cavillaca ate one of the fruit, became instantly pregnant, and was so horrified to be bearing Coniraya's children that she turned herself into a planet, the Earth, and her offspring into continents and **mountains**. Coniraya wandered over her surface, looking for a mate – and everywhere he went new species of plants, insects and animals appeared. By the side of a lake, he courted one of the daughters of the **Sea**, but she rejected him and dived into the water out of reach. Angrily, he picked up the whole lake and hurled it into the sea – and at his touch the water teemed with fish.

Scholars think that this myth predated the Incas, and was probably one of the oldest myth-stories in South America. It is also one of the very few accounts, from anywhere in the world, where creation happens accidentally, even reluctantly: most cultures preferred to believe that the world was made if not for a purpose, at least with conscious will.

COPPER WOMAN
Americas (North)

Copper Woman, in the myths of the peoples of the Northwestern US coast, lived at a time when the Earth was exactly as it is today except that there were no human beings. She lived by hunting seal and fishing for salmon and crabs, but she was desperately lonely. She wept, and her nose began to run – and spirits told her to save the fluid, as a sign that she was mortal. She gathered it in a crab shell – and next morning found that it had formed itself into a wriggling ball, with a grain of sand trapped in it like a tadpole's head. The fluid-creature grew until it metamorphosed into a being half human (from Copper Woman's nose-fluid) and half crab (from the sand in the shell). It had eyes on stalks, pincers for fore-arms and a man's chest-hair and penis. It was unable to speak, and spent every day frolicking with other sea-creatures; but it passed every night making love with Copper Woman in her hut, and her loneliness was over.

*In an ideal world, one might want this myth to end with an act of **creation**, perhaps of the human race. But it stops right here. It was, none the less, popular: some two dozen coastal peoples all told it, with no variation except that in some versions, a clam replaced the crab, and in others Copper Woman also collected her menstrual blood (which did not, however, grow into a living being).*

CORMAC MACAIRT
Europe (North)

Cormac MacAirt ('Cormac, Airt's son'), in Celtic myth, was king of Ireland, ruling in Tara. **Manannan MacLir**, the **sea**-king, visited Tara one May morning, and Cormac hospitably offered an exchange of gifts. He promised Manannan anything he wanted, and Manannan gave him a branch of the tree of **immortality**, hung with golden apples which tinkled when the branch was shaken, lulling everyone who heard them into a sleep which cured all disease and ended all anxiety. But in exchange Manannan took Cormac's beloved wife and daughters, spiriting them away in a sea-mist. Heartbroken, Cormac sailed to find them. In a magic mist he came on an island, and told a passing stranger his troubles before falling into a deep faint. When he recovered the stranger revealed himself as Manannan. He said that Cormac's tears, and his love for his wife and daughters, had moved him so much that he would return them at once – and he also gave Cormac a golden cup which had the property of distinguishing truth from lies: if three lies were spoken into it, it shattered, and if three truths were spoken, it became whole again.

*This story was probably elaborated to honour a real Cormac, a third-century king of Ireland nicknamed 'the Irish Solomon'. Other stories were attached to his name, even less plausible than this one – for anyone with a reputation for wisdom to foster could devise **mysteries** involving self-fragmenting cups and branches with golden apples. His chroniclers claimed that he was raised, like **Romulus and Remus**, by a she-wolf, and that he was a friend of **Finn MacCool** and the other **giants**, advising them on the best design for the Giants'*

Causeway between Ireland and Scotland. ⋙ **heroes**

CORN WOMAN
Americas (North)

Corn Woman, in the myths of the Creek people of the Southeastern US, lived with mortals in the days before people knew anything about **farming**. She seemed just like any other person, but served delicious dishes of corn to the family she lived with. Having no idea what it was or where it came from, they spied on her and found that she scraped boils and sores from her body and gathered them in a pot. Disgusted, they refused to eat any more of her preparations, and as soon as she realized what the matter was she told them to sow the scrapings in prepared ground, harvest them and then husk them to remove any last hint of taint.

The Corn Woman features in dozens of similar myths, and in every case corn comes from her in some unappetizing form: lice, blood-drops, nail-clippings. Usually, as here, she teaches the people to farm and harvest the corn, and to husk it or mill it to remove impurities. But a few myths involve sacrificing her completely, and burying her in the ground, from which corn grows next Spring.

COYOLXAUHQUI
Americas (Central)

Coyolxauhqui ('golden bells'), in Aztec myth, was the beautiful daughter of **Coatlicue**, **Mother Earth**. She got her name because she wore cheek-ornaments of tiny golden bells. When

Coatlicue became mysteriously pregnant with **Huitzilopochtli** and her 400 sons ran to kill her, Coyolxauhqui hurried ahead to warn her. Hearing the warning, Huitzilopochtli was born and grew to full strength in an instant, and started shooting arrows. The first person he killed was Coyolxauhqui. To make amends, when the massacre was over he cut off her head and set it in the night sky as the **Moon** – and the golden bells can still be seen on the cheeks of Coyolxauhqui's face in the full Moon each month.

≫→ **beauty**

COYOTE
Americas (North)

Coyote (Italpas or Sedit), in the myths of many peoples of the Western US, was a primordial god who could have been all-powerful if he hadn't dissipated his energy in playing japes and tricks. For some he symbolized **fire**; for others he was a **shape-changer** who favoured the role of coyote, apparently cringing but always on the lookout for his own advantage, for licking up unconsidered trifles. The Maidu people of California gave him a shape-changing servant, Rattlesnake, who (confusingly) took the form of a small dog and whose bite brought death to the human race – in fact he bit Coyote's own son.

Coyote and Creation. Coyote was often associated with the **creation** of the world or one or other of its peoples. The people of the plains said that originally the **wind** blew unceasingly from all directions, until Coyote, tired of being buffeted, caught the wind-god by one leg and refused to let go until the

Wind agreed to divide himself in four, retire to the compass points, and blow intermittently, from one direction at a time. The Maidu people said that Coyote grew bored with the endless perfection of the original world, and introduced suffering, despair and death to make human life more interesting. The Nez Perce people said that he created their nation, and all other Northwestern peoples, from the body of the huge beaver-monster **Wishpoosh** – but forgot, accidentally or deliberately, to give them proper mouths and noses like the gods, and was forced to add the nostril-holes and lip-gashes which still disfigure the human face.

Coyote the Messenger. Many peoples said that Coyote was a **messenger** between the supernatural world and the mortal world – and the Sioux people said he made himself a wind-horse to ride between the two worlds, and adapted dogs to make horses so that his mortal worshippers could enjoy a small sample of the speed this gave him.

Coyote and the Dead. In the myths of the Wishram people of the Northwestern US, Coyote could have rescued us all from **death**, and didn't. Distressed by the death of his sister, he travelled to the Spirit World to rescue her. He found the spirits dancing and singing all night under the eye of Frog, who was lighting them with the **Moon** as a lantern. He waited until day, when the Spirits all lay down to sleep, then killed Frog, skinned him and put on the skin. That night, when the Spirits danced, suspecting nothing, Coyote blew out the Moon, bundled them into a sack in the darkness and set out for home. But the bag grew heavier and heavier, and the Spirits inside it complained that they were cramped and wanted to stretch their legs in a dance – and in the end Coyote, disgusted, opened the sack and let them go, vanishing like smoke in the wind. At the time he intended to go back the following Spring and try again, but he soon found other distractions and forgot – which is why death still exists.

*At the grander level, Coyote is cousin to **trickster** gods in other traditions, often gods of fire such as **Homasubi** or **Loki** – and like them is prevented from mastering the universe only by his shortness of concentration and his taste for mischief. But he was also a favourite character in folk-tales and children's stories, related less to gods than to such more mundane tricksters as **Anansi**, Brer Rabbit, Reynard or Spider.*

➤➤➔ animal-gods, Ogo

CRAFTS

Crafts were one of the aspects of **justice and universal order** which the gods saw fit to share with human beings – in some cases, crafting us first in order to have someone to share them with. Mortals, however, were allowed only clumsy forms of the gods' craftskills. No human architect, jeweller or weaver was ever the equal of his or her divine teacher, and those who came nearest suffered on Earth for their presumption (though they were often later taken into **Heaven** and granted **immortality**). Unlike **smiths**, who despite their skills were in most traditions treated as second-class citizens by the gods, craft-gods were among the most august and dignified in the pantheon. There was also a sub-class of supernatural craftworkers. In Heaven it consisted of

elves, skilled slaves of the main craft-god; on Earth it consisted of dwarfs and underwater spirits, who had been given this one supernatural attribute at the cost of being condemned never to reproduce and never to see the sky – they made objects of surpassing beauty and dazzling ingenuity, but this gift was all they had, and they resented it even as they used it.

➤➤➔ (Australia): Mangarkungerkunja; (Celtic): Brigid, Lug; (China): Huang Di, Huang Gun, Lu Ban, Sun Bin, Yu; (Egypt): Imhotep, Khnum, Neit, Ptah; (Greece): Arachne, Daedalus, Hephaestus, Pygmalion, Telchines; (India): Dhatar, Ribhus, Tvashtri, Vishvakarman; (Mesopotamia): Kusor; (Nordic): Alvis, Andvari; (general): civilization

CREATION

Devisers of myths tended to ignore the 'Why?' of creation. Gods made the universe by accident, or because they were bored, lonely or filled with uncontrollable generative power. They stocked **Sky** with stars and Earth with plants and animals for similar reasons, or in rivalry with one another. The myth-makers never asked, or answered, any larger questions. But when it comes to the 'How?' of creation, there were no limits to the ingenuity and poetry of the answers given. Gods constructed the universe out of themselves, out of enemies or beloved spouses. They made other gods out of disembodied principles (such as rage or lust, sometimes splitting their own personalities to do so). They made Earth and humans from apparently unpromising materials (such as pebbles, tree-leaves, sludge from the primordial ocean or their own faeces), by **crafts** such as pottery or wood-carving, or by mistake (for example by sneezing). Sometimes they animated all created matter, including **mountains**, rivers and grains of sand, but usually they made a hierarchical distinction between those objects animated with their own breath of life, and those left inanimate.

Primary creation was usually a single-handed job (in some cases literally: the supreme god masturbated); secondary creation often involved many different gods, the original creator's offspring each working in a different area. In most accounts, the task of creation finished when the gods taught wisdom to the human race; in a few, creation still continued, or was a cyclical event, to be repeated when the depredations made on the universe by any particular batch of mortals and **demons** could no longer be tolerated.

With the exception of India, creation-stories are sparse in countries where the great religions thrive. Priests and theologians tend to tease out the philosophical implications of the topic, and to pick and choose which nuts-and-bolts accounts they will give canonical status. But in other areas, especially those inhabited by large numbers of separate peoples, creation-stories are legion – and the objective point of interest here is not how different they all are from one another, but how much they have in common.

≫→ (Africa): Adroa, Ajok, Akongo, Amma, Andriambahomanana and Andriamahilala, Bumba, Chuku, Da, Deng, Dxui, Heitsi-Eibib, Huveane, Imana, Itherther and Achimi, Juok, Kaang, Kalumba, Katonda, Khonvum, Libanza, Mawu-Lisa, Muluku, Mulungu, Ngewowa, Njinji, Nyambe, Nyambi, Olorun, Onyankopon, Ruwa, Unkulunkulu, Wak, Wele, Woyengi, Zamba; (Americas): Ahsonnutli, Aiomum Kondi, Amana, Amotken, Atsehastin and Atseestan, Awonawilona, Baxbakualanuchsiwae, Chinigchinich, Coniraya, Coyote, Dayunsi, Esaugetuh Emissee, Estsanatlehi, Five Sisters, Gucumatz, Gudratrigakwitl, Hahgwehdiyu and Hahgwehdaetgah, Humanmaker, Hunab, Hurukan, Kanassa, Kitshi Manitu, Kloskurbeh, Kodoyanpe, Kokyangwuti, Kononatoo, Kumokum, Kururumany, Kwatee, Maheo, Malsum, Michabo, Nagaitcho, Nanabush, Na'pi, Nocoma, Nokomis, Pachacamac, Page Abe, Raven, Sinaa, Tamusi and Tamulu, Tirawa, Viracocha, Wakan Tanka, Wheememeowah, Wonomi, Xólotl; (Asia): Ahura Mazda, Batara Guru, Naga Pahoda, sPyan-ras-gzigs, Tengri, Zurvan Akarana; (Arctic): Buga, Ulgan; (Australia): Bagadjimbiri, Bildjiwuaroju, Miralaldu and Djanggawul, Julunggul, Kurukadi and Mumba, Minawara and Multultu, Mudungkala, Ngurunderi, Waramurungundju and Wuraka, Wondjina; (China): Fu Xi, Hun Dun, Nü Gua, Pan Gu; (Egypt): Atum, Khnum, Min, Neit, Nun and Naunet, Ptah, Ra, Thoth; (Finnish): Luonnotar; (Greece): Eurynome and Ophion, Gaia, Prometheus; (India): Brahma, Daksha, Indra, Kasyapa, Mithra, Prajapati, Prajapatis, Purusha, Sarasvati, Varaha, Varuna, Viraj, Vishvakarman;

(Japan): In and Yo, Izanami and Izanagi, Okuninushi, Umashiashikabihikoji; (Mesopotamia): Adad, Ea, El, Enki, Marduk, Tengri; (Nordic): Aesir, Honir, Odin, Ve, Vili, Ymir; (Oceania): Areop-Enap and Rigi, Atea, Jugumishanta and Morufonu, Loa, Maui, Nareau, Qat, Rangi, Rangi's and Papa's Immortal Children, Ta'aroa, Tagaro, Tane, Tangaloa, To Kabinana and To Karvuvu; (Slavic): Rod

CREON
Europe (South)

Creon (Kreon, 'wielding power'), in Greek myth, is in fact a title not a name: equivalent to the Egyptian *pharaoh* or the South American *inca*. But the ancient Greek tragedians used it to refer to specific characters (perhaps as we might call them 'His Majesty'), and it has ever since been treated as a proper name.

CREON, KING OF CORINTH
Europe (South)

Creon (Kreon, 'wielding power'), son of **Sisyphus** in Greek myth, was the king of Corinth who gave his daughter Glauce to **Jason**, only to die with her on the day before the wedding, as a result of **Medea**'s poison.

CREON, KING OF THEBES
Europe (South)

Creon (Kreon, 'wielding power'), son of Menoeceus in Greek myth, was a descendant of one of the **Sown Men** of **Thebes**, and the brother of **Jocasta**. When **Oedipus** blinded and exiled

himself, Creon became regent of Thebes. He retired as soon as Oedipus' sons **Eteocles** and **Polynices** were old enough to rule, but returned as regent when they quarrelled over the throne and killed each other. Creon decreed that Polynices (who had led the **Seven Against Thebes**) should be left on the plain to rot, but that Eteocles (who had led the city's defenders) should be buried with honour. When **Antigone**, the dead princes' sister, said that they should be treated with equal honour, and buried Polynices, Creon walled her up in a cave to die. His arrogance destroyed his city. King **Theseus** of Athens arrested him, executed him and buried the dead soldiers, and the Epigoni (sons of the original Seven Against Thebes) sacked the city and sowed its remains with salt.

CRESSIDA: *see* Troilus

CRETAN BULL, THE
Europe (South)

The Cretan Bull, in Greek myth, was a fire-breathing **monster** created by **Poseidon** out of **sea**-foam and given to King Minos of Crete. Poseidon intended Minos to sacrifice it in his honour, but Minos substituted an inferior animal from his own herd. Poseidon punished him by making Queen **Pasiphaë** mate with the bull and give birth to the Minotaur, and then sent the bull mad, so that it rampaged through the Cretan countryside, trampling crops and people and destroying forests and villages with its fiery breath. For **Heracles'** seventh **labour**, King **Eurystheus** of Mycenae ordered him to go to Crete and capture the Bull. Heracles confused the bull by standing with his back to it, wearing his lion-skin cloak. The bull took him for a lion and charged, snorting fire. As soon as Heracles felt its scorching breath, he turned, caught hold of its horns and somersaulted onto its back. Then, however much it arched its back and bucked, he kept fast hold of its horns and rode it until it was as tame as a broken horse. Then he drove it into the sea, forced it to swim to Mycenae and presented it to Eurystheus. Eurystheus wanted to sacrifice the bull to his patron, **Hera**, but it was such a pathetic spectacle, its spirit broken and all the fire gone out of it, that she rejected it and sent it whimpering North, where it took refuge among wild cattle on the plain of Marathon.

CRONUS
Europe (South)

Cronus and Ouranos. Cronus (Kronos, 'crow'; Latin **Saturnus**, Saturn), in Greek and Roman myth, was the first-born of the twelve Titans, children of **Gaia** (**Mother Earth**) and **Ouranos** (Father **Sky**). When Ouranos began attacking his own children, prising open Gaia's body and thrusting them into its innermost crevices, Cronus made a sickle out of diamonds and castrated him. This act of violence tamed Ouranos, who never afterwards interfered with events in **Heaven** or on Earth. Cronus left his giant siblings, the **Cyclopes** and the **Hundred-handed Giants**, imprisoned in the recesses of Mother Earth. He took his sister **Rhea** as queen, and together they and the other Titans ruled the universe.

Cronus and Zeus. However, as the wounded Ouranos withdrew from the Earth, he had cursed his son, prophesying that just as Cronus had dethroned him, so he would be expelled by one of his own children. Whenever Rhea bore a child, therefore, Cronus swallowed it alive: three daughters (**Demeter**, **Hera** and **Hestia**), and two sons (**Hades** and **Poseidon**). To prevent this happening with her sixth child, **Zeus**, Rhea gave the child to **mountain**-nymphs to bring up secretly in Crete, and handed Cronus a stone to swallow, wrapped in baby-clothes. The trick worked. Zeus grew up safely, and when he was adult went to serve his father as cupbearer. He gave Cronus a drink of **nectar** mixed with emetic herbs, and Cronus vomited up Zeus' five sisters and brothers, reborn as full-grown, immortal gods.

War in the universe. As soon as the gods were reborn, they challenged the Titans for control of the universe. The entire universe was engulfed in **war**, and all its creatures took one side or the other. In the end the Titans withdrew to Cronus' citadel on Mount Othrys, the gods besieged it and there was stalemate. Then Mother Earth told Zeus to release the Giants and Cyclopes from imprisonment. The Cyclopes forged invincible weapons for the gods: a helmet of invisibility for Hades, an earth-shaking trident for Poseidon, and for Zeus **thunder**, captured and stored in a thunderbolt. Wearing invisibility, Hades crept into Mount Othrys and stole Cronus' weapons; Poseidon then threatened him with his trident, and while his attention was distracted Zeus hurled a thunderbolt and stunned him. The Hundred-handed Giants streamed up from the Underworld and began tearing the Titans' citadel to pieces. The Titans fled and the gods had won.

In some accounts, Zeus punished Cronus and the other Titans by imprisoning them in the **Underworld**, never allowing them into the Upper World again. In others, he showed mercy. On condition that the Titans never again challenged the gods, he gave them a beautiful country, the Islands of the Blessed in the Far West of the universe, beyond the stars. Here Cronus and Rhea ruled in peace and contentment like the first happiness when the world was newly made – and particularly favoured mortals and immortals were allowed to join them when their time on Earth was done.

CUCULAIN
Europe (North)

Cuculain ('Culain's hound'), in Celtic myth, was the nickname of Setanta, warrior-son of the mortal Dechtire and the **Sun**-god **Lug**. Setanta won the nickname when he killed the fairy watchdog of the **smith** Culain, and agreed himself to guard Culain's fields and byres for a year while a replacement was trained for the job.

Cuculain was born to fight. Rage was his predominant characteristic, so much so that it took three cauldrons of icy water to cool his anger. He proved himself the bravest warrior in Ireland when a **giant** challenged him and two other young men, Laoghaire and Conal, to a test of nerve. Each day, the giant proposed, he would allow one of them to cut off his head if that man, in turn, let the giant behead him. Laoghaire went

first. He beheaded the giant (who simply picked up his head and walked away), but ran away from offering his own neck on the block. The next day Conal did the same, and it was only on the third day when Cuculain bent his own neck for the giant's sword that the giant stepped back and declared him champion of all Ireland.

Cuculain's feats of daring and strength culminated in a huge battle, defending the men of Ulster against the armies of Queen Maeve of Connaught, who were trying to steal the famously potent brown bull of Cooley. In the course of this battle, however, he killed his own foster-brother Ferdiad (who served Maeve), and the war-goddess the **Morrigan** appeared and told him that his own death was near, a fulfilment of the choice he'd made as a boy when the gods offered him the alternatives of long life or everlasting fame. Cuculain, exhausted and seriously wounded by the days-long duel with Ferdiad, strapped himself to a stone column so that his enemies would never beat him to his knees, and challenged them to attack him. They realized that he was dead only when they saw the Morrigan, in her crow disguise, perched on his shoulder.

≫→ **heroes**

CUPAY
Americas (South)

Cupay (or Supay), in Inca myth, was a **death**-god whose speciality was to snatch babies at the moment of birth. Paradoxically, one way to ward off his attentions was to sacrifice live children to him.

CUPID: *see* Eros

CYBELE
Europe (South)

Cybele (Kybele, 'hairy' or 'blade-woman') was a goddess of Phrygia (modern Turkey), the protector of the clefts and chasms of **Gaia** (**Mother Earth**) and the bears and other wild animals which hibernated there. She had a shrine on Mount Ida, near Troy, and when the Greeks returned from the **Trojan War** they brought her worship back with them, attaching it to the goddess **Rhea** (of whom they said Cybele was a particularly fearsome aspect).

Cybele's birth was complex. The **sky** – or in Greek versions of the myth, **Zeus** – masturbated over a stone and fertilized it, so that it was reborn as itself, in the form of the hermaphrodite god Agditis. The gods wanted to kill Agditis, but Zeus refused to let his creation die. So the gods cut off Agditis' penis and allowed its female half, Cybele, to survive. In some versions of the story, the severed penis (or blood from it) was reconstituted as the male god **Attis**, a beautiful youth, or fertilized a tree from which Attis was later born. Cybele lusted after Attis (either as female lusting after male or as the two halves of Agditis longing to be reunited), and Attis was so horrified that he castrated himself.

Ever afterwards, Cybele was the goddess of unrequited lust, and her priests (called Corybantes, 'crested ones' after their headgear) worked themselves up in ecstatic, frenzied dances during which they gashed themselves – and in extreme cases castrated themselves – with sickles. This aspect of the worship of Cybele was never popular in Greece, but became an object of fascination with young aristocratic Romans from the fourth century BCE onwards. They formed secret Cybele societies in Rome and sometimes visited Mount Ida to try the dances, and the ecstasy, on the goddess' original holy ground. In later Rome, the Emperor himself became high priest of the cult (taking little part, one imagines, in the self-mutilation rituals), and presided over an annual ceremony re-enacting the entire bizarre story.

➤ **Great Goddess, mysteries, sex**

CYCLOPES, THE
Europe (South)

The original Cyclopes (Kyklopes, 'round-eyes'), in Greek myth, were three of the first beings in the universe, offspring of **Gaia** (**Mother Earth**) and **Ouranos** (Father **Sky**). They were Arges ('Light-dazzle'), Brontes ('Thunder') and Steropes ('Lightning'), and they were rock and fire blended into human shape. Their strength was enormous: they could tear up hills bare-handed and stack mountain-peaks as mortals stack bricks. They were called 'Round-eyes' because they had one eye each, in the centre of their foreheads.

When the **Titans** took control of the universe, they imprisoned the Cyclopes in the lowest depths of the **Underworld**, out of sight and out of mind. The Cyclopes lay there for a million years guarded by **Campe**. But when the gods were born, and began their battles against the Titans, **Zeus** went to the

Underworld and gave the Cyclopes **nectar** to drink. It brought life back to them as sap brings life to trees. They searched for fire in the roots of their mother Earth, and began to forge weapons for the gods. For **Hades** they made a helmet of invisibility, for **Poseidon** a trident that would part the sea and shake the earth, and for Zeus they made thunderbolts, the sky's explosive power harnessed in lumps of iron.

Using these weapons, the gods defeated the Titans and ruled the universe. Zeus gave the Cyclopes a smithy under the roots of Mount Etna in Sicily. Here they made him thunderbolts, and the flames from their fires and spillage from their smelting spewed out over the countryside. From time to time, they took rests in the upper air, and often when this happened they mated with mortal girls. Eventually a community of huge, one-eyed **giants** lived on the slopes and fields of Etna – and their mothers, the village girls, ashamed to admit that they had had sex with **monsters** from inside the earth, put it about that the father was **Poseidon**. The new Cyclopes were farmers and shepherds, and most were peaceful. But a few – for example **Polyphemus** who attacked the crews of **Odysseus** and **Aeneas** – kept the ungovernable fury of their fathers, and developed a taste for human flesh.

Death (*Medieval European rosary-bead*)

DA
Africa

Da, in the myths of the Fon people of Dahomey, was the serpent who supported the universe. It was of both sexes, and its male identity formed the red end of the spectrum of light, its female identity the blue end. The Earth floated on water, and Da supported this primordial ocean in 3500 coils which were its currents. Above the Earth it formed another 3500 coils (making air-currents), to support the pod-shaped sky with its millions of heavenly bodies.

At the beginning of **creation**, Da took Mawu (female creative component of the double god **Mawu-Lisa**) in its mouth and carried it everywhere across the Earth. Wherever they stopped for the night, Da's dung made mountains, and wherever they passed each day the ground behind them was covered with plants and animals. It was because these creations threatened to sink Earth in the primordial ocean that Mawu asked Da to support it on its coils.

In some versions of these myths, Da made a pyramid-shaped cushion of coils to support the Earth, biting its own tail to keep everything in place. In others, it propped the Earth on four pillars, one at each cardinal compass point, and moved sinuously round and between them, in a continuous supportive flow. It changed colour according to the time of day, and covered all colours of the spectrum. Humans occasionally glimpsed it in full glory, as the rainbow or the pattern of iridescence in a pool or pond; otherwise it was as invisible as a current, and only the stability of the universe guaranteed that it was still in place.

➤ **snakes**

DACTYLS
Europe (South)

The Dactyls ('fingers'), in Greek myth, were sons of the Cretan **mountain-nymph** Anchiale, who gave birth to them not in the usual way but by grasping handfuls of earth, each of which turned into a Dactyl. In most accounts there were only three of them, Acmon, Celmis and Damnameneus, but some stories speak of ten without giving names. When **Rhea** was giving birth to **Zeus** – in the version of the myth which takes place on Mount Ida in Crete – she dug her fingers in the ground as Anchiale had done, and the Dactyls climbed out of the holes to help her. The Dactyls were dwarves, craftsmen and inventors. They lived underground, mining and cutting precious stones, but occasionally came to the surface. They taught **Orpheus music**, and invented poetic metre, beginning with the light-hearted, dancing rhythm (DA-da-da, as in 'Happily') called dactyl after them.

DAEDALUS
Europe (South)

Daedalus (Daidalos, 'dazzling' or 'intricately made'), in Greek myth, was an Athenian craftsman whose skill rivalled that of **Hephaestus**, craftsman of the gods, himself. Until his time, ships had only oar-power; he invented sails in imitation of birds' wings. He showed people how to split logs not with axes but with hammers and wedges. He made beautiful dolls, like miniature statues with flexible, jointed limbs.

Daedalus and Talus. Daedalus' nephew, Talus, was his uncle's apprentice – and as sometimes happens, he was more talented than his master. He looked at the way potters laboriously build up their pots from strips of clay, invented the potter's wheel and gave them a speed and symmetry unknown before. One day, playing with a fish's backbone, he used it to saw a twig in half; he copied the bone's shape in bronze and invented the saw. At this Daedalus, full of jealousy, took him walking on the steep slopes of the Acropolis, and pushed him over. He then took his tools, his blueprints and his young son **Icarus** and fled to Crete, where King **Minos** gave them sanctuary.

Daedalus in Crete. In Crete, Daedalus continued his almost godlike inventive career. In particular, he developed huge, flat-bottomed merchant ships for grain, and ever more complex systems of masts and sailing-oars to control them. He devised the underwater ram, in the shape of a bird's beak, which made Cretan warships the terror of all who faced them.

The labyrinth. Minos' queen, **Pasiphaë**, was tired of her husband's philandering, and rashly blamed the goddess **Aphrodite**. Aphrodite punished her by filling her with lust for an enormous, fire-breathing white bull, a gift to the Cretans from **Poseidon**. Pasiphaë persuaded Daedalus to build her a cow-shaped wooden framework, and hid inside it while he trundled it into the bull's pasture. The bull mounted the framework, and mated with Pasiphaë inside. When Minos discovered what had happened, and that Pasiphaë was pregnant, he ordered

Daedalus to build her a hiding-place where no one would ever see her again. Daedalus designed a vast underground palace, hundreds of rooms linked by a spider's web of passages: a labyrinth, a maze whose secret only he and Minos knew. When it was finished, Pasiphaë was locked inside, deep underground, and there she bore her monstrous child, the **Minotaur**.

Daedalus in Sicily. Since only Minos and Daedalus knew the labyrinth's secret, Daedalus thought it prudent to escape from Crete. Because the ports were guarded, he made enormous wings for himself and Icarus, and one morning they flew away at dawn, soaring high towards the rising Sun. Icarus failed to survive the journey, but Daedalus landed in Sicily and went into hiding. Minos tracked him down by offering a reward to anyone in Greece who could pass a silken thread all the way through a triton-shell. Daedalus smeared honey on the outside of the shell, bored a hole in the closed end and inserted an ant, tied with a silken thread. The ant ran through the shell to find the honey, and Minos had his man. But that night, before Daedalus could be arrested, he poured boiling water down secret pipes into the Cretan king's bath, and scalded him to death. He spent the rest of his life in Sicily, making many wonders, including a golden honeycomb, exact in every detail, for Aphrodite's temple on Mount Eryx. In some accounts, when he died he was taken into Olympus and became a craftsman in Hephaestus' workshop.

This myth seems to have been assembled rather than devised, to explain how certain prized inventions and wonders came about. Daedalus' dolls are direct descendants of the animated puppets Hephaestus was said to have made in Olympus for the gods' amusement. Saws, wedges and sails all came into use in Greece in about the tenth or ninth century BCE – but the myth seems to contain a folk-memory of the (real) ancient Cretan civilization of some 500 years before. One of the high points of that civilization, the palace at Knossos, is thought to have inspired the idea of Daedalus' labyrinth: its hundreds of rooms and maze of corridors must have seemed impenetrable to visitors. (In some versions of the myth, however, Daedalus' labyrinth was not horizontal but vertical: chambers and passages built downwards and outwards from a central shaft, like an upside-down tree carved in the rock.) In modern times, the English artist Michael Ayrton made a golden honeycomb as exact as Daedalus' in Sicily: he set a real honeycomb in plaster, then melted the beeswax, replaced it with gold and broke the plaster mould. If this was how Daedalus made his honeycomb, perhaps the 'lost wax' process should be credited among his inventions.

➤➤ crafts, Lu Ban, Lug

DAGDA, THE
Europe (North)

The Dagda ('good god'), in Celtic myth, was the son of Eladu, god of knowledge, and chief of the original supernatural inhabitants of Ireland, the people of light. As god of life and **death**, he wielded a club so heavy that it needed wheels to carry it, and used it to batter people to death with the knobbed end, or bring them back to life with the other end. His honorific names included Aed ('fire'), Ollathair ('all-father') and Ruad Rofessa ('lord of all knowledge') – and as the last suggests, he was expert at every art and skill, notably castle-building, fighting and harp-playing. (His chord-sequences kept the year progressing and the seasons changing.)

The Dagda was a god of plenty. He was pot-bellied, coarse-mannered and cheery, presiding over a cauldron of plenty which held eighty gallons of milk and a similar quantity of mutton, pork and goat's meat and was never exhausted, an orchard whose trees were always laden with fruit, and two magic pigs, one of which ended each day being roasted and eaten and the other began each day as a newborn piglet, growing fat ready for the next evening's banquet. Inexhaustibly fertile, he was married to Queen Dana, also known as Breng ('lie'), Mabel ('shame') and Meng ('guile'), and their innumerable children included the three goddesses **Brigid**. He also enjoyed **sex** with trees, rivers, humans and even the **war**-goddess the **Morrigan**, with whom he ceremonially mated each New Year's Day.

⋙➤ **justice and universal order**

DAGON
Asia (West)

Dagon, or Dagan ('corn-lord'), in Sumerian myth, was the god who made grain swell on the stalk. He was later confused with Dogon, a fish-god worshipped in towns on the Eastern coasts of the Aegean, where he was shown as half human, half fish. No myths survive from either tradition, but the Bible somewhat lip-smackingly recounts how when the Philistines stored the captured Ark of the Covenant in Dagon's temple in Ashdod, the god's statue fell headlong from its plinth in homage.

⋙➤ **fertility**

DAIKOKU
Asia (East)

Daikoku, in Japanese Buddhist myth, was the god of wealth, one of the **Seven Gods of Good Luck**. He sat on a throne made from bulging rice-bags, or stood, legs apart, on two sacks. Over his shoulder he carried a sack of jewels, and in one hand he held the hammer of prosperity.

DAITYAS
India

Daityas, in the Vedic myths of the Aryans who invaded India in the seventeenth century BCE, were **giants**, children of **Asyapa** and his wife **Diti**. Their enormous strength was essential at the churning of the **Sea** of Milk (see *amrita*), but they refused to take part in sacrifices and feasts with the gods, and **Indra** banished them to the depths of the **Underworld**, where **Varuna** chained them in lightless, rocky cells. Still, occasionally, they stir and mutter – and the world shudders with **earthquakes**.

DAJOJI
Americas (North)

Dajoji ('panther'), in the myths of the Iroquois people of the Northeastern US woodlands, was the spirit of the West Wind. Its roar was so loud that the Sun turned away, and the sky hid its face in the clouds and wept.

DAKSHA
India

Daksha (also known as Pracheta), in the earliest Vedic myths of the Aryans who invaded India in the seventeenth century BCE, was one of the ten **Prajapatis** ('Lords of **Creation**'); he was himself created from **Brahma**'s right thumb. His particular responsibility was to create gods and human beings, and he did so with gusto. But the process was done by meditation and ascetic practice, and Daksha's own sons were more interested in this exercise than in its outcome, and remained childless. He made 1000 sons, and when they died another 1000, and so on. In the end, bored with this, he invented a new method of creating children: sexual intercourse. He and his wife Asikni made use of it to bring 60 daughters into existence, and he married these daughters to male gods (already created by ascetic practice). In one story, 27 of the daughters were married to **Soma**, and Daksha, irritated because Soma preferred one of them above all the others, put a withering curse on him – which is why the **Moon** still wanes. In another, Daksha's most beautiful daughter, **Sati**, fell in love with **Shiva**, much to Daksha's annoyance. He organized a betrothal feast for her, without inviting Shiva, and told her to garland the neck of her chosen bridegroom. Instead, she threw the garland in the air, and Shiva materialized inside it as it fell to earth.

So Sati married Shiva – and Shiva and Daksha began a feud which lasted throughout the rest of time.

DAMBALLAH
Americas (Caribbean)

Damballah, in Voodoo, was the arch of the **sky**, symbolized as a gigantic **snake**. He was gentle and lazy, basking all day in the warmth of the Sun as it rolled along his body, or dropping down to Earth to swim in favourite lakes, coil himself in trees, and feast on the eggs his worshippers laid out for him. (River-channels and valleys were caused by his writhings across the smooth surface of primordial **Mother Earth**.) He and his consort, the rainbow-snake Ayida, also spent much time coupling, and this intercourse guaranteed the **fertility** of the universe and everything in it.

*Mythographers think that Damballah was derived from the West African snake-god **Da**, taken to Haiti by captives in the seventeenth or eighteenth century CE. In later, Christian, myth he was identified with Saint Patrick, the saint who tamed the snakes.*

DANAË
Europe (South)

Danaë ('parched'), in Greek myth, was the only child of King Acrisius of Argos. Acrisius asked the Delphic oracle if he would have a son to succeed him, and the oracle said that Danaë would have a son who would kill his grandfather. To prevent the oracle coming true, Acrisius locked Danaë in an underground dungeon, lined with bronze. She saw only one female slave, who brought her food and water; no one else was allowed near the dungeon on pain of death. This way, Acrisius hoped, Danaë would never meet a man and never conceive a child.

Zeus, who sees and knows everything, looked at Danaë in her dungeon and was filled with lust. He visited her, pouring through the roof in a shower of gold (or some say, golden rain). From this meeting, Danaë conceived and bore a son, **Perseus**. Slaves told Acrisius that they could hear a baby crying in the bowels of the earth, and Acrisius unlocked the room, locked Danaë and Perseus in a wooden chest and threw them in the **sea**.

But no mortal can drown a god's child unless the god so wills. Zeus' brother **Poseidon** carried the chest safely to the island of Seriphos. Here a fisherman, Dictys, caught it in his net, and found Danaë and Perseus sleeping inside. He took them to his brother Polydectes, king of the island. Polydectes gave them a home in his own palace, and there Perseus grew to adulthood.

Several years passed. Polydectes wanted to marry Danaë, but her years underground had made her terrified of men, and she refused. There was no way to force her so long as Perseus was there to protect her: a god's son, he was more powerful than any mortal king. But then, one day, Polydectes and Perseus happened to be boasting about their respective strength, and Perseus said that if Polydectes wanted it, he (Perseus) would kill a **Gorgon** and bring back its head. Gleefully Polydectes held him to his promise, and as soon as Perseus was gone he tried to snatch Danaë. She took sanctuary in the temple of **Athene**, and Polydectes surrounded the temple with armed guards, and waited for her to weaken.

So things remained for several days, until Perseus flew back on the winged horse **Pegasus**, carrying the Gorgon's head. Polydectes and his men heard the whirring of wings overhead, looked up – and were instantly turned to stone by the Gorgon's glance. Danaë, however, who had kept her eyes modestly on the ground throughout, avoided the Gorgon's glance and was safe. Perseus took her away to Argos, leaving Dictys to rule in Seriphos.

DANANN
Europe (North)

Danann, or Danu, in Celtic myth, was the goddess from whose sons Brian, Iuchar and Iucharbar, all the first supernatural inhabitants of Ireland, were descended. The 'People of Danann' fought epic battles against the Fomori, or **demons**; but in the end, lacking **immortality**, they began to age and fade from the world, and are now diminished to fairy presences in woods, fields and caves. Of Danann herself, nothing whatever is known, though her name (connected with *anu*, 'plenty') suggests that she was a **fertility** or earth-goddess.
⟫→ Mother Earth

DARANA
Australia

Darana, in the myths of the Dieri people of Lake Hope, was one of the supernatural beings who shared the world

142

with humans in the Dream Time. During a drought, he sang and chanted spells to make rain, the desert flowered and the ground was covered with witchetty-grubs. Darana hung them in two bags on a branch and went to invite other spirits to join the feast. While he was away two mortals found the bags and split one of them with a boomerang. The witchetty-grubs at once began glowing with a supernatural light; Darana and the other spirits hurried to kill the young men. Darana made their bodies into destiny-stones and gave them to the Dieri people to guard. If the stones were scratched, it would lead to famine; if they broke, it would lead to the destruction of the universe.

This myth was told to explain the presence of the two stones, the Duraulu, among the treasures of the Dieri people. They were kept in a covering of feathers mixed with lard, and brought out only on the most important ceremonial occasions.
≫→ fertility, prophecy

DASARATHA
India

Dasaratha, in Hindu myth, was a descendant (in some accounts, great-grandson) of the **Sun**, and ruled a peaceful, pastoral people in the fertile land between the rivers Son and Ganges. He had three wives, but no children. In some accounts he sacrificed to **Brahma**, who allowed his wives to become pregnant; in others, **Vishnu** gave the wives *soma* to drink, and this made them pregnant with his own avatar **Rama** and Rama's three brothers. Later, Dasaratha agreed to

do a favour for his second wife **Kaikeyi**, and she asked him to banish Rama (his eldest son and heir) and give the throne to her own son **Bharata**. Dasaratha did as she asked, but soon afterwards died of the shame of it.

DAYUNSI
Americas (North)

Dayunsi ('beaver's grandson'), or Water Beetle, in the myths of the Cherokee people of the Southeastern US, made the Earth. In the days when no worlds existed but **Sky** and Ocean, all living beings were crammed together in Sky, and were crying out for living space. Dayunsi alone lived in ocean, and now he dived to the bottom, brought up a mud-speck which the Powerful One, the Creator, hung from Sky on ropes, one at each compass point. As soon as Earth was dry enough, the creatures of Sky let themselves down on ropes to tenant it.
≫→ animal-gods; creation

DAZHBOG
Europe (East)

Dazhbog ('giving god'), also called Dabog and Dadzbog, in Slavic myth, was the **Sun**, giver of happiness, justice, success and wealth. One of the two sons of **Svarog**, he gradually took over his father's position as **supreme deity**. In Serbian myth he lived in a palace in the East, driving his carriage across the sky each morning. In some accounts he had twelve white horses, in others three, made respectively of gold, silver and diamonds. As he rode the sky he aged, dying each evening and being reborn each morning in full youth and strength. In later, Russian myth he lived in the Sun and ruled twelve kingdoms, one for each sign of the Zodiac.

From the tenth century CE onwards, as Christianity spread through the Slavic lands and the old gods were forgotten or demoted, Dazhbog gradually came to be identified with Lucifer, God's light-bringer who fell from the sky to outer darkness. When the ruler of Kiev was converted to Christianity, Dazhbog's huge statue (with others) was ceremonially toppled into the river and humiliated.

≫→ Saule

DEATH

In most myth-traditions, the gods had three possessions denied to human beings: all-knowledge, all-skill and **immortality**. They helped us with the first two, sending us omens and oracles and teaching us as much of their craftskills and understanding of the universe as humans can cope with. But so far as immortality was concerned, they thought that we were past saving. (This is a marked difference between myth and the teaching of the great surviving religions.) The gods offered us immortality once, and we rejected it or spoiled it. We therefore became the prey of Death, and whether we were summoned by a warrior or a **demon**, whether we went to happy new existences or misery, were matters in which the gods took little interest. Death-gods and Death-spirits were a motley crew, ranging from the grandest of **monsters** (the rage of the gods made manifest) to lackeys whose invitations humans could easily evade – or thought they could.

≫→ **(Africa):** Dubiaku, Gauna, Haiuri; **(Americas):** Ah Puch, Cupay, Ixtab, Mama Brigitte; **(Celtic):** Balor, Dagda, Sucellus; **(Finnish):** Kalma; **(Greece):** Thanatos; **(India):** Kali, Kalki, Rudrani, Shiva; **(Mesopotamia):** Ereshkigal, Nergal; **(Oceania):** Hina; **(Rome):** Mors; **(Slavic):** Baba-Yaga

DEIPHOBUS
Europe (South)

Deiphobus (Deiphobos, 'scared of the spoiler, or 'scared of his [own] spoils'), in Greek myth, was one of the younger sons of King **Priam** and Queen **Hecuba** of Troy. When **Helen**'s husband **Paris** was killed by one of **Philoctetes**' poisoned arrows, all Priam's unmarried sons began squabbling over her. She wanted to marry none of them, and one night hung a rope ladder over the city walls and began to climb down. She meant to go to the Greek camp, find **Menelaus** and beg him to take her back. But when she was halfway down, Deiphobus hauled in the ladder and threatened to kill her unless she married him.

The marriage pleased none of Deiphobus' unmarried brothers. Some even began plotting to betray Troy to the Greeks, to ensure the deaths of both Helen and Deiphobus. And Helen herself, irritated at being forced into marriage by a half-grown boy, refused to sleep with Deiphobus and began treating him like a seven-year-old, leading him by the hand round the city and telling him stories. Before anything further could happen, the Greeks built the **Wooden Horse**, the Trojans dragged it into the city, and the destruction of Troy began. Menelaus stormed into Deiphobus' house to kill Helen, and cut Deiphobus to ribbons before he could find his sword. Helen survived only by baring her breasts to Menelaus, filling him with such lust that he sheathed his sword, threw her on the bed and made love to her then and there beside Deiphobus' corpse.

DEIRDRE
Europe (North)

Deirdre (Derdriu), in Celtic myth, was the most beautiful woman in Ireland. Druids prophesied that she would bring sorrow and death to her country, and she was brought up in seclusion. King Concobar of Ulster, ignoring the prophecy, planned to marry her, but she fell in love with a handsome warrior, Naoise, and fled with him to Scotland. Concobar enticed them back to Ireland, promising that he, personally, would never harm them – and then ordered one of his warriors, Eoghan, to kill Naoise. This treachery caused outrage: many of Concobar's own nobles made war against him, and three hundred men were killed before Concobar won the war. He asked Deirdre which two men she most hated in all the world – and when she said Concobar first and Eoghan second, he decreed that she was to spend a year in turn with each of them, as concubine. Deirdre fled, threw herself from her chariot and was killed on the jagged rocks.

≫+ beauty, Savitri

DEMETER
Europe (South)

Demeter ('earth-mother'; Latin Ceres), in Greek and Roman myth, was the daughter of **Cronus** and **Rhea**, and the sister of **Hades, Hera**, Hestia, **Poseidon** and **Zeus**. When her brothers squabbled for control of the universe she took no part or interest: her favourite place was Earth, and her delight was to tend its plants, bringing each to harvest and ensuring that the seeds were planted and tended for each year's new growth. She kept aloof from males, and only ever allowed herself to be seen or worshipped by females. However, none of this exclusivity worked with her own brothers. In some accounts **Zeus** raped her and fathered **Persephone** on her. In others, she was quietly cropping the grass in a water-meadow, having taken the form of a mare to avoid disturbance, when **Poseidon** reared out of the water, disguised as a stallion, and raped her. Their children were a horse called Arion and a beautiful girl called Core ('maiden'). When Core grew up, she caught the eye of Demeter's third brother, **Hades**, who stole her to the **Underworld** to be his queen and renamed her Persephone.

Demeter wandered the world, distraught, looking for her daughter. She held back the harvest, making the Earth barren. She found comfort only in Eleusis, a small town where there was an entrance to the Underworld, and settled there, refusing to have anything further to do with gods or humankind. Eleusis was soon the only place on Earth still fertile. Demeter had given its king, Triptolemus, **immortality** and shown him how to plough fields and sow grain, the first time this was ever done on Earth. In the end Zeus decreed that for half of each year, Persephone was to stay in the Underworld as Hades' queen, and for the other half she was to return to Earth as Core, bringing back the spring.

*Greek women worshipped Demeter and Persephone jointly as 'The Twain', in mystery rituals from which men were barred. Eleusis became the centre of a mystery cult of another kind, blending rituals to renew the **fertility** of the Earth with those designed to let the initiates pass freely between this world and the Underworld, to escape death. Roman women worshipped Ceres/Demeter at a week-long spring festival at which men were forbidden and which featured solemn singing and dancing, torchlight processions and abstinence from meat, wine and milk products – only direct produce from the earth could be consumed.*

*In literature Demeter plays only a small part, the mother grieving over her daughter's kidnapping or the beaming, somewhat brainless dispenser of the fruits and joys of harvest. In art she appears either as a black-robed, veiled mourner (sometimes being comforted by the **Fates**), or as a buxom, apple-cheeked matron carrying a hoe or sickle and surrounded by cornsheaves, baskets of apples, clusters of grapes and garlands and swags of flowers.*
➤ Great Goddess, mysteries

DEMONS

In most myth-cultures, demons were gods, or the offspring of gods, who had been displaced by newer deities and had lost their creative or protective roles in the universe. They turned to darkness, often living in the Earth's caves and crevices instead of in the

sky, and preyed on the gods, animals and humans. Some worked independently, outlaws from all the hierarchies of **creation**; others hunted in bands and companies, rulers or ministers of the **Underworld**. At their simplest they were **monsters**, revolting and slightly ridiculous; at their most complex they were embodiments of Chaos whose depredations might one day destroy all creation. A few Eastern demons did cross over to the enemy, becoming good-natured and using their powers to protect baby animals or children. But most were evil unregenerate, and to face them was to come to terms with the human race's most devastating nightmares.

➤ (Africa): Oduduwa; **(Americas):** Aunyainá, Bossu, Chonchonyi, Dzoavits, Guecufu, Itzpapalotl; **(Arctic):** Disembolweller; **(Celtic):** Bres, Medb; **(Central and Eastern Europe):** Vampires; **(Finnish):** Surma, Tuonnetar; **(Germanic):** Mephistopheles; **(India):** Asuras, Bali, Drumalika, Hiranyakishipu, Hiranyaksha, Jalandhara, Jara, Kansa, Kubera, Kumbhakarna, Mara, Pisakas, Prahlada, Putana, Rahu, Rakshasas and Yakshas, Ravana, Saktasura, Taraka, Trinavarta, Ugrasura, Vibishana, Vritra; **(Japan):** *Kappa*, Kojin, Oni; **(Mesopotamia):** Beelzebub, Ereshkigal, Lilith, Satan; **(Nordic):** Hel; **(Tibetan):** Lhamo

DENG
Africa

Deng, creator-god of the Dinka people of Sudan, made human beings and gave them a lush, fertile country to live in. But one of them, an extrovert called

Abuk, pounded her corn with such energy that the pounding-pole flew up to **Heaven** and bruised the sky, and Deng was so annoyed that he sent drought and famine to make mortal lives as hard as possible – as they have been ever since.

≫→ creation

DEUCALION AND PYRRHA
Europe (South)

Deucalion (Deukalion, 'sailor on new wine'), son of **Prometheus** in Greek myth, visited his father in his agony on Mount Caucasus, and Prometheus told him that **Zeus** was preparing to destroy all life in a **flood**, and that he (Deucalion) should build a boat, place in it food and **fire** and so survive. When the floodwaters subsided, Deucalion and his wife Pyrrha ('blonde'; daughter of Prometheus' brother Epimetheus) beached their boat on Mount Parnassus and stepped out on dry land, into a world empty of life. Not knowing what to do, they sacrificed to **Gaia** (or some say, Zeus), begging for the Earth to be restocked – and at once plants, insects and animals appeared, a bustle of life all round them.

There were still no human beings, and Deucalion prayed again for guidance. This time a voice from the ground told him to gather his mother's bones and throw them. After a moment's bafflement, he realized that his mother was Gaia herself, and that her bones were stones. He began picking up pebbles and tossing them over his shoulders – and as soon as each touched **Mother Earth**, it turned into a young man. Pyrrha followed suit, and her pebbles turned into women. Ever

afterwards Deucalion and Pyrrha were honoured for renewing Prometheus' original creation, for remaking the human race.

*This amiable myth was given a sour gloss by later philosophers. They pointed out that Prometheus' creatures were mud animated by the breath of a god (**Athene**), and so mediated their earthy natures with a vital spark of the divine; Deucalion's and Pyrrha's human race, by contrast, were entirely stone.*

≫→ Atrahis, Doquebuth, Manu, Noah, Nu'u, Utnapishtim

DEVA
India

Deva ('divine one'), in Hindu myth, was the daughter of the farming king and queen **Nanda** and **Yasoda**. As soon as she was born, she was substituted for the infant **Krishna**, whom the **demon**-king **Kansa** had threatened to kill. The gods, however, protected her, and she soared to **Heaven** in front of the angry demon's eyes.

DEVADATTA
India

Devadatta, in Buddhist myth and legend, was **Buddha**'s cousin. He was the exact antithesis of Buddha: dark instead of light, fury instead of calm, evil instead of good.

Devadatta and Siddhartha. While Prince **Siddhartha**, the future Buddha, was growing up, his inseparable companions were Devadatta and **Ananda**. Devadatta was still a child when he first realized that he was Siddhartha's/

Buddha's sworn enemy: he shot a dove and was furious when Siddhartha nursed it back to life. Later, as youths, Devadatta and Siddhartha took part in a contest for the hand of Princess **Yashodhara**. Siddhartha beat Devadatta at horse-racing, chariot-racing, **music**, oratory and poetry. Devadatta fought and killed an elephant, but Siddhartha managed an even greater feat of strength, picking up the carcass with one toe and hurling it two miles outside the palace. Devadatta won at fencing, and the two young men came equal in archery and wrestling – but still, in the end, Yasodhara's father gave her to Siddhartha, and from that moment on Devadatta was Siddhartha's implacable enemy.

Devadatta and Buddha. Devadatta now allied himself with **Mara**, the Evil One. While Buddha was meditating under the *bho* tree, Devadatta stole his rightful throne, and Mara hurried to tell Buddha. They hoped that he would ride to the rescue, and be killed in the fighting – but Buddha ignored them. When Buddha went out in the world to preach, Devadatta set traps and ambushes to kill him, but all came to nothing. Once, he stampeded a drunken elephant directly at Buddha; but instead of attacking, the animal knelt at the Enlightened One's feet and laid its head on the ground in homage. Devadatta bribed thirty-one warriors to murder Buddha, and further arranged that after the murder two would kill the first, four would kill the two, eight would kill the four, and sixteen would kill the eight. (He planned himself to kill the sixteen, leaving no witnesses at all.) But the plan failed as soon as the thirty-one warriors heard Buddha preaching: they

and all Devadatta's followers were instantly converted. Devadatta had no choice but to try to murder Buddha himself – but before he could reach his presence the ground gaped like a fiery mouth and swallowed him.

⟫→ **light and dark**

DEVAKI
India

Devaki, in Hindu myth, was the wife of **Vasudeva** and cousin of the **demon**-king **Kansa**. The gods foretold that Devaki's son would grow up to kill Kansa, and to prevent this Kansa had her first six children murdered. Then **Vishnu** planted two hairs in Devaki's womb: a white one (which was later transferred to Devaki's sister **Rohini**, and was born as **Balarama**), and a black one which developed into **Krishna**. Long afterwards, when Krishna had fulfilled the prophecy and killed Kansa, and it was time for himself to leave the Earth, Devaki threw herself into his funeral pyre and was carried to **Heaven** with him.

DEVI
India

Devi ('goddess'), in Hindu myth, was **Shiva**'s wife and consort. She was his divine energy personified, and the union of her feminine aspect with his masculine aspect was essential to **justice and universal order**. In some accounts, she came before Shiva, indeed before any of the gods, and the heavenly triad of **Brahma**, **Shiva** and **Vishnu** was a personification of *her* divine energy.

Devi's names and natures. Devi had many names, and many natures. She was

the peaceable mother of all **creation**: Gauri ('yellow'), Jagadgauri ('light of the world'), Jaganmatri ('all-mother'), Mahadeva ('great goddess') and **Uma** ('peaceful'). She was Shiva's beautiful consort **Sati** ('virtuous'), and Sati's reincarnation **Parvati** ('chaste wife'). And she was destructive force incarnate, the warrior goddess **Durga** ('unapproachable') and **Kali** ('black'), the fearsome projection of Durga's anger. In this unforgiving form she was given the honorific names Bhairavi ('terrible') and Chandi ('fierce'), she often made herself into lesser goddesses with deadly powers that were more specific (for example **Shitala** goddess of smallpox), and her courtiers were **vampires**, evil spirits, wizards and the spirits of those who died violent deaths.
≫→ **Great Goddess**

DHANVANTARI
India

Dhanvantari, in Hindu myth, emerged from the churning of the **Sea** of Milk (see *amrita*) with the first cup of immortality-giving liquid. He was immediately appointed physician of the gods – not an immortal himself, but a kind of upper servant – and was also given the job of teaching healing skills to mortals.
≫→ **disease and healing**

DHARMA
India

Dharma, in Sanskrit, means 'that which holds together': natural law, the tissue of moral and religious obligation and custom which guarantees **justice and universal order**, the continuity of existence. In Buddhism it was *dharma* which

Buddha formulated during his meditation under the *bho* tree, and which he later expounded to his disciples. In Hindu myth, Dharma was personified: he was **Brahma**'s son and husband of ten (or, in some accounts, thirteen) of the 50 daughters of **Daksha** whose offspring oversaw universal order.

DHARMAPALAS, THE
Asia (Southwest)

The Dharmapalas, in Tibetan Buddhism, were eight **giant** warriors who defended the True Path against **demons**. Their heads extended from horizon to horizon, and were equipped with razor-fangs, **fire**-tongues and, in the middle of their foreheads, third eyes which seared all enemies of Truth with the light of perfect knowledge.

DHATAR
India

Dhatar (or Dhatri, 'organizer'), in the Vedic myths of the Aryans who invaded India in the seventeenth century BCE, was one of the **Adityas**. He was an inventor and technician, and among his creations were the orbs of the **Sun**, **Moon** and planets, and the sky-bag which contains the **rain**.
≫→ **crafts**

DHRITARASHTRA
India

Dhritarashtra, in Hindu myth, was the blind son of Queen **Ambika**. His elder brother **Pandu** (son of the queen senior to Ambika) died when his five sons were babies. Dhritarashtra therefore acted as regent, and brought Pandu's five sons, the **Pandavas**, up with his own hundred children (known as the **Kauravas** after their distant ancestor Kuru). As the boys reached manhood, however, the Kauravas persuaded him to let them inherit the throne and dispossess the Pandavas. The outcome was a war which engulfed every creature in the universe, and ended only with the death of all 100 of Dhritarashtra's sons. The old, blind regent exiled himself in a forest and became a hermit – and two years later the gods sent a forest fire which removed him from the world in a scatter of ash.

DI
Asia (East)

Di ('powerful one'), or Di Mu ('powerful mother'), in Chinese myth, was **Mother Earth**, the first goddess. In earliest times she was believed to nourish all life, and was worshipped with rituals including not only the sprinkling of libations and offering of sacrifice and grain, but also the burying of scrolls with prayers written on them. (Prayers destined for **Heaven**'s ears were burned, and rose up with the smoke.) In later times she was regarded as the consort of **Tian** (**sky**), sitting with him in Heavenly state; later still the two deities were merged into one, **Shang Di** the Power Above All Powers.

DIANA: *see* Artemis

DIAN CECHT
Europe (North)

Dian Cecht, in Celtic myth, was a god of healing and patron of all human doctors and herbalists. Like most ancient healing gods, he worked some of his cures by magic, plunging the injured into a cauldron of healing which sealed up their wounds. But he also, unusually, did surgery, replacing missing eyes with eyes taken from cats.

⟫⟶ disease and healing

DIDO
Europe (South)

Dido's original name, in Greek and Roman myth, was Elissa ('whirling' or 'possessed'). She was a sorceress and prophetess, married to Sicharbas (or Sichaeus), priest of **Heracles** and ruler of Tyre. When Sicharbas died, Elissa's brother Pygmalion (not the sculptor) seized the throne, and Elissa and fifty male attendants left Tyre forever. They landed first on Cyprus, and Elissa asked or persuaded fifty women to join their expedition. They sailed next to North Africa, where Elissa persuaded the locals to give her 'as much land as could be bounded by one bull's hide'. When they agreed, she sliced the hide into strips as thin as hairs, tied them together and outlined a city-sized piece of prime farmland. She consecrated the boundaries with magic spells, and set her people to build the walls and houses of a city: Carthage. Work was hardly under way when refugees from the **Trojan War**, led by **Aeneas**, landed and asked for sanctuary. Elissa planned to make Aeneas co-ruler of Carthage and so secure the city against its neighbours (who had been dispossessed). But after a few months' dalliance Aeneas sailed to pursue his destiny in Italy, and Elissa stabbed herself to death on a funeral pyre – a ritual act of renunciation and purification. The Carthaginians honoured her ever afterwards as one of the guardians of their city, and gave her the cult-name Dido ('highness' or 'brave one').

The Elissa/Dido myth became seminal to Western culture when Virgil built it into the ideological fabric of his **Aeneid** *some time between the third and second decades* BCE. *Virgil was concerned to project Aeneas as ancestor and role-model for the Roman people, the embodiment of those qualities – nobility, steadfastness, duty, leadership – which Romans, and especially Roman men, thought were quintessential national characteristics. If Aeneas were to be deflected from his destiny (which was to found Rome), it could not be by mere dalliance, and his seducer could not be a simple sorceress. To point up Aeneas' greatness of spirit and the extent to which he was prepared to sacrifice his own wishes for the sake of destiny, it was necessary to write Elissa up – in Roman terms – as a person worthy of attention. Virgil accordingly called her Dido throughout, and gave her every quality of regality and nobility save only masculinity (impossible in the circumstances). It is only after the gods sternly remind Aeneas of his destiny, and he sails headlong for Italy, that Elissa/Dido can abandon herself to what the Romans saw as 'feminine' hysteria and irrationality.*

It is hardly surprising that Virgil's Dido should have appealed to audiences of his own day. But the afterlife of the character is amazing. The Aeneid was for centuries one of the most popular books in Europe, and Dido, as Virgil depicted her, became a kind of unstated template for womanhood: beautiful, devoted, spirited, noble, but above all second to the man for whom she existed and devoid of the ultimate qualities of objectivity and awareness of destiny which marked his gender out from hers. There are marked similarities with the Virgin **Mary**, *as depicted by writers and teachers of the same period, and who served as a model for the 'spiritual' side of womanhood.*

From the Middle Ages onwards, Dido was a favourite figure with European artists of all kinds. She was one of the models for Dante's Beatrice, Petrarch's Laura, Shakespeare's Ophelia, even for such heroines as Richardson's Clarissa or the Duchess in Choderlos de Laclos' Les liaisons dangereuses. Queen Christina of Sweden (1626-89) liked to dress as Dido and re-enact the immolation scene. Painters made great play of the pull in the story between 'classical' poise and 'romantic' passion and extravagance. Dido's life and death were favourite subjects for musicians, and works such as Purcell's Dido and Aeneas or Berlioz' The Trojans add glosses of their own (late Renaissance elegance in Purcell's case, Romantic fervour in Berlioz'), remaking the myth – or rather Virgil's descant on the myth – to suit their own purposes.

What happened to Dido, in short, is that she became less a myth-character than a cultural and social icon. Each European generation projected on to her situation or her character its own preoccupations and perceptions – remaking itself (or at least its women) in her image at the same time as recreating her in contemporary terms. This is a classic process with myth, and Dido is exceptional only in that her basic story (as perceived by later generations) is attributable to a single, known creator, and that Virgil's version takes her so very far from the Elissa with whom the original myth began.

≫→ Guinevere, Parvati

DIEVAS
Europe (East)

Dievas ('heaven-shine'), in Baltic myth, was the most ancient of gods, ancestor of all that exists. In Latvian myth (where he is also called Debestevs, 'father of **Heaven**'), he married the **Sun** and controlled all destiny. In Lithuanian myth he surrendered his powers to the **thunder**-god **Pyerun**, but lived on in a kind of retirement-castle beyond the horizon. Each morning he rode his chariot down the hill of **Sky**, being careful to pass only over weeds and not over growing crops. His castle was the home of the Dead, who (if they were lucky) sailed there on the smoke of their own funeral pyres or along the Milky Way, and (if they were unlucky) had to scramble up the sky-hill by their fingernails.

*Scholars derive the name Dievas (and its various derivatives, such as the Lettish dievs), from the Sanskrit word dyut, 'to shine', and relate Dievas both to the early Indian sky-god **Dyaus** and to the Greek **Zeus** (originally Di-eus). The Latin word for 'god', deus, is also derived from it: hence 'deity'. Some mythographers claim that linguistic derivations like these suggest that there was once one single god, creator and sustainer of all – polytheism is a development and not an archetype of religious belief. The original sky-god is always male, so that these theories are in opposition to those claiming that the original deity was female, the Moon or **Mother Earth**.*

DI JUN
Asia (East)

Di Jun, in Chinese myth, was ruler of the Eastern **sky**. His palace was built not on a mountain but in the branches of a huge mulberry tree, 150km high. In the lower branches of this tree roosted his children, the ten Suns, in the form of huge, three-legged birds. They took it in turns to ride the sky until one day all ten tried to rise at once, and the archer **Yi** shot nine of them dead.

DI KANG WANG
Asia (East)

Di Kang Wang ('king of the Earth's womb'), in Chinese myth, was lord of the **Underworld**. He lived on Earth as a mortal, a Buddhist monk (traditional dates are 618-906CE), and spent his nights not sleeping but sitting upright in his own coffin. When he finally died, his body did not decompose, and unlike other souls (which were deprived of bodies), he went to the **Underworld** intact. Instead of meekly accepting the lot of the Dead, he went round the halls of the Underworld banging on every door in sight and demanding the release of his aged mother (who had been condemned to the Underworld for eating meat). He gathered a posse of other monks, winning them to him by inviting them to a banquet, and they made such a racket that Wang's mother was finally allowed back into the Upper World (as an animal), and he himself was given **immortality** and made ruler of the Dead. His immediate entourage, a blend of the comic and the terrifying, included Yen Wang, judge of the Dead, the **demon** jailers Ma Mien ('horse-face') and Niu Tu ('ox-head'), and the two Ghosts of Impermanence whose job it was to harvest the souls of the dead, Yang Wu Zhang collecting everyone under fifty and Yin Wu Zhang all those of middle age or over.

➢➤ Four Kings of Hell, Ten Yama Kings, Yen Lo

DILWICA
Europe (East)

Dilwica, or Devana or Dziewona, was an ancient Polish **hunting** goddess. She galloped with her followers and hunting-dogs through the forests, eternally radiant, beautiful and unapproachable.

*Scholars suggest that Dilwica (a corruption of the Roman name **Diana**) is a kind of folk-memory of the **Great Goddess**, one of the most ancient deities of all, and that the Roman-derived name was given her in myth instead of the secret names known only to her devotees.*

➢➤ mysteries

DIOMEDES, KING OF AETOLIA
Europe (South)

Diomedes ('godlike cunning'), son of Tydeus and Deipyle, was one of the greatest **heroes** in ancient Greek myth. He led the seven sons of the original **Seven Against Thebes**, went to Sparta as one of **Helen**'s suitors, and shortly afterwards joined the Greek expedition which went to fetch her back from Troy. During the **Trojan War** he fought with enormous bravery, wounding mortal champions such as

Hector and not afraid to fight **Aphrodite** and the war-god **Ares**, both of whom he wounded. He went on several expeditions with **Odysseus**, for example raiding **Rhesus**' camp and stealing the **Palladium**. He was one of the warriors chosen to hide inside the **Wooden Horse**.

While Diomedes was fighting in the war, his wife Aegialea was one of those who believed **Nauplius**' story that their husbands had all died and would never return. She took a lover, Cometes — an affair encouraged by Aphrodite, who was still smarting because Diomedes had wounded her. When Diomedes went home after the war, Aegialea and Cometes plotted to murder him, and rather than wage war on a woman he left Aetolia, settled in Southern Italy and married Euippe the daughter of King Daunus. After several years' rule (during which he founded the city later called Brundisium, and later still Brindisi), he died, either of old age or assassinated by Daunus (who couldn't bear a son-in-law greater than himself). The gods took him into **Heaven**, and changed his followers into swans; to this day they sing dirges and weep for him.

DIOMEDES, KING OF THRACE
Europe (South)

Diomedes ('godlike cunning'), in Greek myth, was a son of **Ares** the war-god and King of Thrace who owned four savage mares. He kept them locked in bronze stables and tethered with iron chains; he invited unwary visitors to dinner, killed them and fed the mares their flesh. As the eighth **Labour** imposed on **Heracles**, **Eurystheus** sent him to capture these mares and bring them to Mycenae. He was sure that not even Heracles would be a match for Diomedes' army, let alone his mares. But Heracles had no trouble at all. In some versions he subdued the army single-handed, laying about him with his club, then fed Diomedes to his own mares and, while they were still docile after their meal, harnessed them to Diomedes' chariot and galloped back to Mycenae.

In other accounts, Heracles took a band of **heroes** to help him, among them his friend Abderus. They crept into Diomedes' palace, freed the mares from their stables and drove them warily across the plain down to the coast. When Diomedes and his men came riding after them, Heracles left the mares in Abderus' charge and dealt with the pursuers by tearing open an underground sea-channel and flooding the plain. He came back to find that the mares had fallen on Abderus and eaten him. Furious, Heracles ran round the newly-formed lake, seized Diomedes, dragged him back round the lake and fed *him* to the mares as well. He founded the city of Abdera in Abderus' honour, populated it with the rest of his crewmen, and drove the mares back to Mycenae. Eurystheus, terrified, told him to take the mares to Mount Olympus and offer them to **Hera**, and Heracles warily obliged.

The second version of the story may have been invented in Abdera, to explain the fact that at the annual athletics festival there, horses were strictly banned.

DIONYSUS
Europe (South)

Dionysus' birth and upbringing. Dionysus ('lame god'; Latin Bacchus, 'raging'), in Greek and Roman myth, was the son of **Zeus** and **Semele**. When **Hera** tricked Semele into asking to see Zeus in full divine splendour, and Semele died as a result, **Hermes** (or some say the river-goddess Dirce) rescued her unborn child and carried him to Zeus – and Zeus, lacking a mother's womb, opened his own thigh, placed the child inside and stitched up the wound. In due course Dionysus was born – and Hera, still angry at Zeus' adultery, sent **Titans** to tear the baby to pieces and stew him; just in time, **Rhea** saved Dionysus, reassembled him and brought him back to life. To protect him from Hera, she disguised him as a girl and took him to Earth to be brought up by his aunt Ino and her husband **Athamas**, and then, when Hera discovered this plot, changed his appearance to that of a ram and gave him for safe-keeping to **nymphs** on Mount Nysa.

Recognizing Dionysus. At first, it was hard for mortals to recognize the grown-up Dionysus as a god. In his childhood he had been treated as ram and girl as well as boy; even now his shape deceived people, and they saw him sometimes as an animal (usually fawn, goat or bull), sometimes as a beautiful and seductive youth, sometimes as a god in full glory. He still had in him a portion of mortality inherited from Semele, and this often blinded people to his true godliness as the 'twice-born', son of Zeus. Hera filled him with wandering madness and sent him roaming across the world. His companions were **satyrs** (led by their king **Silenus**), mountain-nymphs and the wild, dancing women known as Bacchae ('revellers') or Maenads ('women possessed'). They wore fawn-skins and each carried a *thyrsus*, a pine pole twined with ivy and tipped with a pine-cone. Dionysus' ecstasy filled them with superhuman strength, so that neither weapons nor **fire** could harm them; as their dances reached climax they ripped to pieces whatever wild beasts lay in their path – fawns, goats, bulls, lions or, in the case of King **Pentheus** of Thebes who tried to stop their revels, His Majesty himself. Dionysus was particularly friendly with **Apollo**, god of music, and the two gods often led their followers in night-long revels on the slopes of Mount Parnassus.

On one of Dionysus' journeys across the world (some say when he was still a youth), Dionysus was captured by pirates, who took him for a beautiful mortal and hoped to sell him in the slave-market. But when the ship was far out to **sea**, it was suddenly overgrown with vines, the sea changed into wine and Dionysus himself became a lion. The terrified pirates threw themselves into the sea and were changed into porpoises, leaping in Dionysus' honour. On another occasion, dancing with his followers on Naxos, Dionysus came on Princess **Ariadne** of Crete, abandoned there by **Theseus**. He took her as his consort, and they had many children, including (some say) **Hymen** god of the marriage-bond.

Dionysus' power. Dionysus' remnant of mortality made him particularly friendly to human beings, and he spent most of his time on Earth, visiting **Olympus** only rarely. He was forbidden to give human beings any of the secrets of the gods, but instead he made mortal imitations, small glimpses of the delights of **Heaven**. Instead of **ambrosia**, food of **immortality**, he showed mortals how to farm bees for honey; instead of **nectar**, he invented wine for them, with its power to grant a few moments' forgetfulness of the cares of life. He invented the orgasm which crowns the sex-act: a taste of the ecstasy which gods feel unceasingly in each others' company. The invulnerability and strength he gave his devotees was a gift of the same kind: all-consuming while it lasted, but transient. He was the god of the exact moment of choice before surrender to the irrational, when we still have the power to draw back, and choose not to do so. To show human beings the power of this moment, the pleasures of making the right kind of surrender and the pains of resisting or making the wrong choice, he invented the art of drama.

*Dionysus was a favourite subject in art and literature. Poets wrote of his adventures – his dances on Parnassus and his discovery of Ariadne on Naxos were popular themes – and of the ecstasy he granted those who surrendered to him. In surviving Greek drama he makes two spectacular appearances: as the seductive, merciless god who takes Pentheus to spy on the maenads in Euripides' Bacchae, and as the buffoon god of drama who descends to the **Underworld** to bring back a 'classy' poet in Aristophanes' Frogs. Artists loved to show him revelling, surrounded by satyrs,* *maenads and wild animals of every exotic kind (panthers and leopards were popular), and the story of the pirates was a favourite scene on drinking-cups.*

≫→ **Odin**

DIOSCURI
Europe (South)

The Dioscuri (Dioskouroi, 'sons of Zeus'), in Greek and Roman myth, were Castor (Kastor, 'beaver') and Pollux (Polydeukes, 'much sweet wine'). They were **twins**, sons of **Leda** queen of Sparta and **Zeus**, who impregnated her in the form of a swan. (Two double-yolked eggs were hatched as a result of this union: in one were Castor and Pollux, in the other **Clytemnestra** and **Helen**.)

As Leda's mortal husband **Tyndareus** had also slept with her on the same night, it was impossible to say which of the four children were mortal and which immortal. Castor and Pollux grew up as mortal princes, athletes and hunters envied by everyone for beauty and strength. They took part eagerly in any kind of adventure, and in sporting events such as the Olympic Games: Pollux was outstanding at boxing, and Castor at riding and taming wild horses.

Castor's death. Castor and Pollux sailed with **Jason** and the **Argonauts** to find the **Golden Fleece**. Throughout the voyage their fiercest rivals were two other twins, Idas and Lynceus. The rivalry began in a friendly way (for example contests to see who could row longest), but led in the end to blows and death. Castor and Pollux stole cattle (or, some say, girls) from Idas and Lynceus, and there was a battle, during which Idas, Lynceus and Castor were all killed. (Clearly, therefore, Castor was the mortal twin and the son of Tyndareus.) Pollux, grief-stricken at the loss of his twin, begged Zeus to let him share his own **immortality** with Castor. Zeus agreed, and ever afterwards they took turn and turn about, spending one day each in **Olympus** and the **Underworld**.

As part of their heavenly duties, the Dioscuri looked after sailors lost at sea. They appeared to them as will-o'-the-wisps, lights flickering across the waves or dancing at mast-tips to guide their sails. (Even so, these lights were often unreliable: the twins' immortal sister Helen also played will-o'-the-wisp – and she used her light to lure men astray.) They can still be seen in the sky as the constellation Gemini.

DISCORD: *see* Eris

DISEASE AND HEALING
Disease was sent to humans either by **demons** (who were jealous because we were nearer to the gods than they were, who wanted to mar the gods' **creation** or who were malevolence pure and simple), or by grudge-bearing gods on the fringes of **Heaven** or outcast from it. Humans could avoid disease themselves, or wish it on others, by appeasing these powers – but given the demons' disturbed personalities, such attempts often failed. The gods healed us sometimes out of feelings of duty or compassion, sometimes in response to prayers and sacrifice, but

usually because healing was a dimension of their creative and constructive role, part of their continuous work to maintain universal order. Some gods specialized in healing particular diseases, or in herbal medicine or surgery. Others – notably the **Sun**, eternal enemy of darkness and its inhabitants – took a grander and more general view, removing all disease in the same way as they eradicated other blemishes on creation. By healing us, they restored to us our own small segment of **immortality**, and several **mysteries**, concerned with giving their devotees full immortality, were therefore associated with healing, both magic and practical.

⧁→ (Americas): Asgaya Gigagei, Itzamná, Ixtlilton, Uaica; (Arctic): Eeyeekalduk; (Celtic): Belenus, Brigid, Dian Cecht, Finn MacCool; (China): Five Plague Demons, Shen Nong; (Egypt): Imhotep, Khonsu, Sekhmet, Serapis, Thoth; (Finnish): Kipu-Tyttö, Loviatar; (Greece): Aesculapius, Apollo; (India): Ashvins, Dhanvantari, Rudra, Rudrani, Shitala; (Iranian): Haoma; (Japan): Gaki, Okuninushi, Oni, Uzume; (Tibet): Lhamo

DISEMBOWELLER, THE
Arctic

The Disemboweller, in Greenland myth, was the **Moon**'s cousin. Condemned to wander Earth instead of the **sky**, she took revenge by preying on human beings. For preference, she attacked her victims alone in the moonlight (where her cousin could watch her at work); but if all else failed she crept up on them indoors, especially at feasts and family celebrations. She whispered jokes into their ears, so funny that they laughed until their bowels gushed out and they died.

⧁→ **demons**

DITAOLANE
Africa

Ditaolane, in the myths of the Basuto people of Lesotho, was born when the **demon** Khodumodumo swarmed across the Earth, eating every living creature. Ditaolane's mother saved herself by smearing her body with ashes so that she looked like a corpse, and burying herself in a dunghill. The heat of the dung brought on Ditaolane's birth, and he no sooner touched the ground than he became a full-grown warrior with shield and spear. He ran after Khodumodumo, killed it and sliced open its belly to free all the animals and humans inside. He ruled as their chief for many years, and when he died his heart fluttered like a bird from his body and flew to **Sky**, from where he watched over them forever afterwards.

⧁→ **heroes**

DITI
India

Diti, in the Vedic myths of the Aryans who invaded India in the seventeenth century BCE, was the mother of the giant **Daityas**. When the gods refused to admit the **giants** to **Heaven** after the churning of the **Sea** of Milk (see *amrita*), and **Indra** banished them to the **Underworld**, Diti planned revenge. She asked her husband **Kasyapa** to give her a child who would grow up to kill Indra, and Kasyapa agreed, provided that her pregnancy lasted for 100 years and that in all that time she remained unblemished in both mind and body.

Diti kept these conditions until the last second of the last day of the hundredth year, when she was so elated at the thought of Indra's coming death that she forgot to wash her feet before going to bed. At once Indra realized what was happening, and sent a thunderbolt to kill the child in Diti's womb, splitting the embryo into seven pieces. In some accounts, the pieces began to cry so bitterly that Indra gave back their lives, splitting each of the seven into seven more and so cloning his servants, the **Maruts** (storm-winds). In other accounts, **Parvati** was so moved by the embryos' tears that she asked **Shiva** to intervene, and it was he who gave them life. As for Diti herself, she was punished by being made utterly forgettable – and she has remained so ever since, the stories of her offspring being the only things that have kept her name alive.

DJANGGAWUL: *see* Bildjiwuaroju, Miralaldu and Djanggawul

DOMOVOI, THE
Europe (East)

The domovoi (from *dom*, 'house'), also known as Kaukas, Majahaldas and Majasgars, in Slavic myth, was the house-spirit who lived behind the fire and protected the home and family. Originally a servant of **Svarog** the creator, he rebelled and fell from **Heaven** to Earth and down the chimney. He had silky fur and a long beard. In daylight he stayed out of sight, or changed his shape and roamed the woods and fields as an animal; at night he patrolled his human hosts' home, eating the bread and salt left out for him or upsetting pots and furniture if he felt ill-treated.

Each home had its own domovoi, linked with the spirits of the family dead – a notion which led Christians to continue celebrating the domovoi well into modern times. In folk-tales, the domovoi was married to another house-spirit, known variously as Domania, Domovikha and Kikimora. She lived in the cellar or hen house, helped good housewives with domestic chores, and annoyed slovenly ones by tickling their children awake in the middle of the night.

DONAR
Europe (North)

Donar ('**thunder**'), or Donner, the original Northern European **thunder**-god, was merged in later myth with **Thor**, to whom he bequeathed the swastika, symbol of the thunderbolt.

DOQUEBUTH
Americas (North)

Doquebuth, in the myths of the Skagit people, a Salish tribe of the Northwestern US, rode in the only canoe to survive the **flood** which engulfed the primordial world. The canoe was crowded: it also contained two of every living creature in creation, as well as Doquebuth's parents and three other adults. While the animals slept or fought or mated, and the humans paddled this way and that across the featureless sea looking for dry land, Doquebuth was taken over by the spirit of the Great Creator, who told him how to remake the Earth and re-establish life.

*Scholars think that this story is the elaboration of an original creation myth, made in the light of Christian teaching. Who the three spare adults were, or what they did after the Earth was re-established, is not recorded; perhaps they became the ancestors of the Skagit people. In the story itself, they seem to have been just friends and neighbours along for the ride (a memory of Shem, Ham and Japhet in the **Noah** story?), and had no supernatural role to play.*

⟫→ Atrahis, Deucalion and Pyrrha, Manu, Noah, Nu'u, Utnapishtim

DORJE PAHMO
Asia (Southwest)

Dorje Pahmo ('diamond sow'), in Tibetan myth, was the **Great Goddess**. She could take any form she chose, and was worshipped especially as consort of the King of Hell, as a wild sow trampling to death all Tibet's Mongol enemies, as wife of the horse-faced **demon** Tamjin and (by Buddhists) as Marici ('shining one'), goddess of dawn.

⟫→ animal-gods

DRAGONS: *see* monsters and dragons

DRAUPADI
India

Draupadi, in Hindu myth, was the daughter of King Draupada of Pancala. In some accounts, she was an avatar

of **Lakshmi**, and was born from the flames of sacrifice. Her father betrothed her to **Arjuna**, one of the **Pandavas**, but the Pandavas' evil cousins burned the Pandava palace, and King Draupada thought that Arjuna and his brothers had died in the flames. He therefore announced an archery contest, saying that the first person to shoot five arrows through a narrow ring would win Draupadi as wife. All the local princes competed, and none succeeded. Then a dirty hermit stepped forward, shot five arrows unerringly through the ring – and threw off his disguise, revealing himself as Arjuna. (The Pandavas had not died, but had hidden in a forest.) The Pandavas' cousins refused to accept the result, but Arjuna raised his bow and they retreated in panic.

Arjuna ran and told his mother, **Kunti**, that he'd won a magnificent prize. But before he could say what it was, Kunti said he must share it with his brothers. Arjuna took this for an omen, the will of the gods, and so Draupadi became the joint wife of all five Pandavas, sleeping with each in turn two nights out of every ten.

The Pandavas' cousins, the **Kauravas**, were still not satisfied. Their leader, **Duryodhana**, challenged the senior Pandava brother, **Yudhishthira**, to a game of dice – and by cheating, won Yudhishthira's kingdom, his brothers, his own self and Draupadi. At once, the Kauravas began treating Draupadi like the slave she now was, using low-class forms of address and demanding that she fetch them food and drink – and she soared to goddess stature, let her hair stream like fire in the wind, and said that it would stay loose until it was washed in Kaurava blood. This prophecy began war between the Pandavas and Kauravas – a war which swelled until it took in every good and evil power in the universe.

At the end of the war, the victorious Pandavas went on pilgrimage to Mount **Meru**, to beg **Indra**'s forgiveness for killing their own cousins. Draupadi went with them, and died on the way, shedding her mortal self and soaring to **Heaven** before the brothers' astonished eyes.

⋙→ **beauty**

DRONA
India

Drona, in Hindu myth, was a wise man who acted as military adviser and trainer to the **Kauravas** while they were growing up. In the war they fought against the **Pandavas** for power in **Bharata**, he supported the Kauravas even though he knew that they represented the forces of evil in the world – and the gods punished him for it. Drona had a son, **Ashvathaman**, and the gods prophesied that he would be safe so long as his father lived. When Drona took command of the Kaurava forces during the war, the Pandavas and their followers began a rumour that Ashvathaman was dead. The distracted Drona went from man to man, and each repeated the story. Finally he asked the Pandava leader, **Yudhishthira**, convinced that such an honourable man would never lie to him. 'Alas yes, Ashvathaman is dead,' said Yudhishthira – and Drona, heart-broken, gave up the fight and allowed himself to be killed, so missing Yudhishthira's muttered addition, 'Ashvathaman the elephant'.

DRUMALIKA
India

Drumalika, in Hindu myth, was a **demon** who raped **Pavanarekha**, wife of King **Ugrasena** and queen of the Yadava people of Northern India. The demons' idea was to plant a child of their own on the Yadava throne, from where he – and therefore they – would take over the world. But the plan failed because the demon-child, **Kansa**, grew up to be so monstrous that **Vishnu** came down to Earth, as **Krishna**, and killed him.

DUAT
Africa (North)

Duat, home of the Dead in Egyptian myth, was not an **Underworld** but a canyon in **Heaven**, gouged over the years by the wheels of the **Sun**-chariot as it travelled the **sky**, and inaccessible to living beings because its sides were too steep to climb.

DUBIAKU
Africa

Dubiaku ('number eleven'), in the myths of the Asante people of Ghana, was the only mortal to outwit **Death**. He was the eleventh son of a poor family, and he and his brothers ate so much that his mother begged the Sky-spirit to let Death harvest some of them. The Sky-spirit sent the boys to visit Death in her hut, telling them to collect four golden items to prove they'd been there: a pipe, a snuff-box, a chewing-stick and a whetstone. Death set out eleven sleeping mats, and on each of them put one of the visitors and one of her own children. She intended to wait until all the visitors were asleep, then eat them.

Dubiaku's brothers fell asleep, but when Death went to the smallest mat and the smallest brother to begin her feasting, she found Dubiaku still awake and asking for a pipe of tobacco. She fetched her golden pipe, and when he'd finished it he asked for a pinch of snuff, then a chewing-stick and finally something to eat. Death lit a fire, striking sparks from her golden whetstone – and while she was outside gathering food to cook, Dubiaku woke up his brothers. They left their clothes bundled on the sleeping-mats, took the golden objects and crept out, so that when Death came back and found all the children sleeping, it was her own eleven sons she ate.

Death ran shrieking after the eleven brothers. But Dubiaku had told them to hide in a tree, and she didn't see them. She stopped underneath Dubiaku to think where the boys might be, and he spat (or in some accounts peed) on her head. She shouted a falling-down spell, and one by one the boys' bodies dropped from the tree like ripe fruit. But before Dubiaku's turn came he jumped down of his own accord, so evading the spell. He lay still until Death climbed into the tree to see if any children had escaped, then shouted the same spell and brought *her* crashing down.

So Death herself was dead. But when Dubiaku revived his brothers with water-of-life, he splashed it so enthusiastically that he revived Death as well. She chased the boys to the river, where the first ten swam safely over, leaving Dubiaku, who couldn't swim, on the same bank as Death. He changed himself into a stone, and

Death picked him up and threw him at the brothers on the other bank.

*This favourite **trickster**-story is capable of infinite expansion, and was told as a kind of competition, each succeeding narrator inventing ever more outrageous turns and twists. Dubiaku became an Asante cult-hero, honoured as ancestor of all the super-natural beings who chose to live not in **Heaven** but on Earth.*

DUDUGERA
Oceania

Dudugera ('leg-child'), in the myths of the Massim area of Papua New Guinea, was conceived when his mortal mother frolicked in the sea with a god disguised as a dolphin; he was called 'leg-child' because he was born from her leg where the dolphin's scales had rubbed it. Throughout his childhood he was mocked and bullied, and when he grew up he told his mother that he would take revenge by burning the world and every-thing in it. Then he soared into the sky as the Sun, and began shooting fire-spears to burn vegetation and destroy all life. For a time his mother cowered in the shadow of a rock, then picked up handfuls of mud and began throwing them into Dudu-gera's face to blind him. She missed, but the mud became clouds and put out some of the Sun's fire-spears – which is why the world survives.

DUGNAI
Europe (East)

Dugnai, in Slavic myth, had one responsibility only, but it was crucial: she made dough rise.

DURGA
India

Durga ('unapproachable'), in Hindu myth, was a warrior goddess, the power and destructive force of the universe made manifest. In some accounts, she was sleep which conquers all, and arose from **Vishnu** when he meditated on the primordial ocean. In others, she was a personification of the anger of **Shiva**'s consort **Parvati** – and her own anger gave rise to an even more savage manifestation, **Kali**, bursting from her forehead like an explosion of torrential fury. In the commonest myth of all, she came into being as a gathering of all the gods' power, to fight **demons** who threatened to destroy the universe.

Durga and the demon Durga. A **demon** king, Durga, had become so powerful that he conquered Earth, Middle Air and **Heaven**, banished the gods, put an end to sacrifice and prayers, and began to plunder and sack the entire universe. The gods sent a deputation to **Devi**, asking her to help. They pooled their strength, each giving her all the authority and weapons he or she could muster, and Devi set out to fight the demon – alone, but holding in her one person the entire power for good in the universe. Her adversary poured out an army against her – 120 million demon elephant-riders, 100 million charioteers, ten million horsemen and foot-soldiers as countless as ants – and she scattered them with a thunderbolt and then made herself into nine million soldiers who ran after the survivors and killed them all.

The demon and Devi now faced each other, one to one. The demon threw a hailstorm, and the hail changed to knives as it fell; Devi made an umbrella from a thunderbolt and scattered the knives like snowflakes. The demon became a mountain-sized elephant; Devi grew ten thousand swords from her own fingernails and sliced him to pieces. The demon hurled mountains; Devi disabled his throwing-arm with a spear, and he grew a thousand more arms and roared to attack her. She grew a thousand arms of her own (one for each god, and full of that god's strength and fury), wrestled him to the ground and stabbed him dead. His blood tinged the primordial ocean scarlet, then gradually faded from pink through rose to nothing as his power disappeared from the universe forever. Devi took his name, Durga, and used it whenever the gods' destructive rage needed to manifest itself.

Durga and Mahisha. A demon-king, Mahisha, took the form of a gigantic buffalo and terrorized the gods. Since no god could defeat him single-handed, they once again concentrated their energy in Durga and sent her to Mahisha's castle to kill him. She grew ten arms (or, some say, eighteen or even a hundred), each wielding an immortal weapon – they included **Agni**'s lightning-flash, **Indra**'s thunderbolt, **Shiva**'s trident and **Vishnu**'s discus – and rode a tiger for war-steed. Mahisha met her in single combat, changing himself (as demons will) into such shapes as bull and elephant as well as the mountain-sized buffalo in which he began. In the end he became a **giant**, with a thousand arms and whirling a club whose shadow darkened the sky – and Durga stabbed him dead with a single spear-thrust, letting his blood drain in torrents to flood the **Underworld**.

Durga, Sumbha and Nisumbha. Durga used different tactics with the demon-brothers Sumbha and Nisumbha. For eleven thousand years they had prayed and sacrificed to Shiva, asking for immunity against all the gods – and in the end he granted their wish, but immediately sent Durga, a goddess, to deal with them. Taking the form of a seductive woman, she promised to marry anyone who could beat her in battle. The demon brothers sent two armies, numerous as ants; Durga stunned the first army dead with a single roar, and licked up the second like an anteater. Sumbha and Nisumbha gathered a third army, and Durga pulled out the hairs from her head and made them into warrior-goddesses which slaughtered the demons and ate their corpses, while she herself killed Sumbha and Nisumbha and gorged on them.

*Thousands of demon-killing stories are told of Durga – and sculptors and painters have made images of most of them. Durga is usually shown as a serene, smiling warrior, with yellow skin and many arms and riding a tiger. Essentially, to conquer demons she has to be more fearsome than they are, and this has led artists to depict in her their all-but-worst nightmares, so neutralizing the fear because Durga always fights on the side of good, not of evil. (Their worst nightmares are reserved for Kali.) But Durga is also venerated in reposeful form, when she is depicted as a warrior-queen sitting on a lotus-throne, with snakes or flames round her head, a necklace of skulls, and many arms, holding such ceremonial objects as drum, shield, sword and sacred **snake**.*

≫→ **Great Goddess**

DURYODHANA
India

Duryodhana, in Hindu myth, was the eldest son of King **Dhritarashtra**, and leader of the **Kauravas** who fought the **Pandavas** for the throne of **Bharata**. He was unscrupulous and devious, trying to win power first by burning the Pandavas' palace round their ears (they were not inside, as he'd hoped), then by cheating at dice to win the throne from the Pandava leader **Yudhishthira**, and finally by enlisting **demons** and wizards to help him in the war. Despite all his efforts the Pandavas gradually killed every man in the Kaurava army, including Duryodhana's own 99 brothers. Duryodhana escaped only because he was magically able to breathe underwater, and hid in a **snake**-lair under a lake.

When the Pandavas discovered Duryodhana's hiding place, he cravenly offered surrender. But Yudhishthira said that the kingdom must be won fairly in battle, and Duryodhana agreed to fight the Pandavas one by one and hand to hand. But **Bhima**, the first to challenge him, shattered his thigh and left him crippled. That night, Duryodhana planned a final act of treachery. He sent **Ashvathaman** into the Pandava camp to cut all their throats in the darkness. But the gods intervened: the five Pandava brothers were spirited out of camp, and **Shiva** filled Ashvathaman with such a murdering madness that he butchered every man in camp, including Duryodhana's own five nephews (whom he took for the Pandavas). He carried their heads back in triumph, swinging them like onions in a bag – and when Duryodhana saw them he was so horrified that he had a stroke and died on the spot.

≫→ heroes

DXUI
Africa

Dxui was the creator-spirit of the Bush-people of the Kalahari Desert, and was known to other Southern African peoples as Thixo and Tsui. It was a **shape-changer**, and made everything in existence by becoming it, one flower or creature at a time, then leaving its imprint as a **snake** sloughs its skin, and moving on to become something else.

≫→ creation

DYAUS
India

Dyaus ('**heaven**-shine'), in the Vedic myths of the Aryans who invaded India in the seventeenth century BCE, was the **sky**-god and god of **fertility**, often depicted as a bull. He mated with **Privithi** (**Mother Earth**), and among their offspring were **Indra** and (some say) **Agni**. In the **Rig Veda** Dyaus also appears as Dyu-piter ('father of light').

≫→ Dyavaprivithi

DYAVAPRIVITHI
India

Dyavaprivithi, in the Vedic myths of the Aryans who invaded India in the seven-teenth century BCE, was a joining of the names **Dyaus** (Father **Sky**) and **Privithi** (**Mother Earth**). Together, they were *janitri*: that is, parents of the gods, and their children included **Indra**, **Ushas** and (some say) **Agni**. In some accounts they also created **Heaven** and Earth.

DZOAVITS
Americas (North)

Dzoavits, in the myths of the Shoshone people of Nevada and Utah, was a **demon**, a malevolent cannibal **giant**. It stole two of Dove's eggs, and Dove recovered them with the help of Eagle. Dzoavits roared across the world to snatch them back, and the animals united to stop it. Crane held out one leg to make a bridge for Dove across a river, then dropped Dzoavits in the water when it tried to cross. Eagle gave Dove a magic lump of tallow, a stomach-pouch and a beakful of feathers – and when Dove dropped them in front of Dzoavits they turned into a ravine, a cliff and a choking fog to slow the demon down. Finally Badger dug a hole, whispered to Dzoavits that this was where Dove was hiding, and as soon as the demon jumped into it threw red-hot rocks on top of him and sealed the entrance. To this day, Dzoavits writhes and wriggles in his prison – and causes **earthquakes**.

EA
Asia (West)

Ea ('house of **water**'), son of **An** and brother of **Enlil** in Mesopotamian myth, threw dice with his father and brother for kingdoms, and won the world of **water**. In some accounts he made human beings by mixing his own essence (water) with that of his brother (dust) – and went on to give them knowledge and to teach them the arts of **civilization**.

*In art, Ea was shown as a being half fish, half human, riding the waves in the company of his consort Damkina (goddess of the glint of **Moon** on water).*
➤ animal-gods, creation

EARTHBORN GIANTS
Europe (South)

The Earthborn **Giants** (Gegeneis), in Greek myth, were 24 monsters created when blood-drops from **Ouranos**' severed penis (see **Cronus**) fertilized **Gaia** (**Mother Earth**). They were creatures of air and rock. Not all had names, but those which had included Agrius ('untamable'), Alcyoneus ('brayer'), Aloeus ('of the threshing-floor'), Clytius ('renowned'), Enceladus ('buzzer'), Ephialtes ('leaper'), Eurytus ('rapids'), Gratium ('grater'), Hippolytus ('stampede'), Mimas ('mocker'), Otus ('resister'), Pallas ('handsome'), Polybutes ('cattle-lord'), Porphyrion ('purple one'), Thoas ('fast') and Tityus ('risker').

When the gods dethroned the **Titans** (who were brothers and sisters of the Earthborn Giants), the Giants determined to attack **Olympus** and take vengeance. Because they were made from Earth, there was no way to destroy them so long as they remained near their place of birth. If they were killed they simply melted into their

Eve tempted by the Serpent (*William Blake, 18th century*)

native soil, were reborn and sprang up again. For this reason they decided to attack Olympus from their actual birth-place, Phlegra in Northern Greece, and to give themselves extra protection they began looking for the magic herb *ephialtion* ('pouncer') which healed the wounds of anyone who chewed it. While some of the Earthborn Giants searched for *ephialtion*, the others be-gan piling mountains and making a tower of stones in Phlegra: when it was high enough they meant to jump across into Olympus and attack the gods.

Unfortunately for the Earthborn Giants, their physical strength was not matched by brains, and they spoiled their surprise attack by pelting Olym-pus with boulders and trees from their tower long before it was finished, trying to terrify the gods. **Hera** told the gods that they would lose the coming fight unless they found *ephialtion* before the Earthborn Giants did, and enlisted the help of a mortal, **Heracles**, the only being in the universe strong enough to outfight the Giants. The **Sun** and **Moon** held back their light, **Athene** hurried to find Heracles, and the other gods began groping for *ephialtion* in all the world's corners and crevices. At last **Zeus** found it and took it to Olympus.

While this was going on, the Earth-born Giants had taken advantage of the darkness to finish their pile of stones. When the Sun and Moon began to shine again, the first thing the gods saw was Alcyoneus on top of it, ready to jump into Olympus. The sudden light dazzled him, and while he teetered on top of the stone-pile, shading his eyes, Heracles shot him and toppled him, then jumped

from Olympus, caught him before he could touch **Mother Earth**, dragged him away from his native Phlegra and clubbed him dead. Meanwhile, the other Earthborn were clambering up the stone-pile and leaping into Olym-pus. Their strength equalled that of the gods: the Olympians could wound them and hold them back, but only Heracles could finish them. Porphyrion tried to strangle Hera; he was slowed down by an arrow from **Eros** and a thunderbolt from Zeus, but it was not until Heracles climbed back from Phlegra and shot him that he finally died. Ephialtes beat **Ares** to his knees and was about to finish him, when he was stopped by an arrow from **Apollo** in his left eye and one from Heracles in his right.

The battle raged on. **Dionysus** fought Eurytus; **Hecate** fought Clytius; Athene fought Pallas (later taking his name as an honorary title); **Hephaestus** fought Mimas with a red-hot ladle; the **Fates** beat back the other Giants with pestles and mortars from the Olympian kitch-ens. Each time one of the Earthborn Giants fell, Heracles was there with arrow or club to finish him. At last the Earthborn Giants gave ground, and began scrabbling down their stone-pile to safety in Phlegra. But the gods ripped up **mountains** and islands and hurled them after them. Athene crushed Enceladus with Sicily; **Posei-don** broke off Nisyros, part of the island of Kos, and used it to smash Polybutes under the sea and drown him. The Earthborn Giants made a last rally at Trapezus, but far from their native region they were no match for Hera-cles' arrows, and were all finally killed. Their huge bodies were buried deep in

Mother Earth, and a volcano was piled high above each of them so that they could never rise again.

In historical times, quantities of dinosaur bones were found in the region of Trapezus, suggesting that this myth was invented in prehistoric times to explain them. In another version, only two Giants attacked Olympus. They were Otus and Ephialtes, and they were the sons not of Ouranos but of Aloeus. They began by capturing Ares, god of war, and imprisoning him in a bronze jar. Then, instead of a stone-pile, they stacked Mount Pelion on Mount Ossa and besieged Olympus. They were defeated not by brawn but by brains: Athene offered to sleep with Otus if he lifted the siege, Otus boasted to Ephialtes and the two giants quarrelled and killed each other.

EARTHQUAKES: *see* Bochica, *Daityas*, Moshiriikkwechep, Poseidon, Qamaits, Ruaumoko, Vasuki, Yambe-Akka

ECHO
Europe (South)

Echo, daughter of **Gaia (Mother Earth)**, in Greek and Roman myth, was one of **Hera**'s handmaids. Hera used her to spy on **Zeus**' love-affairs, and instead of keeping them for Hera's ears alone, she gossiped about them to the other gods. Hera punished her by banishing her to Earth and taking away both her shape and her power of speech, making her a disembodied entity which could only repeat questions put to her. On Earth, Echo fell in love with **Narcissus**, but was unable to make contact with him and pined until Gaia took pity on

her and absorbed her into the stones of rocks and hills – which still echo to this day.

EEYEEKALDUK
Arctic

Eeyeekalduk, in Eskimo myth, was a healing-god. He was a tiny old man, whose face was a speck of jet and who lived inside a pebble. He cured you by looking at you, drawing the sickness out of you along the sightline from his eyes. This meant that it was dangerous for healthy people to gaze into his eyes: all kinds of illnesses might travel in the wrong direction.
➤ **disease and healing**

EGYPTIAN MYTH

Like everything else about ancient Egypt, the nature of the country's myths, and of the religion and society they sustained, was dictated by two factors above all others: geography and enormous, unbroken stretches of time. Egypt may have existed as a single country for some five millennia before the Christian era; even its recorded history reaches back to 2600BCE, the approximate date of the Great Pyramid supposedly designed by **Imhotep**. From those early days until the Roman conquest in the first century BCE, there was a continuous cultural progression, of eighteen royal dynasties stretching over five historical periods. There were upheavals (for example during Akhenaten's brief reign in the fourteenth century BCE, or after the arrival of the Greeks a thousand years later), but by and large a time-traveller from the First

Dynasty would have found much to recognize, in language, religious practice and cultural attitudes, in the Egypt of the Eighteenth Dynasty some 2500 years later.

Conservatism on this scale was one result of Egypt's geographical situation. The country was not entirely insulated from the outside world – Nubians invaded it from the South in earliest times; the Hebrews under Moses escaped from it; Mycenaean, Phoenician and Roman traders did business in the Delta – but it was extremely hard to reach or leave. There were mountains to the South, seas to the North and deserts to East and West. The entire country enfolded the river Nile like the trunk of a tree, habitable on either side for less than a kilometre, until the lush arable lands of the Delta spread out from the river like foliage. It is hardly surprising that Egyptian culture was inward-looking, and that its earliest gods were associated with the river (**Hapi**), with the annual floods (**Khnum**), with the blaze of the Sun (ubiquitous deity of many names, of which **Ra** and **Horus** were merely two of the best-known) and with such implacable desert beasts as lions (**Ammut, Sekhmet**), scorpions (**Serqet**) and snakes (**Aapep, Nehebkau**).

If geography necessitated both isolation and continuity, the annual floods also imposed a recurring pattern on both civic and religious life. It was a small step from building the gods temples in imitation of human houses, and assuming that they might like to leave them and visit their friends and relations, to turning those journeys into ceremonial processions and insisting that the river's annual flooding de-pended on exact ritual duplication every year. The temples of the grandest deities were barred to ordinary mortals: they could be entered only by gods and their families (including the temporal rulers, regarded as gods' children) and by the priests who were their slaves. Priests guarded temple ritual and the myths which upheld it with a scholastic fervour which led to a vast edifice of protocol, sacred knowledge and above all secrecy. Myths grew by a process of accretion, but only parts of them were 'active' at any particular moment, as they were needed for this or that cere-mony. Other details were buried in the dust of archives, or of memory, once-relevant precedents which might or might not ever again see the light of day.

Popular religion, by contrast, was cheerful, open and practical. It treated the gods with an insouciance lacking in the main temple-cults. They were like members of one's own extended family, helpful, irritating, amusing or charming. Creation was not a matter of huge cosmic forces coming together, as in the main cults, but of a weaver (**Neit**) making the universe on her loom, a metal-worker (**Ptah**) forging living beings, or a potter (Khnum) moulding them on his wheel. The power of nature was a **bull** (**Hap**), and its **fertility** was a cow (**Hathor**). A dung-beetle (**Khepri**) rolled the Sun up the sky each morning; a cat (**Bastet**) protected houses against fire; a brick (**Meskhent**) acted as mid-wife to women in labour. The popular pantheon, based on the idea that every-thing, alive, dead or merely a concept, could be a god, contained thousands upon thousands of deities, each of whom had a role in the continuity of life. A frog (**Heqet**) might help with creation, a signpost (**Min**) might acquire new powers as god of sex, a dwarf (**Bes**) might protect against **demons**, and a bird (the **Benu bird**) might carry the Sun's rays from **Heaven** to Earth.

The compendious nature of the temple cults made it possible for many of these popular, local gods to cross over into more 'formal' mythology. It is a feature of Egyptian religion that it was never exclusive, that new deities, and variant accounts of old ones, were welcome side by side with those which had existed for centuries. Egyptian priests had no canon of belief; even ritual, scrupulously observed, used only what it needed. If the stories which accreted over the years were incompatible or inconsistent, that was not a problem for resolution but part of the rich totality of belief. The dozen different creation-stories, for example, involve an assortment of gods and a variety of methods – and no attempt was ever made to harmonize or rank them.

Nevertheless, and inevitably, over the centuries some cults did dominate, and their beliefs and myths spread far beyond their local areas. The reason was political. Since the pharaohs and their families were regarded as incarnations either of already-known deities or of gods who had not previously appeared on Earth, it followed that the grander the dynasty and more impressive its earthly dominion, the more widespread the religious myths with which it was associated. (This preponderance has tended to be repeated in modern times. Archaeologists naturally begin their investigations with sites of 'major' importance, and one fall-out is that the cultures and myths of those areas tend to swamp all others.) One myth-cycle in particular has dominated surviving Egyptian myth: that based on the towns of Yunu (known in the Bible Old Testament as On, to the Greeks as Heliopolis, and now a suburb of Cairo) in the North and Thebes (modern Luxor) in the South.

The cycle centred on nine gods, the **Ennead**: Ra the Sun (in his manifestation as **Atum** the creator) and four pairs of his descendants: **Shu** and **Tefnut**; **Geb** and **Nut**; **Aset** (Isis) and **Osiris**; **Set** and **Nebthet**. Two themes dominated the myths. First, the idea that light was permanently in conflict with darkness led on the one hand to a group of myths concerning the battle between Set (dark), Osiris (light) and Osiris' son Horus after Set killed Osiris, and on the other to a sequence involving the sailing of the Sun above the Earth during the day and through the **Underworld** at night, and the attempts of various demons (led by Aapep, embodiment of chaos) to engulf it. Second, the vexed problem of how, if gods were immortal, they could be killed (as Osiris was by Set) inspired a cult of reincarnation, sustained by a series of stories about **Duat**, the Underworld, what happened to souls when **Anubis** led them there, how they were judged (by Osiris, assisted by **Maat** goddess of truth), and how they were then returned to life.

The other major myth-cycle was less ritual-oriented and more philosophical. It arose in Khemenu (Greek Hermopolis) in Upper Egypt, roughly midway between Yunu and Thebes, a place where the world was held to have come into being. Its heart was a group of eight deities (the **Ogdoad**), not so much beings as abstract ideas embodied. Each had a male and female form: those for wetness were **Nun** and **Naunet** (who became the primordial ocean), those for darkness were Kek and Keket, those for infinity were Heh and Hehet, those for invisibility were **Amun** and **Amaunet**. (Amun later became the supreme power in the Egyptian universe, god of gods, was merged with the Sun and worshipped as Amun-Ra). In common with consistent practice, which allowed all Egyptian gods to take the forms of humans, animals or hybrids as they chose – perhaps a memory of the earliest, animal-spirit gods of all – the Ogdoad were imagined as baboons (symbol of long life and wisdom), and then, when the Yunu-Theban Ra-cult became all-pervasive, as a group of baboons lifting their arms to worship the rising Sun.

One result of the hermeticism and introversion of Egyptian religion, on the one hand, and on the other of its (paradoxical) openness to new ideas, was that it was always fertile ground for cults and **mysteries**. The shortest-lived was that of **Aten**, the One God established by Pharaoh Akhenaten before the arrival of any other monotheistic cults in world religion, and which lasted just one generation before being re-engulfed by the politically stronger Amun-cult. But three others were far more lasting, among the most important mystery-cults of the ancient world. One (the **Serapis** cult) blended worship of Osiris, god of the Underworld, with that of Hap (Greek Apis) the Bull,

who represented the power of universal light, making the single deity Serapis whose devotees were promised eternal life. (The Serapis cult, with its rituals of bull-sacrifice, was popular in Roman Egypt, and spread from there throughout the Roman Empire.) The second, 'Mysteries of Isis', much favoured by upper-class Greek and Roman women, was an ecstatic healing-cult derived from worship of Aset and drawing particularly on the myth of her grief for and reconstitution of her husband Osiris after he was dismembered by Set. Thirdly, one of the earliest Egyptian gods of all, **Thoth**, entered the Hermopolitan pantheon as a creator, was then transformed into the god of scribes, and inspired a mystery-cult based on secret writings which were supposed to contain the secrets of the universe. The cult began in prehistoric times, became prominent in the second millennium BCE, was adapted 1000 years later into the Greek Egyptian mystery-religion of Hermes Trismegistus, Magus of Magi – and still, 2000 years later, has adherents not only in Egypt but throughout Europe and the US, remarkable, if bizarre, testimony to the hold Egyptian myths and beliefs have always had on the imagination of all who encounter them.
»→ Hapy, Imhotep, Mahaf, Mut, Nefertem, Seshat, Taweret

EHECATL
Americas (Central)

Ehecatl, in Aztec myth, was a wind-god who fell in love with a beautiful mortal, Mayahuel. He caught her up in his embrace, laid her on the ground and made love with her. Unfortunately, mating with a god was too much for Mayahuel, who died of it. Ehecatl buried her in the ground, and a tree grew from her grave with branches like outstretched arms. Ever afterwards, Ehecatl moped and searched the world for another woman as beautiful as Mayahuel – and mortals heard his sighing as the wind which stirred the trees, and whose sound gave the god his mortal name.

EIGHT GODS, THE
Asia (East)

The Eight Gods, in Chinese myth, were those annually honoured by the Emperor, on behalf of the whole people, because they were thought to control all existence. They were Earth, **Moon**, the Seasons, **Sky**, **Sun**, Yang, Yin and **War**.

EIGHT IMMORTALS, THE
Asia (East)

The Eight Immortals (Ba Xian), in Chinese Daoist myth, were a group of people who all lived mortal lives on Earth (and in some cases were historically real), who achieved **immortality** in different ways, and then spent eternity together, travelling to see and perform wonders. In myth they were treated as exemplars of those who renounced the world to find the Way; in folk-tale they figured as a kind of travelling circus, their adventures being told with a mixture of wonder and affectionate satire.

The Eight Immortals were Han Xiang, He Xiangu, Kao Guojiu, Lan Kai He, Li Xuan, Lu Dongbin, Zhang Guo and Han Zhongli. Han Xiang, a philosopher of the ninth century CE, achieved immortality by falling out of the Sacred Peach Tree, grabbing a branch to save himself, and being granted immortality just before he hit the ground. He Xiangu was a woman of the seventh century CE who achieved immortality by grinding up a gemstone – or some say a pit from one of the Sacred Peaches – and drinking it. She later became the goddess of housekeepers. Kao Guojiu, brother of the Empress Kao in the eleventh century CE, was so disgusted by corrupt court life that he went to the mountains and learned from two other immortals, Li Xuan and Lu Dongbin, how to achieve immortality.

Lan Kai He has two different stories. In one, she (or he – 'a man who didn't know how to be a man', as the storyteller puts it) was a drunken beggar and busker who was one day carried into **Heaven** and granted immortality, becoming the protector of the destitute. In others, she/he found a beggar and bathed his sores, only to find that he was Li Xuan in disguise. Li Xuan ('iron crutch') in some accounts was given immortality, and his crutch, when the goddess of the Western Paradise found him limping and begging beside her path. In others he received it when the Daoist philosopher Ning Yang (who should have been left seven days between dying and being cremated) was burned to ash a day too early, and assumed the nearest body, that of a dead beggar, to use throughout eternity. He became the god of the disabled. Lu Dong Bin, a prince of the eighth century CE, was warned in a dream that if he continued his royal life he would end up banished in disgrace, and turned instead to the Way, being instructed in immortality by Han Zhongli. Zhang Guo, an eighth-century ascetic, achieved immortality simply by never dying. He rode a magic donkey which, when not in use, could be folded up like a sheet of paper and put in his pocket. Han Zhong Li, an army officer and state official of the first century BCE, retired from public life to become a hermit and to study alchemy, and achieved immortality when the wall of his cave split open and revealed a box containing the elixir of eternal life.

The Eight Immortals were favourite subjects for art, usually a blend of the charming and the comic. Each had his or her own characteristic possession – a tobacco-pipe, a musical instrument, a basket of flowers – and magic steed, and artists used the group to show different types and physiognomies of venerability, beautiful womanhood (in the case of He Xiangu) and above all cheerfulness. A particularly popular story was the folktale telling how the Eight Immortals travelled to see the wonders of the underwater realm of the Dragon Lord of the Sea. They threw their characteristic possessions into the water, where they turned into submersible boats, and reached their destination after a memorable journey during which they were attacked by the Dragon King and his even less friendly son, and drove them off by magic.

EKKEKKO
Americas (South)

Ekkekko, god of good luck in the myths of several peoples from the borders of Bolivia and Peru, was named for his chuckling laugh. He was a fat dwarf who travelled from market to market, carrying on his back a bottomless sack of pots, pans, knives, clothes, combs and every other kind of household good. If you saw him and joked with him, your luck was made for the day; if he gave you one of the goods he carried, you were rich for life.

EL
Asia (West)

El ('that one' or 'the power'), in Canaanite myth, was the supreme being, creator of the universe and everything in it. Originally he was described as king and father – his consort was the **sea**-goddess Asherat and one of his sons was the storm-god **Adad** – and was depicted either as a bull or as a bull-horned, bearded ruler riding a chariot or sitting on a throne. But later myth described him as an aloof, insubstantial figure, more the idea of godhead than its bodily manifestation – and this more philosophical conception led Hebrew scholars to equate him with **Yahweh**, and say that El, so far from being a god, was merely one of the names of God.
⇒ creation, supreme deity

EL DORADO
Americas (South)

El Dorado ('the golden man') was the translation by Spanish explorers of the original name (now lost) of a fabulous golden king who ruled the city of Manoa beyond the Western horizon. Each morning, he was bathed in oil and then covered in gold-dust from head to toe. Modern scholars say that this was a description of the **Sun**; but the

Spaniards (and those English explorers who followed them, including Sir Walter Raleigh), assuming it to be literally true, pushed ever Westwards into South America to find El Dorado's treasure-hoards.

ELECTRA
Europe (South)

Electra (Elektra, 'amber'), in Greek myth, was the daughter of **Agamemnon** and **Clytemnestra**, and the sister of **Iphigenia**, **Chrysothemis** and **Orestes**. When Clytemnestra took **Aegisthus** as lover, Electra smuggled Orestes (the legitimate heir to Agamemnon's throne) out of Mycenae to safety in Phocis. Ten years later, after Aegisthus and Clytemnestra murdered Agamemnon, Electra sent for Orestes, brought him back in disguise and helped him to kill them. After the joint execution, she married Orestes' companion Prince **Pylades** of Phocis, and disappears from myth.

Electra's comparatively shadowy role in the original myth is not matched by her extraordinary status in literature, particularly in tragic drama. The great Greek tragedians depict her as a suffering heroine, loyal to her dead father, and tormented almost beyond endurance by seeing Agamemnon's murderers roistering on his throne. In Aeschylus' Oresteia she completes Orestes' education, so to speak, by 'manning' him to murder Clytemnestra. Sophocles, in his Electra, gives her magnificent arias of despair and longing for vengeance, furious arguments with Chrysothemis and Clytemnestra, and one of the most touching recognition scenes in drama. In Euripides' Electra and Orestes she is like a rudderless ship. The moral and political anarchy created by Agamemnon's murder have all but destroyed her sanity, and much bleak humour is made from her inability to cope with either the grief she suffers, the bloody revenge she and Orestes undertake, or the Fury-ridden madness of Orestes which follows it – they do what they do, and suffer what they suffer, almost by accident, sleepwalking in nightmare. Later writers have tended to follow the Sophoclean portrait: two notable examples are Hofmannstahl (whose Electra was used as the libretto for Strauss' opera) and Henry Treece (who turned the story into a death-haunted historical novel).

ELLAL
Americas (South)

Ellal, in the myths of the Tehaelche people of Patagonia, was the first benefactor of the human race. Before he was born, his father planned to eat him, but Rat saved him and hid him in a hole in the ground, where he grew to maturity. At that time, a race of **demons** ruled the world, and Ellal killed their leader not by force of arms but by letting the demon swallow him alive, then turning into a gadfly and giving him a poisoned sting. Released once more into the world, Ellal bent trees and reeds to his will, making the first bows and arrows. He gave these to his human worshippers, then harnessed a swan and flew on its back up streams of sunshine into the morning **sky**.

ELLI
Europe (North)

Elli ('age') was an old woman with whom **Thor** wrestled in Utgard. Thor lost the match – not surprisingly in view of Elli's real identity.

ELPENOR
Europe (South)

Elpenor ('hope to be a man'), in Greek myth, was **Odysseus**' cabin-boy. He was one of the crew changed into pigs by **Circe** and then freed after the gods helped Odysseus escape her magic. At the banquet which followed, he got drunk for the first time in his life, and went to sleep it off on the flat palace roof. Next morning, Odysseus and the rest of the crew left suddenly, terrified by Circe's prophecies of what would happen when Odysseus visited the **Underworld**. Elpenor heard them, ran to shout to them to wait, fell from the roof and broke his neck. Odysseus was astounded to see his ghost in the Underworld, crying for his lost future as a man and begging for burial, and as soon as he could he hurried back to Aeaea, buried the boy's body on a headland and stuck his oar upright in the grave-mound as a memorial.

ELYSIUM
Europe (South)

Elysium ('relaxation'), sometimes called the Elysian Fields, in Greek and Roman myth, was an island which floated in the deepest swirls and eddies of the **Underworld**. Unlike its surroundings, it was green, fertile and pleasant, filled with bird-song and lit by a **Sun** and stars which were like those on Earth but were its alone. It was the home of dead **heroes** who had lived honourable and blameless lives in the upper world. In Elysium they feasted, exercised their horses, played manly games and sports, enjoyed poetry and **music** and indulged in solemn philosophical conversations. There was no anger, and (since every soul which entered the Underworld drank the water of **Lethe** which made it forget its former life) no enmity: in Elysium, even bitter adversaries became friends.

This agreeable projection onto the after-life of the upper-class (male) Roman's idea of a good time infuriated the early Christians, who depicted Elysium as a kind of never-ending debauch, corrupting the souls of the heathen just as their Godless bodies had been debauched in life. From it came the medieval European notion that one of the torments of Hell was 'perpetual orgy', a state fondly depicted by anonymous sculptors on church walls and woodwork – devils are drunk and pot-bellied and cram their victims with goodies of every unCalvinist kind – and made even more surreal on the canvases of such later artists as the Brueghels and Hieronymus Bosch.
≫→ **Avalon, Heaven, Valhalla**

EMBLA: *see* Ask and Embla

EMPUSA: *see* Lamia

ENDYMION
Europe (South)

Endymion ('seduced'), in Greek myth, was a handsome shepherd, tending flocks on Mount Latmos. One night the **moon**-goddess **Selene** saw him sleeping naked on the mountainside, and fell in love with him. She soared to Earth in her silver chariot, made love with him, and then, to keep him for herself, gently kissed his eyes. From then onwards he was never seen again by mortals, but stayed in a dreamless sleep, never aging and waking up only at night when Selene visited him. They had fifty daughters, star-children still visible in the evening sky.

In some accounts, Endymion's lover was **Artemis***, not Selene – and he led an exhausting double life, spending his days in the mortal world as the husband of a princess and father of a royal dynasty, and his nights on the mountainside with the goddess.*

»→ Adonis, beauty, Ganymede

ENKI
Asia (West)

Enki, in Mesopotamian myth, was a **trickster**-god who created and sustained all life on Earth. He was the lord of **water**, and lived with his wife, the earth-goddess **Ninhursaga**, in a paradise called Dilmun. At the time, they and Dilmun were all that existed, and there was peace in the universe. But then Ninhursaga began to feel desire. She longed to be caressed by Enki, and begged him to let his waters lap into her folds and crevices. Enki did as she asked – and when she gave birth to a daughter, he coupled with her too, and in due course with *her* daughter, his grandchild. He enjoyed **sex** so much that be began creating mountains, valleys, rocks, animals and insects simply for his own pleasure. The water which was his sperm gushed everywhere, and wherever it went, new **creation** happened.

Alarmed at this incessant fecundity, Ninhursaga tried to dam it. She took eight of Enki's sperm from the womb of Spider (whom he'd also created and mated with) and planted them in the ground. They grew into plants, the first ever seen on Earth – and Enki fell on them and ate them ravenously, the first harvest and first meal. Ninhursaga made sure that he at once fell ill with stomach cramps. But the agony killed him, and the only way she could think of bringing him back to life was to bury him in her womb and give birth to him.

Enki created human beings. He worked like a sculptor, shaping a human figure from clay. Then he used that figure to make a mould, and the mould to make replicas which he fired in an oven. His creatures were soon as numberless as stalks of grass in a field, and like a child with a dolls' house, he made a city and peopled it with them. Some were fully baked, and took their place as princes, priestesses, farmers and merchants. Others were half-baked, and since what had been created could not be unmade, Enki taught them skills and gave them roles in life, as dancers, musicians, poets and prostitutes.

*The city built by Enki was identified as the real Eridu, in the marshes of Southern Iraq: the creation-story told above was its foundation-myth. The people of Eridu said that Enki filled their city with treasure – not gold or silver but a pile of gifts such as divinity, families, happiness, honour, kissing and trading – and that other gods kept trying to steal them for their own cities and their own people. In other parts of Mesopotamia, Enki was regarded merely as a trickster who outwitted **giants** and* *demons* and annoyed the gods with pranks. *(When, for example, the gods sent a **flood** to exterminate the human race, he showed **Utnapishtim** how to survive it.) In countries at the upper tip of the Fertile Crescent, he was identified with a much more august divinity: **Ea** the water-lord, son of **An**.*

»→ Chinigchinich, Esaugetuh Emissee, fertility, Humanmaker, Hurukan, Na'pi, Prometheus, Tagaro, Woyengi

ENLIL
Asia (West)

Enlil ('windlord'), in Mesopotamian myth, was the son of **An** and brother of **Ea**. In some accounts he threw dice with his father and brother for kingdoms, and won the world of Earth; in others he prised his father (**Sky**) from his mother (Earth) after he was conceived, usurped his father's place and began gusting round Earth, fertilizing her with storms and **rain**.

Enlil and Cosmic Order. Enlil fathered the **Moon**, the stars and a whole family of gods, and gave each of them a place and a task in the order of the universe. He sent them his orders by a trusted **messenger**, the **giant** Anzu. But his trust was misplaced: Anzu waited until he was bathing, then stole his clothes and the thunderbolts which contained his power. But Anzu, being (like all giants) without brain, had no idea how to use Enlil's powers to guarantee **justice and universal order**, and the universe would have collapsed in chaos if **Ninurta** the war god had not snatched back the thunderbolts and returned them to Enlil.

Enlil and Human Beings. Enlil supervised the Igigi, god-slaves who saw to such menial tasks on Earth as keeping the channels of the rivers Tigris and Euphrates free of sand. But he was a cruel master, and the slaves, led by We-e ('thinks of things') mutinied. Enlil's wife Nintur solved the problem by killing We-e, mixing his blood with sand and creating a new slave-race to dig out the water-channels and till the soil: human beings. To prevent them rising above themselves as the Igigi had done, Enlil denied them **immortality**. But this meant, if he wanted a constant supply of slaves, that he had to allow them reproduction – and over the centuries humans became so numerous, and so noisy, that he decided after all to destroy them. He tried several times to eliminate them: first by sending the plague-god Namtar to cull them, then by preventing animals and plants growing for them to feed on, and finally by flooding the entire world and drowning them. Each time they were saved (helped in some accounts by Enlil's brother Ea, in others by the trickster-god **Enki**), and finally the other gods forced Enlil to let them live and tolerate their noise. Storm-winds and hurricanes, the myth ends, are his snorts of fury whenever our human racket keeps him awake.

ENNEAD, THE
Africa (North)

The Ennead ('group of nine'), in Egyptian myth, was the (Greek) name given by scholars to the gods worshipped at Yunu (Heliopolis): **Ra** the **Sun** (in his manifestation as **Atum**) and his eight lineal descendants. The descendants were grouped in four pairs of **twins**, each containing one male and one female: **Shu** and **Tefnut**, **Geb** and **Nut**, **Aset** (Isis) and **Osiris**, **Set** and **Nebthet**.

ENUMCLAW AND KAPOONIS
Americas (North)

Enumclaw and Kapoonis, in the myths of many peoples of the Northwestern coastal US, were **twins** who went searching for spirit servants who would give them power greater than any other mortals. Enumclaw tamed a fire-spirit, and learned the skill of hurling fragments of fire as if they were spears. Kapoonis found a rock-spirit, and learned the skill of tossing boulders as if they were pebbles. They began swaggering across the land, terrorizing **creation** – and Father Sky was so alarmed that he took them into his kingdom and made them spirits themselves. Enumclaw became **lightning** (which has ever afterwards been called by his name), and Kapoonis became **thunder**.

EOS
Europe (South)

Eos ('dawn', Latin Aurora), in Greek and Roman myth, was the daughter of the **Titans Hyperion** and Theia, and the sister of the **Sun** and **Moon**. In some accounts, she married the Titan Astraeus, and their children were the stars and some of the winds. But Eos was promiscuous, and had affairs with several gods, including **Ares** whom **Aphrodite** loved. Aphrodite punished her by filling her with lust for mortals, not gods, and she had affairs with several

heroes including Cletus, Cephalus and the famous hunter Orion. But her fiercest passion was for Prince Tithonus of Troy. She carried him off to **Olympus** and begged the gods to give him **immortality**. **Zeus** agreed, and for a time they lived happily, even producing sons (Aemathion and Memnon, who later fought at Troy and was killed by **Achilles**). But then Tithonus began to show signs of aging – Eos had asked for immortality, but not eternal youth – and withered before her eyes to a dried-out husk. Disgusted – for the gods abhor old age – she kept him locked in a wooden box, until Zeus rescued him and sent him back to Earth as a cicada.

Poets described Eos as a beautiful woman who opened the gates of the East with her rosy fingers, jumped into a rose-petal chariot and galloped across the sky, sprinkling the Earth with dew and streaking the sky with light in honour of her brother Sun. Night and Sleep scattered before her, and the stars turned down their lights. She was not represented in painting or sculpture, except for a single surviving vase-painting showing her with the cicada Tithonus in a box; but she was a favourite subject for goldsmiths, and in some parts of Greece 'Dawn' bracelets were given as lucky charms to girls as they entered puberty.
≫→ **beauty**

EPONA
Europe (North; South)

Epona, in Celtic myth, was the strength of the Earth made manifest as a horse. People carved horses on chalk hills in her honour, and held ceremonies at which they dressed as horses and performed prancing, curvetting dances. In one particularly gory annual festival, the king symbolically mated each year with a mare, then bathed in her blood or in a soup made from her boiled flesh – thus ensuring that Epona's strength and his were mingled, to guarantee success in the year to come.

The myth of Epona was taken to Rome by the army, and she was worshipped in a cult exclusive to cavalry officers; to this day, its **mysteries** and ceremonies remain unknown.

ERESHKIGAL
Asia (West)

Ereshkigal ('queen of **death**'), in Mesopotamian myth, was darkness personified, the sister of **Inanna** (light). Together they made a wholeness, and neither could exist or be perceived without the other. As Inanna ruled the visible world of the living, so Ereshkigal ruled the invisible world of the dead. Being invisible, she was never shown as herself in art. But she could split off parts of herself and send them to the Upper World as **demons** or **monsters** (usually hybrids of vultures, **snakes** and cats), and these were favourite subjects for artists.

➤➤ **light and dark**

ERH LONG
Asia (East)

Erh Long, nephew of the Jade Emperor of **Heaven** in Chinese myth, was a hunter whose favourite quarry was **demons**. He confused them by never using the same appearance twice. He had seventy-two different forms, and by the time he'd used every one of them the demons had forgotten the first and the rota could begin again.

Erh Long's job made him a popular god for guarding earthly shrines, temples, houses, even fields and allotments, and his image – usually a statuette or a picture – was often found there. His shape-changing magic made him a favourite hero of folk-tales, and of the plays, puppet shows and modern films and cartoons based on them.

➤➤ **guardians, shape-changers**

ERIPHYLE
Europe (South)

Eriphyle ('strife in the family'), in Greek myth, was the sister of King Adrastus of Argos, and wife of the prophet Amphiaraus. When Adrastus was collecting champions to help Polynices (see **Eteocles and Polynices**) win the throne of **Thebes** (see **Seven Against Thebes**), the first person he asked was Amphiaraus. Amphiaraus was reluctant: his knowledge of the future told him that the expedition would fail and that he himself would be killed. But some time before, he and Adrastus had quarrelled, and Eriphyle had prevented them killing each other. In gratitude each of them had promised, by the gods, to consult her in every matter of life and death and to follow whatever advice she gave.

When Polynices heard from Adrastus about this promise he began cultivating Eriphyle. He discovered that she was vain, and was terrified of losing her beauty as she grew older. When Polynices left Thebes, he'd taken with him the golden necklace and dress given by the gods years before as presents for the wedding of **Cadmus** and Harmony – presents which guaranteed eternal youth. He now bribed Eriphyle with the golden necklace to say that Amphiaraus should join the Seven Against Thebes – and Amphiaraus duly went and was killed.

Years later, these events repeated themselves. Thesander, Polynices' son, was gathering a second group of champions to attack Thebes, and the gods said that the expedition would fail unless it was led by **Alcmaeon**, son of Amphiaraus and Eriphyle. Alcmaeon was reluctant, and referred the decision to Eriphyle, just as his father had done before him. Thesander bribed Eriphyle with Harmony's golden wedding-dress, and she said that Alcmaeon should go. After the fall of Thebes, Thesander told Alcmaeon for the first time about this bribery, Alcmaeon asked the Delphic oracle what the punishment should be for a woman who took bribes to send her own husband and son to war, and the oracle answered '**Death**'. Alcmaeon went home to Argos and murdered Eriphyle. To the very moment of her death, her wish for beauty was granted: the golden dress and necklace had kept her as young-looking as when she married Amphiaraus as a young girl. At the instant of death, however, the spell was broken, and she aged forty years in an instant while her soul fled shrieking to the **Underworld**. **Zeus** took the forty years and divided them among Alcmaeon's infant sons, who changed from babies to full-grown warriors in the time it took between leaping out of their cradles and touching the ground.

ERIS
Europe (South)

Eris ('strife', Latin Discordia, Discord), in Greek and Roman myth, was the daughter of Night, sister of **Nemesis** and the **Fates**. She was malevolence personified, and the gods refused to allow her into **Olympus**. In revenge, she waited until the marriage of **Cadmus** and Harmony, and then rolled one of the golden apples of **immortality** across the floor, inscribed 'For the Fairest' – thus beginning the quarrel between **Aphrodite**, **Athene** and **Hera** which led to the judgement of **Paris** and the **Trojan War**.

Painters and sculptors vied to add hideous details to the standard portrait of Eris. She was shown as a conventionally beautiful young girl, wearing flowing clothes and a garland. But when you looked closer her face was white as bone, her eyes were fire, her garland was of snakes, not flowers, her robes were a shroud and at her breast, instead of a choice bloom, she clutched a dagger. Similarly, in literature, her apparent sweetness was belied as soon as she spoke: instead of words snarls, whines and yelps issued from her lips, madness made sound.

ERLIK
Arctic; Europe (North)

Erlik ('first life'), in the myths of the Siberians and Lapps, was the first created being, made by the **sky-god Ulgan** from a speck of mud floating in the primordial ocean. Hoping that by giving Erlik form he could collaborate with him in creating the rest of the universe,

Ulgan sent him to fetch mud from the bottom of the ocean, to make life from it. But Erlik hid a piece of it in his mouth, intending to mould it into a universe of his own. As he chewed it, instead of shrinking the mud grew bigger and bigger, and Erlik was forced to spit it out – chewed gobbets of land, covered in saliva, the marshlands and swamps of the world.

While this was going on, Ulgan had been making mud dolls and giving them life, to create the human race. But he ran out of life-spirit, and went to fetch more, leaving the dolls guarded by an enormous dog. Erlik tried to bribe the dog to give up the dolls, and when the animal refused he spat on them, sliming them with spittle. When Ulgan returned, he turned the dolls inside-out before giving them life – and mortals have been that way ever since, spittle and foulness inside and dry outside. Ulgan banished Erlik to the **Underworld**, and Erlik snatched as many as he could of the mud-dolls to be his people there. He turned them right-side-out again – and the Dead have been inside-out versions of the living ever since.

EROS
Europe (South)

Eros ('desire', Latin Cupido, Cupid), in Greek and Roman myth, was the son of the war-god **Ares** and **Aphrodite**, goddess of love. From his mother he inherited irresistibility and charm; from his father he inherited a love of trouble-making. He was a winged cherub, one of the very few children in **Heaven**, and he flew everywhere, making mischief. He had a bow and unerring arrows of desire, and whoever he shot, god, mortal, animal or even inanimate rock or water-pool, fell irredeemably in love. The gods sometimes persuaded Cupid to help them – or bribed him, for he was a greedy and shameless child – and he fired arrows at chosen mortals with devastating results: at **Helen**, for example, to make her go to Troy with **Paris**. But he also often turned his arrows on the gods themselves, causing havoc and argument in Heaven – and eventually **Zeus** found him a wife, the mortal princess **Psyche**, made him fall in love with her as incurably as if he'd shot himself with one of his own arrows, and refused to let him marry her unless he agreed never again to trouble the gods and used his arrows solely on mortals – as, for example, when he took the form of **Aeneas**' son **Ascanius** in Carthage, and fired the arrow of desire which transfixed **Dido**.

*In earliest myth, Eros was one of the two first beings in the universe, and mated with the other, **Chaos**, to produce the egg from which all **creation** hatched. It was only later that he took the form of a winged cherub, and allowed himself to be reborn as Aphrodite's child. (In some accounts, his parents were not Aphrodite and Ares, but Aphrodite and Zeus, Aphrodite and **Hermes** or Hermes and **Athene**.) He was a favourite figure in Greek art, particularly in miniature sculpture and on gemstones. He was shown as a chubby, winged and naked child, playing with such toys as a hoop or a quoit, chasing butterflies or riding swans. One famous image shows him apologizing to Zeus for breaking one of the thunderbolts – a myth of which no other details survive. In Roman and later art*

– and indeed in the Roman story of Cupid and Psyche – he is depicted not as a mischievous infant but as a boy just over the threshold into adolescence, so that sexual knowingness is added to boyish charm.
»→ archers, sex

ERYMANTHIAN BOAR
Europe (South)

The Erymanthian Boar, in Greek myth, was a flesh-eating monster which terrorized the people who lived beside the river Erymanthus. **Heracles** was sent to capture it as his fourth **Labour** – and it caused him no trouble at all. He startled it with a huge shout (learned from his hunting-master, the god **Pan**), drove it high above the snow-line, fastened it with chains and carried it in triumph back to Mycenae.

*The myth breaks off here. Heracles is carrying the boar to the Lion Gate when a **messenger** arrives asking him to interrupt his labours and join the expedition of the **Argonauts**. The myth gives no information about what happened to the boar – and later travellers filled the gap by saying that a pair of gigantic tusks hanging in **Apollo's** temple in Cumae in Italy belonged to it, and that it had been taken there and sacrificed in honour of the god of **hunting**.*

ERYSICHTHON
Europe (South)

Erysichthon, in Roman myth, ruled Thessaly, a favourite haunt of the wood-**nymphs** and **water**-nymphs who tended trees, kept irrigation-channels clear and looked after growing crops. Knowing nothing of this, Erysichthon thought that his country's wealth came

from the fact that it lay at the foot of Mount **Olympus**, and was enriched by the gold scattered over it by the feet of gods passing to and fro – and he built a toll-gate to charge the gods passage and a fortress to protect it.

Erysichthon's builders cut down all the trees, and choked the rivers and irrigation-channels with barges ferrying stone. Thessaly's prosperity began to die – and Erysichthon, looking for someone to blame, began persecuting the nymphs of woods and fields. His soldiers drove them from hiding-place to hiding-place, until they took shelter in the very last tree in Thessaly: an ancient oak sacred to **Zeus**. Erysichthon ordered his men to chop it down, and when they refused he snatched an axe and felled it himself, despite groans of pain from the branches, and the sap which gushed from the trunk like blood.

As soon as the tree fell, the nymphs ran to Ceres (see **Demeter**) goddess of harvest, and begged her to protect them. She punished Erysichthon by sending the goddess Starvation to feed on him. Starvation, her withered breasts flapping from her chest like pouches and her arms like taloned twigs, flew to Erysichthon's fortress bedroom, locked her arms round him and sank into him, luxuriating in his plumpness as people float in sun-soaked sea. Satisfied at last, she disappeared into the darkness, leaving Erysichthon snoring.

For the rest of that night, Erysichthon was tormented by the same dream: he was at a banquet, but each time he put food into his mouth his teeth ground on wood or ash. His flesh, bones, blood ached for nourishment: Starvation's embrace had turned him from man into hunger-beast. He woke up howling for food, and the more his slaves fetched the more he craved. He ate the candles and crammed his mouth with his own bed-clothes; as the days passed he ate every grain in the royal storehouses and every animal in the royal flocks. At last, when there was nothing else to eat, he crammed his own finger-ends into his mouth, began to chew, and went on ripping and tearing his own impious flesh until every last morsel was consumed.

For all his Greek name and home, Erysichthon features solely in Roman myth, as one of the more gruesome characters in Ovid's Metamorphoses. Hunger-beasts, however, appear in other folk-traditions, from South American to Inuit; perhaps Erysichthon made his way via Northern Europe into the myths of ancient Rome.

ERZULIE
Americas (Caribbean)

Erzulie or Erzilie, in Voodoo myth, is the goddess of love. When she is happy, she gives mortals the gifts of plenty and ecstasy. When she is sad, she weeps for the transience of joy, and sends torments to rack her worshippers. There is no way to predict what aspect she will show you, and she changes from one to the other in an instant: capriciousness is the dark side of her gift of **beauty**, and she can no more control it than she is responsible for her looks.

ESAUGETUH EMISSEE
Americas (North)

Esaugetuh Emissee ('master of breath'), in the myths of the Creek people of the Southeastern US, was the first principle, the creator, the breath of life. The universe began with an all-engulfing **flood**, and he hovered over the surface, waiting for the waters to subside. There were no other beings but birds and insects. He sent two doves to search for dry land, and they brought back news of a mountain-top, marked by a single grass-blade, beginning to emerge. Esaugetuh Emissee waited until the hill was big enough, then built a house of mud there, with a wall of mud-bricks round it. He modelled mud-people, breathed life into them and left them lying on the wall to dry in the sun. The first people were impatient, and jumped down and swam off to start their lives before they were fully dry: they were the white-skins. The rest waited until they were baked fully brown and finished – and Esaugetuh Emissee cut channels in the Earth and separated water from land to provide them with homes and hunting grounds.
»→ **Chinigchinich, creation, Enki, Humanmaker, Hurukan, Na'pi, Prometheus, Tagaro, Woyengi**

ESHU
Africa

Eshu, or Legba, **messenger**-god in the myths of the Yoruba people of Nigeria, spoke the language of every created thing, from wind to elephants, from flowers to poets. He brought the gods' instructions to Earth, and took back the smoke and scent of sacrifice. As he grew older, however, his memory began to be patchy, and the messages were sometimes garbled. In particular, his information about mortal fate, once unambiguous, became unpredictable, and so risk entered human lives.

In addition to carrying messages, Eshu tended the creator-god Fa. Fa had sixteen eyes, each one a window into one of the avenues of past or future time – and every morning it was Eshu's job to ask how many eyes should be opened and consequently how much knowledge would be available to gods or mortals who needed it.

ESTSANATLEHI
Americas (North)

Estsanatlehi as Time. Estsanatlehi ('changing woman'), in the myths of the Navajo people of the Southwestern US desert, was the goddess of time passing. Her parents were Yadilyil, the gulf of space, and Naestan, the horizon; they made her not by mating but by forming her from turquoise. She was discovered as a baby, lying on a mountain-top, by First Man and First Woman, who fostered her, feeding her on pollen brought by the Sun. In eighteen days she was a mature woman, and she has continued the cycle of growth ever since, aging to old woman and then becoming a baby and starting again time after time. Save that she never died, she was the progress of the seasons.

Estsanatlehi lived in a sea-palace in the far West, and entertained the **Sun** there each night from evening to morning. Their offspring were two warrior-twins: **Nayenezgani** (light) and **Tobadzistsini** (dark). But they were too busy slaying **demons** to keep their mother company, and while the Sun rode the sky during the day, Estsanatlehi pined for him. One day, to divert herself, she pulled small pieces of dead skin from her body and breathed life into them, so creating the human race.

*Other versions of this myth say that Estsanatlehi was the **Moon**, and that her unceasing cycle of growth, withering and rebirth was the passage of the months. Still others identify her as **Mother Earth** – and say that the growth-death-growth cycle is the passing from spring to winter and back to spring. In some accounts, she mated with **Tsohanoai**, and their offspring were the hero-twins Nayanezgani and Tobadzistsini.*
»→ creation

ETEOCLES AND POLYNICES
Europe (South)

Eteocles (Eteokles, 'true fame') and Polynices (Polyneikes, 'much strife'), in Greek myth, were the sons of **Oedipus** and **Jocasta**, and the brothers of **Antigone** and **Ismene**. As boys, they insulted their blind father Oedipus, and Oedipus cursed them, praying that they would die together on the same day, each killing the other. When the brothers grew up, Eteocles challenged Polynices (the elder, and true heir) for the throne of **Thebes**, and snatched power. Polynices gathered an army led by seven champions (the **Seven Against Thebes**) to attack the city. He and Eteocles fought single-handed – and each killed the other, exactly as Oedipus had prayed.

EUROPA
Europe (South)

Europa (Europe, 'broad-browed'), in Greek myth, was the daughter of King Agenor of Phoenicia; she had several brothers including **Cadmus**. She and her maids were picking flowers one day in the water-meadows, beside Agenor's cattle-herds, when **Zeus** disguised himself as a bull and let the girls fondle him and garland his horns as if he were tame. Eventually Europa, most daring of them all, climbed on to his back – and he plunged into the sea and swam to Crete, where he dropped Europa on the sand, raped her and disappeared. The king of Crete, Asterius, found her and married her, and she had three children: Minos (Zeus' son), **Rhadamanthus** and Sarpedon (Asterius' sons).

In the middle ages, European scholars claimed that Europa gave her name to their continent. But she never set foot in Europe, and the continent is more likely to have been named either from the Greek word for 'wide' – as opposed to the comparatively tiny land-area of Greece itself – or from the ancient Asian word oorap, 'to the West of us'.

EURYNOME AND OPHION
Europe (South)

In one version of the Greek **creation-myth**, when nothing existed except the emptiness and swirl of **Chaos**, the tumbling elements formed themselves into a spirit of movement, Eurynome ('wide-wandering'). Needing a place to dance, she made the sea, and above it the sky. As she danced, she caught hold of the breeze stirred up by her movement (the North Wind, **Boreas**) and moulded it into a giant **snake**, Ophion ('snake'). She changed her shape to that of a dove, and laid the first egg; Ophion

coiled seven times round it to incubate it. When the egg hatched, all created things were born: the **Sun**, **Moon** and stars, the Earth and everything that grows and lives in it.

For a time, Eurynome and Ophion ruled in **Olympus**. But they quarrelled, and she banished him to the depths of the **Underworld**. Eurynome created the **Titans** to rule the planets, and the first human being Pelasgus to enjoy the fruits of the Earth and rule the sea. (In some accounts she made Pelasgus and his people by sowing Ophion's teeth in the ground, where they sprouted and grew as human beings.) As for Ophion, he coiled himself in the Underworld, sworn enemy of Eurynome, her descendants the Titans and their descendants in turn, the gods. Some accounts identify him with **Typhon**, the monster who challenged **Zeus** and was punished for it. Others say that he was a particular friend to mortals (those beings hated by the gods), and that if they performed specific rituals – those of the Orphic **mysteries** – they would become initiates, and Ophion would grant them power to enter the Underworld and return, alive.
»→ monsters

EURYSTHEUS
Europe (South)

Eurystheus ('wide strength'), in Greek myth, was the son of King Sthenelus and Queen Nicippe of Mycenae. His mother conceived him at the same time as **Zeus** made another local princess, **Alcmena** of Argos, pregnant with **Heracles**. The **Fates** predicted that the first of the children to be born would rule everyone in the area, and would be invulnerable, by mortals and gods alike, so long as he stayed in Mycenae. When Zeus' jealous wife **Hera** heard this, she arranged for Alcmena's womb to be blocked until Nicippe's child was born. Accordingly, Eurystheus was senior to Heracles, was invulnerable so long as he lived in Mycenae, and had power over everyone in the area (though not the nobility or bravery which should have gone with it: he was a coward and a bully).

Eurystheus' chance to use this power came when Heracles reached adulthood. Hera drove Heracles mad and he shot some of his own children dead; to punish him, the gods said that he must carry out exactly whatever ten tasks Eurystheus found for him. Gleefully, Eurystheus set him to fight the most fearsome **monsters** in the world, hoping each time that Heracles would be killed. But after each of his **Labours** – and the additional two which Eurystheus meanly invented for him – Heracles returned safely to Mycenae, bringing trophies or even the monsters themselves, and Eurystheus was so terrified that he had a copper-lined, underground room built, like an enormous vase, and hid inside it whenever Heracles came near.

When Heracles' life on Earth was over and the gods took him into **Olympus**, Eurystheus thought that the clever thing to do would be to kill all the hero's remaining children, so that the Heraclean strain would be wiped forever from the world. Heracles' son Hyllus was protected by King Ceyx of Trachinia, and Eurystheus gathered an army and set out to fight him. In his haste, he forgot that he was invulnerable only so long as he stayed in Mycenae, and Hyllus shot him dead.

EVANDER
Europe (South)

Evander (Greek Euaner, 'good man'), in Roman myth, was the son of **Hermes** and the **nymph** Carmentis. He was a prince of Pallantion in Greece, but accidentally murdered someone and was forced into exile. He took a group of followers to Italy and settled on a hill beside the river Tiber, calling it Pallanteum. His people were surrounded by enemies, and were plagued by the monster **Cacus**. When **Heracles** passed that way after stealing the cattle of the giant **Geryon**, he killed Cacus, and Evander responded by honouring him as a god – the first human being ever to do so. Later, Evander made an alliance with **Aeneas** and the Trojans against the neighbouring peoples, and when Aeneas beat them in battle Evander's original settlement on Mount Pallanteum was incorporated into a new, enlarged town. The hill was renamed the Palatine, and the town was on the site of the future Rome.

EVE: *see* Adam and Eve

EXCALIBUR
Europe (North)

Excalibur (or Caliburn), in Celtic myth, was a magic sword which guaranteed its owner invincibility in battle. In the story of **Arthur**, the young prince proved his worthiness to become king when he was the only person able to pull a sword from the boulder in which **Uther Pendragon** had embedded it. This sword was not Excalibur, and Arthur broke it in a duel with a **giant** who challenged his right to ride through a narrow mountain-pass. **Merlin** took him to the enchanted home of the **Lady of the Lake**, and a hand appeared from the water, brandishing the real Excalibur, and gave it to him for the duration of his rule on Earth. At the end of his reign, Arthur gave the sword to Bedivere to throw back into the lake, and as it vanished into the depths, a boat appeared to take Arthur to the island of **Avalon** where all wounds are healed.

Not unnaturally, many myth-accounts say that both swords were the same, that Excalibur was the sword Arthur pulled from the stone. Probably two different stories have been conflated. One, that of the magic sword Caliburn, originated in Ireland; the other, about a magic sword forged on the isle of Avalon and lent, for a time, to each of the most noble kings to grace the Earth, came from Northern France.

Flora (*Sandro Botticelli, 15th century*)

FAFNIR
Europe (North)

Fafnir (or Fafner) was the second of the three sons of the wizard Hreidmar. His brothers were **Otr** and **Regin**, and all three were **shape-changers**. Otr often made himself into an otter and played in the sea-shallows, and on one of these occasions **Loki** took him for a real otter and killed him. In punishment, Hreidmar and his other sons demanded the lives of three gods: **Honir**, Loki and **Odin**. Loki offered to ransom himself and the other gods by filling Otr's skin with gold. Leaving Odin and Honir as hostages, he stole the gold-hoard of **Andvari**, king of the dwarfs, and handed it over – without telling Hreidmar that the treasure included a ring which would curse anyone who owned it.

As soon as the three gods had gone, the curse took effect. Fafnir stole the gold, turned himself into a dragon and lay sprawled over it in his mountain hiding-place. He refused to let anyone see it or touch it, including his own father Hreidmar (whom he killed) and his brother Regin (whom he exiled). But Regin told the mortal **Sigurd** about the gold, and Sigurd killed Fafnir, ate his heart and took the treasure.

➤ **monsters and dragons**

FAN GUEI
Asia (East)

Fan Guei, in Chinese Daoist myth, was a mortal, a dog-skinner. He discovered the Way, was promoted to **immortality**, and given the most appropriate responsibility which could be found: he was made patron god of butchers.

fARMING

At the beginning of **creation**, farming was often the first skill taught by the gods to humans; indeed, in many traditions the gods regarded the Earth as their garden, and put humans in charge of it. Mortals, however, proved slow learners, either changing the gardens to suit themselves or failing to understand the proper uses of the things which grew there. In those cases, gods came down to give them specific instructions (for example on how to tend trees, grow corn, irrigate fields, which parts of root-vegetables to eat or the management of bees), or themselves took charge of particular processes (such as making grains swell on rice-plants, ripening apples or irrigating the crops). As agriculture was one way for the gods to spread their generative power on Earth, many farming gods also looked after the **fertility** of the whole world, its plants and its creatures – and a few, hampered by permanent erections and heedless of their immortal dignity, took jobs as signposts, gate-guards or scarecrows.

⫸→ (Americas): Azacca, Corn Woman, Mani, Onatah, Paraparawa, Payatamu, Ten Corn Maidens, Utset, White She-Buffalo, Xochipili, Xochiquetzal; (China): Shen Nong; (Egypt): Osiris; (Finnish): Ovda, Tapio; (Greece): Aristaeus, Pan, Priapus; (India): Privithi; (Mesopotamia): Adam and Eve, Telepinu; (Nordic): Gefion; (Oceania): Haumea, Soido, Tane; (Rome): Faunus, Mars, Pomona and Vertumnus, Saturn; (Slavic) Leshy, Zosim; (West Asia): Ba Ja; (general): civilization, fertility, guardians

fATE: *see* Abassi and Atai, Ajysyt, Fates, Mammitu, Norns, Wyrd

fATES
Europe (South)

The Fates (Greek Moirai, 'sharers-out'; Latin Parcae, 'bringers-to-bear'), in Greek and Roman myth, were daughters of Night or, some say, of **Zeus** and Themis. Their names were Atropus ('unbending'), Clotho ('spinner') and Lachesis ('allotter'). They were old women dressed in white and wearing star-crowns. They appeared gentle and serene, but inside their clothes they had no bodies, they were emptiness personified. They spun the threads of all mortal lives. Clotho held the distaff (and sang songs of the present), Lachesis spun the thread (and sang songs of the future), Atropus cut each thread, each life, when its time had come (and sang songs of the past). The Fates were time itself, and against their judgements there was no appeal – everything in **creation**, even Zeus himself was subject to their laws.

⫸→ Ate, Nemesis

fAUNS: *see* Satyrs

fAUNUS
Europe (South)

Faunus ('favourer'), in Roman myth, was a prophetic god, and the god of trees and pastures. In some accounts he was the son of Mercury the **trickster-**god (**Hermes**), and inherited his father's slyness. He pretended to welcome strangers to his kingdom, tricked them to the altar to watch a sacrifice, then butchered them in Mercury's honour. The gods punished him by giving him goat's hind-quarters and horns and imprisoning him in the woods, where he and his descendants the Fauns have hidden ever since. In other accounts, he was the son of Mars (**Ares**) and a mortal princess, and was such a just king that the gods honoured him by giving him **immortality** and making him the guardian spirit of the countryside over which he had so justly ruled. Still others say that he was the son of **Picus**, the young man turned into a woodpecker by **Circe**. It was this ancestry that gave Faunus both his prophetic wisdom – woodpeckers are among the wisest of all birds – and his love of woods and trees.

⮞⮞→ animal-gods, farming, Pan, prophecy, Satyrs, Silenus

fAUST
Europe (Central)

Faust (that is, Faustus, 'blessed'), in Germanic myth, was a wizard who sold his soul to the Devil in exchange for all knowledge and experience on Earth.

*Faust, less than 400 years old, is one of the most recent myth-figures to become important in Western thought and art. In the early sixteenth century a real German doctor, Johannes Faustus, claimed to heal people by magic – and in 1587 his name was used, in Johann Spies' Faust-Book, for a fictional alchemist-scholar who makes a pact with the Devil. The story – and the real Faust's activities before it – grew out of the belief in Medieval Europe that the study of natural phenomena (the prototype of 'science'), because it was hostile to Chris-tian fundamentalist teaching, was Devil-worship. The real Faustus may have been no more than an equivalent of Paracelsus (1493-1541), who rejected standard medical practice (much of which had been handed down, unchanged, for 1500 years) in favour of the then-outlawed practices of herbalism and dissection, and dressed it up in a bedside manner which was psychologically acute (he 'ordered' his patients to get better, saying that their cure was in their own hands, and his, rather than dependent on the goodwill of Saints or the Holy Virgin), but which must have seemed magical to those he healed and was certainly portrayed as Devil-worship by his enemies. From there, in Spies' Faust-Book, it was a short step to add fictional embroidery: Faust in the story, for example, granted sex with any woman he chooses, selects **Helen of Troy**.*

The hold this idea took on people's imagination is shown by the speed with which it travelled. The Faust-Book was known in educated circles (from Marlowe's play Doctor Faustus of 1604, less than twenty years after it appeared, to Da Ponte's and Mozart's Don Giovanni of some 180 years later, using a favourite variant of the story, that of the rake who makes a pact with the supernatural for a joke, and suffers for it). It was even more widespread in the popular arts, where innumerable ballads, farcical interludes and puppet-plays incorporated its ideas. The characters became as familiar as, in later times, such 'literary' creations as Frankenstein's monster, Dracula or Sherlock Holmes – they were known to millions who had never heard of, or read, the originals. (There is a parallel here with the spread of religious myths.)

When Goethe came to the story (his Faust Part I appeared in 1808) he was *able to draw on a vast hoard of popular knowledge of and affection for the story, and could therefore build a complex philosophical and religious edifice on sure foundations. His work gave the Faust story enormous appeal for European intellectuals. In musical circles alone, composers who drew on it included Beethoven, Berlioz, Schumann, Liszt (who was particularly attracted to **Mephistopheles**), Mendelssohn, Brahms, Mahler and Gounod (whose opera Faust was the single most frequently performed work of late-nineteenth-century music-theatre: Gounod was the Lloyd Webber of his day). In our own century, Faust as a character has slipped his hold on the popular imagination (giving way to Dracula and Co), but has continued to appeal to intellectuals, most notably Thomas Mann, whose Doctor Faustus (1947) reincarnates him as an atonal, Schoenbergian composer who symbolizes the creative dilemma of twentieth century artists in general and makes his 'Devil's pact' to counteract creative block.*

ƒAVONIUS: *see* Zephyrus

ƒEI LIAN
Asia (East)

Fei Lian, or Feng Bo ('wind-lord'), in Chinese myth, was the son of **Huang Di**, and had a stag's body with panther-markings, a sparrow's head, a **snake**'s tail and bull's horns. He ruled the winds, holding them in a vast, billowing sack whose mouth he untied to let them rush out across the world. He allied with the **rain**-god Chi Song Zi in an unsuccessful attempt to dethrone Huang Di, and was punished by being banished to a cave on a **mountain**-peak. From here he sent winds

to harry the human race, until **Yi** the archer shot a hole in the wind-bag and hamstrung Fei Lian himself. Ever afterwards, Fei Lian hobbled in front of Huang Di's processions, blowing the dust from in front of his father's feet.

In some accounts, Fei Lian (or Feng Bo) is confused with his wife Feng Bo Bo.

ƒERTILITY

Unlike **sex**, which myths treated as an ungovernable and often ludicrous force, fertility was usually thought of as something orderly, harmonious, a component of universal balance. The world's fertility depended on a merging of opposites, for example Sky's **rain** and Earth's dryness, and conception and growth were encouraged by a myriad godlings and spirits each of whom looked after one particular task (taking water to seed; swelling buds on trees; opening flowers to the **Sun**). When fertility was threatened (as, for example, when its guardian goddess was kidnapped by **giants** or spirits of the **Underworld**), the gods immediately put aside their feuds to restore universal balance, and the orderly progression of the seasons which symbolized it.

➤ (Africa): Ruhanga; (Americas): Adekagagwaa, Chac, Cihuacóatl, Coniraya, Gluskap, Mama Quilla, Nipinoukhe and Pipinoukhe, Onatah, Tláloc, Vaimatse, Xipetotec; (Arctic): Igaluk; (Australia): Darana, Waramurungundju and Wuraka; (Celtic): Cernunnos, Danann; (China): Guan Yin, Mi Lo; (Egypt): Aset, Bastet, Hapi; (Greece): Demeter, Persephone; (India): Parjanya, Prisni,

Sarasvati, Uma; (Japan): Amaterasu, Susano; (Mesopotamia): Anat, Astarte, Dagon, Enki, Inanna, Ninhursaga; (Nordic): Freyja, Sif, Vanir; (Oceania): Sido, Soido, Sosom; (Rome): Flora, Mithras, Pomona and Vertumnus; (Slavic): Mati-Syra-Zemlya, Mokosh, Pyerun, Rod; (general): farming, Mother Earth

fINISHER
Americas (North)

Finisher, the Great Spirit of the Shawnee (an Algonquian tribe from the Midwestern US), created the universe and everything in it.

fINNISH MYTH
Europe (North)

In ancient and medieval times, the population of what is now Finland was both sparse and widely-scattered. Myths were local, confined to small groups or peoples, sometimes only a few dozen in number. Only a handful of gods were widely worshipped, and those that were – **Ukko** the sky-father and his consort **Akka**, **Ilma** the air – were regarded as aloof, insubstantial beings, far less important in the life of their worshippers than the water-sprites, wood-**demons** and **Underworld** creatures which hovered on the fringes of each community's everyday awareness. Despite this isolation, however, the power of Finnish myth guaranteed its spread over a wide area (to the Slavs in the East, say, or the Nordic peoples to the West and South); the Finns also imported gods or stories from such areas.

As well as this core myth tradition, there was an enormous proliferation of folk-stories, poems, ballads, proverbs and other material, most of it much more localized and dealing with the interpenetration of natural and supernatural worlds. Despite the lack of an elaborate cosmology (such as that of the **Nine Worlds** in the Nordic tradition), there was a range of ideas about such matters as the **creation** of the universe and the opposition between the ice-**giants** (trolls) of the North, bringers of winter, and the pastoral gods of the South, guarantors of summer and harvest. In particular, the Underworld was fully imagined: it was **Tuonela**, realm of **Tuoni** and his consort **Tuonetar**, a place tenanted by **diseases** and corpse-eating monsters, in which every concept of the Upper World was reversed, so that time progressed from death to the nothingness before (or in this case, after) conception, hope was replaced by despair, **light** by **dark**, vigour by corruption, warmth by cold and growth by withering.

The coming of Christianity (in some areas, as early as the sixth century CE) further eroded the status of these ideas, fragmenting them in a myriad folk traditions whose persistence is remarkable, given their lack of meaning for people's everyday existence. Then, in the nineteenth century, as part of the upsurge of Finnish nationalism (and the folk-studies which were one of its chief handmaids), the scattered traditions were collected, codified and disseminated nationwide, paradoxically as a way of 'reasserting' an overarching national identity which the country had never actually had. The most important of these works, Elias Lönn-rot's **Kalevala**, became the second most important book in Finland after the Bible. In a way hardly matched in literature since the poems of Homer in ancient Greece, it was thought to enshrine the people's secular soul, to define the nature both of the country and its inhabitants.

Kalevala became a fountainhead and main resource for artists, politicians, folklorists and educationists, providing not only a self-image for Finland and Finnishness but a set of stories and a way of speaking and thinking about them which had the double strength of Lönn-rot's formidable creative personality and the thousands of pieces of folklore he sewed together to make his narrative. Without ever saying so overtly, *Kalevala* makes the story of the god **Väinämöinen** a survey of what might be called the heroic age of Finnish myth, beginning with the **creation**, including a harrowing of the Underworld and ending with a twilight, as Väinämöinen, his work done and his country provided for, recedes from the mortal world to wait until he is needed again. The main characters are few – Väinämöinen's companions **Ilmarinen** and **Lemminkäinen**, the inhabitants of the Underworld, the ice-giants **Joukahainen** and **Louhi**, the doomed hero **Kullervo** – but the book teems with allusion and resonance, and in particular uses such amorphous figures as the creator-goddess **Luonnotar** and the forest-god **Tapio** to give a feeling of all-enveloping Nature, a sentient and life-giving force, which both fits exactly with nineteenth-century Romantic ideas about human relationships with the environment and gives *Kalevala* its par-ticularity, centring it in the lakes, woods and tundra of the Finland whose folk-traditions it enshrines.

⟫→ Ahto, Antero Vipunen, Jumala, Kalma, Kipu-Tyttö, Kuu, Kylliki, Loviatar, Otava, Ovda, Päivä, Pohjola, *Sampo*, Surma

fINN MACCOOL
Europe (North)

Finn MacCool ('fair, noble son of Cumhal'), in Celtic myth, was an Irish prophet, warrior and healer. He learned his skills either by sipping the gods' wine as he served them at table, or by touching **Fintan**, Salmon of Wisdom, as he was cooking it for the gods' banquets. Ever afterwards, he only had to drink wine, or bite the thumb which had touched Fintan, to be granted second hearing and second sight.

⟫→ disease and healing, prophecy

fINTAN
Europe (North)

Fintan, in Celtic myth, was the only Irish survivor of **Noah**'s **flood** – and the reason was that he was a **shape-changer**, able to become a hawk and soar above the waters, or a salmon and live in them. He ate the gods' magic hazelnuts and received all knowledge, but this did him no good as he was netted in a salmon-trap and cooked for the gods' banquet by **Finn MacCool**. (Finn touched Fintan's flesh as he cooked him, and knowledge passed from salmon to scullion, turning Finn into a seer and healer on the spot.)

FIRE: *see* Atar, Agni, Juruma, Kagutsuchi, Kananeski Amaiyehi, Loki, Ogoun, Olifat, Prometheus, Surt, Svarozich, Xiuhtecuhtli

FIRST MADE MAN
Americas (North)

First Made Man, in the myths of the Tewa people of the Southwestern US Pueblos, was one of the human beings who existed in the days before the Earth's surface was inhabitable. The world had been made from mud churned from the bed of the primordial ocean, and had still not dried out sufficiently for life to exist on it. While it did so, humans huddled in two vast underground caves. Summer Mother's cave was fertile, cheerful and bustling with warm-blooded creatures. Winter Mother's cave was icy and filled with cold-blooded creatures.

From time to time, as Earth dried out above their heads, Summer Mother and Winter Mother sent First Made Man to the surface to see if life was possible. The first time he saw nothing but mud and dark; the second time he saw reeds on the land and stars in the sky; the third time he saw blue sky; the fourth time he saw plains rolling to the horizon. But when he returned, each time, he said that life was still not possible. 'Go higher,' Winter Mother and Summer Mother ordered. 'Step out on the surface. Test it.'

Terrified, First Made Man crawled up the underground tunnels to the surface. He lay exhausted, too tired even to defend himself against a group of predators – **Coyote**, Crow, Fox, Mountain-Lion, Vulture and Wolf – which ran up and began tearing and gnawing his flesh. When they saw that he offered no resistance, they drew back, his flesh reconstituted itself, and they told him he'd passed the test and human beings were now permitted to live on Earth. They gave him tokens – a bow and arrows, feathers, an embroidered robe, a bowl, a drum – and sent him back down to fetch his people. First he led the humans from Summer Mother's cave, and on the surface sent them inland, to build settlements in the woods and on the plains. Then he fetched Winter Mother's mortals, and told them to settle along the banks of rivers and seas, and in the frozen North. As soon as all were settled, First Made Man went to live with the animals which had first accepted him. He was Hunt Chief, and acted as intermediary between the two worlds, above and below the Earth.

*This story is repeated, in various forms, in myths from all over the Americas. Human beings are depicted as having emerged from the **Underworld** – often for a brief tenancy of the Upper World before returning. In some accounts, there are Winter and Summer caves, as here. In others there are four levels of existence, and the Guide or Explorer has to lead his/her people from one to the other, in turn. (Those too weak or reluctant to make the journey stay behind, as wraiths and phantoms of the World Below.) Many of these stories have philosophical or psychological overtones; the Tewa version given here, by contrast, treats the emergence of human beings purely as a myth and with essentially realistic detail.*

FIVE AGES OF MORTALS
Europe (South)

In one version of the Greek creation myth, men and women sprang up naturally from **Gaia (Mother Earth)**, created by her like all other animals and plants. From that beginning to the present day, there have been Five Ages of mortals. In the Golden Age, **Cronus** (Saturn) ruled the universe, human beings were untroubled and the world was serene. In the Silver Age mortals were still happy, but were vapid and brainless, a useless species which **Zeus** ended in a huge **flood**. In the first Bronze Age human beings, reborn from **Deucalion and Pyrrha**, thought of nothing but **war**, and eventually all but destroyed themselves. In the second Bronze Age the few survivors prospered, and gods and mortals mated to produce great **heroes** such as **Achilles** and **Heracles**. In this Age, war was still prevalent, and human beings were still wicked, but they had the chance to do good and be happy, and sometimes took it. Most heroic myth-stories take place in this age. The Age of Iron, our present Age, is tenanted by pallid shadows of the **heroes** of the Fourth Age. We are cruel, quarrelsome, greedy and treacherous, destroying more than we create. The gods have abandoned us; but one day, the myth ends, disgusted by our wickedness, they will sweep us away and usher in a Sixth, and possibly New Golden Age.

FIVE BUDDHAS, THE
Asia (East)

The Five Buddhas, in Chinese myth, were the same people as the Great Emperors of the Five Peaks in early myth. Each ruled one of the five **mountains** of which the universe consisted: the Western Peak, the Southern Peak, the Eastern Peak, the Northern Peak and the Central Peak (the Earth).

FIVE ELEMENTS, THE
Asia (East)

The Five Elements, in Chinese Daoist myth, were worshipped separately as gods, and played a large part in both philosophy and alchemy. They were not stable, but in a state of constant flux, which determined the flow and progress of all existence. Each was capable of generating one of the others, and together they formed a ring of **creation** from which everything was made; as each also destroyed one of the others, entropy was also part of the process of existence. Wood was generated by water (in the form of plants) and destroyed Earth (by drawing out its strength); it was associated with the East, spring and the colour blue-green. Fire was generated by wood (as it burned) and destroyed metal (by melting it); it was associated with the South, summer and the colour red. Earth was generated by fire (in the form of ash) and destroyed water (by polluting it); it was associated with the centre (and in particular with China, centre of the universe), all four seasons and the colour yellow. Metal was generated by earth (in the form of ore) and destroyed wood (by cutting it down); it was associated with the West, autumn and the colour white. Water was generated by metal (as it melted) and destroyed fire (by soaking it); it was associated with the North, winter and the colour black.

FIVE EMPERORS, THE
Asia (East)

The Five Emperors, in Chinese myth, succeeded the **Three Sovereigns** as the most important members of a dynasty of half-human, half-divine rulers at the beginning of the civilized world. All had supernatural powers, including the abilities to change their shapes and to live outside human time. In order, the Five Emperors were **Huang Di**, **Zhuan Hu**, Ku, **Yao** and **Shun**.

⟫→ shape-changers

FIVE LANDS, THE
Asia (Southwest)

The Five Lands, in Tibetan myth, were the universe. In the centre was the four-sided **mountain** Rirab Lhumpo, home of the gods. Each side was made from a different precious stone: the North was gold, the East crystal, the South malachite and the West silver. Rirab Lhumpo stood in the ocean of the universe, its peak jutting 100,000km above the surface and its roots planted 100,000km below. Each of the four outer lands floated in Ocean, separated from Rirab Lhumpo by seven golden mountain-ranges and seven seas. Dzambo, the Southern world, was the home of the living, and the Dead lived in Dra Minyen, the Southern world. Balang Chö, the Western world, and Lö Phag, the Eastern world, were inhabited by **giants**, cattle-herders with flat discs for faces and a life-span of 500 years, who took no interest in the affairs of gods or mortals and lived emotionless, religionless and entirely vapid lives.

FIVE PLAGUE DEMONS, THE
Asia (East)

The Five Plague Demons, in Chinese myth, were junior devils sent to Earth to perfect their education. Their supernatural abilities meant that they learned more quickly and thoroughly than anyone else, and when Emperor Li Shin Min announced a competition for knowledge, they set out for his court in certainty of winning. But they took too long on the journey, arrived too late for the competition, and were forced to earn a living by entering Imperial service as musicians. As it happened, **music** was the one skill they'd never mastered, and their performances were excruciating. The Emperor, wanting to punish a Daoist philosopher (Zhang Dao Ling) who had risen so far above the cares of the world that he saw no need to pay his taxes, invited him to a banquet and hid the Five Demons in a secret room, ordering them to play as soon as he gave the signal.

When the racket started, the Emperor told Ling that it was caused by ghosts, and that unless he exorcized them he himself would join them. Ling immediately invoked such strong magic that the **demons** were driven straight back to the **Underworld**. Here they began complaining and moaning so bitterly that Ling was persuaded to allow them back to the Upper World – which he did, on condition that they plagued the tax-greedy Emperor and his court. To rid himself of them, the Emperor offered them eternal lives on Earth providing that they turned their attention to the common people and left the Imperial family alone. He gave each of them an office and a symbol of power – the Fan of Chills, the Fire-gourd of Fever, the Iron Band of Headache, the Wolf-stick of Toothache and the Water-jug of Sweats – and with these they have ever since tormented the entire non-Imperial human race.

≫+ disease and healing

FIVE SISTERS
Americas (North)

Five Sisters, in the myths of the Thompson people of interior British Columbia, were the children of Old One, the creator. Bored with his own company, he made them before the universe, creating them from five hairs from his beard planted in the fog which swirled above the primordial ocean. They grew like saplings in a wood, and as each reached maturity Old One asked her, 'What in all the universe would you like to be?' First Sister said '**Mother Earth**', Second Sister said 'Water', Third Sister said 'Air' – and so it was. They fell from the sky to the ocean, and First Sister at once changed into continents and islands, spreading across the surface. Second Sister and Third Sister ran across her surface, filling her with water-creatures and air-creatures of every kind.

The last two sisters reached maturity together. Old One asked them both what they would like to be, and they answered together. Fourth Sister said 'Mother of the human race: gentle, peace-loving, kind.' Fifth Sister said

'Mother of the human race: proud, cunning, pitiless.' And so it was.
≫+ Amotken

FLOODS

Flood-myths range from stories of the gods who controlled the annual inundations of such great rivers as the Euphrates or Nile, to a remarkably widespread and consistent series of tales of whole-world Floods, cataclysms sent by God or the gods to destroy the human race and start again.
≫+ (Americas): Doquebuth, Ixchel, Szeukha, Tochopa and Hokomata; (China): Yu; (Egypt): Hapi; (Greece): Deucalion and Pyrrha; (India): Manu; (Mesopotamia): Adad, Atrahis, Enki, Noah, Utnapishtim; (Oceania): Nu'u; (General): water

FLORA
Europe (South)

Flora ('flowery'), in Roman myth, was one of the oldest Italian gods; her function was to persuade plants to flower and bear fruit. Originally she was a meadow-**nymph**, Chloris, but the West Wind **Zephyrus** fell in love with her and chased her through woods and meadows. Everywhere she went she scattered flowers to distract him, but still he caught her and married her.

*As a **fertility**-goddess, Flora was worshipped in a spring festival each year, celebrated not only with prayers and sacrifice but with horseplay and ribaldry – the origins, some say, of the 'rustic farces' which influenced later Roman comedy and mime. In more recent times, her most*

*famous appearance is in Botticelli's paint-
ing* La Primavera, *illustrating the myth of her
flirtation with Zephyrus.*

FLYING DUTCHMAN, THE
Europe (North)

The Flying Dutchman story, in Germanic myth, is a variant of the **Faust** myth.
The Dutchman – called in some versions Vanderdecken, in others Falkenberg – bartered his soul to the Devil in
exchange for safe-conduct round the
Cape of Good Hope, but forgot to ask
to make the journey just once, and was
condemned to sail the same seas again
and again forever.

*The best-known appearances of the
Dutchman in European arts are in Wagner's opera* The Flying Dutchman *(where he
is a main character), and Coleridge's* Rime
of the Ancient Mariner *(in which he and his
ship are glimpsed in the distance). The story
is also a variant of the traditional folk-idea
of the Ship of Death, in which damned souls
are doomed to sail stormy seas until the end
of time – a theme painted with devilish glee
by both Bosch and Brueghel.*

FLYING HEAD, THE
Americas (North)

The Flying Head, in the myths of the
Iroquois people of the Northeastern US,
was a giant winged head. It had fire for
eyes, fangs like knives, and its wings
were strands of hair, tossing in the
wind. At night it preyed on wild animals, and when it found a human settlement it fell on the farm animals – and
their owners – like a fox on a chicken-
run. One night, however, it was out-

smarted by a woman. She waited for it,
alone in her hut, and roasted chestnuts
in a fire. She picked them up in a forked
twig, put them into her mouth and
swallowed them with relish. Thinking
that she was eating red-hot stones, the
Head flew into the hut and snatched up
all the stones round the hearthfire, and
the fire itself. Then, having no crop to
store them in or guts to swallow them,
and unable to spit them out because of its
fence of fangs, it was burned to death
from inside, and vanished.

*Flying Heads were common in the myths
and folk-tales of the forest peoples; this is
one of the few stories in which one is
outwitted.*
⫸→ Chonchonyi, demons, monsters
and dragons

FOOD AND DRINK OF
IMMORTALITY: *see ambrosia,
amrita, Haoma, immortality, kvasir,
nectar, soma*

FORSETI
Europe (North)

Forseti, son of **Baldur** and Nanna in
Nordic myth, was the god of **justice
and universal order**. The gods built
him a palace of gold and silver, and
went to him to settle their arguments.
He listened to the evidence, and used
two strategies for judging. Either he
outlined the reasons why one side or
the other was correct, droning on
and on until the combatants accepted
his word out of sheer exhaustion –
or he flatly announced his decision
and said that he would kill anyone
who disagreed with it.

fORTUNA
Europe (South)

Fortuna ('lot-distributor'), in pre-Roman myth, was an Italian goddess who blessed the work of farmers and helped to guarantee the happiness of women in their first marriages. In early Roman times she became amalgamated with a Greek goddess, Tyche ('chance'), whose function was to bring about good luck by chance. The luck of each individual, group in society or state lay in her hands, and she administered it austerely and without favour.

Fortuna's symbol, the wheel which rolls you at one moment to the top and at another to the bottom, was common in ancient Rome, and her statue (showing a beautiful woman with her eyes blindfolded) was worshipped in many houses beside the Lares (see Lar) and Penates, and in the Imperial household was thought to preserve the good luck of the whole city and the Empire. At Fortuna's shrines, people drew lots in the form of cryptic sentences written on slivers of oak-wood, and priests interpreted them to tell the future. In ordinary life, people ate fortune cookies, finding predictions of their future on pieces of wood or skin baked into biscuits or cakes. Some consulted the Sortes Virgilianae – choosing quotations at random from the Aeneid and applying them to their own futures. (This last custom continued long into the Middle Ages, and was also used with the Bible.)

fOUR DIAMOND KINGS, THE
Asia (East)

The Four Diamond Kings, in Chinese Buddhist myth, ruled the four Paradises into which **Heaven** was divided: the Eastern, Northern, Western and Southern Paradises.

fOUR DRAGON KINGS, THE
Asia (East)

The Four Dragon Kings, in Chinese myth, ruled the Four Seas. They were Ao Guang (sometimes known simply as **Long Wang**, 'dragon king'), their chief, Pai Long ('white dragon'), Jang Long ('red dragon') and Zhin Long ('golden dragon'). They were **water**-lords and **rain**-bringers, benefactors and helpers of the human race.

≫→ monsters and dragons, sea

fOUR KINGS Of HELL, THE
Asia (East)

The Four Kings of Hell, in Chinese Buddhist myth, were the **Underworld** equivalents of the **Four Diamond Kings** of **Heaven**. They sat in committee to judge the souls of the Dead, and guarded the Scrolls of Judgement in which all past lives were recorded – and which, on one occasion, Monkey stole from them, causing utter confusion. In non-Buddhist accounts, the Kings were not supreme but were assistants to **Yen Lo**, and there were ten of them, or even fourteen.

≫→ justice and universal order, Ten Yama Kings

fREY
Europe (North)

Frey ('Lord'), in Nordic myth, was the son of the **sea**-god **Njörd** (and, some say, the earth-goddess **Nerthus**); he was the **twin** brother of **Freyja**. Like his sister, he was a god of sexual desire: she ruled the vagina, he the penis. At first, when they lived in Vanaheim, home of the **Vanir**, they had **sex** incestuously with one another. But as part of the settlement after the war between Vanir and **Aesir**, Frey went with his father Njörd to live in **Asgard**, and married the giantess Skirnir, the only female in **creation** able to cope with his incessant lust for sex.

*Frey was a far less important god than his sister. While Freyja guarded the **fertility** of the whole universe, he was merely the god of erections. But this made him the most often depicted of all the gods. Statues and carvings are found all over Northern Europe, and Frey is also the origin of the phallic stick-men carved into chalk hillsides. People carried Frey-statuettes and wore Frey-jewellery for luck, and carved his image into the lintels and jambs of doors.*

»→ Chimatano, guardians, Hermes, Priapus

FREYJA
Europe (North)

Freyja in Vanaheim and Asgard. Freyja ('Lady'), in Nordic myth, was the daughter of the **sea**-god **Njörd** (and, some say) the earth-goddess **Nerthus**; she was the twin sister of **Frey** and goddess of sexual desire. At first she lived in Vanaheim, home of the **Vanir**. But after the war between the Vanir and the **Aesir**, she went to live in **Asgard**. She married **Od**, god of sunshine, and when he vanished she wept tears of gold (corn-seeds) which covered the floors of Asgard. Some

say that after Od's disappearance Freyja never remarried, but had **sex** indifferently with gods, mortals, giants and dwarfs. Others say that she married **Odin**, and is the same person as his wife **Frigg**, queen of the gods. Freyja rode a boar, Hilisvini, or a chariot pulled by a team of cats, she could also put on a hawk-feather cloak and fly through the air.

Freyja and fertility. Freyja often sat with her maids under the branches of **Yggdrasil**, tree of the universe, and her presence there guaranteed the **fertility** of **creation**. On one occasion the giant Beli the Howler kidnapped her and Frey to **Jotunheim**, home of the giants, and there was no new life in the universe until Frey killed Beli and broke through the ice-caves of Jotunheim with Freyja, as spring shoots burst from thawing ground. Freyja wore a dazzling necklace, **Brisingamen**. Some say that **Loki** stole it for her, others that she bought it from its makers the Brisings (four dwarf brothers) by having sex with each in turn. Its possession enhanced her sexual powers, and allowed her to guarantee universal fertility. But its loss stripped the dwarfs – all dwarfs, not just the Brisings – of their powers of reproduction, leaving them no comfort but longevity and the pain of lusting forever for gold, not sex.

Freyja's other powers. Apart from the encouragement of sexual desire, Freyja's responsibilities were magic (which she introduced to Asgard, and controlled), the care of women in **childbirth** and the government of half the mortal **heroes** killed in battle: she was leader of the **Valkyries**, the warriormaidens who carried dead heroes to **Valhalla**, and she supervised their banquets either there or in her own castle

Folkvang. She told favoured mortals the future, and was worshipped by witch-priestesses who could throw themselves into prophetic trances, and work particularly strong magic after turning themselves into mares.

*Freyja, one aspect of the **Great Goddess**, plays a rather passive role in Nordic myth. She is the object of desire by gods, dwarfs and giants rather than an active character in her own right. But she was the most persistent of all the Nordic gods. In the thirteenth century CE, she was the last pagan deity still worshipped in Scandinavia (often, side by side with Christianity), and some of her attributes were later taken over by Christian saints or the Virgin **Mary**. She is the god after whom Friday is named. She was a favourite subject for Viking goldsmiths and silver-smiths. Her image was common in pen-dants, earrings and bracelets. Sometimes she was dressed not in clothes but in her own golden tears, and sometimes Brisinga-men, necklace of desire, was extended to form a circle around her whole figure.*

⫸➔ Loki, shape-changers

FRIGG
Europe (North)

Frigg, in Nordic myth, was the daughter of **Odin** and the giantess Jord, and the sister of **Thor** the Thunderer. She acted as queen and consort (and some say, wife) to her father Odin, ruling the universe. She lived in a palace of her own, Fensalier ('**sea**-hall'), and she and Odin often travelled in state across the sky to stay with one another.

Frigg was the goddess of clouds and **rain**. She wore cloud robes, light or dark according to her mood, and she and her attendants endlessly wove new clouds from threads of mist. She was the god-dess of the marriage-bond, but was also adulterous, having **sex** with the creator-gods **Vili** and **Ve**, her uncles. She could foresee the future, but had no power to change it. On the only occasion she tried, when she begged everything in **creation** to promise not to harm her son **Baldur**, she triggered the very fate she was trying to prevent. She decided not to ask mis-tletoe for promises, on the grounds that it was too slight to do Baldur any harm – and it was from mistletoe that **Loki** made the spear which killed him.

Frigg was sometimes depicted as a wo-man in a billowing cloud-cloak, riding a broom across the sky to sweep away the storms. Some anthropologists think that this is the origin of one, at least, of the medieval European beliefs about witches.

FUJIYAMA
Asia (East)

Fujiyama ('immortal **mountain**', 'blue **rain** mountain' or 'wisteria mountain'), in Japanese myth, was regarded as the symbol of the nation – indeed, as the centre of the world – and pilgrims made a ritual climb to the top each year to pray to its patron god, Kunitokotachi, and to Oanamochi, god of the crater. The mountain grew in a single night, heaving itself in a giant eruption from the Suruga plain. On its slopes was the fountain of the water of life, which was dispensed by the flower-goddess Sen-gen and gave mortals not **immortality** but 300 years of health and happiness.

Two myths explain the mountain's appearance. In one, from the earliest era of Japan, Mioya, ancestor of all gods, was visiting the world, and called on Fuji, god of the mountain. Fuji refused to spend money to entertain him, and Mioya covered the mountain with eternal frost and snow and blighted its **fertility**, so that Fuji would have as few visitors as he deserved. Mioya then visited Tsukuba, god of Mount Tsukuba, and was welcomed – which is why Mount Tsukuba has ever afterwards been covered with greenery.

In the second myth, an old woodcutter found a beautiful child on the lower slopes of Mount Fuji, and brought her up until she married the Emperor. But after seven years she told her husband that she was immortal, and must return to the spirit-world. She gave him a mirror, saying that it would always show him her reflection, and then disappeared. The heartbroken Emperor tried to follow her to **Heaven** by climbing Mount Fuji, the highest mountain in his realm. But even on its peak he found no trace of her, and his love and despair burst out in fire and flames, setting the mirror ablaze. From that time on, the tip of Mount Fuji has been eternally wreathed in smoke.

Mount Fuji is one of the most potent symbols in Japanese life, and has attracted many famous landscape painters and print-makers: a favourite subject is a sequence of pictures showing the mountain in its different aspects at various times of year. In Buddhist paintings it is shown as **Buddha**'s *seat on Earth, and its snows are arranged in the form of eight lotus-petals, symbolizing the eight forms of intelligence: concentration, conduct, contemplation, exertion, language, life, perception and purpose.*

Mount Fuji symbolizes the destiny of Japan, and its top is regarded as the supreme altar of the **Sun**, *ancestor of the Imperial family. (The mountain's very name comes from the ancient Japanese name for the Sun-goddess: Fuchi.) Its eight-sided crater stands for the eight cardinal compass-directions. Pilgrims visit the mountain partly because of the story that from its peak you can (all other things being equal) see into or even pass into* **Heaven**, *and because they believe that somewhere on its slopes springs a fountain of eternal youth.*

➤ **Baucis and Philemon**

FURIES
Europe (South)

The Furies (Erinyes, 'raging ones', or Eumenides, 'kindly ones', Latin Furiae or Dirae, 'dreads'), in Greek and Roman myth, were three monstrous sisters, either daughters of Night and Tartarus or born from blood-drops spilled on to **Gaia (Mother Earth)** after **Cronus** castrated **Ouranos** (Father Sky). Their names were Allecto ('endless'), Megaera ('jealous rage') and Tisiphone ('punishment'). They were aged women with bats' wings, coal-black skin, dogs' heads, rags of clothes and **snakes** for hair. They stank, their eyes, mouths and noses oozed foulness, their voices were halfway between a cackle and a bark. Their home was in Erebus, the lowest depth of the **Underworld**, and their task was to supervise the torments of the wicked. But they also appeared in the Upper World, where they hunted down mortals, such as **Oedipus** and **Orestes**, who had murdered blood-relatives. As well as their nightmare-shapes, they could appear as storm-clouds or as swarms of biting insects.

The Furies appear as walk-on parts in most myths of the torments of the Underworld, and wield iron whips, spears of fire, cups of venom, all the tools of their gruesome trade. Their grandest literary appearance is in Aeschylus' Eumenides, the last play in his Oresteia trilogy. In this, they accuse Orestes before an Athenian court presided over by Athene, and are first defeated, and then persuaded to accept a new position of honour, not hurting mortals but helping them. They are renamed Eumenides, given a home in caves under the Acropolis, and agree to bless the citizens of Athens, keeping plague from the city and pests and diseases from the crops. The first appearance of the Furies in this play was said to have been so terrifying at its original performance that there was a stampede for the exits and women gave birth prematurely – a story which seems as implausible, in its way, as the outcome of Aeschylus' play. In common with most inhabitants of the Underworld, the Furies rarely appeared in fine art, and then usually only as hooded figures in the background of the torments which were the artists' main interest.

≫→ monsters and dragons

fUTEN
Asia (East)

Futen, one of the wind-lords in Japanese myth, was an old man only just in control of his subjects. He stood on mountain-tops as they swirled round him, pulling his long beard and tearing at the banner with which he tried to rally them behind him.

fU XI
Asia (East)

Fu Xi ('bottle gourd'), first of the **Three Sovereigns** in Chinese myth, helped to people the world at the beginning of **creation**. He was born not as a result of normal sexual intercourse (which had not yet been invented), but after his mother became pregnant by the wind. In some accounts he and his sister **Nü Gua** floated in a gourd – hence Fu Xi's name – to escape a **flood** sent to drown the world, and when the waters receded they repopulated the Earth. Nü Gua made human beings, and Fu Xi taught them the ways of **civilization**: how to farm and fish, how to measure land and chart the seasons, how to rear silkworms, and how to tell the future by reading the patterns of lines drawn in the mud.

Fu Xi's lines were a set of eight pa gua: shapes, each of which was formed from three lines, broken (yin) and unbroken (yang), and representing one of the eight elements of the created world: earth, fire, metal, mountain, river, sky, thunder and wind. Fu Xi's successor Shen Nong developed a way of combining these trigrams in 64 different patterns, and gave the human race the skill of reading the future in the combinations. Fu Xi's trigrams and Shen Nong's combinations were later incorporated in the Yijing ('Book of Changes'), and have been used for divination ever since. Fu Xi is also credited with the discovery of the 'magic square' known as Lo Shu ('Book of the River Lo'), which he is said to have found in the shell-patterns on the back of the celestial tortoise. In this square of nine numbers (which represents universal harmony), each line adds up to fifteen, whichever way you total it:

4 9 2
3 5 7
8 1 6

In early myth Fu Xi retired with his sister to **Heaven** after creation was complete. But in later times people claimed that he stayed on Earth to become the first human Emper-

or, the dates of his reign were fixed as 2852BCE-2737BCE. This human Fu Xi was said, plausibly enough, to have invented both **writing** and the first system of law ever known on Earth – and to have had four faces, one looking in each main compass direction, a notion perhaps derived from one of his early statues.

Ganesh (*18th-century French painting*)

GABRIEL
Asia (West)

Gabriel (or Jibril, 'God's power made manifest') was the intermediary between gods and mortals. In Mesopotamian and Iranian myth he was light or sound made manifest: a sunshaft or trumpet-blast. In Hebrew myth he drove **Adam** and **Eve** out of Eden; Christians believed that he announced to **Mary** that she would give birth to Jesus Christ, and that he will blow his trumpet to announce the end of the world. In Muslim belief he dictated the word of God to Mohammed: the Koran.

GAIA
Europe (South)

Gaia (or Ge, '[Mother] Earth'; Latin Terra), in Greek and Roman myth, was one of the two first beings to emerge from **Chaos**: a living organism with clefts, folds and hills like gigantic limbs. Turning and twisting in the swirl of Chaos, she fixed herself in a firm embrace with the other primordial being, **Ouranos** (Father **Sky**). Life-giving rain from Ouranos sought out Gaia's cracks and crevices; streams, rivers and oceans formed; the ground produced plants and creatures of every kind. When this creation was complete, Gaia and Ouranos moved apart. Gaia floated like a huge flat dish; Ouranos soared above like an umbrella of clouds and light. All round, at Gaia's circumference, they touched, and were bound together by a fast-flowing river, Ocean, which whirled in an endless circle, binding everything in place. The entrances to the **Underworld** were at the edge of the circle of Ocean, and there were also cracks and fissures in Gaia's floor itself.

Gaia's children. As well as rivers, beasts and plants, Gaia and Ouranos had children of other kinds. They made three giant sons, blending the shapes of gods and trees: the **Hundred-handed Giants**. Gaia and Ouranos also made the three first **Cyclopes**, blending the shapes of gods, rock and fire. They had many more children, experiments with blending every kind of substance or being in existence – lizards and leaves, water and air, dust and insects. Their children in turn had children, until the bodies of the original parents were tenanted by creatures of every conceivable shape and type.

Most important of all Gaia's and Ouranos' children were the twelve **Titans**. These vast, shapeless beings ruled the universe. They rebelled against their own father, Ouranos, and mutilated him. In turn they were challenged by their own offspring, the gods, and were defeated. Gaia took the Titans' side, sending the **Earthborn Giants** (her offspring with Tartarus, the dark depths below the **Underworld**) to attack the gods' citadels – and the Earthborn Giants lost. After that, like Ouranos, Gaia took little active part in the running of the universe, intervening only when its whole future was threatened (for example when **Demeter**, grieving for **Persephone**, held back the harvests and caused the deaths of most of the world's population).

The idea of the Earth and everything in it or on it as a kind of sentient, organic system which survives so long as everything stays in balance and reacts sharply when the balance is upset, resurfaced in scientific circles in the last third of the twentieth century – and was appropriately named (by its chief proposer, James Lovelock) the Gaia Hypothesis.

>**+ creation, Geb, Rangi**

GAKI
Asia (East)

Gaki ('ghosts'), in Japanese myth, were the spirits of the Dead. After **death**, there were 36 different stages of existence before the spirit was reincarnated on Earth, and the stage you joined was determined by your behaviour in your last existence. The worst sinners of all had to go through all 36 stages, beginning with torments in the **Underworld**. The succeeding stages involved various degrees of penance, at first in the Underworld, then in the Upper World.

Gaki who came to the Upper World suffered the additional hardships of being able to see and smell mortal food and drink but not to taste them, since they had no digestive organs. The only way they could enjoy a square meal was to creep inside humans – through the orifices of the body, or through boils, sores and the bites of insects or animals – and steal whatever nourishment they found there. As they grew plumper and warmer, their human hosts lost weight and suffered from chills and fevers. The only way to drive out *gaki* was to take some medicine they found unpalatable, in which case they left, as silently as they had come, to find another victim.

>**+ disease and healing**

GALAHAD
Europe (North)

Galahad, in medieval Christian myth, was the most perfect human being who ever existed, a kind of shadow-Christ. He was born to rescue the **Holy Grail** and return it to **Heaven** – and in order to do this, in a world which was turning increasingly and inexorably towards evil, he had to be utterly without identity: he was a vessel for the purposes of God, and vessels have no function until they are filled.

Galahad was conceived as the result of a trick. His grandfather **Pelles**, in some accounts magically influenced by the **Lady of the Lake**, arranged matters so that **Lancelot**, the noblest **hero** in Christendom, mistook Pelles' beautiful daughter Elaine for **Guinevere** (**Arthur**'s queen, whom Lancelot loved), and slept with her. Galahad grew up in secret, and then took his place at the Round Table in **Camelot** – a place long kept empty for the knight who would successfully search for the Grail. He gathered a group of knights for the Grail-quest, a kind of crusade against the forces of evil. After many adventures – each account supplies its own; they are usually allegorical and (to non-Christian eyes) both sketchy in detail and predictable in outcome – he found the Grail and took it to Jerusalem, where he died and was taken into Heaven, accompanied by flights of angels playing trumpets and singing hymns.

Galahad and the Grail-quest are the subjects of much devout Christian literature of the European Middle Ages, of which the most substantial are the thirteenth-century romances of Chrétien de Troyes. These follow the form and style of heroic romance, being full of encounters with supernatural beings and phenomena. But they take their tone from the Bible, in particular from the Gospels and the writings of Saint Paul, and constantly interrupt adventure with moralizing, replacing psychological interest with preaching. Galahad has no character whatever: goodness personified, he takes centre-stage without once impressing himself on our consciousness. In particular, he sits ill with the pagan robustness of Camelot, an interloper rather than – as the romancers intended – the culmination and fulfilment of all the Round Table stood for.

Galahad's character in the romances (which were enormously popular) affected much later devotional literature, from the Lives of Saints and Martyrs which proliferated until the Reformation, to such works as Bunyan's Pilgrim's Progress. Other writers vigorously sent up the tradition of the pure hero in a naughty world: the range is from Cervantes' Don Quixote to Grimmelshausen's Simplex Simplicissimus and Voltaire's Candide. Later literature seized on this latter tradition, making the innocent hero-victim a standard character permitting enormous variation in satirical range and purpose: Kafka's Karl (in America), Waugh's Paul Pennyfeather (in Decline and Fall) and Salinger's Holden Caulfield (in The Catcher in the Rye) are all examples.

GAMAG NARA
Asia (East)

Gamag Nara ('land of darkness'), in Korean myth, is one of a multitude of **Heavens**. Its king is guarded by fire-**demons**, shapeless and irrational **monsters** whose light as they squabble is all the inhabitants of Gamag Nara have to see by. Every so often the king sends his demons to steal the **Sun** and **Moon** from Earth. For a time, as they gnaw and bite them, the Earth suffers an eclipse. But the Sun sears the demons' mouths and the Moon freezes them. They spit out the fragments and run home, leaving Gamag Nara as badly-lit as ever.

GANDHARVAS
India

The Gandharvas, in Hindu myth, were the musicians of the gods. They lived at the foot of Mount **Meru**, and entertained at banquets, hunts and festivals. Their city, Gandharvanagara, was shifting, unlocatable, a mirage which none but they could reach. They themselves took many shapes: they were clouds, will-o'-the wisps, mist on mountain pools, birds, winged horses, **satyrs**, **centaurs**. When they were not singing and playing, they made love with the **apsaras**, dancers of the gods. They were spirits of **fertility**, overseeing the moment of conception (and, in a grander role, the moment when each soul transmigrates from life to life). In some accounts, they had special responsibility for **soma**, protecting and guaranteeing its efficacy.

➤➤ **music, shape-changers**

GANESH
India

Ganesh, in Hindu myth, is the god of good luck, the problem-solver. He is also known as Ganapati ('leader of the herd') and Gajanana ('elephant-face'). He is stumpy-legged, pot-bellied, elephant-headed and yellow-skinned. He is the son of **Shiva** and **Parvati**, and rides a **demon**-king reincarnated as a rat. He has four arms, and holds a shell, a discus, a club (or goad) and a lotus.

Ganesh's appearance. Several myths explain Ganesh's unorthodox appearance. In one, he was such a handsome youth that his mother blighted him with ugliness to save him from Shiva's jealousy. In another, he was decapitated to punish his father's crime of killing the **Sun**, and Shiva restored him to life and gave him the head of the first creature that came along, an elephant. In a third, Parvati threw her bath-water into the Ganges, the elephant-goddess Malini drank it and gave birth to a five-elephant-headed son whom Shiva rescued, claimed for Parvati and equipped with just one head. In the best-loved story of all, Parvati, embarrassed at the way Shiva regularly surprised her in her bath and insisted on having sex with her, made Ganesh from her own skin-scrapings and told him to stand guard while she bathed. The young god knew none of Parvati's visitors, and challenged anyone who called – including Shiva, who flew into a rage and cut off his head, then soothed Parvati's tears by restoring Ganesh to life and giving him the first head he could find, that of an elephant. Ganesh's pot-belly is explained either by gluttony (he can never have enough of the food-offerings, especially fruit, which people make him), or as symbolizing the pot of plenty.

Ganesh's missing tusk. One of Ganesh's elephant-tusks is missing, and different myths give different explanations. In one, he was riding his rat in the moonlight when the animal was startled by a snake and threw him. Ganesh's guts burst out all over the ground, and he was forced to scrabble for them, cram them back and fasten them securely using the snake as a belt. The **Moon** watched, hysterical with laughter, and Ganesh tore out one of his own tusks in a tantrum and threw it at her. In another, Ganesh was employed by the sage **Vyasa** to write down the epic **Mahabharata**, and broke off one of his tusks to use as a pen. He made the sage speak slowly, insisting that no sentence of the epic should be written down until he (Ganesh) had pondered and understood every word – and this careful editing is the reason why the *Mahabharata* is the most perfectly-composed epic of them all, and why, among other things, Ganesh is the patron god of literature.

As god of good luck, Ganesh is a favourite figure for people to own, in the form of pictures or figurines. Some show him as an elephant with his foot on a mouse – all creation in one image, from the greatest to the least. Others depict a benignly-smiling, elephant-headed man with four or six arms. Ganesh-statues are often placed at crossroads and in niches on the sides of buildings. He is not regarded as one of the senior gods, but more as a kind of domestic, human-scale (even bumbling) benefactor – characteristic attributes of good-luck gods and spirits in many systems.
»→ **animal-gods, writing**

GANGA
India

Ganga ('swift'), in Hindu myth, was the river Ganges personified as a goddess. In some accounts, she was born from **Vishnu**'s toe and became his wife, until he tired of her and gave her to **Shiva**. In others she was the daughter of the god and goddess of the Himalayas, and was **Agni**'s wife, or was married to the mortal king Santanu, with whom her son was **Bhisma**.

Ganga on Earth. Originally Ganga flowed three times round **Brahma**'s estates on Mount **Meru**; it was to keep her happy in **Heaven** that the gods personified her and gave her divine husbands. Mortals made prolonged efforts to coax her down to Earth as well, but failed, until finally **Bhagiratha** persuaded Brahma to share her. Ganga was reluctant to leave, and threatened to jump to Earth so heavily that she would send it spinning and drown everything on it. But Shiva took her full weight on his head, and she wandered in his matted hair for seven years before flowing in seven more manageable streams to water the world.

Ganga, and the river Ganges, are the Milky Way.
»→ **Hera, water**

GANYMEDE
Europe (South)

Ganymede (Ganymedes, 'rejoicing in his own virility'), in Greek myth, was a Trojan prince so beautiful that **Zeus** took him into **Olympus** to be his lover, and made him the cupbearer of the gods.

Sidestepping the homosexual aspect of this story, Goethe turned it into a poem expressing Ganymede's rapture as he is carried aloft by Zeus' eagle, to be engulfed in and united with the Divine.
»→ **Adonis, beauty, Endymion**

GA-OH
Americas (North)

Ga-oh, in the myths of the Iroquois people of the Northeastern US woodlands, was the **giant** who ruled the winds. His four lieutenants, each of whom patrolled one compass direction, were Bear (North), Panther (West), Fawn (South) and Moose (East) – and the wind from each direction was governed by the character of its ruling animal: North winds were fierce, West winds sly, South winds gentle and East winds wet.

GARUDA
India

Garuda, in Hindu myth, was the son of **Kasyapa** and **Vinata**, daughter of **Daksha**. He was hatched from an egg, and in shape was a human with eagle's head, wings and talons. In colour he was pure gold, and was so dazzling that when he hatched mortals mistook him for **Agni** and worshipped him.

Garuda and the Moon. Garuda's mother Vinata quarrelled with her fellow-wife **Kadru**, mother of serpents, the senior wife of Kasyapa. Kadru's serpent-children kidnapped Vinata and imprisoned her in the **Underworld**. They refused to give her up unless Garuda stole the **Moon** and took it to light the caverns of the Underworld. Garuda tucked the Moon under his wing and flew out of **Heaven** – and it was only when the Underworld began to glow with a pale silver light that the gods realized what had happened. They snatched the Moon back in the nick of time, rescued Vinata and placated Garuda by giving him **immortality** and making him the charioteer (or in some accounts, the steed) of **Vishnu**.

Garuda and *amrita*. In another version of the same story, the **snakes**' price for releasing Vinata was a cup of **amrita**, which would give them **immortality**. In Heaven, the *amrita* was kept on a mountain-peak surrounded by towers of flame and a fire-wheel spoked with knives. Garuda dealt with the flame-towers by sucking up all the rivers in the world and dumping them on the flames. He coped with the fire-wheel by shrinking to the size of an ant and flying unharmed between the knives. He blew dust into the eyes of the *amrita*'s guardians and carried it to the Underworld. In some accounts, Indra tried to stop him on the way, but Garuda beat him, smashed his thunderbolt, delivered the *amrita* and freed his mother. In others, Indra snatched the *amrita* from the Underworld just as the serpents were about to drink. A few drops spilled on the ground, and the serpents divided their tongues to lick up as much as possible – which is why snakes are still immortal (being constantly reborn from themselves as they slough their skins), and why they have forked tongues. The story ends as before, with Garuda (who had gained so much power as stealer of *amrita* that no god dared challenge him) being given immortality and a place of honour as Vishnu's charioteer or steed.

*Garuda was regarded as a personification of the Sun's rays – indeed, the **Rig Veda** calls him the **Sun** itself, made into a bird. Because of his war against snakes, both he and his sacred stone, the emerald,* are considered sure protection against snakebite. He is a major participant in the **Mahabharata** and the Ramayana. In art he is usually shown as a magnificently-robed warrior, hung with gold, and with an eagle's – or sometimes, mysteriously, a parrot's – beak, vast fire-wings and talons instead of nails on his toes and fingers.

≫→ animal-gods

GAUNA
Africa

Gauna (also known as Gawa and Gawama), in the myths of the Bushpeople of Botswana, was **Death**, leader of spirits. He lived in the **Underworld**, and was forever roaming the Upper World to snatch unwary mortals and carry them below. His people were miserable and restless under the Earth, and tried always to escape and take over the Upper World. During the time when **Kaang** lived on Earth, he kept Gauna in check, and in particular taught human beings a series of rituals and taboos which, rigorously observed, would keep the **ghosts** in their graves and stop Gauna from taking over the Upper World.

GAUTAMA: *see* Siddhartha Gautama

GAWAIN
Europe (North)

Gawain, in Celtic and medieval Christian myth, was the son of King Lot of Orkney and **Arthur**'s sister Morgause; his half-brother was **Modred**. In some accounts his real father was not Lot but the **Sun**-god **Lug** (or Lot himself was Lug), and this explained the fact that Gawain's power was like the Sun's: it grew ever greater each morning, reached its peak at noon, and declined towards each evening.

Gawain and the green giant. In **Camelot**, Gawain was one of Arthur's most loyal and noble followers. One year, on New Year's Eve, a green **giant** rode into the hall and challenged the bravest warrior there to cut off his head, and then, one year later, to visit the green giant's castle and have his own head chopped off. Gawain accepted the challenge and decapitated the giant, who picked up his head and galloped away. The following year, Gawain set off to find the giant. He came to the castle of Lord Bertilak, and was royally entertained there for three nights and days. On each night, Bertilak's wife came and tried to seduce him, and he resisted her each time. On the fourth day, alone in the castle grounds, he came across the green giant, and bent his neck three times to the axe. Three times the giant chopped, and each time stopped just before cutting off Gawain's head. Then he disappeared, and Bertilak stood in his place. He told Gawain that the whole adventure had been a test, set by **Morgan le Fay** to find out which of Arthur's followers was the bravest, and Gawain had passed it. Each of the three blows was for one of the nights when he'd resisted seduction; if he had succumbed he would have died.

Gawain, as he survives in the medieval English poem Gawain and the Green Knight *and in the various Arthurian and* **Holy Grail** *sagas, is an invention of medieval chivalry, living by the concepts of bravery, honour and Christian piety which* informed that code. But his origins are pagan, and older: as Gwalchmai ('Mayhawk') in Welsh myth, he derives ultimately from the Irish Celtic **hero Cuculain**, son of **Lug** the Sun-god. Arthurian writers stitched him into the Camelot saga, adapting the original myths to fit – for example in the matter of his birth. They invented suitably chivalric adventures for him: in one account, for example, Lot and Morgause abandoned Gawain as soon as he was born, and he was brought up by the Pope as the epitome of Christian knightliness and honour. Setting off to find his true parents, he came to an enchanted castle, killed its lion-guardian and set free its five hundred women prisoners – and then left it for the real world, to earn by true knightly endeavour and adventure the love of the most beautiful of them all, the Lady Orgeuilleuse.

For all such attempts at unification, Gawain sits as uneasily in medieval Christian myth as do those other made-over figures from paganism, **Lancelot** and **Merlin**. He is presented one minute as the 'pure and perfect knight', the next as dangerously unstable and devious. He is either lecherous or prissy, and when magic occurs he seems more at home in the supernatural world than in the 'reality' of Christian belief and action. He goes in quest of the Grail, long before **Galahad** comes to Camelot – and gets only as far as Carbonek, becoming infatuated with Elaine, the grail-guardian, a surrender to original sin which makes him unworthy to continue.

GAYOMART
Asia (West)

Gayomart ('mortal'), in Iranian myth, was the first mortal. He existed for 3000 years as a spirit, and then **Ahura Mazda** gave him form and placed him on Earth. Gayomart masturbated, and his semen sprouted in the ground to engender Mahsya and Mahsyoi, ancestors of the human race. At first all these beings were immortal, and Gayomart taught his descendants the secrets of the gods. But then human beings fell prey to sexual lust (which was endemic in them because of the way Gayomart had produced their ancestors). They came under the spell of the whore-**demon** Jeh and her master **Ahriman**, the evil one, and didn't complain even when Ahriman murdered Gayomart. For this, Ahura Mazda made them mortal, and condemned them to eternal suffering.

GEB
Africa (North)

Geb ('Earth'), in Egyptian myth, was the son of **Shu** and **Tefnut**, and the twin brother of **Nut** ('Sky'). The **twins** were born locked together in a sexual embrace so tight that nothing could exist between them. **Ra**, their grandfather, ordered Shu ('air') to separate them, and Shu gradually prised them apart, forcing Nut up to form the Sky-arch and Geb down to form the flat Earth. In some accounts, Nut yearned so much for Geb that her vaginal fluids poured down over him – the only time it ever rained in Egypt – and he was so eager for her that his penis lifted in an erection of which Ra took advantage to mate him with a goose. (In this story, the goose went on to lay the egg from which the Sun was hatched.)

⋙→ **creation, Gaia, Rangi**

GEFION
Europe (North)

Gefion ('giver'), daughter of **Odin** in Nordic myth, was a **fertility** goddess, patron of ploughing. She was one of **Frigg**'s handmaids, and like her, had knowledge of the future but no power to change it. In some accounts, she married her half-brother Scyld and lived in his palace in Denmark. In others, she had **sex** with another half-brother, Gylfi, king of Sweden (one of the few mortals allowed to move freely between **Midgard** and **Asgard** and meet with gods as equals). She bore him four sons, and demanded a kingdom for them to rule. Gylfi offered her as much land as she could plough in a single day, and she turned her sons into four giant oxen, harnessed them and ploughed up a vast area, tearing it free of the Swedish mainland and towing it out to sea. It is now the Danish province of Sjaelland (Zealand).
≫→ farming

GEIRRÖD (GIANT)
Europe (North)

Geirröd, in Nordic myth, was a giant determined to punish **Thor** for killing **Hrungnir**. He captured **Loki** (who was flying about **Jotunheim**, land of the **giants**, disguised as a hawk), and tortured him until he agreed to trick Thor into visiting Geirröd's fortress, a castle made entirely of iron. Loki managed to get Thor out of **Asgard** without his belt of strength, iron gloves or giant-killing hammer Mjöllnir. But on the way to Geirröd's castle Thor had **sex** with the sorceress Grid, and she gave him another pair of gloves, a belt of strength and an unbreakable staff.

Geirröd first tried to kill Thor by drowning. He stationed his daughter Gjalp (whose period was just beginning) at the headwaters of a fast-flowing river, Vimur, and menstrual blood gushed from her in such quantities that the river doubled its depth from one second to the next, so that when Thor and Loki tried to cross it (Loki holding tightly to the belt of strength round Thor's waist) they would have drowned if Thor hadn't realized what the problem was and hurled a rock to plug Gjalp's vagina.

The gods reached Geirröd's castle, and instead of being welcomed into the main feast-hall were lodged in a goat-shed. Loki went to wash in a nearby stream, and Thor, left alone, fell asleep on the only chair. He dreamed that he was once again in the river, and the water was rising under him – and awoke suddenly to find that he was indeed rising. Geirröd's daughters Gjalp and Greip had turned themselves into cats and were arching their backs under his chair, pushing it up to crush him against the shed's iron ceiling. Thor took the unbreakable staff given him by Grid and wedged it against the roof. There was a tussle of strength, and at last the giantesses' heaving broke their own backs and they collapsed in a heap, dead, with Thor sprawling all over them.

Next morning, Geirröd summoned Thor and Loki to breakfast as if nothing had happened. But when Thor walked into the feast-hall, instead of coming forward to welcome him Geirröd picked up a lump of red-hot iron from a brazier and hurled it at him. Thor, who was wearing Grid's iron gloves, caught it, whirled it round his head and hurled it back. The iron crashed through one of the iron pillars which supported the roof, seared its way through Geirröd's guts and killed him. Thor chased the giant's servants out of the hall, which was tumbling round their ears, and laid about him with Grid's unbreakable staff until every one of them was dead.

Until this adventure, Thor and Loki had been good friends. But from this time on, though Thor was affable enough with Loki, he never trusted him again – one aspect of the antagonism between Loki and the other gods of Asgard which will flower one day into **Ragnarök**, the cosmic battle which will end this cycle of the universe.

GEIRRÖD (MORTAL)
Europe (North)

Geirröd, in Nordic myth, was a treacherous mortal who tried to dispossess his brother Agnar and steal their father's throne, but was unmasked by **Odin**.

GENDENWITHA
Americas (North)

Gendenwitha, in the myths of the Iroquois people of the Northeastern US, was the morning star. Originally she was a mortal princess. But the hunter Sosondowah, who had been kidnapped into **Heaven** to be the guard and lover of Dawn, fell in love with her and courted her. In spring he appeared as a **bluebird**, in summer as a **blackbird**, and finally in autumn he flew down and carried her to his mistress' house. Dawn was so angry that she turned Gendenwitha into a star and set her as a jewel in the centre of her own forehead.

GERMANIC MYTH

Germanic myth is called after Germania, the Roman name for the region bounded by the rivers Rhine, Danube and Vistula. It was the home of three peoples in particular: Goths, Teutons and Germans. When the Romans conquered them (a process which began under Julius Caesar in the first century BCE, and continued well into the third century of the Christian era), many people remained and accepted Roman cultural and religious domination. Others moved out, taking their cultural ideas North into what is now Scandinavia (the Teutons), East towards the Black Sea (the Goths) and South of the Rhine and West into what are now thought of as the Low Countries and Celtic and Anglo-Saxon Britain (the Germans).

Amalgamation and dispersal, combined with conversion to Christianity (in some areas, as early as the fourth century BCE) had a catastrophic effect on the independence of Germanic myth. It was either marginalized completely (in Christian areas), or submerged in the more powerful traditions of the areas of migration: Nordic myth in particular engulfed it lock, stock and barrel. It thus survives mainly in folk memory (such as the day-name Tuesday, called after Tiw god of war), or as a somewhat hazy part of the myths of other areas. Frija, goddess of love, for example, lent her attributes and cosmological standing first to **Venus** and then to **Freyja** and **Idun**. The **thunder**-god **Donar** became **Thor**. **Woden**/Wotan survived first as **Mercury** and then as **Odin**.

In the medieval period, attempts were made to reassert the Germanness of the Germanic tradition. Epic poems were created, applying to selected ancient stories the style and values of chivalric heroic narrative. These, in turn, were taken up and developed by nineteenth-century German creators such as Wagner, inspired not only by the vigour of the tales but by the glow of Germanic nationalism which infused them. This gave such stories as that of the Nibelungs, Parsifal and Lohengrin a kind of spurious identity – not the real Germanness of the original myths (which lies now mainly in their Nordic versions) but a wished-for, Romantic makeover which, for all the greatness of the works it inspired, is as fake as Sir Walter Scott's Scottishness or the self-conscious Oirishry of *Finian's Rainbow*.

In the present book, some characters from Germanic myth appear under their own names, others under the names, and in the articles, of those gods, **giants** and **demons** into which they metamorphosed in other myth-traditions. Chief among them are Alberich (**Andvari**), **Atli**, Balder (**Baldur**), Brosingamene (**Brisingamen**), Brunhild/Brünnhilde (**Brynhild**), Donar/Thunor/Donner (**Thor**), Fafner (**Fafnir**), **Faust**, Fricka (**Frigg**), Frija (**Freyja**), Götterdämmerung (**Ragnarök**), Hoder (**Höd**), Hoener (**Honir**), Holler/Oller/Uller/Vulder (**Ull**), Loge (**Loki**), **Nibelungs**, **Norns**,

Sigmund, Siegfried (**Sigurd**), **Tiwaz**, Wayland/Weland (**Volund**), Wotan/Woden (**Odin**)

⫸ Flying Dutchman, Mephistopheles, Signy, Sinfiotl

GERYON'S CATTLE
Europe (South)

Geryon ('crane'), in Greek myth, was a **giant**. He had three bodies from the waist up, each with its own arms and head. He lived on the island of Erythea in the river of **Ocean** which girded the world. Here he looked after countless cattle; their hides glowed red like the setting **Sun**, and they were guarded by Geryon's giant herdsman Eurytion and his two-headed dog Orthus. For Heracles' tenth **labour**, King **Eurystheus** of Mycenae sent him to steal some of Geryon's cattle, and drive them all the way back from Erythea to Mycenae.

To reach Erythea, Heracles travelled to the Western edge of the Mediterranean Sea, to the narrow neck of land which joined Africa and Europe. There was no way through to Ocean, so he made one, battering the rocks away, levering the continents apart and setting two massive stone slabs (ever afterwards known as the Pillars of Heracles) at the sides of the channel he gouged. **Helius** the Sun-god, amazed at his efforts, offered to lend him the ship which carried him round the stream of Ocean from West to East each night, and Heracles sailed in it to Geryon's island.

Geryon's cattle were drinking at a river-estuary, their glowing hides almost invisible in the setting sun. As Heracles crept up on them, the watchdog Orthus ran snarling towards him, and he clubbed it dead. Then Eurytion the herdsman shouted for Geryon, and ran to attack. Heracles just had time to kill Eurytion when Geryon appeared: monstrous, vast, a living hill. His three bodies kept him safe from most attacks: if one was injured the other two kept fighting until it recovered. Heracles solved this problem by running round and shooting Geryon from the side. His shot was so powerful that the arrow, poisoned with **Hydra**'s blood, not only passed through all three of Geryon's bodies and left him dead, but also grazed **Hera** (who had come to help him) and sent her weeping back to **Olympus**. Heracles loaded the sun-ship with Geryon's cattle, sailed back to the Pillars of Heracles, returned the ship to Helius and drove the cattle overland to Mycenae.

GEUSH URVAN
Asia (West)

Geush Urvan, in Iranian myth, was the power of **Mother Earth** given form as a **bull**. For the 3000 years it lived on Earth, all the strength of the universe was located there. Then **Mithras** killed it, and its energy was transferred to the **sky**, where universal strength ever afterwards belonged to the gods. The decaying corpse, however, remained on Earth, and the last scraps of Geush Urvan's power were reformed into every species of animal and plant.

⋙→ animal-gods, bulls and cows

GHEDE
Americas (Caribbean)

Ghede, in the original myths of Haiti, was the god of love, **sex** incarnate. In later, Voodoo myth he was amalgamated with Baron Samedi (also called Baron Cimetiere, Baron La Croix and Baron Piquant), god of **death**. He kept his earlier lustful ways, and a fondness for rum and feasting (attributes he shared with his brother the harvest-god **Azacca** and with his wife, **Mama Brigitte**). He was a dandy, always wearing a black tail-coat, a top hat and sunglasses, twirling a cane and smoking a cigar or a cigarette in a long holder. He loved to dance, and swept his followers away into the ecstasy and trance of dancing. But the dance, which originally was a phallic ritual of birth, had now become a dance of death: Baron Samedi's orgies always ended (for his mortal followers) at the crossroads between this world and the **Underworld**, and the way they went was down.

Because Ghede was Guardian of the Crossroads, he knew all the secrets of magic, and had second hearing and second sight. He could be consulted for advice – often on questions of **fertility**, *either of humans, crops or animals. The questioner made blood-sacrifice and asked the priest questions to put to Ghede, and the god answered in the patterns of rum-drops spilled in the dust, or in the fall of dice or the turning of Tarot cards. The advice was often frightening and apparently ridiculous, but it was always true and you neglected it at your peril. Mythographers claim that these rituals, and the whole apparatus of Baron Samedi, are examples (rare in world myth) of 'recent' reality – in this case, the dress and manners of eighteenth-nineteenth-century slave-owners – being successfully grafted on to ideas from earlier, pre-literate times.*

⋙→ prophecy

GHOSTS: *see* bhutas, *gaki, manes,* Russalki

GIANTS

Giants originated at the beginning of **creation**. In some cases they came before the gods, in others they were gods themselves. A few were essential to the establishment of universal order – **Ymir**'s body was dismembered to make the world, **Pan Gu** separated Sky from Earth, **Briareus** rescued **Zeus** when other gods staged a Heavenly *coup*. But most were displaced by the gods (who were physically weaker but far more intelligent), and spent the rest of eternity planning revenge, trying to defeat the other supernatural powers in cosmic battles or to steal their **immortality**, and using their huge strength to help, or more often to prey on, human beings. From their brief heyday at the apex of creation, giants dwindled in importance until they became little more than lurking presences, spirits of mountains, forest-lords or sleepers and prisoners under the Earth whose tossing and turning caused **earthquakes**. Kindly giants exist only in folk-tales; most giants in myth are implacable and dangerous.

»→ (Americas): Bochica, Dzoavits; (Arctic): Sedna; (Celtic): Albion, Bran, Gogmagog; (China): Begdu San, Kuafu, Li No Zha, Pan Gu; (Finnish): Antero Vipunen; (Greece): Briareus, Cyclopes, Earthborn Giants, Hundred-handed Giants, Pallas, Polyphemus, Procrustes; (India): *Daityas*, Hayagriva; (Mesopotamia): Og, Samson; (Nordic): Bergelmir, Bestla, Geirröd, Gilling, Grid, Gunnlod, Hrungnir, Hrym, Hymir, Skadi, Skrymsli, Surt, Suttung, Ymir; (Slavic): Mikula, Svyatogor; (Tibet): Dharmapalas

GILGAMESH
Asia (West)

Gilgamesh, in Mesopotamian myth, was two thirds god (his mother was the sky-goddess Ninsun) and one third mortal (his father, a **demon**, disguised himself as king of Uruk). He succeeded to the throne, and proved his valour by hunting every kind of animal in his kingdom, wild or tame, and his splendour by surrounding Uruk with a wall of 900 defensive towers. Inside this citadel he behaved like a tyrant, enslaving his male subjects and raping the females. The people prayed for help to the gods, and the gods decided to end Gilgamesh's reign by sending a champion who would publicly fight and humiliate him. **Ninhursaga**, **Mother Earth**, created a **giant** called Enkidu, and placed him to live with the wild beasts of the mountains far from **civilization** – and the other gods put a picture of him into Gilgamesh's mind. Gilgamesh decided to catch him and add him to the royal menagerie.

Instead of hunting Enkidu by force, Gilgamesh sent a prostitute to seduce him. Gingerly, she persuaded Enkidu not to hurt her, then went closer and began teaching him the arts of **sex**, washing, wearing clothes and drinking alcohol. After six days and nights of this, Enkidu was ready to follow her anywhere. She took him to Uruk, and inside the city walls. Gilgamesh, thinking that Enkidu must by now be exhausted, went to meet him – and instead of greeting each other normally the two seized each other and began to wrestle. As they fought, however, they began by respecting and ended by loving each other, and eventually they fell to their knees at the same moment, clasped each other's necks and kissed. From that day on they were inseparable friends – and Gilgamesh's people now had two oppressive rulers instead of one. Once more they prayed to the gods, and the gods intervened, putting the idea into Enkidu's head that he was bored with civilization and into Gilgamesh's mind the notion of going on a quest, finding a **monster** (Humbaba, a **fire-breather**) and killing it. The gods intended that Humbaba would kill them both, but after a fierce fight Enkidu held the monster from behind while Gilgamesh stabbed its neck and killed it.

Gilgamesh had now cheated **death** once for each of the two divine thirds of his nature. There remained the third, mortal part, and the gods decided to conquer this by a trick. First **Ishtar**, goddess of desire, went to seduce Gilgamesh, and when he rejected her (preferring Enkidu) she ran to Father **An**, weeping that he'd insulted her. She demanded that An send the Bull of **Heaven** to kill him – and when Gilgamesh and Enkidu took the bull and killed it, exactly as they'd earlier dealt with Humbaba, she gathered the gods together and asked their approval if she personally killed both Enkidu and Gilgamesh.

Ishtar used a simple plague to kill Enkidu. But she made Gilgamesh's death more lingering. First she let him think that Enkidu might be sleeping, not dead, and he wept for seven days and nights by his friend's body before a maggot fell out of Enkidu's nose and showed that it was time for the **giant** to be buried. Then she sent Gilgamesh on a fearsome journey to visit **Utnapishtim** (his ancestor, the only mortal ever granted **immortality**), to ask how to cheat death. Utnapishtim's wife told Gilgamesh of a magic plant, 'eternal youth', growing at the bottom of a lake deep in the **Underworld**. With enormous difficulty, weighting his feet with stones, Gilgamesh dived down, picked the plant and set off for home, intending to share the plant with his people. But on the way he stopped to bathe in a pond, and a **snake** stole the plant and ate it. From that day on snakes were immortal, able to slough their old bodies and put on new ones – and Gilgamesh went home to Uruk to wait for death, destroyed by love exactly as Ishtar had intended.

This story, one of the world's oldest surviving narratives, was compiled some time in the third or second millennium BCE and written down for the library of King Asshurbanipal in the 600s BCE. It took up twelve clay tablets, each containing some 300 lines of verse. As well as the main story, the Epic of Gilgamesh *contained an even older narrative: Tablet Eleven was the story of the great **flood** as a result of which Utnapishtim, the only survivor, was granted immortality.*

Archaeologists have found evidence of a real Gilgamesh, a king of Uruk who fought King Agga of Kish in about 2700 BCE. This leads mythographers to think that the Epic may be based on distant memories of real events, in much the same way as Homer's

Iliad *may have taken as its starting-point the siege of a real city. The real Gilgamesh is also thought to figure in the Bible, as 'Nimrod son of Cush', the 'mighty hunter' mentioned in the Book of Genesis (see* **Babel***), and the ancestor of the Asshurbanipal who had the* Epic *stored in writing.*
⨠ heroes

GILLING
Europe (North)

Gilling, in Nordic myth, was a **giant** treacherously killed by the dwarfs Fjalar and Galar. His son punished them by forcing them to give him the mead of inspiration they'd made from the blood of **Kvasir** (whom they'd also killed). In this way the mead found its way to the giants, and from there back to the gods. Gilling's role in its recovery was passive but crucial.

GINUNGAGAP
Europe (North)

Ginungagap ('the yawn between'), in Nordic myth, was the primeval void. It existed before existence, and was bounded by two huge worlds, **Muspell** and **Niflheim**. When glaciers fingered out from Niflheim across Ginungagap and met flames from Muspell, icy mists were formed, and took shape as the **giant Ymir** to begin **creation**.

GLUSKAP
Americas (North)

Gluskap ('he who conquers by argument, [not by force]': that is, 'liar'), or Glooscap, in the myths of several peoples from North American forests, was a creator-god; he also featured in hundreds of folk-tales as a **trickster**.

Gluskap and Malsum. The Abenaki people say that Gluskap and his twin **Malsum** ('Wolf') were children of **Mother Earth**. Gluskap was air and light, Malsum rock and dark. At first, when their mother died, the **twins** lived harmoniously enough. Gluskap took fragments of Mother Earth's body and made them into the **Moon**, the **Sun**, plains, plants, fish, birds and animals. Malsum made mountains, river-valleys, reptiles and insects. But the harmony was deceptive. There was no way for light and dark to co-exist forever. One day the brothers were discussing their own mortality. Malsum said that nothing but a fern-root could kill him. Gluskap said that only an owl-feather could end his life. At once Malsum stabbed his brother with an owl-feather, and Gluskap fell dead. But this was only his first life lost: he sprang up, plucked a fern and stabbed Malsum dead. Malsum was absorbed into his Mother's body. His spirit still haunts the world below, as a prowling, vengeful wolf.

Gluskap set about peopling the Upper World. He made human beings from handfuls of Mother Earth; he outlawed evil spirits (who flocked to Malsum in the World Below); he battled the Stone **Giants** who ruled the hills. He outwitted Old Man Winter, not by driving him North but by inviting him ever farther South, so that the Lord of Cold began to thaw and melt, and had to retreat to his ice-kingdom and leave Gluskap's people to farm in peace.

Gluskap the trickster. Gluskap was a **shape-changer**, able to make himself whatever he chose to be. He was cloud and dust-in-sunlight; he was water-eddy, arrow, smoke and thorn. He rode whales and eagles; he tried the shapes of all living creatures. His favourite shape was rabbit, and his people worshipped Rabbit the Trickster above all other spirits.

Gluskap and Wasis. Like all tricksters, Gluskap was arrogant. In Algonquian myth, he boasted that no living creature could resist him. But his wife pointed to their infant son Wasis, lying on the floor of their birch-bark tent, and said that Gluskap's power would meet its match in *him*. Gluskap sang a sleep-spell; Wasis laughed and waved his arms. Gluskap danced and changed his shape; the baby slept. 'Get up! Walk! Run!' Gluskap shouted – and Wasis lay still. Gluskap knew that his time in the world was over. He paddled his canoe up the streams of air, East beyond the sunrise, and was never seen on Earth again. But the Algonquians still believe that when the spirits of Evil rise from the World Below to choke the universe, he will come again, paddling down sunshafts to rescue them.

≫→ **animal-gods, Arthur, fertility, Nanabush, tricksters**

GOGMAGOG
Europe (North)

Gogmagog, in Celtic myth, was one of the **giants** who were the original inhabitants of the British Isles. He was killed by **Brit** (a Trojan who'd fled to Britain after the **Trojan War**), cut into two halves and buried not far from what is now Cambridge, where his grave can still be seen in the form of two low hills.

GOLDEN FLEECE, THE
Europe (South)

The Golden Fleece. When Ino, mistress of King **Athamas** of Thebes in Greek myth, tried to bring about the death of Athamas' legitimate son **Phrixus** so that her own children could inherit the throne, the gods flew Phrixus on a golden ram out of danger to the distant Northern country of Colchis, ruled by Aeëtes son of the **Sun**. Aeëtes, hoping that Phrixus would give him the golden ram, let him marry his daughter Chalciope. But Phrixus sacrificed the ram to **Ares**, whose priests hung the Fleece in a garden protected by a dragon – and for this, Aeëtes murdered Phrixus. Phrixus' ghost began wandering on the banks of the river **Styx** begging **Charon** to ferry it into the **Underworld**, or appearing at midnight to Phrixus' relatives in Iolcus, demanding that they bury his body and promising them, as a reward, the Golden Fleece.

Pelias and Jason. The king of Iolcus was Phrixus' cousin **Pelias**. He was an old man, with troubles of his own. Twenty years before he had stolen power, and had consolidated it ever afterwards by murdering every male he thought might ever challenge him. When **Jason** arrived unexpectedly in Iolcus, therefore, Pelias decided to get rid of him by challenging him to sail to Colchis and fetch the Fleece.

The voyage of *Argo*. Jason gathered a crew of fifty **heroes** from all over Greece, and asked Argus, a pupil of the craftsman-god **Hephaestus**, to build a ship. Argus called it *Argo* after himself. The **Argonauts** launched *Argo* and set sail for Colchis. On the way they made landfall several times – and each time brought adventure. In Lemnos the women (who had murdered all their men some months before for bringing mistresses back from another island) made them so welcome that they refused to leave for a year, until **Heracles** (who had broken off his **Labours** to join the expedition and who was eager to finish it), rounded them up and herded them back on board. On Bear Island they helped the human inhabitants kill a tribe of six-armed, bear-headed **giants** – and **Rhea**, the giants' protector, sent storms and gales to delay their sailing. On the shores of Asia Minor they beached to fetch water – and the **water-nymphs** stole Heracles' beautiful page-boy **Hylas**, whereupon Heracles abandoned the expedition and went back to his Labours. In Bebrycus Zeus' son Pollux (see **Dioscuri**) killed King Amycus (who insisted on boxing to the death with the strongest man on every ship that called), and Amycus' people attacked the Argonauts with clubs and knives. In Salmydessus Calais and Zetes put to flight two **Harpies** which were tormenting King **Phineus** – and Phineus showed his gratitude by telling Jason about the **Clashing Rocks** ahead, and how to avoid them.

Jason in Colchis. The Argonauts were the first humans ever to survive the Clashing Rocks and come to Colchis, and Aeëtes was amazed to see them. He was even more amazed when Jason bluntly demanded the Golden Fleece. But instead of killing him outright he set him three impossible tasks: to yoke two fire-breathing bronze bulls and plough the Field of Ares; to sow the ploughed field with dragon's teeth, and

single-handed kill the army of warriors which grew from them; to kill the Fleece's dragon-guardian.

Jason would never have managed these tasks alone, but two goddesses helped him. **Aphrodite** had a grudge to settle with Aeëtes' father **Helius** the Sun-god (who had told her husband Hephaestus that she was having an affair with Ares), and **Hera** was angry with **Poseidon**, and meant to do all in her power to help Jason end the life of Poseidon's son Pelias. Instead of helping Jason openly, the goddesses made use of Aeëtes' daughter **Medea**, a priestess of **Hecate** with magic powers. Aphrodite bribed her son **Eros** to fire an arrow of desire for Jason into Medea's heart, and Medea promised to help Jason if he, in turn, would marry her and take her back to Greece. She told him how to perform the first two tasks, and gave him magic ointment to protect him from the bulls' fiery breath.

Next morning servants brought Jason a helmet filled with dragon's teeth, and led him to the cave where the bulls were kept. Jason stripped off his clothes and plunged into the cave, protected by Medea's ointment. There was a roar and a trampling of bronze on rock, and he reappeared leading the bulls – Medea had told him that their fiery breath was all the power they had, and when it failed their anger would die as fire burns out in smoke. Jason yoked the bulls, ploughed the Field of Ares and sowed the dragon's teeth. At once warriors grew like standing corn in the furrows. Instead of fighting them, Jason threw a stone and hit one of them. The wounded man turned on his neighbour, the neighbour turned on *his* neighbour, and the warriors soon fought each other until all were killed.

Pretending to keep his promise, Aeëtes invited the Argonauts to a feast. Tomorrow, he said, if Jason completed the third task, killing the dragon-guardian, they could take the Fleece and sail away. But Medea warned Jason that Aeëtes meant to sacrifice them all at dawn to his father the Sun. In the darkness of night, therefore, Jason sent the Argonauts to launch *Argo* and prepare to sail, and he, Medea and Medea's brother Apsyrtus went to the Grove of Ares. Medea shook magic drops in the dragon's eyes and sang a sleep-spell, and Jason took the Fleece from its tree and hung it round his shoulders like a golden coat. Then he, Medea and Apsyrtus jumped on board *Argo* and shouted to the crew to row.

The journey home. They had very little start. The priests of Ares found the sleeping dragon and raised the alarm, and Aeëtes came swooping after *Argo* in a fast warship. He would have sunk her and killed her crew, if Medea had not sliced Apsyrtus to pieces and dropped the pieces overboard, one by one. Aeëtes had to stop, each time, to gather them for burial, and so *Argo* slipped easily beyond pursuit.

Outraged by Apsyrtus' murder, the gods snatched *Argo* up in whirlwinds and tossed her from sea to sea. They lashed the crew with sleet and let the ship wallow for days in flat calm and parching sun. At last *Argo* herself rebelled. When she was built, Argus had pegged into her a beam of sacred oak which had the power to speak and prophesy; now she used it for the first and only time. Jason and Medea should go to **Circe**'s floating island, where the goddess would free them from blood-guilt; meanwhile the other Argonauts should wait for them in Drepanum. **Iris** the rainbow-goddess carried Jason and Medea to Circe's island, and **Thetis** took charge of *Argo*, leading her safely past the cliffs where **Scylla and Charybdis** lurked, past the Wandering Reefs and the water-meadows where the Sun's cattle grazed. The Argonauts saw the **Sirens** singing in the distance, and would have been drawn to their deaths if **Orpheus** had not played his lyre and drowned the siren-song. At last they reached Drepanum, where King Alcinous welcomed them.

By the time Iris delivered Jason and Medea to Drepanum, the war-fleet from Colchis had also arrived, demanding back the Fleece. But Alcinous sent them home empty-handed, and the Argonauts sailed safely back to Iolcus. Here Medea tricked Pelias' daughters into murdering their father, and as soon as the tyrant was dead Jason gave the people the Golden Fleece and the priests made offerings so that Phrixus' ghost could rest in peace at last.

GOMMATESHVARA
India

Gommateshvara (or Bahubali), in Jain myth, was the second son of **Rishabha**. When Rishabha renounced his kingdom, he left his throne to his eldest son – and Gommateshvara challenged the decision. For a year the brothers fought, and then Gommateshvara, on the point of winning, suddenly gave up his claim and retreated to meditate as his father had before him. He stood in the same spot for a year, while creepers covered his body and insects, birds and reptiles made their homes on him. His brother was so impressed that he built a statue in his memory, 500 bow-lengths high, and even gods and **demons** bowed down to worship it.

*This myth was probably invented in the tenth or eleventh century CE to explain a huge statue, nineteen metres high, found in the jungle at Sravana Belgola. When the statue was uncovered, it was found to glisten from head to foot. This was explained by another myth: that **Mother Earth**, who had caused the discovery of the statue in the first place, anointed it herself from a cup of immortal milk. Ever since its discovery, the statue has been anointed by mortal worshippers every quarter of a century; the next occasion will be in 2017 CE.*

GONG GONG
Asia (East)

Gong Gong, the **water**-god in Chinese myth, quarrelled with Jurong, god of **fire** at the beginning of **creation**, and lost. In his shame he tried to commit suicide by running full-tilt against one of the four rock-pillars which supported the universe. He himself, being immortal, was unhurt, but the pillar shattered, the universe tilted and everything on it began to slide into the gulf of chaos. **Nü Gua**, goddess of order, hastily repaired the damage, shoring up the pillars with the four legs of an immortal tortoise. Gong Gong was not punished, but lost all status. He has grumbled and muttered about the universe – and been wary of fire – ever since.

GOOD LUCK: *see* Ekkekko, Fortuna, Kui, Laima, Lakshmi, Seven Gods of Good Luck, Silenus, Three Gods of Happiness, Wen Jang

GORGONS, THE
Europe (South)

The three Gorgons ('grim ones'), in Greek myth, were daughters of the Old Man of the **Sea** and his sister Ceto; their sisters were the **Graeae**, and their names were Euryale ('wanderer'), **Medusa** ('ruler') and Sthenno ('strong one'). They were yellow-winged dog-women with snake-hair, bronze talons and copper fish-scales covering their entire bodies, boars' tusks and eyes one glance from which turned mortal flesh to stone. They lived underground in Cisthene, guarded by their sisters the Graeae, and no one dared approach them except **Perseus**, who killed Medusa and took her head.
»+ **monsters and dragons**

GÖTTERDÄMMERUNG: *see* Ragnarök

GRACES, THE
Europe (South)

The Graces (Greek Charites; Latin Gratiae), in Greek and Roman myth, were in some accounts the children of **Zeus**, in others of **Dionysus**, in still others of **Aphrodite**. Most accounts say that there were three of them: Cale (Kale, 'beautiful'), Euphrosyne ('cheerful') and Pasithea ('total goddess'). Some accounts add Aglaea (Aglaia, 'shining') and Thalia ('flowering'), or put one of them in Euphrosyne's place.

The Graces were handmaids of Aphrodite and **Eros**. Their function was to enhance the joy of life, and they often sang and danced with the **Muses**. They filled the world with happiness and sprinkled it with perfume. In some accounts they assisted Dionysus, moderating the effects of too much drinking; in others they breathed on plants to make them grow.

The Graces were a favourite subject for sculptors. There are usually three of them, beautiful women dressed in flowing robes or naked, standing in a circle with their arms round one another. The pose is difficult to balance in stone, and carving the Graces became a challenge for apprentice stone-carvers, who used it as a graduation exercise. The group is therefore one of the commonest in both ancient and Renaissance European sculpture.
≫→ *apsaras*, **beauty**

GRAEAE, THE
Europe (South)

The Graeae (Graiai, 'grey ones'; also known as Phorcides, 'daughters of Phorcys' after their father the sea-spirit Phorcys), in Greek myth, were Pemphredo ('wasp'), Enyo ('warlike') and Deino ('dread'). They were granddaughters of **Sea** and sisters of the **Gorgons**. They had the bodies of swans or beautiful girls, but their hair was lank and grey and they had only one eye and one tooth among them. Their home was a lightless guard-post at the entrance to Cisthene where their Gorgon sisters lived. While two of the Graeae slept, the third took eye and tooth and stayed on guard; when her watch was done she woke one of her sisters and gave her the eye and tooth in turn. When **Perseus** went to Cisthene to kill **Medusa**, he hid in wait until this moment of changeover, then snatched the eye and tooth and refused to return them until the Graeae gave him winged sandals and a helmet of invisibility, and showed him the Gorgons' lair, deep inside the cave.

*The Graeae are a personification of mist, and were also **Underworld** beings, by definition invisible: two good reasons why they were never shown in art.*
≫→ **monsters and dragons**

GREAT GODDESS
Some twentieth-century mythographers have suggested that just as the **supreme deity** was usually thought of as male, and was one and the same person despite his many names in different traditions, so there was a single female deity, the Great Goddess. Her attributes, myths and worship were similar in many parts of the world, although, like her male counterpart, she had many names. She was usually associated with the **Moon**, **Mother Earth** and **fertility**; in some traditions, she also supervised **death**.
≫→ (Egypt): Aset; (Greece): Artemis, Cybele, Demeter, Rhea; (India): Devi, Durga, Kali; (Japan): Amaterasu; (Mesopotamia): Astarte; (Nordic): Freyja; (Oceanic): Hina: (Slavic): Mati-Syra-Zemlya; (Tibet): Dorje Pahmo

GREAT RAINBOW SNAKE
The Great Rainbow Snake was known in West Africa, parts of Polynesia and Melanesia, but mainly in Australia and

Papua New Guinea. In these areas it had as many names as there were peoples: they included Galeru (or Galaru or Kaleru), Karia, Kunmanggur, Langal, Mindi, Muit, Ngalbjod, Taipan, Ungur (or Yurlunggur or Woinunggur), Wollunkwa, Wonambi, Worombi and Yero. In some traditions the Snake was female, and a slit-drum made from a hollowed log symbolized her vagina (and its beating her roaring); in others the Snake was male (and the drum was his penis); in many he/she was of both sexes, or neither.

The Snake was the creator and preserver of life. In some stories, it came down from the sky in the Dream Time (see **Australian Myth**), and its writhing produced river-beds, creeks and waterholes. In others it was the guardian of all **water** on Earth, and hence of **fertility** and survival. When it was treated with respect, it slept. When it was angered – for example when a woman bathed in a waterhole during her period – it sent thunderstorms and floods. In one version of the pollution-story (**Julunggul**), the Snake ate and regurgitated the polluters, time and time again, to populate the world with plants and creatures.

The Snake was disgusted by blood, whether menstrual or not. For this reason, it rejected blood-sacrifice. The way to appease it was the way of soothing all snakes: by singing and repetitive, swaying dances. Australian peoples thought it particularly susceptible to the boom of the didgeridoo – for it had no ears and 'heard' sounds by sensing vibrations in the ground or in the air. Its sky-symbol was the rainbow, and its sacred substances were mother-of-pearl (for its iridescence) and quartz (for its water-drop glitter).

The Snake was a favourite subject in art. It had as many shapes as there were stories, and each story and its associated art belonged to a specific area, often centred on a stream or waterhole. But common to all art was the snake as a vast, multicoloured ribbon of life, surrounding the painting as water surrounds a continent, or coiling through it in serpentine, labyrinthine patterns.

GREEK MYTH

Greek myth is remarkable in three ways. First, it is diverse, and prismatic in detail, to an extent matched only by systems from larger areas and more populous communities: North American myth, for example. Second, it is intellectually consistent, harmonious and rational in a way which makes it seem more than a mere anthology of folk material. Third, it is remarkably undogmatic and unassertive. Elements of myth were used in religious practice (see below), but the vast majority of the myths were secular and open-ended – qualities which make their appeal both general and diverse.

The variety of Greek myth is explainable first by the landscape of Greece itself. Myths arose in several hundred distinct communities – states separated by mountains; islands – and travelled slowly. Each small area had its own stories, and the time and remoteness to develop them. And there is a second explanation: the 'geography' not of real landscape but of the ancient Greek imagination. The

Greeks prided themselves on being intellectually inquisitive and assimilative. They thought of the mind as being like some kind of capacious bag, into which all knowledge, all anecdote, all feeling could be stuffed, and from which one might fish out wonders. Nothing was demanded and nothing prohibited. When people travelled to new places, the first things to be traded (after the exchange of hospitality and names) were ideas. Greeks were the 'chattering class' incarnate – except that they chattered not just about their own local concerns, but about everyone and everything.

A favourite subject for such talk was myth. The stories were compared, added to, developed, in a way not found in other geographically diverse communities, for example Australia or Japan. New ideas, new slants on old ideas, might come from other Greek communities, or be imported from Persia, Egypt, or any of the other places visited by Greeks. This quickly led to the division mentioned above, between sacred and secular use of the myths. At the level of ritual and festival observance, those local myths which had their origins in particular places or religious customs were respected with a fundamentalist rigour as great as (later) Christian adherence to the detail of such stories as those of **Adam** or **Noah**. But in addition to this, and separate from it, the myths (often, the same myths) were enthusiastically revised and embellished, virtually every time they were retold. Some stories – those about the craftsman **Daedalus** or the wind-lord **Aeolus**, for example – exist in dozens of local variants. Others have come down to us in slightly garbled sequence, where a single reteller or a group of tellers have tried to make sense of a mixed bag of tales: the Labours of **Heracles** are an example. Even the best-known cycles of all, for example the story of the House of **Atreus**, were never given canonical form, but were subject to endless new versions, constant recension, incessant tinkering.

At some time early in the first millennium BCE (scholars are not unanimous about dates), this tinkering began to happen on a self-consciously grand and artistic scale. Hesiod, in his *Theogony* ('origin of the gods') collected and retold many of the myths of the birth of the universe, the **creation** and the coming of the gods. Homer, in his 'hymns' (or in hymns attributed to him) collected myths about specific gods, and in the *Iliad* and *Odyssey* organized a huge collection of diverse myths into coherent narratives about (respectively) the origins and events of the **Trojan War**, the greatest unifying event in 'history' until his time, and (in the tale of **Odysseus**' wanderings as he returned home from Troy) myths from the entire geographical area traversed by Greeks. These poems, particularly the *Iliad* and *Odyssey*, were of such compelling artistic and intellectual distinction that they themselves quickly became fundamental works.

The result of this was that Homer became widely regarded as a 'Greek' (that is, pan-Greek) author. Although several states vied for the honour of being remembered as his birthplace, his work was considered the property of all Greeks, a kind of intellectual validation of what it was to *be* Greek. Thus, local myths and attitudes which he incorporated into his stories became the property not just of their own areas, but of all Greek-speakers. The process can be seen in the way the structures of the society depicted by Homer (and, perhaps, for which he composed his poems) became standardized to the point where every real Greek community, and even the imaginary kingdoms of the gods, were assumed to share them. In one form or another, Homer's hierarchies became part of a view of the order of life which permeated Greek thought. They were modified from area to area, but (except in Sparta) were seldom replaced by utterly different systems. The same is true, in a subtler but equally pervasive way, of attitudes. It is impossible, at this distance in time, to decide whether the habits of thought in the bulk of Greek myths are indigenous or learned, whether they reflect the societies in which the myths grew up or are the fruits of a single mind. Certainly, when Western scholars of the past described some myths (such as those of **Dionysus**) as 'exotic' or 'bizarre', what they really meant was 'unHomeric'. (Hesiod's accounts of the attitudes and actions of the powers of the primordial universe were often criticized in this way – and he either predated Homer or knew nothing of his work.)

There are therefore two main types of Greek myths: those mentioned by Homer, and the rest. The Homeric poems were quarried for themes and attitudes by later artists of all kinds, from the great Athenian tragedians to vase-painters, composers and archi-

tects. Later writers treating non-Homeric stories – for example Apollonius retelling the cycle about **Jason** and the **Argonauts** in search of the **Golden Fleece**, or Virgil Romanizing the adventures of **Aeneas** after the Trojan War – often modelled both their work and their attitudes on Homer. The characteristic diversity and bizarreness of myth were squeezed out of the Greek system, being replaced with a feeling, as it were, of intellectual or aesthetic appropriateness, each story fitting some unstated but overarching pattern. (This is perhaps another reason why Greek myth seems such a unified system.) The processes of borrowing and reworking continued throughout Western culture, and to a lesser extent in those areas of the world dominated in the last four centuries by Western cultural imperialism. Paradoxically, however – and although each re-creation leaves in our minds not so much a memory of the basic story (in the way retellings of *Cinderella* or readings of *Bleak House* do), as delight in each particular treatment, exhilaration produced by each artist's individual 'spin' – despite all such plundering, the myths themselves continue undiminished.

⏵ Achates, Achelous, Acheron, Achilles, Adonis, Aegeus, Aegisthus, Aesculapius, Agamemnon, Agave, Ajax, Alcinous, Alcmaeon, Alcmena, Amazons, *ambrosia*, Amphion, Amphitrite, Amphitryon, Andromache, Antigone, Antiope, Aphrodite, Apollo, Arachne, Ares, Arethusa, Argus, Ariadne, Aristaeus, Arne, Artemis, Astyanax, Atalanta, Ate, Athamas, Athene, Atlas, Atropus, Attis, Augeas, Aurora, Autolycus, Bellerophon, Boreas, Briareus, Cadmus, Caeneus, Calchas, Calypso, Campe, Cassandra, centaurs, Cerberus, Chaos, Charon, Chimaera, Chiron, Chrysothemis, Circe, Clashing Rocks, Clytemnestra, Cocytus, Creon, Cretan Bull, Cronus, Cyclopes, Dactyls, Danaë, Deiphobus, Demeter, Deucalion and Pyrrha, Diomedes, Dioscuri, Earthborn Giants, Electra, Elpenor, Elysium, Empusa, Endymion, Eos, Eriphyle, Eris, Eros, Erymanthian Boar, Erysichthon, Eteocles, Europa, Eurynome, Eurystheus, Fates, Five Ages of Mortals, Furies, Gaia, Ganymede, Geryon, Gorgons, Graces, Graeae, Hades, Harpies, Hebe, Hecate, Hecuba, Helen, Helenus, Helius, Helle, Hephaestus, Hera, Heracles, Hermes, Hermione, Hesperides, Hippolyta, Hippolytus, Hundred-handed Giants, Hyacinthus, Hydra, Hylas, Hymen, Hyperion, Hypnus, Hypsipyle, Icarus, Idomeneus, Ilythia, Io, Ion, Iphigenia, Iris, Ismene, Ixion, Jocasta, Keryneian Hind, Laertes, Laius, Lamia, Laomedon, Leda, Lethe, Leo, Lotus-eaters, Lycaon, Lycurgus, Medea, Medusa, Melampus, Menelaus, Metis, Midas, Minotaur, Muses, Narcissus, Nauplius, Nausicaä, *nectar*, Nemean Lion, Nemesis, Neoptolemus, Nephele, Nereus, Nike, Niobe, Nisus and Euryalus, Oenomaus, Olympian Gods, Olympus, Mount, Omphale, Phion, Orestes, Orpheus, Ouranos, Palamedes, Palladium, Pallas, Pan, Pandora, Paris, Pasiphaë, Patroclus, Pegasus, Peleus, Pelias, Pelops, Penelope, Pentheus, Persephone, Perseus, Phaedra, Phaethon, Philoctetes, Phineus, Phlegethon, Phrixus, Pirithous, Polydorus, Polynices, Polyphemus, Polyxena, Poseidon, Priam, Priapus, Procrustes, Prometheus, Proteus, Psyche, Pygmalion, Pylades, Pyrrha, Pyrrhus, Rhadamanthus, Rhea, Rhesus, Salmoneus, Satyrs, Scamander, Scylla and Charybdis, Selene, Semele, Seven Against Thebes, Sibyls, Silenus, Sirens, Sisyphus, Sown Men, Sphinx, Stymphalian Birds, Styx, Tantalus, Telchines, Telemachus, Tereus, Thanatos, Thebes, Tiresias, Titans, Trophonius, Tyndareus, Typhon, Wooden Horse, Zephyrus, Zeus

GRID
Europe (North)

Grid, in Nordic myth, was a **giant** sorceress who possessed the skill of working iron by magic. When the giant **Geirröd** forced **Loki** to fetch **Thor** to his fortress, unarmed, Grid (in exchange for **sex**) gave Thor an iron belt of strength, iron gloves and an unbreakable, iron staff. On another occasion she had sex with **Odin**, and gave birth to **Vidar**, who will be one of the few beings to survive **Ragnarök**, the end of this cycle of the universe.

GU
Africa

Gu, in the myths of the Fon peoples of Dahomey, was a blacksmith-god who took not human shape but the form of a tool. At the beginning of **creation** his parent, the double-god **Mawu-Lisa**, made him in the form of a trowel, using him to mould human beings from the celestial dung-heap. When mortals were establishing themselves on Earth, Mawu-Lisa changed Gu's shape to that of a metal blade embedded in a rock, and sent him to Earth to teach humans how to make and use tools of their own.

The Fon peoples were among the first in Africa to use iron tools, at first for agriculture (making them wealthy) and then for war (making them powerful). Gu, for them, was god of both **fertility** *and* **war** *– and they worshipped him not in human form but as a being present in every tool and weapon.*
➤ **smiths**

GUAN DI
Asia (East)

Guan Di or Guan Gong ('lord Guan'), in Chinese myth, was god of martial arts, and of the diplomacy which prevents or puts an end to fighting. His wisdom came partly from his courteous manner, partly from his knowledge of literature (he was one of the patron gods of scholars), and partly from knowledge of the future – his temples were prophetic shrines.

Guan Di was unofficially worshipped for a millennium, but officially declared a god only in 1594 CE. He was the deification of a real-life general of the third century CE, Guan Yü, apparently a huge man (2.7m tall) who used his size not to dominate enemies on the battlefield but to cow them into avoiding confrontation in the first place. The note about literature possibly refers to the general's education in moral philosophy, not a common accomplishment of army leaders at the time. Before he was deified, Guan Yü was the hero of hundreds of popular stories in which he persuaded the Emperor's enemies not to fight – or if they fought, defeated them. After deification Guan Di became one of the state's main protectors, ready to persuade or force all **demons,** *witches, foreign visitors and other potential adversaries to lay down their arms.*
➤ **prophecy**

GUAN YIN
Asia (East)

Guan Yin, in Chinese Daoist myth, was the **fertility** goddess who made rice edible by humans. Until she intervened, grains of rice were dry and empty, and she squeezed milk from her breasts to fill them – a miracle she repeats each year. In most cases the grains filled only with milk, but in a few plants Guan Yin squeezed so hard that drops of blood were added to the mixture, and 'red rice' was produced.

In Chinese Buddhist myth, Guan Yin was the goddess of mercy, a female form of the **Boddhisattva Avalokiteshvara**. She helped **Tripitaka** to carry the holy books of Buddhism from India to China, and she interceded for prisoners, cured snakebite and sick children and helped the oppressed. In the Western Paradise she stood by the lotus-throne of Emituofo the Compassionate, and dispensed mercy with countless arms.

GUARDIANS: *see* Anubis, Baal, Bes, Campe, Chimatano, farming, Ghede, Graeae, Hang Ha Erh Jiang, Heimdall, household and family, Janus, Mait' Carrefour, Na Kaa, Nehebkau, Taweret, Three Door Gods, Uzume

GUCUMATZ
Americas (Central)

Gucumatz ('feather-snake'), in the myths of the Quiche people, was the god of wind and the breath of life, and hence a creator of life. He was later identified with **Quetzalcóatl**, and their myths were amalgamated.

>>+ creation

GUDRATRIGAKWITL
Americas (North)

Gudratrigakwitl ('old man up there'), in the myths of the Wiyot people of Northern California, created the universe by the unusual method of putting his hands together and then spreading the palms and fingers wide, like wings. The whole created world lies safe between these outspread hands, and despite the evil and cruelty it contains, in his benevolence he has never yet been moved to clap them together and end it.

>>+ creation

GUECUFU
Americas (South)

Guecufu, in the myths of the Araucanian people of Chile, was the king of **demons** and arch-enemy of **Guinechen**. He was always sending plagues, **floods** and other disasters to wipe out Guinechen's mortal creations, and Guinechen's interventions – and therefore the war between the two supernatural beings – guaranteed not only dissension in the universe, but also its continuity.

GUINECHEN
Americas (South)

Guinechen ('ruler of mortals'), or Guienapun ('ruler of Earth'), in the myths of the Araucanian people of Chile, ensured the continuation of life in the universe. He was perpetually at war with **Pillan**

the **thunder**-god and with **Guecufu** king of the **demons**. Their struggle kept the universe in equilibrium, and the myth forecast (chillingly for the Araucanians, for whom it came true when the Spanish invaded) that when that struggle was disturbed, the world would end.

GUINEVERE
Europe (North)

Guinevere, or Guinever, in Celtic and medieval Christian myth, is the French spelling of the Celtic name Gwynhwfar ('white cloud'). Gwynhwfar was a cloud-goddess who often, for mischief, took mortal form and entered the world of humans to cause havoc. Soon after **Arthur** became king of **Camelot**, she entered the womb of a Roman princess whose husband ruled in Britain, and was born as a beautiful mortal: Guinevere. In due course Arthur married her, against the advice of **Merlin** (a fellow **shape-changer**, who knew exactly who she was). Guinevere was the most beautiful woman in the world, and all Arthur's knights would have had **sex** with her if they hadn't been bound by their oaths of chivalry. Only **Lancelot** succumbed, and his and Guinevere's adultery broke Arthur's heart and led to the end of Camelot. When the company of the Round Table was broken up and its heroes disappeared into legend, Guinevere resumed her identity as Gwynhwfar, returned to the sky and has ever since been planning her next earthly manifestation.

The (male) writers from the late Middle Ages who retold the Arthur story had no time for Celtic cloud-goddesses, and re-imagined Guinevere as the typical queen or other grand lady of their own time. They presented her as dignified, serene and gentle, a quiet-spoken, loyal spouse to her noble husband and a respected hostess in Camelot. This led to problems when they went on to tell of her affair with Lancelot: adultery was not part of the chivalric lady's code of behaviour. Some blamed Lancelot (or the Devil who tempted him and made him lose his mind); when Arthur went to **Avalon** at the end of his time on earth he found Guinevere waiting, loyal to the last, and lived happily with her ever after. Others painted Guinevere as momentarily insane, or – suddenly and without motiva-tion – as a kind of Wicked Witch of the North, or blurred the story to the point where it was hardly clear at all what Gui-nevere and Lancelot were up to. The least scrupulous (at least to modern eyes) took the opportunity to dump on Guinevere all the animosity towards women, daughters of **Eve**, characteristic of some fundamental-ist Christian thinking at the time: she did what she did because she was female, wholly corrupt by inheritance from Eve and incapable of the nobler sentiments which govern male behaviour. Modern writers, by contrast, have developed the psychological complexity of the love-triangle between Arthur, his best friend and his wife, and the existential panic events induce in each participant. This, to-day, may seem a more coherent approach than the earlier ones, but it pays just as little heed to Guinevere's myth-origins.

≫→ beauty, Brynhild, Circe, Dido, Morgan le Fay

GUNNLOD
Europe (North)

Gunnlod, in Nordic myth, was a gian-tess. Her father **Suttung** left her to guard the mead of inspiration in a cave in the heart of a mountain – and **Odin** made his way inside and persuaded her to trade the mead for **sex**. Their child was **Bragi**, god of poetry.

GUNNODAYAK
Americas (North)

Gunnodayak, in the myths of the Iro-quois people of the Northeastern US, was a mortal warrior taken into **Heaven** to be the assistant of the **thunder**-god **Hinu**. He returned to Earth to kill the water-**snake** which terrorized the peo-ple of the Great Lakes – and was himself eaten. But Hinu killed the snake, recov-ered Gunnodayak from its belly and breathed new life into him. Ever after-wards, Gunnodayak protected the peo-ple of the Lakes, particularly during thunderstorms.

≫→ heroes

GWYNHWfAR: *see* Guinevere

Hercules and Antaeus (*Roman bronze*)

HACHIMAN
Asia (East)

Hachiman, in Japanese myth, was originally a **fertility**-god, protector of crops and giver of children. But his powers were extended to make him protector of the whole of Japan, and he became the **war**-god, patron of soldiers. In Shinto myth he was identified with the deified Emperor Ojin (fourth century CE), leading armies into battle and using the two **Tide Jewels** (one causing high tides, the other low tides) to baffle enemies at sea. In 783 CE he was taken into Buddhist myth as the **Boddhisattva** Daibosatsu.

HADES
Europe (South)

Hades ('invisible'; also known as Plouton, 'rich', Latin Pluto; Dis, 'rich'), in Greek and Roman myth, was the son of **Cronus** and **Rhea**, and brother of **Demeter**, **Hera**, Hestia, **Poseidon** and **Zeus**. Swallowed by his father at birth, he was released when Zeus gave Cronus emetic drugs to drink. In the war between gods and **Titans** which followed, Hades was given a helmet of invisibility, and wore it to trick his way into Cronus' palace and steal his weapons. After the war he, Poseidon and Zeus cast lots for kingdoms, and Hades won the **Underworld**.

Hades king of the Underworld. As lord of the Underworld, Hades controlled all the riches buried in the Earth, particularly its precious stones and metals: hence his name Plouton. He also ruled the dead as Zeus ruled the living. But he was reclusive, leaving the running of affairs to his assistants Aeacus, Minos and **Rhadamanthus** and staying always in the shadows. His sole venture into the Upper World was to find himself a consort – and when no goddess would agree to marry him and live in emptiness, he snatched **Persephone** and carried her below. He never took part in councils or gatherings of the gods, and never interfered with wars and other affairs in **Heaven** or on Earth. He was aloofness personified, the invisible presence of darkness – and the less he did, the more terrifying he became.

*Hades was never depicted in ancient Greek art, more out of awe than because of the problems of showing an invisible ruler. In Roman art he was presented as a monarch enthroned, holding a toothed sceptre and a bunch of keys, Persephone (Proserpina) beside him, the **Fates** standing by his throne, **Cerberus** at his feet and the **Furies** or **Harpies** flying above his head. He made few appearances in literature, and none of them was benign. He figures in the **Orpheus** story as a stern and unyielding judge, in the Persephone myth as a sudden, all-engulfing force, and even in Aristophanes' comedy Frogs he is not a buffoon (like his lieutenant Aeacus) but a laconic, gloomy host for **Dionysus** and the playwrights he has come to take back to the Upper World.*

HAHGWEHDAETGAH: *see*
Hahgwehdiyu and Hahgwehdaetgah

HAHGWEHDIYU AND HAHGWEHDAETGAH
Americas (North)

Hahgwehdiyu and Hahgwehdaetgah, in the myths of the Iroquois people of the Northeastern US, were **twins**: Hahgwehdiyu was all good, Hahgwehdaetgah all evil. They were born on a tiny island in the primeval ocean, the only land in existence, which Otter and Muskrat had built to receive their grandmother **Ataentsic** when she was thrown out of **Heaven**. Ataentsic's daughter, the twins' mother Wind-breath, died when they were born – some say because they quarrelled from the moment of conception, tearing her womb to pieces with their fighting – and Hahgwehdiyu used her body to build the universe: from her face he made the **Sun**, from her breasts the **Moon** and stars, from her body the fertile Earth. Hahgwehdaetgah, trying to imitate his brother's craftsmanship, only managed to make dark reflections of each creation: instead of light darkness, instead of **fertility** destruction, instead of hope fear.

When the universe was complete the brothers fought for sole rule. (Since weapons had not yet been created, they used thorns from the crab-apple tree.) In the end Hahgwehdaetgah, defeated, hid from his brother in the caves and tunnels of the **Underworld**, where he made himself a people of **demons** and spectres to rule. From time to time he leads his forces out for skirmishes against Hahgwehdiyu and the armies of light; so far they have been unsuccessful, but one day they will culminate in a vast universal battle, like the first battle – and who knows how that will end?

In some accounts the twins were children not of Wind-breath but of her mother Ataentsic. The Huron people, telling the same creation story, rename the brothers **Ioskeha and Tawiskara**.

≫→ **creation, light and dark**

HA'IAKA
Oceania

Ha'iaka, in Hawaiian myth, was the younger sister of the **fire**-goddess Pele. She was born as an egg, and Pele carried her in her armpit until she hatched. She was devoted to her sister, and ran errands for her. Once, Pele fell in love with a handsome mortal prince. She sent Ha'iaka to fetch the young man to her volcano kingdom. But on the way all kinds of **demons** attacked Ha'iaka and the prince. Ha'iaka, being immortal, survived each time, and managed to catch the prince's soul (as a butterfly, a wisp of smoke, a perfume on the breeze) before it escaped and so was able to reconstitute him. These adventures made the journey so long that Pele, back in her volcano, thought that Ha'iaka must be having an affair with the young man – and when they finally reached her she erupted and engulfed them in burning lava. For the last time Ha'iaka reconstituted her prince, and this time she took him back to his island home, across the sea where Pele could not follow, and married him herself.

HAIURI
Africa

Haiuri, messenger of **death** in the myths of the Khoisan (Hottentot) peoples of Southern Africa, was only half a being: one ear, one eye, one arm, one leg. It hopped after its victims, seized them in its half-mouth and carried them to the **Underworld** – and you stood only half a chance of avoiding it, since it was half invisible.

➤ **Adroa**

HANA AND NI
Oceania

Hana and Ni, in the myths of the Huli people of Papua New Guinea, were sister and brother. Ni had fully-functioning genitals, but Hana was sexless. She satisfied her sexual urges by rubbing her body against a tree – and Ni was so disgusted that he hid a sharp stone in the bark, so that the next time Hana rubbed against the tree, her body was gashed open to form a vagina. Ashamed, she hid in the women's house, but when after a few days the bleeding stopped Ni asked to see the wound, and was so aroused that he mated with her on the spot. So **creation** began. But Hana and Ni were so ashamed of their incest that they took no interest in their offspring, but left the Earth and lived in the sky. Hana became the **Moon** and Ni became the **Sun**.

HANG HA ERH JIANG
Asia (East)

Hang Ha Erh Jiang ('Hang and Ha, the generals'), in Chinese Buddhist myth, were two mortal generals, They did a favour for a magician, Tu O, who rewarded them by giving Hang the power to send out laser-like light-streams from his nostrils, and Ha the ability to breathe out poison-gas. With these they easily routed their enemies, and when they died they were taken into **Heaven** and promoted to be **Buddha**'s bodyguards. On Earth, their images were painted on the double-doors of Buddhist shrines.

➤ **guardians**

HANUMAN
India

Hanuman's parentage. Hanuman (or more correctly Hanumat, 'heavy-jawed'), in Hindu myth, was the son of **Anjana**, a cloud-**nymph** who had offended a seer and been turned into a monkey. In one version, his father was **Vayu** the wind-lord, who raped Anjana in the forest. In another, the gods gave the mortal king **Dasaratha** three cakes, saying that if each of his three wives ate one, they would conceive children. Dasaratha's third wife **Kaikeyi** refused her cake because she was offered it last instead of first, and a kite flew off with it into the forest, where Anjana ate it.

Hanuman's jaw. Hanuman was born starving. He saw the **Sun** hanging in the sky, and sprang up to devour it. The Sun ran to hide in **Indra**'s **Heaven**, and Indra knocked Hanuman back to Earth with a thunderbolt which smashed his jaw. This made his father Vayu so furious that he cloned himself and slid into the god's guts, gripping and twisting them until **Vishnu** agreed to give Hanuman **immortality** (or, in some versions, one million years of life and invulnerability). Hanuman kept his deformed jaw, but in every other way was lithe and fast, a combination of monkey dexterity and the swiftness of the wind.

Hanuman and Rama. During Rama's war with the **demon**-king **Ravana** who had kidnapped his wife **Sita**, Hanuman served as a combination of **trickster** and warrior. His skills were speed and cunning, and he also had the devastating power of his wind-god father. During the last battle, when Rama fell wounded and exhausted, Hanuman flew to the Himalayas to find healing herbs – and when Indra (who was still angry because Hanuman had tried to eat the Sun) kept hindering the search, he ripped up the entire mountain and carried it off in a whirlwind. Seeing the **Moon** about to rise (an event which would destroy the healing-herb's magic) he swallowed the mountain, herbs and all, and so carried the cure safely and efficaciously to Rama.

*Hanuman is a major character in the Ramayana, alternating between godlike adventures like the one described above and buffoonish episodes like the one in which he was captured by Ravana and paraded through town with his tail on fire. He is also incarnated as Monkey, the jester-magician who accompanies **Tripitaka** on his journey from India to China. Because of his unorthodox conception, he was – and in some places still is – regarded as the giver of **fertility**, and childless couples pin his image on walls or paste it on lampshades to win his favour. In art he is a shown as a monkey with a red face, white fangs, a flower-mane, no neck and an enormous tail coiled like a spring.*
➤ **animal-gods, Balin**

HAOMA
Asia (West)

Haoma ('life'), in Iranian myth, was both a drink and a god. The drink was made by crushing and distilling the milky sap of the tree of life. It gave the gods **immortality**, but in mortals it produced merely illusions of immortality, in the forms of drunkenness or hallucinations. The god Haoma was created from the plant by **Ahura**

Mazda to be his son. He was the gods' physician, and could be prevailed on to come to Earth to cure mortal disease and drive out sin.

»→ *ambrosia, disease and healing, soma*

HAP
Africa (North)

Hap ('bull', Greek Apis), in Egyptian myth, was the power of the god **Ptah**, symbolized by a bull and born when Ptah's thunderbolt made **Isis** pregnant. (Greek accounts said that the bull-god's father was **Zeus** and his mother was **Io**). Hap acted as messenger between gods and mortals, carrying the gods' messages to Earth in the form of oracles, and travelling beside each soul as it made the perilous journey from this world to the next.

*The Hap cult, in Ptah's sacred city of Memphis, centred on the choice of a sacred animal, the god reincarnated as a black bull with a white crescent on its flank and a white patch on its forehead. The miracle happened every twenty-five years – numerologically important, as there were twenty-five letters in the priestly alphabet, and all the phases of the Moon returned on the same day only once every twenty-five years. The new Hap was crowned and welcomed to the court where it was to be worshipped as a god and honoured as a king for the next twenty-five years. The previous Hap was sacrificed (or was disinterred if it had died in the meantime), and seventy-four days' mourning were decreed. During these, the Hap was embalmed and its mummy was buried in a marble sarcophagus. In Roman times believers thought that when the Hap reached the **Underworld** its godhead merged with that of **Osiris**, to form a new god: Osirap (Greek **Serapis**).*
»→ *animal-gods, bulls and cows, Hermes, Itherther and Achimi, Nandi, prophecy*

HAPI
Africa (North)

Hapi, god of the flooding Nile in Egyptian myth, lived in the cave where the river was born. His job was not to start or control the **floods**, but to ensure that the waters were fertile – something he did in some accounts by masturbating into them, and in others by scattering seeds and plants into them as they surged out of his sluice-gates.

Hapi had no temples of his own, but all other gods respected him and he had statues and images in many of their temples. He was shown naked, with a fat belly, erect penis and pendulous breasts (all signifying **fertility**), a crown of papyrus (symbolizing Lower Egypt) and lotus (symbolizing Upper Egypt), and holding a winnowing-fan in one hand and a tray of plants and birds in the other.
»→ *water*

HAPY
Africa (North)

Hapy, in Egyptian myth, was leader of the team of gods who assisted in the embalming of the dead. Their main responsibility was the soft insides of the body, which were removed without damage and stored in jars, ready for use in the afterlife. Hapy saw to the lungs, and his colleagues Mesta, Tuamutef and

Qebhsnuf took charge, respectively, of the liver, stomach and intestines.

HARIHARA
India; Indochina

Harihara ('maker-destroyer'), in Hindu and Cambodian myth, was a single god made from an amalgam of **Vishnu** (Hari) and **Shiva** (Hara). In some accounts, Vishnu took the form of a beautiful woman during the churning of the Sea of Milk (see *amrita*), Shiva made love with him/her, and their offspring was Harihara. In others, the **demon** Guha attacked the gods, and Vishnu and Shiva united to destroy him.

In Indian art, Harihara was a popular figure because he presented an unusual technical challenge: his left half had to show all Vishnu's attributes, his right half all those of Shiva. In Harihara temples, worship was a (sometimes uneasy) blend of the rituals of the two gods.

HARPIES
Europe (South)

In some accounts, the Harpies ('snatchers'), in Greek myth, were daughters of **Gaia** (**Mother Earth**) and the Old Man of the **Sea**, a failed experiment in the making of life from a blend of feathers, bronze and flesh. In others, they were the Sea's grandchildren, born of incest between two of his children, and cousins of the **Graeae** and the **Gorgons**. No one ever knew how many Harpies there were, but four at least had names: Aello ('hurricane'), Celaeno ('dark one'), Ocypete ('swift') and Podarge ('racer'). They had women's faces, vultures' bodies and bronze talons; their wings darkened the sky, their droppings were poisonous and their beaks and talons were strong enough to splinter rock.

The Harpies were so hideous that their own parents were disgusted by them, and hid them deep in the **Underworld**, in the crevices of Gaia which were the home of misshapen **monsters** of every kind. But when the prophet **Phineus** angered the gods (either by allowing the blinding of the children of his mistress Cleopatra, or by revealing the whereabouts of the secret palace where the Sun rested each night and was reborn each morning), the gods summoned the Harpies to torment him. They pecked out his eyes and snatched the food from the table each time he sat down to eat, filling the palace with poisonous slime.

Unfortunately, once the Harpies were released into the Upper World, not even the gods could force them back. But Calais and Zetes, sons of **Boreas** the North Wind, drove them away to the Whirling Islands on the edge of the world, and would have killed them there if **Helius** had not agreed to pardon Phineus in exchange for their lives. Instead, they left them there – and for most of each year the Islands whirled like humming-tops, creating a vortex which imprisoned the Harpies as securely as a dungeon. Every so often, when the islands came to rest, the Harpies were briefly set free to prey on unwary mortals – including **Aeneas** and his crew on their journey South from Troy.

HATHOR
Africa (North)

Hathor ('mansion of Horus'), in Egyptian myth, was originally a Nubian war-goddess, who took the same lioness-form as **Sekhmet** and drank her enemies' blood. She was one aspect of the **Great Goddess**, and her Nubian name was never spoken – it was the secret which gave her power. When **Isis** gave birth to **Horus**, **Ra** sent **Shu** and **Thoth** to bring Hathor to Egypt. She abandoned her original fierceness (leaving it to Sekhmet), and instead of a lioness became a cow of plenty whose milk fed the infant Horus. When Horus grew up she married him, and her milk became the food of the gods, guaranteeing their **fertility** and prosperity.

At first Hathor lived in **Heaven** with the other gods. She delighted them by singing and dancing, on one occasion dancing a striptease to seduce Ra himself from a depression which was plunging the universe in darkness. But when **Set** gouged out Horus' eyes during their cosmic duel, she restored Horus' sight, and Set punished her taking the form of a ram and raping her, then tried to carry her off to his palace of darkness. Horus rescued her and gave her a new home at Yunet (modern Dendera) beside the Nile. She turned her attention from gods to mortals, who worshipped her as goddess of love and music, protector of mothers and babies during **childbirth**.

*As Horus' wife, Hathor was also involved with the **Underworld**. She entertained Ra on his nightly voyage through the world of darkness, and guided deserving souls past the Island of Fire to **Osiris'** court. She could divide herself into seven – the 'seven cows of prosperity' Joseph saw in his dream retold in the Bible – and met with herself in a kind of council of fate before each child was born, deciding what kind of person it would be and what its life would be like. In art these cows are often shown either as a group or melded together, seven images in one, standing guard at the doorway of the inner tomb. In Dendera, paintings show Hathor as a benign, golden-horned cow decorated with flowers and surrounded by attendants who dance and play two sacred instruments: the sistrum (a kind of rattle) and the menat (a string of beads shaken to accompany ecstatic dancing). In Dendera, too, is an upstairs room oriented to catch the rays of the rising Sun: in this, myth said, Hathor bathed each morning in Ra's brightness as he climbed the sky.*

»+ beauty, bulls and cows, Kamadhenu

HAUMEA
Oceania

Haumea, in Hawaiian myth, was the goddess of **childbirth**. At the start of **creation** there was no birth: instead, Haumea owned an orchard of trees, and creatures grew on them like leaves, pigs on the pig tree, fish on the fish tree and so on. Haumea herself grew leaves, and one day, as one of them fell to the ground, it changed into a handsome young man. Haumea lusted after him, grew a vagina and mated with him. In due course, as leaves do, he aged, died and was reabsorbed into **Mother Earth**. Haumea, heartbroken, died with him – only to be reborn, grow more leaves and start the whole process again.

≫→ farming

HAYAGRIVA
Asia (Central); India

Hayagriva ('horse-necked'), in Hindu myth, was a horse-headed **giant** who stole the sacred writings while **Brahma** slept, and was hunted down and killed by **Vishnu** in his avatar as the fish **Matsya**. In other accounts he was an avatar of Vishnu himself: demons had stolen the sacred writings, and he took the horse-giant form to recover them. Some of these accounts go on to say that he will be reborn as the white horse which carries **Kalki** (that is, himself in his tenth avatar) at the end of this cycle of the universe.

In versions of the story told by Tibetan Buddhists, Hayagriva was not killed but escaped to become the Lord of Wrath. Buddhists in Mongolia (who were converted by missionaries from Tibet) said that he was the protector of horses, and therefore of the strength of the universe which they embodied.

HEAVEN

'Heaven' originally was no more than the estates and gardens of a particular god. The word's meaning was then extended to the gods' realm in general, barred to mortals: in Indian myth, this was sited on Mount **Meru**, in Greek myth on Mount **Olympus**. Finally, a few cultures imagined Heavens to which favoured mortals were admitted after death, to share the gods' privileges and pleasures: characteristic are the Christian Heaven, where worshippers spend eternity singing God's praises and basking in his presence, and **Valhalla**, where Nordic **heroes** killed in battle spend eternity drinking mead, feasting on roast pork and listening to sagas.

≫→ **(Celtic): Avalon; (China): Penglai Shan; (Greece): Elysium, Thebes; (Nordic): Asgard; (Slavic): Buyan**

HEBE
Europe (South)

Hebe ('youth'; Latin Iuventus), the beautiful daughter of **Hera** and **Zeus** in Greek and Roman myth, had charge of **ambrosia** and **nectar**, the food and drink of **immortality**, and served them at the gods' banquets. However, Zeus fell in love with a beautiful mortal, **Ganymede**, and wanted to make him his cupbearer. He waited for an opportunity to banish Hebe to the Olympian kitchens – and his chance came when she slipped one day on some spilled nectar, and her dress rode up revealing her vagina. Pretending outrage, Zeus promoted Ganymede in her place. Later, to soothe Hebe's mother Hera, he let Hebe marry **Heracles**, and she lived happily ever afterwards.

≫→ **beauty**

HECATE
Europe (South)

Hecate ('she who works from afar'), in Greek and Roman myth, was a **Moon**-goddess, daughter of Asterie (goddess of the starry heavens) and either **Perseus** or **Zeus** in the form of an eagle. In the days when **Titans** ruled the universe, she had three-fold power, in land, sea and sky, and when Zeus defeated **Cronus** he let her keep her authority. Often mortals saw her galloping her Moon-chariot across the sky, holding in her hand a torch which blazed with cold, unearthly light; her gifts to those she favoured were wealth, sporting skill, victory in battle and common sense. She was connected with the Earth's **fertility**, and together with **Artemis** helped women in **childbirth**.

Hecate also had a dark side. She was the goddess of black magic and queen of ghosts, more feared than any other spirit of the **Underworld**. Often she danced across the plains of Hell, whip in hand, a pack of ghosts howling at her heels. Sometimes her dance spiralled into the Upper World, and was seen in lonely places at dead of night. She was the goddess of crossroads, and her statues were placed on guard wherever three roads met. (Each had a serpent's body and neck with three faces, lion, dog and mare, one for each direction.) Travellers in daylight often found the remains of sacrifices at these statues' feet (puppies or new-born lambs were common), and knew that ghosts had walked and magic ceremonies had taken place. Hecate's other offerings were wild bees' honey, corn and milk, and her worshippers muttered spells in a language only they could understand.

The difference between Hecate's two aspects suggests that two quite separate goddesses have been confused under the same name. The first aspect was common in the most ancient myths, the second common in later times. Some myths also confuse

*Hecate with two other goddesses, **Selene** the Moon and **Persephone** queen of the Underworld.*

>>+ mysteries

HECTOR
Europe (South)

Hector (Hektor, 'prop'), in Greek myth, was the eldest son of King **Priam** and Queen **Hecuba** of Troy, the senior prince and heir to the throne. During the **Trojan War** he led the forces of Troy, and no one could stand against him. He killed nineteen Greek leaders, and wounded even such **heroes** as **Agamemnon**, **Ajax**, **Diomedes** and **Odysseus**, forcing them to withdraw (or be spirited away from the fighting by the gods who sponsored them) before he killed them too.

The only hero Hector never faced was **Achilles**. The gods knew that their duel would begin the final moments of the war, and kept them apart for ten long years. At last, having decided to topple Troy, they blurred Hector's mind with fury and made him attack and kill **Patroclus**, who was wearing Achilles' armour to encourage his men after Achilles had withdrawn from the fighting because of a quarrel with Agamemnon. Hector carried Achilles' armour into Troy in triumph; Odysseus and Ajax rescued Patroclus' body and carried it back to the Greek camp.

Patroclus' death brought Achilles back into the fighting; he swore not to rest until Hector lay dead at his feet. The gods gave him new armour, made by **Hephaestus**, and he strode out across the plain and challenged Hector to single combat. They were equally matched – and **Zeus** ordered the gods (who had so far taken sides in the fighting) not to interfere. Hector, realizing that the loser in the duel would be whoever tired first, began running from Achilles, round the plain outside the walls of Troy, taunting him. He hoped that Achilles, weighed down by the gods' armour, would exhaust himself and lay himself open for the death-blow. But Achilles, son of a goddess, had more than mortal strength. He kept pace with Hector, chased him three times round the walls, and finally caught him and killed him. He stripped the corpse, cut holes in its heels and threaded through them the purple belt which Ajax had given Hector the day before. Then he fastened the belt to his chariot and drove three times round Troy, dragging Hector's body through the dust.

Every morning thereafter Achilles harnessed his chariot and dragged Hector's body three times round Patroclus' grave, jeering at the Trojans. At last Zeus put an end to it. He sent Priam, Hector's aged father, to the Greek camp to beg for his son's body. Achilles demanded, as a ransom, Hector's full weight in treasure. Scales were brought, and the weighing began. The corpse outweighed all the treasures of Troy, and it was not until Hector's sister **Polyxena** added her gold earrings to the pile that the scales balanced and Priam was able to take Hector's body back to Troy. He gave it a prince's burial – and (the story ends) the mingled noise of tears from Troy and celebration from the Greeks was so loud that birds fell stunned from the sky like stones.

In the original myth, Hector is a comparatively minor figure. His eminence began with Homer, who made him one of the two heroes of the Iliad, a mirror-image and completion of Achilles. All subsequent views of Hector, from the many vase-paintings of him arming or fighting to his Henry V-like nobility and regality in Shakespeare's Troilus and Cressida, derive not from myth but from Homer.

HECUBA
Europe (South)

Hecuba (Hekabe, 'distant mover'), in Greek myth, was the chief wife of King **Priam** of Troy. She ruled over a large harem of wives and concubines, and bore Priam twelve (or some say nineteen) daughters including **Cassandra** and **Polyxena**, and fifty sons including **Helenus**, **Paris**, **Polydorus**, **Troilus** and Priam's heir **Hector** – though in some accounts, **Apollo** was the actual father of Hector and Troilus.

During the **Trojan War** Hecuba, by then an elderly and respected lady, watched the fighting from the battlements, setting an example of modest triumph whenever her sons and the other Trojans won any advantage, and of dignified sorrow when they lost. After the war, however, her character completely changed. She was put in charge of the other female prisoners, awaiting selection by the victorious Greeks. She watched with impotent rage as her daughter Cassandra was torn from her to become **Agamemnon**'s bedmate, her grandson **Astyanax** was hurled to his death from the battlements, and her youngest daughter Polyxena was sacrificed on **Achilles**' grave.

Through all these events, Hecuba was buoyed up by secret hope. Before the war began she had sent her youngest son, the child Polydorus, to safety with King Polymnestor of Thrace, hoping that if Troy fell he would grow up to rebuild the city and take revenge on Greece. But now, when she found that Polymnestor had killed Polydorus to gratify the Greeks, she broke out of the women's quarters, gouged out Polymnestor's eyes and murdered his own two sons.

Mad with grief, Hecuba was by now beyond human control, and when **Odysseus** (who had won her as his war-booty) came to load her in his ship to take her home to Ithaca, she fought and snarled so much that he gave up the attempt and killed her. She turned into a dog, one of the hounds that snarl after **Hecate** goddess of black magic, ran to the shore (or some say, up the mast of Odysseus' ship), jumped into the sea and was never seen again. The Greeks built a lighthouse on the headland, calling it Kynossema ('bitch-monument'), and from then on any ship which went too close was shattered on hidden rocks, while howls of ghostly glee could be heard in the surrounding dark.

*Hecuba's supposed monument, Kynossema, was a real lighthouse, at the entrance to the Dardanelles, still in use in Roman times. (A modern lighthouse marks the same spot.) She is chiefly famous because of four appearances in classical literature. In Homer's Iliad she is Priam's dignified queen, mother of Hector and Paris, mother-in-law of Astyanax. In Virgil's **Aeneid** she has a magnificently pathetic*
scene in which (aged over eighty) she first comforts her children and servants at the family altar as the city is destroyed about them – they are like a flock of doves trembling before a hawk, says Virgil – and then pleads with **Neoptolemus** (Pyrrhus in Virgil) not to kill her husband. Euripides' Women of Troy shows her leading the grief for the fallen city, and for all people dead in war, as one by one her privileges and relatives are stripped from her. Euripides' Hecuba tells the story of the sacrifice of Polyxena and Hecuba's revenge on Polymnestor for killing Polydorus, and presents her as a woman driven by suffering first to the extremes of grief and then over the edge into insanity and bloodlust – an unnerving metamorphosis from Deirdre of the Sorrows to Lady Macbeth.*

HEIMDALL
Europe (North)

Heimdall's birth. At the beginning of **creation**, in the Nordic account of how the world was made, **Odin** was walking on the shore when he came across Atla, Augeia, Aurgiafa, Egia, Gjalp, Greip, Jarnsaxa, Sindur and Ulfrun, the **nine wave-maidens**, daughters of the sea-god **Aegir**. Idly, Odin wondered what it would be like to have **sex** with all nine simultaneously – and his thought was so powerful that it was like action itself. The wave-girls went into corporate labour and produced a single child among them: Heimdall ('shedder of light', spirit of the rising **Sun**).

Heimdall was half **giant**, half god. He needed sleep no more than a gull on the wing, could see for a hundred leagues, as clearly by night as by day, and had such acute hearing that he could hear grass sprouting in the fields and wool growing on a sheep's back. However, like all children of thought alone, he was dumb. Odin made him sentry of the gods, built him a castle (Himinbjorg, 'heaven-cliffs') not far from the bridge **Bifröst** between **Midgard** and **Asgard**, and in compensation for his dumbness gave him a hunting horn, Gjall ('shrieker'). Gjall was so loud that its calls could be heard throughout creation, and in some accounts Heimdall left it lying by the well of Mimir in Midgard until the time came to blow it to announce the beginning of **Ragnarök**, end of the universe.

Heimdall and mortals. In one account, Heimdall was responsible for social hierarchy among human beings. He was a **shape-changer**, and often disguised himself and visited worlds other than Asgard. Once, disguised as a human being, Rig, he wandered the fields and hills of Midgard. He stayed first with the oldest human beings in creation, Ai and Edda (Great-grandfather and Great-grandmother), and as their custom was they shared their own bed with him. Three days later, when he left them, Edda was pregnant, and in due course produced a black-haired child called Thrall. When Thrall grew up he married Thir, and they became the ancestors of every serf ever born on Earth.

In the same way, Heimdall stayed with Afi and Amma (Grandfather and Grandmother), and nine months after he left a son was born: Karl. When Karl grew up he married Snör, and they became the ancestors of all free labourers ever born on Earth. Finally Heimdall stayed with Fathir and Mothir

(Father and Mother), whose child, nine months later, was Jarl. Jarl grew up and married Jerna, and their descendants were all the lords and ladies ever born on Earth.

*Heimdall was a regular minor character in many myths and stories, usually offering the gods strong, silent advice. He seems to have been an enemy of **Loki**: fragments of stories tell of him wrestling with him, or fighting shape-changing duels, and at Ragnarök he will finally confront Loki in a sword-fight from which both will die. He is shown in art as a warrior in armour, with Gjall either hanging at his belt or – more apocalyptically – lifted to his lips to blow. Christians assimilated him with the angel **Gabriel**, another warrior-lord of light whose chief task was to blow his trumpet for the end of time.*

HEITSI-EIBIB
Africa

Heitsi-Eibib, in the myths of the Khoisan (Hottentot) peoples of Southern Africa, was the god of difference. He was born miraculously, in some accounts to a cow who was fertilized by a handful of magic grass she was eating (and which turned to semen inside her), or to a virgin human being. This magic birth was possible because, when all creatures were made at the beginning of **creation**, they lacked specific qualities. Each assumed attributes at random: lions built nests in trees, fish lived in the desert, mice ate snakes. Heitsi-Eibib took each animal in turn and gave it the nature it was to have forever. The only one which escaped was Hare, who ran from him – and he gave Hare, for eternity, the attributes of fear and running.

Heitsi-Eibib chose not to give human beings any one defining characteristic. He allowed them to remain emotional and temperamental **shape-changers**, and to choose what characteristics they wanted either at any one moment or to use throughout their lives. This gave them power over all other creatures on Earth, and he symbolized it by showing them how to control the moods of Fire. Fire let them dominate the whole of creation – except for Gagorib, demon of darkness. Ga-gorib caught his prey by digging a pit in the floor of **Mother Earth**, and eating anything which stumbled into it. Heitsi-Eibib defeated him by shape-shifting. In some accounts he made himself the most powerful wrestler in creation, strangled Ga-gorib and threw him into his own hole. In others he fell into the pit himself, and when Ga-gorib jumped in to eat him he made himself darkness, engulfed the monster and choked him.

Heitsi-Eibib never left Earth for **Heaven**. He stayed with human beings, and used his powers to help them. Because he was a shape-changer, varying his appearance to suit the kind of assistance he meant to give, they never saw him or recognized him, but knew he'd been there only after the help was given and Heitsi-Eibib had long moved on.

⫸ civilization

HEL
Europe (North)

Hel, in Nordic myth, was the daughter of **Loki** and the giantess Angboda. Her siblings were the wolf-**giant** Fenrir and the world-serpent **Jormungand**. She ruled the Dead, from her palace Helheim ('Hel's home'), a huge walled estate in **Niflheim**, near one of the roots of **Yggdrasil**. Her bed was Disease and its cover was Misery; her servants Hunger and Slow moved so imperceptibly that no one could tell if they were paralyzed living beings or animated corpses. Hel herself was monstrous. Her upper half was alive and beautiful, but her lower half was dead and putrid, so black that in the shadows of Niflheim it was invisible, detectable only by its stink. She ruled the **monsters** of the **Underworld** (sometimes called Hel after her), in preparation for the day when her father Loki would summon them to fight at **Ragnarök**.

⫸ Baldur, demons, Hades, Osiris, Sedna, Tuoni

HELEN
Europe (South)

Helen (Helene, '**Moon**'), in Greek myth, was the daughter of **Zeus** and **Leda** (wife of King **Tyndareus** of Sparta). Her brothers were Castor and Pollux, the **Dioscuri**, and her twin sister was **Clytemnestra**. Some say that Leda was doubly fertilized, so that Helen inherited Zeus's immortal nature, Clytemnestra Tyndareus' mortal weakness and arrogance. Certainly Helen had more than ordinary human beauty – she was the most beautiful woman ever seen on Earth – and she was also unconfined by human morality in a way characteristic of all children of one mortal and one immortal parent.

Helen, Theseus and Menelaus. When Helen was twelve years old, King **Theseus** of Athens, distraught at the death of his wife **Phaedra**, went disguised to Sparta, kidnapped her and took her to Athens. He hid her in a village, Aphidnae, intending to marry her as soon as he'd visited the **Underworld** and stolen Queen **Persephone** as a bride for his friend **Pirithous**. But while he was in the Underworld, Helen's brothers Castor and Pollux invaded Athens and rescued her.

News of this adventure travelled all over Greece – and with it, word of Helen's beauty. So many princes flocked to Sparta to ask for her hand in marriage that there would have been a Greece-wide war if **Odysseus** had not persuaded them, first to let Helen choose a husband for herself (something unheard-of), and second to abide by whatever she decided. Helen chose handsome **Menelaus**, brother of her sister's husband **Agamemnon** of Argos, and invited her former suitors to stay in Sparta as wedding-guests. The **heroes** had agreed to accept her decision, but they still grumbled, and forever afterwards, even before the **Trojan War**, neither she nor Menelaus had friends in Greece. Nonetheless, they ruled peacefully for a time in Sparta, and had one daughter, **Hermione**, a child blessed with both her mother's and father's beauty.

Helen in Troy. While this was happening in Greece, in Troy three goddesses had asked Prince **Paris** to judge which was most beautiful, and **Aphrodite** had won by offering him Helen as a bribe. In some accounts, Paris sailed to Greece and seduced Helen into going back to Troy with him. In others, **Hera**, goddess of marriages, unwilling to have Helen break her wedding-vows to Menelaus, spirited her away to Egypt, leaving a phantom Helen in her place for Paris to take to Troy. As soon as she was gone, Menelaus left his daughter Hermione in Argos, and he and Agamemnon sailed from Troy with a huge Greek force to bring Helen back.

During the ten years of the Trojan War, Helen – or her phantom – lived in Troy as Paris' wife, a member of the royal harem. In some accounts she was desolate, longing for Menelaus and moping and sobbing round the city. When Paris was killed, and his unmarried brothers all began courting her, rather than marry again she tried to hang herself – and **Deiphobus** cut her down and forced her to marry him. (His jealous brothers at once started looking for ways to betray Troy to the Greeks.) In others, she supported the Trojans avidly, cheering them on from the battlements and weeping whenever the Greeks won any advantage. When the Greek heroes entered Troy in the **Wooden Horse**, she knew they were inside, and ran about outside the Horse, calling each of them by name and imitating the voices of their wives, trying to make them answer and betray themselves.

After the Trojan War. As soon as Troy fell, the Greeks put Helen on trial and found her guilty. But instead of killing her there and then they gave her to Menelaus to punish as soon as he reached home. In some accounts he took her straight back to Greece – and his intention to punish her evaporated on the first night on board ship, when he took her in his arms; in others (those claiming that the 'Helen' in Troy was actually a phantom) the false Helen disappeared en route, and the gods blew Menelaus' ship off-course to Egypt, where he found the real Helen and took her home. They landed at Argos, where **Orestes** and **Electra**, fresh from the murder of Clytemnestra, demanded protection against the angry townspeople. Menelaus and Helen refused, and Orestes snatched the child Hermione and threatened to kill her. The gods intervened, carrying Hermione out of danger (in fact, marring her to **Achilles'** son **Neoptolemus**), sending Orestes to Delphi for purification, and returning Helen and Menelaus safely to Sparta, where they lived in pomp but obscurity until they died.

In some accounts, Helen, being immortal, was taken up into **Heaven** at the end of her mortal existence. Like her brothers Castor and Pollux, she became a will-o'-the-wisp, a flickering light to guide sailors lost at sea. But unlike her more stolid brothers, she was flirtatious and coy, so that the light was as likely to drown you as to save your life.

*The challenge of depicting the most beautiful woman who ever lived defeated fine artists rather than inspiring them: pictures of Helen, from any period at all of Western art, are almost non-existent. By contrast, she is a favourite character in literature, either as a simple icon of **beauty** (as when Mephistopheles makes her tempt Faustus in Marlowe's play), a serene middle-aged queen (as in Homer's Odyssey), or a vain, arrogant seductress, trying (and failing) to flirt her way out of trouble (as she*

appears in play after play, from Euripides to Giraudoux).
≫→ **twins**

HELENUS
Europe (South)

Helenus (Helenos, '**Moon**-man'), in Greek myth, was the son of King **Priam** and Queen **Hecuba** of Troy, and a prophet of **Apollo**: lying in his cradle as a baby with his **twin Cassandra**, he had been caressed by sacred snakes, which had licked his ears and eyes and given him second hearing and second sight. Throughout the ten years of the **Trojan War** he helped his fellow-citizens with wise advice, and when **Paris** was killed he hoped that they would reward him by letting him marry **Helen**. Helen, however, married his brother **Deiphobus**, and Helenus, disgusted, left the city to become a hermit on Mount Ida. **Odysseus** pursued him there and took him prisoner, forcing him to reveal what more the gods required before Troy was to fall: the stealing of the **Palladium** and the arrival in Troy of Achilles' son **Neoptolemus**.

After the city fell, Helenus was allotted as spoils-of-war to Neoptolemus, together with **Hector**'s widow **Andromache**. Helenus warned Neoptolemus that if he went home by sea he would drown, and the grateful Neoptolemus, having travelled home overland, made him his trusted adviser and counsellor. After Neoptolemus died Helenus married Andromache, and ruled Neoptolemus' former kingdom until he died.
≫→ **prophecy**

HELIUS
Europe (South)

Helius (Helios, 'warty'; Latin Sol), in Greek and Roman myth, was the son of the **Titan Hyperion**, and the brother of **Eos** and **Selene**. He was the god of the **Sun**-disc, and galloped across the sky each day in a golden chariot, roistered each evening with his children (especially Aeëtes) and spent the night recovering before springing back to work next morning when Eos called him out of bed. He owned a herd of supernatural cattle, the Sun's energy transformed into tawny-hided beasts, and gave them to the giant **Geryon** to protect against thieves and rustlers. Helius went everywhere, saw everything, and was a gossip and a busybody – it was he, for example, who told **Hephaestus** about **Aphrodite**'s love-affair with **Ares**. But although he was officious and omnipresent, he was a minor god, and the main work of the Sun, bringing light and health to mortals, was done by **Apollo**, god of the Sun-shaft.

➤ **Ra**

HELLE
Europe (South)

Helle ('bright'), in Greek myth, was the daughter of **Athamas** and **Nephele**. When her father tried to sacrifice her brother **Phrixus**, and **Zeus** saved Phrixus by telling him to fly North on the back of a winged ram with a golden fleece, Helle asked to go with him. Halfway through the journey she lost her hold, fell into the narrow stretch of sea between Europe and Asia and drowned. Ever since, the strip of water has been called Hellespont ('Helle's sea') after her.

HENG O
Asia (East)

Heng O, or Jang E, goddess of the **Moon** in Chinese myth, was the sister of Ho Po, god of the Yellow River, and the most beautiful female, mortal or immortal, who ever existed. She had **sex** with **Yi** when he was still a mortal, and when he was given one of the Peaches of **Immortality** (or, some say, a cup of peach-juice), she stole it from him and escaped his anger to hide in the Moon. Yi later became the **Sun**-god, and he and Heng O patched up their quarrel. But although they slept together twice a month when Yi visited the Moon, for the rest of their time they lived apart. Yi ruled the day from his Sun-palace, the Palace of the Lonely Park, and Heng O ruled the night from her Moon-palace, the Palace of Great Cold made from cinnamon-trees.

HENG XI: *see* Xi He and Heng Xi

HEPHAESTUS
Europe (South)

Hephaestus (Hephaistos, 'dayshine'; Latin Vulcanus, Vulcan, 'volcano-god'), in Greek and Roman myth, was the son of **Zeus** and **Hera** – or, some say, the result of an attempt by Hera to have a child without a partner, as Zeus later had **Athene**. He was such an ugly baby that Hera, in disgust, hurled him headlong out of **Olympus**. (Other accounts say that Zeus threw him out for supporting

Hera in her revolt against Zeus' power.) He fell into the **sea**, and the goddesses **Eurynome** and **Thetis** rescued him and brought him up. He set up a workshop under the sea (where jewel-setting and coral-working were favourite arts), and made necklaces and ornaments so beautiful that his parents invited him back to Olympus to create **beauty** there as well.

Hephaestus the craftsman. Hephaestus was the god of **fire**, particularly of the natural fires that issue from the ground. He was quickly accepted as the blacksmith of the gods, and used hammers and anvils from his smithy to drive off the **Earthborn Giants** when they attacked Olympus. His servants were the **Cyclopes** who made Zeus' thunderbolts, and he set up workshops for them under volcanoes all over the Earth. Apart from thunderbolts, he made all kinds of ingenious and beautiful things: wheeled tables that ran about of their own accord, robots which moved as if alive, a necklace which gave the wearer eternal youth (the gods presented it to Harmony when she married **Cadmus**), a sceptre which gave the wielder all-power (later given to **Agamemnon**), and armour which gave the wearer invincibility (one set for **Achilles**, another for **Aeneas**). He built golden villas, surrounded by beautiful gardens, for the gods who lived on Olympus.

Hephaestus and Aphrodite. When Zeus was told that any son **Metis** bore him would be greater than his father, he ate Metis and was immediately affected not with stomach-ache but with agonizing pains in the head. Hephaestus cured him by splitting his forehead open with a wedge and hammer. The wound healed immediately (as all gods' wounds did), but not before Athene was born and Zeus' headache ended. In gratitude, Zeus offered to let Hephaestus marry any goddess he chose, so long as the goddess agreed.

Hephaestus first paid court to Athene. But she was sworn to eternal virginity, and rejected him. (In some accounts, he tried to rape her, and she brushed his sperm angrily off and down to Earth, where it fertilized the soil of Attica and engendered Erichthonius.) Hephaestus next tried one of the **Graces**, and was again rejected. Finally, most ambitiously of all, he paid court to **Aphrodite**, and she accepted him (some say because she was charmed by the love-gifts he made her, others because she thought it a joke to marry the ugliest god on Olympus).

Aphrodite's eye soon began to wander, and Hephaestus became a notorious cuckold. The joke was even greater because he was blissfully unaware of Aphrodite's affairs. Finally **Helius**, the gossiping **Sun**-god, told him that every time he went to work in his smithy, Aphrodite hurried to make love with **Ares** in the beautiful bedchamber Hephaestus had built for her as a wedding-present. Hephaestus made a golden net so fine that it was invisible and so strong that not even Ares could snap its threads. He hung this above the bed, caught the lovers *in flagrante* and summoned the gods to laugh at them – only to be baffled when he realized that they were mocking not them but him.

The story of Hephaestus and Aphrodite was a favourite comic interlude in ancient times, and received its grandest telling in Homer's Odyssey, *where the bard*

Demodocus recounts it to amuse the court of King **Alcinous** of Phaeacia. Hephaestus, as patron of arts and **crafts**, inspired a huge number of plaques and statuettes, most showing him as a dwarfish blacksmith holding such tools of his trade as hammer, tongs and water-ladle, or working the bellows to blow up the fire. The story that **Dionysus** got him drunk to trick him back to Olympus was popular with painters of vases and wine-cups. Even where he was more seriously treated, for example in the accounts of his forging thunderbolts, or making armour for Achilles and Aeneas, he was hardly described, detailed attention being reserved for the marvels he created.
≫→ **Lu Ban, Lug, smiths**

HEQET

Africa (North)

Heqet, in Egyptian myth, was one of the frogs which lived in the primordial mud before **creation**. After the gods of the **Ogdoad** gathered to create the egg from which **Ra** the Sun was hatched, Heqet made sure that his entry into existence was easy. She later assisted at the rebirth of **Horus**, and as rewards for these services she was given **immortality** and allowed to be midwife at the Sun's rebirth each morning. She became the goddess of **childbirth**, and her frog-headed image, carved on a pendant or bracelet, was a favourite lucky charm among pregnant women.
≫→ **animal-gods**

HERA

Europe (South)

Hera (Here, 'protector'; Latin Juno), in Greek and Roman myth, was the daughter of **Cronus** and **Rhea**, and the sister of **Demeter, Hades**, Hestia, **Poseidon** and **Zeus**. When her brothers defeated the **Titans** and divided universal power among themselves, she was left out, and this induced in her a state of jealousy which persisted throughout eternity and sat somewhat uncomfortably with her position as Zeus' queen and consort, First Lady of the universe. She joined **Apollo** and Poseidon in leading a revolt against Zeus, and was defeated. She took part in a beauty contest with **Aphrodite** and **Athene**, and when she lost was so angry that she stirred up the **Trojan War** to punish **Paris**, the contest's judge. But her chief jealousies were caused by the philandering of her husband, Zeus. Unable to punish him personally, she was merciless to the **nymphs** or women he slept with and to their offspring, so that women like **Semele** (mother of **Dionysus**) and **Alcmena** (mother of **Heracles**) suffered for their affairs with Zeus, and it took aeons of persuasion before Hera would let their offspring enter **Heaven** as fully-accredited **Olympian** gods.

Early mythographers, all male, claimed, in their brisk, politically incorrect way, that Hera was the incarnation of womanhood: inconsistent, emotional and irrational. Women, by contrast, honoured her as the overseer of oaths and promises, particularly those made between husbands and wives. She was also a goddess of prophecy, and the guardian of stability and balance in the affairs of the universe.

In art, Hera was usually depicted as a mature, dignified queen, enthroned or riding a chariot pulled by a team of peacocks.

She wore a golden crown, carried a sceptre on which perched a cuckoo (a bird she especially protected), and was attended by **Iris** with her rainbow cloak. The Roman Juno was similarly represented, except that she was veiled from head to foot in the manner of Roman matrons when they appeared in public. In literature she was depicted either as a kind of irritable Olympian head girl, or as a vengeful, wronged wife. Some mythographers claim that she was the original Great Mother, creator and ruling spirit of the universe, and that it was not so much that she chose to become Zeus' consort as that he supplanted and betrayed her.

HERACLES
Europe (South)

Heracles' birth. Heracles (Herakles, 'glory of Hera'; Latin Hercules), in Greek and Roman myth, was the son of **Zeus** and the mortal queen **Alcmena**. Zeus kept Alcmena's pregnancy secret from his jealous wife **Hera** for almost nine months. But then **Ate** fuddled his wits and he boasted that the man-child about to be born in Mycenae would be the prince of everyone around him. Hera immediately sent **Ilythia**, goddess of **childbirth**, to block Alcmena's womb, until another child – **Eurystheus** son of Nicippe – was born ahead of Heracles. Soon afterwards Alcmena herself bore **twins**: Heracles, Zeus' immortal son, and Iphicles, his mortal brother, fathered by Alcmena's mortal husband **Amphitryon** on the same night as Zeus engendered Heracles.

The first Hera knew of Heracles' birth was when she woke up one night and found him in her arms, sucking from her breast. **Hermes** had secretly put him there, on Zeus' orders: for any baby who sucks a goddess' milk is guaranteed **immortality**. Angrily Hera flung Heracles away; drops of her milk splashed across the sky, and became the Milky Way. Zeus laid Heracles in a cradle beside his twin Iphicles. Later that night Hera sent a pair of **snakes** sliding into the cradle to eat the children. Iphicles' screams woke the palace; but when the servants came running, they found the infant Heracles waving a strangled snake in each chubby fist.

Heracles and his children. Heracles grew up on one of Amphitryon's cattle-farms in the foothills of Mount Cithaeron. When he was eighteen, his neighbours, herdsmen of King Thespius of Thespiae, told him of a fierce lion on a nearby mountain, which savaged the king's cattle and had eluded every hunting-party sent to track it down. Heracles immediately made himself a club (from a wild olive-tree ripped up roots and all), went to Thespius and offered to kill the lion.

Thespius had fifty daughters, and wanted each of them to bear a child fathered by a god's son. So he arranged for every one of them to sleep with Heracles. In some accounts, Heracles managed this feat in a single night; in others, each night when he returned from hunting the lion, he was welcomed by a different girl. Forty-nine princesses slept with him (the fiftieth refused, and ended her days as a virgin priestess); each bore sons – twins, in the cases of the eldest and youngest – and when the children grew up, there were enough of them to colonize Sardinia.

Having killed the lion and fathered the children, Heracles set out to find more adventure. On the road to **Thebes** he dealt, single-handed, with an invading army, and in gratitude the king of Thebes married him to his daughter Megara. Heracles and Megara settled in Thebes and had several children. But Hera had not finished with Heracles. She could not kill him, since he had sucked immortality from her own breast, but she could hinder and harass his mortal life. She clouded his mind with madness, so that he raged through the palace killing everyone who stood in his way. His children were wrestling in the palace yard, watched by their mother Megara; Heracles set arrows to bow and shot them dead.

The twelve labours. After such a crime, the Delphic oracle itself pronounced Heracles' fate. He was to serve King **Eurystheus** of Mycenae (the child born ahead of him as a result of Hera's plotting), and carry out whatever ten tasks Eurystheus chose for him. Heracles was furious: Eurystheus was a coward and blusterer, protected from harm only by Zeus' promise that he would be prince over everyone around, and with Hera's help he would think up tasks as difficult, dangerous and insulting as possible. But there was no choice, and he sulkily took his club and his unerring bow and went to Mycenae.

As Heracles had imagined, Eurystheus found him ten **Labours**, each more difficult or dangerous than the one before. They were: to skin the **Nemean Lion**; to kill **Hydra**; to catch the **Keryneian Hind**; to kill the man-eating **Erymanthian Boar**; to clean out the stables of King **Augeas** of Elis; to drive out the **Stymphalian Birds**; to tame the fire-breathing **Cretan Bull**, sire of the **Minotaur**; to steal **Diomedes'** flesh-eating horses; to steal the golden belt of **Hippolyta**, queen of the **Amazons**; to steal the cattle of the **giant Geryon** who lived in the river of Ocean that girds the world.

Heracles found these tasks easy. He even took time off, after catching the Erymanthian Boar, to sail with **Jason** and the **Argonauts** on their journey to steal the **Golden Fleece**; but on the way his page-boy **Hylas** was drowned, and Heracles left the expedition and went back to see what else Eurystheus had devised for him. When the tenth Labour was done, he expected to be set free. But Eurystheus said that Heracles had had help with two of the Labours (killing Hydra and cleaning out Augeas' stables), and set him two more, the most impossible-seeming of all: to steal the Golden Apples of Immortality, and to capture **Cerberus**, guard-dog of the **Underworld**, and bring him to Mycenae. These labours, too, gave Heracles no trouble.

Heracles and Laomedon. By successfully carrying out Eurystheus' tasks, Heracles proved his immortal powers and purified himself from the crime of murdering his children. He now began settling old scores. The first was with King **Laomedon** of Troy. Heracles had rescued Laomedon's daughter Hesione from a **sea-monster**, and Laomedon had first promised him a reward of two immortal chariot-horses and then broken his word. Heracles now went back to Troy, battered a hole in the walls, and killed

Laomedon and all his sons except **Priam**, a baby, whom he placed on the throne, a helpless king for a helpless state.

Heracles and Augeas. As his fifth Labour, Heracles had been sent to clean the stables of King Augeas – and had bet Augeas one tenth of all his cattle that he could do it in a single day. But when the job was done, Augeas said that Heracles had cheated (by letting a river do the work) and refused to pay. Augeas thought himself safe: he had giant protectors, Eurytus and Cteatus, born from a single silver egg and joined at the waist. But Heracles shot the twins dead with a single arrow, killed Augeas and – some say – used his share of Augeas' cattle to establish a huge athletics festival, the Olympic Games. (At the first Games, no one dared challenge him, so he won every event; it was only later that the Games became a festival open to all-comers.)

Heracles and Omphale. Heracles next entered a shooting contest, whose prize was Eurytus' daughter Princess Iole. But although Heracles won, Eurytus refused him the prize on the grounds that he was a madman and a child-murderer. Heracles' old madness boiled up in his mind, and he took Eurytus' son Iphitus up to a high tower and hurled him to his death. Once again he had to be purified, and once again he went to the Delphic oracle. But Apollo was angry at the death of Iphitus (his grandson), and refused to answer – and Heracles, carried away by madness, tried to steal the holy tripod. He and Apollo began a superhuman tug-of-war, dragging the tripod back and forth across the shrine as the worshippers scattered. At last Zeus threw a thunderbolt to end it, and decreed Heracles' punishment He was to be sold as a slave and serve his new owner for a year, doing whatever he was ordered. Queen **Omphale** of Lydia bought him, dressed him as a woman and made him sit spinning with the female slaves, or carry her parasol when she walked outdoors.

The shirt of Nessus. After this year's service, Heracles had only a short time left on Earth. He was finding it harder and harder to contain immortal strength in a mortal body. And he no longer had Hera's enmity to face. One day he had killed some drunken **satyrs** who were trying to rape her, and she had agreed, at last, to accept him as Zeus' son. Oracles predicted that the end of his time on Earth would come when he was killed by his own dead enemy.

Heracles had just married Deianira, daughter of King Oeneus of Pleuron. (He won her by wrestling another suitor, the river-god **Achelous**.) They set out for Thebes, and on the way a passing **Centaur**, Nessus, offered to carry Deianira across the river Euenus on his back. When they reached the far bank, thinking he was out of Heracles' reach, Nessus threw Deianira on the ground and tried to rape her – and Heracles shot an unerring arrow and killed him. With his dying breaths, Nessus begged Deianira to gather the blood-soaked hair from his chest and weave it into a shirt for Heracles – if Heracles wore it, Nessus promised, he would never abandon Deianira for another woman.

Leaving Deianira at home in Thebes, Heracles went to punish Eurytus for the insults at the archery-contest when he won Iole's hand. Afterwards, he prepared a thanksgiving sacrifice – and put on the shirt Deianira had woven from Nessus' hair. At once his flesh blistered and began to bubble as if on fire. Grinding his teeth in agony, Heracles went to Mount Oeta, built a funeral-pyre and begged a passing shepherd, **Philoctetes**, to lay him on it and set it on fire, to burn away his flesh and end his pain. As a reward, he offered him his bow and unerring arrows.

Philoctetes (who some say was not a shepherd but one of Heracles' fellow-Argonauts from years before) did as he was asked, and as soon as the first smoke from the funeral-pyre reached **Olympus**, Zeus threw a thunderbolt to end Heracles' agony. Pyre, lion-skin, club and armour were consumed, and Heracles slipped from his mortal flesh as a snake casts off its skin, and soared up to Olympus to take his hard-won place at the banquets of the gods.

*Unlike such sagas as those of **Jason**, **Odysseus**, the **Trojan War** or the dynasties of Thebes or Argos, the Heracles myth-cycle was never given coherent literary treatment in ancient times. It remains a ragbag, more like a loosely-strung collection of folk-tales than a single narrative. In ancient times, writers and artists tended to concentrate on single episodes – Euripides, for example, dealt with Heracles killing his children, Sophocles with the Deianira story – and depicted Heracles as a larger-than-life buffoon, a glutton for food, sex and honour. In later times, the Labours eclipsed all other parts of the story. In ancient times Heracles was one of the most popular of all Greek gods; but he was always a Player rather than a Gentleman – and so, in artistic terms, he has remained.*

≫→ **archers, heroes**

HERCULES: *see* Heracles

HERMES
Europe (South)

Hermes ('pillar'; Latin Mercurius, Mercury), in Greek and Roman myth, was the son of **Zeus** and of Maia daughter of **Atlas**. From the moment he was born he was full of pranks. He was born at dawn; three hours later he was running about; at noon he slipped away from his mother to explore the world. He found a discarded tortoise-shell, stretched three strings of plaited grass across the hollow side and plucked them, so inventing the lyre – and when Maia tried to scold him for straying, he played such sweet **music** on it that he charmed her anger away.

Hermes and Apollo. Grass strings, however, were not strong enough. That evening, Hermes slipped away again, this time to the fields where the gods' cattle pastured. The cattle were in the care of Hermes' half-brother **Apollo**, who had left them overnight penned and watched by guard-dogs. Hermes drugged the dogs, covered the hooves of fifty of the finest cattle with shoes of plaited grass and dragged them tails-first to Pylos, where he hid them in a cave. He sacrificed the two finest, divided their meat in honour of the gods and kept for himself only the hides and the gut, to make strings for his lyre.

When Apollo found fifty cattle missing next morning, he could find no trace except the prints of two hundred shod feet, apparently walking up to the edge of the field and then disappearing into thin air. He'd have been none the wiser, except that as Hermes drove the cattle the previous night, he'd been so pleased with himself that he'd boasted about his trick to an old man by the roadside. He swore the old man to silence, but he should have saved his breath, as he was talking to Battus ('blabberer'), god of gossips. Apollo stormed to the cave, confronted Hermes and took him and the stolen cattle to **Olympus**. But even as he was making a formal complaint to Zeus, Hermes charmed him and the other gods by sneaking behind him and stealing his bow and arrows. Hermes paid for the cattle by giving Apollo the lyre and showing him how to play, and in return Apollo brought the boy up as if he were his own son, making him guardian of the gods' cattle in his place, giving him persuasiveness, eloquence and a golden shepherd's staff, and teaching him how to tell the future by swirling pebbles in a bowl of water and reading the patterns they made. Hermes invented the game of knucklebones (jacks), and the two gods often played.

Hermes grown up. When Hermes grew up he became the gods' **messenger**, running their errands and flying on winged sandals between Heaven, Earth and the **Underworld**. Because, as a **trickster** supreme, it was impossible to cheat him and win a second life, he was also given the job of escorting the souls of the Dead on their last journey to the Underworld. He invented many other things as well as the lyre: a shepherd's pipe cut from a hollow reed, astronomy, boxing, gym-

nastics and **writing**. He was an easy-going, high-spirited god, and as well as enjoying his mischief mortals chose him to guard their homes, putting a small Hermes-statue (called a Herm) on a pedestal just outside the door.

*Hermes the winged messenger was a favourite figure in ancient art: an elegant, slim youth with winged sandals and a winged helmet. In sterner guise, he appeared as the guide of the Dead, in white robes (for mourning) and carrying the magic wand with which he opened the gates of the Underworld. He was the patron god of markets and merchants, and statues were placed in niches or plaques were pinned to walls to bring good luck. Statuettes showing his childish exploits were popular children's toys, and his adventures (like those of **Krishna** in India or **Loki** in Northern Europe) also inspired hundreds of children's rhymes and nursery stories. In adult literature he features as a god of music and happiness in pastoral poetry, and in comedy as a camp buffoon, always hungry and out to grab any advantage – prototype of the scheming slave or servant so common in later comedy.*

HERMIONE
Europe (South)

Hermione in Argos. Hermione ('pillar-queen'), in Greek myth, was the daughter of **Menelaus** and **Helen**, and inherited all her parents' beauty. When Menelaus sailed for the **Trojan War**, he left Hermione to be brought up by his sister-in-law **Clytemnestra** in Argos. After the war, when Clytemnestra murdered her husband **Agamemnon**, and their son **Orestes** avenged Agamemnon's death by killing

Clytemnestra, Orestes kidnapped Hermione and held her hostage until Menelaus, Agamemnon's brother, agreed not to execute him for matricide. Menelaus went so far as to promise Hermione's hand in marriage to Orestes. But he had already agreed that she should marry **Neoptolemus** King of Epirus, and as soon as Orestes released her he smuggled her from Argos to Epirus.

Hermione in Epirus. In Epirus, Hermione was honoured as Neoptolemus' future queen – by everyone except Neoptolemus himself, who was infatuated with Princess **Andromache** of Troy, given to him as a concubine after the war. Hermione tried unsuccessfully to murder Andromache, and then, when Orestes secretly arrived in Epirus, persuaded him to kill Neoptolemus and carry her home to Sparta. Here they married, and Hermione spent the rest of her life as his consort and queen, ruling the combined kingdoms of Sparta, Argos and Arcadia.

HEROES

In Greek myth, 'hero' specifically meant the offspring of one mortal and one immortal parent. Heroes lived mortal lives, but often had difficulty containing the immortal half of their natures inside a mortal body. In other myth traditions the derivation was not so explicit. Heroes were fully mortal, or were gods who took mortal form. They had some supernatural abilities (such as shapechanging) and were able to mingle with supernatural beings on all-but-equal terms. In all traditions heroes led the human communities in which they lived, and swaggered about the world fighting battles and undertaking quests. Most existed exclusively in this macho dimension: only a very few (**Arjuna, Lancelot, Odysseus**) engaged in any kind of self-questioning or showed psychological complexity.

⧓➤ (Africa): Ditaolane; (Americas): Gunnodayak, Nayanezgani and Tobadzistsini; (Celtic): Arthur, Beowulf, Brit, Cormac MacAirt, Cuculain, Galahad, Gawain, Lancelot, Lleu Llaw Gyffes, Perceval, Pwyll; (Finnish): Väinämöinen; (Greece): Achilles, Agamemnon, Argonauts, Bellerophon, Diomedes, Hector, Heracles, Jason, Menelaus, Neoptolemus, Odysseus, Orestes, Paris, Patroclus, Perseus, Theseus; (India): Arjuna, Ashvathaman, Balarama, Bhima, Bhisma, Duryodhana, Kauravas, Lakshmana, Nakula, Pandavas, Rama, Sahadeva, Yudhishthira; (Japan): Ninigi, Okuninushi, Yuriwaka; (Mesopotamia): Gilgamesh; (Nordic): Sigmund, Sigurd; (Rome): Aeneas, Horatius Cocles, Turnus; (Slavic): *bogatiri*, Ilya Muromets, Potok-Mikhailo Ivanovich, Sadko, Volkh; (Western Europe): Roland

HERSILIA
Europe (South)

Hersilia ('dewy'), in Roman myth, was **Romulus'** wife. After he was taken into **Heaven** and became the god Quirinus, she was inconsolable, begging the gods to carry her to **Olympus** and grant her a place beside her husband. At last Juno (see **Hera**) sent the **rainbow**-goddess **Iris** to touch Hersilia with one finger, the **Fates** snipped the thread of Hersilia's mortal life, and her immortal self flew to Olympus, her hair blazing in the sun like a comet-tail. She became one of the Horae, goddesses of the hours, and lived happily with Quirinus ever afterwards.

Scholars think that this story may have been invented to explain an appearance of Halley's Comet over Italy some time in the 750s BCE, not long after the traditional date for the founding of Rome. Whatever its origin, by the heyday of the Roman republic worship of Hersilia/Hora was an integral part of the Quirinus-cult at the heart of state religion.

HESPERIDES, THE
Europe (South)

The Hesperides ('nymphs of the West'), in Greek myth, were the three (or some say four) daughters of **Atlas** who tended the tree on which grew the Golden Apples of **Immortality**, **Mother Earth**'s wedding present to **Hera** when she married **Zeus**. Their names were Aegle ('shiner'), Arethusa ('waterer'), Erythia ('blusher') and (some say) Hestia (Roman Vesta; 'hearth' or 'flower-bed'), and they looked after the apple-tree in a beautiful garden on the slopes of Mount Atlas beyond the river of Ocean which surrounds the world.

HINA
Oceania

Hina ('girl'), or Ina, in Polynesian myth, was the feminine principle incarnate, an aspect of the universal **Great Goddess**. In Maori myth she was Hine Ahu One, the sand-woman **Tane** made to be his wife; in Tahitian myth she lived with her brother Ru, often went exploring with him, and one day visited the **Moon** and decided to stay there. Other stories say that she was the wife of **Tangaroa** the sea god, and left him for the Moon when he lost his temper because she was beating bark cloth when he had a hang-over, and sent a servant to stun her with her own mallet. Still other stories make her the wife of the eel-monster Te Tuna, and say that she became so bored with him that she mated with Maui; still others identify her with Hine Nui Te Po, goddess of **death**.

HINU
Americas (North)

Hinu, or Hino, in the myths of the Iroquois people of the Northeastern US, was the god of **thunder** and chief guardian of the **sky**. He lived in a cloud-fortress in the far West, and was peaceful and benign – except when evil threatened his people, and he sent his anger cracking across the sky in **lightning** and thunder to deal with it. He twice appeared on Earth to help his human worshippers: once to kill the water-snake **demon** which polluted the Great Lakes – its shattered body became a series of floating islands – and once to end the power of the Stone **Giants**, whose bodies he smashed to rubble and threw into a pit below the Earth.

HIPPOLYTA
Europe (South)

Hippolyta ('horse-broken'), in Greek myth, was the daughter of **Ares** the war god and was queen of the **Amazons**. She wore a golden belt, given her by Ares as proof that she was the most powerful woman in the world – and as one of the **Labours** King **Eurystheus** of Mycenae devised for **Heracles**, he ordered him to steal it. To reach the Amazons' country, Heracles built a ship and gathered a crew of **heroes**, just as **Jason** had done when he went for the **Golden Fleece**. They sailed North, and after many adventures reached the Amazons' shores. Heracles' men were astonished when the Amazons, instead of fighting, welcomed them and took them as lovers. But Heracles knew that the Amazons always ended by killing or enslaving the men they slept with, so he took hostages and demanded Hippolyta's golden belt as ransom. The Amazons attacked, there was a pitched battle, the Greeks won and Heracles took Hippolyta's belt in triumph back to Mycenae.

Accounts differ about what happened to Hippolyta herself. Some say that in the battle between Heracles' warriors and the Amazons, she fought Heracles in person, hand-to-hand, and he killed her. In others, she fell in love with **Theseus**, one of the heroes who went with Heracles, and willingly surrendered the belt and went back to Athens as Theseus' mistress. (These accounts confuse her with **Antiope**.) Still others say that **Zeus** snatched Hippolyta up out of the fighting, dropped her golden belt in front of Heracles, and then, when the Greeks sailed for home, restored Hippolyta miraculously to her people.

HIPPOLYTUS
Europe (South)

Hippolytus ('horse-broken'), in Greek and Roman myth, was the son of **Theseus** and Theseus' mistress **Antiope**.

When Theseus married **Phaedra**, and killed Antiope when she tried to prevent the wedding, Hippolytus was a child. He grew up in the palace, but refused to behave like a royal prince, instead devoting himself to the service of **Artemis**, the patron goddess of his mother's people the **Amazons**. The gods were waiting to punish Theseus for killing Antiope, and Hippolytus was one of the means they chose. As soon as he was old enough, they drove his step-mother Phaedra mad. She asked Hippolytus to have **sex** with her, and when he refused – since all Artemis' servants swear eternal virginity – she told Theseus that Hippolytus had tried to rape her. Theseus sent guards to arrest Hippolytus; the boy jumped into his chariot and galloped off along the coast road from Athens; Theseus prayed to the gods to stop him, and **Poseidon** sent a wave which startled Hippolytus' horses, so that the chariot crashed and Hippolytus broke his neck.

This was by no means the end of Hippolytus' story. His patron Artemis went to the gods and demanded that since he was entirely innocent, he should be allowed to live again. **Apollo**'s son **Aesculapius** went to the site of the chariot-crash and revived Hippolytus by letting him taste **ambrosia**, the immortal gods' food. The **Fates**, angry at this usurping of their authority to control human destiny, complained to **Zeus**, who killed Aesculapius with a thunderbolt. But Hippolytus had been revived by a god, and no other god could unrevive him. Artemis left a wraith of his body where it lay – the local people later buried it and honoured Hippolytus as a god – but wrapped the real Hippolytus in a cloud and carried him away to Italy. Here she gave him a new body, that of an ancient peasant. She called him Virbius ('twice-man'), and married him to the nymph Egeria – and in this incarnation Hippolytus has lived ever since, in the obscurity and seclusion he craved from childhood.

HIRANYAKASHIPU
India

Hiranyakashipu ('golden-robed') was a **demon**. Like his brother, **Hiranyaksha**, he was granted what he took to be total invulnerability by the gods, and used it to terrorize the universe. In the end **Vishnu** rescued **creation** by changing himself into the man-lion **Narasimha** (against whom it had never occurred to Hiranyakashipu to request invulnerability) and killed him.
➽➔ **Prahlada**

HIRANYAKSHA
India

Hiranyaksha ('golden-eyed') was a **demon** who dragged the Earth and its creatures to the depths of the primordial ocean. He was invulnerable to all creatures except boars, so **Vishnu** changed himself into a boar (**Varaha**), killed him and brought the Earth back to the surface before any living thing was harmed.

HLIN
Europe (North)

Hlin, one of **Frigg**'s handmaids in Nordic myth, was the goddess of consolation.

She looked out for people in distress, flew down and kissed their tears away.

HÖD
Europe (North)

Höd, in Nordic myth, was the son of **Odin** and **Frigg**, and **Baldur**'s twin brother. In some accounts, he was also Baldur's mirror-image – just as Baldur was all-light, so Höd was all darkness. Baldur's radiance streamed out across the world; Höd was blind and introverted. When Baldur began dreaming of his own death, and Frigg begged everything in the universe (save only mistletoe) to agree not to harm him, the gods began entertaining themselves by pelting Baldur with stones, spears and other weapons and watching them bounce harmlessly away. Höd asked **Loki** to help him join in the fun, and Loki gave him a sharpened mistletoe twig and guided his hand so that he stabbed Baldur dead.

In other accounts, Höd was the radiant, virtuous twin, and Baldur was a tyrannical extrovert, the harshness of light made manifest. No beings in **creation** could face Baldur directly, because they were dazzled by the light-spears from his eyes. But Höd was blind, and Loki persuaded him to take a magic sword (named Mistellteinn, 'mistletoe') and kill his twin for the good of the universe – not telling him that Baldur's death would start the process which would one day lead to **Ragnarök**, the end of this cycle of creation.

The myths of Höd and his warring twin gave rise, in Gesta Danorum by Saxo the Grammarian, to an extraordinary tale of skulduggery and derring-do, in which Höd and Baldur were both evil, bandits favoured by warrior-nymphs and fed on snake-venom to insulate them against poison. They robbed, pillaged – and above all fought each other for Nanna, Freyja's beautiful handmaid. Höd won this fight, married Nanna – and not content with that, stole the magic sword Mistellteinn and killed his twin. For this, Odin fathered a son, Boe, whose only role in creation was to grow up and kill Höd, which he duly did.

»»→ light and dark, twins

HOLAWAKA
Africa

Holawaka, in the myths of the Galla people of Ethiopia, was the **messenger** between Earth and **Heaven**. He was sent by the Sky-spirit to tell human beings the secret of **immortality**: that they should take off their skins like clothes when they were old, and put on new ones. To make the journey, Holawaka changed himself into a bird. But the way was long and he grew hungry. He found a snake swallowing a dead mouse, and offered to trade the secret of immortality for a share of the carcass. This is why snakes live forever, sloughing their skins whenever they start growing old – and why Holawaka birds exist on Earth, gods punished by the Sky-spirit for their ancestor's disobedience, and condemned to live among mortals and eat carrion throughout eternity.

HOLY GRAIL
Europe (North)

The Holy Grail (from the medieval French *san gréal*, perhaps a misreading of *sang réal*, 'royal blood'), in medieval Christian myth, was the cup used by Christ at the Last Supper, or the bowl which gathered his blood as he hung on the cross. It was given to Joseph of Arimathea for safe keeping, and when he disappeared from the world its whereabouts became unknown. It also had the property of vanishing when anyone impure went near it. It contained a secret known only to a few; only males were allowed to talk of it, and then only with absolute accuracy, as mistakes brought them disease and death. King **Arthur**'s knights went in quest of it, but only one of them, **Galahad**, was judged worthy enough to find it, and he carried it into **Heaven**.

*The Grail-myth survives not in its own right, but as the basis of Christian religious allegory. The medieval allegorists (of whom the most assiduous, and most successful, was Chrétien de Troyes) made **Galahad** the epitome of Christian obedience and purity – some even identified him with Christ himself – and explained at length why each of the other knights (**Gawain**, **Lancelot**, Ector and others) was unfit to find it. Such allegorizing excellently served its religious purposes, but had the side-effect of bleaching character from the Grail-knights themselves. Even Galahad became no more than a lay-figure, morally impeccable, priggish and predictable. The myths were also sliced down to fit the allegory, so that each encounter became little more than a single conflict between good and evil, a test of Christian fortitude passed or failed according to the character of the protagonist; the variety and unpredictability of myth were almost entirely lost.*

There is a small body of Holy-Grail art, consisting mainly of contemporary illustrations to medieval retellings of the story, and an amount of nineteenth-century European illustration resulting from William Morris' discovery and reprinting of Malory's Morte d'Arthur. This art tends to be moralizing and sententious in style, as if the artists (of whom the greatest was Burne-Jones) had neither the vision nor the technique to render perfect purity. None the less, it has been a norm for religious popular art in Europe for over 150 years. In modern times, Grail-quests have been favourite subjects for romantic adventure stories, from novels by Rider Haggard and Frank G. Slaughter to the film Indiana Jones and the Last Crusade by Steven Spielberg.

From the tenth century onwards, the Grail had an existence outside the arts, as the object of esoteric cults and quests. People identified it not only as the cup of Christ's Last Supper, but as the Jewish Ark of the Covenant, the Cauldron of Immortality owned by the ancient Druids and the gold-hoard of the Cathar people exterminated in Southern France in the thirteenth century – each of them a treasure guaranteed to enrich the finder more than any other worldly hoard. Mystic writings were combed for clues to the Grail's whereabouts, and the secret was held to be known by followers of cults of all kinds, from Cathars to Freemasons, from Rosicrucians to Satanists. To this day devotees continue the search, and Grail-quests belong in the same assiduously-investigated fringe of the paranormal as the Bermuda Triangle and UFOs.

HONEYBIRD: *see* Leza and Honeybird

HONIR
Europe (North)

Honir (also known as Hoenir and Hoener), in Nordic myth, was a tall, handsome and always silent god, **Odin**'s shadow. In the **creation** account which says that Odin made human beings, it was Honir who breathed into **Ask and Embla** to give them souls. After the war between **Aesir** and **Vanir**, Honir was one of the two Aesir who went to live with the Vanir, but without his companion **Mimir** (whose head they cut off and sent back to the Aesir) he was of no use to them, merely standing there tongue-tied. However, although Honir plays only a marginal role in the myths of **Asgard**, his time will come. He will, the **Ragnarök** myth assures us, be one of the very few survivors of the end of the world, and will help to inaugurate the new cycle of the universe, as he helped with the creation of this one.

HONOYETA
Oceania

Honoyeta, in the myths of Goodenough Island, Papua New Guinea, was the **demon** who brought mortality to human beings. He had two wives, who mated with him as an enormous **snake**. But when they went to work each morning, he sloughed his snakeskin, became a handsome human and enjoyed **sex** with every pretty girl he found. One day the wives found out, and burned his snakeskin. Honoyeta, condemned to human form for the rest of eternity, retaliated by introducing **death** to humans.
≫→ shape-changers

HORATIUS COCLES
Europe (South)

When Lars Porsena, king of Clusium, invaded Rome in Roman myth, his only access to the city was a wooden bridge across the Tiber. Horatius Cocles, with two companions, held off the enemy while the Romans chopped the bridge down behind him. At the last moment, just as it collapsed, he hurled his sword at the enemy, dived into the Tiber and swam to safety. His exploit became one of the best-known heroic legends in Roman history.

≫→ heroes

HORUS
Africa (North)

Horus the Sun. Horus, in Egyptian myth, was originally a Sun-god, **Ra**'s strength made manifest. His honorary titles included Harakhty ('Horus of the horizon'), Harsamtaui ('Horus uniter of Egypt') and Horkhentiirti ('Horus of the two eyes', that is lord of the **Sun** and **Moon**). He was often shown as a small child (Herupakhret, 'Horus the child', Greek Harpocrates), suckling at his mother's breast, gazing out with one finger in his mouth, playing with tame snakes and scorpions, or riding crocodiles and lions.

Horus, son of Aset and Osiris. In later myth, from the region of the Nile Delta, Horus was said to be the child of **Aset** (Isis) and **Osiris**. He was conceived when Aset took the form of a hawk, or kite, and beat her wings to try to restore the breath of life to Osiris after his brother **Set** murdered him. In these accounts Horus was a hawk, or a hawk-headed warrior, and his Egyptian name Har was derived from the bird's call. Since hawks symbolize the immensity of the sky, this Horus was merged with the earlier Sun-god to become a single deity, and was regarded as Osiris' representative in the World Above after his father became ruler of the **Underworld**. Horus mediated between the two worlds, guiding the souls of the Dead to judgement before Osiris' throne and giving especial protection to pharaohs and their households. (Pharaohs acknowledged this relationship by taking the title 'living Horus'.)

Horus and Set. The Delta myth-cycle tells of Horus' efforts to punish Set for killing his father and usurping his power on Earth. The battle began when Horus claimed his inheritance from the divine court, and Ra refused to listen because Set made the boy-god's breath smell as foul as a crocodile's. They continued with trials of magic. When Set suggested a race in stone boats, Horus won by making his boat of plaster on a wicker framework. Then Horus suggested that they change themselves into hippos and see who could stay longest underwater. He tried to persuade Aset to spear Set underwater, but Aset refused to kill her own brother and Horus was forced to hide for his life in the desert. Set found him and gouged out his eyes; light disappeared from the world, and was returned only when **Hathor** dribbled gazelle's milk into the sockets and new eyes grew. In some accounts Horus ended the struggle by ripping off Set's testicles and so destroying his power. In others, Set brought about his own downfall by raping Horus, a crime which Aset used to Horus' advantage before the celestial court (see Aset).

In some accounts, perhaps a version of the story of Ra's eye (the Moon), only one of Horus' eyes was restored after Set gouged them out – and his benefactor was not Hathor but **Thoth** the healer. The other eye was left rolling about the darkness which was Set's domain, and became the Moon. However this myth arose, it inspired the cult of Horus' remaining eye, the udjat, which began as a good-luck charm (either worn as an amulet on the forehead, where it gave insight into the past and future as well as the present, or painted on doors, chests and above all, coffins) and ended up as a god worshipped in its own right and depicted as a heavily-made-up eye with a coiled hawk-feather hanging below it to one side and a pair of arms at the other holding a pot containing the two reeds which symbolized Upper and Lower Egypt. These rather portentous artistic representations are, however, outnumbered by the charmingly domestic portraits of Horus as a young child, and by the affectionate way he is shown as guide and protector of the Dead – the only deity in Underworld scenes to be given any glimmer of human warmth.

HOURIS
Asia (West)

Houris ('maidens'), in Islamic myth, were dark-eyed females who, in Paradise, provided sexual services for the glorious male dead. (Female dead had no equivalent.) Seventy-two of them attended each man, and their virginity was endlessly renewed.

The earthly – and earthy – equivalent of houris gave a new slang word to Western soldiers who visited Arabic countries, and it has become standard English: 'whores'.
⟫+ apsaras, beauty, nymphs, Valhalla

HOUSEHOLD AND FAMILY: see
Bastet, Chantico, Domovoi, Dugnai, Lakshmi, Lar, Penates, Tsao Jun, Vesta

HRAESVELG
Europe (North)

Hraesvelg ('corpse-tearer'), in Nordic myth, was a gigantic eagle whose eyrie was the ice-mountains in the extreme North of the universe. All winds were its children, sent out across **creation** by the flapping of its wings.

HRUNGNIR
Europe (North)

Hrungnir, in Nordic myth, was the strongest of the **giants**, a living mountain. His flesh was clay, his head and heart were stone. He was always getting drunk and challenging the gods to races, trials of strength and other contests. He tried to out-gallop **Odin**'s horse Sleipnir, and failed – and rather than take warning, he boasted that he would smash **Asgard** to pieces and take **Freyja** and **Sif** for wives. Thor challenged him to a duel, and smashed him to rubble.

HRYM
Europe (North)

Hrym, in Nordic myth, was one of the few **giants** at home on **water**. He was a boat-builder and navigator – and when **Ragnarök** comes he will load the ice-giants into his boat (Naglfar, made from corpses' fingernails and toenails) and row to attack the gods.

HUAI NAN ZU
Asia (East)

Huai Nan Zu, in Chinese Daoist myth, was a mortal prince. The **Eight Immortals** visited him and offered him three wishes. He asked for **immortality**, omniscience and omnipotence. They told him to work for one at a time, and to begin with immortality. He began to study magic and alchemy, and eventually succeeded in distilling a potion identical to the juice of the Peaches of Immortality, the elixir of life. He tried to gulp it down, but no sooner had the first drops passed his lips than he was carried up towards **Heaven**. He was so surprised that he dropped the glass, which smashed. So mortals were denied immortality, and only a few dogs, who licked up the spilt dregs from the earth, passed into Heaven.

As for Huai Nan Zu, he hammered arrogantly on the doors of Heaven and demanded imperial privileges to equal those of **Yu Huang**, the Jade Emperor, himself. Yu Huang said that he was not ready yet for immortality, and would have to be reincarnated on Earth. But the Eight Immortals interceded, and promised to teach Huai Nan Zu the Way. He gave up his Imperial ambitions, spent the rest of existence as a humble Daoist philosopher – and discovered, the story ends, that omniscience and omnipotence are not as we perceive them in worldly terms, but part of the acceptance and understanding that are the Way.

HUANG DI
Asia (East)

Huang Di ('yellow emperor'), in Chinese myth, was the first of the **Five Emperors** who brought **civilization** to Earth. He was born equipped with all the languages and knowledge of the world. He taught his people how to hunt, fish and build roads; he invented the wheel, armour, weapons, ships, coinage and the compass, criss-crossed his kingdom with roads, and devised systems of law and government. In his spare time he invented the arts, especially **music** and pottery.

In addition to all his other gifts, Huang Di was able to communicate directly with the gods, climbing the holy mountain Tai Shan to speak to them in prayers and sacrifices. His rode in an ivory chariot pulled by six dragons and an elephant and driven by a green-feathered crane with a human face. Tigers, wolves and snakes accompanied it in procession, and squadrons of phoenixes filled the sky. Huang Di sat in the centre, his four faces gazing out serenely, one in each direction across the Earth.

Not surprisingly, Huang Di's reign was generally regarded as a golden age. Only one god rebelled against him, Chi Yu son of **Shen Nong**, who took as allies Chi Song Zi the **rain**-lord and Huang Di's own son **Fei Lian**, the wind-lord. They sent fogs to disorient Huang Di's armies and rain-storms to drown them. But Huang Di's daughter Ba ('drought') went out alone to fight them, drying up their clouds and withering them until they capitulated. Chi Yu was demoted in rank, and Chi Song Zi and Fei Lian were given slaves' jobs. They preceded Huang Di in his processions to Tai Shan, the holy mountain; Fei Lian swept the ground ahead of him and Chi Song Zi sprinkled it to lay the dust. For many mortal years after this victory – some say fifteen generations – the world was calm and prosperous, and Huang Di presided over an unending sequence of feasts and jollity.

Accounts differ about what happened next. In some, Huang Di ascended in state to **Heaven** and lived there with as much ceremony as he had on Earth. In Daoist accounts, however, he began at last to age, and the effects of an over-indulgent life made him paunchy, sallow and sluggish. He abandoned luxury, went to live in a hut in the palace yard and spent his days fasting and praying. One night he dreamed of an ascetic paradise ruled by Hua Xu, mother of the first of the **Three Sovereigns**, **Fu Xi**; its inhabitants felt neither pain, emotion nor longing, and spent their time in the pure joy of the spirit. When Huang Di woke up he told his courtiers that he had discovered the *dao*, or Way. He ruled for one more generation, the story ends, and when he died he ascended into Heaven and was worshipped as a god; his human followers mourned his passing for 200 years.

The Daoist end to Huang Di's story turned him almost exclusively into a moral leader, but in popular belief he remained the universal benefactor from earlier stories, Lord of the Golden Age. Later Emperors, beginning with Shi Huang Di in the third century BCE, claimed that he had been a real person, ruling in the third millennium BCE, and that just as he had been deified after death, so would they be, ascending into Heaven to join his entourage. His inventive skills were thought to have rubbed off on those around him: his chief wife perfected the process of silk-making and his most senior court official invented **writing**.

⁂→ **crafts**

HUANG GUN
Asia (East)

Huang Gun, in Chinese myth, was the patron god of incense-makers. In the time of the Emperor **Yao**, a branch fell from one of the trees of **Heaven** to Earth, and smelled so sweet that Huang Gun presented it to the Emperor, saying that if he burned it, it would return to Heaven and delight the gods. This was the origin both of the idea of burning incense-sticks in temples, and of Huang Gun's **immortality**.

⁂→ **crafts**

HUITZILOPOCHTLI
Americas (Central)

Huitzilopochtli, god of war in Aztec myth, represented the **Sun** at its zenith, and the vigour of young men in the prime of life. His name, literally 'blue humming-bird on the left', means 'killed in battle': the Aztecs believed that dead warriors' souls turned into humming-birds, and flew leftwards to the **Underworld**.

Huitzilopochtli was born miraculously to **Coatlicue (Mother Earth)**, and sprang fully-formed from the womb to defend her against her 400 sons, the Night Stars, who were coming to kill her. He cut out their hearts and hung them round Coatlicue's neck like ornaments, and ever afterwards the hearts of human victims were offered to him, and to her, in bloody sacrifices – annually to Coatlicue to bring **fertility** to the soil, daily at dawn to Huitzilopochtli to coax the Sun to rise in the **sky**.

*Huitzilopochtli was the central god in the Aztec pantheon, regarded as chief guide and father of the nation. Originally a simple, vegetarian god of plenty, **Xochipili**, enjoying sacrifices of flowers and fruit, he advised the nomadic Aztecs to gather together and invade Mexico, and his reward (so his priests claimed) was to be given blood to feed his undying thirst. Daily sacrifice brought him soaring into the sky as the Sun, and the ascendancy in war of the Aztec people was guaranteed by regular feasts and celebrations at which young men fought mock (and sometimes real, gladiatorial) battles, and thousands of victims were offered to him (70,000 alone at one ceremony, to mark the dedication of a new temple in Tenochtitlán). Some accounts claim that these victims were mainly animals, but the Spanish conquerors of Mexico said – and although they are unlikely to have been reliable witnesses, no one has satisfactorily disproved their claims – that they were human, that the Aztecs were cannibals and that after Huitzilopochtli had drunk the victims' blood and Coatlicue had been offered their hearts, hands and heads, the flesh was distributed city-wide.*

HUMAN ANCESTORS: *see* Adam and Eve, Adapa, Ask and Embla, Atsehastin and Atseestan, Bachue, Deucalion and Pyrrha, Gayomart, Jari and Kamarong, Kintu and Nambi, Lif, Manu, Mwambu and Sela, Mwuetsi, Massassi and Morongo, Quaayayp, Parsu, Yima

HUMANMAKER
Americas (North)

Humanmaker, in the myths of the Pima people of the Southwestern US desert, decided to create human beings by making clay models and baking them in an oven. He moulded the first doll, then left it on a wall to harden – and while he wasn't looking **Coyote** ran up and sniffed it. When the doll was baked, it came out not as a human but as a dog. Humanmaker tried again, this time making two dolls. He wasn't satisfied with the look of them, and asked Coyote's advice. 'They're identical,' Coyote told him. 'They won't be able to breed.' He nuzzled the man doll's loins until there was a small piece of clay left dangling, and Humanmaker nicked the female's doll's loins with his thumbnail. Then he put them in the oven to bake. After a while Coyote said, 'They're done' – and Humanmaker took them out, only to find that they were still white and soft. He put them aside, and they scampered away. He tried a second batch, and this time Coyote distracted him at the time they should be taken out, so that they emerged burned black. Humanmaker put them aside, and they ran away. He made a third batch, and this time kicked Coyote out of the way till they were done. The third batch of dolls, taken out exactly in time and baked to perfection, were the ancestors of all the native peoples of North America.

Variants of this myth were told throughout the Americas, Asia and Polynesia – but curiously, by none of the black-skinned or white-skinned peoples of the world, a fact which leads some authorities to surmise that it may be one of the oldest of all creation-stories, dating back to the inter-continental migrations of the last Ice Age.

➤ Chinigchinich, creation, Enki, Esaugetuh Emissee, Hurukan, Na'pi, Prometheus, Tagaro, Woyengi

HUNAB
Americas (Central)

Hunab ('One'), or Hunab Ku ('the only one'), in Mayan myth, was the oldest of gods, the creator of humankind. His other names included Kinebahan ('eyes and mouth of the **Sun**'), which suggests that he personified the Sun-shaft. He tried several times to make a perfect race to inhabit Earth, and sent a **flood** each time to wipe out his botched attempts. The first inhabitants were dwarfs, and the survivors from Hunab's flood still lurk in underground holes and crannies. The second inhabitants were human-shaped but entirely wicked, and those that survived the flood became **demons** in the **Underworld**. The third inhabitants were humans – and we are still waiting to see if Hunab is satisfied, or if our existence is to end in another all-engulfing flood.

➤ creation, Hurukan

HUNDRED-HANDED GIANTS, THE
Europe (South)

The Hundred-handed **Giants** (Hekatoncheires), in Greek myth, were three sons of **Gaia** (**Mother Earth**) and **Ouranos** (Father **Sky**), among the first creatures in the universe. Their names were **Briareus** ('strong'), Gyges ('son of Earth') and Cottus (Kottos, 'son of the Great Mother'), and their shapes were a blend of human and tree: each had fifty heads and a hundred branching arms and hands. They were squat, brutish, brawn without brain, baleful as toads, and revolted their father Ouranos so much that he hurled them into the darkness of Tartarus below the **Underworld**, as far out of sight as possible.

Too unintelligent to realize what had happened, or that there was any alternative, the Hundred-handed Giants lay where they were for a thousand aeons. Over their heads **Cronus**, leader of the **Titans**, castrated their father Ouranos and drove him into retirement in the heavens, and the Titans in turn had children, the gods, who plotted to dethrone them and seize power in the universe. Civil war began, **Zeus** and the gods battling the Titans for supremacy – and the Hundred-handed Giants knew nothing of it. It was not until the war had all but destroyed the universe that Gaia, tired of being ripped and torn by the fighting, told Zeus of their existence, and he gave them **nectar** and **ambrosia** to stir them back to life, and took them to the Upper World as allies of the gods. As soon as the war was over, however, and the gods had won, he banished the Titans to Tartarus, and gave the Hundred-handed Giants the job of guarding them – and the Giants, thinking this promotion, eagerly took on the task and remained out of sight and out of mind throughout eternity.

HUN DUN
Asia (East)

Hun Dun ('chaos'), in Chinese myth, was the primordial substance from which the universe was formed. It contained all that was, is or shall be, and as time passed it formed itself into the shape of an egg. The egg hatched, the shell forming *Yin*, the Earth, the fluid *Yang*, the **sky**. In between them lay **Pan Gu**, god of shaping, and he separated them to begin **creation**.

In other accounts, Hun Dun was one of three Emperors who ruled the universe before **creation**. He was the Emperor of the Centre, and the others were Hu (Emperor of the Northern Ocean) and Ju (Emperor of the Southern Ocean). The three Emperors, the only beings in existence, used to socialize in Hun Dun's palace (the void of space), and it occurred to Hu and Ju that they owed their host a favour. Separately they were powerless, but when they came together they made **lightning**, and used it to cut holes in Hun Dun, who had until then been shape without body. They intended to give him the seven orifices which all animate bodies would one day possess. Cutting the holes took seven days, and as they finished the seventh hole Hun Dun died and his body simultaneously imploded and exploded to form the universe.

*These are the two most coherent accounts of Hun Dun. Others exist only in fragments. In some, he was the wicked son of one of the Emperors who existed before existence, or of **Huang Di**, and it was when he was banished that he formed himself into the yin/yang egg and began creation. In another, he was imagined as a four-winged, six-legged, faceless bird whose body was 'a red-coloured, yellow bag' – possibly a poetic, not to say wildly fanciful, description of the innards of an egg.*

HUNTING: *see* Anat, Artemis, Dilwica, Erh Long, Jara, Leib-Olmai, Mixcóatl, Ogun, Oisin, Pinga, Sraosha, Yamasachi

HURUKAN
Americas (Central)

Hurukan ('one-legged'), in Guatemalan myth, was the god of hurricanes (called after him). He created everything in existence. He made fire by rubbing his sandals together – the myth fails to explain why a one-legged god needed more than one sandal. He swept through the mists which covered the primeval ocean, calling out 'Earth, Earth, Earth' until the Earth rose from the sea. With the help of other gods, he set about peopling it, making doll-figures and breathing life into them. The first creatures were animals, fish, insects and reptiles. But in his zest for finding ever-new shapes and forms for them, Hurukan forgot to give them language, and instead of paying him proper worship they bayed, squeaked and howled. He punished them by making them eat each other, and set out to make a superior race. He began by making human-shaped dolls of clay, but their minds were inert and they refused to pray at all. He tried whittling wood and weaving reeds. The wooden figures were as slack-witted as the clay-people, and the reed-figures had only the suppleness to run, no brains to pray. (Hurukan turned them into monkeys.) Finally he made people by stripping the husks from corn-kernels and giving them life – and the human race was born. Hurukan gave them knowledge (beginning with the power to control fire) and looked forward to enjoying their songs of praise for the rest of eternity.

Unfortunately, the **Sun**, **Moon** and stars did not yet exist, and humans lived on the surface of the Earth in darkness. They scattered, terrified, developed a thousand different languages and habits of life, and began attacking each other. Hurukan made heavenly bodies to enlighten them – but too late. Our race knows about the gods, prays to them and worships them – but we are also tainted with darkness, and our second concern, after paying homage to the spirits of light, is to make life as difficult and brutish for each other as we can.

*Mayan myth says that **Hunab**, not Huru-kan, was the original creator, but then goes on to tell the Hurukan story as if Hunab didn't exist. Mythographers suggest that the two traditions come from different peoples, conquered by or amalgamated into the Mayan empire, and that the Hunab story (by far the less sophisticated) is the oldest.*

≫→ Chinigchinich, creation, Enki, Esaugetuh Emissee, Humanmaker, Na'pi, Prometheus, Tagaro, Woyengi

HUVEANE
Africa

Huveane, in the myths of the Basuto people of Lesotho, made the world and everything in it. He intended that there should be one immortal generation only, but people and animals discovered **sex** and began breeding, and soon the world was so noisy that Huveane starting climbing the Sky-hill, hammering pegs into it as a mountaineer puts footholds in a cliffside. Every so often he stopped and listened, to see if the racket had abated; then, disappointed, he moved even higher – and he is still climbing.

≫→ creation

HYACINTHUS
Europe (South)

Hyacinthus (Hyakinthos, 'hyacinth'), in Greek myth, was a handsome Spartan prince, and **Apollo** fell in love with him. But Hyacinthus already had a lover, the musician Thamyras. To get rid of Thamyras, Apollo told the **Muses** of his boast that he could out-sing them, and the Muses punished Thamyras by stealing his voice, eyes and memory. This left the field clear for Apollo's love-affair with Hyacinthus, and he showered the boy with presents and taught him athletics, **hunting**, poetry and **prophecy**. He kept him hidden from the other gods; but one day the West Wind **Zephyrus** caught a glimpse of Hyacinthus and fell in love. He gusted round Apollo and Hyacinthus as they practised athletics, trying to slip past Apollo and caress Hyacinthus' cheek. One day he blew too hard: his breath spun away a discus Apollo was teaching Hyacinthus to throw, and it cracked the boy's skull and killed him. From his blood Apollo created the purple hyacinth, which forever droops its head and is marked with the letters AI ('Alas!') for grief.

HYDRA
Europe (South)

Hydra ('water-creature'), in Greek myth, was the **monster** killed by **Heracles** as the second of his **Labours**. She was the offspring of **Typhon** and Echidna, and had a dog's body, a dragon's tail and nine snapping heads on serpents' necks. One of the heads was immortal and safeguarded Hydra's life. The others were mortal – but whenever one was cut off, two more grew in its place. Hydra's breath and blood were poisonous, able instantly to freeze mortal blood and even to chill the ichor in gods' veins.

Heracles and Iolaus tackled Hydra together. They crept through the swamp at Lerna where the monster lived, and Heracles fell on her, battering her with his club. But for each head he crushed, two more grew, and Hydra forced him backwards to the lip of the bottomless lake at the heart of the swamp. **Hera** sent a giant crab to nip his ankles and drag him in, but in the nick of time Iolaus drove Hydra back with a blazing branch for just long enough for Heracles to stamp the crab dead and run to firmer ground. Then,

each time Heracles crushed one of Hydra's heads Iolaus ran in and seared the stump before any more could grow.

At last only Hydra's immortal head was left. Heracles snatched Iolaus' sword and sliced through the slimy – and mortal – neck. The head hissed on the ground in front of him, still alive; but without limbs it was harmless, and he buried it under a boulder, chopped up Hydra's body and threw the pieces in the swamp. He dipped his arrows in Hydra's blood: from that moment even their slightest graze was fatal, to mortals and gods alike.

Later, **Eurystheus** (who was setting Heracles' tasks) complained that killing the Hydra did not count, as Heracles had been helped by Iolaus. He set an alternative Labour: stealing three of the Golden Apples guarded by the **Hesperides**.

After Heracles' battle with Hydra, Hera set the crab as a constellation in the sky and made it a sign of the zodiac: Cancer, the Crab.

HYLAS
Europe (South)

Hylas ('wood-child'), in Greek myth, was the son of Thiodamas (who farmed the foothills of Mount Parnassus) and the **nymph** Menedice. He was stolen by **Heracles** when he was still a baby. He grew into a beautiful boy, and Heracles made him his squire and bedfellow, and took him on all his adventures. During the expedition to steal the **Golden Fleece**, the **Argonauts** landed in Asia Minor to fetch **water**, and when Hylas bent over a stream to fill his jug, the water-nymphs were so charmed by his **beauty** that they pulled him underwater to live with them. Heracles quartered the woods to find him, and when he failed abandoned the expedition and went back, broken-hearted, to continue his **Labours** for **Eurystheus**.

HYMEN
Europe (South)

Hymen, in Greek and Roman myth, was the son of **Aphrodite** and **Dionysus** (or, some say, of **Apollo** and Terpsichore, **Muse** of dancing). He was the god of wedding-ceremonies, and he often disguised himself as a guest (sometimes male, sometimes female) and led the singing and dancing. In Rome he was often called Hymenaeus, after a misunderstanding of the Greek words sung to invite him to join processions: they began 'Hymen Hymenaios' (which mean, roughly, 'Hymen, Hymen-ish').

HYMIR
Europe (North)

Hymir ('dark one'), in Nordic myth, was a **giant** who owned a cooking-pot the size of the universe. When **Aegir**, the **sea**-god who brewed beer and mead for the gods, explained a shortage by saying that his pots weren't big enough, **Thor** went to fetch Hymir's pot. There was no wrangling, nothing but good manners on both sides; but it was a trial of strength, and both Thor and Hymir knew it. First Thor and Hymir went fishing, using one of Hymir's prize **bulls** as bait. Hymir fished up two whales, and Thor hooked the world-serpent **Jormungand** himself.

In some accounts, Hymir gave up the struggle at this point and drowned himself, or Thor threw him overboard. In others, the two of them went back to Hymir's palace and feasted on the whales. Hymir challenged Thor to smash his drinking-cup – and Thor tried shattering it on every surface in the place before finding the only one hard enough: the giant's own forehead. After that Hymir said that he could have the cooking-pot. But as Thor was leaving, Hymir led a band of other giants to attack him, and Thor took his hammer and killed them all.

HYPERION
Europe (South)

Hyperion ('strider on high'), in Greek myth, was a **Titan** who mated with his sister Theia and fathered three children: **Eos** the Dawn, **Helius** the **Sun** and **Selene** the **Moon**.

*In pre-Greek times Hyperion was himself the Sun-god, the most important god in the pantheon, but in Greek times he was displaced first by **Helius** and then by **Apollo**.*

HYPNUS
Europe (South)

Hypnus (Hypnos, 'sleep'; Latin Somnus), in Greek and Roman myth, was the son of Night and brother of **Death**. He helped Death carry dead warriors to their graves, and gave gods and mortals rest by pouring it from a horn, brushing them with his wings or touching them with a wand.

HYPSIPYLE
Europe (South)

Hypsipyle ('high gate'), queen of Lemnos in Greek myth, ruled a matriarchal society devoted to **Aphrodite**, whose priestess she was. The Lemnian men resented the power of their women, refused to sleep with them and set up house with a group of prostitutes captured during a raid in Thrace. Aphrodite, insulted, stirred up the women to murder their husbands – and all the Lemnian men were killed on the same night, except for Hypsipyle's aged father Thoas, who had taken no interest in prostitutes and whose life she spared.

Soon after this massacre, **Jason** and the **Argonauts** visited Lemnos on their way to find the **Golden Fleece**, and the Lemnian women, anxious to restock their island with children, gave them a warm welcome. Hypsipyle married Jason and bore him **twins**, Euneus and Thoas (junior). But after a year the Argonauts set sail, and the Lemnian women rounded on Hypsipyle, said that Aphrodite had caused this desertion to punish them because Hypsipyle had spared her father's life, and banished her.

Pirates now captured Hypsipyle and sold her to **Lycurgus** king of Nemea, who made her wetnurse to his baby son Archemorus. She was airing the baby one day in the fields when the seven Argive champions (see **Seven Against Thebes**) passed by on their way to Thebes. They asked where they could find fresh water, and she put the baby down to point the way. A snake reared from the ground and ate the child, and Hypsipyle was saved from death only when Adrastus, the Argive leader, bought her from the furious Lycurgus. She served as a slave in Argos for two decades, after which her sons by Jason, Euneus and Thoas rescued her and took her home to Lemnos to live the rest of her life in peace.

IAE: *see* Kuat and Iae

IARBAS
Europe (South)

Iarbas, son of **Jupiter** in Roman myth, ruled Libya in North Africa. When **Dido** fled from Tyre to escape her murderous brother Pygmalion, Iarbas welcomed her and gave her land for a city – or some say, sold it for the treasure she had brought with her. Dido promised Iarbas that as soon as the city (Carthage) was built she would marry him, but when **Aeneas** came to Carthage from Troy, she deserted Iarbas and began a love-affair with him. Iarbas complained to Jupiter, and the gods took action, beginning the chain of events which ended in Dido's suicide.

ICARUS
Europe (South)

Icarus (Ikaros, 'servant of the goddess Kar'), in Greek myth, was the son of **Daedalus**, and went with his father to Crete. When King Minos refused to let them leave the island by ship, Daedalus invented an ingenious alternative, stitching feathers to ribs of willow and jointing them with wax to make huge wings. He and Icarus strapped them on, and as the first upcurrents of air climbed with the morning sun, they soared into the sky. The islanders mistook them for gods and worshipped them.

Unfortunately, Icarus imagined himself as a god as well. The joy of flying bubbled up in him, and he banked and spiralled upwards in the heat haze. He came closer and closer to the **Sun**, and

The Fall of Icarus (*Jugend, c1900*)

the heat softened and loosened the wax that held his wings together. The wings collapsed and Icarus fell like a stone and drowned, in that part of the Mediterranean **Sea** still called 'Icarian' after him.

ICTINIKE
Americas (North)

Ictinike ('spider'), also known as Ikto, Iktome and Unktome, in the myths of the Sioux people of the US plains, was the son of the **Sun** and a notable **trickster**. His main adversary was Rabbit, and hundreds of folk-tales tell of their contests and japes and pranks. In one of the best-known, Ictinike tricked Rabbit out of his own skin, put it on and went to marry Rabbit's chosen wife, a chief's daughter. Rabbit bided his time until the skin was worn-out, and then offered Ictinike a blanket of cow-hide. What he didn't tell him was that the rest of the hide had been made into war-drums, so that whenever the drums beat Ictinike's blanket jerked and thudded in concert with them. Ictinike was forced to jump about with it, and eventually fell so awkwardly that he broke his neck. Ever since, the Sun his father has veiled his face for half of each day in mourning.
»+ animal-gods

IDA
India

Ida, in Hindu myth, was a nourishing food which floated in the **flood**-waters on which **Manu's** ship sailed. When the ship was safely moored, Manu gathered the *ida* (fragments of curds and butter left from the churning of the **Sea** of Milk: see **amrita**), and it nourished him while he remade the world. In some accounts the gods personified Ida as a cow of plenty, or as Manu's own daughter, who later was taken into **Heaven** as a kind of waitress on the gods.

IDOMENEUS
Europe (South)

Idomeneus ('the one who knows'), a King of Crete of Greek myth, was the grandson of Minos – and one of the least-sensibly named of all Greek heroes, since he was a fool. He was one of the suitors of **Helen** of Sparta, and later offered to take 100 ships to join the Greek expedition to fetch her back from Troy, if **Agamemnon** made him joint grand-admiral. Agamemnon agreed, knowing that Idomeneus was too stupid to pose any threat to his own leadership. Idomeneus swaggered through the **Trojan War**, defeating enemies more because of the vast number of his followers than through any personal qualities – and while he was away **Nauplius**, taking revenge on all the Greek commanders for executing his son **Palamedes**, persuaded Idomeneus' wife Meda to take a lover, Leucus, who responded by killing her and usurping Idomeneus' throne.

After the war, **Poseidon** tried to keep Idomeneus from returning to Crete, by harassing his ships with storms and contrary winds. Idomeneus promised, if he reached home, to sacrifice the first living thing that met him on the island – and Poseidon, realizing that nothing could save him from his own folly, calmed the winds. As soon as Idomeneus set foot on shore, his young son (or, some say, daughter) ran to greet him, and Idomeneus glumly prepared to sacrifice the child. In some accounts, he completed the sacrifice; in others, it was interrupted by a sudden plague or a **sea-monster** which ravaged the island; but all accounts agree that Leucus took advantage of the sacrifice to claim that Idomeneus was unfit to rule, and the Cretans exiled Idomeneus to Southern Italy, where he died as futilely as he had lived.

IDUN
Europe (North)

Idun ('youth'), or Ithun, in Nordic myth, was **Bragi**'s wife and the goddess of spring. She kept a basket of golden apples which conferred **immortality** on all who ate them, and she reserved them for the gods, serving them at banquets in **Asgard**. However many apples were taken from the basket, it filled itself again of its own accord.

Since immortality was the secret of the gods' power, other beings tried to kidnap Idun or steal the golden apples. The **giants**, in particular, were always trying to find ways of forcing or enticing her out of Asgard. Once, **Thiazi**, a **giant shape-changer** who spent most of his time as an eagle, came on **Odin**, **Honir** and **Loki** when they were encamped during a trip to **Midgard**, trying unsuccessfully to roast an enormous ox for dinner. The ox was bewitched, and eagle-Thiazi offered to remove the spell if the gods then let him eat as much as he wanted of the carcass. But when he tore off all the choicest meat, leaving only bones and guts, Loki stabbed him with a sharpened branch, and Thiazi

soared into the sky, taking with him the branch – and also Loki, whose hands had magically fused to the other end. He agreed to let Loki go only if he smuggled Idun out of Asgard.

Without Idun, the gods suddenly began to feel the chill of approaching death. They gathered in Odin's feast-hall to decide what to do – a conference of shaky-limbed grey-beards – and **Heimdall** reported that the last time he'd seen Idun, she was walking with Loki over the bridge **Bifröst**, in the direction of **Jotunheim**, land of the giants. Odin summoned Loki, and threatened him that unless he brought Idun back before a single immortal died, he would be the first to discover what death was like. Loki borrowed **Freyja**'s hawk-skin cloak and flew to Thiazi's fortress in Jotunheim. There he perched, waiting until Thiazi went out hunting – then he changed Idun into a nut, picked her up in one claw and flew back to Asgard.

As soon as Thiazi found that Idun was gone, he knew what had happened. He changed into an eagle and soared after Loki. But the gods foiled him. They built a bonfire of branches on Asgard's battlements, and as soon as hawk-Loki settled inside, exhausted, with Idun still safely in one claw, they lit it. Flames roared up just as eagle-Thiazi flew overhead. They singed his flight-feathers and sent him crashing to the ground, where **Thor** crushed his skull with a hammer-blow. Loki changed Idun back to her usual beautiful shape, she distributed golden apples to the gods (in small pieces so that they could chew them despite their toothless gums), and the danger was over.

It was to avenge the death of Thiazi, her father, that the giantess **Skadi** visited Asgard, demanding a god for husband.

Surprisingly, the story of Idun, Thiazi and Loki is the only substantial surviving myth about the Nordic goddess of spring. Hints and suggestions abound – that she was promiscuous, that she killed one of her (unnamed) brothers, that she was forever sulking and threatening to leave Asgard and live with giants, mortals or the Dead – but none of these ideas remains as a full-blown myth. Similarly, and most unusually for a goddess of spring, Idun hardly features in fine art, except as a dumpy serving-wench handing round apples at a celestial banquet.

≫→ **beauty, Hebe, Xochiquetzal**

IGALUK
Americas (North), Greenland

Igaluk, in Eskimo myth, took part in a **sex**-orgy in the darkness of an igloo. When the fun was over and the participants lit torches, Igaluk found that his partner had been his own sister. She tore off her breasts and threw them at his feet, grabbed a blazing torch and disappeared into the sky. He lit his own torch to follow her, but when he bent to pick up the breasts the torch went out. She became the **Sun** and he became the **Moon** – and this myth explains why the one is only a pale reflection of the other. Igaluk's sister was so disgusted with mortals that she hid her light entirely from them for half the year, and had to be persuaded by prayers and offerings to burn for the other six months. Igaluk, by contrast, always looked after human

beings, guaranteeing the ebb and flow of the seasons and the cycle of women's **fertility**.

ILAMATECUHTLI
Americas (Central)

Ilamatecuhtli ('old goddess'), in Aztec myth, was the original name for **Coatlicue (Mother Earth)**. In her version of the story, she bore her husband **Mixcóatl** not hundreds of children but seven sons only, and they founded the seven cities of the earliest human inhabitants of Mexico, later absorbed (like Ilamatecuhtli herself) into the Aztec state. In some accounts, Ilamatecuhtli was one of the aspects of **Cihuacóatl**, the Great Mother. She was depicted in statues as a toad (Tlatecuhtli) swallowing a knife.

ILLUYANKAS
Asia (West)

Illuyankas, in ancient Syrian myth, was a form of the serpent **Leviathan** which symbolized primordial chaos. Two myths tell how he was conquered, so that order came into the universe. In one, he was insatiably greedy, swallowing everything in his way – and the goddess Inaras trapped him by setting before him a banquet which renewed itself as fast as he ate it, until he was too bloated to move or defend himself when he was tied up and killed. In the other, he conquered the gods, one by one, by wrapping them in his coils and eating their hearts and eyes. **Telepinu**, however, son of Taru the weather-god, seduced Illuyankas' daughter and persuaded her to give him the hearts and eyes as love-gifts – only to hand them back to the gods who then proceeded to kill the **monster** and rebuild the universe.

ILMA
Europe (North)

Ilma ('air'), in Finnish myth, was one of the two elements which existed before **creation**; the other was **Ahto**, ocean. Impelled by the creative principle **Jumala**, Ilma formed her own gusts and breezes into a child, **Luonnotar**, and sent her to lie like a mist-bank on the surface of the sea. So **creation** began.

ILMARINEN
Europe (North)

Ilmarinen, in Finnish myth, was a blacksmith-god or blacksmith-sorcerer. His name is connected with **Ilma** ('air'), and some accounts make him her son and the god of **thunder** and **lightning**. Others say that he was the brother of **Väinämöinen**, or possibly one half of Väinämöinen's dual personality. In **Kalevala**, he courts the daughter of Princess **Louhi** of **Pohjola**, forges the **sampo** to win her, and later goes with Väinämöinen and **Lemminkäinen** to fetch it back to Finland.
➤ heroes, smiths, tricksters

ILYA MUROMETS
Europe (East)

Ilya Muromets, in Slavic myth, was one of the *bogatiri*: his pre-Christian identity was **Svyatogor**. In ancient myth he fought **monsters**, notably the **demon** Nightingale, a bird-headed human whose weapons were hurricanes. In Christian times his enemies became those of the true faith, and he was particularly famous for building the cathedral at Kiev, becoming the last stone laid as the work was completed.
➤ heroes

ILYAP'A
Americas (South)

Ilyap'a, in Inca myth, was the god of **thunder**. He was a warrior, and strode the sky shooting with his sling. His target was a water-pot carried by his sister. When he fired the stone from the sling, the thwack of the leather made thunder, the stone's flight made **lightning**, and the water pouring from the pot made **rain**.

ILYTHIA
Europe (South)

Ilythia (Eileithuia, 'midwife'), in Greek myth, was one of the oldest of all powers in the universe. In some accounts she laid the cosmic egg which began **creation**, in others she was the sister and equal of **Gaia** (**Mother Earth**), but unlike Gaia chose to have no form or shape, to be merely power. Her symbols and her servants were **snakes**, and her reward to snakes was the ability to produce their young without pain. Her power was to help in **childbirth** – and she could lessen or increase the length and pain of delivery according to the way she was treated. Mortal women often wore snake-amulets of Ilythia to help them in childbirth, or put saucers of wine and milk in front of her image in the delivery-room.
➤ Alcmena, animal-gods, Lucina

IMANA
Africa

Imana ('all-powerful one'), in the myths of the Banyarwanda people of Rwanda, was the creator and supporter of the universe. He ruled all living beings, and guaranteed them immortality by hunting **Death**, a savage wild animal. When he was hunting, his orders were that everything in **creation** was to stay in hiding, so that Death would have no refuge. But one day, in the quietness of the hunt, an old woman crept out to hoe her vegetable-garden – and Death hid under her skirt and was taken inside with her. Imana tried a second way of cheating Death, by telling the old woman's relatives to bury her body but leave cracks in the earth above her, so that she could hear him calling her back to life. But the old woman's daughter-in-law, who hated her, filled the cracks with earth and banged the surface hard with her pounding-stick – and Death became endemic.

Even now, Imana helped mortals. He split the world into three lands, like dishes propped on sticks one above the other. The highest land was his alone, and no mortal creatures were admitted. The centre land was **Mother Earth**, home of mortals and other death-bound creatures. The lowest land belonged to Death, and was the home of spirits; Death spent his time climbing to the Middle Land, eating any living creatures he could catch and taking their spirits below. As time passed, the inhabitants of Death's kingdom began to outnumber those on Earth, and they started climbing up ladders and crawling through cracks in the floor of Mother Earth to colonize it. Only Imana could

force them back down, and he spent his time distractedly running from place to place as his mortal worshippers prayed to him. Since the structure of the universe was fragile, and he was in charge of maintaining it, it became ever more rickety and ramshackle – and one day, when Imana's concentration or strength fail for a single moment, the entire edifice will collapse and Death's triumph will be complete.

⏵ **creation**

IMDUGUD
Asia (West)

Imdugud, in Mesopotamian myth, was a lion-headed eagle which brought the rains that ended desert drought. The beating of its wings made **thunder**, the wings themselves were storm-clouds, and raindrops were pieces of down and feather shaken out as Imdugud flew overhead.

IMHOTEP
Africa (North)

Imhotep (Greek Imouthes), in Egyptian myth, was one of the few mortals ever to be deified. A leading courtier of Pharaoh Djoser in the third millennium BCE, he supervised the construction of the Step Pyramid at Sakkara, the oldest stone building in Egypt, and was ever afterwards credited as the inventor of architecture. He was deified, however, as god of medical knowledge, and healing shrines were built in his honour all over Egypt. In Greek Egypt he was identified with **Apollo**'s son **Aesculapius** (who had the power to descend to the **Underworld** and be reborn), and was the centre of a mystery-cult which claimed healing-magic and the ability to raise the dead.

⟫→ **crafts, disease and healing, mysteries**

IMILOZI
Africa

Imilozi ('whistlers'), in the myths of the Zulu people of South Africa, were spirits who used a language of hoots and whistles to tell human beings the secrets of the gods. Unfortunately, few of us could speak their language, and so we remained ignorant of what the gods wanted of us.

IMMORTALITY

Few subjects have exercised the human mind more than the nature of, and reasons for, immortality. Explaining **death** is a psychological need, part of the grieving process – and myths about mortality often validate and guide such explanations. Some myth-systems went further, insisting that death was not the end of our existence but merely of one phase of it, that we were in truth immortal. Most animist religions believed in a continuum of existence, in which those of us in the mortal world were one part of a whole which included every creature born in the past or to be born in the future, every natural phenomenon, the entire essence and structure of the universe. A similar idea, underlying Indian and some Far Eastern belief, was that all existence was a spinning wheel, endless, and that each life we led was merely one among many. To others, this mortal world was merely the threshold to the real world, which was the next one and was eternal; some Eastern thinkers elaborated this idea into the notion that our present existence was all illusion, that we lived in someone else's dream and that even as we thought such thoughts, someone was dreaming us thinking them.

Such views of the endlessness of existence often contained in-built systems of ethics and morality. To live a 'good' life in the present ensured happiness in the future, or a 'better' reincarnation; to live a 'bad' life ensured misery. This idea led to some of the most extravagant imaginings in all myth, pictures of the afterlife ranging from the **Valhalla** roisterings of Nordic **heroes** after their mortal deaths to the harp-plucking, psalm-singing ecstasies of the Christian redeemed praising their creator, from the torments or bliss of the Dead after judgement in the ancient Greek and Egyptian afterworlds to the hierarchical system of rebirths favoured by early Hinduism (a more 'lowly' existence for the 'bad', a more 'exalted' one for the 'good'). Many belief-systems reinforced such teaching by claiming that there were those in the afterlife clamouring to tell us about it, and that there were mortals in this life who were able, after suitable preparation, to hear and transmit their messages.

At a different level, many myth-systems omitted teaching about the afterlife, were content bluntly to explain why human beings were mortal, and left it at that. The Yoruba people of Nigeria said that we were once immortal. We never stopped growing, and became bigger and bigger, older and older, more and more pitiful, until **Olorun** the Creator took pity on us and gave us limits to both growth and life. This idea of the unbearableness of immortality was paralleled in the Roman story of the **Sibyl** of Cumae, a mortal granted immortality without eternal youth, who grew older and more shrivelled with every year that passed. The Juruña people of Brazil said that there was only one immortal creature, **Sinaa**, ancestor of all creation. He sloughed his mortality each time he bathed, pulling it over his head like a sack – and it is because human beings cannot do this that we are mortal. In a similar story, told by many peoples including the Ojaga of East Africa, old people once had the gift of sloughing their mortality like a skin each night, so long as no one saw them, but an inquisitive child once spied on her grandfather and the gift was withdrawn.

Na'pi and First Woman. One of the most wistful of such stories was told by the Blackfoot people of North America. **Na'pi** the creator sat down by a river to mould the first human beings from clay. As soon as First Woman had a mouth – this is a myth to reinforce feminist ideas of patriarchy – she began asking questions, and the first questions were 'How will it be for us? Will it always be?' Na'pi said, 'I've no idea. I'll toss this dung into the water. If it floats, death will last four days only. If it sinks, death will last forever.' He did so, and the dung floated. But First Woman, not satisfied, insisted on verifying the experiment using a stone – and the stone sank, bringing mortality to humans. First Woman had no concept of what she had done until she bore a child

which died – and grief (the myth ends) has been the lot of womankind ever afterwards.

Guilt. This idea of human guilt was common. Sometimes the guilt was a single individual's. A mother in the Solomon Islands, in the days when human beings were immortal, asked the snake spirit Kahausibwara to baby-sit for her. The baby cried; Kahausibwara coiled round it to soothe it, and choked it to death; the mother furiously attacked Kahausibwara with a knife, and Kahausibwara soared into the sky forever, taking human immortality with it. The Hausa people of North Africa say that humans originally lived for as long as they chose. One 500-year-old woman died, and the prophet Moses pined for her beauty and asked God to resurrect her. God did so, and the woman immediately started complaining that she had died from choice, because she was sick and tired of living. So Moses begged God to give mortals shorter and more predictably final existences, and God now sends Azra'il, angel of death, to 'gather' us after some three-score years and ten.

In other myths, the guilt for death was communal. The Upoto people of Central Africa said that **Libanza** the Creator called a huge meeting of all his people. The Moon-people hurried there, and the Earth-people dawdled – not realizing that the prize for first arrival was immortality. In a similar story, the Koko people of Nigeria say that **Nyambe** the Creator planted a tree of life under which humans could gather to praise him – and when they found more interesting things to do, he uprooted the tree and planted it in **Heaven**. The

Masai say that 'Ngai the Creator gave us a charm of immortality to say over our children, and when we were too slow in using it, he took it back. **Kururumany**, the male Creator in Arawak myths from South America, made men, and the female creator Kulimina made women. Peaceful, gentle divinities, they expected their creations to be like them, but when mortals turned out deceitful, licentious and quarrelsome, they punished them by inventing **snakes**, lizards, fleas – and death.

Foolish messengers. A whole group of myths, mostly from Africa, blamed our mortality on foolish messengers from Heaven. The Creator sent humans the good news about immortality, but it failed to arrive. The Galla people told of **Holawaka**, a flesh-eating bird who found a snake eating a carcass, asked for a share, and paid with the immortality it was supposed to be carrying to mortals. In a story similar to the **Pandora**'s-box tale of ancient Greece, the Kaonda tell of a honeybird sent to mortals with three containers, the third of which was not to be opened. The bird could not control its inquisitiveness, and though the first two containers held only the seeds of all plants and animals, the third held **disease** and death. The Ekoi people say that the Creator sent Duck and Frog in a race. Duck was to announce immortality, Frog was to announce mortality – and because Duck got drunk on palm-wine, Frog reached humans first. Zulu people told a similar story, though this time it was Chameleon who stopped to feed and Lizard who brought news that we must die. Nyankopon, the Asante Creator, sent Goat with the clear message

'Death will not be the end for humans'. But Goat stopped to browse, and Sheep, who had half heard the message, went instead, crying 'Death will be the end'. The Ogamba told a similar tale. Humans sent Dog to Wuni the Creator to beg deliverance from the slavery of existence. Dog hung about by a cooking-fire, waiting for some stew – and Goat, who had half-heard the message, ran to Wuni and said that mortals craved delivery from existence.

How to become immortal. In some religious systems, immortality could be achieved by asceticism or by occult practices. In Daoism and the Egyptian cult of **Thoth**, for example, a select few could find immortality by trying to acquire all knowledge, practising all virtue and eliminating all spiritual indiscipline. Several South American and Oceanian peoples told of another way, less morally commendable but no less strenuous: **sex** with as many partners as possible. At the moment of orgasm, the stronger individual in a couple took a small portion of the life of the weaker person. Therefore, by having sex with as many people as possible, invariably weaker than yourself (something you could ensure by black magic), you could gradually build up enough of a stolen life-store to become immortal.

Equally extraordinary, though less likely to annoy the puritanical, was the view, common everywhere, that immortality was a substance contained in specific plants or animals, and that you acquired it by eating or drinking them. In most cases, such food and drink was reserved for the gods, though they sometimes allowed humans a tiny sample of it. **Soma**, for instance, the drink which gave the gods immortality in ancient Indian myth, was available only to them – but all human alcoholic drinks, distilled from earthly plants, gave us a brief insight into the ecstasy and oblivion of which true immortality consisted. **Dionysus**, Greek god of ecstasy, similarly showed humans how to make not **nectar**, the immortality-confirming drink of the gods, but its pallid simulacrum wine. The Sumerian hero **Adapa** was summoned to Heaven after he tore off the wings of the South Wind in a quarrel. **An** king of the gods admired him and offered him the 'food of life' and 'water of life' – but Adapa refused, saying that he preferred life on Earth to life in Heaven. Chinese gods feasted on peaches of immortality, which grew in Heaven once every three thousand years; the ordinary peaches we enjoy on Earth do not cancel our coming death, but delay it a little, granting us a momentary vision of the pleasures of Paradise. Paradise, in the form of a beautiful garden, often contained the Tree of Life, and its human gardeners had to be banished from Paradise before they broke God's commands and tasted the fruit of the tree. **Adam and Eve**, having eaten the fruit of the Tree of Knowledge, were expelled from Eden before they could try those of the Tree of Life. Kumu-Honua, the Hawaiian Adam, similarly picked one of the apples of immortality, and was hastily banished before he could bite into it.

Apples of immortality. Apples of immortality featured in two myth-cycles above all. In ancient Greek myth, the Golden Apples of Immortality grew in a secret orchard at the edge of the world, tended by the **Hesperides**. Their mere existence, and their possession by the gods, guaranteed immortality: there was no need actually to eat them. The **giants**, primordial powers of the universe, were jealous of the gods' immortality, and longed to steal the apples, but could never find them. Exactly the same idea appeared in Nordic myth, where the apples were guarded by **Idun**, and the giants were forever scheming unsuccessfully to steal them. In a combination of these stories, British myth told how the giants did succeed in stealing the Golden Apples, so ending the immortality of the gods. The giants took their prize to Britain – but then, in typically brainless fashion, mislaid them, so that the Golden Apples still lie in some unknown spot, a guarantee of immortality for whoever finds them. ≫→ **food and drink of immortality, Li Papai**

IN AND YO
Asia (East)

In and Yo, in Japanese myth, were the original principles of the universe, and it was when they assumed substantial form that **creation** began. To begin with they swirled in the cosmic soup of chaos, then gradually came together to form an enormous egg, at whose centre was the embryo of life. This embryo grew, and at last split the egg in two. The heavier part, In (the masculine principle, *yang*) floated like a medusa jellyfish in the cosmic ocean – it was the beginning of the Earth – and the lighter part, Yo (the feminine principle, *yin*) rose up to form the firmament. The embryo itself, floating in the form of a white cloud, gradually separated and split to form the first three of the Separate Heavenly Deities (**Kotoamatsukami**). From then on, In and Yo ceased having form of their own, but continued to play their part in the existence of the universe: no life was possible without one or other being present, and no generation of new life was possible unless they came together. »→ **Hun Dun, Pan Gu, Umashiashi-kabihikoji**

INANNA
Asia (West)

Inanna ('sky-lady'), in Sumerian myth, was the daughter either of **An** the Sky or of his son the wind-god **Enlil**. She was the goddess of **sex** and **fertility**, overseeing the reproduction of all plants and animals on Earth. She married a shepherd, Dumuzi, and built him the city of Uruk to rule.

Inanna, all light, was one half of a dual goddess: her **twin** was **Ereshkigal**, darkness, ruler of the **Underworld**. Inanna missed Ereshkigal, and made plans to go to the Underworld to visit her. She dressed in her richest clothes, and told her maid Ninshubur to keep watch and rescue her if she failed to return. Then she went down to the Invisible Land and knocked on the gate. There were seven concentric circles of Invisibility, each with its own gate – and Inanna was allowed to pass through each one only if she took off one garment or jewel. In this way, as she penetrated the Underworld, her light and the life it symbolized were gradually stripped from her, so that when she finally reached

Ereshkigal, heart of darkness, she was like a naked corpse. She went to hug Ereshkigal, but the judges of the Dead, thinking that she was trying to drag their queen from her throne, took Inanna and hung her on a butcher's hook to rot.

In the Upper World, Ninshubur waited for three days and nights – it was later to become the usual period of mourning. Then she began praying to the gods for help: Love was dead in the world, and **creation** would be doomed without it. Although the gods pitied her, they were helpless, since no being filled with the life-spark could visit the Underworld and survive. Then **Enki** the **trickster** found an answer. He created two beings, entities without minds, internal organs or sexual powers (the three attributes which hold the spark of life). He gave one of them a cup of the water of **immortality**, and the other a dish of the gods' immortal food, and sent them to the Underworld. Having no life in them, they passed easily through the gates, found Inanna rotting on her hook and revived her with the immortal food and drink.

Inanna, restored, went to her sister and asked to return to the world of light. Ereshkigal agreed, on condition that Inanna found someone to send to the Underworld in her place. If not, she must return forever. Inanna passed to the Upper World, putting on her garments of light one by one as she passed each gate. In Uruk, she found that her husband Dumuzi, so far from mourning her loss, had spent his time sleeping with another of her sisters, Geshtinanna lady of the grape, and carousing on her invention (wine) and his own clumsy mortal imitation (beer). Without a second thought she banished them both to the Underworld, Geshtinanna during the six winter months and Dumuzi during the six summer months each year.

Geshtinanna's appearance in the story strikes some scholars as a late addition, explaining why beer and wine were not produced in the same months each year in Uruk. In the straightforward version, only Dumuzi was sent to the Underworld – and his death was re-enacted every spring, as each succeeding king of Uruk was sacrificed (literally at first, then figuratively) and his blood was offered to the gods of the Dead to ensure the return of the Earth's fertility.

»→ Anat, Astarte, Cybele, Great Goddess, Ishtar, light and dark, mysteries

INARI
Asia (East)

Inari, in Japanese myth, was the blacksmith husband of the food-goddess **Ukemochi**. When the Moon-god **Tsukuyomi** killed Ukemochi, Inari was put in charge of all the good things she had given the world, in particular rice, and became god of prosperity.

Inari is a favourite figure in art, where he is depicted as a benign old person dispensing food or sitting on a bulging grain-sack and with two foxes for familiars. In some versions, he is so closely identified with his wife that he is shown as hermaphrodite, or female.

»→ creation, smiths

INDIAN MYTH

Indian myth is unique among world myth-systems, and the reason is the nature of the Hindu religion and the Vedic beliefs from which it developed. (All other Indian religions, except such imports as Islam and Christianity, draw on this tradition.) Most faith-systems depend on dogma and tradition: the boundaries for belief and action may be large, but they are also, for the most part, set and unchanging. Hinduism, by contrast, has always been open, non-prescriptive and assimilative. To be sure, there are some fixed tenets, and fundamentalists adhere to them as vehemently as those of any other religious system. But the essential factor in Hindu religious thought is and always has been tolerance rather than assertion. If Islam (say) or Christianity are like cliffs of granite, Hinduism is a coral reef, new ideas constantly growing on and modifying what was there before.

This characteristic, which is partly due to the enormous size and diversity of the sub-continent, but is mainly caused by the nature of Indian religious thought itself, materially affects the myths. There are no core myths, established in unvarying traditions and universally accepted. Each myth-story is subject to a thousand variants, has innumerable inflexions and overtones. The sacred texts – the **Rig Veda**, the *Puranas*, the **Mahabharata**, the *Ramayana* – give many different accounts of the same stories, and their versions shade and blur into one another. Every Indian myth-story comes with a nimbus of poetic resonance, its keynotes are suggestion and metaphor rather than certainty, and each new telling, each recension, is as valid as all others, part of a continuum of tradition in which the present informs the past as much as the past illuminates the present.

Scholars think that the earliest surviving Indian myth-ideas date from before 4000 BCE. They are that the Earth is a universal mother, that the *lingam* or phallic pole symbolizes both **fire** and generation, that the gods' cosmic dance both creates and destroys, and that meditation is a way to accumulate power (and therefore that intellectual strength equals or surpasses physical energy). All these ideas are represented in artefacts found at Harappa, Mohenjodaro and other ancient sites – and they have not only survived the arrival of later myths, but have been assimilated into them and have transformed them.

It is a universal feature of world myth that when new gods arrive, their predecessors either retreat to the farthest reaches of the universe, become **demons** or both. This happened to the gods of the pastoral inhabitants of northern India when waves of invaders arrived from Iran in the seventeenth and sixteenth centuries BCE. 'Demons' were dispersed throughout India – not only as creatures of darkness routed by the gods of light, but often as water-spirits, inimical to the generative heat and fire of the **Sun**. **Surya** the Sun-god, **Agni** the fire-god, **Indra** the storm-god, **Vayu** the wind-god and the other invaders formed a large, loose family, busy about their business of managing the universe, and as happy to welcome respectful incomers – such as the mysterious sages and seers, those beings

with godlike powers but without the gods' unique possession, **immortality** – as they were merciless to the **giants** and demons who challenged them. The complex universal order they oversaw is codified for us in the *Vedas* ('hymns'), and underlies all later Indian religious and myth-ideas.

In order to deal with incomers, challengers and their own unruly relatives, the Vedic gods were often forced to abandon their comfortable amorphousness – they were originally 'thought' or 'fire' or 'storm', ideas rather than shapes – and to assume specific forms and characteristics. They sprouted torsos, heads, arms and legs after the human model, or became **shape-changers**, turning at will into animals, plants, rocks, breezes or waterfalls. The band of stars we call the Milky Way, for example, was at one time or another a speckled **snake**, a waterfall of milk, a beautiful goddess (**Ganga**), and finally the river Ganges compelled (by the attentions of a dynasty of insistent mortals or demons) to flow on Earth as well as in **Heaven**. Sometimes such metamorphoses were temporary, undertaken for a specific purpose and abandoned as soon as it was achieved. But often they 'took', and remained all or part of a god's individuality. As this happened, the 'family' webs of marriage, **childbirth**, dynastic obligation and feud became ever more important, until the gods' private intrigues became almost as important as their cosmological duties.

Already, in the Vedic period, there was busy two-way traffic between the three regions of Heaven, Earth and Middle Air. (Outer Space and the

Underworld were excluded. Their beings could travel to the other regions, but movement in the reverse direction was dangerous and usually irrevocable.) A mortal might take the appropriate steps to enter Heaven and converse with or mate with gods as easily as gods might assume mortal shape and visit Earth. Some places were thought to exist in the three regions simultaneously. Rivers, for example, were parts of a single cosmic water-system, flowing into or out of the primordial ocean which supported, and was, the universe. The gods owned mountain-top palaces, with beautiful gardens, and entry was available to any mortal able to make the climb.

As the Vedic gods began to humanize themselves in these ways, there occurred another of the shifts and blurrings so characteristic of Indian myth. It was not so much that the older gods disappeared or were supplanted by new ones, as in a large family, rather that previously obscure or unknown members took on new prominence and new responsibilities, incomers brought fresh strengths and tensions, and the older members either maintained their former position, took a back seat, or alternated between the two. For example, instead of the universe being controlled (as previously) by a mass of deities each with his or her own responsibilities, it became a hierarchical system dominated by the triad of **Vishnu** (creative energy), **Shiva** (destructive energy) and **Brahma** (the absolute, universal balance). Within the hierarchy, gods moved up or down according to circumstances, character and mood – and many also continued shape-shifting, to

the point where many of the 'new' gods in the cosmic family were, so to speak, no more than refractions or poetic reinterpretations of the old ones, made manifest.

Central to all this process of coalescence and accretion were two concepts: those of time and reality. In most myth-systems, time does not exist or is an unvarying and measurable sequence (in which, for example, parents are older than their children). But in Indian myth, time is inconsequential. It is a continuum in which past, present and future are the same thing, and the only certainty is that everything is cyclical: whatever happens has already happened and will happen many times again. Vishnu is one of many Vishnus, the universe has been created and destroyed countless times, and will be so again. What we think we know now is merely one of a myriad possible 'nows', a momentary and illusory coming-into-focus, a viewpoint, not so much reality as a metaphor for reality. In such a system, nothing is real, and yet (because we perceive things as 'real') everything is real. There are, for example, no such things as human beings or gods or demons – and yet, because we think they exist, and they think we exist, they and we have 'reality'. This philosophical paradox underlies all Indian myth, and gives it its unique fluidity.

Attempts to articulate, if not to codify, myths in the light of these circumstances, to make them serve the multifarious purposes of the Hindu religion, began in the first millennium BCE, and led to many of the stories being given distinct and specific form. The *Puranas* (fifth century BCE and beyond) set the main myths of the Vedic and Hindu gods in order, and with the *Vedas* are the main source for most stories of the creation, establishment and maintenance of the universe. They are, however, not uniform but prismatic, often telling half a dozen versions of the same event, or viewing it from a dozen different perspectives. The *Ramayana* (codified in the same period, but possibly collating oral traditions from many centuries before) drew on these stories and others to present a vision of the life of mortals and supernatural beings in rural South India, and centred on the relationship between Rama and his wife Sita, and his battle to rescue her after she was kidnapped by the demon-king Ravana. The *Mahabharata* (compiled in the third or second century BCE) used the story of the epic battle between the Pandava and Kaurava dynasties to weave a tapestry of inter-related myth and legend of every kind.

From the sixth century BCE onwards, the philosophical underpinning of Indian myth began to be removed and made the basis for specific systems of moral and ethical teaching which came to have religious or quasi-religious force – Buddhism is the prime example, but there were a dozen others. The founders of such systems had no need of myth, being concerned to investigate the enigmas of time and reality in an intellectual way – and eventually, by meditation and the abnegation of the flesh, to break utterly free of 'reality' into whatever 'truth' actually is. Many of their followers took a similarly austere approach, but others, either for their own purposes or to help in teaching, felt the need to adapt and remake the myths in the form of parables and sermon-texts. Some went further still, mythologizing the lives of the founders themselves, so that real-life individuals such as **Buddha** or **Mahavira** were placed, somewhat uneasily, in the company of the supernatural tenants of the mythological universe.

The final stage in the process was when Buddhism, Jainism and other philosophical systems travelled abroad, complete with their mythological penumbras. Buddhism, in particular, was engrafted into the myths of non-Indian nations from Tibet to Japan, from Cambodia to China, and in the process myths which had begun as part of the Vedic or Hindu canon became transformed. In India itself, later Hinduism took account of the stories of such newly imported faiths as Islam and Christianity, showing the same accretive faculty and willingness to accept the idea of 'all truth as part of the one truth' which had been one of its most genial characteristics since earliest times.

➤ Aditi, Agastya, Ages of Brahma, Airavata, Ambalika, Ambika, Amitabha, *amrita*, Ananda, Anjana, *apsaras*, Ardhanarishvara, Arjuna, Ashvathaman, Ashvins, *Asuras*, Atri, Avalokiteshvara, Balarama, Bali, Balin, Bhagiratha, Bharata, Bhima, Bhisma, *Bhutas*, *boddhisattvas*, Brighu, Brighus, Brihaspati, Candramus, Chandra, Chyavana, *Daityas*, Daksha, Dasaratha, Deva, Devadatta, Devaki, *devas* and *devis*, Devi, Dhanvantari, Dharma, Dhatar, Dhritarashtra, Diti, Draupadi, Drona, Drumalika, Durga, Dyaus, Dyavaprivithi, Gandharvas, Ganesh, Garuda, Gommateshvara, Hanuman, Harihara, Hayagriva, Hiranyakishipu,

Hiranyaksha, Ida, Jaganath, Jaland-hara, Jambavan, Janaka, Jara, Jarasandha, Jatayu, Kadru, Kaikeyi, Kalanemi, Kali, Kaliya, Kalki, Kama, Kamadhenu, Kansa, Karttikeya, Kasyapa, Kauravas, Kausalya, Krishna, Kubera, Kumbhaka, Kunti, Kurma, Lakshma, Lakshmi, Madri, Maitreya, Manasa, Manu, Mara, Maruts, Matsya, Maya, Meru, Mount, Mithra, Muchalinda, *nagas* and *naginis*, Nakula, Nanda, Nandi, Narasimha, Pandavas, Pandu, Parashurama, Parjanya, Parshva, Parsu, Parvati, Pavanareka, Pisakas, Prahlada, Prajapati, Prisni, Privithi, Purusha, Pushan, Putana, Radha, Rahu, *Rakshasas*, Rama, Rashnu, Rati, Ratri, Ravana, Ribhus, Rishabha, Rishis, Rohini, Rudra, Rudrani, Rukmini, Sagara, Sahadeva, Saktasura, Sandhya, Saranyu, Sarasvati, Sati, Savitri, Seven Seers, Shashti, Shatrughna, Shesha, Shitala, Siddhartha Gautama, Sisupala, Sita, Skanda, *soma*, Sugriva, Tara, Taraka, *tirkanthara*, Trinavarta, Tripitaka, Tvashtri, Ugrasena, Ugrasura, Uma, Urvashi, Ushas, Vamana, Varaha, Varuna, Varuni, Vashishtra, Vasudeva, Vasuki, Vasus, Vibishana, Vinata, Viraj, Vishvakarman, Vivasvat, Vritra, Vyasa, Yama, Yashodhara, Yasoda, Yudhishthira

INDRA
India

Indra's names. Indra was the chief god of the Aryan people who invaded India in the seventeenth century BCE, and he held his position at the centre of Indian religious myth for over 1000 years. He was the Thunderer, wielder of the Thunderstone and god of **rain**. With **Varuna**, he shared the name Samraj ('supreme ruler'); in fact, the two gods formed a duality, Varuna embodying the power of moral principle in the world, Indra the power of amoral (not to say immoral) principle. Indra's other titles included Meghavahana ('cloud-rider'), Shakra ('powerful'), Shachipati ('lord of might'), Svargapati ('**Heaven**-lord'), Vajri ('thunderer'), Verethragna (in Iran, where he was worshipped as god of war) and Purandara ('wall-smasher', perhaps because the Aryans thought that he led their onslaughts on the fortified cities they attacked).

Indra, lord of water. Indra was the son of **Dyaus** (Father **Sky**) and **Privithi** (**Mother Earth**), or, in some versions, of Father Sky and a sacred cow. He was born as a full-grown warrior, and immediately went to rescue the world from Ahi, the serpent which had swallowed all **water**, creating drought and death everywhere. Indra cut open Ahi's head and belly with the Thunderstone, and water (the monster's blood) gushed all over the world, bringing back **fertility** and life. This battle was repeated every mortal year, Ahi sucking the life from the world during the dry season and Indra releasing it with the beginning of the rains. After the first battle he also created a new universe, separating **Heaven** from Earth and propping it on gold pillars. For human beings he created time, made the ox and horse to carry their burdens, gave cows the power to produce milk and women the first human fertility known on Earth. He also had power over **mountains**. Originally they were living beings, flying above the plains on enormous wings. Indra sliced off their wings and anchored them to Mother Earth, ordering them to gather rain from the sky and funnel it to Earth in waterfalls and rivers. If a mountain kept water for itself, Indra split it open with the Thunderstone to release a life-giving, fertile flood.

Indra's train. Indra's arrival in the world was signalled by a rainbow, and by the rumble of a gathering storm – either the sound of his chariot-wheels or the tread of his war-elephant **Airavata**. In some stories his chariot was the **Sun**, and was pulled by a pair of russet horses. His servants were *ribhus* (horse-taming spirits), and his battle-companions were the healing twins the **Ashvins**, and a company of **Maruts**, gold-clad paladins who sang his praise as they strewed his path with **earthquakes**, **rain** and **lightning**.

Indra's nature. Unlike many Indian gods, which were spirits or ideas embodied, Indra had human characteristics, morals and failings. He was a bad son (in some stories he even murdered his father), a lecher and a glutton; he was arrogant and boastful. Before each exploit he prepared himself by eating a million buffalo and drinking a lakeful of *soma*. He then stormed out across the universe, killing rebels, hurling down fortifications and hunting **demons** as humans hunted lizards. He also seduced every female he clapped eyes on – until his comeuppance at the hands of the sage Gautama (not Gautama **Buddha**). Indra had **sex** with Gautama's wife Ahalya, and Gautama cursed him with the 'thousand marks' all over his body: almond-shaped blotches which earned him the nickname Sa-yoni ('thousand-cunts') and made him a laughing-stock, until the other gods persuaded Gautama to change

them into eyes. (In some versions, Indra lost his testicles after this rape, and was also imprisoned by **Ravana** the **demon**-king of Sri Lanka, being set free only at the request of **Brahma** himself.)

Indra and Vritra. The Sa-yoni story marks the beginning of Indra's decline as leader of the gods. As other gods (notably **Vishnu**) grew more powerful, he lost his taste for rule, and contented himself with roaring about the universe, intoxicated equally by *soma* and by his own ungovernable energy. He made enemies, among them the sage Tvashtri (not the same person as **Tvashtri**, god of craftsmanship). Tvashtri had a son so pious, and so admirable, that every creature in the universe worshipped him. The boy had three heads: one to use for meditation, one for eating and one for scanning the universe. Indra, irritated by his sanctimonious perfection, tried to spoil him by sending females to seduce him, and when this failed he killed him with a thunderbolt and cut off his heads, sending a beautiful radiance and a flock of white doves out across the world. In revenge, Tvashtri created a demon: Vritra, a clone of the world-snake Ahi. It ate all the gods' cattle alive, and when Indra went to rescue them it swallowed him, too. It was not until the gods choked Vritra, and it opened its jaws to gasp for breath, that Indra was able to jump out. Vishnu proposed a truce. If Vritra released the cattle, Indra would attack him 'neither by night nor by day, nor with anything dry nor wet'. Vritra let the cattle go, and Vishnu made himself into a knife of solidified foam (neither wet water nor dry air), and gave himself to Indra to cut off Vritra's head at dusk (that is, neither night nor day). (Some versions of these stories say that Vritra is Ahi; others name the monster Namuci – and say that it was able to swallow Indra only by first getting him drunk on *soma*.)

Indra is the chief god to whom hymns are addressed in the **Rig Veda**, *the oldest surviving Indian religious texts. Out of over 1000 hymns, 250 honour Indra's powers, attributes, fearsomeness and generosity to humans, and recount his exploits. In art he is shown as a handsome, athletic warrior, with a heavily-muscled neck and arms, often a full beard and a jaw made of gold. Some artists give him two arms (the right hand holding the Thunderstone, the left a bow); others show four arms (the third holding a spear or elephant goad, the fourth a 1000-pointed mace made from jet). The thousand eyes are seldom shown, and neither are his thousand testicles (which no myth explains, but his character amply justifies). When Indra is depicted as a god, he is often shown riding in his sun-chariot, or on horseback; when he is shown as a warrior-prince, he is usually riding his elephant-steed* **Airavata**. *His uncontrollable appetites for food, drink and sex made him a favourite subject for joky dance and drama, not to mention the hero of thousands of bawdy anecdotes, too numerous and too transient to qualify as myth.*

⋙→ **creation**

INTI
Americas (South)

Inti, in Inca myth, was the sun-god. Taking pity on the wretchedness of mortals, he sent them his son Manco Capac and daughter Mama Occlo to teach them civilization – the beginning of the Inca ruling dynasty. Inti's name was so sacred that only members of this dynasty were ever allowed to utter it, and then only soundlessly.

IO
Europe (South)

Io ('moon'), in Greek myth, was a river-**nymph** and priestess of **Hera**. **Zeus** raped her, and to save her from Hera's jealousy changed her into a white cow. But Hera knew very well who the cow really was, and asked Zeus to give it to her as a present – an innocent gift he could hardly refuse. Hera's first punishment for Io was to keep her tethered forever, a cow among all the other cows. She left **Argus** of the Hundred Eyes on guard to stop Zeus rescuing Io. Zeus asked **Hermes** to help, and Hermes lulled Argus asleep with **music** and stole Io from the herd.

As soon as Hera realized that she'd been cheated, she sent a stinging fly to torment Io (as flies in fields have tormented cows ever since). Maddened with pain, Io ran from the fly all over the surface of the Earth. Her wanderings even took her as far as Mount Caucasus, where she saw **Prometheus** hanging in agony as a punishment for stealing **fire**. Finally, when her punishment was complete, she came to Egypt and was set free from the fly at last. Zeus also restored her to human shape – and at his touch she conceived and bore a calf-child called Epaphus ('touch'). Io and Epaphus were later worshipped as gods in Egypt, Io as the goddess **Isis**, Epaphus as the bull-god **Hap** (Greek Apis).

Io's most spectacular appearance in ancient literature is in Aeschylus' Prometheus Bound, when she appears in agony from the fly and, raving, asks Prometheus to foretell the end of her wanderings.

⟫→ bulls and cows

ION
Europe (South)

Ion ('strider'), in Greek myth, was the son of **Apollo** and the Athenian princess Creusa, whom Apollo raped on the Acropolis. Creusa abandoned Ion at birth, and Apollo took the child to Delphi, where he was brought up in ignorance of his true parentage. In the meantime, Creusa married King Xuthus. After several years' childlessness, they went to Delphi to ask advice. Apollo told Xuthus that the first person he met on leaving the shrine would be his son — and that person was Ion. Furious that Xuthus was adopting someone she took to be a stranger, Creusa tried to kill Ion, but Apollo (or in some accounts, **Athene**) appeared and explained the situation. They all went back to Athens, and in due course Ion sailed North and became the ancestor of the Ionian nation.

This strangely perfunctory myth survives largely because of Euripides' play Ion, and it is impossible to say how much of the story is traditional and how much is Euripides' own invention. It may date back to an age of myth when Apollo and Athene were at loggerheads — and this would explain one of the main questions asked in Euripides' play, how we can trust a supposedly infallible god who rapes someone and then
gives her husband what seems to be a false **prophecy**. (In the play, the dilemma is unresolved: Athene appears and ends the argument before it gets too blasphemous.)

IOSKEHA
Americas (North)

Ioskeha ('sapling'), in the myths of the Huron people of the Eastern US woodlands, was the grandson of **Ataentsic**. He was all-good, and his twin Tawiskara ('flint') was all-evil. The brothers duelled for control of the world, each snatching up whatever weapons he could find. Tawiskara fought with a rose-twig, but Ioskeha used a stag's antlers, and won. Tawiskara fled into exile, weeping flint tears, and Ioskeha celebrated his victory, and his power in the world, by creating the Huron people.

⟫→ twins

IPHIGENIA
Europe (South)

Iphigenia in Aulis. Iphigenia (Iphigeneia, 'strong mother', or Iphianassa, 'strong princess'), in Greek myth, was the eldest child of **Agamemnon** and **Clytemnestra**. When the Greek fleet assembled at Aulis to sail for Troy, and the gods held back the winds, **Calchas** the prophet told Agamemnon that the only way to release them was to sacrifice Iphigenia. (Different myths give different reasons. In some, Agamemnon had rashly sworn an oath, just before Iphigenia was born, to sacrifice to **Artemis** the most beautiful creature in his kingdom. In others, he had rashly shot a stag sacred to Artemis, and killing Iphigenia was his punishment.) Agamemnon sent messengers to Mycenae with a story that Iphigenia was to marry **Achilles**, and Clytemnestra gladly sent the child to Aulis. Here the sacrifice was completed, the gods unlocked the winds and the Greeks sailed for Troy.

Iphigenia in Tauris. In most versions of the story, it was Iphigenia herself who was sacrificed at Aulis, and her death overshadowed the Greek expedition and began a sequence of murders which later involved all Agamemnon's family. But in some versions, even as Agamemnon lifted his knife to kill Iphigenia, Artemis substituted a doe and carried the child away to Tauris (the modern Crimea, a place Greeks considered beyond the ends of the Earth). Here Iphigenia grew up as Artemis' priestess, supervising a barbaric ritual by which any Greeks who visited the country were sacrificed.

After Orestes killed Clytemnestra, the gods sent him to Tauris to steal a wooden statue of Artemis which had miraculously fallen from the sky and was now the hub of her worship there. After considerable confusion – Iphigenia at first tried to sacrifice **Orestes** to Artemis – they outwitted or killed King **Thoas** and escaped with the statue to Greece, where it was set up in a shrine near Athens, and Iphigenia served as its priestess until the day she died.

Few stories in Greek myth are more confused than this one. Homer calls Iphigenia Iphianassa (a standard word for 'Princess'), and says nothing of the sacrifice at Aulis or Iphigenia's time in Tauris.

*The word Iphigenia ('strong mother') strikes some scholars as an odd description of Iphigenia (who was a virgin priestess). But it was a standard description of Artemis herself, goddess of **childbirth**, and this leads them to suggest that the myths were invented to explain how the statue of Artemis found its way from the Northern Black Sea to Greece – and in Roman times, Italy – or that it arose from a simple confusion of the goddess with her priestess (who, on ceremonial occasions, was thought to be possessed by the deity she served).*

However dubious the origin of these myths, they are central to the work of the great Athenian tragedians and writers and artists who followed them. Iphigenia's murder by Agamemnon outraged the gods, and was the first step on a road of kin-murder which led to his own death, Clytemnestra's murder and the madness and expiation of Orestes which followed. Euripides' Iphigenia in Tauris, exploring the story of Iphigenia's miraculous escape to Tauris, her service as priestess there, and her and Orestes' theft of the holy statue, was popular in ancient times, and also became one of the most influential of all ancient dramas on post-Renaissance European romantics. Among creators attracted by its blend of high tragedy, romantic adventure and pellucid poetry were Vivaldi and Boccherini (each of whom made the story into a highly descriptive piece of music, Vivaldi's a violin concerto and Boccherini's a symphony), Gluck and Haydn (who wrote operas with highly Euripidean librettos), Goethe, Keats and Cocteau. The story has been less generally popular with fine artists. In both ancient and modern times they have concentrated on one aspect only, the moments before sacrifice. Vase-pictures, for example, often show Agamemnon raising his sword to sacrifice Iphigenia over the altar at Aulis, or Iphigenia doing the same over Orestes in Tauris – each time with a god in the background, rushing to the rescue. European romantic artists similarly show these moments, set not in the abstract locations favoured by ancient painters but in spectacularly moody landscapes of rocks, seashores and thorn-bushes, overseen by lowering skies and tenanted by lions, serpents, bears and wolves.

IRIS
Europe (South)

Iris ('rainbow'), in Greek and Roman myth, was the daughter of Thaumas and the **Titan** Electra, an ocean-**nymph** and the wife of **Zephyrus** the West Wind. She was beautiful, with wings as iridescent as a dragonfly's, and **Hera** took her into **Heaven** to be her handmaid. Iris' tasks were to keep the clouds filled with **rain**, and to help mortals who were having a difficult time dying, by flying down and severing the last clinging threads of life.

In literature, Iris appears occasionally as a messenger from Heaven to Earth: she helps the Argonauts in Apollonius' Argonautica, cuts the last thread of Dido's life in Virgil's Aeneid – and in Aristophanes' Birds tries to arrange a truce between the gods and the birds, only to be insulted (among other things, being compared to a watering-can) and threatened with rape. Lack of sufficiently varied pigments made it hard for her to be depicted in paintings in the ancient world, but relief sculptures survive, showing her as an attendant beside Hera's throne, the tracery of her wings as

delicate as that of the fossil dragonflies discovered in later ages.

ISHTAR
Asia (West)

Ishtar (whose myriad other names included Ashtart, Ashtoreth, **Astarte**, **Inanna** and **Isis**) was worshipped all over the Mesopotamian region, from Nineveh to Egyptian Thebes, from Cyprus to Babylon. She was the Evening Star and goddess of **sex**. Eternally promiscuous, she bathed in a sacred lake each evening to restore her virginity. She was the goddess of **music**, and her slaves played instruments and sang wherever she went. In Assyria she was also a **war**-goddess: her songs of lust became warcries which froze the enemies' blood, her arrows of desire became weapons of destruction, and her priest-kings honoured her by offering her the flayed skin and severed hands of prisoners-of-war.

Ishtar and Tammuz. In Sumerian myth, Ishtar loved Tammuz, a particularly handsome mortal (or in some accounts a tree-god who accepted mortality to live on Earth in his beloved forests). When he died she was heartbroken, and went down to the **Underworld** to fetch him back. While she was away from the Upper World, **fertility** died, and it was only when the gods allowed her to bring Tammuz back to life that animals and plants were able once more to reproduce.

In some accounts of the story of Ishtar and Tammuz, Tammuz was still alive when Ishtar went alone to the Underworld to visit her sister Ereshkigal, and she was imprisoned there until she agreed to let Tammuz

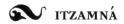

die for her – an almost exact parallel to the myth of **Inanna** *and Dumuzi.*

⟫+ Anat, Aphrodite, Cybele, Helen

ISIS: *see* Aset

ISMENE
Europe (South)

Ismene ('she who knows'), in Greek myth, was the youngest child of **Oedipus** and **Jocasta**, and the sister of **Antigone**, **Eteocles** and **Polynices**. When Antigone proposed to bury Polynices against King Creon of Thebes' orders, Ismene refused to help, but when Antigone was arrested and charged with the burial, she tried to share the blame, only to be rejected contemptuously by her sister.

Ismene features in none of the early accounts of the myth. Her first appearance is in Sophocles' Antigone, and some scholars think that he invented her. Whether or not this is so, she is now an indelible part of the Antigone story, playing a similar role to Chrysothemis in dramatic treatments of the Electra myth. She is the origin of the confidante figure in later European tragedy: a colourless friend, relative or servant of the heroine, to whom plans, feelings and reactions can be expressed without our ever worrying how her reaction will affect the plot.

ITHERTHER AND ACHIMI
Africa

Itherther and Achimi, in the myths of the Kalyl people of Algeria, were buffaloes. Itherther and his mate Thamuatz emerged from the primeval mud before it crumbled into desert, and Achimi was

their calf. At this time buffaloes, insects and humans were the only creatures on Earth, and all of them survived solely by eating plants. But Achimi was restless, wandered away from his parents and found a village of mortals. Ant crawled into his ear and whispered that humans were forever leaving crumbs of food lying around, and that if an insect or animal chose to live with them, a secure living could be made with no trouble. Achimi hurried back to tell his parents. But in the time he'd been away he'd grown to sexual maturity, and as soon as he saw his mother and his newly-born sister he was filled with lust, drove away Itherther his father and mated with them.

Achimi was now the dominant male, and his mother and sister were the first herd-females. Itherther wandered alone, in exile, and pined for his mate. Each time he thought of her he had an orgasm, and his semen spilled on the ground, fertilizing it and engendering antelopes, camels, goats, zebras and other animals of all kinds. A few mortals decided that these animals might be good to eat and began hunting them – and in the course of time they evolved into hyenas, foxes and other predators, including the largest, lions, big enough to prey on Achimi, his mother and sister and the other buffaloes. So hunting and meat-eating came into the world, and Itherther left Earth for **Sky** and has never visited us again.

⟫+ animal-gods, creation

ITZAMNÁ
Americas (Central)

Itzamná ('iguana house'), in Mayan myth, was the son of the **Sun**, and god of healing. He was so busy with good works that he neglected his own appearance: he was old, toothless and dressed in rags; the only things about him that glowed were his bulbous nose and one red-hot, healing hand. By teaching his human worshippers how to build irrigation channels, he healed the land from the scorching of his father. He helped women in **childbirth** and showed his priests how to use medicinal herbs and potions. When he saw that humans needed a cure for boredom, he invented the arts for them.

≫→ civilization, disease and healing

ITZPAPALOTL
Americas (Central)

Itzpapalotl ('flint butterfly'), in Aztec myth, was a **demon**. She looked like a beautiful, desirable woman, but any man who fell for her seduction soon regretted it, as flint knives flashed from her eyes, mouth and vagina, and her embrace squeezed blood from him like water from a rag. She was one aspect of **Cihuacóatl**, goddess of goddesses, the **Great Goddess**.

IULUS: *see* Ascanius

IXCHEL
Americas (Central)

Ixchel ('rainbow lady'), in Mayan myth, was the goddess of **flood** and storm. **Itzamná**'s wife, she was a mixture of **snake** and waterfall, with talons for fingers and snakes for hair. Her palace was filled with enormous jars and pots of water, and unless she was kept happy

with sacrifice, she poured them out on the world below.

IXION
Europe (South)

Ixion ('strong'), in Greek myth, was king of the Lapiths in Thessaly. He was a criminal, who outdid even his own father Phlegyas in wickedness. No rich men's goods, wives or daughters were safe from him. In the end, not content with stealing Dia, daughter of Eioneus, he committed outrage on top of crime. He promised Eioneus a huge bride-price if he came to the wedding, but when the old man arrived at Ixion's palace he walked into a trap: a fire-pit dug in the ground and hidden with earth and branches. So Ixion not only avoided paying the bride-price, but also roasted Eioneus to death.

After this murder Ixion was an outcast. No mortal dared speak to him or touch him until the gods purified his blood-guilt – and the gods refused. Then, mysteriously, **Zeus** favoured Ixion. He answered his prayers and not only freed him from blood-guilt, but invited him to a banquet in **Olympus**. This was an unheard-of honour for any mortal, let alone a rapist and a murderer. The gods muttered, and they were right: for Ixion got drunk and tried to seduce **Hera** herself. In the nick of time, Zeus (who sees and knows all) replaced Hera with a phantom moulded from mist, and while Ixion was grappling with this the gods seized him. For betraying Zeus, he was chained to a blazing wheel which hurtled like a shooting star from Olympus to the **Underworld**. On it, in letters of fire, was written 'Kindness deserves gratitude', and as the wheel revolved this message burned into Ixion's flesh. No end was fixed for his agony: Zeus set the wheel rolling in the Underworld until the end of time.

IXTAB
Americas (Central)

Ixtab, in Mayan myth, was the goddess of suicide. She spent her time dangling from the sky with a noose round her neck – except when she came down to Earth to gather the souls of suicides. (This was not a bad end for them: the Maya thought that suicides went not to Hell but to Paradise.)
»+ death

IXTLILTON
Americas (Central)

Ixtlilton, in Mayan myth, was the god of medicine. If the right prayers and sacrifices were made, he would bring cups of healing drink to cure the sick. He was especially generous to children.
»+ disease and healing

IZANAGI: *see* Izanami and Izanagi

IZANAMI AND IZANAGI
Asia (East)

The beginning of Creation. Izanami ('she who invites') and Izanagi ('he who invites'), in Japanese myth, were the last pair of deities to grow on **Umashiashikabihikoji** the celestial reed at the beginning of the universe. The other deities ordered them to 'invite' the world into being, and they

stood on the Heavenly Floating Bridge (in some accounts a rainbow, in others the Milky Way) in the cloud-swirl above the primordial ocean. While Izanami exerted creative will, Izanagi took the Heavenly Jewelled Spear and with it stirred Ocean like porridge in a pot. When he lifted the spear, a drop of water fell from the point and formed an island. Izanami and Izanagi stepped down on to this, built a pillar in the centre to anchor it to the seabed below and the sky above, and stood back to survey it: the first land.

Monsters. Izanami and Izanagi had no idea how to continue **creation**. But as they looked at each other it became apparent, as sacred writings later put it, that her body was 'a little less' than it should be, and his was 'a little more', and they decided to merge into one being to make a wholeness. To create sufficient energy to do this, they ran in opposite directions round the sky-pillar, intending to merge when they met. As they approached each other, Izanami was so struck by Izanagi's appearance that she cried, 'What a handsome man!', and he in turn said, 'What a handsome woman!' They then mated, and their first child appeared. Instead of being beautiful like its parents, it was a **monster** – a gigantic version of the leeches which were to appear when creation was further advanced – and they dumped it in a boat and set it adrift on Ocean before they became fond of it. They repeated the mating ritual, together with the cries about handsomeness, and this time their child was a lump of earth, which they also set adrift.

The second Creation. Sure that something was wrong with their mating, Izanami and Izanagi asked the celestial council for advice. They were told that the male should speak first, and that by pre-empting this privilege Izanami had corrupted herself so that she would be the mother not only of 'noble' creations but of monsters. They were, however, not allowed to stop the process of creation, and went back down to their island and repeated the ritual, correctly, another fifty-four times, bringing into being the fourteen islands of Japan and forty deities including those of fresh and salt water, **mountains**, pastures, **sex** and the winds. The last-born was **Kagutsuchi**, spirit of **fire**, and he scorched Izanami's vagina so badly that she died and went down to **Yomi**, the **Underworld**.

Divorce between life and death. After punishing Kagutsuchi by beheading him (and creating five volcanoes in the process), Izanagi went to Yomi to beg Izanami to return. In the darkness of the Underworld he could not see her, but only hear her. She said that she had eaten the food of Yomi and become one with Yomi, but would ask the spirits of the Underworld to release her, on condition that Izanagi waited where he was without trying to see her. He stood patiently in the darkness for a long time, then, convinced that she was gone forever, broke a tooth from his hair-comb and breathed on it to make a torch. In the torchlight he saw Izanami: putrid flesh crawling with maggots and with thunder-snakes coiled in the hollows of her bones. Izanagi jumped back, revolted – and Izanami was so affronted that she turned the snakes into warriors and sent them to kill him. He ran to the entrance of the Underworld, slowing

the snake-warriors down by leaving them first a bunch of grapes and then three peaches, fruits of light and life, and blocked the gate with an enormous stone. Izanami stood on one side, inside the Underworld, and Izanagi stood outside. They spoke words of divorce, and Izanami said, 'Every morning I'll kill a thousand of your mortals'. He answered, 'In that case, every evening I'll create fifteen hundred more.'

So the divorce was complete between the world of the living and the world of the dead – and overpopulation was also guaranteed. Izanami stayed in Yomi, and the maggots from her flesh became its teeming **demons**. Izanagi went back to the surface, and washed to rid himself of the pollution of the Underworld. As he did so, still more deities were created, from his clothes as he took them off, and from the water-drops which fell from his left eye (**Amaterasu** the **Sun**), his right eye (**Tsukuyomi** the **Moon**) and his nose (**Susano** the storm-god).

*This story was given formal shape in the Kojiki ('Book of Ancient Matters'), a Shinto account of Japanese myth written in 712 CE. Modern mythographers say that the story as we have it may be a garbled form of an early **Great Goddess** myth, casting her as god both of birth and death, and that parallels can be made between Izanami and such other Great-Mother manifestations as **Artemis** in Greece or **Kali** in India. In Japan itself Izanami was feared and worshipped as one of the gods of death, but Izanagi never acquired comprehensive rites of his own, being revered chiefly as father of Amaterasu and ancestor of the Imperial dynasty. In art, the stirring of the primeval ocean was a favourite subject in* the eighteenth century, showing two elegant young people in a delicate cloudscape over a lowering sea; Izanagi's attempts to rescue Izanami from the Underworld, were shown in cartoons and popular prints, including all manner of hideous monsters and teeming maggots. They were also a subject for popular theatre and puppet-plays, full of spooks, demon-warriors, spells and enthusiastic fights.

Jason steers *Argo* past the Clashing Rocks (*B. Picart, 18th century*)

JAGANATH
India

Jaganath ('lord of the world'), in Hindu myth, was a hideously ugly god worshipped in the huge temple at Puri, Orissa. He was made from **Krishna**'s bones, after the god's spirit returned to **Heaven**. In some accounts, **Vishvakarman** made a statue to contain the bones – and because he was disturbed as he worked, left it an unfinished torso without head, arms or legs. In others, people wandering in the forest found the bones and put them in a box, which immediately became a god.

Jaganath (or 'juggernaut') myths relate only to this one temple, and are connected with an annual festival in which the huge, uncouth statue of the god is put on wheels and trundled round the town. Devotees rush to touch it as it passes, and some of the most devout once used to throw themselves under the wheels to be crushed to death.

JALANDHARA
India

Jalandhara, in Hindu myth, was the **demon**-son of the river Ganges and the primordial ocean. He made himself so strong by prayers and sacrifice that he defeated the gods, and prepared to take his throne in **Heaven** and rule the universe. To delay him, **Shiva** sent **Parvati** to flirt with him, while the gods concentrated their waning energies into a single weapon, a razor-edged **Sun**-disc so radiant with destruction that Shiva had to keep it hidden in his armpit, to prevent it destroying any other god it touched.

While Jalandhara was flirting with Parvati, **Vishnu** turned himself into Jalandhara's clone and had **sex** with

303

Jalandhara's demon-wife Vrindha, who was so embarrassed when she realized what had happened that she killed herself. The furious Jalandhara now surged to attack the gods again, and Shiva faced him with the Sun-disc. But each time the disc cut off Jaland-hara's head, a drop of the demon's blood fell into the primordial ocean and he was reconstituted as good as new. It was not until the goddesses ran up in a troop, disguised as demons, and licked up Jalandhara's blood before it could touch the ocean that the demon died and the universe was saved.

JAMBAVAN
India

Jambavan (more correctly Jambavat), in Hindu myth, was king of the bears. Before the churning of the Sea of Milk (see *amrita*) he roamed the entire sur-face of the Earth 21 times, gathering herbs. He tossed them into the Sea of Milk, and when it was churned they became *amrita*.

When **Vishnu** came to Earth as **Rama**, and the **demon**-king **Ravana** kidnapped Rama's wife **Sita**, Jambavan was one of Rama's helpers in the huge war against the **demons**. But this was no help to him when Vishnu was later reincarnated as **Krishna**. Jambavan had killed a lion which had stolen the **Sun**'s light concentrated in a ruby. Krishna coveted the ruby, and Jamba-van, not realizing who he was, refused to give it up. They fought for 21 days before Jambavan recognized the god, and quickly surrendered, gave him the stone, offered him his own daugh-ter Jambavati as wife, and retreated to

his cave, where he has hidden from Vishnu/Krishna ever since.

⋙→ **animal-gods**

JANAKA
India

Janaka, in Hindu myth, was a childless king who decided to sacrifice to the gods to bring himself offspring. He began marking a groove in the ground to mark the sacrificial hearth – and **Mother Earth** created a woman from her own self, and sent her to become Janaka's daughter. Her name was **Sita** ('furrow'), and she later became **Rama**'s wife.

JANG XIEN
Asia (East)

Jang Xien ('Jang the archer'), in Chinese myth, was the god who brought chil-dren. In ancient times, a double eclipse struck the human race and was followed immediately by infertility for which there seemed to be no cure. Then a young man with his face powdered white like a prostitute's visited the Emperor and told him that Black Dog (the Dog Star) had imprisoned the **Sun** and **Moon**, come down to Earth and was eating babies before they were even conceived. Jang Xien shot arrows to scare off the dog, the eclipse van-ished, and **fertility** returned. The Em-peror rewarded him for this service by making him immortal, and ever after-wards women wanting children carried pictures of Jang Xien and prayed to him.

Scholars say that the myth of Jang Xien is derived from a pun: Jang kong jia tan means both 'Jang shoots with his bow' and 'Jang increases the birth-rate'. The Dog Star, in the most ancient of Chinese beliefs, was held to be malignant, bringing sterility and death to Earth – but in modern terms, the metaphor in Jang's name, of the shooting of arrows, also has its point.

≫⊦ archers, childbirth and infant care, Eros

JANUS
Europe (South)

Janus ('door-jamb'), in Roman myth, was created by **Ouranos** (Father **Sky**), in the earliest days of the universe, as a love-gift for **Hecate** goddess of black magic. Ouranos took handfuls of earth, air, darkness and **water**, moulded them into a ball and rolled them down the crack in the Earth's crust to the **Underworld** where Hecate lurked. As the ball rolled, its sides flattened and its ends bulged, until it was like a cylindrical pillar rumbling through the Underworld. The friction of its movement heated it and gave it life, so that by the time it reached Hecate's lair it was a creature able to breathe, think and move for itself. Hecate called it Janus, wrapped it in her monstrous coils and tried to feed it puppy's entrails, warm lamb's blood and woodlice plucked from the earth like sweets. Revolted, Janus wriggled off her lap and plunged into the river **Styx**, which carried him back to the Upper World and deposited him on the bank of the icy river Eridanus in Italy.

As Janus lay on the bank, the **Sun** – the first he'd ever known – worked on his body as on a growing plant, and he began to sprout legs, arms, eyes, ears and noses. He ran through the woods and hills, a multiform monster – and it was seven centuries before the creatures and peoples of Italy overcame their fear of his appearance and began to treat him as god and friend. Janus lived in peace until the huge war between gods and **Titans** for control of the universe, when his half-brother Saturn (see **Cronus**), leader of the Titans, fled to Italy and begged for shelter. The gods, furious, began blasting Italy with thunderbolts, until Janus had no option but to agree to tell them where Saturn was, if they promised to show him mercy.

The gods kept their promise. They rounded up Saturn and the other Titans for judgement, but instead of harming them gave them a new home, the Islands of the Blessed. As for Janus, **Jupiter** rewarded him by making him a god and promoting him to **Olympus**. But at the same time he punished him for his treachery by making him no more than two-faced and by taking away his power of movement. Janus stood forever as **Heaven**'s doorkeeper, and the Hours, his children, fed him and cared for him. He was rooted to the spot like the pillar he so much resembled, one face fixed ahead and one behind.

In some accounts, Jupiter also punished Janus by putting him in charge of a single moment in time, endlessly repeated: the instant when the old year dies and the new year is born. He thus had **immortality** *without being able to enjoy it. In other accounts, Janus was the child not of Sky but of the Sun, and was a mortal ruler given immortality and the ability to see both ways as a reward for his wisdom and a symbol of his prophetic powers. His temple on the*

Janiculum Hill was one of the main shrines of Rome, and his place at the year's turning-point made the Romans regard him as doorkeeper, or janitor, of the seasons. Statues of Janus were common at the doors of Roman houses, sometimes carved directly from the door-jambs themselves.
»»+ guardians

JAPANESE MYTH

In the fourth century CE, the Japanese fleet – helped or not by supernatural forces, the **Tide Jewels** – conquered the nearmost parts of Korea. One effect was to open Japan, for the first time, to religious and cultural influences from the mainland. In the next two centuries Confucianism and Buddhism, with their attendant systems of philosophy and social morality, were imported and adapted to suit local conditions and ways of thought.

So far as myth is concerned, the first result of this assimilation was the arrival in Japan of a whole range of Buddhist supernatural ideas. In particular, gods and their stories were imported wholesale from China and India. **Buddha** himself became Shaka Muni; Kannon Bosatsu (deity of mercy, sometimes male but more usually female) was a Japanese form of the **boddhisattva Guan Yin** in Chinese Buddhism; the Japanese Amida was the Indian Amitabha, ruler of the Western Paradise; the Japanese **Jizo** was an amalgam of the Indian Ksitigarbha, who guided souls in the **Underworld**, and an aboriginal Japanese god whose main concern was children; the Japanese Yakushi Nyorai was the Indian Bhaishajyaguru, Buddha of Healing; the Japanese Miroku

Bosatsu was **Maitreya**, the Buddha Still to Be. As in Chinese Buddhism, Japanese Buddhism often grouped powers by functions: examples are the Four Heavenly Kings, the Five Wisdom Buddhas and the **Seven Gods of Good Luck**.

A second result of the assimilation of supernatural ideas from the mainland was to trigger a re-examination and codification of Japan's own aboriginal myths. In the eighth century CE two substantial collections were published: *Kojiki* ('Book of Ancient Matters'), grouping myths from the creation of the universe to the reign of the Emperor Suiko (mid-seventh century CE), and *Nihoshoki* ('Chronicle of Japan'), placing the same local stories in a wider spectrum of myths brought from China and India, and in the process blurring both their incidental details and their underlying Japaneseness. Both collections were also pieces of propaganda, equalled only in the West by Roman retellings of ancient Greek and Etruscan myth, and made for the same reason: to dignify the then ruling class by removing the distinction between myth and history, so that current Emperors could be traced back in an unbroken line to the gods themselves. (In Japan's case, this line began with Jimmu, 'son of Heaven', claimed both to be a great-great-grandson of **Amaterasu** the **Sun** and to have lived on Earth in the seventh century BCE.)

This deliberate blurring of supernatural and secular was the most overt form of a process characteristic of *Shinto* ('Way of the Gods'), the native Japanese religion, from earliest times. *Shinto* demanded respect for the whole of creation, since everything which existed had its own indwelling spirit, or *kami*. *Shinto* followers believed that there were 'eight hundred myriad' gods, grouped in a hierarchy as complex as anything in mortal society. (This made the system fertile ground for Confucian ideas.) *Shinto* myths, many dating back to the prehistoric inhabitants of Japan, teem with beings of every kind, from predatory ghosts and demons (**Gaki**, **Kappa**, **Oni**) to gods of weather (**Ajisukitakahikone** the **thunder**-spirit, **Futen** the windlord; the **lightning**-deities **Raiden** and **Raiju**) and of **fertility** (**Chimatano**, phallic god of crossroads; the ricedeities **Inari** and **Ukemochi**). Characteristically 'Japanese' supernatural beings, among the oldest in the entire world pantheon, include **Moshirikkwechep** the primordial trout and **Umashiashikabihikoji**, the reed from which the creator-gods sprouted at the beginning of time. *Shinto* was a system in which not only mortals could become gods – the war god **Hachiman**, for example, was originally the son of Empress Jingo who defeated the Koreans – but also mountains (**Fujiyama**), philosophical concepts (**In** and **Yo**, the principles of maleness and femaleness which underlie all creation), facets of appearance (**Bimbogami**, god of poverty, was emaciation made animate) and even inanimate objects (the divine sword Kusanagi; the Tide Jewels which drank or spewed back the **sea**).

Despite such apparent richness, the central core of *Shinto* myth, as handed down in the *Kojiki* and *Nihoshoki*, is as sparse as it is lucid: a dynastic sequence beginning with the appearance of **Izanami and Izanagi**, creators of the world, continuing with the quarrels between Izanagi's offspring Amaterasu the Sun, **Tsukuyomi** the **Moon** and **Susano** lord of storms, and reaching a climax with the colonization of the world of mortals by Susano's son-in-law **Okuninushi** (who later became god of medicine) and Amaterasu's son Ninigi and grandson **Yamasachi** (grandfather of Jimmu). With the arrival of a god-sponsored Imperial dynasty, *Shinto* myth acquired a core of canonical belief which stayed intact, despite a flurry of coming and going on the fringes – as Emperors were deified or gods, saints or even storybook heroes (such as **Odysseus**, who became the Japanese arrow-lord **Yuriwaka**) were welcomed into the system – right down to Japan's opening up to the contemporary world after the Second World War, an event symbolized in 1946 CE by Emperor Hirohito's renunciation of any claims to divine status.

≫→ Daikoku, Kagutsuchi, Kojin, Kotoamatsukami, Musubi, Ninigi, Yomi

JARA (DEMON)
India

Jara, in Hindu myth, was a schizophrenic **demon**. She was a beautiful, gentle girl, good with children, and looked after the prosperity of households and families. But at night, in secret, she changed into a withered crone and walked the dark paths, sniffing out the remains of corpses and eating them.

JARA (GODDESS)
India

Jara, in Hindu myth, was Old Age, the daughter of **Death**.

JARA (HUNTER)
India

Jara, in Hindu myth, was a hunter who mistook **Krishna** for a deer in the forest and killed him. He is generally said to be the same person (despite the change of gender) as the goddess **Jara**.

JARASANDHA
India

Jarasandha, in Hindu myth, was King of Magadha and a sworn enemy of the Yadava people ruled by King **Ugrasena**. When Ugrasena's **demon**-stepson **Kansa** usurped the Yadava throne, Jarasandha sent him two of his own daughters as wives, hoping to merge the Magadhans and Yadavas into a single, all-powerful nation. But the gods thwarted these plans. **Vishnu**, horrified at Kansa's growing power and the thought that if he conquered the world, demons might make war on **Heaven** itself, came to Earth as **Krishna**, killed Kansa and restored Ugrasena to power. Soon afterwards, Jarasandha was challenged by another powerful dynasty, the **Pandava** princes, who demanded that he accept the eldest Pandava brother, **Yudhishthira**, as emperor. When Jarasandha refused, another brother, **Bhima**, tore him to pieces with his bare hands, and divided the kingdom. This forcible enlargement of Pandava power alarmed their cousins

the **Kauravas**, and led to the huge war described in the **Mahabharata**.

JARI AND KAMARONG
Oceania

Jari, in the myths of the Wogeo people of Melanesia, was the daughter of the primordial **snake**-goddess Gogo. She married a snake-man, but when he killed Gogo and ate her she left him and wandered the world looking for a mortal husband. The best she could find was the lizard-man Kamarong. He had no penis and no anus: he shed sperm from all over his body, and expelled faeces through his mouth. Jari set about making improvements. She pierced an anus at the end of his body, as far from his mouth as possible, and moulded him a penis from breadfruit and crushed betel nuts. She built a hut for the two of them to live in, and showed Kamarong how to fish, gather food and grow tobacco. She took some of her own menstrual blood, made fire of it and taught him how to use it for cooking. This couple, Jari and Kamarong, were the ancestors of all civilized people in the world.

➤➤ civilization, crafts, creation, human ancestors

JASON
Europe (South)

Jason's name. Jason (Iason, 'healer'), in Greek myth, was the son of King Aeson and Queen Alcimede of Iolcus. His birth-name was Diomedes ('godlike cunning'), but while he was still an infant his uncle **Pelias** usurped the throne, exiled Aeson and killed all his children except Diomedes, who was spirited away by the gods. They gave him to **Chiron** to bring up, and Chiron renamed him Jason.

Jason and Hera. As soon as Jason was old enough, he set out to ask the Delphic oracle whose son he really was. On the way he came to the river Enipeus, swollen by flood-water. An old woman on the bank asked him to carry her across, and he took her on his shoulders and waded into the stream. The old woman was **Hera** in disguise, and the weight of an immortal goddess made Jason stumble and slip, losing one sandal in the swift-flowing water. When they reached the other bank, Hera rewarded him by telling him that Pelias had stolen his father's throne, and that she would protect him if he went to Iolcus and demanded it back.

Jason and Pelias. The gods had warned Pelias to beware of a stranger wearing only one sandal, because the young man would bring about his death. Accordingly, he agreed to surrender the throne of Iolcus on one condition: that Jason go to Colchis, beyond the edge of the mortal world, and steal the **Golden Fleece**. Jason commissioned the building of a boat (*Argo*), gathered a crew of **heroes** (the **Argonauts**) from all over Greece, and sailed to Colchis. Helped by **Medea**, he stole the Fleece and brought it – and her – back to Iolcus. He intended to display the Fleece to the people and claim the throne for his father Aeson (by now an old man). But Medea forestalled him. She persuaded Pelias' daughters that the way to rejuvenate their father was to boil him alive – and when they tried this and Pelias

died in agony, she and Jason were forced to run from Iolcus for their lives.

Jason and Medea. Jason and Medea settled next in Corinth. They lived there for several years, and had two children, Mermerus and Pheres. But Jason, still anxious for a throne, made plans to divorce Medea and marry Princess Glauce – and Medea punished him first by poisoning Glauce and her father, and then by murdering Mermerus and Pheres and carrying their bodies away from Corinth in the chariot of her grandfather the **Sun**.

Jason's Death. Accounts differ about what happened next. In some, Jason lived on in Corinth, as the demoralized leader of a mourning people – and several years later Medea, having tried to murder the son and heir of King **Aegeus** of Athens (with whom she had taken sanctuary after escaping from Corinth), went back to him and bewitched him with magic spells into making her his queen again. In others, he left Corinth for Iolcus, where he recovered the Golden Fleece, was acclaimed king and ruled peacefully until he died. Others again say that his life ended in futility and misery. Driven mad by the deaths of his sons, he took to beach-combing, sleeping at night under the stern of his ship *Argo*. The ship had been built with ordinary timbers, pines from Mount Pelion – except for one beam, taken from an oak sacred to **Zeus** and therefore immortal. As the years passed, the pine timbers gradually rotted away, while the oak beam remained as fresh and strong as ever – and one night as Jason slept, *Argo* collapsed into dust and the oak beam fell on his head and killed him.

JATAYU

India

Jatayu (or Jatayus), king of the vultures in Hindu myth, tried to stop **Ravana** abducting **Rama**'s wife **Sita**. Ravana tore out his flight-feathers and bit off chunks of his flesh, leaving him dying on the forest floor. When Rama and **Lakshmana** (alerted by the winds and forest streams) found Jatayu, he just had strength to tell them where Ravana and Sita had gone, before he died. Rama and Lakshmana burned his body on a funeral-pyre, and his spirit soared up from it in a golden chariot to **Heaven**.

≫→ animal-gods

JIZO

Asia (East)

Jizo, in Japanese Buddhist myth, was the **boddhisattva** of mercy. He comforted the bereft and cared for the souls of the Dead, making sure that they found the right section of the **Underworld** after judgement, and protecting them against **demons** on their journey. He was especially kind to dead children, gathering their souls like grasshoppers in his sleeves to hide them from **oni**, and keeping guard each night while they played beside the River of Souls.

JOCASTA

Europe (South)

Jocasta (Iokaste, 'shining moon', also called Epikaste, 'upset'), daughter of Menoeceus in Greek myth, belonged to one of the leading dynasties of Thebes, descendants of the **Sown Man** Echion. She married **Laius** and bore him a son. But the oracle had told Laius that the child would grow up to murder him, so he exposed it at birth. However, the baby, **Oedipus**, was rescued and grew up as a prince of Corinth. In adulthood Oedipus went to the Delphic oracle to ask his true identity, and at a crossroads on the way back quarrelled with an old man – Laius – and killed him.

Oedipus now went to Thebes, and rescued it from the clutches of the **Sphinx**. When news came that Laius had been mysteriously killed, he married Jocasta and they had four children, **Antigone**, **Ismene**, **Eteocles** and **Polynices**. Jocasta lived contentedly as queen and mother, and her presence on the throne ensured Oedipus the loyalty of the descendants of the Sown Men. But then the gods took action, sending a plague on Thebes and announcing that it would be lifted only when the murderer of Laius was found and punished. Oedipus himself conducted the enquiry – and convicted himself. In most accounts, Jocasta was so horrified to hear that she'd had children by her own son that she hanged herself. In others, she lived on after the blinding and exile of Oedipus, but her power was taken over by her brother **Creon, King of Thebes**, and she survived to see her sons Eteocles and Polynices murder each other in their rivalry for the throne, an event which made her kill herself from grief. After the sack of Thebes, visitors to the **Underworld** saw her ghost weeping and wringing its hands, one of the few souls of the Dead tormented by unending memory of what had happened to them in life.

JORMUNGAND
Europe (North)

Jormungand ('world snake'), in Nordic myth, was one of the three children of **Loki** and the giantess Angboda. His brother was the wolf-**giant** Fenrir and his sister was **Hel**, half alive, half dead. The gods, appalled by the children's brutishness, hurled them from **Asgard**. Jormungand fell to the bottom of the ocean surrounding **Midgard**, home of mortals. In the muddy depths he lurked and grew, until he was so huge that he coiled all round Midgard, an ocean-filling serpent who bit his own tail. His presence held Midgard in position, but this was not his intention: he had no reason for existence, except to hate the gods and brood on their downfall.

Jormungand and Thor. Jormungand had inherited his father's shape-changing skill, and from time to time sloughed his snake-skin and ventured into the upper world. A favourite disguise was as a cat, and in this form he sometimes walked as Loki's familiar. On one occasion, in Asgard, Loki fuddled **Thor** with wine and challenged him to lift the cat. The more Thor struggled, the more Jormungand resisted, and in the end Thor could lift only a single paw. In one of the bouts, Jormungand arched his back, as cats do, and the arch became a rainbow that filled the sky.

On another occasion, Thor challenged the **giant Hymir** at fishing. They rowed out on the ocean that surrounds Midgard, and started fishing. Their bait was gobbets of a whole ox, impaled on the hooks like maggots. Hymir fished up a pair of whales, and Thor, not to be outdone, rammed the ox's head on his hook and fished up Jormungand himself. The ocean-snake writhed and roared, shaking the universe, and Thor pummelled his head with his hammer to try and quieten him. Some versions say that he killed Jormungand, thus earning the title 'Serpent-Slayer'. But this conflicts with the **Ragnarök**-story (see next paragraph). In most versions of the story, Hymir panicked at the sight of Jormungand and cut the line – and Jormungand swam down to the ocean depths and resumed his glowering hatred of the gods. It took an age of the world for the tidal wave of his catching to subside.

Jormungand at Ragnarök. At Ragnarök, the end of the world, Jormungand will writhe up from the depths and come to land. With his brother Fenrir he will advance on the gods, roaring and spewing poison. His old enemy Thor will tackle him, and they will kill each other, Thor by battering Jormungand with his hammer and Jormungand by engulfing Thor with venom. Thus Jormungand will have fulfilled his existence, as one essential partner in the destruction of this age of the world and the beginning of the next.

⟫‣ **Aapep, snakes, shape-changers**

JOTUNHEIM
Europe (North)

Jotunheim ('giant-home'), in Nordic myth, was the realm of the **giants**, a plateau fringed by mountains at the

Eastern edge of the ocean that surrounded the world. The giants lived in caves in the rock, and also in a vast fortified citadel, Utgard ('out-place'). They had banqueting-halls and council-chambers like those of the gods in **Asgard** or mortals in **Midgard**, but they tilled no fields, grew no crops and bred no animals. They hunted on skis, eating the flesh of mountain-goats, bears and birds, and for drink they broke off and melted chunks of ice, the covering of their mother Earth and one of the elements of which they themselves were made.

JOUKAHAINEN
Europe (North)

Joukahainen ('thin son of the North'), in Finnish myth, was one of the first beings in **creation**: an icicle given life, a frost-**giant** who ruled the Far North. When **Väinämöinen** was born and started using magic to thaw, plough and plant the tundra, Joukahainen tried to stop him. He sang spells to make **sky**, **sea** and earth shake with terror – only to be outwitted when Väinämöinen's own spells turned his sword into **lightning**, his bow to a rainbow, his arrows to hawks, and Joukahainen himself to a column of ice up to his ears in a bog and melting. Joukahainen escaped only by promising that Väinämöinen could marry his sister Aino. Aino, however, committed suicide rather than marry the stranger, and Väinämöinen sailed North to **Pohjola**, country of the ice-giants, to find another wife. On the way Joukahainen sank his boat and threw him into the sea to drown. When Väinämöinen was rescued, Joukahainen gave up

trying to kill him, left him to the mercy of **Louhi**, witch-princess of Pohjola, and retreated to his castle on the icy fringes of the universe.

JOU WANG
Asia (East)

Jou Wang, in Chinese history, was the last Shang Emperor (ruled 1154-1121BCE). He and his concubine Ta Ji were famed for the debauchery and brutality of their court – they butchered relatives, tortured priests and conducted orgies in which people went skinny-dipping in a wine-lake – and ruled unchecked until gods and humans fought a huge battle to dislodge them. Unfortunately this was not the end of Jou Wang. He was entitled to **immortality** and demanded his prerogatives. The Heavenly Emperor appointed him god of sodomy, with a single temple at Ji Hsien – and the debauches which grew up there, in the name of religious ritual, became as notorious as anything from Jou Wang's mortal court.

JUGUMISHANTA AND MORUfONU
Oceania

Jugumishanta, in the myths of the Fore people of Vanuatu, was **Mother Earth**, the first being. She made a husband, Morufonu, by moulding him from part of herself. Having nowhere to lie down for **sex**, they made islands from their own faeces, and then travelled between them, creating human beings, plants and animals.

In some accounts, Jugumishanta gave the new creations life by playing a flute, and when she was not using it she hid it in her pubic hair. Morufonu, curious, reached for it one day when she was sleeping – and as soon as he touched her pubic hair his own genitals, armpits and chin, which had until then been naked, sprouted hair. The Fore people told this story at the puberty initiation-ceremonies of young males; what stories the females told are not recorded.

»+ **creation**

JULUNGGUL
Australia

Julunggul, or Yurlunggur, in the myths of several peoples of Arnhem Land in Northern Australia, was the **Great Rainbow Snake**. In the Dream Time, its home was a waterhole called Muruwul (or Miraramuinar). One day two sisters, Waimariwi and Boaliri (in some accounts called the Wawilak sisters or Wawalug sisters), on a journey with their two sons and two dogs, stopped to rest by the waterhole, and while Boaliri made a fire and began gathering food for a meal, Waimariwi went to fetch water. She was in the middle of her period, and some menstrual blood fell into the water; Julunggul accidentally opened his mouth and swallowed it. In a rage, he surged from the waterhole to **Heaven**, sending a tidal wave surging over the Earth, and swallowed the sisters, their sons, their dogs and all the plants and animals Boaliri had gathered for supper.

That would have been the end of it, except that when Julunggul reached Heaven an ant-spirit bit him and he writhed so violently that he regurgitated everything he'd swallowed. The sisters, children, dogs and other creatures and plants fell back to Earth. Julunggul slithered after them and swallowed them again – this time everything but the children. Again and again he regurgitated and swallowed, and each time left some creature alive on Earth. Eventually, exhausted, he left everything where it was and vanished into Heaven, leaving Earth stocked with the ancestors of every plant, insect, animal and human we see today.

The Yolngu people of Arnhem Land, whose rituals and myth-ceremonies are particularly complex and well-documented, re-enacted this story once a year as part of the puberty-rites of adolescent boys. While the women sang songs recounting the journey of the Wawilak sisters across the desert to the waterhole, the men took the part of Julunggul, carrying the boys away to a sacred initiation area forbidden to women. After a while the boys came back, as if regurgitated by the snake, and initiation was complete.

»+ **animal-gods, creation**

JUMALA
Europe (North)

Jumala ('darkening sky'), in Finnish myth, was the first **sky**-god. It had no shape or identity, but was creative impulse only. Its existence caused **Luonnotar**, daughter of **creation**, to fall from the embrace of her mother, air, into the primordial ocean, where a duck settled on her knee and laid eggs which were to become the **Sun**, **Moon** and stars. In later myth, Jumala became, or was identified with, a more pro-active version of itself: **Ukko**, king of the gods.

JUN DI
Asia (East)

Jun Di, goddess of dawn and war in Chinese Buddhist myth, lived in the Pole Star. She had three faces (one a sow's) and innumerable arms, two of which supported the **Sun** and **Moon** in the sky and the others held all or some of a battleaxe, a bow, a chariot, a dragon's head, a lotus flower, a pagoda, a pennant, a spear, a sword and a wheel. The seven stars of the Great Bear were harnessed to her chariot, and pulled it in the guise of horses or (more usually) pigs.

Jun Di was also worshipped as Tin Hau, the Evening Star and protector of sailors, and as Tin Fei, **Heaven**'s Concubine (because she was thought to sleep with **Sky**).

JUNO: *see* Hera

JUOK
Africa

Juok the creator, in the myths of the Shilluk people of the Upper Nile, made human beings by mixing sand or dust with river-water (or, some say, his own spittle, blood or semen). The colour of the people he made depended where he was on Earth and on the type of the sand: white sand made white people, brown brown and the rich dark mud of the Upper Nile made Shilluk people. The first human beings were nothing more than rolls of mud, like logs, and lay inert on the ground. Juok gave them

legs to move about on, arms to plant crops, eyes to see what they were doing and mouths to eat with. Finally, to save himself the endless labour of rolling out new humans, he gave them sexual organs – and as soon as the human race was complete, he left us to get on with our lives.

≫+ **creation**

JUPITER
Europe (South)

Jupiter ('sky-father'), in Roman myth, was an amalgam of the Etruscan god Tinia ('thunderer') and the Greek **Zeus**. When the Romans consolidated their mythology they made him supreme ruler of the universe – a title he held alone until Imperial times, when he shared it with the Emperor, ruling the sky as the Emperor ruled on Earth. His other honorific titles included Optimus Maximus ('best and greatest'), and a huge statue of him in this guise presided at his temple on the Capitoline Hill, hub of the Roman state.

Although the Romans attributed to Jupiter many of the myths of Zeus, they imagined him ruling as the chief figure in a celestial committee analogous to the triumvirates of aristocratic Rome. Jupiter's fellow-deciders were Juno (see **Hera**) and **Minerva**, and between them they oversaw all supernatural activity. Jupiter's supremacy in this trio came from his wielding of the thunderbolts, and even that was conditional. There were three categories of thunderbolts (in some accounts, just three actual thunderbolts). The first he could use at will, to warn. The second he could use – also to warn –

only with the agreement of twelve other gods. The third – to punish – was available to him only with the permission of the 'superior' or 'hidden' gods: that is, the oldest powers in the universe, those in existence before the **Olympians**.

In addition to his rather severe official functions, Jupiter had a relaxed, smiling personality – not the lecherous prankster of Greek myth but a kind of beaming father-figure, self-conscious as a slumming prince. The Latin word for this quality, jovialitas, 'Jupiterness', gives English 'joviality', and suggests exactly the kind of wary geniality exuded by the king of the gods when he let himself relax.

≫→ supreme deity

JURAWADBAD
Australia

Jurawadbad ('snake-man'), in the myths of the Gunwinggu people of Arnhem Land in Northern Australia, was one of the supernatural creatures who shared the world with mortals in the Dream Time. In the spirit-world he was a **snake**, in the mortal world a man, and he arranged to marry a woman called Gulanundoidj. But she took a lover, a water-snake-man called Bulugu, and Jurawadbad punished her. He put a hollow log on the ground, changed into snake form and curled up inside it. When Gulanundoidj came that way she saw the log, and felt round the hole with one arm. Jurawadbad bit her, then resumed his mortal shape and went on his way.

*In Gunwinggu ceremonies, this story is re-enacted as part of a rain-bringing ritual involving the urbar, a drum made from a hollowed-out log. The Maung people of Goulbourn Island also beat the urbar to bring rain, but their myth is quite different. The drum symbolizes both the vagina of **Mother Earth** and the penis of the **Great Rainbow Snake** – and beating it causes them to mate and renews Earth's **fertility** (symbolized by rain).*

JURUMU
Australia

Jurumu, in the myths of the Tiwi people of Melville Island in Northern Australia, was the grandson of **Mudungkala**, the spirit-mother who crawled from Underearth to Overearth and made it habitable for humans. Until his time, although Overearth was a paradise, plentifully stocked with plants and creatures of every kind, it was lightless. But one day Jurumu was sitting in the forest with his brother Mudati, idly rubbing two sticks together – and **fire** was born. Thinking that he had created an ungovernable, new predator, Jurumu threw the sticks down, and they landed in a heap of leaves and twigs, setting it ablaze. Jurumu ran in terror to his father, **Purukapali**. Purukapali explained what fire was and how to control it by digging a pit-hearth and feeding the flames with wood.

Ever since then, fire has been the servant of human beings – and of no other creatures, since none dared approach it. Fire also benefited the Earth in another way. Purukapali told Jurumu to give blazing torches to the two women who had come with Mudungkala from Underearth. Taking the torches, the old women soared into the sky to light the world. The elder sister, Jurumu's mother, became the **Sun**, and the younger sister became the **Moon**.

JUSTICE AND UNIVERSAL ORDER

To most creatures in the universe, including humans, justice was not natural: it had to be taught to them or imposed on them by gods. The gods realized that universal order and the continuation of existence depended on a precise balance between opposing forces – indeed discovering the balance-point (either accidentally or deliberately) was, in several traditions, the moment when creation began. All cultures believed that the creator, or some other god or gods, oversaw universal balance, and that part of this responsibility was to make sure that the rest of creation adhered to it. In some traditions spirit-beings, humans and animals, worked together moment-by-moment in a collaboration which ensured universal well-being; in others, the gods had hierarchies and laws in **Heaven**, gave human beings versions adapted for life on Earth, and set up courts and judges in the **Underworld** to assess each individual's contribution to universal well-being, punishing or rewarding according to laws which only the judges fully understood. Humans had no redress against the laws of Heaven; the question was much debated of which laws – if any – bound the gods with equal force, and the gods thought to embody such laws were among the oldest and most mysterious in myth.

≫→ **(Celtic): Dagda; (China): Four Kings of Hell; (Egypt): Aset, Maat; (Finnish): Akka; (Greece): Styx, Themis, Zeus; (India): Brahma, Dharma, Privithi, Shiva, Vishnu; (Iranian): Rashnu; (Mesopotamia): Shamash, Utu; (Nordic): Forseti, Tiwaz; (Slavic): Radigast**

KAANG
Africa

Kaang (also known as Cagn, Kho and Thora), in the myths of the Bushpeople of Botswana, created the world and everything in it – among other things, making the Moon by throwing an old shoe into the sky. At first he lived in harmony with human beings: his sons Cogaz and Gewi married mortal wives, and one of his daughters married a human chief. He spent his time fighting **Gauna**, lord of **death**, and showed his followers how to achieve **immortality** – killed by Gauna's creatures the thorns (at that time living beings) and left for ants to pick his bones clean, he reassembled his own skeleton and lived again. But as the number of people grew in the world, they began to forget Kaang's importance – and one day, treated disrespectfully by a group of children, he decided to leave **Mother Earth** for good. He abandoned any shape recognizable to mortals, and went to live in **Sky** as disembodied spirit. He took the secret of immortality with him, and humans have been Gauna's prey ever since.

Although Kaang himself remained aloof from **creation**, he did leave parts of himself to guide and help humanity. His sons and their descendants owned a portion of his wisdom, and were the chiefs and elders of generations of mortals. One of his daughters married a snake, and Kaang-wisdom was ever afterwards embodied in **snakes**, if any human being could be found wise enough to understand their language. And finally, Kaang used Caterpillar and Mantis as his messengers on Earth, and their movements and behaviour told human beings his wishes.
⫸ **creation**

Krishna arriving at Radha's house (*Indian miniature painting*)

KABUNDUNGULU: *see* Sudika-Mbambi and Kabundungulu

KADLU
Arctic

The Kadlu, in the myths of the people of Baffin Island, were three sisters who lived in the sky and made **thunder** and **lightning** by scrubbing sealskins together.

KADRU
India

Kadru, in Hindu myth, was a **snake-goddess**, one of the two wives of **Kasyapa**. The other wife was **Vinata**. Each wanted power over the other, and when their husband, a powerful sage, promised them as many children as they wanted, Kadru asked for a thousand, and Vinata asked for two only – specifying that they should outrank all of Kadru's. In due course the children were born. Kadru's included the world-snake **Shesha** and **Vasuki** the serpent-king. Vinata's sons were **Varuna**, charioteer of the Sun, and **Garuda** king of eagles – both of whom were remorseless enemies of Kadru's snake-children ever afterwards.

Kadru now turned to magic of her own. Whenever she could, she took advantage of her snake-form to wriggle inside the wombs of pregnant mortal women and lay her own eggs. Unless the women sacrificed to **Brahma** at exactly the right moment of their pregnancy, their children would be born as snakes, or would have mortal forms but serpentine ruthlessness and cunning. Brahma later cancelled the first part of this magic, but the second still applies – and Kadru's children, snakes in human form, still swarm in the world today.

KAGUTSUCHI
Asia (East)

Kagutsuchi ('fire shining swift male'), or Homasubi, in Japanese myth, was the spirit of fire, the god of destructive and purifying fire and of summer heat. When he was born he scorched the vagina of his mother **Izanami** so badly that she died. His father **Izanagi** cut him into five pieces, and when his blood touched the ground it became five mountain spirits. Fire, however, has the power to rekindle itself, and so it was with Kagutsuchi. He settled on the peak of Mount Atago, and was ever afterwards associated with **mountains**. People made pilgrimages to mountain-peaks to worship him, believing that if they placated him they would avert forest fires.

➤ **creation; Osiris; Paris; Ragnarök**

KAIKEYI
India

Kaikeyi ('princess of the Kaikeya people'), in Hindu myth, was the youngest wife of King **Dasaratha**. She was obsessed with her own importance, and jealous of Dasaratha's senior wives. When Dasaratha (who was childless) gave each wife a cake sent by the gods to make them pregnant, she refused to eat hers because she was given it last – and a kite carried it away into the forest, where **Anjana** ate it and became pregnant with **Hanuman**. Kaikeyi did accept Dasaratha's next gift, a drink of *soma* – and became pregnant with **Bharata**.

Then, because Bharata would be the king's second son, subordinate to **Rama**, the royal heir, Kaikeyi used her **beauty** to seduce her husband into banishing Rama and making Bharata king in his place. This plot failed – Bharata refused to act as anything but Rama's regent – and Kaikeyi had the further humiliation of causing her husband's death, for Dasaratha was so mortified at what had happened that he pined away to nothing.

KALANEMI
India

Kalanemi, in Hindu myth, was a **demon**. He supported his nephew **Ravana** in the war against **Rama**, and Ravana offered him half the demon-kingdom if he killed Rama's monkey-general **Hanuman**. Seeing Hanuman in the forest, Kalanemi disguised himself as a hermit and invited the monkey-king to join him for a meal. Hanuman went first to a pool to wash, killed a crocodile which surged out and grabbed his foot – and the crocodile changed into a forest-**nymph** and warned Hanuman of what Kalanemi was planning. Hanuman picked Kalanemi up with his tail and flicked him so high that he bounced on the underside of **Heaven** and fell back to Earth, dead, at his uncle Ravana's feet.

In some accounts, Kalanemi is confused with **Kansa**, the demon who tried to kill **Krishna**.

KALEVALA
Europe (North)

Kalevala ('land of heroes', that is, Finland) is an epic poem first published in 1835 and brought out complete (at 22,800 lines long) in 1849. Its author, the scholar and folklorist Elias Lönnrot (1802-84), assembled it from thousands of folk-poems, ballads, nursery tales, proverbs and other traditional material, adding elements of his own and giving it an over-riding form in the same way as his idol Homer had done with traditional material to create the *Iliad* and *Odyssey*.

Kalevala is an account of the myths and heroic legends of pre-Christian Finland. It centres on the story of the god-**hero Väinämöinen**, his brother **Ilmarinen** and their jester companion **Lemminkäinen**, in their battles to defeat or outwit the frost-giants of **Pohjola**, the Far North, and win wives from Princess **Louhi** by making the magic mill **sampo**. But in passing it describes an entire cosmology, beginning with the **creation** of the world by Väinämöinen's mother **Luonnotar**, including information about such early gods as **Ukko** and **Akka**, rulers of the **sky**, the **sea**-god **Ahto** and the forest-god **Tapio**. Two central episodes add still more material: the dark, self-contained story of **Kullervo** and the tale of Väinämöinen's journey to **Tuonela**, the **Underworld**, and his encounters with its rulers **Tuoni** and **Tuonetar** and their entourage of goblins, diseases and **monsters**.

When Lönnrot assembled *Kalevala*, his intention was scholarly: to record Finland's ancient traditions and songs before they disappeared. His work was part of a Europe-wide upsurge in the collection of traditional material – Asbjörnsen in Norway and the Grimm brothers in Germany, for example, had already published influential collections of folktales, and folk-studies had been added to the curricula of universities in Bohemia, Italy, Scotland and Switzerland. But events gave *Kalevala* an importance in Finland far beyond such amiable but fustian endeavour. Finland spent much of the nineteenth century reasserting its national identity and throwing off the domination of such other countries as Sweden and Russia – and the nationalist movement recruited Lönnrot and *Kalevala* to the cause. The book ran through dozens of editions, both in its original form and in retellings. It was a main factor in re-establishing Finnish as the national language in place of Swedish, and after self-determination became a standard text taught in every school.

Kalevala's swaggering events, and its evocation of the Finnish landscape (and character-in-landscape) appealed to writers and artists of all kinds. Ibsen in *Peer Gynt* (and in the US Longfellow in *Hiawatha*) imitated its characteristic eight-syllable, heavily-accented lines. Finnish fine artists made illustrations of all the stories, sometimes (as with the painter A. Gallen-Kallela, perhaps the best-known outside Finland) in a stridently-coloured style blending mysterious content (brooding lakes, wolves, dark stands of trees) with melodramatic poses and photographic realism in the figures, and sometimes rediscovering pre-Christian Finnish styles of metalwork, woodcarving and tapestry. The greatest artist to use *Kalevala*, the composer Sibelius, wrote so many works inspired by it (over 60, ranging from songs and theatre music to such grand symphonic poems as *Pohjola's Daughter*, *Luonnotar*, the *Lemminkäinen Legends* and *Tapiola*) that the government gave him a lifetime pension for his services to 'national' (that is, 'nationalist') cultural life.

KALI
India

Kali ('black', short for *Kali Ma*, 'black mother'), goddess of **death** in Hindu myth, was the personification either of one of the seven tongues of **Agni** the **fire**-god, or of the fury of **Durga**, **Shiva**'s consort. (In this version she burst from Durga's forehead, roaring.)

Kali and Raktabija. Raktabija was a **demon** who had the power to clone himself from every drop of his blood which spilled on the ground. When Shiva sent Durga to fight him, Durga made seven clones of herself, the *Matrikas* ('little mothers'), to slice him to pieces. But each time his blood touched the ground, he cloned himself and grew even stronger. At last Durga became so angry that Kali exploded from her forehead and dealt with the demon by gulping his blood before it could reach the ground, draining him dry and then licking up his surviving clones like ants. Unfortunately, she became so drunk on all the blood that she began dancing Shiva's cosmic dance of destruction, and knocked Shiva himself down when he tried to stop her. Ever afterwards the gods have been wary of her, and have kept her under control by prayers and sacrifice.

Kali is shown in art as the embodiment of horror. She is hideous, withered, with matt-black flesh, fangs, a fire-tongue and halo of flames and a necklace of skulls. Her four arms carry a noose, a skull-headed club, a sword and a severed head. She wears a tiger-skin, and her eyes (including in some images a third eye like Shiva's) are blood-shot and glaring. She was the patron god-dess of the Thagna (Thuggee) sect, who picked strangers and killed them in her honour, originally by spilling their blood on her altar to waken her, but later by garrotting. The Thagna was a secret so-ciety, a mystery cult, and one of the most frightening things about it, to non-devotees, was that its members were unknown and seemed like ordinary members of society, just as a person can often mask all-consum-ing rage by pretending to be perfectly normal.

≫→ **Great Goddess**

KALIYA
India

Kaliya, in Hindu myth, was a five-headed **snake-demon** who lived in the depths of the Yamuna river. One day the child **Krishna** was swimming in the river when Kaliya and his followers swarmed round him, trying to pull him under-water and drown him. Unperturbed, Krishna jumped on to Kaliya's middle head and began dancing, until the snake-king was so cowed that he agreed not only to release the young god, but to swim downstream with all his followers and settle in the sea, leaving the Yamuna pure and clean forever.

KALKI
India

Kalki or Kalkin, in Hindu myth, is the tenth avatar of **Vishnu**. At the end of this cycle of the universe – a moment which is imminent but still in the future – the world will have become totally degenerate. The process will have be-gun as worship of the gods lapses, rulers govern with cruelty and venality instead of compassion and honour, greed and sensuality replace modera-tion. It will culminate in a society where human beings live in pitch darkness, on all fours like animals, wear bark and tear each other to pieces. At this point Kalki, radiant as the **Sun**, will gallop through the world with his sword glittering in his hand. He will end this present cycle of existence, purifying the universe so that **creation** can begin anew.

Kalki is both a horse-god and a Sun-god, and his representations in art reflect this. He is often shown as a warrior, wielding the sun-sword and a sun-disk shield, and pre-paring to mount or galloping on a white wind-horse. Sometimes he has four arms, and carries a sword, conch-shell, wheel of fate and arrow or club. Or he is himself a white horse, radiating sun-shafts like ar-rows; or he is a **giant***, human from the neck down, horse-headed and with four arms sprouting from his elbows.*

≫→ **light and dark**

KALMA
Europe (North)

Kalma ('corpse-stink'), in Finnish myth, was the goddess of **Death** and decay. In the Upper World she haunted graves, snatching the flesh of the dead; in **Tuonela**, the **Underworld**, she lived in an invisible country guarded by the flesh-eating monster **Surma**. No one ever saw her: she made her presence felt in smell alone, and turned the bodies of her victims from visible flesh and bone to a breath of corruption which hovered briefly above the grave before vanishing forever.

KALUMBA
Africa

Kalumba the creator, in the myths of the Lumba people of Zaïre, built a single road from **Heaven** to Earth, and set Dog and Goat to guard it. Their instructions were to watch for two travellers in particular, **Death** and Life: Life was to be let through but Death turned back. Unfortunately, Kalumba also divided the attributes of watchmen between the two road-guards: Dog had intelligence and Goat had strength. As they sat on guard, Dog grew bored and wandered off – and while he was gone, Death disguised himself as a bundle of dirty clothes tied to a pole, and had his servants carry him safely past Goat. Soon afterwards, Life strolled down the road, only to have Goat jump on her and hold her until Dog ran up and told him his mistake. There was nothing Kalumba could do to recall Death. He closed the road, taking Life back into Heaven and leaving Death to stalk the Earth. As for Dog and Goat, they were never allowed back into Heaven.

KALVAITIS
Europe (East)

Kalvaitis, in Lithuanian myth, was the blacksmith-god who each day remade the Sun-disc, sending it red-hot across the sky. He made golden belts and stirrups for the Sun god and his sons, and a wedding-ring for Sun's consort Dawn.
➨ **smiths**

KAMA
India

Kama ('desire'), in Hindu myth, was the god of erotic desire. Originally, he was a winged archer, flying everywhere in **Heaven**, Earth and Middle Air shooting arrows of passion at gods, mortals and all other living beings. But once, finding that **Shiva** was neglecting his wife **Parvati**, Kama fired at him – and before the arrow reached its target Shiva charred it and Kama to ash with a single glance from his third eye. Kama's wife **Rati** begged Shiva to restore him, and Shiva, won over by her beauty, agreed. But from then on Kama was allowed no physical form, and lived as a bodiless idea only: the flash of desire which passes between a pair of lovers.
➨ **sex**

KAMADHENU
India

Kamadhenu, in Hindu myth, was the cow of plenty. In some accounts, she was the daughter of the Sun-goddess **Rohini**, in others she was the first creature formed from the churning of the Sea of Milk (see **amrita**). She symbolized and supervised the **fertility** of **creation**.
➨ **bulls and cows; Hathor**

KAMAPUA'A
Oceania

Kamapua'a ('pig-child'), in Hawaiian myth, was a **shape-changer**, able to appear as plant, fish, rock, human or pig (the shape he favoured). At the beginning of **creation** he rooted up the Earth from the mud at the bottom of the primordial ocean, and then worried it with his snout and hooves, producing mountains, lakes and rivers. Ever eager for **sex**, he pursued goddesses and human women. The humans produced hoggish offspring, the goddesses usually escaped. But when Pele the **fire**-goddess refused to have anything to do with Kamapua'a, he sent an army of pigs to trample out her flames. In the nick of time, before fire disappeared from the world forever, the gods intervened, leaving human beings their cooking fires and sending Pele to live in the hills (volcanoes) and Kamapua'a in the lowlands. The two gods lived apart thereafter, but met occasionally for quarrelsome, violent sex which caused **earthquakes** throughout the Hawaiian islands.

Mythographers explain Kamapua'a as a water-god, saying that this explains his endlessly-changing shape, his creation of streams and lakes and the antagonism between him and Pele. They also draw parallels with Vishnu, who as a boar heaved the Earth from primordial mud. But the original stories give no hint either of philosophical explanations or of links with India; Kamapua'a is a simple trickster, hoggishness incarnate, and his exploits need no other rationale.

KAMARONG: *see* Jari and Kamarong

KANANESKI ANAYEHI
Americas (North)

Kananeski Anayehi ('water-spider'), in the myths of the Cherokee people of the Southeastern US, lived in the time before warmth came to the world.

Everything in creation cowered in the grip of frost and **rain**. Then the **thunder**-spirits sent **lightning** to kindle fire deep among the roots of a sycamore tree. The fire glowed underground, but the roots were too close-packed and tangled for any creature to pull it to the surface. Kananeski Anayehi wove a basket and attached it to her back with sticky thread. Then she spun a line of silk down through a reed-hole in the earth to the roots of the sycamore, gathered fire in the basket and brought it to the surface. Ever afterwards, her descendants have carried magic fire on their backs, in the form of streaks of reddish-orange hairs.
➤➤ **animal-gods**

KANASSA
Americas (South)

Kanassa, in the myths of the Kuikuru people of the Xingu river in Brazil, created the world and brought light to warm it by catching the vulture-god (who hoarded it in **Heaven**) and refusing to free him until he delivered blazing branches from his store: the **Sun** and **Moon**.
➤➤ **Kuat and Iae**

KANATI
Americas (North)

Kanati, the Lucky Hunter of Cherokee mythology, was the husband of Grandmother Corn (Selu), and the father of Wild Boy.

KANSA
India

Kansa (or Kamsa), in Hindu myth, was the **demon** king of Mathura. In some myths he was the son of **Kasyapa**, creator of all living creatures; in others he was a personification of the wheel of fate. In the best-known story of all he was the son of Queen **Pavanarekha** of Mathura, after she was raped by a demon in a forest. Pavanarekha pretended that he was the child of her husband **Ugrasena** – and when Kansa grew up he dethroned Ugrasena and murdered him. He then began a reign of such atrocity that **Mother Earth** herself begged the gods to put an end to it. **Vishnu** made plans to descend to Earth as **Krishna**, to kill Kansa and restore **justice and universal order**.

Kansa, warned that Krishna would one day murder him, tried every way to kill him first. He locked Krishna's future parents **Devaki** and **Vasudeva** in a cell to stop the child ever being born; he sent demons to tear the toddler to pieces; he laid traps for the young man, and commissioned more demons to finish him. Finally he invited Krishna to a palace festival in honour of **Shiva**, and arranged for demons – a wild elephant, a thousand thousand guards and a company of wrestlers – to attack him on the way. Krishna finished them all, bent the bow of Shiva so hard that he broke it, and then, with the help of his half-brother **Balarama**, fought Kansa and his eight demon-brothers and killed them all.

In some accounts, Kansa is mistakenly confused with another demon-prince, **Kalanemi**.

KAPOONIS: *see* Enumclaw and Kapoonis

KAPPA
Asia (East)

Kappa, in Japanese myth, were water-**demons**. When they appeared to mortals they took the form of human beings with round faces and bowl-shaped depressions on top of their heads. These depressions were filled with water, and if the *kappa* succeeded in picking you up it immediately grew huge, changed into its normal appearance – green skin, webbed feet and hands, turtle-shell – drowned you in the water, then made itself small enough to crawl up your anus and eat your intestines. Anyone who reacted with terror to *kappa* or challenged them was doomed. But there were two ways to disarm them. One was to throw cucumbers into the nearest open water, in which case they dived after them and left you in peace. The other was to bow politely, in which case they bowed back, the water gushed out of their heads, and they lost their power. When this happened, they fawned on you, trying to teach you the only other skills they knew, how to duel with a sword and how to set broken bones – but you still had to be wary if you were anywhere near a pond or river, in case they ducked under the surface, refilled their head-cavities and pounced on you.

KARTTIKEYA
India

Karttikeya (or Skanda, 'attacker'), in Hindu myth, was the god of armies rushing into battle. He had six heads, and was **Shiva**'s fierceness personified. There are various accounts of his birth. He was formed from the mind of **Brahma**, or he was the son of the six **Pleiades**, or he was born when **Shiva** masturbated and semen first spattered the **fire**-god **Agni** and then fell, blazing, into the primordial ocean. In the best-known myth of all, he was one of six sons born from sparks that fell from Shiva's eyes when the god grew six heads to roar at demons who had attacked the gods. Shiva's wife **Parvati** thought the babies adorable, gathered them into her arms and hugged them so hard that they became a single, six-headed child.

*In some accounts, when Karttikeya grew up he married Sena, the personification of an army's power as it marches, or took as his consort Kaumari, the corpse-garlanded crone who was one of the most hideous forms of **Kali**. He is usually shown as a six-headed warrior riding a peacock at the head of countless followers.*

KASOGONAGA
Americas (South)

Kasogonaga, in the myths of the Chaco people, was the **rain**-goddess. In the sky she took the form of a woman, and made rain by urinating. But in her dealings with humans she took the form of an ant-eater – beginning with the first occasion of all, when humans were created not as distinct sexes but as a single androgynous lump, and Kasogonaga used her ant-eater's claws to separate men from women.
≫→ **animal-gods, creation**

KASYAPA
India

Kasyapa, in one Hindu **creation**-myth, was the husband of **Daksha**'s thirteen

daughters (the lunar months), and by them the father of every living creature on Earth, warm-blooded or cold-blooded. His well-behaved children included birds and animals; his badly-behaved children included reptiles, insects and **demons**. His human children were sometimes good, sometimes bad – which accounts for the way the human race squabbles to this day. His other children (by his wife **Diti**) included the **giant Daityas**, the demons **Hiranyaksha** and **Hiranyakashipu**, and the 49 **Maturs**, originally intended to be a single hero who would murder **Indra** himself.

The Sanskrit word Kasyapa means 'tortoise', and paintings and sculpture often show Kasyapa as the primordial tortoise, from which all things were born as an inexhaustible clutch of eggs. Poetry uses a more elegant image. Kasyapa is time, creeping tortoise-like across the sky – but he is like a tortoise, as sure as he is slow.

KATONDA
Africa

Katonda ('creator'), in Ugandan myth, established an enormous bureaucracy to run the universe. He himself was all-father, king and judge, and lived in state, rejoicing in such titles as Gguludene ('biggest'), Kagingo ('life-master'), Lugaba ('giver') and Namuginga ('shaper'). When mortals died, he ranked their spirits according to merit, giving them positions as arbiters, councillors, prophets, slaves or warriors. The two principal spirits, Kalumba's deputies, were Kibuka (war) and Walumbe (death), and a rabble of unallocated spirits, too unimportant or evil to be given ranks, swarmed in Other World as ordinary people did in This World. Spirits of rank were allowed to pass from Other World to This World, where they took the form of animals and were well treated by humans; the unranked spirits, by contrast, were barred from This World, and mortals had to keep ceaseless watch, and carry out endless rituals, to stop them infiltrating. Having established the hierarchy, Katonda left his subordinates to administer the universe, and spent his time in contemplation of his own magnificence, passing judgement only in particularly interesting or difficult cases.

»»+ creation, supreme deity

KAURAVAS
India

The Kauravas, in Hindu myth, were **heroes**, the hundred sons of the blind King **Dhritarashtra**. (They were called Kauravas after a distant ancestor, Kuru.) Their father Dhritarashtra was the elder of two half-brothers, and it would have seemed logical for his sons to take precedence in inheriting the kingdom. But the children nominally of his half-brother **Pandu**, the five **Pandavas**, were in fact all sons of gods, and so outranked the Kauravas. The cousins were all brought up together, and wrangled – at first amicably, but with ever greater savagery as the issue of succession became more prominent. Finally their rivalry broke out in the epic war recounted in the *Mahabharata*, in which the forces for good in the universe took the Pandavas' side and the forces of darkness favoured the Kauravas.

KAUSALYA
India

Kausalya, in Hindu myth, was the senior wife of King **Dasaratha**. She drank one third of the *soma* provided by **Vishnu** in answer to Dasaratha's prayer for sons, and the son she conceived, **Rama**, possessed one half of the god's attributes, powers and nature.

KAVA
Oceania

Kava, throughout Oceania, is a fermented drink made from the roots of the *kava* plant (a species of pepper). In early times it was prepared by women who chewed the roots to soften them, then added water; after Europeans arrived in Oceania, it was made by pounding the roots. It was drunk with sugarcane as a relish.

Myths of the origin of *kava* all concern cannibalism. The god Loau was visiting mortals incognito, and went to stay with a couple called Fevanga and Fefafa. Having no food to offer him – some accounts say because of famine, others because of poverty – they cooked and served their own child. They buried her head in the vegetable-patch, and Loau (who knew very well what had happened) blessed it so that it grew into the *kava* plant. Every time *kava* is prepared and drunk, the child is remembered and so lives on.

KERYNEIAN HIND
Europe (South)

The Keryneian Hind, in Greek myth, was a deer, sacred to **Artemis**, which lived on Mount Keryneia in Arcadia. Its golden antlers made many hunters mistake it for a stag, and its bronze hooves allowed it to outrun any living thing. **Heracles**, for his third **Labour**, was sent to catch it and take it back to Mycenae. He could easily have shot it to slow it down, but his orders were to carry it back unharmed. He tracked it for a year, across the world from the Garden of the **Hesperides** in the South to the land of the Hyperboreans in the North. At last, thinking him far behind, the deer lay down to rest – and Heracles caught it, tied its legs and carried it to Mycenae slung across his shoulders as shepherds carry lambs. He showed it to **Eurystheus** (who had ordered him to catch it), then set it free to run back to her mistress Artemis.

This simple myth gave rise to some of the most beautiful of all ancient painting and sculpture. Vase-paintings show the deer delicately browsing on the leaves of the golden-apple trees of the Hesperides, and one of the commonest cult-statuettes of Heracles, found in hundreds throughout the Greek world, shows him carrying the deer slung round his shoulders – a contrast between grace and strength which greatly appealed to artists in ancient Greece, and an image later adopted by Christian artists showing Christ as the Good Shepherd carrying a lamb.

KHEPRI
Africa (North)

Khepri ('he who is coming into being'), in Egyptian myth, was an early creator-god who took the form of a scarab (dung-beetle, *scarab* is a Greek derivative of

'Khepri') and made the world by rolling a ball of his own spittle, or semen. In later myth, Khepri was identified with **Ra** the Sun, renamed Khepra, and imagined as the god in the morning, taking the form of a dung-beetle to roll the Sun-ball up across the sky.
≫→ **animal-gods**

KHNUM
Africa (North)

Khnum, in Egyptian myth, was one of the oldest of all creator-gods, worshipped at Esna on the island of Elephantine. He moulded gods and mortals on a potter's wheel, and then gave them the breath of life. He took the form of a ram, or a ram-headed human, and controlled the rising and falling of the river Nile, starting and ending the annual flood by opening and closing sluices in **Hapy**'s underwater palace. He and his frog-wife **Heqet** seldom visited **Heaven** or spent time with the gods of light, but in their palace on Elephantine they often gave feasts for gods and goddesses from Lower Egypt and Nubia. One of their most frequent guests was the hunting-goddess, **Neit**.
≫→ **crafts, creation**

KHONSU
Africa (North)

Khonsu ('wanderer'), or Khensu or Khens, the Moon-god in Egyptian myth, was in some accounts the son of **Amun** and **Mut**, in others of **Hathor** and the crocodile-god Sobek, in one account he was said to have grown spontaneously from one of **Osiris'** legs after **Set** dismembered the god. Just as the Moon waxes and wanes in the sky, he grew from infant to adult during the first half of each month, and then aged in the second half from adult to infant. He oversaw human lives, making sure that they lived the full span allotted to them in the **Underworld** before each reincarnation.

Khonsu's name at first arose because of the **Moon**'s journey across the sky each night. But he was also regarded as a healer, and people believed that he could pour his power (in shafts of moonlight) into the statue in his temple in Thebes (modern Luxor), and then send it travelling to sick people's bedsides. In one story, the statue took seventeen months to reach the bedside of a stricken princess, and after she was cured her father kept it for three years, until Khonsu appeared to him in a dream as a golden hawk flying free, and he decided to return it.

In Thebes Khonsu was worshipped as one of the Heavenly trinity with Amun and Mut, and an elaborate mythology – including the story of the travelling statue – was invented to glorify him. He was also said to be the pharaoh's double, a kind of shadow-king formed from the royal after-birth, just as the Moon was the shadow-double of the Sun. He was a hunter, helping the pharaoh bring down prey in the hunting-field and enemies in battle.

➤ **disease and healing**

KHONVUM
Africa

Khonvum, in the myths of the Pygmy peoples of East Africa, created the world and its creatures, then peopled it by lowering humans – Pygmies – from the sky on ropes. Having done so, he left **creation** to its own purposes, merely ensuring its survival by gathering star-fragments and hurling them at the Sun each morning to wake it up.

➤ **creation**

KILYA
Americas (South)

Kilya, in Inca myth, was the **Moon**, wife of the **Sun**. She was originally more dazzling than he was, but he darkened her face with ashes, the marks of which can still be seen.

KINTU AND NAMBI
Africa

Kintu and Nambi, in the myths of the Baganda people of Uganda, were the first people in the world. In the beginning, Nambi lived in **Heaven** with her father Gulu the **sky**-god and her brothers. Kintu lived alone on Earth, except for a magic cow which provided all he needed. When Kintu asked to marry Nambi, Gulu set him a test: he stole the cow and hid it in his own heavenly herd. For a time Kintu lived uncomplainingly on leaves instead of milk, then Nambi told him that his cow was in Heaven, and he set off to the sky to find it. Gulu set him four more tests. In the first, he was put in a hut containing enough food for a hundred people, and told to empty it by morning. He ate what he could, then dug holes in the floor and dropped the rest of the food to Earth (where it filled land and sea with goodness), and called Gulu's servants to take away the empty bowls.

In the second test, Gulu told him to split rocks for firewood, giving him no tools but an axe of soft copper – and Kintu hammered wooden wedges into cracks and wet them until they expanded and broke the rock. In the third test, he was told to fill a bottomless water-pot with dew – and he did this by leaving the pot in the midst of the clouds, which filled it and clung to its sides and lid. In the final test, he was told to pick out his cow from Gulu's herd, identical cattle stretching as far as the horizon. Nambi herself helped in this. She told Gulu to drive his cattle past Kintu, then disguised herself as a bee and whispered to Kintu that he should choose the animals whose horns she settled on – not just Kintu's own cow, but the three calves born to her while she was in Heaven.

So Kintu passed all the tests, and set off down to Earth with his new wife and their cattle. Unfortunately for them, Gulu had asked permission for the marriage from all his sons save one, **Death**. He warned Kintu to walk straight down to Earth without returning, but Kintu ignored him, hurrying back to Heaven for some corn-meal for his chickens. Death saw him for the first time, chased him back down to Earth – and has made war on Kintu's and Nambi's descendants ever since.

KIPU-TYTTÖ
Europe (North)

Kipu-Tyttö, in Finnish myth, was the goddess of illness. She lived in **Tuonela**, the **Underworld**, in the palace of her father **Tuoni** and mother **Tuonetar**, and sang songs so evilly seductive that

mortals who heard them longed to visit the Underworld and live with her.
»» disease and healing

KITSHI MANITO
Americas (North)

Kitshi Manito ('master of life' or 'great mystery') was the name given in the myths of many Algonquian peoples of the Great Lakes and Northeastern US to the universal sky-spirit, lord of **Heaven** and creator of the universe. In some accounts the universe was his teepee, centred on his staff of power, the **Sun** was its hearthfire and it sheltered all creatures from the dark void of space outside. In others, Kitshi Manito wandered the primordial ocean before **creation**, smoking his pipe and looking for somewhere to make the world. Finding none, he asked Duck and Terrapin to help. They dived to the depths and brought back lumps of mud which Kitshi Manito dried on the bowl of his pipe, set floating on the ocean and covered with plants, trees and animals. He made humans from mud-blobs and left them running about the new land like ants.

Kitshi Manito is called Gitchee Manitou in Longfellow's Hiawatha – an immensely appealing deity to Longfellow's Christian readers, since he seemed to equate with their own One God. Manito, however, simply means 'spirit', and the Algonquian Indians believed that everything in existence had its own manito: every stone, grass-blade, breath of wind, plant, animal, lake, mountain or other natural feature. Kitshi Manito was the most important of these spirits, symbolizing abstract creative energy – but he was one spirit among many, first among equals and by no means unique.

KLOSKURBEH
Americas (North)

Kloskurbeh ('all-maker'), in the myths of the Hopi people of the Southwestern US Pueblos, lived alone on **Mother Earth** at the beginning of time. But then his wind-breath made a shape from sea-foam, the **Sun** warmed the shape into life and Youth was born. Kloskurbeh and Youth made plants, animals, insects – everything on Earth except human beings. Then one day, Kloskurbeh's eye watered, a drop fell into a leaf, Sun warmed it, and Love was born. Youth and Love mated to become First Father and First Mother of the human race, and Kloskurbeh, Grandfather, taught the new people the skills and arts of life.

As soon as Kloskurbeh's teaching was done, the myth ends, he withdrew from **creation** *to the far North of the universe. There he waits, benign and attentive, and when his people most need him he will come South once again to advise them.*
≫→ **civilization, creation**

KODOYANPE
Americas (North)

Kodoyanpe, the **Sun**, in the myths of the Western US coast, worked with **Coyote** to create the world. They then set about making human beings to enjoy it, whittling them from pieces of wood. But the dolls were spoiled each time, and Kodoyanpe and Coyote made them into animals instead. After a while

Kodoyanpe began to suspect that Coyote didn't want humans to be created, and was making his knife slip each time. The two spirits began arguing, and Coyote went off to fetch an army of **demons** to wipe Kodoyanpe out for good and all. Unfortunately for him, while he was away Kodoyanpe fathered a sky-warrior, All-Conqueror, Son of the Sun, and Coyote's demons ran back to their holes and were never seen in daylight again. Kodoyanpe now dug in the ground, took a cache of whittled dolls he'd hidden earlier, and breathed life into them to make the human race.

For reasons no anthropologist has yet explained, the same myth is told by the Chinook people, but with the names changed round to make Coyote the spirit of Light and Kodoyanpe lord of Dark.
≫→ **creation**

KOJIN
Asia (East)

Kojin, in Japanese myth, was a child-eating **demon** converted to become their protector. Before her change of heart, she used her thousands of arms to snatch them and crush them; afterwards, she cradled them. She lived in the celestial *enoki* tree, and humans honoured her by leaving dolls in the branches and at the feet of *enoki* trees on Earth.
≫→ **childbirth and infant care**

KOKO
Americas (North)

Koko, in the myths of the Zuni Indians of the Southwestern US, were ancestral spirits whose task was to ensure rain.

KOKYANGWUTI
Americas (North)

Kokyangwuti or Kahyangwuti ('spider woman'), in the myths of the Hopi people of the Southwestern US Pueblos, was the daughter of Sotuknang the First Power and grand-daughter of Taiowa the Creator. The first task they gave her, in the bowels of the First World, was to create the human race. She mixed dust with spittle and sang a **creation**-spell to give it life. So human beings were born. For a long time they lived in the First World in a Golden Age, but after a while their humble origins made them give way to lust and crime, and Sotuknang decided to wipe them out by flooding the whole First World. As the waters rose, Kokyangwuti showed the people the only way to safety: climbing a reed which led from the First World to the surface of **Mother Earth**.

As the people emerged into daylight, Mockingbird gave each of them a name and an identity. The first-comers mounted horses and galloped off East to find the source of the **Sun**: the wind of their passing kept their skins white and pock-marked. The next-comers stayed where they were, under the heat of the noonday Sun – and its rays burned their skins brown. By the time the last-comers were struggling up the reed, Mockingbird had run out of names. Exhausted, he flew away – and the Nameless Ones fell back down the hole into the flood, and lived there in soggy misery ever afterwards.

Kokyangwuti looked at her puny humans and decided to help them once more. She mixed dust and spittle, sang a creation-spell and made **twin** heroes,

Poquanghoya and Palongwhoya. Their tasks were to fight **demons** and act as protectors of humankind.

After this grand beginning, the myth degenerates into folk-tale. Once humans were established, Kokyangwuti spun herself a web on the highest of two needle-thin mountains, Spider Rock. Talking God made a home on the next tallest mountain, and from there spied on human children. He told Kokyangwuti who was well-behaved and who was naughty, and there was always a danger that Kokyangwuti would swoop down in the night, bundle bad children in her sticky threads and carry them off to the heart of her web to eat them.
≫+ **animal-gods, floods**

KOMOKWA
Americas (North)

Komokwa the **sea**-god, in the myths of the Kwakiutl and Haida people of the Northwestern coast (Canada), lived in a vast underwater palace whose roof was supported by sealions. He took no part in the life of the universe: his existence was devoted entirely to his own pleasure, and he spent his days and nights feasting (on whales) with his followers, or riding out across the land in what mortals took to be tidal waves and violent storms.

KONONATOO
Americas (South)

Kononatoo ('our maker'), in the myths of the Warau people of Guiana, created human beings but kept them as slaves in **Heaven**. Hearing rumours from the birds about a beautiful, lush land below the clouds, one enterprising human,

Okonorote, dug a hole in the floor of Heaven and let the human race down on ropes to Earth. They used the fattest woman in existence as a kind of anchor, holding the rope at the top – and when she tried to squeeze through, last of all, she stuck and blocked the hole. The humans tried to persuade Kononatoo to dig another hole and let them back into Heaven, but in the meantime the human females had discovered the pleasures of **sex** down on Earth, and Kononatoo, disgusted, refused to let them or their species ever rejoin the gods.

>>+ creation

KOTOAMATSUKAMI
Asia (East)

Kotoamatsukami ('the separate heavenly deities') in Japanese myth, were the first five powers which came spontaneously into existence at the **creation** of the universe. They were **Sky** (Amenominakanushi), two gods of the generative power in Nature (Takamimusubi, 'high producer', and Kamimusubi, 'divine producer'), Reed (**Umashiashikabihikoji**), from whom the next generation of gods was born, and **Heaven** (Amenotokotachi, 'eternal high-stander').

KREMARA: *see* Priparchis and Kremara

KRISHNA
India

Krishna's birth. Krishna ('black') was the eighth avatar (earthly form) of **Vishnu**. He went into the world to kill the **demon**-king **Kansa**, who had outlawed Vishnu-worship and upset the universal balance between good and evil. Kansa's cousin **Vasudeva** had married a seventh wife, **Devaki**, and Kansa had been warned that their son would grow up to kill him. So each time one of their children was born, he killed it. This happened six times. The seventh child, **Balarama**, was magical, created from a white hair from the world-serpent **Shesha**, and was transferred at the last moment from Devaki's womb to that of **Rohini**, another of Vasudeva's wives. After Balarama's birth Kansa locked Vasudeva and Devaki in a dungeon, chained and guarded by soldiers, dogs, lions and elephants. Vishnu, however, took a black hair from his own body and placed it in Devaki's womb, and in due course it was born as Krishna.

As soon as Krishna was born, he spoke to his parents in the form of Vishnu. Vasudeva was to take him from the prison and substitute him for the child of his friend **Nanda** and Nanda's wife **Yasoda**. The chains fell off, the guardians slept and the doors swung open. Vasudeva did as the god ordered – and on the way Krishna helped him to ford the swollen river Jumna, pressing the waters down with one small foot. Vasudeva left him with Yasoda, and brought her newborn daughter back to the prison, where the doors locked, the guards woke up and the chains refastened of their own accord. Knowing nothing of the substitution, Kansa assumed that the child was Devaki's and tried to kill it by dashing it against the wall. But the baby soared into the sky, told Kansa that Krishna was still alive and would kill him, and then passed into heaven as the goddess **Deva**.

Krishna's childhood. Nanda and Yasoda brought Krishna up as their own son. Their people were cowherds and milkmaids, and Krishna played endless pranks on them, upsetting milking-pails, stealing curds and butter, knocking pots from shelves, waylaying the milkmaids on their way to market and demanding kisses to let them pass. He told the cowherds that they were fools to worship **Indra** the rain-god – and when Indra sent a rainstorm to drown them Krishna uprooted Mount Govardhana and balanced it on one finger, using it as an umbrella for seven days and seven nights.

The child Krishna also had **demons** to fight: for Kansa, determined that no child of Devaki's would live to kill him, sent minions to murder every infant and toddler in the kingdom. **Putana** disguised herself as a wet-nurse, smeared her nipples with poison and went to suckle the infant Krishna – but he sucked all the human essence out of her and turned her back into a screeching, baffled demon. **Saktasura** landed on a farm cart under which the toddler was lying – and was himself crushed to death when Krishna kicked cart and contents clear over on top of him. The whirlwind-demon **Trinavarta** snatched Krishna up from Yasoda's arms – and Krishna dashed him to a whisper of breezes against a rock. The **snake**-demon **Ugrasura** swallowed Krishna alive – and Krishna grew to god-size inside him and burst him apart. Another snake-demon, **Kaliya**, was outwitted when the boy Krishna emulated **Shiva** and danced on his serpent-heads.

'**Krishna stealer of hearts**'. As Krishna grew up, he began to steal the heart of every milkmaid in the kingdom. In the cool evening, he played his flute in the woods and water-meadows, and they ran to dance with him. Once, he found a group of girls bathing in the river, stole their clothes and refused to return them until they came out of the water, one by one, and worshipped him. Finding it impossible to dance with all the girls who were in love with him, he multiplied himself ten thousandfold, so that each girl thought that he was dancing with her, holding her, enrapturing her alone. But in the end Hari Krishna ('Krishna stealer of hearts') found pleasure in one girl above all others, **Radha**. One soft summer evening he slipped away with her into a garden by the river, and they played amorous games while birds sang and flowers breathed perfume to bless their love.

Krishna the warrior. Kansa, still determined to kill Krishna before Krishna killed him, sent demons to finish him, but Krishna outwitted them all. Kansa invited Krishna to a festival, and set demons on the path to waylay him. Once again, Krishna killed them all, including a wild elephant on guard at the city gates, whose tusks he took as spears. Everyone flocked to honour him, and he proved his power by accepting the challenge to bend the great bow of Shiva, pulling it so hard that it shattered in his hand. He routed Kansa's guards, and finally he and his brother Balarama faced Kansa and his eight demon-brothers, and killed them all.

Kansa's death led to a cosmic struggle against demons of every kind, as Krishna and the forces of light battled to restore universal harmony. In particular, he fought demons who opposed each of his marriages – and as he married 16,108 wives, this was a never-ending chore. Each wife bore him ten sons and one daughter, all were children of light, and between them they guaranteed peace and goodness in the universe. Krishna also took part in a huge human struggle, between the **Pandavas** and their cousins and enemies the **Kauravas**. Krishna acted as chariot-driver to the Pandava prince **Arjuna**, helping him not by supernatural intervention – the war had to be won by mortals alone – but by wise advice.

Krishna's death. A group of boys dressed Krishna's son **Samba** as a pregnant girl, and he began taunting a group of Brahmins, asking which of them was the father. The angry Brahmins laid a curse on him, saying that he would give birth to an iron club which would kill his father and destroy his people. In due course Samba's belly split open and the club was born. Although it was immediately broken up and thrown into the sea, it survived. Some of it grew into reeds, sharp as spears, and another fragment was swallowed by a fish and later found and made into an arrow-head.

The gods sent portents, warning Krishna's people of imminent destruction. They went on a panic-stricken pilgrimage to avert disaster, but on the way fell into a drunken fight by the seashore, pulled up spear-sharp reeds and killed each other. Krishna himself was sitting under a fig-tree, in lotus position, meditating. His left heel pointed outwards – the only part of him which was mortal and vulnerable. A passing hunter shot at a deer, missed, and hit Krishna's ankle with an arrow tipped by the iron point made from the fragment of Samba's club. So Krishna returned to **Heaven** and was reabsorbed into Vishnu's radiance.

For many believers, Krishna is the supreme god, for others the one God. He is the object of bhakti worship: relinquishment of the self in unity with God. His innocent, pastoral side is celebrated in pictures showing him as a butter-stealing child or a shepherd playing the flute. His skin is sometimes black, but more usually a serene, dark blue, pellucid as the sky. For centuries, favourite scenes have been his stealing the milkmaids' clothes and his dancing and dalliance with them in the forest. His love for Radha has inspired many fine paintings, usually showing the couple in intimate conversation on a carpet of banana leaves by a stream, while birds sing among the trees and flowers of all kinds blossom around them. Their love is also celebrated in literature, particularly in the Gitagovinda, a serene erotic poem. Other pictures show Krishna enthralling all creation with his flute-playing, or being shot by the lotus-blossom arrows of the love-god Kama.

*Krishna's warlike aspect is celebrated in a range of paintings and – especially – sculptures, showing him as a boy fighting demons, or as an adult warrior driving Arjuna's chariot. His adventures are told in the Puranas, a collection of myths and other writings from Vedic times, and in the **Mahabharata** he features as Arjuna's charioteer. The Bhagavad Gita ('Song of the Blessed Lord') from the Mahabharata contains a long conversation between Krishna and Arjuna. Arjuna is reluctant to fight,* *since friends and enemies alike will be killed for no good reason, Krishna tells him that fighting, death and honour are illusions, and that human beings should do their duty without question, leaving philosophy to the gods.*

≫→ **Apollo, beauty, Hermes, justice and universal order**

KUA FU
Asia (East)

Kua Fu, in Chinese myth, was a primordial **giant**. Determined to catch the **Sun** and so stop it disappearing each evening, he lay in wait one morning, then chased it all day across the whole of China. He was just about to snatch it when he was overcome by thirst, and retraced his steps, draining streams, lakes and even the Yangtze and Yellow Rivers to soothe himself. At last, as the Sun sank below the horizon, he hurled his stick at it and fell into exhausted sleep – and when the Sun returned next morning he had turned into a **mountain**, Mount Chiyu in Shan Xi province, and his stick had grown into a tree on which hung the first crop of the Peaches of **Immortality**, food of the gods.

KUAT AND IAE
Americas (South)

Kuat and Iae, in the myths of the Mamaiuran people of the Xingu river in Brazil, were **twins**. Like all other beings of the primeval universe, they lived in total darkness, and the reason was that Urubutsin, vulture-king of the birds, possessed all light and jealously hoarded it. Kuat and Iae sent Urubutsin a present: a rotting carcass crawling with maggots. Urubutsin feasted on the maggots and asked for more. This time Kuat and Iae hid themselves inside the carcass, and instead of sending it to Urubutsin left it lying on the river-bank. When Urubutsin flapped down to feast, they grabbed him and refused to release him until he gave them light. Urubutsin, after struggling until all his head-feathers were torn out and he was shamed and naked, finally agreed to give them half his store. Kuat and Iae tossed it into the sky in handfuls, and soared up after it. Kuat made his home on the largest piece of light, the **Sun**, and Iae chose the **Moon**. Their power still keeps Urubutsin's darkness at bay, at least for half of each day. But as each month progresses, the brothers grow sleepy as they sit on guard, and darkness begins seeping and bleeding into light. It is only when they start awake that it retreats, and the Earth basks in its full share of light.

≫→ **light and dark**

KUBERA
India

Kubera (or Kuvera), in Hindu myth, was that rare thing, a peaceable **demon**-king. He was dethroned and exiled by his half-brother **Ravana**, who built himself a stronghold on the island of Sri Lanka and tried to win himself a queen by kidnapping **Sita**, **Rama**'s wife. When Rama made war on Ravana, Kubera sided with him – and when the war was won Rama rewarded him by making him shepherd of all the precious stones in the world. The stones had minds of their own, and wandered freely in the space between the mortal world and the **Underworld**, passing as easily through rock and earth as humans do through air. Kubera watched over them, and sometimes let a few of them visit the mortal world for a while – where some spent their holiday giving pleasure, and others spent it causing arguments and wars.

Because Kubera was a demon, artists showed him as hideous: a pot-bellied, three-legged, one-eyed dwarf with eight snaggle-teeth. But because he was lord of wealth, they coloured him gold, and studded his skin with gems. (Statues were made of real jewels, real gold.) Kubera's palace, a building all of precious stones set in beautiful gardens, is described in the Ramayana (in which accounts of his service to Rama also appear), and is the subject of many delicate paintings.

KUI
Asia (East)

Kui, in Chinese myth, was the god who brought success in examinations. Originally he was a mortal youth who combined vast intelligence with a face so hideous that although he came top in the civil service exams, the Emperor refused to employ him and he committed suicide. The gods set him in the sky as a star, overseeing all examination candidates.

Kui is one of the stars in the Big Dipper, and Kui was regarded as one of the servants of Bei Dou Xing, goddess of that constellation. He was also identified as the Chinese letter Kui, which looks like a manic stick-person – and this dominated his representation in art. Good wishes for examinations were and still are exchanged in

the form of Kui cards or pendants, and the letter Kui is a common icon on brushes and inkstones. In some representations, Kui or his letter are shown next to a carp – a fish which leaps upstream from one level to another, as candidates hope to do in their exams.

KUKULKAN
Americas (Central)

Kukulkan ('feathered snake'), in Mayan myth, was an exact equivalent of the Aztec **Quetzalcóatl**: a real person taken into the pantheon and identified as god of the winds.

KUL
Europe (Northeast)

Kul, in the myths of the Siryan people, was a **monster**, half fish, half human, which lurked in the mud at the bottom of lakes, and whose progeny infested wells, poisoning the water unless they were appeased. They were susceptible to both singing and flattery, so that with praise-songs you could hardly fail.

KULLERVO
Europe (North)

Kullervo, in Finnish myth, was Kalervo's son. Kalervo was murdered by his brother Untamo, who then married his queen and sold his children into slavery – in Kullervo's case, to **Ilmarinen**'s wife, the frost-**giant** daughter of Princess **Louhi** of **Pohjola**. She taunted and tormented the boy, until one day Kullervo changed all her cattle to wolves and bears which tore her to pieces. Kullervo fled, and lived in exile for years before making his way back towards his ancestral castle. On the way, he met and had **sex** with an unknown slave-girl, only to discover that she was the sister he hadn't seen since childhood. She killed herself – and Kullervo also committed suicide, after finding his wicked uncle Untamo and mother and killing *them*.

The Kullervo story, a self-contained narrative in the manner of an Icelandic saga, is sewn into the Kalevala because Kullervo causes the death of Ilmarinen's first wife and all the events which follow it. The story inspired, or closely resembles, the medieval tale of Amleth, one of the sources for Shakespeare's Hamlet.

KUMBHAKARNA
India

Kumbhakarna ('pot-ears'), in Hindu myth, was a **demon**, one of **Ravana**'s brothers. He was a hunger-**giant**, ravenously hungry from the moment he was born. He performed a sacrifice which committed **Brahma** to granting any wish he asked. Brahma knew that he was about to ask for 'eternal life', but twisted the demon's tongue at the key moment so that Kumbhakarna actually asked for 'eternal sleep'. Ever afterwards, Kumbhakarna hibernated – in one account for six months, followed by one day of waking and eating, in another for six months, followed by six months of waking – and while he was awake he roamed the universe stocking up with food. He ate 500 *apsaras* at a single sitting, or 5000 mortal women, or enjoyed a more varied menu of 400 buffalo-cows, 6000 cows, 10,000 she-goats and 10,000 ewes – his taste was for female flesh.

When **Rama** made war on Ravana's citadel in Sri Lanka, one of Kumbhakarna's hibernation-periods had just begun. Ravana sent servants to wake his brother up. They decided to do it with the smell of food, piling outside his cave a mountain of rice garnished with buffalo cows and does. Kumbhakarna slept on. They threw rocks and trees at him, but his snores sent them flying back again. Finally they stampeded a herd of ten thousand (male) elephants through the cave, and Kumbhakarna awoke. He swallowed the rice, buffalo and does in a single gulp, washed them down with two thousand jars of wine, then stormed out to finish his dinner by eating Rama's monkey-soldiers. Rama and the monkey-general **Sugriva** dealt with him by cutting him down to size, slicing off his ears, nose and limbs and trimming his body until he was mortal-size, then cutting off his head.

KUMOKUM
Americas (North)

Kumokum, in the myths of the Modoc people of California, was the only creature in existence. He sat alone by the shores of a lake which was all there was. After a while, feeling lonely, he dived to the bottom of the lake, brought up a handful of mud, scattered it all round to make the universe, and stocked it with plants, animals and humans. When **creation** was complete, he hollowed out an underground sleeping-place, and retired from his own creation. He still sleeps there: despite all the evil and suffering in the world, it is still not time

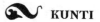

for him to come back and unmake or change creation.

KUMUSH
Americas (North)

Kumush, or Kemush, the Old Man of the Ancients in the myths of the Modoc people of California, brought human beings to Earth. Visiting the spirit-world, he watched the spirits singing and dancing all night, and was sad to see that when day came they turned into dry bones and lay inert. Determined to give them a daytime existence as well, he carried a sack of bones to the surface, scattered them across the land and sorted them into the various peoples of Earth. (The best and biggest bones made the Modoc.) Humans quickly adapted to life in the upper world, but they never forgot their cousins, left behind in the spirit-world: they always consulted them, offered them food and drink and – at the end of each life on Earth – went back to the spirit-world to join them. As for Kumush, he built himself a sky-palace with an observation-stone, on which he could sit and watch benignly as his **creation** scurried about below.

KUNApIpI
Australia

Kunapipi, or Gunapipi, in the myths of many peoples of the Northern Territory, was a **monster** who lurked in water-holes and ate boys on the brink of puberty. If she could be caught and opened up, however, she regurgitated them as adults, taller and stronger than when she swallowed them. In one story,

Yalungur caught her and thrashed her to make her release her prey. Her screams went to live in the trees round the waterhole – and it has been dangerous ever since for boys to sleep under trees, in case the screams grow jaws and swallow them. In the puberty-rituals of several peoples, boys are segregated from the rest of the group and taken away. The group chants and sings the story of Kunapipi, and at the end of the ceremony the boys return, smeared with blood as if they have just been rescued from the monster's belly.

≫→ **Julunggul**

KUNTI
India

Kunti, in Hindu myth, was the sister of **Vasudeva**, **Krishna**'s mortal father. Her birth-name was Prithi, but she called herself Kunti in honour of her first husband Kuntibhoja. She was a singer and dancer, and entertained her husband's visitors so delightfully that many gave her presents – including the sage Durvasas, who said that she would bear five children, each of them fathered by a god: all she had to do was pray, and the god would make her pregnant. Kunti tested the gift by praying for a child to the **Sun**-god **Surya** – and she was so embarrassed when a son was born that she left him secretly to die on the banks of the river Yamuna. (In fact the child was saved: a passing charioteer rescued him and brought him up as his own son, Karna.)

When Kunti's first husband died, she married King **Pandu** of **Bharata**. But he had been cursed by a sage whom he'd accidentally shot: if he ever had sex with his wife, he'd die. In order to become pregnant, therefore, Kunti was forced to invoke the gift Durvasas had long ago given her. She prayed to three gods in turn, and they gave her sons: **Dharma** gave her **Yudhishthira**, **Vayu** gave her **Bhima** and **Indra** gave her **Arjuna**. Kunti then gave the last part of her gift to Pandu's second wife **Madri**, who prayed to the **Ashvins** and bore **twins**, **Nakula** and **Sahadeva**. The five godly sons were brought up as Pandu's children, and were known as the **Pandavas**.

When war broke out between the Pandavas and their cousins the **Kauravas**, Karna (the son Kunti had left to die by the river) enlisted as charioteer for the Kauravas. He formed a particular hatred for the Pandava Arjuna, not realizing that he was his half-brother. In the last days of the war, Arjuna and Karna met in single combat, and Arjuna shot Karna dead. The heart-broken Kunti now revealed Karna's true identity, and the Pandavas realized that their victory in the war had been tainted by fratricide. They set out on a pilgrimage of atonement, and Kunti went to spend the rest of her life in exile in the woods. But the gods knew where she was, and Surya, the Sun-god and Karna's father, charred her to ash in a forest fire and scattered her remains.

KURMA
India

Kurma ('tortoise'), in one of the **creation**-myths of the Aryan people who invaded India in the seventeenth century BCE, was the world, and was formed from a cosmic egg. **Prajapati** the creator

squeezed the egg, and its contents oozed out to form a tortoise shape. The tortoise's upper shell was the **sky**, its lower shell the Earth and its hollow interior the middle air.

In Hindu myth, Kurma was the second avatar of **Vishnu**. When gods and **demons** united to churn the primordial ocean and give rise to all creation (see *amrita*), they used Mount Mandara as a pole and the serpent **Vasuki** as a rope, churning the sea as one might churn butter in a bowl. Since the world did not yet exist, it was necessary to set Mount Mandara firmly on something else, and Vishnu turned himself into a tortoise and volunteered his back.

These myths led to wonderfully fanciful maps in ancient times. India was shown as tortoise-shaped, with its head facing East, its tail West and its front flippers North and South. Alternatively, India was shown as a continent floating on a tortoise's back in the dead centre of the cosmic ocean, with all the other known countries of the world, the stars and the constellations, swimming round it as pilot fish accompany a real ocean-swimming turtle.

➤ animal-gods

KURUKADI AND MUMBA
Australia

Kurukadi ('white iguana') and Mumba ('black iguana'), also known as Wati-Kutjara ('two-men'), in the myths of many peoples of Central Australia, were **twins**, supernatural beings of the Dream Time. Before **creation** they slept under the Earth, but then woke up and wandered the world, creating rock-formations, waterholes, plants and animals. They rescued a group of women who were being pursued by Kulu, a **Moon**-spirit who had descended to Earth in search of human mates. The women ran to Kurukadi and Mumba for help, and the twins killed Kulu with their boomerang. His spirit went back to the Moon (which has ever afterwards been colourless and drained of blood), the women went to live in the sky as the constellation white people call the Pleiades, and Kurukadi and Mumba, when their time on Earth ended, became the constellation later known as Gemini.

»+ animal-gods, Bagadjimbiri, Minawara and Multultu

KURURUMANY
Americas (South)

Kururumany, in the myths of the Arawak people of the Orinoco river, created the human race. He made males only, intending them to be a complete **creation**, but his wife Kulimina imitated him as best she could, and made females. This flawed Kururumany's creation, who grew ever more greedy, treacherous and quarrelsome – and he plagued humankind by making biting insects, snakes, poisonous plants and animals, and by sending them sickness and **death**.

»+ creation

KUSOR
Asia (West)

Kusor, or Kusorhasisu, in Mesopotamian myth, was a craft-god who, at the beginning of the universe, was assigned the job of making windows in the cube that was the created world. The harvest-god Aleyin, however, was afraid that if windows were built in the cube's sides **rain** would gush out and flood his crops, and he persuaded Kusor to build them in the roof instead, as skylights. Kusor opened these when it was time to let rain through, and closed them before the crops were ruined. In his spare time he befriended human beings, foretelling their futures and teaching them the skills of boat-building, navigation and sea-fishing.

»+ civilization, crafts, Daedalus, prophecy

KUU
Europe (North)

Kuu, in Finnish myth, was the **Moon**, formed from the whites of the celestial duck-eggs laid in the crook of **Luonnotar**'s knee. Kuu's light streamed across the world, glittering on the ice-fields, and its glitter passed into the ground as silver.

KVASIR
Europe (North)

Kvasir ('potent liquor'), in Nordic myth, was a god created at the end of the war between **Aesir** and **Vanir**. All the gods spat into a bowl, and Kvasir was made from their spittle, so embodying all the knowledge of all the gods. He was treacherously murdered by dwarfs, who collected his blood in vats and mixed it with honey to make the mead of inspiration. For what happened next, see **Odin**.

KWATEE
Americas (North)

Kwatee ('changer'), or Kivati, in the myths of the Quinault people of the Northwest US coast, brought human beings into the world and made it a fit place for them to live in. At the start of **creation**, the Earth was tenanted by giant animals: Ant, Beaver, **Coyote**, Fox, Hawk, Salmon, Spider and others. Kwatee literally cut them down to size, slicing them into smaller replicas of themselves to make room for humans. Then he started making new people, first from balls of dust and sweat rolled from his own body, then from dogs, lizards and other small creatures (which accounts for our different human characteristics). He taught the new humans how to make weapons for hunting and how to manage **fire**. When the day of creation ended and his work was done, he sat on the ground, covered his face with his blanket and turned himself to stone. (No one knows which of the mountains he became, but people still claim to be able to see his veiled face in this or that rocky outcrop.)

⋙→ **creation**

KYLLIKI
Europe (North)

Kylliki, in Finnish myth, was one of the goddesses of love, and the mother of **Lemminkäinen**.

⋙→ **beauty**

LABOURS Of HERACLES
Europe (South)

The Labours of **Heracles**, in Greek myth, were imposed on him by **Hera**, as a punishment for killing his own children during a fit of madness. Hera left the selection to King **Eurystheus** of Mycenae, Heracles' adversary, knowing that he would find tasks as difficult and dangerous as possible. Eurystheus originally set ten Labours: to kill the **Nemean Lion**; to kill **Hydra**; to capture the **Keryneian Hind**, the fastest animal in the world; to capture the **Erymanthian Boar**; to clean out the stables of King **Augeas** of Elis; to kill or drive away the **Stymphalian Birds**; to capture the fire-breathing **Cretan Bull**; to steal the flesh-eating mares of King **Diomedes** of Thrace; to steal the belt of **Hippolyta**, queen of the **Amazons**; to steal the cattle of the three-headed giant **Geryon**. But when these ten tasks were done, Eurystheus complained that Heracles had had help with two of them: Iolaus helped him to kill Hydra, and the river Alpheus helped him to clean out Augeas' stables. Eurystheus therefore set two more Labours, each of which Heracles fulfilled: to steal six of the Golden Apples of **immortality**, and to capture **Cerberus**, guard-dog of the **Underworld**.

LACHESIS: *see* Fates

LADY Of THE LAKE, THE
Europe (North)

The Lady of the Lake (also known as **Nimue** the Enchantress), in Celtic and medieval Christian myth, lived in an underwater castle in the enchanted lake surrounding the isle of **Avalon**. In some accounts, she was the same

Leda and the Swan (*L Flamenc, 18th century*)

person as **Morgan le Fay**, and her ambition was to destroy the human race. In others, she was a **shape-changer** banished to live underwater, who took revenge by preying on mortals who swam in the lake or sailed on its surface; only **Merlin**, her fellow-shape-changer, could thwart her plans. In the commonest accounts, however, she was a benefactor, not a harmer, of humanity. She gave Arthur the magic sword **Excalibur**, and protected him and his knights against Morgan le Fay's plots against them. When it seemed as if the **Holy Grail** was doomed to leave the mortal world forever, she took human shape, married **Pelles** its guardian, and arranged for her foster-son **Lancelot** to sleep with Elaine and father **Galahad**. Then, when Morgan le Fay finally succeeded in toppling Camelot (using Lancelot's love of **Guinevere** to break up the Round Table companionship), she rescued Arthur from death and took him to Avalon.

LAERTES
Europe (South)

Laertes ('ant'), in Greek myth, was an Ithacan. In his youth he went with **Jason** to find the **Golden Fleece**, but this persuaded him that high adventure was not for him. He married Anticlea, daughter of the bandit-king **Autolycus**, and settled peacefully as king of Ithaca. When his heir **Odysseus** (who was not in fact his son, but the child of **Sisyphus** who had slept with Anticlea on the morning of her marriage) grew up, he was happy to give up royal power to him and retire to an upcountry farm in peace. During the twenty years Odys-

seus was away he left management of royal affairs to Odysseus' wife **Penelope** and son **Telemachus**, not even intervening when a gang of rowdy suitors made their homes in Penelope's palace. Few retirements in myth have ever been so single-minded.

LAIMA
Europe (East)

Laima ('happiness') was the Baltic goddess of good luck. Originally she and her sisters Karta and Dekla controlled the destinies of all living things, and her particular function was to choose the moment of **death**. She specialized in protecting women, from the moment when they were conceived, through their birth, growing up and marriage to the point where they had children of their own. (These were the limits of the life she supervised for them – and she went further, favouring 'modest' young women and pinching and poking those she, or the village gossips, judged 'unchaste'.)
»→ childbirth and infant care

LAIUS
Europe (South)

Laius (Laios, 'herdsman of his people'), in Greek myth, was the son of King Labdacus of **Thebes**. Labdacus died when Laius was only a year old, and the descendants of the **Sown Men** (the most powerful families in Thebes) gave the throne to Nycteus (son of the Sown Man Chthonius), and banished Laius to Pisa in Southern Greece, where he was brought up by King **Pelops**.

Laius and Chrysippus. In Pisa, Laius was educated in all princely sports, including archery, wrestling and chariot-racing. As he grew older he came to prefer the company of drivers and charioteers to that of anyone else. He fell in love with a handsome charioteer called Chrysippus, Pelops' bastard son, and scandalized everyone by giving him presents and sending him love-poems as if he were a girl. (At this time homosexuality was a privilege allowed only to the gods.) Even worse, when news came that the usurpers of the Theban throne were dead, and that power was Laius' for the taking, he asked Chrysippus to marry him and go with him to be queen of Thebes – and when the boy refused he threw him into a chariot and galloped off with him. Chrysippus struggled free, jumped from the chariot and broke his neck. Laius fled to Thebes – and Pelops cursed him, calling on the gods to prevent him ever having a son, or if he did, to make that son his murderer.

Laius in Thebes. In Thebes, Laius was acclaimed as king. To ensure the loyalty of the Sown Men, he married **Jocasta**, great-great-grand-daughter of **Pentheus** son of Echion. But the marriage was childless, and as time went on the descendants of the Sown Men, led by Jocasta's brother **Creon**, began demanding that Laius should either provide an heir or give up the throne. Laius went to Delphi for advice, and the oracle told him that Jocasta was pregnant, but that if the child ever grew to manhood he would murder his father and marry his mother. To cheat this prophecy, Laius took his and Jocasta's baby, fastened his ankles with a golden pin, put him in an earthenware pot and left him on Mount Cithaeron to freeze to death

(or, in some accounts, took him to the coast and floated him out to sea in a barrel).

But no mortal, warned by an oracle or not, can cheat the gods. The child was rescued, named **Oedipus** and brought up by foster-parents in Corinth. In adulthood Oedipus visited the Delphic oracle to ask his true identity – and on the way back met an old man at a crossroads, argued about who should pass first, and killed him. The old man was Laius, and so Pelops' curse, and the oracle Laius had been given years before in Delphi, were fulfilled.

LAKSHMANA
India

Lakshmana, in Hindu myth, was the son of King **Dasaratha** and Queen **Sumitra**, and Rama's step-brother. He went with **Rama** into exile, and acted as his loyal lieutenant during the mighty battle against King **Ravana** of Sri Lanka. In Jain versions of the story, it was he and not Rama who finally met Ravana in single combat, and killed him.

➤➤ heroes

LAKSHMI
India

Lakshmi's names. Lakshmi ('sign'), in Hindu myth, was the goddess of good luck. In Vedic myth, from the time of the Aryans who invaded India in the seventeenth century BCE, she was known as Shri ('prosperity'), and in later times her names included Ksirabdhitanya ('daughter of the sea of milk'), Lokamata ('mother of the world') and Padma ('lotus').

Lakshmi's birth. In Vedic myth, Lakshmi was **Prajapati**'s daughter, born fully-formed and smiling from her father's body, like a ray of sunshine breaking through clouds. In Hindu myth, she was one of the daughters of the sage **Brighu**. When the gods were exiled from their sky-kingdom (in punishment for offending a seer), she hid in the primordial ocean – and when the gods churned it to begin creation (see *amrita*), she was one of the fourteen blessings which arose from it, milk-foam moulded to a being so beautiful that all the male gods lusted after her. She chose **Vishnu**, and was his faithful consort ever afterwards.

Lakshmi and Vishnu. In the sky-kingdom, Lakshmi reclined with Vishnu in the petals of a lotus, or rode with him through the sky on **Garuda**'s back. Whenever he rested, she was active; when he was angry, she was serene; when he smiled, she smiled with him. Whenever he took human form and went to the mortal world, she followed him. Some of these avatars are sketchily reported in the myths, but two are particularly important: when Vishnu was **Rama** she was **Sita**, and when he was **Krishna** she was **Radha**, the most beautiful being ever seen.

Lakshmi and mortals. Lakshmi had the power to divide herself, sending her essence to live with favoured mortals throughout the world. She loved light, and people often put candles in their windows to welcome her. She sat on the lintels and doors of houses, bringing good luck. She stationed herself in human bodies, and your luck depended on which of the seven 'stations' she chose. If she was in your feet, it meant good luck with a house; if in your thigh, wealth; if in your genitals, a wife or husband; if in your bosom, children; if in your heart, the granting of your heart's desire; if in your neck, contact with loved ones; if in your face, physical beauty and artistic inspiration. (By contrast, if she stationed herself on your head, it meant bad luck.) She was particularly concerned with brides, and they dressed in beautiful robes and decorated themselves with gold and jewels to honour her.

*As **beauty** personified, Lakshmi – either as herself or as one of her avatars – is a favourite subject for art. She is shown with Vishnu, sometimes as a doll-sized figure sitting on his knee, or tenderly massaging his feet as he sits enthroned on the world-serpent **Shesha**, sometimes as a full-grown woman gazing rapt at him, her hair covered with jewels and her breasts plump with the milk of life; she caresses him, and he holds her close. Sometimes they ride Garuda, or sit or stand on a spreading lotus. Lakshmi wears fine clothes and jewels, and is surrounded by such good things of life as musical instruments and pets; or she is lotus-eyed, lotus-coloured and wears lotuses for clothing – a symbol that she is the universal mother, linked with the primordial lotus from which **Brahma** himself was born.*

LAMIA
Europe (South)

Lamia ('greedy'), in Greek myth, was a beautiful **sea-nymph**, **Poseidon**'s grand-daughter. **Zeus** made her his mistress, and built her a palace carved from a secret cave in Africa, hoping to hide her existence from his jealous consort **Hera**. He gave her an unusual love-gift: she could take out her eyes while she slept and leave them wide awake beside the bed. No amount of watchfulness, however, helped Lamia against Hera – because instead of attacking her, Hera killed all the children she had had with Zeus. She spared only **Scylla**, because, as goddess of **prophecy**, she knew every detail of Scylla's future suffering.

Losing her children turned Lamia from a serene princess into a vengeful **monster**. She swooped about the world at night, looking for other people's children to devour. Grownups were not safe from her, either: in her uncontrollable lust for children she fell on sleeping men, trying to force them to have **sex**, and the ferocity of her passion sucked all the life from them. If she was cornered, she changed her shape, wriggling and twisting into a thousand forms until she broke free. (But if you held on until she was exhausted, you could force her to disgorge your child.)

In the course of time, Lamia became far less grand: she was made the subject of nursery stories and old wives' tales, each of which contained an even more revolting transformation. The most repulsive of all – said to be Lamia's favourite – was Empusa, a jumble of cow, mule, woman and rabid dog, with fire for face and feet of brass. This was the form in which she most often haunted children's dreams.

LANCELOT
Europe (North)

Lancelot, in medieval Christian myth, was the son of the French King Ban, but was stolen as a baby and brought up by the **Lady of the Lake**. He became the leading knight of King **Arthur**'s Round Table, and served with matchless devotion and bravery. But his childhood, poised between the natural and supernatural worlds, gave him a destructive duality of character. Like all fairy beings he was sexually insatiable, and his mortal self was disgusted by this failing and tried to sublimate it by self-mortification and other spiritual exercises. He had an affair with Arthur's queen **Guinevere**; then, horrified by this betrayal of his friend, he tried to atone by undertaking the quest for the **Holy Grail**. At the beginning of his journey he visited the castle of King **Pelles** of Carbonek, and was tricked into sleeping with his daughter (whom he took for Guinevere).

The child of this liaison grew up to be **Galahad** who rescued the Grail. But Lancelot himself, because of his flawed nature, was denied sight of the Grail. Afflicted by supernatural illness, he retired to his estates in France. Arthur's son **Modred**, ambitious for the throne of Camelot, told his father about Lancelot's affair with Guinevere, and Arthur took an army to France to kill his old friend. But then Modred usurped the throne, and Arthur hurried home to face his own son in civil war. Lancelot gathered an army and went to help, but before he arrived Arthur and Modred had met in single combat and both were fatally wounded. Grief-stricken, Lancelot gave all his lands and property to the church, took holy orders, and served as a monk in the monastery at Glastonbury until he died.

Lancelot is a purely medieval creation, grafted into the Arthurian and Grail cycles and with no existence outside them. Attempts were made at the time to give him a genuine historical pedigree: his father Ban was claimed as a descendant of the Biblical King David. Equally fanciful modern scholars have linked him with the Celtic sun-god Lug. In fact he is a fictional invention, one of the most psychologically complex and satisfying characters in medieval literature. He, not the prissy and unflawed Galahad, is the true hero of the romances of Chrétien de Troyes, and Malory's Morte d'Arthur is his story as much as Arthur's. In later literature, however, he loses this pre-eminence: writers are more fascinated with Camelot and the Round Table themselves, or with Merlin, and Lancelot becomes merely the most noble and dashing of a courtful of knightly clones.
⟫→ heroes

LAOCOÖN
Europe (South)

Laocoön (Laokoön, 'vast-vision'), in Greek and Roman myth, was one of the fifty sons of King **Priam** and Queen **Hecuba** of Troy. He was a prophet, serving **Apollo**, but angered the god when he broke his vow of chastity by taking a wife and breeding sons. Punishment was inevitable, but the gods bided their time, waiting until the Greeks devised the strategy of the **Wooden Horse** to capture Troy. Pretending to sail away, they left the Horse on the shore in front of Troy. It was full of armed men, but the Trojans took it for an offering to **Athene** and shouted that it should be dragged into the city and dedicated in her temple.

Like all Priam's prophetic sons and daughters, Laocoön was blessed with infallible knowledge, and cursed by the fact that no one ever believed a word he said. Now he announced that the Horse was full of soldiers, and said that if it was dragged into the city it would destroy them all. He and his sons set up an altar on the shore to sacrifice for guidance – and a pair of sea-serpents, sent by **Poseidon**, coiled round them and ate them alive before slithering into the city and disappearing behind Athene's altar in the temple. Not realizing that this was punishment for Laocoön's breaking of his oath of chastity, the Trojans took it as proof that he was wrong about the Horse, dragged it into the city – and destroyed their city.

*The Laocoön story is most famously told in Virgil's **Aeneid**. In the first century BCE three Greek sculptors working in Rome, Athenodoros, Hagesandros and Polydoros, collaborated on a statue showing Laocoön and his sons struggling in the serpents' coils. It made a sensation, and was claimed to be the finest artwork ever made. Nero took it and housed it in the imperial collection. When Rome fell some 400 years later, it was lost, but was rediscovered in the Renaissance and placed by Pope Julius II in the Vatican museum, where it still remains: one of the Western world's most cherished sculptures.*

LAOMEDON
Europe (South)

Laomedon ('ruler of the people'), King of Troy in Greek myth, was the son of Ilus and father of Podarces (later **Priam**) and Hesione. When **Zeus** punished

Apollo and Poseidon for plotting against him, he made them serve Laomedon for one year as hired labourers, and Laomedon made them build walls for a new citadel at Troy. (The parts of the walls they built were impregnable; the section Laomedon himself built was vulnerable, and was later broken down to let in the **Trojan Horse**.)

When the work was finished, Laomedon refused to pay the gods their agreed wages – the first-born of every cow, sheep and goat in the kingdom, sacrificed on their altars each year – and they retaliated by sending a **sea-monster** which ravaged the land once a year at harvest-time, and saying that it would be appeased only if Laomedon chose a virgin by lot each time, and sacrificed her to it. In the sixth year, the lot fell for Laomedon's own daughter Hesione – but instead of feeding her to the monster, he asked **Heracles** to kill it, offering him in return his immortal chariot-horses. However, as he had with Apollo and Poseidon, he broke his word as soon as the work was done, fobbing Heracles off with ordinary horses. Heracles sacked Troy (clubbing his way through the section of wall built by Laomedon), killed Laomedon and all his sons except the baby Podarces (Priam), and put the child up for sale in the slave-market.

LAR
Europe (South)

Lar, in Roman myth, was an ancient Italian god of **farming** and travel. Each farm had its own personal Lar, who saw to its **fertility** and the safe journey of its produce to market. When people moved into towns, they took their Lares with them, and the Lares of bride and groom were worshipped at the family hearth, together with the **Penates** and **Vesta**.

LATINUS
Europe (South)

Latinus, in Roman myth, was the son of **Faunus** and the **nymph** Marica. He ruled the original inhabitants of Italy, who were called Latins after him. He promised his beautiful daughter **Lavinia** to **Turnus**, king of the neighbouring Rutulians – and was disconcerted when the gods told him instead to marry her to a visiting foreign prince. Until that time, no foreigners had ever landed in Latinus' kingdom, but now **Aeneas** and his followers arrived from Carthage, and Latinus promised Lavinia to him. This began a war between Latins and Rutulians, which ended only when Aeneas killed Turnus, married Lavinia and became Latinus' heir.

LATONA: *see* Leto

LAVINIA
Europe (South)

Lavinia, in Roman myth, was the daughter of King **Latinus** of Latium and his queen Amata. She was promised in marriage to **Turnus**, prince of the Rutulians, but when **Aeneas** and his followers landed in Italy the gods told Latinus to marry her to a prince from abroad, and he chose Aeneas. This sparked war between Latins and Rutulians, and it ended only when Aeneas killed Turnus. He married Lavinia and made her pregnant. Then he died, or disappeared, and Lavinia, afraid of her step-son **Ascanius** (Aeneas' son born in Troy who had come to Italy with him), fled to the woods to bear her child. She called the boy Aeneas Silvius ('Aeneas of the forests'), and lived with him in exile until Ascanius died, when he inherited the kingdom.

LEDA
Europe (South)

Leda ('lady'), in Greek myth, was the beautiful wife of King **Tyndareus** of Sparta. One day **Zeus** saw her bathing in the river Eurotas, and was filled with lust. Knowing that Leda was faithful to Tyndareus (whose child she was carrying), and would have to be tricked into making love, he persuaded **Aphrodite** to help him. Aphrodite became an eagle and Zeus became a swan. They spiralled through the air like hunter and hunted, and flew down to the bank of Leda's pool, where Zeus lay fluttering as Aphrodite soared away like an eagle cheated of its prey. Leda, taking pity on what she thought was a helpless swan, nestled it in her lap and stroked its neck to revive it. At once Zeus had sex with her, soared into the air and disappeared.

Some time afterwards, Leda gave birth to two identical swan-eggs. From each hatched a pair of human **twins**: two girls, **Clytemnestra** and **Helen**, and two boys, Castor and Pollux (**Dioscuri**). The problem was, who was the father? It was thought at first that Clytemnestra and Castor were mortal (children of Tyndareus), and Helen and Pollux were immortal (children of Zeus). But when the children grew up, Castor and Pollux were treated as immortals and taken into **Heaven**, while Helen and Clytemnestra remained on Earth. As for Leda herself, when she died she was taken to Heaven and became an attendant of (or some say merged into) **Nemesis**, goddess of vengeance.

Although Leda was a minor figure in classical myth – Homer, for example, never mentions her – she became one of the most celebrated of all Greek characters in later European art. The nineteenth-century Romantics, in particular, took full advantage of the opportunity to paint a superb white swan in conjunction with a naked, wet female, and their sly eroticism was echoed in poems by authors as diverse as Goethe, Yeats and Gide. Jung considered that the Leda story gave form to one of the archetypes of human dream-memory, and mythographers ever since have found parallels in many cultures, most of them (for example the American myth of the warrior who mated with a swan-woman, or the Celtic tale of the Children of Lir) about as far as it would be possible to go from the simple (and characteristically Greek) story of Zeus' escapade with Leda.

LEGBA
Americas (Caribbean)

Legba, in Voodoo myth, is the all-powerful ruler of light, the dazzle of knowledge and the enemy of the powers of night and darkness (led by **Mait' Carrefour**). He is an old man, leaning on a stick – and his stick props up the universe. He wanders the world, smoking his pipe and carrying a sunshade, and he is to be found wherever the road of life forks, one way continuing the Path Above and the other leading to the Land Below.

»+ light and dark

LEIB-OLMAI
Europe (North)

Leib-Olmai ('alder-being'), in Lapp myth, was the god of good luck in **hunting**. He lived in alder trees, but when hunters danced for him he appeared as a bear and gave them good luck – especially against bears. At festivals, people painted their faces in his honour with a brownish-red mixture made from ground-up alder bark and water.

LEI GONG
Asia (East)

Lei Gong ('thunder-lord'), the storm-god in Chinese myth, was a blue-skinned warrior with fangs and talons. He rode a chariot pulled by six boys, and carried a drum, a chisel and a hammer. He hammered the drum to make **thunder**, and the chisel to send **lightning**-bolts. The noise of thunder told mortals that he was riding the sky looking for evil-doers, and the lightning-blast found them out however hard they tried to hide.

LEI JEN ZU
Asia (East)

Lei Jen Zu, son of Lei the **thunder**-dragon in Chinese myth, was hatched on Earth from an egg found after a **lightning**-bolt struck the ground. The soldiers who found him gave him to their general Wen Wang. Wen Wang,

who already had ninety-nine other children, had the child brought up by a Daoist hermit. Then Wen Wang was captured by his enemies, and the Thunder-dragon sent his son two apricots to eat. As soon as Lei Jen Zu spat out the pits, he changed from a human prince to a green-faced dragon with mirror-eyes, boar's tusks and an ant-eater's snout, and went to rescue Wang.

»+ monsters and dragons

LEMMINKÄINEN
Europe (North)

Lemminkäinen, in Finnish myth, was the handsome son of the love-goddess **Kylliki**. He was a **shape-changer**, **trickster** and seducer. He travelled the world looking for a wife, and used the quest as an excuse to have **sex** with every girl he met. In **Pohjola**, he courted the daughter of Princess **Louhi**. The ice-castle was thronged with suitors, and Lemminkäinen put on a display of magic to drive them away, flashing flames from his eyes and whirling his fiery hair round his head. All fled except Markhättu, who was blind and could not see the magic.

Louhi set Lemminkäinen three tasks: to outrun the fastest creature in the universe, the elk of the **demon** Hiisi, to bridle a fire-breathing horse and to shoot the black swan which swam in the river which surrounded **Tuonela** the **Underworld**. The first tasks were easy, but when Lemminkäinen went to Tuonela his rival Markhättu was waiting, and sent a water-**snake** to choke the life from him. Lemminkäinen's magic was too weak to protect him, and he died, was cut into pieces by the son of **Tuoni** god of the Dead, and thrown into the river. His mother Kylliki reassembled the fragments on the river-bank, using honey from **Heaven** to glue them together.

While Lemminkäinen was in the Underworld, Louhi took the opportunity to betroth her daughter to **Ilmarinen**. Lemminkäinen, reconstituted, came to the Upper World in time to find that he had not been invited to the wedding feast. He sailed to Pohjola with another disappointed suitor, **Väinämöinen**, and they would have destroyed the country and everyone in it if Louhi hadn't sent her ice-giant army against them. The sea froze round their ship, and Lemminkäinen had to use all his seductive magic to melt the waters and set them free. After this he gave up all ambition to marry a frost-giantess, and continued instead as Väinämöinen's companion in the quest for vengeance against Louhi.

Like Monkey in the story of Tripitaka, Lemminkäinen is a somewhat uneasy blend of fertility god and folksy trickster. His story as we have it dates from the Christian era, by which time the old gods had either disappeared or been converted into heroes and demons of fairy tales. To become a seducer, and then a feckless and charming rogue, was a characteristic fate for pagan love-gods in countries which became Christian – a later stage of the process which is seen beginning in such (entirely pagan) tales as that of Eros/Cupid and Psyche in the Graeco-Roman tradition.
≫→ **Jason, Osiris**

LESHY, THE
Europe (East)

The Leshy (from *les*, 'forest'), or the Ljeschi, in Slavic myth, was the spirit of the forest, much feared by people who had hacked their farmsteads from vast wooded areas. The Leshy was jealous of his forest kingdom, always trying to lose travellers in its depths. He was a **shape-changer**, deceiving his victims by making himself as tall as a tree or as small as a grass-blade, or becoming bird, animal or human. But however he changed, he could always be recognized because his face remained blue (the colour of his blood), his eyes and beard were green, he wore his clothes and shoes back to front, and he cast no shadow. The Leshy, his wife (the Leshachikha) and their children went on holiday each winter, but returned in spring, shrieking and shouting among the trees.
≫→ **farming, Ovda**

LETHE
Europe (South)

Lethe ('oblivion'), in Greek and Roman myth, was one of the rivers of the **Underworld**, a tributary of the river **Styx**. Dead souls drank its waters, which wiped out all memory of former lives.

*There was a river Lethe in the Upper World, not far from the shrine of the prophet **Trophonius**. Before consulting the oracle, people drank from the river, hoping that it would clear their minds ready for the prophet's message. Whether the Underworld Lethe gave its name to that of the Upper World, or vice versa, is not recorded.*

LETO
Europe (South)

Leto ('lady'; Latin Latona), in Greek and Roman myth, was the daughter of the **Titan** Coeus and Phoebe, a ray of sunlight. **Zeus** raped her, and then, to hide her from **Hera**'s jealousy, he changed her into a quail before her children were born, but Hera still recognized her and threw her out of **Heaven**. Distraught, Leto wandered the world looking for a place to give birth, and eventually **Poseidon** took pity on her and anchored the floating island of Delos so that she could flutter ashore and have her children there. Leto gave birth to **twin** gods, **Apollo** and **Artemis**, as painlessly as a quail-hen lays an egg.

LEVIATHAN
Asia (West)

Leviathan ('coiled'), in Canaanite myth, was the personification of the chaos at the beginning of the universe: a seven-headed, fire-breathing crocodile-dragon, the power of the primordial ocean given form. He lurked in the depths of the sea which was himself, waiting his moment to surge up and snatch his victims. **Anat** fought him and chained him, bringing order to the universe – but, the myth ends, Leviathan is not dead but merely sleeping, and one day will return to destroy us all.

*Hebrew and Christian teachers fell joyfully on this myth, using Leviathan as a metaphor for everything which threatened the stability of **Yahweh** and his worshippers, from the Babylonian and Egyptian nations which enslaved them to the power of **Satan** which God's angels will destroy on the Day of Judgement.*
➤ Da, Illuyankas, snakes, water

LEZA AND HONEYBIRD
Africa

Leza ('cherisher'), creator-god in the myths of the Baila, Tonga and other peoples of Southern Africa, sent Honeybird to mortals with three sealed calabashes. The first two held the seeds of every plant in creation. The contents of the third were secret. Needless to say, Honeybird opened all three calabashes on the way from **Heaven** to Earth – and therefore, instead of being under mortal control as Leza had intended, the seeds from the first two scattered at random across the world. The third calabash was full of disease, famine, poisonous animals, predators and **death**. Since neither mortals nor Honeybird knew how to coax them back into the calabash, and Leza refused to tell, they have been the lot of Earth's creatures ever since.

Leza was once close to mortals, but this disaster, and increasing age – he was immortal but not timeless – made him ever more aloof. He spent his time in **Heaven**, spring-cleaning the **Sky**-hut (in which case thunder was the sound of him beating his rugs) or gazing out over **creation** with rheumy, runny eyes (in which case, it rained).
➤ messengers, supreme deity

LHAMO
Asia (Central; South)

Lhamo, in Singhalese and Tibetan myth, was the queen of all **demons** and mistress of all **disease**. She originally came to Earth as a mortal, consort of King Shisrte of Lanka. But she was a Buddhist and Shisrte was not. He banned the religion and brought his son up to hate all Buddhists – and Lhamo killed the boy, drank his blood, flayed him and made his skin into a leather saddle. She took the best horse in Shisrte's stable and galloped with it all over India, China, Mongolia and Tibet, before settling in Lake Lhamo Latson in the Himalayas. As she rode, Shisrte galloped after her, firing poison-arrows – and she caught them in the air and stored them in her quiver of diseases.

Lhamo killed humans by firing arrows of disease at them as she rode across the world. She ate her victims' brains, drank their blood – her cups their skulls – and wore their skins for clothes. At first her fury was implacable, and she killed every human she came on. But as time passed she softened, and turned her anger only on evildoers and those who refused to accept the faith. She protected successive Dalai Lamas, and gave oracles in the ripples of the water and the sighing of wind on the surface of the lake she lived in.

⨠→ **disease and healing**

LIBANZA
Africa

Libanza, creator-god of the Upoto people of the Congo, began by making **Sky** and its inhabitants the gods, and the **Sun** that contains the fire of life. Then he made Moon, Earth and all their inhabitants. At first these were equal, but when he called them all together the Moon-people hurried and the Earth-people dawdled. Libanza rewarded the Moon-people by giving them **immortality**, and punished the Earth-people by sending **Death**. However, the Moon-people

begged him to change his mind, and he relented sufficiently to grant Earth-people immortality in his Heavenly court, but only after they'd served a lifetime of pain and toil on Earth.

LIF AND LIFDRASIR
Europe (North)

Lif ('life') and his wife Lifdrasir ('eager for life'), in Nordic myth, are the only two humans who will survive **Ragnarök**, the end of this cycle of the universe. In some accounts, they will take shelter among the leaves of **Yggdrasil**. In others, they will be stored, as seeds, within the tree itself, and when the last battles are over and the fires and earthquakes have subsided, they will emerge to begin the human race anew.

LIFDRASIR (OR LIFTHRASIR):
see Lif and Lifdrasir

LIGHT AND DARK
Myth-makers assumed that the universe was made from, and continued to exist because of, a precise balance of opposites. Perhaps because of the endless progression of night and day, the most important of these was the balance between light and dark. Light (again hardly surprisingly, since it was the dimension of the humans who made the myths) was thought to be wholesome, unsecret, comprehensible; dark was the dimension of **demons**, dead people, **monsters**, everything which was inexplicit and dangerous. All myth-traditions embodied these ideas in specific gods and stories, and the range was from grand matters (for

example the idea that humans currently lived in a 'light' phase of universal history, and that a 'dark' phase was imminent, either because the powers of dark were outwitting those of light, or because human wickedness was upsetting universal balance), to less serious ones (tales of squabbling siblings, or rivalries between **tricksters** who put on attributes of light and dark like clothes, to outwit one another).

⇛ (Africa): Zanahary; (Americas): Black God, Hahgwehdiyu and Hahgwehdaetgah, Kuat and Iae, Legba, Mait' Carrefour, Raven, Snoqalm and Beaver, Tamusi and Tamulu, Tezcatlipoca; (Arctic): Alklha; (Celtic): Lug; (Egypt): Benu Bird, Set; (Finnish): Otava; (India): Agni; Devadatta, *devas* and *devis*, Kalki, Vishnu; (Iranian): Ahriman, Ahura Mazda; (Mesopotamia): Inanna; (Nordic): Baldur, Höd; (Slavic): Byelobog and Chernobog

LIGHTNING: *see* Borak, Catequil, Enumclaw and Kapoonis, Kadlu, Raiden and Raiju, Shango, thunder, Unkulunkulu

LILITH
Asia (West)

Lilith (Lilitu, 'storm-lady' or 'owl-hag'), in Hebrew myth, was a **demon** who preyed on men, draining their sperm while they slept and so stealing their offspring to turn into demons. In some accounts, she tried to mate with **Adam** before Eve was created (and before he ate the fruit of All-knowledge and discovered **sex**) and **Yahweh** punished her by banishing her to the void of space –

from which she made her subsequent raids on Adam's male descendants.

LI NO ZHA
Asia (East)

Li No Zha, foster-son of Li Jing, gate-keeper of **Heaven** in Chinese myth, was actually the child of the Unicorn of Heaven, implanted in the womb of Li Jing's wife and born the following morning. When Li Jing went into the birth-room, he found no baby but a flesh-ball rolling across the floor. He sliced it open and Li No Zha was born. The child immediately became full-grown, and began to fight other gods, including the son of **Long Wang** the Dragon-king. His parents begged him to calm down, and filled him with such shame that he committed suicide, only to be reborn immediately as a **giant** 20m tall, with three heads, nine eyes and eight arms each brandishing a weapon. Not knowing what else to do, Li Jing attacked him and tried to kill him – and it was only when the gods intervened that the two of them made peace. Li Jing was soothed by being given higher rank, and Li No Zha was promoted to be the shield-bearer of **Yu Huang**, the Jade Emperor himself.

LI PAPAI
Asia (East)

Li Papai ('eight hundred plums'), in Chinese myth, was a sage whose body was entirely covered with plum-coloured boils. An official, Tang Gong Fang, asked him to teach him the secret of eternal youth, and Li Papai said that first he must be cured of his boils, and that the only way to do it was to lick them from his body. Tang ordered his servants to do this, without result – and Li Papai said that the job had to be done by someone of noble rank. Tang ordered his wife to lick the boils, and this too failed. Li Papai now said that an alternative was for him to bathe in wine from a million bottles. With enormous difficulty, Tang assembled the wine, and Li Papai was cured. He told Tang and his wife to bathe in the wine themselves, and when they emerged their old age had been stripped from them and they were young again.

This myth was used as a moral tale in Daoist teaching. It led to the conclusions that enormous effort is required to achieve our mortal desires, and that they may not be worth it, since true self-fulfilment is to be found in other ways. The story most probably survives, however, for its own extravagant sake, as does the claim (derived from the fact that the word li, as well as 'plum', means a distance, some 500m) that Li's method of disciplining his body took the form of walking 800 li, 400km, every day.

LIR
Europe (North)

Lir (or Lleyr), in Celtic myth, was the Old Man of the **Sea**. He had four beautiful children, **Manannan MacLir** and three daughters, and doted on them. But his wife died and he married her sister, who hated him and turned his children into swans, voiceless and aloof from him. By the time Lir discovered what had happened and reversed the spell, the children had aged from beautiful youth to withered age.

This bizarre story may be the ultimate origin of the story of King Lear and his three daughters, as used by Shakespeare. Shakespeare's actual source, in Geoffrey of Monmouth's History of the Kings of Britain and Holinshed's Chronicle, tells of King Leir of Leicester, whose two elder daughters treated him with scorn but whose youngest, Cordeil, honoured him even though he had divided his property between her sisters, leaving her nothing. But Holinshed followed Geoffrey, and Geoffrey notoriously used half-remembered ancient myths to flesh out his tales: hence the scholarly speculation sparked by the coincidence of the names and circumstances of the two unhappy fathers.

LLEU LLAW GYFFES
Europe (North)

Lleu Llaw Gyffes ('lion with steady hand'), in Celtic myth, was the son of the virgin goddess Arianrhod, after she was raped by Gwydion, a **shape-changer**. (Gwydion, interviewing her for the post of foot-warmer in his castle, had said that virginity was a pre-condition of employment, and had asked her to prove it by stepping over his magic wand. As soon as she'd done so, she'd given birth.) Arianrhod refused to name or help the child, and withdrew to her palace in the Aurora Borealis (or some say, on Anglesey). But Gwydion twice tricked her, letting her see her son carry out a feat of skill or strength – and when she exclaimed 'Lleu' the first time and 'Llaw Gyffes' the second time, he told her she'd named the boy.

Arianrhod responded to these tricks by cursing the boy, saying that he would marry no mortal woman – and the curse brought about Lleu's death. Gwydion made him a wife of woven flower-petals, and called her Bloddeuedd ('flower-face'). Bloddeuedd, however, hated Lleu and plotted with her lover Goronwy to murder him. As son of a goddess, Lleu was invulnerable to mortal weapons – but his mother had added the rider 'Unless he's stabbed in a thatch-roofed bath-house beside a running river, standing with one foot on the edge of the bath and the other on a roebuck he's just killed'. Bloddeuedd wheedled this secret out of Lleu and told it to Goronwy, who waited (one imagines for some time) until the conditions were fulfilled, then stabbed Lleu with a poisoned spear. Lleu's mortal body fell dead in the bath, and his soul flew into the sky as an eagle.

There was only one way for Gwydion to bring Lleu back to life: by arranging a duel between him and Goronwy. Foolishly, Goronwy agreed that each contestant could strike one blow – and even more foolishly, agreed to let Lleu go first. He thought he would outwit him by standing behind a solid boulder. But Lleu hurled a sunshaft which shattered the rock and burned Goronwy's body to ash. Gwydion punished Bloddeuedd, his own creation, by turning her into an owl, and she has wept and mourned for Goronwy ever since.

*Lleu is a Welsh form of **Lug**, god of light, and a Celtic counterpart to **Loki** in **Nordic** myth*.
➤ **heroes**

LOA
Oceania

Loa, a Northern Pacific equivalent of the Tahitian **Ta-aroa**, was the first being in creation, and a simpleton. For aeons of time he drifted alone in the primordial **sea**; then he grew bored and began fidgeting. As he was creative power incarnate, every movement made something: an island, a coral reef, a bird, a fish, a plant. Even when he sat back to admire his efforts, his leg twitched and produced the first man and first woman. This couple immediately started producing children of their own, and Loa watched in amazement as the human race spilled out across the world, singing, dancing and enjoying **sex**. But then they started squabbling and fighting, and killed their own ancestors. Terrified in case he might be next, Loa jumped up, meaning to abandon the world forever – and his movement engendered both a tidal wave which drowned the first race of humans, and a second ancestor, Edao, who was to begin the race anew.
➤ **creation**

LOKI
Europe (North)

Loki's nature. Loki ('allure' or 'fire'; also known as Loder, Loke, Lokkju, Lopter and Lopti; German Loge), in Nordic myth, was both the oldest and the youngest of the gods. He existed before existence, as an idea: the principle of irrationality, of mischief, which subverts every attempt by others to make an ordered universe. In some accounts he was the brother of **Odin** and **Honir**, one of the three creator-gods, and his gifts to **Ask and Embla**, the first human beings in the world, were like those of the wicked step-mother in later fairy-tales: desire and passion. Other accounts say that he was able to take shape, to slip into bodily existence, only long after the other gods – and then by cunning and despite all their efforts to prevent it. His father Farbauti struck stone on flint, a spark leapt into the underbrush of his mother, the wooded island Laufey, and Loki took on the shape of the resulting **fire** as a human being shrugs on a garment. Like fire, he remained unpredictable and hard to control. Sometimes he was ingratiating and helpful, as well-mannered as a cooking-fire; at other times his mischievous, conscienceless trickery, unstoppable as forest-fire, engulfed everything it touched. His charm made him irresistible to goddesses and mortal women alike. But he was fickle, and passed from encounter to encounter as eagerly and as irrevocably as flames sweep through cornfields.

Loki the shape-changer. Loki was a **shape-changer**, able to take on the appearance of whatever he chose: a puff of smoke, the blush on a girl's face, fish, bird, insect or animal. As Asgard-Loki (when he lived in **Asgard** with the **Aesir**) he was a seducer; as Utgard-Loki (when he lived in **Utgard** with the **giants**) he was a **monster**. His disguises included flea, fly, giantess, salmon, seal and bird – and he worked the last change by stealing **Freyja**'s feather-cloak. Few other gods shared the skill of shape-changing – most had one attribute only, for example youth, **wisdom**, strength or **beauty**, and could assume others only with difficulty – and Loki basked in it. He used it sometimes to benefit others, sometimes to trick them, sometimes to save his own skin, but always with delight.

Loki and Svadilfari. After the war between Aesir and **Vanir**, when the Aesir wanted the wall rebuilt round their citadel Asgard, Loki tricked a rock-giant into doing the work. He said that if the wall were finished by the first day of spring, the giant's rewards would be the Sun, the Moon and Freyja, the love-goddess. Horrified at the thought of losing Freyja, and hence the pleasures of love, the gods tried to refuse the bargain; but Loki promised them that there was no way for any giant, however strong, to build the wall in a single winter. The giant, however, was helped by his stallion Svadilfari, who worked tirelessly to haul boulders and build the wall.

Three days before the end of winter, only the gate-pillars were needed to complete the wall, and the gods were already beginning to feel intimations of love-loss, chill as a shadow. But Loki cheerfully told them to trust him. He took on the appearance of a seductive mare, prancing before Svadilfari and leading the stallion away from the stone-pile into the woods. The rock-giant, furious, was forced himself to lug boulders for the gate-pillars, and failed to finish the wall in time. He stormed before the gods, and roared that he would take his rewards by force. But **Thor** smashed his skull with a single blow, and tossed its fragments out of Asgard. Soon afterwards, Loki trotted into Asgard, still in the shape of a mare, and beside him was the eight-legged foal Sleipnir, Loki's child and the fastest animal in creation. Loki gave him to **Odin**. So the king of the gods got a charger which could outride the winds, the gods got their wall and kept Freyja, and Loki had the pleasure of knowing how a mare feels when she mates with a stallion and gives birth to a foal.

Loki's marriages. Loki was sexually insatiable, and mated with gods, humans, giants, animals, rocks and trees. He married three wives. The first, Glut ('glow'), bore him two daughters: Esia ('ember') and Einmyria ('ashes'). The second, the giantess Angboda ('grief-bringer'), bore him monsters: the wolf-giant Fenrir, **Hel**, ruler of the Dead, and the world-serpent **Jormungand**. The third, Sigyn, bore him two sons: Narve and Vali.

Loki and Ragnarök. By nature, Loki was fickle and easily bored. For most of the life of the universe he was happy to live with the gods, soothing his restlessness by inventing adventures, trying new disguises and playing practical jokes. But gradually, as time passed, he began to resent the fact that he was never respected as much as some of the other gods, particularly Odin. This resentment turned first to bitterness, then to fury. He arranged to hurt Odin not by playing a trick on him but by causing the death of **Baldur**, the Beautiful, Odin's son – and when Baldur was dead he refused to mourn him, so preventing him rising again from **Niflheim** to Asgard.

Odin tried to persuade Loki to change his mind by banishing him from banquets in Asgard – but Loki turned up anyway and spent his time killing servants and insulting the gods by reminding them of past failures and failings, one by one. Finally persuaded that Loki was beyond control and should be locked away before he destroyed the universe, the gods turned Loki's son

Vali into a wolf and set him on his brother Narve; then they used Narve's entrails to bind Loki deep in the cave-kingdom of the giantess **Skadi**, who hung a serpent above Loki's head, forever dripping venom. Only the loyalty of Loki's wife Sigyn stopped Loki being eaten away by the venom. She sat by his side in the darkness, catching the drops in a wooden dish, and only when she turned away to empty the dish did drops fall into Loki's eyes, causing him to writhe in agony: the origin of earthquakes.

Ragnarök, the end of this cycle of time, will begin, the myth ends, when Loki at last escapes from the cave. His wolf-child Fenrir will jump from Earth to Sky and eat the **Sun**, and his serpent-son Jormungand will stir up a tidal wave and spit venom-showers to drown the stars. Loki, fire, and the giant Hrymir, frost, will jointly lead the forces of darkness against the gods, and the battle which follows will destroy all living things. At the end of the battle only Loki and Hrymir will be left: fire and ice, as at the beginning of the first creation – and from their merging a new cycle will begin.

*It was characteristic of Nordic society that people thought it possible to ward off danger by using jokes and irony. This applied to Loki. Ignoring his savagery and his future role as destroyer of creation, people concentrated on his lighter side, so that hundreds of myths and tales survive showing him as **trickster** and anti-hero, feckless rather than dangerous – the story of him outwitting the giant **Skrymsli** is typical. Even when he causes real trouble (as in the myths of **Sif**'s hair or the death of*

Otr) he is shown as seductive rather than vindictive: a main part of the pleasure seems to have been to place him in impossible situations and see how cleverly he would wriggle out of them. His shape-changing meant that there was no standard image of him in fine art: representations ranged from flames, a fish and a hawk to a handsome, youthful warrior. After Christianity came to Northern Europe, however, there was no such problem. Loki was identified with the Devil, and shown as a kind of bound gargoyle, at the foot of Christ's cross or with Christ standing over him in triumph.

LONG WANG
Asia (East)

Long Wang ('dragon king'), in Chinese myth, was a god of **water**, and like water he could divide himself into a myriad forms, as small as dewdrops or as large as **floods**. When he appeared to humans he borrowed shape from a variety of Earth's creatures: camel's or lion's head with stag's antlers, **snake**'s neck, clam's body, carp's scales, tiger's legs and eagle's talons. He was aggressive towards **demons**, and hated the **Sun**, which he often tried to bite, rearing up like a striking snake. But with mortals he was generous, the **rain**-bringer.
≫→ monsters and dragons

LOTUS-EATERS
Europe (South)

The Lotus-eaters, in Greek myth, lived on a pair of sandbanks in a river-estuary near Carthage in North Africa. The river was tidal, and the sandbanks constantly changed position, so that once you left

them it was impossible to find them again. The Lotus-eaters ate the fruit of the lotus: not the Egyptian water-lily, but a bean-like plant whose roots grew all the way down into the **Underworld** and sucked water from the river **Lethe**. In the Underworld, drinking Lethe-water destroys memory – and lotus-fruit had the same property in the Upper World. The Lotus-eaters had a present but no past and no future; the lotus was all they knew.

When **Odysseus** sailed from Troy, he landed on one of the sandbanks, and sent three men to explore. They found the Lotus-eaters, ate some of the fruit and lost all memory. Odysseus went to find them, fought off the Lotus-eaters who were trying hospitably to offer him fruit, dragged his men back to the ship and hastily rowed away while they wept and cried to be left behind and the Lotus-eaters gazed after them with empty eyes, not knowing or caring who they were.

LOUHI
Europe (North)

Louhi, in Finnish myth, was a magic-working ice-giantess, Princess of **Pohjola**. When **Väinämöinen**, **Ilmarinen**, **Lemminkäinen** and other suitors from the warm South came courting her daughters, she set them impossible conditions (such as outrunning the fastest creature in the universe, the elk of the demon Hiisi) – and if these were met, sent her army of frost-**giants** to kill them. She tricked Väinämöinen and Ilmarinen into making for her the *sampo*, a magic mill of prosperity, and it would have enriched her realm and made her queen of the entire universe if the heroes, for all her magic, had not snatched it back and escaped with it to the South.

LOVE: *see* Aphrodite, Aset, Erzulie, Freyja, Frigg, Hathor, Ishtar, Kamadeva, Krishna, Mama Brigitte, Musubi

LOVIATAR
Europe (North)

Loviatar, in Finnish myth, was the goddess of plagues. She was the hideous daughter of **Tuoni** and **Tuonetar**, king and queen of the **Underworld**, and her body was ravaged by all the diseases to which it was host, every plague ever known. She mated with the wind, and her nine terrible children gusted out across the universe: black death, cancer, colic, consumption, fits, gangrene, gout, ulcers and 'the ninth, the nameless, envy-gnawed, **death**-dealing', the worst of all.
≫→ **disease and healing**

LU BAN
Asia (East)

Lu Ban, in Chinese myth, was a mortal carpenter. When his father was executed for a crime of which he was innocent, Lu Ban carved a wooden statue whose arm lifted of its own accord to denounce the governor who'd condemned him, and laid a curse of drought on the whole state, lifted only when Lu Ban cut off the pointing hand and spread the sawdust on the ground. The gods were so impressed that they gave him **immortality** and made him **Heaven**'s woodworker.

Even so, he preferred Earth to Heaven, and wandered about in disguise, revealing himself only by the things he made for favoured worshippers. These included useful objects – he invented the adze, the ball-and-socket joint and the carpenter's bench – and wonders, among them a wooden hawk which could flap its wings and fly.
≫→ **crafts, Daedalus, Hephaestus, Lug**

LUCRETIA
Europe (South)

Lucretia, wife of Collatinus in Roman myth, was famous for her virtue at a time when, under the tyranny of Tarquin the Proud, most Roman aristocrats were debauched and shameless. Once, when Collatinus and other young nobles were taking part in a siege of Ardea, an hour's ride from Rome, they argued about whose wife was the most virtuous – and Collatinus suggested that they gallop back home to find out. They found all the other wives drinking and enjoying **sex** in their husbands' absence, but Lucretia sitting quietly spinning with her maids. The young men rode back to Ardea, but one of them, Tarquin's son Sextus, was so overcome with lust for Lucretia that he galloped secretly back to Rome, broke into her house, and threatened, unless she slept with him there and then, to kill a slave and put him in her bed, thus shaming her forever. Lucretia gave way to him, but next morning summoned her father and Collatinus her husband, told them what had happened, and stabbed herself dead.

This incident, a mirror-image variant of a standard Mediterranean folktale (which also inspired the Biblical story of Joseph and Potiphar's wife) was retold 500 years after the supposed events by Roman historians as if it were real, not myth. They claimed, further, that it triggered the uprising against Tarquin which led to the overthrow of the monarchy and the establishment of republican rule in Rome.

LUG
Europe (North)

Lug ('light'), in Celtic myth, was the **Sun**-god and the master of all skills and **crafts**. His honorific titles include Find ('blond'), Lamfada ('longhand'), Lonbemlech ('of mighty blows') and Samildanach ('all-skilled'). He was the grandson of the **demon**-king **Balor**. Terrified by a prophecy that his own grandson would kill him, Balor locked his daughter Ethlin in a transparent glass tower, and set watchers to ensure that no male ever went near her. But Cian, god of medicine, disguised himself as a woman, slipped into the tower and impregnated Ethlin under the watchers' very eyes. Lug was born, and Balor threw him into the sea to drown. But he was rescued by **Manannan MacLir** the sea god, and brought up either in Mannanan's underwater kingdom or by Cian's brother the blacksmith-god Goibniu, who taught him all arts and crafts.

As soon as Lug grew up, he went to take his place among the gods. The doorkeeper asked what skills he had, and at first refused to accept him: each skill Lug claimed was already possessed by some other god. But then Lug pointed out that no one but he possessed every single one of them, and the gods took him in. He led them in huge battles against the **demons**, and eventually killed Balor by shooting him in the eye with a fireball from a sling. He also spent time with mortals, carrying messages from **Heaven** to Earth, assisting mortal armies against the demons, and sleeping with their women (one of whom, Queen Dechtire of Connaught, bore him the hero **Cuculain**).

Although, by mortal standards, the gods were enormously long-lived, they were not immortal, and after aeons of existence they began to age. Unable to sustain their celestial palaces and courts, many of them came down to Earth and lived with mortals. New enemies arrived to weaken them still further. In the end they retreated to dens and warrens underground, and over time began to shrink and stoop until they became indistinguishable from dwarfs, craftsmen of the **Underworld**. Lug taught them his craftsman's skills, and became their leader. He took another honorific title, Lug Chromain ('bent light') – origin of the modern word 'leprechaun'. He stored the remains of his sunlight, the last reminder of the gods' former glory, as gold-hoards in fields and on hillsides, marking the spot each time with a rainbow's end.

In some accounts, Lug is the same person as the Welsh god **Lleu**.

The end of Lug's story shows him, like many Celtic gods in the Christian era, losing status and becoming little more than a subject of fairy-tale. In early times he was far more substantial. The Romans identified *him with **Mercury**, the winged messenger who embodies the shaft of illuminating sunlight – and he was worshipped all over Celtic lands, from Ireland in the North (where his cult seems to have originated) as far as Leiden in what is now Holland and Lyon in France, both towns named after him.*

≫→ **Daedalus, Hephaestus, light and dark, Lu Ban, smiths**

LUNA: *see* Selene

LUONNOTAR
Europe (North)

Luonnotar ('daughter of **creation**') or Ilmatar ('daughter of air'), in Finnish myth, existed before the universe. There was nothing but her mother **Ilma** ('air') and the primordial ocean. Luonnotar wandered in the cloud-deserts which were her mother for uncountable time, then fell exhausted into the ocean. She floated there for another 700 years, and the sea caressed every fold and curve of her body, making her boundlessly fertile, pregnant with creativity.

A duck appeared, looking for a place to lay eggs. It found the crook of Luonnotar's knee, laid its eggs and settled there to hatch them. The heat of its body scorched Luonnotar out of her lethargy, and she wriggled to find a new position. The duck flew away and the eggs rolled into the sea and through it into the void below. Here they broke, and their pieces made the universe. The upper halves of the shells made the sky, the lower halves the Earth. The yolks made the **Sun** and the whites the **Moon**; flecks of albumen made stars and pla-

nets. Ripples in the primordial ocean, made when Luonnotar changed position, lapped against the new Earth, shaking it like a blanket and making mountain-ranges, valleys and continents.

In all the 700 years while Luonnotar was floating in the sea, the water had made her pregnant without her knowing it. Her child **Väinämöinen** had grown to adulthood inside her womb, and was now ready to be born. But Luonnotar was a virgin, with no knowledge of **sex** or **childbirth**; she was creativity without intelligence, life without instinct. Väinämöinen had to bring about his own birth, without her help. He sat and pondered for thirty years, then clambered out of her womb and up her vagina as a man might climb out of a pothole, broke through her hymen and dived into the sea. As soon as he was born, Luonnotar's part in **creation** was complete.

≫→ **Päivä**

LYCAON
Europe (South)

Lycaon (Lykaon, 'wolfish'), in Greek myth, was the king of Thessaly at the time when **Zeus**, sickened by the wickedness of mortals, was planning to drown them in a **flood** and re-people the Earth. Before opening the floodgates, Zeus visited the Earth in disguise, hoping to find one single mortal whose honesty might persuade him to change his mind. He found none: wild beasts in their lairs were more god-fearing than the human race. When he came to Thessaly, he threw off his mortal disguise to try and shock Lycaon into worshipping him – and Lycaon called it a conjuring trick and said he would find ways of his own to test the god's **immortality**. First he butchered Zeus' companion and served him in a stew, certain that if Zeus were really a god he would know at once what he was eating. Then, when Zeus kicked back the table and refused to eat, Lycaon devised an even more impious test. He crept in Zeus' bedroom that night and began stabbing the throat and chest of the sleeping god. The knife-blade crumpled at the first touch of Zeus' immortal skin, and the god woke with a roar of **thunder** and felled Lycaon's palace in ruins. Lycaon recognized Zeus as a god at last and fell on his knees for mercy. But even as he whined for forgiveness, the words changed to yelps in his throat, his arms and legs grew bristles and his nose and mouth changed into a muzzle. He fell on all fours and ran into the woods – and his people were transformed into wolves and ran after him, the first wolf-pack ever seen on Earth.

LYCURGUS
Europe (South)

Lycurgus (Lykourgos, 'wolf-work'), king of the Edonians in Greek myth, insulted **Dionysus** and was savagely punished. Until Dionysus came to Edonia, wine was unknown there, but as soon as the god arrived vines grew wherever he set foot, and Lycurgus was horrified to see the Edonian women make wine of the grapes and begin indulging in what they called 'sacred rites'. He banned Dionysus-worship, imprisoned the women and ordered every vine in the kingdom to be chopped down and burned – and for this Dionysus drove him mad. Mistaking his son Dryas, and then his own legs, for vines, Lycurgus snatched up an axe and hacked them to pieces. Dionysus told the Edonian women that unless they punished Lycurgus' madness they would never taste wine again – and they harnessed wild mares to Lycurgus' arms and neck, had him torn apart and fed the fragments to the mares.

Merlin and Nimue (*19th century*)

MAAT
Africa (North)

Maat ('truth'; 'balance'), goddess of truth in Egyptian myth, was the daughter of **Ra** from whom nothing was hidden. She wore a single ostrich-feather in her crown, and its lightness was deceptive. It was undeviating exactitude, and if you weighed yourself against it and lied, it grew heavier and heavier until you stood condemned. At the judging of souls in the **Underworld**, Maat's feather was placed in one pan of a pair of scales, and the heart of any claimant to sinlessness was placed in the other. On Earth, pharaohs administered in Maat's name, and she was often shown as a doll-like figure sitting or standing in the pharaoh's hand as he held it out to the gods, offering them his justice. In **Heaven**, her role was even more important, as her laws guaranteed the stability of the entire universe, and it was in her name that gods swore oaths and promises.

≫→ **justice and universal order**

MABINOGION, THE
Europe (North)

The *Mabinogion* ('tales') was a collection of Welsh stories translated and published by Charlotte Guest in the 1830s. The tales came from two fourteenth-century collections, *The White Book* and *The Red Book*, and contain myth-material from far earlier times. The heart of the *Mabinogion* is four long stories, or 'branches', giving accounts of the early Celtic gods and heroes in a particularly folksy and flowery manner. (In this present book, the chief stories are told under the names of **Arawn**, **Bran**, **Cormac**, **Lleu Llaw Gyffes** and **Pwyll**.) The remaining seven stories are shorter: Welsh variants of episodes from the Arthurian legends.

MACUILXÓCHITL
Americas (Central)

Macuilxóchitl ('five-flowers'), in Aztec myth, was the god of **music** and dance, a benign deity who supervised the gentler pleasures of life.

Some scholars says that Macuilxóchitl was such an unlikely member of the puritanical, blood-soaked Aztec pantheon that he must have come into it from far more ancient myth – but there is no evidence either way.

MADRI
India

Madri, in Hindu myth, was the beautiful second wife of King **Pandu**. Her husband, mistaking a sage in a forest for a deer, wounded him fatally, and the sage cursed him saying that if he ever had **sex** with his wife, he would die. Madri desperately wanted children, and Pandu's senior wife **Kunti** shared with her a gift which she (Kunti) had received from the gods: if she prayed to any particular male god, that god would give her children. Madri prayed to the twin **Ashvins**, and in due course gave birth to twins of her own: **Nakula** and **Sahadeva**.

Some time afterwards, Madri and Pandu were walking in the forest, when they felt a sudden surge of desire for each other. They lay down to make love, but unhappily for Pandu it was in the very place where he'd shot the sage

years earlier, and as soon as he entered his wife he died.

MAHABHARATA, THE
India

The *Mahabharata* is an epic poem in Sanskrit, 180,000 lines long, assembled in the third century BCE. It is attributed to a sage called **Vyasa** ('collector'), who is said in some versions to have dictated it line by line to **Ganesh** himself. It tells of the war between the **Pandavas** and **Kauravas** for the country then known as **Bharata** and later as Upper India – possibly a real war of the fifteenth century BCE. But its human characters mingle freely with gods and **demons**, and it is a repository of myths, poems, philosophical reflections (for example the *Bhagavad Gita*, in which the god **Krishna** and the Pandava hero **Arjuna** debate the nature of duty, justice and fate) and straightforward folk tale. Ever since its compilation, it has permeated Hindu culture, from paintings and sculpture to comic strips, from dance-dramas and poetry to present-day musical films and TV soap operas.

MAHAf
Africa (North)

Mahaf, in Egyptian myth, was **Ra**'s boatman in the **Underworld**. Every night he steered the Sun-ship along the serpentine canals of darkness (in some accounts they were the coils of the world-snake **Aapep**), and every morning he delivered it safely to the world of light.

MAHAVIRA
India

Mahavira ('great hero'), in the Jain religion, was a real person: Vardhamana (c540-468BCE). The child of aristocratic parents, he lived a normal life until the age of 32, when he distributed his possessions to the poor and began a life of austerity and meditation, eventually starving himself to death in the ritual called *sallekhana*. His followers quickly surrounded his life with a halo of myth. Before he was born his mother had sixteen dreams forecasting the coming of a **tirkanthara** (a being greater than gods, who possesses all knowledge and spends time on earth teaching and practising austerities). Gods came to Earth to welcome his birth, and **demons** filled his parents' palace with precious stones and every beautiful flower or fruit in **creation**. As a boy he earned his title Mahavira by heroic deeds: taming a wild elephant, pulling out the hair of a god who tried to draw him up to **Heaven**. On the day he gave up worldly possessions the universe glowed with lotus-light, and at the moment of his enlightenment the gods themselves gathered to honour him. His **death** was marked by universal darkness, and his followers fell into a magic sleep, so that none saw him ascend to a diamond throne in Heaven, endowed with all-knowledge and free from the cycle of birth and rebirth which affects every other being in the universe.

MAHEO
Americas (North)

Maheo ('all-spirit'), in the myths of the Cheyenne people of the US Great Plains, existed before existence. By thought alone, he made the primordial ocean, and birds to fly over it. For a time the birds flew about happily enough, but eventually they needed land to rest on. One by one, they tried diving into the ocean to find mud or weeds to bring to the surface. All failed except Coot, who brought up a beakful of mud and placed it in Maheo's open palm. Maheo worked it, as potters in later times were to work lumps of clay, and it expanded and grew until it became the whole Earth. Maheo floated it on the surface of the ocean, but it was too heavy and began to sink. One by one, sea-creatures tried to support it on their backs – and all of them, even the great whales, were too weak. At last, Turtle, the oldest created being, took it on her back as she swam through space, and as soon as Maheo saw that it was safe, he clothed it with plants and created animals and human beings to live on it.

*This is one characteristic version of a common **creation**-story, known to mythographers as the 'Earth-diver Story': that the world was made from lumps of mud fished up from the bottom of the primordial ocean. In most accounts the fisher is a single being, the Great Diver or one of the animals – Beaver, **Coyote**, Otter, Rabbit – sacred to the particular people telling the story. This version is unusual in claiming that all existing creatures united to make our world.*

MAIT' CARREFOUR
Americas (Caribbean)

Mait' Carrefour ('lord of the crossroads'), in Voodoo myth, is **Ghede**'s younger brother, ruler of the powers of darkness and implacable enemy of **Legba** lord of light. He is young, virile and irresponsible, a magician and **shapechanger**. During the day he is weakened by sunlight, but when the **Moon** rises he drinks its light and redoubles his energy. During the night, he takes over from Legba as **guardian** of the crossroads between this world and the next, being and non-being – but unlike Legba, he is not placated by prayers and offerings, and is to be avoided rather than sought.

➺ **light and dark**

MAITREYA
Asia; India

Maitreya, in Buddhist myth and belief, is the **boddhisattva** who is to become the next **Buddha**. He waits, meditating, in **Heaven** (or, some say, in a secret place independent of the cycle of birth and rebirth), and will be born into the world 5000 years after the passing of **Siddhartha**. In some parts of the world, devotees claim that he already lives among us, but we are too blind to recognize him.

MALSUM
Americas (North)

Malsum, in the myths of a number of Iroquois and Algonquian peoples from the North American forests, was the twin brother of **Gluskap** – and just as Gluskap ruled light, so he ruled darkness. He created monsters and plagues to torment humankind, gave plants spines, insects stings and animals teeth and claws to hurt them, and fought a huge battle with Gluskap for control of the universe. Gluskap won, killing Malsum with a fern, and Malsum retreated to the **Underworld**, where he took wolfform and ruled all the **demons** of darkness.

➺ **creation, light and dark, twins**

MAMA BRIGITTE
Americas (Caribbean)

Mama Brigitte, in Voodoo myth, is the goddess of love – and since love is transient, she also rules **death**. She is kind, not malevolent: as dead souls travel to the **Underworld**, she falls in step with them, chatting and laughing to ease their journey.

MAMA QUILLA
Americas (South)

Mama Quilla, in Inca myth, was the **Moon** goddess: her face can be seen when the **Moon** is full. She married her brother the **Sun**, but lived apart from him, ruling night as he ruled day. She was the guardian of marriage promises and married women, supervising their monthly cycle and guaranteeing **fertility**.

➺ **Artemis**

MAMMITU
Asia (West)

Mammitu ('mother of fate'), in Mesopotamian myth, knew the life of every creature in the universe, from birth to **death** – and if you made the right sacrifice and paid the right price, her priests could be persuaded to consult her and tell you your future.

➺ **prophecy**

MANANNAN MACLIR
Europe (North)

Manannan MacLir ('Manannan son of **Lir**'), or Manawydan ab Llyr, in Celtic myth, was the god of the **sea**. He ruled either from an underwater palace or from the heart of a beautiful magic island, Tir Tairnigiri ('land of promise') or the Isle named Man after him. His beautiful wife Fand had an affair with **Cuculain**, and Manannan forced the lovers to part and gave each of them a potion of forgetfulness – the result of which was that although Fand could never remember the reason, she was forever resentful and discontented with Manannan. For his own part, Manannan often took the form of a heron, or put on his cloak of invisibility (mist) and visited mortal women: their children were always recognizable because their fingers and toes were webbed.

Manannan sailed his kingdom in a magic copper coracle, 'Wave-sweeper', a clone of the **Sun**-ship, and his rowing stirred up or calmed the waters. He owned a cup of truth (see **Cormac**), and a branch of the tree of the golden apples of **immortality**, whose tinkling twigs he shook to soothe the rage of dead souls on their way to the **Underworld**. Although he kept aloof from the other gods, he favoured the forces of light against **demons** of darkness, fostering **Lug** when his father **Balor** tried to kill him and, as the powers of the sky-gods declined, helping them to find new lives as the fairies and leprechauns of folk-tale.

This somewhat catch-all biography was formulated for Manannan by a ninth-century writer from the Isle of Man, who went on to say that Manannan later became a famous (real) wizard, priest and navigator, Manannan son of Oirbsen, one of the island's earliest rulers. The three-legged symbol of the Isle of Man is supposed to refer to Manannan, but no myth explains why – it actually originated as a depiction of the Sun-orb with rays flashing from it.

MANASA
India

Manasa, in Hindu myth, was the sister of **Shesha** the world serpent, or was born from **Shiva**'s semen after he masturbated over a lotus blossom. When the **snake-demon Vasuki** tried to poison **amrita** at the churning of the Sea of Milk, and Shiva sucked the venom into his own throat, Manasa saved Shiva's life by kissing him, taking the poison into her own mouth, and spitting it in small doses into the mouths of every snake and venomous insect and lizard in **creation**. For this she was given the honorific title Vishadhari ('controller of poison') and was granted power to cure the bite of venomous creatures of all kinds – or, if she was dissatisfied with the prayers and sacrifices made to her, to let the poison do its work.

MANCO CAPAC
Americas (South)

Manco Capac, in Inca myth, was the son of the **Sun**-god **Inti**, and founder of the Inca nation. There are two versions of his story. In one, Inti took pity on the misery of mortals, and sent Manco

Capac and his sister Mama Ocllo, to help them. Manco Capac and Mama Ocllo carried with them a huge lump of gold, broken off from the Sun: where it became too heavy to carry and fell to the ground, they were to build a city and found a nation. That place was Cuzco in Peru, and they made it the heart of the Inca empire.

In the second story (possibly older), Manco Capac, or Ayar Manco ('Father Manco'), was the youngest and most ambitious of Inti's four sons. (His brothers were Ayar Cachi, Ayar Oco and Ayar Ayca.) The four sons and their sisters strode across the world looking for a kingdom, and Manco plotted to get rid of each of his brothers in turn. He led Cachi, the eldest and most powerful, to a cave, saying that it might make a suitable palace – and as soon as Cachi was inside he piled stones across the entrance, walling him up forever. When the second brother, Oco, asked where Cachi was, Manco said he'd show him, but instead he took him to the edge of a precipice in the Andes and pushed him over. At this point the third brother, Ayca, ran away from the mountains to the plains and contented himself by ruling not people but plants (he became god of farming). Manco and his sisters travelled on to Cuzco, where Manco built a palace, married his eldest sister Mama Ocllo, and founded the Inca nation.

≫→ heroes

MANES
Europe (South)

Manes, in Roman myth, were **ghosts**. Their name comes either from **Mania**, thought to be their mother, or from *manare* ('to flow') because they flowed through the **Underworld** like an unending stream of bats or moths. They roosted in the Underworld, and people thought that if they ever escaped into the Upper World they would choke it and poison it. They were kept at bay by prayers, spells and offerings of fresh blood, poured on the ground at sacrifices. In later times, people believed that unless they kept statues or pictures of their own dead relatives, including them in family celebrations and daily prayers, those relatives' spirits would join the Manes, and would swarm into hearth and home with particular malevolence.

MANGARKUNGERKUNJA
Australia

Mangarkungerkunja ('flycatcher'), in the myths of the Aranda people of Central Australia, was one of the supernatural beings of the Dream Time. At that time the whole of Central Australia was **sea**, and no animals lived there but fish, birds, insects and amphibians. Mangarkungerkunja was an enormous lizard.

In due course the water receded, leaving desert. On the sand floor lay the first human beings, locked together as one single being. They were like logs: they had no features, no navels or genitals, and their arms and legs were fused to their bodies. Mangarkungerkunja prized them apart with his jaws, in the process tearing a small strip from the female's body (leaving a scar: the vagina) and attaching it to the male (the penis), and making seven holes in each of their heads (two eyes, two nostrils, two ears and a mouth) and one in each of their rumps (the anus). Finally he nibbled and worried until he had freed their arms and legs, and sent them scampering away to colonize the desert.

The myth goes on to say that Mangar-kungerkunja taught the descendants of these first humans all the arts and skills of survival, and ways of worshipping the spirits. In his honour, the Aranda people ever afterwards respected lizards above all other creatures. If you killed one, even accidentally, you were filled with such all-consuming lust that you died of it.

»→ animal-gods, civilization, crafts

MANI
Americas (South)

Mani, in the myths of the Amazon peoples of Brazil, was a beloved mortal elder. When he was about to leave the world he told his distraught followers that he would come back to sustain them in another form. One year after his departure, they were to dig in the ground. When they did so, they found Mani's body transformed into the *manioc* plant – and it has been a staple food ever since.

»→ farming

MANIA
Europe (South)

Mania ('madness', also known as Lara, 'babbler'), in Roman myth, was a **nymph** who prattled endlessly, until **Jupiter**, in exasperation, cut out her tongue. This fate was often used to warn noisy Roman children – and those who kept on chattering might be reminded that Mania was also the mother of the **Manes**, who were drawn irresistibly by the sound of babbling voices, and might come up from the **Underworld** at any moment.

MANJUSHRI
Asia (Central; East)

Manjushri, in Buddhist myth and belief, is the **boddhisattva** who converted the Chinese to Buddhism and who brought **civilization** to Tibet. He turns the wheel of **dharma**, enlightens suffering humanity, and annihilates **death**.

In art, Manjushri is shown holding a blue lotus, a book (symbolizing knowledge) and a sword (symbolizing truth).

MANU
India

Manu ('man'), in the Vedic myths of the Aryans who invaded India in the seventeenth century BCE, was the first human being, the creator of all other humans. **Manu and the flood.** Manu was washing his hands, when he found a tiny fish in the bowl. The fish asked for its life, and said that in return it would save Manu from death. Manu put it in a separate bowl of water. But it began to grow, and he was forced to move it, first to a tank, then to a lake, then to the **sea**. The fish told him that the world was about to be flooded, and advised him to build a boat. When the flood came, Manu tethered his boat to a horn on the fish's snout, and the fish towed it safely through the waters, finally anchoring it to a mountain-peak in the (still submerged) Himalayas. When the water receded, the fish revealed itself as **Vishnu** (or in some versions, **Brahma**) and ordered Manu to set about peopling the world.

Manu the Creator. Manu had stocked his boat with the seeds of every plant on Earth, and with one male and one female of every species of animal. But he was the only human being in existence, and at first there was no way for him to fill the world with creatures: being mortal, he lacked the gods' power to create beings by meditation alone. He sacrificed milk, clarified butter, curds and whey to the gods. In some accounts these offerings grew into a beautiful woman, **Parsu**, who became Manu's mate and co-parent of humanity; in others, the gods told him to how to make himself a wife from one of his own ribs.

Fourteen Manus. Hindu cosmology says that the cycle of **creation** and dissolution (including the flood and the restocking of the world) will be repeated fourteen times. Each cycle will last for 4,320 million years, and will include fourteen **floods**, each survived by a new Manu. There are therefore fourteen Manus in our present cycle – and the Manu of whom the stories above are told is the seventh, the initiator of our portion of human history. In some accounts he is identified with Vaivasvata, son of the Sun-god **Vivasvat**.

*Manu is said to have written the Laws of Manu, a collection of teachings, hymns, prayers, instructions for ritual and philosophical reflections which also retells several myths. Brahma himself is said to have dictated the Laws to Manu, who passed them in turn to the ten sages, one of whom, **Brighu**, gave it the form in which it survives today.*

⟫→ Atrahis, Deucalion and Pyrrha, Doquebuth, Noah, Nu'u, Utnapishtim

MARA
India

Mara ('destroyer', '**death**'), in Buddhist myth and legend, was the king of the **demons**. When **Buddha** settled to meditate under the *bho* tree, Mara realized that the eclipse of his own powers was imminent, and set out to distract Buddha in any way he could. He sent **maya** (delusion) to put into Buddha's mind that **Devadatta**, his princely rival, had stolen the royal throne; Buddha heard nothing. He flailed Buddha with **rain**, rocks, swords and burning coals; Buddha was unaffected. He sent Delight, Discontent and Thirst, his own daughters, to seduce him or torment him; Buddha ignored them. He hurled an army of demons at Buddha, thousand-mouthed, pot-bellied, howling and swallowing live **snakes** – and they rolled on the ground, harmless, paralyzed, their arms tied to their sides, as helpless as flies in a spider's larder. Finally Mara came himself, riding his storm-chariot and hurling his thunderbolt – and the bolt changed into a flower-garland and hung harmlessly above Buddha's head.

This myth, like most Buddhist stories, ends with teaching. Mara knew that although Buddha had attained enlightenment, and was beyond his reach, there was still the rest of humankind. Buddha had two paths open to him: to enter nirvana, or to

stay on Earth and preach the way of salva-
tion. Mara began whispering in Buddha's
ear, trying to persuade him to abandon the
world and go at once to experience nirva-
na's joys – and for the last time, Buddha
ignored him. Now, therefore, although
Mara lurks in ambush for every human
being ever born, we have Buddha's teach-
ing and example to guide us, and if we
follow it we, like him, can bypass Death.
≫→ Varuni

MARDUK
Asia (West)

Marduk ('bull-calf of the **Sun**'), son of
Ea the water-lord in Mesopotamian
myth, created the universe and everything in it.

Marduk and Tiamat. In the days
before **creation**, there was tension between the old generation of gods, led
by **Tiamat** (salt water) and her consort
Apsu (sweet water), and the younger
gods led by **An**, **Ea** and **Enlil**. Finally
Ea killed Apsu, and the old gods gathered an army of **monsters** and sent it,
under Tiamat's leadership, to overwhelm
the new gods. After some argument, the
new gods agreed to give Marduk supreme
power if he defeated Tiamat for them.
Marduk and Tiamat met in single combat:
she took the form of a dragon, he took the
form of wind. She swallowed him, and he
gusted inside her and swelled her like a
bullfrog. Then he stabbed her dead, and
her **demon**-army, not to mention the old
gods who sponsored it, vanished into the
darkness of space where they have
skulked ever since.

Marduk and Creation. Marduk
chopped Tiamat's body in two like an
enormous fish. From one half he made

the vault of **Heaven**, and built sky-palaces
for An, Ea and Enlil. From the other half
he made the world, piling mountains on
Tiamat's head, building cities and temples
on her chest and letting the rivers Tigris
and Euphrates run in tear-streams from
her eyes. He filled **Sky** with stars and
Earth with plants, established the seasons and invented time. Finally, he took
the demon Kingu, Tiamat's helper in the
challenge against the gods, slit his veins
and mixed the blood with dust to make
human beings.

The Babylonians were the chief people
to worship Marduk. They claimed that the
new gods built the city as a thank-offering
to Marduk, and that the ziggurat in the
centre of the city, the pillar which kept
Earth and Sky together, was both Mar-
duk's temple and the god himself, symbol
of universal stability. Other peoples said
that Marduk supported the universe as he
sat on his throne in majesty, and that if he
ever stood up (for example when tricked
into it by Erra, god of death), the stars
would run backwards in their courses,
time would be reversed and the world
of humans would be destroyed as Tiamat
rose again from the dead in storms and
earthquakes.

In art, Marduk was usually shown as a
warrior-king wielding the curved sword of
justice, sometimes with a gilded bull's
head to symbolize the power of the Sun.
≫→ Babel, civilization, creation, justice and universal order

MARINDI AND ADNOARTINA
Australia

Marindi and Adnoartina, in the myths of
the Pitjandjara people of the Gibson

Desert in West Central Australia, were rivals in the Dream Time. They hunted the same prey, were equal in strength and constantly bickered and fought. In the end Adnoartina took the form of a lizard, and challenged Marindi to fight him on the desert floor, not far from the outcrop white people later called Ayers Rock. Marindi took the form of a wild dog and accepted the challenge. They fought all day without advantage, and when darkness fell Marindi suggested that they stop until morning when they could see better. Adnoartina mocked him, saying that a true wild dog could see as well in darkness as in daylight. The fight began again, and Adnoartina snatched Marindi by the throat and choked him to death. He then dragged the carcass on to the Rock and ate it. Marindi's blood ran all over the Rock, which is why it is red to this day, and why it glows like blood in the evening sun.

≫→ animal-gods, Uluru

MARS
Europe (South)

Mars ('war'), in Roman myth, was one of the oldest gods of Italy, a spirit of **farming** from times from which no mythology survives. In later times he was identified with the Greek war god **Ares**, and Ares' myths were retold about him. But unlike the brainless and uncontrollable Ares, he was a dignified and thoughtful god, notable not only for his invincible power but for the self-control with which he managed it. He was the father of **Romulus and Remus**, the founder of the Roman state, the symbol of Roman might, majesty and fair-dealing, and the god most venerated throughout the Roman world after **Jupiter** and (in Imperial times) the Emperor himself.

MARUTS
India

The Maruts ('marchers'), in the Vedic myths of the Aryans who invaded India in the seventeenth century BCE, were storm-gods, associates of **Agni** the **fire**-god and **Vayu** the wind-god. In some accounts they were the children of **Diti** and **Kasyapa**. **Indra** sliced the embryo in their mother's womb into 49 parts – and they were born as clones, seven times seven troops of storm-gods. Other accounts give them different parents – the **sky**, the winds, the oceans, **lightning** – or say that they were self-generating. Equally, numbers vary: from seven, through eleven and 33 to 'three times sixty'. They had iron teeth, roared like lions, and patrolled the sky as Indra's storm-troops, hurling lightning-bolts and shooting **rain**-arrows.

MARY
Asia (West)

It is a commonplace of myth that the union of deities and mortals produces special individuals, often with particular affection for the human race. The Christian tradition varied this pattern chiefly by making Mary, mother of Jesus, not a princess but an ordinary woman, and stressing her normality to make her the epitome of human innocence and simplicity in the face of God. Early Christian writers went further, demystifying the miraculous aspects of Jesus' conception and birth by stressing the domestic problems of Mary's pregnancy, her journey on mule-back to a crowded village, her childbirth in a stable, and so on.

However, from the first century CE onwards, many Christian theorists (usually men and celibate) and the devout women who followed them used this framework to support an elaborate edifice of ideas about the nature, place in God's society and 'duties' of women. For some, it was not sufficient that Mary should have been a virgin mother. She herself had to be born from a sexless union, to be the 'thornless rose' who embodied a renunciation of carnality. (This denial of the corporeal for the elevation of the spiritual, though a traditional idea in many **mysteries** and meditative religions of the Middle and Far East, is rare in myth-accounts of virgin mothers.) For the edification of 'all Christian wives', Mary began to be treated as an icon of feminine 'honesty' and 'nobility', and was given either a semi-divine, miracle-working status which sat ill with previous accounts of her ordinariness, or a symbolic role as Mother and Intercessor in ideal form.

The final element in the creation of the Mary-myth was that, in a religious system otherwise dominated by males (from God 'himself' to the majority of martyrs and miracle-working saints), Mary was a convenient peg for all the residual beliefs and folk-practices associated with the **Great Goddess**. In newly Christianized societies, people could go on worshipping the Mother as they had always done, except that she was now dressed in Christian clothes. This kind of transformation is characteristic of Mother-worship in all traditions. No other deity more often changes aspects, form, name and attributes, remaking herself, or being remade, to suit the needs of each new group of worshippers. Followers of Mary – among the most fervent of all Christian believers – reject any suggestion that the accounts given of Mary in the Bible and by later Church writers are anything but facts. Viewed from the wider world of myth, however, they seem like pious invention in one of its most systematic and egregious forms.

➤ **Dido**

MASSASSI: *see* Mwuetsi, Massassi and Morongo

MATI-SYRA-ZEMLYA
Europe (East)

Mati-Syra-Zemlya ('mother-Earth-moist'), also known as Zemes Màte ('**Mother Earth**') or Zemyna, in Slavic myth, was worshipped not as a goddess in human shape, but as herself: the land beneath our feet. People communicated with her by digging a hole in the ground, speaking into it and then listening for her answer, or by kissing her at the beginning and end of journeys. She always answered immediately – and she helped everyone, especially mothers, and oversaw the world's **fertility** each spring (when people poured her wine or beer to drink, and buried bread for her to eat), and autumn. In times of plague, if you ploughed a furrow round your house at night, Mother Earth would fill it with power to keep infection out.

*In Christian times, priests responded pragmatically to continued worship of Mati-Syra-Zemlya by identifying her with the Virgin **Mary**. Even so, in times of plague, people often reverted to pre-Christian practice. The village women dug a furrow round the houses secretly at night, while carrying scythes. The furrow was to let out Mati-Syra-Zemlya's power to drive out the infection, and the scythes were to kill any men who met the procession.*
≫+ **Great Goddess, Mokosh**

MATSYA
India

Matsya, in Hindu myth, was the first avatar of **Vishnu**: the fish which warned **Manu** of the flood that was coming to drown the world, and which later towed his boat to safe anchorage on the only mountain-peak which was still visible above the water.
≫+ **animal-gods**

MAUI
Oceania

Maui's birth. Maui the **trickster** appears in more stories, from a wider area, than any other Polynesian god. He was twice-born. He was conceived by the human queen Taranga, secret mistress of Makea king of the **Underworld**. In some accounts he was her only son, in others her fourth (though the only one with an immortal father), in others the lucky seventh. Born prematurely when she was walking by the **sea** one day, he

was as unformed as a jellyfish and had no signs of life. She wrapped the body in strands of her hair and threw him into the sea – and the Sky-god Tama rescued him, hung him to dry like a spider's bundle from the rafters of the sky-house, then breathed life into him and gave him to sea-**nymphs** to carry safely back to shore, by now a fully-formed, mischievous young boy. Maui made his way to his mother's house, where she was blessing her children at the end of a feast, one by one in order, from oldest to youngest. He joined the end of the line and she blessed him unawares. Then he told her who she was, and she welcomed him and named him Maui Tikitiki a Taranga, 'Maui, Taranga's topknot'.

Maui and the Sun. Maui was an affectionate son, and worried that the days were too short and the nights too long: his mother had to begin weaving and preparing food in darkness, and it was night long before she finished. He decided that the reasons for this were that the sky was too low, almost touching Earth, and that the **Sun** had too many legs (rays), and ran too quickly across the sky. He dealt with the first problem by sticking a poker (or in some accounts, his own erect penis) into the sky, lifting it away from Earth as one prises open a clamshell, and propping it on mountain-tops. To deal with the Sun he took a club (some say the jawbone of his long-dead grandmother) and a noose, and tried to lassoo the Sun. But the rope was a single strand of dry flax, and the Sun easily burned through it and escaped. Maui made a new rope, this time twisting together strands of wet flax (or, some say, hair from his sister Hina Ika), lassooed the Sun and thrashed him with the club (or in some versions, cut off his legs, one by one) until the god promised to move more slowly across the sky.

Maui and fire. As the youngest child, Maui slept in his mother's bedroom. He woke one night and discovered that she was missing, but by daylight she was back. The same thing happened night after night, and he decided to investigate. He put on his mother's apron, changed into a pigeon and flew after her as she left the house. She went to a clump of reeds by a pool, pulled them up like a trapdoor and walked down into the gardens of the Underworld to spend the night with Makea her secret lover. Maui perched on the ground before them, threw off the apron and was revealed as himself: not a child any longer, but a full-grown young man. (In some accounts he grew from childhood to maturity in the time it took to shed the apron, and also took on the appearance of the war god Tu Matauenga.)

Maui's father, king of the Underworld, was happy to accept him as his son. But instead of giving him a new, secret name which would guarantee **immortality**, he offered him a present to take back to the Upper World: the secret of **fire**. In some accounts, he said that the secret was known only to a family of mud-hens, who used fire to roast bananas and scrabbled out the flames with their feet as soon as the cooking was done. Maui caught the smallest hen and forced her to say where fire went when it was scratched out – and she told him it hid in the wood of the *waimea* tree, and how to find it by drilling the soft flesh of the

tree with a spike of harder wood. In other accounts, fire belonged to the underworld goddess Mahu Ika: it was her fingernails and toenails. Maui went to the goddess, said that he was tired of eating his fish raw, and asked for a share of fire. Mahu Ika pulled out one of her fingernails and gave it to him. He went out of sight down the track, threw the nail in a puddle and went back to say that the fire had died. Mahu Ika gave him another nail, and he did the same thing. This happened nineteen times – the goddess moved from fingers to toes – and on the twentieth she was so angry that she hurled her last nail up into the Upper World, where it started a forest fire that took all Maui's efforts to tame before it engulfed the world. (In some accounts he used a **rain**-spell. In others he turned himself into an eagle and soared above the flames dropping cropfuls of water. The fire singed his feathers, and eagles are still brown and black today.) From the coming of fire onwards, Upper World beings have had light and heat and have enjoyed their fish cooked, and the Underworld inhabitants have eaten raw fish in dark and cold.

Maui goes fishing. Maui was an expert fisherman. He invented sails, fish baskets and barbed fish-hooks and taught his brothers to sail farther out from shore, where the fish were fatter. One day he took his magic club (or some say, sickle), made from the jawbone of his grandmother, baited it with blood from his own nose, and lowered it on a rope deeper than anyone had ever fished before. When he pulled up the catch it was a fish so huge that it seemed to fill the sea from horizon to horizon. In some accounts, Maui tied it behind the canoe and told his brothers to row home without looking back – but they looked, the rope parted and the fish broke up, the pieces forming a thousand islands scattered across the sea. In another, the fish became a single island, shaped like an enormous stingray, and Maui's brothers jumped on to its back, thrashing it into submission as it writhed and twisted under their feet, breaking it in two pieces and humping its back with mountains and gullies. Maui anchored it in the sea, and it has been called Ika a Maui ('Maui's fish') ever since, except by white settlers who named it New Zealand.

Maui and death. Maui heard that a woman of the Tuamotu islands, east of Tahiti, was tired of her husband Te Tuna. Te Tuna was a water-**monster**, an enormous eel, and she complained that she wanted sex with a man, a real man, and not a fish. Taking a flock of songbirds for companions, Maui strode across to the woman's home, stepping from island to island as people use stones in a stream, and enjoyed three days and nights of **sex**. Then Te Tuna appeared, heaving himself out of the sea, flailing his coils and surrounded by an army of smaller eel-monsters. Maui, undaunted, uncoiled his penis and used it to thrash the monsters until the sea ran red with blood. In some accounts, Te Tuna gave up the fight at last and slid back under the sea, where he has lurked in the depths ever since. In others Maui killed him and buried him on the beach; his penis grew into the first coconut palm – or, in some versions, Maui buried his head and grew the palm on top of it.

In some accounts, this was the end of the story. But in others the woman's name was Hine Nui Te Po, and she was the goddess of **death**. Maui, who was still trying to win the immortality his father had denied him, boasted to his songbird-companions that if he could conquer Te Tuna, he could easily outwit death. If he could crawl through Hine Nui as she slept, he would become fully immortal, and would share the secret with all creation. The only thing he asked was that the birds watch in silence: the slightest sound would break the spell. He parted Hine Nui's vagina as she slept, and plunged inside. The birds watched in silence until all of him had disappeared except his feet. Then the smallest bird, seeing Maui's toes twitching and wriggling like maggots, gave a single explosive cheep of a laugh, Hine Nui woke up in an instant, clenched her muscles and crushed Maui to death.

Apart from the substantial myth-stories told above, there are hundreds of trickster-tales involving Maui: virtually no Polynesian island is without. They show him not as a benevolent god but as a prankster, flying kites to blot out the Sun on a feast-day, inventing darts which then go astray like angry hornets, reincarnating a mischievous spirit as a dog. In one Hawaiian tale (a tradition quite different from the story of Maui and Hine Nui), he became such a nuisance that the people killed him and threw his body into the sea – and because shrimps fed on his blood, they have been rose-pink ever since.

≫→ **civilization, crafts, creation**

MAWU-LISA
Africa

Mawu-Lisa, in the myths of the Fon people of Dahomey, began as two separate gods, the female Mawu and the male Lisa. They were children of the first god of all, Nana Buluku, which contained in itself all creativity, but divided its female from its male self and gave them separate identities. Mawu and Lisa then combined into a single being, symbolizing the wholeness of the universe which they proceeded to create. (They first came together during an eclipse, and each eclipse thereafter led – and leads – to a new act of creation.) They were not gods in the sense that they had forms and required priests or worship; they were, rather, the principle of unity which guarantees stability and continuance in life. None the less they were associated with particular phenomena or qualities – Mawu with the **Moon**, darkness, **fertility**, forgiveness, gentleness and rest, Lisa with the **Sun**, heat, light, power, work and war – and when they created offspring, they gave them a share in some or all of these attributes. Their immortal children, who did have form and did require worship, included **Da**, the snake who supports the universe, the desert-god Age, the water-god twins-in-one Agbe-Naete, the thunder-god Heyvoso – and, most important for mortals, the smith-god **Gu**. Their mortal descendants, the human race, all sprang from seven pairs of **twins**, born to them at the seven first eclipses in universal history.

➳ creation

MAYA
India

Maya, in Buddhist myth and legend, was **Buddha**'s mother. Before he was born she dreamed that her womb became a miniature palace of crystal, and that Buddha entered it in the form of a beautiful white elephant. Seven days after his birth – which occurred miraculously, from her side – she died from the sheer joy of his existence, and was reborn in **Heaven**, where the infant Buddha joined her for three months, preaching and consoling her.

The word maya means 'delusion': that is, not reality but what the mind makes of it. One explanation of Maya's ***death*** *is that in order for Buddha to achieve enlightenment, he had to be freed from the trappings of delusion – an explanation reinforced by stories of the period he spent meditating under the* bho *tree, during which* ***Mara*** *the Destroyer sent maya (or in some accounts Maya) to seduce him from the true path of meditation.*

MAYAUEL
Americas (Central)

Mayauel, in Aztec myth, discovered alcohol. Seeing a mouse staggering about one day, she realized that it had eaten *agave* seeds, and she increased the power of the plant by boiling the seeds and distilling them. She became a favourite god with ordinary people, and was credited with every kind of benefaction from soothing the pains of **childbirth** to keeping ghosts away at night. Upper-class Incas, who never drank, tried to stamp out her cult, but it outlived them.

MEDB
Europe (North)

Medb ('intoxication'), in Celtic myth, was the goddess of sovereignty, granting legitimate rule to any king she slept with. Unfortunately for mortals, she was also sexually ravenous, coupling with every man she saw – and to stop all men quarreling for rule, she forced them to fight to the **death**, so that she was also a goddess of **war** and blood.

*Christian mythographers made Medb a neat personification of the evils of alcohol. But in pagan myth she was more sinister, a relation of the **Morrigan** and her war-goddess sisters, and the dark force at the heart of all mortal pomp and kingship. She sponsored the war between the people of Ulster and Connaught, during which **Cuchulain** was killed, and she later allowed nine of her human paramours to survive and form kingdoms in Ireland: the nine kingdoms, source of much later civil war. In later times, like most Celtic gods, she diminished in importance and became a character in folktales: Mab (later called Titania), the malevolent and nymphomaniac queen of the fairies.*

»→ demons

MEDEA
Europe (South)

Medea in Colchis. Medea (Medeia, 'cunning'), in Greek myth, was the daughter of King Aeëtes of Colchis, and grand-daughter of the **Sun**. In some accounts her mother was a **mountain-nymph**, in others **Hecate** goddess of midnight, from whom she learned black magic. When **Jason** and the **Argonauts** came to Colchis to steal the **Golden Fleece**, **Eros** fired an arrow of desire for Jason into her heart, and she used her magic to help him complete the tasks Aeëtes set him, to steal the Fleece and to escape to Greece, where she married him. (She slowed down pursuit by cutting her brother Apsyrtus into pieces and throwing them overboard, so that Aeëtes had to stop and gather them each time for burial.)

Medea in Iolcus and Corinth. Back in Greece, Medea's first idea was to make Jason king of Iolcus, by killing **Pelias** who had usurped his throne years before. Pelias was an old man, and she pretended to his daughters that it was possible to rejuvenate him by magic. She boiled an old ram in a pot of herbs, miraculously produced a frisking lamb – and said that the same change would happen to Pelias if *he* were boiled. When the rejuvenation failed, Medea and Jason fled from Iolcus to Corinth, where they lived for several years and had two children, Mermerus and Pheres. But Jason still coveted a throne. He planned to divorce Medea and marry Princess Glauce of Corinth, and Medea punished him by sending Glauce a poisoned wedding dress and crown which killed both her and her father, and then by stabbing Mermerus and Pheres dead. Jason sent soldiers to arrest her, but she flew out of reach overhead in the chariot of the Sun, her dead children at her feet.

Medea in Athens. Before Medea committed all these murders, she had promised King **Aegeus** of Athens that if he gave her sanctuary she would end his childlessness. She now went to

Athens and lived for a time as Aegeus' mistress. They had a son, Medus. But then Aegeus' elder son **Theseus**, whom his father had never known, arrived in Athens, and Medea, realizing who he was, tried to poison him to prevent him taking Medus' place as Aegeus' heir. Just in time Aegeus dashed the poison-cup from Theseus' lips, and once again Medea was forced to mount the Sun's chariot and flee for her life. In some accounts she went to Colchis and bewitched Jason into remarrying her; in others she went to the **Underworld** and married **Achilles**' ghost.

The story of Medea's part in the expedition of the Argonauts is told by Apollonius of Rhodes in his Argonautica, *and Valerius Flaccus, in his otherwise turgid book of the same name, gives a magnificent portrait of Medea as a woman driven mad by the conflicting claims of love for Jason and addiction to black magic. This aspect of her personality fascinated male Roman writers – perhaps because it was so far removed from their ideal of matronhood and motherhood – and she was a favourite character (for example in Ovid's* Heroides*) and the model for a thousand accounts of witches, madwomen, murderers and seers, in works by such authors as Catullus, Horace, Propertius and Virgil (whose* **Dido** *is a fascinating blend of witch-woman, dignified queen and pathetic heroine).*

The greatest artwork of ancient times to deal with Medea is Euripides' tragedy. Some claim – with a somewhat disingenuous failure to separate reality and fiction – that he wrote it at the request of the people of Colchis (and for a large fee) to blame Medea for the deaths of Mermerus and Pheres, whom the Corinthians had themselves butchered. Euripides' play is the character-study of a lover betrayed by the man she loves, a mother forcing herself to kill her own children, a foreigner at odds with the customs of the people she lives among – and not least an immortal (grand-daughter of the Sun) who chooses to accept the feelings and constraints of mortality, and is as unable to cope with them as the mortals around her are unable to cope with her. Her soliloquies in this play, of panic, hate, revenge and suffering, set models which influenced every later dramatist.

Ancient artists, with their delight in the gruesome, depicted especially the boiling of Pelias (pop-eyed in his cauldron while his daughters look on aghast and Medea stands serenely in the background), Glauce dying in agony from the poisoned wedding-dress, and above all Medea putting her sons to the sword. Curiously, the very power of ancient treatments of the story seems to have frightened off more recent creators. Apart from an opera by Cherubini, a tragedy by Grillparzer, a novel by Henry Treece (and some scenes in Robert Graves' novel The Golden Fleece*) and a ballet written by Samuel Barber for the mesmeric Martha Graham, Medea has made few post-classical appearances.*

MEDUSA
Europe (South)

Medusa ('ruler'), in Greek and Roman myth, was the eldest of the three **Gorgons**, and the favourite of her father the Old Man of the **Sea**. He showed his favour by allowing her now and again to shed her hideousness and appear as a beautiful mortal woman – making one condition only, that on these occasions she should take on actual mortality, shedding **immortality** for a moment. Once, when Medusa was disporting herself as a mortal, **Poseidon** lusted after her, and made love to her in a temple of **Artemis**. Furious, Artemis cancelled Medusa's beauty, took away her immortality forever and banished her to her lair with her sisters in Cisthene. (In some accounts she also changed Medusa's hair to snakes. Until then it had been long and beautiful, the only part of her untouched by hideousness.) It was because Medusa was cursed with mortality that **Perseus** was able to steal into Cisthene, kill her and cut off her head.

MELAMPUS
Europe (South)

Melampus (Melampous, 'black-foot'), son of Amythaon and Idomenea in Greek myth, was the first human being to be given second hearing and second sight. One day his slaves were cutting down a tree when they found a nest of **snakes** in the hollow trunk. Before Melampus could stop them they killed the parents, and he was only just in time to save the young snakes. Remembering that snakes are servants of **Gaia** (**Mother Earth**), he burned the adults' bodies and buried the ashes, then took the young home to rear. That night he felt them licking his ears, and realized that he could understand every word they said: Gaia had rewarded him with the ability to understand the language of every living creature in the world. Later, **Apollo** gave him the power of seeing into the past and future as easily as the present.

Melampus soon had a chance to put his new powers to work. His brother Bias wanted to marry a girl called Pero. Her father had promised her to any man who stole the cattle of Phylacus, a nearby landowner, and Bias asked Melampus to steal the cattle for him. Anyone else would have thought this a crime, but Melampus' special powers told him that if he stole the cattle he would be imprisoned for one year only, but would then be set free, hailed as a hero and given the cattle as a gift. Accordingly, he stole the cattle and was duly caught and thrown into prison.

For three hundred and sixty four days Melampus sat in his prison-cell, eavesdropping on the conversations of ants, spiders and other insects. That night he heard two woodworms congratulating each other on a job well done. They had gnawed through the beam supporting Phylacus' palace roof, and next morning it would fall in and kill everyone inside. Melampus told Phylacus this conversation. At first Phylacus thought that a year in prison had driven Melampus mad, but when he evacuated the palace and the roof fell in as prophesied, he immediately set him free. Melampus now told him the conversation of a pair of vultures, who happened to know how Phylacus' son, until then childless, could father children – and when this, too, happened as prophesied, Phylacus gave Melampus all his cattle in gratitude. Melampus gave Bias the cattle, and Bias married Pero.

Later, Melampus offered to cure the two daughters of King Proetus of Argolis. They had offended **Hera** (or some say, **Dionysus**), and had been driven mad for it – they thought they were cattle, and ran about the fields like cows plagued by flies, lowing, shrieking and trying to trample passers-by. Melampus offered to cure them for one third of Proetus' kingdom. Proetus refused – as Melampus knew he would – and only relented when all the women of the kingdom went mad and also began behaving like cattle. Melampus now said that the price had changed. He wanted a third of the kingdom for himself and another third for Bias. Reluctantly Proetus agreed, and Melampus and Bias led all the cattle-women to drink in a stream which Melampus' powers told him originated in the river **Styx** in the **Underworld** (or, in some accounts, fed them with hellebore, a plant whose roots grow all the way down to the Styx). So they were cured, and Melampus and Bias ruled Argolis jointly with Proetus until the day they died.

≫→ **prophecy**

MENELAUS
Europe (South)

Menelaus as a young man. Menelaus (Menelaos, 'leader of the people'), in Greek myth, was the son of **Atreus** and Aerope, and **Agamemnon**'s younger brother. Unlike Agamemnon, who was a brisk martinet, Menelaus was soft and easy-going: handsome, good at singing and dancing and fond of flirting. After **Aegisthus** murdered Atreus and usurped the throne of Mycenae, Agamemnon and Menelaus were exiled to the court of King **Tyndareus** of Sparta. Here Agamemnon married Tyndareus' daughter **Clytemnestra**, and Menelaus married her sister **Helen**, the most beautiful woman in the world. Agamemnon and Clytemnestra raised an army and went to drive out Aegisthus and rule in Mycenae. Menelaus and Helen stayed in Sparta, where Tyndareus abdicated in Menelaus' favour.

The Trojan War. Menelaus and Helen ruled Sparta for several years, and had several children including **Hermione**. Then Prince **Paris**, encouraged by the goddess **Aphrodite**, stole Helen and took her to Troy – or, some say, the gods spirited Helen away to Egypt, and gave Paris a phantom-Helen to take to Troy – and Menelaus and Agamemnon organized a huge Greek army to win her back. During the ten years of the war, Menelaus was famous for the showiness and dazzle of his forays against the enemy – his well-coiffed red hair, ornate war-cry and polished golden armour made him conspicuous wherever he showed himself. On one occasion he came face-to-face with Paris, and the war would have ended in a duel if Aphrodite had not intervened and spirited Paris out of harm's way.

After the sack of Troy, Menelaus took Helen home – or, in accounts involving the phantom-Helen, sailed for home alone, only to be blown off-course to Egypt, where he found and rescued the real Helen. His intention was to execute her in Sparta, for causing the deaths of so many thousand Greeks. But she easily won him round, and he spent the rest of his life in uxorious bliss, a man whose existence, from first to last, had been as futile as it was gaudy.

Menelaus is a noble character in Homer's Iliad *and* Odyssey: *a brave and*

heroic prince battling for his wife, a serious and worthy king of Sparta. His reputation as fop and fool begins with Euripides (especially in Women of Troy, Orestes and Helen) – and it is this side of him, or the duality between it and the other, which fascinates most later writers, from Apollodorus to Goethe, from Virgil to Giraudoux.
≫→ heroes

MENESS
Europe (East)

Meness, or Menulis, the **Moon** in Baltic myth, rode the sky in a grey chariot and wore a cloak of stars. He married **Saule** the **Sun**, but almost immediately was unfaithful with Ausrine the Morning Star, and was sliced in two by Saule's father Perkunas. Instead of learning from this experience, Meness repeated the adultery every month, and suffered the same punishment.

MEPHISTOPHELES
Europe (Central)

Mephistopheles ('hater of the light'), in the **Faust** story, is either the Devil himself or his cynical, shape-changing lieutenant, sent to Earth to catch Faust's soul.
≫→ demons

MERCURY: *see* Hermes

MERLIN
Europe (North)

Merlin (or Myrrdin), in Celtic and medieval Christian myth, was the child of a nun and a **demon**. From his mother (who plunged him in holy water as soon as he was born) he inherited a love of the mortal world and a desire to help it, from his father the restlessness and sexual insatiability of the **shape-changer**. Often he took human form, either as a wizard advising such kings as Vortigern or **Arthur** (whose education he supervised, and for whom he made the Round Table), or as a handsome young man seducing every girl he met. But equally often he disappeared from the mortal world, spending time as a breeze, a water-current, a cloud or in suspended animation as thought itself.

At the time of the quest for the **Holy Grail**, Merlin's advice would have been invaluable to **Galahad** and the other Grail-knights. But some time before, he had become ensnared with another shape-changer, **Nimue** (called Vivien in some accounts). She fostered him as a child, and as he grew up fell in love with him. But he rejected her and left her for the mortal world, and her love soured into hate. She took on every imaginable shape to try to catch him, and each time he outwitted her. But finally she became a beautiful mortal woman, and seduced him. Merlin's lust made him blind to her true identity, he mounted her – and when he was deep in the ecstasy of intercourse, she changed into a drop of amber and engulfed him. Immortal, they remain trapped together forever. Each knows all the other's secrets, and neither can escape.

*In other accounts, it was the **Lady of the Lake** who loved Merlin, and she trapped him by a double illusion, surrounding him with a cloud which he took for a thorn-bush or a hollow oak-tree – and from which he is still, now, fighting to break free. In these* accounts (most of which are late, and Christian), the Lady of the Lake then abjured her shape-changing nature, retreated to her castle on the isle of **Avalon**, and lived on there as a kind of abbess, welcoming with sober banquets and austere entertainments the souls of such deserving mortal **heroes** as Arthur.

≫→ prophecy

MERU, MOUNT
India

Mount Meru (or Sumeru), in Hindu and Buddhist myth, was the home of the gods. It was a lotus-shaped **mountain**, built of gold and so vast that only **Brahma** could comprehend it. It rested on seven lower worlds, which lay on top of one another like concentric wheels of ever-decreasing size, and the whole edifice was supported by the serpent **Vasuki** (or, in other accounts, **Shesha**, four elephants or four **giants**). Brahma's palace and gardens were built on the summit, 252,000 miles above the surface of the Earth, and were enfolded by the waters of the Ganges. The palaces and gardens of **Vishnu** and **Krishna** were built on levels lower down. Mount Meru's honorific names included Devaparvata ('Mountain of the Gods'), Hemadri ('Golden Mountain'), Karnikacala ('Lotus Mountain') and Ratnasanu ('Jewel Peak').

MESKHENT
Africa (North)

Meskhent, or Meskhenet ('brick'), in Egyptian myth, was the goddess of **childbirth**. In the world of the living she assisted mothers in labour and saw that the correct destiny was allocated to each newborn child. In the **Underworld** she helped souls in their rebirth into the afterlife.

Meskhent's name comes from the fact that Egyptian women squatted on small raised platforms (called 'bricks') to give birth. She was shown in art as a brick with a woman's head or a woman with a brick for a crown.

MESOPOTAMIAN MYTH

Mesopotamia ('land between the rivers', that is the flood-plain of the rivers Tigris and Euphrates) contained some of the earliest **farming** and city settlements in the world, dating back to 3000BCE or earlier. They centred on a number of vast cities, each with its satellites and provinces: Erech and Ur in the South, Babylon in the centre, Ashur, Nineveh and Carchemish in the North. Over the years Mesopotamian influence spread to the mountains of what we now think of as Kurdistan and the coastal region East of the Aegean Sea; there was cultural movement East into Persia, and to some extent West into Egypt.

Given the vastness of the area and the harshness of much of its geography, the city-plus-satellite political structure was inevitable, and each of the great centres of **civilization** developed the core myths in its own individual way. (The myth of the Tower of **Babel**, an egregious, late creation, fictionalizes this dispersal in a particularly elegant way.) A characteristic example is the way **Inanna**, goddess of **fertility** in some regions, becomes in others the war-goddess **Ishtar** – and then, in most of the traditions which have come down to us, blends the two aspects. The **Flood** story, typical of a region whose fertility depended on annual inundations, was told in many different places, each time with almost identical details but attached to the name of a different, local cult-figure: **Atrahis** king of Shurupak, **Noah** of Ur, **Utnapishtim** of Babylon.

One problem for mythographers is that the region was also the birthplace of four of the world's great monotheistic religions: Judaism and Christianity in the West, Islam in the South and Zoroastrianism in the East. In each case, dogmatic belief-systems took what they wanted from the original myths, and destroyed or vilified the rest. For example, knowledge of many of the ancient gods and myths of the Eastern Aegean area was dominated until the 1930s (when a cache of tablets was found telling many ancient Canaanite myths) by the attitudes taken towards them in the Bible Old Testament. In this, all gods but **Yahweh** became 'false gods' (and many – **Baal**, for example – were run together into one), or were turned into angels or **demons** (**Gabriel**; **Satan**). Other myth-figures were received into the religious canon with a new (and in mythographers' eyes, somewhat perverted) identity: **Adam and Eve** and **Noah** are examples, reinvented as human ancestors and given family trees of descendants stretching down to the time of the priests and teachers who codified the new religions.

This process of evolution and assimilation is common throughout the world. The Aryan invaders of India and Christian missionaries to Celtic and Slavic Europe, for example, did exactly the same thing to the aboriginal gods they found. But in the Mesopotamian area it was done with unequalled single-mindedness, and was backed up very early by the production of sacred writings which gave canonical force to the religious interpretation of the stories. The result, for Mesopotamian myth, is that many tales have vanished altogether, and others survive either in fragments (Baal-stories are particularly prone to this) or as self-standing narratives like the story of **Gilgamesh**, complex but isolated, amputated both from the cultures they once adorned and from later developments.

The basic structure of Mesopotamian mythology is a hierarchical pantheon of gods, led by such abstract and aloof forces as **An** or **El** and dominated by groups of gods which stabilize and control the universe by keeping their conflicting powers in balance. Some of these were triads, for example that between Space (usually named An), Water (usually named **Ea**) and Storm (usually named **Enlil**). Others were dyads, *yin*-and-*yang* pairings such as fresh water (Apsu) and salt water (**Tiamat**), chaos (**Leviathan**; **Ninurta**; Tiamat) and order (**Anat**; **Ninhursaga**; **Marduk**) or **light** (Inanna; Ahura Mazda) and **dark** (**Ereshkigal**; **Ahriman**) – this last a duality later imported into religious thinking and given philosophical and ethical force, as for example between Yahweh and Satan or **Ahura Mazda** and Ahriman. Other gods – **Shamash** the **Sun**, **Sin** the **Moon**, **Enki** the **trickster**, **Nabu** the scribe, **Telepinu** lord of agriculture – play lesser parts, while human beings tend to cower on the sidelines, made originally in the divine image but doomed to mortality either because of some squabble between the gods (as in the pre-Judaic version of the myth of the Garden of Eden) or because of their own stupidity (as in the Judaic version of the Eden myth, or the story of **Yima** in Zoroastrian belief).

➤➤→ Adad, Adapa, Ashur, Astarte, Beelzebub, Borak, Cain, Dagon, houris, Illuyankas, Imdugud, Kusor, Lilith, Mammitu, Mary, Nabu, Nanna, Nergal, Og, Samson, Sheol, Tengri, Teshub, Utu

MESSENGERS: *see* Anansi, Bragi, *brighus*, Coyote, Eshu, Gabriel, Haiuri, Hermes, Holawaka, Horus, Imilozi, Iris, Kalumba, Leza and Honeybird, Sraosha

METAMORPHOSES

Metamorphoses ('Changes') was a collection of myths and folk-tales made by the Roman poet Ovid some time between 2BCE and 8CE. Ovid took his tales from ancient classical and Middle Eastern stories about gods and mortals who underwent mysterious transformations – a subject of endless fascination to the Greeks and Romans, and seminal to their myths – and told them with a blend of tongue-in-cheek wit and romantic detail, humanizing even the most bizarre beings by making them bustle and fuss about domestic detail. In medieval Europe, *Metamorphoses* became one of the most influential of all ancient books, inspiring such writers as Chaucer, Boccaccio and the authors of the *Hexameron*,

and spreading East with the Crusaders to influence the style of such Arabian collections as *The Thousand and One Nights*. Many of Ovid's stories – **Jason** and **Medea**, **Orpheus** and Eurydice, **Polyphemus**, **Persephone**, **Tereus** and Procne, **Venus** and **Adonis** – are also retold by others, but some, including **Baucis and Philemon**, **Echo** and **Narcissus**, **Midas**, reach the modern world from his pen alone.

METIS
Europe (South)

Metis ('counsel'), in Greek myth, was the daughter of **Gaia** (**Mother Earth**) and Air (or, some say, of Gaia and **Ocean**). She told **Zeus** how to rescue his brothers and sisters who had been swallowed by their father **Cronus**, and Zeus rewarded her by making her his first queen and consort (this was before he married **Hera**). However, as soon as Metis became pregnant, Gaia told Zeus that if the child was a boy, he would grow up to be stronger than his father. To prevent this, Zeus ate Metis alive – exactly as Cronus had done when told that his children would dethrone him. The result was a headache so appalling that he asked **Prometheus** to help him, and Prometheus held his head while **Hephaestus** split it open with wedge and hammer. At once **Athene** sprang out: the goddess of wisdom and war, fully-formed. She was not Zeus' son, and was therefore no threat to his power. As for Metis, she retreated to a far corner of the sky, where she was given the planet Mercury to govern.

MEZENTIUS
Europe (South)

Mezentius, in Roman myth, was an Etruscan king who ruled by fear. His pleasure was devising ever more excruciating tortures and testing them on his subjects, not to mention such methods of execution as tying a living person to a corpse and watching them decay together. In the end his people banished him, and when **Aeneas** and the Trojans came to Italy, he allied with **Turnus** against them, hoping to be restored to power and to be given the chance of reprisals against those who banished him. For their part, the Etruscans allied with Aeneas.

Mezentius' only weakness was his love for his young son Lausus. The boy insisted on wearing armour and fighting, and his father reluctantly allowed him. But in the last battle between the Trojans and Mezentius' army, Aeneas wounded Mezentius, and Lausus ran between them to give his father time to escape. Aeneas gestured at the boy to keep out of the way – and accidentally caught him in the stomach with his sword-point and killed him. Mezentius, mad with rage, jumped on his war-horse to ride Aeneas down. Aeneas stabbed the horse dead, and it rolled on top of Mezentius, killing him and sending his soul to the **Underworld**, where the **Furies** gleefully began practising on him the tortures he had himself devised on Earth.

MICHABO
Americas (North)

Michabo ('Lord Hare'), in the myths of many Algonquian peoples of the Northern US forests, was lord of the East Wind. Mist and cloud were the smoke of his pipe, and his anger flashed from him in **thunder** and **lightning**. He lived in a sky-palace far above **Mother Earth**, and let Dawn gallop from his stables there each morning. In some accounts, he feuded with his father West Wind, and their arguing scoured the world with hurricanes.

Michabo often went down to Earth to hunt. He was a **shape-changer**, and could take the forms of more than a thousand animals, but usually went as a human huntsman, using wolves for hunting-dogs. One day his pack ran into a lake (Lake Superior) and vanished. Michabo waded out to look for them, and caused such turbulence that the water overflowed and covered the whole of Mother Earth. Michabo sent **Raven** to look for a grain of dust, out of which he could reconstruct dry land. But there was none. Michabo sent an otter swimming through the water to look for floating weed, with the same result. Finally, Michabo sent Muskrat diving to the bottom, and Muskrat brought up just enough land for Michabo to mould in his fingers and remake Mother Earth. Michabo covered it with grass, trees and other plants, and mated with Muskrat to create the human race.

A pendant to this myth, possibly post-Christian, says that Michabo's companions are the souls of the righteous, and that they spend eternity holding banquets in his palace, singing and dancing in his honour.

▶▶▶ **animal-gods, creation, Gluskap, Nanabush**

MICTLAN
Americas (Central)

Mictlan ('land of the dead'), in Aztec myth, was a kingdom in the far North of the universe. To reach it, the dead soul made a terrifying journey through eight forests of predatory trees, across eight deserts filled with poisonous snakes, over eight mountains where the wind hurled knives, and over a fast-flowing river. Once over the river, the soul spent four years working its way through the first eight layers of the **Underworld**, losing a little more of its remaining mortality each time, until it was pure essence and ready to take its place in the ninth region, Mictlan proper.

In contrast to the bustle and pain of the mortal world, Mictlan was a place of absence: no suffering, no shadows, no sound, no movement. It was as if the dead were hibernating – except that their stillness was forever, and no return to activity was possible. In a way hard for the Spanish conquerors of the Aztecs to understand (since Mictlan was a place without moral or ethical resonance, in no way resembling the Christian paradise), human beings longed for it, as the goal to which all mortal life was leading: **death** for them was not an end, but the opening of a door.
≫→ Tuonela

MIDAS
Europe (South)

The Golden Touch. Midas (Meidas, 'seed'), son of the goddess **Cybele** in Greek myth, was a fool, never content with good luck when he found it. In some accounts, he was a rose-grower who stumbled across a treasure in his garden while planting new stock. Overnight he became the richest person in the land (Macedonia) and the people made him king. He still went on tending his roses, and one morning found **Silenus**, king of **Dionysus'** followers the **Satyrs**, snoring in a flower-bed, sleeping off the revels of the night before. Midas entertained Silenus for five days as an honoured guest, and Dionysus offered him any reward he cared to name.

Greed drove every sensible request out of Midas' head. He asked that everything he touched should be turned to gold, and Dionysus agreed. For the next few hours Midas was as happy as a child, turning grass, trees, stones and especially his finest rose-blooms to gold. But when he found himself at the evening meal chewing gold for meat and drinking gold for wine, he begged Dionysus to take back the gift. (In some accounts, his young daughter also ran to sit on his lap – and was turned to gold.) Dionysus told him to go and wash in the river Pactolus, in the distant Asian kingdom of Phrygia – and after a long journey, during which he could neither eat nor drink, and the ground he trod on turned to a golden path under his feet, Midas reached the river and plunged in. At once the golden touch was washed away (and to this day, the Pactolus still abounds in grains and lumps of gold).

Ass's ears. King Gordius of Phrygia, fascinated by Midas' story, offered him half his kingdom to stay, and Midas, delighted not to have to return to

Macedonia and his jeering people, founded the city of Ancyra and settled there. Once again he had the chance of happiness, and threw it away by stupidity. He was walking one day by the river when he overheard **Pan** and **Apollo** arguing about who was the better musician. Midas hid in the reeds to listen while they played in turn to Tmolus the river-god. But when Tmolus declared Apollo the winner, Midas rushed out of hiding and shouted that *he* thought Pan's **music** best. Apollo punished him by giving him ass's ears.

Ashamed and embarrassed, Midas covered his head with a turban. No one knew of his ass's ears except his barber, and Midas forbade him, on pain of death, to tell another human being. For years the barber kept the secret, but then one night, tormented beyond endurance, he crept into a field, dug a hole and whispered into it, 'Midas has ass's ears', confiding the secret to **Mother Earth** before hastily filling in the hole. Time passed. A bank of reeds (or some say, a field of corn) grew where the hole had been. And whenever the wind blew, the stalks bent their heads together and whispered 'Midas has ass's ears' until the whole of Phrygia knew. Not even executing the barber soothed Midas' embarrassment. In the end he drank hot bull's blood (an old Macedonian way of committing suicide) and choked to death.

MIDGARD
Europe (North)

Midgard ('middle world'), in Nordic myth, was the home of mortals. At the beginning of **creation**, **Odin**, **Vili** and **Ve** made it from the eyebrows of the **giant Ymir**. It was the world as we know it, and was a vast, fertile country in the centre of the universe, flanked to the East by **Jotunheim**, home of the giants, to the South by Svartalfheim, home of the dark elves, and to the West by Nidavellir, home of dwarfs. It was joined to Asgard by the rainbow-bridge **Bifröst**, but although gods could travel from Asgard to Midgard, no mortals were ever allowed to pass the other way, except for the souls of dead **heroes**, carried by the **Valkyries** to **Valhalla**.

MI HUNG TANG
Asia (East)

Mi Hung Tang ('potion of forgetting'), in Chinese myth, was made by Lady Meng, who lived just outside the gates of the **Underworld**. Dead souls who had passed through Hell, been judged and were now returning to new lives in the Upper World drank Mi Hung Tang, and all memory of their former lives was wiped from their minds. All that was left was pain – something which not even a drink distilled from the Water of Oblivion could make them forget.
➤ **Lethe**

MIKULA
Europe (East)

Mikula, in Russian myth, was the favourite of **Mati-Syra-Zemlya**, (**Mother Earth**). She gave him giant strength – no one else could lift his plough – and let him gallop across her faster than any other living being. Originally a god, he was downgraded in Christian times to

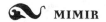

become one of the **bogatiri**, but never stopped using his strength and goodwill to help those who prayed to him.

≫→ **giants**

MI LO
Asia (East)

Mi Lo, in Chinese myth, was an ancient **fertility** god taken over by Buddhists and identified with **Maitreya**, the **Buddha** still to come. So far from being an ascetic intellectual, he was jovial, fat and fertile, the father of countless children. He sat on his throne listening to prayers, and you could tell that he was concerned because however much his lower face beamed, his forehead always frowned.

MIME: *see* Regin

MIMI
Australia

Mimi, in the myths of the peoples of West Arnhem Land in Northern Australia, were spirits which lived deep in rock crevices, and took the form of human figures so thin that they were afraid to come out in case they snapped like grass-stalks in the wind. Although their favourite food was yams, they also attacked and ate strangers who wandered near their homes. For this reason, people in lonely, rocky places constantly sang and shouted to warn the Mimi they were there – and also took care not to hurt wallabies they found there, the Mimi's pets. On windless days and nights, when no one was about, the Mimi sometimes did venture out of shelter, and decorated the rocks with delicate self-portraits.

≫→ **monsters and dragons**

MIMIR
Europe (North)

Mimir, in Nordic myth, was one of the oldest and wisest of the **Aesir**. At the end of the war between the Aesir and the **Vanir**, he went with **Honir** as hostage to the Vanir. The Vanir tried to persuade them to tell the secrets of the Aesir, but Honir was dumb and Mimir refused to speak. In fury, the Vanir cut off Mimir's head and sent it in a parcel back to **Odin**, king of the Aesir. He kept it alive with magic herbs, and planted it in a shrine beside the root of **Yggdrasil** which grew out of **Asgard**. Ever afterwards, a spring of knowledge flowed from this spot. It was known as Mimir's Spring, and Odin often galloped there on his eight-legged horse Sleipnir to ask advice. He was allowed to drink the waters of knowledge only once, and had to pay with one of his own eyes. On every other occasion he put questions to Mimir's head, and it told him the secrets of the universe.

*This is the only substantial story in world mythology in which a talking head reveals all-knowledge. But the idea is common in folk-tales: often, giants' or witches' heads are cut off by **heroes** or heroines and thrown into or planted in the ground near wells, and their presence gives the water magic powers. In some accounts Mimir's head is planted not in Asgard, but beside the Well of Urd in **Midgard**.*

≫→ **Bran, prophecy**

MIN
Africa (North)

Min, in Egyptian myth, was one of the most ancient desert gods, a protector of hunters and travellers. His weapon was the thunderbolt, and some accounts made him either the god of war, or the creator, or both. He was originally shown not in human form but as a barbed arrow (the thunderbolt?), then as a feathered penis, and finally as a stick-man with a large erection. He entered the Nile pantheon as god of **sex**, and was shown as a king in splendour with an enormous jutting penis.

The lettuce, Min's sacred plant, gave white sap when its stems were broken: the god's semen. It was widely considered an aphrodisiac. Min himself was one of the most popular of all gods, and thousands of images have been found, some in the form of phallic amulets or statuettes, others as jugs for vinegar or oil, where the top of the god's head is the spout and his penis the handle.

⟫→ Chimatano, Hermes, Priapus

MINAWARA AND MULTULTU
Australia

Minawara and Multultu, in the myths of the Nambutji people of Central Australia, were supernatural beings from the Dream Time. When the primordial ocean sank, leaving the world a desert, Minawara and Multultu grew from a heap of rubbish on the sand, took the form of kangaroos and travelled everywhere, carving out watercourses with their tails, making trees, plants, insects, birds and animals. Human beings were only one of their creations, and just as they armed insects with stings and wild dogs with teeth, so they gave us spears.

⟫→ animal-gods, Bagadjimbiri, the, creation, Kurukadi and Mumba

MINERVA: *see* Athene

MINOTAUR
Europe (South)

The Minotaur (Minotauros, 'Minos bull'), in Greek myth, was a **monster** born from the mating of **Pasiphaë** and the fire-breathing **Cretan bull**. It had a human body and a bull's head; its home was the Cretan labyrinth made by **Daedalus**, and it ate human flesh. Each year young men and women, sent to Crete as tribute, danced with bulls in honour of the Minotaur and then entered the labyrinth, never to be seen again. This custom continued until Prince **Theseus** of Athens took the place of one of the bull-leapers, found his way to the heart of the labyrinth and killed the Minotaur.

Like many Cretan myths, this one was later rationalized. The Minotaur, scholars explained, was a priest wearing a bull-mask – perhaps the Minos, or god-king, himself. The labyrinth was the royal palace with its myriad rooms and corridors. The victims were not eaten after their bull-dancing, but were taken into the sanctuary and sacrificed by Minos in honour of some ancient bull-god of the island, or made temple slaves. It was this custom, rather than the life of any actual Minotaur, which Theseus ended.

⟫→ bulls and cows

MIRALALDU: *see* Bildjiwuaroju, Miralaldu and Djanggawul

MITHRA
Asia (West); India

Mithra in Iran. In ancient Iranian myth, Mithra ('friend') was the son of **Ahura Mazda**, god of light. At first he shared his father's powers equally, but when Ahura Mazda became supreme ruler of the universe he was made, so to speak, second-in-command. He was driver of the **Sun**-chariot, dispelling the darkness each morning to usher in the dawn. He was god of war, driving a four-horse golden chariot and using as his weapons an enormous mace, a battery of incurable diseases and a huge wild boar, Verethragna, which specialized in smashing the backbones of Mithra's enemies and tearing apart their spinal cords.

Mithra was a creator-god. He was born full-grown from a rock, armed with a pine-torch and a knife. At once he fought and killed the primeval bull, and from the bull's blood and bone-marrow sprang up all fruits, flowers and herbs. Mithra was all-knowledge and all-truth. He saw the suffering of humanity, and made himself mortal to share it – he was born as a human on 25th December, a miracle witnessed by shepherds in the fields. On humanity's behalf, he constantly mediates with his father Ahura Mazda, and does battle with **Ahriman**, the power of darkness – a battle which will end in triumph on the Day of Judgement.

Mitra in India. In the Vedic myths of the Aryans, who invaded India in the seventeenth century BCE, Mithra became Mitra. With his brothers **Varuna** and Aryaman, he was one of the chief Adityas (children of **Aditi**) who oversaw order in the universe. In particular, he formed a duality with Varuna: Varuna was stern, unbending, the god of oaths and promises; Mitra was pliable, patient, the god of friendship. He was the Sun as Varuna was the Moon. He had no shape, but was Sun-dazzle incarnate. He had 1000 eyes and 1000 ears, so that no secrets were hidden from him. People thought that if you stared fixedly at anything ('with the eye of Mitra') you destroyed all evil emanating from it. As one of the judges of the Dead, Mitra will restore the good to life at the end of the universe.

In ancient Rome, Mithra was the centre of a mystery cult: see **Mithras**. ➤➤ **bulls and cows, creation, war**

MITHRAS
Europe (South)

Mithras, in ancient Rome, was the centre of a mystery-cult practised especially by soldiers, and possibly brought back by them from the Middle East. Initiates – all men – worshipped Mithras as Bull-killer, and thought that the sacred bull's blood and bone-marrow guaranteed the **fertility** of the universe. (They claimed that its marrow turned into bread and its blood into wine, staples of the ceremonial meal at the centre of Mithraic ritual.) One of the main events of a Mithraic ceremony was the sacrifice of a bull – sometimes over a grating under which initiates lay to be sprinkled with the life-giving blood. Mithras was the god of resurrection, and full initiation was thought to guarantee **immortality**.

At Mithraic ceremonies, which took place in cave-like buildings to represent the rock from which Mithras himself was born, worshippers took part in ceremonies including the bull-sacrifice, and ate the ceremonial meal. They wore masks signifying the seven stages of initiation: crow, griffin, warrior, lion, Persian, **Sun-messenger**, father. There were higher stages than these, but they were reserved for senior officers and aristocrats, and led to the topmost stage of all, King of Kings, which was available only to the Emperor. (He was thus the only Mithraic initiate to complete the whole series, and be guaranteed immortality.)

The Mithras cult was attacked by Christians who said that its beliefs parodied their religion (though in fact Mithraism came first), and its exclusivity and secrecy – telling the **mysteries** to non-believers brought **death** – meant that it never became wide-spread among ordinary people. But for soldiers, especially officers, it was an important binding-force, guaranteeing not so much immortality as respectability and a secure career.

>>+ **animal-gods, bulls and cows**

MIXCÓATL
Americas (Central)

Mixcóatl ('cloud-**snake**'), in Aztec myth, was the god of hunting, husband of **Coatlicue**. He was a **shape-changer**, who sometimes took the form of the scudding clouds which gave him his name, and sometimes appeared as a **giant** with a striped body, long black hair and the face of a deer or a rabbit.

MM
Europe (North)

Mm, in Celtic myth, was the goddess of thought of the independent peoples of Northern England. She never appeared alone, but always followed deferentially after her more impetuous husband **Aywell**, to whose flashes of uncontrolled energy she supplied a necessary dash of caution. Their names are still common, together, in the area today.

MODIMO AND BADIMO
Africa

Modimo, in Zimbabwean myth, was totality, all supernatural powers rolled into one – earth, fire, root, seed, sky, water, wind. It was so awesome that only shamans, prophets and small children (who were as yet morally un-formed and were therefore still innocent) could speak its name. Others who did so became *badimo* – spirits who lost their moral and ethical identity, and whose power to rationalize the world and take part in its affairs ever afterwards depended on the attentions of human worshippers: in effect, they were children in adult bodies.

MODRED
Europe (North)

Modred (or Mordred and Medraut), in Celtic myth, was **Arthur**'s son, con-ceived when Arthur slept with the wife of King Lot of Orkney, not realizing that she was his own half-sister Morgause. **Merlin** announced that 'the child born on Mayday' would grow up to destroy **Camelot**, and Arthur ordered all babies born on that day to be killed. But Modred was rescued, grew up and later went to Camelot as one of Arthur's knights. When Arthur went to France to fight **Lancelot** (after Lancelot's adultery with **Guinevere**), Modred forged a letter in which Arthur told his knights that he (Arthur) was mortally wounded, and that Modred should marry Guinevere and take the throne. Guinevere sent word to Arthur, who hurried his army back, engaging Modred in a bloody civil war which ended only when they met in single combat and each mortally wounded the other.

MOKOSH
Europe (East)

Mokosh or Makosh (from *mokosi*, 'moist'), in Slavic myth, was a **fertility** goddess widely worshipped north of the Black Sea. She made sure that semen was rich in sperm, and protected women and lambs during birth. She was close to **Mati-Syra-Zemlya**, and in Christian times her functions were handed over to the Virgin **Mary**.

⨠ **childbirth and infant care; Great Goddess**

MONSTERS AND DRAGONS

Monsters lived in the hinterland between myth and folk-tale. They were generally the result of botched matings – in grand stories, between such things as rocks and air, or fire and god; in less grand stories, hybrids of humans and animals, **demons** and plants or fish and fury. The two things they had in common were hideous appearance and an insatiable taste for humans (as sex-partners, food, or both).

Dragons, by contrast, were generally well-disposed to human beings. They were water-creatures, descendants of the giant **snakes** which embodied the primordial ocean or the rivers and lakes of Earth. Often, these snake-beings mated with other animals, so that dragons might have snakes' bodies but the heads of lions, lizards' legs with eagles' claws and the tails of crocodiles or scorpions. In Eastern myth, dragons were benign and gentle, welcome at human celebrations and happy to perform dances of **fertility** and **prosperity**. In Western myth they were less kindly disposed. Many still lived in pools and wells, but their watery ancestry also made them immune to fire, which they swallowed with dire effects on their constitutions. Irascible and unpredictable, they amassed treasure-hoards (the glint of the gold and jewels mirroring the fire in their own eyes), and they were merciless to dwarfs, gods and humans who disturbed them. At one level, this hostility came down into fairy-tale; at another, it was taken over into religion, in the dozens of stories of holy men and devout warriors who killed the dragons of superstition (often embodied as maiden-munching monsters).

⨠ **(Africa): Aigamuxa; (Americas): Flying Head, Underwater Panthers; (Arctic): Alklha; (Australia): Mimi, Namorodo; (Central and Eastern Europe): Werewolves; (China): Four Dragon Kings, Lei Jen Zu, Long Wang, Yu; (Egypt): Ammut; (Greece): Chimaera, Furies, Gorgons, Graeae, Harpies, Hydra, Lamia, Minotaur,**

Nemean Lion, Scylla and Charybdis, Sphinx, Stymphalian Birds, Typhon; (India): *bhutas*, Sisupala; (Iranian): Azhi Dahaka, Kul; (Nordic): Fafnir, Nidhogg; (Oceania): Totoima; (Rome): Cacus; (Slavic): Simarghu

MOON: *see* Auchimalgen, Candramus, Chandra, Cihuacóatl, Coyolxauhqui, Hana and Ni, Hecate, Hina, Heng O, Igaluk, Khonsu, Kilya, Kuu, Mama Quilla, Meness, Nanna, Pah, Rohini, Selene, Sin, Snoqalm and Beaver, Soma, Tsukuyomi, Yalungur

MORGAN LE FAY
Europe (North)

Morgan le Fay ('Morgan the Fairy') is variously identified. In Celtic myth she is one aspect of the **Morrigan**, taking the form not of crow or hag but of a beautiful queen, archetype of the malevolent godmother or stepmother of fairy tale. In some versions of the Arthurian myth-cycle she is the same person as **Nimue** (or Vivien), the **shape-changer** who fosters **Merlin**, falls in love with him and traps him. In Christian accounts of the **Arthur** stories she has two conflicting identities. She is **Arthur**'s half-sister and implacable enemy, endlessly plotting the destruction of **Camelot**. Or else she is leader of the nine mysterious guardians of **Avalon**, and lives either in a palace under the lake which surrounds the magic island, or on the island itself. In these accounts, she is guardian of the magic sword **Excalibur**, gives it to **Arthur** for the duration of his time on Earth, and receives it and him into Avalon when that time ends.
≫→ beauty, Circe

MORONGO: *see* Mwuetsi, Massassi and Morongo

MORRIGAN, THE
Europe (North)

The Morrigan ('great queen'), in Celtic myth, was one of three supernatural sisters: the others were Badb and Macha. Taking the form of huge crows, the sisters perched on the gables of houses forecasting war, and when it came they swooped on the battlefield to gorge themselves on corpses. In some accounts, the Morrigan was said to be a **shape-changer**, turning herself into a beautiful woman and seducing mortal heroes. In others, she was the same person as **Morgan le Fay**.

*The Morrigan features in the myths of **Cuculain**, as the hero's lover and implacable enemy. In Gawain and the Green Knight she appears to **Gawain** first as a hideous hag, begging him to sleep with her, and then as the wife of the Green Knight himself. She and her sisters later became identified with the **Fates**, or the Wyrd (or 'Weird') sisters: a gaggle of witches who foretold the future, as for example to Macbeth in Shakespeare's play.*

MORS
Europe (South)

Mors ('**death**'), in Roman myth, was the child of Night and the sister of Sleep. She was a warrior whose task was to collect mortals whose time on Earth was over and take them for judgement to the **Underworld**. She had no body, but wore a skeleton as if it were a suit of clothes, and carried a reaping hook to gaff any mortals rash enough to try escaping. She was the same person as the (male) Greek god **Thanatos**.

MORUfONU: *see* Jugumishanta and Morufonu

MOSHIRIIKKWECHEP
Asia (East)

Moshiriikkwechep ('world backbone trout'), in Japanese myth, was a **monster** made by the gods at the beginning of **creation**. It was so huge that when it flicked its tail or rippled its fins, the whole universe shook. Two sea-gods were therefore given the task, throughout eternity, of holding it down in the mud at the bottom of the primeval ocean. The passing of water across its gills made tides, and every so often it broke free, causing **earthquakes** and tidal waves until the gods caught it and held it down again.

MOTHER EARTH
In the 1970s a British scientist, James Lovelock, put forward the '**Gaia**' theory: that the Earth is a single, living organism able to defend and heal itself. The idea had been current in myth for millennia, and from traditions as far apart as those of Oceania and Northern Europe, China and Central America. Myth-makers in these areas assumed that the Earth was female, a goddess who dismembered herself or was dismembered to give living creatures a home, and that she was fertilized by her male partner Sky. In some versions, Mother Earth was placid and forgiving, cherishing her own creations; in others, anticipating Lovelock's theory of a self-protective organism, she was furious and restless, always ready to assume a destructive form and prey on her own unruly children.

➤➤ **(Americas): Coatlicue, Ilamatecuhtli, Nokomis; (Celtic): Danann; (China): Di; (India): Privithi; (Mesopotamia): Ninhursaga; (Nordic): Nerthus; (Oceania): Jugumishanta and Morufonu, Papa; (Slavic): Mati-Syra-Zemlya; (Tibet): sGrolma; (general): fertility, Great Goddess**

MOUNTAIN SPIRITS
Americas (North)

The Mountain Spirits (*gan*), in the myths of the Apache people of the American Southwest, protected both humans and animals against sickness and evil spirits; they are the custodians of animals. Ritual dancers (called Mountain Spirit Dancers, or Crown Dancers from their wooden head dresses) impersonated the *gan* at the puberty rituals of young girls.

MOUNTAINS: *see* Atlas, Begdu San, Fujiyama, Kagutsuchi, Kuafu, Kwatee, Meru, Olympus

MUCHALINDA
India

Muchalinda, in Buddhist myth, was a gigantic cobra, a **snake**-king and a relation or manifestation of the world-serpent **Shesha**. Muchalinda's palace was in the roots of the *bho* tree where **Buddha** sat to meditate. While the world-saviour was meditating, a super-natural storm blew up and battered the universe for seven days. Muchalinda reared up, coiled seven times round the tree and the Enlightened One, and spread his hood like an umbrella to keep Buddha dry and undisturbed. When the storm died, Muchalinda turned into a young man and bowed low to Buddha, the first being in **creation** to recognize him.

MUDUNGKALA
Australia

Mudungkala, in the myths of the Tiwi people of Melville Island, lived under the Earth in the Dream Time, with her two daughters and her son **Purukapali**. At this time Underearth was dark and cheerless, equalled only by the muddy wilderness which was Overearth. Nonetheless, Mudungkala was anxious to leave it. She stood up and pressed with her shoulders against the roof of Underearth until it split. Then she climbed through the hole with her children in her arms. She crawled blindly, on hands and knees, across the mud-plains, and her passage made mountains, watercourses and finally the sea-channel between Melville Island and the mainland. Mudungkala filled Melville Island with plants and creatures of every kind, and laid Purukapali and her daughters gently down on the surface: the first humans. Then, content at last, she disappeared back into Underearth and was never seen again.
➣➤ **creation, Jurumu**

MULTULTU: *see* Minawara and Multultu

MULUKU
Africa

Muluku the creator, in the myths of the Macua and Banayi peoples of the Zambesi, created the world and filled it with plants and animals. To tend it like gardeners, he pulled humans from two holes in the ground: one hole for the woman, the other for the man. He told them how to build, farm, plant and cook millet and live civilized lives. But they ignored him, eating the millet-seed raw, breaking the cooking-pots and hiding from him in the jungle. Muluku took a pair of monkeys and gave them the same instructions – and when they behaved like good, sober citizens, he cut off their tails, stuck them on the humans and banished the humans to the trees. Monkeys, therefore, are actually humans and humans are actually monkeys – that's how it is.
➣➤ **creation**

MULUNGU
Africa

Mulungu, also known as Kube ('all-embracer'), Likubala ('step-counter') and Lima ('Sun'), in the myths of the Nyamwezi people of Tanzania, created the world and everything in it. But he had neither form nor shape, and was unable to form any relationship with his **creation**. He was delighted when he saw First Man and First Woman appear on Earth, for he thought that they would one day join him in the Sky-kingdom. But Woman persuaded Man to reject **immortality** – on the grounds that the life they'd had as spirits was better than their present life, and if they died they might return to it – and so Mulungu was cheated of companionship. He remained remote from the world, so high above it that ordinary prayers and sacrifices failed to reach him, and messages had to be passed to and from him along an almost endless line of priests, angels and other intermediaries, a form of Chinese whispers which guaranteed that his answers to prayers were as garbled as the prayers themselves.

≫→ supreme deity

MUMBA: *see Kurukadi and Mumba*

MUSES, THE
Europe (South)

The Muses (Mousai, 'mountain spirits'), in Greek and Roman myth, were the daughters of **Zeus** and Mnemosyne (Memory). They lived on mountains all over the world, and danced and sang to the delight of any mortals who chanced to find them. There were innumerable Muses, but the best known are the nine Pierides ('daughters of Pierus'; but see below), who were born on Mount Pierus and became handmaids of **Apollo**, dancing with him on the slopes of Mount Parnassus at Delphi. Their names, and the arts they taught, were: Calliope ('beautiful voice'; poetic inspiration), Clio ('proclaimer'; history), Erato ('passionate'; lyric poetry), Euterpe ('rejoicing'; instrumental **music**), Melpomene ('leading the lament'; tragedy), Polyhymnia ('many voices'; harmony), Terpsichore ('lover of dance'; dancing), Thalia ('festival'; comedy) and Urania ('heavenly'; astronomy and learning in general). Three other

Muses are also sometimes mentioned, predecessors of these nine: Aoide ('melody'), Melete ('meditation') and Mneme ('memory').

In one account, the Pierides were daughters of a mortal king, Pierus, who challenged the Muses to a song-contest, were defeated and turned into magpies. In others, the Muses were called Pierides after Pieria, the country where they were born.

MUSIC AND DANCE: *see* Apollo, Dionysus, Gandharvas, Hermes, houris, Kali, Macuilxóchitl, Muses, Orpheus, Sarasvati, Shiva, Thoth, Valhalla, Uzume, Xochipili, Xochiquetzal

MUSPELL
Europe (North)

Muspell (or Muspellheim, 'fire-home'), in Nordic myth, was one of the two worlds which existed before existence. It was a fire-continent, mirror-image of the ice-continent **Niflheim**. Its flames licked out across the void between it and Niflheim, and met glaciers extending their fingers into the emptiness. Fire thawed ice into frozen mist, and this gradually took form as the **giant Ymir**, the first being. So creation began.

After the universe was created, and gods and mortals were made to tenant it, Muspell was forgotten. Its rulers, the fire-giant **Surt** and his sons, bided their time – and they bide it still. But at **Ragnarök**, the myth ends, they will join all other forces of evil and ride out to destroy the gods. This cycle of existence will end, and creation will begin again.

MUSUBI
Asia (East)

Musubi, in Japanese myth, was the deity of love, sometimes female (goddess of marriage-vows), sometimes male (god of desire). He/she lived in **Heaven**, but from time to time visited the Earth once a year, taking up residence in the cherry-blossom in the shrine of Kagami.

MUT
Africa (North)

Mut ('mother'), in Egyptian myth, was **Amun**'s queen and the mother of **Khonsu**, god of the Moon. Although with Amun and Khonsu she formed the ruling trinity of gods in Thebes (modern Luxor), no myths were associated with her, and her main function was to stand or sit by her consort's side, the epitome of womanly dignity.

Mut's name refers not to her Heavenly role, but to the idea that she was thought to take human form as the mortal queen at the moment of birth, and personally give birth to each new pharaoh. Perhaps because of the sketchiness of her personal myths, scribes and painters sometimes amalgamated her with Amaunet (see **Nun** *and* **Naunet***)*, **Hathor** *or* **Bastet** *the cat-goddess, and imagined her as a princess from the waist up and water from the waist down, as a cow or as a lion-headed queen savaging pharaoh's enemies. But her chief attribute was dignity, and what she represented was greater than what she was.*

≫→ Juno

MWAMBU AND SELA
Africa

Mwambu and Sela, in the myths of the Abaluia people of Kenya, were First Man and First Woman. Their father, **Wele** the creator, made them so that the **Sun** would have people to shine for. They lived with Wele in a **Heaven**-hut built on stilts to keep it from the Earth. But they asked for a home of their own, and Wele let down a ladder for them to climb down to Earth. Here they built a stilt-house of their own, and engendered a brood of children. They were vegetarians – Wele had forbidden them to eat any of his animal creation. But as the children grew older they began to experiment with meat-eating, and Mwambu and Sela let down a ladder and sent them to settle far and wide across the Earth. They pulled up the ladder to stop their offspring ever returning – and when they went to find the ladder Wele had let down for *them*, they found that he'd done exactly the same.

MWUETSI, MASSASSI AND MORONGO
Africa

Mwuetsi, in the myths of the Makoni people of Zimbabwe, was the first human being. He was put on Earth by the creator-god Maori – not on the ground, but at the bottom of a lake – and given a horn of *ngona* oil, the most fertile substance in existence. The oil's presence made the lake-water teem with life, but Mwuetsi found it cold and clammy and insisted on being allowed ashore. He found land even worse, for there were no plants, no animals, nothing but rock, as empty as the **Moon**. Mwuetsi complained to Maori, who sent the first woman, Massassi, for him to mate with. Their union, and the presence of the *ngona* oil, made the Earth teem with plants, a jungle of fertility. Then Maori sent another woman, Morongo. Her offspring with Mwuetsi were animals, including human beings – and once again the *ngona* oil ensured that enough were born to colonize the entire world.

At this point Maori warned Mwuetsi that there had been enough **sex**, and that if he mated with either of the women again, it would lead to trouble. Mwuetsi abstained for a while, but the *ngona* oil induced such sexual longing in him that he raped Morongo. As soon as he penetrated her, she began giving birth to hyenas, leopards, lions, stinging insects, poisonous lizards and **snakes** – and the last-born bit Mwuetsi and killed him. So pain and **death** came into the world, and also the custom of burial, for Mwuetsi's children, reluctant to throw his body back into the primordial lake in case they polluted it, dug a grave in the ground (or, in some accounts, cut open the body of their own mother Morongo) and hid him there.

*The myth is usually told as rationally and drily as here, leaving open the metaphorical identity of Maori (Sky), Massassi and Morongo (two aspects of **Mother Earth**), the horn of fertility (lightning; the phallus) and even Mwuetsi himself. However, one version of the story says that Mwuetsi was not killed by the snake-bite but merely sickened (since death had not yet been created), but that his disobedience of Maori brought such famine and drought to the world that his children strangled him and buried him to rid the Earth of pollution. They buried the horn of oil with him, and at once fertility returned. In later ritual, ngona oil was used to tend the sacred fire.*

MYSTERIES

Mysteries were religious or magic cults which arose from the worship of specific gods, particularly healers. Devotees conducted secret rites, often based on myth-stories, designed to help them to pass freely between the natural and supernatural worlds. Often these rites were embodied in coded writings, supposedly bequeathed by the god who inspired the cult, and containing the secrets of **immortality** and universal order. With a very few exceptions, all the mystery-cults about which anything is known were prevalent in Egypt, Greece or the Roman Empire; people in other areas either had no need of them (since their entire way of life depended on a symbiosis between natural and supernatural), or obeyed the injunction that mysteries should not be revealed.

≫→ (Americas): Nanabush, Yacatecuhtli; (Arctic): Pinga; (Egypt): Aset, Imhotep, Osiris, Ra, Serapis, Thoth; (Greece): Demeter, Orpheus, Persephone; (Mesopotamia): Inanna; (Rome): Mithras

NABU
Asia (West)

Nabu, in Mesopotamian myth, was **Marduk**'s son and the god of scribes. He invented **writing**, and used it as a kind of magic net to trap all the knowledge of the gods on clay tablets. (When he had no idea what to use for a pen, his wife Tashmetrum showed him how to sharpen a reed from the same river-bank as provided the clay.) The tablets of destiny became the gods' greatest treasure, and Nabu and Tashmetrum were their keepers in **Heaven**.

NAGAITCHO
Americas (North)

Nagaitcho, creator-god of the Kato (or Cahto) people of Northwestern California, raised the sky from the primordial ocean and propped it on pillars, one at each of the four compass points. He then sat between the horns of an enormous water-buffalo. The buffalo walked across the floor of the primordial ocean, occasionally looking up to see the sky – and each time it did so, a speck of dust settled on its head. Finally, in the South of the universe, the buffalo lay down to rest, and Nagaitcho moulded the dust-grains into mountains, rocks and fields, clothed them with vegetation and peopled them. The Earth was born.
≫→ creation

NAGA PAHODA
Indonesia

Naga Pahoda, in Indonesian myth, was the serpent-king of the primordial ocean, in the days when nothing existed but ocean and **Heaven** above it. One day the daughter of **Batara Guru**,

404

Narcissus (*17th-century French engraving*)

lord of Heaven, fell out of the sky into the ocean, and to prevent her drowning Batara Guru threw down handfuls of dust and made an island. Naga Pahoda reared up to swamp the island and the child, but Batara Guru weighted the island down by tossing crumbs of iron down to join the dust. Naga Pahoda was unable to drown the new world, but his writhing and bucking underneath furrowed, humped and split it into the mountains, valleys, continents and islands we know today.

≫→ creation

NAGAS AND NAGINIS
India

Nagas and Naginis ('powerful ones'; *Nagas* are male and *Naginis* are female), in Hindu myth, were **snake**-gods descended from **Brahma**'s grand-daughter **Kadru** and her husband the sage **Kasyapa**, from whom they inherited supernatural wisdom. They were **shape-changers**, able to appear as any kind of human or snake they chose, and they also took the forms of warriors with snake-necks or beautiful women from the waist up, snakes from the waist down. Their ways mirrored those of human society, and their rulers lived in fabulously jewelled palaces in the air, under ground or under the **sea**. (The jewels were because the Nagas and Naginis were servants of **Indra**, bringer of **rain**: the jewels were crystalline water-drops.) Often, they left their palaces, took human form and mated with favoured mortals, producing children who grew up to be human kings and queens.

Naga character. Like humans, the Nagas were neither good nor bad. They could behave with sagacity and altruism, or with cowardice, bluster and injustice. They generally oversaw the distribution of rain on Earth, but sometimes they withheld it, and only released it when they were attacked by the eagle-god **Garuda** and his servants. When **Vishnu** sleeps, and the universe is at rest, he lies on the coiled body of the chief Naga, the world-serpent **Sesha**, whose seven heads fan their hoods above him to give him shade. When a storm threatened **Buddha**, meditating under the *bho* tree, Naga **Muchalinda** enfolded the Enlightened One seven times in his coils and spread his cobra hood to shelter him.

Takshaka and Parikshit. In the **Mahabharata**, by contrast, the Naga king **Takshaka** was devious, unprincipled and fearsome. Once Parikshit, a proud mortal king, insulted a hermit, and the hermit's son called Takshaka's vengeance down on him. Parikshit built a fortress in the middle of a lake, snapping his fingers at Takshaka and daring him to find a way to harm him. A company of wandering monks appeared, with gifts of fruit – and in the last fruit to be cut open was a red insect with glittering eyes. The monks were Nagas and the insect was Takshaka, who changed back into a snake, choked the life from the boastful king and burned fortress and lake before soaring into the sky like the line of red which parts the hair of a bride in all her finery.

≫→ **snakes, Underworld, water**

NA KAA
Oceania

Na Kaa, in Micronesian myth, was one of the first two beings in **creation**, made when **Sky** and Earth rubbed against each other like two enormous hands being washed. (The other being was Na Kaa's brother Tabakea.) Na Kaa lived in a beautiful garden, in which grew two trees. When the gods created humans, only men were allowed to live in the shade of one of the trees, only women in that of the other. They had no idea of each other's existence. Then, one day, Na Kaa called them all together and told them he was going on a journey, but would return: they were to go back to their respective trees and wait for him. Unfortunately, as soon and men and women saw each other they were filled with lust, and all hurried back to the same tree – and Na Kaa told them that they had chosen not the Tree of Life but the Tree of **Death**. He drove them out of the garden, and as they went he wrapped illnesses and the pains of old age in leaves from the tree and threw them after them.

Ever afterwards, human beings have been mortal. After death, their spirits struggle up the steep mountain to reach Na Kaa's paradise, and he sits at the gate with an enormous net, letting past the souls of good people but keeping bad souls trapped forever.

Despite similarities with the Garden of Eden story in West Asian myth, this account predates the arrival of Western missionaries in Micronesia. The trees were pandannus palms, and the Tree of Life, after humans were expelled from Na Kaa's garden, was reserved for gods. In a characteristically Oceanian detail from this story, when men and women first discovered **sex** *under the Tree of Death, they went about it so enthusiastically that their hair turned grey: the first sign that they had been snared by death.*

NAKULA
India

Nakula, in Hindu myth, was one of the twin sons of the **Ashvins** and the mortal **Madri**, second wife of King **Pandu**. (His twin brother was **Sahadeva**.) Nakula fought with his **Pandava** brothers in their war against the **Kauravas**, and was famous as a dandy, as fussy about his appearance as he was invincible in battle.

⋙→ **heroes**

NAMBI: *see* Kintu and Nambi

NAMORODO, THE
Australia

The Namorodo, in the myths of the peoples of West Arnhem Land in Northern Australia, were predatory **monsters**: the rags of human beings, skeletons held together by sinews and skin-shreds. They flew at night and made no sound, but the wind whistled through them making a sound like sighing. They were impotent, and could only increase their numbers by sucking the juice from living humans and turning them into Namorodo too.

NANABUSH
Americas (North)

Nanabush, or Nanabozho or Manabozho ('big rabbit'), in the myths of many Algonquian peoples of the Northeastern and Midwestern US, was a **trickster**-god, a **shape-changer** whose favourite form was that of a rabbit: hence his name. He is a form of the god known to other Algonquian tribes as **Gluskap**, Great Hare, Winabozho and Wisaaka. In folk-tale he was amoral, cheerful and gluttonous, the hero of hundreds of adventures, outwitting **demons**, **giants**, humans, animals and especially other tricksters. In religious myth, however, he was an altogether grander and darker figure. He was the grandson of **Nokomis**, **Mother Earth**, and the enemy of the **Underwater Panthers** who, with their allies the **Thunderbirds**, wanted to destroy the world. The Panthers sent a flood to drown Nokomis, and Nanabush climbed a tree, calling down to swimming beavers, otters and diving birds to bring mud up from his grandmother's body as quickly as possible to make land for the other creatures who would otherwise drown. Originally Nokomis was complete, and her skin was all the Earth there was. It was only after she was reconstituted in these gobbets and fragments that the Earth became continents and islands, floating in the sea as she is today.

*In some versions of this story, Nanabush's quarrel with the Panthers began when they kidnapped and killed his brother, Chibiabos. No one knew what had happened to Chibiabos except **Raven**, who in those days was pure white – and Nanabush caught him and held him over a fire, scorching his feathers black until he told the truth.*

The story of how Nanabush saved the human race from extinction is perhaps one explanation of how he came to be the heart

of the Mide mystery-cult, whose ceremonies (still largely unknown) seem to have been concerned with the raising of the Dead.

≫→ animal-gods, creation, mysteries

NANDA (BUDDHA'S HALf-BROTHER)
India

Nanda, in Buddhist myth and legend, was **Buddha**'s half-brother. A touching story makes the point that it is not always easy to renounce the world and follow the austere path which leads to enlightenment. Nanda was much younger than Buddha, and grew up long after Buddha began preaching and converting. One day Buddha called at Nanda's house. The young man had just married a particularly beautiful wife, and, without recognizing his half-brother, tried to give him alms and send him on his way. Instead he found himself drawn mysteriously after Buddha, and ended up in a monastery where his head was shaved and he became a monk.

From that moment, Nanda was torn between memories of the world (symbolized by the beautiful wife he'd abandoned) and the monkish life of meditation and devotion. One day his worldly memories became too much for him, and he tried to give up the monkish life. Buddha showed him a blind old monkey and asked, 'Is your wife as beautiful?' Nanda indignantly said 'No', but Buddha carried him to **Heaven** and showed him that by contrast with the gods, his wife was indeed no prettier than a monkey. Nanda now began practising ever more severe austerities, hoping to enter Heaven and bask in the radiance of the gods. So Buddha carried him to Hell, showed him a vat of boiling water and said that this was what awaited him, to scald away his devotion to the appetites of the senses. At last Nanda understood. For the rest of his time on Earth, he devoted himself to the Way and to the Teaching which embodied it, forgetting his wife and the world she symbolized, and ignoring the half-remembered delights he had seen in Heaven. His self-denial, the story ends, is an object-lesson to us all.

In some accounts, Nanda is the same person as Buddha's childhood companion and first disciple **Ananda**.

NANDA (KRISHNA'S FOSTER-FATHER)
India

Nanda, in Hindu myth, was the cowherd (or cowherd king) who fostered **Krishna** after the young god was smuggled out of the dungeons of **Kansa**, the **demon**-king.

NANDI
India

Nandi ('happy') was a snow-white **bull**, the symbol of **Shiva's** **fertility** and strength, and the war-charger on which he sometimes rode against his enemies.
⋙→ animal-gods, bulls and cows, Hap

NANNA
Asia (West)

Nanna, the **Moon**-god in Sumerian myth, was the son of Ninlil, goddess of harvest, and the storm-god **Enlil**. Enlil raped Ninlil, and was punished with banishment to the **Underworld**. But Ninlil went down there after him, so that he could watch his son being born. Because Nanna was born in the darkness of Hell, his light was not warm like that of the **Sun** but pale and cold – and he was always the prey of **demons** and **monsters** from the Underworld, who snapped at his heels as he rode the sky, and would have gnawed him to pieces if humans hadn't made sacrifices each month to restore him to fullness.

NANOOK
Americas (North); Arctic

Nanook, in the myths of many peoples of the Northeastern US and Canada, also known to the Eskimos as Nanue, was the Great Bear. He was a benevolent spirit who lived for most of the time in the sky with his attendants, the Pleiades, but occasionally came down to Earth and helped human hunters.

NA'PI
Americas (North)

Na'pi and the Firstborn. Na'pi ('old man'), in the myths of the Blackfoot people of the Northern Plains (US and Canada), created the world before he himself was born. He made dolls of clay and animated them: man and woman, the Firstborn. The man was content with the world and his place in it, but the woman was restless. She asked Na'pi if what she had was all there was, if life would be just like this for all eternity. Na'pi tried to amuse her by suggesting a test. He threw a piece of buffalo dung into a river, saying that if it floated humans would die for four days and then live again, and if it sank death would be forever. It floated. The woman insisted on trying the test herself, but in her brainlessness used a stone instead of dung. It sank, and ever since death has been forever.

Na'pi's Birth. Some time afterwards, when the Firstborn had reproduced and there were human beings all over the world, Na'pi decided that it was time for him, himself, to take form, to experience birth as plants and people did. He arranged for a woman to make regular visits to a nest of rattlesnakes not far from her village, and for one of the **snakes** to mate with her and make her pregnant. The woman's jealous husband trapped her in a net when she next came back from her 'lover', and cut off her head. The headless body at once jumped up and began chasing him across the earth and up into the sky. (He runs from her still, round and round the world, and the speed of his flight has turned him into a blazing star, the **Sun**. She is the **Moon**.) The bodiless head, meantime, pursued the woman's two children, and they were saved only when they threw in front of it a piece of magic moss which turned into a river and drowned it. The story ends in the characteristic way of **trickster**-tales. Na'pi was not the embryo in the woman's womb, fathered by the rattlesnake – there was no such child. Instead, he was the elder of the two children saved from the bodiless head, and went on, in human form, to experience life on earth, and death, before disappearing behind the mountains, as the Sun does each evening. (And as the Sun returns each morning, he will come back one day. Although for the mortals he created, death is forever, he himself is not bound by it.)

Confusion exists over who exactly Na'pi was. Some mythographers identify him with the Sun, and say that his name meant 'Dawn-coloured one'. There was, however, another Blackfoot sun-god, Natos, married to Kokomikeis the Moon. This suggests that stories of Na'pi the creator are from earlier myth, that he was supplanted by Natos, and that he lived on not as supreme sky-god but as a simple trickster. Certainly hundreds of folktales tell of his shape-changing adventures, and none of them give him divinity, let alone supremacy.

⟫→ Chinigchinich, creation, Enki, Esaugetuh Emissee, Humanmaker, Hurukan, Prometheus, Tagaro, Woyengi

NARASIMHA
India

Narasimha ('man-lion'), in Hindu myth, was the fourth avatar of **Vishnu**. A **demon**, **Hiranyakashipu**, by prayer and sacrifice had won from the gods the gift of invulnerability: he could be killed neither by day nor night, neither inside his house nor outside it, neither by human being, beast nor god. Armed with these powers, he had terrorized the world, grabbing all its wealth, enslaving humans and forcing them to worship him instead of the gods. When his own son **Prahlada**, a devout worshipper of Vishnu, refused to give up his faith, he tortured him, stampeding elephants over him, plunging him into barrels of snakes, holding him underwater and tossing him over cliffs on to sharpened rocks – all to no avail. 'Vishnu is everywhere,' Prahlada insisted. 'Even in that roof-pillar over there?' scoffed Hiranyakashipu – and immediately Vishnu, as Narasimha, surged out of the pillar and tore him to pieces. The time was dusk (neither day nor night); the place was the palace doorway (neither inside nor out); Vishnu was neither god, beast nor human being, but a blend of all three. The god crowned Prahlada king in his father's place, and true worship and goodness were restored.

»+ animal-gods

NARCISSUS
Europe (South)

Narcissus (Narkissos, 'bewitching'), in Greek and Roman myth, was a beautiful youth, son of the river-god Cephisus and the **nymph** Liriope. Everyone who met him, including **Hera**'s handmaid **Echo**, fell in love with him, but he ignored them all. In some accounts, he loved only his own sister, and was inconsolable at her death. In others he loved no one but himself. He spent his time moping in the woods and hills, and one day caught sight of his own reflection in a pool, and fell in love with it. The image, however, refused to leave the pool, and he pined away and died. When the nymphs, his mother's companions, came to bury his body, they found that the gods had changed him into a beautiful flower; its descendants, his offspring, are still called narcissus after him and still lean over as if to admire their own reflections.

»+ **beauty**

NAREAU
Oceania

Nareau ('lord spider'), in the myths of Kiribati, was two people. Old Nareau, first being in **creation**, made the gods by moulding wet sand, and then left his son Young Nareau to make the universe and all its creatures. Lacking building materials, Young Nareau dismembered Na Atibu (the first god created by Old Nareau), and made his right eye the **Sun**, his left the **Moon**, his brains clouds, his bones islands, his flesh vegetation and his fleas animals and humans. Na Kika the octopus-god gathered the new creations and set them in position, tenanting the universe. In some accounts, the sky made from Na Atibu's brain was at first too heavy to hang in air unsupported, and pressed down on the land made from his bones, and Nareau persuaded Riiki ('eel') to push them apart and hold them until Sky became accustomed to its new position.

*Young Nareau figures not only in this creation-myth, but in countless folktales as the fount of all wisdom and guide of human beings – and as **trickster** supreme.*
»+ animal-gods, Areop-Enap and Rigi, tricksters

NAUNET: *see* Nun and Naunet

NAUPLIUS
Europe (Southern)

Nauplius (Nauplios, 'navigator'), in Greek myth, was a son of **Poseidon** and the **sea-nymph** Amymone. He was one of the **Argonauts**, and later settled on the island of Evia, ruling from a town called Nauplia after him. During the **Trojan War**, when the Greek lords executed his son **Palamedes** he decided to take revenge not openly but deviously. He visited all the queens of Greece, telling them that the war was lost and their husbands were dead and encouraging them to make new marriages. Then he waited gleefully to see what would happen when the war actually did end and the real husbands went home to claim their wives and kingdoms. Some queens, for example **Penelope**, **Odysseus**' wife in Ithaca, ignored him – though it was Nauplius' news, in her case, which encouraged hordes of suitors to besiege her palace. Others succumbed: in one account it was Nauplius' false news of **Agamemnon**'s death, not fury or revenge-lust of any kind, which persuaded **Clytemnestra** to take a lover, **Aegisthus**, and usurp her husband's rightful throne in Mycenae.

After the war, Nauplius harassed the commanders by a second trick. Building on his reputation as the most experienced navigator in all Greece, he said that their safest way home was along the coast of Evia, his island kingdom, and that he would light fires on the coast to show the safest passages. He then lit the narrowest channels, with the most jagged underwater reefs and rocks, and watched gleefully from the shore as the fleet was wrecked. But his joy turned to rage when the gods rescued Odysseus and **Diomedes** (King of Aetolia) – his greatest enemies, those who had engineered Palamedes' execution – and he hurled himself into the sea among the broken spars and bodies, and drowned.

NAUSICAÄ
Europe (South)

Nausicaä ('ship-burner'), in Greek myth, was the daughter of King **Alcinous** of Phaeacia. She was the only daughter in a large family of sons, and was courted by princes from all over Greece. One day the gods put it into her mind to take all the clothes from the palace down to the shore and supervise the slaves while they washed them and laid them on the shingle to dry in the sun. When the work was finished, she and her maids threw off their head-dresses and began playing with a ball – and **Odysseus**, who had been shipwrecked the night before, came to them and begged for help. Nausicaä took him home and Alcinous welcomed him with honour.

*Nausicaä drops out of myth at this point. Some authorities say that she later married Odysseus' son **Telemachus**, but this is contradicted by the main myth-story, in which Telemachus marries **Circe** after Odysseus' death. For obvious reasons, the story of Nausicaä (which owes its detail to a charming telling in Homer's Odyssey) has attracted painters of every era, most notably Roman fresco painters in the first century CE and English Pre-Raphaelite painters of some 1800 years later. In England, too, there has been a long-standing fancy – based on the human warmth, charm and domestic detail of the narrative itself – that the Odyssey was written by a woman, not a man. Samuel Butler put it forward in the late nineteenth century, and half a century later Robert Graves wrote a historical novel,* Homer's Daughter, *elaborating it* *and retelling the story of the Odyssey from Nausicaä's point of view.*

NAYENEZGANI AND TOBADZISTSINI
Americas (North)

Nayenezgani ('killer of foreign gods' or, in some languages, 'older twin') and Tobadzistsini ('child of water' or, in some languages, 'younger twin'), in the myths of the Navajo people of the Southwestern US desert, were brothers: Nayenezgani was the god of light, Tobadzistsini the god of dark. They were the sons of **Etsanatlehi** ('She who Changes', variously identified as **Mother Earth**, the **Moon** and Time Passing) and **Tsohanoai**, the **Sun**-carrier. Their father was too busy travelling the sky even to know of their existence, and one day they set out to find him. They came across a hole in the ground, climbed into it, and found that it was the smoke-hole of the underground house of Nasteetsan (or Naackjeii esdzaa), Spider Woman. She warned them of four dangers on their journey, and gave them a magic feather each to protect them.

Nayenezgani and Tobadzistsini climbed back to Earth's surface, went on their way, and were immediately kidnapped and taken before a fiery-eyed chief who put them through a series of ordeals – being spitted on spikes, smoking a poison-pipe, being steamed alive – all of which they survived thanks to the feathers. At last he told them his name, Tsohanoai, and they explained that they were his sons. They said that all they wanted in the world was to fight **demons**, and begged weapons. He gave Nayenezgani sunshaft-spears and Tobadzistsini **lightning**, and they went on their way. For the rest of time they have been fighting demons – and each one they kill turns into another harmless species of insect or animal. Neither they nor their father and mother have ever met each other again.

➤ **heroes, twins**

NEBTHET
Africa (North)

Nebthet ('palace-basket') or Nebhut ('lady of the palace'; Greek Nephthys), in Egyptian myth, was the daughter of **Geb** and **Nut** and sister of **Aset** (Isis), **Osiris** and **Set**. She was Set's consort, but seduced Osiris by getting him drunk, and later gave birth to **Anubis**.

*Nebthet is one of the most shadowy of all Egyptian funerary goddesses. Each succeeding pharaoh was her menstrual blood given human form; she suckled him as a baby; her hair was the bandages which wrapped his mummy, and from which he had to break free to enter the **Underworld**. In the Osiris myth she went with Aset to reconstitute Osiris after Set butchered him, and the image was common of the two goddesses as a pair of hawks or kites grieving over his body. (At funerals, two women mourners often took the goddesses' parts, wearing hawk-masks and crying for the dead.) But, in sum, Nebthet was so spectral that some authorities say that she and Aset were one and the same, and that she was given a separate identity in myth merely for symmetry – so that Set could have a female twin just as Osiris had Aset.*

NECTAR
Europe (South)

Nectar ('fragrant'), in Greek myth, was the drink of the gods, which guaranteed and renewed their **immortality**. It was unknown on Earth, but **Dionysus** gave mortals a poor imitation in the form of wine – a drink which conferred not true immortality but (if you drank enough of it) the brief illusion that you lived beyond the reach of human time.
≫→ **ambrosia, soma**

NEFERTEM
Africa (North)

Nefertem ('perfection'), or Nefertum, son of **Ptah** and **Sekhmet** in Egyptian myth, was the sacred blue lotus (a symbol of sky or sea) from which, in some accounts, **Ra** the **Sun** rose each morning as if from a bed.

NEHEBKAU
Africa (North)

Nehebkau ('spirit-harnesser'), in Egyptian myth, had human arms and legs, or in some accounts (which say that he was a son of **Serqet** the scorpion-goddess) a **snake**'s head (or two heads), a human torso and a scorpion's tail. He was born in human form, and sprouted his other attributes when he ate seven coils of the world-snake **Aapep** and was banished to the **Underworld**. Despite his fearsome appearance, he was well-disposed, and used his venom as an antidote against snakebite and scorpion-stings. In the Underworld, he was one of the first creatures seen by the soul of the newly-arrived pharaoh, but instead of attacking he welcomed him and served him food.

Because the Egyptians believed that all snakes and scorpions were immune to flames, they hung Nehebkau's image on their houses as a form of fire insurance.

NEIT
Africa (North)

Neit ('what is'), or Neith, in Egyptian myth, was originally an aspect of the **Great Goddess**, creator-goddess of Sais (modern Sa el-Hagar) in the Nile Delta. She was a warrior, a hunter, and later Greek Egyptians identified her with **Athene**. In the Delta myth-cycle she arose spontaneously from the primeval ocean, invented **childbirth** and created gods, mortals and animals, and then invented weaving and made the universe for them to live in. She was never fully admitted to other myth-cycles, instead being regarded as a kind of dangerous but fortunately distant relative. In some accounts she created **Aapep**, the snake of darkness, by spitting at **Nun**; in others she was the mother of crocodiles. When **Set** and **Horus** fought for supremacy, the gods wrote to ask which should be allowed to win, and she replied, first, that both should live, Set because he protected the Sun-boat and Horus because he mediated between mortals and immortals; second, that Set should be given two foreign goddesses, **Anat** and **Astarte**, as compensation for yielding to his own nephew – and third, that if the gods ignored her advice she would unpick her woven universe and destroy **creation**.

*In another aspect, Neit was known as Tehenut ('the African'), and was said to come not from the Delta but from the Mountains of the **Moon**. Her symbol in this manifestation, a lion-skin shield crossed by two arrows, was one of her depictions in art; in others she was shown as a queen wearing the red crown which symbolized Upper Egypt, the Delta area. The identification with weaving may have arisen because the ideogram for her name, Neit, looked like a shuttle.*

⋙⊦ **creation**

NEMEAN LION, THE
Europe (South)

The Nemean Lion, in Greek myth, was the **monster** killed by **Heracles** as the first of his **Labours**. In some accounts, it was the offspring of **Typhon** and Echidna, in others a creation of the **Moon**-goddess **Selene**, who moulded sea-foam into a lion's shape and breathed life into it. Its claws were razors, its skin was weapon-proof and it was a man-eater, feasting on the people of Nemea. It took Heracles thirty days to track the lion to its lair, where he found it sleepy after a meal of human flesh. He clubbed it hard – not on its weapon-proof skin but on the end of its nose. The lion sneezed in surprise and backed into its cave – and Heracles ran after it, strangled it, skinned it with its own razor-claws (the only things sharp enough to cut the hide), flung the skin round his shoulders as a cloak of invulnerability and made a cap from its gaping jaws.

After the lion's death **Hera** set it as a constellation in the sky and made it a sign of the Zodiac: Leo.

NEMESIS
Europe (South)

Nemesis ('retribution'), in Greek and Roman myth, was the daughter of Night and sister of the **Fates**. She saw to it that no crimes committed by gods or humans went unpunished. In the Upper World she tracked the guilty down; in the **Underworld** she stood by the judges of the Dead, insisting that punishment should fit the crime. She had no fixed shape, but took on the form in which each criminal imagined her: she was conscience personified and vindictive. The Romans sacrificed to her, in her temple on the Capitol, before setting off for war; as states have done throughout history, they sought God's approval in advance.

NEOPTOLEMUS
Europe (South)

Neoptolemus at Troy. Neoptolemus (Neoptolemos, 'new war'), son of **Achilles** and Deidamia in Greek and Roman myth, was a small child when his father went to fight at Troy, and stayed at home with his mother throughout the war. But when Achilles was killed by **Hector**, the gods prophesied that the Greeks would never take Troy unless they brought Neoptolemus (by now adolescent) to the city. The Greeks sent **Odysseus** and **Diomedes** to fetch him, and changed his name from Pyrrhus ('fair-haired', the one his parents gave him) to Neoptolemus. (Some accounts say that he was killed by another Pyrrhus, his own half-brother, who then usurped his name: see **Pyrrhus**.)

From the moment Neoptolemus/Pyrrhus went to Troy, he showed more ruthlessness and savagery than any other Greek soldier. He helped **Odysseus** trick **Philoctetes** into leaving Lemnos and taking his unerring bow to Troy. He was the first man into the Wooden Horse, and the first to attack the royal palace, butchering slaves, women, children, priests and guards indiscriminately until he found **Priam** cowering by the altar, cut his throat and carried his head in triumph through the city on a spear-point. When no other Greek could bring himself to murder the baby **Astyanax**, Neoptolemus volunteered, and he sacrificed Priam's young daughter **Polyxena**, and poured her blood on Achilles' grave for his father's ghost to drink.

After the Trojan War. As battle-spoils, Neoptolemus was allotted Hector's former wife **Andromache** (mother of Astyanax, the baby he had murdered), and Priam's son **Helenus**, a prophet. Helenus advised him that if he set sail with the other Greeks, he would never return home alive, so Neoptolemus went back to Greece overland, crossing the Bosphorus and then fighting his way South with unrivalled savagery. In some accounts, he and Andromache settled near **Zeus'** oracle at Dodona, and lived there peaceably until Neoptolemus tried to sack **Apollo's** treasury at Delphi and was struck miraculously dead – not merely for this blasphemy, but for killing Priam at the gods' altar years before in the sack of Troy.

Other accounts of Neoptolemus' death involve him with **Hermione**, daughter of **Helen** and **Menelaus** of Sparta. During the fighting at Troy, Menelaus was so impressed with Neoptolemus that he agreed to let him marry Hermione. But during the time it took Neoptolemus to make his way home to Greece, Hermione herself agreed to marry **Orestes**. Ignoring this, Menelaus sent her to Neoptolemus – and either she organized Neoptolemus' murder, at the gods' altar just as he had killed Priam, or else Orestes killed him before taking Hermione back to Argos.

≫→ **heroes**

NEPHELE
Europe (South)

Nephele ('cloud'), in Greek myth, as her name suggests, was a cloud-goddess. When **Ixion**, the wickedest mortal in the world, repaid **Zeus'** invitation to a banquet in **Olympus** by trying to rape **Hera**, Zeus moulded an exact image of her from clouds to cheat him – and this was Nephele. After Ixion was punished, however, there was no way to unmake Nephele: she was the immortal creation of an immortal god. She floated about Olympus, lonely and tearful, confusing everyone by her likeness to Hera. At last Hera found a solution: she married Nephele to **Athamas**, the stupidest mortal in the world, and made her queen of Boeotia.

At first Athamas was delighted. He and Nephele had two children: a son, **Phrixus**, and a daughter, **Helle**. But as time passed the marriage soured. Nephele, who had lived in Olympus, found Boeotia dull by contrast, and moped about the palace filling every room with drizzle. Athamas, for his part, grew tired of embracing a cloud instead of a wife of flesh and blood, and took a mistress, Ino, building her a hiding-place so secret that Zeus later used it to hide his infant son **Dionysus** (child of Ino's sister **Semele**) from Hera's jealousy.

Unfortunately for Athamas, Hera found out about Dionysus. She drove Ino mad, and punished Athamas by taking Nephele back into Olympus, where she sat her on permanent watch above a water-butt in the stables of the Sun. So Athamas was left without wife or mistress, and Nephele found a vocation at last, squeezing out tears and wringing her hands to provide fresh water for the **Sun**'s winged horses.

≫→ **Rati**

NEPTUNE: *see* Poseidon

NEREUS
Europe (South)

Nereus ('wet'), son of **Gaia (Mother Earth)** and **Ouranos** (Father **Sky**) in Greek myth, was all the water in the universe. He married the **Titan** Doris, and lived with her in a palace under the Aegean Sea. He spent his time frolicking and dancing with his fifty daughters, the Nereids, and took little interest in the affairs of gods or mortals. However, like all **sea**-beings, he had second sight, and if you could catch him and hold him for long enough – he wriggled and changed shape, like his half-brother **Proteus** – he would reluctantly answer your questions. He told **Heracles** where to find the Golden Apples of **Immortality**, and warned **Paris** about what would happen if he abducted **Helen**.

In some accounts, Nereus and not **Chaos** was the primal being, the ocean from which the universe arose.

NERGAL
Asia (West)

Nergal (Ne-iri-gal, 'power of the terrible abode'), son of **Enlil** in Mesopotamian myth, was amorality personified – and since his father gave him human beings to play with, he also symbolized the unpredictability and risk in mortal life, and in particular brought **death**. He roared about the universe in the form of an enormous bull, creating havoc and mating with any females, mortal or immortal, that caught his eye.

Ereshkigal, Enlil's sister, darkness personified, had been banished from the world of light, and lived in an **Underworld** palace which the gods were forbidden to enter and which she never left. But she still demanded royal privileges, and whenever the gods held banquets in **Heaven** she sent her servant to fetch her share of immortal food and drink. On one of these occasions Nergal was present, and refused to sit down to eat until he'd thrown the servant out of Heaven. Ereshkigal summoned him to the Underworld to explain – and instead of being terrified he sprang up on her throne and raped her. He escaped back to Heaven, and Ereshkigal went after him to hunt him down. But **An**, ruler of the gods, seeing that darkness was about to engulf the universe, ordered Nergal back to the Underworld. This time, instead of raping Ereshkigal, he wrestled her to the ground and refused to let go unless she married him and gave him equal power.

From then on, the myth ends, Nergal and Ereshkigal held equal power. She stayed in the Underworld forever, but he often visited the Upper World with his **demon** followers, racketing across the sky and seeking out mortals to drag down to death. On one occasion he persuaded **Marduk** to take a rest from supporting the sky – and as soon as Nergal sat down on Marduk's throne **justice and universal order** ended and chaos and catastrophe engulfed the world. In some accounts, Marduk hastily displaced him and the Golden Age returned. In others, Nergal has never yet given back the throne, and rules us still.

NERTHUS
Europe (North)

Nerthus, in Nordic myth, was a Danish earth-goddess, the object of a mystery-cult so secret that little is now known of her except her name and her symbol: a round, nude stick-woman with exaggerated **sex**-organs. Some say that she was the same person as the sea-god **Njörd**, who changed his sex whenever he wanted to venture on (or become) land; others that she was Njörd's sexual companion, ceaselessly mating with him as the waters lapped the shore, and that their children were **Frey** and **Freyja**.

⋙→ **Mother Earth, mysteries**

NGEWOWA
Africa

Ngewowa's name. Ngewowa, or Leve ('up-there-person'), in the myths of the Mende people of Sierra Leone, created the universe and all its creatures. His last creations were mortals, a man and a woman. He lived with them on Earth, and they called him Grandfather and respected him. He doted on them, giving them everything they asked with the cheerful 'Nge-e' ('It's yours'). After a long time, however, he decided that it was time for them to stand on their own feet, and one night stole away into the sky, far out of reach. When the humans woke next morning they could see him but not touch him, and he put into their minds that he was now spreading his generosity more widely, across the whole of **creation**. They accordingly gave him a new name, Nge-e-wo-lo-nga-wa-le ('grandfather-universal-it's-yours'), shortened to Ngewowa.

Ngewowa all-present. Although Ngewowa lived in the sky, his goodness irradiated all creation: he was present in every pebble, rivulet, insect, plant and animal. This radiance was more apparent in some things than in others, and a few chose to mask it even more. This, too, was done with Ngewowa's approval. Because he was present in everything, he needed no direct worship or offerings from living beings. But he listened to the spirits of the Dead – and this sometimes brought disaster to creatures on Earth, for the spirits were as fond of deception and cruelty as anyone else, and unless they were given the right gifts of food and tobacco by the living, they garbled any messages entrusted to them. The most perverse spirits of all, white-skinned and bearded, had only one aim in mind, to conquer and rule all humanity – and Ngewowa never lifted a hand to stop them.

This myth was first written down by Western Christian missionaries, emissaries of colonial powers, and the sting in its tail is not the only suggestion that it may have been ironically inflected by the tellers, with more than one eye on the gullibility of their audience.

≫→ supreme deity

NGURUNDERI
Australia

Ngurunderi, in the myths of the Jaraldi people of the Murray River in South-eastern Australia, was the creator-spirit who stocked the **sea** with fish. He went hunting cod one day – and because at that time there were no sea-creatures, the cod he hunted was a huge land-monster. It wriggled and struggled to escape him, and its writhings gouged out the channel which became the Murray River. At last, just as the cod reached the sea, Ngurunderi caught it. He cut it into five pieces, gave each piece the name of a different type of fish and threw them into the sea, where they came to life and swam away. Having finished his fishing, Ngurunderi beached his canoe into the sky (where it became the Milky Way), dived into the sea to wash off any trace of the mortal world, and ascended to the sky-kingdom, where he has lived ever since and where all his Jaraldi subjects join him after death.

≫→ creation

NIBELUNGS
Europe (North)

The Nibelungs, in Nordic myth, were originally the 'elves of light' who lived in Alfheim, an underground kingdom where they worked and hoarded light in the form of gold. In later, Germanic myth, they were identified with a mortal people living in Central or Southern Europe. In the first part of the thirteenth-century *Nibelung Poem* they farm the lands at the southern end of the river Rhine, and are led by the hero Siegfried (**Sigurd**). In the second half of the poem they become or merge into a people from further West (modern Burgundy), ruled by Queen Kriemhild. Finally, in Wagner's *The Ring of the Nibelungs* they stand for all Germanic peoples, the Rhine is their symbol and Siegfried is their prince and champion.

NIDHOGG
Europe (North)

Nidhogg ('corpse-tearer'), in Nordic myth, was a dragon who lived in **Niflheim**. It stripped the flesh from corpses, and also gnawed endlessly at the root of **Yggdrasil**, tree of the universe, trying to destroy it. In this task it was hampered by the squirrel Ratatosk (who arrived each day with fresh challenges and insults from an eagle which lived in Yggdrasil's upper branches), and by the three **Norns**, who watered the tree and plastered its wounds with clay to heal them.

≫→ monsters and dragons

NIFLHEIM
Europe (North)

Niflheim ('mist-home'), in Nordic myth, existed before existence. It was a world of ice and darkness, centred on an icy spring, Hvergelmir, whose waters poured out in eleven glaciers across its barren surface. When they reached the edges of Niflheim, they reached out into the void beyond, were gradually thawed by fire spilling from the other huge primeval world, **Muspell**, and formed the **giant Ymir**, the first being. So **creation** began.

After the universe was created, and gods and mortals were made to tenant it, Niflheim became the world of the Dead, on the lowest of the three levels of existence (see **Yggdrasil**). It remained barren, frozen and lightless, and was dominated by a vast mountain-range on which was the citadel of **Hel**, ruler of the Dead. One of the three roots of Yggdrasil, tree of the universe, grew there, by the spring Hvergelmir, where a darkness-dragon, **Nidhogg**, ceaselessly gnawed it. In some accounts, all human beings when they died passed into Hel's halls for judgement. The **Valkyries** carried **heroes** up to **Valhalla** in the realm of the immortals, where they were entertained like gods. Hel cast sinners over the cliffs of her citadel into the depths of Niflheim, where they died a second time, vanishing forever from sight and memory.

NIKE
Europe (South)

Nike ('conqueror'; Latin Victoria), in Greek and Roman myth, was one of the four daughters of **Styx** who helped the gods in their battle against the **Titans**. **Zeus** rewarded her by making her goddess of victory. She had no personal power, but went with one of the other gods as a kind of good luck charm, often riding in the god's sleeve or perched on his or her arm. She was a particular favourite of **Athene**. In Roman mystery cults she had a special place of honour, standing not only for might in war but for the victory over death which due observance of the **mysteries** was thought to bring.

Nike was a favourite subject for painters and sculptors. She was shown either as a winged female figure, naked or in full armour, or as a tiny figure peeping out from the clothes of another god or flying above like a benign, winged doll, or the good fairy in later children's story-books.

NIMUE
Europe (North)

Nimue, in Celtic myth, was a **shape-changer**, in some accounts the same person as the **Lady of the Lake**. She fell in love with **Merlin**, and after a contest of magic captured him forever by turning herself into a drop of amber and engulfing him.

➤ **Morgan Le Fay**

NINE WAVE-MAIDENS, THE
Europe (North)

The nine wave-maidens, daughters of the sea-god **Aegir** in Nordic myth, were Atla, Augeia, Aurgiafa, Egia, Gjalp, Greip, Jarnsaxa, Sindur and Ulfrun. They were playing on the shore one day when **Odin** passed by, wondered what it would be like to have **sex** with all nine simultaneously – and engendered, by thought alone, their joint child **Heimdall**.

➤ **beauty**

NINE WORLDS, THE
Europe (North)

The nine worlds, in Nordic myth, were the divisions of the three realms of the universe each of which nourished a root of the world-tree **Yggdrasil**. The lowest realm, the **Underworld**, was divided into **Hel** (fortress of Hel herself, ruler of the Underworld) and **Niflheim** (land of the Dead). The central realm contained **Jotunheim** (land of the **giants**), **Midgard** (land of mortals), Nidavellir (land of dwarfs) and Svartalfheim (land of the elves of darkness). The topmost realm contained Alfheim (land of the elves of light), **Asgard** (land of the **Aesir**) and Vanaheim (land of the **Vanir**). In some accounts Hel and Niflheim were amalgamated into a single division, and the ninth world was **Muspell**, the 'world which existed before all other worlds', that is, before **creation**.

NINHURSAGA
Asia (West)

Ninhursaga ('lady of stony ground'), eldest child and first consort of the **sky**-god **An** in Mesopotamian myth, was a form of **Mother Earth**. She was called by different names in different regions: her honorific titles included Aruru ('loosener'), Belit-illi ('lady of the gods'), Belitis ('ladyship') and Nintur ('form-giver'). When she was the consort of **Enki** she was known as Ninki, and their mating created everything in existence. As queen of **Enlil** the storm-lord she was known as Ninlil and was mother of the **war**-god **Ninurta**. As Damkina she was consort of the **water**-lord **Ea**. In some accounts, she abjured

sex altogether and created beings by spontaneous generation. One of them was the giant Enkidu, made to destroy **Gilgamesh**. In all her aspects, she was a goddess of **fertility** and birth, particularly associated with growing plants, with the young of wild animals and with cattle.

Ninhursaga was shown in as many different forms as she had names: they included a cow-faced, many-breasted woman, a hunter and a midwife carrying a water-pot. The kings of Sumeria claimed that as babies they sucked the milk of divinity from her.

⇛ Artemis, childbirth and infant care, creation, Great Goddess

NINIGI
Asia (East)

Ninigi, in Japanese myth, was the grandson of **Amaterasu** the **Sun**. In Heaven his task was to direct her rays to swell the rice in the celestial paddies, food of the gods. But Amaterasu had more ambitious plans for him. At this time, **Okuninushi**'s children were teeming all over the Earth. Many were peaceable, but a few were violent, oppressing their brothers and sisters and challenging their father's rule. Amaterasu gave Ninigi a bag of rice-grains, and three other gifts: the mirror and star-necklace the gods had made long before to entice her from the cave when she fled from **Susano**, and the sword Kusanagi which Susano took from the water-**monster** before he married Kushinada. She told him to take these down to Earth, where Okuninushi would abdicate and let him rule. Led by gods of light, Ninigi walked in procession down the Celestial Bridge to Mount Takachiho on Earth. From here he began his campaigns against Okuninushi's bandit-sons, and defeated them. Okuninushi abdicated and Ninigi became ruler of all the Earth, increasing its prosperity by planting the rice-grains, and so bringing mortals a share in the food of the gods.

When Ninigi first came to Earth, the god of Mount Takachiho introduced him to his two daughters and said that he could marry whichever he chose. The elder (Iwanaga, 'enduring rock'), was ugly, the younger (Konohana, 'blossom') beautiful – and Ninigi chose the younger, not realizing that if he wanted a long life as well as a happy one, he should have married both. None the less, Konohana bore him three children, one of whom, **Yamasachi**, went on to become the grandfather of Jimmu, first human Emperor of Japan.

The three treasures – mirror, necklace and sword – which Amaterasu gave Ninigi later became the most sacred items in the regalia of the Japanese Imperial family, proving its descent, right until modern times, from Jimmu, and therefore from the gods.

NINURTA
Asia (West)

Ninurta, in Sumerian myth, was the war god son of **Enlil** (the wind) and **Ninhursaga** (lady of stony ground). When he first appeared, he was power without shape, and Ninhursaga struggled to give him a form which would contain his energy. She first made him into a gigantic eagle, whose wings covered the sky,

then added a lion's head, then gave him a human body with an eagle's head and wings, and finally turned him into a human warrior with eagle's wings. He was irresistibly handsome, and his war cry was so loud that it terrified all creation.

Ninurta and Ninhursaga. Ninurta galloped his chariot through the universe, hurling thunderbolts and killing anyone who opposed him. Gradually he alienated everything in creation, until even his own mother rose against him. Taking the form of all the rocks in existence, she hurled herself at him in a shower of mountains, boulders and stones. Only a few small pebbles refused to fight, cowering on the featureless Earth until the battle was over. Ninurta hurled thunderbolts and battered the rocks into submission, littering **Mother Earth** with fragments until at last Ninhursaga was defeated and admitted that storm was superior to stone. Ninurta punished the stones which had attacked him by taking the life from them, leaving their corpses strewn on Mother Earth. He rewarded the stones which had refused to fight by leaving their life intact, and they glowed as diamonds, rubies and other precious crystals ever afterwards.

Ninurta and Zu. Ninurta's father Enlil owned a treasury of clay tablets, on which were written all the secrets of creation. These gave him power, as written tablets gave power to mortal kings, and with their help he ruled the universe – until Zu, a lion-headed, eagle-winged **demon** stole them and hid them in his eyrie. Zu had no idea how to release the power locked in the tablets, but clucked over them and incubated

them like a hen with eggs. The gods sent Ninurta to fetch them back. He surrounded himself with storm-winds, galloped his chariot to the mountain-top and roared that he wanted the tablets. Zu, glowing with the light reflected from the tablets, saw nothing but a storm-cloud shouting demands, and took no notice. Ninurta hurled a thunderbolt, but when it reached the aura of light from the tablets it fell to the ground, harmless as a reed plucked from a swamp. Ninurta, outwitted, went to his father (or, some say, to the **trickster Enki**) for advice. The solution was simple. He galloped back to the mountain-top, and this time instead of hiding in the storm-clouds he threw them round Zu like a net, tore off the demon's wings and beheaded him. The tablets of destiny were restored to Enlil, who rewarded Ninurta by letting him share some of their secrets with human beings. (They were the skills of **civilization**, especially how to govern cities and how to turn ore to metal.)
»→ **animal-gods**

NIOBE
Europe (South)

Niobe ('snowy'), wife of King **Amphion** of **Thebes** in Greek myth, boasted that her children were the most beautiful ever born – indeed, that they outdid even **Apollo** himself and his sister **Artemis**. Apollo responded by shooting the children dead, and Artemis turned Niobe into a mountainside, forever weeping waterfalls of tears in memory of her children and for her boasting which caused their deaths.

NIPINOUKHE AND PIPINOUKHE
Americas (North)

Nipinoukhe and Pipinoukhe, in the myths of the Montagnais, an Algonquian people of the Northeastern Canadian forests, were friends and brothers. Nipinoukhe was cheerful and extrovert, Pipinoukhe introvert and morose. They shared rule of the universe, spending six months of each year alternately in the North and the South. When Nipinoukhe ruled it was summer, and when Pipinoukhe took his turn, winter came.
»→ **fertility**

NISUS
Europe (South)

Nisus ('brightness'), in Greek and Roman myth, was a huntsman from Mount Ida, the area near Troy where **Paris** judged the contest between three goddesses which led indirectly to the **Trojan War**. Nisus fought in the war, and formed a close friendship – some say a homosexual union – with another young Trojan, Euryalus. After the sack of Troy, he and Euryalus sailed south with **Aeneas**, impressing everyone with their devotion to one another.

The only being unimpressed was Discord, goddess of quarrels. She waited until the Trojans were fighting the Rutulians in central Italy. The Rutulians were besieging the Trojan citadel on the banks of the river Tiber, and one cloudy, star-less night, when Nisus and Euryalus were on guard together, she put it into Nisus' mind that if he and Euryalus crept together through the besiegers' camp they could get word to Aeneas and his troops, encamped some distance away, and bring them to the rescue.

Nisus and Euryalus let themselves down on ropes from the walls of the citadel and crept into the sleeping camp. Their original idea had been to slip through unobserved, but Discord filled them with madness, and they began slaughtering sleeping Rutulians: Abaris, Fadus, Herbesus, Lamus, La- myrus, Rhamnes the prophet, Rhoetes the drunkard and Serranus. Euryalus stole the golden helmet of the Rutulian general Messapus, and put it on.

The Rutulians, roused by the noise, tried to find the killers. Even then, Nisus and Euryalus would have got away, except that Discord parted the clouds and set a moonbeam glinting full on Messapus' stolen helmet. The two young Trojans were surrounded and killed – and were renowned ever after- wards as a couple, in Roman myth, whose affection for each other was matched only by their bravery.

NJINJI
Africa

Njinji ('he's everywhere'), creator-god in the myths of the Babum people of Cameroon, made human beings in his own image: strong, healthy, immortal. He sent them to Earth to live, and when he looked down from **Sky** to see how they were doing he was horrified to see them lying on the ground, as inert as logs. He asked **Death** what had hap- pened, and Death said that they weren't dead but sulking. He carried Njinji all over the Earth, disguised as a banana, so

that he could overhear the humans complaining about the boredom and misery of their endless lives, and pray- ing to die. Njinji threw up his hands in disgust, and abandoned his creations to Death, who fell on them and answered their prayers.

NJÖRD
Europe (North)

Njörd, the Old Man of the **Sea** in Nordic myth, looked after all the waters on Earth, all ships and all sailors. In some accounts he was the same god as **Nerthus**, the Earth, and changed **sex** from male to female to become Earth, from female to male to become Sea. In others he mated with Nerthus inces- santly, his waves lapping her shores, and their children were **Frey** and **Freyja**.

Njörd and Skadi. Njörd was origin- ally ruler of the **Vanir**, ancient **fertility** gods, but after the war between the Vanir and the **Aesir** (war gods) ended with an exchange of leaders, he and Frey went to live in **Asgard**. Njörd's arrival brought peace and prosperity to the universe, a golden age. But he himself was restless, unsatisfied with Asgard. At first he thought he wanted a queen. **Skadi**, a giantess from **Jotun- heim**, came looking for a husband. The gods of Vanaheim lined up behind a curtain, nothing showing but their bare feet. Skadi walked up and down the line, hoping to recognize the feet of **Baldur** the Beautiful. But Njörd's feet were even more shapely than Baldur's, and she chose him. He went with her to Jotun- heim, high in the snow-hills. But after a time he said he could not bear to live there, to be woken each morning by the howls of wolves and the whistling of the wind. Skadi went with him to his sea-palace, but after a time she left, saying that she could not bear the warmth of the waves and the morning serenade of seagulls. So they separated, and Njörd has patrolled his kingdom ever since, sometimes at peace, sometimes restless and raging when he thinks of the happiness he might have had if he had preferred wife to home.

In some accounts, instead of separating, Njörd and Skadi agreed to spend time alternately in each other's kingdoms – just as Njörd had agreed to spend some of his time in Asgard after the war between the Aesir and the Vanir. This agreement, the writers claim, was the origin of the seasons: the dark, cold half of each year when Njörd lived with the ice-giants, the light, warm half when he was happy in his own sea-kingdom.

NOAH
Asia (West)

Noah and the Flood. Noah ('comforter'), in Hebrew myth, was a pious mortal allowed to escape the **flood** sent by **Yahweh** to wipe out the human race. Warned in advance, he built a boat and filled it, despite the jeers of his neighbours, with one male and one female of every creature on Earth, with plants and seeds and with his own quarrelsome family (his wife and three sons Shem, Ham and Japhet). The flood covered the Earth for 150 days before Noah opened a porthole in his boat and sent out a raven to find dry land. It returned exhausted, and he waited a week before sending out a dove. On the first occasion it returned,

but on the second it came back with an olive-twig in its beak, and Noah knew that the waters were receding. He beached the boat (in some accounts, on Mount Ararat), and released all the creatures.

Noah and wine. In some accounts, Noah found the Earth covered with plants, growing again in the mud left by the floodwaters. In others, he restocked the land with seeds and plants stored in his boat – and the first thing he planted was a vine. Grapes miraculously grew that same night, and when he inspected the vine next morning he accidentally trampled some of them, making the first wine ever known. He drank it, got drunk, and had to endure the laughter of his family. The Bible account of this story says that Ham, Noah's youngest son, ran to fetch his brothers to see their father naked and in his cups, and Shem and Japhet primly covered the old man up until he recovered. When Noah's head cleared he punished Ham by making him and his descendants servants of the families of Shem and Japhet forever.

*Mythographers suggest that the story of Noah and the Flood is directly derived from the account of **Utnapishtim** in Babylonian myth, and that the story of his drunkenness, grafted on to it, may come from a different tradition entirely, the myths of some otherwise long-forgotten harvest-god.*
➤ Atrahis, Deucalion and Pyrrha, Doquebuth, Manu, Nu'u, Utnapishtim

NOCOMA
Americas (North)

Nocoma ('grandfather'), in the myths of the Luiseño (Acagchemem) people of the Southern Californian coast, created the world from a speck of dust lying on a boulder in a stream. Originally these objects were all that existed apart from the fish that filled the stream, but the fish prised open the boulder to find more living-space, and salt water gushed out to form the primordial ocean. Nocoma's Earth grew in a similar way, from a single dust-speck to an entire planet. Earth created trees and plants to dress herself, and Nocoma filled her with animal-spirits of every kind. Finally he moulded two spirit-humans from mud, a male (Ejoni) and a female (Ae), and they mated to produce the human race.

≫→ creation, Owiot

NOKOMIS

Americas (North)

Nokomis ('grandmother'), in the myths of many peoples of the Northeastern US woodlands, was **Mother Earth**. She was originally a love-goddess, one of the most beautiful in **Heaven**. But she had jealous rivals, and one day, when she was swinging on a vine hanging from the sky, one of those rivals sliced it through and sent her plunging into the primordial ocean far below. Here she floated, unable to climb back into the sky. In due time, the movement of wind and waves made her pregnant, and she gave birth to all living creatures – and when she saw that there was nowhere for them to live, she turned herself into an enormous land-mass, floating in the ocean: Earth.

≫→ creation

NORDIC MYTH

Nordic myth is so-called because it survived chiefly among the Nordic peoples, in the folk-literature of Scandinavia and the folk- and art-literature of medieval Iceland. But its origins lie farther South, in the triangle of Europe bounded by the Rhine to the West, the Danube to the South and the Vistula to the East. From the third century BCE onwards, invaders from this area moved North into what is now Scandinavia, taking their myths with them. From the eighth-eleventh centuries the Scandinavians ('Vikings') travelled the world, colonizing Iceland, parts of Britain and the fringes of the Carolingian Empire in Europe, travelling along the rivers Dnieper and Volga as far South as the Black Sea and Byzantium and as far East as the Caspian Sea, and crossing the Atlantic to North America.

All this activity was in the names of trade and the conquest which facilitated it. Culturally speaking, the Vikings were almost entirely self-contained. Their customs and the myths which enshrined them were hardly affected by the huge range of peoples and ideas with whom they came into contact. Even when they became nominally Christian (in the eleventh century everywhere but Sweden; in Sweden two centuries later), they grafted the beliefs and practices of the new religion on to their old ways, without substantially altering them. The co-existence of a non-Christian mindset among 'ordinary' people and a learned, clerky culture centred on cathedrals and monasteries is characteristic of Medieval Europe, but the distinction was nowhere as unblurred as in Scandinavia: it was as if ordinary life and religious life were two different species of creature sharing the same habitat.

This insulation of 'ordinary' culture means that the myths of pre-Christian Nordic peoples survive in a remarkably unadulterated form. Their vigour, originally derived from and sanctioned by religion, remained even when – or perhaps because – religious belief was amputated from them and transferred to Christianity. Because **Odin, Thor, Freyja** and the other gods were never felt as threats by the incumbent religious establishment, they were never marginalized and demonized in the way of, say, **Baal** in the Middle East or the Celtic gods of Western Europe (so effectively made non-persons that even their names are now blurred into locutions such as 'Great Father' or 'Old One'). Nordic cosmology is as pure, and simultaneously as complex, as those of the great cultures which escaped contact with Christianity: Egypt, Greece, India, Japan.

Nordic myths survive, as do most pre-literate traditions, first of all in artwork and folk festivals and customs, and then in a vast number of proverbs, nursery rhymes, ballads, tales, snatches of metaphor and simile, the mindset embodied in the languages people speak. There is also a substantial 'art' literature, covering the myths of the entire area but most of it created in Iceland in the eleventh-fourteenth centuries. Its chief components are *Eddas* ('poems'), *Sagas* ('recitations') and more formal works of history, mythography and literary criticism by such

scholars as Snorri Sturluson. The *Eddas* vary in length from a handful of lines to several hundreds; they are by many hands, some anonymous some known; they use folk forms (such as riddles or prophetic 'kenning') to allude to episodes and ideas from the ancient myths. The *Sagas* (some 700 in all) are prose narratives, again by named as well as anonymous writers, and each tells a specific adventure, either heroic (the story of one particular person or dynasty) or mythic. The scholarly work, of which the most important for later students of Nordic myth are Sturluson's writings (notably *Heimskringla*, a history of Iceland from mythical times to his own day, and the *Prose Edda*, a literary and critical guide to the ancient myths), looks back at the past, and at myth, with a Christian certainty about the present which seldom obtrudes but which allows the authors marvellous academic detachment – save in a few cases (for example when Sturluson claims that the Norse people were descended from settlers from Troy, fleeing North after the **Trojan War** just as **Aeneas** and his followers fled South) they avoid speculation, and confine themselves to documenting what was actually there.

To modern eyes, there are a few signs in the surviving myths that several traditions must have been intermingled at some early stage. The creation-myths, for example, are confused: did the fire-giants of **Muspell** (led by **Surt**) and the ice-giants of **Niflheim** exist before **Yggdrasil**, ash-tree of the universe – and if so, where? Where do really ancient gods like **Donar** and **Tyr** (duplicating some of the functions of later gods like

Odin and Thor) fit into the cosmological scheme? Do the **Vanir** belong to a different tradition from the **Aesir**, so that the story of the war between them is an allegory of the mingling of two traditions? There is enormous confusion over the Golden Apples of **Immortality** – and about their keeper **Idun**, a pale replica of both **Freyja** and **Frigg** (who are in any case, some scholars think, the same goddess under different names). Elves, dwarfs and **demons** seem to play the same kind of marginalized role in the myths as displaced gods in other cultures do when a more powerful myth-system takes over – examples are the ancient South Indian gods who became **Underworld** monsters or countryside spirits after the Aryan invasions. Above all, there is more uneasiness about status among the gods than in most pantheons. Odin and Thor, for example, continually jockey for supreme authority, and **Loki**'s position is so consistently equivocal that he seems to be half a dozen gods, from court jester to ultimate enemy, rolled into one.

»+ Aegir, Agnar, Alvis, Andvari, Asegeir, Asgard, Ask and Embla, Audumla, Baldur, Bergelmir, Berserkers, Bestla, Bifröst, Bor, Bragi, Brisingamen, Brynhild, Buri, Elli, Fafnir, Forseti, Frey, Gefion, Geirröd (giant), Geirröd (mortal), Gilling, Ginungagap, Grid, Gunnlod, Heimdall, Hel, Hlin, Höd, Honir, Hraesvelg, Hrungnir, Hrym, Hymir, Jormungand, Kvasir, Lif, Midgard, Mimir, Nerthus, Nidhogg, Nine Wave-maidens, Nine Worlds, Njörd, Norns, Od, Odin, Otr, Ragnarök, Ran, Regin, Sif, Sigmund, Sigurd, Skadi, Skrymsli, Sleipnir, Suttung, Thiazi, Thor, Tiwaz, Ull, Utgard, Valhalla, Valkyries, Ve, Vidar, Vili, Wyrd, Yambe-akka, Ymir

NORNS
Europe (North)

The three Norns, in Nordic myth, were Skuld ('being'), Urd ('fate') and Verdandi ('necessity'). They sat by the spring of Urd in **Asgard**, watering **Yggdrasil**, ash-tree of the universe, and plastering its wounds with magic clay to keep it and the universe healthy. Urd was older than time itself; Verdandi was young and beautiful; Skuld was middle-aged and crabby. The Norns wove tapestries of human destiny. They made patterns of the utmost intricacy, so involved that not even they could understand them – and this determined the pattern of human lives. A further complication, for humans at least, was that Skuld was forever taking offence at some slight, real or imagined, and when she did so she ripped each tapestry to pieces, so throwing humanity into utter confusion. This is why, the myth ends, our lives seem so chaotic. If the Norns ever finish a tapestry, our existence will be defined forever, and we will live in unending peace and certainty.

»+ Fates

NÜ GUA
Asia (East)

Nü Gua ('gourd-woman'), or Nü Wa ('snail-woman'), goddess of order in Chinese myth, helped to people the world at the beginning of **creation**. In some accounts she and her brother **Fu**

Xi were the only survivors of a huge **flood** sent to drown the world after one of the original human beings tried to imprison **Thunder**. They floated on the waters in a gourd – hence the name Nü Gua – and as soon as the land dried out they set about restoring the world to what it had been before. In some accounts they became a pair of **snakes** with human heads, and mated – and their amorous coilings, all over the surface of the Earth, restocked it with plants and animals.

As for human beings, accounts differ. In one version, Nü Gua gave birth to a round ball of flesh, and just before she and Fu Xi climbed the ladder into **Heaven** and disappeared forever, they sliced it into pieces and scattered them on the Earth – the first humans. In another, Nü Gua (now a snail with a woman's torso and head, hence the name) began making us from handfuls of mud, but grew bored long before the job was done and began flicking mud-balls out of the river-bed with her stick (or some say, a vine). The carefully-rolled mud became aristocrats, the mud-balls ordinary people.

For yet another Chinese account of the creation of human beings, see **Pan Gu**.

≫→ Gong Gong

NUM
Europe (Northeast)

Num, in the myths of the Samoyed people, was the **sky**-god. He had no shape, and was the air itself. He sent his servants, the birds, to look for anything unusual in the primordial ocean (all that existed apart from himself), and

created the universe from a beakful of mud which one of them brought back.

NUN AND NAUNET
Africa (North)

Nun and Naunet, in Egyptian myth, were two aspects of the primeval ocean, worshipped as gods. Nun was male, Naunet female. In some accounts, they were the primordial substance of the universe, and their coming together engendered **Atum** who went on to create the gods; in another, Naunet looked on admiringly while Nun hurled the Sun-ship into the sky each day to begin its journey. On the few occasions when Nun and Naunet were shown in art, they were ocean from the waist down, human from the waist up. All temple pools and **Underworld** rivers were sacred to them.

≫→ creation, sea, water

NUT
Africa (North)

Nut ('**Sky**'), in Egyptian myth, was the daughter of **Shu** and **Tefnut**, and the twin sister of **Geb** ('Earth'). She and he were born locked together in a tight sexual embrace, and **Ra**, their grandfather, ordered Shu ('air') to separate them. Shu found a space and began prising Nut away from Geb. She clung until the last moment, her toes and fingers resting on Geb and the rest of her body arched above him like a bow. She became the sky-arch across which Ra was later to travel in the Sun-ship each day, from horizon to horizon.

In some accounts, Nut and Geb were not forever linked in primordial space: they separated briefly four times, long enough for Nut to give birth, and then resumed their embrace. The gods Nut bore were **Aset, Nebthet, Osiris** and **Seth** – and later, when they became rulers of the **Underworld**, she was also worshipped as receiver of the Dead, opening her arms to accept their souls as a mother enfolds a baby. For the most part, though, she was honoured as the goddess of the sky, and her arched back (or, in some accounts, her upraised arms) kept the universe in being. These ideas – the goddess standing on all fours above the Earth, or standing erect and holding it aloft – were favourite images in Egyptian art. Others, associating her with the cow-goddess **Hathor**, show her, in a bizarre piece of iconography, brandishing a cow above her head while milk streams from its udders to fertilize the Earth.

⇛ twins

NU'U
Oceania

Nu'u, or Nu'u Pule ('praying Nu'u'), in Hawaiian myth, heard from the gods that Kane (that is, **Tane**) was going to swamp the world in a tidal wave. He built a house on a ship, stocked it with pigs, coconuts, plantains and **kava**, and when the flood came sailed on the water-surface until he beached on a mountain-top.

Mythographers think that although flood-survivor stories may have existed before the arrival of missionaries from Europe, the details of this one, including Nu'u's name, are post-Christian embellishments.

⇛ **Atrahis, Deucalion and Pyrrha, Doquebuth, Manu, Noah, Utnapishtim**

NYAMBE
Africa

Nyambe, in the myths of the Koko people of Nigeria, created Earth and human beings, and lived peacefully there with all his followers. At first there was no death, because Nyambe had in his garden the Life-Tree, and anyone who felt old or sick had merely to embrace it to be restored to vigour. But as time went on, the grandchildren and great-grandchildren of the original humans began to ignore Nyambe, paying him no respect and drifting away to set up homes of their own. In the end, having called a meeting of the entire human race to explain just what was happening, he uprooted the Life-Tree, stalked off to **Heaven** and was never seen again.

NYAMBI
Africa

Nyambi, creator-god of the Barotse people of the Upper Zambesi, lived on Earth with his wife Nasilele. At first everything was peaceful, and he revelled in his own **creation**. But then he began to be pestered by a neighbour, Kamonu. Kamonu visited him a dozen times each day, borrowed pots and pans and copied his way of eating, walking, talking, even pissing and farting. In the end he went too far. Seeing Nyambi forging iron, he imitated him, but instead of beating out ploughshares and scythes he made spears and knives and began killing both animals and people.

Nyambi decided that it was time to leave the world. He sailed with Nasilele to an island in the middle of the primordial lake – and found that Kamonu had stowed away in the same boat. He strode up the highest mountain on Earth, and two years later Kamonu came panting after him. Irritated to desperation, Nyambi took Spider, forced her to spin a rope, climbed up it with Nasilele and pulled it up after him. Before he left Earth he blinded Spider – his one cruel action since the beginning of creation – so that she could never tell Kamonu where exactly Nyambi and Nasilele had penetrated the clouds. Ever since then, Kamonu and his mortal descendants have spent their time gazing up at the sky, trying to glimpse Nyambi. When the **Sun** comes up they mistake it for the god and worship it; when the **Moon** comes up they take it for Nasilele. One day, the myth ends, Nyambi will return in person, and instead of having to guess what God is like and how to emulate him, we will know.

NYMPHS
Europe (South)

Nymphs ('maidens'), in Greek and Roman myth, were the daughters of **Zeus** and such natural phenomena as rivers, trees, waterfalls, the **sea**, air and **fire**. They were beautiful, innumerable, and peopled every part of **creation**. Some were demure and shy, others as eager for **sex** as their insatiable father. Many found mates among rivers, trees, animals, gods and mortals, and the result was an even larger colony of nymphs.

Often, groups of particular nymphs were given names reflecting their special haunts. *Dryads*, once oak-tree nymphs, were wood and forest nymphs of all kinds. *Hamadryads* were dryads who had surrendered their **immortality** to live with, or in, particular trees, and who died when their host-trees died. *Leimoniads* were meadow nymphs, *Naiads* **water** nymphs and *Orestiads* **mountain** nymphs. Among the best-known nymphs of all were the *Nereids* (fifty **sea**-nymph daughters of the water-god **Nereus** and the nymph Doris), the **Muses** and the *Oceanides* (3000 daughters of **Ocean** and the nymph Tethys).

➤ *apsaras*

Orestes, Electra and the Furies (*18th-century French engraving*)

OBERON

Europe (Central)

Oberon, in medieval European myth and folk-tale, was the king of the Fairies. In some accounts he was the same person as **Andvari**, and was solely of the supernatural dimension. In others he was the son of a mortal (Julius Caesar) and an enchantress (**Morgan le Fay**), and was tormented by the duality in his nature between mortal emotions and fairy ruthlessness. (This is the root of his character in his best-known appearance, as a racked lover and jealous, tyrannical **trickster** in Shakespeare's *A Midsummer Night's Dream*.)

OCEANIAN MYTH

Oceania is an artificial grouping of Pacific islands, consisting of dozens of independent states and three large regions: Melanesia (centred on Papua New Guinea, Vanuatu and the Fijian Islands), Micronesia (a shoal of small island groups including those named after Europeans, the Carolines, the Marshalls, the Gilberts), and Polynesia (a triangle whose corners are New Zealand to the South, the Hawaiian and Midway Islands 8000km away to the North and Easter Island a similar distance East). There are over 1000 languages – some 700 in Papua New Guinea alone – and the area is one of the most heterogeneous and most sparsely populated on Earth.

Perhaps unexpectedly, the huge distances separating one community from another, and the smallness of many of the communities – sometimes an individual language was spoken by only a few dozen families – do not lead to vast myth-proliferation. The Native Americans, similarly scattered (but over land not sea), evolved far more varied systems. In practice, from the time when the first settlers travelled from Indonesia to Melanesia some 2000 years ago, most communities have taken an easygoing, assimilative view of other people's stories and religions, merely adapting them to local conditions. At times it seems as if ideas (whether cosmic, for example that Father **Sky** and **Mother Earth** mated to begin **creation**, or merely colourful, for example that the strength of the universe might be embodied in a pig or that generative power might be symbolized by a male-god's penis whirled like a bullroarer) were able to travel, and occupy, the whole area almost faster than the humans who devised them.

The Oceanian universe begins with acts of individual creation, either by the Father Sky-Mother Earth couple **Rangi** (**Atea**; Vatea) and **Papa** and their children (most commonly **Tane** and the **sea** god variously known as **Ta'aroa**, **Tagaroa**, **Tangaloa** and **Tangaroa**). A few ornately individual myths survive alongside this tradition: examples are those of the creator-spiders **Areop-Enap** and **Nareau**, **Loa** or **Qat** who made the universe largely by accident, or the quarrelling creator-twins **To Kabinana** and **To Karvuvu**. There are gods of natural phenomena (**Dudugera** the Sun; the volcano-gods **Pele** and **Ruaumoko**), and a host of **fertility**-gods ranging from **Haumea** the universal mother to **Kamapua'a** who made lakes and rivers, from **Totoima** the boar to the **sex**-god known variously as **Soido**, **Sosom** and **Sido** (in which manifestation he is also the House of Death). Several stories (for example those of **Hina**, **Honoyeta** and **Na Kaa**) explain why human beings die, and there is a scattering of old myths made over in the light of teaching by Christian missionaries, for example the story of **Nu'u** who built and stocked a boat to escape a universal **flood**. Widest-ranging of all are **trickster**-myths and stories: those concerning **Maui** and **Olifat**, for example, are found, hardly changed, in every corner of Oceania.

If the world-view of Oceanian myth is remarkably consistent – a consistency which extends to matters of ritual practice, for example the observance of *tapu* (taboo) or the idea that spirits talk to us through the sounds made by musical instruments – the physical survival of the stories has varied enormously from century to century. Originally they were passed on by oral tradition, associated with particular feasts or ceremonies. After the coming of Europeans (beginning with Magellan, who visited Guam in 1521) they were recorded in writing for the first time, but with glosses by the Westerners who heard them – and who were sometimes unfamiliar with local languages or practices (as late as the twentieth century, people in Samoa cheerfully told the anthropologist Margaret Mead exactly what they thought she wanted to hear). Finally, as communities regained independence after interludes of colonial domination, many myths were remade as political propaganda, not to bind the community (one of their original purposes) but to assert its given identity to the outside world. This last metamorphosis, into dogma, is regrettable (at least by mythographers) in view of the way it conflicts with the adaptable, open-ended nature both of the original stories and the societies they served.

»→ Ha'iaka, Jari and Kamarong, Jugumishanta and Morufonu, Kava, Rangi's and Papa's Immortal Children

OD
Europe (North)

Od, or Odur ('passionate'), in Nordic myth, is one of the most mysterious of all gods whose names survive. **Freyja** married him, but he left her to go to **Midgard** (some say, in search of beautiful mortal women), and ever afterwards she wept golden tears for him. Nothing else is known.

ODIN
Europe (North)

Odin's names and powers. Odin ('rager'), also known as Wotan and Woden, was the Nordic and Germanic god of storms and battle, and particularly ruled the moment of no return: the point where the spear-cast is complete and the weapon leaves your hand, the instant when sexual orgasm is unstoppable, the moment when poetic inspiration begins. His honorary names included Bileyg ('shifty-eyed'), Galgagram ('gallows-lord'), Glapsvidir ('swift-tricker'), Sidfodir ('victory-giver') and Valfodr ('father of the slain'). He was a **shape-changer**, able to enter any place or condition he chose, and to conquer **death**, but his chief function was as lawgiver and ruler of gods and mortals – none of whom shared his wisdom or could stand against his dwarf-crafted spear Gungnir, with which he stirred up or quelled universal strife. He led favoured mortals to victory – and when brave **heroes** were killed in the fighting, he sent his warrior-maidens the **Valkyries** to fetch them to **Valhalla**, where he led them in roistering, listening to martial poetry and practising warskills. (The heroes ate roast pork, but Odin took none of it. He never needed food, nourishing himself on his own power and wisdom and on occasional sips of the mead of poetic inspiration.)

Odin and creation. Odin was one of the sons of **Bor**, father of the gods. He and his brothers **Vili** and **Ve** killed the frost-**giant Ymir**, and used his flesh, blood and bones to make the physical universe. They built worlds for the Dead, the living and the gods, and hung stars and constellations in the sky. They made dwarfs, elves and mortals, and begat gods. The only creatures they had no hand in making were giants, creatures of frost and ice – and, throughout eternity, the giants fought Odin and his descendants for universal power.

Odin and wisdom. Odin searched perpetually for the all-knowledge that was one of the secrets of his power. He used his shape-changing skills to discover what life was like as an insect, smoke, water, as a leaf, a fish, an animal, fire, a serpent, wind. He understood the languages of all living creatures, especially birds, and had two raven-servants, Hugin ('thought') and Munin ('memory'). Hugin flew round the world of the living, collecting information; Munin did the same round the world of the dead, and every evening they perched on Odin's shoulders and told him all they had discovered.

Odin often disguised himself as a mortal traveller, wandering the world in search of the kind of adventures ordinary heroes enjoyed. He asked to drink from the well of **Mimir**, which drew wisdom from the dew which ran into it from one of the roots of **Yggdrasil**, and plucked out his own eye to pay for it. He stabbed himself with his own spear and hung himself, dead, on Yggdrasil for nine days to let the dew seep into his bones – and then, filled with wisdom (the kind carried in writing, rune-magic), brought himself back to life. This feat brought him two other honorary names, Geigud ('dangler') and Hangagud ('hanging god').

The mead of inspiration. When the war was settled between **Aesir** and **Vanir**, each of the gods spat into a bowl, and from their spittle they fashioned a being, **Kvasir**, filled with all the knowledge of the universe. But Kvasir was tricked by the dwarves, who invited him to a feast, stabbed him dead, then gathered his blood in jars and mixed it with honey to form a miraculous mead: whoever drank of it was filled with wisdom and the power to make poetry. The giant **Suttung**, in turn, took the jars of mead from the dwarfs and hid them in the heart of a mountain, guarded by his daughter **Gunnlod**.

Odin set out to recover the mead for the gods. Disguised as a man, Bolverk, he visited Baugi, Suttung's brother, at harvest-time. He killed all Baugi's farmhands and then offered to harvest all the grain himself, single-handed, in return for one drink of Suttung's mead. Baugi agreed, and at the end of harvest, when Suttung refused to part with any of the mead, he bored a hole through the mountainside to the inner chamber. It was less than a thumb's-breadth wide, but Bolverk changed himself into a snake and wriggled through it, then stood in front of Gunnlod in the disguise of the handsomest giant she had ever seen. He sang to her, told her jokes and stories, flirted with her and finally agreed to **sex** with her in exchange for three sips of the magic mead. There were three jars, and he emptied each of them with a single sip. Then, holding the mead in his mouth, he changed himself into an eagle, flew back to **Asgard** and spat it out into jars and basins which the gods held waiting. Only a little was spilled – the mead of inspiration which sometimes fills mortals' souls – and ever afterwards the magic drink remained in Asgard as the property of the gods and the especial privilege of Odin who had used his shape-changing powers to rescue it.

Odin, Agnar and Geirröd. Odin played with two mortal brothers, **Agnar** and **Geirröd**, on an island when they were children. But when the boys rowed the boat back to shore, Geirröd suddenly jumped out on to dry land and shoved the boat out to sea, then went to his father and said that Agnar had been drowned. In due course, he succeeded to his father's throne. Years later, a man called Grimnir visited Geirröd's court and Geirröd, afraid that he was a sorcerer, chained him over two fires to roast to death. Agnar, however (who had not been drowned but had survived and come to work in his brother's court, disguised as a pot-boy), pitied Grimnir and gave him ale to drink. Grimnir prophesied that Geirröd would kill himself with his own sword – and at once the fires sputtered out, the chains fell away and Grimnir shed his disguise as a snake sloughs its skin, revealing himself as Odin. Geirröd snatched his sword to kill him, but tripped and stabbed himself dead. Odin set Agnar on the throne, promised him a lifetime of prosperity, and disappeared back to Asgard.

*Although Odin's shape-changing was a gift to story-tellers – of all Northern European gods, only **Loki** features in more tales – it made him a difficult god to depict in fine art. The images most favoured show him as a bearded, middle-aged warrior riding his eight-legged charger **Sleipnir** (sometimes at the head of his **Berserkers** on mortal battlefields, or leading the hosts of the Dead across the sky) and sometimes as a wanderer wearing a blue cloak, a broad-brimmed hat and an eye-patch, and carrying his spear Gungnir. His roles as leader of the Dead and holder of all wisdom led to a mystery-cult, widespread in Europe for three millennia. It was thought that anyone who was stabbed (as Odin stabbed himself) and hung nine days on an ash-tree (as Odin hung himself on Yggdrasil) would achieve all-knowledge and conquer death (as Odin did): the body-husk would be discarded and the soul would float free for all eternity. Many images survive showing this practice, and buried remains suggest that it was common well into Christian times. Otherwise, Odin was chiefly remembered in the tradition of the 'Wild Hunt': a belief that on stormy nights the Dead rose from their graves and galloped across the sky behind Sleipnir, his eight-legged, mist-coloured charger. His name (as Woden) survives today mainly as patron deity of Wednesday.*

≫→ creation, Dionysus, prophecy, supreme deity

ODUDUWA
Africa

Oduduwa, in Yoruba myth, was involved in **creation**. In some versions of the creation-story, the god sent by **Olorun** to grow trees and plants got drunk and fell asleep in the shade of the first tree he planted, and Olorun sent Oduduwa down to finish creation. However, Oduduwa was ambitious, and determined to find out how Olorun gave the breath of life to the mud-shapes of animals and humans he moulded for him, and so make creatures of his own. He hid behind a wood-pile to spy on Olorun. But the creator knew exactly what he planned, and sang a sleep-spell to make him doze. Oduduwa never did find out how to make perfect human beings – and his botched attempts, as soon as he woke up, were the ancestors of **demons**, predators and poison-animals.

ODYSSEUS
Europe (South)

Odysseus' youth. Odysseus ('angry'; Latin Ulysses or Ulixes), in Greek and Roman myth, was the son of Anticlea (daughter of the **trickster Autolycus**) and either **Laertes** King of Ithaca or another trickster, **Sisyphus**. He was educated by the **centaur Chiron**, and Laertes abdicated in his favour as soon as the boy was old enough to rule Ithaca. Like every other young hero in Greece, Odysseus wanted to marry **Helen** of Sparta, but because Ithaca was the poorest kingdom in Greece and because there were so many other suitors, he avoided the humiliation of rejection by marrying someone else instead: Helen's cousin **Penelope**.

Odysseus at Troy. Odysseus advised Helen's father, **Tyndareus**, that the rejected suitors would wage civil war in Greece unless he made them swear an oath to support whoever actually married her. Tyndareus did so – and it was this oath which later compelled every Greek hero to go to the **Trojan War**, to help **Menelaus** after **Paris** abducted Helen. Only Odysseus resisted. An oracle had told him that if he went to war he would be twenty years away and would return a beggar, so when the kings came recruiting he feigned madness, yoking an ass and an ox to the same plough and sowing his fields with salt. **Palamedes** revealed the trick: he dropped Odysseus' baby son **Telemachus** on the ground ahead of the plough, and Odysseus stopped to prevent the child being trampled to death, something no madman would have done. Odysseus was forced to go to war, and never forgave Palamedes, later engineering his death.

Once Odysseus joined the expedition, he put all his cunning to work for it. He showed the Greek leaders where **Achilles** was hiding (on Scyros, disguised as a woman), and tricked **Philoctetes**, who owned the unerring bow of **Heracles**, into giving up his quarrel with the Greeks and going to fight. Instead of the head-on heroics favoured by other Greek leaders (for example Achilles) he used strategy, attacking the camp of the Thracians (Trojan allies) in the middle of the

night and killing their king **Rhesus**, or slipping into the city through the drains and stealing the **Palladium**, the statue of **Athene** which symbolized the luck of Troy. His slyness made him as many enemies as friends among the Greeks, and there was a furious row after Achilles' death, when some of the leaders wanted to give Odysseus Achilles' god-made armour, and others (led by Achilles' son **Neoptolemus**) opposed the idea. 'Great' **Ajax** demanded a duel to the death for the armour; Odysseus suggested a vote, and persuaded the army to give him the arms – a decision which drove Ajax to madness and suicide. Finally, Odysseus' cunning ended the war. Athene suggested to him, or he himself devised, the strategy of the **Wooden Horse**, and he led the expeditionary force which hid inside it while the other Greeks pretended to sail away.

After the Trojan War. Odysseus' character divided gods as well as mortals. His chief supporter was Athene, goddess of wisdom, and his most implacable opponent was **Poseidon**, who had built the walls of Troy which Odysseus' slyness had destroyed. Poseidon set about delaying his return to Ithaca, and although Athene gave Odysseus her support, the journey took ten years, carried him at the winds' whim over every ocean and sea on Earth, and stripped him of his Trojan treasure, his captured slaves and all his companions. Time after time he faced supernatural enemies, and defeated them by cunning, bravery or both. He visited the **Lotuseaters** and heard the **Sirens**' song (the only mortal ever to do so and survive). He outwitted **Polyphemus**, king of the

438

Cyclopes, and the enchantresses **Circe** and **Calypso**. He escaped **Scylla** and **Charybdis** and visited the **Underworld**. Finally, naked and alone, he was washed up on the shores of Phaeacia, where Princess **Nausicaä** rescued him and King **Alcinous**, after hearing the story of his wanderings, gave him a ship and crew to take him safely home to Ithaca.

King Odysseus. During Odysseus' twenty-year absence, suitors had swarmed round his wife Penelope. She had remained loyal to him, at the expense of keeping a gang of lords roistering in her palace day in, day out. Odysseus now crept into the palace, disguised as a beggar. (The only living beings to recognize him were his faithful old dog **Argus** and the pig-herd Eumaeus.) The gods put it into Penelope's mind to suggest a trial of strength. Whoever strung Odysseus' huge war-bow, and shot an arrow through the loops of a dozen axe-hafts set in a row in the ground, would be her husband. One by one, the suitors tried and failed. Then Odysseus stepped up, despite the suitors' jeers, strung the bow, shot the arrow and claimed his prize. He and Telemachus, helped by the gods, barred the doors of the palace and shot all the suitors dead in a single night. Penelope recognized her husband at last, and the people welcomed him as their king, returned.

Odysseus' death. There was still the matter of Poseidon's anger. The god told Odysseus that he must find a country where no one had ever heard of **sea** or standing **water**, and build Poseidon a temple there. Odysseus made Telemachus regent in Ithaca,

and set off on another enormous journey. He went alone, rowing first from Ithaca to the mainland and then walking inland, carrying an oar over one shoulder. For ten years, wherever he went, people jeeringly asked 'Stranger, why are you carrying an oar so far from the sea?' Then at last, in Thesprotia, far to the North, people asked 'Stranger, why are you carrying that winnowing-fan?' – and he knew his search was over, planted the oar in the ground and built a temple to Poseidon.

Safe at last from Poseidon's anger, Odysseus set off for Ithaca. On his way he consulted the Delphic oracle (or, some say, the prophet **Tiresias**), and was told that his own son would kill him. When he reached home, therefore, he immediately banished Telemachus. Characteristically, however, the oracle had only partially revealed the truth. The death-dealing son was not Telemachus but Telegonus, whom Odysseus had fathered on Circe years before, leaving her without even knowing that she was pregnant. Telegonus, equally, had no idea who his father was. He sailed the seas of the world, trying to find his father, and landed by chance on Ithaca. Odysseus took him and his men for pirates, and led armed soldiers to the shore to drive them off. There was a battle, and Telegonus killed Odysseus with a spear made from a sting-ray's spine.

Other myths. Some myth-tellers decorate this narrative with even more fanciful additions. In one account, when Odysseus was coming back from Delphi, he stayed with the king of Epirus, and rewarded him by raping his daughter Erippe. She had a son,

Euryalus (not the Euryalus of other myths), and when he was grownup sent him to Ithaca to avenge the rape. Penelope, however, discovered the plot and told Odysseus that Euryalus had tried to seduce her. Odysseus executed Euryalus, who therefore lived and died without his father ever knowing who he really was. Other accounts embroider the very end of Odysseus' story, saying that after Telegonus killed him he married Penelope and ruled Ithaca, leaving Telemachus to sail to Circe's island, marry her and found a new royal dynasty there.

Of all ancient classical literature, only Sophocles' Antigone and Virgil's **Aeneid** *have ever rivalled the popularity and influence of Homer's Odyssey – and the Aeneid is itself modelled on the Odyssey. Homer makes Odysseus' journey home, and the dangers he faces, parables for the philosophical and psychological growth of a human being, and endows Odysseus not only with cunning but with long-suffering, heroism and nobility. These are not Odysseus' qualities in the* Iliad *– indeed his character is so different there that people suggest that the two poems might be by different authors. In the* Iliad *he is arrogant, devious, a politician and – if there is no alternative – a skilful if unscrupulous fighter. Other ancient authors, notably Sophocles and Euripides, use these same qualities, giving Odysseus a kind of shifty grandeur which endears him to no one. Later writers pick and choose among qualities, much as they plunder individual moments from the stories, so that to this day few myth characters, in any tradition, are more elusive or enigmatic.*

The events of the Odyssey are a gift to fine artists, and Odysseus' supernatural adventures, not to mention his stringing of the great bow and battle with the suitors, have been depicted by potters, sculptors and painters of all kinds from geometric vase-painters of the ninth century BCE *(a couple of centuries or so after the Odyssey is thought to have been written) to such people as Picasso, Dalí and de Chirico in our own time. Odysseus has also appeared as the hero of operas (by Monteverdi and Dallapiccola among others), in an important strand of Jungian philosophy, in epic Hollywood movies and innumerable children's stories. The combination of trickster and long-suffering heroic wanderer seems irresistible.*

≫→ **heroes**

OEDIPUS
Europe (South)

Oedipus (Oidipous, 'swell-foot'), in Greek myth, was the son of King **Laius** and Queen **Jocasta** of **Thebes**. Before he was born, the Delphic oracle prophesied that he would one day murder his father and marry his mother, and Laius and Jocasta therefore exposed the newborn baby, fastening his ankles with a golden pin and leaving him to die on Mount Cithaeron. Shepherds rescued him, named him Oedipus after his swollen ankles, and took him to safety in Corinth, where Queen Periboea (or, in some accounts, Merope) and King Polybus brought him up as their own son.

Oedipus grew up convinced that Periboea and Polybus were his parents. He was horrified when a drunken banquet-guest one day jeered at him for being a foundling. He went to Delphi to ask the oracle who he was, and Apollo answered 'You are the man fated to murder his father and marry his mother'. Just as Laius had done before him, Oedipus determined to cheat the oracle. He left Delphi, vowing never to see Polybus and Periboea again, and went East towards Thebes instead of South towards Corinth. He came to a narrow track, where the road passed between cliffs before forking at a crossroads to Daulia and Phocis. An old man in a chariot was coming the other way, and shouted to Oedipus to make room. Oedipus refused; they quarrelled; Oedipus killed the old man and went on his way.

Some days later, Oedipus came to Thebes. He found the city tormented by **Sphinx**, a **monster** sent there by **Hera**. Each day, she asked the Thebans the same riddle, and each day they failed to answer she snatched up a Theban child and devoured it. Oedipus realized that the answer had been shown him in **Apollo**'s shrine, and shouted it full in Sphinx's face. The monster flew up in a rage, then crashed to the ground and broke her neck. Oedipus was proclaimed saviour of Thebes – and when word came that King Laius had mysteriously disappeared, he married Queen Jocasta and took the throne.

Oedipus and Jocasta ruled happily for several years, and had four children: **Antigone**, **Ismene**, **Eteocles** and **Polynices**. But then the gods sent plague, and announced that the reason was the murder of Laius. His killer was still in Thebes, and unless he was found and punished, the plague would not be lifted. Oedipus ordered the prophet **Tiresias** to consult the gods and name the guilty man. At that moment a messenger from Corinth, an old man, brought news that Polybus and Periboea were dead. Oedipus was delighted: there was no more risk from the oracle that he would murder his father and marry his mother. But Jocasta laughed at his fears. All oracles were false, she said. Laius had been told that his own son would murder him, and in fact he had been killed by strangers at a crossroads. The word 'crossroads' awoke memories in Oedipus' mind, and the old Corinthian made matters worse by identifying Oedipus, by the scars on his ankles, as the baby long ago rescued from Mount Cithaeron and taken to Corinth. Finally Tiresias spoke and made all plain: Oedipus was the son of Laius and Jocasta; his wife was his mother, and his children were his brothers and sisters.

When Jocasta heard the news she ran into the palace and hanged herself – and Oedipus took one of the gold pins from her dress, an exact match for the one which had pinned his ankles long ago, and stabbed his eyes again and again until he was blind. For a time, afterwards, he lived on in Thebes. But his sons Eteocles and Polynices despised him – and one day, instead of serving him the king's portion of meat from a sacrifice, they gave him a slave's helping instead. Oedipus threw down the meat and cursed them, praying that they would dispute their inheritance with iron, and go to the **Underworld** on a single day, each killing the other. Then, leaning on a beggar's stick, he picked his way out of Thebes into exile.

Oedipus wandered for years, tormented by the **Furies** and guided by his daughter Antigone. At last he came to Athens, where the Delphic oracle had foretold that his life would end. King **Theseus** welcomed him in a grove of trees at Colonus on the outskirts of the city: a crossroads between the Upper World and the Underworld. The Thebans, led by Jocasta's brother **Creon**, demanded Oedipus back: he embodied the luck of Thebes, and unless he lived (or died) in Thebes the city would never prosper. While Creon and Theseus were still arguing, Oedipus went alone to the heart of the sacred grove, and to the accompaniment of supernatural voices and peals of thunder from below the earth, passed from human sight forever.

This story gave rise to two of the noblest of all surviving Greek tragedies, Sophocles' King Oedipus and Oedipus at Colonus. Sophocles used the myth to tease out aspects of the relationship between human beings and the supernatural world, in particular our ideas of what 'knowledge' and 'ignorance', 'sight' and 'blindness' are. (The blind prophet sees more truthfully than the king who thinks he sees; our attempts to cheat fate lead us down blind alleys and increase our suffering; only when true knowledge comes to Oedipus (in Colonus, after he has blinded himself) is he able to transcend his own mortality.) A century after Sophocles, Aristotle used King Oedipus as a model of how Greek tragedy should be written, and this gave it enormous respect, and influence, through the next two millennia of European dramaturgy, right down to the present time. In the twentieth century it gained even greater currency because Freud used Oedipus' name for the complex by which all infant males (according to Freud) long to displace their fathers in their mothers' affections, 'murdering the father and lying with the mother'.

The reputation of Sophocles' play, whether thus superficially achieved or not, has meant that all other versions of the myth – for example Euripides' Phoenician Women or Cocteau's The Infernal Machine – or such artworks using its themes as O'Neill's Long Day's Journey Into Night or Frisch's I'm Not Stiller, tend to live in its shadow; only two, Sophocles' Antigone and Shakespeare's Hamlet, exist entirely free from it. Its overwhelming power as drama (perhaps the main result of Sophocles' magisterial treatment) is not matched in other media: it is, for example, one of the rarest of Greek myth-stories to be illustrated in the fine arts of any age, and where musical setting is attempted – two notable examples are by Stravinsky and Orff – the text and story tend to swamp the music.

OENOMAUS
Europe (South)

Oenomaus (Oinomaos, 'roaring drunk'), in Greek myth, was the son of **Atlas'** daughter Sterope and **Ares** god of war, and king of Pisa in southern Greece. Suitors came from all over Greece asking to marry his beautiful daughter Hippodamia. But the gods had warned Oenomaus that although he was the son of a god, by choosing to live and rule in the world he had forfeited his **immortality**, and would one day be killed by his own son-in-law. To prevent this he put all

Hippodamia's suitors to a test they were bound to fail. He challenged each of them to a chariot-race, all the way from Pisa to the Isthmus of Corinth. The would-be husband took Hippodamia as his driver, and was given half an hour's start; then Oenomaus and his charioteer set out after him in a war-chariot.

The agreement was that if the suitor reached the Isthmus first, he would marry Hippodamia; if Oenomaus won, the suitor would die. And Oenomaus always won: his chariot-horses were a gift from his father Ares, and could outrun the winds. Twelve princes risked the race, and their heads rotted on poles at Oenomaus' palace gates. Oenomaus celebrated each time with a drunken banquet, shouting that that one day there would be enough skulls to build Ares a temple – a boast which disgusted the gods and made his death even more certain.

Hippodamia's thirteenth suitor, **Pelops**, had a chariot and winged horses given him by **Poseidon**, easily able to outride Ares' team. But even so, he made sure of the race by cheating. He bribed Myrtilus, Oenomaus' charioteer, to replace Oenomaus' axle-pins with wax, which melted as soon as the race began; Oenomaus' chariot-wheels spun away and he was thrown and killed. So Pelops won the race and Hippodamia's hand – and Zeus shattered Oenomaus' palace with a thunderbolt and buried the remains of the twelve murdered suitors as they deserved.

OG
Asia (West)

Og, in Hebrew myth, was the only **giant** not to be drowned in the **flood** sent by **Yahweh** to destroy the world. In some accounts, he was so huge that the water reached only to his ankles; in others, he sat on the roof of **Noah**'s ark until the storm subsided. Og settled in the **mountains** of Jordan, and tried to persuade Sarah, Abraham's wife, to join him there as queen. When she refused, he became an implacable enemy of the Jewish people, and when Moses tried to lead them from Egypt to the Promised Land he blocked their way and picked up an enormous boulder to crush them. But Yahweh made the stone slip in his hands, and it fell on to his upturned face and stuck in his teeth. While he was struggling to free it, Moses chopped through his ankles with an axe, and Og toppled to the ground. His bones changed to rock and his flesh to soil: he became the mountain-range which Moses climbed to survey the Promised Land.

In the Bible, Og was reinvented as King of Bashan, ruler of giants and possessor of a vast iron bed. Scholars claim that this story arose when someone mistook the coffin of a real king (made many times life-size) for a bed, and its polished black basalt for metal. In the Bible account, no mention is made of Og's supernatural end (which is recounted in Canaanite myth-tablets discovered only in the 1930s); the Old Testament merely says that 'the Lord delivered him and his people into our hands...and we utterly destroyed them'.

OGDOAD, THE
Africa (North)

The Ogdoad ('group of eight'), in Egyptian myth, is the Greek name given by

443

scholars to a group of eight gods worshipped at Khemenu (Hermopolis), the place where the world was thought to have come into existence. The Ogdoad consisted of four pairs, each of one male and one female deity: **Nun** and **Naunet** (water), Kek and Keket (darkness), **Amun** and Amaunet (invisibility), Heh and Hehet (infinity). In one version of the creation-myth, they came together in the primordial chaos to form the egg from which **Ra** the Sun was hatched to begin creation. Some accounts treat them as powers without form; others say that the males were frogs and the female **snakes**, wriggling in the primordial mud; others again depict them as an octet of baboons, lifting their hands to greet the newly-hatched, rising **Sun**.

⫸ **Heqet**

OGMIOS
Europe (North)

Ogmios was the Celtic god of eloquence. He was an old, bald man, and wore a lion-skin which grew stronger, not weaker with age. By words alone, he spun a gold chain (or, in some accounts, made a necklace of pearls) which passed from his tongue to the ears of his listeners, and drew them after him like puppies on a lead. In Ireland, where he was called Ogma, he gave human beings a small version of his eloquence, in the form of the Ogham runes, a script so powerful that if spells were written in it they paralyzed anyone who saw them.

Perhaps unexpectedly for a god of words, Ogmios is better known in fine art than in literature. He is often shown on plaques, bracelets and other ornaments, surrounded by emblems of strength such as bears, lions or boars, and with chains of gold or pearls issuing from his mouth. The Ogham pendant to the myth probably reflects no more than the awe felt by illiterate people towards written script – an awe exploited by early Christian missionaries in their teachings about the Bible.

OGO
Africa

Ogo ('jackal'), in the myths of the Dogon people of Mali, was the son of the creator-spirit **Amma**. In some accounts he was hatched from the primordial egg. The egg was double-yolked, and each yolk contained **twins**. Ogo, the male twin, tried to rape his sister, but Amma hid her in the other egg, so that all Ogo copulated with was the placenta which had nourished them. Disgusted, he hurled it into space, where it became **Mother Earth**.

While Amma was busy populating Earth – in some accounts by mating with her, in others by sacrificing the second pair of twins to create beasts and plants, and then reconstituting them as ancestors of the human race – Ogo plotted to climb the sky and dethrone his father. To do this he had to gather as much power as possible – and power resided in semen, stored in the very tip of the penis. Ogo waited until his half-brother, the male human ancestor, was sleeping, then fellated him and stole his semen. But before he could invade **Sky**, his brother's human descendants crowded round him, bit off the end of his penis and also cut out his tongue (which was wrapped round his brother's semen). So Ogo was deprived simultaneously of universal power and of the ability to speak – and his descendants, jackals, have cowered silently ever since on the fringes of earthly life. His followers are **demons**, **monsters** and such qualities of darkness as **death**, drought and famine, mirror-images of the qualities of light which Amma and his human descendants seek to maintain on Earth.

This story, which combines philosophical and mythopoeic ideas to a degree unmatched in any African system, for good measure stirs in explanations of the Dogon practice of male and female circumcision. (Male Dogon were circumcised to offer back to Amma the divine portion of creativity which Ogo had tried to steal; female Dogon were circumcised to facilitate sexual intercourse and ensure fertility.)
≫→ animal-gods, Coyote

OGOUN
Americas (Caribbean)

Ogoun, in Voodoo myth, is the warrior-god whose symbol is fire. When he shouts 'My balls are cold!' his worshippers pour rum on the ground and set it alight to warm him. He is lecherous, and spends much time in **sex**-orgies with the love-goddess **Erzulie**. With humans he likes performing such circus tricks as balancing on sharp points and fire-eating; but he is also a **trickster** and wheeler-dealer, patron of gangsters, politicians and anyone else who lives by making deals.

Ogoun is a comparatively modern invention, and his myths are still growing.

Scholars say that he probably originated as **Ogun**, *the West African god brought to Haiti by captives for the slave trade in the eighteenth century* CE.

OGUN
Africa

Ogun, the Yoruba war-god, led the other gods on a hunting-expedition, climbing down from **Heaven** to Earth on a spider-thread. They found themselves entangled in jungle, and Ogun turned himself into an iron machete and chopped a way through. Ever afterwards, mortals worshipped him as the power of iron, and as god not only of hunting and war but also of blacksmiths, who sacrificed dogs to persuade him to bless their work.

Ogun is the African ancestor of **Ogoun**, the Haitian Voodoo god of fire.
≫→ smiths

OISIN
Europe (North)

Oisin ('fawn'), in Celtic myth, was the son of the famous hunter, **Finn Mac-Cool**, and a **shape-changer**. One day, in the woods, Finn kissed a pig-snouted woman, so lifting a spell from her. She was the queen of the Fairies, took him to Tir nan Nog (the fairy kingdom) and made him its ruler. After a while he began longing to visit the mortal world once more. She gave him a fast white horse, and told him that it would carry him home and back like the wind, but that if he fell off fairyland would be barred to him forever. He galloped through the barrier between the mortal and immortal worlds, but slipped from the horse – and lay on the ground, blind and aged. What had seemed moments in Tir nan Nog had been three hundred mortal years, and now he had lost his youth, his queen, his magic steed and his kingdom, all for nothing.

*This story is typical of hundreds of tales about people who stray into fairy time and regret it. Its extra point of interest is that the eighteenth-century Scots poet James Macpherson claimed to have discovered, and translated, two epic poems by Oisin (whom he called 'Ossian'), giving first-hand accounts of the **giants** and fairies of ancient myth. 'Ossian's' Fingal and Temora were best-sellers, but their success was their undoing, since they triggered further research into ancient Celtic literature and myth which proved, almost immediately, that they were forgeries. None the less, they affected people's ideas about pre-Christian British myth for generations. Sir Walter Scott and Mendelssohn, for examples, were still propagating Macpherson's view of ancient Scotland sixty years after 'Ossian' was exploded.*

OKUNINUSHI
Asia (East)

Okuninushi ('earth-ruler'), in Japanese myth, was the god of healing and sorcery; in some accounts he was one of **Susano**'s sons, in others the same person as Daikoku god of wealth. He was the youngest of eighty brothers, who treated him like a slave. They all wanted to marry the beautiful princess Yagami, and set off to march to her castle, forcing Okuninushi to carry all the bags. On the way they found a flayed hare lying by the roadside. It said that its skin had been stripped by a crocodile, and begged them to help – but instead of curing it they cast spells which tore off ten more layers of flesh. But when Okuninushi came up he spoke a healing-spell, and the hare's skin grew completely back, and in gratitude it forecast that Yagami would reject all his brothers and marry him.

The brothers decided that Okuninushi would never even reach Yagami, let alone marry her. They told him to catch a red-hided boar hiding on a **mountain**-side – and then, instead of driving a boar towards him, rolled a lump of red-hot iron down the slope so that he was burned to death. His mother prayed to **Musubi** the marriage-god, asking him to bring Okuninushi back to life for Yagami's sake. Musubi answered her prayer. Okuninushi's brothers laid ambush for him, chopping down a tree as he passed underneath and crushing him to death. Once again Musubi restored him to life, and this time he suggested that he ask help from Susano the wind-god (in some accounts, his own father).

In Susano's palace, before Okuninushi could even speak to the storm-lord, he met and was immediately attracted to Susano's daughter Suseribime (in some accounts, his own sister). Instead of merely begging protection on his journey to Yagami, therefore, he also asked Susano if he could marry Suseribime. Susano said that he needed time to make his decision, and offered Okuninushi the best guest-room in the palace. But in the middle of the night he sent **snakes** to kill Okuninushi, who was saved only because Suseribime had warned him and given him a potion to counteract their poison. The same thing happened the next night, except that instead of snakes Susano sent a swarm of insects with poison-stings. The following morning Susano said that if Okuninushi fetched an arrow shot into the middle of a cornfield, Suseribime would be his. As soon as Okuninushi went into the field, Susano set it on fire – and Okuninushi was saved only because a mouse (or, in some accounts, the hare whose skin he had earlier restored) showed him an underground tunnel to escape the fire.

Susano now claimed to be satisfied, and gave a banquet in Okuninushi's honour. But Okuninushi still suspected him, and when Susano fell asleep, full of *sake*, he tied his long hair to the rafters, strand by strand, before blocking the palace door with a huge boulder and escaping with Suseribime on his back and in his arms Susano's finest treasures: a bow, magic arrows, a sword and a harp. As he hurried through the trees, trailing branches brushed the harp-strings and woke Susano up. But by the time the storm-god had untied each strand of hair from the rafters and moved the boulder from the door, Okuninushi and Suseribime were safe outside the borders of his kingdom. He shouted after them that they were now free to marry, and that the magic sword, bow and arrows would help Okuni-nushi defeat his eighty brothers and rule the Earth. Okuninushi made Yaga-mi his second wife, and married dozens of others; his offspring gradually spread across the entire world: the human race.
≫+ **creation, disease and healing, heroes**

OLIfAT
Oceania

Olifat, or Olofat, Olofath, Orofat or Yelafath, in Micronesian myth, was a **trickster**, in some accounts identified with the mischievous, uncontrollable aspect of **fire**. He was the son of the trickster-god Luk (or Lugeilan) and a mortal woman. Luk fathered him and then abandoned him on Earth, and when Olifat visited him in **Heaven** (riding up on a column of rising smoke) he first smothered him, then took such pity at the look of surprise on his face that he reanimated him and let him live. (In memory of this event, fire is the only substance in the universe which can be still be reborn each time it dies.)

Olifat spent the rest of eternity sliding down to Earth on **lightning**-flashes, or riding up again on smoke-plumes. In Heaven he plagued the gods, knocking over cooking-pots, singing when they were trying to sleep, trying to rape their daughters. On Earth he was dangerous as well as tricky. Just for the fun of it, he gave sharks teeth and scorpions stings. He liked sitting on top of or underneath the beams which supported house-roofs. When he sat on top, he often cracked his knuckles and sent out sparks which set the whole roof on fire. When he sat underneath, in the holes where the beams were set, he sometimes scratched his back, and the movement widened the hole so that the house fell down, or the skin-scratchings turned into red ants which nibbled away the beams. Only when humans died were they free of him – and as soon as they realized how dull **death** was, they longed for him.

OLORUN
Africa

Olorun, king of gods. Olorun ('owner'), or Olodumare, in the myths of the Edo and Yoruba peoples of Nigeria, was **Sky**, one of the two original gods; the other was his brother Olokun, **Water**. There were 1698 less senior gods, and they met to choose a supreme ruler. It was agreed that the throne should go to whichever of Olorun and Olokun appeared in greater splendour. In some accounts Olokun dressed himself in ever richer finery, only to be discomforted seven times when Olorun's messenger (Chameleon) came in even greater splendour to fetch him. Finally he admitted defeat and surrendered the throne to Olorun.

In other accounts, the two gods contested the throne in person. At first it was touch and go: when Olorun appeared in blue robes, Olokun immediately matched him; when Olorun clothed himself in clouds, Olokun at once tipped his waves with white. But then Olorun pointed out that he was the original and Olokun merely the reflection – and when the gods asked Olokun to justify himself, and all he could do was echo Olorun's words, the matter was decided.

Even then, the 1698 junior gods were dissatisfied. They demanded that supreme power be passed round them all, a day each in rotation, again and again throughout eternity. Olorun suggested a trial period – and it took only eight days for all supernatural activity to grind to a halt and for them to accept his rule.

Olorun, creator of the universe. Olorun was no sooner secure on his throne than he created the universe. He gave himself, Sky, to the gods for their kingdom and stocked Olokun, Sea, with fish. In between was a swamp, the Earth. It was barren, and the gods let themselves down on spider-threads and used it for water-sports. But then Olorun sent the leader of the junior gods down to Earth with a snail-shell of soil, a pigeon and a hen, and told him to make land. The god shook the soil from the snail-shell, and the pigeon and hen scrabbled their feet in it until it filled in enough of the swamps to support life. Olorun then gave his assistant seeds of every tree and plant, and told him how to mould animals and human beings from clay. (The assistant indulged his own fancy, which is why there are so many species of animals and so many different human shapes.)

At this point in **creation**, all Earth's animals and humans were **giants**, immortal and able to deal with gods as equals. But Olorun imposed on them something absent from **Heaven**: the passage of time. They began to age, and as they grew older they shrank. Before long they were creeping like termites on Earth's surface, crying out for an end to the miseries of senility. Olorun took pity on them, sent **Death** to gather the feeblest, and gave the others fixed terms of life. It has been so ever since – and mortality, coupled with the fact that Earth's creatures have never grown back to their original giant sizes, means that we have never again been able to meet or talk on equal terms with gods.

≫+ **Oduduwa**

OLYMPIANS, THE TWELVE
Europe (South)

The twelve Olympians, in Greek and Roman myth, were the gods who had homes on Mount **Olympus**, and were the most senior gods in **Heaven**. Their ruler was **Zeus** (confusingly called 'Olympian Zeus' not because he was an Olympian but because his principal shrine was at Olympia in Southern Greece, home of the Olympic Games), and their names were **Aphrodite**, **Apollo**, **Ares**, **Artemis**, **Athene**, **Demeter**, **Dionysus**, **Hephaestus**, **Hera**, **Hermes**, Hestia and **Poseidon**.

OLYMPUS
Europe (South)

Olympus is the highest **mountain** in Greece. Its peak is permanently in cloud, which led to the idea in myth that it was a pathway between Earth and **Heaven**. The gods used all Heaven as their kingdom, but lived in a kind of exclusive estate on the upper slopes of the mountain, in villas of gold and silver designed by **Hephaestus**. Zeus' mansion, on the uppermost peak, was the administrative centre of the supernatural world, containing among other things his treasury, his arsenal of thunderbolts (to which only he and **Athene** had keys), the banqueting-rooms to which favoured mortals (such as **Ixion** and **Tantalus**) were invited, usually with drastic results, the conference room and Zeus' audience-chamber and judgement-room.

The weather on Olympus was perpetual spring, and its temperateness extended down to the lower slopes (where **nymphs** and **satyrs** lived) and to the homes of mortals in the Vale of Tempe at its feet. But despite this lushness, the supernatural domain was ring-fenced from the mortal world by a barrier of snow and ice. Gods never noticed it as they passed between the two realms, but without divine permission – rarely granted – no mortal could enter it and survive.

OMETECUHTLI
Americas (Central)

Ometecuhtli ('supreme duality'), in Aztec myth, was the first principle of the universe, on which all existence depended. To Ometecuhtli, the universe was no more than a grain of corn in a water-drop in the palm of the hand, arousing no interest and causing no concern: its management was left to lesser beings, particularly **Quetzalcóatl** and **Tezcatlipoca**, whose rivalry kept it in balance. **Ometecuhtli** contained everything, and whatever was a duality on Earth was at one in Ometecuhtli: chaos/order, **death**/life, **light**/**dark**, movement/stillness, self/other.

The Spanish conquerors, in their anxiety to portray the Aztecs as barbarians, neglected the philosophical and metaphysical components of Aztec belief, among them the Ometecuhtli cult. The serenity of absence, the calm of stasis, were concepts with which they were unfamiliar – and to this day, some Western scholars of the Aztecs still find them hard to grasp.
⋙→ **supreme deity**

OMPHALE
Europe (South)

Omphale ('navel'), queen of Lydia in Greek myth, bought **Heracles** at a slave-auction. The gods had ordained that Heracles was to serve a mortal for a year as slave, and Omphale dressed him as a woman and made him spin, or carry her parasol when she went walking. Predictably, she fell in love with him, and delighted in wearing his clothes when they went walking, swaggering in his lion-skin and threatening passers-by with his club as he tagged behind her in dress and veil. On one occasion, having made love in a grotto on Mount Tmolus, they fell asleep – and **Pan**, who had lusted after Omphale for years, found a nightdress on the floor beside the bed, took it for Omphale's, leapt in to rape her, and found himself tangling with Heracles, who kicked him angrily out of the cave and gave him a limp which stayed with him for evermore.

ONATAH
Americas (North)

Onatah the corn-goddess in the myths of the Iroquois people of the North-eastern US woodlands, was the daughter of Eithinoha (**Mother Earth**). One morning, when she was gathering dew, she was snatched and taken by the ruler of the **Underworld**. Eithinoha searched everywhere for her, and while she pined, no crops could be grown on Earth. Finally, the **Sun** realized where Onatah was, split open the ground and rescued her. Spring and **fertility** returned to Earth. But the Underworld spirits still longed for Onatah, and each year, when the Sun slept, they stole her back again and a vast human effort, in ceremonies and offerings, was needed to waken the Sun and rescue her.

➤ **farming, Persephone**

ONI
Asia (Southeast)

Oni, in Japanese myth, were **demons** with **snakes**' horns, human bodies and eagles' legs and talons. They carried plague to mortals, and then swooped on those about to die and snatched their souls.

➤ **disease and healing**

ONYANKOPON
Africa

Onyankopon ('great one'), also known as Anansi Kokroko ('wise spider') and Bore-bore ('creator'), in the myths of the Ghanaian Asante people, once lived on Earth with human beings, his favourite **creation**. He was the arch of the **sky**, and crouched over them as a mother hen broods chicks, nourishing them with his radiance. Unfortunately, among the many things he taught them was how to mash yams by pounding them with long poles in mortars – and one old woman did this so vigorously that her pole kept banging Onyankopon in the guts and bruising him (or in some accounts poking him in the eye): the origin of storm-clouds. Gradually he lifted himself higher and higher, but the higher he went the harder she poled, and there was no end to it until he lifted himself entirely out of reach, to the place where the sky-arch stands today.

Aghast, Onyankopon's humans wondered how they could ever reach him in future, to whisper prayers in his ears. The old woman suggested that they pile yam-mortars into a tower to reach the sky. So they did, until the teetering pile was just one mortar's height away from Onyankopon. All the mortars were used up, and the old woman shouted to Onyankopon to ask what to do. 'Climb down and fetch the mortar at the bottom,' he answered – and when she did so the entire pile collapsed, killing hundreds of the crowd below and bringing death to mortals.

*Some accounts add a **death-messenger** story to this myth. Seeing how distressed his people were at the thought of death, Onyankopon sent Goat to tell them that it was not the end of existence, but that their spirits would rise to spend eternity with him. Goat, however, stopped on the way to browse in a thistle-patch, and Oyankopon sent Sheep with the same message. Sheep misremembered his instructions, and said that death would be oblivion and that mortals would never spend eternity with Onyankopon – and since the message once delivered could not be revoked, things have been thus ever since.*

*Tower-stories are told by many African peoples. In the myths of the Bambala people of the Congo river, humans built a tower to reach the **Moon** and find out what it was made of. One man began the tower by holding a pole upright on the riverbank. A second man climbed the pole and tied a second pole to it, holding it tight while a third climbed to the top of that pole, and so on until the whole contraption fell into the river (where the Moon's reflection was waiting, and mocking them).*

OPHION: *see* Eurynome and Ophion

ORESTES
Europe (South)

Orestes ('mountain-man'), in Greek myth, was the youngest child of **Agamemnon** and **Clytemnestra**. When Clytemnestra and **Aegisthus** murdered his father, he was smuggled out of Argos to safety in Phocis, where he grew up at the court of King Strophius. **Apollo** then urged him back to Argos, where he entered the palace in secret and butchered Aegisthus and Clytemnestra. The **Furies** drove him mad for these murders and hunted him across the world until he came at last to Delphi, where Apollo freed him from guilt by saying that he (Apollo) had ordered Clytemnestra's death.

Orestes went home to rule in Argos. He married **Hermione**, the daughter of **Helen** and **Menelaus** of Sparta – in some accounts, first assassinating **Achilles**' son **Neoptolemus** to whom she was betrothed. But he was still restless and unsatisfied. He began wandering again, founding colonies on the islands of Lesbos and Tenedos, and ruling for a time in Arcadia. Finally, at the age of ninety, he went to die on Apollo's sacred island, Delos. Apollo ordered the removal of his bones to Sparta, where they were revered well into historical times.

The elements of the Orestes myth are simply told in Homer's Odyssey, and are elaborated in the work of Aeschylus, Sophocles and Euripides into some of the finest of all surviving Greek tragedy.

Aeschylus' Oresteia concentrates on the tangled sequence of murders and the ethical and moral dilemmas which underlie it. Sophocles' Electra explores the plight of Orestes' sister, her hysterical joy when Orestes returns and her passionate urging of him to kill Clytemnestra. Euripides, in his Electra and Orestes, treats the whole story with a kind of flippant irony, exploring the various states of anarchy which the murders of Agamemnon and Clytemnestra unlock in Argos itself and in the souls of the murderers. The same writer's Iphigenia in Tauris is a fanciful (perhaps original) new episode, unrelated to the main myth: see Iphigenia. Greek painters and sculptors favoured two scenes from the story above all others: Electra recognizing Orestes beside Agamemnon's tomb (on which he has just left a lock of shorn hair), and Orestes murdering Clytemnestra, either with a sword or with the axe she used on Agamemnon. In modern times, the Orestes story has been reworked by several dramatists, from Sartre (who gave it existential underpinnings in The Flies) to O'Neill and T.S. Eliot (who explored the idea of a latent family curse suddenly impinging on one particular individual). The idea of the family curse also underlies Faulkner's The Sound and the Fury and his other novels about the Sartoris family, which transpose the Orestes myth to the post-Civil War United States. Dostoevsky's Crime and Punishment explores the effects of guilt on the mind and soul of a murderer in ways directly influenced by Aeschylus.

⟫⟫→ heroes

ORMAHZD: *see* Ahura Mazda

ORPHEUS
Europe (South)

Orpheus' early life. Orpheus ('of the river bank'), in Greek myth, was the son of King Oeagrus of Thrace and Calliope, **Muse** of poetry. He learned **music** from **Apollo** himself, and his playing and singing attracted not only human listeners, but also the beasts of hills and woods. When he sang, rivers changed their courses, and trees and boulders uprooted themselves and came to hear. As a young man he visited Egypt, where the temple priests taught him their mysteries. He was one of the **Argonauts** who sailed to fetch the **Golden Fleece**; on this journey he became a follower of **Dionysus**, expert in all the god's rituals. When he returned to Thrace he became king of Ciconia and took as his queen the wood-**nymph** Eurydice.

Orpheus and Eurydice. Orpheus' cousin was Aristaeus, son of Apollo and the river-**nymph** Cyrene. Aristaeus was brought up by **Hermes'** daughters the myrtle-tree nymphs, who taught him such country skills as cheese-making, pressing olive-oil and above all beekeeping. Aristaeus wandered all over Greece, teaching these skills to the grateful inhabitants. One day he came by chance on Eurydice, bathing in the river Peneus. Overcome with lust, he plunged into the water to rape her, and Eurydice fled in such alarm that she trod accidentally on a snake. At once **Hades** sent Death to fetch her to the **Underworld**. By the time word reached Orpheus, Eurydice was nowhere to be seen (for the Dead are invisible to mortal eyes). Distracted, Orpheus quartered Greece for her, calling her name and playing his lyre in case its music wooed her back to life. At last Hermes pitied him and told him where she was.

Orpheus' grief led him to attempt what only a handful of mortals had ever dared before him: to harrow Hell. Lyre in hand, he plunged down the dank tunnels which led from the Upper World to the Underworld. He reached the banks of the river **Styx**, and charmed **Charon** with his music into ferrying him across. **Cerberus**, the three-headed watchdog of the Underworld, was also soothed by song, and eventually Orpheus reached the judgement-seat of Hades and his queen **Persephone**. He began to play and sing so sweetly that all Hell's torments ceased. The Dead flocked to hear him, weeping for the beauty of the Upper World which they, no less than Eurydice, had lost. When the song was done, Hades announced his decision. Orpheus could lead Eurydice back to the Upper World and life, on condition that he never once looked back at her. In the kingdom of invisibility, one glance from living eyes would condemn Eurydice to eternal darkness. Hermes, guide of souls, led Orpheus and Eurydice on the slow climb to the Upper World. Orpheus' resolution held as far as the very lip of the Upper World, the brink of light. Then, with his foot on the threshold of Greece, he glanced back at Eurydice. Hades' irrevocable law took effect, and Hermes led Eurydice back to eternal death.

For seven days Orpheus wandered the caverns and tunnels of the Underworld, calling Eurydice's name. He begged Charon to pole him a second time across the Styx; the old ferryman

refused. Orpheus stumbled to the Upper World, his wits distracted both by grief for Eurydice and by the sights and smells of the Underworld – for in his torment he had omitted to drink **Lethe**-water (which wipes out remembrance) before returning, and the memory of his experiences flowered like lichen in his mind. He lived on Mount Pangaeum in a hermit-cave, and every night he climbed the peak to worship Apollo in the rising **Sun**. Word spread among mortals that he had returned from the Dead, and groups of disciples made pilgrimages to his cave, to sit at his feet and learn the secrets of the grave. They were all young men. From the moment of his return, Orpheus forswore the company of women. Indeed, some accounts say that it was he who introduced male homosexuality – formerly practised only by the gods – to the human race.

Orpheus' death. There are several accounts of Orpheus' death. Some say that **Zeus**, angry that Orpheus was teaching mortals the secret knowledge of the structure of the universe which the gods had learned from **Gaia (Mother Earth)**, the first being, blasted him with a thunderbolt. Others say that the women of Thrace came on him one night, in the midst of an orgy with his followers on Mount Pangaeum, and tore him to pieces. The best-known account, however, says that his worship of Apollo and his disdain for women aroused the hostility of Eurydice's fellow-nymphs, who had in the meantime become Maenads, devotees of Dionysus. They came in a pack like hunting-dogs to the cave where Orpheus taught his **mysteries**. As was customary,

Orpheus' disciples had stacked their knives and other weapons at the cave-entrance, and the Maenads snatched them and hacked Orpheus to pieces. They threw the scraps of his body into the sea, nailed his head to his lyre and tossed it into the river Hebrus. To their astonishment, instead of sinking the lyre began to play and the head to sing, floating gently down-river and out to sea. The Muses, led by Orpheus' mother Calliope, gathered the fragments of his body and buried them at Libethra on Mount **Olympus**; ever afterwards nightingales sang more sweetly there than anywhere else on Earth. As for the head and lyre, they floated to the island of Lesbos. The islanders buried the head in Dionysus' temple, to appease the god's anger against Orpheus, and Apollo hung the lyre as a star-constellation in the sky. From that time on, the myth concludes, both Dionysus and Apollo blessed Lesbos, and it was renowned ever afterwards for its wine (the gift of Dionysus) and its music and poetry (Apollo's gifts).

*The Orpheus myth was widely retold in ancient times. It features more in verse and prose than in pictures (because the Greeks never depicted the Underworld in art). In later times, it inspired thousands of artworks, by creators as varied as Monteverdi and Stravinsky, Offenbach and Henry Miller, Sullivan and Cocteau. (As this list implies, musicians found it particularly resonant.) In ancient Greece, it was the heart of a mystery cult, whose devotees believed that initiation would allow them to pass freely from the Upper World to the Underworld, as Orpheus had done: to cheat **death**. There survives a body of Orphic writings, mysterious utterances which may have been part of the ceremonies or teachings of the cult. Devotees attributed them to Orpheus himself. They survive in fragments, as gibberish.*

OSHADAGEA
Americas (North)

Oshadagea ('giant dew-eagle'), in the myths of the Iroquois people of the Northeastern US woodlands, was the bringer of **rain**. When **demons** tried to wipe out human beings by starting forest fires, Oshadagea scooped up oceans in the hollow between his wings, flew over the fires and doused them.

OSIRIS
Africa (North)

Osiris (or Oser, 'lord'), in Egyptian myth, was the son of **Nut** and **Geb** and the brother of **Aset** (Isis), **Nebthet** and **Set**. He gave the Earth plants and established the seasons. He gave order to human communities, showing mortals how to rule their secular lives by laws and civilized manners, and their religious lives by rituals and respect for the gods. Leaving his consort Aset to rule Egypt as his regent, he often travelled the world to spread these teachings, and was honoured everywhere as *wennefer* ('forever good').

During one of Osiris' absences, his jealous brother Set made a plot to kill him. He built a box-like bed of cedar wood, beautifully carved and painted, and made to Osiris' exact measurements. Then, when Osiris came home, Set held a feast in his honour and invited him to try the gift. As soon as Osiris lay down in it, Set and his fellow-conspirators nailed a lid on the bed – making it the first-ever coffin – and sank it in the Nile, weighted with lead. The river washed the coffin out to sea, to Lebanon, where it lodged in a myrrh-tree whose trunk gradually grew round it, hiding it.

Aset quartered the world to find Osiris' body. At last, drawn by the scent of the myrrh-tree, she persuaded the king of Lebanon to let her cut it down and release Osiris' coffin. She took the coffin back to Egypt, opened it, and tried to revive Osiris by disguising herself as a hawk (or in some versions a kite) and fluttering her wings to fill his lungs with air. All that revived, however, was his penis, which ejaculated the last essence of the living god into Aset's womb before life entirely left the body. Aset fled to the Delta with Osiris' corpse, and there she bore their child, the hawk-god **Horus**. Set, meantime, stole the coffin and chopped Osiris' body into fourteen pieces. He scattered thirteen of them round the provinces of Egypt, and threw the fourteenth (the penis) into the Nile, where it was eaten by a fish (some say a crab).

Once more Aset laboriously searched for Osiris' body. She reassembled the thirteen remaining pieces on the river-bank, and tried to bring them back to life by washing them with perfumed oils and wrapping them with bandages. Although the process worked, the gods decreed that Osiris should live not in the world of mortals but in the **Underworld**. They appointed him judge of the Dead, and when dead souls reached him – after the bodies they had discarded from the upper world had been anointed and bandaged as he had been – he cast up the accounts of their mortal lives and sent them to be punished or rewarded.

In some accounts, the conception of Horus took place not when Aset first brought Osiris back from the Lebanon but when she reconstituted him after Set's dismemberment. In religious art, concerned almost exclusively with Osiris' role as ruler of the Underworld, he was imagined as an earthly pharaoh, with similar insignia, throne and court, and with particular concern for the souls of the ruling mortal dynasty. In the last 500 years or so BCE, his cult – and that of Aset – eclipsed all others in Egypt, and spread throughout the Mediterranean and into Northern Europe as a mystery-religion concerned with rebirth after death and the return of spring which symbolizes it each year.

»→ **civilization, farming, mysteries**

OTAVA
Europe (North)

Otava, in Finnish myth, was the Great Bear, one of the constellations formed from specks of albumen in duck-eggs laid in the crook of **Luonnotar**'s knee at the beginning of **creation**. Light from Otava reached the Earth after lumbering round the universe for many years, and warmed the ground, fertilizing it to produce bear-offspring.

»→ **light and dark**

OTR
Europe (North)

Otr ('otter'), in Nordic myth, was the brother of **Fafnir** and **Regin**. The brothers were **shape-changers**, and one day Otr took otter form to catch a salmon. As he was eating it, **Loki** and **Odin** passed by, and Loki killed Otr with a stone and skinned him, delighted at having made two catches with one throw, a fresh salmon and a fine otter-pelt. But when he and Odin stayed that night with Hreidmar, their host, horrified to recognize his son's flayed skin, forced them to pay for the murder by stealing gold from the dwarves. For what happened next, see **Fafnir**, **Sigurd**.

OURANOS
Europe (South)

Ouranos ('[Father] **Sky**', Latin Uranus), in Greek and Roman myth, was one of the two first beings to emerge from **Chaos**: a living organism made of air and light. His life-giving rain sought out the cracks and crevices of the other primordial being, **Gaia** (**Mother Earth**); streams, rivers and oceans formed; the ground produced plants and creatures of every kind.

Ouranos' children. Ouranos and Gaia had children of other kinds: the **Hundred-handed Giants**, the first **Cyclopes**, the twelve **Titans** and others blending every kind of substance or being in existence. Ouranos was a remote, uncaring father, and came to detest both the act of **creation** and the sight of his own offspring. He took the Hundred-handed Giants and the Cyclopes and hurled them down to Tartarus, the darkness of space below the **Underworld** which itself lay below the body of his consort Gaia. Then he began prising Gaia open, thrusting his other

offspring into her deepest clefts and chasms. In agony, Gaia asked her Titan-son **Cronus** to end it, and Cronus castrated Ouranos with a sickle made from diamonds mined from Gaia's innermost recesses.

Castration ended both Ouranos' incessant urge to procreate and his hatred of his offspring. He abandoned all shape and became the amorphous atmosphere which drifts with Gaia in space. He took no further interest in the universe – the storms and calms which affect the world were caused by gods and other beings, and were not of his volition. From the blood-drops from his severed penis Gaia created more children: the twenty-four **Earthborn Giants** and the **Furies**. From the foam created when the penis fell into the sea was born **Aphrodite**, goddess of desire.

➤➤ **Rangi**

OVDA
Europe (North)

Ovda, in Finnish myth, was the god of the darkness of deep forests. Its gender depended on whom it was preying – female for men, male for women. It appeared to people wandering alone in woods, and took the form of a naked human figure, normal in every way except that the feet pointed backwards. It danced or tickled its prey to death, and then ate them.

➤➤ **farming**, **Leshy**

OWIOT
Americas (North)

Owiot ('master'), in the myths of the Luiseño (Acagchemem) people of

Southern California, was created by two spirits, Sirout ('pinch of tobacco') and Ycaiut ('up there'). They intended him to rule a blameless race of beings: humankind. Unfortunately, he was a tyrant, and his subjects began to imitate his bullying ways. But by chance, Sirout and Ycaiut had never given him **immortality**, and were able to poison him while he slept. The first human race, sharing his mortality, died with him. So the spirits continued to rule the world, and it was left to **Chinigchinich** to re-create the human race.

Poseidon at the sea-battle of Salamis (*17th-century engraving*)

PACHACAMAC
Americas (South)

Pachacamac ('earth-maker') was the creator-god of the peoples who lived in Peru before the Inca conquest. He was taken into the Inca pantheon, but somewhat reluctantly, being seen mainly as an ineffective rival of **Viracocha**. His myths are sparse and confused: some accounts, for example, identify him as Manco Capac's cowardly brother Ayca, while others say that he, Manco Capac and Viracocha were the sole three sons of **Inti** the Sun-god. Another story says that he made the first man and first woman, but forgot to give them food – and when the man died and the woman prayed over Pachacamac's head to his father Inti to make her the mother of all the peoples of Earth, Pachacamac was furious. One by one, as her children were born, he tried to kill them – only to be beaten and thrown into the **sea** by her **hero**-son Wichama, after which he gave up the struggle and contented himself by becoming supreme god of fish.

PAGE ABE
Americas (South)

Page Abe ('father **Sun**'), in the myths of the Tukaño people of the upper Amazon, was the Sun, and ruled the day. His brother, Nyami Abe, ruled the night. At first the night was as bright as the day. But then Nyami Abe tried to rape Page Abe's wife, and Page Abe beat him and dimmed his light forever. Page Abe created the world and all its creatures, then sent his daughter Abe Mango to teach mortals the use of **fire**, **hunting**, cooking, pottery, **music** and the other skills of **civilization**.

≫+ creation

PAH
Americas (North)

Pah ('father'), in the myths of the Pawnee people of the US Great Plains, was the **Moon**. He and his consort **Sun** had a son, who mated with the daughter of the Morning and Evening Stars and produced the human race.

PÄIVÄ
Europe (North)

Päivä, in Finnish myth, was the **Sun**, formed from the yolks of the celestial duck-eggs laid in the crook of **Luonnotar**'s knee. Päivä's light-rays warmed every corner and crevice of the Earth, passing into the ground as gold. They were also the immortals' highway between Earth and **Heaven**, and the gods sailed up them in golden ships or galloped on horses borrowed from Päivä's stables.

PALAMEDES
Europe (South)

Palamedes ('age-old wisdom'), in Greek myth, was the son of King **Nauplius** of Evia. He was an inventor, devising such ingenuities as the letters of the alphabet and the game of draughts. When **Odysseus** feigned madness to trick his way out of going to the **Trojan War**, ploughing his fields in an insane manner, Palamedes laid Odysseus' baby son **Telemachus** on the ground in front of him, so forcing him to stop (something no lunatic would have done). Odysseus was forced to go to war, and never forgave Palamedes.

Later, during the war, Palamedes began boasting that he was a better war-leader than Odysseus because he sent home regular shiploads of booty, whereas Odysseus captured only glory. This hardly improved Odysseus' temper, and in the end he forged a letter from King **Priam** of Troy, offering Palamedes a fortune to betray the Greeks. Then he buried a pile of gold beside Palamedes' tent, and arranged for the Greeks to find both it and the letter. Palamedes was arrested and imprisoned. While waiting for trial, he tried to bring his father Nauplius to the rescue by writing messages on oar-blades and floating them towards Evia on the waters of his grandfather **Poseidon**. But none of them reached Nauplius, and eventually Palamedes was tried for treason – Odysseus and **Diomedes** were his chief prosecutors – and was stoned to death.

PALLADIUM
Europe (South)

The Palladium (Palladion, 'little Pallas'), in Greek and Roman myth, was a statue of **Athene**. In most accounts it was said to have fallen from the sky, perhaps from the workshop of **Hephaestus** himself. (The most fanciful accounts say that he made it from the bones of **Pelops** after **Tantalus** fed him to the gods, but this conflicts with the story that Pelops was reconstituted and returned to the mortal world.) Some writers say that that the Palladium was like an enormous pine-cone, a torso hung with innumerable breasts (or eyes, or eggs). Others describe it as a metre-high statue showing Athene enthroned, holding a war-spear in one hand and a distaff in the other – and add that after Hephaestus finished it Athene breathed life into it, so that it had the power to move and speak.

When the Palladium fell from the sky, it landed beside Ilus, founder of the original city of Troy. He put it in a shrine, and it became the city's most sacred object, guardian of its survival. Towards the end of the **Trojan War**, the gods said that Troy would never be captured so long as the Palladium was safe in its temple – and **Odysseus** and **Diomedes** crept into the city and stole it. In some accounts, Odysseus carried the statue on his shoulders, covered with his cloak, so that from a distance it looked as if Athene herself was running from the stricken city. In other accounts Odysseus and Diomedes stole not the real Palladium, but one of dozens of replicas placed all over the shrine to confuse robbers. The true Palladium, the Luck of Troy, was saved until **Aeneas** carried it South to Italy and placed it at the heart of the reborn Troy, the settlement which later became Rome.

*The discrepancies between these myths are explained by the different Greek and Roman versions of the fall of Troy. To the Greeks, Troy was totally destroyed, and Odysseus' and Diomedes' capture of the Palladium was essential for this to happen. (Some Greek writers describe how the statue resisted capture, flashing fire and leaping and bouncing as they tried to subdue it.) This statue was the pine-cone-shaped lump, similar to (and by some, confused with) the even more famous statue of **Artemis** at Ephesus. Modern scholars say that if it really existed, it may have been a meteorite.*

*Roman authorities, by contrast, anxious to validate Rome as a reborn Troy, elaborated the story of the moving, living statue, showing the goddess as like a queen on her throne, a Roman matriarch. An actual statue of this kind was worshipped in Rome as the Palladium for centuries, only to be lost (or converted, some say, into a statue of the Virgin **Mary**) in the Christian era.*

PALLAS (GIANT)
Europe (South)

Pallas ('brandisher'), in Greek myth, was one of the **giants**, sons of **Gaia** (**Mother Earth**), who fought the gods at the beginning of the universe. **Athene** killed him and skinned him. In some accounts she made his hide into a cloak, in others into a covering for her shield. In both cases, the skin gave her invulnerability (though it had signally failed to do the same for Pallas himself), and she added Pallas' name to her own in memory of her victory.

PALLAS, SON OF EVANDER
Europe (South)

Pallas, in Roman myth, was a boy at the time of the war between **Aeneas** and the Rutulians for possession of the countryside round the mouth of the river Tiber. Rashly, he challenged **Turnus**, king of the Rutulians, to single combat, and Turnus killed him and took his belt for trophy. At the end of the war, when Aeneas and Turnus faced each other, to end the fighting by single combat, Aeneas had Turnus at his mercy and was about to spare him when he saw Pallas' belt round Turnus' waist, and was so angry that he stabbed him dead.

PAN
Europe (South)

Pan ('everything', Latin **Faunus**), in Greek myth, was the god of flocks and shepherds. In some accounts he was the son of the Cretan **nymph** Amalthea, and was **Zeus**' foster-brother in the Dictean Cave. In others, he was Zeus' own son, or the son of **Hermes** and the nymph Callisto. One of the wildest accounts of all claims that he was the son of Hermes and **Penelope**, **Odysseus**' wife. From the waist downwards he was a goat, from the waist up a mortal (save for goat's ears and horns). He lived in woods and water-meadows, and led a group of similar beings, half human half goat, the **Satyrs**. He was an expert dancer and musician, playing on the pan-pipes, an instrument he made himself from the nymph Syrinx, after the gods changed her into a bank of reeds to save her from his attempts to rape her. His other main attributes were gargantuan sexuality and an ear-splitting shout, able to shatter castles and rout armies – the cause of the irrational fear called 'panic' after him.

Pan was a favourite figure in fine art, both in statuettes and paintings. He figures in lyric and pastoral poetry as a kind of genial, amoral forest-spirit, the essence of the countryside. In the first century CE, passengers on a ship passing the island of Paxos heard a huge shout, 'Pan is dead'. At the time Christians claimed that this was an acknowledgment by the whole community of gods that Christ had ascended into **Heaven** *and that they therefore had no place left in the world. Later believers (and non-believers) have extended or disproved this assertion by identifying Pan with the Devil, and making his goat-horned, goat-eared head a focus for Satanic ritual – a far cry from the pastoral simplicity of his existence in ancient myth.* ➤➤ **animal-gods, farming, Faunus, sex**

PANDAVAS
India

The Pandavas, in Hindu myth, were **heroes**, nominally the five sons of **Pandu** but actually the children of gods and Pandu's mortal wives **Kunti** and **Madri**. They fought their cousins the **Kauravas** in the epic war described in the *Mahabharata*. Their names were **Arjuna**, **Bhima**, **Nakula**, **Sahadeva** and **Yudhishthira**. In some accounts, **Indra** favoured them by allowing them to use his Thunderstone. In others, they took an ordinary spear and, by prayer and sacrifice, elevated it to the status of a divine and unerring thunderbolt.

Pandavas and Kauravas. While the cousins were growing up, the rivalry between them was chiefly in sport: contests of wrestling or archery regularly degenerated into brawls. Matters became more serious when the Kauravas stole the throne of Hastinapur from Yudhishthira, forcing the Pandavas to live in hiding in a forest. Then an archery contest was held for the hand of Princess **Draupadi** – and the Pandavas entered in disguise, and won it. War was only averted when the Pandavas and Kauravas agreed to divide the kingdom equally; but soon afterwards **Duryodhana**, senior brother of the Kauravas, challenged Yudhishthira to a dice-game, and (by cheating) won

Yudhishthira's half of the kingdom, his palace, his wife Draupadi and all his brothers as slaves. The Pandavas once again retreated to the forest, and war was declared.

By this time, both sides had recruited support, including that of **Krishna**. He offered each group a choice: they could have either himself alone, or a large army. The Kauravas chose an army; the Pandavas chose Krishna, who served in the war as Arjuna's charioteer. **Demons**, by and large, saw that the struggle would be epic and would result in possession of the whole mortal world. They enlisted on the side of the larger army, led by the Kauravas. **Shiva** also took their part. The rest of the gods either stayed aloof or favoured the Pandavas.

Despite the presence of gods and demons, and the use of supernatural weapons, the war in the end boiled down to a long series of chivalric contests, often hand-to-hand and usually involving one or other of the Pandava brothers and a Kaurava enemy. In the end the Pandavas won, and Yudhishthira was re-established on his throne. But the Pandavas' victory gave them no pleasure, since it had involved murdering their own kinsfolk and indulging in treachery and deceitful strategy. Feeling that their moral and ethical integrity was fatally impaired, the brothers and Draupadi made a pilgrimage of atonement to **Indra**'s **Heaven** on Mount Meru. On the way all died except for Yudhishthira – and when he reached Indra's Heaven he was aghast to discover that it contained the spirits not of his family but of all his Kaurava enemies, dead in battle. It was only after he visited the **Underworld**, saw the torments of the damned, and was allowed to wash away his sins in the Ganges and become an immortal, that he was able to enter Heaven properly at last – and found there his wife, his brothers and all their dead followers, as well as their former opponents, all enmity forgotten in the radiance of the gods.

*The Pandava-Kaurava war is the subject of the huge epic poem the Mahabharata, which has for 2000 years been an inexhaustible source of material for poetry, art, drama and – in modern times – films, TV series and comic strips. Historians theorize that the stories mythologize a real war, between a mountain-dwelling people (the Pandavas) and their plain-dwelling rivals, perhaps for the fertile lands of Upper India (the area called **Bharata** in the poem – hence its title). But as we have it, the war and its protagonists have long passed from actuality to myth, and only the Mahabharata's stressing of the human dimension, giving the supernatural a markedly second place, now distinguishes it from most other myth-cycles, both Indian and from other cultures round the world.*

PANDORA
Europe (South)

Pandora ('all-gifts'), in Greek myth, was a beautiful mortal. **Zeus** made her from mud in the same way as **Prometheus** moulded the rest of humankind – and his intention was to use her to make trouble for Prometheus' creations, whom he hated but could not destroy. All the gods gave her gifts – **Aphrodite** showed her how to make herself irresistible, **Apollo** taught her **music**, the

Muses taught her dancing, and so on. When she was ready, Zeus gave her a treasure-box for dowry and sent her to marry Prometheus. But Prometheus, as his name 'forethought' suggests, was wary and refused to have anything to do with her. His brother Epimetheus ('afterthought') had no qualms: he married her and took her down to Earth. But when he opened the dowry-box, a swarm of plagues, miseries and disasters flew out, tenanting the world and blighting all human lives. Nothing was left inside but Hope, and this remained ever afterwards the only palliative for all the pains Zeus wished on human existence.

PANDU
India

Pandu ('pale'), in Hindu myth, was the son of **Ambalika**. Ambalika's husband Vichitravirya died before she had children, and according to custom she agreed to have sex with his brother in order to bear her dead husband a legitimate heir. She expected Vichitravirya's handsome brother, the sage **Bhisma**, to come to her bed; but Bhisma had forsworn sex and sent instead his brother **Vyasa**, an unkempt hermit. Ambalika turned pale at Vyasa's embrace – and at that moment Vyasa ejaculated inside her, fathering Pandu. Because she had turned pale, her son Pandu was born albino.

When Pandu grew up he married two wives, **Kunti** and **Madri**. But before he could give them children, disaster struck. Out hunting one day, he mistook a sage and his wife (who were making love in the forest) for deer, and shot them. The dying sage cursed Pandu, saying that if he ever made love with either of his wives, he would die. Pandu therefore refused sex with Kunti and Madri, and they compensated by having children with gods. Five sons were born, jointly called the **Pandavas** after Pandu, who brought them up as children of his own.

One day, Pandu, strolling with Madri in the forest, felt a sudden arrow of desire for her. They lay down to make love – and at the precise moment of penetration, Pandu's heart burst and he died. His and Madri's love-bower was the exact spot where he had killed the sage and his wife years before, and the sage's curse had now come true. Pandu's brother now accepted the throne, and brought up Pandu's children, the Pandavas, as if they were his own sons. But from the moment of Pandu's death the young princes began quarreling with their cousins the **Kauravas** – and hostility between them eventually led to a war which engulfed the world.

PAN GU
Asia (East)

Pan Gu, creator of the world in Chinese myth, was formed when *Yang* and *Yin* came together at the beginning of **creation**. For 18,000 years he lay in **Hun Dun** (Chaos), inside the primeval egg. He began as a dwarf, but grew until he split the shell and hatched. The egg-fluid became **Sky** and the shell became Earth, and Pan Gu lay between them. He continued to grow, 3m a day for another 18,000 years, and as he grew he worked on Sky and Earth with his chisel, forcing them apart and shaping them until they reached the positions and appearance they hold today. As soon as they were fixed in place, he died, and his body divided. In some accounts his head became the mountain that bounds the world to the East (Taishan, 'Eastern Peak'), his feet Huashan ('Western Peak'), his arms the twin Hengshan ('Northern' and 'Southern Peaks') and his stomach Songshan ('Central Peak'), anchoring creation. In others, his breath became wind, his voice **thunder**, his eyes the **Sun** and **Moon** (opening and closing in alternation), his blood seas and rivers, his sweat **rain**, his hair and eyebrows stars, his flesh soil, his bones rock, his semen pearls, his marrow jade, and his body-hair vegetation.

In some accounts, human beings, least of all creation, were not made from Pan Gu's body but evolved from the fleas which fell out of his beard. In others, he modelled them from clay and left them to dry in the sun, but was forced by a sudden rain-shower to bundle them under cover. (In the process some fell and were damaged – which is why disabled people exist on Earth.)

For another Chinese account of the making of human beings, see **Nü Gua**.

In art, Pan Gu is shown as a bearded dwarf dressed in a bearskin or a leaf-skirt and accompanied by the four celestial beasts, a dragon, a phoenix, a tortoise and a unicorn.
≫⁺ giants

PAPA
Oceania

Papa ('flat'), in the Maori **creation** myth, was **Mother Earth**, consort of **Rangi** (Father **Sky**). She and he lay in an embrace so tight that all created beings, their children, were trapped in her womb, and it was not until the gods, led by **Tane**, prised Rangi away from her that the world was fully formed.

In Hawaiian myth, Papa was the first woman. She came to the world as a bird, and laid an egg in the ocean which cracked open and became the island of Hawaii. She married Wakea, the first man, and they created first a huge calabash (which Wakea threw into space above their heads to become the sky), and then the human race. Wakea, however, raped their daughter, and Papa retaliated by cursing the human race with mortality and leaving the world forever.

PARAPARAWA
Americas (South)

Paraparawa, in the myths of the Trio people of Brazil and Surinam, lived in a time before **farming**, when human beings lived only on flesh. One day he caught a *waraku* fish, and was about to eat it when it changed into a beautiful woman. He asked her to be his wife, and she called her father from the river for the marriage-meal. He surged from the depths, in the form of an alligator (or some say, an anaconda), and brought with him a feast of bananas, sweet potatoes, yams and yucca. Instead of eating them, however, Paraparawa's wife told him to plant them in the ground, and as soon as he did so each plant divided itself, sprang up a hundredfold, and provided food for all Paraparawa's people. At the end of the feast, Paraparawa gathered the remains and planted them – and the miracle happened again. So **farming** was discovered.

PARASHURAMA
India

Parashurama's axe. Parashurama ('Rama with the battleaxe'), in Hindu myth, was the sixth avatar of **Vishnu**. A forest-dwelling hermit had a family of sons, and the youngest was both a devout servant of the gods and a keen huntsman. In reward for his prayers and sacrifices, the gods gave him unerring skill with the bow. But **demons**, afraid that he would use archery against them, stole his bow, leaving him weaponless. Alone on a mountain, the young man prayed and sacrificed – in some accounts, for a whole mortal generation – and in return Vishnu entered him, so taking mortal form on Earth, and **Shiva** gave him a battle-axe and told him to use it to fight the enemies of the gods.

Parashurama and his mother. One day, while Parashurama was still on the mountain, his mother was walking in the forest when she saw a young couple making love in a forest pool. The sight filled her with sexual excitement, and when she went home her hermit-husband saw that impure thoughts had entered her head and ordered his cowherd sons, one after another as they came home that evening, to remove them by cutting off her head. All refused, and their father punished them by making them as witless as the cattle they herded. Finally Vishnu-Parashurama came home. He realized the true purpose of the beheading, and used Shiva's axe to do as his father

ordered. As soon as his mother's head touched the ground she was restored to life, cleansed of impurity – and Parashurama's father rewarded him by granting him immunity from death in war.

Parashurama and the warrior-kings. Parashurama's father and brothers owned cattle, pasturing them in the forest. When the gods wanted to protect **Kamadhenu**, the cow of plenty, from demons and mortals who were trying to steal her, they hid her among his herds, coming each morning and evening to collect her miraculous milk (the wealth of **creation**). A mortal king, Kartavirya of the thousand arms, was hunting one day in the forest when he saw Kamadhenu, realized what she was and stole her from Parashurama's brainless brothers, stampeding her out of the forest ahead of his hunting-party. Parashurama stopped him in a clearing by a lake and challenged him to single combat. Each of Kartavirya's thousand arms held a different weapon, and he whirled his swords, brandished his clubs and fired volleys of arrows like a one-man army. But Parashurama, armed with Shiva's axe, chopped off his arms one by one, cutting him down to size, and finally removed his head.

Kartavirya's twenty-one warrior sons, each as powerful as his father, now gathered an army and swarmed into the forest like a column of driver ants. They killed everything in their path, **demons**, humans, animals, insects, and finally chopped Parashurama's father to pieces beside his own altar. Parashurama set out after them for vengeance. He fought twenty-one campaigns, each against a different son, and beheaded each of them with Shiva's invincible axe. The bones of the sons' myriad soldiers littered the ground like trees after a hurricane, and their blood filled five lakes as big as inland seas. Parashurama gave the cow of plenty to **Kasyapa**, father of Vishnu's former avatar **Vamana**, and so prosperity returned to the world.

Parashurama and Rama. As soon as the twenty-one kings were dead, Vishnu returned to **Heaven**, leaving Parashurama's mortal self once more on Earth. Parashurama still had Shiva's immortal axe, and his bow recovered from the demons. Human ambition welled up in his mind, and he demanded that the gods reward him for rescuing the cow of plenty: they were to let him rule as much land as he could cover in a single bowshot. Alarmed, **Varuna** summoned **Yama**, lord of the dead, from the **Underworld** and changed him into an ant. Yama chewed Parashurama's bow-string, fraying it so that when he fired it snapped, and instead of the arrow covering the whole world, as Parashurama intended, it merely covered Malabar.

Despite this reduction in his power, Parashurama was still the most powerful human warrior on Earth. He took part in the early stages of the war between the **Pandavas** and the **Kauravas**, teaching the Pandava prince **Arjuna** all the skills of archery and fighting a fierce duel with the Kauravas' war-leader **Bhisma**. But his human arrogance led him to challenge the gods – and not just the gods, but Vishnu himself, who had once used his body as a mortal avatar. When Vishnu came to Earth as **Rama**, and took part in the archery-contest for the hand of **Sita**, daughter of King Janaka, Parashurama was another of the suitors. Rama not only strung and drew the bow of Shiva, but broke it, and Parashurama indignantly challenged him to a duel. He backed down as soon as Vishnu revealed himself in Rama – but he had still challenged a god, and Vishnu punished him by barring him from **immortality** in Heaven, condemning him to take part forever in the cycle of human life and death on Earth.

*Parashurama's story is told in the **Mahabharata** and **Ramayana**. In southern India, he was worshipped as a god in his own right, and is still a favourite avatar of Vishnu, being shown in art as a smiling warrior in full armour and brandishing Shiva's axe.*

PARIS
Europe (South)

Paris on Mount Ida. Paris ('wallet' or 'scrotum'), in Greek myth, was one of the fifty sons of King **Priam** and Queen **Hecuba** of Troy. On the night before he was born his mother dreamed that she gave birth not to a human child but to a blazing torch whose flames engulfed all Troy. The prophets advised Priam to have the baby killed at birth, and Priam gave the job to his herdsman Agelaus, and told him to bring back the child's tongue as proof that he was dead. Agelaus left Paris to die on Mount Ida, but when he came back next morning found him alive and well, being suckled by a she-bear. Impressed by this sign of the gods' favour, he took Priam a dog's tongue to make him think that the baby was dead, and brought

Paris up as his own child, renaming him Alexander ('defender').

When Paris grew up he married the mountain-nymph Oenone, and together they herded Agelaus' cattle on the mountainside. On one occasion, Ares disguised himself as a bull and fought a locked-horns contest with Paris' prize bull. Paris awarded Ares the prize, and this proof of his good judgement made Zeus choose him to decide the contest of beauty between Aphrodite, Athene and Hera (see below). Soon after the contest, Priam sent for a choice bull for sacrifice at a lavish funeral games, and Paris personally drove his best bull (the one which Ares had defeated) into Troy, competed in the Games and won every event. Priam's sons attacked him and would have killed him, but Agelaus ran to tell Priam who he really was, and Priam was so delighted to have his son restored that he welcomed him to Troy and ignored all the prophets who warned him that if Paris lived Troy would die.

The judgement of Paris. At the wedding of **Peleus** and **Thetis**, **Eris** goddess of quarrels, who had not been invited, rolled a golden apple between Aphrodite, Athene and Hera. On it was written 'For the Fairest', and the three goddesses asked Zeus to choose which of them was meant. He refused, saying that only a mortal could make an unbiased choice and that Paris was the man to do it. **Hermes** took the goddesses to Mount Ida. At first Paris was reluctant to judge, suggesting instead that the goddesses divide the apple among them; but Hermes threatened him with a thunderbolt and he agreed. One by one the goddesses appeared before him – and each offered him a bribe to place her first. Hera offered royal power; Athene offered wisdom; Aphrodite offered **Helen** of Sparta, the most beautiful woman in the world. Paris chose Helen, and Athene and Hera flew back to **Olympus** in a rage and began to plan trouble for Paris and doom for Troy – exactly as Zeus had known would happen.

Paris and Helen. As soon as Paris was accepted as a prince of Troy, he asked his father Priam for a fast ship, and Aphrodite gave him safe journey to Sparta. **Menelaus**, Helen's husband, happened to be away in Crete (for the funeral of his grandfather Catreus), and Helen welcomed the visitors in his place. Aphrodite made her seem even more desirable to Paris in the flesh than in report, and **Eros** buried an arrow of love for Paris deep in Helen's heart. They loaded their ship with half the treasure in Sparta, including gold from **Apollo**'s temple (which made them another immortal enemy) and sailed for Troy. Hera saw their ship far out to sea and sent a storm to sink it, but Aphrodite snatched it from danger and beached it on her sacred island, Cyprus. From there they sailed to Egypt. In some accounts, they made their way directly from there to Troy, stopping in Phoenicia on the way. In others, King **Proteus** of Egypt arrested them, sent Paris packing and kept Helen safe until his friend Menelaus could come and take her back to Sparta. Zeus, however, afraid that there would be no **Trojan War**, made a phantom Helen and sent it to Troy at Paris' side, leaving the real Helen in Egypt for Menelaus to rescue when the war was done.

The Trojan War. During the war Paris fought with more show than flair. He loved parading in front of the army in his golden armour, or appearing on the battlements to be cheered by his men, but he was terrified of hand-to-hand combat. On one occasion, having boasted that he was easily a match for Menelaus, he was forced by **Hector** to fight him, and survived only because Aphrodite snatched him away from the duel in the nick of time and dumped him in Helen's bedroom. His favourite weapons, from his boyhood on Mount Ida, were bow and poisoned arrows, and with these he wounded **Diomedes**, Euryphilus and Machaon the physician. In some accounts, he shot and killed **Achilles**, the gods guiding his arrow to Achilles' one vulnerable place, his heel. In others, Paris' sister **Polyxena** tricked Achilles into Troy by promising to marry him, and at the ceremony Paris, who had been hiding behind the altar, slipped out and killed Achilles by stabbing him in the heel.

Paris' death. **Calchas** the prophet told the Greeks that Troy would not fall unless they brought **Philoctetes** back from exile on Lemnos. They did this, and with him came the bow and unerring arrows of **Heracles**. Philoctetes challenged Paris to a duel, bowman against bowman, and Paris, trusting in his poisoned arrows and the favour of Aphrodite, readily agreed. Paris shot first, and missed. Then Philoctetes fired one of Heracles' arrows and hit Paris in the heel. The Trojans dragged him into the city and tried to ease his pain, without success. Finally they took him to

Mount Ida, and begged Oenone (who had invented the poison used on Paris' own arrows) to pick herbs and make some antidote for Heracles' poison. She refused. 'He preferred Helen to me; let him ask her for help!' So Paris died – and Oenone, frenzied with grief, threw herself on his funeral-pyre. Her angry ghost flew down with his to the **Underworld**, where she reproached him for faithlessness ever afterwards.

≫→ **heroes**

PARJANYA
India

Parjanya, in the Vedic myths of the Aryans who invaded India in the seventeenth century BCE, was the son of the sky-god **Dyaus**. He was the god of rain-clouds, and drove a cart across the sky, laden with bags and buckets of rain which he poured out on the Earth below – and because he sent rain to fertilize the ground, he also oversaw the **fertility** of animals (especially horses and cattle) and of human beings.

PARSHVA
India

Parshva (or Parshvanatha), in Jain myth, was the twenty-third **tirkanthara**, and lived some two centuries before **Mahavira**. He was an avatar of **Vishnu**, and showed his divine knowledge at the age of eight when he warned a king who was about to chop a log in two that if he did so he'd harm the world-serpent **Shesha**. As an adult, Parshva devoted himself to teaching, and to ever more self-denying austerities, until finally he freed himself of his mortal body by starving himself to death.

PARSU
India

Parsu, in the myths of the Aryan people who invaded India in the seventeenth century BCE, was the first female human being. She was either created from the rib of **Manu**, the first man, or grew from the milk, clarified butter, curds and whey he offered to the gods when he was saved from the primordial **flood**. She mated with Manu, and they became the ancestors of the entire human race.

PARVATI
India

Parvati, in Hindu myth, was **Shiva**'s beautiful wife. In some accounts she was the daughter of the goddess of the Himalayas, in others she was a reincarnation of **Sati**, created by **Vishnu** to stop Shiva's destructive dance after Sati committed suicide.

⧁➔ **beauty**

PASIPHAË
Europe (South)

Pasiphaë ('light of all'), in Greek myth, daughter of **Helius** the Sun-god and the ocean-**nymph** Perseis, married King Minos of Crete, and they had several children, including **Ariadne**, **Hecate** and **Phaedra** (daughters) and Androgeus, **Deucalion** and Glaucus (sons). But then Minos offended **Poseidon**, and the god punished him by driving Pasiphaë mad. Minos had begged Poseidon to send a bull from the **sea** as a sign of

favour, and promised to sacrifice it to him as soon as it came to land. But when he saw the bull he kept it for himself, hiding it in the royal herds and fobbing Poseidon off with the best animal he could find. Poseidon punished him by making Pasiphaë lust after the sea-born bull. She bribed **Daedalus** to make a cow-shaped framework, covered in hide. Then she climbed inside it, Daedalus pushed it into the byre, and the sea-born bull mated with it – and with Pasiphaë inside.

When Minos discovered that Pasiphaë was pregnant by the bull, he made Daedalus build an impregnable prison – the Cretan labyrinth – for her and her eventual offspring. Here Pasiphaë gave birth to the monstrous **Minotaur**: human body and limbs, bull's head, and with a taste for human flesh. No one knows what happened to Pasiphaë after the monster was born. Some accounts say that it ate her, others that her father the Sun rescued her and absorbed her into his own radiance, others again that she wandered, distracted, in the corridors and corners of the labyrinth, and was never seen again.

This is one of the few Greek myths which have encouraged later writers to rationalize. The labyrinth is claimed as a metaphor for the palace of the kings of Crete, with its many corridors and underground rooms. Pasiphaë's bull-passion is prosaically explained as a love-affair with a man called Taurus ('Bull'), an officer in the royal guard who met her secretly in Daedalus' house. In this version, there was no Minotaur. Is supposed bellowing was wind roaring through the subterranean chambers of the palace, and its taste for human victims was a handy way to explain an ages-old Cretan tradition of human sacrifice. Still other 'authorities', cleaving more closely to the idea of a miraculous bull, tie themselves in knots by saying that the bull was not Poseidon's creation but was the white bull whose form **Zeus** took in order to mate with **Europa**. When Zeus abandoned it, the form was left as a kind of immortal wraith, skimming the surface of the sea and eventually splashing ashore on Crete to be corralled by Minos and seduced by Pasiphaë. In this version, the bull went mad after mating with Pasiphaë, and rampaged all over the island until it was tamed by **Heracles** and returned harmlessly to the royal herds.

PATROCLUS
Europe (South)

Patroclus (Patroklos, 'his father's glory'), in Greek myth, was the son of King Menoetius and Queen Sthenele (or some say Philomela) of Opus. As a boy he accidentally killed Clysonymus son of Amphidamus, and was forced to fly for safety to the court of King **Peleus** of Phthia, where he was brought up with the young prince **Achilles**. He and Achilles became close friends, then lovers, and when Achilles went to fight in the **Trojan War** Patroclus accompanied him as his squire. Achilles, like all children of sea-creatures (his mother was the sea-**nymph Thetis**), was bisexual, and at Troy took Briseis as his mistress, sleeping with her and with Patroclus on alternate nights. Then **Agamemnon** took Briseis from Achilles by force, Achilles withdrew from the fighting in a sulk, and the Greeks began to lose the war.

To hearten Achilles' men, Patroclus put on his friend's armour and led the soldiers against the Trojans, who scattered in terror before him. Only the intervention of **Apollo** stopped Patroclus breaking down the walls and entering Troy itself: the god blocked Patroclus' path and brought **Hector** to challenge him and kill him. Patroclus' death brought Achilles back into the fighting. He sacrificed twelve young Trojans over his friend's funeral pyre, and began hunting Hector down – exactly the turn of events planned by the gods to bring the war to its final phase.

Patroclus is a major character in Homer's Iliad, *and appears often in art as a dignified, princely companion in Achilles' battles. His funeral pyre, with Achilles grieving beside it, was a favourite subject for Greek vase-painters.*
≫→ **heroes**

PAVANAREKHA
India

Pavanarekha, in Hindu myth, was the wife of King **Ugrasena** and queen of the Yadava people of Northern India. She was raped by the **demon Drumalika**, and gave birth to **Kansa**, whom she later persuaded Ugrasena to bring up as his own son.

PAYATAMU
Americas (North)

Payatamu, in the myths of the Hopi people of the Southwestern US pueblos, was a flute-playing, pastoral god, invisible to mortals. He settled like a butterfly on flowers, which opened their petals to welcome him.

≫→ **farming, music**

PEGASUS
Europe (South)

Pegasus (Pegasos, 'water-spirit'), in Greek myth, was the winged stallion which grew from the blood spurting from **Medusa**'s neck after she was beheaded by **Perseus**. He served Perseus faithfully throughout Perseus' life, then flew to Mount Helicon, home of the **Muses**. He found the Muses in despair. All the streams on the mountain had run dry, including the waters of their inspiration. Pegasus created a spring by stamping his hoof on the ground, and the grateful Muses called it Hippocrene ('horse-spring') to honour him. He often went back to the mountain to browse in the meadows watered by the stream – and he created several other water-springs in the same way, notably Pirene in Corinth, which he visited at night, invisible to mortals, sipping the **water**, cropping the grass and whinnying with pleasure.

When **Bellerophon** was ordered by King Iobates to kill the monstrous **Chimaera**, the gods helped him by giving him supernatural **weapons** and leading him to Pirene, where he coaxed Pegasus into accepting him on his back and soaring through the **sky** to Chimaera's lair. When the monster was dead, Bellerophon kept Pegasus for himself, and one day tried to ride him up to **Olympus** and visit the gods. But **Zeus** sent a fly to sting Pegasus, who reared and sent Bellerophon crashing back to earth. The gods opened Olympus' doors for Pegasus (who was immortal), and put him to work in Zeus' chariot-team, pulling his new master about the sky to hurl his thunderbolts.

PELEUS
Europe (South)

Peleus ('Muddy'), son of King Aeacus of Aegina in Greek myth, was one of the unluckiest mortals who ever lived. He and his brother Telamon were jealous of their third brother, the handsome, gifted Phocus. They challenged him to an athletics match, and killed him in the course of it – either deliberately (when Telamon threw a discus at his head), or accidentally (when Peleus misthrew an axe). Their father banished them from Aegina, Telamon to Salamis and Peleus to Phthia.

Peleus in Phthia. Peleus' bad luck continued in Phthia. First he killed a fellow-prince in a hunting accident; then one of the palace women, Cretheis, angry because he refused to have sex with her, told her husband that Peleus had raped her. The husband challenged Peleus to a trial-by-hunting on Mount Pelion. If he killed more game than anyone else, he would be proved innocent. The gods gave Peleus a magic sword, and he killed a huge pile of game. But he celebrated too lavishly, fell into a drunken sleep, and his companions stole all his game and left him on the mountain as prey for the wild **Centaurs** who lived there.

Peleus and Thetis. Peleus was rescued by **Chiron**, king of the Centaurs, who told him how to win the hand of the sea-**nymph Thetis**. The gods wanted this marriage, partly because **Zeus** had courted Thetis himself, been rebuffed and had sworn that she would never marry an immortal, and partly because the **Fates** had prophesied that Thetis' son would grow up to be greater than his father. Every day, Chiron said, Thetis rode on a dolphin's back to her favourite bay, Haemonia in Thessaly. Here, in a myrtle grove by a sandy beach, she slept in a cave during the heat of the day. All Peleus had to do was catch her and hold her, and she would agree to marry him. Peleus did as instructed, clinging to Thetis despite all her changes of shape: before she agreed to marry him, she became lioness, snake, waterfall, fire and cuttlefish.

The wedding was held on Mount Pelion, lit as bright as day by the **Moon**, stars and constellations who came as guests. The feasting and dancing lasted until dawn. It was the twinkling of an eye for the gods, but they had to keep the party short for the sake of Peleus, who, being mortal, would not have lived to see the end of a full-scale, 300-mortal-year Olympian wedding-night. There was one sour moment. **Eris**, goddess of quarrels, had not been invited, and rolled a golden apple across the floor, inscribed 'For the fairest'. Peleus picked it up – and at once regretted it, as he could not decide which goddess to give it to: **Hera**, **Aphrodite** or **Athene**. He asked Zeus' advice, and Zeus said that the goddesses must ask another mortal to judge between them: Prince **Paris** of Troy. Thus, in all innocence, Peleus started the chain of events which led to the **Trojan War**.

Peleus' bad luck continued after his marriage. Thetis was determined to make her children immortal. Each time a son was born, therefore, she burned his flesh from his bones, rubbed the bones with **ambrosia** and boiled them to remove any trace of mortality inherited from Peleus. Six of his children were made immortal in this way, and vanished into Heaven out of his sight. When the seventh son was born, he rushed in on Thetis before she had time to complete the spell. The mortal part of the child was all charred away except for one ankle-bone. Peleus snatched it and so prevented his son from becoming fully immortal. Thetis, infuriated, left Peleus and went to live in her underwater palace, where he could never follow. The child grew up as **Achilles**, and – as the Fates had prophesied – lived to be greater than his father. (In some accounts, Thetis dipped Achilles in the Styx instead of burning him, and his mortal heel was the only part untouched by the water.)

Peleus' end. When Thetis left Peleus, he went back to Phthia. Zeus gave him an army of ants which grew into men (the Myrmidons), and with them he defeated his enemies and made himself king. He ruled until he was an old man, protected by immortal weapons which the gods had given him as wedding-presents. But when Achilles at last sailed for the Trojan War, he gave him the weapons – and immediately Peleus' enemies rose up and banished him.

At this point Thetis took pity on Peleus. She promised that if he waited in the cave where they had first made love, she would make him immortal and take him into her sea-kingdom. Unfortunately for Peleus, his bad luck still held. While waiting in the cave, he heard news that Troy had fallen and that his grandson **Neoptolemus**, Achilles' child, was travelling home. He set out to meet him, but died on the journey, and so was denied the **immortality** Thetis had promised him.

PELIAS
Europe (South)

Pelias (Peleias, 'bruised'), in Greek myth, was the son of **Poseidon** and the mortal princess Tyro. Ashamed of her love-affair, Tyro exposed Pelias at birth, and he was brought up by shepherds, who gave him his name because of a port-wine birthmark on his face. Tyro meanwhile married King Cretheus of Iolcus and had three more children, of whom Aeson, the eldest, was made Cretheus' heir. But when Cretheus died Pelias suddenly appeared, snatched the throne, exiled Aeson and killed all his children except one – the infant **Jason**, whom the gods removed for safety and gave to **Chiron** to bring up.

Pelias reigned in triumph for twenty years. Then Jason appeared, fully grown, and demanded the throne for his father Aeson. Pelias agreed to give it up if Jason sailed to Colchis, beyond the edge of the mortal world, and stole the **Golden Fleece** – a task he thought impossible. After Jason left, he continued his tyranny for many more years, thinking himself safe. Then Jason came back with the Golden Fleece and with a Colchian wife, the witch-priestess **Medea**.

Jason's plan was to storm the palace, kill Pelias and prove his claim to the throne by showing the Golden Fleece. But Medea pointed out that Pelias, being a god's son, could be killed only by trickery, not force. She went into the palace alone, dressed as a priestess of **Hecate**, and offered to show Pelias' daughters how to rejuvenate their father. She cut an aged ram in pieces and boiled them, produced by sleight of hand a lamb, and said that the same treatment would have the same effect on Pelias. Pelias' daughters fell on him with knives, and Poseidon saw that the time had come to end his son's life, stripped Pelias' **immortality** and sent his soul to the **Underworld**.

PELLES
Europe (North)

Pelles, or Amfortas, in medieval Christian myth, was lord of the magic kingdom of Carbonek, a place which had no fixed location: you found it by searching for the **Holy Grail** and proving yourself worthy to find it. Pelles was guardian of the Grail, but was tainted by human frailty and therefore doomed to surrender the Grail when a true and pure guardian appeared to claim it. His disability was symbolized by lameness – in some versions, a wound which prevented him riding a horse or indulging in any activities more strenuous than fishing, and earned him the nickname 'Fisher King'. When **Lancelot** came to Carbonek, Pelles tricked him into sleeping with his daughter Elaine. This trick tainted Lancelot himself with mortality, so that he was unworthy to find the Grail; but his and Elaine's son **Galahad** eventually became its guardian and took it into **Heaven** – and in the course of that quest he absolved the guilt of his grandfather Pelles and the old king's wound was healed.

≫+ **Morgan le Fay**

pelops
Europe (South)

Pelops and the gods. Pelops ('mud-face'), in Greek myth, was the son of **Atlas**' daughter Dione and **Tantalus** king of Phrygia. When he was a baby, his father served him up as a meal for the gods. Some accounts say that Tantalus had no other food fit for immortals, others that he was testing them, others that he was insane – but whatever the reason, he invited them to a banquet and served them stew made from Pelops' chopped-up flesh. **Demeter**, whose mind was clouded with grief for lost **Persephone**, ate a piece of meat; but the other gods pushed back their plates in horror, and **Zeus** hurled **Tantalus** to the depths of the **Underworld**, where he was punished for all eternity. **Hermes** gathered the pieces of Pelops' flesh and boiled them in the cauldron of rebirth. Then the **Fate** Clotho reassembled them into human form, and Demeter brought an ivory shoulder (carved by **Hephaestus**) to replace what she had eaten. **Rhea** breathed life into Pelops, and he was reborn. **Poseidon** took him to **Olympus** and gave him a team of winged horses and a chariot so light that it could skim the sea dry-wheeled.

Pelops and Myrtilus. Pelops grew up in Olympus until it was time for him to find a mortal kingdom and a wife. He chose Hippodamia, daughter of King **Oenomaus** of Pisa in Southern Greece. Oenomaus challenged all his daughter's suitors to a chariot-race, and killed those who lost. Pelops took no chances. He had immortal horses, faster than Oenomaus', but he made sure of victory by cheating. He knew that Myrtilus, Oenomaus' charioteer, was in love with Hippodamia, but was too frightened of Oenomaus to challenge his master to a race. Pelops bribed Myrtilus: if he made sure that Pelops won the race, he could sleep with Hippodamia on the wedding night. Myrtilus eagerly replaced the metal axle-pins of Oenomaus' chariot with pins of wax.

The race began. Oenomaus gave Pelops and Hippodamia half an hour's start, and then streamed after him with Myrtilus, in **Ares**' war-chariot. The friction began to melt the wax axle-pins of Oenomaus' chariot, and just as the wheels spun away from it Myrtilus jumped clear and left his master to crash. So Pelops won the race and Hippodamia's hand – and he, Hippodamia and Myrtilus set out in Poseidon's chariot on a victory-ride. They galloped across country and then turned out to sea, skimming the waves. Pelops waited until they were out of reach of land, then kicked Myrtilus into the sea and hovered overhead to watch him drown. Myrtilus choked and sank – and with his last breath cursed Pelops and all his descendants.

Pelops' dynasty. Pelops and Hippodamia rode to the bank of Ocean, set up an altar and prayed to be cleansed of guilt for Myrtilus' death, on the grounds that he had deserved to die for killing his master Oenomaus. Hephaestus, whose favourite Pelops had been ever since the carving of the ivory shoulder which allowed him life, granted their prayer. They rode back to Southern Greece, and settled as king and queen of Pisa. They had six daughters and sixteen sons, and their children eventually ruled the entire region – which Pelops renamed 'the Peloponnese' after himself.

At this time, the gods were trying to end mortal squabbling and wickedness, to unite them peacefully under a single ruler, as Olympus was united under Zeus. They chose Pelops, the mortal they had themselves remade, to be this king. Hephaestus made a royal sceptre, the gods' gift of authority, and Zeus gave it to Pelops, hoping that his descendants would rule evermore in peace. Pelops himself spent the rest of his life in happiness, and when he died he was buried at Olympia (where some say the Olympic Games were later developed from the funeral games in his memory). The gods took him into Olympus and granted him **immortality**.

No such happiness – either on Earth or in **Heaven** after death – awaited Pelops' descendants. They had inherited a tendency to evil from their ancestor Tantalus, and been tainted by Myrtilus' dying curse. Three generations, therefore – Pelops' sons **Atreus** and **Thyestes**, his grandsons **Agamemnon** and **Menelaus**, his great-grandchildren **Orestes** and **Electra** – chose war instead of peace, evil instead of good and suffered for it, until at last, after the **Furies** pursued Orestes for murdering his mother, the gods ended the cycle and let succeeding generations live out their lives in peace. But in the course of the family's travails the sceptre of authority was lost, and the human race never found the unity or serenity the gods had planned for it.

PENATES
Europe (South)

Penates (from *penus*, 'store-cupboard'), in Roman myth, were the gods who looked after a family's food and drink. They were worshipped at the hearth with the **Lares** and **Vesta**, and were personal to each family.

*The Penates of the Imperial family were held in particular honour. It was thought that they were the patron gods of Troy, brought to Italy in prehistoric times by **Aeneas**, and guaranteed that Rome would never suffer famine or drought.*

PENELOPE
Europe (South)

Penelope in Sparta. Penelope, in Greek myth, was the daughter of the Spartan prince Icarius. Icarius wanted a son, and when Penelope was born her mother concealed the fact for several days, calling her Arnaea ('lambkin') and hiding her in the royal flocks. Then Icarius found out, and threw his daughter into the sea to drown. But she was rescued by a family of ducks, and Icarius was so impressed by the omen that he renamed her Penelope (after the word *penelops*, 'duck') and she became his favourite child.

Penelope was the same age as **Helen**. When suitors began arriving for Helen from all parts of Greece, Penelope despaired of ever finding a husband; but **Odysseus** saw her and immediately asked to marry her. Icarius, reluctant to part with his darling child, asked Odysseus to settle in Sparta, and Odysseus, who was eager to be off home to Ithaca, asked Penelope to choose where she would like to live. Embarrassed, she blushed and covered her head with her veil – and Icarius realized that this was another omen, let her go to Ithaca and built a temple to the goddess Modesty in her honour. He visited it every day, but her going had broken his heart and he died soon afterwards.

Penelope in Ithaca. Unlike the marriages of some royal couples in myth, that of Penelope and Odysseus was a love-match. Odysseus was so devoted to Penelope that he was reluctant to leave her and fight in the **Trojan War**; it was not until **Palamedes** tricked him that he forced himself to go. Throughout the ten years of the war, and the ten years which followed (during which Odysseus was struggling home from Troy), Penelope remained faithful to him. She was courted by swarms of suitors, and entertained them civilly enough. But she refused to believe that Odysseus was dead, and accepted none of their presents or advances.

Towards the end of Odysseus' absence, when the suitors became even more pressing, she announced that she was weaving a linen shroud for her father-in-law **Laertes**, and would choose a husband as soon as it was finished. Every day she wove, every night she unpicked the weaving – and it was months before one of her maids gave the game away and she was forced to finish the shroud. She announced that the following morning her slaves would take a dozen axe-heads, and

Odysseus' great war-bow, from the armoury. Each axe was a wedge of metal with a leather loop at the top to fasten it to the wooden shaft. The slaves would set up the axes in a row in the ground, loops uppermost. Then whichever suitor could string Odysseus' bow and shoot a single arrow through all twelve loops, would be the man she would marry.

One by one, the suitors tried and failed. Then a decrepit beggar asked to take his turn, strung the bow and fired an arrow through all twelve loops. He turned the bow on the suitors, and he, **Telemachus** (Odysseus' and Penelope's son) and the swineherd Eumaeus fought a pitched battle in the palace hall until all the suitors were dead. No one but Eumaeus and the old nurse Euryclea knew that the beggar was really Odysseus returned, disguised by the gods; and the gods hid his true identity even from Penelope. Even when he had bathed, dressed in royal clothes and the gods had stripped his disguise from him, she was still suspicious. She called to the slaves to pull the royal bed from the bedroom and make it up on the landing outside – and only when Odysseus showed that he knew its secret (he'd built it himself years before, carving it from the trunk of a tree which supported the palace roof, so that the bed was part of the room and could not be moved) did she recognize him at last. The gods held back the dawn for them, granting them a second wedding-night, of supernatural length – a moment of **immortality** after all their suffering.

After Odysseus' return. One reason for this gift was that the gods knew what else was left for Penelope to endure. Soon after Odysseus returned, the gods sent him wandering again, this time to find a country whose people had never heard of **Poseidon**, god of the **sea**, and build him a temple there. Leaving Penelope in Ithaca, he wandered the world for another sixteen years. On his way he seduced Princess Erippe of Epirus, and she bore him a son, Euryalus, and sent the boy to Ithaca to await his father's return. Penelope, furious, decided to take revenge – and when Odysseus came home, years later, she said that Euryalus (now adolescent) had tried to rape her, and watched with grim satisfaction as the father killed the son he had no idea he'd had.

The Delphic oracle (or, some say, the prophet **Tiresias**) had told Odysseus that his own son would one day murder him. As soon as he came home, therefore, he banished Telemachus (who went to marry **Circe** and found a royal dynasty). At this point Penelope would have gone home to Sparta, to her father Icarius. But the old man was long dead, and she was forced to live on in Ithaca with a husband she'd known only for a handful of months out of a 36-year marriage, and who was edgy and suspicious of all strangers. Telegonus, Odysseus' son by Circe (another child he'd no idea he'd fathered) came to Ithaca, and Odysseus took him for a pirate, fought him and was killed by him, so fulfilling the oracle.

Penelope's descendants. The gods now intervened for the last time in Penelope's life. They told her to marry Telegonus, and miraculously restored her youth, so that she was a young woman again, but still endowed with all the wisdom learned as queen of Ithaca. She and Telegonus ruled for a time in Ithaca, then sailed South, where their son Italus gave his name to the new country they discovered: Italy.

*Some writers give an extraordinary twist to the beginning of this story. They say that far from being modest and chaste, Penelope slept in turn with each of Helen's suitors before choosing Odysseus, and that she also made love with the god **Hermes**, by whom she became pregnant with **Pan**. Hermes, to prevent her telling whose son Pan was, removed her forever from mortal sight and sent a wraith-Penelope to Ithaca as Odysseus' loyal wife. The long-suffering wife and queen, therefore, was no more than a mirage, a mirror-image of the wraith-Helen the same myth-writers claim was stolen away to Troy.*

PENGLAI SHAN
Asia (East)

Penglai Shan ('mount Penglai'), in Chinese myth, was one of 108 Daoist paradises. It had eight peaks, on each of which was the palace of one of the **Eight Immortals**. Its air was scented by a million million flowers, its trees were coral and their fruits were pearls, and all its birds and animals were as white as clouds. To stop mortals finding their way accidentally to Penglai, it was surrounded by what looked like water but was in fact an element too insubstantial to take the weight of boats or swimmers. The only way to reach Penglai was through the air, so that only birds, insects and immortals ever saw it. The Dew of Eternal Life flowed in all Penglai's streams and fountains,

ensuring the **immortality** of anyone who drank it.
≫→ Heaven

PENTHEUS
Europe (South)

Pentheus ('pain'), in Greek myth, was the son of **Cadmus**' daughter **Agave** and Echion, one of the **Sown Men** of **Thebes**. He succeeded Echion as king of Thebes, and ruled with a puritanical zeal characteristic of all the Sown Men's descendants. When the god **Dionysus** brought his ecstatic worship to Thebes, all the women of Thebes, including Pentheus' mother Agave, went up to Mount Cithaeron to worship and commune with the god. Pentheus at once assumed that they were holding orgies. He rounded up the women and shut them in their homes, and imprisoned Dionysus in chains in an underground cell. But the chains turned to vine-tendrils twining round the god's limbs, the cell became a leafy arbour, and Dionysus soared out of Thebes back to the mountain, with the women dancing after him.

Pentheus decided that the only way to stop the perversion was to kill all those taking part in it. He was gathering his soldiers when Dionysus appeared to him, disguised as a handsome priest. He charmed Pentheus, hypnotizing him into agreeing to go alone up the mountain to sit in a high pine-tree and spy on the women, gathering evidence of their orgies. In his trance, Pentheus even agreed to wear women's clothes and a wig so that he wouldn't be recognized – or, some say, the god changed him

into a woman. He climbed the tree, and Dionysus at once revealed him to the women not as man or woman but as a wild beast. Led by Agave, they tore the tree from the ground, ripped Pentheus to pieces and played catch with lumps of his flesh. Agave spiked his head on her thyrsus (the wool-tipped stick carried by all Dionysus' dancers) and carried it in triumph back to Thebes – and to the realization of what she'd done.

This myth is the starting point of Euripides' play Bacchae, *which centres on confrontation between Dionysus and Pentheus. It is one of the few ancient Greek plays – one of the few ancient Greek writings of any kind – to discuss the nature of transcendental religious feelings, the ecstasy of divine possession, and as such was utterly deplored and sidelined during the two thousand years of Christian religious hegemony in Europe. It was not until the return of rationalism in the nineteenth century, and the rise of comparative religious and anthropological studies, that its extraordinary power was recognized, and it is now regarded as one of the finest, and most disturbing, of all ancient plays.*

In fine art, two scenes from the myth were popular above all others, particularly on vase-paintings: the transformation of Dionysus' chains and prison cell, and Agave dancing with Pentheus' head. Christian disapproval meant that the play's themes were not used by fine artists from ancient times to the nineteenth century, but it then became popular, allowing as it did large panoramas of naked and half-naked women dancing in (often somewhat lumpenly-depicted) ecstasy on a romantic mountainside.

PERCEVAL
Europe (North)

Perceval ('pierce-veil'), or Parsifal, in medieval Christian myth, was **Galahad**'s companion on the quest for the **Holy Grail**. He was the seventh son of King Eburac of York, but his father abandoned the world for a monastery soon after he was born, and Perceval's mother brought him up alone in the forest, utterly ignorant of chivalry, religion, social hierarchy and **sex** – all staples of a gentleman's education at the time. She wanted him to remain throughout his life as pure and innocent as a child, to save him from original sin – but as soon as he met **Arthur** and some of the warriors of the Round Table in the woods, he espoused chivalry and went to **Camelot**, where he quickly proved himself one of the bravest and noblest warriors there. At the beginning of the Grail-quest, Perceval's qualities made him an apparently ideal companion for Galahad. But when he left the forest he had broken his mother's heart, and although he was allowed a vision of the Grail (hence his name), he was not allowed to accompany it to Paradise.

In some accounts, Perceval is the same person as the Celtic prince Peredur.

In a variant of the Perceval story, Perceval (now named Perlesvaus) was the son of the Grail-guardian, and should have inherited his father's sacred office. But when the guardian died his wicked brother (inspired by the Devil, and aided by demons and monsters) snatched both his castle and the Grail, and it was only with the help of the Knights Templar that Perlesvaus was able to storm the castle, kill his uncle and recover the Grail. This version inspired two thirteenth-century epics – one of which, Parzival, by Wolfram von Eschenbach, became the source of Wagner's opera Parsifal.

≫→ **heroes**

PERSEPHONE
Europe (South)

Persephone and Zeus. Persephone (Fersefassa, 'teller of destruction'; Latin Proserpina), in Greek myth, was the daughter of **Zeus** and **Demeter**. She was originally called Core (Koure, 'virgin'), and was the most beautiful being in **Olympus**. Every god lusted after her, and she was safe only because her mother protected her. Then one day her own father, Zeus, turned himself into an enormous **snake** and had **sex** with her, enfolding her in his coils. Demeter, furious, snatched her from **Heaven** to Earth, changed her name to Fersefassa and placed her on the island of Sicily, where she spent her days picking flowers and singing with her serving-**nymphs**.

Hades and Persephone. Hades, ruler of the **Underworld**, asked his brother Zeus for permission to marry Persephone. The two gods went to Demeter, and Demeter, horrified to think of Persephone leaving the sunny Earth for the shadows of the Underworld, refused. There was nothing for Hades to do but kidnap Persephone. One day Persephone was picnicking in the water-meadows of Sicily, when she saw a particularly beautiful hesperis. Its roots supported a hundred flowers; its scent filled the air throughout all Earth and Heaven. Persephone bent to sniff it – and at once the earth gaped open and Hades galloped up from the Underworld in a golden chariot pulled by coal-black horses, and snatched her into the darkness. The Earth's wound healed at once, and the water-meadows rippled in the sun as if nothing had happened.

No one knew where Persephone had gone or who had kidnapped her. Hades had been wearing his helmet of invisibility; all Persephone's nymphs could tell Demeter was of the ground splitting and of a roar like a whirling wind. Frantic, Demeter searched for nine days everywhere across the world, a pine-torch blazing in each hand, stopping neither to eat nor drink. At last **Helius** the **Sun**-god, who goes everywhere and sees everything, told her that the thief was Hades, that Persephone now lived in his dark kingdom, and that Zeus knew and approved of what had happened.

Demeter swore to have nothing more to do with Zeus or with any other god. She threw off her immortal shape, disguised herself as an old woman and went out into the world of mortals, a beggar. She wandered from town to town, village to village, and at last was welcomed by King Celeus and Queen Metanira of Eleusis.

Without Demeter's protection, nothing grew. Across the whole world crops withered, trees died and the ground grew sour. It was as if the barrenness of the Underworld were reaching up to corrupt all healthiness above. Human beings began to starve. At last Zeus sent the **messenger**-goddess **Iris** to make terms with Demeter. If she would bring back life to living things, she would beg Hades in turn to let Persephone go.

Unexpectedly, Hades listened to Demeter's appeal. For all his grimness, he was fairness personified, and he pitied human suffering. He agreed to let Persephone go; the black horses were harnessed, and the Earth gaped open ready for Persephone to leave. As she parted from Hades – sadly, for she had come to love both him and his sad people – he gave her a last gift, a pomegranate. In all her time in the Underworld, Persephone had neither eaten nor drunk; now, on the point of leaving, she ate a single pomegranate seed.

It was the gods' unbreakable law that if anyone ate food of the Underworld they were bound to live there forever. What could Persephone do? On the one hand, she was bound to Hades and his kingdom; on the other, she felt pity for her mother and the starving people in the world above. At last Zeus settled it. For six months of each year Persephone was to live in the Upper World and bring spring and summer to the Earth; for the other six months she was to live in the Underworld as Hades' queen, co-ruler of the shadow-world. From that day on the pattern of growth and withering, the cycle of the seasons, was forever fixed.

This was one of the most potent of all myths in the ancient Greek world. Demeter and Persephone were worshipped together as 'The Twain', especially by women, and were thought to represent the essential dualities which ensured the continuity of existence: light/dark, impetus/stasis, birth/death. In the Underworld, Persephone was a kind of mediator between the Dead and the gods of darkness –

and this role, worked up in cult terms in Roman times, was transmuted by the early Christian church into one aspect of the Virgin **Mary**, who intercedes for human souls before God's judgement seat as Persephone did before Hades.

»+ farming, fertility, mysteries, Onatah

PERSEUS
Europe (South)

Perseus ('sacker'), in Greek myth, was the son of **Zeus** and **Danaë**. His mortal grandfather Acrisius, afraid of an oracle that Danaë's child would grow up to kill him, locked mother and child in a box soon after Perseus was born, and threw it into the sea. A fisherman rescued them, and Perseus was brought up by Polydectes, king of the tiny island of Seriphos. Polydectes wanted to marry Danaë, but she refused, and so long as Perseus was there to protect her, there was no way to force her. But one day, when Perseus (now grown-up) and Polydectes were trying to out-boast each other, Perseus rashly said that if Polydectes ordered it, he would go at once, cut off a **Gorgon**'s head and bring it back. Delighted, Polydectes agreed at once.

Perseus and Medusa. Of the three Gorgons, the only one with a trace of mortality was **Medusa**. But she could turn a man to stone with a single glance, and Perseus could think of no way to get near enough to cut off her head. The gods lent him prized possessions: **Hades**' helmet of invisibility, **Hermes**' winged sandals, **Athene**'s shield (polished as dazzling as a mirror) and **Hephaestus**' sickle made entirely of

diamonds. Wearing Hermes' sandals, Perseus was able to run in air as easily as people run on land. Athene guided him to Cisthene, the land, beyond the river Ocean that girds the world, where the Gorgons lived.

The Gorgons' lair was part of a vast underground cave-system, pitch-black and cold as death. There they slept, snuffling like dreaming dogs. Their sisters the **Graeae** guarded the entrance. They had only one eye and one tooth among them, and while two of them slept, the third took the eye and tooth and stayed on guard; then, when her watch was over, she woke one of her sisters and handed over the eye and tooth. Wearing Hades' helmet of invisibility, Perseus waited until this moment of changeover, then snatched eye and tooth and hurried down the cave-corridor into pitch darkness, leaving the Graeae fumbling and cursing behind him.

The three Gorgons slept in a heap. To make sure that he never looked once into Medusa's eyes, Perseus avoided facing her directly and worked behind his back, with Athene's mirror-shield to guide him. Reversing every normal movement, he lifted Hephaestus' sickle and severed Medusa's neck. Her head bumped on the ground, and he snatched it up by the nearest snake-hairs and crammed it into a bag. Blood spurted from Medusa's neck, and where it touched the ground it grew into a winged horse, **Pegasus**. Perseus leapt on its back and flew out of the cave and away from Cisthene before Medusa's Gorgon-sisters even realized what had happened. On his way, he tossed down the eye and tooth which belonged to the

Graeae: they fell into Lake Tritonis in Africa, leaving the Graeae blind and defenceless forever.

Perseus and Andromeda. On his way from Cisthene home to Seriphos, Perseus landed twice. The first time was at the feet of **Atlas**, the **giant** condemned by the gods to support the sky forever. Perseus showed him the Gorgon's head and turned him to stone – the Atlas **Mountains**, whose peaks still support the sky. Later, looking down at the North African coast, Perseus saw a woman chained to the rocks. Her name was **Andromeda**, and she was fastened there as food for a sea-**monster**. (Her mother Cassiope had boasted that she and Andromeda were more beautiful than the sea-nymphs, **Poseidon**'s servants, and this was the punishment Poseidon had decreed.) Perseus drew his diamond-sickle, plunged into the sea on Pegasus and killed the monster just as it reared up to snatch Andromeda. He asked to marry Andromeda – and when her parents refused and sent soldiers against him, he showed them the Gorgon's head and turned them all to stone before taking Andromeda on Pegasus and soaring away to Seriphos.

Perseus and Polydectes. While Perseus had been killing Medusa, Polydectes had tried to force Danaë to marry him. She had taken refuge in Athene's temple, and Polydectes and his guards stood in a ring round it, waiting for her to weaken. When Perseus and Andromeda soared overhead on Pegasus, Polydectes and his soldiers looked up to see what was approaching – and Perseus showed them Medusa' head and turned them to a circle of stones which can still be seen.

Perseus returned the helmet, sickle, winged sandals and mirror-shield to the gods, and gave Athene Medusa's head to fix on the front of her shield. He and Andromeda flew on Pegasus to find a new kingdom. On the way, he dropped his sword, and decided to build a city on the place where it fell. He called his new citadel Mycenae after the word *myces* (sword-hilt), and ruled there until the day he died and was taken into **Olympus**. The people of Seriphos and Mycenae soon began to worship him as a god, and he often appeared to them in the form of a warrior seven times mortal size.

≫→ heroes

PHAEDRA
Europe (South)

Phaedra (Phaidra, 'bright'), in Greek myth, was the daughter of King Minos and Queen **Pasiphaë** of Crete, and the sister of **Ariadne**. She married King **Theseus** of Athens, and bore him two children, Acamas and Demophoön. But during the wedding Theseus and his guests had been attacked by a group of **Amazons** led by **Antiope**, the mistress Theseus had abandoned to marry Phaedra, and Theseus had killed Antiope. The gods waited to punish him until his and Antiope's son **Hippolytus** was grown-up. Then they used the innocent Phaedra as instrument of their vengeance. Driven momentarily insane, Phaedra asked Hippolytus to have **sex** with her, and when he refused she told Theseus that Hippolytus had tried to rape her. Theseus prayed to the gods to punish his son, and **Poseidon** killed the boy in a chariot crash.

Phaedra realized what she'd done, and hanged herself.

PHAETHON
Europe (South)

Phaethon (Greek Phaithon, 'blazing'), in Roman myth, was the son of the **Sun** and the **ocean-nymph** Clymene. An arrogant youth, he demanded proof of his paternity, and when the Sun asked what proof would be enough said that if he could harness the Sun's horses and gallop his fiery chariot across the **sky**, he would be satisfied. His father said that he himself was the only being able to control the horses; not even **Jupiter** could manage them, and if Phaethon tried he would be killed. But Phaethon insisted, yoked the horses and galloped away across the sky.

Phaethon's ride was disastrous. The horses galloped out of control, night turned to day and the chariot one minute spun into outer space and seared the stars, the next skimmed the surface of **Gaia** (**Mother Earth**), charring tilled land to desert and drying up the seas. At last Gaia complained to Jupiter, who toppled Phaethon from the chariot with a thunderbolt and sent him plummeting into the river Po, where he drowned. The Sun's horses galloped home to their master, and Clymene and her nymphs gathered Phaethon's body from the river and buried it. They stood on the banks, weeping for him, until the Sun took pity on them and turned them into alders.

*This myth was invented, soon after the first Roman expeditions to the interior of Africa, to explain the deserts and dark-skinned people the Romans found there. Its origins lie in the Egyptian story of **Sekhmet**, from the Upper Nile – which may explain the apparent standoff in power between the Sun (**Ra**) and Jupiter, not a standard feature of the kind of Greek myth this purports to be. Its definitive version, in Ovid's **Metamorphoses**, is notable for the lively characterization of Phaethon and his father.*

PHILEMON: *see* Baucis and Philemon

PHILOCTETES
Europe (South)

Philoctetes (Philoktetes, 'loves possessions'), in Greek myth, was, in some accounts, an **Argonaut**, the son of Poeas and Demonassa and a friend of **Heracles**. At the end of Heracles' time on earth, it was Philoctetes who lit the funeral pyre which burned away the hero's mortality and made it possible for him to enter **Olympus** as a god, and in gratitude Heracles gave him his bow and unerring arrows. In other accounts, Philoctetes was a passing shepherd who saw Heracles' agony, lit the pyre and was rewarded with the bow.

Armed with the bow, Philoctetes joined the group of princes who went to Sparta as suitors for **Helen**, and later arrived in Aulis to take part in the expedition to bring her back from Troy. But he was not allowed to sail. Some say that the cause was **Hera**, angry with him for helping Heracles enter **Olympus**; others that he broke an oath he had sworn to Heracles not to reveal where the **hero**'s mortal ashes were buried – broke it by tapping one foot on the ground above the spot. Whatever the reason, one of the poisoned arrows slipped from the quiver and stabbed his foot, and the stench of the wound was such that the Greeks marooned him on an island – either Lemnos or the sacred island of Chryse – and sailed without him.

During the ten years of the **Trojan War**, Philoctetes sat on the island nursing his wound and feeding his hatred of the Greeks. Meanwhile, in Troy, the gods ordained that the city would not fall except with the help of Heracles' bow and arrows. **Odysseus** and **Diomedes** (or, in some accounts, Odysseus and **Neoptolemus**) set out to persuade Philoctetes to give up his anger and go to Troy with them. At first he spat at them, furious and disdainful, but the gods intervened and at last he agreed to what they asked. Outside Troy, the doctors Machaon and Podalirius laid him in Apollo's sanctuary, and drugged him asleep while they cleaned his wounded foot and poulticed it. The gods – who were as anxious as the Greeks to end the war – saw to it that the medicine worked at once, and when Philoctetes awoke next day he found both his health and his wits restored.

Philoctetes challenged **Paris** to a duel, bow against bow. Paris shot first, and missed. Then Philoctetes set one of Heracles' unerring arrows to his string and fired. The arrow hit Paris in the ankle, poison flowed into his body, and he died. This was the end of Philoctetes' moment of glory. He had done what the gods intended him to do, starting the chain of events which ended the war.

He tried to swagger his way into the councils of the Greek leaders, and once again they would have none of him. Sulkily, he set sail before the final onslaught against the city. He landed in Southern Italy, founded a small town, Petilia, and lived there in obscurity until he died, boasting to the end about his immortal friend and his part in the greatest adventure the world had ever seen – boasting to people who had no idea what he was talking about, or what it meant.

➤ **archers**

PHINEUS
Europe (South)

Phineus ('sea-eagle'), King of Salmydessus in Greek myth, married the North Wind's daughter Cleopatra, and they had two sons. When the boys were full-grown, Cleopatra died, and Phineus' second wife Idaea, afraid that they would take the succession from her own children, accused the young men of trying to rape her, and – since no blind person could inherit the throne – persuaded Phineus to let her punish them by putting out their eyes. For allowing this atrocity, **Zeus** told Phineus to choose between **death** and blindness, and when he chose blindness sent **Harpies** to peck out his eyes and steal his food. It was not until Calais and Zetes, sons of the North Wind, called at Salmydessus with the **Argonauts** that the Harpies were finally driven away, Idaea was punished and Phineus was restored to health. Because he could never recover his lost eyes, Zeus compensated by giving him second hearing and second sight.

In another version of the story, Cleopatra and Idaea played no part. Phineus had second sight from childhood, but rashly used it to tell the gods' secrets to strangers. When **Phrixus** landed in Salmydessus after **Helle** fell from the golden ram, Phineus told him how to get to Colchis and find the secret palace of Aeëtes, son of the **Sun** – and **Helius** the Sun-god punished him by blinding him.

PHLEGETHON
Europe (South)

Phlegethon ('blazing'), in Greek and Roman myth, was one of the rivers of the **Underworld** – a torrent not of **water** but of **fire**.

PHRIXUS
Europe (South)

Phrixus (Phrixos, 'spiky-haired'), in Greek myth, was the son of **Athamas** and **Nephele**. His father was ordered to sacrifice him to end a blight on the crops, but **Zeus** intervened and sent **Heracles** to the rescue, riding a winged ram with a golden fleece. Phrixus and his sister **Helle** flew on the ram out of danger. Helle was killed on the journey, but Phrixus landed safely in Colchis, where he sacrificed the ram to Zeus and hung its fleece in a temple guarded by a dragon. He married Chalciope, daughter of King Aeëtes, and they lived happily for a time and had several children. But Aeëtes coveted the **Golden Fleece**, murdered Phrixus and stole it – the crime which later gave **Jason** and the **Argonauts** an excuse to sail North and steal the Fleece.

PICUS AND CANENS
Europe (South)

Picus ('woodpecker'), in Roman myth, was the son of Saturn (**Cronus**), and was chosen by the gods to be the new king of Latium in Italy after **Janus** left **Mother Earth** for **Olympus**. He was a horse-breeder and huntsman: his pleasures were galloping his thoroughbreds along the Milky Way, and searching Italy's forests and fields for game. He was young and handsome, and every wood-**nymph** in Italy fell in love with him; even **Pomona**, the orchard-goddess, languished for him for a whole growing-season, while the fruit hung wizened and untended on her trees.

In the end Picus married Janus' daughter Venilia, and the other nymphs had to hide their jealousy. Venilia was a river-nymph, and her singing was like a magic spell, taming wild beasts, soothing storms, drawing animals, birds, even rocks and trees to hear her. Her nickname was *Canens,* 'singing', and while Picus was away hunting or horse-riding she spent the time singing, until her maids dropped what they were doing and ran to listen.

One day Picus was hunting in the marshes beside the river **Tiber**. He wore a purple cloak fastened with a golden chain, and carried two broad-bladed boar-spears – and the **Sun**, glinting on the metal, caught the attention of **Circe**, witch-daughter of the Sun, who took it for a signal from her father and ran to it. As soon as she saw Picus she was transfixed, determined to have **sex** with him. She moulded a wisp of mist into a boar which only Picus could see or hear. He galloped after it, and it drew him farther and farther from his companions into the marshes. At last Circe confronted him. She begged him to forget Canens and make love with her: she was Circe, a god's child like himself. Picus angrily refused, and Circe changed him into a woodpecker and left him banging his head on a tree-trunk in despair.

As for Canens, when Picus failed to come home she ran to the marshes and searched for six days and nights, calling his name, neither eating nor sleeping. In the end she threw herself on a patch of grass beside the Tiber, and the river-god himself took pity on her, and turned her from a woman to a disembodied spirit. Her flesh and bones melted away, and all that was left was a voice, hovering and calling. She has wandered the fields and woods ever since, settling in the throats of this bird or that and lending them her song.

This myth, told here in a version derived from Ovid's **Metamorphoses**, *is paralleled by another, quite different, account of how Picus came to be connected with woodpeckers. In that, he was the son not of Saturn but of the baker-god Pilumnus. He gave his people oracles by tapping on the wooden arms of his throne – and after his death the gods, impressed by their accuracy, turned him into a woodpecker and gave all his woodpecker-descendants prophetic powers.*
≫→ prophecy

PILIRIN: *see* Tjinimin and Pilirin

PILLAN
Americas (South)

Pillan the **thunder**-god, in the myths of the Araucanian people of Chile, was barely in control of his own anger, and was forever hurling boulders and blazing torches about the sky, or racketing over the Earth's surface at the head of his gang of **demons** (**snake**-headed shooting stars), tearing up houses and flooding fields. He swarmed through the world of the Dead, picking up the seeds of crop-blight and human disease and carrying them to the upper world. His only benefit to mortals was accidental: by hurling a torch into a forest one day, he gave them **fire**.

PINGA
Arctic

Pinga, in Eskimo myth, was a hunting-goddess, the centre of shamanistic **mysteries** designed not to bridge the gap between life and **death** but to ensure plenty in this world. She herded animals, both on land and in the sea, and if the right ceremonies had been performed in her honour, she shepherded them towards the hunters.

PIPINOUKHE: *see* Nipinoukhe and Pipinoukhe

PIRITHOUS
Europe (South)

Pirithous and Theseus. Pirithous (Peirithoös, 'prancer'), in Greek myth, was the son either of **Ixion** and **Nephele** (the cloud made into a goddess by **Zeus** to prevent Ixion raping **Hera**), or of Dia and Zeus, who courted her in the form of a stallion, prancing round her and whinnying (hence Pirithous' name). He was still young and ambitious when he became king of the **Lapiths**, and set about making himself and his people famous. He first tried to do this by conquest, gathering an army and setting out to invade Athens – but when he and **Theseus** saw each other at the head of their soldiers, they abandoned all idea of fighting, ran to shake each others' hands and became as close friends as if they'd been **twins**.

The Lapiths and the Centaurs. Pirithous next tried to win honour by marrying Princess Hippodamia (not the Hippodamia who married **Pelops**). He invited to the wedding every **hero** in Greece, the entire herd of **Centaurs** (the people who lived next door to the Lapiths), and every god in **Olympus** – except **Ares**, who had caused such trouble at the wedding of **Peleus** and **Thetis**. Ares punished him by making sure that the Centaurs tasted wine (something entirely new to them) and then encouraging one of them, Eurytion or Eurytus, to try to kidnap Hippodamia. A battle ensued; the gods left in disgust and Pirithous, Theseus and **Heracles** routed the Centaurs, who ever afterwards remained the Lapiths' implacable enemies.

Pirithous in the Underworld. After this catastrophic beginning to his reign, Pirithous reduced his ambition, contenting himself with occasional adventures with Theseus and regular arguments and skirmishes with the Centaurs. But when Hippodamia died, he once again lost all reason. Theseus (also newly widowed) suggested that they each kidnap a daughter of Zeus and make her queen. They stole **Helen** of Sparta for Theseus, and then Pirithous suggested that, for him, they visit the **Underworld** and demand Queen **Persephone** herself.

They made their way to Hell, and demanded that **Hades** give them Persephone or suffer the consequences. Hades politely invited them to a banquet – but placed them on the Thrones of **Lethe**, which turned all who sat on them to stone. Heracles (who was in the Underworld at the same time, to steal **Cerberus**) rescued Theseus, but was too late to save Pirithous. In some accounts, the ground gaped open and swallowed him. In others, Cerberus tore him to pieces. In others again, Heracles begged Persephone to pardon Pirithous – and Persephone did so, allowing Heracles to take him to the Upper World, only to find that he had turned to stone on the way.

PISAKAS
India

Pisakas, in Hindu myth, were **demons** who haunted cemeteries and cremation grounds. The gods allowed them only the most unappetizing parts of sacrifices – hide, hair, hooves – and they therefore ate bits of corpses whenever they got the chance, regarding as particular delicacies the faeces left in a body's intestines. If they were really starving they crept into the bodies of the living mourners, though you could avoid this by covering your mouth and nose, snapping your fingers to frighten them off, and above all not farting.

PLUTO: *see* Hades

POHJOLA
Europe (North)

Pohjola ('far-land'), or Pohja, in Finnish myth, was the country of the ice-**giants** in the Far North, realm of the evil queen **Louhi**. Later Finns identified it as the part of their country, and of Lapland, which lay in the Arctic Circle, but in earlier myth it was utterly remote, a frozen continent in the no-man's-land between Earth and stars.

POIA
Americas (North)

Poia ('scar-face'), in the myths of the Blackfoot people of the Northern Plains (US and Canada), was the son of the Morning Star and the mortal woman Soatsaki. The Morning Star took Soatsaki to the court of his father the **Sun** in **Heaven**, hoping to grant her **immortality**. But she preferred Earth to Heaven and the Sun, insulted, sent her back to Earth to bear her son, and then let her die. The child was born with a port-wine birthmark – hence his name – and grew up with the Blackfoot people. He asked to marry the chief's daughter, but was rejected as 'blemished'. He set out to find his grandfather the Sun and ask for help, leaving the land and walking West across the sea on the path made by the Sun's reflection on the water. In Heaven he rescued his father Morning Star from seven birds of darkness, and the Sun rewarded him by removing his birthmark. He hurried down to Earth, along the **Milky Way**, and took his mortal beloved back into Heaven just as his father had fetched his mother there long before.

This myth lies at the heart of one of the core rituals of the Blackfoot people, the Sun Dance, taught to them by Poia when he returned to Earth.

POLLUX: *see* Dioscuri

POLUDNITSA
Europe (East)

The Poludnitsa (from *poluden* or *polden*, 'noon'), in Slavic and Russian myth, was a mischievous spirit who tormented people working in the fields, especially at midday in summer. She pinched them and pulled their hair, and if they failed to greet her politely, she took their children into the standing corn and lost them.

POLYDEUKES: *see* Dioscuri

POLYDORUS
Europe (South)

Polydorus (Polydoros, 'many gifts'), in Greek myth, was the youngest son of King **Priam** and Queen **Hecuba** of Troy. Before the **Trojan War**, Hecuba sent him for safety to King Polymnestor of Thrace and his queen Ilione, Hecuba's sister. She gave Polymnestor half the treasure of Troy to pay for the child's upbringing, hoping that when Polydorus was grown he would avenge the fall of Troy.

In some accounts, as soon as word reached Polymnestor that Priam was dead he butchered Polydorus and kept the treasure. Polydorus' ghost appeared to Hecuba (or, in some accounts, his bones were washed up on the shore near where the Trojan prisoners-of-war were waiting to be shipped back to Greece), and she took revenge on Polymnestor by blinding him and killing his sons. In other accounts, the baby Polydorus was substituted, as soon as he arrived in Thrace, for Polymnestor's newborn son Deiphilus; it was therefore Deiphilus whom Polymnestor killed, and when Polydorus (now grown-up) heard from the Delphic oracle who he really was, he punished Polymnestor's treachery by killing him. (What happened to Polydorus next is not recorded.)

Another tradition entirely says that during the war itself Polymnestor changed sides, and brought the child Polydorus to the Greek camp outside Troy. The Greeks flaunted the child outside the gates of Troy, and told Priam that they would exchange him for **Helen**. Priam refused, and they butchered Polydorus before his father's eyes. Yet another says that Polydorus never went to Thrace at all, but was a grown man who fought at Troy and was killed by **Achilles** – and indeed that he was not Priam's son by Hecuba at all, but by the Thracian princess Laothoë.

POLYNICES: *see* Eteocles and Polynices

POLYPHEMUS
Europe (South)

Polyphemus, Galatea and Acis. Polyphemus ('famous'), in Greek myth, was a **Cyclops**, son of a Sicilian **nymph** and either **Poseidon** or one of the Cyclopes who lived under Mount Etna and made thunderbolts for **Zeus**. He began as a peaceful shepherd, pasturing his flocks and herds in the water-meadows and making up songs and pipe-tunes to amuse them. What changed him was his unrequited passion for the sea-nymph Galatea. She was terrified of being wooed by a one-eyed, tree-sized **giant**, however gentle, and she already had a lover: the shepherd Acis. One day, Polyphemus found them together and crushed Acis' skull with a boulder. The gods changed Acis into a rippling stream whose waters carried Galatea out to sea, far out of Polyphemus' reach.

Polyphemus and Odysseus. Losing Galatea changed Polyphemus from shepherd to **monster**, sworn to destroy every member of the human race. For generations, no sailor who landed on Sicily lived to tell the tale. Then **Odysseus** passed that way on his journey home from the **Trojan War**. He went foraging with twelve crewmen, found Polyphemus' cave, made a meal there and politely waited until the Cyclops came home to thank him for his hospitality. For answer, Polyphemus blocked the cave-mouth, seized two crewmen and ate them alive. Next morning he ate two more for breakfast before sealing the cave-mouth and going off with his sheep to pasture.

While Polyphemus was away, Odysseus sharpened a green olive-branch and hardened it in the fire. Then he took beside him some skins of wine he'd brought from the ship, and waited. At evening Polyphemus returned, milked his ewes, stirred up the fire and killed two more men for supper. Odysseus offered him one of the wineskins. Polyphemus drank it dry and demanded another, and another –

this was the first wine he had ever tasted. He offered Odysseus a present in return, if Odysseus told him his name, and when Odysseus answered 'Nobody' he said, 'Your present is, I'll eat you last.' Then he fell into a drunken stupor, and Odysseus and his surviving crewmen heated the olive-pole red-hot and ground it into his eye, which bubbled and sizzled until all its sight was gone.

Polyphemus' screams brought the other Cyclopes running. 'What's the matter?' they called. 'Nobody's hurt me!' he answered. 'Well in that case, go back to sleep.' Polyphemus lay groaning until dawn. Then he lifted the stone to let his sheep out to pasture. He sat by the cave-mouth, feeling them as they passed to make sure that they were sheep not men. But Odysseus fastened each of his men to three fleecy sheep and covered them with wool, so that as the sheep passed out of the cave Polyphemus felt nothing but matted fleece. Odysseus himself went last, clinging under the belly of Polyphemus' fattest ram. Once he was back on board ship, instead of slipping quietly away, he shouted back to Polyphemus, taunting him and boasting that the Nobody who had tricked him was really Odysseus of Ithaca, greatest of **heroes**. For answer, Polyphemus hurled a rock the size of a house after them, then lifted his arms and prayed to Poseidon to drown Odysseus and all his men, or if their death was forbidden to make Odysseus' journey home the most dangerous any mortal had ever made.

Polyphemus and Aeneas. Months later, when **Aeneas** and his crew visited Sicily, also journeying from Troy, they found Achaemenides, one of Odysseus' crewmen, hiding terrified in the woods. In haste to leave, Odysseus had left him behind, and he'd spent the next months lurking in holes and hollow trees and only daring to come out at night. He'd hardly finished his story when the Trojans saw Polyphemus himself on the hillside: a vast, blind giant feeling his way with a pine-trunk. They splashed to their ships, taking Achaemenides with them, and rowed for deep water. At first Polyphemus didn't hear them. He came down to the shore and began to bathe the festering socket where his eye had been. Aeneas signed to his crew to row, and Polyphemus turned his face in their direction like a hound sniffing the air, then gave a shout which brought the whole group of Cyclopes running from their lairs. They roared and hurled rocks, and the Trojans bent to their oars and rowed for their lives.

POLYXENA
Europe (South)

Polyxena ('hospitable'), in Greek myth, was the youngest daughter of King **Priam** and Queen **Hecuba** of Troy. In some versions of her story she was a child. When the Trojans were ransoming **Hector**'s body, all Priam's treasure was exhausted before the scales balanced, and Polyxena offered **Achilles** her golden earrings to make up the weight. At this, Achilles offered Priam Hector's body and all the treasure back, in exchange for Polyxena's hand in marriage when she was old enough. It was meant lightly, but the story still spread through the Greek camp that

Priam had offered Polyxena to Achilles if he deserted the Greeks and fought for Troy, and when Achilles was finally killed many Greeks rejoiced.

In other versions, Polyxena was a grown woman. She hated Achilles for killing her brother **Troilus**, and pretended to admire him in order to trap him and kill him. She took him into Troy at night, slept with him – and wheedled out of him the secret of his immortal skin and its one vulnerable place, his heel. Then she arranged for Priam to invite Achilles to marry her; **Paris** was hiding behind the altar, and when Achilles came to the wedding he stabbed him or shot him in the heel and killed him.

Two different accounts are also given of Polyxena's death. In one, she was so distraught at Achilles' death that after the fall of Troy she took his sword and stabbed herself over his grave. In the other, the Greeks gave her as prisoner-of-war to Achilles' son **Neoptolemus**, and he sacrificed her on the grave and invited his father's ghost to drink her blood.

POMONA AND VERTUMNUS
Europe (South)

Pomona, a beautiful wood-**nymph** in Roman myth, lived in an orchard on the Palatine Hill beside the river **Tiber**, and was so busy with her trees that she had no time to spare for all the fauns, **satyrs** and tree-spirits who courted her. Her shyest suitor was the woodland-god Vertumnus. His task each autumn was to turn leaves from green to gold and float them to the ground to make new growth. But for the rest of the year he had nothing to do but watch Pomona working in the orchard, and hide behind a tree each time she looked his way. A thousand times Vertumnus plucked up his courage to declare his love, and a thousand times he drew back at the last moment. In the end he asked advice from Pales, the goddess of pastures after whom the Palatine Hill was named. 'You change the leaves in autumn,' she answered. 'Why not change yourself, from shy to bold, and see what she makes of that?'

Vertumnus tried every kind of transformation. He made himself a ploughman, a soldier, a fisherman, a beekeeper and a fruit-farmer, without success. He disguised himself as an old woman, and hobbled into the orchard in the heat of noon, carrying a cup of cool water. He offered Pomona a drink, but when she put the cup to her lips he was so overcome with love that he hugged her in a way no old woman ever would. Furiously she ordered him out of the orchard. He walked dejectedly through the trees, shaking the old-woman disguise from him as a dog shakes water – and was astounded to find Pomona gazing after him. She'd never seen him before as he really was, and now was transfixed with love.

From that moment on, the story ends, Pomona and Vertumnus have been inseparable. They have worked together in orchards, making ripe apples, instead of just green, a sunburst of autumn russets, yellows, golds and reds.

*In Ovid's **Metamorphoses**, from which this account is adapted, Vertumnus also tries to woo Pomona (in his old-woman* disguise) by telling her a myth within a myth. 'Iphis, a poor peasant, fell in love with Princess Anaxarete. But she refused him because of his humble birth, and made her heart as hard as stone. In despair, he hanged himself, and when Anaxarete found his body the stone in her heart engulfed her whole body and turned her into a statue.' It was when this story was no more successful than the transformations that Vertumnus shook off his old-woman disguise and Pomona recognized him for what he truly was. The Renaissance Italian painter Archimboldo, illustrating the main story, made Vertumnus' and Pomona's faces from a mass of different fruits, assembled into human shapes – and invented a whole new style of painting.

≫→ farming, fertility

POSEIDON
Europe (South)

Poseidon ('drink-giver' or 'master'; Latin Neptunus, Neptune), in Greek and Roman myth, was the son of **Cronus** and **Rhea**, and the brother of **Demeter**, **Hades**, **Hera**, Hestia and **Zeus**. In some accounts he was the original lord of the universe, and was supplanted by Zeus who banished him to the underwater kingdom. Poseidon hurled waves at Zeus' sky-kingdom, but was unable to reach it; he threw them at the land, and eroded it except where **Mother Earth** built cliffs to keep him at bay. In other accounts he was swallowed at birth by his father, was rescued by Zeus and joined him and the other gods in battle against the **Titans** for universal power. When the war was won Zeus, Poseidon and Hades cast lots for kingdoms, and Poseidon won the **sea**. He revolted briefly against Zeus, but was defeated and punished by being made to serve one year as slave to the mortal King **Laomedon** of Troy. After that he kept to his sea-kingdom, and there was generally peace between him and Zeus.

Poseidon's powers. To arm Poseidon in the battle against the Titans, the **Cyclopes** made him a trident with which he could fork up whole continents and islands. This became the instrument of his power. He used it to raise up new land from the seabed, or to sink existing countries below the waters – and often, exasperated by human wickedness, he hurled it at the mainland, causing **earthquakes**. He used it to stir the sea to fury, churning the foam into white horses. Poseidon himself could calm the waters with a single, horizon-spanning glance: to persuade him to do this, mortals sacrificed horses or bulls and threw them into the sea. When he came to shore to mate with mortal creatures, usually mares or women – which he often did – it was in the form of a stallion, and he gave all horses the power to open up new water-springs by stamping their hooves on the ground.

Poseidon's quarrels. Poseidon was never entirely satisfied with his sea-kingdom. Unwilling to challenge Zeus, he turned his attention to the land. He argued with **Athene** for power over Athens and Troezen, with Zeus over Aegina, with **Dionysus** over Naxos, with the **Sun** over Corinth and with Hera over Argolis. Three river-gods judged the last case, and when they supported Hera, Poseidon sealed their waters with a single trident-blow, so that to this day they are dusty and dry in summer.

Poseidon's queen. Looking for a consort to live with him under the sea as Hera lived in the sky with Zeus, Poseidon first approached his sister Demeter. But as his idea of wooing was to rape her in a water-meadow in Arcadia (where she was mourning the loss of **Persephone**), she rejected him. He next planned to marry the sea-**nymph Thetis**, daughter of **Nereus**, but just in time was told the secret held by **Prometheus** (that she was fated to bear a son greater than his father), and hastily abandoned her to a mortal husband, **Peleus**.

Finally Poseidon chose **Amphitrite**, grand-daughter of Ocean. The wedding was held with great pomp – mortals who glimpsed it told of a moonlight procession of stags, panthers, lions, horses, bulls, rams, tigers and every kind of sea-creature, each ridden by a sea-nymph, escorting bride, groom and their guests the gods across the wide, calm sea. Marriage to Amphitrite finally reconciled Poseidon to his underwater realm. He still kept aloof from the other gods; his anger still burst out from time to time and shook land or sea. But by and large he was content with his authority, and saved his fury for those who challenged it (for example **Odysseus**, who blinded his son **Polyphemus**). To most mortals he was generous, guiding their ships and filling their nets with fish. He and Amphitrite lived in an underwater palace near the island of Evia, had many children (most of them Tritons, that is merpeople with human bodies and fishes' tails) and ruled innumerable subjects, the creatures of the sea.

In ancient literature, Poseidon generally appeared either as an irascible senior god, Zeus' testy elder brother, or to mortals as a terrifying figure able to cross the universe in three strides and cause havoc with a single trident-throw. His amours were dreamlike and otherworldly, as often homosexual as heterosexual and combining the dignity and grace of a stallion with the violence of rape – Amphitrite was the only partner he ever wooed with gentleness. In art he is usually shown as a king in splendour, in a chariot pulled by dolphins and with Triton outriders, or standing with his courtiers on a throne mounted on a giant clam-shell. His hair, beard and clothes are water-streams, his eyes glare and he brandishes his trident. One of the most famous statues of all from ancient Greece shows him as a huge, naked warrior, with jutting beard and piercing eyes, his right arm bent back to hurl the trident (which will follow the line of his gaze). This statue was once thought to represent Zeus about to hurl a thunderbolt – the actual weapon is missing – but recent scholarship has identified it as Poseidon, and it is now a symbol of ancient Greek culture as universally recognized as the so-called 'funeral mask of Agamemnon' or the Parthenon themselves.

POSHAIYANKAYO
Americas (North)

Poshaiyankayo, in the myths of the Zuñi people of the Southwestern US Pueblos, was one of the countless creatures planted in the four cave-wombs of **Mother Earth** by the creator-spirit **Awonawilona**. Alone of all such creatures, he possessed intelligence, and he longed to leave the dark slime of Earth's womb for the bright sunlight of the surface. He tunnelled his way up, stood on the shore of the primordial ocean and prayed to Awonawilona (the rising **Sun**) to release his fellow-creatures into the light of day. Awonawilona sent sun-shafts to break open the Earth, and the creatures spilled out and stood on the green earth, howling and whining with terror. Gradually, as they accustomed themselves to the light, they scattered into the forests and hills: all the animals of creation. Some aspired higher, and soared into the air as birds; others stayed afraid of the light, and hid in the rivers and oceans as fish, or lurked in cracks as reptiles. A few waited with Poshaiyankayo to pray to Awonawilona – and they became the ancestors of the Zuñi. As soon as the people were established in their new home, Poshaiyankayo left them – some say that he sailed up a sun-shaft to be united with Awonawilona, others that he was absorbed into Mother Earth. He has not been seen again on Earth, but the myth ends by saying that when his people have desperate need of him, he will return.

In other versions of this myth, Poshaiyankayo is called Poseyemu, and he is the brother of the corn-goddess, formed from a seed placed inside a nutshell.

POTOK-MIKHAILO IVANOVICH
Europe (East)

Potok-Mikhailo Ivanovich, in Slavic myth, was one of the *bogatiri*. He and his wife each vowed to commit suicide if the other died. Soon after the wedding, she died and Potok buried her in a tomb with a secret entrance, and a rope connected to the cathedral bell. He led his horse into the tomb and waited until dark. At midnight he was surrounded by snake-**demons**, and a fiery serpent appeared and threatened him. Potok cut off its head with his sword and anointed his wife's body with its blood. At once she came to life, he pulled the rope and the sound of the cathedral bell brought everyone running to rescue them.

⋙→ **heroes**

PRAHLADA
India

Prahlada, in Hindu myth, was the son of the **demon Hiranyakashipu**. His father tried to usurp the powers and honours of the gods, and Prahlada was the only being in the universe still to stay loyal to **Vishnu**. His father tried to torture him into submission, and then to kill him, but Vishnu protected him against each attack. In the end, when Hiranyakashipu mocked Prahlada's assertion that Vishnu was all-powerful and everywhere in the universe, Vishnu took the form of **Narasimha** the man-lion, surged out of a pillar in Hiranyakashipu's palace and tore him to pieces. The god then crowned Prahlada king in Hiranyakashipu's place, and order and harmony returned, for a time, to the mortal world.

PRAJAPATI (BUDDHA'S FOSTER-MOTHER)
India

Prajapati, in Buddhist myth, was the sister and fellow-queen of **Buddha**'s mother **Maya**. When Maya died of joy seven days after Buddha's birth, Prajapati nursed the infant as her own. Her own son **Ananda** became Buddha's inseparable companion and, later, chief disciple.

PRAJAPATI (CREATOR)
India

Prajapati the Creator. Prajapati ('lord of **creation**') was already an ancient god at the time of the Aryan invasions of India in the seventeenth century BCE, and survived in shadowy form right through to the Hindu period, when he became merged with **Brahma**. There were 33 Vedic gods (eleven for each of the three kingdoms, **Sky**, Earth and Middle Air); Prajapati was the 34th, the entity which encompassed them all. In some accounts, he made himself from the primordial **sea**, and wept to see the emptiness. Those of his teardrops which fell into the ocean made continents and islands; those he dashed from his eyes flew into the sky to make stars and planets. Prajapati then unpeeled his own body like an onion, and the pieces made (in order) darkness and its creatures the **demons**, moonlight and its creatures human beings, twilight and the seasons, daylight and its creatures the gods, and last of all **death**.

Prajapati and Ushas. In another creation-myth, Prajapati made the first gods not by sexual union (for there was no other being to mate with) but by meditation, fasting and contemplation. Among the first gods was his daughter, **Ushas** the dawn, and she was so beautiful that when he saw her he had an immediate erection, the first in the universe. Terrified, she turned into a doe, whereupon he became a rampant stag, and his semen spilled on Earth and made human beings. In another version of this myth, Prajapati physically mated with Ushas, and their offspring were all created things, born in pairs, male and female in due sequence.

Prajapati the creative principle. In later Hindu thought, Prajapati was rationalized as one half of the principle of creation. He symbolized potency, the primal creative urge. (The other half was **Vishvakarman**, creator and shaper.) Sometimes he was given his own name, Prajapati; sometimes he was Brahma; sometimes he was a nameless, bodiless entity, an idea known as Ka ('who?').

PRAJAPATIS, THE
India

The Prajapatis ('lords of **creation**'), in some of the Vedic myths of the Aryans who invaded India in the seventeenth century BCE, were ten spirits brought into being by **Brahma** to see to the detailed creation of the world. Their names were Angiras, Atri, **Brighu**, **Daksha** (also called Pracheta), Kratu, Marichi, Narada, Pulaha, Pulastya, Vashishta, and they made or fathered everything in existence, from gods to flowers, from **demons** to the **Sun**, **Moon** and stars.

PRIAM
Europe (South)

Priam's name. Priam ('bought'), in Greek myth, was the son of King **Laomedon** of Troy and Placia, daughter of the river-god Strymon. He was originally called Podarces ('bear-foot'), and was still a baby when his father promised his sister Hesione to **Heracles** and then broke his word. Heracles sacked Troy, killed Laomedon and all his sons except for Podarces, whom he sold in the slave-market. Hesione bought her brother and changed his name to Priam – and Heracles derisively put the baby on the throne of the devastated city, a helpless king for a helpless state.

Priam's family. Priam reigned for three generations, and made Troy the most glittering and powerful city in the area. He had a harem of wives, led by Queen **Hecuba**, and innumerable children (including fifty sons by Hecuba alone). His children included **Cassandra** the prophet (and her **twin Helenus**), **Laocoön** the priest, the **heroes Hector** and **Paris**, and the young children **Polyxena** and **Polydorus**, both of whom were sacrificed after the fall of Troy.

Priam and the Trojan War. Priam never forgot his sister Hesione, who had bought him from the slave-market as a baby. Heracles had taken her to Greece and married her to his friend Telamon – and seventy years later (by which time Hesione was well into her eighties) Priam sent his son Paris with a warfleet to bring her back (or, some say, to steal a Greek princess in recompense). Paris returned not with Hesione but with **Helen** of Sparta, and shortly afterwards the Greeks sent a fleet crammed with heroes to sack Troy and rescue her.

By the time of the **Trojan War**, Priam was old and feeble. His sons, and in particular Prince Hector, managed state affairs, and he ruled in name only. He took no part in the fighting, and his main contributions to the war were lamentation when his children were killed and pathetic attention to the exact details of recovering and burying their bodies, so that their souls would have peace in the **Underworld**. After the trick of the **Wooden Horse**, when the Greeks were sacking Troy, **Neoptolemus** killed Priam's son Polites at Priam's feet, and the aged king found a last spark of fury and hurled a spear at Neoptolemus. The spear-cast was too weak to do harm, but Neoptolemus responded by dragging Priam to the family altar, butchering him there and carrying his head back to the Greek camp in triumph.

PRIAPUS
Europe (South)

Priapus ('pruner'), in Greek myth, was **Aphrodite**'s son, fathered either by **Adonis** or by **Zeus**. **Hera**, still smarting because Aphrodite had been judged more beautiful by **Paris**, blighted the child in her womb, with the result that he was born impotent, ugly and so foulnatured that the gods refused to have him in **Olympus** and threw him down to Earth, where he was brought up by shepherds or orchard-**nymphs**.

Priapus became a companion of **Pan** and the **satyrs**, a spirit of **fertility** and growth. But Hera's curse of impotence made him always more eager than able to consummate his lust. Once, for example, he tried to rape the sleeping nymph Lotis – and just as he was about to enter her a donkey brayed (or in some accounts, howled with laughter) and his erection disappeared. In the end lust gave him a permanent erection, and his penis grew so large that he was unable to move. He stood at the entrance to the woods where Pan and the satyrs were revelling, and frightened off unwanted visitors by lifting his tunic and brandishing his penis like an angry-looking club.

Priapus-statues were common everywhere in ancient Greece and Rome, standing on guard at doorways, crossroads and gateways into fields. (In Athens, Priapus was confused with **Hermes**, *so that the door-guarding statue was a god with winged helmet and sandals and a huge erection.) To propitiate Priapus, you stroked his penis as you passed.*
≫→ **farming, sex**

PRIPARCHIS AND KREMARA
Europe (East)

Priparchis and Kremara, in Slavic myth, had one crucial function: to protect domestic pigs. Priparchis made sure that piglets were successfully born and weaned, and Kremara looked after them from then until they were slaughtered. Priparchis had no particular ceremonies of worship, but to invoke Kremara you poured beer into the fire – a pungent smell he loved.

PRISNI
India

Prisni ('speckled'), in the Vedic myths of the Aryans who invaded India in the seventeenth century BCE, was the goddess of soil and compost. In some accounts she took the form of a cow

(see **bulls and cows**), and her continuous supply of milk symbolized and guaranteed the ground's **fertility**.

In some accounts, Prisni, not **Diti**, was the mother of the **Maruts**.
≫→ **bulls and cows**

PRIVITHI
India

Privithi ('earth'), in the Vedic myths of the Aryans who invaded India in the seventeenth century BCE, was **Mother Earth**. She was the consort of **Dyaus** (Father **Sky**), and their children included **Ushas** (Dawn), **Indra** (**Rain**) and some say **Agni** (**Fire**). Privithi was particularly associated with agriculture and the problems of everyday life. Once, she complained to **Brahma** that she was overpopulated: humankind swarmed on her like termites. Brahma sent **Death**, a beautiful woman whose tears were deadly diseases, and the human race was culled. Privithi was also the goddess of purity and honesty. She was the last judge when all other appeals failed; **Shiva**, for example, appealed to her when he was accused of adultery.
≫→ **Dyavaprivithi, farming, justice and universal order**

PROCRUSTES
Europe (South)

Procrustes ('stretcher'), in Greek myth, was a **giant** who lived beside the river Cephisus near Athens. He welcomed travellers, feasting them and offering them a bed for the night. But he had only one guest-bed, and if his visitors were too long for it, he cut off their legs to make them fit; if they were too short he lengthened them on a rack. **Theseus**, travelling from Troezen to Athens, stayed with him – and turned the tables on him, first stretching him on his own rack and then chopping him into pieces. The phrase 'Procrustean bed' became proverbial for a situation with only two ways out, each as bad as the other.

PROMETHEUS
Europe (South)

Prometheus ('forethought'), in Greek myth, was the son of the **Titan** Iapetus and the **sea-nymph** Clymene (or, some say, the Titan **Themis**). His half-brother **Atlas** helped the Titans in their war against the gods, and was punished for it. But Prometheus supported the gods, and was favoured by them. He also held **Zeus**' aching head for **Hephaestus** to split open and release **Athene**, and in gratitude she taught him all arts and sciences, the knowledge of the gods.

Prometheus makes mortals. Prometheus moulded mud into dolls, small statues of the gods. They were the first fine art, the first copies of reality made for no other reason than to give delight – and they were also the origin of humankind, for Athene was so charmed by them that she breathed on them and gave them life. Prometheus, equally delighted, planned to teach them all-knowledge, but Zeus refused permission. The human race had been created by gods and could not be uncreated, but Zeus decreed that they were to be confined to Earth, not to be allowed into **Heaven** or the **Underworld**). Denied **immortality** and knowledge, they were to be as ignorant as plants or brute beasts.

Mortals and fire. Prometheus pitied his **creation**, but could find no way to give them knowledge. To help them in other ways, he strengthened their diet by making them meat-eaters. He took one of the **Sun**'s magnificent bulls, slaughtered it, skinned it and divided the meat. He wrapped the bones and fat in the hide, and the meat in the foul-smelling stomach. Then he invited Zeus to choose: one bag for the gods, one for mortals, to fix the way of sacrifice for all eternity. Zeus chose the hide – and when Prometheus revealed that this meant that mortals were allowed the meat of sacrifice, while the gods were permitted only the waste parts, he said, 'So be it. But they must eat their meat raw. From now on, they are forbidden fire.' He also sent them **Pandora** with her boxful of plagues.

Prometheus waited until the gods were feasting on **Olympus**, then went to the smithies where **Hephaestus** and the **Cyclopes** forged thunderbolts for Zeus. He stole a spark of fire, hid it in a hollow fennel-stalk, and carried it down to mortals. Fire gave them power over all other creatures on Earth, a fragment of the gods' authority; they became in reality what they had so far only been in image, little models of the gods. In a rage, Zeus stunned Prometheus with a thunderbolt, then had him pegged to a rock on Mount Caucasus on the boundary of Earth (being) and **Chaos** (nothingness) – or, some say, in the lowest depths of the Underworld. Every day a vulture gorged itself on his liver; every night the liver renewed itself. Zeus ordained no end for

Prometheus' torment unless another immortal agreed to take on his suffering, and unless he revealed a secret about the future of the universe which he alone knew.

Prometheus freed. Prometheus suffered on Mount Caucasus for 30,000 mortal years. Ocean-nymphs (his mother's sisters) and gods begged him to reveal the secret, bow to Zeus and win his freedom, but he refused. Then **Chiron** the **Centaur** was accidentally wounded by one of **Heracles'** poisoned arrows, and begged Zeus for death. Zeus asked if he would trade agonies with Prometheus, and Chiron said he would; then Zeus offered Prometheus forgiveness and freedom if he revealed the secret. **Mother Earth** in person begged Prometheus to give way, and her prayers persuaded him. He told the secret: it was that **Thetis** the sea-nymph was fated to bear a son greater than his father – important information, as Zeus' brother **Poseidon** was preparing to marry her – and the gods hastily gave her instead to a mortal, **Peleus**. Chiron stood ready to take Prometheus' place on Mount Caucasus, but Zeus turned him into a constellation of stars instead and sent Heracles to kill the vulture and set Prometheus free.

In some accounts, Prometheus made the mud for mortals by mixing dust with his own tears or semen. In others, he used clay from the area which later became the town of Chaeronea in Boeotia. The ground there is mainly thick, brown clay, and it is often baked by the sun into distorted shapes like half-completed sculptures. There are also many stones, human-size, scattered

about. These were said to be petrified lumps of clay discarded by Prometheus as he worked.

The Prometheus myth received its grandest ancient treatment at the hands of Aeschylus, who wrote several plays about it, of which one alone survives: Prometheus Bound, *describing Prometheus' imprisonment and his railing against the injustice of Zeus. Some modern scholars dispute the Aeschylean authorship of this play, but it remains one of the seminal works of European drama, and was especially popular in the nineteenth century, when its outbursts against tyranny and hymns to the freedom of the soul struck chords with revolutionary sentiment. In fine art, only the tearing of Prometheus' liver has been frequently depicted: the idea of a colossus in chains, heroically suffering, has had power down the ages. In ancient Greece, however, the slang name for children's toy dolls (like the figures in a more modern farm scene or townscape) was 'Prometheus' babies.'*

≫→ Chinigchinich, civilization, Enki, Esaugetuh Emissee, Humanmaker, Hurukan, Na'pi, Tagaro, Woyengi

PROPHECY

One of the gods' attributes most envied by mortals was freedom from time. To an immortal, time was not progressive but a continuum, a landscape which could be surveyed in its entirety from any point and in any direction. (One god, **Odin** in Nordic myth, had to learn the secrets of eternity in a highly painful manner; another, **Zeus** in Greek myth, had to be told his own future by **Prometheus**; but they were exceptions.) Most gods were reluctant to share all-knowledge with humans, and punished any mortals (such as **Adam and Eve** in

Mesopotamian myth) who tried to usurp it. Others took a malicious delight in letting us see only a fraction of the pattern and watching the devastation this caused us. A few, however, did risk their colleagues' displeasure by sharing everything they knew, albeit usually in garbled forms which only chosen priests could interpret. Sometimes they walked the Earth in person, entrancing chosen humans and revealing **mysteries**, or filling the air with sounds and sensations which specially-gifted mortals could interpret. A few humans learned or were given the skills of second hearing (understanding every language and sound in creation) and second sight (being able to see into the past and future as easily as into the present). Others used magic and potions to make themselves receptive to the secrets of the gods. But to learn the gods' secrets was to surrender part of one's own mortality, and human prophets seldom lived comfortable lives.

≫→ (Americas): Ghede, Tezcatlipoca; (Australia): Darana; (Celtic): Bran, Finn MacCool, Merlin, Taliesin; (China): Guan Di; (Egypt): Hap: (Greece): Apollo, Calchas, Cassandra, Helenus, Melampus, Proteus, Sibyls, Tiresias, Trophonius; (Japan): Tsukuyomi; (Mesopotamia): Kusor, Mammitu; (Nordic): Mimir, Odin; (Rome): Picus and Canens; (Slavic): Svarozich

PROSE EDDA, THE
Europe (North)

The *Prose Edda* (c 1220) by Snorri Sturluson (1179-1241) is one of the prime sources for surviving Nordic myth. 'Edda', connected with the English word 'ode', is a poetical work dealing with matters from myth or religion, and Snorri's book is a critical discussion of what the ancient Eddas were, how they were written and what they contained. In the course of it he quotes the earlier poems and retells many of their stories with a mixture of his own scholarly precision and the heady metaphor of the originals – qualities which give Norse myth the unique flavour preserved in most later retellings.

PROSERPINA: *see* Persephone

PROSPERITY: *see* Dagda, El Dorado, Four Dragon Kings, Inari, Lakshmi, Rosmerta, Ruhanga, Shou Lao, Tsai Shen, Ukemochi, Yacatecuhtli, Yu

PROTEUS
Europe (South)

Proteus ('first one'), the Old Man of the Sea in Greek myth, was one of the oldest beings in the universe. His father was Ocean, the river which binds **Heaven** and Earth. He herded and protected sea-creatures as a land-shepherd herds sheep, and as a reward **Poseidon** gave him the gift of unerring **prophecy**. Any mortal who could find him and ask him about the future was sure of a true reply. The problem was catching him. Like all ancient gods he had no fixed form, but changed shape at will, becoming smoke, a tiger, a whirlwind or a water-spout in enquirers' hands.

Proteus' daughter Eidothea was the only person in the universe who knew the secret of how to catch Proteus, and she told it to a few favoured mortals. Every day at noon he rested on the island of Pharos at the mouth of the River Nile; he counted the seals basking there, and when he was sure all were safe he settled down for a nap. Eidothea told mortals that they should dress in sealskins, lie among the seals and wait until Proteus dozed, then creep up on him and hold him however he transformed himself. Eventually he would assume manageable, human shape and answer their questions. **Menelaus**, affected by flat calm while sailing home from the **Trojan War**, made use of this strategy to discover how to raise a wind, and **Aristaeus** also used it when he was trying to find how to restock his hives with bees.

In some accounts, Proteus is identified with the first Egyptian pharaoh Menes – presumably because of Menes' reputation for wisdom, and the belief that all Egyptian rulers were also gods. Euripides, in Helen, *explains that Proteus took the title 'pharaoh' after the island Pharos on which he built his palace.*

➤ **shape-changers**

PSYCHE
Europe (South)

Psyche ('soul'), in Roman myth, was the youngest daughter of the king and queen of Sicily. She was the most beautiful person on the island, and suitors flocked to ask for her hand. In the end she boasted that she was more beautiful even than Venus (see **Aphrodite**) herself, and Venus sent Cupid (see **Eros**) to transfix her with an arrow of desire and make her fall in love with the nearest person or thing available. But even Cupid fell in love with her. He took her to a secret palace, in a flowery valley surrounded by needle-cliffs. Every day invisible attendants saw to her every need, and every night in the darkness the god came to her bed and made love with her. He told her never on any account to look at him, for on the day she did so she would die.

Psyche was the happiest person in the world, and the loneliest. One night she persuaded Cupid to let her sisters visit her, and he sent the West Wind to waft them to her palace. They admired Psyche's home, clothes, garden, life of luxury – but told her that the reason her husband refused to let her see him must be because he was a **monster**. They gave her a knife and a lamp and told her to wait until he was asleep that night, then light the lamp and kill him. Psyche did as she was told, lighting the lamp and lifting the knife – but when instead of a monster she saw Cupid in all his glory lying in the bed, her hands shook in surprise, and a drop of boiling oil fell from the lamp and scalded Cupid's shoulder. Psyche fainted, and when she recovered the palace and gardens had vanished, and she was alone in a country she had never seen before.

Desperately, Psyche wandered the countryside, begging help. She asked Ceres (**Demeter**), and the harvest-goddess said that she was not allowed to interfere between husband and wife. Psyche asked **Pan**, and the herdsman-god said that he understood only sheep and goats, not people. Finally Psyche asked Venus herself, and Venus set her a series of impossible tasks. First she took her to a barn filled with a mess of millet, wheat and barley grains, and told her to sort them by morning. Ceres sent ants, who collected the grains and placed them in three neat piles. Next Venus told Psyche to catch a ram with a golden fleece, pluck its wool and weave a headdress by morning. This time Pan helped, and the job was done. Furious, Venus gave Psyche the third task: to fetch a cup of water from the river **Lethe** in the **Underworld** – something no mortal had ever done before and lived.

At this point **Jupiter** intervened. He sent his eagle to fly down to the Underworld and fill the cup. Then he went to Cupid's bedroom, where the god was tossing in agony from his oil-burned shoulder. Jupiter rubbed the place with **ambrosia**, and Cupid leapt up cured and restored to his former vigour. Jupiter summoned Psyche, Venus and Cupid for judgement. He said that all Psyche's tasks were done, and therefore Venus must allow her to enter **Olympus**. But the prophecy that if Psyche ever saw her secret husband she would die must also be fulfilled. Psyche must forfeit her mortality. At this point Cupid begged for Psyche to be allowed to marry him, and Jupiter gave permission, on condition that Cupid settled down and stopped firing arrows of desire at the gods, saving his havoc solely for the human race.

The judgement over, Jupiter gave Psyche **ambrosia** to eat, and mortality fell from her like a cloak. She married Cupid, settled in Olympus and in due course bore an immortal child, the goddess Pleasure. As for Psyche's

sisters, Cupid punished them by filling them with insatiable desire not for other mortals but for Psyche's golden palace. They searched all over Sicily, came to the cliffs overlooking the palace in its valley – and instead of waiting for the West Wind to waft them down, threw themselves over and were dashed to pieces.

This variant on the folk-story of Beauty and the Beast was given literary form by Apuleius in his The Golden Ass *(second century CE), and the style he used to tell it – a mixture of sentimental, pastoral description and ironical characterization – became standard in retellings of folk tales and fairy tales throughout Europe, influencing writers as disparate as Boccaccio, Chaucer, Perrault and Hans Andersen.*
≫→ **beauty**

ᴘᴛᴀʜ
Africa (North)

Ptah ('sculptor', Greek Phtha), in Egyptian myth, was the chief god of the pantheon worshipped at Memphis. Originally a creator-god, son of **Nun and Naunet** (male and female aspects of the primordial ocean), he made the first gods by imagining them and then naming them, so that they were creations of both intention and breath-of-life. (The heartbeat and voice were considered Ptah's presences on Earth: the heartbeat because the heart was regarded as the seat of thought, the voice because it was breath-of-life given form.)

In some accounts Ptah went on to finish **creation** by metal-working (a skill he invented for the purpose), or by chiselling creatures from stone and wood. He became the god of all crafts and skills, **guardian** of all knowledge.

In temple art, Ptah was shown as a dignified, priestly figure wearing close-fitting clothes, a skull-cap and – unusually for gods – leather sandals. In less formal art he was shown as a blacksmith or metal-worker, and also as a hollow, womb-like amulet which, because it contained air, was thought to hold the breath of life and so to protect the wearer.

»→ smiths

PURUKAPALI
Australia

Purukapali, in the myths of the Tiwi people of Melville Island, was the son of **Mudungkala**, who brought him to the surface from Underearth at the beginning of **creation**. He had several children, including **Jurumu** and Mudati who discovered fire. But when his last child was still an infant, his wife went into the forest to enjoy **sex** with her lover Tjapara, and left the baby lying in full sunlight in the heat of the day. The child died – the first human ever to do so – and Purukapali was so angry that he refused Tjapara's offer to regenerate the body, took his son and dived into the sea, never to be seen again. So **death** came to mortals.

PURUSHA
India

Purusha ('maleness'), in one **creation-myth** of the Aryans who invaded India in the seventeenth century BCE, was the first being in the universe. A golden egg (**fire**) floated in the primordial ocean, and cracked open to give birth to Purusha. He had already been alone in the egg for 1000 god-years (1,576,800,000,000 mortal years) and felt lonely. In one version of the myth, he split himself in two, a male half (Purusha) and a female half (Viraj, 'female' and 'universal power'). The two halves mated, and gave birth to all living beings. They made them in pairs, male and female, and the pairs went on to breed. In another version, Purusha sacrificed and dismembered himself – or was sacrificed and dismembered – to bring about creation. His mouth became *brahman*, the universal power, his eye became the **Sun**, his breath the wind, his head the sky, his arms aristocrats, his thighs artisans, and so on. Nothing was wasted, and he is part of everything which exists or ever has existed.

Later myth identified Purusha either with **Brahma** or with **Prajapati**. He also symbolized sacrifice: the purification and offering by fire which guarantees universal order.

*Engagingly, because of the story of Purusha's dismemberment, he is depicted both in poetry and art as a maimed but still all-powerful being. He has literally been cut down to size, so that he is no bigger now than a human thumb – and still he embraces all **Heaven** and all Earth. He has no eyes, but can still see, no ears but can hear, no feet but can walk. Because he is in everything, and is everything, the survival of all creation depends on his goodwill – if he ever gathered all his parts and reassembled himself, the universe would end.*

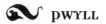

PUSHAN
India

Pushan ('nourisher'), in the Vedic myths of the Aryans who invaded India in the seventeenth century BCE, and then in Hindu myth, was one of the twelve Adityas, sons of the **sky**-goddess **Aditi**. He nourished all **creation** with his regard, gazing benignly out across it. In particular, he controlled the progression of night and day, looked after cattle (the wealth of the universe), and guided souls of the dead to the **Underworld**.

Pushan's teeth. When **Daksha** held a banquet for all the gods except his hated son-in-law **Shiva**, Shiva stormed to the feast and attacked everyone in sight. Pushan had just taken a bite of meat, and Shiva kicked him so hard that he knocked out all his teeth. The teeth became stars in the Milky Way, and the unfortunate Pushan had to spend the rest of eternity toothless, fed on pap and unable ever to eat meat again. (This is why he was the ideal god to look after cattle.)

Pushan the Nourisher was a welcome god at weddings and childbirth. His images show him as a plump, bearded prince, riding a chariot pulled by goats and carrying a spear, goad and leatherworker's awl.

PUTANA
India

Putana, in Hindu myth, was a **demon** who tried to kill the infant **Krishna** by smearing poison on her nipples and then suckling him. Krishna was not only immune, but sucked so hard that

he drew all Putana's essence out of her and left her as dry as a sloughed snake-skin.

PWYLL
Europe (North)

Pwyll and Arawn. Pwyll, in Celtic myth, was a **shape-changer** and the king of Dyfed in Wales. Out hunting one day, he saw a stag being chased by a pack of dogs, drove them off and set his own dogs to kill it. The owner of the first pack, **Arawn** prince of the **Underworld**, demanded recompense, and Pwyll agreed to change identities with him, go to the Underworld and kill his rival Havgan. After a year and a day he and Arawn met again, recovered their own identities and went back to their own kingdoms – and Pwyll was astonished to find that the Lord of the Underworld had been a far wiser and gentler ruler of Dyfed than he had.

Pwyll and Rhiannon. Pwyll was the only person able to catch and court Rhiannon, a human form of the horse-goddess **Epona** who galloped as fast as the wind. (Pwyll caught her by changing himself into the wind and whispering in her ear.) They married, and Pwyll defended her against Gwawl, the suitor her family preferred for her. Rhiannon's family, and her maids, never accepted the marriage, and when Rhiannon had a baby son, Pryderi, they hid the child, smeared Rhiannon with puppy's blood and claimed that she'd eaten her own child alive. She was forced to sit and beg at the palace gate, telling visitors the details of her crime. Meanwhile Pwyll, visiting a neighbouring prince to investigate the nightly loss of all foals born in the royal stables, cut off the arm of the supernatural thief who was stealing them, and chased the **monster** into the darkness. At dawn, when he came back to the stables, he found his son Pryderi lying in the straw, and took him triumphantly home.

*The origins of this inconsequential and folksy story lie in matters much more serious. Pwyll is a form of the healer-god who visits the Underworld, cheats **death** and returns, Rhiannon/Epona symbolizes both sexual energy and the potency of the entire universe, and Gwawl is a form of the god of light. All this being so, it is unexpected to find good and bad moral qualities so evenly shared among the characters. Pwyll is both a **trickster** and a **hero**; Rhiannon is both imperious and put-upon; Gwawl is both noble and devious. A mass of proliferating detail, omitted in the outline above, surrounds every event of the story. This is a characteristic of all tales in the **Mabinogion**, from which the story comes – and it suggests that, to Welsh bards and their audiences, embroideries in the telling were at least as important as the basic narrative elements.*

PYERUN
Europe (East)

Pyerun was the Russian name for the **thunder**-god; people in other regions called him Perkonis, Perkunas, Perkons, Perom, Peron, Perun, Perusan, Pikker and Piorun. Each of these names has its own meaning – Perusan is Bulgarian for 'thunder', Peron is Slovak for 'curse', and so on – but scholars think that the word-derivations come from the asso-ciation with Pyerun, not the other way round, and that his name came originally from the same Indo-European root as Paranjanya, one of the names of the Indian storm-god **Indra**.

As **rain**-god, Pyerun controlled the world's **fertility** – people thought that his thunderbolt awoke the Earth from its winter sleep. As **lightning**-wielder he was the god of war, riding the sky in an iron chariot pulled by an enormous billy-goat, throwing his axe to kill **demons** (it always returned to his hand). When Darkness took the **Sun** prisoner, he blasted open the cell door to set it free – an action symbolically repeated every morning.

In Stone-Age times, at spring festivals, young girls danced themselves to death in Pyerun's honour – the origin of the story of Stravinsky's The Rite of Spring. *Later, this ceremony was modified to a ceremonial ring-dance for all the virgins of a village or nomadic group. In many Slavic regions Pyerun was the king of the gods, and Christian missionaries had enormous difficulty dislodging his worship. In Novgorod his statues were solemnly thrashed with sticks each year, to rid them of demons; in other areas he was amalgamated with Saint Ilya (the prophet Elijah) or reinvented as the **bogatyr Ilya Muromets**.*

PYGMALION
Europe (South)

Pygmalion ('stone-carver'), in Greek myth, was a Cypriot sculptor who refused to marry, pouring all his love instead into his work. But then he made a statue so beautiful that he begged **Aphrodite** to let him have **sex** with it,

and the goddess, fearing for his sanity, turned the statue into a mortal woman, Galatea, and let Pygmalion marry her.
≫→ crafts

PYLADES
Europe (South)

Pylades, in Greek myth, was the son of King Strophius of Phocis and **Agamemnon**'s sister Anaxibia. He was **Orestes'** cousin, and when Orestes escaped from Argos after the murder of Agamemnon, he and Pylades grew up together. Pylades returned with Orestes to Argos, and helped him to murder **Clytemnestra**. When the **Furies** drove Orestes mad, Pylades looked after him, accompanying him on all his wanderings. His reward for all this devotion was to marry Orestes' sister **Electra**; he set up court with her in Phocis after his father's death (or, some say, in Sparta after **Menelaus'** death), and they had two sons, Medon and Strophius junior.

In all surviving versions of the Orestes myth except those of Euripides (where Pylades is a garrulous, if colourless, character) Pylades is as notable for his silence as for his devotion – in the whole of Aeschylus' Oresteia, for example, he speaks just a single line, and in art he is always the spear-carrier in the background of great events. In classical times and later, however, he was the epitome of loyal friendship. Ancient philosophers claimed him as origin for the Athenian custom of older men befriending and tutoring younger men in

the arts of adulthood – a practice pilloried by comedians – and in medieval chivalry the relationship of knight and squire was consciously patterned on his and Orestes' mutual devotion.

PYRRHA: *see* Deucalion and Pyrrha

PYRRHUS
Europe (South)

Pyrrhus (Pyrrhos, 'fair-haired'), in Greek myth, was the birth-name of **Achilles'** son, who was renamed **Neoptolemus** when he went to Troy. Some accounts, taking the line that Neoptolemus was just a boy, too young for the exploits attributed to him at Troy, say that those deeds were actually done by another Pyrrhus, also Achilles' son, who was one of the most savage of all the Greeks at Troy – and indeed that one of Pyrrhus' first outrages was to murder the child Neoptolemus and usurp his name. (For what he did at Troy, see Neoptolemus.)

*Roman myth-writers and historians claimed that after the **Trojan War**, instead of returning to Greece, Pyrrhus went to Epirus (modern Albania) and founded a piratical royal dynasty. Another, real-life Pyrrhus, king of Epirus, centuries later, was claimed to be his descendant. This man was one of the fiercest enemies of Rome, but lost so many men in battle that even when he won his power was totally destroyed – the origin of the phrase 'a Pyrrhic victory'.*

Building of the Tower of Babel (*Gustave Doré, 19th century*)

QAMAITS
Americas (North)

Qamaits (or Qamaye, 'dear one'), in the myths of the Bella Coola people of the Northwest coast (Canada), was a warrior-goddess. At the beginning of time she fought a battle against the **giants** who ruled the Earth and swarmed in such numbers that there was no room for any other life. She killed them all, and from their bodies made mountains and hills. In this way, she inadvertently made room for other life on Earth, including the human race. But she had no interest in mortal species, or indeed in the planet they lived on, and on the rare occasions she visited Earth, her presence was so terrible that **earthquakes**, forest fires, plagues and **death** were all she caused.

QAT
Oceania

Qat, in the myths of the people of the Banks Islands of Vanuatu, was the first being in the world, born when a vagina-shaped rock split open, and immediately grew to adulthood. He began creating at once, fishing up islands from the bottom of the sea and covering them with trees, animals and plants. He made human beings by carving three female and three male dolls from wood, then hid them for three days, brought them out again and spent three more days dancing and singing life into them. (Marawa the spider tried to copy him, but foolishly left *his* dolls buried for six days, so that when he dug them up they were decomposing – which is how **death** came to humans.)

At the beginning of **creation**, there was no alternation of night and day: darkness ruled half the world, light the other half. Qat's people grew ever more exhausted, until at last he went to Night and traded pigs for a share of darkness. When he came back, he spread darkness across the sky like a cloak, and laboriously taught his people how to lie down, close their eyes and sleep. At the end of the first night he reached up with his sickle, cut a hole in the darkness-cloak and let dawn shine through.

Western settlers in Melanesia ended their telling of this myth in a way paralleled in other parts of the world (for example in the story of Quetzalcóatl). When Qat had taught human beings all the skills they needed – fishing, farming, cooking, weaving, singing – and they seemed able to survive without him, he loaded his canoe and paddled away along the rays of the setting Sun. Ever afterwards, his followers believed that he would one day return – and when Captain Cook landed – the first white man they had ever seen – they took him for the god.
⋙→ civilization, crafts, farming, music

QIAN NIU AND ZHI NU
Asia (East)

Qian Niu ('ox boy'), a mortal herdsman, and Zhi Nu ('weaving girl'), the goddess who wove the clouds, fell in love when Zhi Nu bathed in a pool on Earth and Qian Nu hid her clothes. They married, but then Zhi Nu found her clothes and was compelled to return to **Heaven**. Separated, they pined – and the gods took pity on them. They appointed Qian Niu cowherd of Heaven and set him on the star Altair. Zhi Nu was sent to the star Vega. In between, so that they would not neglect their work, the gods put a river of stars, the Milky Way. On the seventh day of the seventh month each year, however, they gave Qian Niu and Zhi Nu a holiday and let magpies build a stick-bridge across the river so that they could meet. On this day on Earth it always rains – a sign that the lovers are reunited and happy.

QI YU
Asia (East)

Qi Yu the **rain**-god, in Chinese myth, was the son, grandson or chief minister of **Shen Nong**, second of the **Three Sovereigns** who ruled the universe at the beginning of time. He was half **bull**, half **giant**, and his head was fronted with iron. When **Huang Di** became ruler of the universe, Qi Yu opposed him, and allied himself with Huang Di's son, the **wind**-lord **Fei Lian** and with the rain-lord Chi Song Zi, to dethrone him. Huang Di sent a vast army to attack them, and they disoriented it with fog and cloud, picking off the confused soldiers one by one. But Huang Di's daughter Ba ('drought') drank up the cloud and Qi Yu was defeated. Reduced in rank in the heavenly hierarchy, he compensated by inventing weapons and **war** and giving them to the human race.

QUAAYAYP
Americas (North)

Quaayayp ('human'), in the myths of the Pericu people of California, was the son of the Creator Spirit Niparaya and his wife Amayicoyondi. Quaayayp went from **Heaven** to live on **Mother Earth**, taking an enormous retinue of servants, both animals and spirits, and became chief of an ever-increasing group of his own offspring. Many generations after this event, his descendants grew jealous of his wisdom and his pomp and tried to murder him. But all they killed was his mortality – an act which made human beings ever afterwards subject to **Death**. His spirit returned to his father Niparaya, and his body remained on Earth as a mountain-range fed constantly by underwater streams (his blood) and so never subject to decay. Animals could talk to it and share its secrets, but to humans it was dumb.

QUETZALCÓATL
Americas (Central)

Quetzalcóatl, in Aztec myth, was the god of the spirit of life, symbolized in the breath of the wind. His name means either 'precious twin' (and refers to his relationship with **Xólotl** (see below), or 'winged snake' (and refers to his dual nature as earth-serpent and wind-soarer). He was the son of the **Sun** and of **Coatlicue**, **Mother Earth**, and was usually shown either, literally, as a **snake** with wings or as a bearded warrior wearing earrings, a conical crown, a green jade pendant (the 'wind jewel') and a loin-cloth which barely concealed the erect penis which symbolized his generative power. He carried a rubber ball to symbolize that he was as unpredictable, as playful, as the bounce of a ball in the 'game of life'

– and also, since he was the Morning Star, to stand for the elliptical orbit of the planets.

Quetzalcóatl and human bzeings. In some accounts, Quetzalcóatl and his twin Xólotl rescued human beings and restored them to the upper world. The entire human race had died out because the gods had not given them the power to reproduce. Their bones lay scattered in the **Underworld**, and Quetzalcóatl collected them, took them to the upper world, ground them to dust and mixed them with his own blood. Xólotl moulded them into doll-shapes and Quetzalcóatl breathed life into them and taught them **sex**. Ever afterwards, he protected his creation, teaching them astronomy, **farming**, **music**, technology, **writing** and the measurement of time which allowed them, if not to cheat **death**, at least to anticipate the day of its arrival.

Quetzalcóatl and Tezcatlipoca. As helper and benefactor of humanity, Quetzalcóatl was permanently at war with the war god **Tezcatlipoca**. Unable to defeat him by force, Tezcatlipoca used trickery. He went to Quetzalcóatl's court, got Quetzalcóatl drunk, then showed him his own reflection in a mirror – the 'smoking mirror' of Tezcatlipoca's own face. Quetzalcóatl, horrified at the image of drunkenness and sensuality the mirror showed, vowed to go into exile until his imperfections were purged. He built a pyre, dressed in his finest robes and walked into the flames. His finery burned away, a flock of birds streamed out of the flames and flew towards the Sun, and in the middle of them Quetzalcóatl's heart left his bones and soared into the sky (some say as a *quetzal* bird, others on a boat carried on serpents' backs) to become the Morning Star.

Some scholars speculate that the story of rivalry between Quetzalcóatl and Tezcatlipoca was a late invention, to explain hostility between the priests of the two gods. Eventually, Quetzalcóatl's devotees left the city of Tenochtitlán and founded a new, holy city at Chichen Itza. The myth of his return one day took hold of popular imagination, and he came to be regarded as a saviour who would come in his people's darkest hour to save them as he had rescued the human race before. The priests said that in this return, he would appear as a tall, old man with a white face, black beard, long cloak and jewels – a description which inspired the Spanish adventurer Hernán Cortés to impersonate the god when he rode into Mexico in 1519, with fatal results for Aztec culture.

The conquering Spaniards, in their accounts of the wars which followed this deception, and of the people they conquered, identified Quetzalcóatl with a real, if by then legendary, person, a king of the city of Tollan who had been renowned for his civilized ways and the generosity of his laws. The truth is probably that Quetzalcóatl was the creator-god of the original Toltec people of Mexico, made over, for their own purposes, by the conquering Aztecs. In some parts of Mexico there is still a Quetzalcóatl cult, associating the god's return with the end of centuries of oppression and the revival of his people.

As Koloowisi, god of plenty, the plumed snake was also worshipped by the Zuñi people of the Southwestern US, but there are no substantial myth-stories, and (seemingly) there is no connection with Quetzalcóatl.

➤ civilization, crafts, Kukulkan, twins

RA

Africa (North)

Ra the Supreme. Ra ('creator'), or Re or Phra, the **Sun**-god in Egyptian myth, was the supreme power in the universe, giver and sustainer of life. In some accounts he was ruler of the gods, in others he was the only supernatural being: all other gods were merely his various aspects. Originally he was a god local to Yunu (Greek Heliopolis, 'Sun-city'), now a suburb of Cairo. But as his cult grew his power challenged that of cult-gods from other areas, notably Aton of Thebes (modern Luxor), and he was amalgamated with them to make a single, all-encompassing deity.

Light and Dark. Ra's first assimilation, in myth, was to the earlier Yunu cult of **Atum** the creator, so that he came to be regarded as father of **Shu** (Air) and **Tefnut** (Moisture), whose children **Geb** (Earth) and **Nut** (Sky) mated to produce the universe. Since Atum was primordial Chaos, this amalgamation involved saying that Ra, as Light, had gathered all the brightness latent in Chaos and made it into himself. The darkness which remained, the myth continued, formed itself into the **snake Aapep**, whose one desire was open its gullet and swallow Light and all Light's creations. Ra sailed above the world each day in a golden ship, travelling along the arched body of his grand-daughter Nut (which lay like an invisible roadway through the blue-sky 'sea'). As he travelled, he gazed down on Earth below, and brought warmth and fertility to all its creatures. At night, having evaded the maw of Aapep (who waited on the Western Mountains each evening to swallow him), Ra sailed through the **Underworld**, bringing light to the darkness of the Dead.

Rama and Sita in the forest (*Indian miniature painting*)

Ra's Journey. In most accounts, Ra's journey was a majestic procession, serene and untroubled except when his servants the gods did battle with Aapep each evening and scattered the clouds each morning. But some versions gave him a more laborious journey. In one he was compared to a scarab (dung-beetle), rolling the Sun-disc up the arch of **Heaven** as a beetle rolls its ball of dung: it was not until midday, at the zenith, that he metamorphosed into a falcon and soared high and free. In another he was born each day, as a helpless baby, from the womb of his own grand-daughter Nut, and the prayers and sacrifice of both gods and mortals gave him strength to survive. He grew steadily until midday, then his powers slowly declined until by evening he was old and exhausted, so that new offerings were needed to help him escape Aapep and gather strength enough to survive the night and be reborn next morning.

The Eye of Ra. In one myth-cycle, Ra first ruled the universe in a golden age. Wherever he travelled, whatever he saw was perfection. In the end it dazzled him, tears dropped from his eyes to the Earth below and grew into tiny models of the gods – human beings – or, in some versions, living creatures of every kind. Just as a water-drop which falls into the desert quickly dries up and dies, so Ra's tear-creatures were mortal, disappearing underground. But in their time on Earth they had free will, and as time passed some grew violent and heedless of Ra their creator. Eventually he was so angry with them that he tore out his own (single) eye, turned it into a goddess (**Hathor**) and hurled it at the Earth to wipe his creatures from

existence, then changed his mind and was forced to fuddle her with alcohol to stop the destruction. (This myth was also told, in slightly different terms, of Ra and another goddess, **Sekhmet**.)

In another myth, Ra had, quite literally, a roving eye. It stayed in its socket throughout the day, but at night it left him sailing the Underworld and tried to roll across the sky under its own momentum. It left some of Ra's radiance in the Underworld, and took some of the Underworld's darkness with it, so that what appeared in the sky was a pale reflection of the daytime Sun: the **Moon**. Ra sent **Thoth** to fetch it back, ready for the next day's dawn, and the **Eye** agreed to return only if it was allowed to do its own wandering, and its own shining, every night.

*Devotees of the Mysteries of Isis (**Aset**), a widespread mystery cult in Greek Egypt and Rome from the first century BCE to the coming of the Christian Empire (fourth century CE), believed that 'Ra' was not a name but the description of a function. Ra's real name, his identity, was a secret shared by no other being in creation, and the facts that it existed, and that no one knew it, were what kept the entire universe in balance. But although Ra was immortal – and in particular, his eye the Sun never weakened – he was subject to aging, and eventually, worn out with concern for universal order, he allowed Aset to trick out of him the secret of his name. Knowledge of the name gave Aset Ra's former responsibility for maintaining universal balance, and he retired to the far reaches of the sky, becoming the serene, uninvolved and distant Sun we still know today.*

⋙▸ creation, mysteries, supreme deity

RADHA
India

Radha, in Hindu myth, was a beautiful milkmaid with whom **Krishna** fell in love, preferring her above all other women.

The love of Krishna and Radha, a central theme in present-day Krishna-worship, is told in a twelfth-century pastoral play, Gitagovinda, and is the subject of some of the finest and gentlest Indian painting. In some philosophical systems Radha symbolizes woman as Krishna symbolizes man, and their union is attained when each enters into the condition of the other.

≫+ **beauty**

RADIGAST
Europe (East)

Radigast was the Baltic god of good advice, sound thinking and the keeping of promises. He carried a two-headed axe, and wore a flying swan on his head (symbolizing thought) and a bull's head on his chest (symbolizing unshakeability).

≫+ **justice and universal order**

RAGNARÖK
Europe (North)

Ragnarök ('destruction of the powers'), in Nordic myth, also known by its German translation *Götterdämmerung*, is the end of this cycle of **creation**. It has not yet happened, but the chain of events has begun which will lead to it. Ragnarök will be caused by the implacable hatred **Loki** feels for the rest of the gods. Once, he played harmless pranks on them, but over time these hardened into serious mischief, until he angered them past endurance by arranging the death of **Odin**'s son **Baldur**, and then refusing to save him from the **Underworld** by shedding tears for him. In punishment, the gods tied Loki in an underground cave, using chains made from the entrails of his own son, and set a serpent to drip venom into his upturned face. (This last punishment is eased by Sigyn, Loki's loyal wife, who catches the venom in a dish.)

For the present, Loki writhes in agony, causing **earthquakes** and volcanic eruptions everywhere on Earth. In the meantime, the death of Baldur has ended **beauty** in the world, which is gradually turning more and more evil, beyond the power of the gods to cure it. One day, Loki will break free, and Ragnarök will begin. He will sail to fight the gods, with the frost-**giants**, in a ship made from corpses' fingernails. The fire-giants, led by **Surt**, will swarm over **Bifröst**, the rainbow bridge, toppling it behind them, and will mass on the plains of **Asgard** to fight the powers of light. Loki's wolf-offspring Fenrir will lead the spirits of chaos to swallow the Sun and Moon, his serpent-offspring **Jormungand** will surge from the sea that girds creation and engulf the Earth, and his daughter **Hel** will come from the Underworld with her army of ghosts and **monsters**. There will be a huge battle, in which good will destroy evil and evil good. Only Surt will survive it, and he will burn the corpses in a huge fire, engulfing creation and drowning its ashes in the sea of chaos.

Ragnarök is not, however, the final end. The world-tree **Yggdrasil** will survive, as will two human beings (**Lif and Lifdrasir**) and the few animals and birds which have sheltered in its branches or its hollow trunk. They will tenant the Earth, reborn out of chaos, and will begin a new age of the universe, ruled by **Baldur** and the **Sun**-god's beautiful daughter. All giants, imps and **demons**, all evil and ugliness, will have been swept from memory forever.

The most all-engulfing depiction in any artwork of the events of Ragnarök is Götterdämmerung, the cataclysmic last section of Wagner's Ring of the Nibelungs. Wagner depicts the crumbling of all creation in fire and storm and the passing of the old gods – a triumph of musical synthesis (in the orchestra) and of stage design (in the collapse of the set onstage, which he organized meticulously in terms of the stagecraft of his own time, so that it made the entire theatre seem to totter round the audience).

RAHU
India

Rahu ('grabber'), in Hindu myth, was a **demon** who disguised himself as a god during the churning of the Sea of Milk (see **amrita**), drank some *amrita* and became immortal. But before he could pass himself off completely as a god, **Surya** the **Sun** and **Soma** the **Moon** recognized him and **Vishnu** sliced off his head. The gods tossed his body into the **Underworld**, but his head soared into the sky and has stayed there ever since. The head, trailing a tail of fire (that is, demon's blood), gallops about in a chariot pulled by eight storm-horses, and its

32 comet-sons appear and gloat whenever disaster is about to strike the Earth. Rahu himself is perpetually at war with the Sun and Moon, and periodically snatches them and tries to eat them: on Earth, we call these moments eclipses.

RAIDEN AND RAIJU
Asia (Southeast)

Raiden, in Japanese myth, was the god of **lightning**, a warrior with flames for skin, a **demon**'s head and eagle's claws. He sat on his cloud-throne showering **fire**-arrows on the world below. His familiar Raiju ('thunder-beast') ran about on Earth, sometimes jumping from tree to tree (in which case its claw-marks could be seen in the bark when the storm died down), sometimes hurtling across fields and through buildings (the phenomenon some humans called ball lightning). It rested by curling up in the navels of human beings rash enough to sleep out-of-doors in thunderstorms – and Raiden woke it up by shooting fire-arrows, against which not even the most tightly-curled navel was protection.
≫→ Ajisukitakahikone, animal-gods, archers

RAIJU: *see* Raiden and Raiju

RAIN: *see* Adad, Chac, fertility, Four Dragon Kings, Ilyap'a, Imdugud, Frigg, Indra, Kasogonaga, Oshadagea, Parjanya, Pyerun, Qi Yu, Rod, Shi Zong Di, Sosom, Tláloc, Tonenili, Yu Zu and Yun Tun

RAKSHASAS AND YAKSHAS
India

Rakshasas and *Yakshas* were **demons**; *Rakshasas* were spirits of purest evil, *Yakshas* only slightly less malevolent. (These are the male forms; Rakshasis and Yakshis are female.) When **Brahma** set about creating the universe, he began by making Ignorance – and when he threw her away in disgust she turned into Night and began spawning creatures of her own. They were ravenous, and since there was no other food in existence except their mother and grandfather, and since eating Night was out of the question, they debated whether to fall on Brahma and tear him to pieces. The *Rakshasas* were all for it; the *Yakshas* hesitated. In that moment of hesitation Brahma created gods and other light-beings, and the opportunity was lost.

Ever afterwards, the *Rakshasas* and *Yakshas* skulked about the world, hiding from the gods and preying on humankind. The *Yakshas* could be bought off with sacrifice, and sometimes they even heeded prayers made to their better nature, but the *Rakshasas* were implacable. They could take any form they chose – dog, dwarf, eagle, lover, owl, vulture – but their lolling red tongues and fiery eyes always gave them away. They hid in the folds of their mother, Night, and slipped into the orifices of the human body as people ate, drank, listened, looked, made love or defecated. They feared only mustard and fire; if neither of those were to hand, the best thing to do was throw sticks at them to blind them.

»+ shape-changers

RAMA
India

Rama's birth. Rama (short for Rama-chandra, 'Rama the Moon' or 'Rama the radiant'), in Hindu myth, was the seventh avatar of **Vishnu**. Brahma and Shiva, persuaded by sacrifice and austere practice, had made **Ravana**, demon-king of Sri Lanka, invulnerable against all supernatural beings. At once Ravana began attacking the gods, and they had no defence against him. They decided that since he had been too disdainful of mortals to bother asking for immunity against them, the best way to deal with him was for one of the gods to take mortal form and kill him. Vishnu volunteered. He took a jar of *soma* to Earth, and let the three wives of King **Dasaratha** drink from it. **Kausalya**, the senior wife, drank half the *soma*, and gave birth to Ramachandra, a mortal with half of Vishnu's supernatural powers. **Kaikeyi**, the next senior wife, drank half of what was left, and her child **Bharata** had a quarter of Vishnu's supernatural powers. The third wife, **Sumitra**, drank what was left, and her sons **Lakshmana** and **Shatrughna** had one-eighth each of Vishnu's supernatural powers.

Rama and Sita. The four mortal princes grew up together, close friends and brothers – unsurprisingly, since together they were Vishnu. They hunted, made **music**, danced and feasted in the time of peace and harmony which the world then enjoyed. Rama was particularly good at archery, and the bow became his favourite weapon, both for sport and when he went (reluctantly) to war. A sage, **Vishvamitra**, asked Rama and his brothers to help him conquer the demon-queen **Taraka**. At first Rama was unwilling to fight a female, but Vishvamitra persuaded him, and he killed Taraka. Vishvamitra then introduced him at the court of King **Janaka**, whose daughter **Sita** (an avatar of Vishnu's wife **Lakshmi**) was the most beautiful woman on earth. Her father held a contest for her hand: her suitors were to try to bend a bow given him by Shiva himself, and the winner would become her husband. Every suitor failed but Rama, who bent the bow so far that he broke it.

Rama's exile. Soon after Rama's marriage, King Dasaratha planned to abdicate in his favour. But Queen Kaikeyi, his second wife, wheedled a favour out of him: to exile Rama and make her son Bharata king. Rama, Sita and Lakshmana went into exile in the Dandaka Forest. Soon afterwards, Dasaratha died – and when Bharata (who had been away during all these events) came home, he agreed to reign only as Rama's regent during the time of exile, and enthroned a pair of Rama's shoes to show who was the rightful king.

Rama and Surpanakha. Surpanakha was a demon, Ravana's sister. She asked Rama to marry her, but Rama said that he was satisfied with the wife he had: Sita. Lakshmana also refused to marry Surpanakha, and the furious demon soared to **giant**-height and attacked Sita as a windstorm attacks a lake, opening her gullet to swallow her alive. Rama and Lakshmana drove her off, and in the fight sliced off her nose, ears and breasts. Mutilated and furious, Surpanakha retreated to her brother's kingdom Sri Lanka – and deviously, instead of

filling his mind with rage against Rama and Lakshmana, seduced him instead with descriptions of Sita's **beauty**.

The capture of Sita. Ravana, mad with lust for Sita, plotted to kidnap her. Sita spent her days in the forest, in a clearing by a stream. Ravana sent a magic deer to this clearing, and Sita asked Rama and Lakshmana to catch it as a pet for her. The deer led them far into the forest, out of hearing, and Ravana snatched Sita up in his sky-chariot and carried her off to Sri Lanka. She cried out to the forest, to the air and to the water-streams, to tell Rama what had happened. The vulture-king **Jatayu** (an avatar of **Garuda**, Vishnu's heavenly mount) tried to hinder the kidnap, but Ravana wounded him so badly that he was able only to flutter to Rama and tell him the whole story before he died.

Rama and Ravana. In the forest, Rama had helped **Sugriva** the monkey-king recover his throne from his wicked half-brother, and in return Sugriva now gave him an army of bears and monkeys, led by **Hanuman** (son of the wind-god **Vayu**). Hanuman flew across the sea to Sri Lanka, saw Sita alone in the palace gardens, spied out the defences and flew back to tell Rama. Rama tried to persuade the sea to divide and allow his army across, but the waters refused. So **Nala**, son of the architect-god **Vishvakarman**, led a band of monkey-builders and made a bridge, supported on floating rocks, all the way across the straits. (The gods later anchored the rocks to the sea-bed: they still survive, and are known as Nala's Bridge, Rama's Bridge or Adam's Bridge.)

A huge battle now began, one of the cosmic struggles of the universe. Demons watched from the cracks of Earth, or from their undersea lairs which Rama's architects had disturbed when they built their bridge. The gods watched from **Heaven**, like spectators in a theatre. (They were powerless to help: Ravana could be harmed only by a mortal, not by a god.) Ravana's son Indrajit injured both Rama and Lakshmana, and Hanuman revived them with draughts of *soma* from the Himalayas. Ravana's brother, the giant **Kumbhakarna**, feasted on Rama's monkey-soldiers as an ant-eater licks up ants.

Finally, Rama and Ravana faced each other in single combat. Rama shot arrows, knocking off each of Ravana's ten heads; but new heads sprouted immediately, redoubling Ravana's strength. Then Rama fired his most deadly weapon, the 'arrow of Brahma' whose feathers were winds, whose points were **sun** and flame, and whose shaft was Mount **Meru**, hub of the universe. It burst Ravana's chest, passed right through his body and flew back to Rama's quiver, as obedient as a hunting-dog. Ravana fell dead, and the gods showered Rama with flower-garlands of victory. On the battlefield, their servants bustled about tossing demon-corpses into the **Underworld** and restoring life to Rama's monkey-army.

The end of the story. Rama and Sita went home in triumph, and Rama accepted the throne which had been kept for him so long. But there was a last residue of demon-poison in Rama's mind, and it caused coldness between him and Sita. He was not convinced that she had not had **sex** with Ravana, and demanded proof of her faithfulness. **Agni** the **fire**-god himself spoke for her, and Rama took her back. But his people still muttered, and he was forced to send her into exile, even though she was pregnant with his children. Fifteen years passed, and Sita's and Rama's sons, now grown, demanded that he take her back. Rama gathered the people, and before them Sita asked the gods for a sign that she was pure, that Rama was indeed the children's father. For answer, **Mother Earth** gaped open and swallowed her alive – and Rama, heartbroken, followed her to eternity by walking into the river Sarayu, ending his mortal life and returning to Vishnu whose avatar he was.

Rama is the subject of the Ramayana, *the Hindu myth-epic compiled in the eleventh-sixth centuries* BCE. *The* Ramayana *is in part a picture of an age of harmony, with gods and goddesses, mortal men and women, living contentedly and in full understanding with one another: a golden age. But it also tells of Rama's adventures against the demons, and in particularly of his quest to win Sita back from Ravana. Thus it is both a vision of what life should be, intended for emulation, and a well of stories and anecdotes about adventures, derring-do and the working-out of destiny. Over the centuries, apart from its devotional uses, it has been the source of a million children's books, adults' adventure stories, films, TV series and other artworks.*

In fine art, Rama's adventures – and those of the comic Hanuman – are popular subjects for paintings and sculpture, both on temples and in secular art, where the range is from illustrated manuscripts to modern strip cartoons. Rama the warrior is a favourite figure for makers of bronze figurines – almost a branch of the art in himself. He is shown in armour, with a royal scarf flying from his helmet, the gods' bow in his hand and the quiver of immortal arrows at his side.

≫→ heroes

RAN
Europe (North)

Ran ('snatcher'), in Nordic myth, was the wife of the sea-god **Aegir**. Sexually voracious, she surged from the bottom of the sea whenever handsome mortals ventured out on the surface, netted them and dragged them down to have **sex** with them – only to discover, each time, that drowning destroyed their vigour.

RANGI
Oceania

Rangi ('sky'), or Raki, Langi or Vatea ('wide expanse') and his consort **Papa** ('flat'; that is, **Mother Earth**), in Maori myth, were the first beings in the universe, created from such abstract entities as 'emptiness' and 'shapelessness'. They lay together, locked in permanent mating, and engendered vast numbers of offspring: the whole of **creation**. After a while, because of the tightness of Rangi's and Papa's embrace, there was no room for their children, who lay wriggling and squirming in Papa's womb, with neither space to move nor light to see by. The first six children, gods, met in council to decide what to do. Tu the war god suggested killing Rangi and Papa, but **Tane**, god of forests, said that it would be better to

separate them, and the other gods agreed.

The gods took it in turn to try to prise their parents apart. Rongo, god of **farming**, and Haumia, god of wild plants, each had countless arms, plant-stalks, but neither was strong enough to lift Rangi's weight. **Tangaroa**, god of the primordial ocean, and Tawhiri the wind-god tried to wash or blow the parents apart, but failed. Tu hacked them with knives, and succeeded only in turning Papa's soil-flesh red with blood. Finally Tane planted his feet in Papa, held up his branching arms to Rangi, and let himself grow. Nowadays, mortals think that trees grow immeasurably slowly; but this is nothing compared to the aeons-long growth of Tane, which finally lifted Rangi free of Papa and flooded the space between with light. The teeming offspring of the first couple poured out of Papa's womb, scattered all over her body and began mating and filling the world with life.

Rangi was heartbroken at losing Papa. His tears flowed down, and covered her with a rising flood of salt water which began to drown creation. The gods turned Papa over so that he could no longer see her face, and the tears stopped – apart from a misty sigh each morning, which lay on Papa's back until the Sun dispelled it and which mortals called morning dew. Apart from those sighs, from that time on Rangi took no more interest in the world or its creatures, ignoring both the bustle of life far below on Papa and the storms of his god-children which racketed across the gulf between him and them.

≫→ **Atea, creation, Gaia, Geb**

RANGI'S AND PAPA'S IMMORTAL CHILDREN
Oceania

Rangi's and **Papa**'s immortal children, in Maori myth, were the infant **Ruaumoko** and the six adult gods Haumia (wild plants), Rongo (**farming**), **Tane** (forests), **Tangaroa** (**sea**), Tawhiri (winds) and Tu or Ku (**war**). At the beginning of the universe the six gods worked together to separate their parents Rangi and Papa from the embrace which was holding all **creation** trapped in Papa's womb, bereft of both light and space. But as soon as the parents were separated, the gods began squabbling. Tangaroa sucked all the salt water of Rangi's tears to form oceans, and stocked them with fish and crustaceans (which until then had lived in the forests). Tane, furious at losing so many of his subjects, taught human beings how to make dugout canoes, sail on the sea and catch fish. Tangaroa retaliated by hurling himself at the Earth twice each day in tides, trying to pull Tane's forests down to his underwater kingdom. Tu (who had first suggested killing the primordial parents, and had then attacked the other gods for prising Rangi and Papa apart) fought for supremacy with the wind-god Tawhiri, and their quarrel raged across the sky in storms and hurricanes. As for Haumia and Rongo, they each claimed power over all growing plants; Haumia sent weeds to choke Rongo's neat fields and vegetable patches, and Rongo taught mortals to hack down Haumia's luxuriant undergrowth and burn it.

RASHNU
Asia (West)

Rashnu, in Iranian myth, was the judge of the Dead. He was impartial, knew everything and could not be challenged. He judged people at the precise moment of **death**, while they still had breath left in their bodies. Their souls then passed to the bridge between life and death. Good people were helped across by beautiful attendants; bad people felt the bridge turn to a razor beneath their feet, and fell shrieking to eternal punishment. When the last breath left a dying person's body on Earth, those watching knew that the bridge had been crossed, for good or ill.
⧉ justice and universal order

RATI
India

Rati ('lust'), in Hindu myth, was the wife of **Kama**, god of erotic desire. She was a beautiful cloud-goddess, and danced for her husband. When **Shiva** seared Kama to ash, Rati danced for him, seducing him into restoring her husband's life. But Shiva granted Kama life only as a disembodied idea, and the disappointed Rati became promiscuous, enjoying **sex** with any god, mortal, beast, river, plant or tree that took her fancy.
⧉ beauty, Nephele

RATRI
India

Ratri ('Night'), in the Vedic myths of the Aryans who invaded India in the seventeenth century BCE, was **Prajapati**'s

522

daughter and the sister of **Ushas** (Dawn). She wore a black star-cloak and shadowed all **creation**. But she was not to be feared: she was benevolent and gentle, looking after the universe while its creatures slept.

RAVANA
India

Ravana, in Hindu myth, was a **demon** king who had originally been an angel in **Heaven**, but had insulted **Brahma** and been offered the choice of being reborn on Earth seven times as **Vishnu**'s friend or three times as Vishnu's enemy. He chose the second option, thinking that this would make his punishment lighter, as Vishnu would deal more quickly with his enemies than with his friends. Accordingly, he was granted three mortal lives on Earth. His first avatar, **Hiranyakashipu**, tortured and murdered everyone, demons or mortals, who respected the gods – until he was killed by Vishnu's avatar Ramasimha.

Ravana, king of Sri Lanka. Ravana's second avatar (the one actually called Ravana) was a **monster** of all-evil. He could soar in an instant from human-size to mountain-size, and had ten heads, twenty arms, red eyes and buck teeth like knives. He hurled hills about like chickpeas, churned sea as a woman churns milk. He lived in a golden palace in Sri Lanka, and roared about the universe raping, pillaging and committing atrocities so foul that the **Sun** shrank in its course, the wind held its breath and the tide was afraid to flow. He was immune from **death** at the hands of gods or demons, and

although his body was hideously scarred from the gods' weapons (**Indra**'s thunderbolt, **Airavata**'s tusks, **Vishnu**'s discus) he remained unharmed. In the end the gods realized that only a mortal could kill him, and Vishnu's avatar **Rama** was born on Earth to do it.

Sisupala. Ravana's third avatar, **Sisupala**, was born with three eyes and four arms, and only intervention by **Krishna** (Vishnu's ninth avatar) restored him to human shape. He was less of a physical threat to Krishna than a loudmouthed nuisance, dogging his footsteps and forever muttering in the shadows. In the end, however, he went too far, threatening to kill an aged king who had honoured Krishna before him. The Sun-disc fell from the sky and split him in two, his soul left his body in a gush of flames and was absorbed into Krishna's body. So, finally, Ravana became part of his enemy, and was forgiven and allowed back into Heaven.

RAVEN
Americas (North)

Raven the Creator. Raven (Yehl – called after its cry), in the myths of the Kwakiutl and many other tribes of the Northwest coast (both US and Canada), was one of the magic-animal spirits who created the world. He flew over the primordial ocean, carrying pebbles in his beak, and dropped them one by one in the sea to make stars and planets. He skimmed the surface of the largest planet, Earth, and the wind of his wings made river-beds, mountains and valleys. His droppings fertilized the ground, and from it grew every kind of plant and animal in **creation** except human beings. Raven knew that he wanted to make us, but had no idea how to do it. He tried dropping stones and beaksful of water together on the ground, and failed. He tried wafting air into human shape, and it blew away again as soon as he stilled his wings. In the end he turned himself into human shape, whittled a piece of wood into a man and moulded a lump of clay into a woman – and as soon as they were finished, breathed life into them, turned back into a raven and flew to join his own bird-offspring in the sky.

Raven and Light. The Tsimshian people say that the world, as originally created, had no light. High in the hills, a chief kept it for himself, hoarded in a box. No one knew how to get it back, until Raven found a way. He flew high into the hills, then changed into a cedar-leaf and fluttered into the cup from which the chief's daughter was just about to drink. She swallowed him, and in due course she became pregnant. When the child was born he was raven-black, had coals for eyes and cried incessantly. The chief's entire household tried to pacify him with songs and presents, without success. Finally, they gave him a bag of star-rocks to play with – and he picked them out one by one, tossed them through the smoke-hole in the roof to stick on the roof of the sky, and as soon as the bag was empty began to cry even more loudly. There was nothing left to offer him but the boxful of light, and as soon as he had it he turned back into Raven, flew high into the air and set it in the sky as the **Sun** to light the world.

»→ animal-gods, light and dark

REGIN
Europe (North)

Regin, in Nordic myth, was the brother of **Fafnir** and **Otr**. When **Loki** killed Otr, Regin and Fafnir demanded that he steal for them the hoard of dwarf-gold which constituted the wealth of the universe. Fafnir, transformed into a dragon, lay on the hoard to guard it – and Regin, full of jealousy, began making plans to steal it for himself. He fostered **Odin**'s great-great-grandson, the hero **Sigurd**, and persuaded him to kill Fafnir and take the gold. As soon as the theft was made, he intended to catch Sigurd unawares; but Sigurd, warned by birds, struck first and killed him.

In the Nibelung Poem *and Wagner's* Ring of the Nibelung, *derived from it,* *Regin is renamed Mime.*

REMUS: *see* Romulus and Remus

RHADAMANTHUS
Europe (South)

Rhadamanthus (Rhadamanthys, 'prophet using rods'), son of **Zeus** and **Europa** in Greek myth, was such a just king in life that when he died he was given **immortality** and made one of the judges of the Dead, sitting on a tribunal with his brother Minos.

»→ Underworld

RHEA
Europe (South)

Rhea ('earth'), in Greek myth, was a **Titan**. She became the consort of her brother **Cronus**, and bore him five children: **Demeter, Hades, Hera**, Hestia and **Poseidon**. Each time a child was born, Cronus (afraid that it would grow up to dethrone him) swallowed it alive. When Rhea's sixth child, **Zeus**, was born, therefore, she hid the child on Crete and gave her husband a stone wrapped in baby-clothes. In due course Zeus grew up and dethroned his father, exactly as Cronus had feared. Rhea and Cronus led a huge war between Titans and gods, and lost. In some accounts they were banished to the lowest depths of the **Underworld**. In others they were pardoned and made rulers of two beautiful kingdoms, Italy on Earth and the Islands of the Blessed in the Far West of the universe, on condition that they never troubled the gods again.

*Some anthropologists identify Rhea as the **Great Goddess**, the female deity who existed before any of the male gods, who was dethroned by them and who survived in myriad forms in all cultures. Greek and Roman scholars claimed, variously, that she was the same person as **Artemis, Cybele**, Demeter, **Gaia, Selene** and a dozen other goddesses, or simply 'The Great Mother'. But there is no agreement, and study of the Great Goddess remains one of the most self-contained and contentious branches of both mythology and anthropology.*

RHESUS
Europe (South)

Rhesus (Rhesos, 'breaker'), in Greek myth, son of the Thracian river-god Strymon and the **Muse** Terpsichore, was famous for his herds of horses (descendants of the white horses of his protector **Poseidon**). He trained a special team of chariot-horses to use in the **Trojan War**, and went to join the Trojans. The gods prophesied that once the horses had eaten hay from Trojan mangers, and drunk the water of the river Xanthus in Troy, the city would never be taken. Before entering the city, Rhesus camped overnight on the plain outside the walls – and **Odysseus** and **Diomedes** crept into his camp, killed him and stole his horses.

RIBHUS
India

The Ribhus ('craftsman-elves'), in the Vedic myths of the Aryans who invaded India in the seventeenth century BCE, were twin sons of **Indra** and **Saranyu**, daughter of the smith-god **Tvashtri**. They bustled about the world, making useful devices of all kinds, including grass, the celestial cow which granted all blessings, chariots and chariot-horses for the gods, and four cups to contain *soma*, the drink of **immortality**. (In some accounts they crafted **Heaven** and Earth themselves.) They were originally mortal, but their cheerfulness and usefulness led the gods to allow them each a sip of *soma*, and hence **immortality**. Unable to share this with mortals, they devised an alternative: posterity, the idea that human beings live on in their children, bequeathing their nature and memory to later generations. In some accounts, the Ribhus were the same people as the **Ashvins**.
≫ **crafts, smiths**

RIGI: *see* Areop-Enap and Rigi

RIG VEDA, THE
India

The *Rig Veda* is the oldest of the four *Vedas*, or 'sacred knowledge', of the Aryans who invaded India in the seventeenth century BCE. It consists of some 1000 hymns in honour of such gods as **Agni** and **Indra**, and is a prime source not only for later religion and ritual, but for information on the myths and beliefs of the Aryan people.

RISHABHA
India

Rishabha, in Jain myth, was the first **tirkanthara**. He was a wealthy king with 100 sons. At the height of his prosperity he abdicated in favour of his eldest son, entered a monastery, and began a system of meditation and austerity which let him acquire all the knowledge of the universe and so free himself from the trappings of passion and worldly concern.

Rishabha is worshipped as the founder of Jainism, and Jain ascetics often use his image (real or imagined) as a focus for meditation. When he is shown in art, he is often standing on or trampling a bull, symbolizing the passions which the true ascetic conquers.

RISHIS
India

The Rishis ('seers'), in the Vedic myths of the Aryans who invaded India in the seventeenth century BCE, were beings who, though not gods, maintained the universe through their total knowledge and vision of cosmic unity. Their intellectual binding-power equalled and balanced the gods' material and martial power. In some accounts, the Rishis were also **Prajapatis**, creating the universe by the power of thought alone. Two of them, **Daksha** and **Brighu**, were particularly august, and were granted the status of full gods. The others, the **Seven Seers**, remained on the divine sidelines, forming a group as testy as they were omniscient.

ROD
Europe (East)

Rod, also known as Rodú ('kin') and Chur, in Slavic myth, was an ancient **rain**-god, controller of **fertility**. Gradually, instead of merely watering the Earth, he was assumed to have created it and to have filled it with children by tossing pieces of gravel or dust on to the surface.

Rod was the Eastern Slavic equivalent of the Baltic **Svandovit**.

➤ creation

ROHINI (MOON-GODDESS)
India

Rohini ('red'), in the Vedic myths of the Aryans who invaded India in the seventeenth century BCE, was one of **Daksha**'s 27 daughters, married to **Soma** the **Moon**-god. It was she who cheated the **demons** out of their share of **amrita** after the churning of the Sea of Milk, and so guaranteed **immortality** exclusively to the gods. Soma liked her better than all Daksha's other daughters, and when they sulked and went back to their father, Daksha placed a wasting-spell on

526

Soma until he agreed to treat all his wives equally. This is why the Moon still wanes and waxes.

Rohini is identified with one of the red stars in the constellation Taurus.

ROHINI (MORTAL PRINCESS)
India

Rohini ('red'), in Hindu myth, was **Devaki**'s and **Vasudeva**'s wife. When **Vishnu** reincarnated himself as a mortal, he placed two hairs in Devaki's womb. One, his own black hair, was to grow into **Krishna**. The other, a white hair from the world-serpent **Shesha**, was to grow into **Balarama**. When the demon-king **Kansa**, hearing a prophecy that one of Devaki's sons would grow up to kill him, began murdering babies, Vishnu smuggled Balarama's embryo out of Devaki's womb and placed it in Rohini's, then sent Rohini to safety in the kingdom of the cattle-lord **Nanda**. Here Balarama was born and grew up, one part god (the part inherited from Shesha) and two parts mortal (those inherited from his first mother, Devaki, and his second, Rohini). The Balarama myth tells nothing further about Rohini, though other myths suggest that she was taken up into **Heaven** after death and merged with one of her heavenly namesakes, **Rohini** the **Moon**-goddess or **Rohini** the **Sun**-goddess.
➤➤ **beauty**

ROHINI (SUN-GODDESS)
India

Rohini ('red'), in the Vedic myths of the Aryans who invaded India in the seventeenth century BCE, was the goddess of the rising **Sun**. Later myths identified her as **Savitri**, **Surya** or the dawn-goddess **Ushas**. Unusually for a Sun-goddess, she was cow-shaped: she was either the daughter or (in other accounts) the mother of **Kamadhenu**, the cow-goddess who represented the **fertility** of **creation**, and her appearance in the **sky** each morning guaranteed that that fertility would continue.
➤➤ **bulls and cows**

ROLAND
Europe (North)

Roland was a real person, a follower of Charlemagne who died fighting the Saracens in 778CE. Three centuries after his death he was made the subject of an epic poem, the *Chanson de Roland*, and entered Christian myth. The poem shows him as the epitome of chivalric virtue – to modern eyes, to the point of seeming ridiculous. As a young man, he challenged a colleague to a duel. Neither knew who the other was, they fought in full armour, and they duelled for no less than five days before realizing that Roland was fighting his best friend, Oliver. (They agreed peace, and honours were exactly even.) In a similar display of how to put chivalric dignity before common sense, Roland later in the poem was overwhelmed by Saracen forces, but refused to blow his war-horn for reinforcements until it was too late, and so died a heroic but pointless death.
➤➤ **heroes**

ROMAN MYTH
Roman myth was largely an official creation, a codification for national

political, social and religious purposes of a heterogeneous body of stories and beliefs from all the peoples ruled by Rome. At its peak, the Roman empire consisted of the whole of Europe, much of North Africa and the Middle East, and had contacts as far North as the Crimea and as far South as the Straits of Hormuz.

The peoples ruled or influenced by Rome spoke some hundred different languages, worshipped thousands of gods and had innumerable customs and habits of mind, all conditioned by local myths. It was Roman policy not to replace these indigenous ways with an imposed central structure, but to incorporate and assimilate them. So long as subject peoples followed Roman law, paid Roman taxes and gave at least lip-service to the Emperor-centred Roman religion, they were free to believe as they chose, and if myths and influence travelled, it was from outside to the heart of the Empire rather than from the centre outwards. **Jupiter**, for example, **sky**-god and leader of the Roman pantheon, was worshipped in Egypt as **Ammon**, in Greece as **Zeus**, in Persia as **Ahura Mazda**, in Celtic Europe as 'the Good God' – and stories and attributes from each of these manifestations were carried back to Rome, Latinized and attached to an increasingly multi-faceted and omni-functional Jupiter.

The earliest myths assimilated into what became the 'Roman' canon – and it *was* a canon, officially codified and annotated – were tales of pastoral gods and spirits indigenous to Italy. **Mars** himself, later the god of **war** and one of the major guaranteeing powers of Rome, began as a central Italian spirit of fields and **farming**. **Janus** the year-keeper began as a North Italian god able to roll between the Upper World and the **Underworld**. Juno, consort of Jupiter, was an amalgam of a dozen local goddesses of **fertility**, growth and harvest. When the Romans conquered Greece, they embraced the entire Olympian religious system, changing the gods' names and giving them additional attributes and functions, but otherwise incorporating their myths bodily into Roman belief. (Mars, for example, somewhat uncomfortably added to his pastoral role the attributes and myths of **Ares**, god of war.) With the gods came a whole train of other Greek myth-beings – **nymphs**, **ghosts**, **heroes**, **monsters** – and all, however remote or arcane their origins, were taken into the story of Rome and became part of what Romans knew.

An egregious example of this incorporation is the Roman view of the **Trojan War**. From one small detail of the original Greek myth-cycle – the story that some Trojans survived the sack of Troy and sailed South to found a second Troy – the Romans elaborated the entire saga of **Aeneas**' voyage South, his landing in Carthage and Italy, his battles and his founding of the settlement from which Rome would ultimately grow. At a stroke this gave Rome a myth-history, a dynastic line traceable back to the gods (Venus, Aeneas' mother, Greek **Aphrodite**), and a pattern and standard of heroic behaviour – not to mention a collection of supplementary myths and legends about all the Greeks and Trojans, gods and humans, involved in the Trojan War. They then propelled this story forwards, generation by generation, until they linked Aeneas to **Romulus and Remus**, sons of Mars and founders of the city of Rome – and from them, by a process which gradually blended myth into legend and legend into 'real' history, to the current ruling dynasties of the city and the Empire. Virgil and Livy are the best-known authors involved in this process, but they were not inventing what they wrote so much as codifying what every educated Roman, and many uneducated Romans, already knew.

In this book, to save unnecessary duplication, where the same stories are told both about Roman-named characters and characters from other traditions, they come under the participants' original names – usually Greek, though characters from more remote traditions such as **Cybele** and **Mithras** make appearances. Roman names appear in the index, and refer to these entries: thus, for example, Latona is referred to the article on **Leto**, Pluto to **Hades**, Venus to **Aphrodite**. Other main parallels are as follows (article-headword in brackets): **Aesculapius** (Asclepius), Aurora (**Eos**); Bacchus (**Dionysus**), Ceres (**Demeter**), Cupido (**Eros**), Diana (**Artemis**), Juno (**Hera**), **Jupiter** (**Zeus**), Mars (**Ares**), Mercurius (**Hermes**), Minerva (**Athene**), Neptunus (**Poseidon**), Saturnus (**Cronus**), Terra (**Gaia**), Uranus (**Ouranos**), Venus (**Aphrodite**), Vulcan (**Hephaestus**). ⋙→ Achates, *Aeneid*, Anchises, Angerona, Baucis and Philemon, Bellona, Cacus, Dido, Epona, Faunus, Flora, Fortuna, Hersilia, Horatius

Cocles, Lar, Latinus, Lavinia, Lucretia, Mania, *manes*, *Metamorphoses*, Mors, Nisus and Euryalus, Penates, Picus and Canens, Pomona and Vertumnus, Psyche, Pylades, Pyrrhus, Saturnus, Tiber, Troilus and Cressida, Turnus

ROMULUS AND REMUS
Europe (South)

Two brothers in Roman myth, Numitor and Amulius, ruled the town of Alba Longa, founded twelve generations before by Trojan settlers led by **Ascanius**, son of **Aeneas**. Numitor was the lawmaker, Amulius the warlord. After several years' joint rule, the brothers quarrelled, and Amulius deposed Numitor and took full control. To prevent the rise of a rival royal dynasty, he imprisoned Numitor and made Numitor's daughter Rhea Silvia a Vestal Virgin, sworn to eternal celibacy.

The gods, however, had other plans for Alba Longa. **Mars** raped Rhea Silvia on the banks of the **Tiber**, and in due course she gave birth to **twins**, Romulus and Remus. Amulius was furious. He killed Rhea Silvia by burying her alive (a standard punishment for spoiled Vestals), and ordered that Romulus and Remus be drowned in the Tiber. But the river-god floated the babies to safety in a basket, washing it up on the shore under a fig-tree (later called Ruminal) beside a grotto (later called Lupercal). A she-wolf found and suckled the twins, until they were rescued and brought up by the royal shepherd Faustulus and his wife Larentia. When Romulus and Remus were fully-grown, Mars appeared to them and told them the story of their birth. They led an uprising of shepherds and farmhands, killed Amulius and restored their grandfather Numitor to the throne.

Rome. In the next few years, overcrowding in Alba Longa led Romulus and Remus to found a new town, on the shores of the Tiber where they had once been left to die. While Romulus marked out boundaries, ploughing furrows to mark the line of new fields and walls, Remus and his men went hunting. On Remus' return, the brothers quarrelled. One account says that Remus mocked the new 'walls', jumping scornfully over them, and Romulus or one of his followers killed him. Another says that the brothers took bird-auguries to decide who would rule the new city. Remus saw six vultures on the right (the favourable side), Romulus twelve on the unlucky left. The brothers argued about which augury was better, there was a skirmish and Remus was killed. The new settlement was named Rome, and Romulus was its king.

Rape of the Sabines. Despite early military and mercantile success, Rome seemed doomed to die in a single generation. It was a town of men, without women. Romulus invited the people of neighbouring towns and villages to a festival in honour of Neptune (see **Poseidon**), declaring (as at all religious events) a sacred truce and welcoming women and children as well as men. But when the signal was sounded for the Games, instead of lining up to race the young Romans took out concealed weapons and abducted the visiting women. This incident – known ever afterwards as the Rape of the Sabines, after the most numerous of the visiting peoples – led to several years of inter-communal war, ended only when the women marched between their Roman husbands and their parents and insisted that peace be made.

Romulus' departure from the world. Romulus ruled for forty years. He was presiding one day at an athletics festival when the gods shrouded the area with cloud and took him up to **Olympus**. He was made immortal – some say as the war-god Quirinus, a follower of Mars whose temple was on the Quirinal Hill in Rome – and was worshipped throughout Roman history as creator and protector of his people.

The main surviving sources for this story are the Roman writers Livy and Ovid. Livy was a historian, concerned – in the manner of his time – to tell the story of his people from mythical times, and to give legitimacy to contemporary rulers and practices by finding, or inventing, precedents in the distant and supernatural past. Ovid was more interested in telling a good story, but projected contemporary habits of speech, dress and custom back on the people of the past (rather as Shakespeare did later). The origins of the myth – it is akin in some details to the wolf-children stories characteristic of Northern and Central Europe, and in others to many world myths about quarrelling twins – are thus lost under a later Roman gloss. Subsequent tellings, and all depictions in art, take Livy or Ovid as their starting points.

The she-wolf suckling human babies became a main symbol of the city of Rome, and a statue of the scene (not all of which is authentic) survives to this day in the Capitoline Museum. Ancient Roman artists, however, avoided later events of the myth, preferring to depict Romulus in his godly

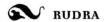

transformation, and Remus hardly at all – and more modern artists, for examples Rubens and the Pre-Raphaelites, followed this trend, so that the part of the story most favoured in art is the Rape of the Sabines, with its opportunities for showing huge panoramas of warrior males in uniform and nubile females half (or more) undressed.

ROSMERTA
Europe (North)

Rosmerta ('great provider'), in Celtic myth, was the goddess of plenty. Originally a goddess of **fertility** and harvest, when the Romans conquered Celtic lands she was made the consort of Mercury (see **Hermes**) god of markets, and became the guarantor of success in business.

RUAUMOKO
Oceania

Ruaumoko, in Maori myth, was the youngest immortal child of **Rangi** (Sky) and **Papa** (Earth). When the gods split Rangi and Papa apart, and turned Papa face down so that Rangi would not see her face from above and weep oceans of tears for her, Ruaumoko was still an infant, suckling at Papa's breast. He fell into the darkness of the **Underworld**, and his brothers, gods of the Upper World, were unable to rescue him. But they pitied his crying, and Tawhiri the windlord took a **lightning**-bolt from his brother Tu, god of **war**, and blew it down to the Underworld to warm Ruaumoko. This lightning was the ancestor of all Underworld fires, and when Ruaumoko grew up he

spent his time stoking them, causing **earthquakes** and sending molten rock and flame streaming through vent-holes to the world above.

RUDRA
India

Rudra's birth. Rudra ('howler' or 'red') came to India with the Aryan invaders of the seventeenth century BCE. In some accounts he was the son of **Prajapati** the creator and **Ushas** the dawn. Horrified that Prajapati and Ushas should have committed incest, the gods gathered the most terrible attributes of each of them and gave them to Rudra. The child began to cry, and his father immediately named him 'Howler'. This was a mistake, as one of the Rudra's first acts was set arrow to bow and shoot him. In another account, Rudra was the joint child of Ushas and her four brothers **Aditya**, **Agni**, **Candramus** and **Vayu**. When the brothers saw Ushas for the first time, they became so sexually excited that they spilled semen across the universe – and Prajapati gathered it and made from it a power with 1000 eyes and 1000 feet: Rudra. In yet another version, Rudra was **Brahma**'s son, born in an explosion of anger from his father's forehead.

Rudra's nature and powers. Rudra was the god of storm-winds, thieves and murderers, and raged through the universe in imitation of **Agni**, god of fire. His food was corpses, and he drank the blood of bulls. To appease him, people worshipped him as *shiva*, 'kindly' – and this led to his later merging with the god **Shiva**, who took over his attributes and powers. Like most gods of disease, he was his own mirror-image, healer as well as killer, and he was also worshipped as the scouring heat of the **Sun** and as the wind of artistic inspiration. His children, sometimes called Rudras after him, were the **Maruts** or storm-winds.

Rudra usually appears in art as a blue-necked man with many red faces, a black belly, innumerable arms and legs and a furious temper. He wears shaggy animal-skins, rides a wild boar, spits with rage and shoots arrows of death at anyone in his path. In some paintings and sculptures he is shown as a huge, roaring bull.

➤ disease and healing, Rudrani

RUDRANI
India

Rudrani ('red princess') came to India with the Aryan invaders of the seventeenth century BCE. She was **Rudra**'s wife, bringer of **death** and disease, a monster who gorged on the blood of battle and lapped it from the edges of sacrifice. (In later, Hindu myth she became identified with **Durga**.) She ended the gods' **fertility**. When she and Rudra first mated, they were locked together for so long that the gods, alarmed at the kind of monster such a union might produce, begged Rudra to withdraw without ejaculating semen. He did so, and swore that he would never have **sex** again. Rudrani cursed the gods with infertility – and they never again had offspring. The only exception was **Agni**, who was not there when Rudrani made her curse.

➤ disease and healing

RUGIEVIT
Europe (East)

Rugievit was an ancient **war** god of the Western Baltic, particularly associated with the island of Riigen. He was chiefly remembered for his savagery, symbolized by his wearing seven swords and brandishing an eighth, and by the savage glances from his seven faces.

RUHANGA
Africa

Ruhanga, in the myths of the Banyoro people of Uganda, was the god of **fertility** and prosperity. He gave people health and happiness, and in his kindness even promised that they would be immortal, rising from the grave – on condition that no one ever mourned for a dead relative, but put on festive clothes and danced. The whole human race accepted this condition except for one woman, who refused to dance and sing when her daughter (or in some accounts, her pet dog) died – and Ruhanga had no choice but to make **death** the end of our existence.

RUKMINI
India

Rukmini, in Hindu myth, was one of the avatars of **Lakshmi**. When **Vishnu** went to Earth as **Krishna**, Lakshmi followed him, becoming Rukmini, sister of Prince Rukmin of Vidarbha. Rukmin wanted to marry his sister to the **demon**-prince **Sisupala**, a sworn enemy of Krishna, but Rukmini wrote Krishna a letter begging him to rescue her, and he kidnapped her from the wedding-ceremony and married her himself. She became the first and most important of his 16,108 wives, and bore him a mortal son: Pradyumna, an avatar of the love-god **Kama**.

RUSSALKI, THE
Europe (East)

The Russalki (plural of Russalka) were the souls of unbaptized babies or of young girls who had accidentally drowned or died on their wedding nights. (Some mythologists associate the name with Rosa, the Latin for 'rose', and say that the Russalki were named after the wedding-garlands they wore.) They sang seductively over ponds and rivers, luring male hearers to disaster. In Southern Slavic lands the Russalki were long-haired and beautiful, nesting in trees hanging over the water, dancing in water-meadows to make the ground fertile, and tickling their prey to death. In Northern Slavic lands they were ugly and cold, roosting like bats in lakeside trees.
≫→ **water**

RUWA
Africa

Ruwa, creator-god in the myths of the Djaga people of Kenya, made human beings and planted a paradise-garden for them to live in. He gave them **immortality**, on condition that they avoided picking or eating the fruit of just one plant in the garden, a yam called Ukaho. Every morning and evening he sent an angel to make sure that this condition had been kept. One night, as the angel came down to Earth, he smelled yam cooking – not just any yam, but Ukaho itself. In the cool of the afternoon **Death** had visited the garden and told the people that Ruwa had made a special exception: for him, and him alone, they could prepare Ukaho. The angel took Ukaho's remains, in their pot, back to Ruwa, who reconstituted Ukaho in **Heaven** for the gods alone. He left mortals their garden, but they were now Death's prey.

*This myth is one of the oldest in all Africa, and predates the **Adam and Eve** story in the Bible. The similarities between them – and indeed the prevalence of myths in which immortality is contained in a fruit forbidden to mortals – have suggested to some mythographers that all such stories have a common ancestor, and the possibility is that it came from this region of Kenya, where the human race first evolved.*

*In another Djaga myth, also of a type common throughout Africa, Ruwa told mortals that they could keep ever-young by taking off their aged hides as **snakes** and other reptiles sloughed their skins. The method worked until a young girl who knew nothing of it burst in by accident on her grandfather while he was half-undressed, and the spell was forever broken.*

Satan and the Rebel Angels (*William Blake, 18th century*)

SADKO
Europe (East)

Sadko, originally a pagan **water**-god in Slavic myth, was reinvented in Christian times as one of the **bogatiri** associated with the city of Novgorod. He was a merchant trading overseas. One day his boat was becalmed in mid-ocean, and Sadko took three cups, filled one with gold, one with silver and one with jewels, and floated them on the sea-surface on a plank, for the servants of the Tsar of the Sea to carry to their master. But the plank stayed where it was, and Sadko realized that the Tsar demanded human sacrifice. He and his crew drew lots, and Sadko himself was chosen. He took his *gusli* (a string instrument) – and in more pious accounts, an icon of Saint Nicholas calmer of storms – climbed on to the plank and was drawn down to the Sea-Tsar's underwater palace. He played his *gusli*, and the Tsar was delighted and began to dance, faster and faster until the sea boiled overhead. Realizing that it was about to drown the world, Sadko broke the strings of his *gusli*, took firm hold of Saint Nicholas and escaped to the surface.

The storm had left Sadko penniless. For twelve years he worked as a barge-hand on the river Volga, eating nothing but bread and salt. Then he decided to go back to Novgorod, and at the end of his last day on the Volga he gave the river a gift of salted bread and a prayer of thanks. The river-spirit answered, asking Sadko to take a greeting to its brother, Lake Ilmen. Sadko did so, and the lake-spirit told him to cast fishing-nets in the deepest part of the water. Sadko hauled in three huge nets, bursting with fish – and when he carried them back to land they turned into silver coins, making him rich again.

This favourite story is best-known outside Russia in the form of Rimsky-Korsakov's opera Sadko, and the 'symphonic picture' he derived from its music.
»+ **heroes**

SAGARA
India

Sagara, in Hindu myth, was a mortal king ambitious to become a god. By prayer and sacrifice he won the gift that one of his wives would have one son, the other 60,000. The first son was conceived by sexual intercourse in the normal way, the others when Sagara masturbated over a gourd held by his second wife and containing 60,000 seeds. However the sons were conceived, they were all worthless, as Sagara had forgotten to ask that they be noble or heroic.

Sagara set out to dethrone **Indra**. He planned to sacrifice the celestial horse which symbolized the strength of the universe, and so to gather that strength for himself. Indra hid the horse deep in the womb of **Mother Earth**, and Sagara set 60,000 of his sons to dig down and find it. Mother Earth complained to the gods, and they turned the sons into burrowing termites before they could do more harm. Indra said that the sons would come back to human form if, and only if, the river Ganges left **Heaven** and flowed down to Earth. This was equivalent to saying 'Never' — but Sagara persisted. He ruled for 30,000 years, perpetually sacrificing and praying to **Brahma** to order the Ganges down to

Earth. Brahma at first refused to listen, but after Sagara's surviving son, grandson and great-grandson also plagued his ears with prayers and sapped his will with sacrifice, he agreed. He intended the Ganges to fall like a meteorite and destroy the Earth, but **Shiva** took the river's weight on his head and made it flow more gently.

Sagara is the personification of ocean, and his 60,001 sons are the world's various seas and lakes. He asked for the Ganges to flow on Earth to make sure that his own strength was constantly replenished — and Shiva's weakening of the flow of the Ganges was essential to prevent Sagara/Ocean from brimming up and swamping all creation.

SAHADEVA
India

Sahadeva, in Hindu myth, was one of the twin sons of the **Ashvins** and the mortal **Madri**, second wife of King **Pandu**. (His twin brother was **Nakula**.) Sahadeva fought with his **Pandava** brothers in their war against the **Kauravas**, and was famous as much for his peppery pride as for his fighting skill.
»+ **heroes**

SAKTASURA
India

Saktasura, in Hindu myth, was a **demon** who tried to kill the infant **Krishna** by crushing him. The child was lying in the shade under a wagon. Saktasura took the form of a dove and alighted on the wagon — and just as he did so, changed back to his full size and mountainous weight. The cart collapsed, but Krishna underneath lifted one tiny foot and kicked it up so that it rolled on top of Saktasura and killed him.

SALMONEUS
Europe (South)

Salmoneus ('loved by the goddess Salma'), in Greek myth, was the son of **Aeolus** the wind-lord and the mortal Enaratta. His brothers were **Athamas** and **Sisyphus**. He ruled in Thessaly, with extreme cruelty, until he was forced out by his people, after Sisyphus his brother claimed that he had slept incestuously with his own daughter Tyro. Salmoneus went to Elis, where he founded a new city, Salmonia. Here his arrogance reigned unchecked, until one day he went too far, announcing that he was no longer a mortal but had changed into **Zeus** himself and was ready to receive his people's worship. He drove through the streets in a chariot, dragging a bundle of copper cooking pots: their clattering, he claimed, was how Zeus made **thunder** in the sky. For thunderbolts he lit oak-branches at a brazier in the chariot and hurled them at his subjects. In the end Zeus hurled a real thunderbolt at him and dashed him to the **Underworld**.

SAMBA
India

Samba, in Hindu myth, was **Krishna's** son. He inherited his father's delight in pranks and tricks, but had none of the god's compassion or common sense. Rather than win a bride in the usual way, for example, he chose the adventurous method of abduction, kidnapping the daughter of the **Kaurava** prince **Duryodhana** and so prolonging the huge war related in the **Mahabharata**. His impishness eventually led to his own father's departure from Earth. He dressed as a pregnant woman and taunted some Brahmins, asking which of them would admit to being the baby's father. They cursed him: he was to bear an iron club which would kill his father. In due course the club was 'born', and Samba immediately had it broken up and thrown in the sea. But a fish swallowed one piece of it, and when the fish was caught the fragment was found and made into an arrowhead – the very one by which, later, Krishna was accidentally killed.

SAMPO, THE
Europe (North)

The *sampo*, in Finnish myth, was a magic mill demanded by Princess **Louhi** of **Pohjola** as the bride-price for her daughter. She said that whoever made the mill would marry the girl. **Väinämöinen**, who had originally courted Louhi's daughter, forgot this condition, and asked his brother **Ilmarinen** to make the *sampo*. Ilmarinen threw into his furnace swansdown, milk from a barren cow, sheep's wool and barley, and sang moulding-spells as he worked the bellows. On the first day a golden bowl appeared, on the second a copper ship, on the third a cow with golden horns and on the fourth a plough made of precious metals. Each was a guarantor of prosperity, but Ilmarinen threw them back into the furnace and waited.

On the fifth day the *sampo* appeared: a mill shaped like a pyramid. Out of the first side came endless supplies of salt, out of the second flour and out of the third gold.

Ilmarinen took it to Louhi and duly married her daughter. The *sampo* brought prosperity to Pohjola, and Väinämöinen coveted it for his own people in Finland. His chance to steal it came when Ilmarinen's wife died and her mother Louhi refused to let Ilmarinen marry her younger sister. Väinämöinen, Ilmarinen and **Lemminkäinen** sailed to Pohjola, made the people fall asleep by playing music on a magic zither, and stole the *sampo*. On the way home, their ship was battered by a storm sent by Louhi, and the *sampo* was smashed and washed overboard. But Väinämöinen managed to rescue enough of the pieces to take home to Finland, and their magic made his country the prosperous, peaceful place it remains to this day.

SAMSON
Asia (West)

Samson (Shimshon, 'Sun-man'), in Hebrew myth, was a **giant** trapped in a normal-sized human body. His superhuman strength (which he used to fight the Philistines) depended on strict devotion to **Yahweh**, and was symbolized by his refusal to drink alcohol or cut his hair. The Philistines sent Delilah to seduce him, and when he got drunk and told her his secret she cut off his hair so that the enemy soldiers could lead him away, as helpless as a child. They blinded him, chained him between the pillars of their temple, and set him to work the mill like an animal. He endured this until his hair grew again, then exerted all his strength and pulled down the pillars and the temple, killing his enemies and himself.

Mythographers regard this story as a devotional reworking of an original Sun-myth, now otherwise lost. Samson is the strength of the Sun, and his long hair symbolizes its rays at midday. Cutting the hair and blinding are forms of emasculation – a humiliation Sun-men undergo in myths of all cultures. Samson's devotion to Yahweh and ritual forms of self-denial, the heart of the story to the Hebrew teachers who reworked it, are regarded by myth-experts as pious embroideries.

SANDHYA
India

Sandhya, in Hindu myth, was **Brahma**'s daughter. She was so beautiful that her own father lusted after her. In some accounts, Brahma got drunk and raped Sandhya, and **Shiva** punished him by cutting off his fifth head. In others, Sandhya was Shiva's wife, and Shiva prevented the rape by turning her into a doe and shooting her before Brahma (now changed into a stag) could mount her.

⋙→ beauty

SANJNA: *see* Surya (Sun)

SAOSHYANT
Asia (West)

Saoshyant ('saviour'), in ancient Iranian myth, was the saviour whose coming would inaugurate the last age of the world, the Golden Age restored when **Ahura Mazda**, spirit of light, finally routed the power of darkness (**Ahriman**). He has not yet come.

SARANYU
India

Saranyu, in the Vedic myths of the Aryans who invaded India in the seventeenth century BCE, was the daughter of the smith-god **Tvashtri**. She married **Vivasvat**, god of the rising **Sun**, and bore him twin children, **Yama** and Yami, the first human beings. Then, afraid of her husband's dazzling radiance, she hid among the clouds, leaving in her place an exact replica of herself (some say fashioned by her father). Vivasvat fathered **Manu** on this clone before she told him who she was. Vivasvat searched **Heaven**, Earth and Middle Air for Saranyu, and eventually found her in the shape of a mare. He became a stallion and reared to mount her, but was so excited that he prematurely ejaculated. His semen spilled from the clouds onto **Mother Earth**; Saranyu sniffed it and at once became pregnant. In time she gave birth to the twin **Ashvins**.

SARASVATI
India

Sarasvati ('she who flows'), in Hindu myth, was originally a river-goddess, and devotees still sometimes claim to see her at the confluence of the rivers Ganges and Yamuna, the most sacred place in India. Her other names include Brahmi ('[female] first principle'), Shatarupa ('hundred-formed'), Savitri ('life-giver') and Vac ('speech').

Sarasvati and Brahma. In one version of the Hindu **creation**-myth, Sarasvati was the first being created by **Brahma**. Either he divided himself in two, making her the female half, or she was born in a gush of **water** from his side and turned at once into a goddess. She was so beautiful that he lusted after her – the first lust ever felt. Shyly she drew back, walking slowly round him in a circle; or, some say, she danced round him in delight at being in his presence. As she walked, or danced, he remained sitting where he was, but grew a second, third and fourth face to gaze at her with eyes of love. She soared above him, and he grew a fifth face on top of his head to see her. (This was later burned off by the rays of **Shiva**.) Sarasvati and Brahma retired into seclusion for 100 divine years (147,688,000 mortal years), and during that immortal honeymoon they created everything which exists.

In another, far less complimentary myth, Sarasvati was originally one of the three wives of **Vishnu**, the others being **Lakshmi** and **Ganga**. But the three squabbled ceaselessly, and Vishnu gave Sarasvati to Brahma and Ganga to Shiva, keeping Lakshmi for himself. In this myth, Sarasvati was vain and lazy, and Brahma took a second wife, Gayatri, who was more interested in intellectual pursuits. Sarasvati insisted that she was the senior wife, but the dispute between intellectuality and **beauty** in females has – males say – never been resolved from that time to this.

Sarasvati and the arts. Sarasvati is the goddess of the arts, particularly poetry and **music**, and inspires all science and scholarship. She invented writing, and put order into musical sounds. When Brahma's four faces gave birth to the four *Vedas* (sacred writings), she took charge of them. Sarasvati forms Brahma's inspirations and gives them to humans. She is worshipped with gifts of flowers, fruit and incense, and her shrines are often found in libraries.

Sarasvati is second only to Lakshmi in the beauty of the art she has inspired. She is usually shown as a voluptuous, serenely-smiling woman sitting on a lotus, riding a peacock or swan, or gazing enraptured at Brahma. Her skin is ivory, her forehead is a crescent moon, and her four arms hold objects connected with the arts or with **beauty***: a musical instrument, a pen, a necklace, a perfume-box.*

➤ civilization, fertility

SATAN
Asia (West)

Satan (Shaitan, 'adversary'), in Hebrew myth, was originally an angel, a lord of light. (Later Christian theologians, writing in Latin, identified him as Lucifer, 'light-bringer', the morning star.) But he despised **Yahweh**'s son **Adam**, not only refusing to honour him but tempting him to disobey his creator by eating the fruit of the Tree of All-knowledge in the Garden of Eden. Yahweh punished Satan for this by hurling him from **Heaven** to Hell, where Satan became Prince of Darkness just as Yahweh was Prince of Light. His original courtiers were other fallen angels (for example Azazel, who lusted after a mortal and fathered on her the monstrous Asmodaeus), but he soon gathered an army of imps and **demons** (many of them spawned from matings between angels and humans, angels and animals or animals and humans), and began using them to tempt or torment the human beings he hated.

On this simple myth-foundation Jewish and Christian writers built an enormous philosophical and psychological edifice, in which Satan became not merely an embodiment of evil but the Other, the negative image of ourselves with which, with God's help, we must come to terms. In the Middle Ages, however, ordinary people in Europe sidestepped such intellectual ideas and reverted to the idea that Satan was a physical rather than a spiritual adversary. Satanic cults and demon-worship became endemic and a vast literature of rituals, spells and prophetic utterances, much of it in numerological code, began to be compiled. This literature and the practices it serviced, in their turn, richly fed the imagination of tale-tellers, painters, playwrights and writers: everything from Hieronymus Bosch's depictions of Hell to such stories as Faust *or* Little Red Riding Hood, *at one level, and at another the whole horror-genre from* Dracula *or* Doctor Jeckyll and Mr Hyde *to such films as* Friday the Thirteenth *or* Nightmare on Elm Street, *sucks power from it.*

SATI
India

Sati, in Hindu myth, was the daughter of **Daksha**. She was in love with **Shiva**, but her father opposed the marriage, until Sati forced his hand by throwing a bouquet of flowers into the air at a betrothal-banquet – for Shiva to catch.

Afterwards, Daksha lost no opportunity of insulting Shiva, and finally Sati grew so angry that she threw herself into a sacrificial **fire** and died. The grief-stricken Shiva took her body and began dancing – his dance of death which would destroy the universe. Vishnu hastily brought Sati back to life, reincarnating her as **Parvati**, and she spent the rest of eternity as Shiva's beautiful, playful and loving wife.

Some authorities say that the myth of Sati's self-sacrifice for love was devised to explain the custom of wives throwing themselves (actually or symbolically) on their dead husbands' funeral-pyres – a custom named sati (or 'suttee') after her.

SATURNUS
Europe (South)

Saturnus ('sower'), in Roman myth, was one of the oldest of the gods. When the Romans incorporated their myths with those of the Greeks, they identified him with **Cronus**, and the stories of Cronus' mutilation of his father **Ouranos** (Roman Uranus or Coelus) and his battle with his children (led by **Zeus**, Roman **Jupiter**) were told of Saturnus too. The main change was at the end of the story. Instead of sending Saturnus with the other **Titans** to punishment in the **Underworld** or to live in the Islands of the Blessed in the Far West, Jupiter allowed him to escape to Italy, where he ruled jointly with **Janus**. Saturnus taught the Italians such skills as **farming**, architecture and engineering, and during his reign the world enjoyed peace and prosperity unknown before or since. (It was the first of the **Five Ages**: the Golden Age.) At the end of his time on Earth he went to live forever in the sky: the planet Saturn.

Because Saturnus was pardoned by Jupiter, he was the patron god of freed slaves, and his temples were full of miniature manacles and leg-chains of gold and silver, thank-offerings from grateful freedmen. He supervised the Saturnalia, held at the turn of every year: a carnival during which slaves and owners symbolically changed places for a day or two, there was a legal amnesty, a series of bank holidays, no business was carried on and there was eating, drinking and high-spirited enjoyment. The celebrations climaxed on December 25 – the day accordingly chosen by the early Christians as Christ's official birthday.
≫→ civilization

SATYRS
Europe (South)

Satyrs (Latin Fauni, 'fauns' or Silvani, 'forest-people'), in Greek and Roman myth, were the offspring of mountain nymphs and goats. From the waist up they were human, from the waist down goat, and some had horses' tails into the bargain. They served **Dionysus**, and were famous for drunkenness and the lasciviousness of their dancing.
≫→ Faunus, Pan, sex, Silenus

SAULE
Europe (East)

Saule, the **Sun** in Baltic myth, was courted by **Sky** but then became the consort of **Meness** the **Moon**. The stars and Earth were their children. However, Saule still spent half of each day with Sky, and there was constant bickering between her and Meness. What mortals called an eclipse was when she and Meness had just made up, and hung a sheet of darkness to hide them from the world while they made love. They would have separated except that they couldn't decide who should have custody of Earth, their favourite child. In the end **Pyerun** said that he would chase away whichever of Sky and Moon lingered too long with her. Saule got up so early that Meness got bored and went to make love with the Morning Star.

Every morning, Saule left Moon's bed and harnessed her gleaming copper chariot. She rode across Sky to the sea, where she washed her horses and then either sat on the Sky-hill or sailed a copper boat across the sea. Sometimes she wept, and her tears turned to red berries and fell to Earth.

In some Baltic traditions, the sexes of Saule and Meness are reversed.

SAVITRI (GOD)
India

Savitri (or Savitar, 'life-giver'), in the Vedic myths of the Aryans who invaded India in the seventeenth century BCE, was **Aditi**'s son and the god of movement: he caused the rotation of day and night, supervised the seasons and managed the turning year. He was the morning and evening **Sun**, and was shown as a fire-haired prince riding a golden chariot pulled by white horses whose manes streamed **fire**.

SAVITRI (PRINCESS)
India

Savitri, in Hindu myth, was a mortal princess named after the goddess **Sarasvati**. She fell in love with Prince Satyavan, who lived as a forest hermit with his blind father, exiled King Dyumatsena. She married Satyavan, despite being told that he had only one year to live. At the end of the year she went with her husband into the forest, where **Yama**, judge of the dead, was waiting. Savitri followed Yama as he dragged Satyavan towards the **Underworld**. Three times Yama turned, praised her faithfulness, and promised to reward it with any gift she asked. First, she wished that Dyumatsena's sight would be restored. Second, she wished that Dyumatsena be restored to power. Third, she wished that she might become the mother of a thousand children – and when Yama agreed, pointed out that this would be impossible unless her husband came back to life. Yama, as amused by her trick as he'd been charmed by her devotion, granted her wish.

≫→ **beauty**

SCAMANDER
Europe (South)

Scamander (Skamandros, 'twisted'), son of the Cretan priest Corybas in Greek myth, was a worshipper of **Cybele**, goddess of **fertility**, whose followers danced themselves into ecstatic trances during which they mutilated themselves with knives. Scamander sailed from Crete to take the rites of Cybele to other countries, and settled at the foot

of Mount Ida (near the future site of Troy). He began to teach the local people Cybele's worship, and was demonstrating the ecstatic dance when he fell into the river Xanthus and drowned. Cybele granted him **immortality** on Earth, making him god of the river (whose name she changed to Scamander after him) and giving him the power to ensure the fertility of any young female who bathed in his waters. Ever afterwards, farmers used to dip their sheep and cattle in the water, young women used to swim there on the night before their marriages – and when **Aphrodite**, **Athene** and **Hera** were preparing to appear before **Paris**, asking him to say who was most beautiful, they made sure to bathe in Scamander first.
≫→ **water**

SCYLLA AND CHARYBDIS
Europe (South)

Scylla (Skulle, 'bitch') and Charybdis ('sucker-down'), in Greek myth, were **sea-monsters**. Scylla was the daughter of the sea-god Phorcys and the witch-goddess **Hecate** (or, some say, the monster **Lamia**). She was originally a beautiful sea-sprite, but **Poseidon** had **sex** with her, and his jealous wife **Amphitrite** filled Scylla's favourite pool with poisonous herbs, so that the next time Scylla bathed there she was turned into a revolting monster. In another version of the story, the transformation was worked by **Circe**, who was jealous because the sea god Glaucus preferred Scylla to herself. But whoever changed Scylla, the result was the same. From the waist up she kept human form, but from her waist sprouted twelve dogs' legs and

six yapping heads with razor teeth and snaky necks. Charybdis was the daughter of Poseidon and a sea-**nymph**, and was as beautiful as Scylla until she, too, offended the gods.

Scylla and Charybdis went hunting together, eating seals, sealions, dolphins and anything else that came their way. But one day they went too far, attacking and eating the herd of cattle **Heracles** had stolen from **Geryon**. It was time for the gods to punish them. Heracles killed Scylla, and her father Phorcys quickly burned the body and boiled the ash, to bring her back to life. He gave her a new home, in a cave on a cliff whose peak pierced the skies and whose sides were washed glass-smooth by waves. Zeus stole Charybdis' beautiful body from her, leaving her nothing but a toothless, ravenous mouth just under the surface of the sea.

The lairs of Scylla and Charybdis were on opposite sides of the narrow sea-channel between Italy and Sicily. Three times a day Charybdis opened her gullet and swallowed the sea overhead and anything in it. Scylla waited on guard above, reaching down and eating alive whatever passed her way: seagulls, fish and – as the crews of **Odysseus** and **Aeneas** found to their cost – human beings.

SEA

The sea and its gods played an equivocal part in many myth-traditions. The sea was often thought to have existed before the rest of the universe, as the primordial ocean from which all life began. But **creation** itself was usually done by **Sky** and Earth, and their gods took precedence over those of the ocean. In some traditions Sea then fought Sky and Earth for a share of power, or they divided it by agreement. In others, sea-gods lived aloof from the rest of the pantheon, rulers of an element filled with beings like no others in creation, and endowed with knowledge of the universe's primordial secrets, predating all other gods and the source of a power as overwhelming as it was mysterious.

⟫→ (Americas): Komokwa, Pachacamac; (Arctic): Aulanerk; (Celtic): Lir, Manannan MacLir; (China): Four Dragon Kings; (Egypt): Nun and Naunet; (Finnish): Ahto; (Greece): Amphitrite, Nereus, Poseidon, Proteus, Telchines, Thetis; (India): Tara; (Japan): Tide Jewels; (Mesopotamia): Tiamat; (Nordic) Aegir, Njörd, Ran; (Oceania): Tangaroa

SEDNA
Arctic

Sedna, or Arnarquagssaq, or Nerrivik, or Nuliajuk, in Eskimo myth, was the daughter of the creator-god Anguta and his wife. In some accounts she was so huge, and so hungry, that she ate everything in her parents' home, and even gnawed off one of her father's arms as he slept. In others, she refused to marry the suitor Anguta chose for her and instead took a dog for husband. (Their children were all the human beings and animals on Earth.) Some accounts go on to say that she was then kidnapped by Petrel, and when her father rescued her in a canoe, Petrel sank it in a storm. Others say that her father was so angry at her marrying a dog that he threw her overboard. She clung to the sides of the canoe, and he chopped her fingers off one by one until she sank to the depths. She lives there still, queen of all the **monsters** and **demons** of the **Underworld** – and her huge fingers are the origin of seals, sea-lions and whales.

⟫→ **giants**

SEKHMET
Africa (North)

Sekhmet (or Sakhmet, 'powerful'), in Egyptian myth, was consort of **Ptah** the craftsman-god and daughter of **Ra**, the Sun. She was lion-headed and carried a fire-spitting cobra. When she was at rest, she was a figure of calm, royal dignity. But when she was angry, she transformed herself into the Eye of Ra, and became a war-goddess so fierce that even the world-snake **Aapep** cowered before her. Fire-arrows darted from her eyes, she breathed flames, and searing heat – the parching winds of the desert – radiated from her body. She charred her enemies' bodies and gulped their blood.

Ra and Sekhmet. In the beginning, Ra created the world and all its people. He was the Sun, but he also took human shape, as the pharaoh, so that humans could see him and worship him. But human shape also meant that, although he was immortal, he was subject to aging. He began to wither and stoop, as the Sun does at evening, and his people turned away from him and worshipped Aapep instead. Enraged, Ra sent Sekhmet his Eye (or some say Sekhmet and **Hathor**) to punish mortals. Sekhmet raged across the land, parching the crops, searing the earth and greedily feasting on human blood. She slaughtered all Aapep's followers, and then turned on the innocent. The Nile foamed red with blood; the human race seemed doomed.

Not even Ra could control Sekhmet in her rage. The only way to stop her was trickery. While she was rampaging in the Delta, Ra sent servants to the island of Elephantine, to gather red ochre or, some say, pomegranates. Meanwhile, other servants fetched beer from the royal cellar. They mixed the red ochre (or the pomegranate juice) with the beer, and poured it over the land – seven thousand jarsful. When Sekhmet came hissing and snarling down the sky, she took the red mess for blood, lapped it up, and became so fuddled that her fires were banked, her eyes closed, and she laid her lion's muzzle on her paws and slept like a cat.

Sekhmet the healer. From the time of this 'taming' onwards, Sekhmet turned her rage mainly on Egypt's enemies, particularly the Nubians: their dark colour was caused by the searing of her breath, and she reduced their country to desert. For her own people she became a healer, using her skill in sorcery (learned because no darkness was too great for her piercing eyes to search out) and scorching with her fire-arrows the disease-**demons** that attacked humans. She ruled with her husband Ptah and son Nefertem in Memphis, where her priests formed a centuries-long dynasty of healers (specializing, some authorities say, in diseases of the heart), and she was worshipped everywhere in statues of black basalt, which can still be found all over Egypt.

➤➤ Bastet, disease and healing

SELA: *see* Mwambu and Sela

SELENE
Europe (South)

Selene (Latin Luna), '**Moon**', in Greek and Roman myth, was the third child of the **Titans Hyperion** and Theia. Unlike her brother **Helius** (**Sun**) and sister **Eos** (Dawn), she was secretive and shy. She loved the darkness of Night, and galloped through it on horseback or in a chariot pulled by pearl-white horses or silvery oxen. Soundless and aloof, she soared above the clouds. She hoarded her light: it was often pale and thin, and sometimes she veiled her face altogether and let Night's darkness rule.

In some accounts, Selene was not born shy, but withdrew from the world after her abortive love-affair with the mortal **Endymion**. In others, the reason for her shyness was that human beings were always trying to catch her and pull her down to Earth. In particular, people thought that if her reflection could be trapped in water, like a fish in a pool, she would become the slave of whoever caught it, and that if you prayed quietly enough she would creep nearer and nearer to hear you, and you could pick the right moment to snatch her from the sky. For this reason, her true worshippers banged cymbals and drums, shrieked and blew trumpets, to drown out her enemies' whispered prayers.

In most accounts, Selene is a different goddess from **Artemis** (Diana), but some myths treat them as the same.

545

SEMELE
Europe (South)

Semele ('Moon', Latin Luna), daughter of **Cadmus** and Harmonia in Greek myth, caught **Zeus'** eye, and he sent word that he wanted to sleep with her, promising in the name of the river **Styx** to give her any reward she asked. **Hera** intercepted the message, took the form of Semele's aged servant Beroe, and told her to demand a high price: she would submit to Zeus only if he came to her in all his immortal glory. Semele made her demand, and Zeus was forced to grant it, as not even gods can swear by Styx and break their word. He appeared to Semele in full glory – it was as if the sky itself were bearing down on her – and entered her in the form of a thunderbolt. Semele was scorched to ashes, and Zeus just had time to snatch up the embryonic child in her womb, **Dionysus**, before **Mother Earth** gaped open and Semele's remains disappeared into the **Underworld** forever.

SERAPIS
Africa (North)

Serapis, in Egyptian myth, is the Greek form of the name Osirap, 'Osiris-Hap'. Until the time of Alexander the Great, he was a **fertility**-god, a merging of the bull-god **Hap** and the **Underworld** ruler **Osiris**. But when Alexander the Great was on his deathbed, in 323 BCE, he called out to Serapis (the only deity he invoked), and after his death Ptolemy, who inherited power in Egypt, began a Serapis cult, centred on a statue which he claimed had miraculously fallen from the sky and which he

housed in a grandiose temple in Alexandria. In the time of Ptolemy's descendant Cleopatra, when all things Egyptian fascinated the Romans, Roman army officers were drawn to the Serapis cult, and took its **mysteries** to Rome. Serapis' initiates claimed that the god was able to cure all illnesses, and gave his worshippers easy passage between the worlds of Life and **Death**.
⋙→ **disease and healing, Mithras, mysteries**

SERQET
Africa (North)

Serqet (short for *Serqet hetyt*, 'she who lets the throat breathe'), the scorpion-goddess in Egyptian myth, was named to ward off evil: scorpion-venom paralyses the breathing instead of easing it. One of **Aset's** serving-maids, she helped to reassemble **Osiris** after **Set** cut him to pieces. She was an expert bandager, and was given the task of helping with the embalming of bodies for burial. (She was quickly promoted from bandage-nurse to chief embalmer of entrails.) In some accounts, the gods sent her to fasten the coils of the world-snake **Aapep** in a multiple S-bend pattern which would stop him moving fast enough to attack the Sun-ship.
⋙→ **animal-gods**

SESHAT
Africa (North)

Seshat ('queen of the bookroom'), in Egyptian myth, was the wife of **Ptah** god of **writing**, and the divine archivist. She noted the passage of time and the movements of the stars, made blueprints for temples and palaces, and kept a tally of all taxes, gifts and war-spoils in **Heaven** and on Earth. Her priests – unusually for Egypt, women as well as men – were site-engineers, historians and mathematicians; above all, they kept records of land-holdings and the annual levels of the Nile-floods.

SET
Africa (North)

Set (or Seth or Seti; Greek **Typhon**), in Egyptian myth, was the storm-god son of **Geb** and **Nut**. He was so impatient to be born that he ripped himself from Nut's womb before he was fully formed, and consequently had no fixed shape. To give himself body he borrowed pieces of animals, or inhabited animal bodies as a hermit-crab takes shells. Most often he had an ant-eater's head, donkey's ears and a scorpion's tail, or appeared as a hippo with a crocodile's jaws and tail; he also entered the bodies of unwary humans, and drove them mad.

Ra made Set watchman on the prow of the Sun-ship, where he fought and killed **Aapep** every evening. But he was jealous of the gods of light and lusted after their women, causing havoc in **Heaven**. In particular, he killed his own twin brother **Osiris** and then fought a prolonged battle with Osiris' son **Horus**, ending only when Horus and **Isis** humiliated him in front of the celestial court. Castrated and impotent, he gave up his ambitions to be anything more than a slave of the light-gods, Ra's figurehead, and spent eternity harassing the mortal world instead.

➤ **light and dark, twins**

SEVEN AGAINST THEBES
Europe (South)

The throne of Thebes. In Greek myth, after **Oedipus'** banishment from **Thebes**, his brother-in-law **Creon** became regent while Oedipus' sons **Eteocles** and **Polynices** grew up. As soon as the princes were old enough, they began a bitter quarrel for the throne. They could have ruled Thebes jointly, but neither would agree to share. Eteocles (the eldest) proposed that they should take turns, ruling for one year each and spending one year in exile. Polynices refused, saying that he could never trust Eteocles to hand over the throne when his year was up. He went to Argos and asked King Adrastus for help to win the throne. Adrastus gathered an army, led by seven champions, the Seven Against Thebes: Adrastus and Polynices, Amphiaraus, Capaneus, Hippomedon, Tydeus and Parthenopaeus.

Seven Against Thebes. The Seven marched their army up and ringed Thebes with spears. There were seven city gates, and each champion led the attack on one of them. Inside the city, seven Theban champions led the defence: Actor, Hyperbius, Lasthenes, Megareus, Melanippus, Polyphontes and Prince Eteocles. There would have been an eighth champion, Creon's son Menoeceus, taking Eteocles' place while Eteocles led the whole defence. But just before the battle, the prophet **Tiresias** said that the Thebans would win if a royal prince sacrificed his own life for the city, and Menoeceus jumped from the battlements and killed himself.

The battle began, and Capaneus, fieriest of the seven Argive champions, was driven mad by blood-lust. He climbed a scaling-ladder, and was boasting that he would fall on the city like a thunderbolt, so hot that in comparison **Zeus**' thunderbolts would seem like rays of winter sun, when Zeus threw a real thunderbolt and toppled him. The omen encouraged the Thebans, who threw open four of the gates and surged out to attack. Two of the seven champions, Hippomedon and Parthenopaeus, were killed at once in the fighting, and a third, Tydeus, was wounded in the belly. His supporter **Athene** ran to save him, but at the last moment Amphiaraus cut off the head of the spears-man who had wounded Tydeus and gave it to him saying 'Suck the brains' – and when Tydeus sucked out his enemy's brains Athene hurried back to **Olympus** and left him to die. The Theban hero Periclymenus ran to kill Amphiaraus, who jumped into his chariot and fled. He prayed to Zeus to spare him the dishonour of being stabbed in the back, and Zeus split open the earth so that Amphiaraus and his chariot plunged headlong into the **Underworld**. When Adrastus saw this, and realized that with five of his champions dead the expedition was doomed, he leapt onto his winged horse (a gift from his father **Poseidon**), shook the reins and soared from the battlefield. The Argive army fled.

Eteocles and Polynices. Now, on the plain, only the brothers Eteocles and Polynices were left, facing each other in single combat. Before Oedipus left Thebes, he had cursed them, praying that they would decide their inheritance with iron and go to the Underworld on a single day, each killing the other – and in the same moment, after battering each other for hours, they lunged, dealt each other mortal wounds and fulfilled the prayer.

The Epigoni. In Thebes, Creon was now king. He issued an edict that all the dead Thebans, including Eteocles, were to be buried with honour, but that all the dead Argives, including Polynices, were to be left to rot. This proclamation not only set Creon against his own niece **Antigone** (who buried Polynices knowing that it would lead to her own death), but disgusted all Greece. King **Theseus** of Athens led an army against the city, executed Creon and saw that all the dead soldiers, on both sides, received equal funeral honours. This done, he left.

Enfeebled and powerless, the city of Thebes carried on a ragged existence for a couple of decades. But then another group of seven warriors, the Epigoni or Second Champions, descendants of the original Seven, decided that for honour's sake it should be obliterated forever. Led by Alcmaeon son of Amphiaraus, they were Aegialeus son of Adrastus, **Diomedes** (King of Aetolia), son of Tydeus, Sthenelus son of Capaneus, Polydorus son of Hippomedon, Promachus son of Parthenopaeus and Thesander son of Polynices. They set siege, intending to starve the people into submission. But in the night Tiresias warned the Thebans that their city was doomed, and they packed their belongings and crept away – so that next morning the Epigoni found the gates swinging open and the city deserted.

SEVEN GODS OF GOOD LUCK, THE
Asia (East)

The Seven Gods of Good Luck (*Schichi Fukujin*, 'seven happiness beings'), in Japanese myth, were Benzai goddess of love, Bishamon god of success in war, Daikoku god of wealth, Ebisu god of fishing, Fukurokoju god of good health, Hotei Osho god of generosity and large families, and Jurojin god of long life.

SEVEN SEERS, THE
India

The Seven Seers, in Hindu myth, were star-lords of the constellation of the Great Bear. They were **Atri**, Bharadwaja, Gautama, Jamadagni, Kasyapa, **Vashishtra** and **Vishvamitra**. They protected gods and human beings, and fought ceaseless wars against **demons**. But they were touchy, quarrelsome and unpredictable, and neither the gods, mortals, nor other Seers were safe from their bad tempered magic.

SEX

The sex-urge, the impulse to mate, appeared in two ways in most myth-traditions. At the beginning of the universe, it was a physical equivalent of the irresistible mental urge which started the process of **creation**, and it remained only just controllable, female spirits endlessly receiving and welcoming fertilization, males spraying **fertility** in unstoppable floods. (In some accounts, creation-gods were so fertile that whenever they stirred, or breathed, or moved, new life appeared.) Later, charge of the sex-urge was given to particular gods, who combined seductiveness with unpredictability and danger, and who oversaw the fertility of the gods, the universe and all creation except **demons**, **monsters** and creatures of the **Underworld**. In many accounts, sex-gods guarded or embodied **immortality** itself, and **giants** and others, deprived of it, were always trying to kidnap them or rape them. A rollicking side-branch of sex-myths concerned gods inadvertently trapped on Earth, who spent eternity obsessively mating with everything in sight, from trees to nymphs, from stones to horses – or, if all else failed, standing in endless erection as signposts, scarecrows or doorguards.

»→ (Americas): Ghede, Tlazoltéotl, Wahari and Buoka; (Australia): Bildjiwuaroju, Miralaldu and Djanggawul; (Egypt): Min; (Greece): Aphrodite, Cybele, Eros, Pan, Priapus, Satyrs; (India): Kama, Rati, Shiva; (Mesopotamia): Inanna, Ishtar; (Nordic): Frey, Freyja; (Oceania): Kamapua'a; (Slavic): Yarilo

sGROLMA
Asia (Southwest)

sGrolma, in Tibetan myth, was **Mother Earth**, one of the two first beings in the world. She took the form of a rock-giantess and mated with the other primordial being, the monkey-god **sPyan-ras-gzigs**, and their offspring were all created beings.

SHAMASH
Asia (West)

Shamash ('**Sun**'), in Sumerian myth, was the son of the **Moon**-god **Sin** and brother of **Ishtar**, goddess of **fertility** and **war**. He lived in a palace called Efabbar ('shining house') with his wife Aya ('youth') and his sons Giru ('fire'), Kittum ('truth'), Mesharum ('justice') and Nusku ('light'). Because nothing could hide from the radiance which streamed from his eyes, he oversaw **justice and universal order**, using a knife (or in some accounts a saw or a sickle) to slice truth from lies. He and his sons spent their days riding their chariot across the sky, and at night they threw open a gate in the mountains and galloped into their palace to rest.

In art, Shamash was shown sometimes in symbolic form, as the Sun-disc or wheel of truth, and sometimes as a king sitting in splendour, wearing a four-horned crown and holding the staff of justice and the wheel of truth.

SHANG DI
Asia (East)

Shang Di ('great god'), in Chinese myth, was the supreme being. He personified the power which generates life and causes growth. This power energized the universe at the beginning of **creation** and keeps it in existence, by the continual rebirth of plants and animals. In the earliest times, Shang Di was regarded as a Heavenly equivalent of the Emperor on Earth, presiding over a vast court of functionaries and lesser gods. In Confucian times he was made more abstract, an august and somewhat disembodied power to whom no myths were attached. In Daoist times (in fact as late as the eleventh century CE) he was merged with a new figure, **Yu Huang**, to become the single supreme being in a monotheistic and largely philosophical system; anyone who didn't follow the Dao, however, continued to regard him as the benevolent ruler of a **Heaven** teeming with deities, the long-bearded, smiling grandfather so often shown in art.

⟫→ justice and universal order, supreme deity

SHANGO
Africa

Shango, in Yoruba myth, ruled the people in the days when gods still walked the Earth. He was the son of **Ogun** the **war**-god, a **lightning**-bolt in human form, and when he was angry **fire**-arrows shot from every orifice and burst through his skin. His wives were three rivers, Niger, Oba and Oshun, but not even their coolness could soothe his rage. In the end his temper made his people turn against him and banish him. Instead of leaving the kingdom, he hanged himself – and when the people went to bury his body all they found was an iron chain dangling from a hole. Priests interpreted this to mean that the king had become a god, but the people disagreed and there was furious argument until Shango settled it by sending a lightning-storm which destroyed the houses of everyone who'd refused to worship him. Ever afterwards he was revered as god of **thunder**.

Shango's animal-familiar was the lion, and when Yoruba slaves took his worship to Brazil in the nineteenth century CE, their Christian masters identified him as Saint Jerome (who also had a lion as his symbol) – a somewhat unexpected new role for the saint previously remembered chiefly for translating the Bible into Latin.

SHAPE-CHANGERS

At the beginning of the universe, the gods and spirits who oversaw **creation** were usually shape-changers, trying on different forms to find those they liked or were most suitable for their work. They were creative energy or intellectual thought incarnate, and to imagine a thing was to become it. Usually thereafter, when something was created it was given a stable form, and kept it; the exceptions were **tricksters** and wizards, who kept their shape-changing powers, sometimes to help human beings (especially as they roamed the world finishing the task of creation), sometimes as ways to discover new knowledge (for example what it was like to be an ant or a sea-current), and sometimes just for the fun of it.

After the coming of the great monotheistic religions, when the establishment of a scriptural canon involved much selection and editing of myth, shape-changing was allowed only to the supreme deity, and other shape-changers were downgraded – in some traditions into **devils** and **monsters**, in others into the fairies, goblins, sprites and witches of folk-tale. But in other traditions, including some of the most ancient, shape-changers were among the grandest and most awesome deities in the pantheon: **Heitsi-Eibib**, **Tezcatlipoca**, **Odin** and **Zeus** are typical examples.

»→ (Africa): Dxui; (Americas): Annency, Mixcóatl; (Australia): Wondjina; (Celtic): Cernunnos, Fintan, Lady of the Lake, Merlin, Morgan le Fay, Nimue, Pwyll, Uther Pendragon; (China): Erh Long, Five Emperors, Yu; (Finnish): Lemminkäinen; (Greece): Proteus, Telchines, Titans; (India): apsaras, nagas and naginis, Sisupala; (Japan): Ukemochi; (Nordic): Fafnir, Heimdall, Loki, Otr, Thiazi; (Oceania): Honoyeta, Kamapua'a; (Slavic): Vodyanoi, Volkh

SHASHTI
India

Shashti, in Indian myth, was the goddess of **childbirth**. **Demons** were particularly active on the sixth day after a child was born, trying to snatch it to the **Underworld** – and Shashti rode to the rescue on her sacred cat, or in cat-form herself, driving them off as a cat drives off snakes. In some accounts, she was one form of **Durga**, in others of Shri, goddess of prosperity.

»→ animal-gods

SHATRUGHNA
India

Shatrughna, in Hindu myth, was the son of King **Dasaratha** and Queen **Sumitra**. He was a loyal supporter of his brother **Bharata**, and acted as his lieutenant in the same way as Shatrughna's twin **Lakshmana** served their elder brother **Rama**.

SHEN NONG
Asia (East)

Shen Nong, in Chinese myth, was the second of the **Three Sovereigns**, successor to **Fu Xi**. He was the son of a mortal princess and the Sky-dragon, and was a **shape-changer**. Usually he took the form of an ox-headed human, but he also made himself into the scorching wind which produces forest-fires – a shape which, in some accounts, earned him the honorary name Yen Ti ('burning emperor'). He taught human beings the 'slash-and-burn' technique of land-clearance, invented the plough and showed our ancestors the properties of all plants on Earth, distinguishing between those which nourished, those which cured illness and those which poisoned.

In some versions, Yen Ti was an entirely separate Emperor, Shen Nong's successor and the third of the Three Sovereigns. But no stories are told of him, and scholars now think that he and Shen Nong were the same individual. Accounts which try to give historical identities to myth-characters say that Shen Nong ruled from 2737-2697 BCE. Myth accounts, more exuberantly, claim that he ruled for seventeen mortal generations. The herb-lore of ancient Chinese medicine is still claimed to have been largely his invention – and myth says that he had a transparent stomach, and used it to test plants. The testing went well until one particularly poisonous herb shredded his insides and ended his mortal life.

⟫→ **disease and healing, farming**

SHEOL
Asia (West)

Sheol ('pit'), in Hebrew myth, was the **Underworld**, a vast cavern filled with the dead of all creatures which had once lived in the Upper World. It was the mirror-image of the Upper World, except that its hierarchies depended on whether people had been 'good' or 'bad' in earlier lives. Instead of light its inhabitants had darkness, instead of body they had non-entity – and crucially, instead of knowledge-of-God they had absence-of-God.

SHESHA
India

Shesha ('all that's left'), also known as Ananta ('endless one'), in Hindu myth, was the huge **snake** which encompassed the universe. **Vishnu** slept on Shesha's coils, which floated on the primordial ocean, and the snake raised its thousand heads like a canopy to protect him. At the end of each cycle of existence, Shesha spews forth fire which destroys **creation**.

Shesha and Balarama. In some accounts, when Vishnu was incarnated as **Rama**, Shesha joined him, taking the human form of **Balarama**. When the time came for Balarama to die, Shesha turned back into a snake and wriggled out of his body, before cloning himself a thousand-thousand-fold to make every snake on Earth.

Scholars explain Shesha as the infinity of time.

SHITALA
India

Shitala ('shivering'), in Indian myth, is the goddess of skin diseases, particularly smallpox. She is the eldest and most virulent of seven unholy sisters (each of them manifestations of **Devi**,

552

goddess of disease), and either flogs the skin of her victims raw with iron reeds, or creeps into their bodies and kisses the pestilence into them from inside.

≫→ disease and healing

SHIVA
India

Shiva's origin and names. Shiva ('auspicious'), in Hindu myth, is one of the triad of gods who oversee **justice and universal order**. He is the destroyer, the force which sucks everything towards the centre; **Vishnu** is the preserver, the force which radiates outwards from a still centre; **Brahma** is the equilibrium between them. The name Shiva, in the Vedic prayers and poems of the Aryans who invaded India in the seventeenth century BCE, was a description of **Rudra** the storm-god, given him to placate his fury; Shiva became an independent god in the second century BCE. His own honorific names include Bhaivara ('who enjoys dancing' – a reference to his presence in cremation-grounds, dancing among the pyres), Digambara ('sky-clad' – that is, naked), Gangadhara ('upholder of the Ganges' – see below), Hara ('ravisher'), Ishvara ('lord'), Kala (**'death'**), Lingodbhava ('lord of the phallus' – see below), Mahadeva ('great god'), Nataraja ('lord of the dance' – see below), Natesa ('dancer' – when he slays **demons** by dancing on their heads) and Pashupa ('lord of animals').

Shiva's birth. Brahma and Vishnu were discussing which of them was the supreme power in the universe, when they were interrupted by the sudden appearance of a vast penis, a pillar which shone with star-brightness and whose roots were as far out of sight below as its tip was invisible above. Brahma changed into a wild goose and flew up to find the tip; Vishnu changed into a boar and grubbed in the **Underworld** to find the roots. Both gods returned, defeated – and a vagina-shaped opening appeared in the penis' side and gave birth to Shiva. Brahma and Vishnu, recognizing his power, at once accepted him as third member of the triad which ruled the universe.

Shiva's appearance and attributes. Shiva was the reconciliation of apparent opposites: he was a destroyer who created, a scatterer who unified, an implacable judge who showed mercy, and his twin attributes were meditation and ferocious dance. He sided with such outcasts as demons and **vampires** – and often slouched into **Heaven** as a matted-haired beggar, his body and head streaked with ash from the mortal funerals he enjoyed. Or he sat for years, brooding, and none of the gods dared approach him. He was knowledge, unflinching and essential: his third eye (see 'Shiva's weapons', below) and his fearsome dance banished ignorance and darkness because those things were part of him, because he understood them from within. His dance, which was Truth, so delighted the world-serpent **Shesha**, who saw it by chance one day, that he abandoned Vishnu for years and tried every kind of prayer and sacrifice to be allowed another glimpse.

Shiva's strength. Ceaseless meditation gave Shiva enormous strength – and he increased it by trickery. Demons once persuaded Brahma, by prayer and sacrifice, to give them three castles which could be destroyed only by a god, and then not unless he fired a single arrow. Safe in these castles, they made war on Heaven, and none of the gods had a bow powerful enough to fire such an arrow, or was strong enough to draw it if they had. They asked Shiva's help, and he offered to lend them half his strength. But none of them could control it, and he proposed instead that they pool all their own strength and lend him half. When the gods agreed, Shiva fired a single arrow and dealt with the demons – and then refused to return the gods' strength. Their strength combined with his made him the most powerful being in the universe.

Shiva's weapons. As eternity progressed, Shiva acquired a miscellany of weapons, into each of which he distilled some of his power, making them invincible. He was armed with a stubby mace whose tip was a skull, a sword and trident fashioned from thunderbolts, a bow made from a rainbow, and above all his terrible, third eye. Originally he had just two eyes, and their calm gaze illuminated the entire universe. But one day his wife **Parvati** crept up behind him and playfully covered his eyes. The universe went pitch-dark, and demons clambered eagerly out of the Underworld to take control. But Shiva opened a third eye in the centre of his forehead, and concentrated all his inner light to shine from it. It scattered the darkness and seared the demons dead. Ever afterwards the eye remained in Shiva's forehead. Usually it was closed, but at the end of each cycle of the universe he opens it as he dances, and destroys gods,

mortals, demons and everything in **creation**.

Shiva and the thousand atheists. A thousand seers once thought themselves so powerful that they had no need of gods. The gods asked Shiva to deal with them. He walked into the seers' stronghold, disguised as a naked tramp, and said, 'There are gods: worship them.' The seers combined their magic powers and made a tiger as big as a mountain – and Shiva extended the nail of one little finger, skinned it alive, threw the skin round him like a cloak and said, 'There are gods: worship them.' The seers conjured up a demon-dwarf of black rock, armed with a thunder-mace: ignorance personified. Shiva jumped on its head and began to dance – and the seers gaped at the beauty and terror of the dance. Then Shiva said, 'There are gods: worship them', and parted the sky to show the gods in Heaven, watching like spectators at a show. The seers fell to their knees in homage, and never questioned the gods again.

Shiva Gangadhara. All water in the universe came from the river Ganges, flowing eternally to fill the primordial ocean. At first, the Ganges watered only Heaven, making it green and lush, and there was no water at all on Earth. The ashes of the dead began to choke the land and destroy the world's **fertility**. A sage, **Bhagiratha**, persuaded Brahma to solve the problem by diverting the Ganges from Heaven to Earth. But the river was so powerful that if it fell from the sky it would shatter the Earth and drown it and everything on it. Shiva sat in meditation under Mount Kailasa in the Himalayas, and let the river wash over him. It spewed out of Heaven and became lost in the tangle of hair on top of his head. For seven years it wandered, trying to find a path through his matted locks – and finally ran to Earth, tamed, in seven broad streams, to water all the world. Shiva built himself a palace on Mount Kailasa, and it has been his home ever since.

Shiva and Daksha. Shiva's all-knowledge made him implacable: wherever he found wickedness, he punished it. On one occasion he went too far, cutting off one of Brahma's heads (see 'Shiva Linghodbhava' below), and the gods retaliated by banishing him from Heaven. This exile began a long quarrel, which flared up particularly in a feud between Shiva and Brahma's son **Daksha**. Daksha held a betrothal-feast for his daughter **Sati**, inviting all the gods except Shiva, and invited Sati to choose her future husband. Sati threw a garland into the air – and Shiva materialized in the middle of the room and caught it. Daksha shouted that Shiva was an outcast, mad, a dancer in cemeteries and a consorter with demons – and every time he saw Shiva or held another feast at which the god was not invited, he repeated these accusations.

Finally Sati could stand it no more: she threw herself into the sacrificial fire and was consumed. Shiva, furious with grief, sliced off Daksha's head, plucked demons out of his hair like lice and sent them scampering through Heaven, grabbed Sati's body and began dancing with it, his dance of destruction which would end creation. Vishnu hastily intervened, causing Sati to be reborn as Parvati, even more beautiful than before. In return, Shiva gave Daksha back

his life. But the demons had stolen Daksha's head, and Shiva could only replace it with the head of the first creature which came along: a goat. This hardly improved Daksha's temper, and he continued to hold feasts without inviting Shiva – something which caused trouble whenever Shiva found out (see **Pushan**).

Shiva Lingodbhava. Two myths explain Shiva's title 'lord of the phallus'. One is the story of his birth: see above. (In some accounts, Brahma claimed to have reached the tip of the penis, and Shiva in a fury cut off one of his heads – the deed for which the gods later banished him from Heaven.) In the second myth, he was wandering in a forest when he saw the beautiful wives of a group of sages. He changed himself into a youth so handsome that all the wives began swooning with desire for him. The furious sages put a spell on him which caused his penis to wither away – and he retaliated by blighting the universe with darkness, until they hastily made an artificial penis, garlanded it with flowers and planted it in the ground for their wives to worship. From that moment the penis-column, or *lingam*, became one of Shiva's aspects, and the regeneration of his penis symbolized the springtime rebirth of fertility for all the world.

*No gods are more often represented in art than Shiva, or in so many different forms. Sometimes he is a smiling prince with four arms and four faces (one of which contains the third eye); in paintings his skin is fair and his neck is blue (from the poison he sucked from **Vasuki**, who tried to spit it into the **amrita** churned from the Sea of*

Milk); he wears a tiger-skin and a necklace of skulls and bones, or has snakes coiling round his neck or arching above his head to strike. Sometimes he rides Nandi, his milk-white bull; sometimes he is Yogeshvara, 'prince of ascetics', meditating, covered in ash, with his matted hair lank and straggling. As Lingodbhava, 'lord of the phallus', he is shown either as a man with a huge erect penis, or as a flower-garlanded penis jutting from the ground. In the commonest image of all he is shown as Nataraja, 'lord of the dance': surrounded by a ring of fire, with snakes fanning from his head, he stands with one leg raised in the dance. One hand holds a drum (or sometimes a gazelle), another a flame (or sometimes an axe), the third hand blesses, and the fourth points down towards the dancing foot, to symbolize salvation.

≫→ sex

SHI ZONG DI
Asia (East)

Shi Zong Di, in Chinese myth, was one of the ministers of **Shen Nong**, second of the **Three Sovereigns**. Shen Nong, lord of the scorching wind, travelled with such force over **Mother Earth** that he dried up the ground and parched vegetation without realizing it – and in the nick of time, before the whole of **creation** withered and died, Shi Zong Di poured water in a bowl, dipped a branch in it and scattered it over the Earth: the first **rain**. For this he was rewarded with **immortality** and the title Rain-Master. He was an important official in the celestial court until he rashly supported Qi Yu's *coup* against the Emperor **Huang Di**. The revolt was crushed and Shi Zong Di was

demoted. The administration of rain was given to others, and instead of dipping his branch to water the whole Earth, he was allowed to use it only to sprinkle the dust ahead of Huang Di as he walked in procession.

SHOU LAO
Asia (East)

Shou Lao ('star of long life'), in Chinese myth, was in some accounts the home of the Old Man of the South Pole, in others the god himself in the form of a star. He was a favourite figure in art, being shown as a smiling, bald old man carrying a peach (symbolizing long life) and a gourd (symbolizing prosperity), sitting on the ground or riding a stag and with a bat and crane in attendance. (Stags, bats and cranes were symbols of happiness.)

≫→ **Three Gods of Happiness**

SHU
Africa (North)

Shu ('air'), in Egyptian myth, was the son of **Atum** and brother of **Tefnut**. In some accounts he was born after Atum masturbated; in others (perhaps influenced by the sound of his name), he was sneezed out of Atum's nose. He and Tefnut mated to produce the interlocking **twins Geb** (Earth) and **Nut** (Sky), and Shu then separated them, leaving Geb floating in the primordial ocean and arching Nut's body high above as a pathway for the **Sun** to travel each day from horizon to horizon.

In art Shu takes two forms. As god of light, he is shown kneeling, facing us, holding the Sky-arch on his shoulders and upraised arms. As one of the deities of darkness, he is leader of a gang of glee-fully-drawn **demons** *who butcher the wicked in the* **Underworld**.

SHUN
Asia (East)

Shun, in Chinese myth, was the fifth of the **Five Emperors**. From his birth, to humble parents, he was outstandingly sweet-natured and patient. His father, brothers and step-mother hated him and tried to kill him, but he gradually wore them down until, like everyone else, they loved him. The aged Emperor **Yao** was so impressed by tales of his uprightness that he married him to one of the Imperial daughters and then sent him, as royal son-in-law, to pass a series of tests – finding his way in jungle, adjudicating between quarrelling farmers, showing potters how to improve their work – and when they were done, he appointed the young man his heir, preferring him above his own legitimate sons.

As soon as Shun took the throne, the chaos always latent in nature rebelled. There were ten Suns in the sky, and every day they took the form of birds and flew up into the sky. Nine roosted in trees, and the tenth soared on high to warm the Earth. After Shun's enthronement all ten rose simultaneously, and their heat would have scorched Earth's inhabitants dead if Shun had not sent the archer **Yi** to shoot nine of the Sun-birds dead – which is why there is only one Sun today. Shun then sent **Yu** the Dragon Lord to control disastrous **floods** which were engulfing the

Earth, and as soon as the land was dry divided it into twelve administrative regions and ruled in peace and harmony until the day he died.

In some accounts, Shun is said to be the same person as **Zhuan Hu**, the second of the Five Emperors.

Shun's golden age, somewhat anodyne compared to the roistering of his predecessor **Huang Di**, *was held to have taken place at the end of the third millennium BCE, and to have been a time of consolidation and order whose benefits stayed with China for thousands of years. Shun himself was a roi fainéant, setting a good example but leaving strenuous good deeds to others (such as Yi and Yu). He was, however, held in such reverence that when the list of Twenty-four Examples of Hsiao was compiled in historical times, his name came first. (Hsiao, the quality of acceptance and fulfilment of one's duty – as parent to child or child to parent, and as ruler to ruled or ruled to ruler – is akin to the Roman quality of pietas attributed by Virgil to* **Aeneas**, *and is therefore usually, and inadequately, translated as 'piety' in English.)*

SIBYLS
Europe (South)

Sibyls, in Greek and Roman myth, were prophetesses. They were ordinary girls, taken from their families and trained for their work from infancy. When worshippers asked questions of the gods, the Sibyls put themselves in trances – for example by chewing sacred plants or allowing sacred snakes to bite them – and uttered sounds supposed to be the gods' words, which priests then wrote down and translated into prophecies.

The best known Sibyls served at shrines close to supposed gateways between **Heaven** and Earth or Earth and the **Underworld**. The Sibyl at Delphi, for example, presided at Mount Parnassus, a favourite bridge for the gods between Heaven and Earth. The Sibyl of Cumae guarded one of the entrances to the Underworld. The last Sibyl of Cumae was the most respected of all. Her birthname was Deiphobe ('god-fearing'), and she was so beautiful that **Apollo** not only told her the future but offered her any gift she chose if she would have **sex** with him. In some accounts she asked for **immortality**, in others to live one year for each grain of sand she was holding in her cupped hands. But in each case as soon as the wish was granted she refused to have sex, and Apollo punished her. She had forgotten to ask to keep her youth and beauty forever, and as the years passed she became ever more shrivelled, until in the end the priests hung her on the wall in a bottle, and when travellers asked 'Sibyl, what do you want?' she answered 'I want to die'.

*The Sibyl of Cumae was highly regarded in Roman myth and legend. When Aeneas visited her, she took him to the Underworld where his father **Anchises** showed him the whole future destiny of Rome, the generations of Romans yet unborn. (Roman writers computed that at this time the Sibyl was a mere 700 years old.) Later, she took nine books of prophecies to King Tarquin, saying that they contained every secret of Rome's future, that it would last forever, and offering to sell them to him if he agreed to take over her immortality and supervise that future. He refused, and she burned*

*three books before offering him the others at the same price. Once again he said no, and she burned three more. Tarquin bought the last three books, and the Sibyl disappeared and was never seen again. The prophecies in the books turned out to be gibberish, but none the less Tarquin had a temple built for them and the 'Sibylline verses' were ever afterwards consulted by the priests in times of civic trouble. But by allowing six of the original nine books to be burned, Tarquin had foreshortened not only his own life but the future destiny of Rome. Its glory was great but finite, and – the story ends – wherever the Sibyl now is, living out her agonized immortality, she has the dubious satisfaction of knowing that in this **prophecy**, as in all others, she spoke exact and literal truth.*

SIDDHARTHA GAUTAMA
India

Siddhartha Gautama, in Buddhist myth and belief, was the mortal prince who became **Buddha**. Born miraculously to **Maya**, he was kept from all the evil and misery of the world throughout his youth. He grew up rich, carefree and happy, married the beautiful **Yashodhara** and had a son. But one day by accident he saw an old man, and the sorrows of the world suddenly flooded his consciousness. He left his family and his palace to wander the world, and after six years, and five weeks' meditation under a *bho* (wild fig) tree, he achieved enlightenment about the causes of human misery, and how to avoid it.

Siddhartha (c563-479 BCE) was a historical figure, and artwork shows him as a

typical prince of the time, riding his chariot, hunting, seated at court, surrounded
by friends and servants. His face usually
shows anxiety and alarm at the state of
the world, in marked and deliberate contrast to the serenity which always char-
acterizes Buddha.
⫸ **Ananda, Devadatta, Mara,
Nanda**

SIDO
Oceania

Sido, in the myths of the Kiwai and
Toaripi peoples of Melanesia, was
born to a pair of Siamese-**twin** goddesses, and as soon as he was born he
separated them. Generative power
sprayed from his penis like rain, clothing the naked Earth with plants. Sido's
mothers taught him the secret of **immortality**: to slough his skin like a
snake each night. But a group of
children disturbed him halfway
through the change, and the spell
was broken. His spirit continued to
wander the world, but his body rotted
– and his mothers washed his skull
and used it as a cup for the water of
immortality (a gift available to every
god but Sido, who was unable to drink
from his own skull). Sido's restless
spirit married a mortal girl (and gave
her fire as a wedding-gift), and when
she died it transformed itself first into
a gigantic pig (which mourners ate at
her funeral-feast) and then into the
vast, dark House of **Death** where all
mortals are doomed to go.
⫸ **fertility**

SIEGFRIED: *see* Sigurd

SIf
Europe (North)

Sif the harvest-goddess, **Thor**'s wife in
Nordic myth, had hair like ripe wheat,
flowing to the ground. One night as she
slept, **Loki** cut it all off for a prank,
leaving her bald and the world grain-
less. Thor threatened to kill Loki unless
he replaced the hair, and Loki went to
the dwarf Dvalin, master-goldsmith,
and promised him that if he made Sif
a headful of new hair he would have the
thanks and favour of the gods forever.
Dvalin and his brother forged hair from
gold, working it with rune-magic, and
used the spare gold to make two other
presents for the gods, an unerring spear
for **Odin** and for **Frey** a ship big enough
to hold all the gods, but which could be
folded up like a handkerchief when not
in use and kept in Frey's pocket.

Armed with these presents, Loki now
bet two other dwarfs that they could
never surpass them. If they did, he said,
he'd let them cut off his head. The
dwarfs set to work, and Loki realized
at once that they were better goldsmiths
even than Dvalin. The first dwarf stayed
at the forge, working the bellows and
keeping the fire at a constant tempera-
ture – essential for the magic – while the
other went out of the room to cast his
spells. When he left for the first time
Loki changed himself into a fly and bit
the first dwarf on the hand, trying to
distract him. But the dwarf took no
notice, and when his brother returned
they pulled out of the fire the golden
boar Gullinbursti, destined to be Frey's
charger as he rode the sky. The second
time, Loki bit the bellows-dwarf on the
cheek, and again failed to distract him:

the treasure this time was a golden armlet for Odin which had the property of cloning itself eight times every ninth night. The third time, Loki stung the bellows-dwarf on the eyelid, and the dwarf let go the bellows for an instant to brush him away. The treasure this time, a golden hammer, was short in the handle and seemed imperfect. But when Loki took all six presents to the gods, they told him that the hammer, Mjöllnir, was in fact the greatest treasure of all, since Thor would use it to kill all their enemies. The dwarf-brothers now demanded Loki's head, as promised – and when he said they could have it so long as they didn't take any part of his neck (which was not included in the bargain), they sewed up his lips instead, using a magic awl to cut through his immortal skin.

The dwarfs now gave Thor his hammer, and sewed the golden hair to Sif's head, where it immediately began to grow. So the gods got protection from their enemies, mortals got back their harvest, and Loki got a twisted mouth and the laughter of all **Asgard**.

>>→ **crafts, fertility, smiths**

SIGMUND
Europe (North)

Sigmund ('victory-mouth'), in Nordic myth, was the great-grandson of **Odin**'s son Sigi. Odin stuck a magic sword in a tree (some say in **Yggdrasil**), and declared that whoever pulled it out would be the greatest hero mortals had ever seen. Sigmund was the only man strong enough to perform the feat. He led his people to victory in battle after battle, and when the time came for

him to leave the mortal world for **Valhalla**, Odin smashed the sword to fragments. Sigmund's widow Hjördis gathered them and gave them to the smith **Regin**, to whom she also entrusted her and Sigmund's newborn son **Sigurd**. Regin was to foster Sigurd, and when the boy came of age he was to refashion the sword and give it to him, so that Sigurd would lead his people with the same bravery and distinction as Sigmund had done. (Unfortunately for Hjördis' plans, the gods had other ideas: see **Andvari**, **Fafnir**, **Regin**, **Sigurd**.)

>>→ **heroes**

SIGNY
Europe (North)

Signy, Volsung's daughter and **Sigmund**'s **twin** sister in Germanic myth, was married to Siggeir, who had killed her other nine brothers and her father in order to seize the throne. Determined to bear a son who would be one of the greatest warriors ever seen on earth, she sent her firstborn for Sigmund to train in the arts of **war**. Sigmund found him an effeminate weakling, and killed him. Signy sent her second son – and Sigmund scornfully returned him, saying that he wasn't worth even the trouble of killing. At this point Signy decided that the fault must be Siggeir's and that he was unworthy to sire the grandson of Volsung. She changed her appearance by magic, took Sigmund to bed for three nights and days of continuous intercourse, and then disappeared, returning to her own shape. Nine months later **Sinfiotl** was born, and Signy claimed that he was Siggeir's son.

SIGURD
Europe (North)

Sigurd ('victory-peace'), in Nordic myth (or, in Germanic myth, Siegfried) was a member of the Volsung family, descendants of **Odin** and a mortal. He was the son of **Sigmund**, born after his father's death and brought up by the smith **Regin**, who reforged for him a magic sword which had symbolized his father's kingship until it was smashed by Odin. Using this sword, Sigurd killed Regin's dragon-brother **Fafnir** and stole his hoard of gold (the wealth of the universe). He also bathed in Fafnir's blood, which made him invulnerable except for one place, where a leaf fluttered down and stuck to the skin of his shoulder.

By eating Fafnir's heart, Sigurd acquired second hearing, the ability to understand the languages of birds, animals and insects. The birds told him that Regin intended to murder him and take the gold – and before this could happen he killed Regin. He took from the treasure a single gold ring (not realizing that it had been cursed by its dwarf-maker, **Andvari**, with the power to destroy all who owned it), and set out to find adventure. Crossing the rainbow-bridge **Bifröst**, he came to the hilltop where the **Valkyrie Brynhild** lay sleeping in a ring of fire, waiting until a hero braved the flames and woke her. Sigurd gave her the ring as a sign of betrothal, and continued on his journey.

In the land of the **Nibelungs**, Sigurd was given a magic potion to make him forget his promise to Brynhild, and prepared to marry princess Gudrun. Remembering only that Brynhild had his ring, he first sent Gudrun's brother Gunnar to exchange it for another, and then (when Gunnar was driven back by the fire-circle) disguised himself as Gunnar, agreed to marry Brynhild and exchanged rings with her. He gave the magic ring to Gunnar who married Gudrun. Brynhild, scorned and mocked, made her brother-in-law Guttorm murder Sigurd as he slept – and then, filled with guilt, threw herself on Sigurd's funeral-pyre and died.

These are the bare bones of the story, as told in the Norse Volsung Saga. The German Nibelung Poem from the same period (thirteenth century CE) tells much the same story, changing some of the names (Andvari becomes Alberich; Gudrun becomes Kriemhild; Gunnar becomes Gunther; Guttorm becomes Hagen; Regin becomes Mime; Sigurd becomes Siegfried) and makes Brynhild (Brünnhilde) an Icelandic princess. Hagen kills Siegfried by stabbing him with his own sword, in the one vulnerable spot on his skin. The gold-hoard, including the baleful ring, is thrown into the Rhine and lost to mortals forever. The poem continues with Kriemhild leading her armies against Hagen, to avenge his murder of Siegfried, and ends with her death in battle.

In the nineteenth century, the Volsung Saga and Nibelung Poem inspired Wagner's four-part music-drama The Ring of the Nibelungs. Wagner took elements from both stories and added ideas from other Norse and Germanic myths – gods, dwarfs and other supernatural beings play leading parts, and Brünnhilde's (Brynhild's) suicide triggers nothing less than *Götterdämmerung* (**Ragnarök**), the end of the universe. He also gave the characters psychological complexity, and used musical 'leading motifs' (tags of melody or harmony, each with a specific referent, for example 'love', 'destiny' or 'the sword') to weave webs of meaning and relationships latent in the myths, perhaps, but outside the scope of the medieval works which inspired him. In its way, the Ring is as 'definitive' a myth-based work as Homer's Iliad or Virgil's **Aeneid** – and our feeling that Wagner has taken more liberties than Homer or Virgil might vanish if we knew as much about their sources as we do of his.

⫸ heroes

SILENUS
Europe (South)

Silenus (Sileinos, 'moony'), in Greek myth, son of **Mother Earth** (or, some say, of **Hermes** or **Pan**) was renowned for his wisdom. He was made tutor to the young god **Dionysus**, and filled him with good advice. In return, Dionysus filled Silenus with his new invention, wine, and Silenus became a jovial drunk. He grew too fat to take part in ecstatic Dionysian dancing, preferring to sit on the sidelines swilling wine and urging on the dancers. In processions, he always rode last, on a donkey, crowned with flowers, holding a parasol or a wineskin in one hand and stroking his paunch with the other. He was Dionysus' good luck personified, and the gods honoured him by making him king of the **Satyrs** and giving him **immortality** so long as he stayed on Earth.

⫸ Faunus, Pan

SIMARGHU
Asia (West); Europe (East)

Simarghu (Iranian) or Simorg (Slavic) was a dragon who guarded the tree of life, on which could be found seeds of every plant on earth. This tree looked like all other trees, and Simarghu itself was invisible, so that no human could ever know which was the tree of life. To fell any tree at all was therefore dangerous. In Iran all trees were left standing until they collapsed of their own accord, in the Slavic forests tree-felling took place only after elaborate rituals to propitiate Simarghu.

⫸ monsters and dragons

SIMORG: *see Simarghu*

SIN
Asia (West)

Sin ('moon'), also known as Asimbabba, **Nanna**, Nannar, Suen and Zuen, was the **Moon**, son of **Enlil** (air) and father of **Ishtar** (**fertility**) and **Shamash** (the **Sun**). He was the power of the sky embodied in bull form. In some accounts, **demons** tried to nibble him to nothing, but **Marduk** stopped them before he was utterly destroyed, and Sin recreated himself, growing to full strength – a miracle repeated each month. This event began the process of time, and Sin was its guardian. In other accounts he was invisible, neither light nor dark. He sailed the sky in his ship (the crescent Moon) looking for demons, and when he found them he expanded the ship to a full light-disc and scattered them to the **Underworld**.

SINAA
Americas (South)

Sinaa, in the myths of the Juruña people of Brazil, was the creator-spirit, half man half jaguar. He made the world, propped the sky on a stick, and peopled Earth with creatures. Alone of all **creation**, he could defy time, taking off his skin (and with it age) every night to bathe, and being restored to youth. But he controlled human time – and he will end the world whenever he chooses, by kicking away the sky-stick.
➠ **animal-gods**

SINfIOTL
Europe (North)

Sinfiotl, in Germanic myth, was the son **Signy** conceived with her brother **Sigmund**, and passed off as the child of her husband Siggeir. Determined to make the boy the bravest mortal ever born, she toughened him up from infancy, sewing his clothes to his skin each morning and ripping them off each night. The child's 'uncle' Sigmund taught him the arts of war and of shape-changing. Every night, the two of them changed into wolves and roamed the countryside slaughtering everything in their path.

When Sinfiotl was old enough, Signy persuaded him to murder his two elder brothers (Siggeir's legitimate children). Siggeir punished Sinfiotl by burying him alive, but Sinfiotl dug his way to freedom with a magic sword, and he and Signy burned the palace round Siggeir's ears. Signy, as was the custom, threw herself into the flames which were destroying her husband –

and as she died she shouted to Sigmund that he was Sinfiotl's true father. The story would have ended here, happily (at least for Sigmund and Sinfiotl), except that Sinfiotl had an argument with the brother of Sigmund's wife Borgild, and killed him – and Borgild retaliated by poisoning him.

This whole sequence of events was manipulated by the gods. Sinfiotl was, so to speak, no more than a first attempt at creating the greatest of mortal **heroes** – and he was clearly flawed. The gods therefore put it into Sigmund's mind to divorce Borgild for killing him, and marry a new wife. This wife was Hjördis, and the gods intended her and Sigmund's son **Sigurd** to be not only as heroic as Sinfiotl, but also just and pure. (Thanks to Sigurd's upbringing, these plans failed: see **Regin**, Sigurd.)

SIRENS
Europe (South)

The Sirens (Seirenes, 'binders'), in Greek myth, were the three daughters of the river-god **Achelous** and the **Muse** Calliope (or, some say, Melpomene or Terpsichore). They were beautiful girls with sweet voices (inherited from their mother), and served **Persephone**. When **Hades** opened the ground and stole Persephone to the **Underworld**, the Sirens failed to help her. In some accounts, Persephone's mother **Demeter** changed them into **monsters**. In others, they begged the gods to give them wings so that they could fly across the world to find her. Whatever the reason, they became birds with women's heads and lions' claws.

The Sirens lived on a barren island, one of the entrances to the Underworld, and whenever ships passed they sang, hoping to entice Persephone. Their singing was so beautiful that no human being could resist them, and sailed closer and closer to the lip of Hell. Each time, when the Sirens realized that Persephone was not on board, they swooped on the ship and its sailors, tearing them limb from limb and sending their souls unburied to the Underworld. The only mortal to hear them and live was **Odysseus**. He stopped his crews' ears with wax, and told them to keep on rowing whatever instructions he shouted at them in his desperation. Then he strapped himself to the ship's mast, heard the Sirens' song, and remained unscathed.

SISIUTL
Americas (North)

Sisiutl, in the myths of the Kwakiutl and Bella Coola peoples of the Northwest coast (Canada), was a water-**snake** with three heads: snake, human, snake. Its skin was so tough that no knife could pierce it: only a holly-leaf had sufficient magic. Sisiutl lived in a pool behind the home of the sky-goddess **Qamaits**, and could be seduced from it down to Earth by magic rituals – to help or harm human beings, depending on the kind of magic.

SISUPALA
India

Sisupala, in Hindu myth, was a **monster**: in some accounts, the son of **Shiva** and a mortal queen, in others, an avatar of the **demon Ravana**. He was born with four arms and three eyes, and the gods told his terrified mortal parents that these were signs of good luck, and that he would live happy and adored until he sat on the knee of the person who would kill him – at which point the extra eye and arms would shrivel away, and with them his luck. One day **Krishna** visited the palace, and the child Sisupala ran to sit on his knee. At once the extra arms and eye disappeared, and he was a child like all other children. His mother begged Krishna not to kill him but spare his life a hundred times, and Krishna promised.

From that day on, Sisupala spent all his time brooding about Krishna and plotting ways to kill him. His fury was not eased when Krishna stole his bride-to-be **Rukmini**. (She had written to Krishna, saying that she hated her future husband and begging him to stop the wedding – and Krishna rode to the rescue, kidnapping Rukmini from the wedding-procession and marrying her himself.) But whatever ambushes Sisupala prepared, and whatever disguises he assumed, he was no match for Krishna. A hundred attacks all ended in forgiveness, as Krishna kept his promise to Sisupala's mortal mother.

Sisupala's hundred-and-first attack came when Krishna was the honoured guest at a sacrifice held by King **Yudhishthira**. Sisupala insulted him before the crowd, calling him a cowherd and a yokel. He then drew his sword and went to kill Yudhishthira – and Krishna called down the discus of the Sun, which fell on Sisupala's head and split him in two from crown to toes. The two halves of the demon's body fell apart like segments from an orange, and Sisupala's soul gushed out in a pool of fire. It surged round Krishna's feet, and then was absorbed into the god's own being: Sisupala had spent so long brooding on his enemy that he had become inseparably part of him.

The details of this story were probably elaborated for moral teaching: however often you sin, if you keep God in mind at all times, you will eventually be freed from the trammels of mortality and be absorbed in him.

≫→ shape-changers

SISYPHUS
Europe (South)

Sisyphus and Autolycus. Sisyphus (Sisyphos, 'too clever'), in Greek myth, was the son of **Aeolus** the wind-lord; his brothers were **Athamas** and **Salmoneus**. He was a cattle-farmer on the Isthmus of Corinth, and a rogue, rivalled only by his neighbour **Autolycus**. Autolycus asked his father **Hermes** (god of **tricksters**) for the power to make black seem white and white seem black. He used it to steal Sisyphus' cattle: when Sisyphus' men came looking for black cows in Autolycus' herds, they found only white ones, and vice versa. To prove who was stealing his cattle, Sisyphus had to think up a trick of his own. He branded all his cattle with his initial (C, the Greek capital S) – not on the hide, but on the underside of the hooves. The next time Autolycus' men raided Sisyphus' herd, a trail of Ss next morning led to Autolycus' byres, and the stolen cattle could be identified despite their colour-change.

Sisyphus and Salmoneus. Sisyphus won a kingdom by treachery. His brother Salmoneus was king of Thessaly. Sisyphus raped Salmoneus' daughter Tyro, and she was so ashamed that she killed her sons as soon as they were born. Sisyphus called the Thessalians together, showed them the bodies and said that they were Salmoneus' and Tyro's children, the result of incest. The people were so disgusted that they banished Salmoneus and made Sisyphus king. (In some accounts, he later claimed that the Delphic oracle had made him lie about the incest, to punish Salmoneus' crimes against his own people; but as he was just as much of a tyrant himself, this claim was hardly credible.)

Sisyphus and Zeus. In Thessaly, Sisyphus revelled in cruelty. His method of executing enemies – not to mention rich travellers rash enough to risk his hospitality – was to peg them on the ground and build stone-piles on top of them. In the end, he went too far and cheated **Zeus**. When Zeus stole the river-**nymph** Aegina from her father and hid her, Sisyphus was the only person on Earth who knew where she was, and he promised Zeus to keep it secret. But Aegina's father, the river-god Asopus, offered to pay for the information by creating a spring of pure water in Sisyphus' citadel; Sisyphus immediately broke his word to Zeus and told Asopus where to find the lovers. His reward from Asopus was the spring called Pirene; his reward from Zeus was death.

Even then, Sisyphus nearly managed to cheat **Death** himself. Zeus sent his brother **Hades** to make sure that Sisyphus actually reached the **Underworld**. Hades told Sisyphus to hold out his wrists to be tied. Sisyphus pretended to be fascinated by the knot, and asked Hades to show him how to tie it. Hades held out his wrists, and Sisyphus tied him up and locked him in a dungeon. For days, now that Hades was a prisoner, no mortal in the world could die. This was particularly awkward for **Ares**, god of war: all over the world men were being killed in battle, only to spring back to life and fight again. In the end Ares went to Thessaly and untied Hades, and the two of them frogmarched Sisyphus to the Underworld. On the way, Sisyphus called out to his wife that she was on no account to bury his body; then, when he reached the Underworld, he complained to **Persephone** that he had been dragged down to Hell alive and unburied. He asked her to allow him three more days in the Upper World to arrange his own funeral. Suspecting nothing, she agreed – and Sisyphus went back to Corinth and took up his old life exactly as before. Zeus realized that the only person who could outwit such a rogue was an even greater rogue, and sent **Hermes** himself to deal with Sisyphus. Hermes devised the cleverest trick of all: no trick at all. Sisyphus was expecting argument or lies, and was on his guard against words. But instead of speaking, Hermes simply took him by the scruff of the neck and bundled him down to Hell.

The judges of the dead gave Sisyphus a punishment to suit both his trickery and his method of killing people with boulders. They placed a huge boulder just above him on a steep hillside. The only way he could prevent it rolling back and crushing him was to push it up the hill, and they promised that if he ever reached the top and pushed it down the other side his punishment would end. With immense effort, time after time, Sisyphus heaved the boulder to the lip of the downward slope – and each time, just as one more push would have toppled it, it slipped out of his grasp and rolled all the way back down the hill. So he was doomed to make desperate efforts, and to be cheated, until the end of time.

SITA
India

Sita ('furrow'), in Hindu myth, was born fully-formed from **Mother Earth** when the mortal King **Janaka** marked out a line in the ground before sacrificing and asking the gods to send him children. Some accounts say that she was Mother Earth's own child, others that she was an avatar of **Lakshmi**, **Vishnu**'s wife, placed by the goddess on Mother Earth to share the earthly life of **Rama** (Vishnu's avatar) as she, Lakshmi, shared her husband's existence in **Heaven**.

Janaka treated Sita as his beloved daughter, and suitors flocked to court her from all parts of the country. Janaka set up a competition: she would marry whichever of them succeeded in bending a huge bow given him by **Shiva**. Prince Rama not only bent the bow but shattered it, and so Sita married him. Soon afterwards, the demon-king **Ravana** kidnapped her and carried her off to his fortress in Sri Lanka. Rama won her back after a huge war between **demons** and mortals. But his subjects refused to accept her as queen, saying that because she'd spent time in another king's harem, she was spoiled. Sita appealed to Mother Earth to prove her faithfulness, and the earth-goddess rose up, seated on a golden throne, took Sita in her arms and carried her from mortal sight forever.

»+ Balin, beauty

SKADI
Europe (North)

Skadi ('hurt' or 'shadow'), in Nordic myth, was the daughter of the **giant Thiazi**, who stole **Idun** from the gods and was killed for it. Skadi went to **Asgard** to avenge his death – and the gods, unwilling to fight a female, asked her instead to take as a husband whichever of them she chose. Skadi, full of desire for **Baldur**, agreed, and the male gods lined up behind a curtain, only their bare feet showing, and asked her to choose. Unfortunately for Skadi, Baldur's feet were less beautiful than those of **Njörd**, the Old Man of the Sea, and she chose him instead.

The marriage was a disaster. Njörd refused to live in Skadi's icy mountain home, and Skadi refused to live in Njörd's sea-palace. They agreed to separate, and she went back to her skiing and hunting. In some accounts, however, they had sex just once before they parted, and their children were the **twins Frey** and **Freyja**, gods of desire. (In others, Frey and Freyja were born to **Nerthus**, the earth-goddess against whose shores Njörd lapped to comfort himself after Skadi left him.)

Alone in her mountain-lair, or on her rare visits to Asgard (to which, as Njörd's wife, she now had access), Skadi still pined for Baldur. When he was killed, as a result of **Loki**'s plotting, the gods took Loki to her fastness and pinioned him there with the entrails of his own son Narvi. Skadi hung a snake high in the roof above his head, hoping that its venom would drip into his eyes until **Ragnarök**, the end of time. Being a giantess, however, and not a god equipped with all-knowledge, she didn't realize that Sigun, Loki's faithful wife, had also crept into the cave, and now sat by her imprisoned husband, protecting him by catching the venom-drops in a wooden bowl.

SKANDA: *see* Karttikeya

SKILI
Americas (North)

Skili, in the myths of the Eastern Cherokee people of North Carolina, were witches that preyed on humans. They travelled at night, and often disguised themselves as owls.

SKRYMSLI
Europe (North)

Skrymsli, a **giant** in Nordic myth, was challenged by a mortal to a chess-game. If he won, he was to eat the mortal's son, unless the child could be hidden in such a way he could never find him. Skrymsli won the game, and the boy's father begged the gods to help hide his son. First **Odin** changed the child into a single grain in a field of standing corn – and Skrymsli mowed the field and ate the corn, grain by grain. At the last moment, **Honir** snatched the child, turned him into a feather and hid it in the down on a swan's head. Skrymsli took the swan and began eating it, down and all.

Loki now took a hand. He turned the child into one egg in the roe of a huge turbot, which he set swimming in a school of fish in the deepest part of the ocean. Skrymsli launched his boat and started fishing, and as soon as he was gone Loki set up a spiked trap in the boat-house, hidden in a pile of rope. Skrymsli fished his way through all the turbot in the ocean until he caught the one with the child in it. While he was picking through the roe, trying to find the child, Loki snatched the boy, changed him back to human shape, put him on shore and told him to run for safety. Skrymsli rowed back to the boathouse and fell over the hidden trap. At once Loki cut off his leg – but it grew again, twice as strong as before. Loki cut off the other leg, and this time, before it grew back, placed a spark of fire on the stump. Skrymsli bled to death, and the child was safe.

SKY

Sky, in most traditions, was the originator of **creation**: its arising from the primordial ocean and mating with Earth began the universe. Sky itself began as a god, but in most traditions gave way to its own offspring or was dispossessed by them, retreating to an elder-statesman-like serenity far beyond the squabbles of the rest of creation. The chief god in many traditions took over the powers of Sky, and ruled the entire world of **light**, usually in opposition to the powers of darkness and in uneasy alliance with the gods and spirits of the **sea**.

≫→ (Africa): Olorun; (Americas): Ataentsic, Damballah; (China): Di Jun, Tian; (Egypt): Nut; (Finnish): Jumala; (Greece): Atlas, Ouranos, Zeus; (India): Aditi, Aruna, Dyaus; (Mesopotamia): An; (Nordic): Thor, Tyr; (Northern Europe): Num; (Oceania): Rangi; (Slavic): Dievas

SLAVIC MYTH

Slavs, migrants from Central Asia and such areas as Turkey, Iran and as far South as the Indus Valley, settled on the Western shore and hinterland of the Black Sea in the sixth century CE. In the next 200 years they spread in all directions: to Poland and the Baltic, Macedonia, the former Czechoslovakia, Russia and the Ukraine. Each of these regions developed its own distinctive language, and the peoples turned from being nomads to living in settled agricultural communities, but many of the ancient myths remained, a bedrock of universal Slavic culture. (There were, none the less, a few important additions, borrowed from neighbouring traditions. The Baltic god Perkunas (**Pyerun**), for example, has affinity with the neighbouring Norse god **Thor**; **Simorg** was the Iranian god **Simarghu** in Slavic dress.)

The pre-Christian Slavs had no knowledge of **writing**, and all we know about their myths is based on the writings of outsiders. When Christianity came (in the ninth century CE), missionaries brought a script and the new

religious system it codified, and began
organizing offensives against the ancient Slavic gods. Some gods disappeared; others changed their identity
– Volos the farming-god, for example,
became a shepherd figure identified
with Saint Vlas; others again were
downgraded into the folk-heroes
known as *bogatiri*. (Notable examples
were **Ilya Muromets**, originally the war-
god Pyerun, **Miktula**, **Potok-Mikhailo
Ivanovich**, **Sadko** and **Svyatogor**.) A
few gods lived on: examples are **Mati-
Syra-Zemlya** (**Mother Earth**) and the
death-goddess **Baba Yaga**. The missionaries either went on fulminating for
centuries against pagan beliefs – as late
as 1618 the Jesuits cut down a sacred
oak to prevent its being worshipped –
or took them bodily into Christianity,
for example when the ancient Slavic
belief in the cleansing power of **fire**,
originally denounced, was incorporated
in Orthodox belief.

In early Slavic myth there were two
gods, one black (Chernobog), one
white (**Byelobog**) for **light and dark**,
good and evil. Later, gods of individual
peoples (for example **Rod**) arose, and
were assisted by ancestor spirits. The
Slavs believed that the soul lived on
after death. They took great care of
ancestral burial places, putting luxuries
into the graves, leaving food there – a
habit that persisted into the twentieth
century – and holding feasts in honour
of the dead. At a domestic level each
place or activity had its own spirit: the
Domovoi, Domania or Kikimora looked
after the home, the Dvorovoi the yard,
the **Bannik** the bath-house, the Ovinnik
the barn, **Dugnai** bread-rising, **Priparchis and Kremera** pigs, Kurwaichin

sheep, Walgino cattle, the **Polevik** fields,
the **Russalki** and the **Vodyanoi** water.
Complex cosmogenies developed, with
deities for the **Sun** (**Dazhbog**; **Saule**),
the **Moon** (**Meness**), Dawn and Sunset
(the **Zoryas**), **Sky** (Rod and **Yarilo**),
Earth (Mati-Syra-Zemlya), fire (**Svarozich** and Gabijia), water (Kupala), the
home (Zemepatis), pasture (Pudnuitsa),
the forests (the **Leshy**; Zuttibur), war
(Pyerun, **Rugievit** and Yarovit), wind
(**Stribog** and **Varpulis**), even bees
(**Zosim**), blacksmiths and different
kinds of fruit.

SLEIPNIR
Europe (North)

Sleipnir, in Nordic myth, was the eight-
legged, flying horse sired by the stallion
Svadilfari and born to **Loki** disguised as
a mare. Loki gave him to **Odin**, and he
became the warrior-god's charger, carrying him about the sky at the head of
his hosts of the Dead. Odin used him to
leap the walls of **Niflheim** and consult
the prophetesses of the **Underworld** –
and he once lent him to Hermod to go
to Niflheim and try to rescue **Baldur**.
≫→ Borak, Pegasus

SMITHS

Most myth-systems were conceived and
elaborated before metal-working was
widely known. This means that smiths
made late appearances in myth, and
indeed were absent from many traditions. In systems where smiths did
appear, they often had lower status
than other supernatural beings, and
were tolerated as servants rather than
honoured as equals. Indeed, some

human smiths whose skills earned them promotion to **Heaven** never properly lost their mortality, never achieved the status of ranking gods.

Smith-stories, whether about mortals or immortals, tended to peter out as soon as the main event – forging invincible weapons for a hero, building a golden palace, repairing a Sun-ship – was complete. Often, smiths were imagined as lame and ugly, their shoulders grotesquely over-developed from their work. They were associated with dwarfs, those secretive miners of the Earth's interior and hoarders of its gold. Sometimes they made good marriages – **Hephaestus** married **Aphrodite**, goddess of **beauty**; **Ptah** married **Sekhmet**, daughter of the Sun – but such unions were seldom happy, and the smith-god was often cuckolded by one of his own most important customers, the god of war.

In early Indian myth, the smith-god **Tvashtri** crafted the chalice which held the immortal drink *soma*, made thunderbolts for **Indra**, built cities, taught human beings arts and **crafts** – and was also moody and a buffoon. Ancient Irish myth told of three craft-gods, Goibhniu the smith, Luchta the wright and Creidhne the metal-worker. They forged unfailing weapons, Goibhniu making the blades, Luchta the shafts and Creidhne the rivets. (In Goibhniu's spare time he presided at feasts in the Otherworld, for which, like his Welsh counterpart Govannon, he brewed ale of **immortality**.) Irish myth also told of the lordly smith Culain – but only in the context that the boy-hero Setanta killed his guard-dog and was forced to work for six months as the new guard-dog,

which earned him the nickname 'Culain's hound,' **Cuculain**. In Finnish myth the smith-god **Ilmarinen** won the hand of a sorcerer's daughter by making magic presents, and then acted as a kind of supernatural Sancho Panza to the hero **Väinämöinen**. The Phoenician god Hiyon made bull-statues for **Baal**. Other smiths, from various traditions, made wind-cloaks, jewels (in Indian myth, from raindrops) and fabulous steeds (such as flying horses or saddled eagles) which senior gods then endowed with life.

Many myth-systems linked smiths with intelligence. **Fire** was a symbol of **wisdom**; the sparks from the smiths' anvils were like shafts of insight; the smiths were therefore custodians or granters of knowledge. (In the Greek myth of **Prometheus**, for example, the fire Prometheus stole to give to mortals was a spark from Hephaestus' anvil.) Sadly, smiths themselves, in myth, seem regularly to have been bypassed by the wisdom they controlled. They were often wily, but seldom wise.

⟫→ (Africa): Gu, Ogun; (Celtic): Oberon, Volund; (Greece): Cyclopes; (India): Vishvakarman; (Japan): Inari; (Slavic): Kalvaitis; (Mesopotamia): Cain; (Nordic): Thor

SNAKES

Snakes were central to most myth-systems, perhaps because of their perceived quality of being at once familiar and exotic. The look of their faces (for example their unblinking, lidless eyes), and their behaviour, seemed to imply that they were intelligent, that they lived by reason rather than instinct; and yet their thought-processes were as alien to those of humans as their ways of movement.

In some cultures (for example in Australia and among the African Bush-people) snakes were phallic symbols. The Hopi people of North America danced an annual snake dance, to celebrate the union of Snake Youth (a **Sky** spirit) and Snake Girl (an **Underworld** spirit) and renew the **fertility** of Nature. During the dance live snakes were handled, and at its end they were released into the fields to guarantee good crops. In other cultures snakes symbolized the umbilical cord, joining all human beings to **Mother Earth**. The **Great Goddess** often had snakes as her familiars – sometimes, as in ancient Crete, twining round her sacred wand – and they were worshipped as guardians of her mysteries of birth and regeneration.

Snakes and immortality. Many cultures regarded snakes as immortal, because they appeared to be reincarnated from themselves when they sloughed their skins. In a similar way, the snake was often associated with **immortality** because when it coils it forms a spiral, and when it bites its tail – which few people in real life can have seen a snake do – it formed a circle, and spirals and circles were symbols of eternity. The circle was particularly important in Dahomeyan myth (where the snake-god Danh circled the world like a belt, corseting it and preventing it flying apart in splinters) and in ancient Egypt (where a serpent biting its tail symbolized the **sea**, the eternal ring which enclosed the world).

Snakes and creation. Snakes were a common feature of **creation** myths. Many peoples in Africa and Australia told of a **Rainbow Snake**, either Mother Earth herself who gave birth to all animals, or a water-god whose writhings made rivers, creeks and oceans. In ancient Indian myth, the drought-serpent **Ahi** swallowed the primordial ocean, and it was not until **Indra** split her stomach with a thunderbolt that all created beings were released. In another myth, **Brahma** creator of all slept on the coils of the world-serpent **Shesha** (or **Ananta**, 'endless', one part of Vishnu the child of the primordial waters); Shesha in turn was supported on **Kurma** (another part of Vishnu) – and when Kurma moved, Shesha stirred and yawned, and the gaping of its jaws caused **earthquakes**. One of the oldest Greek cosmological myths tells of Ophion, the snake which incubated the primordial egg from which all created things were born. In Egyptian myth, the state of existence before being was symbolized as Amduat, a many-coiled serpent from which **Ra** the Sun, and all creation with him, arose, returning each night and being reborn each morning.

Snakes and the Underworld. Because snakes lived in cracks and holes in the ground, they were regularly thought to be guardians of the Underworld, or **messengers** between the Upper and Lower Worlds. The **Gorgons** of Greek myth were snake-women (a common hybrid), whose gaze turned flesh to stone. In Indian myth, *nagas* and *naginis* were human-headed snakes whose kings and queens ruled jewel-encrusted underground or underwater paradises and who were perpetually at war with **Garuda**, bird of the Sun. In Nordic myth Evil was symbolized as a snake, **Nidhogg** the 'Dread Biter', who coiled round one of the three roots of **Yggdrasil**, Tree of Life, and tried to choke (or in some versions, gnaw) the life from it. In Egyptian myth, similarly, **Aapep** the serpent (symbolizing chaos) each morning attacked the Sun-ship (symbolizing order). Aapep tried to engulf the ship, and the sky was drenched red at dawn and dusk with its blood as the Sun defeated it.

The idea of snake-people below the Earth was particularly prominent in American myth. The Aztec Underworld, **Mictlan**, was protected by python-trees, a gigantic alligator and a snake, and spirits had to evade them (by physical ducking and weaving, or by cunning) before they could begin their journey towards immortality. In North America, the Brule Sioux people told of three brothers transformed into rattlesnakes which permanently helped and guided their human relatives. The Pomo people told of a woman who married a rattlesnake prince and gave birth to four snake-children who were able to pass freely between the worlds of their two parents. The Hopi people told of a young man who ventured to the Underworld and married a snake princess, and the Navajo people told of Glispa, a girl who lived for two years with the Snake People by the Lake of Emergence in the Underworld, and returned with magic healing lore. Healing and snakes were similarly associated in ancient Greek myth. **Aesculapius** had snake-familiars which crawled over the bodies of sick people asleep at night in his shrines, and licked them back to health.

Snakes and water. As well as with the Earth, snakes were commonly associated with water. The primordial ocean was a coiled snake – examples are Ahi in early Indian myth and **Jormungand** in Nordic myth. Sea monsters, from Greek **Scylla** with her twelve snake-necks to Koloowisi the sea-god of the Zuñi people of North America or **Leviathan**, the seven-headed crocodile-serpent of Hebrew myth, lived in every ocean, and in some cultures eels (which spend some of their lives in fresh water before returning as adults to the sea) were regarded as magic creatures. Rivers and lakes often had snake-gods or snake-guardians – a typical example is Untekhi, the fearsome water-spirit of the Missouri River. Until very recently, Northern Europeans held 'well-dressing' ceremonies to appease the snake-spirits of village wells, and told legends of Saints vanquishing malevolent lake-snakes – Saint George, for example, in a story exactly paralleled among the Colombian people of Guatavita, killed a maiden-devouring serpent, and Saint Columba rebuked the Loch Ness Monster, which at once gave up its taste for human flesh and became shy of human visitors.

Snake gods. The anthropomorphic bias of most religions made it rare for gods to be depicted solely in the shape of snakes. (Exceptions were Ndengei, the Fijian creator-god; the dozen or so creator-snakes of the Solomon Islands, each with different responsibilities;

Coatlicue, the Aztec Mother Earth; and **Damballah**, Simbi and Petro, snake-spirits in Voodoo belief.) More commonly, snake-gods were hybrids or **shape-changers**. North American snake-spirits, for example, could shift at will between human and serpentine appearance, retaining in each form the attributes of both. The most important American snake-god of all, **Quetzal-cóatl** ('Plumed Serpent'), spirit of wind and intelligence, was balanced in Aztec myth by the Serpent of Obsidian Knives, the evil spirit of sacrifice and one of the four pillars supporting the sky – but in each case, the association with snakes seems more to do with imagery than with particularly snakish qualities. The Mayan sky-goddess I had snake-hair – a common attribute, except that in her case the snakes leaned into her ears and whispered the secrets of the universe (which is to say, the secrets of herself). **Shiva**, in Indian myth, had a cobra coiled on his head and another at rest on his right shoulder, ready to rear and strike his enemies. Egyptian myth included snake-gods of many kinds, from the two-headed **Nehebkau** who was one of the guardians of the Underworld, to 'the coiled one' Mehen, who sailed on Ra's sun-boat and helped to fight Aapep and maintain the diurnal cycle.

Snakes and wisdom. Snakes were associated with wisdom in most myth-systems – perhaps because they appear to ponder their actions as they stalk or prepare to pounce, and because of their hissing – which West African medicine men imitated as a preliminary to prophesying. Some-times their wisdom was of the ages and non-human, indeed directed against humans. But usually they were beneficent. This was particularly so in East Asia, where snake-dragons oversaw such things as the cycle of the seasons, good harvest, **rain**, weddings, **fertility** and the making of money. In ancient Greece and India, snakes were regarded as lucky, and snake-amulets and pet snakes were talismans against evil. Snakes were associated with healing in West Asia and Northern Europe, and in South Asia were – and in some places still are – considered to have aphrodisiac qualities. In Greek myth, if a snake licked your eyes or ears you acquired second sight or second hearing (this happened to Melampus); **Tiresias** acquired his insight into the supernatural world, and his dual nature as man and woman, as a result of killing a pair of snakes coupling in a wood. In Hebrew myth, a snake guarded the Tree of Knowledge in the Garden of Eden, and it is the extension of this story (the corruption of Eve) in Judaic and Christian teaching that leads to the idea now common in the Western world that snakes and humans are eternal enemies – a view shared by few other myth-cultures across the world.

⇒ **(Africa): Da; (Americas): Bachue, Sisiutl, Umai-huhlya-wit, Uncegila; (Australia): Bobbi-Bobbi, Djulunggul, Jurawadbad, Kunapipi; (Egypt): Atum, Tefnut; (India): Kadru, Manasa, Muchalinda, Vasuki, Vritra; (Indonesia): Naga Pahoda; (Mesopotamia): Illuyankas; (Oceania): Honoyeta**

SNOQALM AND BEAVER
Americas (North)

Snoqalm ('**moon**'), in the myths of the peoples of the Northwestern American coast, ruled the **sky**. At that time Sky was an exact reflection of **Mother Earth**, except that Sky was all-light and Earth all-dark, because Snoqalm hoarded the **Sun** in a fire-box, taking out only as much as he or his people needed. One day, curious about the dark of Earth, he told Spider to weave a rope so that he could climb down through the clouds and see what was to be seen. Unfortunately, he forgot that if he could climb down, Earth-creatures could climb up – and this is what happened. Beaver climbed up the rope, clambered into Snoqalm's village while Snoqalm was asleep, and stole not only the glowing Sun-orb from its box but also Snoqalm's fire-making tools. He climbed back down the rope, on the way hanging the Sun in the sky like a lamp, to light Mother Earth. As soon as he reached the surface he showed human beings how to use flint and tinder to make fire. Snoqalm woke up to find the Earth glowing far beneath him, and his own kingdom lit by no more than a pale reflection.

This myth is told by several Northeastern peoples. The Snoqalmie people of Washington State add details. In their version, it was Fox who climbed into Sky; he changed himself into Beaver when he clambered through the hole in Sky and found himself at the bottom of a lake, and when he went back down to Earth he carried not just fire but also trees, ancestors of the forests of the Cascade Mountains of the Northwestern US. Snoqalm pursued him down the rope, but was too heavy and crashed to Earth – and became Mount Si, not far from modern Seattle.

➤ **light and dark**

SOIDO
Oceania

Soido, a Melanesian **fertility**-god, married a mortal wife. She was not able to sustain the love-making of a god, and died as soon as he entered her. But her womb teemed with his sperm, and when he buried her taros, yams, sweet potatoes and bananas grew from her grave – the first ever seen on Earth. Soido travelled the world looking for a new wife, masturbating endlessly to ease his frustration (and in the process clothing the Earth with plants). Eventually he found a woman, Pekai, who could tolerate love-making with a supernatural being, and settled happily with her as god of agriculture.

➤ **farming**

SOL: *see* Helius

SOMA (DRINK)
India

Soma, in the Vedic myths of the Aryans who invaded India in the seventeenth century BCE, was the drink which guaranteed the gods' **immortality**. It was a companion to their celestial food **amrita**, and if mortals could somehow make their own supply and drink it, they would be granted not full immortality but temporary communion with the gods and the universe. **Demons**, too lazy to make *soma* of their own, were always trying to steal the gods' supply, so that they could become immortal and usurp the gods' privileges in **Heaven**.

The origin of *soma*. In some myth-stories, *soma* was pressed out for the gods through a gigantic sieve, the **sky**. The noise of the pressing was **thunder**, and the milky liquid was **rain** – the semen of the sky which guaranteed the Earth's **fertility**. In other accounts, **Indra** discovered the plant *soma* in the Himalayas and took it to Heaven; in others, *soma* was made during the churning of the **Sea** of Milk (see **amrita**), from every healing or magic herb in the universe, tossed into the primordial ocean.

In the most elaborate myth of all, *soma* existed in Heaven at a time when the gods still lived on Earth. They asked **Suparni**, goddess of poetry, to send messengers to fetch it down for them. Suparni had three children, each a four-syllable line of poetry made into a goddess. The eldest child, Jagati, turned herself into a bird and flew to Heaven. But the journey tired her so much that she lost three syllables and had to limp back, exhausted. The second daughter, Tristubh, lost only one syllable, but still came back without *soma*. The third child, Gayatari, brought back not only *soma* but also the syllables shed by her sisters. (This is why the eight-syllable line, *gayatari*, was later chosen for writing the sacred hymns, the *Vedas*.)

In later, Hindu myth, *soma* was personified as a god: see next entry.

SOMA (GOD)
India

Soma (also called Chandra, 'radiant'), in Hindu myth, was the god of the waning and waxing **Moon**. Two different myths explain his waxing and waning. In one, for half of each month, he is consumed by 36,300 gods, guaranteeing their **immortality** – this is why the Moon wanes in the sky. For the other half, he is fed by water from the celestial ocean fetched for him by **Surya** (either Surya the **Sun** or a female Surya, Soma's wife) – this is why the Moon waxes in the sky. In the second, he irritated his father-in-law **Daksha** by preferring one of his 27 wives (Daksha's daughters) above all the others, and Daksha put a withering curse on him, only to be persuaded by the entreaties of the other 26 wives to make it not inexorable but cyclical.

Soma and Tara. Tara was the beautiful wife of **Brihaspati**, teacher of the gods. Soma lusted after her and abducted her. There was war in the universe, and stalemate: the gods on one side, Soma and the **demons** of darkness on the other. At last **Brahma** forced Soma to return Tara – and Brihaspati found that she was pregnant. He refused to accept her back, until a child was born so beautiful that he claimed it as his own son. Soma made a counter-claim, and war once again seemed imminent. Brahma settled it by asking Tara who the father was, and she named Soma. Brahma gave Tara back to Brihaspati, pardoned Soma, and made the child father of all lunar dynasties – a settlement which sacrificed equity in the interests of universal harmony.

Although Soma the god is an individual personality, it is easy to see how his myths developed from those of the immortal drink soma (see separate entry). He is a favourite *god of poets: Indian religious verse is full of his praise, and tells of his powers and exploits. In art he has many forms, most of them hallucinatory and blurred: they include bird, bull, embryo, milk, plant with milky leaves and water-**giant**.*

SOMNUS: *see* Hypnus

SONG JIANG
Asia (East)

Song Jiang, in Chinese myth, was a master criminal on Earth who wangled his way into **Heaven** and procured for himself the post of patron god of thieves.

SOSOM
Oceania

Sosom, in the myths of Southern Papua New Guinea, was the **Sun**'s brother and the god of **fertility**. He whirled his penis like a bullroarer, and even its noise in the distance (the rumble of coming **rain**) was enough to stock the Earth with produce.

Needless to say, Sosom was the spirit invoked during the puberty-rites for adolescent boys. When the rituals began and the bullroarer sounded, women and girls knew that the god was present, and stayed away.
➤ fertility

SOWN MEN
Europe (South)

When **Cadmus**, in Greek myth, killed the earth-serpent which guarded the plain on which the city of **Thebes** was to be built, he gathered its teeth and sowed them like seed-corn. An army of soldiers instantly grew; Cadmus tossed a pebble among them, and they fell on each other and fought until all but five were dead. The five knelt and promised Cadmus obedience. Their names were Chthonius ('earthman'), Echion ('snakeman'), Hyperenor ('more than man'), Oudaeus ('born from the soil') and Pelorus ('giant snake'). Together they were called the Spartoi ('sown men'), and they were the ancestors of Thebes.

SPHINX
Europe (South)

Sphinx ('throttler'), in Greek myth, was the monstrous offspring of Echidna and **Typhon**; her siblings included **Cerberus**, **Chimaera**, **Hydra** and the **Nemean Lion**. She was woman from the waist up, dog from the waist down and had vulture's wings. **Hera** sent her to punish **Thebes** for hiding **Zeus**' bastard child **Dionysus**. Every day the Sphinx posed the same riddle – 'Four-legs morning, two-legs noon, three-legs evening, most legs weakest – what am I?' – and when the Thebans failed to answer she ate one of their children. Then **Oedipus** arrived, fresh from visiting the Delphic oracle, and realized that the inscription carved above **Apollo**'s temple there, 'Remember you are mortal', contained the answer to the riddle. Four-legs morning: crawling, as a baby; two-legs noon: walking upright, in the prime of life; three-legs evening: walking propped on a stick – the answer is a human being. When he shouted this answer, Sphinx was so startled that she flew straight up in the air, crashed down on a jagged rock (later named Sphikion after her) and broke her neck.

Apart from the name, there is no connection between Sphinx in Greek myth and the Egyptian sphinx – in fact the Egyptian sphinx was given that name in recent times, by archaeologists conversant with Greek myth. The Egyptian sphinx was male, symbolizing royal power in the form of the pharaoh's head on the body of a crouching lion (which in turn stood for the power of the rising Sun). It was unwinged, tame and (except to enemies of the state) entirely benevolent. Its Egyptian name was Harmakhis, 'Horus in the Horizon' (that is, 'Rising Sun'), and its statues were placed on guard outside temples and monuments (such as the pyramid complex at Giza), or in avenues like that which links the temples of Egyptian Thebes (modern Luxor) and Karnak, three kilometres away.
≫→ monsters and dragons

sPYAN-RAS-GZIGS
Asia (Southwest)

sPyan-ras-gzigs, in Tibetan myth, was a monkey-god, one of the two first beings in the world. He mated with the other, the rock-giantess **sGrolma**, and their offspring were all created beings. In Tibetan Buddhism sPyan-ras-gzigs became identified with **Avalokiteshvara**, who still repeatedly takes human form (as the Dalai Lama) to guide his people.
≫→ animal-gods, creation

SRAOSHA
Asia (West)

Sraosha ('listen'), in ancient Iranian myth, was the mediator between gods and mortals. During the day he stood by **Ahura Mazda**'s throne, listening for human prayers and relaying them to his master. At night he went down to Earth to hunt **demons**, in particular Aeshma lord of anger. In later myth Sraosha became Surush, and from there he passed into Muslim belief as the angel Jibril (**Gabriel**).
≫→ messengers

STAR COUNTRY
Americas (North)

Star Country, in the myths of the Hopi people of the Southwestern US Pueblos, was the sky. It was an exact reflection of **Mother Earth**, with lakes, rivers, **mountains** and fields, and in it the star-people lived and hunted as mortals did on Earth. Their elders were the **Sun** and **Moon**, and they lived placid and uneventful lives. When they felt like travelling, Spider spun them ropes down which they climbed to explore their reflected world, the Earth. Sometimes, they became trapped in pools and lakes, and had to wait there until Spider noticed and came down to haul them home again.

STORMS: see *brighus*, Indra, Ixchel, Maruts, Rudra, Susano

STRIBOG
Europe (East)

Stribog ('wind-lord'), in Eastern Slavic myth, was the grandfather of all other winds. In some areas he was also the god of wealth, spreading it as widely and as randomly as the winds blow. In others, less poetically, he was winter-king, and his gusts distributed snow and chilled the bones of **Mother Earth**.

STYMPHALIAN BIRDS
Europe (South)

The Stymphalian Birds, in Greek myth, infested the Stymphalian Marshes in Arcadia, and **Heracles**, for his sixth **Labour**, was sent to kill them or drive them away. The birds ate human flesh; they had bronze beaks, talons and feathers, and killed their prey by dropping razor-sharp feathers from above and then tearing it to pieces with their talons. So long as Heracles wore the skin of the **Nemean Lion**, he was safe from their attacks, but he could find no way to dislodge them from their nests. He could only shoot one at a time, and there were countless thousands. In the end all his arrows were fired, and he angrily shook his empty quiver at the birds. Its bronze casing rattled against the bow, and at once the birds rose in a dense cloud, clattering their metal wings. Heracles began running up and down, shouting the terrible hunting cry taught him by **Pan** and rattling his god-given weapons (or, some say, a special bird-scarer given him by **Athene**). The birds flew off in a bronze cloud, glinting in the sun, settled on a barren island in the river which girds the world, and were never seen again by mortals, except for the **Argonauts** on their way to Colchis to steal the **Golden Fleece**.

⨠➔ **monsters and dragons**

STYX
Europe (South)

Styx ('hate'), in Greek myth, was a river-goddess, daughter of Ocean whose waters girded all **creation**. She had four children, Force, Might, Victory and Zeal, and when the gods were fighting the **giants** for control of the universe, she sent her children to help them. In gratitude, **Hades** built her a palace in his **Underworld** kingdom, **Poseidon** gave her power over all other waters in the world, and **Zeus** allowed her authority over the gods themselves: it was in her name that they swore their oaths.

Styx lived in a rock-palace at the edge of the Underworld. From its peak gushed a river of icy water, called after her. It spread out in ten streams, **Acheron**, **Cocytus**, **Phlegethon** and others, and held the Underworld in its grip as Ocean gripped the Upper World. The last of the ten streams was called Oath of the Gods, and any god who swore an oath had to drink from it. If mortals drank Styx water, it turned their blood to ice and killed them.

⨠➔ **justice and universal order**

SUCELLUS
Europe (North)

Sucellus ('good striker'), in Celtic myth, was the king of the gods. He wore a wolf-skin cap, traveller's boots and tunic, and carried a pot (from which he dispensed benefits to the human race) and a hammer (which he used both to strike plenty from the ground, and to hit dying people on the forehead, so granting them a quick **death** and an easy passage to the **Underworld**).

⨠➔ **supreme deity**

SUDIKA-MBAMBI AND KABUNDUNGULU
Africa

Sudika-Mbambi ('thunderbolt') and Ka-bundungulu ('thunder-from-the-West'), in the myths of the Mbundu people of Angola, were miraculous **twins**. They were born fully formed, Sudika-Mbambi (the elder by an eye-blink) as a warrior armed with a knife and the tree of life, and Kabundungulu as his companion. They made war on the **demons** of darkness, killing monsters, mating with witches and pillaging the **Underworld**. Finally they quarrelled over the two daughters of the king of the Underworld. They fought, briefly, then agreed to a stand-off. Sudika-Mbambi married the elder daughter and set up his castle in the East; Kabundungulu married her sister and set up his castle in the West. The **thunder** we hear rolling round the sky is the brothers calling to each other.

SUGRIVA
India

Sugriva, in Hindu myth, was the mon-key-king, a son of **Surya** the **Sun**. Dethroned by his half-brother **Balin**, he was helped back to his throne by **Rama**, and repaid him by gathering the huge army of monkeys and bears which fought the **demon**-king **Ravana** who had kidnapped Rama's wife **Sita**. Sugri-va went on to become the ancestor of every ape and monkey in the world.

SUMITRA
India

Sumitra, in Hindu myth, was the third wife of King **Dasaratha**. She drank one third of the *soma* provided by **Vishnu** in answer to Dasaratha's prayer for sons, and conceived **twins**, **Lakshma-na** and **Shatrughna**, each of whom possessed one quarter of the god's attributes, powers and nature.

SUN: *see* Amaterasu, Apollo, Aten, Belenus, Dazhbog, Dudugera, Hana and Ni, Helius, Horus, Hyperion, Inti, Kodoyanpe, Lug, Marduk, Mithra, Ninhursaga, Ninurta, Page Abe, Päivä, Ra, Sarasvati, Shamash, Surya, Tonatiuh, Tsohanoai, Unelanuki, Viracocha, Vivasvat, Yi

SUN BIN
Asia (East)

Sun Bin, in Chinese myth, was a mortal general who, when his toes were sliced off in a battle, invented shoes to cover them – and was promptly promoted to **Heaven** and made patron god of cobblers.
➤ **crafts**

SUPREME DEITY
In some accounts, the supreme deity was the original creator of the universe, or was the universe itself, conceived either as an abstraction or as an active, sentient force. In others, the supreme deity was merely the first among gods, and reached that position either by creating all the others, by might or awesomeness, or because his or her weapons were more powerful than those of any other god. (In several traditions, those weapons were thun-derbolts, and the supreme deity ruled the sky.)

A few myths said that once the supreme deity made and tenanted the universe, he or she lost interest and withdrew to some region beyond the reach of human imaginings – or, in disrespectful accounts, became so senile that retirement was imposed. This idea was particularly common in areas where one group of myths had superseded another: the chief god or gods of the older system, displaced by newer powers, abandoned the bustle of ordinary existence, most of them forever, others to await the coming of some dire emergency such as the imminent destruction of **creation**. Most myths, however, imagined the supreme deity as an active absolute ruler, emperor of the supernatural world, head of an enormous hierarchy, final arbiter, patriarch of a large (and usually quarrelsome) extended family, and in some cases not only grand but tetchy, lecherous and cunning. These imperial deities were almost always light-gods or sky-gods (some *were* the sky), and were locked in conflict with their eternal enemy, the ruler of darkness. (In Western myth, this was a straightforward conflict; in Eastern myth, **light and dark** were aspects of *yin* and *yang*, and their harmonious co-existence was essential if the universe was not to collapse into chaos.)

➤ (Africa): Akongo, Katonda, Leza and Honeybird, Mulungu, Ngewowa; (Americas): Aiomum Kondi, Kitshi Manito, Ometecuhtli, Wakonda; (Arctic): Torngarsak; (Celtic): Sucellus; (China): Shang Di, Yu Huang; (Egypt): Amun, Aten, Ra; (Finnish): Ukko; (Greece): Zeus; (India): Amitabha, Brahma, Vishnu; (Mesopotamia): Adad, Ashur, El, Yahweh; (Nordic): Odin; (Rome): Jupiter; (Slavic): Svandovit, Svarog

SURMA
Europe (North)

Surma, in Finnish myth, was the monster which guarded the gate to the realm of **Kalma**, goddess of **death** in the **Underworld**. Surma was a bodiless pair of jaws with rows of fangs like swords and an endless, hungry gullet. It allowed the Dead to pass unharmed, but any living being which tried to enter the Underworld was snatched by the jaws, torn to pieces by the teeth and dispatched down the gullet into oblivion.
➤ demons

SURT
Europe (North)

Surt ('soot') was the **giant** ruler of **Muspell**, the fire-world which existed before the **creation** of the universe. At **Ragnarök**, he will erupt in volcanic frenzy, hurling fire until all creation is destroyed.

SURYA (DAUGHTER OF SAVITRI)
India

Surya ('shiner'), in the Vedic myths of the Aryans who invaded India in the seventeenth century BCE, was the daughter of **Savitri**, a portion of the **Sun**'s radiance turned into a serene, beautiful goddess. She was the shared wife of the **Ashvins**, the horse-lord healers who were also her cousins.
➤ beauty

SURYA (THE SUN)
India

Surya (also called Savitar, 'shiner'), in the Vedic myths of the Aryans who invaded India in the seventeenth century BCE, was the god of the Sun's disc. In Vedic myth he was one of **Dyaus'** sons, and formed a heavenly triad with **Indra** and **Agni**. He upheld the universe during the day, handing it over to **Varuna** at night. He knew all, saw all, and gave mortals disease, healing and the glow of intelligence.

Surya in Hindu myth. In Hindu myth Surya was the son either of **Brahma**, or of **Aditi** and **Kasyapa**. His symbol was the swastika, sign of plenty. The best-known story about him is a variant of the Vedic myth of **Vivasvat** and **Saranyu**. He married Sanjna, daughter of the smith-god **Vishvakarman**, and their children included Vaivasvata, **Manu**, **Yama** and Yami. But Sanjna found his radiance insupportable, left her servant Shaya ('Shadow') in her place and hid in the woods as a mare. Surya found her, changed to a stallion and fathered the **Ashvins** on her. For a time he and Sanjna lived as horses, but then they returned to their palace. Surya agreed that Vishvakarman should reduce his radiance by one eighth, shaving him down on the smith-god's lathe. So he and Sanjna lived happily ever after – and from the shavings Vishvakarman made weapons for the gods.

In art based on Vedic myth, Surya the Sun is shown as a dwarfish warrior with a body of polished copper, riding a golden, one-wheeled chariot drawn by seven mares (or one seven-headed mare) representing the days of the week. In Hindu art he is shown as a prince with dark red skin, three eyes and four arms. Two of his hands hold water-lilies, the third beckons and the fourth blesses. Sometimes he rides the Sun-chariot, sometimes he sits on a red lotus, smiling seraphically, light-beams radiating from his body.

SUSANO
Asia (East)

Susano, the storm-god in Japanese myth, was born from the water-drops when **Izanagi** washed his nose to rid himself of the pollution of the **Underworld**. (In some accounts he was created when Izanagi blew his nose.) Izanagi gave rule of the **Sun** to Susano's sister **Amaterasu** and rule of the **Moon** to his brother **Tsukuyomi**. Susano was given rule of the sea, or some say of Earth, and refused to accept it. He roared and raged about **creation**, constantly harassing Amaterasu. In the end he went too far, causing the death of her sister Wakahirume (Dawn), and Amaterasu retreated from the world to a cave, taking her light with her. The gods eventually enticed her into coming out again, and punished Susano by cutting off his beard, fingernails and toenails, fining him and banishing him from **Heaven** forever.

This punishment chastened Susano. He retreated to Earth, and began using his powers for good, not bad. In particular, he sucked up **water** from the **sea** and carried it to land in the form of **rain**, which brought the world its first **fertility**. When he shaved or cut his hair he planted the strands on mountain-slopes to grow as trees. At this time water-snakes and other **monsters** sent from the Underworld by **Izanami** were terrorizing human beings, mortal children of Susano's father Izanagi. (Although Izanagi created 1500 new humans each day, Izanami killed 1000.) Susano harnessed his storms to fight the monsters.

In Izumo province, where the gods met once every year to discuss human affairs, Susano rescued a beautiful girl, Kushinada, from the fiercest of all Izanami's water-monsters. It had already eaten her seven sisters; it had fire for eyes, eight heads and eight tails, and was so vast that its body covered eight valleys and eight mountain-peaks and trees grew on its back. Susano saved Kushinada by turning her into an ornamental comb which he stuck in his hair. He told her parents to fill eight barrels with *sake* (rice-wine), and offered one of the barrels to each of the monster's eight heads. As soon as the beast was drunk – this was the first alcohol it had ever tasted – he cut off its heads and chopped its body into tiny pieces. Then he turned Kushinada back into a woman, made her his consort, and settled down to rule the world.

The Shinto priests who retold this myth added a detail with vital religio-political importance. When Susano chopped up the monster's tails, buried in one of them he found the magic sword Kusanaginotsur-ugi ('harvests enemies like grass'), and presented it to his sister Amaterasu. She later gave the sword to her grandson Ninigi when she sent him from Heaven to rule the Earth, and from him it descended from generation to generation of the royal

house, one of the most sacred objects in the Imperial regalia.

≫→ Okuninushi, Izanami and Izanagi

SUTTUNG
Europe (North)

Suttung, in Nordic myth, was a **giant**. His father **Gilling** was murdered by two dwarfs, Fjalar and Galar, who had previously brewed the mead of inspiration from the blood of another of their murder-victims, **Kvasir**. Suttung forced them to give him the mead, and stored it in a cave in the heart of a mountain, guarded by his daughter **Gunnlod** – from whom **Odin** rescued it for the gods.

SVANDOVIT
Europe (East)

Svandovit, or Svetovid, in Baltic myth, was the father of all gods, in particular **Sun** and **Fire**. He controlled the world's **fertility** and was lord of **prophecy** and **war**.

Svandovit's prophecies were given in two ways. His statues held drinking-horns, and at the end of each year priests saw how much liquor was left and foretold from it the size of the following year's harvest. In his temple in Arcona lived a sacred white war-horse. Each year, it was driven through an obstacle course of spears – and the fewer 'hits', the better the future. Svandovit's statues had four faces (one for each cardinal compass point), and the inner shrines of his temples were so sacred that they were guarded by armed soldiers day and night, and the high priests (the only

people ever admitted) had to hold their breath while cleaning them.
»»→ **Dazhbog, Radigast, Rod, Rugievit, supreme deity**

SVAROG
Europe (East)

Svarog ('very hot'), in Slavic myth, was **Sky**, father of all other gods. When his sons **Dazhbog** (the **Sun**) and **Svarozich** (Fire) became more powerful, he surrendered his powers to them, remaining a benevolent but remote presence in the universe.

*The name Svarog is close to the Sanskrit word svar ('bright'), and suggests to some mythographers that Svarog came originally from North India. Other scholars trace a succession in chief Slavic gods, from the original **Byelobog** to Svarog, and from Svarog to Dazhbog. In Baltic myth, Svarog's equivalent was **Svandovit**.*
»»→ **Pyerun, supreme deity**

SVAROZICH
Europe (East)

Svarozich (from *svarog*, 'very hot'), son of **Svarog** and brother of **Dazhbog** in Slavic myth, was the god of **fire** and of **prophecy** – the glow of inspiration allowing glimpses into non-mortal time and space.

SVYATOGOR
Europe (East)

Svyatogor, a **giant** in Slavic myth, boasted that he could lift the whole weight of **Mother Earth**. One day, riding along, he saw a bag on the ground. He tried to lift it with his stick, and failed. He leaned down to pick it up, and it was too heavy. He dismounted and used both hands; he thought he'd raised the bag to his knees, then realized that it had stayed where it was while his legs had sunk knee-deep into the ground. He tried to climb out of the hole, straining until he wept tears of blood; but he was stuck, and starved.

In later stories, Svyatogor was identified as **Ilya Muromets**, one of the *bogatiri*.

SZEUKHA
Americas (North)

Szeukha, Earth-maker's son in the myths of the Pima people of the Southwestern US desert, lived on Earth with the humans his father had created from balls of mud and sweat. Great Eagle, lord of water, had no time for humans. He began by preying on them, snatching them to his mountain-eyrie and eating them alive. Then he sent a **flood** to engulf **creation** and end them. Only Szeukha survived, floating among the flotsam and jetsam on a lump of pine resin. As soon as the waters began to recede, he stepped out on the top of a mountain – by chance, right into Great Eagle's eyrie. A magic duel ensued, and Szeukha won only by enlisting the spirits of rock and mud, **Mother Earth**'s own children, to fight for him. As soon as Great Eagle was dead, Szeukha gathered bones and skin-scraps from the debris round the eyrie, laid them on the ground and breathed life into them. So humankind was reconstituted: not the first creation, imbued with existence by Earth-maker himself, but a degenerate version made from its own remains.

The Wooden Horse (*P. Lombault, 18th century*)

TA'AROA
Oceania

Ta'aroa, in some Polynesian **creation-**myths, was the first and only being. At the beginning of creation, he hatched from an egg which floated in chaos. Finding that the time was not right to be born, he formed a second egg and waited inside it until the time again came to be hatched. Then he made the shell of the first egg into **Atea**, **Sky**, and the shell of the second into Fa'ahotu, Earth. To complete creation, he used his own body, turning his flesh into soil, his internal organs into clouds, his bones into mountains, his feathers into plants, his intestines into eels and his blood into birds. Thus, when creation was finished he was simultaneously nowhere and everywhere, part of all that was.

*In some accounts, Ta'aroa later reconstituted himself as **Tangaroa** or **Tangaloa**, god of the **sea**. The sea was his own sweat, caused by the exertions of creation. He was therefore both the sea and lord of it.*

TAGARO
Oceania

Tagaro, in the myths of the people of Vanuatu, modelled the first human beings from mud. There were ten of them, all images of himself, and he stood them in a row and played skittles with them, throwing fruit at them. One fruit stuck to the penis of one of the mud-men, and when Tagaro pulled it away, the penis came with it. So the first woman was created, and she married one of the men and had children of her own.

⟫⟶ **creation, Chinigchinich, Enki, Esaugetuh Emissee, Humanmaker,**

Hurukan, Na'pi, Prometheus, Woyengi

TALIESIN
Europe (North)

Taliesin ('shining brow'), in Celtic myth, was a powerful wizard and bard. He was born as Gwion, a humble farm-boy, without inspiration. But Caridwen, a witch who had borne an unbelievably ugly son, determined to compensate the child by giving him all the knowledge in the world, filled a pot with magic herbs and set it to boil for a year and a day. This boiling would reduce it to three drops, which would contain all-knowledge. Caridwen asked Gwion to watch the mixture, and one day as he was stirring it a drop of the liquid fell on his finger and he licked it off. At once he was given one third of all the world's knowledge, including the fact that Caridwen meant to kill him as soon as the boiling was finished.

Caridwen chased Gwion to kill him. Among the skills he'd learned was that of shape-changing, and he made himself a hare, a fish, a bird and a grain of corn. Caridwen pursued him as greyhound, otter, hawk – and finally as a hen, eating the corn-grain. Nine months later, having resumed her normal shape, she gave birth to another child – Gwion, reborn – and this time tried to kill him by sewing him in a bag and throwing him into the river. River-currents carried the bag downstream to the salmon-leap owned by Prince Elphin, who opened it and was dazzled by the radiance streaming from Gwion's face, a glow like golden corn. 'Taliesin!' he exclaimed – and took the child to his own palace, where Taliesin/Gwion grew up to be the seer, prophet and chief entertainer of his people.

This tale seems to have been told in honour of a real bard called Taliesin, who lived at the Welsh court in the sixth century CE, and is said to be buried at the village still called after him. No surviving poems are known actually to be by him, though a large fourteenth-century collection of poetry in Welsh, by miscellaneous hands, was named The Book of Taliesin after him. (This includes a set of 'Taliesin's riddles', and an account of his shape-changing and of such miraculous exploits as visiting Noah in his ark, Jonah in his whale, God on his throne, Satan in his kitchen and Romulus and Remus building the walls of Rome.) Some French accounts of the Arthur myth attribute the story of his encounter with Caridwen to the young Merlin, but Welsh sources insist that they were two quite different people, and that the only occasion when Taliesin came into contact with Arthur was when he guided him to Annwn, the Underworld, to recover stolen treasure.

≫→ prophecy, shape-changers

TAMENDONARE: *see* Ariconte and Tamendonare

TAMULU: *see* Tamusi and Tamulu

TAMUSI AND TAMULU
Americas (South)

Tamusi and Tamulu, in the myths of the Caliña people of South America, were sons of **Amana** the creator, sent from her sea-kingdom in the Milky Way to protect Earth against the fire-serpents of her enemy the **Sun**. Tamusi, Light, was born in the morning before the day's heat began; Tamulu, Dark, was born in the evening when it was done. The brothers hated each other, but were inextricably linked, since Light and Darkness cannot exist without one another. They divided their responsibilities rigorously: Tamusi slept while Tamulu ruled, and although Tamulu sometimes lingered for a while in the sky when his brother rose in the morning, he very soon gave way.

The Sun attacked the Earth with **fire-serpents**, sending them snaking up through vents in the surface. During the day, Tamusi sliced them to pieces with his **lightning**-sword and tossed the fragments into the sky, where they made shooting-stars and comets. Tamulu smothered them in his cloak of darkness.

As soon as the Earth was safe from the Sun, Amana told Tamusi and Tamulu to people it. Tamusi's creations, children of light, were animals, insects and human beings. Tamulu's creations, children of darkness, were **monsters**, dreams and phantoms.

>>→ creation, light and dark

TANE
Oceania

Tane, or Kane, in Polynesian myth, was the son of **Rangi** (Father Sky) and **Papa** (**Mother Earth**). At the beginning of the universe, **Sky** and Earth were united in such a close sexual embrace that all **creation** was trapped in Papa's womb. Tane, god of forests, planted his feet in Papa, lifted his arms to Rangi and grew

until he had separated them. He clothed Sky in a cloak of darkness studded with jewels (the stars, the Milky Way) and lined with red (Dawn); he clothed Earth with shrubs and trees – at first planting them upside down (mangroves), but then right way up. He taught Earth's people, the human race, all knowledge, in two branches: the Upper Jaw (information about the gods, space and time, the order of the universe) and the Lower Jaw (everything needed for life on Earth, from **farming** methods to **music**, from law to myth).

Tane favoured human beings so much that he decided to live with them. He tried to find a mate. Because no human woman could have **sex** with a god and live, he was forced to mate with trees, plants, stones and pools, fathering all kinds of creatures including **snakes** and dragons. He asked his mother Papa what to do, and she told him, first, that he should mould himself a wife from sand (or, in some accounts, carve her from sandstone), and second, that the union would bring disaster. Ignoring the warning, Tane made himself a wife, Hine Ahu One ('Earth-girl') and breathed life into her. The result of their first, botched mating was an egg – which hatched to produce the ancestor of all birds on Earth. At their second attempt Hine Ahu One was transformed into her own daughter, Hine Titama ('Dawn-girl') or Tikikapakapa. When this child grew up, Tane married her, and they had another daughter, Hine Titamauri. But then Hine Titama asked Tane who her father was, and when he answered by pointing to his penis, she was so ashamed to have committed incest with her own father that she fled to the **Underworld**. She became Hine Nui Te Po, goddess of death, and dragged all members of Tane's human race down to her kingdom when their time on Earth was done.

In some accounts, the coming of **death** into the world made Tane abandon his attempts to live with humans. He became aloof, as his father Rangi had done before him, and left mortals to live their own (now foreshortened) lives and make their own mistakes. In other accounts, he remained on Earth, but retreated to the high hills, where he married a new wife (Hine Tu A Muana, 'mountain-girl'), born of the dew which was his father Rangi's tears; their offspring were mountain springs, streams and the water-**monsters** that live in them.

≫→ Atea, civilization, crafts, creation, farming

TANGALOA
Oceania

Tangaloa, in Samoan myth, was the first god in existence. He saw a stone floating in the primordial ocean, carried it into space and carved a wife from it. He threw the remains of the stone into the sea, where they formed the Polynesian islands. Tangaloa told his daughter Tuli ('snipe') to fly down and plant a vine on the largest island. The vine divided itself into plants and vegetation of every kind. Grubs scrabbled round its roots, and Tangaloa transformed them into animals, birds, fish, and finally human beings, to complete **creation**.

≫→ Ta'aroa

TANGAROA
Oceania

Tangaroa the sea-god. Tangaroa, in Polynesian myth, was the eldest son of **Papa** (**Mother Earth**) and Vatea (that is **Rangi**, Father Sky). In some accounts he took part in the council of gods which tried to separate Papa and Rangi from their stifling, incessant sexual embrace, and later quarrelled with **Tane**, god of trees, forever attacking dry land (in tides), biting holes in the shoreline and snatching people and animals into the **sea**-kingdom. His wives were Faumea, who loved him enough to magic a nest of male-swallowing **monsters** out of her vagina and allow him intercourse, and Hina A Rauriki, whom he rescued from the octopus-**demon** Rogo Tumu Here.

Tangaroa and Rongo. In one Mangaian myth – a story so biased towards red-haired people that one wonders who invented it – Tangaroa and Rongo were **twins**, the eldest children of Papa and Vatea. Tangaroa was the elder, but generously allowed Rongo to be born first, and himself arrived later from a boil on his mother's arm. He knew all the secrets of the universe, and taught Rongo (who was less intelligent as well as junior) how to look after growing plants. As elder, he should have been sole ruler, but Vatea said that his saltiness would kill all life on land, and ordered that Rongo be given it instead to rule. Tangaroa agreed, asking only that he be allowed rule of everything red in creation: red birds, red fish, red-leaved trees, red vegetables and fruit, red-haired people. Rongo agreed, and the result was that, although red creatures and produce are the minority in creation, they are also the choicest.

Tangaroa appears in many different traditions, and his name is sometimes spelled Ta'aroa, Tagaro or Tagaroa.
≫→ sea

TANTALUS
Europe (South)

Tantalus (Tantalos, 'all wretched'), in Greek myth, was the son of **Zeus** and the **Titan** Pluto (not the same person as the king of the **Underworld**). Although he chose to live with mortals on Earth, his immortal parentage guaranteed him regular access to **Olympus**, and he was a frequent visitor at banquets of the gods. He married **Atlas'** daughter Dione, and their children were **Niobe** and **Pelops**.

Tantalus either cared nothing for right and wrong, or was a fool. He did what he wanted, regardless of the consequences – and suffered for it. On one occasion, he stole **ambrosia** and **nectar**, the gods' food and drink of **immortality**, and would have shared them with his mortal friends if the gods had not snatched them back in time. On another, he gave a banquet for the gods – and fed them a stew made from his own son Pelops. His third crime was smaller than either of these, but still the last straw for the gods. Tantalus' friend Pandareus stole a golden guard-dog made long before to protect the infant Zeus – and Tantalus hid it, suspecting (rightly) that no one would question a son of Zeus. No one, that is, but Zeus himself, who soon found out what had happened. He punished Pandareus by turning him to stone, and hurled him at Tantalus – a boulder which toppled Tantalus from **Heaven** to the Underworld.

In the Underworld, Tantalus was tied fast and surrounded by luscious fruit and a pool of clear water. As the centuries passed he became ever more hungry and thirsty – but whenever he tried to eat or drink the food and the pool slipped out of reach, leaving him forever tantalized. The boulder which had dashed him to the Underworld hung overhead, half-slipping and threatening to crush him to even lower depths – and he was condemned to endure these not-quite-punishments throughout eternity.

TAPIO
Europe (North)

Tapio, in Finnish myth, was the god of forests. He was himself without shape or substance, but his beard and clothes were made entirely of trees, and he had bottomless lakes for eyes. He lay sleeping across the countryside of Finland (which some called Tapiola after him); occasionally he stirred uneasily as he dreamed, sending storms rippling through his tree-cloak. Mortals sometimes settled among his trees, as ticks live in a sheep's fleece – and gradually, over time, as they listened to the rustling and whispering of the branches, they heard tiny echoes of Tapio's secrets, the knowledge of the gods.
≫→ farming

TARA
Asia (Southwest); India

Tara in Hindu myth. Tara was the beautiful wife of **Brihaspati** who was abducted and made pregnant by **Soma**.

Tara in Buddhist myth. Tara was a **sea**-goddess, and her mood changed in the same way as the sea: sometimes she was calm and serene, sometimes stormy and destructive. Like a squid or an octopus, she revealed her mood by the way her colour changed: when she was angry she turned blue, red or yellow, and when she was calm she turned green or white. She led a company of sea-**nymphs** who rescued sailors in danger.

Tara in Tibetan myth. In Tibetan myth the sea-aspect of Tara's character was, of necessity, turned into metaphor. Born from the Sea of Wisdom, she was Perfect Understanding, and ferried worshippers over the River of Experience to the Shore of Enlightenment. She was the wife of **Avalokiteshvara**, and the mother of all human beings on Earth.

Images of Tara are often painted on or pinned to boats. They show her as a serene, smiling woman, sometimes carrying a lotus and usually sitting on a lion (symbolizing the stormy water she has tamed).

TARAKA
India

Taraka ('star'), in Hindu myth, was a **demon**-queen who used to bite off mountain-tops with her teeth and hurl them at people she disliked. While **Rama** and his brothers were growing up, the sage **Vishvamitra** asked them to kill her. At first Rama was reluctant to fight a female, but he finally agreed. He and **Lakshmana** fought Taraka. Lakshmana cut off her nose and her ears to stop her sniffing them out or hearing

their approach, and Rama cut off her arms to stop her hurling rocks. But she went on biting mountains and spitting boulders until Rama fired an unerring arrow and shot her dead.

TARANIS
Europe (North)

Taranis, in Celtic myth, was the god of **thunder**. Its rumblings were caused by the wheels of Taranis' war-chariot rolling across the **sky**, and **lightning** was the sparks from his horses' hooves. Taranis was savage and destructive, but if he was appeased (by human sacrifice, the victims being drowned or burned), he sent prosperity to the earth in the form of **rain**.

TAWERET
Africa (North)

Taweret ('great one', Greek Thoueris), **Set**'s wife in Egyptian myth, was as benign as her husband was savage. She helped mortal women in **childbirth**, frightening off evil spirits at the instant the child entered the world of light – and she did this not by actual ferocity but by her appearance, as she had a hippo's head, the body of a pregnant lioness (but with human breasts), standing upright, and a crocodile's tail.

Taweret was popular with ordinary people. Women wore Taweret-bracelets and pendants, and put her statuettes beside their beds. There were Taweret jugs, hollowed out so that the goddess' pregnant belly held the liquid, her tail was the handle, and one breast was pierced to make *the spout. Her popularity persuaded the priests to incorporate her in the **Underworld** pantheon, and she was married off to **Horus** (who won her from Set, in a newly-invented myth, during their cosmic duel) and placed at one of the gates of the Underworld, where she eased the passage not of souls coming in but of those going out, on their way to be reborn.*

≫→ animal-gods

TAWISKARA: *see* Ioskeha

TAWISKARON
Americas (North)

Tawiskaron, in the myths of the Mohawk people of the Northeastern US woodlands, was a **demon** who shepherded wild beasts as ordinary people kept goats or chickens. He and his pets lived in a corner of the **sky**, and from time to time he let down a bridge of cloud and sent his animals to Earth to prey on mortals.

TEFNUT
Africa (North)

Tefnut (or Tefenet, 'wetness'), in Egyptian myth, was the daughter of **Atum** and sister of **Shu**. She was either born from semen after her father masturbated, or (as the sound of her name suggests) from his spittle when he spat. She mated with Shu to engender **Geb** (Earth) and **Nut** (Air), but thereafter played little part in myth. In some accounts she quarrelled with **Ra**, left Egypt for Nubia and had to be enticed back by **Thoth**; in others, morning dew is her vaginal fluid.

*In art, Tefnut was shown sometimes as a pair of spitting lips, and occasionally – perhaps because the Nubia story led her to be confused with **Sekhmet** or **Hathor** – as a lioness. She was also shown as a snake coiling round the pharaoh's sceptre: a guarantee that so long as pharaoh ruled and Tefnut supported him, there would be no drought.*

TELCHINES
Europe (South)

The Telchines ('enchanters'), in Greek myth, were nine of the earliest and most elusive sea-**monsters** of all. They were the children of Sea, the first creatures ever able to breathe both on land and in water. They had dogs' heads, and flippered, stumpy arms like sealions; if they were angered, poisonous mist flashed from their eyes and killed any animal or mortal who came within range. They were craftsmen who made (some said) the sickle used by **Cronus** to attack Uranus (see **Ouranos**), and who invented the art of sculpture.

At first the Telchines settled in Rhodes (or some say Crete). But like many of the older gods, they cared nothing for the **Olympians**. They were not powerful enough to cause real trouble, but loved playing practical jokes and pranks. They interfered with the weather, to **Zeus**' irritation. They insulted **Aphrodite** so much, on one of her visits to Rhodes, that she lost her temper and sent them mad, so that they rioted across the island, fouling and breaking everything in sight. In the end **Poseidon** decided to rid his kingdom of them forever. He sent a **flood** to swallow them, but they scattered and escaped. Ever afterwards, they appeared briefly and unexpectedly all over the world, and every time they did they caused havoc. Sailors often claimed to have been attacked by them, in the shape of sea-**demons** surging on the wings of the East Wind. On land, like all supernatural sea-beings, they could assume any form they chose – and on one occasion they disguised themselves as hunting-dogs, and led the pack which tore Actaeon to pieces.

≫→ **crafts, shape-changers, tricksters**

TELEMACHUS
Europe (South)

Telemachus ('late-battle'), son of **Odysseus** and **Penelope**, in Greek myth, was born just before Odysseus sailed to take part in the **Trojan War**, and grew up during the twenty years of his father's absence. When Odysseus came home, Telemachus helped him to kill the suitors who were pestering Penelope. But an oracle told Odysseus that his own son would one day murder him, and – not knowing of the existence of any sons except Telemachus – he banished the boy from Ithaca forever. Telemachus went first to Sparta (which he had visited some years earlier, to ask **Helen** and **Menelaus** if they had news of Odysseus' adventures after the Trojan War), and then to the floating island of Aeaea, where he married **Circe**, or in some accounts her daughter Cassiphone, and founded a royal dynasty.

Soon after this, Telemachus left Aeaea. Some say that he accidentally killed Circe and was banished, others that he inherited his father's wanderlust, and that he and Circe joined Penelope

and Telegonus (who had married Penelope after Odysseus' death) and sailed South to a country previously unknown to Greeks. They called it Italy after Telegonus' and Penelope's son Italus, and Telemachus' and Circe's son **Latinus** later founded a dynasty, becoming the ancestor of the Latin people.

TELEPINU
Asia (West)

Telepinu, god of **farming** in ancient Syrian myth, was temperamental, liable to take offence at small slights (such as a frown from his father Taru, the weather-god) and to hold back or blight the crops. On one occasion he lost his temper altogether, threw on his clothes so quickly that he put his boots on the wrong feet, and disappeared. All over the world plants died, crops failed, human beings began to starve and the gods were denied their sacrifices. **Demons** swarmed from the **Underworld** to feast on corpses. The gods quartered the universe to find Telepinu and persuade him back. The **Sun** smashed down the gate of his palace and ran through the corridors and courtyards looking for him, but they were empty.

Then Hannahanna, Mother of All, sent a bee to find Telepinu's hiding place and sting him into reappearing. Instead of looking in palaces and cities, the bee went where bees go, and found Telepinu hiding among the flowers of a meadow. It stung him on the nose, knees and elbows, but instead of bringing him to his senses the pain made him even angrier, and he began jumping up and down and roaring at the gods.

Hannahanna sent Kamrusepas, goddess of magic healing, to poultice his stings with the herb of **immortality** and soothe the pain. Reluctantly Telepinu let himself be wooed back to work and the order of the universe was saved.

*Gods of agriculture are often comic in myth, particularly in traditions where city-dwelling story-tellers have reworked stories from more ancient times. (Agriculture-gods in animist traditions seldom undergo such revisionism.) In Telepinu's case, another cause of mirth seems to have been that he was not the first god in his family to indulge in frets and sulks: a similar myth (now surviving only in fragments) seems to have been told of his father Taru. Other myths, however, suggest that Telepinu was not entirely a buffoon: in one, when the dragon **Illuyankas** stole the gods' eyes and hearts, it was Telepinu who seduced the dragon's daughter and persuaded her to get them back.*

TEMAZCALTECI
Americas (Central)

Temazcalteci ('grandmother of the sweatbath'), in Aztec myth, was the goddess of cleanness and patron of bath-houses. She protected people inside while they made themselves vulnerable to **demons** by stripping and washing. In some accounts, she was one aspect of **Cihuacóatl**, the **Great Goddess**.
≫→ water

TEN CORN MAIDENS
Americas (North)

The Ten Corn Maidens, in the myths of the Zuñi people of the Southwestern US Pueblos, were beautiful dancers who came to the Upper World with the human race. They themselves were invisible, but their presence could be seen as they danced with corn-plants in the breeze. Witches transformed them into human girls, and imprisoned them, causing famine all over Zuñi lands. Then the harvest-god **Payatamu**, who was in love with Yellow Corn Maiden, rescued them and took them back to the Zuñi, where they danced and restored the harvest.
≫→ beauty, farming

TENGRI
Asia (Central)

Tengri ('power'), also known as Od and Odlek, in Mongolian myth, created the universe by wresting order from chaos. He gathered **fire**, wind and **water** and moulded them to make human beings. He himself, universal power, galloped in a disembodied form through the world on the horses of the storm to right wrongs and punish evil-doers. His wife was Itugen, **Mother Earth**, or Umai, Mother of All, and their children (also called Tengri) went to live on Earth as the spirits of everything in existence, both of visible entities such as trees, rivers, **mountains** and flames, and of such abstract notions as order, law and virtue.
≫→ civilization, creation

TEN YAMA KINGS, THE
Asia (East)

The Ten Yama Kings, in Chinese myth, were judges of the Dead. Each presided over a different court. The first King weighed each soul to see if it was heavy with guilt and should go to another court for judgement, or was light enough to pass straight to the Wheel of Transmigration and return to the mortal world in a new body. The second King judged greedy business-men and incompetent doctors, the third liars and politicians, the fourth blasphemers and misers, the fifth mur-derers and rapists, the sixth atheists, the seventh cannibals and slave-tra-ders, the eighth those who failed to honour their parents and the ninth arsonists and people killed in acci-dents. In all these courts, the Yama Kings had at their disposal an arsenal of punishments ranging from pillory and stocks to impaling, roasting, boil-ing in oil and throwing to wild beasts. Finally, the souls reached the tenth court, where appropriate new lives were settled before they passed at last to the Wheel of Transmigration and their new lives as aristocrats, paupers or animals.

➤ Underworld

TEREUS
Europe (South)

Tereus ('on guard'), son of **Ares** in Greek myth, was a king of Thrace who helped King Pandion of Athens in a war against **Thebes** (or, some say, Megara). In gratitude, Pandion let Tereus marry his daughter Procne. Procne pined for her sister Philomela, and Tereus went South to bring Philo-mela to Thrace. As soon as he saw her, however, he was filled with lust, raped her, cut out her tongue to prevent her telling anyone, shut her in a remote castle and went home to tell Procne that she was dead.

Unfortunately for Tereus, the gods were so outraged that they helped Phi-lomela and Procne to take vengeance. Philomela embroidered the story of her rape on a tapestry and sent it to Procne, and Procne rescued her and took her to Thrace, with the gods' help, before Tereus arrived home. They butchered Tereus' infant son Itys, and when Ter-eus arrived Philomela served him the child's flesh in a stew of welcome. At the end of the meal Philomela appeared from behind a curtain, gibbering, and threw Itys' severed head on the table in front of Tereus. He drew his sword to kill the sisters – and the gods intervened for the last time, turning all four hu-mans into birds. Tereus became a hoo-poe (or, in some accounts, an owl – forever watchful), Philomela a nightin-gale (sweetly singing forever in recom-pense for her severed mortal tongue), Itys a pheasant (or, some say, a sand-piper) and Procne a swallow.

This gory myth gave rise to some of the most beautiful of all Greek lyric poetry. Ignoring the rape and child-murder, poets concentrated on the transformation, and on the way in which the nightingale and swallow have mourned for Itys ever since, the sweetness of their singing only enhan-cing the heartbreak which inspires it. The 'Lament for Itys' was a favourite subject for lyric poets, and was often set for competitions; the phrase 'Itys, Itys' ('ee-tun, eetun') became a kind of vocalization of grief, similar to English 'Alas', and features in poems otherwise unconnected with the myth. Sophocles wrote a tragedy about the original myth (now lost), and

Aristophanes' Birds *parodies parts of it, introducing Tereus as a tattered bird-king, full of regret for his glorious past and of a mock-tragic, seedy arrogance.*

TERRA: *see* Gaia

TESHUB
Asia (West)

Teshub, the ancient Syrian storm-lord, was the son of two male gods. When Kumarbi and **An** fought for the throne of **Heaven**, Kumarbi bit off An's penis, was fertilized by it and gave birth to three full-grown offspring, **Rain**, **Lightning** and **Thunder**, of which Teshub, Thunder, was the most fearsome. He rode the sky on a bull, brandishing an axe in one hand and a thunderbolt in the other, and was surrounded by a group of admiring goddesses, all of them so concerned with the **fertility** of the universe that they were determined to mate with him.

As soon as Teshub and his brothers were born, they dethroned their parent Kumarbi. He retaliated by masturbating over a stone and engendering a **giant**, Ullikummi. Ullikummi was made of green quartz, and never stopped growing. His weight gradually made **Mother Earth** sink into the primordial ocean, and he began to push the sky-arch ever higher, threatening to smash the gods' palaces and spill the stars into the gulf of space. Teshub and his brothers attacked him with rain, lightning and thunder, but he was impervious. **Ishtar**, Teshub's sister, tried to seduce him, but he had no sexual organs and ignored her. At the last possible moment, just as Ullikummi was about to break

open the sky, blotting out the gods, Teshub dived deep into Ocean, found where the giant's feet were planted in Mother Earth and hacked them off at the ankles. Ullikummi toppled into Ocean, Mother Earth and Heaven were restored to their proper places, and the universe continued as if he had never existed.

This myth survives only in fragments, and the account is incomplete – for example, what happened to Kumarbi is not recorded. An interesting feature is the proliferation of storm-gods. In the **mountains** *where the story originated, storms were thought to be caused not by single deities but by whole armies racketing across the sky. It was only in later myth that the various attributes of Teshub, his brothers and his followers were gathered and given to a single deity, usually known just as* **Baal** *('lord').*

TEUTATIS
Europe (North)

Teutatis or Toutatis ('people') was the Gallic war god – and as his name suggests, he also symbolized the strength of the entire Gallic nation. With his companions **Taranis** and the mysterious Esus (about whom nothing else is known) he was worshipped with human sacrifice, the victims being ceremonially drowned or burned.

TEZCATLIPOCA
Americas (Central)

Tezcatlipoca ('smoking mirror'), in Aztec myth, was the original **Sun**-god, but was toppled from the sky (in some accounts, by **Quetzalcóatl**) and became the god of darkness and sorcery, afraid of daylight. His other names included Telpochtli ('young man'), Yaotl ('warrior') and Yoalli Ehecatl ('wind of the night'). He was one of the gods who existed before **creation**, and he plunged into the primordial ocean to wrestle with **Coatlicue** (in her guise as Cipactli the crocodile), tearing off her lower jaw to make the Earth. (In some accounts, she bit off one of his feet, and he replaced it with a mirror of polished flint, which reflected not just the present but the past and future. In others, he lost his foot by trapping it in one of the doors of the **Underworld**). When he was first hurled from the sky he had neither form nor shape, but was the all-present 'wind of the night', the invisible presence which terrifies human beings alone at night. Then he put his shape-changing powers to work, and became a black jaguar on Earth and in the sky the star-constellation the Great Bear. He also retained his invisible nature, gazing with four unseen faces in each of the four cardinal compass directions. His servants were wizards, **demons** and soothsayers, and he had power over wind and stillness, darkness and silence.

Tezcatlipoca took other forms as well. As consort of Tlazoltéotl, goddess of lust, he often appeared as a nude young man and set girls' hearts racing. To armies in the field he appeared as a warrior in full armour, recognizable as himself by his mirror-foot and a diagonal black stripe across his face. Another favoured form was that of a skeleton, gibbering in lonely woods, with a heart throbbing inside ribs which flapped open and shut like the doors of a cage. To conquer him, you thrust your arm between the ribs and tore out the heart – and at once he offered you riches to put it back. (He usually lied.) These depredations weakened him, and once every year he died and had to be revived at a bloody ceremony in which the heart of a living man was torn out and offered, still pulsing, at his altar.

Tezcatlipoca's mirror worked both ways. It showed the future to those of his worshippers who could read its secrets, and it gave him all-knowledge of human wishes and intentions. However, and perhaps unexpectedly in view of his unceasing thirst for human blood, he used his knowledge to help mortals, not harm them. He rewarded the good and punished the wicked, taking particular care of slaves, widows and orphans. His malevolence was chiefly directed towards the gods who had dethroned him as lord of creation, and he especially hated Quetzalcóatl. In the end he tricked Quetzalcóatl into self-disgust and self-immolation; light left the world, the Golden Age came to an end, and in the darkness and cruelty which filled human hearts thereafter, Tezcatlipoca once more ruled supreme.

*The Tezcatlipoca cult gave the invading Spaniards their chief defence for exterminating the Aztecs. Claiming that his dark secrets and bloodthirsty rituals were typical of the whole people, they set about butchering an entire nation in the name of their own redemptive God. It was as if visitors from Mars were to exterminate a nation of fundamentalist Christians on the grounds that they believed in **Satan**.*

»→ light and dark, prophecy, shape-changers, twins

THANATOS
Europe (South)

Thanatos ('death'), in Greek myth, was the child of Night and the brother of Sleep. He was a warrior whose task was to collect mortals whose time on Earth was over and take them to the gates of the Underworld, after which Hermes led them below for judgement. Thanatos is the same person as the (female) Roman Mors.

THEBES
Europe (South)

Thebes, in Greek myth, a city on the banks of the river Ismenus on the Boeotian plain, was one of the most beautiful places in the world. The gods chose it as the site of their earthly paradise, and sent Prince Cadmus of Phoenicia to build a city there. But Cadmus killed the sacred guardian of the place, Mother Earth's own serpent-offspring, and polluted the ground by spilling its blood. Mother Earth took her revenge by demanding the blood of each generation of the royal line of Thebes, and ever afterwards, while the city lasted, Theban kings and queens duly slaughtered one another and gave the ground their blood. Agave, Cadmus' daughter, tore her own son Pentheus to pieces. Zethus' (see Amphion and Zethus) wife, creeping into the nursery to murder the children of her sister-in-law Niobe, killed her own child by mistake in the darkness. Laius tried to kill his infant son Oedipus, to prevent

an oracle that the child would grow up to murder him – and failed. Oedipus killed Laius. Oedipus' sons Eteocles and Polynices killed each other, fighting for the throne. Creon executed Antigone, and caused the death of his own son Haemon.

After seven generations of slaughter, the rest of Greece at last rose up to put an end to Thebes. They sacked the city, smashed the walls, ploughed the rubble and sowed salt. The soil, already rank with blood, was poisoned: nothing ever grew there again, and the gods' dream of making Thebes an earthly paradise was frustrated forever.

»→ Heaven, Seven Against Thebes

THEMIS
Europe (South)

Themis ('justice'), in Greek myth, was a Titan. Zeus mated with her, and their offspring were the Fates and the Seasons. In some accounts, it was she and not Clymene who mated with her fellow-Titan Iapetus and gave birth to Prometheus. She was always depicted as a beautiful woman with bandaged eyes, or blind, and holding a sword in one hand and a pair of scales in the other.

»→ justice and universal order

THESEUS
Europe (South)

Theseus and Athens. Theseus ('layer-down'), in Greek myth, was the son of King Aegeus of Athens and Princess Aethra of Troezen. Aegeus, visiting Troezen, got drunk, slept with Aethra and left in a hurry. He left a golden sword and a pair of sandals under a rock, and told Aethra that if she bore a son, and the son grew up, she should tell him what had happened, and then if the gods gave the boy strength to lift the rock and find the sword, he should come to Athens as Aegeus' heir.

In due course Theseus was born, grew up, recovered the sword and sandals and set out for Athens. In the meantime, however, **Medea** had settled there, having fled to Aegeus after killing her children by **Jason**. Black magic told her who Theseus was, and she tried to poison him before Aegeus recognized him and made him his heir instead of Medea's own son Medus. But Aegeus recognized his sword and sandals from years before, and dashed the poison-cup from Theseus' hand. (Medea fled to the **Underworld**, where **Hades** welcomed her; Medus fled to Asia Minor.) Theseus next killed the fifty sons of Aegeus' brother Pallas, who were besieging Athens, and tamed a miraculous white bull (in some accounts the bull that fathered the Cretan **Minotaur**), which had swum ashore at Marathon not far from Athens; the Athenians hailed him as saviour and king-in-waiting.

Theseus and the Minotaur. Every year, as tribute to King Minos, the Athenians sent seven young men and seven young women to Crete. They became bull-leapers, and at the end of the season were sent into the Labyrinth where the Minotaur devoured them. Determined to end this custom, Theseus sailed to Crete in place of one of the young men, and began training as a bull-leaper. Minos' daughter **Ariadne** promised to help him kill the Minotaur if he took her away from Crete afterwards. She gave him a spindle wound with wool, and led him through corridors and chambers of the Labyrinth, while he unwound the wool to mark his way. They came to the den where the Minotaur slept, and Theseus killed it with his golden sword. They retraced their steps, winding up the wool, and freed the other Athenians from their cells. It was night, and there were no guards – for Crete was an island, and who but **Daedalus** had ever escaped from it? The Athenians scuttled the ships of the Cretan fleet, jumped into their own ship and rowed for home.

Theseus, Ariadne and Dionysus. Theseus planned to marry Ariadne as soon as they reached Athens. But on the way they landed on the island of Naxos for water, and while the Athenians went to the stream, Ariadne fell asleep on the beach – and **Dionysus** caught sight of her and lusted after her. He blurred the minds of Theseus and his companions with forgetfulness, so that they sailed away without Ariadne. She woke up alone on a deserted shore. Then Dionysus appeared, dancing over the sand-dunes with his maenads and **satyrs**; he spoke gently to her, charmed all memory of Theseus from her mind, and made her his consort.

Dionysus' forgetfulness-spell still clouded Theseus' mind. Before he sailed for Crete, he had promised Aegeus he would hoist a purple-red sail (or some say a white sail) to show success, and to tell his men to hoist a black sail for failure. He now forgot to change the sails, and when Aegeus, watching anxiously for news, saw a black sail on the horizon, he jumped from the Acropolis wall and killed himself.

Theseus, Antiope and Phaedra. After Aegeus' death the Athenians made Theseus king. He began to join other **heroes** on their expeditions and adventures. He was invited to the wedding of **Pirithous**, king of the Lapiths, and helped him in the battle which followed against the **Centaurs**. He and Pirithous became close friends, and had many adventures together. They went with **Heracles** to steal the belt of **Hippolyta**, queen of the **Amazons**. On the way they besieged the Amazon town of Themiscyra, and Princess **Antiope**, watching from the battlements, fell in love with Theseus and opened the gates for him. He took her to Athens as his mistress, and fought off a huge force of Amazons which tried to win her back. They lived happily for several years, and had a son, **Hippolytus**. But then King Minos died in Crete, and Theseus planned to make an alliance with the new king, Catreus, and to celebrate it by marrying **Phaedra**, **Ariadne**'s sister. Antiope burst in on the wedding ceremony with a band of Amazons to stop it, and in the battle which followed Theseus killed her.

Antiope's father, **Ares** god of war, and her patron, **Artemis**, waited to punish Theseus until his son Hippolytus was grown-up. Then they made Phaedra fall in love with the young man – and when he refused to have anything to do with her, they made her send a letter to Theseus claiming that Hippolytus had raped her, and then hang herself. Theseus sent soldiers to arrest Hippolytus, and Hippolytus jumped in a chariot and fled down the road beside the shore. In his fury, Theseus prayed to the gods to kill his son, and Poseidon sent a tidal wave which terrified Hippolytus' horses and made them rear; the chariot crashed and Hippolytus broke his neck.

Theseus' madness and death. The deaths of Phaedra and Hippolytus drove Theseus mad. He and Pirithous planned to kidnap and marry two daughters of **Zeus**, one for each of them. They stole twelve-year-old **Helen** from Sparta, then made their way into the **Underworld** and demanded no less a person than Queen **Persephone** herself. **Hades** pretended to welcome them and invited them to sit at a banquet. But the seats he offered were the Thrones of **Lethe**, which fused with the flesh of whoever sat on them, holding them in the Underworld forever. Theseus and Pirithous would have sat until they were totally engulfed in stone, if Heracles, on his quest to steal **Cerberus**, had not seen his old friends' torment. He tore Theseus from his throne, ripping all the flesh from Theseus' legs. Then he turned to help Pirithous – too late, for the ground gaped open and swallowed Pirithous to the lowest depths of Hell.

Theseus hobbled back to the Upper World on his rags and bones of legs. He had been four years in the Underworld, and during that time Castor and Pollux (see **Dioscuri**), Helen's brothers, had rescued her, conquered Athens and set up a new king there. None of Theseus' former people recognized him, and he limped away, a discarded beggar. A captain bound for Crete took pity on him, and gave him free passage. But on the way they landed on the island of Scyros, and Artemis whispered to

Lycomedes, king of the island, who Theseus really was and told him to kill him for murdering her servant Antiope. Lycomedes threw Theseus over a precipice and drowned him.

In ancient Athens, Theseus was regarded as not mythical but real. At the battle of Marathon, fought by the Greeks against the Persians in 490 BCE, Athenian soldiers reported that his ghost had come fully armed to help them, and had scattered a whole wing of the invading army. The Athenians asked the Delphic oracle what this meant, and the oracle advised them to collect Theseus' bones from Scyros and bury them. In an ancient burial-mound on Scyros they found a gigantic human skeleton and an ornate golden sword, carried them back to Athens and placed them in the temple called the Theseum, where they were thought to protect the city ever afterwards.

In myth, Theseus lacks the psychological complexity and emblematic force of such other **heroes** *as* **Odysseus** *or* **Orestes***. He is a reactive figure, at the mercy of events rather than controlling them – and his story seems to tell us little, to have no point except the interest of the adventures themselves. No creative artist in ancient times – and none later until Mary Renault in her novels* The Bull from the Sea *and* The King Must Die *– treated his story as a unified whole and made coherent sense of it. Instead, single episodes were given individual treatment, ranging from the Minotaur story (which was a favourite of ancient Greek vase-painters, and became a standard hero-kills-monster tale in later children's literature) to events in which Theseus' own part is peripheral, for example the abandonment of Ariadne – Monteverdi's*

Ariadne's Lament, to take just one treatment, was one of the best-known of all Renaissance compositions based on ancient Greek stories – or Phaedra's passion for Hippolytus, which inspired playwrights from Euripides (who described it from Hippolytus' point of view) to Racine (whose Phèdre became a pinnacle of the French tragic repertoire). Twentieth-century fine artists and sculptors, notably Ayrton, Lipchitz and Picasso, have been especially fascinated by the Minotaur – and once again Theseus has been marginalized.

THETIS
Europe (South)

Thetis ('disposer'), daughter of **Nereus** in Greek myth, was a beautiful **sea-nymph** whom both **Zeus** and **Poseidon** wanted to make their consort. But **Prometheus** revealed a secret told him by the **Fates**, that she would bear a son greater than his father, and the gods hastily found other consorts and married Thetis instead to a mortal, **Peleus**.

Thetis was determined to make her children immortal. Accordingly, when each child was born, she burned it in fire to remove its mortal flesh and then sprinkled the ashes into the sea. When her last child, **Achilles**, was born, Peleus rushed in and stopped her, so she took the child instead to the **Underworld** and dipped him in the River **Styx**. This made him immortal – except for the heel by which she'd held him, and into which **Paris** was later to fire the arrow which killed him.

When the **Trojan War** began, Thetis (who, like all sea-creatures, had second sight) knew that Achilles was fated to die in it. She tried to stop him going by dressing him as a woman and hiding him in the harem of King Lycomedes – but the plan failed when he heard the trumpet-call of the recruiting party and ran out shouting his war-cry. At the end of the Trojan War, after Paris killed him, she gathered his ashes in a golden urn and scattered them on the sea, as unlucky with her last child as she'd been with all the others.

THIAZI
Europe (Northern)

Thiazi, in Nordic myth, was a **giant shape-changer** who spent much of his time as an enormous black eagle. He tricked **Loki** into bringing him **Idun**, goddess of youth, guardian of the golden apples of **immortality**, and the gods would have aged and died if Loki hadn't found another trick to fetch her back again. (*see* Idun.) Thiazi's daughter **Skadi** married the **sea**-god **Njörd**.

THOR
Europe (North)

Thor ('thunder') or Thunor or Donner, in Nordic myth, in some accounts was the son of **Odin** and Fjörgyn; in others, he derived his identity from the older **thunder**-god Donar. He was the god of the **sky**, generally a sunny, chuckling **giant** (in which case the weather was fine), but uncontrollable when angry. His weapon was the stubby-handled hammer Mjöllnir ('crusher'), made for him by dwarfs. Nothing withstood its blows, and it returned to his hand like a boomerang every time he threw it. Often, it glowed red-hot, and he wore a pair of iron gloves to hold it. He also owned a magic belt, which doubled his strength every time he put it on.

Thor and Thrym. Thor was the gods' champion against the **giants**, and hunted them mercilessly. On one occasion giant Thrym stole Mjöllnir, and refused to give it back unless the gods let him marry **Freyja**, goddess of desire. When Freyja refused, **Heimdall** suggested that Thor himself dress as a bride. Reluctantly, Thor did so, and he and **Loki** went to Thrym's feast-hall for the wedding-reception. Here Thor astonished the giants by eating a whole ox, eight salmon and the cakes and sweets made for the entire female group of giants, washed down with three barrels of mead. (Loki explained that the bride had been so eager for the wedding that she'd not eaten for a week.) Thrym bent to kiss his bride and was astonished to see eyes glowing red like coals: Loki explained that the bride had been so excited that she hadn't slept for weeks. Finally Thrym laid the phallic Mjöllnir in Thor's lap to symbolize the wedding, and Thor threw off his headdress and began hurling Mjöllnir round the room until Thrym and all the other giants were dead.

Thor and Hrungnir. At a banquet in **Asgard** (to which he had been invited without Thor knowing), the giant Hrungnir got drunk on mead and boasted that he would destroy Asgard, topple the gods and steal both Freyja and Thor's own wife **Sif**. He challenged Thor to a duel. Thor's weapon was Mjöllnir, Hrungnir's an enormous whetstone. They hurled them at the same moment, and Mjöllnir smashed the whetstone to pieces in midair.

Some of the fragments killed Hrungnir, but one embedded itself in Thor's own forehead. The witch Groa tried to say a spell to pull it out, but Thor distracted her by boasting how he'd once rescued her husband from the giants' kingdom, and she was so enthralled that she lost the thread of her magic. Ever afterwards, the lump of stone stayed embedded in Thor's head.

Thor and Skrymir. Thor and Loki were travelling, as they often did, in **Jotunheim**, land of the giants, when they stopped to shelter in a building so huge in the darkness that the gulf of eternity itself seemed to stretch between its entrance and the nearest wall. It was not until daylight that they discovered that it was the thumb of one glove of the giant Skrymir, who walked off with their provisions, taking such enormous strides that he was out of sight before they even noticed he'd been there. They hurried after him, and caught up with him at nightfall, only to find him sleeping. Thor hit him on the head three times with Mjöllnir: the first time Skrymir took it for a falling leaf, the second for an acorn, the third for bird-droppings. He told the gods to hurry to **Utgard**, where even bigger and fiercer giants were waiting.

In Utgard, the giants challenged Thor and Loki to trials of strength. Loki and the giant Logi held an eating contest – and Logi won by eating not just the meat of the cattle but their bones, the wooden trenchers they lay on, and even the table. Thor tried to drain a drinking-horn – but it was filled with water from the primordial ocean, and welled full each time he drank from it. He wrestled the pet cat of Utgard-Loki, lord of Utgard, and succeeded only in lifting one of its paws from the ground. Finally he wrestled Utgard-Loki's foster-mother **Elli**, an aged, bent crone who nevertheless made him sink to his knees and would have finished him if Utgard-Loki had not ordered the contest to stop. Utgard-Loki now claimed that the contests had proved giants superior to gods – and this was hardly surprising, since Logi was not really a giant at all but Fire, the cat was **Jormungand** the world-serpent in disguise, and the crone was Old Age (against whom not even gods could defend themselves once they left Asgard and the Golden Apples of **immortality**). Thor snatched up Mjöllnir to kill Utgard-Loki – and the entire kingdom and everyone in it disappeared before his eyes. Everything, from Skrymir and his glove to the feast-hall and the wrestling-opponents had been illusions, conjured up by the giants who were too terrified to face the gods in person.

Thor and Jormungand. Thor had no particular dislike of Jormungand, but the Fates decreed that they were to meet and fight throughout this cycle of the universe. When Thor challenged the giant **Hymir** to a fishing-competition, it was Jormungand he hauled up from the depths. In fantasy-Utgard he wrestled the world-serpent Jormungand, disguised as a cat. And at **Ragnarök** he and Jormungand will fight to the death. Thor's weapon will be Mjöllnir, and Jormungand will use his coils and his venom. They will kill each other, Thor smashing the world-serpent's skull only to drown in the poison that pours out of it.

Thor was one of the most popular of the Nordic gods, and his worship survived well into Christian times: as late as the eleventh century CE he was Christ's main rival in Northern Europe, displacing even **Odin**. In Scandinavia his sacred tree was the rowan (because of its flame-red berries); in Germany it was the oak, and lightning-blasted oaks were regarded as particularly holy. In art he was shown as a burly, flame-bearded warrior, riding a chariot hung with pots and pans (whose rattling made **thunder**) and pulled by two winged goats, Tanngrisn ('tooth-grinder') and Tanngniort ('tooth-gnasher'). When he was hungry he ate the goats, then hammered their bones back to life with Mjöllnir.

Thor's hammer, shaped like a letter T with a cross-bar at the bottom, was a common symbol, in rock-carvings, paintings and above all in metalwork: hammer-amulets, rings and pendants range from simple everyday wear to the finest ancient Nordic craftsmanship. People made the 'sign of the hammer' as they prayed to Thor, for example over a baby's head at its naming-ceremony – an action readily converted by conquering Christians into the sign of the cross. Another symbol, the swastika (perhaps representing a ring of flickering flames) was also associated with Thor-worship, and may have reached Europe originally from India. Hitler's Baltic brigade took it to Germany, where it was adopted as the Nazi emblem and acquired connotations quite different from any it had before.

Thor is Thursday's name-god.

≫+ Geirröd (giant)

THOTH
Africa (North)

Thoth (or Djeheuty, 'he of Djehut'), god of wisdom in Egyptian myth, was in some accounts born from **Set**'s fore-head after Set (a god who enjoyed fellatio) swallowed some of **Horus**' semen. Having no form of his own, he entered the body of the baboon god Hedjwer, and was given the task of supporting the Moon-disc in the sky. In other accounts Thoth was the son – or perhaps the heart or tongue – of **Ra** the Sun, and was himself the Moon. He had a portion of his father's all-knowledge, understanding time and truth; in some versions this knowledge was intuitive, in others it was contained in books from his father's library which only he knew how to read. He invented every intellectual skill which required organization: astronomy, fine art, geometry, law, magic, medicine, music, and especially writing. In later times he was even credited with creating the world by naming it (a skill which had once belonged to **Ptah**).

Thoth was the patron of one of the ancient world's main **mysteries**, that of Trismegistus, 'the Thrice-Greatest' whom Greeks identified with **Hermes**. Cult members believed that Thoth's magic books, or portions of them, were owned by his priests, and that devotees could learn to read them and decipher in them the secrets of the universe.

In less hermetic worship, Thoth was the patron god of scribes and doctors. His temple at Ashmunen (Greek Hermopolis, 'Hermes-city') was a healing-shrine for three millennia. In art he is shown either as a baboon (or baboon-headed man) dictating to a scribe who sits cross-legged before him, or as an ibis-headed warrior trampling his enemies. This image arose partly because the curved beak of the ibis represented the crescent moon, and partly

because of a pun – more apparent in Egyptian than in English – between hib ('ibis') and hab ('tread on').
»→ animal-gods, creation, disease and healing, Underworld

THREE DOOR GODS, THE
Asia (East)

The Three Door Gods, in Chinese myth, were Qin Shupo, Hu Jingte and We Jeng. Many other gods and spirits protected doors and those who passed in or out through them, but these three were the main deities, and their pictures were often painted or hung on doors, and were replaced each year. The gods were originally mortals, ministers of Emperor Tai Song of the seventh century CE. He fell ill, dreaming that he was being tormented by **demons**, and the ministers took turns to stay awake at his bedroom doors each night until he recovered. He was so impressed that he had their pictures hung on doors throughout the kingdom, and the gods also rewarded them by granting them **immortality**.
»→ guardians

THREE GODS OF HAPPINESS, THE
Asia (East)

The Three Gods of Happiness, in Chinese myth, all began as mortals but were promoted to **immortality** for their extreme goodness while on Earth. They lived in the Palace of Immortality in the Happy Isles, but often sailed from there in their ceremonial barge to bring good luck to mortals. They were Fu Xing god of happiness, Lu Xing god of salaries and Shou Lao god of long life.

THREE LAVATORY LADIES, THE
Asia (East)

The Three Lavatory Ladies, in Chinese myth, were goddesses of **childbirth**. They were originally mortal princesses, and won their name and **immortality** by using a privy-bucket and its contents as a weapon during a supernatural battle. In later times, a red privy-bucket, known as the 'golden bushel of troubled origins', was given to each married couple as a wedding-present, and was used not only as a privy but during childbirth – hence the Lavatory Ladies' main prerogative.

THREE SOVEREIGNS, THE
Asia (East)

The Three Sovereigns, in Chinese myth, inaugurated civilized life on Earth. In order, they were **Fu Xi**, **Shen Nong** and Yen Ti.
»→ civilization, crafts

THUNDER
Thunder-gods. Thunder, one of the most awesome forces of Nature, was treated with appropriate respect by most peoples – but not by all. One Melanesian tale said that Thunder, as a foetus, racketed round his mother's womb so noisily that the gods were appalled and gave him the power of instant growth. But although he leapt to physical maturity as soon as he entered the light of day, his mind

remained that of an irritable baby, and he has been howling and squalling round the world ever since. Similarly, **Ajisukitakahikone**, the Japanese thunder god, was so rowdy that the gods set him sailing in a boat sent eternally round Japan – which is why the sound of thunder still advances and recedes. The North American Wyandot thunder-god, Heng, was a butterfingers, so destructive that his relatives threw him out and forced him to live eternally on his own.

The Cherokee people of North America depicted Thunder as **Lightning**'s twin brother. They called him Tame Boy, and said that he played rumbling games of ball across the sky with his brother, Wild Boy. For the Chibcha people of Colombia, Thunder's fury was caused by pain when the Sun God kicked him in the testicles, rendering him impotent; he has raged round the world, smarting, ever since. Kadaklan, the thunder-god of the Tinguian people of the Philippines, lived in a tree with his dog Kimat, lightning, and sent him to bite people he disliked. **Enumclaw**, the thunder-god of several peoples of Washington State, US, was a mortal who grew so skilled at hurling fireballs that the sky-spirit, afraid for his own position, promoted him to **immortality** and found him celestial work to do.

Most thunder-myths, however, avoided such knockabout. Unlike the Tame Boy and Enumclaw stories, for example, most thunder-myths from North America – in common with those of ancient Siberia – imagined the god as a powerful, eagle-like bird which was both creator and destroyer.

The Japanese pantheon included not only the buffoon Ajisukitakahikone, but also a gigantic, rook-like **thunderbird** which guarded the gates of **Heaven**. The Sumerian storm-bird Zu had a lion's head (its roars were thunder) and was the servant of **Ninurta** the war god. The Sioux thunder-gods were five fierce brothers who, when mortal, refused to give up cannibalism and who ever afterwards craved human flesh. Other thunder-gods were equally implacable to humans. The Maori thunder-spirit Taohirimatea defended his father **Rangi** (the sky-spirit) against his brothers and sisters who were set to dethrone him, and killed them all save Tumataunega, spirit of human aggression – since when thunder and humans have always been enemies. **Lei Gong**, the Chinese thunder-god, carried a drum for noise, and a chisel to hurl at evildoers. Pillan, thunder-god of the Araucanian people of Chile, had a hatred for humans as unexplained as it was implacable, and employed an army of human-headed snakes to blight their crops. The thunder-god of ancient Peru was summoned to help mortals – and appeased from harming them – by an annual festival culminating in the sacrifice of white llamas (symbolizing fleecy clouds).

Other thunder-gods were beneficial to humans. The roaring and teethgnashing of the Mayan **Chac** heralded his tears, which watered the Earth with **fertility**; the same god among the Inca, **Tlaloc**, took dead souls to the earthly paradise Tlalocan. Hinun, the Iroquois thunder-god, used his invincible bow and fire-arrows to destroy evil – not least, at the beginning of time, the giant water-snake which preyed on humans. **Vajrasattva**, the Tibetan ur-**Buddha**, origin of the other six Buddhas and known as 'adamantine' and 'thunder-hurler', protected devotees seeking enlightenment by sending thunder, lightning, rain and snow to fight the **demons** which might distract them.

Thunder as a weapon. Thunder was often imagined as a weapon, a visible sign of a god's power and anger, and as something which could be handed on or stolen. When **Athene**, in **Greek myth**, wanted to borrow one of **Zeus'** thunderbolts, she begged him to unlock the cupboard where they were kept, and had to convince him that she had a legitimate need for it, and would not use it in a revolt against him. **Teshub**, the ancient Babylonian storm-god, used thunder and lightning first to fight his brother and sister (who were seeking to dethrone their father **Anu** the **Sky**), then turned his weapons on Anu himself. (Teshub was the same person as the Sumerian storm-god **Baal**, who however was beneficial to mortals, using thunder and lightning to vanquish Mot, god of desert dryness, and to bring water to growing crops.) The youthful Polynesian god Tuamoto, on growing up, borrowed the long-forgotten weapon of his ancient ancestors, thunder, and used it to dethrone his father **Atea**, Sky. In Indian myth, **Shiva** (known as Rudra, 'thunderer'), shot lightning-flashes of anger to consume his enemies. Adad, the Sumerian thunder-bringer, and **Jumala**, the original Finnish sky-god, wielded thunderbolts in the shape of jagged lightning-spears. **Thor**, the Norse blacksmith-god, carried the hammer which was the thunderbolt; he inherited it from his predecessor **Donar**, and it was the gods' sole protection against the **giants**. He honed his skills with it by hunting trolls, and hurled it in epic battles against all who would unseat the gods.

Thunder and creation. Thunder played a central part in three creation-myths. The Pawnee people told how **Tirawa** the creator sent his servant Lightning to hang constellations in the sky. Lightning carried a bag of stars and constellations, fragments of his own body – and also filled with their opposing medium, darkness. While he was busy hanging stars, **Coyote** the **trickster** prevailed on Wolf to rummage in the sack – and light and darkness spilled out, tussling for supremacy, and filled the sky. So thunder was born, and with it plague, blight and death arrived on Earth. In a more genial myth, part of the ancient Indian tradition, Vritra (or Ahi), serpent of drought, drank the primordial oceans and everything they contained, and **Indra**, lord of thunder, sent a thunderbolt to split its belly and so release all life. And in the Greek creation-myth, when the gods tried to unseat the **Titans**, civil war lasted for forty seasons of the world. The immortal combatants were unharmed; the chief victim was **Mother Earth**, who from being placid and beautiful became a ragged no-god's-land. In the end she whispered to Zeus a way to end the war. He crept to the inner recesses of the **Underworld**, where Mother Earth's giant-children the blacksmith-**Cyclopes** had long been imprisoned. He gave them **nectar** to drink, and it filled them with godlike intelligence. At once they set to work to forge weapons for him: thunder, trapped and stored in thunderbolts. Thereafter Zeus used thunderbolts to control the universe, and the Cyclopes, working in forges under Mount Etna, constantly renewed the supply.

In a pendant to thunder-stories, the Chinese for centuries revered Li T'ien, a real person of the eleventh century CE who was the first ever to use firecrackers to scare evil spirits from processions and festivals – a miniature version of thunder which quickly became a standard part of all religious celebrations. »+ (Africa): Sudika-Mbambi and Kabundungulu; (Americas): Catequil, Hinu, Ilyap'a, Pillan, Tupan, Valedjád; (Celtic): Taranis; (Finnish): Ilmarinen; (Mesopotamia): Ada, Imdugud; (Rome): Jupiter; (Slavic): Pyerun, Varpulis; (general): creation, rain, war

THUNDERBIRDS

Thunderbirds were an entire species of supernatural beings. They were known in Siberia (as ducks whose sneezing brings rain), but were otherwise virtually exclusive to the peoples of Northern America. They controlled **thunder**, **lightning**, **rain**, **fire** and truth – if you lied or broke your word, they sent a lightning bolt to punish you. They were ruled by the Great Thunderbird. He was the most senior of four elders; the others were the Red Thunderbird of the North, the Yellow Thunderbird of the East and the White (or some say Blue) Thunderbird of the South. Between them they guarded the nest of bones in which a giant egg was incubated – the egg from which all small

thunderbirds, storms and parching winds, were hatched.

The appearance of thunderbirds. Thunderbirds were often shown in statues and on totem-poles as eagle-headed human beings with wings for arms and talons instead of toes. In some cases, they had second, human heads in their bellies and enormous penises in the shape of forked lightning. The Crow people said that they wore eagle-feather cloaks, and Pacific-coast peoples said that the Great Thunderbird carried a lake on his back and ate whole whales. But all such depictions differ from the most widely-accepted myth. In this, thunderbirds had no form. Their bodies billowed like clouds. They had claws but no feet, fanged beaks but no heads, wings but no shoulders. The flapping of their wings made storms, and they created lightning by tearing trees open with their beaks or by opening and shutting their eyes (or what would have been their eyes if they'd had eyes).

In contrast to the rest of the world, which had a clockwise rotation and moved forwards in time, Thunderbirds existed in an anti-clockwise dimension and communicated in backwards-speech. These powers gave them their authority. Entranced mortals could enter their dimension briefly, listen to their speech and learn some of their secrets; but to stay too long was dangerous.

Thunderbirds and creation. The Algonquian people of the Northeastern US believed that thunderbirds were the supernatural ancestors of the human race, 'our grandparents'. Others connected them with the **creation** of the universe or the coming of **justice and universal order**. In many myths, thunderbirds were the enemies of **snakes** (which symbolized evil and anarchy.) In one Sioux creation myth, for example (from the US Great Plains), the Great Thunderbird Wakan Tanka was the grandson of the Sky-spirit who made the world. The Sky-spirit created human beings and put them on the fertile Earth, where they scurried about like ants. Unktehi, the water-spirit of the Missouri River, a gigantic, horned water-snake with a horde of smaller offspring, took them for lice. She and her followers spouted water from their horns to flood the countryside and drown human beings.

In the flood which followed, most of our ancestors perished; the survivors scrambled to a mountain-top as the waters continued to rise, and prayed for survival. Wakan Tanka and his thunderbird followers set out to save them. For many ages of the world they battled Unktehi and her wriggling spawn. Each creature picked an enemy of its own rank and size. Fire fought water, and though fearful wounds were dealt, neither side won. Then Wakan Tanka soared with his followers high in the sky, out of reach of the water-monsters. They concentrated their lightning and sent it crashing down. The water-monsters cowered in the crevices of Earth – and the thunderbirds' lightning began to sear and scorch **Mother Earth** herself. The ground baked hard and cracked open, and the monsters' water-flesh dripped from their bones and drained away. At last nothing was left but parched bones – and they can still be seen in the regions humans call the Badlands.

This battle, the story ends, gave the thunderbirds power over water as well as fire. It originated the first Age of the World, and ever afterwards the thunderbirds have used their powers to help human beings, and humans have responded by honouring them, and the Great Thunderbird especially, as rulers of the universe.

⟫➔ **animal-gods, creators**

THYESTES
Europe (South)

Thyestes ('beater' or 'sacrificer'), in Greek myth, was one of the sixteen sons of **Pelops** and Hippodamia. Jointly with his brother **Atreus**, he ruled the small town of Midea near Mycenae. When King **Eurystheus** of Mycenae died, the gods told his people to let Atreus and Thyestes decide among themselves which of them should rule. Atreus owned the fleece of a golden ram which he had stolen from **Artemis** and hidden in a box. But unknown to him, Thyestes had been having an affair with Atreus' wife Aerope, and she had given him the fleece as a love-token. He now suggested that whichever brother owned the fleece should rule – and when Atreus agreed, triumphantly produced it and took the throne.

At once the gods sent omens. The **Sun** and stars reversed their courses and the Earth shrieked. Terrified, Thyestes admitted what he'd done, and Atreus took power and banished him. But his revenge was not finished.

He invited Thyestes to a banquet of reconciliation – and served him his own children, cooked in a stew. Thyestes cursed his brother and fled to Sicyon, where his daughter Pelopia was a priestess of **Athene**.

In Sicyon, Thyestes asked the gods how his dead children might be avenged, and the oracle told him to father a child on Pelopia: the fruit of incest would avenge the murder. Thyestes hid beside Athene's temple, and when Pelopia came out to wash her dress (which she'd stained in the blood of a sacrifice) he jumped out, masking his face in his cloak, raped her and fled. Pelopia had no clue about her attacker except for his sword, which fell from his belt in the struggle.

Pelopia's baby was born, and she gave him to goatherds to bring up. But the child's uncle Atreus discovered him and took him to Mycenae to grow to manhood with the royal princes **Agamemnon** and **Menelaus**. Not knowing who he really was, they called him **Aegisthus** ('strength of goats'). While the boys were growing up, Thyestes spent his life in exile, begging. But then the gods sent plague on Mycenae, and said that only the death of a 'son of Pelops' would end it. Agamemnon and Menelaus arrested Thyestes and took him to Mycenae, thinking that he was the man they meant.

To avoid the taint of killing a blood-relative, Atreus ordered Aegisthus, the son of unknown parents, to butcher Thyestes. Aegisthus raised his sword – and Thyestes recognized it as the one he had dropped years before in Sicyon. He embraced Aegisthus as his son, told him how Atreus had butchered

his brothers and sisters, and begged him to take revenge. Aegisthus murdered Atreus, and Thyestes seized power and banished Agamemnon and Menelaus. They, however, went straight to King **Tyndareus** of Sparta, and Agamemnon raised an army, captured Mycenae and sent Thyestes once more into beggary, in which condition the old man died.

TIAMAT
Asia (West)

Tiamat, in Mesopotamian myth, was salt **water**, one half of the chaos which existed before **creation**. The other half was Apsu, fresh water. When Tiamat mingled with Apsu, gods were created, generation after generation. At first they all shared the universe in harmony. But then **Ea**, the young gods' waterlord, challenged the power of Apsu and killed him. Tiamat, his consort, formed herself into a dragon with an eagle's head, and led an army of **monsters** to take revenge. But Ea's son **Marduk** puffed her up with wind and shot her dead, then split her in two and used her carcass to build the universe.

≫+ creation, sea

TIAN
Asia (East)

Tian, in Chinese myth, was the **sky**. In some myths, dating from most ancient times, it was worshipped as a god, consort of **Di (Mother Earth)**, but generally it was imagined as a dome (*pi*) with a hole in the centre through which **rain** and **lightning** fell to Earth.

The pi disc was a favourite good luck charm, and hundreds of thousands have been found from earliest times to the present: those carved from jade or other precious stones are commonest.

TIBER
Europe (South)

The river Tiber, in Roman myth, was originally called Albula ('white') after the brightness of its waters. But when King Tiberinus of Alba drowned in the floodwaters, and **Jupiter** made him a god and guardian spirit of the river, it was renamed Tiber after him. (It was also called Volturnus, 'rolling water', and this name was sometimes also applied to Tiberinus.)

This myth explains why the Tiber was always shown as a virile, reclining prince, with streams of water flowing from his hair and beard – a favourite sculptural theme in ancient Rome, and one which influenced river-god statues, and images of river-gods in fountains, ever afterwards.

≫→ **water**

TIDE JEWELS, THE
Asia (East)

The Tide Jewels, in Japanese myth, were carved by the jewel-workers of Ryujin, Emperor of the **sea**. The Low Tide Jewel sucked up the entire ocean, leaving the bottom exposed; the High Tide Jewel returned the waters to their former height. Ryujin gave the jewels to his young son, the beach-god Isora, and Isora played with them, sending tides surging up and down the shores of the world's oceans. When a Japanese fleet attacked Korea, Isora lent the jewels to the Empress Jingo, who used them first to drain the sea in front of the Korean navy, then to drown the ships as they floundered on the sea-bottom. In some accounts, Isora next presented the jewels to Jingo's son Ojin (later deified as the **war**-god **Hachiman**); in others he went back to his seashore games with them.

TIME: *see* Ages of Brahma, Estsanatlehi, Five Ages of Mortals, immortality, Janus, Ushas, Zurvan Akarana

TIRAWA
Americas (North)

Tirawa, or Tirawahat ('arch of Heaven' or 'this expanse'), in the myths of the Pawnee people of the US Great Plains, created the world in the shape of a bowl floating in space. He gave the stars the tasks of supporting the world and protecting it. Four of them churned the surface of the primordial ocean to make land, and Tirawa stocked it with plants and creatures. Then he ordered the **Moon** and **Sun** to mate and produce a son, and the Evening and Morning Stars to mate and produce a daughter: parents of the human race.

When the Earth was finished, Tirawa sent **Lightning** to inspect it. On his back Lightning carried a sack full of minor stars and constellations, and as he crossed the Earth he hung them one by one in the sky to light his path. Wolf (or, in some accounts, **Coyote**) snatched the sack and turned it out, not only scattering a Milky Way of stars in the sky but dropping crumbs and fragments of light on the Earth, where they took the form of storms, diseases and death. So Paradise was polluted, and Tirawa and the other gods disdained it, leaving it for mortals and never visiting it personally but sending only **messengers**. They taught humans **hunting**, **farming**, religious rituals and the arts of **civilization** – but what comfort were those to humans, if **immortality** was denied them? ⫸→ **creation**

TIRESIAS
Europe (South)

How Tiresias became a prophet. Tiresias (Teiresias, 'delighter in omens') of **Thebes**, son of Everus and Chariclo in Greek myth, was an ordinary man blessed – or cursed – with prophetic powers by a chain of bizarre events. One day when he was hunting he found two **snakes** coupling in a clearing. He hit them with a stick and killed the female. At once, **Gaia** (**Mother Earth**, protector of snakes) changed him into a woman, and he remained female for seven years. Then, by chance, in the same clearing, he found another pair of snakes. This time he killed the male, and immediately changed back into a man.

While Tiresias was a woman, he had several lovers; as a man, he made love with several women. This made him the ideal person to settle an argument between **Zeus** and **Hera** about whether sex gives more pleasure to the female or the male. (Zeus said that the male gives more pleasure than he gets; Hera said the opposite.) They asked Tiresias, and from personal experience he agreed with Zeus, saying that the male gives

nine times more pleasure than he gets. Hera was so angry that she blinded Tiresias; but Zeus rewarded him with the prophet's gifts of second hearing and second sight, and a life-span of seven mortal generations.

Tiresias, Aphrodite and Athene. Other accounts give completely different explanations. Some say that Tiresias' change of sex was caused by **Aphrodite**. She was arguing with the three **Graces** about which of them was most beautiful, and asked Tiresias to judge. He chose the Grace Kale, and Aphrodite punished him by changing him into an old woman. Even after he turned back into a man (thanks to Zeus' help after the argument with Hera), he still kept wrinkled, old-woman's breasts.

In still another account, the argument between Zeus and Hera never happened. Tiresias lost his sight because one day on Mount Helicon he saw **Athene** bathing in the spring called Hippocrene. The punishment for any mortal who saw a goddess naked was blindness, and could not be avoided. But Chariclo, Tiresias' mother, was one of Athene's servant-**nymphs**, and pleaded so eloquently for her son that Athene compensated Tiresias for his lost sight by giving him prophetic powers, and a cornel-wood stick which guided his steps as clearly as if he could see.

Tiresias' life and death. Tiresias spent most of his long life in Thebes, where his prophecies helped the townspeople steer a path between their own wishes and the edicts of the gods. (This sometimes brought him into conflict with those who thought that they understood oracles and omens better than he did: an example is **Oedipus**, whose blindness to the truth made him accuse Tiresias of taking bribes to bring about his downfall.) He had two special skills: he understood the language of birds, and he could talk without fear to the ghosts of the **Underworld**. In the last days of Thebes, after the Epigoni besieged the city (see **Seven Against Thebes**), he warned the people of the coming destruction and helped them escape from the city under cover of darkness.

After the fall of Thebes, Tiresias wandered, led by his daughter Manto, looking not for a home on Earth but for death. In the afternoon heat he felt thirsty, and drank a handful of water from a spring. The spring was Tilphussa, which drew its icy waters directly from the river **Styx** in the Underworld. The chill froze Tiresias' blood, and he died and passed to the Underworld. Even there, the gods still favoured him: he kept his knowledge of the future, and any person bold enough to consult his ghost was rewarded with accurate prophecies. (For example, he told **Odysseus** every detail of his coming adventures on the journey home from Troy to Ithaca.) Even after death, he still appeared and gave prophecies at two shrines on earth: on Mount Tilphussa beside the icy spring, and at Orchomenus near Thebes.

≫→ **prophecy**

TIRKANTHARAS
India

Tirkantharas ('those who make the crossing', or 'teachers'), in Jain religious teaching, were beings who practised physical and mental austerities to the point where they freed themselves from all passions and distractions from true knowledge. Because they possessed all the knowledge in the universe, including the secrets of the gods, they were superior to or equal to gods, but they chose to take human form and teach the way which had made them Jaina ('conquerors'). Since this age of the world began, there have been twenty-four tirkantharas, the best-known of which are **Rishabha** (of unknowable date), the first, **Parshva** (eighth century BCE), the twenty-third, and **Mahavira** (sixth century BCE), the twenty-fourth.

TITANS
Europe (South)

The Titans ('lords'), in Greek myth, were the twelve original gods, offspring of **Ouranos** (Father Sky) and **Gaia** (**Mother Earth**). The six females were Mnemosyne (Memory), Phoebe (Phoibe, 'brightness'), **Rhea** (Earth), Thia (Theia, 'divine'), **Themis** (Right) and Tethys (Settler). The six males were Coeus (Koios, 'intelligent'), Crius (Krios, 'ram'), **Cronus** (Kronos, 'crow'), **Hyperion** ('dweller-on-high'), Iapetus ('racer') and Oceanus ('swift'). Like their parents, the Titans were living beings but had no fixed shape. Sometimes they took on human form; sometimes they patterned themselves after water, rocks or fire; sometimes they abandoned shape altogether and spread their essence invisibly across the universe.

When Cronus' children the gods were born, they began a cosmic war with the Titans for control of the universe. **Prometheus**, son of Tethys, went to them with the secret of intelligence, a sure way to win the war, but they ignored him and he took it to the gods instead. In due course the gods won the war. In some accounts, the Titans were banished to the depths of space or the **Underworld**, or abandoned shape altogether and survived as entities with no location, brooding endlessly on their own folly and the power it had lost them. In others, they were pardoned, and given a beautiful home in the Far West of the universe, the Islands of the Blessed – on condition that they never troubled the gods, or the universe, again.

»→ shape-changers

TIWAZ
Europe (North)

Tiwaz (also known as Tiw, from which we get 'Tuesday'), in Nordic myth, was an ancient sky-god: one-armed, stern but just, oath-guarder and battle-lord. In some accounts he was a pillar of wood, an enormous totem-pole or a tree which supported the universe. In prehistoric times, his functions were taken over by **Odin** and **Thor**, and he retired from myth except as a memory – and, here and there, as a spirit of darkness who lurked in dark woods and could be appeased only by human sacrifice.

»→ justice and universal order

TJINIMIN AND ÞILIRIN
Australia

Tjinimin ('bat'), in the myths of the Murinbata people of the Northern Ter-

ritory, was a **trickster** of the Dream Time. Like all other spirits, he teemed with creative energy – but instead of its being productive (as theirs was) it took the form of endless, insatiable lust. His particular obsessions were the Green Parrot Girls, consorts of the **Great Rainbow Snake**, and nothing deterred him from trying to rape them. They drove him off with bees, sent a river to wash him out to sea, and finally dropped him over a cliff on to jagged rocks. Summoning up all his magic, he regenerated himself (testing the spell by cutting off his own nose and recreating it) – but then turned his magic into a spear and used it to stab the Rainbow Snake itself. The Snake writhed in agony across the land, gouging rivers and waterholes, and finally gathered up all the fire in the world and dived with it to the bottom of the sea. Only one charred stick was left, and neither Tjinimin nor anyone else knew what to do to bring back fire, light and heat.

It was at this point that Þilirin ('kestrel') came to the rescue. He showed human beings how to use fire-sticks to call up the spark-spirits which slept in wood. So the world, and the human race, were saved. But Tjinimin ever afterwards stayed well away from the world of light, coming out only at night; he also foreswore **sex**, even roosting upside-down so that he could see only the barren sky above and not the world and its teeming life below. His magic waned, and as it did so his recreated nose fell off – which is why bats are still snub-nosed.

This story is one of the few to treat the spirits of the Dream Time with knockabout humour – and *Tjinimin's wooing of the Green Parrot Girls* is ribaldly embroidered at each new telling. As recorded here, it is more rounded and self-contained than most Australian myth-stories; some (white) scholars suggest that it may have this 'literary' form because it was one of the first tales to be retold by Westerners.

≫→ animal-gods, tricksters

TLÁLOC
Americas (Central)

Tláloc ('growth-maker'), the Aztec **rain-god**, was responsible for the **fertility** of **Mother Earth**. His tools, **lightning** and **thunder**, were the divine equivalents of a mortal ploughshare and axe, and he kept four brimming water-tubs in each of his mountain-top palaces: the nourishing morning rain, blighting mid-day showers, frost-bringing evening drizzle and – for when he really lost his temper – storms. His consorts were Chalcitlicue, goddess of fresh water, and Uixtocijuatl, goddess of salt water, and when he mated with them, morning and evening, their sexual juices replenished the water-bowls. Rain itself was delivered to the Earth by Tláloc's cloud-servants, the Tlaloques, and if they missed your farm or fields you could attract Tláloc's attention by burning rubber, whose pungent smell he savoured as other gods enjoyed the meat-scents of sacrifice.

Tláloc's garden, Tlálocan, was a hilltop paradise in the far South. It was filled with plants and birds, and its orchards and pastures were fed by the unceasing marriage of sun and rain. Tláloc welcomed there the spirits of mortals dead from disease (especially leprosy and smallpox), drowning and the fury of his own lightning-strikes.

Despite Tláloc's apparent gentleness, he became the centre of a particularly blood-thirsty practice: in dry seasons, the priests killed and ate babies, whose tears – if they cried before dying – meant that rain was sure to follow. Some scholars suggest that there was no distinction in Aztec minds between the gods' two aspects, that human sacrifice and cruelty were necessary components of Aztec worship, without moral overtones. Others, more prosaically, suggest that two ancient gods, a savage thunderer (possibly one of the gods of the Toltecs whose culture the Aztecs overwhelmed) and a mild bringer of **fertility** *(from a different native tradition), were run together and given Tláloc's name.*

TLAZOLTÉOTL
Americas (Central)

Tlazoltéotl ('dirty woman'), in Aztec myth, was the goddess of all kinds of uncleanness, and especially of lust (which the Aztecs thought created a moral miasma, a stench which only gods could smell). She was also known as Tlaelquarni ('cleanser'), because, as goddess of confession and absolution, she could eradicate filth as well as cause it.

The cult of Tlazoltéotl roused the Christian Spaniards' disgust more than any other save that of **Tezcatlipoca**. *They claimed that her temples were centres of prostitution, where young girls, torn from their families, were taught every kind of sexual perversion before being sent into the barracks of young army recruits and then, when they* were 'used up', sacrificed to their grim mistress. Once a year, at each of her temples, a chosen young man was flayed alive, and his skin was used to clothe the goddess' statue. For the rest of the year she was naked, and was – at least in the Spaniards' accounts – a witch-hag who rode a broomstick and carried a sacrificial knife, a severed snake's head and a pulsing human heart. All this fits oddly with her other attributes: she was the goddess of **beauty** (wearing a mask because her face was so beautiful that no human could see it and survive), the patron of fidelity in marriage and of demure femininity (symbolized by her holding a distaff and spindle), and the goddess of the Aztec equivalent of the sauna.

»+ sex

TOBADZISTSINI: *see* Nayenezgani and Tobadzistsini

TOCHOPA AND HOKOMATA
Americas (Central)

Tochopa and Hokomata, in the myths of the Walapai people of Mexico, were twin sons of **Mother Earth**. When the human race was formed, Tochopa played with them as a child plays with dolls, teaching them the arts of **civilization**. Hokomata was jealous, and tried to destroy them. First he taught them to fight, and when they failed to exterminate each other he sent a **flood** to wash them from the Earth. Just in time, Tochopa saved his daughter Pukeheh by hiding her in a hollow tree (or some say, a dugout canoe). When the water receded, Tochopa sent two other gods, Sunshaft and Waterfall, to mate with her, and she became pregnant with a second human race. However, even

though we are the descendants of gods, we are still at the mercy of the heavenly **twins**' rivalry, forever torn between Tochopa's urgings towards good and Hokomata's attempts either to kill us or to make us destroy ourselves.

TO KABINANA AND TO KARVUVU
Oceania

To Kabinana and To Karvuvu, in the myths of the Tolai people of Vanuatu, were twin brothers created from sand at the beginning of time. To Kabinana, the Sun, was sensible; To Karvuvu, the Moon, was a fool. To Kabinana made a woman by breathing life into a coconut; To Karvuvu tried to do the same, but picked a bad nut so that the woman was dead. (This is why human beings die.) To Kabinana carved fish to feed his children, and when To Karvuvu tried to do the same, he made sharks. To Kabinana said that the brothers should take it in turns to 'look after' the first woman when she grew too old for child-bearing. When To Karvuvu's turn came, the only way he could think of 'looking after' her was killing her and eating her – the origin of cannibalism.

»+ creation, twins

TO KARVUVU: *see* To Kabinana and To Karvuvu

TONATIUH
Americas (Central)

Tonatiuh, in Aztec myth, also known as Pilzintecuhtli ('majesty'), was the latest of four **Sun**-gods to light the sky down the ages. Supporting the universe exhausted his strength, and he died each evening. To bring him to life each morning, it was necessary to offer him human hearts still pumping blood. He owned a paradise, Tollan, where the souls of those victims whose blood he had drunk, of dead warriors, and of women dead in **childbirth**, feasted throughout eternity.

TONENILI
Americas (Northern)

Tonenili ('waterer'), in the myths of the Navajo people of the Southwestern US desert, was the god who brought **rain**. He was a jester, fond of dancing and capering – and the Navajo rain-dance, intended to catch his attention, used similar movements.

TORNGARSAK
Arctic

Torngarsak ('good one'), the supreme being in Eskimo myth, was a remarkable collection of cancelling opposites. He had no shape, or was a bear, a one-armed warrior or a finger-sized midget. He was all-**creation**, but created nothing. He was immortal, but could be killed by the **Thunder**-god. Later mythographers have had a fine time psychologizing him as (for example) 'What Is' or 'The Human Condition'; the Eskimo peoples, more pragmatically, simply paid him respect.
≫→ supreme deity

TOTOIMA
Oceania

Totoima, in the myths of the Orokaiva people of Papua New Guinea, was a monster who married a mortal woman. While they had intercourse he took human shape, but every time she bore children he changed into a wild boar and ate them. Eventually she bore **twins**, a boy and a girl, and hid them. Totoima rooted after them, found them and ate the boy. He was just about to kill the girl when his wife ran up with a shaman who brought the son to life in his father's belly. The boy grew to adulthood in an instant, burst his father's belly and was reborn. The shaman married the daughter, and Totoima's wife divided the boar's huge body among all the people for the marriage-feast.

This story was re-enacted annually, on the occasion of a huge pig-feast. The Orokaiva people believed that boars were universal power in animal shape, and that if you ate them, you shared in it.
≫→ animal-gods

TRICKSTERS

In many stories, both myths and folktales, tricksters were morally neutral: their quick-wittedness was simply an attribute like physical strength or artistic ability, and other people expected and accepted it without overmuch admiration or condemnation. The victims of **Odysseus**, arch-trickster of Greek myth, for example, complained about what he did to them, but everyone else treated him as hero, king and lord – at least until he turned his trickery on them. Many tricksters helped in the process of creating mortals – and if their cleverness got in the way and 'changed' things (for example when they nicked the groins of the mud-doll humans and so accidentally created sexual organs), this was no more blameworthy than if a clumsy god had dropped them or an artistic god given them extra hands to play lyres and flutes. Trickster-gods were often put in charge of asking humans whether they wanted to be mortal or immortal – and curiosity distracted them on the journey from **Heaven** to Earth, with the result that we are mortal. (Often, the trickster repaid us for this by teaching us **civilization**.) Even the most destructive trickster of all, **Loki** who constantly threatened universal balance in Nordic myth and who will one day bring about **Ragnarök**, universal cataclysm, was told about in a matter-of-fact manner, without overtones of regret or blame.

The coming of the great monotheistic religions, however, changed perception. In systems where truth was an absolute, the possession only of God and those who surrendered themselves to God, trickery and deception became undesirable qualities, and in some cases were even associated with God's enemies, the **demons** and devils of darkness. This led on the one hand to some highly suspect readings of ancient stories – Christian mythographers in medieval Scandinavia, for example, identified Loki with **Satan** – and on the other to a general downgrading of tricksters, to become the pixies and other supernatural pranksters of children's stories. **Anansi**, **Gluskap** and **Maui** are examples: originally spirits who helped to set the entire universe in order, they became the heroes of thousands of jokes and anecdotes, surviving not because of their importance in myth but because they were almost entirely divorced from it.

»→ (Africa): Dubiaku; (Americas): Annency, Coyote, Gluskap, Ictinike, Ogoun; (Australia): Tjinimin and Pilirin; (Finnish): Lemminkäinen; (Greece): Autolycus, Hermes, Odysseus, Sisyphus; (India): Hanuman; (Mesopotamia): Enki; (Oceania): Olifat

TRINAVARTA
India

Trinavarta, in Hindu myth, was a **demon** who tried to kill the baby **Krishna** by turning himself into a whirlwind and snatching him from his mother's arms. Just as he caught hold of the child, however, Krishna gave him a god-sized kick which sent him spiralling into a cliff and killed him.

TRIPITAKA
Asia (East)

Tripitaka, in Chinese Buddhism, was a real person: the monk Hsuan-Tsang who travelled from China to India and back in 629-640 CE, bringing back accurate copies of the holy scriptures. His journey was later used by the sixteenth-century writer Wu Cheng-en as the basis for a rip-roaring picaresque narrative, *Pilgrimage to the West*, part novel part folktale-collection, in which Tripitaka and his companions **Hanuman** (or 'Monkey') the **trickster**, Chu Pa Chieh ('Pig') the lecherous glutton and the priest Sha Ho-shang outwitted **demons** of all kinds, sometimes by magic or martial arts but more often by a combination of slyness and intellectual sleight-of-hand which was totally beyond the demons' slower wits.

Pilgrimage to the West remains one of the most popular books in Chinese literature, the source of a thousand films, TV series and comic strips. Many Chinese artists have produced sets of paintings either illustrating Wu's stories or inventing new adventures, and the saga grows by accretion, so that Tripitaka's (or, equally often, Monkey's) adventures are known to millions who have never heard either of the original book or of Hsuan-Tsang's Buddhist pilgrimage which inspired it.

TRISTAN AND ISOLDE: *see* Tristram and Yseult

TRISTRAM AND YSEULT
Europe (North)

Tristram ('sad soul'), in Celtic myth, was the son of Queen Elizabeth of Lyonesse, and was named because his mother died when she bore him. He was brought up by his uncle, King Mark of Cornwall, and defended the kingdom against a band of Irish raiders who came to demand tribute, led by the **giant** Morholt. Tristram killed Morholt, half-brother of the king of Ireland. Soon afterwards, Mark sent him to Ireland to fetch Yseult the Beautiful back to Cornwall to be Mark's queen. On the voyage home, on a particularly hot day, Tristram and Yseult quenched their thirst with the nearest drink they could find – a love-potion made by Yseult's sorceress-mother for her daughter to give to Mark. They fell passionately and hopelessly in love.

Back in Cornwall, Yseult and Mark were married. On the wedding night, Yseult's maid Brangen took her place in the marriage-bed – and Mark suspected nothing. But in the days that followed, when he saw Tristram and Yseult together, he did grow suspicious, and his courtiers, jealous of Tristram, told him that they were having an affair. He prepared to burn them alive, but they escaped and hid in the woods. Pursuing them, Mark found them asleep together, but with a drawn sword between them. This convinced him that their love was innocent, and he agreed to take Yseult back so long as Tristram left Cornwall forever.

Tristram went to France and married another Yseult, Yseult White-hands. But he pined for his real love, and never consummated the marriage. Yseult White-hands planned revenge. Her chance came when Tristram was wounded by a poisoned spear. On his deathbed he sent Brangen to fetch Yseult the Beautiful from Cornwall, so that he could see her for the last time. If Yseult agreed to come, Brangen was to return in a white-sailed ship; if she refused, Brangen was to hoist black sails. Brangen did as she was asked – but when she and Yseult the Beautiful returned, Yseult White-hands treacherously told Tristram that the sails were black. He died, and when Yseult the Beautiful found his body she, too, died of grief. Recognizing the strength of their love at last, Mark selflessly took their bodies back to Cornwall and buried them in the same grave. He planted two trees above the grave, and as time went on – the myth ends – the trunks leaned together and the branches intertwined.

The bones of this story are references in the Arthurian myth-cycle and the **Mabinogion** – both of which concentrate on Tristram's early giant-killing exploits. The tale of his and Yseult's doomed love was first told by the medieval German poet Gottfried of Strassburg, and his Tristan is the basis for Wagner's Tristan and Isolde, in which the passion and romantic coincidences of the plot are transfigured by the headiness of the music.

≫→ Adonis, beauty, Brynhild

TROILUS
Europe (South)

Troilus (Troilos, 'Trojan from Ilium'), son of King **Priam** and Queen **Hecuba** in Greek myth, was an adolescent when the **Trojan War** began, and the gods decreed that if he reached the age of twenty safely, Troy would never fall. But **Achilles** came up against him in single combat, and, overcome with lust, offered to spare his life if Troilus made love with him. Some accounts say that Troilus indignantly refused, whereupon Achilles cut off his head; others that Achilles raped him, still in full armour, and crushed him to death even as he penetrated him.

In medieval Europe, this story was embroidered in ways which had no foundation whatever in ancient times. Troilus fell in love with Cressida (that is, with Chryseis the beautiful daughter of Chryses; she was called Cressida in these versions because the medieval Latin for 'Once Troilus loved Chryseis' is Olim Troilus Cressida amavit). Cressida's uncle Pandarus offered to arrange assignations between them. But Cressida's father Chryses (or in Shakespeare's

version, confusingly, **Calchas**) meanwhile arranged an exchange: Cressida was to be taken to the Greek camp and married to **Diomedes**, and the captured Trojan prince Antenor was to be returned to Troy. Troilus raged out across the plain, trying to find Diomedes and kill him – and it was then that he met Achilles, with fatal results. (Shakespeare's Troilus and Cressida, whose subtext concerns the mind-numbing futility of war, breaks off before this dénouement, taking Achilles to fight **Hector** and leaving Troilus raging at the injustice of the world.)

TROJAN WAR
Europe (South)

Heroes. In Greek myth, at the end of the heroic age of the world, the human race was thriving, but for the first time in its existence it was also beginning to squabble and argue. A main cause – as the name 'heroic age' suggests – was the gods' own children, the **heroes**, whom they had fathered or mothered with human partners. The heroes swaggered and lorded it over lesser beings, strong, fearless, always in search of challenges (such as fighting the **Erymanthian Boar** or sailing as **Argonauts** to steal the **Golden Fleece**) – and happy, if no other excitement could be found, to invent causes and fight wars just for the sake of it. **Zeus** decided to cut down the heroes' numbers by setting up the fiercest war mortals had ever seen. It would be fought by princes from every state – and when it was all over and the most arrogant heroes were dead and gone, the world would return to its former peace.

Troy and Greece. Zeus chose as battle-ground the city of Troy, beside the Bosphorus on the westernmost edge of the continent of Asia. He sent a Trojan raiding-party to Sparta in Greece; their leader was Prince **Paris** of Troy, and they stole half the treasure in Sparta – and Queen **Helen**, Zeus' daughter, the most beautiful woman in the world. The Greeks assembled a war-fleet to win her back. Heroes gathered from every Greek state, each bringing ships and soldiers. They waited at Aulis until their leader **Agamemnon** won favourable winds from the gods by sacrificing his own daughter **Iphigenia**, then sailed for Troy.

The two sides were equally matched. The Trojan defenders were led by Prince **Hector**, eldest of **Priam**'s fifty sons, and their city was protected by walls built long ago by two gods, **Apollo** and **Poseidon** – walls which could not be breached by mortals except in one place, a narrow section built by the mortal king **Laomedon**. The Greeks, led by Agamemnon and his brother, Helen's husband **Menelaus**, included such heroes as **Achilles**, **Ajax**, **Diomedes** and **Odysseus**, the most cunning man in the world. (Another Greek hero, **Philoctetes**, owned the bow and unerring arrows which had once belonged to **Heracles** himself. But because he had offended the goddess **Artemis**, he was kept in exile on the island of Lemnos until the very last days of the war.) Gods themselves took sides. Some, including **Aphrodite** and **Poseidon**, favoured the Trojans throughout the war. Others, including **Apollo**, **Athene** and **Hera**, favoured the Greeks. Others again, notably **Ares** the war god himself, changed sides many times as the war went on. Only Zeus remained impartial.

Achilles and Hector. The fighting lasted for ten years. Every skirmish ended in a small victory for one side or the other, but there was no overall advantage, and no sign that the fighting would ever end. At last Zeus brought matters to a head by organizing a quarrel between the Greek heroes Achilles and Agamemnon. Achilles had given a beautiful girl, Chryseis, to Agamemnon, a prisoner-of-war. But she was the daughter of a priest, and Zeus sent plague into the Greek camp and refused to lift it until Agamemnon sent Chryseis back to her father. Agamemnon immediately found himself another mistress, Achilles' own concubine Briseis – and Achilles retreated to his camp and sulked, refusing to have anything more to do with the battle. At once, with Achilles out of the fighting, the Trojans began to win the war – and Achilles' friend and squire **Patroclus** put on Achilles' armour, went out to lead the Greeks against the Trojans, and was killed by Hector. Achilles, enraged, surged back into the fighting, killed Hector and dragged his body three times round the walls of Troy.

End of the war. At this point the gods moved decisively for Greece and against Troy. They told the Greeks to fetch Philoctetes from Lemnos: his bow and arrows were essential if the city was to be captured. They told them to steal the **Palladium**: the statue of Athene which was worshipped in a shrine at the heart of Troy and symbolized the city's luck. And Athene suggested to Odysseus the trick of the **Wooden Horse**. Philoctetes fought and killed Paris; Odysseus and Diomedes stole the Palladium; the Wooden Horse was built, manned with soldiers and left on the beach while the rest of the Greeks pretended to sail away. Thinking that the war was over, the Trojans dragged the Horse into the city and set it up in Athene's temple – and that night the soldiers hidden inside let themselves down on ropes, opened the gates and sent a signal to their companions to sail back to Troy and capture the city.

The aftermath. After the sack of Troy, the victorious Greeks divided up the spoils and the prisoners and set out for home. They had been ten years away, and many had made enemies of particular gods, who now took delight in delaying their return still longer. Many came back to find that their wives had taken lovers, or that enemies had seized their thrones. The **Underworld** was thronged with the ghosts of heroes killed in the fighting, squabbling or brooding as if the war had never ended. As for the Trojans, their city was destroyed, their wealth was stolen and their people were dead or slaves. A small band of refugees, led by **Aeneas**, took the statues of the city's gods and sailed South to find a new homeland, a new Troy, first in Africa and then in Italy.

TROPHONIUS
Europe (South)

Trophonius and Agamedes. Trophonius (Trophoneios, 'nurturer'), son of the **Argonaut** Erginus in Greek myth, was one of the stonemasons who built **Apollo**'s first temple at Delphi. His collaborator was his brother Agamedes ('much praise'). There are two accounts of how they died. In one, instead of

paying them the wages they asked for, Apollo invited them to a week of wining and dining in **Olympus**, at the end of which they were found dead in bed. This, however, was not a trick: it was not until after death that they could receive his reward, the gift of **prophecy**. In another, King Hyrieus of Boeotia commissioned them to build a treasury, and they made it totally secure apart from one removable stone in the wall. Every night thereafter they crept in and stole as much gold as they could carry. One night Agamedes took too much and stuck fast. To keep their secret Trophonius cut off his head, and was immediately punished when **Gaia** (**Mother Earth**) gaped open at his feet and swallowed him.

Trophonius' oracle. Soon after Trophonius disappeared from the world, the people of Boeotia asked the Delphic oracle how they could end a drought that was threatening their lives. Apollo told them to follow the road from Delphi to **Thebes** until they found a forest cave overhung with bees. There, Trophonius' spirit would tell them what to do. They found the cave and the oracle told them how to channel an underwater stream to irrigate their parched land. Ever afterwards, Trophonius was honoured as a god, Apollo's adopted son, and his oracle was renowned for its reliability.

As the oracle of Trophonius lay on the road between Thebes and Delphi, it built up a thriving trade as a kind of antechamber to the Delphic oracle, offering to tell pilgrims whether their questions to Apollo would be answered or not. The priests made the consultation process as elaborate and impressive as they could. At most oracles, all you had to do was ask your question and wait for the answer. But if you wanted Trophonius' advice you had to spend several days at the shrine, fasting and sacrificing. Then, on the day of the consultation, you bathed, rubbed yourself with oil, put on sackcloth and drank from two ice-cold fountains, the Spring of Memory and the Spring of Forgetfulness (said to be tributaries of the river Lethe in the Underworld). Then two boys took you to the cave of the oracle, an eight-metre-deep hole in the forest floor. In the centre of the floor was another hole, just wide enough to admit one person at a time. You wriggled into this and lay waiting in the pitch-black cavern beyond until the oracle spoke to you, then squeezed back through the hole and up to the surface, where priests were waiting on the Throne of Memory to explain what the oracle's words meant. People who went through this ordeal believed that they'd visited the Underworld and spoken with Trophonius' ghost. Despite all this apparent charlatanry, the oracle was famous for its accuracy, and for centuries people visited it from all over Greece.

TSAI SHEN
Asia (East)

Tsai Shen, god of wealth in Chinese myth, began as a mortal hermit and magician called Jao Gong Ming. He tamed a black tiger, and rode it into battle, hurling diamonds and pearls like bombs to scatter the enemy. The enemy general made a statue of Jao Gong Ming and shot it in the eyes and heart – and at that moment Jao died and was taken into **Heaven**. Because of his easy way with precious stones, he was made Heavenly Treasurer-in-Chief and god

of wealth. He was shown in art as a fat-bellied, cheerful man, sometimes riding his tiger, and was particularly worshipped by merchants.

TSAO JUN
Asia (East)

Tsao Jun ('kitchen god'), in Chinese myth, began as a mortal called Jang who divorced his wife and married his mistress. The gods stole his sight and his money, and his mistress left him. He wandered the streets as a blind beggar, and one day came by chance to the house of his first wife, who gave him a plate of his favourite dish, noodles. As soon as he tasted them he realized where he was, and was so ashamed that he jumped into the stove and was burnt to ash – all except for one leg, by which his ex-wife tried to pull him out. (Stove-rakes have been called 'Jang's legs' ever since.)

At this point the gods took pity on Jang, carrying him into **Heaven**, giving him **immortality** and appointing him god of the kitchen. Because of his past life, they made him overseer of the morals of each household, and once a year he had to report to the celestial court on the behaviour of each family member. To sweeten his accounts, people made him offerings of honey or honey-cakes – and if they were unsure that this would work, another way was to leave gifts of drink, enough to make him tipsy.

TSOHANOAI
Americas (North)

Tsohanoai ('Sun-bearer') the Sun-god, in the myths of the Navajo people of the

Southwestern US desert, was no grand ruler but a humble porter. Every day he struggled across the sky, with the **Sun** in a bundle on his back; every night when he went home, he hung it thankfully on a peg and went to bed. In some accounts, he mated with **Estsanatlehi** and their children were **Nayanezgani** and **Tobadzistsini**.

TSUKUYOMI
Asia (East)

Tsukuyomi ('moon-counter') or Tsukiyomi ('moon-bow'), in Japanese myth, was created from the **water-drops** which fell from **Izanagi**'s right eye when he washed himself after visiting **Yomi**, the **Underworld**. Izanagi made Tsukuyomi god of the **Moon**, consort of **Amaterasu** the **Sun**-god. For a time they lived peaceably together, but when Tsukuyomi killed **Ukemochi** the rice-goddess, Amaterasu refused to have anything more to do with him – which is why night and day are forever separate.

*Tsukuyomi's connection with rice is explained by a pun in Japanese: the symbols for 'Moon' and 'rice-pounding' are similar. The association, coupled with the identification of hares and rabbits with the Moon, common in many cultures from China to North America, leads to his symbolic image in Japanese ritual painting: a hare pounding rice – a reference which no surviving myth explains. The Moon's regular waxing and waning led to Tsukuyomi being regarded as a god of **prophecy**, and his priests foretold the future by examining and measuring the Moon's reflection in huge mirrors. (Looking at it directly was*

dangerous, for although Tsukuyomi never blinded those who stared him in the face, as Amaterasu the Sun did, he filled their minds with delusion and sent them mad.)

TUONELA
Europe (North)

Tuonela ('Tuoni's realm'), in Finnish myth, was the **Underworld**. It was an exact mirror-image of the Upper World. Its inhabitants were dead, not living – instead of moving from birth to death their lives progressed from adulthood to infancy and thence to non-existence. Instead of light they had darkness, instead of hope despair, instead of conversation silence, instead of presence absence.

Only **demons** and diseases, children of **Tuoni** and **Tuonetar**, were ever allowed out of Tuonela. And only the Dead were allowed to enter it. Living mortals who tried to reach it had to travel for a week through thorn-thickets, a week through empty woods and a week through forests, swim an icy river of darkness on whose surface a black swan sang binding-spells of **death**, and finally face **Surma**, the flesh-tearing monster that guarded **Kalma**, goddess of decay. Any visitors who survived were then welcomed by Tuonetar, who offered them beer of oblivion to make them forget their former lives – and while they drank, her children threw iron nets across the river to stop them ever returning to the world of life.

TUONETAR
Europe (North)

Tuonetar ('Tuoni's wife'), in Finnish myth, was the consort of **Tuoni**. She was queen of the **Underworld**, matriarch of an enormous family of **demons**, plagues and diseases.

TUONI
Europe (North)

Tuoni, in Finnish myth, was darkness personified, not a visible being but the quintessence of nothing. He ruled **Tuonela**, the **Underworld**, and fathered an enormous population of **monsters**, plagues and diseases.

TUPAN
Americas (South)

Tupan ('his holiness'), in the myths of the Guaraร่i people of Argentina, was the son of the sky-goddess. When a flood swamped the universe, he escaped by climbing a tree. Every day thereafter, he set out in his canoe to visit his mother, and what mortals took to be **thunder** was in fact the splashing of his paddles in the ocean of space.

TURNUS
Europe (South)

Turnus, in Roman myth, was the son of King Daunus and the **nymph** Venilia. He was a favourite of the goddess **Juno**, who granted him invulnerability in battle so long as he was pure, honourable and steadfast. In the war between Turnus' people, the Rutulians, and the Trojan settlers led by **Aeneas**, Turnus showed all these qualities, leading his troops with as much dignity and honour as Aeneas himself. But he let his guard slip for an instant, killing the young prince **Pallas** who had rashly challenged him to single combat, and wearing his belt as a trophy. At once Juno withdrew her protection, and when Aeneas and Turnus faced each other in hand-to-hand combat, and Aeneas saw the belt, Turnus' death was certain.

≫→ **heroes**

TVASHTRI
India

Tvashtri (originally Tvashtar, 'shaper'), in the Vedic myths of the Aryans who invaded India in the seventeenth century BCE, was the craftsman-god. In the earliest myths of all he was thought to contain the seeds or embryos of everything in **creation**, and to grant them existence as he chose: he was thus the universal creator, the single principle from which all arose. This idea survived only partially in later times: Tvashtri was regarded as the god of human **fertility**. He gave human beings embryos, and supervised the birth of healthy children. Only creatures with testicles were allowed to approach him: male priests, male offerings (which were not sacrificed, but set free when the ritual was done), no plants or flowers.

Tvashtri as craftsman-god. In his diminished role in later myth, Tvashtri was a kind of supernatural handyman. For the gods' supply of *soma*, he made a cup which replenished the drink even as they drank it. He made weapons and chariots for the war-gods, most notably **Vishnu**'s discus, **Indra**'s thunderbolts and **Shiva**'s trident. (The trident and thunderbolts were made from shavings from the Sun-god **Surya**, whom

Tvashtri turned on his lathe to reduce his dazzle.) He built palaces for Indra and for **Varuna**: Varuna's underwater, a dazzling white building studded with jewels and golden flowers, Indra's on Mount **Meru**, a cloud-palace where the spirits of **heroes** dead in battle were welcomed, and which had the power to vanish and resite itself at will.

In some later accounts, Tvashtri was identified with **Vishvakarman**, architect of the gods.

Tvashtri figures in poetry less as a being than a principle: the matrix, all-power, the generator. He is rarely shown in art: in painting sometimes as a swirl, a kind of soup of all matter, and in carvings as a disembodied hand.
≫→ crafts

TWINS

Twins offered an excellent way to embody the pairs of balancing opposites of which the myth-universe and its beings were made: good and bad, **light and dark**, male and female and so on. In several stories, after the Earth was first created, twins were sent to stock it, and rivalry between them was why both bad and good later existed in the world, and why it was sometimes hard to tell them apart. Twins often featured in the myth-cycles of important cities and states, as founders – and after their work was done many were promoted to the sky, either as full gods or as pairs of stars.

≫→ (Americas): Ariconte and Tamendonare, Enumclaw and Kapoonis, Gluskap, Hahgwehdiyu and Hahgwehdaetgah, Ioskeha, Kuat and Iae, Malsum, Nayanezgani and Tobadzistsini, Quetzalcóatl, Tezcatlipoca; **(Australia): Kurukadi and Mumba; (Egypt): Geb, Nut, Set; (Greece): Amphion and Zethus, Clytemnestra, Dioscuri, Helen; (Iranian): Ahriman, Ahura Mazda; (Rome): Romulus and Remus; (Oceania): To Kabinana and To Karvuvu**

TYCHE: *see* Fortuna

TYNDAREUS
Europe (South)

Tyndareus ('pounder'), King of Sparta in Greek myth, was noted more for his devotion to the women of his family than for his common sense. His wife **Leda** was seduced by **Zeus** in the form of a swan, and Tyndareus showed no irritation when she gave birth to bird's eggs instead of children. He forgave her adultery and brought up the four offspring (the **Dioscuri** Castor and Pollux; **Clytemnestra** and **Helen**) as if they were his own. (In some accounts two of them actually were his own: each pair of **twins** included one immortal child, descended from Zeus, and one mortal, descended from Tyndareus. His son was Pollux and his daughter was Clytemnestra.)

When suitors from all over Greece came asking for the hand of Tyndareus' daughter Helen, he refused to choose one of them – a father's prerogative and duty – and instead did something as unheard-of as it was indulgent: let her select her own husband. (She chose **Menelaus**, the handsomest man there.) Soon after the wedding, Tyndareus, whose other daughter had married

Agamemnon and gone to Mycenae (and whose wife and sons had been taken to **Heaven** by the gods long ago), let Helen wheedle him into handing his throne over to Menelaus and living a lonely, pensioned-off existence in a corner of the royal estates.

TYPHON
Europe (South)

Typhon ('smoke' or 'hurricane', also known as Typhoeus), in Greek myth, was a **monster**, the offspring of **Gaia** (**Mother Earth**) and Tartarus (the fathomless gulf below the **Underworld**). When he stretched himself out fully he covered the whole of Greece like a cloak of darkness. His body was formless smoke, out of which sprouted a hundred dragons' heads; his countless arms and legs were snakes; his eyes flashed flame and his mouths spat molten rock.

Gaia bore Typhon to punish the gods for defeating the **Earthborn Giants** in the battle for power in the Universe. As soon as Typhon was created, he surged up and began battering the ramparts of **Olympus**. The gods, terrified, fled to Egypt, where they disguised themselves as animals and cowered: **Apollo** pretended to be a crow, **Aphrodite** a fish, **Artemis** a cat, **Dionysus** a goat, **Hermes** an ibis, and **Zeus** a ram. Only **Athene** stayed in Olympus, and she jeered at Zeus until she shamed him into flying back to fight. He sent Typhon reeling with a thunderbolt, and ran to finish him off with the diamond-sickle **Cronus** had used to mutilate **Ouranos**. But Typhon, even weakened by a thunderbolt, was more than a match for

Zeus. He entwined him in his serpent-hands and flew to a cave on Mount Casius in Syria. There he took the sickle and hacked out the sinews of Zeus' hands and feet. Zeus' immortal flesh soon healed, but without the sinews he lay helpless, unable to move. Typhon gave the sinews to a she-monster, Delphyne, to guard, and flew off to deal with the other gods.

In the meantime, however, Athene had persuaded Hermes and **Pan** to leave Egypt and come and fight. They crept to Delphyne's cave. Pan sent his terrible cry echoing across the countryside, and while Delphyne shrank back in panic, Hermes replaced the sinews in Zeus' arms and legs. Zeus snatched up his thunderbolts and raged after Typhon. Typhon had gone to Mount Nysa in Greece (where Dionysus had once invented wine) and demanded food and drink. The three **Fates** were waiting there; they enticed him and flattered him, but instead of giving him immortal food they fuddled him with wine and gave him a fruit called 'for a day' – mortal nourishment which would weaken him and sap his strength. Satisfied, he flew out across Mount Haemus in Thrace, and the battle with Zeus began.

Even weakened by mortal food, Typhon still had the strength of a thousand gods. His weapons were **mountains**, ripped up and hurled at Zeus. There was no defeating him by force: the only weapon was cleverness. So, instead of aiming his thunderbolts at Typhon, Zeus hurled them at the rocks he threw. The blast turned the rocks in mid-air, sending them crashing back on Typhon. Jagged splinters tore the monster's flesh; his blood dyed the mountain red (and gave it its name: 'Mount Blood'); roaring in agony, he picked up his ragged body and fluttered to Sicily. Now Zeus used strength. He picked up Mount Etna and flung it at Typhon. In some versions of the myth, the weight of the mountain pushed Typhon through the Earth's crust, through the Underworld, down to the dark chasms of his father Tartarus where he lay, Zeus' prisoner forever. In others, the fight was beaten out of him, and he either went to live peaceably in Olympus (where he fathered a number of destructive winds, called typhoons after him), or lay for all eternity under Mount Etna, where his gasps of pain provided **fire** for the furnaces of Zeus' blacksmith-**Cyclopes**.

TYR
Europe (North)

Tyr ('dayshine' or 'god'), in Nordic myths, was in some accounts the original **sky**-god, precursor of **Odin**; in others he was the son of Odin and Frigg, or Frigg and the **giant Hymir**; in others again he was the same person as **Tiwaz**. He presided over the gods' councils of war, and was their commander in battle.

Tyr was fearless. When **Loki**'s wolf-offspring Fenrir was brought to **Asgard**, he looked after it, feeding it haunches of meat and exercising it as if it were a tame puppy. Fenrir kept growing, and soon terrified all Asgard. The gods decided that it must be bound before it destroyed the universe. They begged from the dwarfs a magic rope (made from cat's stealth, woman's beard, mountain-root, bear-sinews, fish's breath and bird-spittle), and challenged Fenrir to break it. Fenrir agreed to be bound, so long as he could hold one of the gods' arms in his jaws to guard against treachery. Tyr volunteered, and when the wolf found that the rope was as unbreakable as it was invisible, it bit off Tyr's arm. So Fenrir was bound for this cycle of the universe, safe until **Ragnarök** – and Tyr fought one-handed from that day on.

Venus (*Roman bronze*)

UAICA
Americas (South)

Uaica, in the myths of the Juruña people of the Xingu river, was given healing powers by **Sinaa** the creator, and used them to help his people. He brewed potions, made poultices from herbs and insects, set bones and sang spells to keep mortality at bay. But his powers depended on sexual abstinence, and they waned, first when his people gave him a wife and then when the wife took a lover. Finally the lover tried to kill Uaica, and Uaica disappeared into the ground forever, taking his healing powers with him. Before he went, he offered his people one last chance, if they followed him to the shadow-world; but they refused, and from that day on, human beings have been plagued by disease and **death**.

≫+ **disease and healing**

UGRASENA
India

Ugrasena, in Hindu myth, ruled the Yadava people of northern India. When his wife **Pavanarekha** was raped by the **demon Drumalika**, and gave birth to **Kansa**, Ugrasena brought the young demon up as his own son, only to be dethroned as soon as Kansa was old enough to rule. Later, **Krishna** led the Yadava people against Kansa, killed him and restored Ugrasena to his throne. But Ugrasena's remaining time on Earth was short: when Krishna was killed, he was so distraught that he threw himself on the god's funeral pyre and was carried with him into **Heaven**.

UGRASURA
India

Ugrasura, in Hindu myth, was a snake-demon who tried to kill the boy **Krishna** by swallowing him as a cobra swallows a frog. Krishna rescued himself by growing to full god-size inside the demon's gullet and bursting it apart.

UKEMOCHI
Asia (Southeast)

Ukemochi, in Japanese myth, was a **fertility** goddess, married to the blacksmith-spirit **Inari**. Tsukuyomi, god of the **Moon**, paid them a visit, and Ukemochi laid a feast before him: meat, fish and piles of rice. However, Tsukuyomi had glimpsed her preparing the dishes, apparently by vomiting up the food, and he was so disgusted that he killed her. Because what she'd made could not be unmade, he filled a sack with the rice, gave the animals and fish back their lives, stocked the Earth with animals and the sea with fish, and put Inari in charge of all of them.

There is enormous confusion over both Ukemochi and Inari. Sometimes they are treated as husband and wife, sometimes as the same person – so that Inari, the partner most usually shown in art, can be male or female – and sometimes as forms of a third deity, Ugonomitama goddess of agriculture. Ukemochi is also sometimes shown as a fox, bringer of good luck. Possibly she was a **shape-changer**, *and what Tsukuyomi saw was not her vomiting but turning herself into the food she then offered him – but the cults of Ukemochi are among the most ancient in Japan, the myths which survive are fragmentary, and none takes this line.*

UKKO
Europe (North)

Ukko ('old one'), in Finnish myth, was

king of the gods, successor to the first sky-god **Jumala**. He was an elder of the universe, and his existence kept it in being and guaranteed its survival. He stayed aloof: the only signs of his presence mortals ever saw were rain-clouds. He was the supreme authority, to be invoked only when all other prayers had failed.
≫→ **supreme deity**

ULGAN
Europe (North)

Ulgan, or Yryn-ai-tojon, the Siberian and Lapp **sky**-god, created the Earth by setting a vast saucer of land on the backs of three fish frisking on the surface of the primordial ocean. The leaping of the fish caused **earthquakes**, and pieces of the Earth-disc broke off and floated free, until Ulgan anchored them as continents and islands. He was startled when one of the smallest specks suddenly spoke, announcing that it had no intention of letting plants grow on it – and he took it at its word and instead of making it into land he turned it into **Erlik**, the first created being.
≫→ **creation**

ULL
Europe (North)

Ull ('dazzler'), also known as Holler, Oller, Uller and Vulder, in Nordic myth, was the god of frost-glitter. **Thor**'s wife **Sif** bore him to a frost-giant, and he later married the giantess **Skadi**. (In some accounts he was promiscuous, and had **sex** with his own mother and with **Frigg**). A powerful archer, Ull was able to track down his prey and escape his enemies by skiing: he invented the skill, and refused to share it with any other god. He was a show-off, streaking the whole Northern sky with firework-displays of his own radiance – the lights mortals called the Aurora Borealis.

In some accounts, Ull was **Odin**'s rival (not least for the favours of **Frigg**), and they challenged each other for universal power. In the end **Forseti** persuaded them to accept a standoff: for six months of each year, Ull and Odin would share rule of **Midgard** and **Asgard**, and there would be winter; for the rest of the year Ull would live with **Hel** in **Niflheim**, leaving Odin to fill the upper worlds with summer.
≫→ archers

ULURU
Australia

Uluru, in the myths of the Pitjandjara people of the Gibson Desert in West Central Australia, is the area centred on what white Australians now call Ayers Rock. Originally the Rock was a sandhill beside a waterhole. In the Dream Time, a group of harmless snake-people, the Woma and Kunia, settled there, and lived peacefully until they were attacked by the venomous-snake Liru people. There was an enormous battle, the Woma and Kunia males were all killed and the females were raped and murdered. Their bodies made rocks and boulders, and their pubic hair made brush and shrubs. The sandhill heaved itself from the ground and solidified, becoming the Rock which is there today.

ULYSSES: *see* Odysseus

UMA
India

Uma, in Hindu myth, was a mysterious mother-goddess who had no form of her own, but slipped into the bodies of other goddesses whenever she wanted to enjoy a few hours' material existence. Her 'hosts' included **Ambika**, **Devi**, **Durga**, **Rudrani** and above all **Parvati**, in whose body she seduced **Shiva** from meditation. In some accounts she was the daughter of the Himalayan **mountains**, and saved human beings from starvation after a long drought by miraculously producing fruits and vegetables from her body after it was fertilized by the **rain**.
≫→ fertility

UMAI-HULHLYA-WIT
Americas (North)

Umai-hulhlya-wit ('big **snake**'), in the myths of the Diegueño people of Southern California, was a water-monster which existed before **creation**. Then two creator-spirits, Chacopá and Chacomát, made and peopled the universe, and Umai-hulhlya-wit went from his den in the gulf of space to see what it was like. He was so enormous that he threatened to swallow all creation. But guided by Chacopá and Chacomát, the people welcomed him and invited him to sleep in a sacred enclosure made of brushwood. He coiled himself small enough to get inside – it took three mortal days – and as soon as he was in, the people set the wood on fire. The heat turned Umai-hulhlya-wit's water-blood to steam, and he gradually swelled and exploded. The force of the blast sent pieces of his skin and flesh flying everywhere in creation – and they were languages, songs, religious rituals, laws, customs and stories of the gods.

UMASHIASHIKABIHIKOJI
Asia (Southeast)

Umashiashikabihikoji ('pleasant reed sprout prince elder'), in Japanese myth, was the fourth of the five primordial deities to come into existence at the beginning of **creation** (see **Kotoamatsukami**). When it appeared, the Earth floated in the primeval ocean like a medusa jellyfish, the changing colours, like oil on its iridescent surface, showing where future continents and islands would exist. As time passed, one part of the substance of Earth began to sprout and grow like a stalagmite of molten glass. As it hardened, it turned into a reed, Umashiashikabihikoji, and grew six branches. Each branch in turn produced a pair of gods, one male and one female: the invisible Kuninotokotati and Toyokumono (spirits of majesty and awe which remained eternally aloof from universal concerns), Upidini ('lord mud') and Supidini ('lady mud'), Tunogupi ('seed coordinator') and Ikugupi ('life coordinator'), Opotonodi ('great place elder') and Opotonobe ('lady great place elder'), Omodaru ('perfect face') and Ayakasikone ('awesome lady'), and last of all **Izanami and Izanagi**, who acted on the instructions of all the others to complete creation.

UNCEGILA
Americas (North)

Uncegila, or Unktehi, in the myths of the Sioux people of the US Great Plains, was a giant water-**snake**. In the days when **Mother Earth** was young, the plains of Nebraska and Dakota were marshy, crossed by rivers and covered with jungle. They would have been a paradise for the humans who lived there – if it hadn't been for Uncegila. She spent most of her time swimming through the oceans of the world, but once or twice each year she swam up into the Nebraska swamplands, polluting them with salt water and making the level rise so that it flooded and poisoned the land. Her eyes were fire, her scales were flint and her heart was crystal.

Two boys, **twins**, went to hunt Uncegila, armed both by magic and by information that there was only one vulnerable place in her flint hide: the seventh spot down from her head. As soon as she reared out of the swamp to attack them, one fired an arrow while the other said a magic word of guidance. The arrow struck Uncegila's seventh spot and killed her. With her dying spasms she wriggled out of the water and spread her huge body across the plain – and the Sun, grateful that his old enemy was dead at last, seared all the flesh from her, sucked up all the water from horizon to horizon and burned off the vegetation, so that nothing was left but Uncegila's enormous bones, bleaching in a desert.

Meanwhile, the twins had taken Uncegila's heart back to their village, where they placed it in an underground chamber. The place became holy and they became its guardians; the heart granted them powers of **prophecy** and healing. But one day they rashly allowed ordinary people to see the heart, and it screamed like a living thing, exploded and burned to ash.

This is one of many similar myths explaining the bleached rock-formations of the Nebraska and Dakota Badlands.

UNDERWATER PANTHERS
Americas (North)

Underwater Panthers, in the myths of many peoples of the Eastern US woodlands, were creatures of destruction. Some were the mirror-images of creatures from the Upper World, like reflections seen in water. Others were **snakes**, bison, toads – or panthers with snakes', bisons' or toads' horns. They lived in the Underwater World, and sought either to drag Upper World beings into it, or to drown the entire Upper World by sending **floods**, usually in conjunction with the **Great Thunderbird** and his storm-birds.

➤➤ **animal-gods, monsters and dragons**

UNDERWORLD, THE

The universe existed as a balance of equal and opposite forces, and one of the most important was that between 'our' world and the 'other' world. Our world was one of light and clarity, overseen by gods and spirits who shared it with us; the other world was dark and mysterious, and its creatures were hostile and predatory. In the human view of them – theirs of us is not

imagined or recorded – they were jealous of our main possession, life, and endlessly surged from their darkness to prey on us and snatch it. In many traditions the Underworld – the name was common, even though many 'underworlds' were not 'under' our own at all, and others had no physical location whatever – was filled with dead humans, expiating their lives in the Upper World before being allowed to return there or to pass on to some other future existence. It was also a kind of dumping-ground for **giants**, **monsters** and **demons** who had opposed the gods and been punished for it, and who spent their time spawning creatures even more hideous and deadly (to humans) than themselves.

Baroque ideas of this kind were prevalent in most myths – and led to a shoal of stories in which Upper-World **heroes** visited the Underworld or Underworld creatures came to the Upper World, and spectacular battles took place. A few myths, however, explored the idea of another world in more philosophical, objective ways. Their Underworlds were mirror-images of ours: places of non-being, non-consciousness, non-emotion, non-striving. Some traditions also made them cold instead of warm, inert instead of energetic, blank instead of multiform. In one Chinese myth, the Underworld was the 'real' world, and our existence was merely a dream in its inhabitants' minds; in Egyptian and Indian myth the Underworld was a way-station through which souls pass on their way to a new existence; in one Mayan myth (surviving tantalizingly in fragments), the Underworld was a place of peace and rest, and lack was viewed not (as elsewhere) as something negative, but as positive, blessed and to be wished-for.

»+ (Arctic): Sedna; Yambe-Akka; (Celtic): Annwn; (China): Di Kang Wang, Ten Yama Kings, Yen Lo; (Egypt): Anubis, Osiris, Serapis, Thoth; (Finnish): Tuonela; (Greece): Acheron, Cerberus, Cocytus, Furies, Hades, Hermes, Lethe, Orpheus, Persephone, Phlegethon, Rhadamanthus, Styx; (India): Yama; (Japan): Yomi; (Mesopotamia): Inanna, Sheol; (Nordic): Hel

UNELANUKI
Americas (North)

Unelanuki ('appointer'), the **Sun**-goddess in the myths of the Cherokee people of the Southeastern US, seduced her brother the **Moon**. He had no idea who he was sleeping with, but when he went to wash later he discovered that his face was smeared with sun-ash, and realized what had happened. Ever since then he has avoided her, shrinking out of the way every time she approaches – and he has never entirely removed the ash, which is why his light is less than hers.

UNKULUNKULU
Africa

Unkulunkulu ('ancient of days'), in the myths of the Amazulu people of South Africa, and known to the Ndebele people of Zimbabwe as Nkulnkulu, was the first power in existence. He had no shape, but was the immanent power of **creation**. He made the first human beings by plucking two reeds from a swamp, and gave them the Earth to live on. He sent Chameleon to tell them that they would live forever, but unfortunately Lizard darted to them first and mischievously told them that they would certainly die. Unkulunkulu could not change the message, but gave mortals the gift of **sex**, so that they could achieve a kind of **immortality** through their offspring. He showered them with other gifts – control of fire, farming, hunting, medical skills, music – hoping that these would compensate for the loss of eternity. When they or their children died he sent them to the Land of the Dead, **Heaven**, from where they still look down on their descendants with shining eyes – the stars.

Since Unkulunkulu was all-present and all-controlling, he was also the god of war, expressing his rage in thunder and lightning. His many honorific titles included uGobungquonqo ('dethroner'), uGuqabadele ('all-conquering') uKqili ('all-wise'), uMabongakutukiziwezonke ('terror-roarer') and uZivelele ('all-that-is, in one').

URANUS: *see* Ouranos

URVASHI
India

Urvashi, in the Vedic myths of the Aryans who invaded India in the seventeenth century BCE, was an **apsara**, or heavenly dancing-girl, so beautiful that none could resist her. Once, she danced for **Varuna** and **Mitra** (or, some say, **Surya**), and they were so aroused that

they had orgasms on the spot. Their sperm, collected in a jar, grew into a sage: in some accounts **Agastya**, in others **Vishvamitra**.
≫→ **beauty**

USHAS
India

Ushas, in the Vedic myths of the Aryans who invaded India in the seventeenth century BCE, was the dawn-goddess, the daughter either of **Aditi** or of **Dyaus** (Father **Sky**) and **Privithi** (**Mother Earth**). Every day she opened the doors of **Heaven**, showing off her carmine clothes and bringing light and wealth to mortals. She bustled about the world, waking all good creatures to their daily activity, but leaving the wicked to sleep forever. There was just one dark aspect to her generosity: among her gifts to mortals was time, and with time came old age and **death**.

UTGARD
Europe (North)

Utgard ('out-castle'), in Nordic myth, was a stronghold of the **giants**, visited by **Thor** and **Loki**. It seemed to be a vast castle, deep in the giant kingdom of **Jotunheim**, a Kafkaesque edifice in which every room led into another, every wall towered higher the more your eyes reached the top of it, every horizon merged into the next as you approached. In fact both Utgard and its ruler Utgard-Loki were illusions, conjured out of air by the giants who were too terrified of Thor and Loki to face them in person.

UTHER PENDRAGON
Europe (North)

Uther Pendragon ('cruel dragon-chief'), in Celtic myth, was a Welsh (or in some versions, French) prince ambitious to rule all Britain. He asked **Merlin** for supernatural help, only to be told that he would fail and that his ambition would destroy his entire dynasty. Dismissing this prophecy, Uther demanded shape-shifting powers, and Merlin briefly granted them. Taking the form of his rival King Gorlois of Cornwall, Uther slept with Ygern, Gorlois' queen, making her pregnant with the child that was to become King **Arthur**.

At this point, Uther largely disappears from myth. In some accounts, he was killed in battle, or assassinated, and was buried in the centre of Stonehenge. In others, he stuck a sword in a boulder, and announced that the man who pulled it out would rule all Britain; Merlin took charge of the education of Arthur, the 'once and future king', and when Arthur was fifteen he pulled the sword from the stone and assumed his father's throne. Other, sketchier, accounts identify Uther with the willow-tree god Bel, saying that he came into the mortal world specifically to father Arthur, and left it soon after the child was born.
≫→ **shape-changers**

UTNAPISHTIM
Asia (West)

Utnapishtim or Utanapishtim, in Babylonian myth, was one of **Gilgamesh's** ancestors who survived the great **flood** sent by the gods to wipe out the human race. Warned by **Enki**, he filled a cube-shaped boat with treasure and with plants and creatures of every kind, then as the waters rose set sail in it with his wife and family. After seven days he sent out a dove to look for dry land, and it came back exhausted. On the eighth day he sent a swallow, with the same result. On the ninth day he sent a raven, and when it failed to come back he beached his boat, released the animals and planted the plants. The gods, seeing his simple goodness, rewarded him and his wife by granting them **immortality** and making them ancestors of the reborn human race.

In Tablet Eleven of The Epic of Gilgamesh *Utnapishtim tells this story when Gilgamesh asks him how to achieve immortality.*
≫→ Atrahis, Deucalion and Pyrrha, Doquebuth, Manu, Noah, Nu'u

UTSET
Americas (North)

Utset, in the myths of the Cherokee Indians, peopled the world. When the Lower World was drowned in the primordial **flood**, she led people and animals to safety up a hollow reed, and gave them the Upper World to live on. She carried the stars in a sack, but gave it to Beetle for safe-keeping, and he opened it, spilling the stars across the sky. Utset ran to pick them up, but had rescued only a few (the planets) when she realized that her people, back on Earth, were starving because she'd never taught them how or what to eat. She left the rest of the stars where they were, hurried back to Earth and

planted pieces of her own heart to make crops for her people: the first corn.
≫→ farming

UTU
Asia (West)

Utu, in Sumerian myth, was the brother of **Inanna** and god of justice. He went with the **Sun** on his journey round the heavens, judging the living during the day and the Dead at night – and his decisions were sunshafts, hurled like spears: unerring, irrevocable and impossible to argue away.
≫→ justice and universal order

UZUME
Asia (East)

Uzume ('twirling'), in Japanese myth, was the goddess of happiness expressed in dance. When **Amaterasu** barricaded herself into a cave because she was disgusted with **Susano**, Uzume danced to entice her out. As she performed, she began whirling faster and faster, and her clothes fell off one by one – causing such whoops and howls from the male deities that Amaterasu, wondering how it was possible to have such a good time while she was still in hiding, stuck her head out of the cave and was caught and dragged back to the light. The deities rewarded Uzume by making her guardian of the spring of pure water which lies at the foot of the Floating Bridge between Earth and **Heaven** (in some accounts, the Milky Way, in others, a rainbow). Ever afterwards, she let favoured mortals drink its waters, which gave them a brief taste of **immortality**. Her priests on Earth brewed potions to imitate this water, and the herb-lore they learned led to Uzume being worshipped as goddess of good health, and her temples becoming healing-shrines.

The myths give various accounts of who exactly Uzume was. In some, she was Amaterasu's daughter, sister of Wakahir- *ume the Dawn-goddess whose death made Amaterasu retreat from the world in the first place. In others Uzume herself was Dawn, and in still others she was the sister and/or consort of **Ninigi**, and travelled with him to Earth when he went to rule and found the Imperial dynasty.*

➤ disease and healing

Valkyries gathering dead heroes (*19th-century German engraving*)

VAHAGN
Europe (Southeast)

Vahagn, the warrior-god in Armenian myth, was born accidentally at the beginning of **creation**. Sky and Earth were copulating, trying vainly to find ways of engendering life, and their writhings caused a reed which had been floating on the surface of the primordial ocean to fly up into the gulf of space. The reed was red, and as it whirled through space its redness concentrated at one end like a comet-tail, and formed itself into a fire-being: Vahagn. Vahagn went on to fill Sky with stars – in some accounts, the Milky Way was wisps of straw dropped from the bale he gathered to feed his chariot-horses – and to cover Earth with plants, animals and human beings.

*Vahagn is a somewhat shadowy figure in myth, but he is identified in Iranian folk-stories with the **giant**-killer and **demon**-smiter Rustem, and in Zoroastrian belief was merged with no less a deity than **Ahura Mazda** himself. His wives were Astlik, star-maker, and the **fertility**-goddess Anahit.*
≫→ creation

VAIMATSE
Americas (South)

Vaimatse ('beast-lord'), in the myths of the Tukaño people of the upper Amazon, was the spirit of forest **fertility**. He was present at every act of **sex** between humans, animals or plants, and usually took part, guaranteeing offspring. If mating took place while he was somewhere else, he blighted it, making the union infertile or giving the female involved an uncomfortable and sometimes fatal pregnancy.

VÄINÄMÖINEN
Europe (North)

Väinämöinen's birth. Väinämöinen, in Finnish myth, was the son of the fertilizing sea and the **creation**-goddess **Luonnotar**. He spent 700 years reaching maturity in Luonnotar's womb, and a further 30 years as a grown man sitting there, becoming ever more bored and shouting vainly to the **Sun** and stars to help him out. But the Sun and stars could not hear him, and Luonnotar, utterly innocent in the ways of **sex** and **childbirth**, had no idea even that she was pregnant. Finally, in desperation, Väinämöinen began hauling himself hand over hand out of her womb and up the tunnel of her vagina. He hammered on the vast membrane of her virginity, tore a hole with his left big toe, and clambered out as a man emerges from a pothole.

Väinämöinen and Joukahainen. Väinämöinen swam ashore in the country that was to become Finland. He began felling trees and clearing land for farming. Lacking tools and draught-animals, he used magic spells and songs – and these attracted the attention of the frost-**giant Joukahainen**, who sledged over the ice from the far North to challenge the intruder. Joukahainen's magic made the Earth shake, the sky cower and the mountains shudder. But he was no match for Väinämöinen, who changed his sledge into a lake, his horse to a boulder, his bow to a rainbow, his arrows to hawks, and his clothes into cloud, then planted him up to his armpits in a swamp. Joukahainen hastily offered a truce, and agreed to let Väinämöinen married his sister Aino if

Väinämöinen first set him free. Unfortunately for Väinämöinen, as soon as Aino saw him, she shrieked that he was too old and decrepit for a husband, threw herself into the sea and drowned.

Väinämöinen in Pohjola. Aino's rejection made Väinämöinen all the more eager to marry and sow children before it was too late. He set out for **Pohjola**, the Northland, to see if any of the frost-giantesses would have him, but Joukahainen ambushed him and threw him into the freezing sea. He swam for eight days, growing ever weaker, until an eagle scooped him up like a fish and took him to shore. Here Princess **Louhi** offered him her daughter in exchange for a *sampo*, a magic mill able to churn out endless supplies of salt from one side, flour from the second and gold from the third. When Väinämöinen said that no one had ever made a *sampo*, Louhi answered 'Only the one who does so will have my daughter.'

Louhi sent Väinämöinen home to Finland to make the *sampo*, telling him that he would have an untroubled journey if he neither stopped nor looked up on his journey. But Väinämöinen forgot these conditions. He heard singing, looked up and saw Louhi's daughter sitting on a rainbow spinning gold. He begged her to marry him without the *sampo,* and she agreed providing that he first split a hair with a blunt knife, knotted an egg, peeled a stone, broke a lump of ice without making splinters and carved a boat from her shuttle. Väinämöinen had no problems with the first four tasks, but when he was shaping the boat with a magic axe, three evil spirits (sent by Louhi) made him lose concentration, drive the axe into his own knee and sever the ligaments. None of his own magic was strong enough to heal this wound, and by the time he'd found a magician who knew the appropriate spell, the shaped part of the boat was lost and he had to start again. **Väinämöinen in Tuonela.** This time, instead of using an axe Väinämöinen made the boat by magic. He remembered the chopping-spells and smoothing-spells for the wood, the weaving-spells for the sail and the bubbling-spell for the pitch to caulk the timbers – every piece of magic except the binding-spells needed to make the boat leap together and become complete. He searched the Upper World, listening to songs and rejecting them, and finally went to look for magic in **Tuonela**, the **Underworld**. He walked for a week through thickets, a week through woods and a week through forests, and persuaded the daughters of **Tuoni**, king of the Underworld, to ferry him across the River of Weeping to Manala, land of the Dead. Here Queen **Tuonetar** offered the beer of oblivion, and he refused it just in time. Her son dropped an iron net into the river to stop him swimming for safety – and Väinämöinen escaped only by turning himself into an eel and wriggling through the grid.

Väinämöinen and Antero Vipunen. A shepherd told Väinämöinen that the only being who knew the binding-spell was **Antero Vipunen**, a giant who slept underground with the earth as his blanket. He had been asleep so long that trees had grown from his face and body. Väinämöinen hacked them down, and woke Antero Vipunen by sticking his iron staff down his throat. The giant

yawned, swallowed Väinämöinen and went back to sleep. Inside his belly, Väinämöinen made his shirt into a forge, his coat into bellows, his knee into an anvil and his elbow into a hammer, and began hammering and banging until Antero Vipunen woke up, growling with heartburn, and spewed out of his mouth not only Väinämöinen but every spell and binding-song he knew.

Väinämöinen and Ilmarinen. Väinämöinen set to work to finish his ship, and in the meantime asked his brother, the **smith Ilmarinen**, to forge a *sampo* for Princess Louhi. Ilmarinen threw into his furnace swansdown, milk from a barren cow, sheep's wool and barley, blew up the flames and waited to see what would happen. On the first day a golden bowl was forged, on the second a copper ship, on the third a cow with golden horns, on the fourth a plough of gold, silver and bronze. Ilmarinen threw them all back into the flames, and on the fifth day the *sampo* appeared. He took it to Princess Louhi – and at once the promise came true, the promise Väinämöinen had forgotten: Louhi's daughter would marry whoever forged the *sampo*.

Väinämöinen and Louhi. Unfortunately for Ilmarinen, Louhi's daughter died soon after the marriage, torn to pieces by her own cattle for ill-treating the magic-working hero **Kullervo**. Ilmarinen asked Louhi for her other daughter's hand, and Louhi refused. Ilmarinen went back to Finland, made his peace with Väinämöinen, and asked him to go with him to Pohjola and steal the *sampo* – if there were no wives for the gods in Pohjola, at least prosperity could be found there for the people of

Finland. They took as companion the jester **Lemminkäinen**, and sailed to Pohjola in Väinämöinen's magic boat. On the way Väinämöinen caught a pike and made from its backbone a zither whose music had the power to charm rocks, stones, trees, rivers, and living beings into a magic sleep. With this he lulled Louhi and her people and stole the *sampo*. Just as they sailed away, however, Lemminkäinen started singing a triumph-song, and Louhi woke up and sent storm-winds and icebergs to sink the gods' ship and destroy them.

The storm washed Väinämöinen's zither to the bottom of the sea (where its melancholy music can still sometimes be heard). It smashed the *sampo*, but Väinämöinen was able to collect enough fragments to guarantee prosperity to the people of Finland forever. He also bequeathed to them his magic, breathing it into the lakes and forests, so that however often Louhi attacked the country from Pohjola with frost and ice, they were safe in the knowledge that spring would come again. Väinämöinen then sailed from the mortal world in a bronze boat, gliding up the sunshafts to settle in the no-man's-land between Earth and Heaven. There he still lives, the myth ends, ready whenever his people need him to sail on the shafts of the morning sun and help them.

*In the **Kalevala**, Elias Lönnrot stitched together the story of Väinämöinen from thousands of poems, songs, ballads, proverbs and other items of folk culture. The character is both unique and elusive, an amalgam of god, shaman and folk-hero. Some parts of the story suggest familiarity with non-Finnish traditions – the beer of oblivion, for example, is reminiscent of the water of **Lethe** in Greek myth, the magic zither recalls **Orpheus'** lute, the tests are like those given to **Gilgamesh**, the spell-bound boat has Amerindian and Polynesian parallels, and the end of the story is similar to accounts of **Arthur** and his knights sleeping 'under the mountain'. Whether these similarities are coincidence, the result of Lönnrot's own wide reading or a remarkable example of the widespread cross-fertilization of folk cultures in pre-literate times, scholars have never determined. The fact that Väinämöinen is so often a loser also makes him rare in myth and legend; some scholars have suggested that he and Ilmarinen were originally not separate individuals but two aspects of the same god.*
≫→ heroes, shape-changers, tricksters

VAJRASATTVA
Asia (Southwest)

Vajrasattva, in Tibetan Buddhist myth, was the primordial **Buddha** from whom all others came. He was fiery-tempered, and his anger sent thunderstorms and **earthquakes**. But he was also amorous, and his loving embraces of his wife both symbolized and guaranteed **justice and universal order**.

VALEDJÁD
Americas (South)

Valedjád, in the myths of the Tupari people of Brazil, was the first human being, born when a vagina-shaped rock on the surface of **Mother Earth** suddenly split apart. As soon as he was born he tried to kill his own mother and all her creatures by opening the flood-gates of the sea. Earth cried out to the Sun, who dried up the waters and sent a wizard called Arkoayó to make Valedjád harmless. Arkoayó waited until the giant was asleep, then blocked his eyes, ears and nose with beeswax and stuck his fingers together to stop him unblocking them. Then he bound him with holly (whose magic no stone-giant can break) and called the birds to carry him to the Mountains of the North and leave him there. Valedjád has lain there ever since, writhing and trying to free himself. His rage flickers in a red cloud above his head – the Aurora Borealis – and his roars and groans fill the sky with **thunder**.

VALHALLA
Europe (North)

Valhalla ('hall of the slain'), in Nordic and Germanic myth, was **Odin**'s feast-hall in **Asgard**. Its roof was of shields, supported on rafters made from spears. It had 450 doors, each of which was wide enough to admit a column of 800 marching men. Here the **Valkyries** took all mortal **heroes** killed in battle (and, some say, all wives or mistresses sacrificed on their menfolk's funeral pyres). Their wounds healed magically, and they spent their days exercising martial arts and their nights feasting. When **Ragnarök** comes, the myth ends, they will march out to battle on the side of the gods.

VALKYRIES
Europe (North)

The Valkyries ('gatherers of the slain'), in Nordic and Germanic myth, were warrior-women, servants of **Odin**. In some accounts there were three of them, all immortal; in others there were three times nine, and some were mortal. White-skinned and golden-haired, they rode above the battlefield in full armour, singing war-songs, and gathered the souls of dead **heroes** to take them to **Valhalla**. There, dressed in pure white robes, they looked after heroes as they feasted: serving food and drink, singing and dancing, and – unless they were sworn virgins – providing **sex**.

VAMANA
India

Vamana ('dwarf'), in Hindu myth, was the fifth avatar of **Vishnu**. King **Bali**, great-grandson of **Hiranyakashipu**, shared his great-grandfather's ambition to rule the entire universe. Having conquered Earth and Middle Air, he began gathering his powers to attack **Heaven** itself. Vishnu made himself into a dwarf, crept into Bali's court and begged a tiny strip of territory to live on – as much as he could cover in three steps. In some accounts, when Bali agreed to this, Vishnu soared to god-height and in three steps traversed the entire universe, before treading on Bali's head and trampling him down to the **Underworld**. In others, Vishnu traversed the universe in two steps, and then gave up his right to a third step, allowing Bali to keep dominion over the world below.

This avatar of Vishnu is a favourite subject for statuettes, making the contrast between Bali, enthroned in royal splendour, and the misshapen, cringing figure of Vishnu-Vamana. The story is also popular as a subject for dance-drama, the scene where Vishnu dances his enemy down to the Underworld making an imposing effect.

VAMPIRES
Europe (Central; East)

Vampires (from an ancient Slavic word *vampir*, related to the Turkish *ubir*, 'undead'), in European myth, were corpses which refused to surrender their lives. Their origin may be in ancient Black Sea myths about ghosts, who could be persuaded to come from the **Underworld** by feasts of warm blood poured on the ground. Vampires, similarly, required fresh blood to keep them from the corruption of death, and found it by rising from their graves and sucking it from sleeping human victims. In sixteenth-century Central and Eastern Europe, vampires were held to be the spirits of suicides, and they could be killed only by being exposed to full daylight or stabbed through the heart with a sharpened crucifix – after both of which treatments they crumbled in seconds from living beings to heaps of dust. In the witch-hungry atmosphere of the times, they were also thought to be as sexually voracious as any other emissary of **Satan**, and to rape their virgin victims even as they drank their blood. Suspected victims were executed just as often as suspected vampires.

The vampire myth lay dormant in the European imagination until the end of the nineteenth century, when it was given huge new impetus by Bram Stoker's novel Dracula, *based in part on the story of the fourteenth-century Transylvanian warlord Vlad 'the Impaler'. Stoker added the idea that vampires were half bat, half human, and his creation has more or less taken over the entire vampire industry, a staple of horror comics, novels and films ever since. In particular, his depiction of the typical vampire as a devilishly handsome, witty and tormented aristocrat completely ousted the former view of vampires: that they were walking corpses, smelling of putrefaction and incapable of any human emotion or thought save the needs to copulate and to survive by drinking blood – Western equivalents of Zombies, the Undead in Voodoo myth.*

⫸ **demons, Flying Head, Namorodo**

VANIR
Europe (North)

The Vanir ('beautiful ones'), in Nordic myth, were a family of **fertility**-gods led by **Njörd** (the Old Man of the **Sea**) and his twin children **Frey** and **Freyja**. They guarded the fruitfulness of Sea and Earth, and the mating of every living creature in existence. They were gentle and creative, and distrusted the other family of gods who shared the universe, the **Aesir**.

One of the Vanir – some say it was Gullveig, others Freyja herself disguised as Gullveig – visited **Asgard**, the citadel of the Aesir. She never stopped talking of gold, the warmth and glow of gold, and the Aesir, irritated, burned her three times in fire, only to see her reborn each time. When the Vanir heard of it, they declared war on the Aesir, who eagerly snatched the chance of eliminating their rivals for supreme authority in the universe. The war raged for centuries of mortal time. The Aesir laid waste Vanaheim, home of the Vanir; the Vanir reduced Asgard, home of the Aesir, to a heap of rubble. In the end, since neither side was winning, the Aesir and Vanir made an uneasy truce, and agreed to exchange hostages to ensure its survival. Njörd and Frey went to live for part of each year among the Aesir, and **Honir** and **Mimir** went from Asgard to live with the Vanir.

Although this settlement brought peace, it failed to reconcile the gods. Ever afterwards, the Aesir and Vanir regarded each other with suspicion. The Vanir thought that in some way the Aesir had tricked them, that Honir and Mimir were living with them not as friends but as spies. They hacked off Mimir's head and sent it back to Asgard. This move was disastrous for the Vanir. Mimir's head carried all the wisdom of the gods, and Odin rubbed it with herbs of **immortality** and kept it to speak and advise the Aesir. So the Aesir had all-knowledge, and they also had all-power (in the shape of **Thor** and his thunderbolts) and, in Njörd, Frey and Freyja, the regenerative power once controlled by the Vanir. As for the Vanir, they rebuilt Vanaheim and lived on, but without power or authority, an ever-fading memory of what they once had been.

Later scholars explained this myth as an allegory of the conflict in the universe, and in human nature, between the opposing forces of generation and destruction. In such a view, the Vanir came to symbolize a kind of lost Golden Age, and the Aesir stood for the hard-faced cruelty of present existence. Some writers said that so long as the Vanir continued to exist, even as shadows of their former selves, there was still hope of a return to Golden Age peace and prosperity, before the final battle of Ragnarök when all creation would be destroyed. Others used the current stalemate between the two families of gods as a springboard for preaching the new religion which swept Northern Europe in the tenth-fourteenth centuries CE: redemptive Christianity.

VARAHA
India

Varaha in Vedic myth. Varaha ('boar'), in the Vedic **creation**-myths of the Aryan people who invaded India in the seventeenth century BCE, was a form taken by **Brahma** to bring the world from the depths of the primordial ocean to the surface. When no land, no sky, no middle air existed, Brahma noticed a lotus growing on the surface, and swam down to see what was anchoring its stem. He discovered the Earth, deep in the ocean depths, formed himself into a gigantic boar and heaved it to the surface with his tusks. In some versions the Earth was as we know it: mountains, forests, plains. In others it was a beautiful goddess, **Privithi** Mother of All, riding serenely on Varaha's forehead.

Varaha in Hindu myth. In a Hindu version of the same **creation**-myth, Varaha was the third avatar of **Vishnu**. The Earth had already been created and stocked with plants, animals, people – and **demons**. One demon, **Hiranyaksha**, by sacrifice and prayers, had

645

persuaded the gods to make him invulnerable, and had listed everything on Earth against which he wanted protection – except one, the boar. Once the gift was granted, he terrorized all creation, and finally pulled the Earth deep under the primordial ocean and held it there to drown everything on it. Vishnu changed himself into a boar: his size was a mountain's, his roar was **thunder**, his hide radiated heat-arrows like those of the **Sun** and his eyes flashed **lightning**. He dived into the ocean, killed Hiranyaksha and tossed the Earth safely to the surface with his tusks before a single insect, animal, plant or human drowned.

≫→ animal-gods

VARPULIS
Europe (East)

Varpulis, in Southern Czech myth, was a wind-god who ran beside **Pyerun**'s chariot as it galloped across the sky. His panting was the grumble and mutter of thunderstorms.

VARUNA
India

Varuna ('encompasser'), in the Vedic myths of the Aryans who invaded India in the seventeenth century BCE, was the god of the **sky**. He was known as Aditya ('**Aditi**'s son', that is 'light of **Heaven**'), and his other names included Pasabhrit ('noose-carrier'), Pasi ('judge') and Prasetas ('all-wise'). After something like 1000 years his power and functions changed. He became the god of **water**, and his honorary second names included Kesa ('liquid-lord'), Variloma ('water-hair') and Yadhapati ('ruler of water-creatures').

Varuna the Creator. Varuna oversaw, and indeed embodied, *rita* ('world-order'): the truth, the ultimate reality against which all other realities were matched. One of the earliest **creation**-myths says that he stood in emptiness and made three worlds simply by exercise of will: **Heaven**, Middle Air and Earth. He then continued to create, or sustain, the universe by unceasing effort of will – and if that effort ever slackens, the universe will end. In some accounts he physically supported the sky, surveying it sternly, unceasingly, with his eye the **Sun**. In others he lived in a sky-palace with a thousand doors, and his agent the Sun travelled about the firmament and returned to him each evening to report on the doings of gods and mortals.

Varuna the Encompasser. In later Aryan myth, Varuna shared his power with his brothers Mithra and Aryaman. Aryaman's powers are hardly remembered – he was some kind of sky-god. But with Mithra, Varuna the Encompasser formed a duality. He was sternness, Mithra was compassion; he was rigidity, Mithra was flexibility; he was night, Mithra was day. Varuna lived in the middle of the sky, in void – and he was that void. He was the god of the Moon, and protected *soma*, the **nectar** of the gods. Because of his impartial judgement, he conferred, or removed, **immortality**. On Earth, he oversaw good government, the rule of law, the hierarchies of society and families – and above all, the correct forms and rituals for sacrifice. He himself accepted offerings of horses, symbolizing the life-force. When he was angry, he sent disease and earthquakes; when he was pleased, he sent healing and peace.

Varuna Lord of Water. In early Aryan myth, **Heaven** was imagined as a celestial **sea**, and it was this which Varuna ruled. At first his power was all-encompassing. But there was a cataclysmic war between gods and **demons**, and when it was over the gods reorganized their powers. Varuna's influence declined, and he ruled only the Western quadrant of the sky, above the Indian Ocean on Earth. He was, however, made supreme lord of Earthly oceans, and therefore supervisor of the demons who lived in them. His palace was built on an underwater mountain, Pushpagiri, and from it he rode out on his sea-charger Makara, a fish with a deer's head and antelope's legs. His retinue of river-warriors and waves streamed after him, as he galloped across the sea, noose in hand, to catch and punish demons who challenged the gods.

Varuna the Regulator. As water-lord, Varuna kept a few of his former powers. He scooped out river-beds on Earth, and gathered rain-clouds to fill them. He controlled the tides, using them to regulate the depth of the oceans. He was a god of fishers and sailors, and took special care of drowned people, welcoming them to his underwater kingdom. If mortals offended him, he filled their joints and limbs with liquid, in a particularly painful form of dropsy.

As 'encompasser', Varuna had no shape. He was the personification of the night sky; the wind was his breath, his eyes were stars. He was rarely depicted in art, and then usually as a prince dressed in a cloud-cloak, riding a tortoise and carrying a noosed rope (symbol of his status as binder, knot-master). As 'water-lord', he was depicted either as a prince with foam-white skin, riding his sea-charger, or as a creature, part crocodile, part dolphin, part shark.
⋙→ justice and universal order

VARUNI
India

Varuni (also known as Mara, 'destroyer'; 'intoxication' – not the same person as **Mara**, mother of **Buddha**), in Hindu myth, was the goddess of wine. She was either the daughter of **Varuna**, or was born from the churning of the Sea of Milk (see *amrita*). She had big, rolling eyes, and whoever once enjoyed her favours, whether god, **demon** or mortal, could never resist her afterwards.

VASHISHTRA
India

Vashishtra, in Hindu myth, was one of the **Seven Seers**. He was priest of King **Dasaratha**, **Rama**'s mortal father, and owned Nandini the cow of plenty. He is chiefly remembered, however, as the Seer who opposed the promotion of **Vishvamitra** and suffered for it.

VASUDEVA
India

Vasudeva ('good god'), in Hindu myth, began as an honorific name for **Krishna**, and then became used for the mortal prince whose wife, **Devaki**, gave birth to Krishna and his brother **Balarama**. In the myth, when Krishna later died and returned to **Heaven**, Vasudeva threw himself on the god's funeral pyre and ascended with him.

In Jain myth, each cycle of the universe is led by 24 Saviours, 12 Emperors and nine triads of heroes. One third of each triad is a 'Vasudeva', and there are therefore nine of them in each universal cycle.

≫→ **Vasus**

VASUKI
India

Vasuki, in Hindu myth, was the son of the world-**snake Shesha**. When the gods churned the Sea of Milk to produce *amrita*, they used a mountain as a churning-pole and Vasuki as a rope. Vasuki tried to poison the *amrita* by spitting venom into it, but **Shiva** caught the venom in his mouth and so stopped the gods' **immortality** from being forever tainted. Vasuki was punished by being made to support the entire weight of the Earth on his many heads. Whenever he stirs, he causes an **earthquake**.

VASUS
India

Vasus ('good ones'), in Hindu myth, were eight minor deities who bustled about the universe doing good. Their names were Anala ('fire'), Anila ('air'), Apa ('water'), Dhara ('contemplation'), Dhruva ('sacrificial ladle'), Prabhasa ('radiance'), Pratyusa ('holder of the sacrificial dish') and **Soma**. They had no special functions, but listened to prayers and did their best to help them come true. In one account they took pieces of the **Sun** and moulded them into a golden horse which pulled **Indra's** storm-chariot; in another, unable to get hold of the Sun, they made themselves into a team of horses instead and presented themselves to Indra.

VAYU
Asia (West); India

Vayu in Iranian myth. Vayu ('breath') was originally one of the grandest of Iranian gods. He ruled – and indeed was – the middle air, and was equal in rank to **Ahura Mazda** and **Ahriman**. But when Ahura Mazda became supreme ruler of the universe, Vayu was demoted to being wind-lord and god of storms. -

Vayu in Vedic Indian myth. Vayu came to India from Iran with the Aryan invasions of the seventeenth century BCE. With **Agni**, god of **fire**, and **Surya** the **Sun**-god, he formed a triad which ruled the universe. But new gods came into being, there was a power-struggle, and Vayu once again lost status, taking the position of charioteer to **Indra** god of storms. He was barred from the sky-palace on the summit of Mount **Meru**, and lived in its foothills among the **Gandharvas**. He made war on the sky-citadel, trying to blow down its defences. But **Garuda**, king of the birds, protected it with outspread wings, and it was a year before Vayu was able to rip off the mountain-tip and hurl it into the sea. It became the island of Sri Lanka, home of Vayu's son the monkey-god **Hanuman**.

Vayu in Hindu myth. In later myth, Vayu lost even more status. In some accounts he remained an uncontrolled buccaneer among the gods, blustering round the sky, fathering illegitimate offspring and attacking anything in his path. In others he was a servant of **Vishnu** and **Lakshmi**, sometimes raging but often gentle and balmy, breathing perfumes across the world. In his most undignified manifestation of all, he is wind trapped in the human gut, and we fart him out.

VE
Europe (North)

Ve and his brothers **Odin** and **Vili**, in Nordic myth, were sons of **Bor**, father of the gods. They fought the frost-**giants** and then dismembered **Ymir** to create the universe. After this Odin went on to rule the gods, and Ve and Vili retired from myth.

»→ creation

VECHERNYAYA ZVEZDA AND ZVEZDA DENNITSA
Europe (East)

Vechernyaya Zvezda ('evening star') and Zvezda Dennitsa ('morning star'), in Slavic myth, were the daughters of **Dahzbog** the **Sun**, and in some myths one or the other, or both, married **Meness** the **Moon**. They supervised the Sun's chariot-horses, keeping them overnight in the Moon's stables and harnessing them for their father each morning.

VENUS: *see Aphrodite*

VERTUMNUS: *see Pomona and Vertumnus*

VESTA
Europe (South)

Vesta ('hearth'), in Roman myth, was one of the four **Hesperides** who tended the Golden Apples of **Immortality**. She also tended immortality in the form of fire, in a wheel of **fire** or in an undying flame constantly tended in an open hearth. The Romans thought that the immortality of their state depended on such an eternally-burning fire, built a temple to her in Rome and founded a sisterhood of high-born priestesses, the Vestal Virgins, to tend it.

Vesta is identified with the Greek goddess Hestia, though parts of her story (for example her parentage) are quite different.

VIBISHANA
India

Vibishana ('terrifying'), in Hindu myth, was the good brother of the **demons Ravana** and **Kumbhakarna**. He won **Brahma**'s favour with sacrifice, then asked him to ensure that he (Vibishana) never did 'anything unworthy'. He tried to persuade Ravana not to kidnap **Rama**'s wife **Sita**, and when Ravana refused, he soared across the sea from Sri Lanka and joined Rama's army. After Rama killed Ravana, the gods rewarded Vibishana by making him king of Sri Lanka and granting him **immortality**.

VICTORIA: *see Nike*

VIDAR
Europe (North)

Vidar, in Nordic myth, was the son of **Odin** and the metal-working sorceress **Grid**. His mother equipped him with iron weapons made invincible by magic, including an enormous shoe with which he could trample any created thing to death. Armed with these, Vidar will kill the wolf Fenrir at **Ragnarök**. He will be one of the few survivors of the end of this cycle of the universe, and one of the rulers of the next.

VILI
Europe (North)

Vili and his brothers **Odin** and **Ve**, in Nordic myth, were sons of **Bor**, father of the gods. They fought the frost-**giants** and then dismembered **Ymir** to create the universe. After this Odin went on to rule the gods, and Vili and Ve retired from myth.
≫→ **creation**

VINATA
India

Vinata, in Hindu myth, was the second wife of **Kasyapa**. Kasyapa's senior wife was the **snake**-queen **Kadru**, and Vinata was jealous. Kasyapa, a powerful sage, offered each of them as many children as they wanted, and when Kadru asked for a thousand, Vinata asked for two sons only, but specified that they should outrank all of Kadru's children. In due course the children were born: a thousand snakes to Kadru, and to Vinata the **Sun**-charioteer **Varuna** and the eagle-king **Garuda**.

Kadru, furious, used her serpent's cunning to hypnotize Vinata, and persuaded her to agree to become her slave. She made Vinata's existence a misery, and refused to set her free unless one of her children stole some **amrita**, **immortality**, from **Heaven**. With enormous difficulty, Garuda did this, and Kadru drank it and freed

Vinata. At once Vinata's children declared war on all Kadru's descendants, and eagles and the Sun have been enemies of snakes from that day on.

VIRACOCHA
Americas (South)

Viracocha ('lake of creation'), in the myths of the pre-Inca peoples of Peru and then in Inca myth, was the god of the **Sun**, storms and **creation**. His other names included Illa ('light') and Tici ('birth'). He rose from Lake Titicaca at the dawn of the universe, and made the Earth, Sky, **Sun**, **Moon** and stars. He peopled the Earth with creatures, and then set about making human beings by breathing life into stones. The first people were brainless giants, and he swept them away in a **flood** and made a second human race, this time from pebbles. He scattered them all over the Earth. Ever afterwards, to give them knowledge and goodness above that of wild beasts, he regularly disguised himself as a beggar and wandered the world to teach and work miracles. Because so many of his humans refused to listen to this teaching, preferring crime and war, Viracocha always returned from these trips in tears – and if we ever become all-wicked, those tears will turn into a second flood and drown us as the giants were drowned.

*In another account, Viracocha was one of three sons of **Inti** the sun god, and brother of **Manco Capac** and **Pachacamac**. In others, he and his brothers were not separate entities at all, but three different aspects of the sun-god. At the height of Inca*

650

civilization, at his temple in the heart of Cuzco, he was worshipped in a huge, gold-covered statue of a king in splendour, crowned with the Sun, carrying thunder-bolt-spears and weeping rivers of golden tears. After the Spanish conquest many surviving Incas believed that he put on his beggar's disguise and disappeared into the West, walking over the sea as if it were dry land – and that he will come back one day, either to redeem the human race or drown us.

»→ civilization, Deucalion and Pyrrha

VIRAJ
India

Viraj ('femaleness'), in one **creation-myth** of the Aryans who invaded India in the seventeenth century BCE, was the second being in the universe. She came into being when **Purusha**, the first being, divided himself in two, and she then mated with him to produce everything in existence.

VISHNU
India

Vishnu in Vedic myth. Vishnu ('all-pervader' or 'many-shaped'), in the myths of the Aryan people who invaded India in the seventeenth century BCE, was the power of light, the first force in the universe. His beams danced in the ripples of the primordial ocean, or he rested on the surface, floating on the thousand-headed cosmic **snake** Shesha, until **Brahma** was born from a lotus which grew in his navel. His names included Ananta ('infinite'), Kesava ('hairy', because light-beams streamed from his head like hair) and Mukunda ('liberator'). When gods and **demons** argued about who should rule the universe, Vishnu changed into a dwarf and proposed that the gods should rule as much territory as he could cover in three strides, and the demons should take the rest. When the demons agreed, he took three steps which covered, in turn, Earth, Middle Air and **Heaven**.

Vishnu in Hindu myth. In Hindu myth, Vishnu is one of a triad of gods who oversee and maintain **justice and universal order**. He is the preserver, the force which radiates from a still centre; **Shiva** is the destroyer, the force which sucks everything inwards like a whirlpool; Brahma is the equilibrium between them. As Preserver, Vishnu personifies sacrifice. His existence, and the continuance of ritual offerings for which he stands, guarantee universal stability. He and his wife **Lakshmi** live in a Heaven, Vaikuntha, made entirely of gold and jewels, and with a garden centred on five lotus-filled, world-spanning pools; they sit enthroned on white lotuses, while the Ganges flows from Vishnu's right foot.

Vishnu's avatars. Vishnu's concern for creation leads him to leave Vaikuntha at moments of extreme tension in the universe, when the equilibrium between light and dark seems about to tip towards dark. On each of these occasions he makes a descent (*avatar*) into the world, taking the form either of a hero or a creature or object filled with his own power and radiance. There have been innumerable such avatars, too many even for gods to count. But ten are of particular significance for mortals. In order, they are: **Matsya** the fish, **Kurma** the tortoise, **Varaha** the boar, **Narasimha** the man-lion, **Vamana** the dwarf, **Parashurama** the axe-wielder, **Rama**, **Krishna**, the **Buddha** and **Kalki** the destroyer. (The last is still to come.)

Vishnu is a favourite subject for paintings and sculptures of all kinds. He is often shown asleep on Shesha, in the peace before **creation**, *or sitting enthroned on a white lotus, his head haloed with Sun-radiance and his four hands holding sacred objects: a conch-shell (symbolizing the origin of existence), a wheel (symbolizing the Universal Mind and the cycle from creation to destruction), a club (symbolizing power, both physical and intellectual) and a lotus (symbolizing purity). Sometimes his wife Lakshmi is beside him, in earlier art one quarter his size, in later art of equal stature. Other favourite subjects are panels or discs showing Vishnu and his avatars, or Vishnu (sometimes with Lakshmi) riding* **Garuda**, *king of birds and with his outrider* **Hanuman** *the monkey-king. In most such pictures he is a smiling prince, with blue skin and robes of golden yellow.*

≫→ **light and dark, supreme deity**

VISHVAKARMAN
India

Vishvakarman or Visvakarma ('all-creator'), in the earliest Vedic myths of the Aryans who invaded India in the seventeenth century BCE, created the universe and everything in it. He was a totality, all things in one, and made the world by dismembering himself and scattering the pieces. By the time of the Aryan invasions, this myth had been superseded by those of **Brahma**, the universal principle, and **Tvashtri**, in whom all seeds or embryos resided.

In later, Hindu, myth, Vishvakarman was reduced in status to the architect of the gods. His daughter Sanjna married the Sun-god **Surya**, and Vishvakarman turned the Sun on his lathe to reduce his dazzle, forging the shavings into weapons for the gods. (In earlier myth this feat was attributed to Tvashtri.) He built chariots and palaces for the gods, and also constructed a bridge across the sea to Lanka, which was ruled by his son Nala. The Lankans gave Nala the credit for this, calling the bridge Nala's Bridge and claiming that he had the power to make stones float on water.

≫→ **crafts; creation; smiths**

VISHVAMITRA
India

Vishvamitra, in Hindu myth, was one of the **Seven Seers**. He was born a mortal king, but prayed and sacrificed so diligently that he persuaded **Brahma** to grant him magical powers. Five of the other Seers welcomed him to their number, but the sixth, **Vashishtra**, refused and the two became enemies. The *Mahabharata*, parts of which Vishvamitra is said to have written, tells of the Seers' battles on behalf of gods and mortal **heroes** against the **demons** – but it also, endearingly, keeps breaking off to tell anecdotes of the feud between Vashishtra and Vishvamitra – who on one typical occasion fed his rival's hundred sons to a hungry demon, so causing them to lose caste for 700 future births.

VIVASVAT
India

Vivasvat ('dazzle'), in the Vedic myths of the Aryans who invaded India in the seventeenth century BCE, was god of the rising **Sun**, father of the healing-**twins** the **Ashvins** and of **Yama** and Yami, the first human beings. Despite such splendour, he features in myth as one of **Heaven**'s unfortunates. Under his original name, Marttanda ('born from an unfertilized egg'), he was the eighth son of **Aditi**. He was born as a lump of shapeless matter, and his horrified mother threw him out of Heaven. **Tvashtri**, smith of the gods, rescued him and moulded him into a god (throwing away unwanted scraps which fell to Earth and were regenerated as elephants). The gods honoured Marttanda's new identity by giving him a new name, Vivasvat, and the job of a Sun-god, and marrying him to Tvashtri's daughter **Saranyu**. But the bride disappeared just after the wedding-feast, and Tvashtri hastily created an exact double, who went on to be the mother of Vivasvat's children. In later myth, Vivasvat surrendered his status as Sun-god to his brother **Surya**, and became his charioteer.

VODYANOI
Europe (East)

The Vodyanoi (from *voda*, 'water'), or Vodnik, in Slavic myth, were **water-spirits** and **shape-changers**. They appeared sometimes as beautiful girls, sometimes as floating logs, sometimes as themselves – green-skinned, weed-slimed and covered with bumps and warts. They prowled lake-sides and river-banks at nights, particularly favouring mill-races, and dragged unwary humans underwater to be their slaves.

VOLKH
Europe (East)

Volkh, in Slavic myth, was a **shape-changer**, one of the *bogatiri*. He used his powers in a huge battle to save the churches of Kiev from invading infidels led by the Tsar of India. His name hedges its bets between paganism and Christianity: it means both 'priest' and 'sorcerer'.

≫→ heroes

VOLUND
Europe (North)

Volund (or Wieland or Wayland), in Nordic and Celtic myth, was a blacksmith-god, expert at forging weapons. (In some accounts, he made King **Arthur**'s **Excalibur**.) He was bent and lame, and the reason was that after living with the three daughters of the mortal king Nidud on a remote island for seven years, Nidud punished him by stealing his immortal weapons, hamstringing him and marooning him. Volund retaliated by turning the daughters into swans, killing their brothers (and sending their skulls to Nidud as fantastically bejewelled and gold-embossed drinking-goblets), and then soaring into **Heaven** on wings he had made himself. Ever afterwards the gods made him a laughing-stock for what he had let a mortal do to him.

In Denmark and England especially, Volund/Wayland was regarded not so much as a god to be feared as a kindly, supernatural uncle who supervised the growing of crops, the building of houses and men's and women's **fertility**. He was said to have built all stone circles, barrows and other prehistoric remains, and to have carved, for fun, all the giants, horses and other figures in the chalk downlands of Southern England.

VRITRA
India

Vritra ('holder-back' or 'choker'), in the Vedic myths of the Aryans who invaded India in the seventeenth century BCE, was a drought-**demon**, a gigantic **snake** which swallowed the clouds and stopped the **rain**, or (in some accounts) lay in coils which entirely filled the space between **Heaven** and Earth, so blocking out the rain. **Indra** killed him, water gushed from his corpse like horses galloping, and **fertility** was restored to Earth.

VULCAN: *see* Hephaestus

VYASA
India

Vyasa, in Hindu myth, was a sage, son of the **apsara** Satyavati and the holy man Parasara. He spent his life meditating in the forest, and never cut his hair, shaved or washed. His mother married King Santanu, and bore two sons who grew up and married but died before they could have children. According to the custom that a dead husband's near male relative could have **sex** with his wives and give them children which would count as his, Vyasa was summoned to bed with his nieces **Ambika** and **Ambalika**. Their horrified reactions to his appearance affected the sons they conceived. Ambika shut her eyes, and her son **Dhritarashtra** was born blind; Ambalika turned pale, and her son **Pandu** was born an albino.

Some myths say that Vyasa went on to compose the **Mahabharata**, the account of the epic war fought for the kingdom of **Bharata** by the **Pandavas** (grandsons of Ambika and Ambalika) and their cousins the **Kauravas** – and that he dictated it to **Ganesh**, who wrote it down using one of his own elephant-tusks as a pen. But this may be simple confusion, since the Sanskrit word Vyasa simply means 'editor' or 'assembler'. Vyasa narrates the Mahabharata, but need not also be one of its characters – unless we take the allusions to his uncouth appearance to be self-mockery.

WAHARI AND BUOKA
Americas (South)

Wahari and his brother Buoka, in the myths of the Piaroa people of Venezuela, shared the sexual favours of a large family of women. One day, the women were swinging on a liana across a ravine in the jungle, and while each one swung, Buoka wrapped the others, one at a time, in his long, **snake**-like penis, drew them down to the ravine floor and mated with them. Instead of exhausting Buoka, the **sex** excited him more and more – and when Wahari came along he wrapped his penis round him and tried to find an orifice to mate with him. Irritated, Wahari chopped Buoka's penis down to normal size – it was so long that he had to cut it into five sections – and Buoka hobbled back to the village and lay in his hammock, bleeding.

The women, who had seen none of this, asked Wahari where Buoka was. 'At home. It's that time of the month,' answered Wahari. The women didn't know what this meant, as periods were then unknown. But they soon found out. One by one, they crept into Buoka's hut and seduced him into making love with them. The blood from his penis entered their vaginas – and from that time onwards, both they and all other women bled every month, and each Piaroa woman spent the first day of her period alone in her hammock in her hut. As for the chopped-off parts of Buoka's penis, they wriggled off into the ravine and hid there, lively as snakes, on the lookout for unwary females to mate with.

WAK
Africa

Wak, the Ethiopian creator-god, made

The death of Beowulf (*N. Vogel, 19th century*)

the sky by propping a bowl upside-down over the flat plate of the Earth, and studding it with stars. In a fit of absent-mindedness, he created the first human being before Earth was finished, and had to bury him in a coffin while he made mountains, seas and forests. (As a result of this incarceration, human beings have ever since spent half of their lives in the spirit-world, asleep, and the other half awake.) When First Man emerged from the coffin, Wak took a drop of his blood and made First Woman. He gave Man and Woman the gift of **sex**, and left them alone for a time to enjoy it – which they did so enthusiastically that thirty children were born. They heard Wak coming back, and, embarrassed at their own fecundity, hid fifteen of their offspring in holes in the ground. Wak blessed the other fifteen, who became ancestors of all the peoples of the world – and from the hidden fifteen he created the ancestors of every wild predator, poisonous **snake** and **demon** ever born.
≫→ **creation**

WAKAN TANKA
Americas (North)

Wakan Tanka ('great mystery'), in the myths of the Dakota people of the US Great Plains, existed alone in the void before existence. He was lonely, and made company for himself by dividing himself into four. He began by gathering his energy into a single enormous force: Inyan (Rock). From this he made Maka (Earth), and mated with her to produce Skan (Sky). Skan then mated with Inyan and Maka to make Wi (the **Sun**). After this, **creation** continued to

grow from Wakan Tanka as leaves, twigs and branches grow on trees. Inyan, Maka, Skan and Wi, the four High Ones, made four Companions to help them create and people the universe: **Moon**, Wind, Falling Star and the **Great Thunderbird**. The four Companions, in turn, made four Related Ones: Whirlwind, Four-Winds, Four-legs and Two-legs. After the four Related Ones came four Godlike Ones: Nagi (spirit of **death**), Nagila (shadow), Niya (breath-of-life) and Sicun (Thought). All sixteen of these beings were aspects of Wakan Tanka, who was in all of them and was composed of all of them – and between them they created and oversaw all that exists.

This is an elaborate version of a common creation-account, in which the Great Spirit, the original principle, makes the universe and everything in it by a process of organic self-division. These systems explain the presence in the world of such things as evil, suffering and death by saying that division was interrupted or diverted by some chance event, or that merging took place between two incompatible beings, such as fire and whirlwind – and the result was a trickster (Spider, in Dakota myth; Coyote, in many other Plains accounts) or a destructive power such as hail. But the point of all the stories is the same: that all creation, everything which exists, is part of a single organic and interdependent whole.

WAKONDA
Americas (North)

Wakonda ('power above'), in the myths of the Sioux people of the US Great Plains, was the supreme authority in

the universe, keeping it in balance and revealing its secrets only to a few favoured shamans. In Dakota myth he was incarnated as the Great Thunderbird who ruled the world of light and led his flocks of **thunderbirds** in endless battles with the **demon** water-snakes of darkness.
»→ supreme **deity**

WAR: see Adad, Aesir, Ares, Athene, Bellona, Cihuacóatl, Durga, Eris, Hachiman, Huitzilopochtli, Ishtar, Jun Di, Kali, Karttikeya, Krishna, Mars, Min, Morrigan, Nike, Ninurta, Ogoun, Ogun, Qi Nu, Rugievit, Sekhmet, Teutatis, Thor, Tyr, Unkulunkulu

WARAMURUNGUNDJU AND WURAKA
Australia

Waramurungundju (or Imberombera, 'mother who made us all') and her consort Wuraka, in the myths of many coastal peoples of Arnhem Land in Northern Australia, walked out of the **sea** in the Dream Time. Waramurungundju was aching with **fertility**, but had no means of making herself pregnant or giving birth. For his part, Wuraka had a penis so long that he carried it in coils round his neck and it bent his back like an old man's. But when they reached the shore, the penis began to uncoil and stiffen. It searched out Waramurungundju's vagina and impregnated her. Instantly she began giving birth, filling land and sea with creatures which Wuraka then named and taught their various languages. When **creation** finished, the two spirits turned and walked back into the sea, never to be seen again.

WATER

From the primordial ocean to the smallest well or pool on Earth, water and its gods and creatures were treated, in most myth-traditions, as entirely separate from the rest of **creation**. Sometimes they were at war with the rest of us, sometimes friendly and life-giving, sometimes aloof. Each river or lake had its own inhabitants (often imagined as **snakes** or hybrids of gods and snakes), and the **sea** was a realm as vast and varied as **Sky** or Earth themselves. Water-snakes in many traditions made the landscape of **Mother Earth**, and clothed her with vegetation; water-creatures were full of generative power, endlessly lustful and hopeful for mates – something which made them particularly dangerous to mortals, since they never understood why we drowned in their embraces or died in their underwater dens. They were also susceptible to flattery – more so than any other supernatural beings – and could be persuaded, with the right offerings and ceremonies, to help human beings instead of harming them.
»→ (Americas): Agwe, Temazcalteci; (China): Gong Gong, Long Wang, Yao; (Egypt): Hapi, Nun and Naunet; (Greece): Achelous, Acheron, Arethusa, Ocean, Scamander; (India): Ganga, Indra, *nagas* and *naginis*, Sarasvati, Varuna; (Mesopotamia): Leviathan, Tiamat; (Rome): Tiber; (Slavic): *Bannik*, Russalki, Vodyanoi; (general): floods, rain

WAYLAND: *see* Volund

WELE
Africa

Wele ('high one'), also known as Isaiwa ('honoured in ritual') and Khakaba ('distributor'), creator-god in the myths of the Abaluia people of Kenya, built himself a house on stilts (**Heaven**), and then created **Sun** and **Moon**. Sun and Moon were originally **twins**, with equal radiance, but they fought and Sun spattered Moon with mud to reduce his brightness. Wele gave Sun the day to rule and Moon the night. He then made stars, clouds, lightning (in the form of a crowing cock), rain (and rainbows to control it), frost, the Earth and finally plants, animals and the first human beings **Mwambu and Sela**, whom he settled in a stilt-house of their own on Earth. All this activity took six days, and on the seventh day Wele rested, beginning a sabbatical from the affairs of Earth which has lasted ever since.
≫→ creation

WEN JANG
Asia (East)

Wen Jang ('god of literature'), in Chinese myth, was the deification of a scholar and administrator of the eighth century CE who disappeared without trace during a battle and was assumed to have been taken into **Heaven**. He was worshipped as a dwarf with a demon's face – perhaps because of his association with **Kui**, the phenomenally ugly god of success in examinations – and supervised everyone involved with literature, especially writers, students and stationers. He gave his secrets generously to honest worshippers, but there

was no hope for cheats trying to winkle them out of his attendants, since one (Tien Long) was deaf and therefore never heard the prayers and the other (Ti Ya) was mute and never answered them.

WEREWOLVES
Europe (East; North)

Werewolves (Vlkodlaks or Vookodlaks, 'wolf-hairs'; the English name comes from the Saxon *wer*, 'man' and *wulf*, 'wolf') were widely feared throughout Northern and Eastern Europe. They were born to human mothers but out of human time, and harked back to an age when shape-changing animals (in this case, wolves) roamed the world. Werewolf-children were particularly hairy at birth, or had extra cauls of skin on their heads. They sometimes had wolf-claws and fangs, biting their mothers as they suckled. Often, they were often **twins** (as in the cases of such mythic pairs as **Romulus and Remus**), and in human form, at least, they were sexually as attractive to women as they were voracious. They were associated with the **Moon** (in ancient myth, the Moon-goddess' hunting dogs were often humans miraculously turned into wolves), and changed into wolves each full Moon. Some were invulnerable to mortal weapons; others could be hurt by silver arrows (or later, silver bullets); others again could be wounded in the ordinary way, but slunk to their human homes and resumed their human shapes to die – after which their immortal selves were reborn to another human mother.

Although belief in werewolves is recorded as far back as the first millennium BCE, and in all Northern regions of the world including Canada and the Siberian Arctic, their greatest upsurge was in late medieval and Renaissance Europe. Here, they were ranked with witches and de-mons, emissaries of Satan, and anyone suspected of lycanthropy – all werewolves were male, and the signs were hairiness, the port-wine birthmark known as the 'mark of Cain', stubby fingers with sharp nails, threatening sexuality and in extreme cases cannibalism – was persecuted. In France alone between 1520 and 1630, over 30,000 suspected werewolves (all in human form) are known to have been executed. The werewolf, or 'Big Bad Wolf', of fairy-tale has been their enduring legacy, though they had a resurgence in the 1920s, in adult horror stories such as those of E.W. Hornung, and in Hollywood.

Fearsome human-animal hybrids were common in other cultures. Those which shared all the characteristics of werewolves include werebears (North America), wereboars (Greece – the Ery-manthian Boar is now best-known), were-crocodiles (Africa and Australia), werepanthers (South America), weres-nakes (China) and weretigers (India).
»+ monsters and dragons

WHEEMEMEOWAH
Americas

Wheememeowah ('great high chief'), in the myths of the Yakima people of the US Plateau region, lived alone in the Sky at the start of **creation**. Nothing existed but him, Sky and the primordial ocean. Bored, he went down to the shallowest part of the ocean and began playing in the mud. He tossed it up in handfuls – and it stuck to Sky or floated, making continents and islands. He shaped the surface, moulding river-beds and mountains. Finally, he breathed life into mud-droplets to make plants, animals and our ancestors, First Man and First Woman.

A somewhat preachy pendant to this myth, added after the European conquest, says that human beings were no sooner made than they began to quarrel, and the time will come when Wheememeo-wah grows tired of them and returns them to primordial mud. He has sent floods and earthquakes as warnings, and we have taken no notice. Already the spirits are leaving the world, and unless we change our ways and woo them back, our destruction is assured.

WHITE SHE-BUFFALO
Americas (North)

White She-Buffalo (also known as White Buffalo Calf-Woman), in the myths of the Lakota people of the US plains, taught the people how to plant and farm corn. Hunters on the plain one day saw a beautiful stranger, and went closer, hoping that she would agree to **sex**. But she told them that she was not their plaything; they should go home and prepare to welcome her as a queen deserved. They hurried to build a lodge for her in the village – and when it was ready she appeared. She gave them a ceremonial tobacco-pipe, and a package which she said contained four drops of her milk. The drops, if planted, would grow into corn-stalks, and feed the people. (Corn grains are milky to this day.) She went on to teach them **mysteries**: the winds' secrets and seven life-prolonging rituals. These were all associated with the pipe, her first gift to them. When she'd finished her teaching she changed into a buffalo and disappeared.

»→ **farming**

WIDJINGARA
Australia

Widjingara, in the myths of the Worora people of the Kimberleys in Northern Australia, was the first human being ever to die. In the Dream Time, he protected a woman against the **Wondjina**, who retaliated by killing him. His wife wrapped his body in bark, shaved her head, smeared her face with ashes and mourned for him. This was the first time anyone on Earth had ever mourned, and when Widjingara came back from the Dead after three days (as custom was) he was so angry at his wife's changed appearance that he went straight back again – and **death** and mourning have ever since been part of the human condition.

WIND: *see* Aeolus, Boreas, Dajoji, Ehecatl, Enki, Fei Lian, Futen, Ga-oh, Gucumatz, Hraesvelg, Hurukan, Ilma, Kukulkan, Michabo, Quetzalcóatl, Stribog, Varpulis, Vayu, Zephyrus

WISDOM: *see* Agastya, Athene, Atri, Bhagiratha, Bhisma, Brighu, Chiron, Chyavana, Drona, mysteries, Prometheus, prophecy, Rishis, Thoth, Vashishtra, Vishvamitra, Vyasa, writing

WISHPOOSH
Americas (North)

Wishpoosh, in the myths of the Nez Perce people of the Northwestern US, was a monstrous beaver which ruled the primeval lake and refused access to any other creatures. **Coyote** the **trickster** went to the lakeside to fish, and Wishpoosh attacked him. They fought, and as they rolled and wrestled among the mountains they gouged out canyons and river-gorges. Wishpoosh swam into the sea and began gulping down whales to give himself strength. Coyote turned into a fir-branch and floated, resting – until Wishpoosh realized who he was and swallowed him. Inside the monster, Coyote swam up Wishpoosh's veins and arteries and stabbed his heart. He floated the huge carcass to shore, hacked it to pieces, and used the fragments to make the first human beings.

»→ **animal-gods**

WONDJINA, THE
Australia

The Wondjina, in the myths of the Worora and Ungarinjin people of the Kimberleys in Northwestern Australia, were **rain**-spirits of the Dream Time who helped to shape the world and everything in it. They were **shape-changers**, taking the forms of giant owls, pigeons and hawks, or of humans. They were so disgusted with the lawlessness and lust of the first human beings that they opened their mouths and vomited huge **floods** which drowned them all. The Wondjina then remade the human race and taught them civilized behaviour. They used to fly round their creation, enjoying its praise, or bask on the rocks in human shape. They kept their mouths shut to prevent any further floods, and in due course the mouths disappeared altogether. (Fortunately the Wondjina, like all supernatural creatures, had no need to eat or drink.) When in due course the Wondjina abandoned visible shape, their spirits went to live in water-holes and creeks and the image of their bodies remained as paintings on the rocks where they used to sunbathe. Every year those paintings were refurbished at the end of the dry season, and the Wondjina responded by sending rain.

≫→ animal-gods, civilization, creation

WONOMI
Americas (North)

Wonomi ('no **death**'), in the myths of the Southwestern and Western US, created the universe and everything in it, and gave them their names. He ruled serenely and peacefully until **Coyote** the **trickster** came and started renaming everything. Giving new identities brought Coyote all-power, and he even persuaded human beings to give up their **immortality** for the pleasures of the world. From then on, Coyote ruled our mortal bodies on Earth, but Wonomi took our souls to his sky-kingdom after death, restored their immortality and ruled them.

≫→ creation

WOODEN HORSE, THE
Europe (South)

The Wooden Horse, in Greek myth, was a trick devised by **Athene** to get Greeks inside the walls of Troy and end the **Trojan War**. She told the trick to **Odysseus**, and he proposed it to a council of the Greek commanders. They should build a huge pinewood horse, with a hollow belly large enough to hide twenty-four armed men, and trick the Trojans into dragging it into the city. Then, at night, the men inside should open the city gates and let in the rest of the army.

To build the Horse, the Greeks chose Epeus the shipwright. He was as cowardly as he was skilful, and agreed to build the Horse only if no one made him ride in it. He made it of pineplanks, pegged like ship's timbers; it rode on solid wooden wheels, and on its side he carved 'Offered to Athene, to grant the Greeks safe voyage home'. In one flank he made a trapdoor, carefully concealed – and he was so carried away with his own craftsmanship that he made a fastening which no one but himself could work. Unfortunately for him, this meant that the Greeks had to take him with them after all, and he sat, whimpering, with the twenty-three **heroes** in the Horse's belly while the next part of the trick was played.

As soon as the heroes were in place and the trapdoor was shut, the rest of the Greeks made a bonfire of all their tents, animal-pens and the other paraphernalia of a ten-year siege, and, taking nothing but their weapons, launched their ships and sailed away – not to Greece, as the Trojans immediately assumed, but to the far side of the island of Tenedos, out of sight of Troy. There was nothing left on the plain but the smouldering bonfire, scattered debris, and the Wooden Horse pregnant with armed men.

Convinced that the Greeks had gone, the Trojans poured out of the city to inspect the Horse. The Trojan leaders immediately began arguing about what to do with it. **Priam** and his warrior-sons thought it harmless, and wanted to drag it into the city and offer it to Athene to whom it was dedicated. Others, including Priam's prophet-children, said that if it entered the city Troy would fall, and wanted to drag it down to the shore and burn it in honour of **Poseidon**. Priam's son **Laocoön** led this second group, and nearly convinced the Trojans, hurling a spear which jarred into the Horse (its point narrowly missed **Neoptolemus'** head, inside) and made the hollow belly boom and roar. But the gods sent a portent – sea-serpents which ate Laocoön and his sons alive – and the Greek **trickster** Sinon, who had been hiding for this very purpose in the marshes, persuaded the Trojans that if the Horse were dragged into Athene's temple, the Greeks would never get home alive.

Convinced, the Trojans knocked down part of the city walls and dragged the Horse into Troy. As they did so, **Cassandra** ran wildly round them, screaming that the Horse was full of armed men and would eat the city – and, as always, no one believed her. The gods put it into **Helen's** mind to walk round the Horse with her young husband **Deiphobus**, telling him about each of the great Greek heroes (the ones inside the Horse) and their wives, imitating their voices and the way they talked. Several of the heroes inside the Horse thought that their wives were actually there, and groaned and sweated to think that they were prisoners in

Troy. One man, Antielus, was even about to call out when Odysseus grabbed him by the throat to silence him (some say so fiercely that he broke his neck).

The Trojans placed the Horse in the courtyard of Athene's temple, decorated it with flowers, and spent the day in an orgy of celebration for the end of the war. That night, no guards were posted – there was no need, now that the war was done – and while the Trojans slept, Epeus opened the secret trapdoor and let his companions down on ropes. They took possession of the gates and guard-posts, Helen lit a beacon to summon back the Greeks waiting at Tenedos, and the Trojans awoke to find their city swarming with armed men.

WOTAN: *see* Odin

WOYENGI
Africa

Woyengi the creator, in the myths of the Ijaw people of Nigeria, stepped down from **Heaven** to Earth in a lightning-storm. Nothing existed there except a chair, a table and a flat creation-stone. Woyengi scooped up handfuls of mud and put them on the table. Then she sat on the chair, rested her feet on the creation-stone, and shaped the mud into dolls. As she finished each one she picked it up, gently opened its eyes, gave it the breath of life. She asked them, 'What would you like to be, man or woman' – and gave them sexual organs according to their answers.

When all the dolls were finished, and the table-top was covered with them, she told them, 'Your first gift was life and your second was gender. Now choose a profession to keep throughout your lives.' The dolls made a thousand choices, everything from baker to warrior, from farmer to poet, and when they'd finished Woyengi gathered them in handfuls and put them on the ground. There were two streams leading to the horizon, and she said, 'One leads to luxury, the other to ordinariness. You've chosen the life you want to lead; now let the correct stream carry you to where you chose to be.' The people who'd chosen high-ranking lives stepped into the first stream, and found it fast-flowing and full of rapids. The people who'd chosen the second stream found it clean and clear but shallow. Each group shouted its discoveries back to those still on the bank, and some drew back and asked Woyengi if they could change their minds. But she refused: they'd made their choices, and those choices were irrevocable. So the dolls all waded into the water, and the streams carried them away, irrigating the world with the human race.

>>+ Chinigchinich, creation, Enki, Esaugetuh Emissee, Humanmaker, Hurukan, Na'pi, Prometheus, Tagaro

WRITING: *see* Bragi, Fu Xi, Ganesh, Guan Di, Nabu, Ogmios, Sarasvati, Seshat, Thoth, Wen Jang

WURAKA: *see* Waramurungundju and Wuraka

WYRD
Europe (North)

Wyrd ('fate'), in Nordic myth, was in some accounts mother of the three **Norns**. In others, she was the same person as the Norn Urd, and in others again she was all three Norns, merged into an unknowable, unconquerable, trinity-in-unity.

One of the best-known literary appearances of Wyrd is as the 'three weird sisters', the Witches in Shakespeare's Macbeth who tell him his destiny.

XI HE AND HENG XI
Asia (East)

Xi He and Heng Xi, in Chinese myth, were the wives of **Di Jun**, Emperor of the Eastern sky. Each bore him ten children. Xi He's children, born in the morning, were the ten **Suns**, and she bathed them before dawn each day in a pool at the foot of the 150km-high mulberry tree in the far East of the universe, before taking one of them in turn each day in her chariot to ride the sky. Heng Xi's children, born in the evening, were the ten **Moons**, and she bathed them each evening in a pool at the foot of the *ruo* tree in the far West of the universe, before taking one of them in turn in her chariot to ride the sky each night.

In some accounts, Heng Xi is identified with the moon-goddess **Heng O**.

XIPETOTEC
Americas (Central)

Xipetotec ('flayed lord'), in Aztec myth, was the god of spring **fertility**. When human beings were starving, he skinned himself alive to show how the seed bursts from the bud.

*Scholars think that the Xipetotec spring ritual, which involved shooting victims with arrows, letting their blood drip into the ground like **rain**, then skinning them, began as simple re-enactment of the myth, designed to coax fertility back to the soil. (The victims, had anyone ever bothered to ask them, might have said that their suffering was a form of exaltation, a means of escape from the agony of this world into the peace of **Mictlan**.) Later, however, the cult developed a dark psychological rationale: that no blessing came without suffering, and therefore the greater the suffering,*

Thor (*17th-century engraving*)

the more the blessing. Xipetotec's devotees wore the flayed skins of his victims to give themselves strength in battle, or to cure the huge range of skin ailments, from warts to leprosy, from smallpox to plague, which he was thought to send mortals who offended him. He was also the patron god of goldsmiths – some scholars say because he was originally a **Sun**-god, others (with, one hopes, more imagination than experience) because of the golden-yellow colour of freshly-flayed skin.

⫸ civilization, crafts, disease and healing

XIUTECUHTLI
Americas (Central)

Xiutecuhtli ('**fire**-lord'), or Huehuetéotl ('old god'), in Aztec myth, was the fire-god who sustained the entire universe. His origin was in a hearth in **Mictlan**, the spirit-world, and he soared up from there in a pillar of flame which passed through Earth and **Heaven**, keeping them permanently in place. If ever he died, the entire universe would collapse in ruins. He was also the guide of souls between one plane of existence and another: when sacrificial victims were cremated, he took them from this world to their final homes.

The Aztec cycle of time renewed itself every fifty-four years, and people believed that it was essential, at each turn of this all-but 'century', to renew the compact between gods and mortals. Xiutecuhtli was the centre of this ritual. Every fire in the kingdom was put out, his priests ceremonially lit new fire and distributed it to the people, and the world was safe again.

XOCHIPILI
Americas (Central)

Xochipili ('flower lord'), in Aztec myth, was the god of flowers, **music** and dancing, the male equivalent of **Xochiquetzal**. In particular, he guarded the humming-bird souls of dead warriors. He was spirit personified, and was shown in portraits as red and skinless – his flayed condition symbolizing his indifference to things of the flesh.

One of the oldest of all Aztec gods, Xochipili was later – and somewhat surprisingly – subsumed into the cult of the war-god **Huitzilopochtli**.

⫸ farming

XOCHIQUETZAL
Americas (Central)

Xochiquetzal ('flower feather'), in Aztec myth, was the goddess of flowers, fruit and **music**, the female equivalent of **Xochipili**. Just as he represented pure spirit, so she represented pure body, and was shown as a buxom, beautiful and serene young woman, mother of all. She was, however, also a war-goddess, and ruled a paradise reserved for soldiers dead in battle and women who died giving birth to boys (that is, sacrificed their own lives to provide future warriors).

⫸ beauty, farming, Idun

XÓLOTL
Americas (Central)

Xólotl ('animal'), in Aztec myth, was a deformed dog: his face pointed forwards but his feet ran backwards. He

667

was the Evening Star, and every night he snatched the **Sun** and dragged it to the world of darkness. In some accounts, he created the human race by bringing our ancestors up from the spirit-world and giving them **fire**. But his contradictory nature (symbolized by his shape) meant that he hated his own **creation**, and spent his life bringing us bad luck. Praying to him was problematical, since the way he heard and reacted to each prayer depended on which way his ears were pointing – and until the prayer was finished and its effects were known, who knew?

⫸→ **animal-gods**

YACATECUHTLI
Americas (Central)

Yacatecuhtli ('lord nose'), in Aztec myth, was the god of merchants. His power resided in a bundle of twigs which he carried everywhere, and this was also the symbol of the secret society of his worshippers. He was the hub of a mystery-cult, a mercantile freemasonry about whose practices and influence no information – including the reason for Yacatecuhtli's name – now survives.
≫→ **mysteries**

YAHWEH
Asia (West)

Yahweh, in Judaic belief, is the secret name of God, represented by the four letters YHVH and spoken only by the High Priest once a year in the Holy of Holies in the Temple at Jerusalem. Some scholars associate the name with an ancient volcano-god (Jahu), others with the Hebrew verb to be (so that it means 'Is'). It appears in short form as Yah (for example in the phrase Hallelujah, 'Praise be to Yah'), and its non-Hebrew, perverted form Jehovah led some medieval churchmen to link it, quite wrongly, with Jove (that is **Jupiter** or **Zeus**).

Yahweh, as he survives, belongs entirely to the religions of Judaism and Christianity, and has no place in myth. But the Bible offers glimpses of possible mythic derivations or parallels. He is creative energy; he is protective of his **immortality** and refuses to share it with mortals. He is light, enemy of darkness. He sends a **flood** to wipe human evil from the world. As ultimate arbiter of good and evil, he will judge the universe at the end of time.
≫→ **supreme deity**

Faust tormented with doubts (*19th-century engraving*)

YAKSHAS: see Rakshasas and Yakshas

YALUNGUR
Australia

Yalungur ('eagle-hawk'), in the myths of the Wumunkan people of Cape York Peninsula in North Eastern Australia, was one of the supernatural beings who made the world during the Dream Time. His particular distinction was that he originated the female sex and **childbirth**. Another being, Gidja, lusted after him. To make intercourse easier, Gidja cut off Yalungur's penis, and to make Yalungur pregnant he made a wooden doll and stuffed it inside the wound. Yalungur quickened the doll to life and expelled it from the wound – and so the vagina, and childbirth, were created. As for Gidja, the other Dream Time beings were so disgusted with his behaviour that they tried to kill him; he escaped into the sky and became the **Moon**.

YAMA
India

Yama ('restrainer'), in the Vedic myths of the Aryans who invaded India in the seventeenth century BCE, was the son of **Vivasvat** and **Saranyu**. His **twin**, their daughter, was Yami, and she and Yama were the first beings in the world to experience mortality. When Yama died, he was granted dominion over the **Underworld**, made judge of the Dead and given the task of snatching the souls of the dead from their bodies and dragging them to the Underworld.

Yama is often shown as a black buffalo, or as a crowned king riding a black buffalo. He carries a noose to gather human souls, and a mace to subdue any who resist.

YAMASACHI
Asia (East)

Yamasachi, or Hikohohodemi, son of **Ninigi** and Konohana in Japanese myth, was a hunter-god who used magic arrows to kill his prey. His brother, the fisherman Umisachi, or Hosuseri, used a magic hook. Curious to see what fishing was like, Yamasachi asked Umisachi to exchange weapons – and as soon as he tried fishing, he lost his brother's hook. He offered him a thousand more, made from his own sword, but Umisachi refused. Yamasachi went to ask the sea god Owatatsumi for advice, and the hook was found at last in an enormous fish. But during the three mortal years it took to find it, Yamasachi fell in love with Owatatsumi's daughter Toyotama, and when he returned to land he took her with him. She said that she was pregnant, that she would have to return to her original form to bear her child, and that Yamasachi was not to watch. As he had done earlier, when he wanted to try his brother's fishing magic, he let curiosity overrule common sense, and was horrified to see Toyotama change into a monstrous crocodile to bear her child. He shouted in alarm, and she was so embarrassed that she slithered back into the sea and disappeared. Yamasachi brought up the boy, half god, half **sea-monster**, and when the young man was old enough he married

Tamayori, his mother's sister. The eldest of their four children was Jimmu, founder of the Japanese Imperial dynasty.

≫→ archers

YAMBE-AKKA
Europe (North)

Yambe-akka ('old woman of the dead'), in Lapp myth, was the goddess of the **Underworld**. Her kingdom was a vast ice-realm under the mortal world, and its entrances were where rivers flowed into the frozen Arctic Ocean. In some accounts Yambe-akka supported the mortal world on her own upheld hands, and **earthquakes** happened when old age made her arms tremble.

YANAULUHA
Americas (North)

Yanauluha, in the myths of the Zuñi people of the Southwestern US pueblos, led human beings from the darkness of the **Underworld** to the surface of the Earth. They were misshapen creatures, part termite, part snake, part owl, part frog, and he improved their appearance and their skills (by teaching them **farming**, weaving, dancing and the other skills of **civilization**) until they became tall, elegant and confident, replicas of gods.

YAO
Asia (East)

Yao, or Di Yao ('Emperor Yao') or Dao Dung Shi ('lord of Dao and Dung'), was the fourth of the **Five Emperors** under whose rule the world moved from barbarism to **civilization**. When he inherited the throne the Imperial family lived in a grass-roofed hut and fed on porridge, a tradition of austerity begun by Yao's ancestor **Huang Di**, and Yao continued it throughout his long reign of seventy years. His time on the throne was marked by a series of quarrels with storm-gods and **water-monsters**: **Fei Lian** the storm-demon (formerly Huang Di's own son), Ho Po the river-lord and **Gong Gong** spirit of water. Yao employed the famous archer **Yi** to deal with the first two, but was unable to end the **flood** brought by Gong Gong – a job finished long after his reign by **Yu** son of Kun.

Yao ruled for seventy years, and during that time corruption grew so bad that he could trust no one, not even his own sons. Since one of high rank could be trusted to succeed him, Yao searched the kingdom for the most honest and dutiful man he could find. That man was **Shun**, the most upright individual who ever lived, and Yao married him to his daughter, made him his heir and abdicated in his favour, living on in retirement for another dozen years.

The mythical Yao was transformed in later times into the 'first historical Emperor', and his dates were given as 2357-2255 BCE. Archaeologists have discovered enormous drainage-schemes and patterns of irrigation from this period: possibly the origin of the myths of his battles against water-gods. There also survives a text, Edicts of the Emperor Yao, which among other things claims that he set up the first astronomical observatory ever known, and invented the calendar.

YARILO
Europe (East)

Yarilo (derived from *yary*, 'passionate'), or Erilo, god of **sex** in Slavic myth, supervised not only lust in living creatures but also the ground's eagerness to split open and receive seed in spring. He was a handsome youth who rode a white horse. In many areas, Yarilo festivals were held well into modern times: at the spring festival a beautiful girl was crowned with wild flowers as his queen, and after the harvest his straw image was burned during an orgy of eating, drinking and sex, and the ashes were strewn on the fields to ensure next year's crops.
»+ **fertility, Kama, Soido**

YASHODHARA
India

Yashodhara, in Buddhist myth and legend, was the wife of Prince **Siddhartha**, the future **Buddha**. There are two accounts of how he won her. In one, he won a contest against his childhood companion and enemy **Devadatta**, and she was the prize. In another, Siddhartha's father brought 500 princesses together, and Siddhartha gave each of them a jewel – until he reached the last, Yashodhara, and gave her his ring as a sign of betrothal.

Yashodhara lived happily as Siddhartha's wife for years, and bore him a son. But there was no place for her in Siddhartha's new life as Buddha, and when he renounced the world he also bade farewell to his beloved wife and son, slipping out of the palace while they slept. At first, when Yashodhara discovered what had happened, she was heart-broken. But then she shaved her head, entered a monastery, and served her husband with joy and devotion as a nun until the day she died.

YASODA
India

Yasoda, in Hindu myth, was the wife (or queen) of the cowherd (king) **Nanda**. When **Krishna** was in danger from the **demon**-king **Kansa**, he was smuggled out of Kansa's dungeon to Yasoda, who brought him up as her foster-son. Her own newborn baby was smuggled back to the dungeon in Krishna's place (see **Deva**).

YEN LO
Asia (East)

Yen Lo, in Chinese myth, was originally King of the Dead. His kingdom was divided into several smaller courts – some say four, some ten, some fourteen – each with its own ruler and its own allotted area of expertise in punishment. Yen Lo was the supreme judge, against whose decisions there was no appeal. But the other rulers grumbled that he was too lenient, and when he refused to punish Monkey for coming to Hell and stealing the Scroll of Past Judgements (an essential list of precedents), they rebelled against him and reduced his privileges. He retained jurisdiction only over those who in mortal life had been sexually promiscuous, butchers or cruel to animals.
»+ **Underworld**

673

YGGDRASIL
Europe (North)

Yggdrasil ('ash-tree horse of Ygg'), in Nordic myth, was a giant ash-tree, the hub and support of the universe. It got its name when Ygg (**Odin**) hung himself for nine days and nights on it, 'riding' it in order to learn all the secrets of **creation**. Yggdrasil had three roots. The longest grew from the icy well of Hvergelmir in **Niflheim** home of the Dead, where it was perpetually gnawed by **Nidhogg** the dragon, trying to kill it. The second grew from **Midgard**, where it drew nourishment from the Well of **Mimir**, source of all wisdom. The third grew from the well of Urd in Asgard, where the three **Norns** watered it and plastered it with clay to heal the wounds made by Nidhogg far below.

On Yggdrasil's topmost branch sat Vithofnir, the rooster whose crowing was to announce the beginning of **Ragnarök**, the end of this cycle of the universe. An eagle nested in the tree, and spent its days trying to distract Nidhogg the dragon from its task of destroying the tree; the squirrel Ratatosk scurried endlessly up and down Yggdrasil's branches and trunk, carrying insults between the combatants. Every morning, Yggdrasil's trunk exuded dew which four deer licked and changed into golden mead for the warriors feasting in **Valhalla**. Inside the trunk were the seeds of two human beings. They were to lie dormant until Ragnarök, when Yggdrasil would survive and they would grow into ancestors of a new race of mortals, ready to tenant the world and begin the human race anew.

YI
Asia (East)

Yi ('archer'), the Sun-god in Chinese myth, was originally a mortal soldier, a bowman so expert that he was nicknamed Shen Yi ('divine archer'). In some accounts, he visited the palace of Xi Wang Mu, goddess of the air, and she gave him one of the Peaches of **Immortality**. This was stolen from him by Heng-O, sister of the god of the Yellow River, who soared to the **sky** and hid from him in the **Moon**. Yi travelled the Earth looking for her, riding the wind and feeding on flowers; eventually he was carried back to Xi Wang Mu's palace, and her husband Dong Wang Gong, lord of destiny, took pity on him, granted him immortality and gave him the **Sun** (or rather Suns) to rule.

At first, Yi ruled ten separate Suns. But when the Emperor **Yao** chose **Shun** as his successor instead of his own children, the ten Suns were so outraged that they all tried to appear in the sky at the same moment, which would have destroyed the Earth and everything on it. Yi shot dead nine of the birds which lived in the Suns, and himself took up residence in the tenth: the Sun we know today. He forged its light into unerring arrows, and used them to benefit mortals. When the wind-lord **Fei Lian**, disgraced son of **Huang Di**, gusted in terrible storms across the world, Yi told mortals to make an enormous windbreak from cloth anchored with stones, and when the winds bounced off it he rode on their wings to Fei Lian's mountain-top castle, weakened Fei Lian first by shooting a hole in the sack which contained all the winds and then by hamstringing him with a second arrow, and forced him to surrender. When Ho Po, **Heng O's** brother and lord of the Yellow River, rose from his bed in floods and storms, Yi shot him in the knee and sent him limping back to his underwater lair. In some accounts, he then married Ho Po's wife Fufei, goddess of the river Lo; in others, he settled his differences with Heng O and married her.

≫→ archers

YIMA
Asia (West)

Yima, in ancient Iranian myth, was the first human being. To begin with, his reign on Earth was a Golden Age. Humans shared the gods' **immortality** and powers, and drove out **demons**, conquered darkness and ruled the storms. But Yima spoiled it by killing flesh, and offering the meat of sacrifice not only to **Ahura Mazda** but to other gods as well – and Ahura Mazda punished him by removing his and his descendants' **immortality**. To prove how fragile human life had become, he sent Winter to tear the world to pieces – and has renewed it every year since then. Before the first storm, he told Yima to build an underground shelter, store in it the finest male and female examples of each species of animal and plant on Earth, and wait with them until the time came to restock the world and restore the Golden Age. Somewhere, the myth ends, Yima is still waiting; our human time will come.

YMIR
Europe (North)

Ymir ('two-in-one'), in Nordic myth, was the **giant** formed at the beginning of **creation**, when glaciers from the ice-kingdom **Niflheim** spread out across the void and were thawed by flames from the fire-kingdom **Muspell**. As Ymir's name implies, it was neither male nor female but both at once, and had the power to generate life spontaneously. As Ymir slept, it sweated, and giants were born from the sweat: a male and a female from Ymir's left armpit, and another male where Ymir's thighs touched as it slept.

Ymir's offspring began to mate with one another, spawning a race of ice-giants. But in the meantime a rival race had been created from ice: first the cow **Audumla**, then **Buri**, the first human, then **Bor** his son and Bor's sons **Odin**, **Vili** and **Ve**. These last three attacked the sleeping Ymir, and killed it. Ymir's blood was ice-water: it gushed from the giant's wounds in a flood which drowned all the frost-giants but two (**Bergelmir** and his wife), and bubbled and swirled in the void like an icy ocean. Into the middle of this ocean Odin, Vili and Ve carried Ymir's corpse. They broke it up to make the world. Ymir's flesh made earth, its bones made mountains, its teeth made boulders and its hair made trees. Its skull made the heavens, its brains made clouds, and the brothers set sparks from Muspell in them to make **Sun**, **Moon** and stars.

The brothers gathered the ocean of Ymir's blood into a fathomless, boundless **sea**, girding their creation like a belt. They called their creation **Midgard**, ('middle land'): that is, the one between Muspell and Niflheim. They built themselves a huge citadel, Asgard, and fortified it with a hedge made from Ymir's eyebrows. And finally, seeing maggots swarming in the remaining fragments of the earth-giant's corpse, they made them into dwarfs, burying them deep in the caves and crevices of their giant parent.

*Local details notwithstanding, the story of Ymir being dismembered to create the world is almost exactly paralleled in the Indian myth of **Purusha** – so much so that some scholars think that they have a common source.*

➤ Ask and Embla

YO: *see* In and Yo

YOMI
Asia (East)

Yomi (short for Yomitsukumi, 'heart of night' or 'gloom-land'), the **Underworld** in Japanese myth, was originally no more than a mirror-image of the world of light, without inhabitants or character. But when **Izanami**, scorched to death giving birth to the fire-god **Kagutsuchi**, went to hide in Yomi, her body rotted and the maggots formed into **demon**-hordes, which lived on in the Underworld to torment the Dead.

In Japanese Buddhist myth, Yomi was ruled by Emma-O (the Japanese form of **Yama**). He lived in a castle crafted from all the jewels and precious metals found underground, and judged the Dead.

Their souls were fetched by demons in fiery chariots, or transported once a year by ship across the Sea of Darkness. In the darkness of the Underworld, the last embers of their life-force from the world of light above made them glow like fireflies. Emma-O judged the men, and his sister judged the women. The innocent were dispatched to the Upper World in a new incarnation, and the wicked were punished before being allowed to return to life. The punishments, overseen by Emma-O's **demon**-army of eighteen generals and 80,000 green-skinned or red-skinned warriors, ranged from physical torment (for example being boiled in molten metal or used for target-practice by demons) to the psychological agony of loneliness, wandering Yomi's barren plains and tunnels until they had expiated their crimes. These punishments were ordained by **Buddha**, and could not be changed or evaded except by those blessed with the intercession of Kannon (Japanese version of **Guan Yin**), goddess of mercy.

Although Yomi was a land of darkness, artists used their licence to show it as a kind of Imperial palace, whose chambers, corridors and gardens teemed with the Dead. In the central judgement-room, Emma-O sat on his throne, his advisers on stools beside him and his ink-brushes and scrolls on a desk in front of him. The Dead were paraded with planks round their necks on which their crimes were written. Some pleaded their cases before lesser demons before being allowed to make their last appeals to Emma-O; others, less hopeful, surrendered immediately to their demon-tormentors. *Other paintings showed the tunnels, gardens and barren landscapes of Yomi, tenanted by demons and the Dead, and full of every kind of torment: hair-pulling and toenail-pulling for minor offenders, scourging with chains or snakes for middle-rank sinners, and mutilation or boiling for the guiltiest.*

YSEULT: see Tristram and Yseult

YU
Asia (East)

Yu, in Chinese myth, was the son of Lord Kun, the minister of the Emperor **Yao** who had spent nine years ineffectively trying to control **floods** which were devastating China. In some accounts Yu was born directly from his father's corpse, cut open three years after the old man's death – he soared out as a dragon. In others his mother saw a meteor, swallowed a pearl and in due course gave birth to Yu in the normal way.

Kun had been executed on the orders of **Huang Di**, for going to **Heaven** and trying to steal a handful of magic Swelling Earth (Huang Di's own possession) to soak up the floodwaters. In some accounts, Yu, ordered by Emperor **Shun** to finish his father's work, went himself to Heaven, asked Huang Di politely for some Swelling Earth and used it to make mountains and river-channels which controlled the water. In others, Huang Di (or even, in some versions, **Fu Xi**) was so impressed with Yu's good manners that he not only showed him the Nine-fold Plan which controlled the entire universe, but also

taught him how to modify it to reorganize the movement of water over land.

In the third version of Yu's control of the waters, he discovered something that his father had never known: namely, that floods were caused by malicious water-spirits, evil children of the water-god **Gong Gong**, and that the way to end them was to kill the **monsters**, one by one. Using his shape-changing powers, Yu travelled the length and breadth of the world, battling monsters, cutting water-channels, making islands and marshes for Gong Gong's water-creatures and plains, forests and arable land for animals and humans. To fight water-**snakes** he made himself into a dragon. To tunnel through mountains he made himself into a bear, gouging out rock with his forepaws. To climb the peaks he became an eagle. To clear the undergrowth he became a **fire**.

The work of controlling the water took thirteen years, and the continual shape-changing exhausted Yu's mortal body. When he left home to begin the work he was a virile young man, when he came back he was a dotard. After Shun's death he took the throne, but was so worn out that he ruled for only eight years before he died.

Some scholars claim that this myth was invented to explain real water-engineering, huge works from the third millennium BCE, including a 350km canal-and-tunnel system through the Wu Shan **mountains** *which still bears Yu's name. In later times Yu was claimed as a historical figure, founder of the Xia dynasty, and the dates of his reign were given as 2205-2197 BCE. In historical accounts of his reign, he was said to have invented not only* **farming** *and fishing –*

skills attributed to all early Emperors – but also the first-ever systems for distribution and marketing, which in turn necessitated inventing cities. Myth stories credit him with inventions of a more tangible kind, designed to ease his travels round the country subduing monsters: the first wheeled carriage, the first boat and a pair of magic crampons which helped him walk up vertical mountainsides.

»+ civilization, crafts, shape-changers

YUDHISHTHIRA
India

Yudhishthira, in Hindu myth, was the son of the god **Dharma** and the mortal queen **Kunti**, wife of King **Pandu** of **Bharata**. As the eldest of five brothers, he expected in due course to succeed to his father's throne, but was robbed of it by his cousin **Duryodhana**, eldest of the **Kaurava** brothers, who first tried to kill Yudhishthira and his brothers, the **Pandavas**, by burning their palace, then won the kingdom from Yudhishthira by cheating in a game of dice.

The battle for Bharata. A huge war followed. Gods and other powers for good in the universe supported the Pandavas; **demons** and other powers for evil supported the Kauravas. There was heroism on both sides, but there was also deceit – as when Yudhishthira half-lied to persuade the Kaurava commander **Drona** that his beloved son was dead. Accordingly, although the Pandavas won and Yudhishthira was restored to his throne, he felt morally compromised. As the time approached for him to leave the mortal world, he led his

brothers and their wife **Draupadi** on pilgrimage to **Indra**'s **Heaven** on Mount **Meru**. All died on the journey except Yudhishthira – and when he reached Mount Meru he was horrified to find there the spirits not of his friends and relatives but of his dead enemies the Kauravas.

Yudhishthira in Hell and Heaven. The gods next carried Yudhishthira to the **Underworld**, where he picked his way through pools of blood and piles of severed limbs from evildoers paying for their crimes in mortal life. He saw the tortures and heard the screams – and suddenly recognized the voices of his brothers and their wife. He promised to stay and help them, and at once the scene vanished like smoke before his eyes. It had been a vision sent by the gods. In the Ganges, he washed his mortality away, and so was able at last to enter Indra's Heaven, where he found his brothers, their wife, his followers and all his former enemies at peace in the radiance of the gods.

»+ Arjuna, Bhima, heroes, Mahabharata

YU HUANG
Asia (East)

Yu Huang or Yu Di, short for Yu Huang Shang Di ('supreme jade Emperor'), in Chinese myth, was the Daoist version of the older figure **Shang Di**, supreme ruler of the universe. As a baby, he was given by the gods to human foster-parents, the Emperor Jing Te and his queen Pao Yu, and grew up as a prince before renouncing the world's pomp and spending his time helping the poor and sick. When his time on Earth ended he became supreme Emperor of the Daoist **Heaven**.

Yu Huang was created and given a mythology in the eleventh century CE, when the Emperor Zhen Tsong began ceremonies in his honour and declared him head of the Daoist pantheon. In the twelfth century Tsong's descendant Hui built temples to Yu Huang throughout the empire, and merged his worship with that of the older Shang Di, so that Yu Di (as he became popularly known) became the only supreme being.
≫→ supreme deity

YUN TUN: *see* Yu Zu and Yun Tun

YURIWAKA
Asia (East)

Yuriwaka, a warrior-prince in Japanese myth, owned a quiverful of magic arrows and an iron bow which only he could draw. Two of his lieutenants, Jiro and Taro, were jealous of him, and one day when they were all sailing back from a successful conquest and Yuriwaka fell asleep, they marooned him on a desert island, stole his bow and arrows and sailed home to tell his wife that he was dead. Taro began pestering her to marry him, and she held him at bay only by prolonging the period of mourning for her lost husband. After several years

of this stalemate, Yuriwaka was rescued from his island by passing sailors, hurried home and entered his palace, disguised as a servant, on the very day when the wedding between his wife and Taro was announced. Foolishly, Taro began the proceedings with an archery competition – and Yuriwaka, still disguised, asked to be allowed to try the iron bow and magic arrows, successfully strung the bow and shot Taro dead.

*This adaptation of the story of **Odysseus** reached Japan during one of the brief periods when Japan opened up to the West in the sixteenth century CE. Although a late entry to the canon of Japanese myth, it has remained one of the most popular, inspiring art (paintings, cartoons and comic strips), plays and puppet shows, in many of which Yuriwaka also fights **giants**, **monsters** and **demons** in true Odyssean style.*
≫→ archers, heroes

YU ZU AND YUN TUN
Asia (East)

Yu Zu and Yun Tun, in Chinese myth, were two of the most important of a large contingent of weather-gods. Yu Zu carried the **rain** in a pot and flicked it over the Earth with the end of his sword. Yun Tun, a small boy, piled clouds in the sky like a mortal child playing with snowballs.

Zeus (19th-century engraving, after an ancient vase-painting)

ZAMBA
Africa

Zamba, creator-god of the Yaunde people of the Cameroons, made the Earth and all its creatures except human beings. He left that job to his four sons, Ngi (gorilla) the strong, N'Kokon (mantis) the wise, Otukut (lizard) the fool and Wo (chimpanzee) the curious – and each made human beings in his own image, which is why we are the way we are.

≫→ **creation**

ZANAHARY
Africa

Zanahary, in Madagascan myth, was two gods in one: Light-Zanahary ('him above') and his mirror-image Dark-Zanahary ('him below'). Light-Zanahary was content with his existence, but Dark-Zanahary grew bored and amused himself by making dolls from clay, perfect in every respect except that they were lifeless. He offered to trade some of them with Light-Zanahary in exchange for the light of life. Light-Zanahary looked at the dolls, and was filled with a new emotion: lust. He asked for some of the females, and Dark-Zanahary promised. Light-Zanahary sent down the light of life, a share in his own brightness. But Dark-Zanahary cheated him, sending him first a basket of fish (pretending they were women) and then refusing to part with any of the real females. The two gods never spoke to each other again. Light-Zanahary sat sulking in his Sky-kingdom and Dark-Zanahary pranced about on the Earth below, mocking him and amusing himself by sending illness, pain and death to torment the living dolls.

In another version of this myth, there was originally only one Zanahary, the creator Light. He made the Earth but left it desert. But when he returned to Heaven some of his brightness remained below, and it fertilized the ground until a being formed itself: Ratovoantany ('self-maker'). Ratovoantany made doll-creatures, in the shapes of humans and animals, but could not give them life. Zanahary offered to animate the creatures if he could take them all back to Heaven, but Ratovoantany refused and after some argument Zanahary agreed to lend the creatures life for a short time on Earth, if he could take it back to Heaven on the day they died. This is why our spirits leave our bodies on death: they are going to spend eternity with Zanahary, while our bodies return to the clay from which Ratovoantany first made them.

⟫→ light and dark

ZEPHYRUS
Europe (South)

Zephyrus (Zephyros; Latin Favonius) was the son of Astraeus and the Dawn-goddess **Eos**. He was the West Wind, and his brothers were **Boreas** the North Wind, Notus the South Wind and Apheliotes (Latin Eurus or Vulturnus) the East Wind. As a young wind, Zephyrus was as tempestuous and piratical as his brother Boreas. He snatched whatever he fancied, answering to no one. But after he fell in love with **Apollo**'s darling **Hyacinthus**, and his attempts to snatch a kiss ended in the boy's death, Zephyrus completely changed his character. He became soft and gentle, and devoted his time to filling ships' sails and caressing the earth with his warm breath, bringing **fertility**. He married the **rainbow**-goddess **Iris** (or, some say, the harvest-goddess **Flora**), and had many children, including a family of cherubic windlets (the Zephyrs) and the harvest-spirit Carpus, whose task each year was to put the bloom on fruit as it ripened.

ZETHUS: *see* Amphion and Zethus

ZEUS
Europe (South)

Zeus and Cronus. Zeus ('shining **sky**'; Latin **Jupiter**), in Greek myth, was the youngest child of **Cronus** and **Rhea**. His father had eaten his five elder siblings (**Demeter, Hades, Hera**, Hestia and **Poseidon**) as soon as they were born, and to prevent this happening to Zeus, Rhea gave him to **mountain-nymphs** to bring up secretly in Crete, and handed Cronus a stone wrapped in baby-clothes. On Crete, Zeus grew up in the Dictean Cave, fostered by the mountain-spirit Amalthea (half goddess, half goat; mother of Zeus' foster-brother, the god **Pan**) and taught martial skills by the Curetes, a band of shaven-headed warrior-spirits.

As soon as Zeus was fully-grown, he went to serve as Cronus' cupbearer. He gave his father a drink of **nectar** mixed with emetic herbs, and Cronus vomited up Zeus' brothers and sisters, now full-grown gods. At once there was war in the universe, the gods (led by Zeus) battling the **Titans** (led by Cronus). It ended when the giant children of **Gaia** (**Mother Earth**), came to help the gods. The **Cyclopes** made invincible weapons – a helmet of invisibility for Hades, an earth-shaking trident for Poseidon, and for Zeus the most powerful of all, the thunderbolt – and the **Hundred-handed Giants** stormed the Titans' citadel on Mount Othrys.

The three kingdoms. As soon as the Titans were defeated and banished, Zeus and his siblings met to decide who should rule the universe. Two of them, Hestia and Demeter, were gentle and unambitious, and settled on Earth, content to accept whatever came their way. The three brothers cast lots for kingdoms, and Zeus won the sky, Poseidon the sea and Hades the Underworld; the Earth was common territory, to be enjoyed by all.

Zeus and Hera. This division left Hera unsatisfied. Lacking invincible weapons to match those of her brothers, she retreated to Mount Thornax, a mist-ridden wilderness where she sat and sulked. She saw no other living being, until one day she found in the rain a bedraggled cuckoo, took pity on it and warmed it in her bosom – whereupon it changed into Zeus and mated with her. Zeus persuaded Hera to become his consort, sharing rule of the sky-kingdom. They spent their wedding-night on the island of Samos – a single night to gods, three hundred years to mortals – and then set up court on Mount **Olympus**.

Zeus' children. Zeus and Hera had children: **Ares, Eris, Hebe, Hephaestus, Ilythia** and others. But Zeus was not satisfied with a single partner. He mated with Titans, birds, animals, nymphs, clouds and running water; when **Prometheus** created human beings, and persuaded Zeus to let them survive, he began mating with mortal women too. His offspring began to people the

universe. Some (**Apollo, Artemis, Hermes**) were admitted at once to full Olympian godhead; others (**Dionysus, Heracles**) had to wait until the other gods were prepared to accept them; others again (the **Muses**, the Seasons) remained on Earth.

Revolts against Zeus. Zeus' affairs, together with the memory of the trick he'd played on Mount Thornax, kept Hera furious with resentment. But Zeus alone knew how to wield thunderbolts, and they made him invincible. He made laws for the universe, fixed the stars' courses in the sky and the order of the seasons, and proclaimed the future in omens and oracles. The only times Hera could master him were when she borrowed **Aphrodite**'s girdle of desire (a belt that made the wearer irresistible) and charmed him into making love. In the end she, Apollo and Poseidon began plotting to overthrow him. In order to catch him before he had time to snatch up a thunderbolt, they crept up while he was sleeping, and tied him to his bed with ropes made from the hides of the cattle of the **Sun** and therefore unbreakable, even by an immortal god. They tied a hundred knots; Zeus was helpless.

Hera, Apollo and Poseidon began squabbling about how to divide his power. Earth and **Heaven** shook with the echoes of their rage. Terrified of another civil war, like the one which had raged between gods and Titans, the ocean-nymph **Thetis** crept down to the **Underworld** and freed the **Hundred-handed Giant Briareus**, who swarmed up to Olympus, untied the knots and set Zeus free. Zeus hung Hera from the roof of the sky on golden chains, weighting her ankles with anvils. Then he took his thunderbolt and forced every god in Olympus to kneel before him and swear eternal allegiance. He punished Apollo and Poseidon by making them serve one year as slaves to a mortal (King **Laomedon** of Troy). He cut Hera down, forced her to grovel at his feet and to accept, ever afterwards, subordinate status, female giving way to the male.

Gaia took advantage of the trouble on Olympus to stir the **Earthborn Giants** to revolt against the gods. The giants built a stonepile and climbed up it to attack Olympus, and the gods had to abandon their squabbles and defend themselves. There was a pitched battle, and the giants were defeated by Zeus' half-mortal son **Heracles** – who was later rewarded with full **immortality** and godhead. Mother Earth then sent her last and most hideous offspring, **Typhon**, to attack the gods – and when Zeus defeated him at last (thanks to cunning rather than brute strength), the rest of the gods, and all other beings, accepted his royal authority at last.

Zeus as supreme ruler. Once Zeus' throne was secure, he retreated from active involvement in the affairs of the universe. He was the supreme authority, the first and last decider against whom there was no appeal, and he used thunderbolts only sparingly to warn or punish. He left the running of the universe to the enormous family of gods and goddesses (many of whom were his own offspring), and spent his time supervising their councils and adjudicating their frequent quarrels and arguments. To Hera's irritation, he never abandoned his taste for promiscuous **sex**, and his chief diversion was visiting the Earth, choosing a new partner and taking on some appropriate disguise to enjoy sex with her.

Although Zeus is omnipresent in ancient literature, he is sparsely represented in art. The most famous ancient sculpture to show him in majesty was a 13-metre-high statue at Olympia, one of the seven Wonders of the World, and it was widely available in small copies (some of which may have originated as souvenirs sold at the Olympic Games). His amours were more often shown, in paintings and carvings – but he is there a bull, swan or shower of gold rather than a god. Perhaps the problem was representing daylight as a living thing – a mirror-image of the tabu on showing Hades, darkness and invisibility made immanent. (The Romans had no such problem with Jupiter: he was a prince enthroned, dressed in the clothes and carrying the regalia of a Roman ruler, proud and unequivocal.) In Delphi, the holiest object in Apollo's shrine was a phallic, pillar-shaped stone, the omphalos or 'navel'. It was said to be the stone which Rhea gave Cronus to eat instead of baby Zeus; when the adult Zeus forced his father to regurgitate his swallowed children, he hurled the stone down to Earth and it landed in the exact centre of the world, in the shrine at Delphi. Apollo's priestess sat on this stone to prophesy, and Apollo came down from Heaven and entered her.

»→ justice and universal order, shape-changers, supreme deity

ZHI NU: *see* Qian Niu and Zhi Nu

ZHUAN HU
Asia (East)

Zhuan Hu, second of the **Five Emperors** in Chinese myth, came to power after a seven-year interregnum when **Huang Di** left Earth for **Heaven**. When he took the throne, Heaven and Earth were still accessible to one another. Heaven was propped above Earth on nine pillars (or, some say, on the mountains formed from the body and bones of the primordial giant **Pan Gu**). In Huang Di's reign relations between gods and mortals had been good-mannered and harmonious, but during the interregnum his teachings about how mortals should address gods and vice versa had become perverted to the point where some of the more confused gods were even offering sacrifices to mortals. Zhuan Hu ended this. He gave one of his sons, Chong, the job of organizing the gods into a separate kingdom and a recognizable hierarchy, and told his other son, Li, to do the same for mortals. Chong ruled the South and Li the North, and ever afterwards relationships between the two worlds observed established rules of diplomatic and religious precedent.

In some accounts, Zhuan Hu is the same person as **Shun**, the fifth of the Five Emperors.

ZORYA
Europe (East)

Zorya, in Slavic myth, was originally three goddesses, sisters. Morning Zorya opened the gates of the **Sun**'s palace each day to let him ride out across the sky, Evening Zorya opened them in the evening to welcome him home, and Midnight Zorya oversaw the darkness of night. The sisters also had charge of the dog tied to the Little Bear (or in some accounts, the Great Bear): if it ever broke loose, it would create havoc in the universe. Of the three sisters, the most beautiful and important was Morning Zorya, wife of the war god **Pyerun**. When he rode out to battle she armed herself and went with him, letting her veil down to protect favoured human warriors. In the course of time her worship eclipsed that of her sisters, so that Zorya (originally 'light') came to mean just 'Dawn'.

ZOSIM
Europe (East)

Zosim, god of bees in Slavic myth, was named after their buzzing. He was also the god of mead, and when humans drank enough of it he entered their throats and taught them bawdy songs.

»→ Aristaeus, farming

ZURVAN AKARANA
Asia (West)

Zurvan Akarana ('infinite time'), in Iranian myth, was the primordial being which existed before existence. It was both male and female, and inseminated itself. **Twins** grew in its womb: **Ahriman**, lord of darkness, and **Ahura Mazda**, lord of light. In the endless eons of its pregnancy, Zurvan Akarana idly wondered which twin would be greatest, and murmured 'The firstborn' – whereupon Ahriman ripped open the womb and shouldered his way out ahead of Ahura Mazda. Hastily, Zurvan Akarana finished its thought – 'for a thousand thousand years, until he is destroyed' – and the world has been waiting for this moment, the final destruction of evil, ever since.

≫→ **creation**

ZVEZDA DENNITSA: see Vechernyaya Zvezda and Zvezda Dennitsa

INDEX

Main entries are shown in bold type.

Aapep 1, 368, 414, 513, 544, 546
Abassi 1
Abdera 154
Abderus 154
Abe Mango 459
Abel 108
Abhimani 20
Abraham 443
Abuk 147
Acamas 483
Achaemenides 491
Achates 3
Achelous 3, 27, 255, 563
Acheron River 3, 578
Achilles 4, 24, 32, 109, 243, 295, 383, 438, 469, 471, 473, 490, 491, 600, 619
Achimi 297
Acis 490
Acmon 138
Acrisius 141, 482
Actaeon 56, 592
Actor 547
Acts of King Arthur and His Noble Knights, The 58
Adad 6
Adam 7, 356, 533, 540
Adapa 7
Addad 6
Addu 6
Adekagagwaa 8
Aditi 8, 646, 653
Aditya 531
Adityas 149, 505
Admetus 53
administration, god of 100
Adnoartina 375
Adonis 8
Adrastus 179, 274, 547
Adro 9
Adroa 9

Adroanzi 9
advice-giving god 516
Adyok 25
adze 362
Ae 426
Aeacus 235
Aed 140
Aeëtes 122, 222, 250, 486
Aegeus 9, 382, 597
Aegialea 153
Aegialeus 548
Aegina 565
Aegir 10, 273
aegis 68
Aegisthus 11, 18, 71, 124, 385, 412, 451, 609
Aegle 259
Aello 240 *see also* Harpies
Aemathion 178
Aeneas 3, 11, 13, 43, 49, 59, 116, 150, 240, 275, 350, 390, 423, 461, 476, 491, 528, 543, 557, 558, 621, 624
Aeneas Silvius 351
Aeneid 6, 13, 43, 47, 151, 229, 245, 296, 349, 440, 562
Aeolus 13, 96
Aerope 17, 71, 608
Aeschylus 5, 18, 111, 174, 204, 294, 451, 500, 507
Aesculapius 14, 49, 260, 281
Aeshma 577
Aesir 15, 60, 644
Aeson 474
Aethra 10, 597
Affan 46
Affwys 46
Afi 246
African myth 15
afterlife *see* Dead; Heaven; paradises; supernatural worlds; Underworld
Agamedes 621

Agamemnon 4, 11, **17**, 24, 72, 109, 111, 121, 124, 248, 294, 385, 476, 609
Agasti 19
Agastya **19**, 635
Agave **19**, 108, 479
agave seeds 381
Agbe-Naete 381
Agditis 73, 134
Age 381, 448
Agelaus 467
ages 37 *see also* Bronze Age; Golden Age; Iron Age; Silver Age
Ages of Brahma **19**
of Mortals **196**
Agga 220
Aglaea 225
Agnar **20**, 216, 436
Agnen 54
Agni **20**, 99, 100, 164, 211, 212, 321, 326, 531, 532, 648
agriculture *see* farming; flower deities; plants
Agrius 122, 165
Agwe **22**
Ah Puch **22**
Aha 90
Ahalya 292
Ahi 291, 571
Ahriman **22**, 214
Ahsonnutli **22**
Ahti 23
Ahto **23**, 280
Ahura Mazda 22, **23**, 214, 239, 395, 539, 639, 648
Ai 246
Aigamuxa 17, **23**
ailments 198, 208 *see also* diseases
Aino 312, 640
Aiomum Kondi **23**
Airavana 23
Airavata **23**, 292, 293
Ajax (Great) **24**, 244, 438
Ajax (Little) **25**, 111
Ajisukitakahikone **25**
Ajok **25**
Ajysyt **26**
Akhenaten 66, 171
Akka **26**

Akongo **26**
Alberich 45
albinism 464
Albion **26**
Alcinous (King of Drepanum) 224
Alcinous (King of Phaeacia) **27**, 252, 439
Alcmaeon **27**, 180, 548
Alcmena **28**, 38, 65, 185, 252, 253
alcohol 285, 327, 381, 382 *see also* ale; beer; mead; rum; wine
Alcyoneus 165
alder trees 484
ale 11, 121
Alexander (son of Priam) 468
Alexander (the Great) 5, 546
Aleyin 341
Alfheim 419
Alfrigg 101
Alklha **29**
All-Conqueror 331
Allecto 126, 203 *see also* Furies
alligators 465
Aloeus 165
Alpheus 74
Alpheus River 52
Altair (star) 510
Alvis **29**
Amalthea 682
Amana **29**
Amaterasu **30**, 421, 581, 623
Amaunet 402, 444
Amayicoyondi 511
Amazons **32**, 48, 64, 259-60
Ambalika **33**
amber 386
Ambika **33**
ambrosia **33**, 155, 242, 260, 473, 589
Amduat 571
Amenhotep IV 66
Amenohohi 32
Amenoosimasa 32
Amenowakahiko 32
America 209
American myth **33**, 351
Amfortas 474
Amitabha **36**
Amleth 338

Amma **36**, 246, 444
Ammon 40
Ammut **37**
Amon 40
Amotken **37**
Amphiaraus 179, 547
Amphion **37**
Amphitrite **38**, 494, 543
Amphitryon 28, **38**, 253
amrita 24, **39**, 140, 212, 304, 517, 648,
    650
Amulius 529
Amun **40**, 79, 329, 444
Amun-Ra 41
Amycus 223
An 7, **41**, 220, 375, 417, 421, 595
anacondas 465
Anahit 639
Anala 648
Ananda **41**, 147, 409
Anansi **42**, 46
Anansi Kokroko 450
Ananta 571, 651
Anat 6, **43**, 354, 414
Anaxarete 493
Anchiale 138
Anchises 11, **43**, 558
Andersen, Hans Christian 503
Andriamahilala **44**
Andriambahomanana **44**
Androgeus 470
Andromache **44**, 249, 258, 416
Andromeda 483
Andvari **44**, 101, 189, 433, 561
anemones 9
Angboda 247, 360
Angerona **45**
Anghar 46
Angiras 496
Angra Mainya 22
Anguta 544
Anila 648
animal deities 23-4, 34, 37, **45**, 51, 81,
    84, 85, 128, 190, 210, 212, 238, 239,
    252, 297, 304, 310, 328, 342, 372,
    378, 390, 411, 444, 462, 523, 563,
    577, 579, 590, 607, 613, 633, 645, 667

Anjana **46**, 238, 319
Annency 43, **46**
Annunaki 41
Annwn **46**, 586
Ant 297
Antea 88
ant-eater 326
Antero Vipunen **47**, 641
Anticlea 77, 345
antidotes 414
Antielus 663
Antigone **47**, 131, 297, 440, 442, 548
Antiochus 5
Antiope 32, **48**, 54, 260, 483, 599
Anu 41
Anubis **48**, 413
Anzu 177
Ao Guang 200
Aoide 401 *see also* Muses
apes 579
Apheliotes 682
aphrodisiacs 394, 573
Aphrodite 8, 11, 12, 43, **48**, 52, 138,
    223, 225, 248, 251, 274, 351, 385,
    456, 468, 473, 506, 611, 626, 683
Apis 239
Apkallu 8
Apollo 5, 14, **49**, 88, 109, 110, 125, 155,
    167, 250, 255, 256, 271, 273, 294,
    349, 350, 354, 392, 416, 423, 451,
    454, 468, 558, 621, 626, 683
Apollodorus 386
Apollonian impulse 50
Apollonius 53, 229, 296, 383
Apophis 1
Apoyan Tachi 77
apple trees 236, 328, 492
apples of immortality 15, 26, 58, 61, 64,
    77, 97, 112, 127, 180, 254, 259, 278,
    285, 371, 428 *see also* peaches of
    immortality
apsaras 46, **50**, 210, 634
apsarasas 50
Apsu 375, 609
Apsyrtus 224
Apuleius 503
Aqhat 43

Arachne **51**
Ararat, Mt 425
Arawn 46, **51**, 367, 505
Archemorus 274
archers 32, **51**, 55, 56, 159, 181, 253, 304, 323, 439, 466, 469, 484, 517, 518, 631, 671, 674, 679
Archimboldo 493
architects 652
architecture 281, 541, 546
archivist goddess 546
Arcturus (constellation) 57
Ardhanarishvara **51**
Areop-Enap **51**
Ares 9, **52**, 64, 113, 167, 178, 251, 376, 442, 468, 488, 566, 683
Arethusa **52**, 259
Arges 134
Argo 53, 222, 309
Argonautica 53, 296, 383
Argonauts **53**, 124, 156, 182, 229, 254, 274, 309, 411, 452, 486, 578
arguments 3
Argus (hunting dog) **53**, 439
Argus (shipwright) 53, 222
Argus (watchman) **53**, 293
Ariadne **54**, 155, 470, 598
Arianrhod 357
Ariconte **54**
Arion 145
Aristaeus **55**, 452, 502
Aristophanes 155, 236, 296, 595
Aristotle 442
Arjuna **55**, 93, 159, 335, 340, 368, 462, 467
Ark of the Covenant 263
Arkoayó 643
armour 5, 24, 243, 251, 266, 438
Arnarquagssaq 544
Arne 13
arrows 19, 51, 181, 296, 323
Arsinoe 27
Artemis 18, 38, 43, 49, **56**, 64, 71, 176, 260, 294, 300, 354, 384, 423, 461, 525, 545, 626, 683
Arthur 6, 46, **57**, 98, 186, 232, 345, 348, 386, 396, 480, 586, 635, 642

Artos 57
arts creator deities 266, 297-8, 539, 631-2
arts, goddess of 68
Aruna **58**
Aruru 421
Aryaman 646
Asbjörnsen, Peter Christian 320
Ascanius 12, **59**, 351
Asegeir **59**
Aset **59**, 178, 264, 413, 454, 515
Asgard 15, **60**, 643, 645, 674, 676
Asgaya Gigagei **61**
ash trees 674
Asherat 173
Ashtart 296
Ashtoreth 296
Ashur **61**
Ashvathaman **61**, 160, 163
Ashvins **62**, 121, 340, 368, 525, 539, 580
Asikni 141
Asimbabba 562
Ask **62**, 263
Asmodaeus 540
Asopus 565
asses 392
Asshurbanipal 220
Astarte 43, **62**, 414
Asterius 185
Astlik 639
Astraeus 178
astronomy 401, 511, 546, 603, 672
 see also stars
Astyanax 44, **63**, 416
Asuras **63**
Ataentsic **63**, 236, 294
Atai 1
Atalanta **64**
Ataokoloinona **64**
Atar **65**
Ate **65**, 253
Atea **65**, 585
Aten **66**
Athamas **66**, 154, 416
Athene 14, 25, 51, **68**, 71, 107, 125, 167, 251, 294, 389, 414, 420, 438, 460, 461, 468, 473, 482, 493, 499, 611, 626

Athenodoros 349
Athens 69, 600
Atla 245, 420
Atlantis 69, 70
Atlas **69**, 483, 499
Atlas Mountains 38, 70, 259, 483
Atli **70**
Atrahis **70**
Atreus 11, 17, **71**, 476, 608
Atri **72**, 496, 549
Atropus 190 *see also* Fates
Atseestan **72**
Atsehastin **72**
Attis **73**, 134
Atum **73**, 177, 513, 556
Atum-Ra 74
Auchimalgen **74**
Audumla **74**, 675
Augeas **74**, 255
Augeia 245, 420
Aulanerk **75**
Aulis 295
Aunyainá **75**
Aurgiafa 245, 420
Aurora 178
Aurora Borealis 87, 631, 643
Ausrine 386
Australian myth **75**
Autolycus **76**, 565
Autonoe 55, 108
Avalokiteshvara 36, **77**, 231, 577, 590
Avalon 58, **77**, 187, 343, 387, 398
avatars *see* Kama; Lakshmi; Ravana; Vishnu
Awitelin Tsta 77
Awonawilona **77**, 494
Aya 550
Ayakasikone 632
Ayar Manco 372
Ayca 372, 459
Ayers Rock 376, 631
Ayida 141
Ayrton, Michael 139, 600
Azacca **78**
Azazel 540
Azhi Dahaka **78**
Azra'il 283
Aztec myth 34

Ba 266, 510
Ba Ja **82**
Baal 43, **79**, 88, 595
Baal Berith 79
Baal Gad 79
Baal Hammon 79
Baal Samin 79
Baal Tyre 79
Baal Zebul 79, 87
Baal Zebulon 79
Baba-Yaga **79**
Babel (Tower of) **81**, 387
babies 25, 26, 63, 133, 154, 222, 274, 346, 438, 467
baboons 171
Babylon 81
Bacchae 155, 479
Bacchus 154
Bachue **81**
Badb 398
Badger 73, 164
badimo 396
Badlands 608
Bagadjimbiri **81**
Bahubali 224
bakers, god of 487
balance *see* scales; universal order
Balang Chö 197
Balarama **82**, 148, 325, 333, 527, 552, 647
Baldur 15, **83**, 202, 261, 360, 424, 516, 567
Bali **84**, 643
Balin **84**, 579
ball-and-socket joint 362
Balor **85**, 363
Ban 348
bananas 44, 379, 424, 465, 574
bannik **85**
Barber, Samuel 383
Baron Samedi 218
Bastet **85**, 402
Batara Guru **86**, 404
bath-house, deities of 85, 593
bats 613
battles 113, 509, 516 *see also* war
Battus 257

Baucis **86**
Baugi 436
Baxbakualanuchsiwae **86**
beach god 610
Bear 212, 352, 455 *see also* Great Bear;
  Little Bear
bears 134, 304
beauty 8, 50, **87**, 122, 145, 159, 175,
  179, 183, 211, 225, 232, 247, 271,
  272, 347, 383-4, 411, 468, 502, 516,
  522, 538, 566, 634
beauty, deities of 48, 49, 83, 115, 614
Beaver **574**, 661
Bebrycus 223
Bedivere 187
bee-keeping deities 55, 452, 685
Beelzebub 79, **87**
beer 273, 287, 498, 623
bees 155, 330, 592, 621
Beethoven, Ludwig van 192
Beetle 636
Begdu San **87**
Bei Dou Xing 337
Bel **88**, 635
Belenus 88
Beli (King) 88
Beli the Howler 201
Belinus 88
Belit-illi 421
Belitis 421
Bellerophon **88**, 117, 472
Bellerus 88
Bellini, Vincenzo 111
Bellona **89**
benefactor deities 174, 204, 266, 308,
  331, 342, 373, 381, 511, 634, 660,
  672 *see also* civilization; good luck;
  prosperity
Benu Bird **89**
Benzai 549
Beowulf **90**, 113
Bergelmir **90**, 675
Berling 101
Berlioz, Hector 151, 192
Beroe 9, 546
Berserkers **90**
Bertilak 213

Bes **90**
Bestla 15, **91**, 96
Bhagavad Gita 56, 335, 368
Bhagiratha **91**, 211, 554
Bhairavi 149
bhakti 335
Bharadwaja 549
Bharata (King) **91**, 143, 319, 518
Bharata (place) **91**, 92
Bhima **91**, 308, 462
Bhisma **92**, 211
bho trees 102, 399, 558
Bhutas **93**
Bias 384
Bible, The 200, 209
Biddice 67
Bifröst 61, **93**
Big Dipper (constellation) 337 *see also*
  Great Bear (constellation)
Bildjiwuaroju **94**
Billingsgate 88
Bimbogami **94**
birds 117
Birds 296, 595
birthmarks 108, 474, 489, 660
Bishamon 549
Black God **94**
Black Sea 123
blacksmith deities 43, 230, 251-2, 280,
  323, 363, 445, 606, 653
Bleak House 229
Bloddeuedd 358
Boaliri 313
boars 64, 182, 261, 616, 645
boat-building 341 *see also* ships
Bobbi-Bobbi **95**
Boccaccio, Giovanni 389, 503
Boccherini, Luigi 295
Bochica **95**
Boddhisattvas **95**, 102
bodyguards 237
Boe 262
Boeotia 107
Boeotus 13
bogatiri **96**, 569
boils 356
Bolverk 436

bones 168, 608, 632
Book of Taliesin, The 586
boomerangs 95, 143, 341
Bor 15, 91, **96**, 104, 675
Borak **96**
Boreas **96**, 185, 682
Bore-bore 450
Borgild 563
Bosch, Hieronymus 175, 199, 540
Bossu **96**
Botticelli, Sandro 199
Bragi 15, **97**, 233
Brahma 19, 21, 24, 84, **97**, 100, 141,
    143, 211, 319, 325, 338, 347, 374,
    387, 496, 498, 504, 518, 523, 531,
    538, 539, 553, 555, 645, 649, 652
Brahmi 539
Brahms, Johannes 192
Bralbral 94
Bran **98**, 367
Brangen 618
Branwen 98
bread, goddess of 161
Breng 140
Bres **99**
Bresson 58
Brian 142
Briareus **99**, 269, 683
brides 347
bridges 93
Brighu 21, **99**, 347, 374, 496, 526
Brighus **100**
Brigid 99, **100**, 140
Brihaspati **100**, 575
Brindisi 153
Briseis 4, 18, 471
Brisingamen **101**, 201
Brisings 201
Brit 27, **101**, 222
Britain 26
Brontës 134
Bronze Age 196
Brueghel, Pieter 199
Brünnhilde 561
Brut 101
Brynhild **101**, 561
Bubastis 85

Buddha 36, 42, 77, **102**, 147, 149, 203,
    290, 306, 370, 374, 381, 399, 406,
    408, 495, 558, 642, 652, 673, 676
    see also Boddhisatvas
    avatars of Buddha see Kalki
Buddhas, Five **196**
Buddhism 118, 306
buffaloes 162, 297, 671
Buga **103**
Bull from the Sea, The 600
bull of Cooley 133
bullroarers 576
bulls 45, **103**, 131, 133, 138, 164, 173,
    218, 223, 239, 395, 409, 470
Bulugu 315
Bumba **103**
Bunyan, John 209
Buoka **655**
bureaucracy 266, 326, 423
Buri 74, **103**, 675
Burne-Jones, Edward 263
business deities 531, 669
butchers, god of 189
Butler, Samuel 412
Buyan **104**
Byelobog **104**, 569, 583

Cachi 372
cactus 116
Cacus **105**, 186
Cadmeia 108
Cadmus 19, **107**, 576, 597
Caeneus **108**
Caenis 108
Caesar, Julius 112, 433
Cagn 317
Cain **108**, 660
Cairbe 99
calabashes 354, 465
Calais 53, 96, 223, 240, 485
Calchas **109**, 294, 619
Cale 225
calendars 672
Caliburn 186
Calliope 8, 401, 454, 563 see also Muses
Callirrhoe 27
Calvino, Italo 55

Calydonian Boar 64
Calypso **109**
Cambodian myth 240
Cambridge 222
Camelodunum 110
Camelot 57, 58, **110**
Campe **110**, 134
Cancer (constellation) 272
Candide 209
Candramus **110**, 531
Canens **486**
cannibalism 327, 605, 615
canoes 624
Capaneus 547
Capitoline Hill 314
Carbonek 214, 474
Caridwen 586
Carmentis 186
carp 337
carpenter's bench 362
Carpus 682
carrion 262
Carthage 12, 150, 361
Cassandra 18, 25, 49, **110**, 244, 663
Cassiphone 592
Castor **156**, 247, 351, 599, 625
castration 134
Catcher in the Rye, The 209
Catequil **111**
Caterpillar 317
Cathars 263
cats 85-6, 551
cattle 217, 250, 256, 505, 565
Catullus 73, 383
Cauldron of Immortality 263
Cavillaca 126
Celaeno 240 *see also* Harpies
Celeus 481
Celmis 138
Celtic myth 58, **111**, 351
Centaurs **113**, 120, 488
Centaurus (Centaur) 113
Centaurus (constellation) 120, 500
Cephalus 178
Cerberus **114**, 236, 453
Ceres **145**, 182, 502
Cernunnos **114**

Cervantes Saavedra, Miguel de 209
Ceto 225
Ceucy **115**
Ceyx 186
Chac **115**
Chacomát 631
Chacopá 631
Chalchihuitlicue **115**
Chalciope 222, 486
Chalcitlicue 614
Chameleon 42, 634
Chandra **115**
Chanson de Roland 527
Chantico **116**
Chaos 28, **116**, 181, 185, 207, 417, 456
character, god of 246
Chariclo 611
Charites *see* Graces
Charlemagne 6, 13, 112, 527
Charon 114, **116**, 453
Charybdis **543**
Chaucer, Geoffrey 389, 503
cheese-making 452
Chernobog 104, 569
chess 567
Chi Song Zi 192, 266, 510
Chi Yu 266
Chia 95
Chibchacum 95
Chibiabos 408
Chichen Itza 512
child protectors 331
childbirth 7, 51, **116**, 414, 505, 667, 671
childbirth deities 56, 85, 201, 241, 243,
    252, 280, 298, 300, 381, 387, 397,
    551, 590, 604, 624
child-bringer god 304
child-bringers 238
childcare **116**
Chills, Fan of 198
Chimaera 88, 117, 472
Chimaeros 88
Chimatano **117**
Chiminigagué **117**
chimpanzees 681
Chinese myth **117**
Chinigchinich 120, 457

Chione 96
Chiron 14, 113, **120**, 309, 437, 472, 500
Chiyu, Mt 336
Chloris 198, 682
Chonchonyi **120**
Chong 685
Christ, Jesus 328, 541
Christianity 112, 193, 216, 290, 388, 427, 568
Christina of Sweden 151
Chronicle 357
Chryseis 4, 18, 619
Chryses 4
Chrysippus 346
Chrysothemis 17, **121**, 124, 297
Chthonius 576
Chu Pa-Chieh 617
Chuku **121**
Chur 526
Chyavana **121**
Cian 85, 363
cicadas 178
Cihuacóatl **121**, 279, 298
Cinderella 229
Cinyras 8
Circe **122**, 224, 486, 543, 592
circles 571
circumcision 445
Cisthene 225, 226
Cithaeron, Mt 19, 346
cities 678
civilization **123**, 266, 293, 373, 387, 459, 593, 617
civilization, deities of 37, 72-3, 95, 165, 204, 400, 423, 454, 509-10, 541, 587, 611
clams 51
Clashing Rocks 12, **123**, 223
clay 36, 138, 176, 268, 271, 283, 369, 409, 428, 448, 465, 500, 524, 681
clay tablets 220, 404, 422
cleanliness, deities of 593, 614
Cleopatra (daughter of Boreas) 96, 240, 485
Cleopatra (Queen of Egypt) 546
Cletus 178
Clio 401 *see also* Muses
Clotho 190, 475 *see also* Fates

clouds, deities of 202, 232, 416, 510, 522, 679
Cloven Viscount, The 55
Clymene 484
Clysonymus 471
Clytemnestra 11, 17, **124**, 174, 257, 294, 351, 451, 507, 625
Clytius 165
Coatlicue **125**, 596
cobblers, god of 579
cobras 573 *see also* snakes
coconut palms 380, 615
Cocteau, Jean 295, 442, 454
Cocytus River **125**, 578
cod 419
Coeus 612
Cogaz 317
coins 266
Coleridge, Samuel Taylor 199
Collatinus 362
Comaetho 39
comedy 257, 401 *see also* drama
Cometes 153
comets 517, 587 *see also* Halley's comet
commerce 37, 257, 678
compass points 37, 203, 205, 596
Conal 133
Concobar of Ulster 145
Confucianism 118, 306
Coniraya **126**
Connecticut Yankee in King Arthur's Court, A 58
consolation, goddess of 261
constellations 54, 57, 94, 117, 120, 156, 272, 337, 341, 415, 454, 455, 500, 527, 549, 596, 606, 610
Cook, James 510
cooking 459
Cooley, bull of 133
Coot 369
Copper Woman **126**
Coppersmith 31
Cordeil 357
Core 145, 480
Cormac MacAirt **126**, 367
corn 127, 201, 636, 660
Corn Maidens, Ten **593**

Corn Woman **127**
corn, goddess of 450
Corona Borealis (constellation) 54
corpses 22, 644
Cortés, Hernán 512
Corybantes 134
Cottus 269
Covenant *see* Ark of the Covenant
cowherds 334, 409, 466, 510
cows 40, 45, 54, 62, 74, **103**, 107, 138,
    241, 291, 293, 329, 430, 498, 525, 527
cows of plenty 60, 241, 277, 323, 466,
    467, 647
Coyolxauhqui 125, **127**
Coyote 37, 73, 94, 120, **128**, 195, 268,
    331, 610, 661, 662
crab-apple trees 236
crabs 126, 272
craft deities 100, 251-2, 341, 503, 624,
    652
crafts 44, **129**
craftsmen 108, 135, 138, 362, 506, 525,
    591
crampons 678
Crane 164
creation 89, **129**, 285, 333, 632
creation myths 16, 128, 226-7, 401, 419-
    20, 427, 434, 504, 571
creator deities 15, 16, 42, 97, 128, 164,
    165, 207, 237, 280, 291, 328, 372,
    400, 429, 430, 456, 503, 513, 526,
    631, 651
creators of Earth 22, 29-30, 63-4, 77, 81,
    86, 126, 137, 143, 158, 176, 180-1,
    198, 207, 299, 312, 323-4, 338, 340-
    1, 358, 369, 378-80, 390, 400, 404,
    406, 425-6, 430, 456, 459, 509, 563,
    630, 660, 681
creators of humankind 3, 23, 25, 26, 81,
    103, 120, 141, 146, 176, 181, 183,
    184, 198, 204, 214, 221, 263, 268,
    269, 270, 314, 328, 331, 332, 339,
    341, 342, 358, 373, 381, 409, 418,
    424, 425-6, 429, 430, 450, 459, 460,
    470, 499, 511, 523, 533, 544, 583,
    585, 586-7, 588, 589, 593, 634, 650,
    655, 660, 661, 663, 667-8, 671, 681

creators of life 77, 94, 126, 158-9, 164,
    176, 218, 221, 231, 241, 297, 312,
    313, 326, 331, 354, 369, 373-4, 394,
    395, 400, 425-6, 428-9, 437, 448,
    454, 459, 549, 574, 577, 585, 588,
    658, 661
creators of the universe 9, 36, 37, 51-2,
    65-6, 72, 73, 97, 103, 117, 121, 149,
    164, 173, 177, 185, 193, 232, 236,
    270, 271, 281, 291, 317, 329, 330,
    355, 364, 375, 381, 400, 411, 414,
    418, 419-20, 429, 435, 448, 464, 496,
    504, 521, 523, 539, 550, 593, 609,
    610, 624, 639, 646, 649, 650, 652,
    655-6, 657, 659, 662, 675
Creon (title) **131**
Creon (King of Corinth) **131**
Creon (King of Thebes) 47, **131**, 442, 547
Cressida 619
Cretan Bull **131**
Crete 138, 185, 598
Cretheis 472
Cretheus 474
Creusa 294
Crime and Punishment 452
Crius 612
crocodiles 320
Cronus 120, **132**, 235, 305, 456, 524,
    541, 612, 682
crop blight 487
crossroads, goddess of 243
Crow 195
crystal 197
Cteatus 255
cuckoos 108, 253, 683
Cuculain **133**, 214, 363, 371, 398
cucumbers 325
cucura trees 115
Culain 133
culture *see* arts; civilization; dancing;
    literature; music
Cumae 182
Cumae, Sibyl of 12, 49, 558
Cupay **133**
Cupid **181**, 502
Curetes 682
Cuzco 372, 651

Cybele 43, 73, **134**, 525, 542
Cyclopes 12, 14, 49, 110, 132, **134**, 208,
   251, 456

Da **137**, 141, 381
Da Ponte, Lorenzo 191
Dabog 143
Dactyls **138**
Dadzbog 143
Daedalus **138**, 275
Dagan 140
Dagda **139**
Dagon **140**
Daibosatsu 235
Daikoku **140**, 446, 549
daityas **140**
Dajoji **140**
Daksha 141, 326, 496, 505, 526, 540,
   555, 575
Dalai Lamas 355, 577
Dalí, Salvador 440
Dallapiccola, Luigi 440
Damballah **141**, 573
Damkina 421
Damnameneus 138
Danaë **141**, 482
Danann **142**
dance of death 218, 541
dancing 50, 128, 134, 155, 218, 241,
   321, 399, 401, 553, 593, 667
dancing, deities of 49, 368
Danh 571
Dante, Alighieri 151
Danu 142
Dao Dung Shi 672
Daoism 118, 284
Darana **142**
Dardanelles 124
darkness 29 *see also* light and dark
darkness, deities of 22, 94, 179, 261,
   369-70, 595
Dasaratha **143**, 238, 319, 327, 518
David 349
Dawn 216
dawn, deities of 159, 178, 314, 635, 685
Day of Judgement 395
Dayunsi **143**

Dazhbog **143**, 583
de Chirico, Giorgio 440
de Laclos, Choderlos 151
de Troyes, Chrétien 58, 113, 209, 262, 349
Dead, place of the 94, 104, 152, 160,
   197, 391, 420, 487, 623, 641, 676
Dead, rulers of the 179, 200, 247, 437
Dead, the 65, 114, 116, 181, 208, 257,
   264, 310, 353, 370, 392, 408, 418
death 3, 56, 95, **144**, 263, 273, 300, 305,
   345, 354, 410, 451, 504, 509, 532,
   611, 629 *see also* judgement of the
   Dead
Death 160, 281, 323, 330, 424, 498, 533
death, deities of 6, 22, 79, 85, 133, 139,
   213, 218, 237, 259, 296, 321, 322,
   370, 375, 380, 398, 417, 532, 578,
   588, 597
Death, Ship of 199
Death, Tree of 407
death-watch beetles 94
Debestevs 152
Dechtire 133
Decline and Fall 209
deer 18, 327-8, 674
Deianira 3, 255
Deimos 52
Deino 226 *see also* Graeae
Deiphilus 490
Deiphobe 558
Deiphobus **144**, 248
Deirdre **145**, 245
Dekla 345
Delilah 538
Delos 49, 354
Delphi 49, 125, 558, 621
Delphic oracle 27, 64, 68, 107, 141, 180,
   254, 346, 439, 440, 576, 621
Delphinus 38
Delphyne 626
Demeter 132, **145**, 208, 475, 480, 494,
   525, 563, 683
Demodocus 251
demon-hunters 19, 21, 82, 149, 162,
   179, 280, 308, 332, 334, 363, 413,
   506, 518, 549, 553, 562, 577, 617,
   639, 675

demons 17, 21, 22, 26, 34, 40, 54, 63,
75, 84, 85, 87, 93, 99, 120, 142, **146**,
157, 160, 162, 163, 164, 179, 197,
209, 232, 247, 261, 263, 288, 298,
300, 303, 304, 307, 320, 321, 322,
324-5, 331, 334, 336, 338, 354, 356,
370, 371, 374, 375, 409, 410, 422,
437, 450, 463, 488, 495, 505, 517,
518, 523, 536, 540, 544, 574, 575,
588, 590, 591, 617, 623, 629, 633,
645, 647, 654, 657, 672, 676
Demophoön 483
Deng **146**
desire, deities of 48, 181, 323, 352-3,
402 *see also* love; lust; sex
Desmontes 13
destruction, god of 553
Deucalion 147, 470
Deva (goddess) **147**, 334
Deva (Princess) **147**, 673
Devadatta 102, **147**, 374, 673
Devaki 82, **148**, 325, 333, 527, 647
Devana 153
Devaparvata 387
Devi **148**, 162, 552
Devil 191, 361, 386, 462, 540
devils 197
dew 521, 591
Dew of Eternal Life 478
Dhanvantari 40, **149**
Dharma 20, **149**, 340
Dharmapalas **149**
Dhatar 8, **149**
Dhishana 100
Dhrishtadyumna 62
Dhritarashtra 33, **149**
Dhruva 648
Di **150**, 609
Di Jun **152**, 665
Di Kang Wang **152**
Di Mu 150
Di Yao 672
Dia 298, 487
Diamond Kings, Four **200**
Dian Cecht **150**
Diana 43, 52, **56**, 57
diarrhoea 88

Dictean Cave 682
Dictys 142
didgeridoos 227
Dido 12, 13, **150**, 181, 275, 383
Dido and Aeneas 151
Dievas **152**
Digambara 553
Dilmun 176
Dilwica **153**
Diomedes (King of Aetolia) **153**, 412,
460, 461, 485, 525, 548, 619
Diomedes (King of Thrace) **153**
Dione 589
Dionysian impulse 50
Dionysus 19, 54, 55, 67, **154**, 167, 225,
236, 252, 365, 391, 417, 452, 453,
479, 493, 546, 562, 598, 626, 683
Dioscuri **156** *see also* Castor; Pollux
diplomacy, god of 231
Dirce 154
Dis 235
disability 465
disability, god of 173
disease, deities of 330, 354-5, 362, 531,
552
diseases 49, 93, **156**, 247, 354, 362, 395,
450, 487, 498, 581, 611, 614, 623, 629
Disemboweller **157**
Ditaolane **157**
Diti **157**
Djanggawul **94**
Djeheuty 603
Djoser 281
Doctor Faustus 191
Doctor Jeckyll and Mr Hyde 540
doctors, god of 603
Dodona 416
Dog 284, 323
Dog star 94, 304
Dogon 140
dogs 39, 48, 53, 56, 81, 114, 181, 189,
217, 236, 245, 376, 439, 453, 570,
592, 667, 685
dolphins 38, 161
domovoi **158**
Don Giovanni 191
Don Quixote 209

Donar **158**, 601
Dong Wang Gong 674
Donizetti, Gaetano 111
donkeys 173
Donner 158, 601
Door Gods, Three **604**
door-keeping deities 305, 604
Doquebuth **158**
Doris 417
Dorje Pahmo **159**
Dostoevsky, Fyodor 452
Dove 164
doves 148, 183, 425, 636
Dra Minyen 197
Dracula 191, 540, 644
Dragon King 173
Dragon Kings, Four **200**
dragons 78, 90, 189, 200, 352, 354, 361,
    397, 419, 562, 587, 677
dragon's teeth 107, 185, 223
drainage 672, 677
drama 155, 401
draughts 460
Draupada 159
Draupadi **159**, 462
Dream Time **75**, 631
dredging 177 see also drainage
drinks see alcohol; elixirs
Drona 61, **160**, 678
dropsy 647
drought 70, 147, 631
Drumalika **160**
drums 277, 315
Dryads 431
Dryas 365
Duat **160**
Dubiaku **160**
Duck 330
ducks 313, 364
Dudugera **161**
Duellona 89
Dugnai **161**
Dumuzi 286, 297
dung beetles 328, 515
Duraulu 143
Durga 149, **162**, 321, 551
Durvasas 39, 339

Duryodhana 91, **163**, 462, 537
Dvalin 101, 559
dwarves 29, 44, 201, 643, 676
Dxui 16, **164**
Dyaus 21, **164**
Dyavaprivithi **164**
Dyumatsena 542
Dyu-piter 164
Dzambo 197
Dziewona 153
Dzoavits **164**

Ea 7, 41, **165**, 177, 375, 609
Eagle 164
eagles 265, 281, 351, 379, 422, 436,
    583, 601, 650, 674
Earth, creation of see creators of Earth
Earth (element) 196, 204
earth goddess 498
Earth goddess 126 see also Gaia; Mother
    Earth
Earthborn Giants **165**, 208, 456
    see also Titans
earthquakes 95, 140, 164, 324, 360, 399,
    493, 509, 516, 531, 571, 630, 642,
    648, 660, 672
Ebisu 549
Eburac 480
Echion 19, 53, 310, 576
Echo **168**, 411
eclipses 29, 210, 304, 517
ecstasy, god of 155
Edao 358
Edda 246
Eddas 427
Eden 7, 407
Edicts of the Emperor Yao 672
eels 572
Eeyeekalduk **168**
Efabbar 550
Egeria 261
eggs 24, 124, 156, 185, 212, 237, 255,
    341, 351, 352, 364, 455, 460, 465,
    568, 587, 607, 625
    cosmic 214, 252, 270, 280, 285, 313,
        326, 340, 444, 585
    primordial 36, 181, 444, 464, 504, 571

Egia 245, 420
Egyptian myth 168
Ehecatl 171
Eidothea 501
Eight Gods 172
Eight Immortals 172, 266, 478
Einmyria 360
Eioneus 298
Eitel 70
Eithinoha 450
Ejoni 426
Ekkekko 173
El 43, 173
El Dorado 173
Eladu 139
Elaine 209, 214, 474
Electra (daughter of Agamemnon) 17,
    121, 124, 174, 249, 476, 507
Electra (Euripides) 174, 452
Electra (Hofmannstahl) 174
Electra (Sophocles) 18, 174, 452
Electra (Titan) 296
Electryon 28, 38
elements 37, 196, 204
Elements, Five 196
elephants 24, 102, 148, 162, 210, 381,
    387, 653
Eleusis 145
Elijah 506
Eliot, TS 452
Elissa 150
elixirs 173, 238, 266, 341, 414, 574
Ellal 174
Elli 174
eloquence, deities of 97, 444
Elpenor 123, 175
Elphin 586
Elysian Fields 175
Elysium 175
embalming deities 239, 546
Embla 62, 263
emeralds 212
Emituofo 36
Emma-O 676
Emperors, Five 197
Empusa 348
Enceladus 165

end of the world 20, 65, 232, 281, 322,
    504, 516, 552, 554
Endymion 175, 545
engineering 266, 547, 652, 677
    see also inventors
English language 90
Enipeus 309
Enki 70, 176, 177, 286, 635
Enkidu 219, 421
Enlil 41, 70, 177, 375, 409, 417
Ennead 177
enoki tree 331
Enumclaw 178
Enyo 52, 226 see also Graeae
Eoghan 145
Eos 178
Epaphus 293
Epeus 662
Ephesus 57
Ephialtes 165
ephialtion 167
Epic of Gilgamesh, The 8, 220, 636
Epidaurus 15
Epigoni 27, 180, 548, 612
Epimetheus 69, 147, 464
Epona 178, 505
Erato 401 see also Muses
Erebus 203
Ereshkigal 179, 286, 417
Erginus 621
Erh Long 179
Erichthonius 69, 251
Eridanus 305
Eridu 176
Erilo 673
Eriphyle 27, 179
Erippe 439, 478
Eris 52, 180, 468, 473, 683
Erlik 180, 630
Eros 48, 52, 181, 223, 251, 353, 468
Erp 70
Erra 375
Erymanthian Boar 182
Erysichthon 182
Erythia 259
Erzulie 183
Esaugetuh Emissee 183

Eschenbach, Wolfram von 480
Eset 59
Eshu **183**
Esia 360
Estsanatlehi **184**, 623
Esus 595
Eteocles 47, 131, **184**, 441, 547
Ethlin 85, 363
Etna, Mt 135, 626, 627
Euippe 153
Eumaeus 439
Eumenides 203, 204 *see also* Furies
Euneus 274
Euphrates River 6, 7, 177, 375, 387
Euphrosyne 225
Euripides 5, 10, 18, 44, 50, 111, 155, 174,
    245, 249, 256, 294, 295, 383, 386, 440,
    442, 452, 479, 502, 507, 600
Europa **184**, 524
Eurotas River 351
Euryale 225 *see also* Gorgons
Euryalus (Argonaut) 53
Euryalus (son of Erippe) 440, 478
Euryalus (Trojan) 423
Eurydice 55, 452
Eurynome **185**, 251
Eurystheus 29, 71, 75, 114, **185**, 253,
    254, 272, 328, 343
Eurytion 217, 488
Eurytus 165, 255, 488
Euterpe 401 *see also* Muses
Evander **186**
Eve **7**, 233, 533, 573
Evening Star 296, 314, 668
Everus 611
evil 9, 37, 686
evil, deities of 22, 147
Evnissyen 98
examinations, god of 337
Excalibur **186**, 398, 653
eye of Horus 265
    of Ra 515, 544
eyes 150, 168, 348, 553

Fa 184
Fa'ahotu 66, 585
Fafnir **189**, 524, 561

Falkenberg, Willem 199
Falstaff 114
families, god of 549
famine 147, 338, 354
Fan Guei **189**
Fand 371
Farbauti 359
farming 55, 127, **190**, 215, 308, 373,
    376, 400, 450, 465, 471-2, 498, 511,
    552, 593, 611, 634, 636, 660
farming, deities of 78, 145, 200, 371-2,
    498, 522, 541, 574, 592
farting 488, 649
fate 190, 428
fate, deities of 26, 428
Fates 24, 167, **190**, 236, 260, 398, 597, 626
Father Sky 305, 456 *see also* Ouranos
Fathir 246
Faulkner, William 452
Faumea 588
fauns 541
Faunus **190**
Faust **191**, 199, 540
Faust Part I 191
Faust-Book 191
Faustulus 529
Favonius 682
Fawn 212
feasts 86
feathers 125, 164, 221, 275, 367, 379,
    408, 413, 578
Fefafa 327
Fei Lian **192**, 266, 510, 672, 674
Feng Bo 192
Fenrir 247, 311, 360, 516, 627, 650
Fensalier 202
Ferdiad 133
fern-roots 221
fertility 176, 190, **192**, 243, 291, 403,
    581, 654
fertility deities 8, 50, 59, 61, 62, 85, 114,
    115, 126, 141, 142, 164, 198, 201, 210,
    226-7, 231, 235, 238, 239, 286, 323,
    353, 377, 393, 395, 397, 421, 434, 469,
    498, 506, 526, 527, 532, 546, 555, 559,
    574, 576, 582, 614, 624, 630, 631, 639,
    644, 654, 665, 682 *see also* creators of life

Fevanga 327
Fever, Fire Gourd of 198
figs 109
Find 363
Fingal 446
Finian's Rainbow 217
Finisher 193
Finn MacCool 194
Finnish language 321
Finnish myth 193
Fintan 194
fire 65, 247, 270, 315, 379, 401, 414,
  486, 487, 499, 559, 565, 574, 580,
  608, 613, 634, 649, 668
Fire (element) 196, 204
fire deities 20, 88, 225, 251-2, 319, 324,
  359, 445, 583, 667
fire serpents 587
firmament, goddess of the 29-30
First Made Man 195
First Man 400
First Woman 283, 400
Firstborn 409
fish deities 140, 419, 459
Fisher King 474
fishing 379
fishing, deities of 549
five ages of mortals 196
Five Buddhas 196
Five Elements 196
Five Emperors 197
Five Lands 197
Five Plague Demons 197
Five Sisters 198
Fjalar 221, 582
fleas 465
fleeces see golden fleeces
flies 293
Flies, The 452
floods 6, 23, 69, 70, 72, 82, 86, 95, 147,
  158, 169, 177, 183, 194, 198, 204,
  220, 239, 269, 298, 332, 364, 373,
  378, 388, 390, 408, 425, 429, 430,
  443, 521, 547, 583, 591, 608, 615,
  624, 632, 633, 635, 636, 650, 660,
  661, 669, 677
Flora 198, 682

flower deities 471-2, 667 see also farming;
  fertility
flutes 69, 313
Fly 87
flying 275
Flying Dutchman 199
Flying Dutchman, The 199
flying foxes 95
Flying Head 199
Fomori 85
food 277
food of the gods 33, 39
forest deities 456, 522, 589
forest fires 21
forests 353
Forseti 59, 199, 631
Fortuna 200
Four Diamond Kings 200
Four Dragon Kings 200
four elements 37
Four Kings of Hell 200
Fox 195, 574, 630
foxes 39
foxes, flying 95
Frankenstein, Baron Victor von 191
Freemasons 263
Freud, Sigmund 442
Frey 200, 418, 559, 567, 644
Freyja 61, 101, 201, 265, 418, 435, 567,
  601, 644
Friday the Thirteenth 540
Frigg 15, 83, 201, 202, 261, 627
Frisch, Max 442
Frog 128
frogs 252
Frogs 155, 236
frost giants 90, 91, 320, 361, 489, 630,
  675
frost glitter, god of 631
fruit goddess 667
Fu Xi 204, 677
Fu Xing 604
Fuchi 203
Fufei 675
Fuji, Mt 203
Fujiyama 202
Fukurukoju 549

funerary goddess 413
Furies 27, 125, **203**, 236, 390, 442, 451, 456, 476
Futen **204**

Gabijia 569
Gabriel **207**, 246, 577
gadflies 174
Ga-gorib 247
Gaia 49, 132, 147, 196, **207**, 389, 525, 621 *see also* Mother Earth
Gaia Theory 208, 399
Gajanana 210
gaki **208**
Galahad 57, **208**, 345, 348, 474
Galanthis 29
Galar 221, 582
Galaru 227
Galatea 490, 507
Galeru 227
Gallen-Kallela, Akseli Valdemar 321
Gamag Nara **209**
Games *see* Olympic Games, Pythian Games
Ganapati 100, 210
Gandharvanagara 210
Gandharvas 50, **210**, 648
Ganesh 100, **210**, 368
Ganga **211**, 539
Gangadhara 553
Ganges River 91, 92, 102, 210, 211, 387, 463, 536, 539, 554, 678
gangsters 445
Ganymede **211**, 242
Ga-oh 8, **212**
Garuda **212**, 319, 347, 406, 648, 650
gate-keepers 62, 356
Gauna **213**, 317
Gauri 149
Gautama (Buddha) *see* Siddhartha Gautama
Gautama (sage) 292
Gawa 213
Gawain **213**
Gawain and the Green Knight 58, 213, 398
Gawama 213
Gayatari 575

Gayatri 539
Gayomart **214**
Geb 178, **214**, 429, 556
geese 40, 86, 98, 214
Gefion **215**
Geirröd 20, **215**, **216**, 436
Gemini (constellation) 156, 341
Gendenwitha **216**
Genetrix 49
Geoffrey of Monmouth 26, 357
geometry 603
Germanic myth **216**
Geryon **217**
Geryon's cattle 105, 217, 250, 543
Geshtinanna 286
Gesta Danorum 261
Geush Urvan **218**
Gewi 317
Gguluddene 326
Ghede 78, 97, **218**
ghosts 25, 93, 175, 372, 533
    see also phantoms
Ghosts of Impermanence 153
giants 3, 26, 47, 49, 53, 61, 83, 87, 95, 98, 99, 133, 140, 149, 164, 165, 177, 201, 212, 213, 215, 217, **219**, 222, 230, 233, 242, 255, 259, 265, 269, 273, 311, 312, 336, 338, 356, 359, 435, 443, 461, 465, 490, 498, 509, 538, 567, 580, 582, 583, 595, 601, 602, 618, 635, 650, 675
    see also Cyclops; Earthborn Giants; frost giants; Hundred-handed Giants; Titans
Giants' Causeway 127
Gide, André 351
Gidja 671
Gilgamesh 81, **219**, 388, 421, 642
    see also Epic of Gilgamesh, The
Gilling **221**, 582
Ginungagap **221**
Giraudoux, Jean 249, 386
Giru 550
Gitagovinda 335, 516
Gjall 246
Gjalp 215, 245, 420
Gladsheim 60
Glastonbury 77

Glauce 131, 309, 382
Glaucus 122, 470, 543
Glispa 572
Glooscap 221
Gluck, Christoph Willibald von 295
Gluskap 42, **221**, 408
Glut 360
Goat 323, 451, 555
Gods of Good Luck, Seven 140, **549**
Gods of Happiness, Three **604**
Gods, Eight **172**
Goethe, Johann Wolfgang von 191, 211, 295, 351, 386
Gogmagog **222**
Gogo 308
Gohone 8
Goibniu 363
gold 27, 93, 101, 179, 197, 212, 222, 372, 561
Golden Ages 58, 196, 266, 332, 418, 515, 539, 541, 596, 645, 675
golden apples *see* apples of immortality
Golden Ass, The 503
Golden Fleece, The 383
golden fleeces 67, 71, **222**, 250, 272, 309, 474, 486
goldsmiths 44, 101, 178, 559, 667
Golgus 9
Gommateshvara **224**
Gong Gong **225**, 672, 677
good luck 50, 85, 98, 117, 257, 337, 420, 564, 610, 630
good luck deities 140, 173, 200, 210, 211, 345, 347, 549, 562, 604
Gordius 391
Gorgons 14, 68, 70, 142, **225**, 226, 383, 482
gorillas 681
Gorlois 635
Goronwy 358
Götterdämmerung 516, 517
Gottfried of Strassburg 619
Gounod, Charles 192
gourds 556
Govardhana, Mt 334
Graces **225**, 611
Graeae 225, **226**, 482

Graham, Martha 383
Grail, Holy *see* Holy Grail
grapes 300 *see also* wine
Gratium 165
Graves, Robert 383, 412
Great Bear 409, 685
Great Bear (constellation) 337, 455, 549, 596
Great Eagle 583
Great Goddess 60, 81, 121, 145, 148, 153, 159, 201-2, **226**, 241, 253, 259, 300, 377, 525, 571
  see also Mother Earth
Great Hare 408
Great Rainbow Snake **226**, 313, 315, 571, 613
Great Spirit 657
Great Thunderbird *see* Thunderbirds
Greek myth 12, 15, **227**, 389
Greek/Roman equivalent names 529
Green Giant 213 *see also* giants
Green Parrot Girls 613
Greip 245, 420
Grendel 90
Grendel's mother 90
Grerr 101
Grid 215, **230**, 649
Grihaspati 20
Grillparzer, Franz 383
Grimm brothers 320
Grimmelshausen, Hans von 209
Grimnir 20, 436
Groa 602
grubs 143, 588
Gu **230**, 381
Guan Di **231**
Guan Gong 231
Guan Yin 36, 77, **231**, 676
Guan Yü 231
guardians 62, 110, 114, 179, 226, 370, 604
Gucumatz **231**
Gudratrigakwitl **232**
Gudrun 70, 561
Guecufu **232**
Guernica 113
Guest, Charlotte 367
Guha 240

Guinechen 232
Guinevere 209, 232, 348, 397
Gulanundoidj 315
Gullinbursti 559
Gullveig 644
Gulu 329
Gunapipi 339
Gungnir 435
Gunnar 70, 101, 561
Gunnlod 97, 233, 582
Gunnodayak 233
gusli 535
Guttorm 101, 561
Gwalchmai 214
Gwawl 505
Gwern 98
Gwion 586
Gwydion 357
Gwynhwfar 232
Gyges 269
Gylfi 215

Hachiman 235
Haddad 6
Hades 116, 132, 135, 145, 235, 453,
   480, 482, 488, 563, 566, 683, 684
Hagesandros 349
Haggard, H. Rider 263
Hahgwehdaetgah 64, 236
Hahgwehdiyu 64, 236
Ha'iaka 237
hair 407
Haiuri 17, 237
Halley's Comet 259
Ham 425
Hamadryads 431
Hamlet 338, 442
Han Xiang 172
Han Zhongli 172
Hana 237
Hand of Atum 74
Hang Ha Erh Jiang 237
Hannahanna 592
Hanuman 46, 238, 319, 320, 519, 617, 648
Hanumat 238
Haoma 238
Hap 239, 293

Hapi 239
happiness, goddess of 636
Hapy 239
Har 264
Hara 553
Harappa 288
Hare 246
hares 102, 408, 447, 623
Hari Krishna 334
Harihara 240
Harmony 19, 27, 107, 251, 401
Harpies 223, 236, 240, 485
Harpocrates 264
Harsamtaui 264
harvest deities 145, 341, 492, 559, 593
harvests 6, 176, 193, 582, 673
Hathor 60, 241, 264, 402, 430, 515
Haumea 241
Haumia 521, 522
Havgan 51, 505
Hawaii 465
Hawk 73, 362
hawks 194, 264
Hayagriva 242
Haydn, Joseph 295
hazelnuts 194
He Xiangu 172
headaches 389
Headache, Iron Band of 198
healers 49, 62, 113, 194, 239, 552
healing 33, 88, 104, 156, 403, 572, 581,
   603, 634, 637, 647 see also medicine;
   surgery
healing deities 14-15, 61, 88, 100, 149,
   150, 168, 281, 297-8, 299, 329, 363,
   446, 506, 531-2, 545, 546, 592, 629,
   665-6
health, deities of 549, 637
heartbeat 503
hearts 37, 48, 70, 115, 125, 279, 561,
   596, 615, 616, 632, 636, 644
Heaven 97, 242, 449, 634
Hebe 242, 683
Hecate 122, 167, 242, 245, 305, 470
Hector 24, 243, 471, 491
Hecuba 244, 245, 467, 489, 497
Hedjwer 603

Heh 444
Hehet 444
Heimdall 15, 93, **245**, 420, 601
Heimskringla 427
Heitsi-Eibib **246**
Hel 83, **247**, 311, 360, 420, 516
Helen 386, 502
Helen of Sparta *see* Helen of Troy
Helen of Troy 17, 25, 124, 144, 153, 156,
   191, **247**, 249, 277, 351, 385, 437,
   468, 476, 484, 488, 497, 599, 625, 663
Helenus 44, 110, **249**, 416
Helheim 247
Heligoland 59
Heliopolis 74, 170
Helius 217, 223, **250**, 273, 481
Helle 67, **250**, 416
hellebores 385
Hellespont 250
Hemadri 387
Heng 605
Heng O **250**, 665, 674
Heng Xi **665**
Hengshan 465
Heorot 90
Hephaestus 5, 68, 138, 139, 167, **250**,
   449, 460, 475, 482, 683
Heqet **252**, 328
Hera 28, 49, 50, 52, 53, 67, 132, 168,
   186, 218, 223, 248, 250, **252**, 253,
   255, 293, 298, 309, 343, 348, 354,
   468, 473, 493, 497, 546, 576, 611, 683
Heracles 3, 24, 26, 29, 32, 48, 67, 74,
   79, 105, 114, 116, 120, 131, 154, 167,
   182, 185, 186, 217, 223, 242, **253**,
   260, 272, 328, 350, 415, 417, 449,
   471, 484, 488, 497, 500, 543, 578,
   599, 683, 684
   Labours of 343
herb-lore 552, 637
herbs 238, 304, 575
Hercules 253
Herm 257
Hermes 29, 54, 154, 190, 253, **256**, 453,
   462, 468, 475, 478, 482, 498, 531,
   565, 603, 626, 683
Hermes Trismegistus 171

Hermione 248, **257**, 385, 416, 451
Hermod 569
Hermopolis 170
Hern the Hunter 114
Herodotus 89
heroes 4, 11, 17, 53, 57, 82, 88, 90, 91,
   92, 96, 101, 126-7, 133, 153, 157,
   196, 208-9, 213, 219, 243, 253, **258**,
   264, 277, 280, 308-9, 346, 348, 357-
   8, 415-6, 420-1, 437-8, 451, 462, 466,
   467-8, 471, 482, 495, 505, 518-20,
   527, 535, 560, 561, 597-9, 619, 624,
   640, 653, 662, 679
Heroides 383
herons 89, 371
Hersilia **258**
Herupakhret 264
Hesiod 228
Hesione 254, 350, 497
Hesperides **259**, 328, 649
hesperis 480
Hestia 132, 259, 649, 683
Hexameron 389
Heyvoso 381
Hiawatha 321, 330
hibernation 338
Hiisi 352
Hikohohodemi 671
Hilisvini 201
Himinbjorg 246
Hina **259**
Hina A Rauriki 588
Hina Ika 379
Hindu religion 287
Hine Ahu One 259, 587
Hine Nui Te Po 259, 380, 588
Hine Titama 587
Hine Titamauri 587
Hine Tu A Muana 588
Hino 259
Hinu 8, 233, **259**
Hippocrene 472, 611
Hippodamia (Princess of Argos) 113, 488
Hippodamia (Princess of Pisa) 442, 475
Hippolyta 48, **259**
Hippolytus 14, 48, 49, 165, **260**, 483, 599
Hippomedon 547

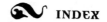

Hippomenes 64
Hipponous 88
hippos 264
Hiranyakashipu **261**, 410, 495, 523
Hiranyaksha **261**, 645
history 401
History of the Kings of Britain 357
Hjördis 560, 563
Hlin **261**
Ho Po 250, 672, 675
Höd 15, 83, **261**
Hoener 263
Hoenir 263
Hofmannstahl 174
Högli 70
Hokomata **615**
Holawaka **262**
Holinshed, Raphael 357
Holler 630
holly trees 564, 643
Holmes, Sherlock 191
Holy Grail 57, 209, **262**, 345, 348, 386, 474, 480
Homasubi 129
home, goddess of 116
Homer 5, 13, 14, 18, 44, 47, 111, 220, 228, 244, 245, 249, 251, 295, 320, 351, 385, 412, 440, 451, 471, 562
Homer's Daughter 412
homosexuality 211, 346, 453
honesty, goddess of 498
honey 155, 353, 622
Honeybird 354
Honir 15, 189, **263**, 393, 568, 645
Honoyeta **263**
hoopoes 594
Hope 464
Horace 383
Horae 259
Horatius Cocles **264**
Horkhentiirti 264
Horn of Plenty 3 *see also* plenty
Hornung, E.W. 660
horses 96, 153, 178, 242, 359, 493, 525, 536, 539, 581, 582, 646
see also Wooden Horse
horses, flying 472, 482, 484, 548, 569

Horus 59, 73, 241, 252, **264**, 414, 455, 577, 591
Hosuseri 671
Hotei Osho 549
Houris **265**
hours, goddesses of 259
House of Death 559
household deities 90-1, 158, 346-7, 350, 476
households 307
housekeeper goddess 172
Hraesvelg **265**
Hreidmar 189
Hrothgar 90
Hrungnir **265**, 602
Hrym **265**
Hsuan-Tsang 617
Hu 270
Hu Jingte 604
Hua Xu 267
Huai Nan Zu **266**
Huang Di **266**, 510, 677
Huang Gun **267**
Huashan 465
Hugin 435
Hui 679
Huitzilopochtli 125, 128, **267**, 667
human ancestors 7, 16, 26, 44, 62, 70-1, 72, 82, 147, 195, 214, 245, **268**, 308, 329-30, 355, 372, 373, 388, 402-3, 409-10, 446, 465, 494-5, 607, 615, 635-6, 655-6, 659, 674, 675
humankind, creation of *see* creators of humankind; creators of life; human ancestors
Humanmaker **268**
Humbaba 220
humming-birds 268, 667
Hun Dun **270**
Hunab **269**, 271
Hundred-handed Giants 99, 132, 208, **269**, 456
Hunger 247
hunger demons 338
Hunger-beast 182-3
hunters 394
hunting 51, 297

hunting deities 49, 56, 153, 352, 396, 409, 487, 671
hurricanes 280, 522 *see also* storms
hurricanes, god of 270 *see also* wind deities
Hurukan **270**
Huveane **271**
Hvergelmir 420, 674
hyacinths 272
Hyacinthus **271**, 682
Hydra **272**
Hyginus 13
Hylas 254, **272**
Hyllus 186, 256
Hymen 155, **273**
Hymenaeus 273
Hymir 11, **273**, 311, 602, 627
Hymn to Aten 66
Hyperbius 547
Hyperenor 576
Hyperion **273**, 612
Hypnus **273**
Hypsipyle **274**
Hyrieus 621

I 573
Iae **336**
Iapetus 597, 612
Iarbas **275**
Iaso 15
Iasus 64
Ibsen, Henrik 321
Icarius 476
Icarus 138, **275**
ice worlds 419
Ictinike **277**
Ida **277**
Ida, Mt 134
Idaea 485
Idas 53, 156
Idomeneus **277**
Idun 15, 97, **278**, 601
Igaluk **279**
Igigi 177
Ika a Maui 380
Ikugupi 632
Ilamatecuhtli **279**
Iliad 5, 13, 18, 44, 221, 228, 244, 245,

320, 385, 440, 471, 562
Illa 650
Illuyankas **279**, 593
Ilma **280**, 364
Ilmarinen **280**, 320, 353, 537, 641
Ilmatar 364
Ilmen, Lake 535
Ilus 461
Ilya Muromets **280**, 506, 583
Ilyap'a **280**
Ilythia 28, 253, **280**, 683
Imana **281**
Imberombera 658
Imdugud **281**
Imhotep **281**
Imilozi **282**
immortality 4, 7, 20, 25, 38, 39, 92, 118, 172, 177, 220, 238, 262, 263, 266, **282**, 305, 317, 341, 355, 356, 400, 457, 473, 479, 533, 559, 571, 574, 611, 634, 636, 669
immortality, goddess of 649
Immortality, Tree of 7
Immortals, Eight **172**, 266, 478
I'm Not Stiller 442
Imouthes 281
impotence, god of 497
In **285**
Ina 259
Inanna 43, 179, **286**, 297, 387
Inaras 279
Inari **287**, 630
Inca myth 34
incense 267
incest 237, 531, 565, 588
Indian myth 19, **287**
Indiana Jones and the Last Crusade 263
Indonesia 86
Indra 8, 20, 21, 24, 84, 93, 102, 140, 157, 164, 212, 238, **291**, 334, 340, 376, 406, 462, 506, 536, 625, 648, 654
Infernal Machine, The 442
infertility 304, 532, 641
Ino 67, 108, 154, 222, 417
intellect, goddess of 100
Inti **293**, 371, 459, 650
inventor deities 539

inventors 138, 149, 266, 379, 460, 677
invisibility 481, 482
invulnerability 24, 108, 261, 415, 624
Inyan 657
Io 53, 54, 239, **293**
Iobates 88
Iolaus 256
Iole 255
Ion **294**
Ioskeha 64, 236, **294**
Iphianassa 294
Iphicles 29, 253
Iphigenia 17, 56, 124, **294**, 452
Iphigenia in Aulis 18
Iphigenia in Tauris 295, 452
Iphis 493
Iphitus 255
Iranian myth 22
Iris 253, 258, **296**, 481, 682
Iron Age 196
irrigation 6, 182, 298, 672
Isaiwa 659
Ischys 14
Ishtar 43, 220, **296**, 388, 595
Ishvara 553
Isis 171, 293, 430 *see also* Aset
Islam 290, 388
Islands of the Blessed 133, 305
Isle of Man 371
Ismene **297**
Isora 610
Italus 478
Ithaca 477
Itha-Irapi 54
Itherther 297
Itugen 593
Itylus 38
Itys 594
Itzamná **297**
Itzpapalotl **298**
Iuchar 142
Iucharbar 142
Iulus 59
Iuventus 242
Iwanaga 422
Ixchel **298**
Ixion **298**

Ixtab **299**
Ixtlilton **299**
Izanagi 30, 117, **299**, 581, 623, 632
Izanami **299**, 582, 632, 676

jackals 48, 445
Jagadgauri 149
Jaganath **303**
Jaganmatri 149
Jagati 575
jaguars 563, 596
Jahu 669
Jain myth 224, 346, 369, 469, 526, 612, 648
Jalandhara **303**
Jamadagni 549
Jambavan **304**
Jambavat 304
Jambavati 304
Janaka **304**, 566
Jang 622
Jang E 250
Jang Long 200
Jang Xien **304**
Janiculum Hill 306
Janus **305**, 486, 541
Jao Gong Ming 622
Japanese myth **306**
Japhet 425
Jara (demon) **307**
Jara (goddess) **308**
Jara (hunter) **308**
Jarasandha **308**
Jari **308**
Jarl 246
Jarnsaxa 245, 420
Jason 53, 274, **308**, 382, 474
Jataka 103
Jatayu **310**, 519
Jeh 214
jellyfish 285, 632
Jerna 246
Jewelmaster 31
jewels 30, 140, 216, 235, 251, 304, 347, 406, 422, 622, 676 *see also* precious stones; Tide Jewels
Jibril 207, 577

Jimmu 306, 422, 672
Jing Te 678
Jingo 610
Jiro 679
Jizo **310**
Jocasta **310**, 346, 441
jokes 157, 360, 591
Jord 202
Jormungand 11, 247, **311**, 360, 516, 602
Joseph (of Arimathea) 77, 262
Joseph (son of Jacob) 241, 363
Jotunheim 93, 201, **311**, 392
Jou Wang **312**
Joukahainen **312**, 640
Ju 270
Judaism 388
judgement of Paris 468, 543
judgement of the Dead 37, 41, 48, 200,
    316, 367, 395, 455, 522, 524, 593,
    636, 671, 676 *see also* Dead
Judgement, Day of 395
judgement, goddess of 415
judges of the dead 566
juggernauts 303
Jugumishanta **312**
Julius II 349
Julunggul **313**
Jumala **313**, 630
Jumna 333
Jun Di **314**
Jung, Carl Gustav 351
Jungian philosophy 440
Juno **252**, 314, 624
Juok **314**
Jupiter 86, 305, **314**, 503, 528, 541
    see also Zeus
Jurawadbad **315**
Jurojin 549
Jurumu **315**, 504
Jurupari 115
justice **316**
justice, deities of 20, 199, 367, 597, 636
    see also judgment of the Dead
Jyeshtharaja 100

Ka 496
Kaang 213, **317**

Kabundungulu **579**
Kadaklan 605
Kadlu **319**
Kadru 212, **319**, 650
Kafka, Franz 209
Kagami 402
Kagingo 326
Kagutsuchi 300, **319**
Kahausibwara 283
Kaikeyi 143, **319**, 518
Kailasa, Mt 24, 554
Kala 553
Kalanemi **320**, 325
Kale 611
Kalervo 337
Kalevala 194, 280, **320**, 642
Kali 149, 162, 300, **321**, 326
Kaliya **322**, 334
Kalki 102, 242, **322**, 652
Kalma **322**, 580, 623
Kalumba **323**
Kalvaitis **323**
Kama **323**, 522
    avatars of Kama 533
Kamadhenu **323**, 466, 527
Kamapua'a **323**
Kamarong **308**
Kamonu 430
Kamrusepas 593
Kamsa 324
Kananeski Anayehi **324**
Kanassa **324**
Kanati **324**
Kane 430, 587
kangaroos 394
Kansa 82, 147, 148, 160, 308, 320, **324**,
    333, 471
Kao Guojiu 172
Kapoonis **178**
kappa **325**
Karia 227
Karl 246
Karna 339
Karnak 40
Karnikacala 387
Karta 345
Kartavirya 466

Karttikeya **325**
Kasogonaga **326**
Kastor 156
Kasyapa 157, 212, 319, 325, **326**, 467,
    549, 650
Katonda **326**
Kaukas 158
Kaumari 326
Kauravas 61, 92, 150, 159, 160, 163,
    308, **327**, 340, 462, 536, 678
Kausalya **327**, 518
kava **327**
Keats, John 295
Kek 444
Keket 444
Keryneian Hind **327**
Kesa 646
Kesava 651
Khakaba 659
Khandava Forest 21
Khemenu 170, 444
Khepra 328
Khepri **328**
Khnum **328**
Kho 317
Khodumodumo 157
Khonsu **328**
Khonvum **329**
Kibuka 326
Kiev 280
Kilya **329**
Kimat 605
King Must Die, The 600
King Oedipus 442
Kings of Hell, Four **200**
Kingu 375
Kintu **329**
Kipu-Tyttö **330**
kitchens, god of 622
Kitshi Manito **330**
Kittum 550
Klehanoai 73
Kloskurbeh **331**
Knossos 139
knowledge 393, 435, 570, 587, 589
knowledge, deities of 341, 603
Knowledge, Tree of 573

knucklebones 257
Kodoyanpe **331**
Kojiki 300, 306
Kojin **331**
Koko 331
Kokomikeis 410
Kokyangwuti **332**
Koloowisi 512, 572
Komokwa **332**
Konohana 422
Kononatoo **332**
Koran, The 207
Koronis 14
Kothar 43
Kotoamatsukami 286, **333**
Kratu 496
Kravyads 22
Kremara **498**
Kriemhild 419
Krishna 56, 82, 93, 147, 148, 160, 257,
    303, 304, 308, 322, 325, **333**, 368,
    387, 463, 505, 516, 523, 527, 532,
    536, 537, 564, 617, 629, 647, 652
Ksirabdhitanya 346
Ku 522
Kua Fu **336**
Kuat **336**
Kube 400
Kubera **336**
Kui **337**, 659
Kukulkan **337**
Kul **337**
Kulimina 341
Kullervo 320, **337**
Kulu 341
Kumarbi 595
Kumbhakarna **338**
Kumokum **338**
Kumush **339**
Kun 677
Kunapipi **339**
Kuninotokotati 632
Kunitokotachi 202
Kunti 159, **339**, 464
Kuntibhoja 339
Kupala 569
Kurma 39, **340**

Kuru 327
Kurukadi **340**
Kururumany **341**
Kurwaichin 569
Kusanagi 32
Kusanaginotsurugi 582
Kushinada 582
Kusor **341**
Kuu **341**
Kuvera 336
Kvasir 221, **341**, 436, 582
Kwatee **342**
Kylliki **342**, 352
Kynossema 245

Labours of Heracles 343
labyrinths 139, 470
Lachesis 190 *see also* Fates
Lady Meng 392
Lady of the Lake 58, 187, 209, **343**, 386
Laelaps 39
Laertes 77, **345**, 437, 477
Laima **345**
Laius 310, **345**, 440
Lakshmana 19, 310, **346**, 518, 590
Lakshmi 40, **346**, 539, 649, 651
avatars of Lakshmi *see* Drampadi; Radha;
   Rukmini; Sita
Lamfada 363
Lamia **347**
Lan Kai He 172
Lancelot 57, 58, 209, 232, **348**, 474
Lancelot du Lac 58
Lands, Five **197**
Langal 227
Langi 521
languages 7, 76, 81, 90, 183, 266, 270,
   282, 321, 435, 501, 631-2, 658
Laocoön **349**, 663
Laoghaire 133
Laomedon 50, 254, **349**, 493, 684
Laothoë 490
Lapiths 113, 298, 488
Lapithus 113
Lar **350**
Lara 373
Larentia 529

Lars Porsena 264
La Sirene 22
Lasthenes 547
Latinus 12, 122, **350**, 592
Latona 353
Lausus 390
lava 237
Lavatory Ladies, Three **604**
Lavinia 12, 350
law 205, 266, 454, 603
Laws of Manu 374
Lear 357
Learchus 67
Leda 156, 247, **351**, 625
Legba 183, **351**, 370
Lei Gong **352**
Lei Jen Zu **352**
Leib-Olmai **352**
Leiden 364
Leimoniads 431
Leir 357
Lemminkäinen 320, **352**, 538, 642
Lemminkäinen Legends 321
Lemnos 223
Leo (constellation) 415
leprechauns 112, 363
leprosy 614, 667
Lesbos 454
Leshachikha 353
Leshy **353**
Lethe River 175, **353**, 361, 453, 599,
   622, 642
Leto 49, 56, **353**
lettuces 60, 394
Leucus 277
Leve 418
Leviathan 279, **354**
Leza **354**
Lhamo **354**
Lhamo Latson, Lake 355
Li 685
Li Jing 356
Li No Zha **356**
Li Papai **356**
Li Shin Min 197
Li T'ien 607
Li Xuan 172

Liaisons dangereuses, Les 151
Libanza **355**
libraries 540
Lif **355**, 517
Lifdrasir **355**, 517
life, creation of *see* creators of life; creators of humankind; human ancestors
Life, Tree of 238, 407, 562
light 207, 271, 336, 347, 524, 574
light and dark 22, 23, 34, 78, 104, 170, 184, 221, 331, **355**, 369, 413, 510, 513, 540, 556-7, 586, 681 *see also* darkness
light, deities of 23, 83, 115, 286, 322, 324, 351, 651, 669
lightning 6, 17, 20, 97, 259, 270, 280, 324, 390, 531, 550, 590, 605, 614, 634 *see also* thunderbolts
lightning deities 111, 178, 280, 319, 517 *see also* storm deities; thunder deities
Lightning 610
Likubala 400
Lilith **356**
Lima 400
linden trees 86
Lingodbhava 553, 556
lions 253, 415, 551
Lipara 14
Lipchitz, Jaques 600
Lir 351, **357**
Liszt, Franz 192
literature 231 *see also* drama; poetry; writing
literature, deities of 211, 659
Little Bear 685
Little Red Riding Hood 540
Livy 59, 529, 530
Lizard 75, 372, 376, 634
lizards 681
Ljeschi 353
llamas 605
Lleu Llaw Gyffes **357**, 363, 367
Lleyr 357
Lo (river) 675
Lö Phag 197
Lo Shu 204
Loa **358**

Loau 327
Loch Ness Monster 572
locusts 82
Loder 358
Loge 358
Logue, Christopher 6
Lokamata 346
Loke 358
Loki 15, 44, 61, 83, 97, 129, 189, 215, 246, 257, 261, 278, 311, **358**, 456, 516, 524, 559, 567, 568, 569, 601
Lokkju 358
Lonbemlech 363
London, Tower of 99
Long Day's Journey Into Night 442
Long Wang 200, **361**
longevity, god of 549
Longfellow, Henry Wadsworth 321, 330
Lönnrot, Elias 194, 320, 642
Lopter 358
Lopti 358
lost wax process 139
Lot of Orkney 213
Lotis 497
lotus 21, 36, 97, 102, 347, 369, 371, 373, 414, 540, 581, 645
Lotus-eaters **361**
lotus-fruit 361
Louhi 280, 312, 337, 352, **361**, 537, 640, 641
Love 331
love deities 59, 183, 241, 333-4, 342, 370, 402, 549
Lovelock, James 208, 399
Loviatar **362**
Lu Ban **362**
Lu Dongbin 172
Lu Xing 604
Lucifer 144, 540
luck 667
luck, god of 417 *see also* good luck deities
Lucretia **362**
Lug 85, 213, 349, 358, **363**
Lugaba 326
Lugeilan 447
Luk 447
Luonnotar 280, 313, 321, **364**, 640

lust 497, 613 *see also* sex
lust, deities of 134, 201, 522, 614, 673
Luxor 170
Lycaon **364**
Lycomedes 4, 600, 601
Lycotherses 19
Lycurgus 274, **365**
Lynceus 53, 156
Lyon 364
Lyre (constellation) 454
lyres 37, 256

Maat **367**
Mab 112, 382
Mabel 140
Mabinogion 46, 113, **367**, 506, 619
MacAirt, Cormac *see* Cormac MacAirt
Macbeth 398, 664
Macbeth, Lady 245
MacCool, Finn *see* Finn MacCool
Macha 398
Machaon 485
MacLir, Manannan *see* Mannannan MacLir
Macpherson, James 446
Macuilxóchitl **368**
Madri 340, **368**, 464
Maenads 155, 453
Maeve 133
Magellan, Ferdinand 434
magic 218, 243, 382, 444 *see also* sorcery
magic square 204
magpies 510
Mahabharata 21, 56, 91, 211, 213, 287,
    290, 308, 327, 335, **368**, 406, 462,
    463, 467, 537, 652, 654
Mahadeva 149, 553
Mahaf **368**
Mahavira 290, **369**, 612
Maheo **369**
Mahisha 162
Mahler, Gustav 192
Mahsya 214
Mahsyoi 214
Mahu Ika 379
Maira Ata 55
Mait' Carrefour **369**
Maitreya **370**, 393

Majasgars 158
Maka 657
Makea 378
Makosh 397
Malabar 467
malachite 197
Malini 210
Malory, Thomas 58, 113, 263, 349
Malsum **370**
Mama Brigitte 218, **370**
Mama Ocllo 293, 372
Mama Quilla **370**
Ma Mien 153
Mammitu **370**
Manabozho 42, 407
Manala 641
Manannan MacLir 127, 363, **371**
Manannan (son of Oirbsen) 371
Manasa **371**
Manawydan ab Llyr 371
Manco Capac 293, **371**, 459, 650
Mandara, Mt 340
Manes **372**, 373
Mangarkungerkunja **372**
mangroves 587
Mani **373**
Mania 372, **373**
manioc 373
Manjushri **373**
Mann, Thomas 192
Manoa 173
Mantis 317
mantises 681
Manto 612
Manu 277, **373**, 470, 539
Maori 402-3
Maori myth 259, 465, 521, 522, 531
maps 340
Mara 148, **374**, 647
Marawa 509
Marduk 41, 81, **375**, 418, 562, 609
Marerewana 23
Marichi 496
Marici 159
Marindi **375**
Mark 618
markets, god of 257

Markhättu 352
Marlowe, Christopher 191, 249
marriage deities 26, 59, 202, 252, 370, 402, 615
Mars 52, 89, **376**, 529
Marsyas 49
martial arts, god of 231
Marttanda 653
Maruts 158, **376**, 498, 532
Mary 151, 202, **376**, 378, 397, 461, 482
Massassi 403
Mati-Syra-Zemlya **377**, 392
Matrikas 321
Matsya 242, **378**
Maui 259, **378**
Mawu 137
Mawu-Lisa 137, 230, **381**
Maya 102, **381**
Mayahuel 171
Mayan myth 22, 34, 115, 269, 297, 298, 299, 337, 633
Mayauel **381**
mead 221, 273, 341, 436, 685
meat-eating 297, 402
Meda 277
Medb **382**
Medea 5, 9, 111, 223, 309, **382**, 383, 474, 598
medicine 15, 59, 603
meditation 72, 98, 102, 141, 224, 290, 292 401, 526, 553, 558
Medon 507
Medraut 396
Medus 10, 383, 598
Medusa 225, 226, **383**, 472, 482
  see also Gorgons
Megaera 203 *see also* Furies
Megara 254
Megareus 547
Meghavahana 291
Mehen 573
Melampus **384**
Melanion 64
Melanippus 547
Melete 401 *see also* Muses
Melicertes 67, 68
Melpomene 401, 563 *see also* Muses

Melville Island 400
Memnon 5, 178
memory 183, 392
Memphis 239
Mendelssohn, Felix 192, 446
Menelaus 17, 44, 72, 124, 144, 248, 249, 258, **385**, 416, 468, 476, 502, 625
Menes 502
Meness **386**, 542
Meng 140
Menoeceus 547
Menoetus 69
menstruation 60, 126, 215, 227, 308, 313, 413, 655
Menulis 386
Mephistopheles 192, 249, **386**
Mercator, Gerhardus 70
merchants, god of 257
Mercury 86, **256**, 389
mercy, deities of 36, 77, 231, 310
Merlin 187, 232, 345, **386**, 586, 635
Mermerus 309, 382
Merope 440
Merry Wives of Windsor, The 114
Meru, Mt 92, 98, 211, **387**, 463, 625, 678
Mesharum 550
Meskhenet 387
Meskhent **387**
Mesomedes 66
Mesopotamian myth **387**
Messapus 424
messenger deities 100, 128, 183, 237, 239, 296, 363, 577
messengers 17, 42, 65, 97, 257, 262, 282, 284
Mesta 239
Metal (element) 196, 204
metal working deities 100, 230, 503
  see also smiths; crafts
metals 423 *see also* gold; silver
Metamorphoses 183, **389**, 484, 487, 492
Metanira 481
Metis 251, **389**
Mezentius **390**
Mi Hung Tang **392**
Mi Lo **393**
Michabo **390**

Mictlan **391**, 667
Midas **391**
Mide 408
Midgard 62, **392**, 674, 676
Midsummer Night's Dream, A 433
midwifery 421 *see also* childbirth
Mikula **392**
military bands, goddess of 69
milk 291, 334, 466, 498
Milky Way 29, 30, 52, 87, 93, 94, 253, 288, 419, 486, 489, 505, 587, 610, 636, 639
Miller, Henry 454
millet 400
Mimas 165
Mime 524
Mimi **393**
Mimir 15, 263, **393**, 645
Min **394**
Minawara **394**
Mindi 227
Minerva **68**, 69, 89, 314
Minos 131, 138, 235, 470, 598
Minotaur 54, 139, **394**, 470, 598
Mioya 203
Miralaldu **94**
Miraramuinar 313
mirrors 623
mischief, deities of 65, 489
Misery 247
Missouri River 608
mistletoe 83, 202, 261
Mithra 8, 19, **395**, 646
Mithras 218, **395**
Mitra 395
Mixcóatl 125, 279, **396**
Mjöllnir 560, 601
Mneme 401 *see also* Muses
Mnemosyne 612
Mockingbird 332
Modimo **396**
Modred 57, 348, **396**
Mohenjodaro 288
Mokosh **397**
Moloch 79
moly 122
Monkey 200, 238, 353, 617, 673
monkeys 46, 75, 102, 238, 400, 577, 579

monsters 23, 29, 88, 105, 114, 117, 131, 182, 191, 199, 203, 225, 226, 272, 299, 305, 337, 339, 347-8, 380, 383, 393, **397**, 399, 407, 415, 543, 564, 572, 576, 578, 580, 582, 587, 591, 616, 626, 631, 644, 659, 677
Monteverdi, Claudio 440, 454, 600
months 326
Moon 29, 34, 52, 141, 167, 211, 212, 226, 237, 242, 264, 316, 336, 341, 410, 451, 515, 603, 659, 665, 671
moon deities 44, 74, 95, 110, 115, 121, 127-8, 184, 242-3, 250, 279, 328, 329, 370, 386, 409, 460, 526, 545, 562, 574, 575, 615, 623, 634, 646
moonbeams 56
Moon-people 355
Moose 212
Mopsus 108, 109
Mordred 396
Morgan le Fay 213, 345, **398**, 433
Morgause 213, 396
Morholt 618
Morning Star 216, 489, 511, 512
Morongo 403
Morrigan 133, 140, 382, **398**
Morris, William 263
Mors **398**, 597
mortality 16, 17, 128, 214, 430, 448, 511, 661, 662, 671 *see also* immortality
Morte d'Arthur 58, 113, 263, 349
Morufonu 312
Moses 283, 443
Moshiriikkwechep **399**
Mot 6, 43, 606
Mother Earth 37, 125, 150, 152, 225, 280, 304, 312, 325, 377, **399**, 413, 418, 421, 444, 465, 498, 521, 536, 549, 566, 611, 631
see also Gaia; Great Goddess
mother-of-pearl 227
Mothir 246
Mountain (element) 204
Mountain Spirits **399**
Mountain-Lion 195
mountains 87, 197, 202, 291, 319, 336, 443, 449

mourning 661
Mozart, Wolfgang Amadeus 191
Muchalinda 102, **399**, 406
Mudati 315, 504
mud-hens 379
Mudungkala **400**
Muit 227
Mukunda 651
mulberry trees 152, 665
Multultu **394**
Muluku **400**
Mulungu **400**
Mumba **340**
Munin 435
Murray River 419
Muruwul 313
Muses 50, 271, **401**, 431, 472
music 50, 66, 88, 226, 257, 266, 296, 401, 434, 452, 459, 511, 603, 631-2, 634, 667
music, deities of 49, 241, 368, 539
musicians 50, 197, 210
Muskrat 63, 236, 390
Muspell 221, **401**, 580, 675
mustard 518
Musubi **402**, 446
Mut 329, **402**
Mwambu **402**, 659
Mwuetsi **402**
Mycenae 71, 483
Myrmidons 473
Myrrdin 386
myrrh 8, 455
Myrtilus 443, 475
mysteries 57, 100, 115, 116, **403**, 487, 603
mystery cults 45, 59-60, 146, 171, 179, 282, 322, 377, 395, 408, 418, 420, 437, 455, 669
myths 631-2 *see also* African; American; Australian; Celtic; Chinese; Egyptian; Finnish; Germanic; Greek; Indian; Japanese; Mesopotamian; Nordic; Oceanian; Roman; Slavic

Na Atibu 411
Nabu **404**
Naestan 184

Naga Pahoda **404**
Nagaitcho **404**
Nagas **406**
Naginis **406**
Naiads 431
Naijok 25
Na Kaa **406**
Na Kika 411
Nakula 368, **407**, 462
Nala 519, 652
Nala's Bridge 519
Nambi 329
Namorodo **407**
Namtar 177
Namuci 293
Namuginga 326
Nana 73
Nana Buluku 381
Nanabozho 407
Nanabush **407**
Nanda 333, **408**, **409**, 527
Nandi **409**
Nandini 647
Nanna 83, 199, 262, **409**, 562
Nannar 562
Nanook **409**
Naoise 145
Na'pi 283, **409**
Narada 496
Narasimha 261, **410**
Narcissus **411**
Nareau **411**
Narve 360
Nasilele 430
Nasteetsan 413
Nataraja 553, 556
Natesa 553
Natos 410
Naunet **429**, 444
Nauplius 277, **411**, 460
Nausicaä 27, **412**, 439
navigation 341
navigators 53, 266, 411-12
Nayenezgani 184, **413**
Ndengei 572
'Ndriananahary 64
Nebhut 413

Nebthet 178, **413**, 430
nectar 135, 242, **414**, 589
Nefertem **414**, 545
Nehebkau **414**
Neit 328, **414**
Neith 414
Nemean Lion 24, **415**
Nemesis 351, **415**
Neoptolemus 5, 44, 245, 249, 258, **415**,
   438, 474, 485, 492, 497, 507, 663
Nephele 67, **416**
Nephthys 413
Neptune 86 *see also* Poseidon
Neptunus 493
Nereids 417, 431
Nereus **417**
Nergal **417**
Nero 349
Nerrivik 544
Nerthus **418**, 424
Nessus 255
New Zealand 380
Ngalbjod 227
Ngewowa **418**
Ngi 681
ngona oil 402
Ngurunderi **419**
Ni **237**
Nibelung Poem 101, 419, 524, 561
Nibelungs **419**
Nicippe 28, 185
Nidavellir 392
Nidhogg **419**, 420, 674
Nidud 653
Niflheim 74, 221, 401, 419, 675
Niger River 550
Night 28, 522-3
nightingales 38, 594
Nightmare on Elm Street 540
Nihoshoki 306
Nike 68, **420**
Nile River 328
Nimrod 221
Nimue 343, 386, 398, **420**
Nine Worlds **421**
Ning Yang 172
Ninhursaga 176, 219, **421**, 422

Ninigi 32, **421**, 637
Ninki 421
Ninlil 409, 421
Ninshubur 286
Ninsun 219
Nintur 177, 421
Ninurta 177, **422**
Niobe 38, **423**, 589
Niparaya 511
Nipinoukhe **423**
Nirvana 103
Nisumbha 163
Nisus **423**
Nisyros 167
Niu Tu 153
Njinji **424**
N'Kokon 681
Njörd 418, **424**, 567, 644
Nkulnkulu 634
Noah 159, **425**
Nocoma **425**
noise 271
Nokomis 408, **426**
noodles 622
Nordic myth **426**, 501
Norns 61, 419, **428**, 664, 674
North Wind 96
Northern Lights 63
Notus 682
Novgorod 506
Nu'u **430**
Nu'u Pule 430
Nü Gua 204, 225, **428**
Nü Wa 428
Nubians 545
Nuliajuk 544
Num **429**
Numitor 529
Nummo 36
Nun 414, **429**, 444
Nusku 550
Nut 178, 214, **429**, 513, 547, 556
Nyambe **430**
Nyambi **430**
Nyami Abe 459
nymphs 225, 259, 401, **431**, 453
Nysa, Mt 626

oak trees 86, 182, 309, 386, 569, 603
Oanamochi 202
Oath of the Gods 578
oaths 232, 252, 294, 349, 367, 395, 438, 484, 578, 613
Oba River 550
Oberon **433**
Ocean 28, 207, 536
Oceanian myth **433**
Oceanides 431
Oceanus 612
Oco 372
Ocypete 240 *see also* Harpies
Od 201, **435**, 593
Odin 15, 20, 62, 90, 91, 97, 101, 189, 201, 202, 230, 245, 263, 359, 360, 392, 393, **435**, 559, 560, 567, 569, 582, 613, 627, 643, 649, 675
Odlek 593
Oduduwa **437**
Odur 435
Odysseus 4, 14, 18, 24, 27, 53, 77, 109, 111, 122, 175, 245, 248, 249, 295, 307, 345, 361, 412, **437**, 460, 461, 476, 485, 490, 494, 525, 543, 564, 662, 679
Odyssey 6, 13, 47, 228, 249, 251, 320, 385, 412, 440, 451
Oedipus 47, 131, 184, 310, 346, **440**, 576, 612
Oedipus at Colonus 442
Oeneus 255
Oenomaus **442**, 475
Oenone 468
Offenbach, Jacques 454
Og **443**
Ogdoad **443**
Ogham runes 444
Ogma 444
Ogmios **444**
Ogo 36, **444**
Ogoun **445**
Ogun 445
Oidipous 440
Oisin **445**
Ojin 235, 610
Okonorote 333

Okuninushi 421, **446**
Old Age 308
Old Man of the Sea 38, 357, 383, 424, 501
Old One 198
Olifat **447**
olive trees 69, 253
olive oil 452
Oliver 527
Ollathair 140
Oller 630
Olodumare 448
Olofat 447
Olofath 447
Olokun 448
Olorun 437, **448**
Olympia 449, 476, 684
Olympian gods 26, **449**
Olympic Games 255, 476
Olympus, Mt 9, 165, 182, **449**, 454
Ometecuhtli **449**
Omodaru 632
Omoigane 31
Omphale 255, **449**
omphalos 684
Onarus 54
Onatah **450**
Once and Future King, The 58
O'Neill, Eugene 442, 452
Oni **450**
Onyankopon **450**
Ophion **185**, 571
Opotonobe 632
Opotonodi 632
oracles 49, 239, 353, 355, 621 *see also* Delphic oracle
Orchomenus 612
order 26, 646 *see also* universal order
order, deities of 225, 428
Oresteia 18, 174, 204, 452, 507
Orestes 11, 17, 121, 124, 174, 249, 257, 295, 386, 416, **451**, 452, 476, 507
Orestiads 431
Orff, Carl 442
orgasms 19, 155, 284, 297, 435, 635 *see also* sex
Orgeuilleuse 214

Orion 56, 178
Ormahzd 23
Orofat 447
Orpheus 138, 224, 236, **452**, 642
Orthus 217
Orythia 96
Oser 454
Oshadagea **454**
Oshun River 550
Osirap 239, 546
Osiris 59, 178, 239, 264, 413, 430, **454**, 546, 547
Ossa, Mt 168
Ossian 446
ostrich feathers 367
Otava **455**
Othrys, Mt 132
Otr 45, 189, 361, **455**
Otter 63, 189, 236, 390
Otukut 681
Otus 165
Oudaeus 576
Ouranos 132, 269, **456**
see also Father Sky
Ovda **456**
overpopulation 271, 300
Ovid 13, 107, 111, 183, 383, 389, 484, 487, 492, 530
Owatatsumi 671
Owiot 120, **456**
owl-feathers 221
owls 69, 358, 594
oxen 278

Pachacamac **459**, 650
Pactolus River 391
Padma 346
Page Abe **459**
Pah **460**
Pai Long 200
Päivä **460**
Palamedes 412, 438, **460**
Palatine Hill 186
Pales 492
Palladium 57, 153, 438, **460**
Pallanteum, Mt 186
Pallas (Athene) 68

Pallas (giant) 165, **461**
Pallas (son of Evander) **461**, 624
Pallas (son of Pandion) 9, 598
Palongwhoya 332
Pan 392, 450, **462**, 478, 497, 502, 626
Pan Gu 270, **464**
Panacea 15
pandannus palms 407
Pandareus 589
Pandarus 619
Pandavas 55, 82, 91, 92, 150, 159, 163, 308, 327, 335, 340, 407, **462**, 464, 467, 536, 678
Pandion 594
Pandora **463**
Pandu 339, 368, **464**
panic 462
pan-pipes 462
Panther 212
Pao Yu 678
Papa 66, **465**, 521, 587, 588
Paracelsus 191
paradises 7, 77, 98, 103, 104, 108, 119, 121, 175, 176, 200, 231, 265, 267, 285, 407, 478, 533, 597, 614, 616, 667 see also heaven
Paranjanya 506
Paraparawa **465**
Parasara 654
Parashurama **466**
Parijata 40
Parikshit 406
Paris 124, 248, 385, 417, **467**, 485, 492
Parjanya **469**
Parnassus, Mt 147, 155
Parrot 75
Parrot Girls, Green 613
Parshva **469**, 612
Parsifal 58, 480
Parsu 374, **470**
Parthenon 113
Parthenopaeus 64, 547
Parvati 149, 158, 162, 210, 303, 323, 326, **470**, 541, 554, 555, 631
Pasabhrit 646
Pasi 646
Pasiphaë 122, 138, **470**

Pasithea 225
Patroclus 5, 243, **471**
Pavanarekha 160, **471**
Payatamu **471**, 593
peaches 300, 556
peaches of immortality 250, 266, 285,
    336, 674 *see also* apples of immortality
peacocks 54, 98, 252
Peer Gynt 321
Pegasus 88, 142, **472**, 482
Pekai 574
Pelagon 107
Pelasgus 185
Pele 237, 324
Peleus 4, **472**, 600
Pelias 222, 308, 382, **474**
Pelion, Mt 168, 309, 472
Pelles 209, 345, 348, **474**
Pelopia 71, 609
Peloponnese 476
Pelops 345, 443, 460, **475**, 589
Pelorus 576
Pemphredo 226 *see also* Graeae
Penates **476**
Pendragon, Uther *see* Uther Pendragon
Penelope 123, 412, 438, 439, 462, **476**
Penglai Shan **478**
penises 48, 59, 66, 74, 82, 134, 165,
    214, 308, 372, 380, 394, 455, 456,
    497, 553, 555, 576, 585, 607, 655,
    658
Penthesilea 32
Pentheus 19, 155, **479**
peppers 327
Perceval 113
Perceval **480**
Percival 58
Peredur 480
Periboea 440
Periclymenus 53
Perkonis 506
Perkons 506
Perkunas 506
Perlesvaus 480
Pero 384
Perom 506
Peron 506

Perrault, Charles 503
Perseis 122
Persephone 8, 145, 236, 243, 248, **480**,
    488, 566
Perseus 70, 142, 225, 226, 242, 384, **482**
Persian myth 104
Perun 506
Perusan 506
Petrarch (Francesco Petrarca) 151
Petrel 544
Petro 573
Phaedra 48, 260, 470, **483**, 599
Phaethon **484**
phallic symbols 117, 201, 288, 394, 555,
    571, 684
phantoms 67, 248, 260, 298, 416, 471,
    478 *see also* ghosts
pharaohs 41, 329, 402, 413, 414, 502, 544
Pharos 502
pheasants 594
Phèdre 600
Phegeus 27
Pheres 309, 382
Phidias 69
Philemon **86**
Philoctetes 109, 256, 416, 438, 469, **484**
Philomela 594
Philyra 120
Phineus 240, **485**
Phlegethon River **486**, 578
Phobos 52
Phocus 472
Phoebe 612
Phoenician Women 442
phoenix 89
Pholus 120
Phorcides 226
Phorcys 383, 543
Phra 513
Phrixus 67, 222, 416, **486**
Phtha 503
Phylacus 384
pi disc 609-10
Picasso, Pablo 113, 440, 600
Picus 122, **486**
Pierides 401
pietas 557

pigs 46, 122, 140, 159, 498
Pikker 506
Pilgrim's Progress 209
Pilgrimage to the West 618
Pilirin **613**
Pillan **487**
Pillars of Heracles 217
Pilumnus 487
Pilzintecuhtli 615
Pinga **487**
Piorun 506
Pipinoukhe **423**
Pirene 472, 565
Pirithous 113, 248, **487**, 599
Pisakas **488**
Pittheus 9
Plague Demons, Five **197**
plagues 25, 70, 377
plants, deities of 145, 522, 559
  see also farming
Plautus 29
Pleasure 503
Pleiades (constellation) 94, 326, 341, 409
plenty, deities of 140, 531
ploughing, goddess of 215
ploughs 82, 552
Plouton 235
Pluto (god) 235
Pluto (Titan) 589
Po River 484
Podalirius 485
Podarces 497
Podarge 240 see also Harpies
poetic inspiration, god of 436
poetic metre 138, 575
poetry 97, 100, 138, 401
poetry, deities of 539, 575
Pohjola 320, **489**
Pohjola's Daughter 321
Poia **489**
Polites 497
politicians 440, 445
Pollux **156**, 223, 247, 351, 599, 625
Poludnitsa **489**
Polybus 440
Polybutes 165
Polydectes 142, 482

Polydeukes 156
Polydoros 349
Polydorus 245, **489**, 548
Polyhymnia 401 see also Muses
Polymnestor 245, 489
Polynices 47, 131, 179, 184, 441, 547
Polyphemus 135, **490**
Polyphontes 547
Polyxena 5, 244, 416, 469, **491**
pomegranates 6, 481, 545
Pomona 486, **492**
Poquanghoya 332
Porphyrion 165
porpoises 155
porridge 672
Poseidon 12, 38, 50, 68, 96, 131, 132,
  135, 142, 145, 167, 260, 277, 349,
  350, 384, 438, 470, 474, 475, **493**,
  543, 591, 683
Poseyemu 495
Poshaiyankayo 77, **494**
Potiphar 363
Potok-Mikhail Ivanovich **495**
potter's wheel 138
pottery 266, 459
poverty, god of 94
Powys, John Cowper 6
Pracheta 141, 496
Pradyumna 533
Prahlada 410, **495**
Prajapati (Buddha's foster mother) **495**
Prajapati (god) 50, 110, 340, 347, **496**,
  504, 531
Prajapatis **496**, 526
Pramati 20
Prasetas 646
Pratyusa 648
precious stones 60, 84, 138, 197, 235, 336
precious stones, goddess of 116
pregnancy 639 see also childbirth
Pre-Raphaelites 412, 531
preserver god 651
Priam 5, 244, 255, 349, 416, 460, 467, **496**
Priapus 9, 52, **497**
prickly-pear trees 115
Primavera, La 199
primordial Chaos 73, 221

primordial ocean 6, 10, 33, 171, 289, 304, 354, 429, 503, 521, 543, 554, 630, 645, 658
Priparchis 498
Prisni 498
Prithi 339
Privithi 21, 164, 498, 645
Procne 594
Procrustes 498
Proetus 88, 384
Promachus 548
Prometheus 69, 120, 147, 293, 463, 464, 499, 597, 613
Prometheus Bound 294, 500
promises 12, 71, 83, 89, 108, 127, 142, 179, 202, 252, 277, 298, 305, 367, 395, 516, 578, 613
Propertius 107, 383
prophecy 98, 204, 346, 393, 487, 500, 557, 595-6
prophecy, deities of 49, 190, 231, 252, 341, 370, 582, 583, 623
prophets 109, 110, 249, 349, 384, 501, 557, 611, 621
Prose Edda 427, 501
Proserpina 480, 563
prosperity 98, 173, 241, 307, 336-7, 424, 537, 556 *see* also plenty
prosperity, deities of 22, 140, 287, 532, 549, 551, 577, 622
prostitution 63, 219, 614
protectors 158
Proteus 38, 55, 468, 501
Pryderi 505
Psyche 48, 181, 353, 502
Ptah 41, 239, 503, 545, 603
Pterelaus 28, 38
Ptolemy 546
pubic hair 313
Pudnuitsa 569
Pukeheh 615
Pulaha 496
Pulastya 496
Puloma 21, 99
Puranas 287, 289, 335
Purandara 291
Purcell, Henry 151

Purukapali 315, 400, 504
Purusha 504, 676
Pushan 505
Pushpagiri 647
Putana 334, 505
Pwyll 51, 367, 505
Pyerun 152, 506, 542
Pygmalion (brother of Dido) 150
Pygmalion (sculptor) 506
Pylades 174, 507
Pyleus 74
Pyrrha 147
Pyrrhic victory 507
Pyrrhus 245, 415, 507
Pythian Games 49

Qamaits 509
Qat 509
Qebhsnuf 240
Qi Yu 510
Qian Niu 510
Qin Shupo 604
Quaayayp 510
quails 354
quarrels, goddess of 423
quartz 227
quests 53, 222, 262, 308-9
Quetzalcóatl 115, 510, 511, 596
Quirinus 258, 530

Ra 1, 40, 60, 66, 74, 89, 177, 214, 264, 328, 368, 414, 444, 484, 513, 544, 547, 591, 603
Rabbit 222, 277
Racine, Jean 44, 600
Radha 334, 335, 347, 516
Radigast 516
Ragnarök 11, 61, 83, 246, 261, 311, 355, 360, 401, 516, 562, 580, 650, 674
Rahu 40, 517
Raiden 517
Raiju 517
rain 65, 103, 143, 341, 581
rain dances 315, 616
rain deities 6, 115, 192, 200, 202, 281, 291-2, 296, 326, 331, 361, 406, 454, 469, 506, 526, 556, 614, 616, 679

Rainbow Snake *see* Great Rainbow Snake
rainbow snakes 141
rainbows 42, 87, 93, 137, 227, 292, 636
rainbows, goddess of 296
Raki 521
Rakshasas **518**
Raktabija 321
Ralegh, Sir Walter 174
Rama 19, 84, 91, 143, 238, 304, 310,
    320, 327, 336, 346, 467, **518**, 523,
    566, 579, 590, 649, 652
Ramachandra 518
Ramasimha 523
Ramayana 21, 213, 238, 287, 290, 337,
    467, 520
rams 22, 40, 67, 154, 328, 486
Ran 11, **521**
Rangi 66, 465, **521**, 587, 588
Rangi's Children **522**
Rashnu **522**
Rat 174
Ratatosk 419, 674
Rati 323, **522**
Ratnasanu 387
Ratovoantany 682
Ratri **522**
Rattlesnake 128
rattlesnakes 572
Rauni 26
Ravana 84, 310, 320, 336, 338, 518,
    523, 566, 649
    avatars of Ravana *see* Sisupala
Raven 390, 408, **523**
ravens 98, 425, 636
Re 513
red 588
Red Book, The 367
reeds 299, 632
Regin 189, **524**, 560, 561
Remus 376, **529**, 659
Renault, Mary 600
resurrection 139, 282
resurrection, god of 395
Rhadamanthus 235, **524**
Rhea 64, 132, 138, 154, 475, **524**, 612, 682
Rhea Silvia 529
Rhesus 153, 438, **525**

Rhiannon 505
Rhine River 45
Ribhus 62, **525**
ribs 7, 374
rice 31, 140, 231, 287, 623
Richardson, Samuel 151
riddles 29, 576
Rig 246
Rig Veda 19, 21, 164, 212, 287, 293, **526**
Rigi **52**
Riiki 411
Rime of the Ancient Mariner 199
Rimmon 7
Rimsky-Korsakov, Nicolai 536
Ring of the Nibelungs, The 45, 101, 419,
    517, 524, 561
rings 44, 189
Rirab Lhumpo 197
Rishabha **526**
Rishis **526**
Rite of Spring, The 506
River (element) 204
river deities 3, 4, 239, 539, 578
rivers 3, 6, 52, 87, 125, 177, 198, 211,
    289, 353, 391, 486, 610
Ro'o 66
Rod **526**, 569
Rodú 526
Rogo Tumu Here 588
Rohini (moon goddess) 40, **526**, 527
Rohini (princess) 82, 333, **527**
Rohini (sun goddess) 527
Roland **527**
Roman myth 12, 389, **527**
Roman/Greek equivalent names 529
Rome 12, 59, 186, 530
Romulus 376, **529**, 659
Rongo 521, 522, 588
Rosicrucians 263
Rosmerta **531**
rowan trees 26, 603
Ru 259
Ruad Rofessa 140
Ruaumoko **531**
rubber 614
Rubens, Peter Paul 531
Rudra 97, **531**, 532, 553

Rudrani **532**
Rugievit **532**
Ruhanga 16, **532**
Rukmini **532**, 564
rum 445
runes 97, 444
ruo tree 665
Russalki **533**
Rustem 639
Ruwa **533**
Ryujin 610

Sabines, rape of the 530
sacred writings 211, 242
sacrifice 20, 40, 100, 125, 133, 183, 210,
    218, 227, 268, 277-8, 294, 303, 372,
    396, 504, 518, 590, 616, 646, 665, 675
Sadasapati 100
Sadko **535**, 536
Sagara **536**
Sagas 427
sages 8, 19, 91, 97, 99
Sages, Seven 8
Sahadeva 368, 462, **536**
sails 139, 379
Sakhmet 544
Sakkara 281
Saktasura 334, **536**
Salinger, J.D. 209
sallekhana 369
salmon 83, 194
Salmoneus **537**
salt 74, 131, 158, 535, 538
Samba 335, **537**
Samildanach 363
sampo 361, **537**, 640
Samraj 291
Samson **538**
Sandhya **538**
Sanjna 581
Santanu 92, 211, 654
Saoshyant **538**
Saphon, Mt 6
Sarah 443
Saranyu **539**, 653
Sarasvati 97, **539**
Sarayu 520

Sardinia 253
Sarigoys 55
Sartre, Jean-Paul 452
Satan 7, 79, **540**
Satanists 263
Sati 141, 149, 470, **540**, 555
satire 99
Saturn (planet) 541
Saturnalia 541
Saturnus 132, **541**
Satyavan 542
Satyavati 654
satyrs 155, 462, **541**, 562
Saule 386, **541**
saunas 615
Savitri (god) 8, 527, 539, **542**
Savitri (Princess) **542**
saws 139
Saxo the Grammarian 261
scales 37, 367
Scamander (priest) **542**
Scamander River 543
scarab beetles 328, 515
scarecrows 82
schizophrenia 307
scholars, god of 231
Schumann, Robert 192
scorpions 56, 414, 447
Scott, Walter 217, 446
screams, living 339
scribes, deities of 211, 404, 603
Scroll of Past Judgements 673
sculptors 506
sculpture 591
Scyld 215
Scylla 122, 348, **543**
Sea **543**
sea deities 10, 75, 332, 371, 417, 424,
    493, 522, 585, 588, 590
Sea of Milk 24, 39
sealions 544
seals 319, 544
seas 521, 591 *see also* oceans; Old Man of
    the Sea; water
seasons 6, 8, 31, **99**, 140, 184, 195, 221,
    279, 336, 423, 425, 450, 454, 481,
    542, 567, 597, 631, 665, 675

second hearing 194, 501, 561, 573, 611
second sight 194, 501, 573, 611
secrecy, goddess of 45
Sedna **544**
seers 59, 417, 485, 554
Seers, Seven 72, 526, **549**, 647, 652
Sekhmet 85, 484, 515, **544**
Sela 402, 659
Selene 175, 243, 525, **545**
Semele 108, 154, 252, **546**
semen 19, 60, 103, 176, 214, 297, 394,
  397, 444, 531, 539, 575
Sena 326
Sengen 202
senility 448
Serapis 239, **546**
Serpent of Obsidian Knives 573
serpents *see* snakes
Serqet **546**
Sesha 406
Seshat **546**
Set 1, 59, 178, 241, 264, 414, 454, **547**,
  603
Setanta 133
Seth 430, 547
Seti 547
Seven Against Thebes 47, 153, 179, 184,
  274, **547**
seven cows of prosperity 241
Seven Gods of Good Luck 140, **549**
Seven Sages 8
Seven Seers 72, 526, **549**, 647, 652
sex 63, 85, 101 140, 170, 176, 284, 286,
  296, 324, 403, **549**, 657, 673
sex, deities of 201, 218, 286, 296, 394
Sextus 362
sexual organs 17, 237, 314, 617, 655,
  663
sGrolma **549**
Sha Ho-shang 617
Shachipati 291
Shaitan 540
Shakespeare, William 18, 111, 151, 244,
  338, 357, 398, 433, 442, 619, 664
Shakra 291
Shamash **550**
Shang Di 150, **550**, 678

Shango **550**
shape-changers 42, 45, 46, 50, 53, 114,
  125, 128, 164, 179, 189, 194, 197,
  210, 221, 232, 246, 247, 263, 278,
  311, 323, 345, 352, 353, 359, 370,
  371, 386, 390, 396, 398, 406, 407,
  420, 435, 455-6, 473, 501, 505, 518,
  551, 552, 563, 573, 586, 591, 595-6,
  601, 612, 630, 640, 653, 659, 661,
  677, 682
sharks 447, 615
Shashti **551**
Shatarupa 539
Shatrughna 518, **551**
Shaya 581
sheep 25, 121, 451, 476
Shem 425
Shen Nong 204, **552**, 556
Shen Yi 674
Sheol **552**
shepherds 175, 256, 286, 395, 440, 474,
  490, 529
Shesha 82, 83, 319, 333, 387, 469, **552**,
  553
Shi Huang Di 267
Shi Zong Di **556**
Shinto 306
Ship of Death 199
ships 53, 138, 266, 678
Shisrte 354
Shitala 149, **552**
Shiva 46, 51, 62, 91, 97, 100, 141, 148,
  158, 163, 210, 211, 240, 303, 321,
  323, 325, 326, 334, 371, 409, 463,
  466, 498, 505, 531, 536, 538, 539,
  540, **553**, 566, 648 *see also* Harihara
shoes 649
shooting-stars 587
Shou Lao **556**, 604
Shri 346, 551
shrimps 380
shrines 15, 38
Shu 73, 178, 214, 429, **556**
Shun **557**, 672, 677
Shutu 7
Si, Mt 574
Sibelius, Jean 321

Sibyls **557** *see also* Cumae, Sibyl of
Sichaeus 150
Sicharbas 150
Sicily 12, 139, 167
Siddhartha Gautama 102, 549, **558**, 673
   see also Buddha
Sido **559**
Siegfried 419, 561
Sif 15, 265, 360, **559**, 601, 630
Siggeir 560, 563
Sigmund **560**, 563
Signy **560**, 563
Sigurd 101, 189, 419, 524, 560, **561**,
   563
Sigyn 360, 516, 567
Silenus 391, **562**
silk 31, 204, 267
silver 197, 341, 536
Silver Age 196
Simarghu **562**
Simbi 573
Simorg 562
Simplex Simplicissimus 209
Sin **562**
Sinaa **563**
Sindur 245, 420
Sinfiotl 560, **563**
Sinon 663
Sirens **563**
Sirius (star) 94
Sirout 457
Sisiutl **564**
Sisters, Five **198**
Sisupala 523, 532, **564**
Sisyphus 77, 88, 537, **565**
Sita 19, 85, 304, 310, 336, 347, 519, **566**
Skadi 279, 360, 424, **567**, 630
Skan 657
Skanda 325
skeletons 107, 317, 398, 407, 596, 600
skiing 631
Skili **567**
Skirnir 201
Skrymir 602
Skrymsli **567**
Skuld 428 *see also* Norns
sky 69, **568**

Sky (element) 204
sky deities 41, 58, 63, 94, 141, 150, 152,
   164, 259, 313, 330, 429, 450, 456,
   601, 609, 613, 627, 646, 683-4
Sky spirit 42, 160
slash and burn 552
Slaughter, Frank G. 263
Slavic myth **568**
sleep, deities of 162, 273
Sleipnir 265, 359, **569**
Slow 247
smallpox 552, 614, 667
smith deities 85, 287
smiths 31, 133, 135, 202, 560, **569**
   see also craft
Smyrna 8
snails 52
snake deities 406
snake demons 495
snakes 1, 45, 73, 91, 95, 108, 137, 141,
   210, 212, 220, 253, 263, 274, 279,
   280, 298, 311, 315, 317, 319, 322,
   371, 384, 397, 399, 414, 436, 533,
   552, 556, 564, **570**, 587, 608, 631,
   648, 650, 654, 657
   see also Great Rainbow Snake
snakes, winged 511
Snoqalm **574**
Snör 246
Soatsaki 489
Sobek 328
sodomy, god of 312
Soido **574**
Sol 250
solstices 45
soma (drink) 21, 39, 72, 210, 327, **574**,
   624
Soma (god) 40, 100, 110, 115, 141, 517,
   526, **575**, 648
Somnus 273
Song Jiang **576**
Songshan 465
Sophocles 18, 47, 174, 256, 297, 440,
   442, 452, 594
sorcery 150, 230, 603 *see also* magic
sorcery, deities of 201, 243, 446, 545,
   596

sortes Virgilianae 200
Sosom **576**
Sosondowah 216
Sotuknang 332
soul guides 210, 505, 591
souls 1
Sound and the Fury, The 452
South Pole 556
Sovereigns, Three **604**
sovereignty, goddess of 382
Sown Men 107, 345, **576**
Spaceman at the Court of King Arthur, A 58
Spartoi 576
Sphinx 310, 441, **576**
Spider 176, 431, 574, 577
Spider Woman 42, 413
spiders 51, 434
Spielberg, Steven 263
Spies, Johann 191
Spoiling of Annwn, The 46
spring, deities of 145, 278, 665
sPyan-ras-gzigs 77, **577**
Sraosha **577**
Sravana Belgola 225
Sri Lanka 648
St Brigid 100
St Columba 112, 572
St David 112
St George 572
St Ilya 506
St Jerome 551
St Nicholas 535
St Patrick 141
St Paul 57, 209
Staphylus 121
Star Country **577**
stars 94, 510, 610, 634, 636, 649 *see also* Dog Star; Evening Star; Morning Star
Starvation 182
Steinbeck, John 58
Steropes 134
Sthenelus 548
Sthenno 225 *see also* Gorgons
Stoker, Bram 644
stone giants 221, 259
Stonehenge 635
stonemasons 621

storm deities 100, 292, 298, 352, 376, 435, 531, 547, 581, 595, 607, 648, 650, 675 *see also* rain; thunder
storms 38, 115, 177, 332, 400, 406, 422, 535, 611, 642
stove-rakes 622
Strauss, Richard 174
Stravinsky, Igor 442, 454, 506
Stribog **577**
Strophius 507
Sturluson, Snorri 15, 427, 501
Stymphalian Birds **578**
Styx (goddess) **578**
Styx River 4, 116, 385, 546, **578**, 600, 612
Sucellus **578**
Sudika-Mbambi **579**
Suen 562
Sugriva 84, 519, **579**
suicide, goddess of 299
Sullivan, Arthur 454
Sumbha 163
Sumeru 387
Sumitra 518, **579**
Summer Mother 195
Sun 8, 29, 30, 34, 71, 72, 74, 122, 167, 173, 203, 212, 237, 238, 264, 316, 336, 378, 410, 484, 493, 574, 587, 646, 648, 659, 665
Sun Bin **579**
sun deities 30-2, 66, 88, 112, 143, 203, 250, 267, 273, 279, 293, 363, 395, 413, 459, 460, 513, 527, 541, 542, 550, 581, 615, 622-3, 634, 650, 653, 674
Sunshaft 615
supernatural worlds 33-4, 46, 75, 118, 124, 170, 193, 242, 282, 288, 306, 326, 339, 388, 403, 434, 569, 580, 633
Supidini 632
supreme deities 23, 26, 36, 40, 61, 66, 88, 97, 143, 152, 173, 267, 291, 314, 326, 330, 435, 448, 513, 550, 568, 578, **579**, 582, 583, 616, 630, 657-8, 669, 678, 683-4
Surabji 40

surgery 150 *see also* medicine
Surma 322, **580**, 623
Surpanakha 519
Surt 401, 516, **580**
Surush 577
Surya (god) 8, 19, 339, 517, 527, 575, 579, **581**, 648
Surya (goddess) **580**
Susano 30, 421, 446, **581**
Suseribime 446
suttee 541
Suttung 233, 436, **582**
Svadilfari 61, 359
Svandovit **582**
Svargapati 291
Svarog 158, **583**
Svarozich **583**
Svartalfheim 392
Svetovid 582
Svyatogor 280, **583**
swallows 594, 636
swans 98, 153, 351, 352, 357, 568, 653
swastikas 158, 581, 603
Sweats, Water-jug of 198
sweet potatoes 465, 574
swords 10, 24, 30, 32, 187, 261, 421, 560, 679
Sybils 50
sycamore trees 324
Syracuse 53
Syrinx 462
Szeukha **583**

Ta'aroa **585**, 589
Ta-aroa 358
Tabakea 407
Tacitus 112
Tagaro **585**, 589
Tagaroa 589
Tahu 66
Tai Song 604
Taiowa 332
Taipan 227
Taishan 465
Ta Ji 312
Takshaka 406
Taliesin 46, **586**

Talking God 332
talking heads 393
Talus 138
Tama 378
Tamayori 672
Tame Boy 605
Tamendonare **54**
Tamjin 159
Tammuz 296
Tamulu **586**
Tamusi **586**
Tane 66, 430, 465, 521, 522, **587**, 588
Tang Gong Fang 356
Tangaloa **588**
Tangaroa 259, 521, 522, 585, **588**
Tanngniort 603
Tanngrisn 603
Tantalus 124, 475, **589**
Tanunapat 20
Taohirimatea 605
Tapio **589**
Tapiola 321, 589
tapu 434
Tara 100, 127, 575, **589**
Taraka 519, **590**
Taranga 378
Taranis **590**
Taro 679
taros 574
Tarquin 558
Tartarus 269, 456, 499, 627
Taru 592
Tashmetrum 404
Tauris 295
Taurus (constellation) 527
Taurus (person) 470
Taweret **590**
Tawhiri 521, 522, 531
Tawiskara 236, 294
Tawiskaron 64, **591**
Te Tuna 259, 380
tears 423
technology 511
Tefenet 591
Tefnut 73, 178, 556, **591**
Tehenut 415
Telamon 472, 497

Telchines **591**
Telegonus 122, 439, 478
Telemachus 123, 412, 438, 439, 460, 477, **592**
Telepinu 279, **592**
Telpochtli 596
Temazcalteci **593**
Temora 446
Tempe, Vale of 449
Ten Corn Maidens **593**
Ten Moons 665
Ten Suns 665
Ten Yama Kings **593**
Tengri **593**
Tenochtitlán 512
Tereus **594**
termites 536
Terpsichore 401, 563 *see also* Muses
Terra **207**
Terrapin 330
Teshub **595**
Tethys 612
Tetoinnan 122
Teutatis **595**
Tezcatlipoca 511, **595**, 614
Thagna sect 322
Thalia 225, 401 *see also* Muses
Thamuatz 297
Thamyras 271
Thanatos **597**
Theaeno 14
Thebe 38
Thebes 37, 40, 108, 170, 329, 402, **597**
Theia 273
Themis **597**, 612
Themisto 67
Theogony 228
Thesander 27, 180, 548
Theseus 10, 32, 48, 54, 113, 116, 131, 248, 260, 383, 394, 442, 483, 488, 499, **597**
Thespius 253
Thesprotia 439
Thetis 4, 24, 224, 251, 472, 494, 500, **600**, 683
Thia 612
Thiazi 278, 567, **601**

thieves, deities of 531, 576
Thir 246
Thixo 164
Thoas (giant) 165
Thoas (King of Lemnos) 274
Thoas (King of Tauris) 295
Thoas (son of Hypsipyle) 274
Thökk 83
Thor 11, 15, 29, 158, 174, 215, 265, 273, 311, 359, 559, **601**, 613
Thora 317
Thoth 265, 284, 515, 591, **603**
Thoueris 590
Thousand and One Nights, The 389
Thrall 246
Three Door Gods **604**
Three Gods of Happiness **604**
Three Lavatory Ladies **604**
Three Sovereigns **604**
Thrud 29
Thrym **601**
thunder 17, 25, 158, 354, 390, 517, 575, 601, **604**, 614, 646, 682
Thunder (element) 204
thunder deities 6, 25, 111, 158, 178, 259, 280, 281, 291, 319, 381, 487, 506, 550, 579, 590, 604, 607, 624, 634, 642-3 *see also* lightning deities; storm deities
Thunderbirds 408, 605, **607**, 658
thunderbolts 132, 251, 314, 374, 422, 550, 606, 683
Thunderstone 21, 291, 293
Thunor **601**
Thyestes 11, 71, 476, **608**
Ti Ya 659
Tiamat 375, **609**
Tian **609**
Tiber 264, 529
Tiber River **610**
Tiberinus 610
Tibet 373
Tibetan myth 149
Tici 650
tidal waves 38, 311, 313, 358, 399, 430
Tide Jewels 235, 306, **610**
tides 522
Tieholtsodi 73

Tien Long 659
tigers 554, 622
Tigris River 6, 177, 375, 387
Tikikapakapa 587
Tilphussa (spring) 612
Tilphussa, Mt 612
time 19, 196, 259, 291, 305, 326, 511, 546, 563
time, deities of 184, 542, 635
Tin Fei 314
Tin Hau 314
Tinia 314
Tir nan Nog 445
Tir Tairnigiri 371
Tirawa 606, **610**
Tirawahat 610
Tiresias 439, 441, 547, 548, **611**
Tirkantharas 369, 526, **612**
Tisiphone 203 see also Furies
Titania 382
Titans 28, 69, 99, 132, 134, 185, 208, 305, 420, **612**, 626
Tithonus 178
Tityus 49, 165
Tiw 613
Tiwaz **613**, 627
Tjapara 504
Tjinimin **613**
Tlaelquarni 614
Tláloc **614**
Tlalocan 614
Tlaloques 614
Tlatecuhtli 125, 279
Tlazoltéotl 596, **614**
Tmolus 392
To Kabinana **615**
To Karvuvu **615**
tobacco-pipes 660
Tobadzistsini 184, **413**
Tochopa **615**
Tollan 616
Tonantzin 122, 125
Tonatiuh **615**
Tonenili **616**
tools 231
Toothache, Wolf-stick of 198
Torngarsak **616**

tortoises 225, 326, 340
totems 34
Totoima **616**
Toutatis 595
Tower of London see London, Tower of
towers 81, 451
Toyokumono 632
Toyotama 671
tragedy 401 see also drama
Trapezus 167
travellers, deities of 117, 394
Tree of Death 407
Tree of Immortality 7
Tree of Knowledge 573
Tree of Life 238, 407, 562
Treece, Henry 174
trees 62, 86, 190, 241, 353, 407, 562, 574, 587, 613, 674
trees, god of 190
tricksters 17, 42, 45, 46, 65, 77, 128, 160-1, 176, 221, 238, 256, 277, 352, 358, 378, 407, 411, 434, 437, 445, 447, 613, **616**, 657
tridents 14, 38, 493
Trinavarta 334, **617**
Tripitaka 231, 238, **617**
Triptolemus 145
Trismegistus 603
Tristan 619
Tristan and Isolde 619
Tristram **618**
Tristubh 575
Triton's Horn shellfish 52
Troilus 492, **619**
Troilus and Cressida 18, 244, 619
Trojan war 3, 12, 18, 24, 32, 44, 48, 109, 111, 124, 144, 153, 222, 243, 244, 248, 249, 277, 385, 416, 423, 438, 460, 461, 469, 471, 473, 477, 485, 489, 491, 497, 507, 525, 600, **619**, 662
Trojans, The 151
Trophonius 353, **621**
Troy 25, 254, 350, 461, 543, 619
True Path 149
truth, deities of 367, 550
Tsai Shen **622**
Tsao Jun **622**

Tsar of the Sea 535
Tsohanoai 73, 184, 413, **622**
Tsui 164
Tsukiyomi 623
Tsukuba 203
Tsukuyomi 30, **623**, 630
Tu 521, 522
Tu Matauenga 379
Tu O 237
Tuamoto 606
Tuamutef 239
Tuli 588
Tumataunega 605
Tumun River 87
Tunogupi 632
Tuonela 320, 322, 330, 352, **623**, 641
Tuonetar 623, 641
Tuoni **624**
Tupan **624**
turbots 568
turmeric 93
Turnus 12, 350, 390, 461, **624**
Turquoise Woman 22
Turtle 29, 63, 369
tusks 211
Tutankhamun 66
Tvashtri (sage) 292
Tvashtri (smith) **624**, 652, 653
Twain, Mark 58
Twenty-four Examples of Hsiao 557
twins 37, 54, 64, 81, 111, 124, 156, 178,
    214, 221, 236, 247, 286, 294, 332,
    336, 340, 370, 413, 434, 444, 511,
    529, 536, 579, 588, 615, **625**, 632, 659
Tyche 200
Tydeus 547
Tyndareus 156, 247, 351, 438, 609, **625**
Typhoeus 626
Typhon 185, 547, **626**, 684
typhoons 627
Tyr 11, 15, **627**
Tyro 474, 537, 565

Uaica **629**
udjat 265
uGobungquonqo 634
Ugonomitama 630

Ugrasena 308, 325, **629**
Ugrasura 334, **629**
uGuqabadele 634
Uixtocijuatl 614
Ukaho 533
Ukemochi 623, **630**
Ukko 314, **630**
uKqili 634
Ulfrun 245, 420
Ulgan 180, **630**
Ull **630**
Uller 630
Ullikummi 595
Uluru **631**
Ulysses 437
Uma 149, **631**
uMabongakutukiziwezonke 634
Umai 593
Umai-hulhlya-wit **631**
Umashiashikabihikoji **632**
Umisachi 671
Uncegila **632**
uncleanliness, goddess of 614
understanding, goddess of 590
Underwater Panthers 408, **633**
Underworld 13, 46, 48, 99, 110, 114,
    116, 125, 146, 175, 195, 203, 212,
    243, 257, 296, 300, 353, 368, 370,
    379, 409, 417, 450, 452, 463, 480,
    486, 488, 511, 513, 524, 531, 552,
    564, 566, 571, 572, 578, 580, 589,
    591, 599, 621, **633**, 678
Underworld, rulers of 22, 51, 59, 84,
    152, 235, 236, 430, 454-5, 624, 671,
    672, 673
Unelanuki **634**
Ungur 227
universal order 60, 148, 149, 177, **316**,
    335, 367, 375, 449, 642, 685
universal order, deities of 61, 97, 139-40,
    550, 553, 646, 651, 682
universe cycles 648
universe, creation of *see* creators of the
    universe; creators of Earth
Unktehi 608, 632
Unkulunkulu **634**
Untamo 337

Untekhi 572
Upidini 632
Urania 401 *see also* Muses
Uranus 456
urbar 315
Urd 61, 428, 664, 674 *see also* Norns
Urubutsin 336
Urvashi **634**
Ushas 496, 527, 531, **635**
Utanapishtim 635
Utgard 312, **635**
Utgard-Loki 602, 635
Uther Pendragon 57, 187, **635**
Utnapishtim 220, 425, **635**
Utset **636**
Utu **636**
uZivelele 634
Uzume 31, **636**

Vac 539
vaginas 62, 82, 94, 215, 227, 237, 298,
    315, 372, 380, 640, 658, 671
Vahagn **639**
Vaicnavara 20
Vaimatse **639**
Väinämöinen 47, 194, 280, 312, 320,
    353, 364, 537, **640**
Vaivasvata 374
Vajrasattva **642**
Vajri 291
Valedjád **642**
Valerius Flaccus 383
Valhalla 61, 83, **643**
Vali 15, 360
Valkyries 61, 101, 201, 420, **643**
Vamana 84, **643**
vampires 120, **644**
Vanaheim 645
Vanderdecken, Willem 199
Vanir 201, 424, **644**
Varaha 261, **645**
Vardhamana 369
Variloma 646
Varpulis 569, **646**
Varuna 8, 19, 291, 319, 395, 467, 625,
    646, 650
Varuni 40, **647**

Vashishta 496
Vashishtra 549, **647**, 652
Vasudeva 325, 333, **647**, 648
Vasuki 39, 319, 371, 387, 555, **648**
Vasus **648**
Vatea 521
Vayu 46, 238, 340, 531, **648**
Ve 15, 62, 91, 202, 392, **649**, 675
Vechernyaya Zvezda **649**
Vedas 288, 290, 540, 575
Vega (star) 510
Venilia 486, 624
venom 371
Venus 12, **48**, 502
Verdandi 428 *see also* Norns
Verethragna 291, 395
Vertumnus 492
Vesta **649**
Vestal Virgins 529, 649
Vibishana **649**
Vichitravirya 33
Victoria 420
victory, goddess of 420
Vidar 230, **649**
Vili 15, 62, 91, 202, 392, 649, **650**, 675
Vinata 212, 319, **650**
vines 365, 425, 479, 588
Viracocha 459, **650**
Viraj 504, **651**
Virbius 261
Virgil 3, 13, 43, 47, 59, 107, 111, 151,
    245, 296, 349, 383, 386, 440, 529,
    557, 562
virgin births 63, 246, 357, 376-7
Virgin Mary *see* Mary
virginity 251, 260, 265, 296, 640
virginity, goddess of 56
Vishadhari 371
Vishnu 8, 39, 84, 97, 100, 143, 148, 160,
    212, 240, 261, 303, 304, 308, 324,
    325, 327, 333, 347, 374, 387, 406,
    495, 517, 523, 539, 541, 552, 553,
    649, **651** *see also* Harihara
  avatars of Vishnu 102, 651 *see also*
    Krishna; Kurma; Matsya; Narasimha;
    Parashurama; Parshva; Rama;
    Vamana; Varaha

Vishvakarman 303, 496, 519, 625, **652**
Vishvamitra 549, 590, 635, 647, **652**
Visvakarma 652
Vithofnir 674
Vivaldi, Antonio 295
Vivasvat 8, 539, **653**
Vivien 386, 398
Vlad the Impaler 644
Vlkodlaks 659
Vodyanoi **653**
voice 503
volcanoes 168, 237, 251, 531
Volga, river 535
Volkh **653**
Volsung 561
Volsung Saga 101, 561
Voltaire, François Marie Arouet de 209
Volturnus River 610
Volund **653**
Voodoo myth 35
Vookodlaks 659
Vrindha 304
Vritra 20, 292, 606, **654**
Vulcan 250
Vulder 630
Vulture 195, 310, 519
vultures 384
Vyasa 211, 368, **654**

Wagner, Richard 45, 101, 199, 217, 419, 480, 517, 524, 561, 619
wagtails 89
Wahari **655**
Waimariwi 313
waimea trees 379
Wak **655**
Wakahirume 31, 581, 637
Wakan Tanka 608, **657**
Wakea 465
Wakonda **657**
Walgino 569
wallabies 393
Walumbe 326
war 132, 180, 462, 520, 522
war deities 15, 52, 68, 89, 133, 162, 230, 231, 235, 296, 314, 325, 333-4, 376, 382, 394, 395, 398, 420, 422, 435,

445, 509, 510, 522, 532, 544, 549, 582, 595, 627, 634, 639
Waramurungundju **658**
warriors 90, 149
warts 667
Wasis 222
water 17, 211, 417, 533, 536, 572, 593, 608, 632, 653, **658**
Water (element) 196
water deities 22, 23, 85, 165, 176, 200, 225, 227, 324, 361, 535, 587, 609, 646
Water of Oblivion 392
water buffaloes 404
water demons 325
Waterfall 615
water snakes 82, 233, 259, 632
Wati-Kutjara 340
Waugh, Evelyn 209
Wave Maidens 245, **420**
Wawalug sisters 313
Wawilak sisters 313
Wayland 653
We Jeng 604
wealth *see* prosperity
weapons 14, 19, 49, 56, 88, 135, 162, 174, 215, 226, 235, 266, 272, 312, 394, 466, 554, 578, 581, 601, 606, 624, 649, 652, 659
see also arrows; swords
weasels 29
weaving 31, 51, 68, 190, 414
weaving goddess 68
weddings, deities of 273, 505
We-e 177
Wele 402, **659**
Well of Mimir 674
Well of Urd 393
well-dressing 572
Wen Jang **659**
Wen Wang 352
werewolves **659**
West Wind 141, 502, 682
whales 273, 544
Wheel of Fate 325
of Life 19,373
of Time 97
of Transmigration 118, 594

wheels 200, 266, 298
Wheememeowah **660**
whetstones 601
whirlpools 23, 543
White Book, The 367
White She-Buffalo **660**
White, T.H. 58
whores 265
Why There Are No More Bogatiri In Holy Russia 96
Wi 657
Wichama 459
Widjingara **661**
Wieland 653
Wiglaf 90
Wild Boy 605
will-o'-the-wisps 156, 249
willow trees 88
Winabozho 408
Winchester 110
Wind (element) 204
Wind Breath 64, 236
wind deities 13-14, 96, 171, 177, 192, 204, 231, 337, 390, 522, 556, 577, 646, 648, 682
winds 141, 212, 265, 511, 552
   see also hurricanes; typhoons
Windsor Great Park 114
wine 113, 155, 287, 365, 414, 425, 562
wine, deities of 155, 647
winter 577 *see also* seasons
Winter 675
Winter Mother 195
Wisaaka 408
wisdom 59, 99, 120, 121, 652, 654
wisdom, goddess of 68
Wishpoosh 128, **661**
witches 202
witchetty-grubs 143
wizards 586
Wo 681
Woden 435
Woinunggur 227
Wolf 195, 610
Wollunkwa 227
wolves 365, 529, 563
women, supremacy of 115

women, goddess of 345
Women of Troy 44, 111, 245, 386
Wonambi 227
Wondjina 661
Wonomi **662**
Wood (element) 196
Wooden Horse 153, 248, 349, 416, **662**
woodpeckers 122, 191, 487
woodworms 384
Worlds, Nine **421**
Worombi 227
Wotan 435
Woyengi **663**
writing 97, 205, 267, 404, 444, 511, 540, 603
Wu Cheng-en 617
Wu Shan 677
Wuraka **658**
Wyrd 112, **664**

Xanthus 543
Xi He **665**
Xi Wang Mu 674
Xipetotec 125, **665**
Xiutecuhtli **667**
Xochipili 268, **667**
Xochiquetzal **667**
Xólotl 511, **667**
Xuthus 294

Yacatecuhtli **669**
Yadhapati 646
Yadilyil 184
Yagami 446
Yahweh 87, 108, 173, 443, 540, **669**
Yakshas **518**
Yalu River 87
Yalungur 339, **671**
Yama 467, 539, 542, **671**, 676
Yama Kings, Ten **593**
Yamasachi **671**
Yambe-akka **672**
Yami 539, 671
yams 393, 450, 465, 533, 574
Yamuna 82, 322, 339
Yamuna River 539
Yanauluha **672**

Yang 270, 285, 464
Yangtze River 336
Yao 267, 557, **672**, 677
Yaotl 596
Yarilo **673**
Yarovit 569
Yashodhara 148, 558, **673**
Yasigi 36
Yasoda 333, **673**
Yasodhara 148
Ycaiut 457
Yeats, W. B. 351
Yehl 523
Yelafath 447
Yellow River 336
Yen Lo 200, **673**
Yen Ti 552
Yen Wang 152
Yero 227
Ygern 57, 635
Ygg **674**
Yggdrasil 61, 201, 393, 419, 420, 428, 516, **674**
Yi 152, 192, 250, 557, 672, **674**
Yijing 204
Yima **675**
Yin 270, 285, 464
Ymir 15, 74, 221, 392, 401, 420, 435, **675**
Yo **285**
Yoalli Ehecatl 596
Yogeshvara 556
Yomi **676**
Yomitsukumi 676
Youth 331
Yryn-ai-tojon 630
Yseult **618**
Yseult White-hands 618
Yu 557, 672, **677**
Yu Di 678
Yu Huang 266, **678**
Yu Huang Shang Di 678
Yu Zu **679**
yucca 465

Yudhishthira 163, 308, 462, 564, **678**
Yun Tun **679**
Yunu 170, 513
Yuriwaka **679**
Yurlunggur 227, 313

Zamba **681**
Zanahary **681**
Zealand (Denmark) 215
Zemepatis 569
Zemes Màte 377
Zemyna 377
Zephyrs **682**
Zephyrus 198, 271, **682**
Zetes 53, 96, 223, 240, 485
Zethus **37**
Zeus 5, 9, 12, 14, 28, 38, 43, 49, 53, 64, 65, 68, 89, 99, 108, 109, 120, 132, 134, 142, 145, 154, 168, 180, 239, 242, 250, 251, 252, 253, 255, 269, 293, 298, 314, 347, 351, 364, 389, 431, 443, 449, 453, 462, 468, 471, 472, 473, 475, 476, 480, 485, 493, 499, 524, 525, 537, 543, 546, 565, 611, 619, 626, **682**
Zhang Dao Ling 197
Zhang Guo 172
Zhen Tsong 679
Zhi Nu **510**
Zhin Long 200
Zhuan Hu 557, **685**
Z'ile Minfort 22
ziggurats 375
zithers 642
Zodiac 144
Zombies 644
Zoroastrianism 22, 388
Zorya **685**
Zosim **685**
Zu 422, 605
Zuen 562
Zurvan Akarana 22, **685**
Zuttibur 569
Zvezda Dennitsa 649